BEING POLAND

A New History of Polish Literature and Culture since 1918

Being Poland offers a unique analysis of the cultural developments that took place in Poland after the First World War, a period marked by Poland's return to independence.

Conceived to address the lack of critical scholarship on Poland's cultural restoration, *Being Poland* illuminates the continuities, paradoxes, and contradictions of Poland's modern and contemporary cultural practices, and challenges the narrative typically prescribed to Polish literature and film. Reflecting the radical changes, rifts, and restorations that swept through Poland, Polish literature and film reveal the multitude of perspectives to emerge after the First World War. Addressing romantic perceptions of the Polish immigrant, the politics of post-war cinema, poetry, and mass media, *Being Poland* is a comprehensive reference work written with the intention of exposing an international audience to the explosion of Polish literature and film that emerged in the twentieth century.

TAMARA TROJANOWSKA is Director for the Centre for Drama, Theatre and Performance Studies at the University of Toronto, and an associate professor in the Department of Slavic Languages and Literature at the University of Toronto.

JOANNA NIŻYŃSKA is an associate professor in the Department of Slavic & East European Languages and Cultures at Indiana University, Bloomington.

PRZEMYSŁAW CZAPLIŃSKI is a professor of Polish literature at Adam Mickiewicz University in Poland.

AGNIESZKA POLAKOWSKA is a freelance editor and translator specialising in academic publications. She holds MAs in Polish language and literature and in English literature, both from the University of Toronto.

Being Poland

A New History of Polish Literature and Culture since 1918

EDITED BY TAMARA TROJANOWSKA, JOANNA NIŻYŃSKA, AND PRZEMYSŁAW CZAPLIŃSKI, WITH THE ASSISTANCE OF AGNIESZKA POLAKOWSKA

UNIVERSITY OF TORONTO PRESS
Toronto Buffalo London

Toronto Buffalo London
utorontopress.com

Reprinted in paperback 2019

ISBN 978-1-4426-5018-3 (cloth) ISBN 978-1-4875-2459-3 (paper)

Library and Archives Canada Cataloguing in Publication

Title: Being Poland : a new history of Polish literature and culture since 1918 / edited by Tamara Trojanowska, Joanna Niżyńska, and Przemysław Czapliński ; with the assistance of Agnieszka Polakowska.
Other titles: New history of Polish literature and culture since 1918
Names: Trojanowska, Tamara, editor. | Niżyńska, Joanna, editor. | Czapliński, Przemysław, editor. | Polakowska, Agnieszka, editor.
Identifiers: Canadiana 20190115548 | ISBN 9781487524593 (softcover)
Subjects: LCSH: Polish literature – History and criticism. | LCSH: Polish literature – 20th century – History and criticism. | LCSH: Polish literature – 21st century – History and criticism.
Classification: LCC PG7051 .B45 2019 | DDC 891.8/509007 – dc23

This publication has been supported by the © POLAND Translation Program and the Adam Mickiewicz Institute.

University of Toronto Press acknowledges the financial assistance to its publishing program of the Canada Council for the Arts and the Ontario Arts Council, an agency of the Government of Ontario.

Canada Council for the Arts Conseil des Arts du Canada

Contents

Part II: Strategies

Part III: Transmissions

Part IV: Genres and Their Discontents

Acknowledgments

A book of this scope could not have appeared without the long-term, ongoing support from numerous institutions and people. Our deep gratitude is due first of all to our sponsors: the Adam Mickiewicz Foundation, the Millennium Foundation, and the Stanisław Reymont Foundation, all in Toronto, as well as the Polish Book Institute (Instytut Książki) in Kraków and the Adam Mickiewicz Institute in Warsaw. We thank their presidents, past and current (including Richard Tyndorf, Marek Malicki, Kazimierz Chrapka, Grzegorz Gauden and Dariusz Jaworski, and Krzysztof Olendzki), as well as their collaborators, in particular Krzysztof Koehler, Marta Jazowska, and Szymon Wróblewski, for supporting this project. We also wholeheartedly thank Joanna Tchorek DeMone of Toronto for her generous private sponsorship.

We are immensely grateful to our former and current graduate students for their help with various editorial tasks throughout this book's journey from idea to print. First and foremost, we thank Agnieszka Polakowska for her unwavering assistance, exquisite translations, and extensive editorial collaboration. We thank Olga Ponichtera for her conscientious checking of facts and bibliographies, and Laine Newman for lending a helping hand in compiling the latter. Our appreciation also goes to Philip Redko for stepping in when his translation skills were needed. Finally, we want to thank Bethany Braley, Edith Krannich, and Caitlin Gowans for their assistance.

We would be amiss not to acknowledge all of the participants at the First International Conference of Polish Studies in North America, "In Search of (Creative) Diversity: New Perspectives in Polish Literary and Cultural Studies Abroad," held at the University of Toronto in 2006. It was there that Tamara Trojanowska's idea of writing a new history of Polish literature and culture for English speakers was first confirmed as having real potential by the international academic community. It was also there that this book's transatlantic editorial team was formed and that many of its future contributors first came on board. We thank them all for their work as well as their faith in the successful completion of this vast project.

There are many other people whose advice and support sustained our resolve to see this book through. We thank German Ritz for discussing with us this project's initial conceptual ideas; Elwira Grossman for inspiring our thinking about its transnational profile; Donna Orwin, Stephanie Sandler, and Julie Buckler for their many helpful comments and suggestions. Finally, we want to express our gratitude to Richard Ratzlaff and Mark Thompson, our acquisitions editors at the University of Toronto Press and steady supporters of this book, as well as to Barb Porter, who saw us through the final stages of its completion. We also want to acknowledge and thank for the time and attention that many other interlocutors have invested in this project over the years, and in particular Eric Foster, for contributing an idea that in the end left an indelible mark on this volume.

This book would also not have been possible without the loving support and patience of our families, whom we thank for understanding the – at times heavy – demands this project had placed on us. As an editorial team, we thank one another for years of faithful and fruitful collaboration. Last but not least, we thank our past and present students at the University of Toronto, Harvard University, and Indiana University for inspiring us to undertake this task and for confirming its usefulness over hours of conversations. We dedicate this book to them and their future generations.

Adam Mickiewicz Institute

The Adam Mickiewicz Institute is a national cultural institute with a mission to build and communicate the cultural dimension of the Poland brand through active participation in international cultural exchange. All of the Institute's projects carry our flagship brand, Culture.pl.

The Institute's Culture.pl portal offers a daily information service covering key events related to Polish culture around the world. In addition to information on events organised in Poland and abroad, the portal features numerous artist profiles, reviews, essays, descriptive articles, and information about cultural institutions. The site is available in three languages: Polish, English and Russian.

Recently, Culture.pl announced a new project: Stories From The Eastern West. It is a new audio show that reveals the hidden history of Central and Eastern Europe. Intertwining in-depth interviews, rich sound design, and original music to build compelling narrative stories, the podcast is the start of a new chapter for Culture.pl.

For more information go to Culture.pl.

Introduction

"Ex Pluribus Plures": Cultural Histories in the Twenty-First Century

A culture roiled with radical changes, a history of greatness and of misery, a society of rifts and restorations – this is Poland, then and now. During the sixteenth century it was the third-mightiest power in Europe; in the seventeenth, it had repelled the Ottoman Invasion of the Old World; and in the eighteenth, it had created Europe's first national constitution – while on the brink of losing its independence. Non-existent as a state throughout the nineteenth century, it was revived at the end of the First World War for a mere two decades and then vanished from the map once again with the onset of the Second World War. A Soviet satellite thereafter, it became a sovereign country – at last – only fifty years later, in 1989. Since then, Poland has been once again injecting its tumultuous legacy and creative potential into the global narrative. This book is part of that process.

This is by no means the first history of Polish literature and culture intended for an English-speaking audience. It has some illustrious predecessors, starting with Manfred Kridl's *A Survey of Polish Literature and Culture* (1956), through *The History of Polish Literature* (1969) by the Nobel Prize–winning poet Czesław Miłosz, and ending with Julian Krzyżanowski's *A History of Polish Literature* (1978). The first two authors taught at American universities and wrote their textbooks with that readership in mind; the third taught briefly in London, but his book was a translation of a Polish text written for Polish university students, whose background made them receptive to the material. All three authors presented Polish literature from its medieval beginnings to various points in the twentieth century: Kridl up to 1918, Krzyżanowski up to 1939, and Miłosz – if the brief epilogue added to the second (1983) edition of his *History* is taken into account – up to 1980.

The present work focuses on modern and postmodern developments in Polish culture, targeting periods that previous volumes either could not address or addressed only briefly. It begins with the end of the First World War, a war that many see as the true beginning of the twentieth century and that, for Poland, marked a return to independence after 123 years of partition. It closes with the most recent developments, which warrant a place in this book despite the uncertainty of their future cultural standing. This trajectory reflects a crucial assumption of this project – that what is happening in Polish culture as this book goes to press is just as relevant as what has been historically validated as canonical. Such a view is rare in most traditional literary histories, as exemplified by the above-mentioned works of Kridl, Miłosz, and Krzyżanowski.

The histories written before this one were also monological; Miłosz's book in particular was a personal and at times even biased account.[1] This book embraces a different model of authorship: it offers a polyphonic model of cultural analysis by engaging close to sixty scholars from Europe and North America. In so doing, it capitalizes on their multiple intellectual, cultural, generational, and institutional perspectives, as well as a variety of theoretical tools and approaches. Our contributors illuminate the paradoxes, contradictions, and occasional inscrutability of Poland's modern and contemporary cultural practices, appealing equally to anglophone scholars, students, and generalist readers interested in Polish and world cultural history.

This internationalization of authorship defies – as it did in *A New History of French Literature* (1989) and *A New History of German Literature* (2004) – the old belief that "literary history has to be written by natives, from within."[2] This view is outdated for many reasons. Over the past century, the accelerating interconnectivity of the globalizing world has changed the modes of both the production and reception of culture and the nature of knowledge. It has reconfigured intellectual communities, including their means of communication and what they can offer one another. The transatlantic distribution of our contributors is a good example of such reconfiguration. In today's multicontextual world, hegemonic interpretations and clearly delineated subjects of inquiry are downplayed, and the territory of academic expertise and ownership is being radically remapped. This is not to say that these global tendencies have discredited the importance of local traditions or the expertise fostered by specific local environments. In our view, the purpose of international academic collaboration is to capitalize on the strengths of such traditions and contexts and on what transpires from their multifocality, while also drawing in new readers, with their multiple interests, frames of reference, and modes of communication. The comparative, interdisciplinary, transcultural approach is as much a way of writing here as it is a way of reading.

The new cultural histories, with their collaborative approach, expect to attract new readers. In the French and German cases, the authors undoubtedly benefited from the centrality of these cultures in the world reception of European history. The Polish case is different in this regard due to its specific history: for two centuries, it was empires that spoke for a non-sovereign and at times non-existent Poland. Its own historical and cultural meta-narratives were outside the mainstream narratives of Western Europe at the time when European nationalisms took centre stage. This process of becoming Europe's "Other" – its silent backwater periphery – only intensified during the Cold War, further entrenching a division first established two centuries previously, as Larry Wolff points out in *Inventing Eastern Europe*.[3] After the Iron Curtain was raised, this sweeping notion of Eastern Europe became naturalized for the broader Western audience.

Moreover, local (Polish) traditions and external (European) influences intertwined with exceptional intensity at times, generating eccentric cultural formations such as Polish Sarmatism (seventeenth century) and Romanticism (nineteenth century). Both these formations are still important in contemporary Polish culture even while remaining at odds with their Western counterparts; both are difficult to understand for students grounded in more dominant and better-known European traditions. The reasons for their idiosyncrasies are culturally and historically specific. Sarmatism dominated Polish culture at a time when Poland was still one of Europe's great powers, and its peculiarities vis-à-vis Western Europe were not viewed as cause for an inferiority complex; on the contrary, Sarmatism was a source of pride for Poles.

Polish culture also appears unique when examined in the context of nineteenth-century modernity. Along with the rest of Europe, Poland participated in two processes of modernity: modernism, which emancipated the individual in all spheres of social and creative life, and modernization, with its advances in commercial, scientific, and technological infrastructures. In the case of Poland (and of other suppressed cultures, such as Czech, Greek, Italian, and Irish), however, the relationship between modernism and modernization translated into especially pronounced tensions between traditionalism and innovation. Poland's national culture felt a relentless pressure to resist colonization by sustaining tradition as the unwavering foundation of collective identity, while at the same time responding to the modern imperative to innovate. In other words, it faced an inherently contradictory demand: to hold on to the past while embracing the future. Furthermore, having been partitioned between three empires, Poland underwent three separate and indeed conflicting processes of modernization, all the while remaining on the margins of the partitioning powers, which were not particularly interested in coordinating the modernization of their colonized provinces. As a result, the Polish version of modernity was inconsistent with the hegemonic European model.

Mapping the Volume

Readers would do well not to rush through this book. It does not have to be read in its entirety, nor does it need to be read in sequence. The approach can be random, with the reader acting like a contemporary *flâneur* on a journey that is open to chance, sensitive to detail, and aimed at discovering not the whole of the "city" but its individual fragments, with all that they entail. Alternatively, one could plan their journey through this book more systematically, using its contents pages and introduction as a guide. In this case, the readers' decisions would follow from their interests and needs. There is yet another way to explore the modern and postmodern Polish culture as presented here, namely by means of associations and in line with the proposal put forth by Jorge Luis Borges in "The Garden of Forking Paths." His short story corresponds well with the underlying structure of this book, which makes possible the passage from a text that speaks of ties between Polish interwar prose and reportage, for instance, to one solely dedicated to the latter, and from there to an essay about Polish film, which in turn could lead to a text about a chosen film director. Indeed, to make the most out of this garden, one may have to become lost in it at least once.

This *History* adopts four intertwining frameworks to allow readers different points of entry into their explorations of Polish culture. The first three parts, under the respective headings of Transitions, Strategies, and Transmissions, complicate historical and typological narratives of traditional histories of literature and culture by foregrounding coordinates that have organized Polish cultural imagination for centuries. Part I, "Transitions," engages with the already mentioned paradigms of Sarmatism and Romanticism, whose various replications and contestations speak to their ongoing meta-narrative vitality in Polish culture. Sarmatism, which took root and flourished in the Commonwealth of Both Nations during the sixteenth and seventeenth centuries, had no equivalent among Western European cultures of that time. It impacted the political system, lifestyle, literature, and material culture of the gentry in the Commonwealth until the eighteenth century. With the nineteenth century came Polish Romanticism, which decisively shaped Polish national identity. A slightly belated peer of European Romanticism, it emerged in an already partitioned Poland and acquired its idiosyncratic character particularly after the November Uprising of 1830–1.

These two somewhat clashing paradigms have channelled much of Polish intellectual life, beginning with the self-questionings of the Romantics themselves and continuing throughout the twentieth century. Polish modernism, for example, would undoubtedly have a different face if Witold Gombrowicz (its main international representative today) had not duelled with both Polish Sarmatism and Romanticism. To give a collectively resonant example, the internationally known and often celebrated phenomenon of civil dissent in Poland had its main features modelled by both of these paradigms.[4] Such examples can be multiplied, and their pervasive cultural presence partly explains the urgency of Polish culture's search for equally strong counter-narratives and its repeated attempts to find new ways of inhabiting the realities of Poland's post-1989 cultural space and identity. Thus, contemporary reimaginings of Poland's lost multi-ethnic culture have new multicultural, globalizing, and transnational discourses as their context, while returns to historical moments of monumental loss find, in their most successful incarnations, a common framework for discussing national particularities.

The six essays of Part I are paired to provide twofold reinterpretations of Sarmatism, Romanticism, and Modernism, respectively. Written by the scholars on both sides of the Atlantic, they explore the intellectual history of these paradigms and make opposing claims about their significance, permutations, and influence. They access Polish modern and contemporary culture through its internal tensions, paradoxes, and contradictions, scrutinizing the factors that have delineated its contours over the centuries. The cultural and historical complexities of Sarmatism are re-examined via a political and socio-economic critique in one essay (Jan Sowa), and from a philosophical and cultural perspective in the other (Ewa Thompson), with these two approaches leading their authors to diametrically opposed conclusions. In the first essay devoted to Romanticism, in turn, Stanley Bill analyses the reception and long-term impact of Romanticism in its diverse modes of popular transmission, while Dariusz Skórczewski's discussion utilizes a postcolonial perspective to reassess both well-known and overlooked aspects of the Romantic paradigm over its long duration in Polish intellectual history. Indeed, the comparative potential of all four essays becomes apparent both in their discussions of local specificities within the broad, European cultural context and in their oppositional relations to one another.

The two essays on modernism build an understanding of what modern and postmodern formations mean in the Polish context. Włodzimierz Bolecki argues for the existence of a specific Eastern European modernism and outlines the modalities and historical specificities of its Polish incarnation. He also analyses the continuities and discontinuities of this Eastern European development vis-à-vis its broader European modernist framework. The second essay by Ryszard Nycz proposes a new typology of Polish literature of the twentieth and twenty-first centuries and formulates four general models of literature by adopting the oppositional notions of the elite and the popular as well as the autonomous and the engaged. Both essays provide a strong historical and theoretical backbone for the systematic discussion of individual genres that constitutes Part IV (Genres and Their Discontents) of the volume.

The second framework of "Strategies," presented in Part II, reconfigures Polish culture from another perspective by proposing four distinct modes of its interpretation: canonical, emancipatory, transgressive, and compensatory. These culturally adapted strategies of engaging with dominant cultural norms and practices serve here as interpretative frameworks for addressing overarching questions about Polish culture and its particularities over the past two centuries. Each strategy uses different means, sets different goals, and performs different functions in relation to these leading cultural paradigms. In engaging with these norms and practices as well as with one another, they form conceptual networks that allow the marginal, the excluded, the suppressed, the silenced, and the "forgotten" to assert their individual positions within or against the mainstream. They also reference and build on arguments raised in Part I regarding the Sarmatian, Romantic, and Modernist paradigms, as well as foreshadow issues of gender, ethnicity, language, trauma, and cultural identity that arise throughout the essays of Part IV.

The first – *canonical* – strategy is a clear point of reference for the other three. It validates the norm but also hides the mechanisms of its creation, thus naturalizing it as a norm. Its function is to stabilize cultural practices while serving as a tool for assessing such stability. The *emancipatory* strategy, in turn, is invested in overcoming old norms and replacing them with new ones, positing its function as liberating and socially progressive. It pushes against everything that is seen as restricting the subject's sovereignty. The *compensatory* strategy, by contrast, focuses on the culture's reading of the canonical. Its goal is to therapeutically (mis)read the canon for the sake of the long-term cultural sustenance of its practitioners, however this sustenance is understood. It separates out the canon's otherness – precisely what the *transgressive* approach privileges – in order to build collective and redemptive narratives; it is based on the replication of sameness and is thus repetitive and compulsive. Transgression challenges the boundaries of the norm without disinheriting or destroying it. The *transgressive* strategy sheds light on the laws that constitute the canon and implicates them in what is transgressed. It also seeks out the hidden places, gaps, fissures, and ruptures that allow chaos through, even if only momentarily. In its function, therefore, the transgressive is anarchic and epiphanic.

The four essays in Part II present different approaches to their respective strategies. Thus, Bożena Shallcross's essay on the canonical proposes a concept of the transatlantic canon – namely, the canon of Polish literature existing outside of Poland – and probes the mechanism of its creation in North America through the production of literary translations and histories available in English. Grażyna Borkowska's essay on emancipation chronologically traces the emancipatory gestures and narratives in Polish prose that attest to the insufficiency and limits of the domestic canon. Joanna Niżyńska's essay on compensation reads Polish cultural responses to the twentieth century's historical traumas, particularly the Second World War, and analyses the paradoxical mechanisms of cultural affective compensation whereby the traumatic is reproduced rather than worked through. Finally, focusing on the idea of sacrifice, Tamara Trojanowska's essay on transgression scrutinizes the intersections between what is individual, personal, and intimate and what is culturally and historically scandalous in the context of twentieth-century Polish theatre projects.

The third framework of "Transmissions," presented in Part III, expands the notion of literary and cultural history further still. It responds to one of the challenges facing national literary histories, as identified already in the 1990s by Linda Hutcheon and Mario Valdès, namely the risk of "marginalizing or even excluding the literary creations of ... those working ... in other languages or other cultural traditions."[5] It also underscores the need for a more flexible and integrative concept of literary history than that implied by a focus on a single language, which is often conceived as a synecdoche of a nation: besides accounting for the obvious fact that people can and often do participate in several language communities at once, it addresses a point of particular significance to Polish studies abroad – that texts as well as ideas and images pass from one language to another through the medium of translation.

The five essays that constitute this part of the volume focus on the multilingual and multi-ethnic fabric of Polish culture, on the one hand, and on cultural transmissions on the other, all the while highlighting their transatlantic perspective. Rafał Moczkodan's essay outlines the formative developments of exilic and diasporic Polish literature and culture. It discusses the most significant waves of exiles and emigrants during the last century, contextualizes their most important contributions to Polish domestic culture as well as to its internationalization, and outlines the impact of émigré cultural institutions on intellectual life in Poland and abroad. Beth Holmgren's discussion invites us to the Warsaw interwar cabaret and tells the exciting story of the extraordinarily fertile Polish-Jewish artistic collaboration. It focuses on Jewish writers of the cabaret songs, some of whom also happened to be exquisite poets, who wrote in Polish while self-consciously popularizing a notion of hybrid Polish-Jewish identity. The essay by Marta Skwara is devoted to the multilingual legacies of Polish culture and their rich history of violent disruptions, recent revivals, and transatlantic transmissions. It undercuts the notion of the homogeneity of Polish literature by charting the history of Poland's multilingual writings, starting with universal Latin, through modern bi- and multi-lingual writers, and ending with the transnational literature of the twenty-first century. The final two essays in Part III explore the multilingual aspects of Polish literature by focusing on translation. Tomasz Bilczewski outlines a history of translation as a model of transcultural osmosis in Polish culture, both domestic and exilic, and theorizes it in the context of historically configured Comparative Studies. Bill Johnston's discussion concerns the relationship between literary translation and cultural institutions, on the one hand, and cultural reception on the other. The questions posed by both authors probe the ways in which translation promotes a certain view of Central/Eastern European identity as well as the kind of "canon" it constructs for a Western audience.

The final part of the volume, "Genres and Their Discontents," recognizes that acts of interpretation are most often governed by generic conventions and assumptions. It is also fully aware, however, that the debate about the problematic status, if not the breakdown, of genres in literary histories is extensive and ongoing. Postmodernist criticism has undermined these assumptions many times while simultaneously recognizing that "it is the paradox of postmodern genre that the more radical the dissolution of traditional generic boundaries, the more important the concept of genericity becomes."[6] Using genres as a governing principle can restrict acts of interpretation, and the category of genre can determine the type of cultural production deemed worthy of institutional support. Nevertheless, building on a certain normative stability of aesthetic determinants and on genres' translatability into different cultural contexts has its benefits, particularly when bringing new literatures into dominant (in this case Western, Anglo-American, academic) contexts. It provides a stable point of reference for the essays that present alternative frameworks for discussing literature and culture in previous parts of the volume.

A historical account of literature must take into account the system of genre elements characteristic of a given time – its basic categories and diagnoses. In his memorable text about "blurred genres," Clifford Geertz drew in particular on the history of the modern European novel. Nevertheless, it would be a mistake to conclude that it was the novel, thanks to the achievements of writers such as Flaubert, Proust, Dostoyevsky, and Conrad, that completely deregulated the genre system.[7] The situation was, and still is, somewhat different. In Europe, genres were the fundamental orientation system for literary histories for most of the twentieth century. To use Levi-Strauss's terms, this system was reminiscent of kinship in its ordering of relations. It allowed readers to situate a given work in a diachronic perspective – for instance, by relating twentieth-century historical prose to the nineteenth-century historical novel. It also permitted a synchronic view of a specific text at a given moment of literature's development – for example, by comparing different approaches to the novel of manners. Differently put, the genre system made legible Harold Bloom's "anxiety of influence" and aided the discovery of tropes that pointed to a work's "murdered fathers" (the influential predecessors that its author was trying to surpass) and its "enemy brothers" (other artists who employed similar literary techniques).[8]

Genre typology has also played a significant role in the reception of Polish culture abroad and has become the most often encountered vehicle of Polish cultural identity. "Polish school of poetry," "Polish film school," and "Polish school of reportage" are all based on genre identification and go hand in hand with genre-dominated, often-taught books such as Czesław Miłosz's *Polish Postwar Poetry* (1965), Jan Kott's *Four Decades of Polish Essay* (1990), and the more recent collections *The Eagle and the Crow: Modern Polish Short Stories* (1996) and *Polish Cinema Now! Focus on Contemporary Polish Cinema* (2010).[9]

This volume builds on this familiar mode of reception and problematizes it by expanding the range of genres to include the essay (Michał Paweł Markowski), diary (Paweł Rodak), reportage (Zygmunt Ziątek), literary theory (Katarzyna Kasztenna), film (Elżbieta Ostrowska), mass media (Edwin Bendyk), popular culture (Marek Krajewski), and the graphic novel (Ewa Stańczyk) in addition to the more traditional categories of poetry (Piotr Śliwiński), prose (Jerzy Jarzębski; Przemysław Czapliński), and drama (Ewa Guderian-Czaplińska; Jerzy Kopciński). With such expansion comes a broadening of the contexts in which these genres are discussed. The reception of Polish literature abroad is one such context, highlighting the often unexpected success of genres that, until recently, received little institutionalized attention in Poland. This is the case with both essay and reportage, which hold a prominent place in this book.

This examination of genres also embraces issues that elsewhere might be addressed in separate thematic entries, such as otherness, ethnic minorities, and historical revisionism. In the Polish context these issues have often been tied to genre. For example, since 1989, prose has been the primary locus of the search for the lost heterogeneity of the Polish provinces (the so-called literature of small homelands), of the revival of interest in the multi-ethnic past of Poland's cities, and of the post-memorial reworking of collective identities. At the beginning of the twenty-first century, in turn, we observe an outburst of post-Holocaust works, mainly in film and drama. All of these issues have been present in Polish literature and culture for decades, recently reaching self-aware crystallizations in genre-specific waves.

The short essays about individual artists included in Part IV offer examples of concrete Polish realizations of different genres. They can also be read, however, in different configurations as sites of possible comparisons and extrapolations; some of these create expected connections, while others reveal surprising links. For instance, the authors of the texts on Bruno Schulz (Karen Underhill), Bolesław Leśmian (Benjamin Paloff), and Julian Przyboś (Bogdana Carpenter) foreground modernist visions of creation and representation that problematize the relationship between art, language, and reality. The essay on Schulz also resonates with Milija Gluhovic's essay on the theatre of Tadeusz Kantor and Artur Grabowski's on that of Sławomir Mrożek, with a common ground established by the pronounced cultural locality of these artists' works, all of which emerge from the Central European imaginaries of Galicia. The focus on the condensed metaphysical dimension that comes up in the articles on Schulz and Leśmian is also at play in the essays of Kazimierz Braun on Juliusz Osterwa and of Allen J. Kuharski on Jerzy Grotowski, both of which discuss these artists' new concepts of theatre, and in Tadeusz Sobolewski's treatment of Krzysztof Kieślowski's films; taken together, all of these essays signal the continued importance of metaphysics in Polish culture.

Many contributors to this volume relate the subjects of their essays to the grand narrative of modernist metaphysics; for others, the national grand narratives (for instance, Romanticism) are the main points of reference. Such is the case in the essays on theatre director Leon Schiller (Ewa Guderian-Czaplińska), literary critic and novelist Karol Irzykowski (Kris van Heuckelom), film director Andrzej Wajda (Janina Falkowska), and novelist, playwright, and essayist Witold Gombrowicz (George Gasyna). Discussions of the novels of Stanisław Lem (Elżbieta Foeller-Pituch), the essay work of Jolanta Brach-Czaina (Eliza Szybowicz), Leszek Kołakowski (Maciej Michalski), and Czesław Miłosz (Marek Zaleski), and the reportage of Melchior Wańkowicz (Beata Nowacka), all provide occasions to explore the borders of literature and philosophy, as well as the hybridity and fluidity of genres. They can also be read through a different lens, for example in terms of the complexities of reception. One can add Ewa Mazierska's interpretation of Jerzy Skolimowski's films to this context for its engagement with the paradoxical dynamics of international and domestic reception. The essay on Brach-Czaina also resonates with Ursula Phillips' text on Zofia Nałkowska's novels, Katarzyna Taras' assessment of films by Wojciech Jerzy Has, and Krystyna Iłłakowicz's look at the film work of Dorota Kędzierzawska. In their specific ways, all of these essays address artists' commitment to existential and psychological investigations of often neglected subjects and experiences, whether they pertain to the aging body, sexuality, substance abuse, or the allusive emotions of children.

Daniel Gerould's discussions of Stanisław Ignacy Witkiewicz (Witkacy) and Stanisława Przybyszewska bring historiosophy into the picture. Paying careful attention to their artistic sensibilities, Gerould views revolutions as the kernel of their *Weltanschauung.* Historiosophy is a common framework for the discussion of many other artists in this volume, including Miłosz, Lem, Kantor, Leopold Buczkowski (Sławomir Buryła), and Tadeusz Różewicz (Andrzej Skrendo; Halina Filipowicz). Różewicz's investment in resuscitating the allegiance between language and experience is echoed in Artur Płaczkiewicz's reading of Miron Białoszewski's work and Andrea Lanoux's discussion of Anna Świrszczyńska, with both essays emphasizing the given poet's commitment to the deeply personal revalidation of the ordinary and the everyday. They point Polish literature away from grand narratives towards the underexplored territories of the individual, bodily experience of everyday reality (e.g., gender, aging) and the colloquial registers of language. These essays could just as well accompany the reader's experience of the already mentioned texts on Brach-Czaina and Kędzierzawska. Just as all of these artists discover a new agent in the overlooked and marginalized subject, the works of Jarosław Iwaszkiewicz (German Ritz), Olga Tokarczuk (Bożena Karwowska), Andrzej Stasiuk (Magdalena Marszałek), and Mariusz Szczygieł (Aleksander Kaczorowski and Przemysław Czapliński) are discussed in the context of new agency in the textual understanding of space. Such grouping points not only to their common framework of geopoetics but also to their generational trajectory from the historically rooted spatial imaginarium of Iwaszkiewicz to the mythical and imaginary explorations of the others.

As with every history of literature and culture in book form, this volume presents a snapshot of Polish culture at a particular moment in time. As such, it does not discuss many important forms of cultural production, for instance music, visual arts, and dance. Their significance in the history of Polish culture notwithstanding, for logistical reasons the scope of this volume is limited to the culture of the word. While other configurations of Polish literature and culture are easily conceivable, this volume's conceptualization emerged in response to the variety of needs encountered by its editors and contributors in their capacity as scholars and teachers. We trust that our readers will find it inspirational as they explore their own interests and forge new paths of thinking about Polish culture.

Tamara Trojanowska, Joanna Niżyńska,
and Przemysław Czapliński

NOTES

1 It is not surprising that Miłosz's history has become the most popular of the three. After all, he was a poet and essayist with an appealing writing style rather than a philologist bound to the prescriptive model of literary history, such as had taken root in nineteenth-century German academia and deeply impacted Polish scholarship.

2 Hollier, *A New History of French Literature*, xxi.

3 Wolff, *Inventing Eastern Europe*, 1–16.

4 Cf. Walicki, "The Three Traditions."

5 Hutcheon and Valdès, "Rethinking Literary History – Comparatively," 3–4.

6 Perloff, ed., *Postmodern Genres*, 4.

7 Geertz, "Blurred Genres," 165–79.

8 See Bloom, *Anxiety of Influence*, xi–xlvii.

9 Miłosz, *Polish Postwar Poetry*; Kott, *Four Decades of Polish Essay*; Halikowska and Hyde, eds., *The Eagle and the Crow*; Werner, ed., *Polish Cinema Now!*.

WORKS CITED

Bloom, Harold. *Anxiety of Influence. A Theory of Poetry*. Oxford: Oxford University Press, 1997.

Geertz, Clifford. "Blurred Genres. The Refiguration of Social Thought." *American Scholar* 49, no. 2 (Spring 1980): 165–79.

Halikowska, Teresa, and George Hyde, eds. *The Eagle and the Crow: Modern Polish Short Stories*. London and New York: Serpent's Tail, 1996.

Hollier, Denis, with R. Howard Bloch et al. *A New History of French Literature*. Cambridge, MA: Harvard University Press, 1989.

Hutcheon, Linda, and Mario Valdès. "Rethinking Literary History – Comparatively." ACLS Occasional Paper 27 (1994).

Kott, Jan. *Four Decades of Polish Essays*. Evanston: Northwestern University Press, 1990.

Miłosz, Czesław. *Polish Postwar Poetry*. Garden City: Doubleday, 1965; 3rd ed., Berkeley: University of California Press, 1983.

Perloff, Marjorie, ed. *Postmodern Genres*. Norman: University of Oklahoma Press, 1989.

Walicki, Andrzej. "The Three Traditions in Polish Patriotism and Their Contemporary Relevance." In *Polish Paradoxes*. Edited by Stanisław Gomułka and Anthony Polonsky. 21–40. London and New York: Routledge, 1990.

Werner, Mateusz, ed. *Polish Cinema Now! Focus on Contemporary Polish Cinema*. London: John Libbey; Warsaw: Adam Mickiewicz Institute, 2010.

Wolff, Larry. *Inventing Eastern Europe: The Map of Civilization on the Mind of the Enlightenment*. Stanford: Stanford University Press, 1994.

PART I

Transitions

Sarmatism, or the Secrets of Polish Essentialism

Sarmatism was a pre-modern Polish cultural episteme built on the belief that at the centre of human endeavours reside metaphysical realities rather than the desire for power, and that all human concerns should play second fiddle to those realities. This belief is central to Christianity, and it was the Christian articulation of it that provided the stimulus for Sarmatian creativity. More specifically, it was the Thomistic view of reality, which was critical of nominalism and its modern transformations, that proved most appealing. While Sarmatism is deeply rooted in metaphysics, its cultural manifestations are exuberantly physical and sensual, easily absorbing both Western European and Oriental elements. In this respect it is a distinctly Catholic phenomenon, one that eschews Calvinist suspicion of worldly pleasures. Sarmatism is grounded in the idea of republicanism and is based on the virtue of the republic's citizens. Virtue and liberty are its key political and social concepts, which links it to Athenian democracy and Roman republicanism. Its historical cousins include the American Southern Agrarianism of the 1930s and the American Republic itself as conceived by the Founding Fathers.[1]

Ever since the fall of the Polish state in 1795, Sarmatism has been criticized by Polish and foreign critics. They have relentlessly condemned the deficient education system and lack of interest in public affairs that Sarmatism supposedly fostered, but without (one suspects) reading many of the books they condemn, while Sarmatism's political traditions have been excoriated for failing to defend Poland from its neighbours. Yet Sarmatian texts, of which there are a multitude, challenge one of Polish history's *idées recues*: that Sarmatian culture rejected learning in favour of mindless religiosity and a monotonous country existence punctuated by pointless duels. Sarmatism bequeathed to Polish culture a tremendous amount of symbolic capital, in Pierre Bourdieu's sense of the word. Writers from Adam Mickiewicz through Henryk Sienkiewicz to Witold Gombrowicz borrowed copiously from its literary riches. Its legacy also includes a language of great vitality, bursting with confidence that its users belong to a strong and dynamic culture.

Sarmatism is regarded by many as Poland's foundational myth, comparable to the Celtic myths of the Irish, the Nibelungen myths of the Germans, and the King Arthur myths of the English. Krzysztof Koehler puts it bluntly: "Owing to historical circumstances, Sarmatism has become the foundational and unchallenged formula of Polish national identity."[2] From this perspective, Czesław Miłosz was wrong when, in "Traktat poetycki" (Treatise on Poetry, 1957), he sought the roots of modern Poland in Kraków's coffee houses that imitated the Viennese cafés. These were but toys of the Polish intelligentsia. The Polish cultural paradigm that influenced all strata of society, from the educated and wealthy to impoverished peasants, had little to do with the genteel atmosphere of fin-de-siècle coffee houses and much to do with the down-to-earth posture of

Sarmatism. This influence has been unevenly distributed, however: different aspects of Sarmatism penetrated diverse strata of society in dissimilar ways.

> During the Renaissance and the Baroque periods, the subject of Polish national consciousness was the elite, understood as the noble *natio Polonorum*, rather than all of the people living within the Polish state. One should follow the same principle when speaking of the nation of Europe: that nation was its intelligentsia. Initially, it was ecclesiastic – *clerici* – and formed the foundations and edifice of the Church, teaching the people of the European continent a sense of kinship, of the unity of earthly and eternal goals, as well as language and insights into their shared past. The next formation of the European nation – *natio Europaea* – was made up of the humanists, the secular intelligentsia, the founders and citizens of *Reipublicae litterarum*.
>
> – Borowski, *Powrót Europy*, 13–14

As is often the case with periodization, only approximate dates can be provided for the beginning and end of Sarmatian culture. The Nestor of Polish cultural history, Alexander Brückner, states that the cultural golden age of the "republic of nobles" was between 1548 and 1648,[3] while the subsequent century spelled its gradual decline. He points out that the number of schools and printing houses decreased in the second half of the seventeenth century and continued to do so in the eighteenth. In Brückner's view, and in the view of most Polish scholars, the second part of the seventeenth century marked the beginning of a corrosion that accelerated in the eighteenth. The civil war in Polish-held Ukraine (1648–54) and the Swedish invasion (1655–60) marked the beginning of the Polish "time of troubles." Notwithstanding, great works of literature were written in the second half of the seventeenth century, and the most Sarmatian of Polish kings, Jan III Sobieski, led the Polish army to victory at Vienna in 1683. The cultural world view that compelled Poles to come to the aid of Austrians attacked by the Ottomans peaked at about the same time. After the victory, Sobieski's letter to Pope Innocent XI began with the words "Venimus, vidimus, Deus vicit."[4] This famous phrase summarizes much of what Sarmatism is about. It is humble (*Deus vicit*) yet proud in its terseness (*Venimus, vidimus*). It contains implicit praise of military valour: without it, Sarmatian Poland would not have survived a single generation. Finally, King Sobieski's announcement takes for granted that Christian countries should help one another. One could claim that this sense of loyalty and generosity was deleterious to the political health of Sarmatian Poland: within a century after the Ottoman Turks who besieged Vienna were defeated by armies under the Polish king's command, Austria participated in the first partition of Poland. One can therefore assign two centuries to cultural Sarmatism, from the mid-sixteenth to the mid-eighteenth, or – using literature as a framework – from the serenity of Jan Kochanowski (1530–84) and mysticism of Mikołaj Sęp-Szarzyński (1550–81) to the good-natured and matter-of-fact eloquence of Jędrzej Kitowicz (1727–1804). In between stands the seventeenth century, in which the characteristics of Sarmatism manifested themselves with particular intensity.

The tacit agreement about the centrality of metaphysics that underpins Sarmatism stemmed from the largely Catholic mores and manners of those who called themselves

"Sarmates." They were members of the Polish nobility (both gentry and aristocracy) with full civil, political, and religious rights, and they constituted about 10 per cent of the country's population – a substantial figure relative to other European countries at that time. Polish nobles used the words "Sarmatia" and "Sarmatian" interchangeably with "Poland" and Polish."

The grounding in the idea of natural law (as opposed to the increasingly nominalistic trends in European philosophy during that period and all the way into modernity) brought about, when viewed from a postmodern philosophical stance, Sarmatism's seemingly contradictory features. It was oriented towards metaphysics, but it also proclaimed the legitimacy of worldly pleasures, from the enjoyment of food, drink, and other gratifications of the flesh, to leisurely country living and *dolce far niente.* Catholic Sarmates viewed themselves as the bulwark of Latin Christianity, yet they tolerated – and indeed accepted into their ranks – representatives of Protestant churches (Calvinist and Arian).[5] In fact, a good part of the Polish nobility turned Protestant at the height of the Reformation, only to change their minds within a couple of generations and return to Catholicism.[6] Sarmatian nobles engaged in public debates concerning the superiority of their respective denominations, a situation rare in Western Europe, which in the sixteenth and seventeenth centuries found itself convulsed by religious wars.[7] These disputes did not end with one of the parties sentenced to be burned at the stake: as Janusz Tazbir rightly notes, Poland was a country "without stakes,"[8] although the level of verbal violence during the debates was sometimes considerable[9] and religious tolerance waned as the country's ability to fend off its enemies diminished. Polish Jews enjoyed self-government and participated actively in economic life of the country, to the point of gaining a virtual monopoly on foreign trade.[10] Their demographic virility was such that they grew in numbers several times faster than the Christians. Sarmatian mores were characterized by both pride and humility: next to the "sarmatization of heaven" (a certain Father Dębołęcki argued that in Paradise they spoke Polish),[11] one senses in the writings of the period a deep awareness of the triviality of all human hierarchies and divisions. The Sarmates saw the world in hierarchical terms in accordance with Christian doctrine, but they also proclaimed equality among members of the "noble nation" regardless of their material status and position. One of the favourite proverbs of the gentry nation was "A rural nobleman on his plot of land is equal to the provincial governor." As Norman Davies points out, the Sarmatian way of living served many generations of Polish gentry well. It seemed to them far superior to what was going on in Muscovy, the Ottoman Empire, or the neighbouring Czech lands,[12] all examples of autocracies.

The Sarmatian space (households, homes, property, fatherland) was not hierarchically organized, and in this it differed from the German and Russian spaces of the period. It was divided into a number of self-governing spaces in which individual families went about their lives limited only by God's commandments and the country's laws. The tsar's decree or the official's whim could not rearrange them from the outside, so to speak; for this to happen, the inhabitants themselves had to give consent.[13] Unfriendly neighbours and commentators routinely equated this lack of "centralization of imagination" with lack of organization. While Poland's neighbours rapidly centralized, thus bestowing power on a single individual who stood above the law, Poland continued to be ruled through the dietines, which gathered in individual voivodships, where they selected parliamentarians to travel to Warsaw to debate and vote in the Sejm. This was a slow and cumbersome process that made it difficult if not impossible to pass appropriate laws on time, especially for new taxes. This last problem was aggravated by excessive attention paid to the minority vote – that is to say, by the *liberum veto.*

For the educated segment of Polish society, Sarmatian Poland provided an opportunity to savour personal and political liberty to a degree unmatched anywhere else in Europe at that time. Indeed, the centrepiece of the "gentry nation's" social doctrine was the idea that liberty was to be cherished more than any other privilege. As Andrzej Walicki has stated, liberty trumped ethnic or religious affiliations in matters political and social.[14] Anna Grześkowiak-Krwawicz puts it this way:

> Starting already in the 16th century, the concept of freedom, love for freedom, concern for preserving freedom, and a constant fear of losing freedom were permanent elements not just of political discussion, but nearly every public statement made in the Republic of the Two Nations. Freedom was perhaps the most frequently appearing catchword in political treatises and propaganda pamphlets, in addresses to the Sejm, *sejmiki,* and courts, in sermons and laudations, where it featured as the supreme value, the most cherished treasure of the Poles.[15]

Liberty was understood in a modern way, as the right of citizens to participate in decisions that concerned the polity as well as the right to one's own pursuits in life. The Polish gentry's motto was the same as the one adopted by the US state of New Hampshire in 1945: "Live free or die." Early-twentieth-century Southern Agrarianism, by the way, has much in common with Sarmatism in its vision of a free citizenry. Sarmatism was born among and practised by the privileged strata of society.[16] Like the Southern Agrarians, Sarmates valued and celebrated the traditional community. A decentralized society was their ideal. The Polish noble could justifiably boast that he was freer than any other noble in Europe. His liberty began with the *neminem captivabimus nisi iure victum* ("we will not arrest anyone without a court verdict") privilege granted by the first Jagiellonian monarch Władysław in 1430. It guaranteed that the king would neither imprison nor punish a nobleman without a court order. (A modern version of the *neminem captivabimus* exists in all modern democratic states. In the United States, the police are not allowed to enter anyone's house without a court order.) This privilege (promptly revoked by the three partitioning powers in 1795) was the most important guarantor of the citizens' liberty, and it stood in direct opposition to the autocratic visions of the state that Russia and Prussia represented. Furthermore, it was taken for granted that the right to liberty stems from natural law rather than originating in a social contract. In 1505 the Sejm adopted the law known in Poland as *nihil novi nisi commune consensu* ("nothing new without common consent"), or the rule that no new taxes or other new obligations could be imposed on the nobility without explicit consent of the Sejm. In 1573 a formal agreement between the nobility and the king (the so-called Henrician Articles) reiterated the electability of kings and the king's obligation to convene the Sejm at least once every two years. Taxation, general mobilization, and declarations of war and of peace were all prerogatives of the Sejm.

Grześkowiak-Krwawicz's book *Queen Liberty* analyses the subtle changes of meaning that consecutive generations of Polish Sarmates assigned to the word *wolność*, which in Polish means both *liberty* and *freedom*. After analysing texts from the Sarmatian period, she points out that in some situations *wolność* was most often understood as the individual's freedom to do what seemed most personally advantageous, which amounted to a libertarian understanding of the term; whereas at other times it was understood in the classically republican way, as "freedom to make decisions concerning the state"[17] under laws that imparted the right shape to freedom. She notes that "significantly earlier than other European countries, the Poles shifted their notion of sovereignty away from institutions such as the monarch and parliament, to the nation itself (albeit only the noble nation)."[18] The significance of this modern definition of nation cannot be overemphasized. Because of it, Ernst Kantorowicz's reflections on "the king's two bodies" do not apply to Poland: here the king played the role of a modern president instead of partaking of the mystical attributes that the medieval understanding of succession to the throne bestowed on monarchs in other countries.[19] As Grześkowiak-Krwawicz states, "distrust of the monarch was one of the most enduring elements of the Polish perception of the state."[20] The Polish state was not dependent on the existence of the king's body, be it physical or symbolic, because each citizen was a fragment of that state. Sarmatian Poles were aware that freedom occupies "a narrow ridge wedged between the precipice of despotism on one side and the chaos of anarchy on the other."[21] After the Polish state fell, however, historians saw only disorder and chaos in a society that had vested the concept of the nation in its citizenry and that had considered individual liberty rather than state power the principal objective of social life. With the condemnation of Sarmatism as a political system came denigration of the cultural achievements of the country's intellectuals, who had been humiliated by the loss of statehood.

The crowning ornament of Sarmatian liberty was the *liberum veto*, a legal device that allowed a single deputy to veto a decision of the entire Sejm. Conceived as a way of protecting minorities from tyranny of the majority, it became a tool of selfish interests and a means for foreign powers to influence the legislative process. It was meant to safeguard the principle of equal participation of all representatives of the Polish–Lithuanian Commonwealth, but instead contributed to its demise. The idea behind the *liberum veto* was that the laws that were passed should satisfy everyone; in this way, minority resentment would be avoided. One seventeenth-century political writer argued in favour of *liberum veto* for still another reason: it allowed a few wise persons in the Sejm to annul the dictatorship of a reckless majority.[22]

Halfway through the Sarmatian period, the political abuses of *liberum veto* and of other gentry privileges increased, while statesmanship and readiness to compromise declined. *Liberum veto* allowed a single voice of dissent to derail important bills, such as those that raised taxes. It thus became a perfect tool for neighbouring countries bent on increasing their influence in Poland to break up Sejms by bribing deputies. During the reign of the Wettins (1698–1763), only five out of thirty-three Sejm sessions passed any legislation at all. Under Augustus III (r. 1733–63), only one Sejm was not annulled by *liberum veto* or other legal procedures.[23] Also important to note here is the lack of statesmanship among the aristocracy (as opposed to the petty nobility), who came close to turning the Polish state into a federation of territories ruled by individual aristocrats, rather than a unitary kingdom.[24] Plenty of individuals proposed various remedies to strengthen the Polish state, but Poland's geographical position between two energetic imperial powers required more than the citizens were able or willing to deliver. Prussia and Russia were highly centralized states, besides being armed with aggressive political philosophies that discounted personal liberty and represented the opposite of the "live and let live" attitude of the Polish gentry. An inability to handle ethnic conflicts within the state also contributed to Poland's decline. Sarmatian Poland eventually yielded to military conquest and to the narration imposed by the victors. As a consequence, its image became a caricature of reality.

Even though the practice was not always consistent with the ideal, the very fact that the country's laws proclaimed political, religious, and civil liberties and considered those liberties central to a healthy society was a remarkable achievement of noble democracy. Already in the sixteenth century, Poles understood that individuals must be able to decide their own fate as well as the direction the state should take; without this, all other advantages of a good life – wealth, security, prestige – would be of little value. The rights that Polish nobles enjoyed precluded the appearance of authoritarian monarchy in Poland and ensured that the king would depend on communal consent. All of this makes Polish Sarmatism stand out among state ideologies prevalent in Europe at that time; it also contributes greatly to the tone of self-assurance that is so prominent in Sarmatian literature.

It bears repeating that the foundation of Polish liberties was the law. All of the privileges enjoyed by the gentry nation had been acquired through negotiations with the king; none had been obtained by violence. The Poles declared that "where there is law, there is liberty."[25] For the laws to be observed, however, virtue had to be taught and practised: hence the abundance of parenetic literature in Sarmatian Poland. Poems, biographies, and treatises ceaselessly repeated that virtue was necessary if the state was to function properly. Jan Kochanowski's "Wykład cnoty" (Treatise on Virtue and Friendship) thus instructed the reader:

> Two things ennoble man: his habits and his mind. The habits come from virtues, and a good mind comes from learning. Both are important to have. But if you can acquire only one of them, take virtue over intelligence; for intelligence without virtue is like a sword held by a madman, whereas virtue, even deprived of intelligence, is useful and praiseworthy.[26]

Kochanowski goes on to explain what it means to give prudently yet lovingly, as well as to consider the nature of friendship. His beautifully worded essay is a model of parenetic writing. His treatise was followed by Andrzej Radawiecki's *Prawy szlachcic* (The Righteous Nobleman, 1614) and Wacław Kunicki's *Obraz szlachcica polskiego* (The Image of the Polish Nobleman, 1615). Both present behavioural models for the nobility. It is worth noting that in matters pertaining to religion, the parenetic authors condemn the act of betrayal of one's faith rather than declaring Catholicism to be the only proper option. Wacław Potocki's poem "Do apostaty" (To the Apostate) tells the story of two Lutheran noblemen sentenced to death for siding with the Swedish king, Gustavus Adolphus, and thus betraying their homeland during his invasion of Poland. A third Lutheran nobleman is apprehended by the Polish king inside a Catholic church. The king asks him how long he has been Catholic, and the nobleman answers, "Since they started hanging Lutherans." The king retorts: "And if they started hanging Catholics tomorrow, you would become a Jew, then a Turk, and then perhaps a pagan. You will do anything to save your skin. Fellow, you actually deserve to be hanged for betraying your religion for personal profit."[27] Here the emphasis is unmistakably placed on fidelity rather than on religious denomination. Potocki's many poems about anger are all parenetic. Here is one that combines common sense with charity:

> I am angry. Who is the guilty party?
> If someone weaker, then I should forgive him,
> Nothing is gained by exerting vengeance on the weak.
> If I do not, I may confirm him in his wrongdoing, which will burden my conscience.

If he is an equal, I should likewise forgive him: it often happens that, like a bee,
A vengeful man places his soul in someone's else wound.
If the offender is greater and stronger than I,
I should forgive myself, and avoid being beaten twice.[28]

Parenesis is but one aspect of the abundant literary production of the period. Sarmatian Poland produced political treatises, dialogues, biographies,[29] memoirs, and essays along with epic poems, songs, sonnets, threnoids, catafalk (funeral) verse, and, last but not least, epigrams on every imaginable subject. Bucolic descriptions of nature and country manors, sometimes spiced with erotic allusions, stand next to majestic poems about warfare. Most of these texts are almost unknown abroad, and this creates a dilemma for an introduction like this one. One inevitably chooses Jan Chryzostom Pasek's *Pamiętniki* (Memoirs, 1690–5) as a subject of commentary, but then the question arises, why not Jędrzej Kitowicz's *Opis obyczajów za panowania Augusta III, 1734–1763* (Description of Social Mores during the Reign of Augustus III, 1771)? Both read well and contain significant information about Polish society. However, the first has been translated into English twice, while the second exists only in the original. Regarding treatises and dialogues, if Stanisław Herakliusz Lubomirski's Platonic dialogue between Artaxes and Evander is foregrounded (*Rozmowy Artaksesa i Ewandra* [Conversations between Artaxes and Evander, 1683]) – Lubomirski's work earned him the nicknames "the Polish Solomon" and "the Polish Tacitus"[30] – then why not Krzysztof Warszewicki's monologue on citizens' freedoms under the Polish political system?[31] And let us not forget Andrzej Maksymilian Fredro and Łukasz Opaliński, two remarkable mid-seventeenth-century theorists. And if Wacław Potocki, why not Wespazjan Kochowski or Samuel Twardowski? The literary wealth of Sarmatian Poland has been explored only superficially in English.

Potocki (1621–96) and Pasek (c. 1636–1701) are perhaps the best known Sarmatian men of letters. Both were warriors, farmers, and writers. Pasek's *Memoirs* is the most frequently read work of the period, partly because Henryk Sienkiewicz (1846–1916), probably the most popular writer of historical fiction in Polish literature, borrowed so copiously from Pasek's vocabulary, syntax, and approach to history, not to mention his unique ability to conjure up three-dimensional men and women who fought, loved, prayed, and died without bitterness.[32] We sometimes forget that the art of narration developed gradually and that it was the nineteenth-century novel that made Europeans routinely capable of expressing the thousands of small details and emotions of life. Those who mastered that art much earlier are exceedingly rare. Pasek is among them. In his account of thirty years of military adventures and country life, he has provided us with an inexhaustible source of factual information about the seventeenth century, while at the same time teaching us how to succinctly express a range of feelings – a range that is not narrower than that of the nineteenth-century novelistic heroes. That he succeeded in charming the reader into following an almost plotless story of one man's life was perhaps the greatest achievement of narrative art in Europe at that time.

A jewel of Sarmatian literature is Potocki's *Transakcja wojny chocimskiej* (The Khotyn War, 1670, published in full only in 1850 and never translated into English), an epic poem in majestic rhymed hexameter that describes Hetman Jan Karol Chodkiewicz's victory over the Ottoman army at the besieged city of Chocim (today Khotyn in Ukraine) in 1621. The battle at Khotyn lasted almost a month, hence the word "war" in the title. Chodkiewicz died during that conflict, and the description of his demise is second to none in epic literature, adding a dimension of tragedy to the victory. Claude Backvis contends that "in *The Khotyn War* human society is depicted as powerfully and richly as in the *Iliad* and the *Odyssey*."[33]

Pride in the nation is evident in this and other texts of the period. Even when they point out the faults of their fellow citizens, these texts are saturated with the belief that Poland is, all in all, the best place to be. "I was born and raised in Poland. / I live in a free country, and I partake of that freedom also," writes Elżbieta Drużbacka (1695–1765), the author of *Punkta dla poprawienia zepsutych obyczajów Polskich, przez pewnego senatora Polskiego do opisania mnie podane* (Pleas for the Improvement of Polish Morals).[34] The self-assurance with which this otherwise undistinguished woman "raises her voice" ("I am proud to raise my voice against actions / of which I do not approve. I shall never praise with a servile pen / The bad habits / Which some people have domesticated in our country / Under this or that guise") indicates that noble women felt free and indeed obligated to instruct those who did not measure up to the standards of virtue expected of nobility.

Confidence in Poland's ability to repel the enemy is reflected in many epic poems written during the Sarmatian period, from the anonymous "Twelve Songs on the Siege of Częstochowa" to Wespazjan Kochowski's *Liryka polskie*.[35] This tone of self-confidence ended with the partitions and has yet to reappear: the most prominent caesura in Polish cultural life came in the year 1795 and with the subsequent failed uprisings to regain liberty.[36]

The most popular literary genre in Sarmatian Poland was the rhymed epigram. These short poems circulated among the gentry nation by the hundreds, both in print and in handwritten or memorized copies. Potocki was the great master of this genre. Here is one of his "tombstone poems" ("nagrobki"– recapitulations of the lives of the deceased). It is dedicated to King Sigismund III (1566–1632):

> When Poles elected their own king they were doing well; but when unwisely they brought one from overseas, immediately they lost two provinces. Hence I propose the following tombstone for Sigismund III: *Here I lie, having lost Curland, Estonia, and the Swedish Crown (I am not even mentioning Muscovy). Here I am turning into dust, having destroyed Poland by generously spilling the blood of Polish soldiers (but who cares, they were not my countrymen) – until I came to the end of my miserable life. May one of my sons turn out better.*[37]

This prose translation does not fully render the poem's gracefulness – and sarcasm – but it does allow for two comments. First, it is a notable example of free speech in the mid-seventeenth century. Indeed, it could be an excerpt from a twenty-first century US election campaign, yet it is a comment about a seventeenth-century European monarch by his subject. Second, Potocki expresses a healthy scepticism about open elections for the title of the King of Poland. He rightly says that a foreign king with royal roots in Sweden may think of the country of his birth first and of Poland second. This is not an example of the xenophobia of which later critics falsely accused the Sarmatian gentry. Remember that Polish open elections differed fundamentally from dynastic arrangements whereby a member of the aristocracy in one country acquired the crown of another, and with it a vested interest in the welfare of the country that now became his. In the Polish open elections the winner had no vested interest in making Poland prosper. (Not surprisingly, it often did not.)

Potocki was the opposite of a prude. In "Spowiedź" (A Confession) a dissatisfied lady is asked by her confessor whether her husband is sufficiently virile. Yes, she says, he shows his virility four or five times a night. "What," exclaims the confessor. "So infrequently? Is he sick?"[38] Potocki wrote dozens of such little rhymed jokes, reminiscent of Chaucer and Rabelais, but he was keenly aware of the difference between his "serious" poems and those that were meant to amuse. In "Na swoje wiersze" (About My Poetry) he compares writing to various culinary creations: some are bitter, some sweet, others sour or tart. They are all good, but they have to be consumed in proper order and served on separate platters.[39]

Potocki wrote about virtually everything that can be experienced in life: spiritual strivings and longings, wars and battles, eating and drinking, communing with nature, visiting neighbours, family, marriage, friends, death, cultivation of the land. His works are reminiscent of a shop where rolls of fabric lie in apparent disorder, the best next to the worst. It is the purchaser's task to sort them out and make a selection according to need and quality. This superabundance signals a certain generosity of spirit, and a lack of interest in playing the role of Poet Laureate or "preparing a face to meet the faces that you meet."[40] Potocki does not write in order to impress; his poems are like the spontaneous songs of a happy person.

Other Sarmatian writers were not as prolific as Potocki, but they shared his confidence that "all is right with the world" on a fundamental level, to use Robert Browning's expression. Their advice is often commonsensical. In Wespazjan Kochowski's epigram about love, we read:

> Whenever you see the winged baby arrive,
> Do not yield to your pride and do not try to combat it.
> This baby is known to conquer crowns and miters, scepter and mace,
> Courage, wisdom, even poverty – yield to it.[41]

In poems like these there is no trace of hypocritical guilt associated with the daily pleasures of life. And for all the seeming anarchy of topics and images, Christian morality is taken seriously. There is quite a bit of concern about the have-nots, especially the smallholders who bore the main burden of taxation in the seventeenth century. Szymon Szymonowic's "Żeńcy" (Reapers), published in *Sielanki* (Pastorals, 1614), expresses deep empathy towards those who do physical labour in the fields. One also observes how surprisingly often these authors reflect on the fate of animals – horses, wolves, birds both wild and domestic. Their views would satisfy today's supporters of PETA. Perhaps most famous in this regard is Pasek's description of a pet otter and her unfortunate demise.

Quite a few poems are calls to arms to defend the country against the Ottomans and, later, the Muscovites. Khotyn is invoked as a symbol of Polish victories over the Turks (later in the century it is replaced by Vienna). Taken together, the seventeenth-century martial poems provide a history lesson; it seems that every generation of petty nobles was called to arms several times in that century, often without being paid because the treasury was empty. Few of the authors were free of material want; most of them were drafted into the army (*pospolite ruszenie*) whenever the need arose. That the Polish Crown was not wealthy is made plain in an episode in Pasek's *Memoirs* where King Jan Casimir frantically searches for the money to pay a faithful soldier. Payments were irregular, and loot was often the only reward, as noted by both Potocki and Pasek. Most of these "warrior texts" call upon God and his saints to help the warriors, and invoke scenes of the harms inflicted by the Turks – not burnt-out manors and raped women, however, but rather burnt-out churches and desecrated Hosts – in order to attract recruits. Around one-third of this literature was written in Latin, the nobles' second language. Some of this poetry has been translated into English directly from Latin – for example, Kazimierz Sarbiewski's volume of sonnets.[42]

What is striking about this huge outpouring of poetry in particular is the ease with which the authors shift from one topic to another, from sadness to joy, oscillating between tragedy and joyful celebration with a distinctly unmodern lack of self-consciousness. Bucolic poems and rhymed plays about country life transition easily to blood-soaked fields of battle; peaceful deaths in bed and horrible deaths on the battlefield are treated with a stoicism befitting a society that routinely has had to fight to defend its borders. The joy of life is present in hundreds of poems celebrating God's world. There is no shortage of bawdy jokes and anecdotes told in verse: such was the entertainment of these farmer-soldiers, who accepted life no matter what it brought. Into descriptions of everyday activities are woven love stories and reports on the election of kings and military campaigns, as well as prayers and invocations to virtue and to Christianity. By the nineteenth century, though, the ease and naturalness with which these topics were addressed together had disappeared. In this regard, postmodernism, with its admittance of new versions of *silvae rerum,* is closer to Sarmatism than to nineteenth- and twentieth-century literary conventions.

Sarmatian Poland possessed a strong sense of community, and its notions about authorship bore little resemblance to modern and postmodern notions of copyright. Poems were copied and recited without regard for authorship – indeed, intellectual property was an empty concept for the literate people of that time. Much of Sarmatian literature was *ad hoc,* written to amuse the family or to be recited at social gatherings. Łukasz Opaliński, a poet, statesman, and political writer, published his text on public ethics titled *De Officiis libri tres* in twenty copies only, meant to be distributed among friends and family.[43] In 1929 a book-length epic poem was discovered in a Gniezno archive, which was written in 1621 by a Polish Silesian and dedicated to the ironworks.[44] The poem testifies not only to the early existence of advanced industries in Poland but also to the fact that Polish was the language of communication in Silesia at that time. The pearl of seventeenth-century literature, Pasek's *Memoirs,* was "discovered" in the late eighteenth century and published only in 1821. Polish seventeenth-century literature can be compared to the chamber music tradition in Germany, where burghers would gather at night to play together without the intention of making a profession out of it.

Few cultural epistemes have worked out an acceptable response to pain, or to the infliction of pain by one human being on another. Physical pain is mentioned in world literature only marginally.[45] Owing to their down-to-earth view of human life, Sarmatian writers take on the subject of pain more often than their counterparts in other parts of Europe. In Pasek's *Memoirs*, the brutality of peasant life is mentioned; indeed, the noble warriors themselves commit what today would be considered war atrocities (slicing open soldiers' stomachs in search of gold ducats). Pasek narrates physical suffering without rejoicing in it, but also without panic or fear for his own life. He is neither angry nor fearful nor scandalized nor approving of cruelty. His attitude is stoic: physical pain is a part of life, and one should narrate it the same way one narrates other events. Threnoids lamenting the death of children were written throughout the seventeenth century (Jan Kochanowski's sixteenth-century *Treny* [Threnoids, 1580] were not an isolated case), but their writers' biographies suggest that family losses did not lead to long-term depression: Sarmatian writers ultimately thought them to be justified.

Krzysztof Koehler has written about another notable characteristic of Sarmatian poetry and credits Ludwik Osiński, a nineteenth-century literary critic, for articulating this unique strength of seventeenth-century Polish verse.[46] Osiński observed that Sarmatian writings show a rare sense of self-sufficiency. In modern times, literary styles tend to be responses to preceding literary styles: they usually defy them and try to be as unlike them as possible. Thus Romanticism reacted to the Classicist mode, which was characterized by strong attention to form rather than to feelings and emotions. Paraphrasing Alasdair MacIntyre, one can say that literary texts usually depend for their modes of argument on contrasts between them and that which they aspire to overcome. Thus, paradoxically, they are derivative, drawing their necessary sustenance from that which they profess to have discarded.[47] They respond to what they are *not,* or to what they do not want to be. Adam Mickiewicz's "Oda do Młodości" (Ode to Youth, 1820), while defiantly claiming a genre that belongs to an earlier epoch in its title, is a manifesto for an approach to poetic form and content that is at odds with the traditional attributes of the ode. It glorifies inexperienced youth rather than sober and wise old age. Thus it throws down a gauntlet at the past – and literary critics have praised it for doing so.

Sarmatian poetry displays none of these dependencies and insecurities. It does not look over its shoulder to see whether it matches up to or surpasses its predecessors. It does not fight with them or compare itself to them. Whether bawdy or religious, whether speaking of love or war, it is self-confident. It is not a response to anything, and it is not an attempt to improve on an earlier literary style. Poems flow out of the author's desire to write rather than from the desire to show his or her superiority over the past or over the audience. This self-assurance manifests itself in characters who accept their place on earth without bitterness or complaint. Modern literature has accustomed us to literary characters who are dissatisfied with the place where they live, the situation they are in, and the present time. Their goal is to leave the present and seek betterment in the future, perhaps in another place. Not so with Sarmatian characters: whether participating in weddings or disasters, whether feeling playful or sad, they seem satisfied with their position in life and do not question God or fate as to why they have been placed here and not somewhere else.

Writers of the Sarmatian period intuitively observed a rule that has been disregarded in modern times: that one should not reach beyond what is one's nature, in line with Saint Paul's admonition "not to be more wise than it behooveth to be wise" (Romans 12:3). The Sarmates seemed to understand that unverifiable social theories conceived by one frail human mind should not be offered to humanity as a panacea for the world's ills. They were the ultimate anti-ideologues. The Sarmates did not believe in ultimate explanations produced by ambitious philosophers whose virtue had not been guaranteed or even tested. They believed in God but not in secular ideologies. Lubomirski in *Conversations between Artax and Evander* praises common sense and moderation and is sceptical of theories aspiring to describe everything that reality contains. He contends that such total explanations are inevitably motivated by "vanity and arrogance"[48] and by implicit contempt for empirical proof. His remarks seem to be a rejoinder to György Lukács's famous opinion that if the facts contradict the theory, "so much the worse for the facts!"[49] I submit that it was the saturation of Polish society with attitudes developed during the Sarmatian period that later made this society so impervious to Soviet Marxism, which tried to inculcate in society theories for which daily life provided no proof.

This brings us back to the aforementioned presence of metaphysics in Sarmatian poetry. In Sarmatian texts, be they Catholic or Protestant, God and his heaven are the background against which human events unfold. Some Sarmatian religious poetry has found its way into the Polish religious consciousness. Many Polish Christmas carols were written in the seventeenth and eighteenth centuries. *Gorzkie żale* – laments on the death of Jesus – are still sung in Polish churches today, and so are poems on the Christian way to begin and end the day. Some of these were authored by the finest poet of the Polish Renaissance, Jan Kochanowski.

Thousands of epigrams, songs, carols, and other poetic genres circulated in the republic of nobles. However, that era's most significant intellectual achievements are to be found in its philosophical, political, and religious dialogues, treatises, and memoirs. These have been neglected largely because of post-Enlightenment prejudice against the deeply religious seventeenth century. Lubomirski and Andrzej Maksymilian Fredro stand out among the seventeenth-century political writers. They compete with several other powerful figures who debated the proper borders of freedom and the pros and cons of various political systems. Besides being writers, Lubomirski and Fredro were prominent in Polish politics: the first was Marshal of the Crown and served as a foreign envoy; the second was a Speaker of the Sejm. Both participated in the defensive war against Sweden, and both were important patrons of the arts. Lubomirski's *magnum opus*, the aforementioned *Conversations between Artax and Evander* (republished in 2011), structured as a lengthy dialogue between two Polish senators, is a treatise on good behaviour, virtue, fortune and vanity, prudence and military valour, rhetoric and the human soul. It is grounded in the conviction that the state in which the two men live has a good foundation – that is to say, it promotes virtue as well as self-development. The two speakers invoke biblical characters and make references to contemporary political events. What strikes one about this dialogue (which is divided into thirteen conversations) is its leisurely tone and pace, as if the speakers had all the time in the world to discuss political issues, as if they were standing in the Athenian *agora* among a group of disciples ready to ask questions and show up the next day as well. It is as if Poland were not in mortal danger of being overrun by the Turks, Tatars, or Muscovites. The dialogue implicitly endorses the view that human beings are rational by nature and inclined to do good (rather than being Hobbesian egoists). The speakers are calm and self-assured: clearly, they both believe in the political system of which they are a part and are happy to be citizens of the Polish state. Lubomirski's *Conversations* is a good example of the Sarmatian vision of the world as a place where human beings are obliged to practise virtue and reflect on the best way to run affairs of state.

One of the most profound Sarmatian authors, though he is seldom read today, was Andrzej Maksymilian Fredro (c. 1620–79). As a conservative Catholic writing largely in Latin and an aristocrat sceptical of ceding to minorities the monopoly on foreign trade,[50] Fredro was disliked by Enlightenment intellectuals, who were eager to blame Sarmatian Poland for the demise of the Polish state. Thus his name was largely scrubbed from textbooks, except as an example of backwardness. The results have been predictable: most Polish children know the title of Andrzej Frycz Modrzewski's work on the improvement of the Polish state, *De Republica emendanda* (1551), yet hardly anyone has heard of Fredro's much more extensive writings on the same topic. His political writings represent attitudes that are at odds with what meets the approval of most of today's political scientists. Fredro does not like democracy, but he also dislikes absolute monarchy. He favours republicanism in its aristocratic form. He is a defender of the *liberum veto*, but his argument in favour of it has little to do with the original intent behind this noble privilege:

protection of minority interests. In Fredro's opinion, *liberum veto* should be used for different purposes. It should allow those who are wise to make the final decisions about affairs of the state. It should safeguard the right of the wise minority to counteract the short-sighted demands of the unwise majority. In other words, Fredro turns the intent of this privilege upside down. His views are somewhat similar to the original (republican) concept of the American polity: he wants the state to be ruled by enlightened aristocrats, and he desires a republic ruled by representatives of the upper class. By "republic" he understands the elective monarchy where the king is subject to the laws of the country instead of being the giver of laws.

Fredro wrote a great deal of parenetic works in Polish, as well as a number of treatises on political matters in Latin. Many of his epigrams have become Polish proverbs: "Virtue rather than a piece of paper nobilitates a man"; "What one fool can destroy often cannot be repaired by a thousand wise men"; "The greatest victory is to conquer oneself."[51] These sayings echo Cicero and Marcus Aurelius – indeed, some are calques from Latin. Nevertheless, the noble republic treated them as their own.

Fredro was also a practical politician, and some of the advice contained in his treatises is comparable to Machiavelli's. In *Scriptorum seu togae et belli notationum fragmenta* (1660),[52] he outlines the reforms that in his view should be introduced in the Polish army. He is aware of the possible consequences of Ruthenian/Ukrainian nationalism (the republic of nobles underestimated it grievously), and his recommendation is that the army consist of Poles rather than members of the Commonwealth's other nationalities. He is mindful that during the Khmelnitsky rebellion many Cossacks deserted the Polish army and joined Khmelnitsky's. Fredro also wrote about the wealth of nations: in his view, Poland's wealth lay in agriculture, which therefore should be favoured by the state. He later expressed a preference for mercantilism. In *Monita Politico-Moralia et Icon Ingenniorum* (1664), he insists that the state should reward private enterprise and inventiveness and that trade should likewise be supported by the state. He calls for the creation of banks and for encouragements to save, and he recommends that the state sponsor the creation of factories and industrial centres. We know from Polish Jewish sources that almost the only institutions in Poland that loaned money at that time were a few Jewish *kahals*;[53] thus Fredro's call for the creation of a Polish banking system was perspicacious – although it went unheeded.

Critiquing Sarmatism

Attempts to discredit Sarmatism as a harmful part of the Polish heritage began, unsurprisingly, during the Enlightenment, when the periodical *Monitor* (1765–85) made Sarmatian culture its favourite "scapegoat," supposedly responsible for all Polish political and social ills, including the incipient loss of sovereignty. For the intelligentsia gathered around the last Polish king, Stanisław Poniatowski, Sarmatism became synonymous with backward religiosity, quarrelsomeness, and a lifestyle unmindful of the common good and dedicated to leisure, entertainment, and personal fulfilment. From Franciszek Zabłocki, who wrote the satirical play *Sarmatism* (1785), through the "progressive" critics of the nineteenth century, to a range of contemporary Marxist historians, Polish and foreign scholars have piled accusations upon the republic of nobles. They contend that the period's political mistakes – the *liberum veto*; the election rather than blood succession of kings, which permitted foreigners to compete for the Polish throne; an inefficient taxation system; reliance on general mobilization rather than on a permanent army; an economic policy called by one historian "fragmentary and devoid of long-term planning"[54] – left the Polish state unable to respond to the dangers of conquest posed by Poland's land-hungry neighbours. To this day, Sarmatism continues to get bad press among the Polish educated classes.

> It was during the Baroque that the Sarmatization and "Europeanization" of Polish literature, particularly of its popular forms, reached a pinnacle. This was the result of the relatively wide-spread popularization of the literary and cultural legacy of the Renaissance, particularly among the gentry and to some extent also the burghers, due mainly to the influence of the schools (Jesuit collegia). Moreover, the Baroque aesthetic shared a lot with Sarmatian culture, which was fairly open to foreign and especially oriental influences, and thus clearly eclectic and prone to eccentricities. It also valued artistic expression and experiment, as well as courageously (if sometimes too fecklessly) emulated classical models. This emulation included not only the postulate to equal but also to rival the classical canon of perfection. Rooted in the culture of rhetoric, it became the universal and dominant component of the Sarmatian attitude to (not only artistic) reality. Here lies one of the sources of Sarmatian "swashbuckling," its disregard for difficulties and its nonchalance toward prevailing aesthetic norms.
>
> – Borowski, *Powrót Europy*, 47–8

These negative assessments, however, confuse politics (including military defeats) with culture. Many critics associate political decline with cultural worthlessness, which is a crudely Marxist assessment. Some Polish scholars treat Sarmatism as largely a political phenomenon, instead of investigating its ability to foster cultural developments. Instead of feeling humbled by the shock of discovery of the seventeenth century – the way T.S. Eliot was humbled by discovery of the English metaphysical poets – critics of the Sarmatian period display a sense of superiority vis-à-vis their subject by dismissing important works because they originate in, or glorify, Sarmatian Poland. This ideological dislike sometimes reaches comic proportions. The Nobel Prize winner Henryk Sienkiewicz, who modelled his bestselling *Trylogia* (Trilogy, 1884–8) on Sarmatian literature, continues to be attacked in post-communist scholarship. Stanisław Brzozowski has referred to him as a "a classic case of Polish unenlightened ignorance" – an assessment echoed in a recent essay in *Gazeta Wyborcza*.[55] Needless to say, the article's author completely fails to bring the culture of Sarmatism back to life and does not even try to make it resonate with contemporary sensibilities.[56]

While the "decentralization of sovereignty"[57] that Sarmatian Poland represented did not work, the oft-expressed accusations of Polish political anarchy overemphasize the shortcomings of the Polish aristocracy (as distinct from the "noble nation"), while underemphasizing the activities of the neighbouring absolute monarchies. If the impecunious petty nobility had not been bribed by foreign powers to block consensus in the Sejm, the Polish system might have continued long enough for the prudent and the patriotic to carry out necessary reforms. Major political changes were indeed finally voted in 1791; however, a coordinated military attack by Russia and Prussia blocked implementation of those reforms, and the second partition of Poland followed. Thus the noble nation can be accused of naivety more than of anything else. It is fair to say that the Polish political system had been designed for an environment in which states were friendly towards one another and in which each nation-state was able to handle its own internal affairs without interference from neighbours. In other words, the nobility's golden liberty presupposed a utopian world that was the opposite of what actually existed. Granted, these were political faults, but they were of a different nature than those imputed to the conquered by the conquerors. It seems that in spite of assurances to the contrary, the main grievance against Sarmatism was that it did not win. In the strong competition for political power, economic advantage, and territory in seventeenth- and eighteenth-century Europe, Sarmatism, with its lack of prudence and its live-and-let-live philosophy, was bound to lose, like a chess player who does not think enough moves in advance. The Sarmatian nobility saw themselves as living according to God's commandments, more or less, and viewed the political disasters of 1772, 1793, and 1795 as the fault of their conspiratorial neighbours.

Sarmatian Poland has been accused of xenophobia. Janusz Tazbir expands on this in *Sarmaci i świat* (Sarmatians and the World).[58] But how can a country that invites foreigners to run for the office of King of Poland be considered xenophobic? The law allowing any nobleman of any nationality to compete for the highest position in the state had implications that challenge such facile critique. Early on, Jędrzej Kitowicz's *Description of Social Mores during the Reign of Augustus III* lists religious denominations and nationalities within the Polish Kingdom in a tone that quashes the notion of discrimination. In chapter 1, titled "About Confessions in Poland under Augustus III," Kitowicz states:

> The prevailing confession is Roman Catholicism, second in numbers is Judaism, third, the Karaim … fourth, Lutheranism … fifth, Calvinism … sixth, Islam … seventh, Greek Orthodox … eighth, Old Believers … ninth, Quakers … tenth, Freemasons … eleventh, Frankists … twelfth, Deists (Unitarians).[59]

That Sarmatism absorbed a number of Oriental features indicates an openness to other nations. The self-confidence that the gentry nation abundantly possessed explains the ease with which it welcomed the trappings of other cultures. It has been noted that the curved Polish sabre resembles Turkish weapons[60] and that some items of clothing (the indoor coat, or *kontusz*) and home decor (a fondness for carpets and kilims) are similar to Turkish ones (although some say that the *kontusz* was modelled on the Roman toga).[61] Scholars in Poland have long delved into the xenophobia of their ancestors, unlike those of many other nations, who have shown little interest in uncovering prejudice against foreigners in the histories of their respective countries.

But the label of xenophobia, once pasted on, stuck to the Poles. Catherine the Great's correspondent and protégé Voltaire had never been to Poland, yet he wrote contemptuously about its stubborn adherence to Catholicism, the oppression of non-Catholics there, its enslavement of peoples, and its lawless anarchy.[62] Voltaire was widely read in eighteenth-century Europe, and his fantasies about Poland congealed into the image held of that country by the enlightened. Voltaire and Diderot, both of whom received financial support from Catherine, used their popularity and prestige to discredit the vulnerable Polish Commonwealth and to proclaim the right of the Russian autocrats to impose order on the unruly Poles. And there were other critical voices to which Poland, busy with defensive wars, was ill-positioned to respond. A Scottish traveller and poet, John Barclay, stated in *Icon animorum* (1614) that Poland was "an abyss for kings, heaven for the nobility, purgatory for the clergy, hell for peasantry, paradise for Jews and a gold mine for merchants."[63] Interestingly, Barclay wrote this shortly after the slaughter of Catholics by Protestants (and vice versa) in England during the Reformation.

The accusation that Sarmatian Poles invented fantastic stories about their origins and paid great attention to them likewise seems based on frail evidence. Legends about the origins of European nations circulated throughout Europe during various epochs without becoming major targets of domestic or foreign criticism. They were marginal offspring of national confidence or attempts to build such confidence.[64] In Poland, too, they were marginal and are virtually forgotten now. Jan Skórski's Latin epos *Lechus, Carmen heroicum* (1745), translated into Polish in 1751, tells the story of the ancestors of the Poles, who supposedly came from territories near the Black Sea. It was republished in 1923, and a xeroxed copy of this edition was reprinted in 2011. Neither has attracted the attention of readers. There is no evidence that such myths played a political or cultural role in Poland – unlike, say, the Nibelungen myths in Nazi and pre-Nazi Germany.[65]

The melancholy angst that marks so many nineteenth- and twentieth-century Polish works of literature is another reason why the literature of the seventeenth century has been pushed aside unread. Sarmatism meant self-assurance, pride, and joy – all in short supply in a nation without a state. As generations of Poles under the partitions came and went, Sarmatism became a convenient scapegoat for Poland's lack of independence, its economic backwardness, and its philosophical and religious traditionalism (Poles retained their Catholicism, while Polish Jews in the Russian and Austrian partitions remained Orthodox and unassimilated).

The heaping of accusations on Sarmatism has a long history. It was especially pronounced during the Enlightenment and in Poland under the Soviet occupation (1945–89). The most recent attempt to discredit Old Poland by distorting the image of Sarmatism can be found in *Fantomowe ciało króla* (The King's Phantom Body, 2012) by a young Marxist historian, Jan Sowa. Having borrowed his argument from the recently dusted-off medieval writings about the king's two bodies, Sowa debases the very notion of the noble republic by arguing that the Polish state lacked continuity – indeed, that it did not exist as an established kingdom. The Polish kingdom with its Sarmatism was an empty term; it had no *signifiés.* In my view, the book raises to the extreme the nominalistic argument about the non-existence of universals, in addition to subscribing to an outdated concept of the nation. In Sowa's text, Sarmatian republicanism is thoroughly misunderstood. His argument is based on the idea that the transfer of power between rulers in Sarmatian Poland should have been no different from the transfer of power in medieval and Renaissance kingdoms, where the state was identified with the king. It was assumed that the king had two bodies: a mortal one, and a transcendent one in which the royal powers resided. Succession to the throne based on family ties ensured that the state never died, for when the king died, the successor automatically ascended to the throne. In the Polish system, there was no automatic successor when the king died, because Polish kings were elected by a vote of the Sejm. One could therefore – and Sowa does – speak of gaps in the existence of the Polish state: every time the king died, the Polish state died also. The second body of the king, the one that never dies, did not exist in Poland. After the death of the last Jagiellonian king, Sigismund Augustus, the *interregnum* lasted four years. Hence the title of Sowa's book.

> **Surrogate hegemon:** What does this phrase signify? To explain it, one has to start with the "real" hegemon in Poland in the twentieth century: the USSR. Even though the Soviets wielded power over Poland … the Polish elite dependent on the Soviets did not respect their foreign hegemon in a way comparable to that in which the Anglo-Saxon hegemon was respected in Ireland or India …
>
> On the other hand, after the partitions a tradition developed in Poland of emigration of the elite to countries that allowed émigrés to conduct their own political discourse … In the course of time the émigré narrative began to be seen in Poland as the model discourse … Out of this practice there emerged a view that Western countries are a model to follow in every way, that one travels westward to enjoy liberty and well-being, and to learn how to interpret history and the present … While under the circumstances some of this reverence was justified, in the long run it ceded to foreigners the right to interpret the world and society, including Polish society … [The] acceptance of the intellectual primacy of France, Germany, Great Britain, or the United States inscribed a sense of "being worse," or at least being less developed intellectually, into the consciousness of the Polish elite, thus confirming the hegemon's narrative about the primacy of metropolis over periphery. The fact that the surrogate hegemon was freely accepted, as it were, made the Polish elite's subjugation to it much deeper than similar internalizations among the Arab, Pakistani, Hindu, or Irish intellectuals.
>
> – Ewa Thompson, "Whose Discourse? Telling the Story in Post-Communist Poland," 5–7

Such an argument, however, points to a fundamental lack of understanding of the nature of sovereignty in the gentry republic of Poland. Polish sovereignty did not reside in the institution of the king or even in the Sejm, but rather in the *nation*. Sarmatism was not the domain of the Polish aristocracy, or of a few dozen families who were wealthier, more influential, and more powerful than the gentry nation, which numbered in the hundreds of thousands.[66] Granted it was only the noble nation, with some participation by the burgher class, but impenetrable to peasantry (except by nobilitation) and with an ambivalent relationship to Poland's sharply rising Jewish population. In spite of these limitations, the noble republic practised what Western Europeans had begun to practice after the French Revolution: the vesting of sovereignty in the nation rather than in the monarch. This Sarmatian custom allowed Poles (whose ranks began to swell as peasantry gained awareness of their Polishness)[67] to survive as a community in the nineteenth and twentieth centuries, when they enjoyed no political recognition.

The Polish kingdom was based on the republican principle. Unfortunately, it is all to common for people to fail to distinguish between the republican model of state (where citizens enact laws to which both they and their kings must submit and which are based on the notion of virtue stemming from natural law) and the liberal model of state (where citizens argue about the extent of personal freedom they should have or the size of the slice of the economic pie they can claim). Marxist nominalism is unable to deal with political systems based on Christian realism; for such nominalism, philosophical realism amounts to a fairytale.[68] Furthermore, Sowa's reliance on the medieval distinction between the "body natural" and the "body politic" of the king[69] is a typical example of a reliance on the "surrogate hegemon" (*hegemon zastępczy*),[70] a frequent practice in Polish scholarship both during and after communism. The postcolonial nations once subjugated by Russia (both pre-Soviet and Soviet) looked up to the free West as the model to be followed, thus coming dangerously close to a self-imposed quasi-colonial dependence that I have called "surrogate hegemony."[71] Yet to uncritically copy patterns that worked in another place under different conditions would be naive. Such naivety, I believe, is clear to see in the complaint that Poland did not put to practice the medieval theory about the symbolic and physical nature of kingship. Just because Ernst Kantorowicz made a cogent argument concerning the two bodies of the king does not make his presentation relevant to Polish republicanism. Similarly, the hierarchical structure of empire whereby power emanates from the centre/capital/king is irrelevant to the Polish case, for Sarmatism did not have such a centre, nor did it strive for one. This lack of understanding of the republican structure is typical of postmodernity, which focuses on relationships between centres of power. In the Polish case, it also amounts to a reliance on the surrogate hegemon to whom generations of Poles living under colonial regimes paid tribute all too often.

The *idées reçues* about Sarmatism, repeated from generation to generation, seem to have abated somewhat in recent years. In "Mitologia sarmacka. Rekonesans badawczy" (Sarmatian Mythology: A Second Look), historian Jan Malicki defines Sarmatism as "a stage of the multigenerational dialogue between the universalism of the traditional European culture and uniqueness of the nations that together made up Europe."[72] Małgorzata Beata Mroz speaks of "enlightened Sarmatism," which she ascribes to King Jan Sobieski; her approach is most helpful in developing a relationship with that part of the Polish literary heritage.[73] Jacek Staszewski points out that much of Sarmatian culture was vital to the continuation of Polish cultural identity,[74] while Krzysztof Koehler has developed a portal in which the "Sarmatian marshes" are systematically explored by him and his students.[75]

Finally, while the political weaknesses of Sarmatism were indisputable, one should not forget G.K. Chesterton's assessment that there is hardly a word ever said against the Polish aristocracy that could not have been said against the English aristocracy. There is scarcely a word against Polish liberty that could not have been said against English liberty. No horrible fate befell Britain because it had considerable strength and security as an island, and happened to be surrounded by very different neighbours than Poland.[76]

Sarmatism's Legacy

Sarmatism was the most influential cultural paradigm that Poland produced. It far surpassed Romanticism, which influenced only the educated part of society. As I pointed out earlier, all social strata in Poland became permeated with at least some of Sarmatism's cultural ways. The fact that those ways survived passionate assaults by Enlightenment critics and then by several generations of left-leaning intellectuals testifies to its remarkable cultural strength. However strongly it has been fought against, Sarmatism has inspired countless artists, writers, and thinkers, and it can be found in the religious and folk customs of the Polish peasantry. One can argue that the vehemence with which it has been criticized is itself a form of homage, because it acknowledges its lasting importance. As indicated earlier, there is a dose of misunderstanding in the attacks that have placed a "=" between the political system based on excessive liberty and the rich daily culture the system produced. The Polish political system relied on the virtue and good will of citizens rather than on the power of central authority and an aggregate of punishments for opposing authority. Its failure has been endlessly analysed. However, under the weak political system there flourished a society that might have found the secret of life that Dostoevsky wrote about in the introductory chapter to *The House of the Dead.* Sarmatian society's capacity to accept life, along with pain and death and disputes about religion and state, and to enjoy its offerings, provides rare lessons to postmodern readers. Any vigorous culture looks into the past to confirm its legitimacy, as attempts to proclaim the end of history turn out to be premature. So it appears that those who accept Sarmatism for what it has to offer are right in allowing themselves to be inundated with its love of life, its unending praise of this world, with its battles, loves, duels and wars, superabundance and virility.[77] Those who cannot liberate themselves from resentment towards the past miss out on the beauty and wisdom of this unique Polish cluster of attitudes, beliefs, and writings.

On the philosophical level, Sarmatian writers have bequeathed to later generations of readers a strong grounding in philosophical realism. As a consequence, the problem of identity continues to be taken very seriously in Polish culture. The Sarmatian debates about virtue (understood in an essentialist way) have morphed into almost obsessive discussions of treason and self-sacrifice in Polish history. Such discussions have almost disappeared from the works of Western historians in the twenty-first century. Moral laws, taken to be universally obligatory, still constitute the ultimate reference point for Polish political debates. Those Polish citizens who created Sarmatian culture shared the belief that human life should be subordinated to the metaphysical realities that give rise to human existence, and that discussions about the forms of this subordination can claim a legitimate presence in the public square. Hence the "impracticality" of the Sarmates; their lack of interest in separating "you" from "me," or stranger from friend; their preference for rural life; and a lack of that curiosity that sent so many Europeans to conquer and subjugate lands outside Europe without pondering the question of the morality or immorality of such undertakings.

Sarmatian insistence on the primacy of metaphysics influenced the (relative) Polish fidelity to Roman Catholicism, but it also manifested itself in other ways. In a secularized society, it morphed into a predilection for celebrating anniversaries, monuments, and rituals of all kinds. Catafalk portraits are not painted any longer, but flowers and votive lights are placed on the graves of both relatives and strangers on All Saints' Day in Poland. The propriety of the various commemorations is hotly debated: much energy is spent discussing who is to be buried where, as demonstrated by the controversy surrounding the burial of poet Czesław Miłosz in the "national Pantheon" in the crypt of the Skałka church, and of Polish President Lech Kaczyński in the Wawel Cathedral. Polish social history is replete with rituals of moving the remnants of historical figures from foreign cemeteries to Poland, and indeed dismembering the body according to the wishes of the deceased. Frederick Chopin's heart is buried in the Warsaw church of the Holy Cross, just as he wished, whereas his body lies in Père Lachaise Cemetery in Paris. Ignacy Paderewski and Henryk Sienkiewicz were disinterred from their respective graves abroad and brought back to Poland in 1992 and 1924, respectively.

Without Sarmatism's prolific literary production, modern Polish literature would have lost much of its lustre. As T.S. Eliot noted, "often not only the best, but the most individual parts of [the poet's] work may be those in which the dead poets, his ancestors, assert their immortality most vigorously."[78] Andrzej Waśko points out that Mickiewicz's epic poem *Pan Tadeusz* (Sir Thaddeus, 1834) borrowed more from Sarmatian Poland than its Romantic and post-Romantic admirers have been willing to admit.[79] Witold Gombrowicz's best novel, *Trans-Atlantyk* (1953) foregrounds the language of Sarmatism in a delightfully ironic way. The tradition of the *gawęda* (oral tale), domesticated in Polish literature by such writers as Melchior Wańkowicz, has its roots in Sarmatism, while the fondness of Polish writers for producing outlines (*szkice*) and notes (*notatki*),[80] rather than works that belong to a well-defined genre, echoes the Sarmatian belief that human life remains an unfinished business.

In the contest between Catholicism and Protestantism, mainly verbal violence was used, and thus Poland made serious advances towards acceptance of freedom of religion in modern society. The high offices in the Polish Commonwealth were occupied by both Catholics and Protestants, and sometimes by Jews, and changes of denomination between Catholics and Protestants were not infrequent.[81]

Sarmatism created two models of life: one represented by bucolic and carefree poetry and oriented towards neighbourhood, family obligations, and a generally peaceful existence; and the other oriented towards the dark side of life, war in particular. When the first kind of poetry began to be written in the mid-sixteenth century, Poland had few competitors in exporting grain through the Baltic ports and was prospering economically. The other model of life became a major topic of literary works in the seventeenth century, when defensive wars multiplied and the Sarmatian farmer was transformed into the Sarmatian warrior. This second part of the Sarmatian literary heritage was suppressed under the partitions, because the three partitioning powers did not wish to cultivate the self-image of Poles as victorious in any wars. In *The Polish Way*, Adam Zamoyski emphasizes that the secret clause to the document sealing the third partition of Poland contained an agreement to stop using the word "Poland" altogether, so that the memory of the Polish state would eventually vanish.[82] Thus Chodkiewicz's victory over the Turks at Chocim, the victorious battles with the Muscovites at Orsza and Kłuszyn, and the Hodyń victory over the Tatars were all to evaporate from school textbooks and from the world's memory.

While originally limited to aristocracy and petty nobility, the Sarmatian models of behaviour and ways of looking at the world were adopted by the nascent Polish burgher class and eventually penetrated all social strata. The contemporary phenomenon of *ludowy katolicyzm* (folk Catholicism), with its fondness for pomp and ritual and its passion for archaic religious songs, goes back to the fondness for ceremony and ritual so characteristic of Sarmatism. A recent look at the financial disclosures of Poles elected to the European Parliament in 2014 shows that regardless of their financial status, they all hold a piece of land somewhere in the country, with a nice house to match if they are well-off, and a shack if they are not.[83] This is an echo of the bond to the land so characteristic of Sarmatism. Military valour, which was an important aspect of Sarmatism, is being honoured in endless "replays" of various battle scenes, which are held in Polish cities and towns on appropriate anniversaries. In the twenty-first century, vocal disagreements between the two main parties in Poland, PiS (Law and Justice) and PO (Citizens' Platform), are new renditions of the often destructive debates that took place in the seventeenth century. The quarrelsomeness of Polish parliamentarians echoes the frequent and infamous Sejm scenes of the seventeenth and eighteenth centuries, when the vanity or greed of individual nobles prevented the passing of important bills. The inability to achieve consensus or to compromise is an unsightly feature of Polish political life in the second decade of the twenty-first century. At the same time, these parliamentary quarrels evidence the passionate desire to be morally "in the right" that Sarmatian culture encouraged and cultivated.

The cultural heritage of Sarmatism is vast and deep. It has been diminished by the Polish loss of sovereignty and liberty to manage its own cultural affairs, as well as by Sarmatian society's lack of attention to image-building. The writers of Sarmatian Poland seem to have disdained engaging in self-promotion of any kind. Alexander Brückner attributes the paucity of seventeenth-century publishing houses to wars and the ensuing financial difficulties, but a lack of care was also a factor. In Jan Kochanowski's words, Sarmatian poets sang to themselves and the muses. The opening lines of Kochanowski's "Muza" (The Muse, ca. 1570) have usually been interpreted as a complaint, but they also contain a dose of consent to the lack of interest in his poetry (Kochanowski does say, however, that he hopes for recognition by future generations). He is content to sit under the linden tree next to his homestead, look at the world, and write. One observes a certain disregard for making oneself known not just in him, but in virtually every Sarmatian poet. One wrote poetry just as one tended the garden: it was a serene occupation that the poet engaged in for his own satisfaction.

Sarmatian writers were unaware of the modern truth that naming an object reinforces its social existence, and that every statement made in the public arena has a positive or negative influence on the prestige not only of the speaker but also of the political entity he or she represents. Their attitude towards creativity and public presence differed from what prevails in the twenty-first century. As a result, many literary and philosophical works written during the period have fallen into oblivion. Scores of notable works generated by Sarmatism should have been carefully edited, published, and used in schools in the nineteenth century, but this did not happen. The aforementioned *Description of Social Mores* by Kitowicz was published in 1840 for the first time, and Warszewicki's treatise was translated from Latin into Polish only in 2010! And, contrary to Bulgakov's famous comment, first editions and manuscripts burn easily. A great number of them went up in smoke in 1944 when the withdrawing German Wehrmacht set fire to the National Library in Warsaw.[84] The systematic printing and reintroduction into the mainstream of Polish literature's accomplishments in the Sarmatian period is thus one of the tasks of post-communist reconstruction.

Ewa Thompson
Rice University

NOTES

1 Southern Agrarianism was based on the republican ideal of independent, virtuous, and politically engaged farmers. The ownership of land was considered crucial. Sarmatism was also republican in spirit (instead of hereditary monarchy, it introduced the election of kings), and it envisaged society as a community of independent landowners. For a recent look at Southern Agrarianism, see McClanahan, "Restoring the Old Order."

2 Koehler, ed., *Słuchaj mię, Sauromatha*, 5.

3 Brückner, *Dzieje kultury polskiej*, vol. 2, 377.

4 In English translation, "We came, we saw, God conquered." Tucker, *Battles That Changed History*, 216.

5 Poets Daniel Naborowski and Zbigniew Morsztyn, as well as political thinker Andrzej Frycz Modrzewski, can serve as examples here.

6 An example of this shift is Wacław Potocki, the greatest poet of Sarmatism and a scion of an Arian family, who eventually converted to Roman Catholicism.
7 See Orzechowski, "Frycz" and "Prosta opowieść"; Modrzewski, "Orzechowski," In *Stanisława Orzechowskiego i Andrzeja Frycza Modrzewskiego spór o wiarę.*
8 Tazbir, *A State without Stakes.*
9 See Wilczek, "Catholics and Heretics."
10 Schiper, *Dzieje handlu żydowskiego na ziemiach polskich*, 167, 174, 212. Schiper states that in the eighteenth century the Jews controlled two-thirds of all import trade that went through Wrocław and the majority of the trade that went through Gdańsk and Toruń (p. 234). In the Białystok region, the ratio of Jewish to non-Jewish merchants was 13:1 (p. 307). See also Weinryb, *The Jews of Poland.*
11 See Koehler, *Palus sarmatica.*
12 Davies, *God's Playground*, 360.
13 This principle has been poignantly described in Stefan Żeromski's novel *Popioły* (Ashes, 1902–4), where the nobleman Nardzewski refuses to give consent to arbitrary demands of the Austrian officials.
14 Walicki, *Idea narodu w polskiej myśli oświeceniowej*, 21.
15 Grześkowiak-Krwawicz, *Queen Liberty*, 25.
16 Wandycz, *The Price of Freedom*, 62.
17 Grześkowiak-Krwawicz, *Queen Liberty*, 50.
18 Ibid., 51.
19 Kantorowicz, *The King's Two Bodies.*
20 Grześkowiak-Krwawicz, *Queen Liberty*, 69.
21 Ibid., 69.
22 Fredro, *Scriptorum seu togae et belli*, 306.
23 Grześkowiak-Krwawicz, *Queen Liberty*, 19–20.
24 Ibid., 20.
25 Ibid., 44.
26 Kochanowski, "Treatise on Virtue and Friendship," 192–3.
27 Potocki, *Dzieła*, vol. 1, 282. Unless otherwise indicated, all translations from the Polish language are mine.
28 Ibid., 376.
29 Hanna Dziechcińska comments on seventy-three biographies written during the period 1476 to 1627 in her comprehensive study *Biografistyka staropolska w latach 1476–1627: Kierunki i odmiany.*
30 Lubomirski, *Rozmowy Artaksesa i Ewandra*, 5.
31 Warszewicki and Anonymous, *Krzysztofa Warszewickiego i Anonima uwagi o wolności szlacheckiej* [1598], 2010.
32 See Pasek, *Memoirs of the Polish Baroque* (*Pamiętniki*).
33 Backvis, "Szczególna próbka historycznego eposu," 287–8.
34 Drużbacka, "Reskrypt na wyżej wyrażone Punkta."
35 Sokołowska. ed., *Poeci polskiego baroku,* vol. 2, 211.
36 See Thompson, "Sarmatyzm i postkolonializm."
37 Potocki, *Dzieła,* vol. 1, 451.
38 Ibid., 346.
39 Ibid., 383.
40 Eliot, "Prufrock and Other Observations," 4.

41 Sokołowska, ed., *Poeci polskiego baroku,* vol. 2, 244.
42 Fordoński and Urbański, eds., *Casimir Britannicus.*
43 Sokołowska, ed., *Poeci polskiego baroku,* vol. 1, 644.
44 An English translation of Roździeński, *Officina Ferraria,* was published by MIT Press in 1976.
45 I know of only one work of fiction whose central subject is pain: Marta Żukowska's short story "Pain."
46 Koehler, Introduction to *Słuchaj mię, Sauromatha,* 13.
47 MacIntyre, *Three Rival Versions of Moral Enquiry,* 215.
48 Lubomirski, *Rozmowy Artaksesa i Ewandra,* 29.
49 Kołakowski, *Main Currents of Marxism,* vol. 3, 265.
50 See n10. Schiper also quotes Robert Johnston's *Travels through parts of the Russian Empire and the Country of Poland along the Southern of the Baltic* (London 1815). According to Schiper, Johnson states that "all retail trade in Poland and Lithuania is in the hands of the Jews." Schiper, *Dzieje handlu,* 365.
51 Fredro, *Przysłowia mów potocznych,* 21, 31, 32.
52 Portions of this and other treatises were translated from Latin to Polish and are available in Ogonowski, ed., *Filozofia i myśl społeczna XVII wieku,* 301–48.
53 Schiper, *Dzieje handlu,* 212, 400.
54 Ibid., 221.
55 Brzozowski, "Sienkiewicz to klasyk polskiej ciemnoty i nieuctwa," 83; repeated by Roman Pawłowski in his attack on Sienkiewicz in *Gazeta Wyborcza,* 8 September 2014.
56 Sarmatism coincided with the European Baroque, indeed was derived from it in several ways. Its energy and vitality blended with the baroque art, replete with rich and untamed structures. There exists an overlap between the two, and much of Sarmatian love of ceremony and pomp could be fitted into the landscape of European Baroque. Some scholars avoid mentioning the very word Sarmatism when dealing with the seventeenth century. In her anthology of Old Polish literature titled *Monumenta Polonica,* Bogdana Carpenter replaces the word "Sarmatism" with "Baroque," and so does Michael Mikoś in *Polish Baroque and Enlightenment Literature: An Anthology.*
57 Leśnodorski's term. Quoted from Wandycz, *The Price of Freedom,* 88.
58 Tazbir, *Sarmaci i świat,* 367–406. See also Tazbir, *Rzeczpospolita i świat,* 185.
59 Kitowicz, *Opis obyczajów za panowania Augusta III,* 4–14.
60 Bogucka, "Obraz Polski i Polaków na przełomie XVI i XVII wieku," 397.
61 Faber, "Das Westliche in Sarmatismus," 83. Andrzej Maksymilian Fredro was also of that opinion.
62 Fiszer, "L'image de la Pologne et des Polonais," 255–60.
63 Brückner, *Dzieje kultury polskiej,* vol. 2, 398.
64 Matusiak, "Z badań nad sarmatyzmem w polskiej myśli literaturoznawczej XX wieku," 125.
65 Kopp, *Germany's Wild East,* 160–201.
66 McEvedy and Jones, *Atlas of World Population History,* 73.
67 On the transformation of Galician peasants into Poles, see Stauter-Halsted, *The Nation in the Village.*
68 In his introduction to *Fantomowe ciało króla,* Sowa takes on mysticism and blissfully opines that, under the cold light of reason, mysticism wilts and disappears.
69 Kantorowicz, *The King's Two Bodies,* 11f.
70 Thompson, "W kolejce po aprobatę."

71 Thompson, "Said a sprawa polska."
72 Malicki, "Mitologia sarmacka," 10.
73 Mróz, "Jan III Sobieski na Kahlenbergu," 356.
74 Staszewski, "Sarmatyzm a Oświecenie," 23.
75 Koehler, *Palus Sarmatica*, http://www.palus-sarmatica.pl.
76 Chesterton, "Preface," Zygmunt Krasiński, *The Un-Divine Comedy*, 6.
77 Koehler, *Palus sarmatica*.
78 Eliot, *Selected Essays*, 4.
79 Waśko, "Sarmatism or the Enlightenment," 453–61.
80 A recent example is Dobosz, *Z różnych półek*.
81 Protestant Walerian Otwinowski held the offices of judge and the honorific office of food taster (*podczaszy*) (Sokołowska, ed., *Poeci polskiego baroku*, vol. 1, 279). From the reign of Mieczysław III (twelfth century) until the partitions of Poland (late eighteenth century), Polish mints were leased to Jewish managers (Koczy, *Dzieje handlu polskiego przed rozbiorami*, 68). Even in neighbouring Slovakia, denomination-based slaughter was not uncommon. http://wpolityce.pl/kosciol/222401-franciszkanie-uczcili-i-upamietnili-zamordowanych-wspolbraci.
82 Zamoyski, *The Polish Way*, 5.
83 http://www.sejm.gov.pl/sejm7.nsf/PoslowiePE.xsp.
84 Pollak, *Wśród literatów staropolskich*, 543.

WORKS CITED

Backvis, Claude. "Szczególna próbka historycznego eposu. *Wojna chocimska* Wacława Potockiego." In *Szkice o kulturze staropolskiej*. Translated and edited by A. Biernacki. Warsaw: PIW, 1975.

Bogucka, Maria. "Obraz Polski i Polaków na przełomie XVI i XVII wieku." In *Christianitas et cultura Europae. Festschrift for Professor Jerzy Kłoczowski*. Lublin: Instytut Europy Srodkowo-Wschodniej, 1998.

Borowski, Andrzej. *Powrót Europy*. Kraków: Księgarnia Akademicka, 1999.

Brzozowski, Stanisław. "Sienkiewicz to klasyk polskiej ciemnoty i nieuctwa." In *Współczesna powieść i krytyka literacka*. Warsaw: PIW, 1971.

Brückner, Aleksander. *Dzieje kultury polskiej*, vol. 2 [1930]. Warsaw: Książka i Wiedza, 1958.

Chesterton, G.K. "Preface." In Zygmunt Krasiński, *The Un-Divine Comedy*. Translated by Harriette E. Kennedy and Zofia Umińska. London: George H. Harrap & Co. and Warsaw: Książnica Polska, 1924.

Carpenter, Bogdana, ed. *Monumenta Polonica: The First Four Centuries of Polish Poetry: A Bilingual Anthology*. Ann Arbor: Michigan Slavic Publications, 1989.

Davies, Norman. *God's Playground: A History of Poland*, vol. 1. New York: Columbia University Press, 1982.

Dobosz, Andrzej. *Z różnych półek*. Warszawa: Teologia Polityczna, 2014.

Drużbacka, Elżbieta. "Punkta dla poprawienia zepsutych obyczajów Polskich, przez pewnego senatora Polskiego do opisania mnie podane." In *Wiersze wybrane*. Edited by Krystyna Stasiewicz. Warszawa: Neriton, 2003.

Dziechcińska, Hanna. *Biografistyka staropolska w latach 1476–1627. Kierunki i odmiany*. Wrocław: Wydawnictwo Polskiej Akademii Nauk, 1971.

Eliot, T.S. "Prufrock and Other Observations." In *The Complete Poems and Plays, 1909–1950*. New York: Harcourt, 1952.

– *Selected Essays of T.S. Eliot.* New York: Harcourt, 1960.
Faber, Martin. "Das Westliche in Sarmatismus." In *Sarmatismus versus Orientalismus in Mitteleuropa.* Edited by Magdalena Długosz and Piotr O. Scholz. Berlin: Frank & Timme, 2012.
Fiszer, Stanislaw. "L'image de la Pologne et des Polonais dans l'oeuvre de Voltaire." *Revue des etudes slaves* 70 (1998): 255–60.
Fordoński, Krzysztof, and Piotr Urbański, eds. *Casimir Britannicus: English Translations, Paraphrases, and Emulations of the Poetry of Maciej Kazimierz Sarbiewski.* Vol. 11 of *Critical Texts.* Edited by John Batchelor. London: Modern Humanities Research Association, 2008.
Fredro, Andrzej Maksymilian. *Przysłowia mów potocznych, albo przestrogi obyczajowe, radne, wojenne.* Sanok: Wydawnictwo Karola Pollaka, 1855. http://www.wbc.poznan.pl/dlibra/doccontent?id=92602.
– *Scriptorum seu togae et belli* [1660]. Translated by F. Wujtewicz. In *Filozofia i myśl społeczna XVII wieku,* vol. 1. Edited by Zbigniew Ogonowski. Warsaw: PWN, 1979.
Grześkowiak-Krwawicz, Anna. *Queen Liberty: The Concept of Freedom in the Polish–Lithuanian Commonwealth.* Translated by Daniel Sax. Leiden and Boston: Brill Academic, 2012.
Kantorowicz, Ernst H. *The King's Two Bodies: A Study in Medieval Political Theology.* Princeton: Princeton University Press, 1957.
Kitowicz, Jędrzej. *Opis obyczajów za panowania Augusta III.* Edited by Roman Pollak. Wrocław: Ossolineum, 1970.
Kochanowski, Jan. "Treatise on Virtue and Friendship." Translated by Cedric Spak. *Sarmatian Review* 13, no. 3 (September 1993): 192–3. http://www.ruf.rice.edu/~sarmatia/993/kochan.html.
Koczy, Leon. *Dzieje handlu polskiego przed rozbiorami.* Lwów: Państwowe Wydawnictwo Książek Szkolnych, 1939.
Koehler, Krzysztof. *Palus sarmatica.* http://palus-sarmatica.pl/index.php/component/content/article/77-palus-sarmatica/84.
– ed. *Słuchaj mię, Sauromatha. Antologia poezji sarmackiej.* Kraków: Arcana, 2012.
Kołakowski, Leszek. *Main Currents of Marxism,* vol. 3. Translated by P.S. Falla. Oxford: Oxford University Press, 1978.
Kopp, Kristin. *Germany's Wild East: Constructing Poland as Colonial Space.* Ann Arbor: University of Michigan Press, 2012.
Lubomirski, Stanisław Herakliusz. *Rozmowy Artaksesa i Ewandra.* Edited by Justyna Dąbkowska-Kujko. Warsaw: IBL, 2006.
MacIntyre, Alasdair. *Three Rival Versions of Moral Enquiry: Encyclopedia, Genealogy, and Tradition.* Notre Dame: University of Notre Dame Press, 1990.
Malicki, Jan. "Mitologia sarmacka. Rekonesans badawczy." In *Wokół Wacława Potockiego.* Edited by Jan Malicki and Dariusz Rott. Katowice: Wydawnictwo Uniwersytetu Śląskiego, 1997.
Matusiak, Małgorzata. "Z badań nad sarmatyzmem w polskiej myśli literaturoznawczej XX wieku." In *Sarmatismus versus Orientalismus in Mitteleuropa.* Edited by Magdalena Długosz and Piotr O. Scholz, 115–30. Berlin: Frank & Timme, 2012.
McClanahan, Brion. "Restoring the Old Order: Who Owns America?" In *The Imaginative Conservative* http://www.theimaginativeconservative.org/2014/09/mass-resurrection-who-owns-america.html.
McEvedy, Colin, and Richard Jones. *Atlas of World Population History.* Middlesex: Penguin, 1978.
Mikoś. Michael J. *Polish Baroque and Enlightenment Literature: An Anthology.* Columbus: Slavic Publishers, 1996.

Mróz, Małgorzata, Beata. "Jan III Sobieski na Kahlenbergu." In *Sarmatismus versus Orientalismus in Mitteleuropa.* Edited by Magdalena Długosz and Piotr O. Scholz, 355–68. Berlin: Frank & Timme, 2012.

Ogonowski, Zbigniew, ed. *Filozofia i myśl społeczna XVII wieku.* Warszawa: PWN, 1979.

Orzechowski, Stanisław, "Frycz" (97–297) and "Prosta opowieść" (51–96); Andrzej Frycz Modrzewski, "Orzechowski." (299-366) In *Stanisława Orzechowskiego i Andrzeja Frycza Modrzewskiego spór o wiarę.* Edited by Krzysztof Koehler. Kraków: Ignatianum–WAM, 2013.

Pasek, Jan Chryzostom. *Memoirs of the Polish Baroque* (*Pamiętniki*). Edited and translated by Catherine Leach. Berkeley: University of California Press, 1976.

Pollak, Roman. *Wśród literatów staropolskich.* Warsaw: PWN, 1966.

Potocki, Wacław. *Dzieła*, vol. 1. Edited by Leszek Kukulski. Warsaw: PIW, 1987.

Roździeński, Walenty. *Officina Ferraria: A Polish Poem of 1612 Describing the Noble Craft of Ironwork.* Translated by Stefan Pluszczewski. Edited by Wacław Różański and Cyril S. Smith. Cambridge, MA: MIT Press, 1976.

Schiper, Ignacy. *Dzieje handlu żydowskiego na ziemiach polskich.* Warsaw: Nakładem Centrali Związku Kupców, 1937.

Sokołowska, Jadwiga, ed. *Poeci polskiego Baroku*, vols. 1 and 2. Warszawa: Państwowy Instytut Wydawniczy, 1965.

Sowa, Jan. *Fantomowe ciało króla. peryferyjne zmagania z nowoczesną formą.* Kraków: Towarzystwo Autorów i Wydawców Prac Naukowych Universitas, 2011.

Staszewski, Jacek. "Sarmatyzm a Oświecenie." In *Kultura literacka połowy XVIII wieku w Polsce. Studia i szkice.* Wrocław: Wiedza o Kulturze, 1992.

Stauter-Halsted, Keely. *The Nation in the Village: The Genesis of Peasant National Identity in Austrian Poland, 1848–1914.* Ithaca: Cornell University Press, 2004.

Tazbir, Janusz. *Rzeczpospolita i świat. Studia z dziejów kultury XVII wieku.* Wrocław: Ossolineum, 1971.

– *Sarmaci i świat.* Kraków: Universitas, 2001.

– *A State without Stakes: Polish Religious Toleration in the Sixteenth and Seventeenth Centuries.* New York: Kosciuszko Foundation, 1973.

Thompson, Ewa. "W kolejce po aprobatę. Kolonialna mentalność polskich elit." *Europa* (*Dziennik*) 180 (14 September 2007).

– "Said a sprawa polska." *Europa-Newsweek,* 28 June 2005, http://www.newsweek.pl/said-a-sprawa-polska,45500,1,1.html.

– "Sarmatyzm i kolonializm." *Newsweek Polska*, 11 November 2006. http://www.newsweek.pl/sarmatyzm-i-postkolonializm,44873,1,1.html.

– "Whose Discourse? Telling the Story in Post-Communist Poland." *The Other Shore* 1, no. 1 (2010): 1–15.

Tucker, Spencer C. *Battles That Changed History: An Encyclopedia of World Conflict.* Santa Barbara: ABC-CLIO, 2010.

Walicki, Andrzej. *Idea narodu w polskiej myśli oświeceniowej.* Warsaw: Polish Academy of Sciences, 2000.

Wandycz, Piotr S. *The Price of Freedom: A History of East Central Europe from the Middle Ages to the Present.* London and New York: Routledge, 1992.

Warszewicki, Krzysztof, and Anonymous. *Krzysztofa Warszewickiego i Anonima uwagi o wolności szlacheckiej* [1598]. Edited by Krzysztof Koehler. Translated from Latin by Krzysztof Nowak. Kraków: WAM, 2010.

Waśko, Andrzej. "Sarmatism or the Enlightenment: The Dilemma of Polish Culture," *Sarmatian Review* 17, no. 2 (April 1997). http://www.ruf.rice.edu/~sarmatia/497/wasko.html.

Weinryb, Bernard D. *The Jews of Poland: A Social and Economic History of the Jewish Community in Poland from 1100.* Philadelphia: Jewish Publication Society of America, 1973.

Wilczek, Piotr. "Catholics and Heretics: Some Aspects of Religious Debates in the Old Polish–Lithuanian Commonwealth." *Sarmatian Review* 19, no. 2 (April 1999). http://www.ruf.rice.edu/~sarmatia/499/wilczek.html.

Zamoyski, Adam. *The Polish Way: A Thousand-Year History of the Poles and Their Culture*. London: John Murray, 1987.

Żukowska, Marta. "Pain" ["Ból," 1942]. Translated by Claire S. Allen. *Sarmatian Review* 9, no. 1 (1989): 10–15.

Spectres of Sarmatism

O! Poland! As long as you imprison
An angelic soul in a boorish skull,
So long your flesh will be hacked by a headsman,
So long your revenge sword will remain dull,
So long a hyena will lie over you
And a grave – your eyes opened in the grave too.

Throw off completely those hideous tatters,
First – that Deianira's burning attire:
And then arise like great shameless sculptures,
Naked – and bathed up in the Stygian mire,
New – brazen in your iron nakedness –
Not embarrassed by anything – deathless.

– Juliusz Słowacki, *Agamemnon's Tomb*[1]

The typical Anglo-American reader may feel puzzled by Sarmatism at first glance. It may well strike them as a bizarre cultural tradition followed by an exotic tribe of Eastern European aristocrats centuries ago, one that blended heterogeneous cultural elements such as Oriental clothes, Far Eastern spices, references to the supposedly Roman origins of the noble elites, tribal democratic institutions, agrarianism, and superstitious Catholicism. Yet those acquainted with the plantation-centred societies of the southern United States and other places around the Americas may find the cultural, social, and economic aspects of Sarmatism easier to understand. Indeed, anyone who saw director Quentin Tarantino's *Django Unchained* (2012) can construct an approximate image of Sarmatian society. Sarmatism was, first and foremost, a culture of slave owners who built their social and political universe around a revamped relic of Medieval Europe: the manorial agricultural plantation (Pol. *folwark*).

A comprehensive picture of the Sarmatian universe in beyond the scope of this text, but its discussion necessitates the reconstruction of at least those of its elements that are prerequisite to understanding its influence on contemporary Polish culture and society. There are two important myths that need to be debunked before we can address Sarmatism as a social and cultural reality, rather than an ideological fetish whose purpose is to cure the afflictions of Polish culture. The first myth presents Sarmatism as an expression of a strong and vigorous state that reached its apogee in the seventeenth century; the second interprets it as a vanguard political movement that preserved democracy and freedom at a time (from the fifteenth to the eighteenth centuries) when the rest of early modern Europe was suffering from "absolutist disease." Deconstructing these myths is not just a matter of ensuring historical accuracy. Sarmatism holds sway over the contemporary Polish social and cultural imagination, and a superficial reconfiguration of its patterns will not reduce its power. The Polish collective consciousness today has been affected by Sarmatism's deeper structures, such as hierarchism, elitism, the affirmation of social inequalities, conservative contempt for emancipatory ideas, agrarianism, a colonial attitude towards Eastern Europe, cheerful machismo, the extreme exploitation of labour in the workplace combined with an authoritarian management style, megalomaniacal self-delusion, and susceptibility to superstition. That is why addressing the social, political, cultural, and (last but not least) economic legacy of our ancestors' follies is an urgent task.

The first myth – that the period of high Sarmatism coincided with the supposed Golden Age of the Polish state – is widespread among Polish scholars. By way of example, one can point to Krzysztof Koehler's conviction, expressed in his forward to an anthology of Sarmatian verse, *Słuchaj mię, Sauromata* (Hear me, Sarmatian), that Sarmatism was a "culture of a strong state."[2] There was indeed a time when Poland held exceptional power as the strongest player in the region. The term "Golden Age" refers mainly to the sixteenth century, although it could be extended back to the fifteenth as well. After its victory over the Teutonic Order at Grunwald (Tannenberg) in 1410, the Kingdom of Poland in a union with the Grand Duchy of Lithuania became the uncontested hegemon of the lands stretching from the Baltic to the Black Sea. That commonwealth prospered into and throughout the sixteenth century: cities flourished, the rule of the Jagiellonian dynasty was uncontested, and the middle nobility prevented wealthy magnates from dominating the state. Some cracks in this regime were visible, especially in the sixteenth century, when the gentry (*szlachta*) consolidated its grip on power and weakened the king's rule. Nevertheless, the Kingdom of Poland at that time deserved the title of a regional empire, which explains contemporary conservative nostalgia for the "Jagiellonian Idea."[3]

> Sarmatism was and is still associated or even quite generally identified with the bygone Polish culture, namely Old Poland, or with its very core, meaning the landed gentry culture. These associations are justified if we agree that Sarmatism was in fact the first entirely native form of national culture and that it was, simultaneously, a form of national consciousness that found its expression in literature … [Sarmatism] can also be understood in a historically refined way, as a term for one of the seventeenth-century Polish literary currents, or it can be counted among the most important ideas that shaped the consciousness and creative output of Poles over several centuries. Indeed, not only of Poles, since Sarmatism – precisely as an idea that impacted stereotypes of various kinds – was influential also outside of the Old Polish cultural realm.
>
> – Borowski, *Powrót Europy*, 42

Interestingly enough, this was not the era of Sarmatism as a *cultural* formation. While the term "Sarmatism" first surfaced in the fifteenth century, it was mainly sixteenth-century historians like Marcin Kromer and Maciej Miechowita who disseminated it to a general audience. However, the peak of Sarmatism's influence was not the fifteenth century, nor was it the sixteenth – times of prosperity for the Polish state; rather, it was the seventeenth, which for Poland was a time not of greatness but of decay. The Polish–Lithuanian Commonwealth, a still powerful political formation at the beginning of the seventeenth century, was bankrupt by its end: after the Great Northern War of 1700–21, Russia became the region's hegemon, with Poland reduced to its pseudo-sovereign puppet. The partitions of the late eighteenth century may have sealed Poland's fate, but its political and military impotence was a fact from the beginning of the century. The same can be said about the internal situation of the commonwealth during the seventeenth century, a time of deteriorating economic performance (as revealed by worsening trade terms)[4] and of growing inequality between the magnates and the rest of society, including the peasants and the poorer nobility (the magnates constituted the elite "1 per cent" of that time). The century was also marked by increasing serfdom, a diminished role for urban dwellers, a general demise of Polish cities, a chronic crisis of Polish parliamentarism that weakened the central political power, and escalating tensions to the east that gave rise to a series of Kozak and Ruthenian revolts, with the so-called Khmelnytsky Uprising being only one of a dozen similar conflicts in Ukraine during the first half of the seventeenth century.[5] It is against this political backdrop and on this social soil that Sarmatism flourished.

Oddly enough, Sarmatism remained highly popular throughout the century that saw the collapse of the Polish–Lithuanian Commonwealth. This situation is captured by English historian Perry Anderson:

> Culturally, the *szlachta* took its revenge on the history which had disappointed it by a morbid mythomania: an astonishing cult of imaginary "Sarmatian" ancestors in the pre-feudal past was combined with provincial Counter-Reformation bigotry, in a country where urban civilization now largely ebbed away. The pseudo-atavistic ideology of Sarmatianism was not a mere aberration: it reflected the state of the whole class, which found its most vivid expression in the constitutional realm proper. For politically, the combined impact of the Ukrainian Revolution and the Swedish Deluge shattered the brittle unity of the Polish Commonwealth.[6]

Anderson's observations are seminal here. The terms "revenge" and "mythomania" help us grasp the nature of Sarmatism as a cultural formation as well as its social function, *then and now*. Sarmatism did not express or reveal any truth about Polish society, culture, or economy; rather, its purposes were aligned with what contemporary psychoanalytical theory tells us about ideology.[7] The principal function of Sarmatism was to compensate for the decline of the Polish state, to hide the inconvenient truth of that decline from its subjects, and to create the illusion that everything was fine. That is why it was so popular. Ideology is a *screen of fantasy* in both meanings of the word "screen": it provides a canvas on which to paint an inadequate, even when soul-inspiring, image of reality (as a cinema screen does), and it adds an additional layer of reality that protects us, like sunscreen, from the desert of the Real, with its burning emptiness.

An attempt to fully illustrate this miserable condition would exceed the scope of this discussion. Nevertheless, for the sake of the argument, I will demonstrate it in the realm of political thought. Expressionist interpretations of Sarmatism posit that there are good reasons why the Sarmatians were enraptured by their state and culture. Yet the high point of Sarmatism did not coincide with actual greatness of the Polish state, but rather with its demise. Sarmatism, viewed as an ideology, was neither concerned about these developments nor saddened by them, because – and here comes the screen – it barely noticed them, and even when it did, it portrayed decay in a way that denoted success. The more the Polish state crumbled into chaos in the seventeenth and eighteenth centuries, the more spectacular Sarmatian eulogies to its purported greatness became. Self-delusions of power and greatness had always been a part of the Sarmatian world view, and over time they only became more entrenched.

A quick tour through this theme park of political and social delusions might begin with a brief diagnosis by Stanisław Orzechowski (1513–66) from *Policya Królestwa Polskiego, na kształt Arystotelesowskich polityk wypisana* (Policy of the Polish Crown, Inspired by Aristotle's "Politics", 1566): "Poland is so perfect that no one can either add to, or take anything away from it."[8] Or with a similar sentiment expressed by Bishop Paweł Piasecki (1579–1649): "The decree of the Commonwealth is the best, most well-founded, formed by God himself, and needs no change, for such would only harm it."[9] Wacław Kunicki was even more eloquent in his *Obraz szlachcica polskiego* (Portrait of a Polish Nobleman, 1615):

> Were we to go round all the Commonwealths, none can nor will equal Poland, but take a second or third place behind it. The Pole has illustrious robes, that is a freedom equal to his Lord. He has a decorative gold ring, that is nobility, by which the highest and the lowest in Poland equal are made. He shares an ox with his Lord, that is the common law, which like an ox serves them both.[10]

The Sarmatian poet Wespazjan Kochowski (1633–1700) nursed an even grander vision, believing that the Poles would push the Turks not only out of the Balkans but also out of Egypt, until "Persians and Blacks, and far-away China, will extend their hands to God."[11] To grasp the ideological nature of this vision, one must remember that it was written around the time that a Swedish invasion was laying ruin to broad swaths of the country and the Ukrainian Revolution was driving the Poles out of eastern Ukraine. The Sarmatians were facing enormous challenges to preventing their overextended nation from falling apart, yet this did not discourage them from dreaming of founding a world empire.

The most misplaced affirmations of Poland's ever-lasting superiority are found in the eighteenth century, which was a time of clear and undeniable decline of the Sarmatian state. In 1724, for instance, Antoni Potocki wrote: "Let the ox of Europe *dites manipulos* earn and amass, the Poles can boast *aquila desuper quatuor eorum* above all the insignia of other kingdoms, almost above the human condition, our eagle soars, for with an inherent loftiness he rises up, *nescit frena pati*."[12] But nothing matches the opinion of Wacław Rzewuski, who in 1756 – only two decades before the partitions and the collapse of the Polish–Lithuanian Commonwealth – wrote:

> There is no nation under the sun that would equal ours in happiness. We count more than twenty years of constant peace, and lack for nothing, Praise be to God; freedom, prosperity, security, harvest, and the heavenly gifts that are most precious to people are generously granted to us, in our homes there are riches, decorations, and collections, money in trunks, silver on the tables, crops on the threshing floor … All of Europe and our neighbours were recently stained with blood, armies of hundreds of thousands were unable to secure their peace, their unsurpassed treasures could not save them, consistent and autocratic rule did not

> prevent their oppression. Our army is perhaps slight, our sejm sessions disorderly, and the treasury impoverished, but since God has us in his grace and the King in his care, we seem to be happiness' only child, free, peaceful, saved, kept safe amid nations that are destroying one another.[13]

The link between Poland's actual social and political condition and the Sarmatian world view articulated by Polish writers and political thinkers does not seem causative, so there is no basis for claiming that Sarmatism expressed the power and the glory of the Polish state of that era. Rather, there seems to be a *reverse relationship* between the two: the worse Poland's actual situation, the more eloquent the declarations of its absolute superiority. This should come as no surprise. A core function of ideology is to mask and suppress reality so that the more problematic it becomes, the stronger the ideological formation must be to keep the truth at bay. Sarmatian literature served this purpose well by maintaining the illusion of the Polish state's superiority, which served to block attempts at modernizing and reforming the country. The status quo remained functional for the magnates and for the upper strata of *szlachta*, but this happened at the expense of the minor gentry (*szlachta zagrodowa, gołota*), the peasants (who remained serfs until mid-nineteenth century), and the Polish state, which became dominated by its powerful neighbours.

The second myth surrounding Sarmatism is that of its supposedly progressive character – its fostering of freedom and democracy in times of dark absolutism. Those who embrace this view often reference "Polish republicanism" as a tradition that offers valuable inspiration for the conduct of politics and social organization. Such a stance is presented, for example, in Zdzisław Krasnodębski's *Demokracja peryferii* (Democracy of the Peripheries), and a similar view is shared by various other writers and scholars, such as Ewa Thompson, Dariusz Skórczewski, Piotr Gliński, and Krzysztof Szczerski.[14] This view of Sarmatism is not new. Józefat Bolesław Ostrowski, a Polish conservative political writer of the early nineteenth century, wrote the following: "Our land, our Poland is the fatherland of political freedom … our liberal principles and institutions preceded all of Europe's nations … We must resurrect these institutions, popularize them, extend them to all citizens, we do not have to imitate anything."[15]

There is no doubt that Polish political and social developments offered an alternative to the mainstream of European culture throughout early modern times. For instance, Poland had no episodes of absolutism; to the contrary, the king's power began to fade after the sixteenth century. Poland also followed unique patterns in social change. Beginning in the late Middle Ages, the West began to evolve from a feudal, serf-based, agrarian economy towards a capitalist regime of waged labour. Yet in the part of Europe east of the river Elbe, social development went in the opposite direction: after a period of weakening, serfdom was reinforced and grew in strength throughout the existence of the Polish–Lithuanian Commonwealth. In the West, cities expanded and filled with peasant migrants in search of work, and this fostered an urban proto-proletariat, while in the East, the importance of cities diminished, with populations trapped in what Marx and Engels called the "isolation of rural life." Likewise, the Polish bourgeoisie could not develop because of hostility from the Polish *szlachta*, who passed dozens of anti-bourgeois laws, including one in 1565 that forbade Polish merchants to conduct foreign trade.

There truly was a "Sarmatian alternative" to Western modernity, but it was one that could not withstand external pressures. Yet it turned out to be a failure not because of outside threats, but due to the internal organization of the state. At the time, there was hardly a country that did not face hostile foreign powers; indeed, all of the European powers were constantly at war – Britain versus France, France versus Italy, Spain versus the Netherlands, Sweden versus Russia, and so on. Sarmatian Poland was no exception. What *was* exceptional was that this vast and resource-rich country was unable to defend itself, which was a logical consequence of decisions taken by the Sarmatians, especially those that eroded the king's authority. The royal standing army, for instance, was limited to four thousand soldiers, in accordance with the *Artykuły henrykowskie* (Henrician Articles, 1573) – a laughable number by the eighteenth century, given that the surrounding powers had standing armies of around 100,000 men. Sarmatian international political and military doctrine was failing, but first and foremost, so was Sarmatian internal political and social organization. It is a misconception to think of Sarmatism as some kind of vanguard democratic experiment undertaken centuries before parliamentary democracy took root in the Western world. First of all, the term "democracy" (as in "parliamentary democracy," or "nobles' democracy" [Pol. *demokracja szlachecka*]) is misleading. Modern democratic regimes have little in common with their much older counterparts, for they are based on the northern European institution of representative councils. They are part of the *liberal* tradition, not the democratic one.

The debates conducted by the Founding Fathers of the United States, especially Alexander Hamilton and James Madison, make this point very clearly: democracy is the rule of the people, whereas the republic – nowadays referred to as "parliamentary" or "liberal" democracy – is the rule of *representatives* of the people.[16] These representatives are not bound by any instructions; they hold a free mandate, and they can make any decisions they deem appropriate. This has important consequences. The French political philosopher Claude Lefort rightly claims that parliamentary democracy is a system in which the site of power remains empty: it is not filled by the people in the absence of a monarch.[17] "The people" as such does not constitute any solid and permanent subject. Instead, at the moment of elections, it is divided into an arithmetical set of equal individuals who are allowed to express not their will as such, but rather their *consent* to be ruled by elected individuals (to channel Joseph Schumpeter's notion of parliamentarism as competitive leadership).[18] Jacques Rancière underscores a similar feature of parliamentary politics when he argues that it does not allow the social to translate into the political through the electoral process. In other words, the social position we hold does not matter in the moment of elections: every person is equal to all others and counts for one vote.[19]

Robert Dahl's theory of democratic politics refers to parliamentarism as a poliarchical regime.[20] In parliamentary societies there are multiple sources of power. It is a myth that sovereignty ultimately rests with the people. While the people exercise some power, of course, parliamentary regimes also include aristocratic and oligarchical components. Thus, apart from elected representatives, other non-democratic subjects such as private corporations, international institutions (e.g., the IMF, the World Bank, and the United Nations), religious associations, lobby groups, and highly respected individuals can all influence the decision-making of "democratic" countries. Lefort's and Dahl's views on parliamentarism, although developed in different intellectual traditions, converge on this point: in parliamentary countries it is impossible to give a single answer to the question "Who rules?" This is not really surprising, for parliamentarism developed as a system of sharing power among the monarch, the aristocrats, and other social agents, especially the bourgeoisie, which often also represented the interests of peasants against the aristocracy as a way of balancing power.[21]

"Power sharing" was fundamentally alien to Sarmatian political culture. The entire political edifice of Sarmatian Poland was erected in such a way that the *szlachta* (nobles) did not have to share even the tiniest sliver of power with anyone: not the king, not the bourgeoisie, not the peasants, not any other social actor. It is when we reverse the above-given description of parliamentary democracy that an accurate image of Sarmatian political culture emerges. The members of the Sejm (parliament) were not free to make decisions they judged appropriate, bound by precise instructions received from their respective *sejmiki* (local constituencies). In practice, after the Jagiellonian dynasty ended in 1572, the local magnates ruled the country. That was the case, for instance, with the infamous *liberum veto*, which was first exercised in 1652 by Władysław Siciński, an MP from Lithuania acting on behalf of Janusz Radziwiłł, a powerful magnate who was playing his own political game against the Polish king. The site of power was not empty, but rather packed full by one subject: the collective body of *szlachta*, who equated the republic with their own estate. In the Polish case, it was easy to answer the question "Who rules?" – it was the *szlachta*. Polish nobles made sure the social translated into the political in a direct and absolute manner.

LIBERUM VETO

[In the Polish parliamentary system] it was taken for granted that the minority would accept the views of the majority not only legally but morally, giving up their separate position and thus saving the unity of the corporate will of the nation; at the same time each member of the Diet had an inalienable right to veto and, if this right was used, the Diet was automatically dissolved and *all* laws voted during the session were annulled. This was based on the belief that, if an individual member of the Diet had the courage to use this right of "free protest," his reasons must be very strong and it would therefore be better to make no decision at all … The ideological justification of this view may be defined as anti-authoritarian collectivism; *anti-authoritarian*, because it recognized that a mechanical majority was not enough, that there could be cases in which the entire collective had to respect the will of one of its members; *collectivism*, because it was assumed that as a rule an individual, or minority, had to bow to majority opinion and accept it as *morally binding*.

– Andrzej Walicki, "The Three Traditions of Polish Patriotism," 29

The second problem with the Sarmatian political regime rested in its exclusiveness. The *szlachta* radically differentiated themselves from the rest of the society. Indeed, the term "Pole" applied solely to members of the nobility and was not used to describe other estates or individuals. The origin myth of the (Polish) Sarmatians portrayed them as an alien tribe that had arrived from the south or southeast and taken control of the region's peasant populations. This colonial aspect of the Sarmatian mentality was strongly articulated in the Ukraine. It erected a barrier between the *szlachta* and the rest of society.[22] The nobles were not just better than the rest: they were substantially *different*, and they constituted a different nation, one that excluded all other groups.[23] The crucial difference between modern parliamentary democracy and the *demokracja szlachecka* of Sarmatian

Poland is that the former is constituted on universal principles: the ideals of full inclusion and popular suffrage.

One might argue that at its birth in the late eighteenth century, parliamentarism was hardly inclusive in practice, for it barred around 90 per cent of the population from the political process.[24] That is true, but it misses the point: the fact that parliamentary democracy articulated the idea of universal rights, even if they remained only theoretical at first, played a crucial role in the later inclusion of the entire population in the political process. While that process took more than 150 years in some cases (African Americans had to wait until 1965 for full inclusion), it ended in success because people wanted their reality to align with the principles written in their constitutions. These principles played an important performative role in changing the political realities of parliamentary democracies.[25] This sort of evolution was impossible under the regime of *demokracja szlachecka*, for it was exclusive not just on a practical level but, first and foremost, on a theoretical level. It did not postulate universal equality; to the contrary, it *affirmed* inequality between social groups, leaving no place for the emancipation of the masses – which was the central project of the Enlightenment and, more recently, of modernity. Before emancipation could come about, the old Sarmatian regime would have to be abandoned. This happened in the eighteenth century with the Constitution of the 3rd of May (1791), which spelled the end of the Sarmatian order in all possible respects: the *liberum veto, liberum rumpo*, and royal election *viritim* were all abandoned, the king's position was strengthened, and the distinction between the nobles and the rest of society was abolished. Clearly, then, it is a misunderstanding to treat that constitution as a triumph of Sarmatian culture.

Presenting *demokracja szlachecka* as a vanguard form of modern democracy and freedom amounts to intellectual abuse. The Sarmatians did all they could to resist modernity, a process described by Jerzy Jedlicki in his book *Jakiej cywlizacji Polacy potrzebują* (The Kind of Civilization That Poles Need).[26] They loathed the universal ideals of the Enlightenment because they found them incompatible with the essence of the Sarmatian political order – a firm and exclusive grip on power. The "freedom" they praised was in fact merely a collective wilfulness, even waywardness, which they exercised as a feudal privilege rooted in their noble origins.[27] Modernity has always worked against the privileges of birth; liberal, parliamentary democracy developed precisely as a means to prevent the exercise of individual or collective wilfulness.

In Sarmatian Poland, the freedom of the few was bought with the enslavement of the many. The serfdom that played a vital role in maintaining the material base of Sarmatian society was not much different from slavery. The only dissimilarity was that people were not bought and sold individually, although villages could be sold to a new owner along with their populations.[28] Apart from this difference, the authority exercised by nobles over their peasants mirrored all aspects of slave owners' power over their subjects. A master could discipline peasants in any way he judged appropriate in order to force them to work, and there was no legal instrument to *effectively* challenge abuses of power, since all courts and administrative positions were controlled by the *szlachta*. The amount of work that peasants were expected to do increased systematically, from two or three days a week in the sixteenth century up to as many as eleven in the eighteenth century, which meant that a peasant's wife and children were also forced to work. In this way, the Sarmatians combined slave and child labour. The *pan* (master)[29] controlled the personal lives and the "free time" of his peasants. He had the authority to tell them how much alcohol they could drink, and he could bar them from buying it from anyone but him (the so-called *propinacja*). He could also decide the fate of their children (allowing them to migrate to a city and become craftsmen, or forcing them to stay at the manor to work in the fields). He could arrange marriages with candidates of his choosing, as well as remarriages of widows. He could even rape newlywed women (the infamous *ius primae noctis*). Physical abuse was widespread and is well documented in literature and arts, from the folk songs gathered and published by Julian Przyboś (1901–70) in *Jabłoneczka* (Little Apple Tree, 1957) to literary texts such as *Zamek kaniowski* (Kaniv Castle, 1828) by the Polish Romantic poet Seweryn Goszczyński (1801–76). In his apt description of post-Sarmatian social relations in nineteenth-century Ukraine,[30] Daniel Beauvois quotes court documents proving that a nobleman's punishment for killing a peasant, even in the most brutal way, was at worst several weeks in prison, and at best – a prayer.

All social arrangements share a common feature: inertia – or hysteresis, as Pierre Bourdieu called it, borrowing the term from the sciences. Social phenomena do not come to an abrupt end unless, of course, a disaster happens and an entire community is rapidly destroyed. Customs, regulations, patterns of social interactions, and values tend to last much longer than the circumstances that brought them to life. Such is the case with Sarmatism. The Polish–Lithuanian Commonwealth ended with the final partition of 1795, but Sarmatism did not, and it is currently enjoying an unexpected renaissance.

Beauvois's comprehensive study shows that Poland's partitions of the late eighteenth century did little to change how the Polish nobles functioned. Important new developments concerned, first of all, taxation. The elites of the Polish–Lithuanian Commonwealth had been unable to undertake much-needed tax reforms, and taxation levels remained very low, oscillating around 5 per cent.[31] As a consequence, the state was notoriously underfunded. In the second half of the seventeenth century, at a moment crucial for the commonwealth's survival, its budget amounted to around 10 million *złoty*, whereas the budget of France at that time stood at an impressive 360 million, England at 240 million, and Turkey at 180 million. Even Denmark, a smaller country with a better geopolitical location, had a budget of 20 million.[32] After the partitions, the new rulers of Poland and Lithuania introduced their own taxation system, thus raising the taxes. The Polish nobles found themselves forced to pay their conquerors what they had been unwilling to pay their own king.

The partitions did not change much with regard to social relations between the nobles and the peasants; serfdom remained in place until the mid-nineteenth century. It was abolished on the initiative of the partitioning powers, since the Poles themselves were unable to undertake this crucial social reform at that time, although it continued in an informal way until the interwar years of the twentieth century. There have been many portrayals of this post/neo-slavery in both literature and scholarly research. One could point to *Ferdydurke* (1937) by Witold Gombrowicz (1904–69), or to the compelling picture of social inequalities in *Wyprawa w dwudziestolecie* (An Excursion through the Twenties and Thirties, 1999) by Czesław Miłosz (1911–2004), which also mentions authors such as Józef Mackiewicz (1902–85) and Maria Milkiewiczowa. *Polesie* (2007), a collection of essays written by Polish ethnographer Józef Obrębski (1905–67), paints a bleak picture of poverty, exploitation, and the extravagance of the nobility in the region of Polesia (eastern Poland until 1945, now Ukraine). Obrębski describes Polesia as "a land of princes and yokels," where extreme social contrasts have continued unchanged since the Sarmatian era. Zofia Chomętowska (1902–91), a pioneer of Polish photography, documented this region around the same time. Her photographs depict a world that had changed little for the peasants since the Middle Ages, along with the opulent life of the aristocrats, with their palaces, garden parties, and art collections.[33]

One might have expected the turbulent events of mid-twentieth century to radically change Poland's social and ideological landscape. The new Polish People's Republic from the start declared itself a workers' and peasants' state. One priority of the new regime was agrarian reform, which included redistributing lands owned by the aristocracy. This was carried out in 1944, before the Second World War ended, by the Polish Committee of National Liberation (PKWN), a puppet quasi-government controlled by Stalin. Notably, Poles had failed to enact basic modernization reforms as an independent state during the interwar years (1918–39). These reforms were badly needed and much welcomed by the peasants, who responded to them by supporting the new state. The Polish elites had learned little from the nineteenth century, during which uprisings against the partitioners gained little traction among the peasantry. Polish attempts to regain independence during the nineteenth century had failed because the nobles were not numerous enough to score a military victory and the peasants were unwilling to fight for a cause they did not recognize as their own. They were correct not to do so. These were the uprisings of *Poles*, and the peasants were not Poles, for Polish national identity was constructed solely by the *naród szlachecki* (nation of nobles). In this way, history took revenge on Sarmatian elitism.

The functionaries of the new Polish state launched vicious attacks on all that was associated with the *ancien régime*. Even so, patterns of Sarmatism made a spectacular comeback in the second half of the twentieth century. Przemysław Czapliński analyses this process in *Resztki nowoczesności* (The Remnants of Modernity, 2011), which describes how Sarmatism made a puzzling comeback in Polish cultural production in the 1970s. The numerous film adaptations of classic Polish historical novels – in particular Henryk Sienkiewicz's *Potop* (The Deluge, 1886) and *Ogniem i mieczem* (With Fire and Sword, 1884) – exemplify this phenomenon.[34] These films brought back the atmosphere and values of the honour-centred, post-warrior Sarmatian universe and became instant blockbusters. Sienkiewicz's novels are vivid proof of the performative force of literature. Polish perceptions of the Khmelnitsky Uprising have been shaped largely by how its leader is represented in *With Fire and Sword*, which eschews historical accuracy. In fact, Khmelnitsky was a law-abiding citizen who tried to settle his conflict with Aleksander Koniecpolski, a local Polish magnate, by legal means. He even managed to secure an audience with the Polish king Władysław IV. The king, after listening to his complaint that the courts controlled by the Polish nobles always ruled in their favour, deprived him of land legally in his possession, asking him sardonically, "Vel no habes frameam stupide?" (Didn't you have a sword, stupid?), thus encouraging him to settle the dispute by force. That is what he did, by starting an uprising that broke the back of the Polish colonial project in Ukraine. This marked the beginning of the decline in Polish rule in the borderlands. Yet in Sienkiewicz's novel, Khmelnitsky is simply a greedy bandit, and this representation has dominated the collective Polish imagination, with important consequences for contemporary Polish–Ukrainian relations.

Another (this time ironic) example of Sarmatism's comeback discussed by Czapliński is the popular television series *Czterdziestolatek* (The Forty-Year-Old, 1974–7), which portrays the private and professional life of a Polish engineer who has just entered middle age. In one episode, the protagonist of the series, Stefan Karwowski, while remodelling his apartment, comes up with a brilliant idea: he will build an arch in one of its doorways to make it look like a noble's manor.[35] Since his apartment is located in a *blokowisko* (communal apartment complex) – an example of a modernist approach to affordable housing and architecture, in both its visual form and social logic – the scene offers a perfect synecdoche: a new, progressive social form, represented by modernist architecture, is penetrated by archaic and regressive content inherited from Sarmatian times.

Why has Sarmatism made a come-back in Polish popular culture? This is probably the most interesting and pertinent question. The Polish cultural philosopher Andrzej Leder wrote a book about this that can be read alongside Czapliński's *The Remnants of Modernity* and that helps answer this question. In *Prześniona rewolucja. Ćwiczenie z logiki historycznej* (The Overslept Revolution: An Exercise from Historical Logic, 2014), Leder argues that the years 1939 to 1956 marked a genuine revolution in Poland, one that brought about the destruction of the symbolic field of Polish, (post-)Sarmatian society and culture. The revolution happened in two steps: Hitler eliminated the Jews, then Soviet and Polish communists destroyed the post-Sarmatian *ziemiaństwo* (landed gentry). The post-Sarmatian symbolic order was thereby replaced by a new one – popular, egalitarian, and emancipatory. However, Leder argues, this change was not accompanied by an adequate formulation of the new social imaginary – that is, by a set of images, beliefs, and values capable of making sense of the world and of complementing the symbolic field.[36] This was mainly because the revolution was conducted by foreign forces, which did not allow the new Polish subject to experience its own agency, although it fulfilled – as Leder demonstrates – the wishes and desires of Polish society. Anti-Semitism was widespread in prewar Poland,[37] as was anti-establishment hatred of the landowning class. The majority of Poles, especially in the countryside and smaller towns, welcomed the disappearance of both Jews and the landed gentry, but in the aftermath, they found themselves bereft of an imaginary: they had "overslept" (over-dreamed) the revolution, as Leder puts it in the title of his book. This is where Czapliński's and Leder's diagnoses link up: both nature and culture abhor a vacuum. Since the void left by Sarmatism was not filled by any comprehensive and coherent imaginary, Sarmatism returned like a sea that floods the land at high tide.

What is the current state of the Third Polish Republic, which replaced the Polish People's Republic twenty-five years ago? It bears many traces of old Sarmatian culture, in that its social arrangements favour inequality, hamper emancipation, and affirm the power of elites over the lower classes, especially of bosses over workers. This has not gone unnoticed by Polish writers and artists. When we look at Dorota Masłowska's celebrated *Wojna polsko-ruska pod flagą biało-czerwoną* (Snow White and Russian Red, 2002) through the lens of the post-Sarmatian predicament, we immediately see its protagonist, Silny (Strong), as a typical representative of the impoverished Polish *gołota* (petty gentry), who combines cultural primitivism with belief in his ultimate superiority. The fictional and surreal Polish–Russian war, named in the original Polish title, echoes the colonial conflict between two empires struggling to control the same strip of land between the Baltic Sea and the Black.

But the best artistic portrait of the endurance of the Sarmatian *ancien régime* is found in the writing of Sławomir Shuty from the early 2000s. In three of his books – *Bełkot* (Gibberish, 2001), *Cukier w normie* (Sugar within Norm, 2002), and his award-winning novel *Zwał* (The Heap, 2004) – he persistently returns to two themes. The first concerns everyday life in the suburbs of Polish cities, with their housing complexes that resemble similar solutions for affordable housing in Pruitt-Igoe (St Louis, Missouri). The second relates to the oppressive reality in many Polish workplaces, be they a small company or a large corporation. Together, these books present a sombre image of modern serfdom. The daily lives of Shuty's protagonists are filled with mindless consumption and rituals such as grilling, which serve as synecdoches for – to add a twist to Marx's original phrase – the "idiocy of urban life." Nowa Huta, a suburb of Kraków portrayed by Shuty, is filled with rural migrants living an echo of earlier village life where peasants, who were systematically denied emancipation by their Sarmatian masters, lived under a cloud of obscurantism and superstitions. The most interesting locus of contemporary post-Sarmatian social arrangements is the workplace, a site of ruthless exploitation equal to that experienced by peasants in rural Poland in Sarmatian times. The bosses in Shuty's novels behave like feudal masters, punishing any form of disobedience and constantly complaining about the laziness of their staff. Another Polish writer, Mariusz Sieniewicz, offers a compelling description of similar problems in his novel *Czwarte niebo* (The Fourth Heaven, 2003).

These artistic diagnoses find confirmation in more systematic academic research. A recent comprehensive investigation of work relations in Polish organizations, conducted by Janusz Hryniewicz, revealed the persistence of Sarmatian-like, serfdom-oriented attitudes in the organizational culture of contemporary Polish enterprises.[38] Upper managers behave like plantation owners, treating employees like slaves who must be disciplined with a whip. There is no space for questioning a superior's decisions, or for any form of resistance, and even doubt is severely punished. The workers thus live in constant fear, preferring not to voice any criticism; their dream is to have a precisely defined scope of tasks to fulfil in order to avoid the wrath of their bosses. So it is no wonder that the Polish economy is not innovative. It never has been, not even when it came to the cash-crop production that was the main source of the nobility's income. Agricultural productivity in Poland lagged behind that of the West throughout the entire Sarmatian period and rose only during the period of partitions.[39] After all, why innovate if it is easier to further exploit a plentiful, slave-like workforce? The question applies to both former and contemporary Poland, where wages are still among the lowest in the European Union despite the growing productivity of labour.

The most important and enduring consequence of Sarmatian arrangements, however, is to be found in the hostile attitude of Polish society, and especially its elites, towards the project of modernity. As I argued earlier, Sarmatism between the sixteenth and eighteenth centuries was both a genuine alternative to modernity and its negation. Back then, modernity was viewed as something alien and hostile that must be opposed at all costs, for it threatened the traditional Polish way of life. Poland's partitions by foreign powers only reinforced this attitude. Many modernizing reforms, such as establishing administrative control and an effective taxation system in the late eighteenth century, abandoning serfdom in mid-nineteenth century, conducting successful land reform in the mid-twentieth century, and passing laws to curb domestic violence in the early twenty-first century, were introduced by foreign powers or as a result of their initiative. It comes as no surprise, then, that adherents to "traditional Polish values" treat modernity with suspicion. Yet at the same time, Poland has embraced a particular form of modernity – neoliberalism – with the unanimous support of the elites.

To address this paradox, we have to consider modernity as such. What is it? In his inspiring book *A Singular Modernity*, Fredric Jameson offers a notion of modernity that is particularly useful in the Polish and Central European contexts. He claims that modernity is an interplay between two distinct notions that operate separately on the levels of material base and cultural superstructure. *Modernization* thus accounts for all that falls within the realm of material economy: highways, the stock exchange, supermarkets, cellular phones, the Internet, computers, and so on. *Modernism* is a set of values, norms, and ideals operating in the sociocultural sphere and linked to the legacy of Enlightenment: equality, social justice, emancipation, the rational organization of society, and so on. According to Jameson, modernity should not be reduced to either one of these two aspects, or components, being a complex combination of both.[40]

What does this interplay look like in present-day Poland? The two approaches that dominate the mainstream of Polish social and political life – conservative and liberal – focus on only one aspect of modernity – namely, modernization. Liberals seem to think that emancipation is a private matter at best, and a necessary evil at worst, and that it should be left therefore outside of collective politics. They focus entirely on modernizing the material base by, for instance, building highways, airports, and stadiums, or by developing a stock exchange. As a result, even though Poland has been governed by so-called liberals for 80 per cent of the time since it joined EU, it has to this day refrained from signing the Charter of Fundamental Rights, which focuses on emancipatory issues. The conservatives, for their part, reject emancipatory politics altogether as alien to both traditional Polish values and the teachings of the Catholic Church.[41] Just like the liberals, the conservatives accept only the material-infrastructural aspects of modernity – modernization, to use Jameson's term.[42] Neoliberalism fits perfectly in this social and cultural configuration. It affirms only the economic aspects of classical liberalism associated with the post-Locke and post-Smith philosophical traditions,[43] leaving aside emancipatory issues that interested liberals such as John Stuart Mill.[44] It is well suited to conservative attitudes, as illustrated by American neoconservatism, which combines neoliberal free market fundamentalism with a conservative stance on social issues. Not surprisingly, its main base of support is found in the post-slavery cultural landscape of southern United States.

The affinity between neoliberalism and post-Sarmatian cultural patterns runs deeper still, however. French sociologist Loïc Wacquant offers the mythical figure of the centaur – a monster with a human upper body and the lower body of a horse – as a metaphor of neoliberalism. Neoliberalism is shaped like a centaur, Wacquant argues – it appears as a pleasant businessman in a suit to the elites, but as a vicious beast to the lower classes.[45] For the elites, it offers an emphasis on individual autonomy, prosperity, and freedom from constraints, while refraining from demands for cultural reforms in customs or manners (e.g., in the treatment of women and sexual minorities, or in childrearing practices). The aim of neoliberals is to weaken the state's ability to intervene in ways that are uncomfortable for the elites. For the lower classes, it brings nothing but the brutal subjection to discipline in the workplace, as well as the destruction of forms of collective care (the welfare state) and collective bargaining (trade unions) – briefly put, the infamous austerity that has recently become the focus of major political debates.

Similarities between the neoliberal agenda and the ideals of Sarmatism are striking, starting with *freedom* – the word that has served as a mantra for both formations. In both cases, this freedom comes with a price tag that is epitomized in the fate of the lower classes, who are compelled to adapt to harsh social realities if those realities are convenient for the elites. In economic terms, it comes down to a form of exploitation corresponding to a particular historical reality: serfdom in older times, an austere and precarious life today. Its result is the modern workplace serfdom portrayed by Sławomir

Shuty in his writing and discussed by Janusz Hryniewicz in his research. Both Sarmatism and neoliberalism are profoundly anti-egalitarian, in that they affirm that the influence of elites on collective policy should be greater than that of the lower classes. The neoliberals achieve this via media, allegedly impartial experts, and lobby groups. The task was easier for the Polish nobility, who controlled the power apparatus directly. Both neoliberalism and Sarmatism are hostile towards the state as such and treat it as a necessary evil that always threatens freedom and that should be constrained as much as possible.[46]

Of course, neoliberalism is a global ideology that has triumphed in many places around the world. As such, it does not derive from Sarmatism and does not need a post-Sarmatian cultural milieu to thrive. This is, however, beside the point. Some of the reasons for neoliberalism's success in other places around the world may bear little significance in the Polish context, and vice versa.[47] What is important is that social arrangements and values typical of Sarmatism proved to be functional in promoting neoliberal ideology and pacifying discontent in Poland. In this respect Poland – and more generally the entire post-Sarmatian region that comprises the Baltic states, Belarus, and Ukraine – differs from other countries. While the neoliberal agenda of austerity faces serious social resistance in Greece, Portugal, Spain, Britain, and France, in Poland it has been enthusiastically embraced.[48] Even the adjacent Czech Republic is significantly more equal as a society.[49] A recent analysis conducted by the *Financial Times* proves that the overall good performance of Polish economy is founded on extreme exploitation: Poland, a crucible of neoliberalism, is the region's uncontested leader when it comes to precarious employment and cheap labour.[50] Interestingly, if sadly, this leaves Poland as a nation in the same place where it has been for centuries: on the periphery of the capitalist world system. Cheap labour is Poland's main export on the global market, since the local workforce has been primed by local elites to accept work conditions that developed nations are not willing to accept – just like in good old Sarmatian times.

Jan Sowa,
Independent Scholar, Poland
Translated by Agnieszka Polakowska

NOTES

1 Słowacki, "Agamemnon's Tomb," 96.
2 Koehler, *Słuchaj mię, Sauromata*, 6.
3 See Chornovol, "The Jagiellonian Idea and Ukrainian Historiography."
4 Kula, *Teoria ekonomiczna ustroju feudalnego*, 141.
5 For a more extensive presentation of this issue, see Sowa, *Fantomowe ciało króla*, 341.
6 Anderson, *Lineages of the Absolutist State*, 292.
7 See Žižek, *The Sublime Object of Ideology*.
8 Orzechowski, *Policya Królestwa Polskiego*, 68.
9 Quoted in Tazbir, "W cudzym i własnym zwierciadle," 18.
10 Kunicki, *Obraz szlachcica polskiego*, 73.
11 Kochowski, "Psalmodia polska," 180, quoted in Bogucka, *Dzieje kultury polskiej do 1918 roku*, 181. This would be a good starting point to explore the discourse of Polish colonial expansion, which I have addressed extensively in my book *Fantomowe ciało króla*.

12 *Mowa Stefana Potockiego referendarza koronnego marszałka poselskiego przy powitaniu JKM-ci w Warszawie 1724*, quoted in Michalski, "Sarmatyzm a europeizacja Polski w XVIII wieku," 122–3.
13 Rzewuski, *Myśli o teraźniejszych okolicznościach*, quoted in Michalski, "Sarmatyzm a europeizacja Polski w XVIII wieku," 139.
14 A good popular summary of this point of view is offered by a website "Polska Wielki Projekt": http://polskawielkiprojekt.pl.
15 Ostrowski, *Przyszły król* quoted in Szacki, *Liberalizm po komunizmie*, 58.
16 Hamilton, "The Union as a Safeguard"; Madison, "The Same Subject Continued" and "The Senate Continued."
17 See Lefort, *Essais sur le politique*.
18 See Schumpeter, *Capitalism, Socialism, and Democracy*.
19 See Rancière, "Ten Thesis on Politics."
20 See Dahl, *Polyarchy*.
21 See Barrington, *Social Origins of Dictatorship and Democracy*.
22 One could also apply here the notion of heterogeneity as it is used by Laclau in *On Populist Reason*.
23 Some scholars believe that not all nations are modern and that there were pre-modern nations, which included Poles along with English, Scots, French, Dutch, Castilians, Portuguese, Danish, Hungarian, and Russians. See Seton-Watson, "Old and New Nations," 134.
24 See my *Ciesz się późny wnuku*, esp. ch. 1, "Od uczestnictwa do reprezentacji" (From Participation to Representation) and ch. 2, "Długie trwanie" (The Long Duration).
25 French philosopher Jacques Rancière devoted a lot of attention to this process. See his *On the Shores of Politics*, esp. ch. 2, "The Uses of Democracy," 39–61.
26 Jedlicki, *Jakiej cywilizacji Polacy potrzebują?*
27 For this reason, Sarmatian arrangements are sometimes confused with anarchism. This is a misconception, since the latter models a horizontal, inclusive, democratic, and egalitarian politics that runs counter to elevating the interests of one class above another. Sarmatism was anarchic with its disdain for state power, but not in putting class privilege over such ideals of anarchism as equality and inclusion. See for example Graeber, *Fragments of an Anarchist Anthropology*.
28 I thank Keely Stauter-Halsted for directing my attention to this fact.
29 This is still the polite form of address in the Polish language, equivalent to the French *vous* or the German *Sie*.
30 See Beauvois, *La bataille de la terre en Ukraine, 1863–1914*.
31 Rutkowski, *Wieś europejska późnego feudalizmu*, 195–6.
32 Wimmer, "Wojsko," 198. See also Mączak, "The Structure of Power," 131.
33 See: *Między kadrami*.
34 Jerzy Hoffman directed the film adaptations of *The Deluge* and *With Fire and Sword* in 1974 and 1999, respectively.
35 The construction of the arch can be viewed in an excerpt from this episode, available online: https://www.youtube.com/watch?v=jD6Z0X3jsXg.
36 Leder refers here to Charles Taylor's use of this notion in *Sources of the Self*.
37 A recent exhibition of anti-Semitic drawings in the Polish press from 1919 to 1939 presented by the Jewish Historical Institute in Warsaw shatters any illusions on the subject. Visit http://www.jhi.pl/en/exhibitions/22.
38 Hryniewicz, *Stosunki pracy w polskich organizacjach*.

39 Kula, *Historia, zacofanie, rozwój*, 161.
40 Jameson, *A Singular Modernity*.
41 In Poland, the latter seems indistinguishable from the figure of John Paul II; the new, more liberal turn offered by Pope Francis has been rejected by the Church and the mainstream of conservative media in Poland.
42 Their attitude is more paradoxical than that of liberals, however, since they want to use modernization against modernism. In other words, they seek material development in order to obtain the means and tools to fight emancipation. An excellent example is provided by the funding scheme of the Polish right-wing conservative and religious media, which are financed to an important extent with profits derived from the banking industry – to be precise, from the Polish credit union system, which is controlled by right-wing conservative politicians. See, for example, Michał Gąsior, "'Milioner, u którego pół prawicy siedzi w kieszeni.'"
43 For a good example see Zakaria, *The Future of Freedom*.
44 See for example Mill, *The Subjection of Women*.
45 Wacquant, "Three Steps to a Historical Anthropology."
46 Taxes are one aspect of the state that they both detest.
47 I argued elsewhere that the neoliberal transformation of the Soviet Bloc played a crucial role in justifying neoliberalism as a universal ideology, in a way that was similar to the impact of the Haitian Revolution on the ideals of the French Enlightenment. See my "An Unexpected Twist of Ideology."
48 Ost, *Defeat of Solidarity*.
49 The GINI coefficient describing material inequalities in Poland is 20 per cent higher than in the Czech Republic (around 0.30 versus 0.25), and the percentage of workers earning the minimum wage is four times higher (10 versus 2.5 per cent).
50 See Romei, "Pole Position." For more on this issue, see Woś, *Dziecięca choroba liberalizmu*.

WORKS CITED

Anderson, Perry. *Lineages of the Absolutist State*. London: New Left Books, 1974.

Barrington, Moore, Jr. *Social Origins of Dictatorship and Democracy: Lord and Peasant in the Making of Modern World*. Boston: Beacon Press, 1967.

Beauvois, Daniel. *La bataille de la terre en Ukraine, 1863–1914: Les Polonais et les conflits socio-ethniques*, Lille: Presses universitaires de Lille, 1993.

Bogucka, Maria. *Dzieje kultury polskiej do 1918 roku*. Wrocław: Zakład Narodowy im. Ossolińskich, 1991.

Borowski, Andrzej. *Powrót Europy*. Kraków: Księgarnia Akademicka, 1999.

Chornovol, Ihor. "The Jagiellonian Idea and Ukrainian Historiography." In *Razem w Europie*. Edited by Irena Mikłaszewicz and Rūstis Kamuntavičius. Kaunas: Česlovo Milošo slavistikos centras, 2006.

Dahl, Robert. *Polyarchy: Participation and Opposition*. New Haven: Yale University Press, 1971.

Gąsior, Michał. "'Milioner, u którego pół prawicy siedzi w kieszeni' – Grzegorz Bierecki, prezes SKOK-ów," http://natemat.pl/31541,milioner-u-ktorego-pol-prawicy-siedzi-w-kieszeni-grzegorz-bierecki-prezes-skok-ow.

Graeber, David. *Fragments of an Anarchist Anthropology*. Chicago: Prickly Paradigm Press, 2004.

Hamilton, Alexander. "The Union as a Safeguard against Domestic Faction and Insurrection." *The Federalist*, no. 9.

Hryniewicz, Janusz. *Stosunki pracy w polskich organizacjach.* Warszawa: Wydawnictwo Naukowe SCHOLAR, 2007.

Jameson, Frederic. *A Singular Modernity: Essay on the Ontology of the Present.* London: Verso, 2002.

Jedlicki, Jerzy. *Jakiej cywilizacji Polacy potrzebują? Studia z dziejów idei i wyobraźni XIX wieku.* Warszawa: PWN, 1988.

Kochowski, Wespezjan. "Psalmodia polska oraz wybór liryków i fraszek." In Maria Bogucka, *Dzieje kultury polskiej do 1918 roku.* Wrocław: Ossolineum, 1987.

Koehler, Krzysztof, ed. *Słuchaj mię, Sauromata. Antologia poezji sarmackiej.* Kraków: Arcana, 2002.

Kula, Witold. *Historia, zacofanie, rozwój.* Warszawa: Czytelnik, 1983.

– *Teoria ekonomiczna ustroju feudalnego. Próba modelu.* Warszawa: PWN, 1963.

Kunicki, Wacław. *Obraz szlachcica polskiego.* Kraków: Officina typographica Francisci Caesarji, 1645.

Laclau, Ernesto. *On Populist Reason.* London: Verso, 2007.

Lefort, Claude. *Essais sur le politique. XIXe–XXe siècle.* Paris: Seuil, coll. Esprit, 1986.

Madison, James. "The Same Subject Continued." *The Federalist*, no. 10.

– "The Senate Continued." *The Federalist*, no. 63.

Mączak, Antoni. "The Structure of Power in the Commonwealth of the Sixteenth and Seventeenth Century." In *A Republic of Nobles: Studies in Polish History to 1864.* Edited by J.K. Fedorowicz, 109–34. Cambridge: CUP Archive, 1982.

Michalski, Jerzy. "Sarmatyzm a europeizacja Polski w XVIII wieku." In *Swojskość i cudzoziemszczyzna w dziejach kultury polskiej.* Edited by Zofia Stefanowska, 113–68. Warszawa: Państwowe Wydawnictwo Naukowe, 1973.

Między kadrami. Fotografie Zofii Chomętowskiej z Polesia 1925–1939. Warszawa: Dom Spotkań z Historią, http://starastrona.dsh.waw.pl/wydarzenia/miedzy-kadrami-fotografie-zofii-chometowskiej-z-polesia-1925-1939.

Mill, John Stuart. *The Subjection of Women.* Mineola: Dover, 1997.

Orzechowski, Stanisław. *Policya Królestwa Polskiego, na kształt Arystotelesowskich polityk wypisana.* Poznań: Biblioteka Kórnicka, 1854.

Ost, David. *Defeat of Solidarity: Anger and Politics in Postcommunist Europe.* Ithaca: Cornell University Press, 2005.

"Polska Wielki Projekt." http://polskawielkiprojekt.pl.

Rancière, Jacques. "Ten Theses on Politics." *Theory and Event* 5, no. 3 (2001): 10–16.

– *On the Shores of Politics.* Translated by Liz Heron. London and New York: Verso, 1995.

Romei, Valentina. "Pole position, Financial Times Data." https://www.ft.com/content/9e4e9a38-3d96-3770-aa0f-8ddd784cfffb?mhq5j=e5.

Rutkowski, Jan. *Wieś europejska późnego feudalizmu.* Warszawa: PWN, 1986.

Schumpeter, Joseph. *Capitalism, Socialism, and Democracy.* New York: Harper Colophon, 1975.

Seton-Watson, Hugh. "Old and New Nations." In *Nationalism.* Edited by John Hutchinson and Anthony D. Smith, 134. Oxford: Oxford University Press, 1994.

Skórczewski, Dariusz. *Teoria – literatura – dyskurs. Pejzaż postkolonialny.* Lublin: KUL, 2013.

Słowacki, Juliusz. "Agamemnon's Tomb." In Juliusz Słowacki, *This Fateful Power: Sesquicentennial Anthology 1809–1849.* Edited and translated by Michael J. Mikoś. Lublin: Norbertinum, 1999.

Sowa, Jan. *Ciesz się późny wnuku. Kolonializm, globalizacja i demokracja radykalna*, Kraków: Korporacja Ha!art, 2007.

– *Fantomowe ciało króla. Peryferyjne zmagania z nowoczesną formą*. Kraków: Universitas, 2012.

– "An Unexpected Twist of Ideology: Neoliberalism and the Collapse of the Soviet Bloc." *Praktyka Teoretyczna* 5 (2012). http://www.praktykateoretyczna.pl/PT_nr5_2012_Logika_sensu/13.Sowa.pdf.

Szacki, Jerzy. *Liberalizm po komunizmie*. Kraków: Znak, 1994.

Taylor, Charles. *Sources of the Self: The Making of Modern Identity*. Cambridge: Cambridge University Press, 1992.

Tazbir, Janusz. "W cudzym i własnym zwierciadle." In *Szlaki kultury polskiej*. Warszawa: PIW, 1986.

Wacquant, Loïc. "Three Steps to a Historical Anthropology of Actually Existing Neoliberalism." *Social Anthropology* 20 (2012): 66–79.

Walicki, Andrzej. "The Three Traditions in Polish Patriotism." In *Polish Paradoxes*. Edited by Stanisław Gomułka and Antony Polonsky, 21–39. London and New York: Routledge, 1990.

Wimmer, Jan. "Wojsko." In *Polska XVII wieku: państwo – społeczeństwo – kultura*. Edited by Janusz Tazbir. 175–229. Warszawa: Wiedza Powszechna, 1974.

Woś, Rafał. *Dziecięca choroba liberalizmu*. Warszawa: Studio EMKA, 2014.

Zakaria, Fareed. *The Future of Freedom: Illiberal Democracy at Home and Abroad*. New York: W.W. Norton, 2007.

Žižek, Slavoj. *The Sublime Object of Ideology*. London: Verso, 2009.

The Splintering of a Myth: Polish Romantic Ideology in the Twentieth and Twenty-First Centuries

At the beginning of the twenty-first century, just over a decade after Poland regained its independence, Marek Koterski's popular comedy film *Dzień świra* (The Day of the Wacko, 2002) unveiled the new condition of the grand old Romantic paradigm in Polish culture. In the film's early scenes, a neurotic high-school literature teacher and aspiring poet named Adam Miauczyński sits on his sofa in a functional modern apartment to read Adam Mickiewicz's *Crimean Sonnets*. As he recites the words of his venerable Romantic predecessor, the contemporary "A.M." imagines himself in the black cape of a nineteenth-century bard, floating – "jak łódka brodzi" (like a boat) – among the charmless buildings of his post-communist housing estate. As the camera pans across the grass and the concrete, poetry infiltrates the banality of a sunny morning in the Polish suburbs. Yet the daydream of this shabby new Romantic soon crashes into the unwelcome cacophony of late capitalist modernity: loud music from a stereo, the clatter of rollerblades in a stairwell, a neighbour practising her karate chops, and the whine of a grass trimmer. As the noise drowns out the hushed words of the poem, the caped protagonist thrusts his head into his hands, exclaiming, "I'm dying here!" The collapse of Miauczyński's fantasy in this hostile reality resonates with Mickiewicz's cultural death in a society no longer interested in poetry. In the Brave New World of post-1989 Poland, the Romantic tradition has been condemned to irrelevance, absurdity, and ultimate extinction.

Koterski's cult film captured in popular form what eminent literary critic Maria Janion had earlier characterized as "the end of a paradigm." In her famous essay of the same title, written between 1990 and 1992, Janion diagnosed "the expiration of a certain historical cycle in Polish culture."[1] The nineteenth-century Romantic paradigm had developed in the context of Poland's struggle for independence, as a cultural expression of the insurrectionary tradition against foreign domination. For much of the twentieth century, this tradition remained painfully relevant, as Poland fought against Nazi Germany and the Soviet Union for its political and cultural survival. Yet the final realization of the central Romantic political aim of national self-determination paradoxically led to a rapid erosion of Romanticism's relevance. As a genuinely independent political community established itself in the 1990s, the need for a defensive "imagined community" rooted in literature evaporated. Janion ironically characterizes this positive shift as yet another national calamity, since the end of the Romantic paradigm in Polish culture also dealt a fatal blow to the collective's highly idealized image of itself. How would Poles define themselves when they had nothing to fight bravely against? What would form the symbolic matrix for Polish culture in the new era of independence, democracy, and the free market? What would be the fate of those great literary works and symbols that had sustained the nation's cultural existence for almost two centuries? Koterski's film answers Janion's questions with a bitterly satirical vision. In *The Day of the Wacko*, post-transition Polish society is shallow, materialistic, envious, and ugly, and the degenerate remnants of the Romantic tradition persist only on the humiliated margins, in the daydreams of an irascible schoolteacher.

This vision offers a valid albeit partial description of contemporary reality in Poland, for Romanticism has also proven to be extraordinarily resilient. Indeed, Janion's announcement of the "end of a paradigm" was never meant to be an anti-Romantic manifesto. Rather, she was proposing a reinvigoration and redirection of the Romantic legacy. Together with Maria Żmigrodzka, Janion was advocating a shift away from national and historical readings of Polish Romantic literature to what the two critics describe as an "existential" interpretation focused on the reconciliation of individual and collective concerns.[2] Various other post-1989 thinkers have also attempted to rework the Romantic legacy for diverse non-political purposes. In the 1990s, the poet Jarosław Marek Rymkiewicz argued for a new emphasis on the Romantic poetry of earthly "being," rooted in everyday life, against its phantasmagorical visions of otherworldly "existence."[3] Agata Bielik-Robson, in turn, developed the concept of "Romantic rationalism" in her book on Romanticism as an "unfinished project" of modernity.[4] More recently, Dariusz Skórczewski has called for a radical reinterpretation of Polish Romantic literature, with a new emphasis on the works of Juliusz Słowacki (1809–49), which would be a departure from the damaging cocktail of messianic self-glorification and postcolonial inferiority complex supposedly inculcated by the Mickiewiczean legacy.[5]

All of these fascinating projects have been decidedly scholarly and correspondingly marginal in their social impact. But when the Polish presidential plane crashed into the forest near Smolensk, Russia, on 10 April 2010, the Romantic paradigm dramatically reasserted its galvanizing power in public life. Polish citizens came out in droves onto the streets of Warsaw to honour the dead. The astonishing symbolic resonance of this event with earlier tragedies on Russian soil led many to suspect foul play, and before long the old narratives of persecution and martyrdom were revived in an atmosphere of intense domestic political conflict. Some looked on in horror, critiquing the collective commemoration of the fallen as "thanato-messianism," an unhealthy national obsession with death and sacrifice inherited from Mickiewicz's drama *Dziady, cz. III* (Forefathers' Eve, Part III, 1832).[6] Others reveled in the renewed collective spirit of this ritual communion with the dead on the streets of the capital and in public discourse. The debate split along political lines, with many of its participants drawing heavily on the vocabulary of the Romantic tradition to characterize it and using Romantic ideas to attack their opponents.

Seven years later, the Romantic paradigm continues to rise from the ashes around the anniversary of the Smolensk disaster, and Poland has a new government with a particular interest in the tragedy. The Romantic legacy remains irrelevant to some, while to others it forms the foundation for their interpretation of contemporary events. But what are the longer-term cultural processes behind this division? Perhaps the Polish Romantic paradigm of purity, suffering, and sacrifice is so deeply rooted that it is bound to re-emerge whenever Poland seems to be threatened, only to sink into irrelevance when the country is stable and thriving. But if so, why has it arisen once again in a period regarded by many as Poland's "second golden age"? Alternatively, when we look at the influence of Romanticism on Polish culture in the twentieth and twenty-first centuries, we are perhaps dealing with repeated attempts to instrumentalize its legacy for political purposes. In this chapter,

I attempt to understand the Romantic legacy by tracing its diverse transformations over the past century.

What Is the Polish Romantic Paradigm?

In her essay on "the end of a paradigm," Maria Janion asserts the existence of a relatively monolithic Romantic "system" in Polish culture, developed largely through works of literature. This system constructed "a sense of national identity" and defended "the symbols of this identity," passing them from generation to generation, while organizing itself around certain "spiritual values" of the national community, including "fatherland, independence, the freedom of the nation and national solidarity."[7] Janion concedes that this system has always been open to interpretation, though she maintains that the core "spiritual values" have generally been understood in "martyrological or messianic" terms. Above all, the Polish Romantic paradigm enshrined the historical suffering experienced by the Polish people, constructing a compensatory myth after the final dismembering of the Polish–Lithuanian Commonwealth by Russia, Prussia, and Austria at the end of the eighteenth century.

Mickiewicz produced the most influential forms of this myth in his play *Forefathers' Eve, Part III* and in the quasi-biblical tract *Księgi narodu polskiego i pielgrzymstwa polskiego* (The Books of the Polish Nation and of the Polish Pilgrimage, 1832). In these key works, he developed the heretical notion of Poland as "the Christ of the Nations," an innocent victim suffering at the hands of the "Satanic trinity" of partitioning powers for the ultimate salvation of a corrupt and indifferent Europe. At the heart of Mickiewicz's project was a poetic rationalization of political weakness. As Witold Gombrowicz observed in 1956, "because we had lost our independence and were weak, [Mickiewicz] decorated our weakness with the plumes of Romanticism … he opposed our Christian virtue to the lawlessness of the partitioners."[8] Gombrowicz interprets the Polish Romantic tradition almost as Friedrich Nietzsche interpreted the development of Christianity itself – as a "revaluation of all values."[9] To be more precise, the Polish Romantic myth embodied what we might call a "revaluation of political values," so that political structures no longer constituted the foundation of national identity, as they had done throughout the period of the Polish–Lithuanian Commonwealth, and catastrophic defeat was a sign of positive virtue. In the absence of a Polish state, the external realities of history and politics gave way to a set of "spiritual" or "inner" realities – a new "homeland of the mind."[10]

This revaluation would carry extraordinary power, rendering Polish national identity almost immune to the political and military aggression of its enemies, but also changing its fundamental nature. As early as 1772, Jean-Jacques Rousseau observed that its main aim would be "to establish the Republic so firmly in the hearts of the Poles that she [would] maintain her existence there in spite of all the efforts of her oppressors."[11] The revaluation of political values ensured that Poland's weakness became a source of strength, while simultaneously remoulding the very concept of the nation from the political identity of the earlier "gentry republic" to a much broader and deeper cultural community – what Mickiewicz called "the Polish pilgrimage." The Polish nation ensured its indestructibility by shifting its existence from the external political world into the internal or "spiritual" consciousness of its constituents, becoming the quintessential "imagined community."[12]

Yet this radical revaluation of political and national values offers only a partial description of Mickiewicz's project and its continuing influence. After all, Mickiewicz was not only a purveyor of spiritual values, but also a revolutionary agitator and activist. Indeed, this analysis emphasizes the positive and constructive resonance of the Romantic myth – namely, its maximalist transformative potential. In both its Mickiewiczean origins and later adaptations, Polish messianism has explained the nation's trials by placing them within broader narratives prophesying the coming of fundamental positive changes to a fallen social and political reality. These narratives have anticipated three primary forms of often interconnected transformation: (1) transformation through the apotheosis of national self-determination, (2) transformation through social revolution, and (3) transformation through a dramatic reordering of political relations in Europe. At the core of the Polish Romantic myth, uncomfortably intertwined, we find nationalism, radical democratic politics, and programmatic internationalism.

Meaning in History – Mickiewicz's poetic mythology ascribes a fundamental meaning and direction to history. More broadly, the philosophy of history formed a central pillar of Polish Romantic thought. Apart from Mickiewicz's historical prophecies, the philosopher August Cieszkowski (1814–94) developed a Hegelian strand of historical dialectics focused on the concept of "action." His ideas exerted a strong influence on the poet Zygmunt Krasiński (1812–59), who painted a dark picture of social revolution and historical apocalypse in his drama *Nie-boska Komedia* (The Un-Divine Comedy, 1835). Meanwhile, Juliusz Słowacki (1809–49) elaborated his own poetic philosophy of history as the evolution of "spirit" through nature, human individuals, and nations in two of his most famous works, *Genezis z Ducha* (Genesis from the Spirit, 1844) and *Król Duch* (The King Spirit, 1845–9).

At the same time, the Romantic era marked the beginning of a crucial transition in the very concept of the nation: from a political category prioritizing social estate over ethnic identity, as in the so-called noble democracy of the old Polish–Lithuanian Commonwealth, to a broader concept embracing a proto-democratic idea of "the people." The motivations for this shift lay in both idealistic commitment and political expediency. On the one hand, freedom fighters like Tadeusz Kościuszko (1746–1817) and poets like Mickiewicz and Słowacki had all absorbed a great deal of the democratic and revolutionary spirit of the era, looking to political developments in France for inspiration. On the other hand, it had become increasingly clear that the struggle for Polish independence against the partitioning powers could not succeed without the broad support of the masses. Here we see a move away from pre-modern ideas of the political nation towards the mass democratic politics that would later be intertwined with the development of modern nationalism.

Yet Mickiewicz's own paradigm was far from nationalist. Instead, he espoused a paradoxical form of nationalist internationalism, whereby the impending resurrection of the crucified Poland would have global consequences, spreading freedom across Europe. Andrzej Walicki characterizes this synthesis as "Romantic universalism," proposing a balanced tension between the national and the international, the particular and the universal, and an ultimate rejection of egoism, or chauvinism among nations, in favour of a spirit of fraternity and self-sacrifice.[13] Mickiewicz viewed the "Polish pilgrimage" as a kind of revolutionary avant-garde, one that would clear the way for the freedom of all through selfless suffering. The final aim was international, though the historical means of achieving it were national.

But this productive tension between the particular and the universal sometimes reached a breaking point. Along with universalism, Mickiewicz's *The Books*, *Forefathers' Eve, Part III*, and even *Pan Tadeusz* (Sir Thaddeus, 1834) include strong doses of petty parochialism, self-glorification and – in the case of *The Books* – xenophobia. In his peculiar quasi-biblical tract, Mickiewicz exhorts his compatriots in exile to stick together and to maintain a healthy suspicion of "foreigners." He presents unflattering stereotypical images of various other nations and peoples, likens non-Poles to "wolves" and "swine," and regularly insists on the moral superiority of his own nation.[14] Mickiewicz's universal salvation project is inseparable from what Stanisław Eile and others have criticized as "national megalomania."[15] The seeds of modern nationalist chauvinism are apparent, even in an ostensibly internationalist project.

I have focused on Mickiewicz in this rough outline of the Polish Romantic paradigm because the continuing influence of his work has been incalculably more significant than that of Słowacki, Zygmunt Krasiński, Cyprian Norwid (1821–83), and others, for reasons I will discuss shortly. Nevertheless, even without considering the varied contributions of these other Romantic writers, we should note that Mickiewicz's oeuvre itself is far from homogeneous or consistent. In his canonical texts, three very different forms of transformation are united in a single grand narrative, which is then weakened by perceptible fault lines. Early modern political ideas of the nation conflict with a rising emphasis on "the people"; traditional religion collides with revolution; universalism clashes with nationalism.

The process I will trace over the twentieth century until today involves the decisive splintering of this fragile unity, as diverse interpreters and political actors have deployed the transformation narratives of national self-determination, social revolution, and universal renewal in very different proportions and combinations. The twentieth century witnessed a disintegration and reconstitution of the Romantic myth into several often competing versions, in a continuation of a process that began in the second half of the nineteenth century.[16] The "Romantic paradigm" in Polish culture has proven to be far from monolithic. Instead, the heterogeneous and contradictory nature of its core content has been exposed, providing fuel for a range of opposing ideological projects in the twentieth century and beyond.

The Splintering Paradigm: Romantic Currents from 1918 to 1945

When we survey the twentieth century in Polish culture, we discover an astonishing range of political projects finding either inspiration or legitimation in Romanticism. The Romantic poets and their works were congenial for traditionalists and progressives, rulers and revolutionaries, reactionaries and rebels, Catholics and communists. Among others, I will point to Józef Piłsudski and the interwar state; Bolesław Bierut and the postwar communist regime; the left-wing student rebels of 1968; Pope John Paul II; and the Solidarity movement. Various sides of the political spectrum made strong claims to the Romantic legacy, effectively splitting it into a set of competing narratives rooted in contradictory aspects of the heterogeneous political mythology developed largely by Mickiewicz.

While the focus of my attention is mainly political here, it is also crucial to address the declining influence of the Romantic legacy on twentieth-century Polish literature, since the political nature of the Romantic paradigm is directly related to this decline. In the earliest years of the century, we still find a form of "neo-Romanticism" in the modernist poetry of "Young Poland."[17] After the rebirth of an independent Poland in 1918, however, very few writers consciously took up the Romantic legacy. As early as 1919, Antoni Słonimski (1895–1976) set the tone in his poem "Czarna wiosna" (Black Spring), linking Poland's new independence with a turn away from the national poetic tradition embodied by the iconic figure of Konrad, the national poet-hero of Mickiewicz's *Forefathers' Eve, Part III*: "My fatherland is free, free … So I hurl Konrad's cape from my shoulders."[18]

Much of the most innovative literature of the interwar period would critique and even mock the "Romantic legend."[19] Admittedly, this was not entirely unprecedented, in that the "Positivist" writers of the late nineteenth century had also taken a critical, if often nostalgic, position towards their Romantic predecessors. The interwar generation brought this critique to a radical new level. Perhaps most memorably, Gombrowicz made merciless fun of the inculcation of Romantic ideology by the interwar school system in the famous classroom scenes of his satirical novel *Ferdydurke* (1937), ridiculing the forced worship of Romantic poets inflicted on disinterested pupils. Even earlier, the poet and translator Tadeusz Boy-Żeleński (1874–1941) had repudiated the official cultural propagandists who turned the Romantic writers into national monuments by emphasizing their patriotic virtues over critical readings of their literary works.[20] In a very different vein, the futurist Bruno Jasieński (1901–38) wrote evocatively of "hauling the stale mummies of mickiewiczes and słowackis off the streets and squares in wheelbarrows."[21]

For Jasieński, the Romantic tradition needed to be swept away to usher in the modern era. Indeed, this opposition between Romanticism and modernity would remain important. However, I will argue that Romanticism manifested itself in Polish literature after 1918 predominantly as the looming spectre of the insufficient autonomy of the aesthetic sphere in Polish culture after 125 years of political non-existence. Above all, the various experimental movements of interwar Polish modernism rejected the Polish Romantic paradigm because it reflected a subordination of aesthetics to politics, and – analogously – of the individual to the collective. However, this was not necessarily true of all the Polish Romantic writers, but rather of a certain set of texts by Mickiewicz.

The culturally dominant "Polish Romantic paradigm" is deeply political precisely because political interpretations of literary texts are much more conducive to social transmission than purely aesthetic readings. Accordingly, Mickiewicz's enormous influence on Polish culture emerged, at least in part, from the amenability of *Forefathers' Eve, Part III*, *The Books of the Polish Nation and of the Polish Pilgrimage*, and certain sections of *Sir Thaddeus* to political interpretation, simplification, and didactic transmission. Słowacki's often obscure metaphysical explorations of history, Krasiński's quasi-Hegelian conservatism, and Norwid's critical perspective could never compete with the rhetorical power of Mickiewicz's literary expressions of the Polish nation's struggle for independence. For the same reason, his own late lyrics and philosophical epigrams have not attracted the same cultural attention. Moreover, his quixotic political activities for the Polish cause in France, Italy, and Constantinople reinforced the legend of Mickiewicz as a figure who had united word and deed, the individual and the collective, aesthetics and politics.

Forefathers' Eve, Part III presents the individual protagonist's integration with the national collective, beginning with his symbolic death at the beginning of the play and culminating in an extraordinary union: "Now is my soul incarnate in my country / And in my body dwells her soul; / My fatherland and I are one great whole."[22] In *Forefathers'*

Eve,[23] the reborn protagonist abandons the private erotic tragedy of his earlier incarnation from Part IV to accept the burden of suffering on behalf of his nation. Janion and Żmigrodzka characterize this transition as a shift from "individual existential experience" to "identification with the collective."[24] Elsewhere, in *Sir Thaddeus*, another headstrong protagonist, Jacek Soplica, effaces his individual identity and devotes his new life to the service of the national community. In these works, individuals dissolve themselves into the collective, while the artistic integrity of the works themselves is potentially compromised by the burden of their political and national content, as one early French critic argued in Mickiewicz's own time.[25]

More recently, an influential contemporary French scholar, Pascale Casanova, has characterized the systematic subordination of the aesthetic to the political as an inevitable literary consequence of colonial oppression or political weakness, providing a useful context for understanding the reception of Romanticism in twentieth-century Polish culture. In her book on "the world republic of letters," Casanova argues that the politicization and nationalization of poetic works is typical of the "small literatures" of nations whose very political existence has remained under threat.[26] Only when this political existence is confirmed and strengthened can such literatures undergo a process of depoliticization, becoming more "pure" or "free."[27] To some extent, this is precisely what happened in the literary sphere after Poland's renewed independence in 1918, at which point many writers rejected the Mickiewiczean national Romantic legacy.

In 1920, Jan Lechoń (1899–1956) made a programmatic call for the autonomy of the aesthetic from political and national concerns in a poem titled "Herostrates": "And in the spring let me see spring, not Poland."[28] Lechoń's symbolic declaration of independence from the patriotic Romantic tradition would come to define literary developments in the interwar period. The "Skamander" movement to which he and Antoni Słonimski belonged became a symbol of conservatism for later avant-gardes; even so, the break with the political and national dimensions of the Romantic legacy would prove decisive.

At the same time, the political content of the Romantic paradigm – with its heterogeneous transformative potential – is precisely what ensured its continued relevance for a host of political projects. As we have seen, Jasieński emphasized the opposition to modernity, but Romanticism can also be productively linked to two modern political projects: nationalism and socialism. In the early years of the century, these two projects were united in the person of Józef Piłsudski (1867–1935), a campaigner for Polish national self-determination and member of the Polish Socialist Party, who became the figurehead of Poland's regained independence in 1918. Raised in a noble family, Piłsudski was steeped in the patriotic traditions of Mickiewicz, and especially of Słowacki, whose works he always kept on his work desk in later years.[29] Even the events of his early life followed the pattern enshrined by Mickiewicz's biography and *Forefathers' Eve, Part III*: conspiracy against tsarist Russia, arrest, and exile.

Another young socialist, Feliks Dzierżyński (1877–1926), a nobleman from the same region and background as Piłsudski, embarked on a very different revolutionary career. He joined the Social Democracy of the Kingdom of Poland and Lithuania and later became the chief of the Soviet Union's secret police. As his biographer Sylwia Frołow reveals, the Polish Romantic tradition profoundly influenced his early ideological development, instilling an early sense of totalizing political commitment and the promise of maximalist transformation. According to Frołow, "Iron Felix," the first head of the *Cheka*, was very much "a child of Polish messianism," though this early fascination would fade as he became a committed Marxist revolutionary.[30]

The very different trajectories of Piłsudski and Dzierżyński illustrate the Polish Romantic tradition's power to inspire diverse transformative visions, while also revealing the limitations inherent in the marriage of national and social revolutionary aspirations. Despite the radical democratic convictions of Mickiewicz and Słowacki, the national tenor of Polish Romanticism could never fully cohere with the internationalist Marxism of Dzierżyński's mature political activities. Conversely, Piłsudski claimed to have treated socialism merely as a convenient ideological vehicle for pursuing the greater aim of national self-determination, alighting from the "red tram" of socialism at "the station marked 'Poland's Independence.'"[31] Yet throughout the twentieth century, the adherents of national and socialist political projects would continue to exploit their putative connections with the Romantic paradigm, however dubious these connections were in the case of socialism. A nationally inflected Romanticism came to underpin the legitimacy of the Second Polish Republic; the socialist thread would re-emerge strongly in the postwar communist era.

As we have seen, the writers of the interwar period were generally critical of the politicized and nationalized legacy of Polish Romanticism in Piłsudski's state. To some extent, this resistance merely underscored the continuing impact of the paradigm, as the need to assert the autonomy of literature was strengthened by the patriotic tone of official culture. This is especially clear in Gombrowicz's satirical depictions of students' classroom indoctrination into the national mythology of "Poland – the Christ of the nations, flame, eternal sacrifice, inspiration, suffering, redemption, heroes, and symbols." For the narrator of *Ferdydurke*, ideological violence ultimately leads to the dissolution of individual identity into imposed collective forms: "Faces … stripped of any notion of a face, seemed ready to assume any face – one could make those faces into anything."[32]

For the first time, the Romantic poets were not simply the apostles of an "imagined community," but the poetic patrons of a new political order. This blending of poetry and politics was especially evident when Piłsudski presided over the interment of Słowacki's ashes at Wawel Castle in 1927 only a year after becoming the virtual dictator of Poland in the May Coup. More broadly, a key foundational myth of the Second Polish Republic cast Piłsudski as a providential man, a great military and even spiritual leader in the Romantic tradition, who had brought his people out of the wilderness of the partitions and defeated the Red Army in the Polish–Soviet War of 1919–21. In an essay titled "Powstają legendy" (The Formation of Legends, 1935), the avant-garde writer Bruno Schulz (1892–1942) captured this sense of Piłsudski as the very emanation of Polish history from the imagination of the Romantic poets: "[Piłsudski] emerged out of the undergrowth of history, out of the mouths of graves, out of the past. He was heavy with the dreams of seers, misty with teeming visions of poets, burdened with the martyrdom of generations. He was sheer continuity. He drew the past behind him like a vast mantle for all of Poland."[33]

Of course, Schulz's essay is not propaganda, but rather a poetic analysis of how national legends develop. Broadly speaking, the most influential writers of the interwar period either did not participate in this process or explicitly attacked it. However, it is worth noting that many writers picked up other dimensions of the Romantic legacy. For instance, the "Skamander" poets emphasized the language of the everyday, adapting a poetic tradition first established by Mickiewicz in his *Ballady i romanse* (Ballads and Romances, 1822), in the wake of earlier German and English attempts to bring the colloquial language of "the people" into the national poetic idiom. Gombrowicz's obsession with authentic individual identity in the face of the overwhelming collective also drew on the Romantic cult of the individual, though Gombrowicz suggested that the individual ultimately could not exist outside social "forms." Even Schulz's poetics are often strongly Romantic, especially in his insistence on the power of words to reveal or construct reality.[34]

In general, interwar writers turned away from Romantic politics, while sometimes continuing to exploit other aspects of Romantic poetics. The brutal German and Soviet occupations that followed the outbreak of the Second World War, however, brought the political and national dimensions of the Romantic heritage to pre-eminence once again, as the Mickiewiczean legend of the poet-hero uniting word and deed assumed new meaning in the most appalling circumstances. The doomed Warsaw Uprising of 1944 took its place in the national insurrectionary tradition of heroic catastrophes, while poets like Krzysztof Kamil Baczyński (1921–44) and Tadeusz Gajcy (1922–44) revived Romantic tropes of personal sacrifice for an idealized Poland – though without Mickiewicz's martyrology, or any faith in a transformed future. Mickiewicz had written poems filled with conviction, but famously never joined his comrades on the barricades of the 1830–1 uprising; Baczyński and Gajcy wrote poems filled with hopeless resignation, and gave their lives in the battle for Warsaw.

At the same time, strongly critical perspectives on the political and national dimensions of the Romantic legacy persisted even in the cauldron of war. One of the poetic speakers of Czesław Miłosz's (1911–2004) wartime collection *Głosy biednych ludzi* (Voices of Poor People) questions those who would seek solace "in the idolatry of country";[35] and the "naïve poems" of *Świat* (The World) function partly as an extended assertion of poetry's autonomy from history through the ironic construction of a timeless idyll in the very eye of the storm. Yet even for Miłosz, the scale of his nation's suffering ultimately necessitates acceptance of certain collective responsibilities. He refuses to submit to the old narratives of national martyrdom and personal sacrifice, but nevertheless must confront the nagging question of poetry's relevance in a time of crisis: "What is poetry that does not save / Nations or people?"[36]

MIŁOSZ AND EUROPEAN ROMANTIC TRADITIONS

Czesław Miłosz's general attitude towards the Romantic tradition was highly critical, but he always maintained a strong attachment to his Polish-Lithuanian predecessor, Adam Mickiewicz. Miłosz attempted to reshape Mickiewicz's legacy by shifting the emphasis away from the emotional and national aspects of his poetry, focusing instead on "classical" form and on religious and metaphysical themes. Miłosz also drew inspiration from various Romantic writers for his own poetic enterprise to resist what he described as "the erosion of the religious imagination." The English Romantic poet William Blake was an especially important figure for this project. Turning away from the sphere of Polish culture towards English poetry perhaps allowed Miłosz to deploy selected Romantic ideas for his own purposes without the political and national baggage he associated with Polish poets of the same era.

The failure of the Warsaw Uprising and the Soviet seizure of power put an end to any hopes for the resurrection of the Second Polish Republic in 1944. After the war, Romantic patriotism of the Piłsudskian strain would survive largely in the émigré circles of London and Paris, while the precipitous decline of Romanticism's influence on literary developments would continue after the brief renaissance of the occupation. At the same time, a new politicization of the Romantic legacy emerged in what would soon become the Polish People's Republic.

Battles over the Bard: Interpreting Mickiewicz in the Communist Era

My overview of the Mickiewiczean "Polish Romantic paradigm" outlines the three main dimensions of a single transformative political myth: national self-determination, social revolution, and universal renewal. The ideology of the interwar Polish republic largely concentrated on the national element, propagating the narrative of a miraculous resurrection partly achieved, but still ongoing in a climate of rising external threats. After the dismantling of the Second Polish Republic and the unprecedented destruction of the Second World War, a new political order set about exploiting the Romantic paradigm, focusing largely on its revolutionary and internationalist dimensions.

In the postwar Polish Republic, the Soviet-imposed communist authorities explicitly identified their social and political project with Mickiewicz's revolutionary rhetoric and patriotic internationalism. In 1950, the communist leader Bolesław Bierut unveiled a reconstructed statue of Mickiewicz in the centre of Warsaw, hailing the "genuinely popular-democratic social and ideological foundation of [Mickiewicz's] creative work."[37] The bard of the Polish nation emerged as a proto-communist whose political values anticipated those of the regime. As the nation reconstructed itself from the ruins, the ruling party espoused an ideology of social transformation, freedom, and equality. However imprecisely these core values matched the oppressive reality, the Romantic paradigm fit the professed ideology rather well. The party itself was ostensibly progressive and revolutionary, and the selective use of Mickiewicz's radical slogans was a convenient means of tying official state ideology to deeply rooted national tradition. Communist leaders like Bierut publicly highlighted the current of revolutionary politics and the idea of "the people" in Mickiewicz's works, supported by Marxist literary scholars like Stefan Żółkiewski.[38]

This propaganda inevitably demanded significant distortions and the elision of undesirable elements, in particular Mickiewicz's metaphysical interests and abiding Christian faith. Nevertheless, the distortions were based on certain unassailable facts. While not a Marxist, Mickiewicz was a Christian socialist who heralded a revolutionary confrontation between the corrupt dynastic monarchies and a religiously inflected socialist solidarity. When he published his manifesto on "Le socialisme" in *La Tribune des Peuples* in 1849, a year after the appearance of *The Communist Manifesto*, his ideas were distinct from those of Marx and Engels, yet they also shared significant common ground. Marx even proclaimed in his passionate defence of "Communism, Revolution and a Free Poland" in 1848 that the Polish revolutionary movement had "set all of Europe a glorious example, because it identified the question of nationalism with democracy and with the liberation of the oppressed class."[39] At least to some extent, Mickiewicz's project fit this description.

Polish Stalinists systematically exaggerated possible parallels between the disparate visions of Mickiewicz, Marx, and Soviet communism, but their falsifications benefited from the existence of a genuine shared intellectual heritage in the radical democratic movements of mid-nineteenth-century Europe. Here we see the simultaneous operation of distortion, simplification, and authentic ideological links. Unsurprisingly, the postwar communists also placed less emphasis on the national aspects of Mickiewicz's Romantic paradigm, preferring to emphasize a combination of patriotism and internationalism that suited the state's similarly mixed propaganda. According to another speech by Bierut, Mickiewicz had inspired the new socialist nation with both "patriotic and universal human feelings," while the People's Republic of Poland was the realization of Mickiewicz's dream of a new age of freedom.[40]

After two decades of communist rule, Mickiewicz's ideological usefulness reached its limits in 1968, when the authorities cancelled Kazimierz Dejmek's production of *Forefathers' Eve, Part III* at the National Theatre in Warsaw. The play's anti-tsarist content had become a rallying point for a protest movement against Soviet domination of Poland. After its final performance in Warsaw, agitated crowds of students gathered around the very statue of Mickiewicz that Bierut had unveiled less than two decades earlier, draping it with patriotic banners and symbolically reclaiming it in a public space. In the weeks that followed, the poet's statues in Kraków, Gliwice, and Poznań became focal points for further protests, as the dissidents clamoured for Romantic literature: "We demand *Forefathers' Eve*."[41] In effect, the students had turned Mickiewicz against the regime.

At this crucial juncture in the development of the democratic opposition, we witness a dramatic contest between the regime and its domestic opponents over the meaning of the Romantic paradigm. First Secretary of the Polish United Workers' Party Władysław Gomułka responded to the protests by seeking to reappropriate the bard in a fiery address at a party meeting, attacking those who would "distort the deepest democratic and progressive sense of Mickiewicz's work" or turn his works into "a banner for anti-Soviet demonstrations."[42] Yet the cancellation of the play amounted to a virtual admission of defeat. Monuments and superficial slogans bearing no relation to reality had their ideological uses, but any deeper analysis of Mickiewicz's works revealed the disjuncture between communist rhetoric and the broader context of his poetry. The critique of Russian imperialism and of treachery among the Polish elite in *Forefathers' Eve, Part III* resonated as a scathing attack on the regime and its Soviet masters; a transformative narrative of authentic national self-determination had been freed from the official interpretations that the Soviets had imposed on it.

Yet the protesters of 1968 shared many of the purported values of the Communist Party, in particular a concern for social justice and a form of patriotic internationalism. Their aim was to force the government to deliver on its own principles, while confirming Poland's right to national autonomy within the system of international socialism. One of the young protesters, Adam Michnik, would later recall how Mickiewicz had inspired their revisionist program: "He suited our state of mind: he allowed us to be both patriots and internationalists."[43] For many of the movement's key figures, including Michnik himself, this "internationalism" had a very specific dimension, since their own background was both Polish and Jewish. As a Polish poet generally regarded as "philo-Semitic" – and, according to legend, part Jewish himself – Mickiewicz symbolized the inclusive potential of Polish culture in the tradition of "Romantic universalism." Ironically, the response of the regime to this crisis was to turn away from its own professed internationalism towards chauvinistic nationalism. An aggressive party faction led by Mieczysław Moczar launched an "anti-Zionist" campaign against the oppositionists, all but burying the official communist Mickiewicz in the process. The protesters held up the poet as a symbol of individual freedom, national self-determination, and universal values; to this, the regime could only respond with censorship of his play, harsh crackdowns on individual freedoms, anti-Semitic nationalism, and renewed subservience to Moscow. The students had won the battle for the bard.

A decade after the events of May 1968, the communist state faced a very different form of Romantically inflected opposition when Cardinal Karol Wojtyła became Pope John Paul II. Michał Masłowski would later describe the pontiff from Wadowice simply as "the last Polish Romantic."[44] In his inauguration homily in St Peter's Square, John Paul II told his compatriots that he prayed "in the words of the poet," quoting directly from the opening invocation of Mickiewicz's *Sir Thaddeus*.[45] He would continue to cite Mickiewicz, Słowacki, and Norwid copiously in numerous public addresses, especially during the 1979 visit to his homeland, weaving their words into a Christian version of patriotic universalism that linked the Polish nation with the Catholic Church and divine Providence. According to the pope, the Polish Church under communist oppression had become "a church of especial witness, towards which the eyes of all the world [were] turned."[46] Like Mickiewicz, he placed the Polish nation at the centre of an integrated earthly and divine history. Unlike Mickiewicz, he did not reach the heretical extremes of national messianism, proposing instead a kind of transformative "missionism." The mission of Catholic Poland was to demonstrate the meaning of faith to a secularizing world by holding firm to its Christian traditions in the face of a hostile atheist regime. Poland was not the redemptive "Christ of the Nations," but divine providence had given the nation a special role in a universal contest between good and evil. Once again, this role demanded suffering.

Like the regime and the student protesters of 1968, John Paul II evoked a form of Romantic patriotic universalism, ascribing a direction and meaning to history, though always within a strongly Christian framework. While the authorities had used Mickiewicz to emphasize Poland's historical participation in the glorious progress towards a communist paradise on earth, and the revisionist protesters attempted to hold the regime to this promise, John Paul II deployed the poet to confirm Poland's special role in Christian salvation history. The combination of this Catholic–Romantic patriotism with the secular legacy of the 1968 protests would go on to inspire the movement described by Janion as the last "culmination of the Romantic ethos": the Solidarity revolution of 1980–1.[47] The Solidarity trade union successfully united these two forms of opposition in a mass movement that captured the collective imagination with new hopes of radical transformation.

The Solidarity movement took up the Romantic legacy on a number of different levels. Bold confrontations with the authorities – especially the barricading of the Lenin Shipyard in Gdańsk – resonated strongly with the spirit of Romantic insurrection, and the iconography of the protests embodied a familiar mix of the national and the religious. The movement even adopted poets like Czesław Miłosz and Zbigniew Herbert as "bards" in the nineteenth-century tradition.[48] At the same time, the Solidarity trade union also evinced strong internationalist aspirations – for instance, in the famous message "to working people in Eastern Europe," which extended greetings and words of support "to the workers of Albania, Bulgaria, Czechoslovakia, the German Democratic Republic, Romania, and all nations of the Soviet Union."[49] Poland's Solidarity movement conceived itself as fighting for a much wider cause of freedom, following the earlier path of Mickiewicz's universalism. In 1989, the movement would bear fruit not with a revolution, but with the peaceful transfer of power negotiated at the Round Table accords between the Solidarity opposition and the party.

In all these uses of the Mickiewiczean paradigm, we find both common threads and significant divergences, as opposing ideological actors recast its core transformative potential by variously combining the three primary modes: national self-determination, social revolution, and universal renewal. Piłsudski's regime had adapted the myth with a primary focus on national self-determination, including some continuation of the legend of Polish sacrifice for universal freedom, but with only limited interest in social reorganization. The communists paid less attention to national autonomy, focusing instead on dubious achievements in social justice and international cooperation. The protesters of 1968 demanded political change and freedom from the Soviet Union's hegemonic power, with some internationalist outreach to other opposition movements in Eastern Europe and beyond. The pope concentrated on national independence and Poland's providential role in universal history, while remaining suspicious of revolutionary politics.

All of these adaptations and appropriations of the Mickiewiczean paradigm – some more than others – involved distortions and reductions of its original content. At the same time, all of them developed certain authentic strands of thought from within the original mythology, so that it is sometimes difficult to determine whether we are dealing with cynical politicization, inspired reinterpretation, or simple elaboration of the source material. One way or another, Feliks Dzierżyński, Józef Piłsudski, Tadeusz Gajcy, Władysław Gomułka, Adam Michnik, John Paul II, and the Solidarity movement were all inheritors of the Romantic legacy. Over the course of the twentieth century, a combination of intentional ideological manipulation and the elaboration of its own heterogeneous content under the pressure of political circumstances splintered the Romantic paradigm into the competing projects of Polish modernity.

"Lava": Smolensk Romanticism and the Collective

In essence, I have advanced two contending though ultimately complementary accounts of Romanticism's continuing political influence: (1) The Romantic paradigm has been so deeply embedded in Polish cultural consciousness that diverse political movements have felt compelled to use its myths and symbols to legitimize their ideas. This has often led to the instrumentalization of the Romantic project, forcing the paradigm into the desired shape of a given ideology. (2) The Romantic paradigm has genuinely constituted a founding discourse for multiple transformative narratives, from conservative nationalism to socialist internationalism. While Mickiewicz's original Romantic paradigm bound nascent versions of these narratives together, however incongruously, this unstable compound disintegrated over the course of the twentieth century as contradictory elements developed in disparate ideological directions. In the meantime, literary writers tended to reject the mainline Romantic paradigm because of its political and national emphasis, while occasionally adapting other Romantic tropes, especially those emphasizing the individual over the collective.

So how has this process evolved in the contemporary Poland of Mickiewicz's neurotic modern successor, Adam Miauczyński from *The Day of the Wacko*? If the core of Romanticism's continued relevance has lain in its radically transformative potential, one might expect to find it irrelevant in an era in which transformative projects appear to be outmoded. While Polish Romanticism and its inheritors have often exhibited utopian inclinations – from Mickiewicz's idea of universal freedom to the idealism of 1968 and even the Solidarity movement – the post-1989 era in Polish history has coincided with a general collapse of the very possibility of transformative politics amidst the apathy of late capitalist consumerism and neoliberalism. In particular, as Russell Jacoby points out in his book *The End of Utopia*, leftist or progressive politics have crumbled in the face of the neoliberal assault, retreating from any claims to forge political or social change.[50]

In the Polish context, this breakdown has been especially stark. After 1989, two utopian visions collapsed in Poland. First, the communist ideal, which had lost credibility and social support many years earlier, disappeared from the political scene, with former members of the communist party reinventing themselves as democrats supporting the transition to a market economy. Second, the Solidarity ideal of a unified Polish society transforming its political reality and marching into a better future evaporated as the Solidarity movement splintered into bitterly competing political factions. The harsh realities of life under post-1989 economic shock therapy led to a dramatic fall in public support even for former heroes like Solidarity leader Lech Wałęsa, who was unable to make the transition from freedom fighter to democratic politician and who lost the 1995 presidential elections to the post-communist neoliberal Aleksander Kwaśniewski.

In *The Day of the Wacko*, as Adam Miauczyński laments his social irrelevance and insulting state salary, he reflects that only Poland's struggle against oppression has raised the status of poets among the people: "Dictatorships have always been shaken by poets! Then they really need us – those despairing masses who can't see further than a slice of sausage." With the new market system theoretically guaranteeing Polish citizens the freedom to pursue their own individual slice of sausage, the transformative visions of poets became superfluous, perhaps even impossible. The great Romantic paradigm in Polish culture was thus doomed to dissipate into the impotent rage of a schoolteacher striving in vain to impart the greatness of Mickiewicz to a new generation of apathetic consumers.

Yet the Romantic myth has not vanished. The tragic deaths of President Lech Kaczyński, his wife, and ninety-four other people at Smolensk in Russia brought various dimensions of the old paradigm back into public discourse. Since the victims were on their way to commemorate Polish officers murdered by the Soviet NKVD in the Katyn Forest during the Second World War, the tragedy took on an uncanny symbolic significance, superimposing almost palimpsestic multiple layers of martyrological memory and "post-memory" on the fresh trauma of the present. Collective memory of the past was deeply intertwined with collective grieving and suspicion of Russian intentions in the present, reactivating the ready-made Romantic tropes of innocent suffering and transformative hopes. The Smolensk catastrophe has even inspired a new wave of neo-Romantic poetry, some of it written by poets of genuine talent and standing, like Jarosław Marek Rymkiewicz and Wojciech Wencel. In a poem addressed to the deceased president's twin brother, Rymkiewicz speaks of a renewed Russian threat ("the tsar of the north") in a passionate polemic with unmistakably Mickiewiczean overtones.[51] Wencel, in turn, has written a whole series of Romantically inflected Smolensk poems, including one referring directly to *Forefathers' Eve, Part III*, and concluding with an Old-Testament renovation of the messianic myth: "Poland in the darkness of birth / you are not the Christ of the nations / you are Jonah in the belly of the whale / go, oh, go to your Nineveh."[52]

ROMANTICISM AND CONTEMPORARY LITERATURE

Romanticism's influence on post-1989 literature has followed a pattern familiar from earlier in the century. Notwithstanding the emergence of "Smolensk Romanticism," very few of the most influential writers have consciously taken up the Romantic tradition in any systematic way. Nevertheless, Romantic tropes have manifested themselves – often rather superficially – as ghosts to be exorcized, with various writers continuing to ironize aspects of the Romantic paradigm. In poetry, critics have noted this strategy in the works of Marcin Świetlicki and Andrzej Sosnowski. In prose, parodies of Romantic ideas appear in novels by Ignacy Karpowicz, Michał Witkowski, and Dorota Masłowska. The persistent need to mock the Romantic paradigm probably does not suggest a strictly literary anxiety of influence, but rather discomfort with Romanticism's continued power as a political ideology.

It would be easy to explain this resurgence of Romantic ideas as yet another political instrumentalization of the paradigm, pointing to the perception of a renewed Russian threat, and especially to conservative hopes for a radical transformation of the post-1989 political order. Indeed, various right-wing political formations have expressed their dissatisfaction with the negotiated exit from communism of the Round Table accords. They argue that the independent Third Polish Republic has been fundamentally illegitimate from its inception, tainted by the alleged political and economic influence of people associated with the former power structures of the communist state.[53] Many have even blamed the recently defeated centrist government for the Smolensk crash. Accordingly, the Romantic myths of present suffering and future transformation have yielded martyrological interpretations of Lech Kaczyński's death as well as hopes for radical change. Time will tell whether the electoral triumph of Jarosław Kaczyński and his party in October 2015 will deliver this change, and whether "Smolensk Romanticism" will find direct expression in the new government's policy.

Yet the continuing relevance of the Romantic paradigm runs much deeper than party politics. The enormous crowds that turned out in Warsaw to pay their respects to the presidential couple and to leave votive candles in the public space of the city suggested a much more profound desire for genuine community rooted in a sense of shared traditions and rituals, even if political divisions soon re-emerged. To some extent, these scenes echoed the earlier outpouring of public grief and national unity upon the death of John Paul II in 2005, when Poles took to the streets to celebrate his life and his contribution to the nation's struggle for independence. The same desire for collective unity expressed itself in different ways in the national symbolism of the 1968 student protests and of the Solidarity movement, but it has arguably become more relevant than ever in the atomized individualist world of neoliberal capitalism that Poland entered in 1989. The Polish Romantic paradigm could offer a powerful response to the breakdown of pre-1989 forms of social solidarity, since its defining feature is precisely the grounding of individual identity in the community.

According to Canadian philosopher Charles Taylor, the two main imaginative ambitions of the European Romantic generation were "the aspiration to radical autonomy on the one hand, and to expressive unity with nature and within society on the other."[54] In the Polish case, the pressures of more than a century of political non-existence entrenched a canon of works, mostly by Mickiewicz, that placed the emphasis firmly on expressive unity with the collective. The individual was to realize the meaning of his or her existence through the nation. Perhaps the most evocative Mickiewiczean description of this collective ethos is a fiery simile from *Forefathers' Eve, Part III*:

> … Our nation is like lava,
> With surface cold and dirty, hard, congealed;
> But there are fires beneath, no years can end;
> Let's spit on this foul crust, and descend into the depths.[55]

The lava nation is not a stratified assemblage of atomized units, with a treacherous elite at the top, but a molten mass into which the individual dissolves himself or herself. Some find this dangerous – the contemporary novelist Olga Tokarczuk, for instance, responded with "a shudder of horror" to the apotheosis of the "collective psyche" after the Smolensk catastrophe.[56] Others have mobilized Mickiewicz's metaphor as an ideal of collective unity and a symbol of their hopes for a new revolutionary transformation, as exemplified by the right-wing intellectuals who published a collection of interviews on the Smolensk crash under the title *Lava: Conversations on Poland*.[57] As we have seen, the Romantic paradigm has inspired diverse understandings of collective unity: the state-building nationalism of the interwar regime; communism's universal narrative of social equality; John Paul II's vision of Poland's sacred mission in history; and Solidarity's experiment in rebellious civil society. All of these narratives – including the most recent – have framed distinct combinations of national, social, and universal transformation, representing a splintering of Mickiewicz's original poetic myth into competing political variants.

But is radical transformation of any kind still possible, or even desirable in the capitalist world of late modernity? For some factions within Poland's conservative movement, the answer to this question is unmistakably affirmative, though twentieth-century Polish history suggests that transformative ideals rarely convert well into political reality. Nevertheless, the recent electoral success of a party ostensibly emphasizing both unified national identity and increased social equality suggests a broader desire for change within Polish society and a profound questioning of the post-1989 order. If Romanticism ultimately represents one of the strongest alternative visions to the prevailing modern ideology of utilitarian rationalism, industrial capitalism, and atomized individualism, as various scholars have claimed,[58] then perhaps some form of the collectivist Romantic paradigm may still offer the most coherent critical response to the post-1989 neoliberal system in Poland.

Romanticism's influence on the development of Polish literature declined sharply over the course of the twentieth century, but Romanticism as a splintered political ideology has retained its imaginative power.

Stanley Bill
University of Cambridge

NOTES

1 Janion, "Zmierzch paradygmatu," 12. Unless otherwise indicated, all translations from the Polish language are my own.

2 See Janion and Żmigrodzka, "Romantyczne tematy egzystencji."
3 "Sernica i nieskończoność," in Janion and Żmigrodzka, *Nasze pojedynki o romantyzm*, 94.
4 See Bielik-Robson, *Romantyzm, niedokończony projekt.*
5 See Skórczewski, *Teoria – literatura – dyskurs.*
6 For instance, see Bielik-Robson, "Polski triumph tanatosa."
7 Janion, "Zmierzch paradygmatu," 9.
8 Gombrowicz, *Diary*, 277.
9 Nietzsche, "The Anti-Christ," 568.
10 Here I adapt Anita Debska's phrase from her book *Country of the Mind.*
11 Rousseau, *The Government of Poland*, 10.
12 Here I refer to Benedict Anderson's famous concept from his influential book on nations and nationalism, *Imagined Communities.*
13 Walicki, *Philosophy and Romantic Nationalism*, 74.
14 Mickiewicz, "The Books of the Polish Pilgrims," 390.
15 Eile, *Literature and Nationalism in Partitioned Poland*, 46.
16 Brian Porter describes certain aspects of this process in his book *When Nationalism Began to Hate.*
17 See Krzyżanowski, *Neoromantyzm polski.*
18 Słonimski, "Czarna wiosna," 62.
19 See Piwińska, *Leganda romantyczna i szydercy.*
20 See Boy-Żeleński, *Brązownicy.*
21 Jasieński, "Do narodu polskiego manifest," vol. 2, 209.
22 Mickiewicz, "Forefathers' Eve, Part III," 107.
23 Mickiewicz wrote Part IV in Kowno in 1820–21, a decade before Part III.
24 Janion and Żmigrodzka, "Romantyczne tematy egzystencji," 18.
25 The critic warned his readers that "despite their beauty … the purely national nature" of Mickiewicz's poetry made it "naïve to the point of puerility." Quoted in Koropeckyj, *Adam Mickiewicz*, 278.
26 Casanova, *La république mondiale des lettres*, 260.
27 Ibid., 123–6.
28 Lechoń, "Herostrates," quoted in English in Miłosz, *The History of Polish Literature*, 385.
29 Jędrzejewicz, *Piłsudski*, 254.
30 Frołow, *Dzierżyński*, 49.
31 Humphrey, *Piłsudski*, 189.
32 Gombrowicz, *Ferdydurke*, 45–6.
33 Schulz, *Letters and Drawings*, xliii.
34 I have written about this in an article on Schulz's conception of writing. See Bill, "Dorożka w lesie."
35 Miłosz, "The Poor Poet," 79.
36 Miłosz, "Dedication," 97.
37 Bierut, speech, quoted in Żółkiewski, *Spór o Mickiewicza*, 5.
38 See ibid.
39 Marx, *Political Writings*, 102.
40 Quoted in Żółkiewski, *Spór o Mickiewicza*, 244.
41 Kemp-Welch, *Poland under Communism*, 154–5.
42 Gomułka, "Przemówienie na spotkaniu."
43 Michnik, *Letters from Freedom*, 42.

44 See Masłowski, "Ostatni polski romantyk."
45 "Homily of His Holiness Pope John Paul II."
46 Quoted in Maliński, *Pope John Paul II*, 145.
47 Janion, *Czy będziesz wiedział co przeżyłeś?*, 11.
48 For instance, an extract from Czesław Miłosz's poem "Który skrzywdziłeś" (You Who Wronged) was inscribed on the monument raised to commemorate the shipyard workers killed by the authorities in the earlier protests of 1970. The government gave permission for the raising of the monument as part of the historic agreement with the Solidarity trade union in August 1980. Miłosz himself did not feel entirely comfortable in his new role as a national "bard."
49 "Posłanie Pierwszego Zjazdu Delegatów NSZZ 'Solidarność,' do ludzi pracy Europy Wschodniej," 55.
50 See Jacoby, *The End of Utopia.*
51 Rymkiewicz, "Do Jarosława Kaczyńskiego."
52 Wencel, "Czterdzieści i cztery."
53 Michael Bernhard and Jan Kubik have discussed this interpretation of the Roundtable accords as one of "five and one-half different interpretations of what happened." See Bernhard and Kubik, "Roundtable Discord," 61–71.
54 Taylor, *Hegel and Modern Society*, 69.
55 Mickiewicz, "Forefathers' Eve, Part III," 139. I have altered the translation slightly to bring it closer to the original Polish.
56 Tokarczuk, "When History's March Is a Funeral Procession."
57 See Dawidowicz, *Lawa.*
58 For instance, see Löwy and Sayre, *Romanticism against the Tide of Modernity*, 57.

WORKS CITED

Anderson, Benedict. *Imagined Communities: Reflections on the Origin and Spread of Nationalism*. London: Verso, 1983.

Bernhard, Michael, and Jan Kubik, "Roundtable Discord: The Contested Legacy of 1989 in Poland." In *Twenty Years after Communism: The Politics of Memory and Commemoration*, 60–84. Oxford: Oxford University Press, 2014.

Bielik-Robson, Agata. "Polski triumf Tanatosa." *Krytyka Polityczna*, 15 April 2010. http://krytykapolityczna.pl/felietony/agata-bielik-robson/polski-triumf-tanatosa.

– *Romantyzm, niedokończony projekt: Eseje*. Kraków: Universitas, 2008.

Bierut, President Bolesław. Speech on the unveiling of the statue of Adam Mickiewicz in Warsaw, 28 January 1950. In Stefan Żółkiewski, *Spór o Mickiewicza*. Wrocław: Wydawnictwo im. Ossolińskich, 1952.

Bill, Stanley. "Dorożka w lesie: Schulz i pisanie." *Schulz / Forum* 2 (2013), 25–34.

Boy-Żeleński, Tadeusz. *Brązownicy i inne szkice o Mickiewiczu*. Warszawa: Państwowy Instytut Wydawniczy, 1957.

Casanova, Pascale. *La république mondiale des lettres*. Paris: Éditions de Seuil, 1999.

Dawidowicz, Zuzanna, ed. *Lawa: Rozmowy o Polsce*. Kraków: Wydawnictwo Arcana, 2010.

Debska, Anita. *Country of the Mind: An Introduction to the Poetry of Adam Mickiewicz*. Warszawa: Burchardt Edition, 2000.

Eile, Stanisław. *Literature and Nationalism in Partitioned Poland, 1795–1918*. New York: St Martin's Press, 2000.

Frołow, Sylwia. *Dzierżyński. Miłość i rewolucja*. Kraków: Znak, 2014.

Gombrowicz, Witold. *Diary*. Translated by Lillian Vallee. New Haven: Yale University Press, 2012.

– *Ferdydurke*. Translated by Danuta Burchardt. New Haven: Yale University Press, 2000.

Gomułka, Władysław. "Przemówienie na spotkaniu z warszawskim aktywem partyjnym wygłoszone 19 marca 1968." *Blog Wiesława*. http://wieslaw1956.blogspot.co.uk/2012/10/przemowienie-na-spotkaniu-z-warszawskim.html.

Homily of His Holiness Pope John Paul II for the Inauguration of His Pontificate. http://w2.vatican.va/content/john-paul-ii/en/homilies/1978/documents/hf_jp-ii_hom_19781022_inizio-pontificato.html.

Humphrey, Grace. *Piłsudski: Builder of Poland*. New York: Scott and More, 1936.

Jacoby, Russell. *The End of Utopia: Politics and Culture in an Age of Apathy*. New York: Basic Books, 1999.

Janion, Maria. "Zmierzch paradygmatu." In *Czy będziesz wiedział co przeżyłeś?* 5–23. Warszawa: Wydawnictwo SIC!, 1996.

Janion, Maria, and Maria Żmigrodzka. "Romantyczne tematy egzystencji." In *Nasze pojedynki o romantyzm*. Edited by Dorota Siwicka and Marek Bieńczyk. 9–26. Warszawa: Instytut Badań Literackich, 1995.

Jasieński, Bruno. "Do narodu polskiego manifest w sprawie natychmiastowej futuryzacji życia." In *Polska awangarda poetycka,* vol. 2. Edited by Andrzej Lam. 208–14. Kraków: Wydawnictwo Literackie, 1969.

Jędrzejewicz, Wacław. *Piłsudski: A Life for Poland*. New York: Hippocrene Books, 1990.

Kemp-Welch, Anthony. *Poland under Communism: A Cold War History*. Cambridge: Cambridge University Press, 2008.

Koropeckyj, Roman. *Adam Mickiewicz: The Life of a Romantic*. Ithaca: Cornell University Press, 2008.

Krzyżanowski, Julian. *Neoromantyzm polski, 1890–1918*. Wrocław: Zakład Narodowy im. Ossolińskich, 1980.

Lechoń, Jan. "Herostrates." In Czesław Miłosz, *The History of Polish Literature*. 385. Berkeley: University of California Press, 1983.

Löwy, Michael, and Robert Sayre. *Romanticism against the Tide of Modernity*. Durham: Duke University Press, 2001.

Maliński, Mieczysław. *Pope John Paul II: The Life of Karol Wojtyła*. New York: Seabury Press, 1979.

Marx, Karl. *Political Writings: The Revolutions of 1848*. Edited by David Fernbach. 102–11. New York: Vintage Books, 1974.

Masłowski, Michał. "Ostatni polski romantyk." In *Problemy tożsamości: Szkice mickiewiczowskie i (post)romantyczne*. 427–48. Lublin: Instytut Europy Środkowo- Wschodniej, 2006.

Michnik, Adam. *Letters from Freedom: Post–Cold War Realities and Perspectives*. Edited by Irena Grudzińska Gross. Berkeley: University of California Press, 1998.

Mickiewicz, Adam. "The Books of the Polish Pilgrims." In *Poems by Adam Mickiewicz*. Translated by George Rapall Noyes. 380–415. New York: Herald Square Press, 1944.

– "Forefathers' Eve, Part III." In *Polish Romantic Drama: Three Plays in English Translation*. Edited by Harold Segel. 73–176. Ithaca: Cornell University Press, 1977.

Miłosz, Czesław. "Dedication." In *Poezje wybrane – Selected Poems*. 97. Kraków: Wydawnictwo Literackie, 1996.

– "The Poor Poet." In *Poezje wybrane – Selected Poems*. 78. Kraków: Wydawnictwo Literackie, 1996.

Nietzsche, Friedrich. "The Anti-Christ." In *The Portable Nietzsche*. Translated by Walter Kaufmann. 565–656. New York: Penguin Books, 1982.

Piwińska, Marta. *Leganda romantyczna i szydercy*. Warszawa: Państwowy Instytut Wydawniczy, 1973.

Porter, Brian. *When Nationalism Began to Hate: Imagining Modern Politics in Nineteenth-Century Poland*. Oxford: Oxford University Press, 2000.

"Posłanie Pierwszego Zjazdu Delegatów NSZZ 'Solidarność' do ludzi pracy Europy Wschodniej." In *Kronika Solidarności: 20 lat dzień za dniem* ... Edited by Leszek Biernacki. Sopot: Pracownia Impuls, 2000.

Rousseau, Jean-Jacques. *The Government of Poland*. Translated by Willmoore Kendall. Indianapolis: Hackett, 1985.

Rymkiewicz, Jarosław Marek. "Do Jarosława Kaczyńskiego." *Rzeczpospolita*, 21 April 2010. http://www.rp.pl/artykul/464644-Do-Jaroslawa-Kaczynskiego.html.

Schulz, Bruno. *Letters and Drawings of Bruno Schulz with Selected Prose*. Translated by Walter Arndt. New York: Fromm International, 1990.

Skórczewski, Dariusz. *Teoria – literatura – dyskurs: Pejzaż postkolonialny*. Lublin: Wydawnictwo KUL, 2013.

Słonimski, Antoni. "Czarna wiosna." In *Poezje zebrane*. 54–6. Warszawa: PIW, 1964.

Taylor, Charles. *Hegel and Modern Society*. Cambridge: Cambridge University Press, 1979.

Tokarczuk, Olga. "When History's March Is a Funeral Procession," *New York Times*, 15 April 2010. http://www.nytimes.com/2010/04/16/opinion/16tokarczuk.html?_r=0.

Walicki, Andrzej. *Philosophy and Romantic Nationalism: The Case of Poland*. Notre Dame: University of Notre Dame Press, 1982.

Wencel, Wojciech. "Czterdzieści i cztery." In *Wiersze o Smoleńsku*. http://wierszeosmolensku.blogspot.co.uk/2010/11/wojciech-wencel.html.

Żółkiewski, Stefan. *Spór o Mickiewicza*. Wrocław: Zakład Narodowy im. Ossolińskich, 1952.

(Polish) Romanticism: From Canon to Agon

History of Polish literature textbooks have consolidated a canonical image of Polish Romanticism, according to which the epoch is defined largely by the great works of three extraordinary, individual, one-of-a-kind poets – the "prophets," "bards," and "priests of the national cause" – namely Adam Mickiewicz (1798–1855), Juliusz Słowacki (1809–49), and Zygmunt Krasiński (1812–59). On the one hand, those textbooks present these writers, along with their peers, imitators, and epigones, as both the beneficiaries of the doctrines of European Romanticism and as their critics who often transformed them in original ways. Thus, as artists they were *par excellence* European, even universal. On the other hand, those same textbooks present these authors as strictly national writers: the children of their geopolitical location who fought with their pens for the sovereignty of a nation that had been stripped of its freedom.

This "Holy Trinity" of Polish Romanticism was to be supplemented with the oeuvre of Cyprian Kamil Norwid (1821–83) – a "late child" and simultaneously a great critic of Romanticism, the first post-Romantic poet, an author not only original but also misunderstood by his contemporaries. He was discovered late, only towards the end of the nineteenth century, and was given the moniker of the "fourth bard" by scholars in the 1930s. In distinction from the other Romantics, however, a diachronic look at Polish literature positions Norwid as a precursor of modern, twentieth-century avant-garde poetics and as a critic of Romanticism rather than a representative and orthodox follower of Romantic ideas. Norwid's work did not enter into wider cultural circulation while he was alive. Overshadowed by three earlier literary "giants" long celebrated both in exile and at home, it remained isolated, unnoticed, and unheeded. That is why Norwid, with his critical attitude towards the historiosophy and aesthetics of the three "bards," could not affect the consciousness of his contemporaries to the same degree as Mickiewicz, Słowacki, and Krasiński.

These four poets – their dramas, long poems, lyrics, and poetic epics ("poetic novels," as they came to be called later), as well as their lectures, letters, and critical writings – constitute the indissoluble core of the Polish literary canon. An elementary knowledge of their work, acquired in school and through cultural osmosis, is the foundation of Polish cultural literacy to this day. Such was the case before Poland's sovereignty was restored after the First World War, as well as afterwards, in the Second Polish Republic (1918–39), during the German and Soviet occupations of the Second World War (1939–45), throughout the years of Soviet hegemony, and even today, in a free, post-1989 Poland. Poles have long used these authors' writings to bond a cohesive national identity. That identity is defined not only negatively, that is reactively, in relation to external dangers, but also positively, with reference to the imagology and rhetoric of Romantic discourse, which is the most "sanctified" of Polish cultural discourses.

The Many Faces of the Syndrome of Loss

Romanticism coincided with the first epoch during which the loss of statehood (i.e., of the gentry commonwealth) as a result of the partitions of 1772, 1793, and 1795 (carried out by Russia, Prussia, and Austria) was a *fait accompli* for Poles and a determining factor for their knowledge and perception of reality. This purely external factor, which was largely military and political in nature – and thus non-literary, non-cultural, and fundamentally non-intellectual – strongly influenced Polish Romanticism, though in an almost invisible manner. Those "inside" Romanticism's cultural development barely noticed its influence. The exception was Norwid, whose awareness of the consequences of foreign domination on the Polish culture and world view far exceeded that of his times.

> In a letter to Alexander Herzen from 1853, Norwid wrote: "No one among us will feel himself, no one will be free and, as a result, no one will reach their full potential, without first acquiring sovereignty – and sovereignty for a nation or for a person encompasses judgement of dependencies, it is a fulfillment ... work can flower and be free only in a sovereign nation."
>
> – Norwid, *Listy 1*, 478

These circumstances led to a peculiar, "schizophrenic" situation. On the one hand, "in so far as the descendants of the citizens of the Polish-Lithuanian Republic were incorporated into the states of Russia, Prussia, or Austria, the material aspects of their lives form subjects not for Polish History but for Russian, Prussian, or Austrian History."[1] As a result, the "Polish Question" was considered in Europe to be an internal affair of the three states within whose borders the Poles found themselves. On the other hand, Poland continued to exist as an *idea* stored in the individual and collective memory of the Polish people. This idea, deposited within a national body, was transmitted and discussed in cultural discourses in the form of allusions or direct references, in poetry as well as political, historical, and philosophical writings. As an idea, it could not and was never intended to be translated into commensurate political actions during the partition period. It did, however, serve this primary function: it cemented the Polish nation, which continued to exist even without statehood. Indeed, "loss of independence, coupled with unfortunate location, in no way diminished the Polish sense of identity and uniqueness; if anything, it increased it."[2]

Poland as an idea maintained its identity all through the nineteenth century and up until 1918 thanks mainly to two forces: the clergy, and literature. Regarding the first, a strong Roman Catholic Church provided Poles throughout the three partitions with a steady sense of national community; it also helped preserve that community despite the harsh politics of subordination aimed at the Church by the three authoritarian empires, and despite the lack of support for the "Polish Question" from the Holy See.[3] Literature in turn, along with other functions, provided a counter-narrative to the anti-Polish narratives of the empires. It was the Romantics who constructed the first great and durable Polish narrative. The idea that Poland was a nation temporarily stripped of its state became especially meaningful for Poles once it became apparent that their loss of political agency constituted the basis for a lasting balance of power in Central Europe – a region that did very well without a sovereign Poland.

Polish Romantic literature thus "came to flower in the looming shadow of a phantom state that had been erased from the map of Europe."[4] It was driven "from below" primarily by a national myth, one that supported the multi-ethnic national body of the former commonwealth in conditions of statelessness, in much the same way that Jewish culture survived thousands of years of diaspora.[5] This explains the frequent use of messianic language when the political was translated into the metaphysical and religious – in other words, the "Christianization of politics."[6] This is noticeable mainly in the later work of Mickiewicz (*Księgi narodu polskiego i pielgrzymstwa polskiego* [Books of the Polish Nation and Pilgrimage], 1832; Paris lectures), Słowacki (*Genezis z Ducha* [Genesis from the Spirit], 1844; *Król-Duch* [The Spirit King], 1847); and Krasiński (*Przedświt* [Daybreak], 1843), as well as in the writings of philosophers August Cieszkowski (1814–94), Józef Hoene-Wroński (1776–1853), and Bronisław Trentowski (1808–69).

Consequently, the world view of Polish Romantics, based as it was on still fresh memories of freedom that had been lost as well as on painfully present experiences of subordination, diverged in many ways from that of the British, German, or French Romantics, even if it was inspired by the same readings. The peoples of western and northern Europe derived a sense of stability and order from the system that had been imposed on the continent by the countries of the Holy Alliance at the Congress of Vienna (1815), even if that order blocked more serious reforms. For Poles, that same order brought a painful awareness of loss, for it "practically eliminated the 'Polish question' from European politics."[7]

The Romantic world view was enriched in the works of Polish writers with singular, "local" elements of the sort that were absent in, for example, German Romanticism. The German Romantics were distinguished by their basic lack of interest in public affairs, by the orphic character of their writings, and by their strong focus on aesthetics.[8] By contrast, Romanticism in Polish lands, while oriented towards the aesthetic, the spiritual, and the psychological, was also marked by strong political engagement. This last quality spoke to the Polish Romantics' desire to forge poetic words into collective action – to bring about an anti-imperial insurrection under the leadership of a prophet-priest. Not surprisingly, therefore, "the cult of love, the obsession with the self and the yearning for heroic action which were such distinctive hallmarks of European Romanticism were not indulged in by the Poles."[9] These characteristics were present in Polish Romanticism, but they were also subordinated to a higher, national cause, especially after the defeat of the November Uprising (1830) and the Polish–Russian War of 1831.

Polish Romanticism was inspired and influenced by its Western European counterparts, mainly German but also French and English. It continued the practice of cultural borrowing that began during the Enlightenment – an epoch that Romanticism openly contested but to which it was indebted. Polish Romantics had been raised in an atmosphere of Enlightenment rationalism before embracing Romanticism. This meant they placed some trust in European thought and ideals, including the ideals of the French Revolution, which had "infected" them during the Napoleonic era. The hope that a great social revolution would bring freedom to nations was a constant motif for Polish writers; however, it must be emphasized that they were ambivalent about revolution itself. They viewed it through the lens of their own, recent historical experience – that of partitions – as a rebellion against despotism, and they accepted it to the extent it might help them realize their own republican ideas. They distanced themselves, however, from revolutionary "madness" (another effect of their memories of a home-grown republican tradition), and they disapproved of violence as a means to bring about a new social order. Such was the basis for the moral dilemmas faced by tragic heroes like Mickiewicz's Konrad Wallenrod (in the eponymous poem from 1828): Did the love of fatherland justify all, even unethical actions? These kinds of questions were not given unequivocal answers. Rebelling against evil – embodied mainly in Russian aggression and the figure of the tsar – Polish Romantic heroes balanced on the precipice of crime, and even committed it. This did not mean that the authors were promoting crime as a means to achieve political ends. To the contrary: the problem of conscience, shaped by the Decalogue, remained a troubling subject of debate for Polish Romantics. Although their consciousness, like that of their Western European contemporaries, was "dominated by a tragic dialectic of revolt and action," their work stopped short of crossing over to the dark side of "Romantic luciferism."[10]

Polish writers, though Romantics *par excellence*, not infrequently expressed political and social traditionalism rather than revolutionary fervour. For example, Mickiewicz was more in awe of the American Revolution, an event that actually transferred power to the people, than of the French Revolution.[11] Polish Romantics were also raised in a cult of Napoleon, who, next to Tadeusz Kościuszko – the leader of the first, failed anti-Russian Uprising in 1794 – became another great, symbolic figure of a leader-saviour, one who was expected to bring liberation and freedom to oppressed Poles. It is no coincidence that memories of the hope felt by Poles when Napoleon's Grand Army marched on Moscow in 1811 are woven into the intrigues of Mickiewicz's *Pan Tadeusz* (Sir Thaddeus, 1834). This masterpiece of the Romantic epic, besides being the national text that serves as the basis of the Poles' cultural alphabet, refers to Napoleon as the "God of War" and consolidates the Napoleonic Myth. That myth explains the Poles' sentimental ties to the French during the nineteenth century and, to some extent, even today.

Poles' fascination with France and its culture took root during the Enlightenment; however, it was primarily German literature (Schiller, Goethe, Novalis), along with English works (Scott, Byron, Shelley, Coleridge), that channelled artistic and intellectual Romanticism to Polish lands during the so-called Romantic Turn (1810–20). Young Mickiewicz and Słowacki, and their contemporaries (members of the Philomath Society and others), absorbed the philosophical and aesthetic ideas of not only Voltaire, Montesquieu, and Kant, but also Fichte, Schelling, and the brothers Schlegel, while studying at the renowned Vilnius University.[12] Zofia Stefanowska, an outstanding scholar of Romanticism, writes: "It is amazing even today to trace the intellectual biography of the Philomath youth. A few years' hurried readings made up for a hundred years' cultural delay to catch up to European modernity."[13] She then cites Mickiewicz, who in a letter from Kaunas in 1820 begs for a dispatch of books: "Have mercy, anything German. For I have nothing more to read."[14] The young poet's obvious intellectual hunger strongly suggests that he saw the West as culturally superior, and that he believed Poles would benefit from the cultural transfer that reading (here, German writers and thinkers) would bring about.

But this transfer had an ambivalent character. It constituted proof not only of the Poles' fervent desire to remain *au courant* with the main currents of Continental thought, but also of their loss of cultural self-orientation, a vector that characterized the work of writers and thinkers in the Polish–Lithuanian Commonwealth during sixteenth and seventeenth centuries. When they encountered the thought and culture of the West at that time, Poles felt no sense of inferiority – they were aware of the universal value of their own culture and its attractiveness to foreigners in Europe and even Asia. The loss of cultural self-orientation was a consequence of losing the feelings of safety, self-esteem, and self-confidence, as is common among the colonized everywhere, in proportion to the scale and forms of violence employed by the hegemon.[15] The yearning to make up for cultural delays stems from the premise that one's own culture is insufficient and lacks vitality, an attitude that can lead to further cultural – and consequently also mental – (self) marginalization. In Poland, that attitude was first embraced by the writers and thinkers of the Enlightenment, who intended to reform society and repair the state by imitating Western social structures and cultural models. Romantics re-formed this idea with reference to ideals shared by Europeans at that time, having discovered within European Romanticism a space that could be filled with native content through links to popular stories and historical narratives.

Polish Romanticism was not simply a derivative of German and British prototypes, in part because of the influence of Catholicism. Remember that Poles' religious devotion was about more than practising the faith; it resonated in their culture through deeply engrained "cultural models" of the Christian world view and ideals. In this regard, Polish Romanticism as encountered in literature was a continuation of an earlier tradition: community-oriented thinking, sensitivity towards human suffering, the ethics of generosity, and alertness to threats to truth and freedom.[16]

> Polish writers showed great inventiveness in placing elements that were peculiar, local, and reflective of their native culture within a general framework shared by the entire European Romantic paradigm. Among these elements were traditional folk rites (Mickiewicz's *Dziady* [Forefathers' Eve]); regional legends (Mickiewicz's ballads); historical and quasi-historical motifs (the epic poems of Mickiewicz, *Grażyna* and *Konrad Wallenrod*; Antoni Malczewski's *Maria*; Seweryn Goszczyński's *Zamek kaniowski* [Kaniv Castle]; and Słowacki's drama *Lilla Weneda*); as well as "Oriental" motifs (Mickiewicz's *Sonety krymskie* [Crimean Sonnets]; Słowacki's *Listy z Egiptu* [Letters from Egypt] and *Ojciec zadżumionych* [Father of the Plague-Stricken]; Krasiński's *Agaj-Han*; and the work of Michał Czajkowski and the "Ukrainian School").

Within the realm of Christian orthodoxy, however, this native, Catholic component was treated with considerable licence by Polish Romantics (the exception being the thoroughly Christian Norwid). This licence was derived in part from the philosophical and religious currents of the epoch. Among these currents were an infatuation with post-Rationalist heterodoxy (a spectacular example being the ambiguous alliance of Mickiewicz and Słowacki with the pseudo-mystic Andrzej Towiański), and fascination with the pre-Christian roots of the Slavs, to say nothing of the common (among Romantics) sense of needing to rely on Hegel and Schelling's "positive philosophy." Even a writer as conservative and ultra-Catholic as Krasiński was tempted by Gnostic inquiries; this "esoteric knowledge," which reached him initially through Goethe, Blake, and Nerval, revealed itself in his writing, including the essay "Gnosis" (1842–4), the poem *Trzy myśli Ligenzy* (Three Thoughts of Henryk Ligenza, 1840), and the treatise *O Trójcy* (On the Trinity, 1883).[17]

The unorthodox approach to Christianity represented by Saint-Martine, Ballanche, Novalis, and other Romantics prompted Mickiewicz and Słowacki to formulate utopian programs of spiritual regeneration at great distance from Catholic dogma. Their programs included the creation of God's Kingdom on earth (see Mickiewicz's Paris lectures and *Zdania i uwagi* [Opinions and Remarks], 1869), as well as mystical metamorphosis (viz. Słowacki's *Genesis of the Spirit* and other works).[18] The myths of primal, pagan, anti-Christian, and anti-Latin Slavic cultures explored in the work of the ethnographer and historian Zorian Dołęga-Chodakowski (1784–1825) fascinated and inspired many of the Romantics.[19] Some Romantic writers, especially in a later phase (1838–48), also worked out historiosophical ideas that formed an original synthesis of the French philosophy of action and criticism of German Idealism (for example, Mickiewicz in the Paris lectures and Słowacki in his mystical writings, with considerable input from philosophers such as Cieszkowski, Karol Libelt, Henryk Kamieński, and Edward Dembowski). For this reason, this period can indeed be seen as a "truly 'philosophical epoch'... It was rightly noted that 'never before, and never afterwards, did the Poles set so many hopes on philosophy – not only cognitive hopes, but moral, social, and national hopes as well.'"[20] This philosophy, in the form of both lectures and artistic representations, was harnessed to the Romantic cause of building a collective subjectivity – the nation as the subject of history.[21] In this manner, philosophy not only served as the main driver of Polish identity discourse but also became a substitute for political self-articulation for a collective denied its own statehood. Its real, meaning institutional, authority, however, was slight at a time when the Hegelian system continued to provide the Prussian state with rationalistic legitimacy.

Thanks to the factors discussed above, Polish Romanticism had a unique, irreproducible quality that is often difficult to translate into other, especially non-Slavic languages. That Polish writers, thinkers, and historiographers chose to follow the same path of cultural development as had been taken by other countries provides food for thought, however. That they sided with the European Romantic project underscores the strength and attractiveness of its Western approach to, and ways of registering, reality. This reminds us, here and today, of the hegemony that the West's cultural centres were able to maintain over the East-Central peripheries of Europe. It also suggests that Polish Romantics were unable to find in the culture of their own nation – by then a culture of a conquered people – an approach strong enough to serve as a fully autonomous alternative to foreign formulas.

In other words, Romanticism was an epoch when Polish culture stopped being a self-sufficient source of its own authority. On the contrary: a new model of cultural activity began to dominate, one that depended on Poles looking into "the mirror of European opinion."[22] This did not undermine, of course, the deeply national character of Polish Romanticism, although Herder's idea of the nation is also, after all, one of the central philosophical themes of European Romanticism. The emergence of this new "mirror mentality" clearly indicates that we are dealing with a significant qualitative change that the transfer of Romanticism onto Polish lands brought about in the history of Polish cultural development. At the base of this change was the experience of loss of sovereignty by the conquered population – an experience that in the language of postcolonial theory "alter[ed] their cultural priorities once and for all."[23] After the advent of Romanticism, not just the literature but the entire culture and mentality of Poles were never again as they had been before.

The Orientalization of Polish Romanticism

The work of Polish Romantics was thus situated between what was taken from European Romanticism and what was, against that background, original. In its individual contributions it variously converged with or diverged from the texts of authors such as Goethe and Schiller, Byron and Scott, Lamartine and Chateaubriand, among many others. Later reception of Polish Romanticism in Europe and the world, however, was influenced by factors other than those responsible for both its European character and its specific, local one. These latter factors were largely political rather than cultural, and as a consequence, the study of Polish culture in general, and of Polish Romanticism in particular, has become bound up with (to use a Foucauldian term) *knowledge/power* relations. In these relations, national egoism played an ever-increasing role. Under its influence, Goethe – who was, incidentally, full of appreciation for Polish culture – not only showed indifference towards the Poles' fight for freedom in 1830, but also publicly supported the Prussian authorities' confiscation of *Polens Untergang* (1832), a work by the German historian Friedrich von Raumer that was sympathetic to the Poles. He did so, he admitted, out of fear that the book would incite antipathy towards Germany.[24]

This was but one example of a broader phenomenon, which can be described as a discursive elimination of the conquered: those who, as a result of military and political defeat, could not longer participate in Europe's public life. The philosophy of Hegel, with its concept of the Slavs' civilizational "delay" and exclusion from European culture, provided intellectual support for an immoral political practice with dangerous consequences. This practice consisted of withholding history – and, later, also the right to narrate it – from nations that were, like Poland, under the political, economic, and military control of aggressive empires.[25] As a result, these nations lost not only their subjectivity and agency but also the means to draw European attention to their writings. This dismissive, paternalistic attitude towards their culture lasted, with periodic fluctuations, through the second half of the nineteenth century and the entire twentieth century.

All of this impacted the image and assessment of Polish Romanticism from comparative and humanistic perspectives. The links between Polish Romanticism and Western European Romanticism were treated as imitations or repetitions unworthy of closer attention. Polish Romanticism's local and singular elements, in turn, for a long time seemed alien and incomprehensible to foreign audiences, especially when they required patient and culturally contextualized readings, which were made difficult by a shortage of adequate literary translations. As a consequence, even in the most significant historical and literary syntheses, the writings of Polish Romantics either have not been considered at all – as with Charles Dédéyan's textbook *Le Drame romantique en Europe* (1982); or they have been evaluated with stunning ignorance by otherwise renowned scholars – as with, for example, Allardyce Nicoll and Arthur Wilmurt's *World Drama: From Aeschylus to Anouilh* (1976), whose authors apparently "cannot rate Słowacki highly as a playwright."[26] Alina Kowalczykowa, a Polish scholar of Słowacki, has rebuked the above statement, declaring that "he [Słowacki] is one of the most outstanding playwrights of

European Romanticism; were it not for national and language barriers, he should take his place along[side] at least Victor Hugo."[27] These kinds of rejoinders and corrections made by scholars from Central and Eastern Europe have often gone unnoticed, however, stripped of their authority by the hegemony of the Western humanistic discourse.

Słowacki's Orientalizing, paternalistic reception by British specialists is metonymic of the overall fate of Polish Romanticism.[28] Słowacki and Mickiewicz, along with other great Polish Romantics (including Krasiński and Norwid), have slowly entered the consciousness of a small group of American experts in Slavic Studies (which usually focus on Russian literature), thanks to the work of American Polonists and Slavists (Wacław Lednicki, Wiktor Weintraub, and their successors), and only recently have taken their place in world literature compilations.[29] The introduction of Polish Romanticism into world cultural circulation is a long process, however, and so far only Chopin's music has taken its rightful place. Where literature is concerned, Polish Romantic writers remain at best an exotic, "Oriental" (in Said's understanding) ornament of popular literature, rather than an integral and valuable part of it, not only in the minds of average readers but also in the consciousness of Humanities graduates of European, American, and Australian universities.

Between Aesthetics and Politics, between Europeanness and Peripherality

According to the time frame commonly accepted in the history of Polish literature, Romanticism began with the publication of Mickiewicz's *Ballady i romanse* (Ballads and Romances, 1822), a volume of poetry in which the ballad "Romantyczność" (Romanticism) manifested the new era, and with the programmatic articles of the literary critic Maurycy Mochnacki. It ended with the outbreak of the tragic January Uprising against Russia (1863), which resulted in the devastation of the territories under Russian partition (central and eastern regions of the former commonwealth), the loss of land and property by the nobility, the death of 20,000 people and the deportation to Siberia of 40,000 more, decades of economic stagnation, and the extinguishment of any hope that national sovereignty would be restored. The sense of defeat and the weakening of faith in being able to change the status quo brought about a long-term social crisis, especially among the most active and idealistic Polish patriots.

Tsar Alexander II's 1864 edict ending peasant serfdom under the Russian partition brought about a *de juro* rather than a *de facto* modernization of Polish lands. Instead of improving Poles' living standards and fostering native capital, it drained the economic resources of Polish lands and deepened social antagonisms. The greatest losses were incurred by the gentry, the social class that had once played a leading role in politics, culture, and the economy. The enfranchisement of peasants on Polish lands was part of a Russian project to pacify the "disobedient" Polish periphery. In part, its purpose was to generate a positive image of Russia as a "caring hegemon" while providing Russian governors with cover as they meted out harsh sanctions against patriotic circles in Polish society. In part, it was meant to deprive the Polish manor house (*dwór*) of economic support and to prevent the formation of any alliance between the nobility and the peasantry – enlightened Poles had been trying to develop such an alliance since the late eighteenth century. This Russian tactic would lead to a complete de-Polonization of the inhabitants of "Priwislinja," which is what Polish lands were called by the Russian Empire after 1863, in accordance with this Russian declaration: "May we not cease in working on the complete unification of Priwislinja with the Russian fatherland until the word 'Pole' acquires the same meaning as 'Breton' or 'Provençal' for a Frenchman, until it becomes one of many branches of one great nation."[30] Repressions were accompanied by a thorough Russification of social life, which symbolically culminated in a ban on the publication of Adam Mickiewicz.

To summarize: The territorial unity of Polish culture was broken in 1795 as a result of partitions. Cultural circulation was weakened further after 1830 by rising emigration and tightened border controls between partitions. Then in 1863, as a result of repressions targeted at both the material base of Polish culture and its spiritual superstructure, the nation's developmental continuity was cut. All of this left its mark on the cultural development of the Romantics and subsequent generations.

Clearly, Polish Romanticism symbolically reflected its era, during which trends in European philosophy, literature, and art intersected on a local level with politics, resulting in a unique cultural blend, albeit one that was little known outside of Poland and other Slavic countries. This blend had been anticipated by sentimental and pre-Romantic tendencies in the arts of the 1790s, when "the heart began to rule the mind just as the ravished motherland was being enslaved."[31] These tendencies had been given a voice in the work of poets such as Franciszek Karpiński, Franciszek Dionizy Kniaźnin, and Prince Adam Czartoryski, who "wrote of the expiring Commonwealth as lovers."[32] In turn, the leitmotif of early Romanticism – namely, rebellion against the philosophy and aesthetics of Enlightenment, described as a conflict between Romantics and Classicists – was treated *ex post* by readers as a metaphor of, or a "cover" for, a geopolitical antagonism that the defeated nation could not discuss openly. After the outbreak of the November Uprising in 1830, a young critic and political activist described the situation in this way:

> Under the banner of Romanticism that tears down old rules in the arts and philosophy, and calls for unlimited freedom of thought, we called for a political revolution. We used disputes about Romanticism and Classicism as blindfolds for our censors, our oppressors, convinced that if we could topple scientific rules, if we could habituate Poles to perceive everything freely, we would easily in so doing reveal to them our political powerlessness, the abuse of our liberties ... The Romantic School was a school of political revolution ... For this reason, the writers of the Romantic School were always critical, always wanted to tear down and topple everything, and this was why their writing stirred up passion, rapture, and sometimes hate.[33]

The birth of Romanticism on Polish lands was to some extent a natural consequence of political circumstances. The Romantic attitude can be interpreted as a rational option, one bordering on paradox, given the programmatic "irrationalism" of Romanticism: it was a choice to "escape into fiction" in a situation where external reality was at odds with the desired state of affairs. The political entanglement of Polish Romanticism does not alter, nor does it counter, the fact that works such as *Ballads and Romances* were a clear manifestation of aesthetic sensitivity and Romantic *Weltanschauung*, with the latter encompassing the following: individualism; historicism; emotionalism and gnoseological scepticism; belief in the formative role played by folklore and popular culture; and, finally, faith in the power of the poetic word. At the time, both Poles and others perceived Polish Romanticism as a phenomenon *par excellence* European, in terms of circulation of both ideas and texts. Translations between Polish and German, Russian, French, and even English were not unusual; on the contrary, they were fairly common, albeit not always in both directions. This was conducive to the spread of a revitalizing intellectual excitement and did not create a sense that the Polish lands were culturally delayed in relation to the West.

Over time, however, in the absence of support from state structures, and with the strengthening of repressive policies by the empires – especially by Russia after 1830 – things changed. All that followed – imprisonments, the deportation of 50,000 insurgents and their families to Siberia, the confiscation of the Warsaw library archives – was an expression of the disciplinary politics of the Russian metropolis. The great symbol of that politics was the Warsaw Citadel, a prison built by order of Tsar Nicholas I "in a capital punished for the rebellion of the Polish peripheries."[34] From this point on, it was clear to all that Russia would be treating Polish lands "as a conquered nation, not suited for assimilation into the Empire, but only to being held by force as a typical conquered colony."[35] This grim picture was completed by the censorship of publications in all of the partitions and by the the Great Emigration, as it is now called – the forced emigration from Polish lands of more than 6,000 of the most intellectually active citizens. This event led to an unprecedented in Polish history split of culture into two branches – domestic (additionally divided among three partitions) and exilic.

From that point on, everything that was of greatest importance to Polish Romanticism transpired beyond the borders of Polish lands – mainly in Paris, which became the great centre of the Polish diaspora. Only there was it possible to freely articulate ideas, and the resulting literary texts, political proclamations, and articles were then smuggled into the defeated nation in support of conspiratorial activities. The greatest of Polish writers took part in this process, along with critics and historians (Lelewel, Mochnacki), as well as philosophers and thinkers (Hoene-Wroński, Trentowski, Towiański). Towiański – "a charlatan who founded a cabalistic sect in Paris," whose "messianic vision took on a political tint" and whose "lectures became openly revolutionary" – was a strong influence on Mickiewicz, who in his lectures at the Collège de France spun delusions of reconciliation between socialism and a Christian concept of history.[36] It was also in Paris that the virtuoso pianist Chopin composed his works.

Poland's intellectual and political elites were displaced mostly to France, England, and Belgium, where they found themselves largely isolated from their compatriots at home and lacked any real influence on European politics. Indeed, they resisted adapting to their host cultures, as the "Epilogue" of Mickiewicz's *Sir Thaddeus* canonically expresses. All of this led to the impoverishment of culture on Polish lands and to the ghettoization of Poles living abroad. This was conducive neither to radical political transformation nor to increased visibility for Polish culture, which was driven not by the desire to propagandize for itself, but rather by a "moral imperative to sustain the collective sense of national identity, dismembered by three foreign powers and deprived of integrative institutions."[37]

The growing disparities in the civilizational, technological, and economic development of Polish lands relative to Western Europe contributed to a diminishing interest in Polish writing in nineteenth-century Europe. This was reflected in a growing asymmetry between the attention paid by Polish scholars and thinkers to the literature and humanistic thought of the West, and the analogous interest of the West in the works of Polish writers.[38] The subsequent writings of Polish historians of literature convey an awareness of this disparity, interpreted in terms of historical injustice, by striking clearly compensatory notes that speak to the lasting trauma of the peripherality complex, as heard in the following example: "We were not at the tail end of Europe then. Mickiewicz, Słowacki,

Norwid – these were not the peripheries of literature, but its centre at that time – their voice as weighty and representative of the creative value of world literature as the voice of their great contemporaries: Schiller, Byron, Pushkin and Lermontov."[39]

Notwithstanding the compensatory consolations formulated in native discourse, the virtual absence of Polish Romanticism in comprehensive history-of-literature textbooks, already evident during the times of colonial expansion by European empires, has lasted more or less to this day. This is worrisome, especially in the case of textbooks that, while seemingly attempting to do justice to artistic production in languages other than English, reduce Eastern European Romanticism to the output of Russian-language poets, dispensing with authors of other nationalities with short commentaries or complete silence.[40] An uninformed reader might conclude that Polish writers of this period, unlike English, German, French, and Russian writers, had nothing significant to share with the world, and that their work deserves at best a passing note.

"Necessary Fictions"

Polish Romanticism sanctified the principle, born with Poland's loss of sovereignty, according to which the "Word" holds precedence over the "Fact" and "more attention is paid to what people would have liked to happen than to what actually occurred."[41] This did not signify the escape of literature from reality, however, but rather a peculiar transformation or "coding" of reality. The Romantics worked out formulas for addressing the condition of colonization – "necessary fictions" of a kind. These fictions were to provide the nation with support in history, as well as in the world of myth that was sovereign and independent of the actual political situation. But they would also make it possible to articulate anti-colonial resistance in a way that was legible to their audience and that challenged their current reality, which negated the past world along with its fantasies. Thanks to these "necessary fictions," an oppressed nation would be able to find the strength to cope with its oppressor – at that time, primarily the Russian Empire. Thus, "necessary fictions" had not only a compensatory but also a political function. Their existence ensured the historical *continuum* of the Polish nation, for a nation exists as long as it is able to generate, adapt, and creatively remake its myths, symbols, and values in confrontation with external circumstances.

> The Romantics worked out a set of formulas for dealing with the condition of colonization. These "necessary fictions," such as the authority of poetry, the national idea, and knowledge of the empire, performed both compensatory and political functions. On the one hand, they provided the nation with the language to write its own history as well as to turn it into myth; on the other hand, they made it possible to articulate anti-colonial resistance.
>
> From today's perspective, the Western world did not recognize the universal human experience in the Polish experience, in its specific variant of colonization of "whites by whites." In this manner, the nineteenth-century experience of Poles living in the territories annexed to three European empires was pushed out of the European consciousness and cultural memory.

For Poles, Romanticism's "necessary fictions" were an integral part of a system of cultural communication – indeed, they were the basis for that system. This "code" allowed Poles dispersed across the three partitions and in exile to understand one another as members of a single "imagined" community. Three of the main elements of this code – the authority of poetry, the national idea, and knowledge of the empire – are briefly characterized below. Among other "necessary fictions" of importance to Polish Romanticism are the Slavic utopia, historical and mythical (re)construction of Polish genealogy, and the idea of solidarity with other peoples who found themselves oppressed by Orientalizing and "othering" discourses. These "fictions," however, are beyond the scope of current discussion.

1. The First Fiction: Absolute Authority of the Poet's Word

The great poets of Polish Romanticism were believed to possess the gift of artistic inspiration and to have a prophetic role to play, one that Mochnacki defined early in the eighteenth century. He wrote in 1825: "Let us dispense with facts, experiences and observation, and use inspiration and free imagination to explore the mysteries and phenomena of intellectual life. As the prophets already knew, what is too complicated and often undiscovered for wise man, the poet-bard's passion [*wieszczy zapał*] can encompass, permeate and grasp."[42]

These poets did not become national "bards," "prophets," and "priests of the national cause" automatically, however. Sheer poetic ability was not enough, even when that gift was supported by profound epistemological insights. The poets' role acquired a new, national aspect only after 1830, when "the scattered and disoriented nation looked to [them] to make sense of things and [they] grew into the role of the spiritual leaders, the oracular high-priests who strove to provide some answers."[43] The desperate search at that time for leaders, spiritual guardians, and moral authorities points to one of the most characteristic qualities of Polish Romanticism – the "literarization" of social and political life. Having been disappointed by their actual leaders when leadership was most needed (the defeat of anti-Russian insurrections was actually caused by an absence of competent leadership), Poles transferred the responsibility for their collective condition into the hands of poets. What other nations attained through public institutions and state apparatus, Poles of the Romantic era hoped to attain by surrendering themselves to literature. In these circumstances, Mickiewicz, Słowacki, and Krasiński took on the role of charismatic, spiritual leaders of a nation. Paradoxically, therefore, these poet-bards rose to this honour by virtue of a national defeat, and they were required to deliver "national themes in their work, patriotic fervor and responsiveness to current historical affairs, as well as tone of speech – full of pathos, dramatic or lyrical."[44]

Mochnacki played a unique role in Polish nineteenth-century thought: "Like no one before him and not many since, Mochnacki was concerned with the problem of originality, a key issue of all cultures that develop under conditions of strong dependence on foreign thought and foreign norms. He did not desire intellectual isolation of Poland by any means ... At the same time, he felt that Polish culture's great opportunity came from difference and not repetition . Creativity and not imitation."[45] Mochnacki created a modern conceptualization of national literature: he saw it as a factor constitutive of national self-awareness, which he referred to as "recognition of oneself in one's being."[46] The nation, according to him, was an independent and sovereign subject of history. To exist as a subject, however, it needed literature to carry its self-knowledge and to articulate itself. According to this concept, which was of enormous significance for the discourse on Polish identity, the decisive factor in the existence of a nation as a real political subject was not the state but literature, with the latter elevated by these means to the status of the conquered peoples' main cultural discourse. In this manner, "Mochnacki's theory of literature became in fact an ontology of national being, a philosophy of national culture."[47] From then on, the diagnoses and prescriptions pertaining to the national condition, as put forward by both Romantic and later generations of poets, attained a status comparable to social or political-scientific analyses. The diagnostic and interventional functions of poets were seen as natural and necessary for regulating public life under the partitions, especially after the defeat of the 1831 uprising. As late as the mid-nineteenth century, Norwid could write about the poet's political role that "the national artist organizes imagination like a national politician organizes state forces."[48]

The "command of souls" (*rząd dusz*) demanded by Mickiewicz's Konrad in *Forefathers Eve, Part III* – for the good of the people, as he claimed – became a metaphor for the aspirations of Romantic poets. That phrase has entered the Polish language permanently as a synonym for the elite's aspirations, which bordered on usurpation, to lead the nation. The intelligentsia's demand for the right to lead the masses is an ambivalent part of its historical ethos, in that the leadership of intellectuals did not always align with ethics of responsibility for, and solidarity with, other social strata. This problem had its roots in the Romantic concept of spiritual command, which was awarded instead of real political power to exceptional individuals who either were nominated for the position by virtue of their creative talent, or viewed themselves as especially predisposed to the task.

The prophetic and commanding model of writing that led the way during Romanticism, and that was most fully realized in poetry and drama, had three weighty implications not only for literature and for the further development of culture, but also for the world view and social life of the Poles. To begin with, it privileged "high" and solemn poetry. In so doing it placed at a disadvantage comedy and humour on the one hand, and prose and the novel on the other, even though these had the potential to be culturally productive and might have broadened the scope for the development of national self-awareness. This explains why, for example, Aleksander Fredro's (1793–1876) comedies were devalued for lacking national character, and why the genre of novel encountered the same fate, despite its potential for building the "narrative of a nation." At a time when English and French novels were flourishing, this privileging of poetry widened the gap between Polish and Western European literatures. Polish culture remained decidedly "poetry-centric," despite the popularity of Henryk Rzewuski's (1791–1866) *Pamiątki Soplicy* (The Memoirs of Soplica, 1839–41; 1844–5), which in its style embraced the gentry oral-tale tradition (*gawęda szlachecka*), and despite the spectacular opus of Józef Ignacy Kraszewski (1812–87), a talented prose craftsman with a gift for tapping modern trends in European literature to build the narrative of a nation (Kraszewski was also the most prolific novelist in Polish history). This remained the case despite the appearance of great novelists after Romanticism, including Bolesław Prus (1847–1912), Eliza Orzeszkowa (1841–1910), and Henryk Sienkiewicz (1846–1916). For this reason, even in the context of two twentieth-century totalitarianisms – German and Soviet – Poles looked primarily to their poets to witness and lead the nation at turning points of history.[49]

Second, the high status of poetry resulting from its leadership function invested the poetic word – referencing Herder's conceptualization of it in *Über den Ursprung der Sprache* (On the Origin of Language, 1771) – with a perlocutionary force and absolute authority, parallel to the power of the divine Word, *logos*. The poet's word was an autonomous act constituting reality and emigrant poetry – the only domain of freedom outside the oppressor's control. Having been vested with the highest authority, the word of the poet was to secure "command of souls," a more noble and moral authority than that based in raw power. This word was to be revered, and the ideas it expressed, including the national idea, were to attain the status of revelations. That status would compensate for poetry's lack of real influence on geopolitics. This "sacralizing," dogmatic model of reception had some side effects: it made it difficult for future generations of readers to undertake an independent, critical analysis of the Romantic legacy in terms of its real intellectual propositions. Attempts to undermine Romantic ideas were seen as attacks on the Polish ethos – indeed, as treasonous.

Third, the authority and position of the "bard" provoked debates about the hierarchy of Polish poets. This hierarchy was not at all clear, especially since Polish culture after 1831 circulated in two realms: emigrant and domestic. The canonical "trinity" of Mickiewicz, Słowacki, and Krasiński belonged to the first group and were joined later by Norwid. The domestic Romantics included Wincenty Pol (1807–72), the author of sentimental songs on national and patriotic subjects; he was not an equal of the émigré poets, but he enjoyed great popularity among readers at home. The domestic group also included Teofil Lenartowicz (1822–93), Kornel Ujejski (1823–97), and many others. One's poetic ranking was not set in stone; rather, it was decided by the opinions of the salons, which admired masterful displays of poetic improvisation, as well as by the opinions of critics. Disputes among readers as to whether Mickiewicz was a better poet than Słowacki, or Słowacki than Krasiński, lasted long after their deaths. Critical reflection about their ideas often gave way to debate over the formal merits of their work: its style, versification, and language. Regardless of all this, during the nineteenth century Poles took their "trinity" for granted. Only in the twentieth century was Norwid promoted to their rank.

2. The Second Fiction: "National Idea"

Confronted first with the loss of their own country, and later, in 1831, with the loss of hope for its quick restoration and with growing indifference of the rest of Europe, Polish Romantics grew increasingly aware that they needed to work out their own realistic national idea. The idea that came out of this effort, however, lacked a uniform character. Although in the minds of its proponents it stemmed from pragmatism, it was expressed both in the form of messianism (by Mickiewicz, Krasiński, and Słowacki in literature, and August Cieszkowski in philosophy), which can hardly be classified as a pragmatic approach today, and in other political concepts that had little to do with messianism even when formulated by the same authors. Regardless of the direction in which it developed, however, the Romantic national idea did not become an ideology for preserving the dominance of a social elite, even though it was proffered by members of this elite. Rather, it aimed at bringing all of society into a horizontal community (modelled on the republican ideal, among other things) that would willingly share the same cultural values and political goals. This puts into question those contemporary theories of the nation that look for its source in nationalism understood as a by-product of modernization and of the centralized efforts of the elites to rule over the masses.[50]

Messianism was neither exclusively Polish nor specifically Romantic. Messianic thought, inspired by the philosophy of Fichte, among others, enjoyed considerable popularity throughout nineteenth-century Europe. In Polish writing, however, it played a unique role, in that it laid down the foundations for comprehensive explanations – based in the philosophy of history – of the Polish historical experience of loss; and for building the national idea on such explanations. Contrary to the irrationalism that supposedly characterized Romanticism, messianism assumed that collective suffering had a rational basis and might be used constructively. In that sense, this ideology was pragmatic despite implying a political utopia. It restored self-agency to the nation; it also actively propounded the national mission, which would entail mastery over suffering and turning defeat into a moral victory over the enemy and one's own weaknesses. It offered conquered peoples hope that they might rejoin the ranks of the world's sovereign nations. It also exposed the immorality of the political law of the survival of the fittest.

In the context of the failed 1831 uprising, the compensatory character of this "necessary fiction" is clear. According to the ideology of Polish messianism, the suffering of the nation could be equated with Christ's sacrifice on behalf of humanity. In an unforeseeable future, as a result of their suffering, the oppressed nations would be redeemed (i.e., liberated) and resurrected. Both male and female literary heroes followed the logic of heroism, absolute sacrifice, and individual lives laid down for the fatherland. This is true, for example, of Mickiewicz's Konrad Wallenrod and Grażyna (in the eponymous works), of Emilia Plater in the poem "Śmierć pułkownika" (Death of the Colonel, 1836), of Konrad, Father Piotr, and the imprisoned patriots in *Forefathers' Eve, Part III*, and of Ordon in "Reduta Ordona" (Ordon's Redoubt, 1833), as well as of Słowacki's Kordian and Sowiński. All of these characters, in line with the narratives in which they appear, serve as allegories of Romantic sacrifice and as emblematic figures in a victimizing discourse.

Messianism was more than a blueprint for a political utopia; it was also a pseudo-Christian political philosophy, and even a "milleniaristic" political religion, one that had little in common with Christian orthodoxy despite being saturated with a theological vocabulary and religious rhetoric. Norwid called it a "mystical radicalism and gnostic spiritual aristocracy of the summoned."[51] The pragmatism of messianism was often called into question when messianistic slogans were confronted with harsh political realities: "Messianism was the main defendant in all of the trials that the Romantic legacy faced in Polish culture. For foreigners, it sometimes provided arguments for creating or popularizing a negative stereotype of Polish national character, in which the lack of a grasp on reality accompanies outbursts of mass megalomania."[52]

From today's perspective, Romantic and post-Romantic messianism can be treated as one of the principal "necessary fictions" of the discourse on Polish identity. It provided, after all, answers to key questions – for Poles as for all colonized people – about who they were and, given their situation, what their historical role was.

Yet this "necessary fiction" was not merely an innocent interpretation of history, a salve that provided the subordinated population with transcendental consolation. It can also be viewed more ambivalently, as reflecting a "refusal to accept the political situation as the reality." On the one hand, it gave an "essential spur to national consciousness"; on the other, it "has tended to cloud the vision of the past."[53] The messianism of the Romantics also had unpredictable political implications, which were pointed out with precision by Roman Dmowski, the creator of modern Polish nationalistic discourse:

> In no other country did the political legacy of the first half of the nineteenth century survive as long as it did in Poland: faith in the rule of justice in international relations and the effectiveness of redressing one's just rights through unbiased European opinion; referring to historical facts as "crimes" and "wrongs"; belief in the final victory of the "just cause"; lack of consideration for actual power relations in international life, and lack of understanding that the outcome of all matters depends primarily on the resultant force of these power relations. This anchoring of political perspectives in entirely illusory foundations, and with it the tendency to undertake political actions without clear determination of their aims and a calculation of resources – is called political Romanticism.[54]

The substitution of political realism with political Romanticism reached a climax in messianism, which rejected *Realpolitik*, given that it was a political theology free of political calculation and national egoism, both of which were seen as morally objectionable. Hence repeated critical readings of Romanticism that accuse it of lacking political realism in some sense fall on stony ground.

Perhaps, as Zdzisław Krasnodębski suggests, the republican tradition explains why Polish Romantic messianism did not evolve into totalitarianism or a demonic nationalism.[55] After all, it did not offer a religious justification for the rule of an individual over the masses, nor did it become a political substitute for religion by eliminating a transcendental perspective. Instead, it provided religious grounds for understanding and accepting the national community's situation.[56] Thus it remained, despite everything – against the background of transformations in political culture in nineteenth- and twentieth-century Germany and Russia – a mild political aberration. This does not mean that this aberration was free of the problematic consequences mentioned earlier. Messianism undoubtedly made it more difficult for Poles to understand the mechanisms of "great" politics that run the world (and its mental residue still has this effect). It did make it easier, though, to activate social emotions around tragedies and defeats, even if its social capital was insufficient for political transformation.

The national idea assumed other forms besides messianism in Polish Romanticism, but these never attained the same popularity; nor, despite disputing it, did they become sufficient counterweights for it.[57] The most radical approach to the issue of the national idea is found in Norwid, who re-evaluated the category of the nation in relation to society, claiming that "Polish society is as inferior as the Polish nation is superior."[58] Norwid's gnomic commentary, which articulated the overcoming of the Romantic legacy's undesirable aspect, achieved the status of a *bon mot* in Polish discourse only in the twentieth century as the main thesis of post-Romantic social critique.

Besides Norwid's, other forms of the national idea outside of the main messianic current remained generally unnoticed; they were seeds of thought that failed to sprout. Słowacki, who cultivated messianic concepts during his mystical phase but was not influenced solely by them, is an interesting example, especially when he anticipates thinking in categories of "organic work," advocated later by Norwid and other writers and thinkers of the second half of the nineteenth century. Słowacki's political thought, which remains underappreciated, tellingly deconstructs social ethics. He subordinates the moral significance of social behaviour to the aims of self-presentation, which is needed so badly in a nation of subalterns denied the right to speak. Słowacki contended that any action that could increase the visibility of the repressed society was positive and desirable. To illustrate this, he offered the hypothetical figure of the extravagant Russian, who fritters away a fortune abroad while testifying to the power of the Russian Empire and "even in boldly throwing down money on a card, in the purchase of the first love of the most famous dancer ... the youngster ... seems to say: 'Look at me here! I'm a milksop and a lunatic! But men akin of spirit, only higher up ... are prepared to thus throw down millions in order to occupy the highest positions in Europe!'"[59] In this passage, the attitude of the citizen of the Russian Empire can serve Poles subjugated by Russians as a strategy of colonial mimicry, through which they will learn to talk back to the metropolis and strengthen their lost subjectivity. At the same time, Słowacki's argument points to the third "necessary fiction" of Polish Romanticism, one that has survived almost unaltered in Polish culture up to the present day.

The Third Fiction: *Spécialité Polonaise* – Knowledge of the Russian Empire

At the beginning of the nineteenth century, Russian and Polish identity discourses centred on two elementary myths that continue to fuel each of these discourses. These myths are, respectively, (1) the Russian myth about Poles, who renounced their Slavic identity by choosing Catholicism in order to mimic the West, and who in the end descended into anarchy; and (2) the Polish myth about Russians, who are not true Europeans, but the descendants of wild Mongol hordes and a continuous threat to the Commonwealth and the entire Western world due to their inherent imperialist ambitions.[60]

While these myths came into conflict in the literatures of the two nations as a result of the dynamic between the Polish periphery and the Russian metropolis, they did not condition each other. What is more, they were not symmetrical in relation to each other. The first depended on an ideological interpretation of religious and political choices, made independently by Poles from the beginning of their statehood and of no threat to the Grand Duchy of Moscow or the later Tsardom of Russia. The second was also based in interpretation, but it had as its subject not the sovereign affairs of Russia, but rather the aggressive imperial politics of the tsars against the Commonwealth of Both Nations, which culminated in the partition of Poland on Catherine the Great's initiative and the anti-Polish politics of the Russian Empire in the annexed peripheries. Both myths significantly affected the development of Polish Romantic (as well as subsequent) thought. The Slavic question is a repercussion of the first myth in Polish culture, and overlaps with ruminations on the historical role of the Slavs that are popular not only in Polish Romanticism, but also its other Eastern European variants. The second myth is the basis of various opinions and stereotypes about Russians as a nation and a people, and about Russia as an empire and as the centre of Orthodox Christianity, and it supplies reasons for the critique of Russian culture and civilization. Notably, it was not the exclusive result of resentment following the defeat of the November Uprising, for the process of "gradual differentiation between Poland and Russia" had begun earlier in Polish culture.[61]

The second myth found emphatic and complex articulation in Mickiewicz's "Ustęp" (Digression) in *Forefathers' Eve, Part III*. On the one hand, Mickiewicz conveyed there the nature of Tsarist absolutism in hyperbolic style; on the other, he took an empathetic stance towards the Russian people, presented as victims of authoritarian rule:

> Poor nation, I deplore thy tragedy!
> Thy heroism is naught but slavery.[62]

Słowacki takes a similar tone in "Hymn (Bogarodzico, Dziewico!)": "there too live people – there too they have a soul." Krasiński consistently took the stance of an implacable enemy of Russia and Russians, which he pointedly expressed in the poem "Do Moskali" (To the Moscovites):

> [...] for I nursed at my mother's breast
> On a great and holy hate for you!
> And this hate is all I now possess.

In Polish Romanticism, the ambivalent image of Russians as "normal people" and, at the same time, as passive or active participants in despotic rule – exemplarily presented also in Norwid's poem "Do wroga" (To the Enemy) – was the result of negotiations between anti-colonial anger and hate and the Christian ethical imperative to love one's neighbour. Polish Romantics did not question this ethic; indeed, they tried to base their political and historiosophical ideas on it. They thus turned their anger not towards the people, but towards the despotic empire, hoping to thereby sway Russian democratic circles to the "Polish cause." In taking this approach, they also established the discursive model for solving the "Russian question." This model was based on the interaction of two stereotypes that would endure in Poland's literature and world view until the fall of communism. The first stereotype was that of the "good Russian." Two of the most beautiful portraits of Russian soldiers in Polish literature – Captain Rykow in *Sir Thaddeus* and Colonel Korff in Norwid's poem "Fulminant" – can serve as examples. They are friends, even brothers, of Poles, as well as their companions in the suffering inflicted by the same oppressor (as in Mickiewicz's "Do przyjaciół Moskali" [To Our Friends Moscovites]). The second stereotype was that of unreformable Russian tyranny that is inherently hostile towards Poland and personified by the tsar and his depraved, blindly obedient *soldati*, whom Mickiewicz calls the "lava of mud" in "Ordon's Redoubt." This stereotype has been raised on many occasions since Romanticism, directly and indirectly, including in the publications of the democratic opposition during 1970s and 1980s.

Polish writing of the Romantic era also focused on the civilizational and cultural border between Europe and Asia – a border that has attracted the world's attention only recently on the heels of Samuel P. Huntington's *The Clash of Civilizations* (1996). Due to their historical experiences, this issue was vital to Poles almost two hundred years before Huntington broached it. They saw this border as a dividing line between two historically antagonistic faiths, on which had been built antithetical cultures, anthropologies, and axiological systems: Catholic, leaning towards Latin civilization; and Orthodox, gravitating towards – as it was said – "Asian barbarism." The issue of Polish–Russian relations was presented from this perspective in Polish literature as well as in historical and philosophical writing, including writing addressed to an international public – for example, in the works of Trentowski and Mickiewicz. The latter's lectures at the Collège de France and his articles in *La Tribune des Peuples* reveal that he was "faithful to his concept of a Russia whose authority is synonymous with every conceivable political and moral evil, and whose ordinary people, isolated from their natural leaders, have not yet found their historical *raison-d-être*."[63] Initiating the world into the mysteries of the Russian soul and politics had become, it seems, part of the Polish cultural mission and, in today's terminology, of the historical and foreign politics of a non-existent state.

Worth noting is the "first-hand" nature of the knowledge that Polish Romantics had of Russians and Russia, which was unmediated and had been analytically deepened through constant contact in a colonial setting. This experience was described by, for example, the authors of memoirs, who included Siberian deportees who had experienced inhuman treatment as prisoners – the Bar confederates, Kosciuszko and the November insurgents, high-ranking officers of the 1831 war, and civilians of both sexes.[64] Their narrations presented a dichotomous image of Russians and Russia in much the same way as high literature did. This confirms that the image of the Russian Empire and its inhabitants in the writing of the Romantics was not simply a literary creation subordinated to a single *a priori* thesis, nor was it an artistic strategy of representation chosen by the principal ideologists of Polish Romanticism. To the contrary, the image corresponded to Poles' common perception of the despotically ruled Russia – a perception rooted in the quotidian realities of life on the empire's periphery as well as in the harsh conditions of Siberian dislocation. That these diarists, like the great poets, attempted to show different aspects of the Eastern neighbours who had conquered their nation speaks to the coherence of Polish culture. That culture's most refined and artistic, as well as common and colloquial, forms of articulation appear to have been rooted in Christian anthropology. The Christian understanding of the human being left room for faith in providentialism and in the eventual triumph of the good, which encourages foregoing the desire for revenge and the dispensation of justice in the here and now, as well as conquering hatred of the enemy with the imperative to "love one's enemies."

In this context – in the face of Russian hegemony – the Polish Romantics' ruminations on Poland's role within the geopolitical arena of the nineteenth century are not surprising. Krasiński referenced the Sarmatian idea of the Bulwark of Christianity (*antemurale christianitatis*), which provided support for messianic beliefs, as he warned against the consequences of that hegemony. His rhetoric conveys well the Poles' determination to restore their state and reveals the rationale behind his interpretation of political events. His arguments also foreground the "Russian question":

> Today [in 1848 – D.S.], Poland's reappearance in the world is the condition of progress in the East, and of the recovery of civilization in the West ... In perishing, Poland will leave the world at the mercy of European anarchy and Eastern barbarity; both will be inevitable. European anarchy, tearing itself apart, will make easier the fulfillment of Eastern barbarity's godless dreams. The Moscovy banner will appear and expand on the horizon, it will grow nearer, and the people in Europe, covered in the blood of their brothers, will come to adore this emblem of the Asian idea among the ruins that they will themselves create.[65]

The problem of the "Russian subject" being a "specialty" of Poles during the Romantic era needs to be seen as a cultural effect of colonization. It was a consequence of imperialism's logic, where imperialism is understood as "the politics of pulling other nations and countries into the circle of influence of the imperializing nation or country."[66] This "pulling in" encompassed both "hard" institutional resources (e.g., economic or military) and "soft" psychological ones, in which trauma played the main part – trauma resulting both from great threats and from minor, quotidian ones, all caused by the colonizer's presence and actions.

As an effect of this trauma, a new and culturally productive factor appeared in the post-partition discourse of Poles – namely, the imperative to take a stance towards the empire, its politics, and its inhabitants. This need intensified with the defeat of the November Uprising. The intellectual and emotional engagement in the study of the "Russian soul" sometimes led Polish writers and thinkers to subtle and intellectually compelling analyses of the empire, its functionaries, and its citizenry. This exploration also fostered among Polish society a sense of superiority – moral, cultural, and civilizational – over all things Russian, however. This only solidified the antagonism between the two nations in Polish discourse; to some extent, it also determined the subsequent development of the Polish culture and world view. This is why, regardless of the form that the "Russian question" took in Polish writing, answering that question was – from the perspective of the development of Polish society and culture – a fruitless undertaking. It wasted the intellectual energies of remarkable individuals, energies that could have been utilized differently – namely, to define and implement positive social change. Polish Romantics and their successors devoted a great deal of energy to studying the Russian hegemon, but the results of this "imperiological" (as opposed to anthropological) work were neither appreciated nor understood abroad, and they did not significantly impact the image of Russia in the West. To the contrary, the (anti)Russian obsession often earned Poles a reputation for intransigent Russophobia, which ironically came to be referred to as the *spécialité polonaise*. Indeed, from a contemporary perspective, it can be treated as a posthumous trap set for the colonized by the colonial system.

Universalism of Polish Romanticism

There are three ways of understanding the universalism of Polish Romanticism. To begin with, its universal aspect stemmed from the national character of Polish Romanticism. This ceases to be paradoxical if we remember the key thesis of Said's final chapter in *Orientalism*. For "national" does not necessarily mean "particular." All of European Romanticism developed in an atmosphere of national sentiment and ambitions; thus, national inclinations were neither eccentric nor isolated. Have the cultures of nations like Poland become better known and understood as a result, however? Has knowledge about them been assimilated and reflected upon by the rest of the world as part of a common human history?

From today's perspective it is apparent that the Western world did not glean a universal human experience from the Polish experience in its specific variant: that is, the colonization of "whites by whites" through the conquest and annexation of Polish territories to three European empires. This accounts for the erasure of the Poles' nineteenth-century experience from European consciousness and cultural memory. As is the case with Said's Orient, the dominant humanistic discourse of the West placed the formally non-existent nineteenth-century Poland and its inhabitants in "a region of the world it considered alien to its own." As a consequence, it failed to to see the Polish experience as "a human experience."[67] If the ethical obligations of the humanities are to be taken seriously, reclaiming this experience as part of the general human experience is a basic necessity.

Second, the universalism of Polish Romanticism was a universalism of freedom, anchored in a sense of co-responsibility for other people and nations that had been deeply interiorized by Polish culture. Polish Romantics extended their efforts at sovereignty to the ideals of freedom and equality for all people. They did not stop at declarations, but took action by participating in, for example, the "Spring of Nations" in 1848 (as General Józef Bem did in Hungary). In doing so, they invoked not only the ideals of the French Revolution but also of the Polish republican idea – that of defending a shared, Christian Europe – with the motto "For your freedom and ours" inspiring Tadeusz Kościuszko and Kazimierz Pułaski to fight for the sovereignty of the United States of America. The relationship between the freedom of fatherland and the freedom of humanity was defined indirectly by Norwid in his commentary on King John III Sobieski's opinion about the nature of homeland: "A noble man could not survive even one day in a Fatherland, if its happiness were to be any more than a percentage of the happiness of humanity. All of the forefathers and fathers of the Polish Commonwealth thus understood the Polish cause."[68]

The universalism of Polish Romanticism has yet another aspect, one that is close to, yet transcends, the last one. Access to it does not demand any historically and politically contextualized knowledge of Romantic writing – in other words, it does not require a reading that considers the "necessary fictions" discussed above. Polish Romanticism was more than a "narration of a nation" on its own subject, to paraphrase Homi Bhaba. It was also at times simply a "human narration" – a story about a human being. Three examples must suffice: Krasiński's play *Nie-Boska Komedia* (The Undivine Comedy, 1835), Mickiewicz's *Lyriki lozańskie* (Lausanne lyrics, 1861) and Norwid's ideas.

The Undivine Comedy, which was Krasiński's answer to Mickiewicz's *Forefathers' Eve, Part III*, continues to strike readers as a poignantly pessimistic diagnosis and extremely perceptive study of revolutionary movements "as the consequence of the crisis of Christian civilization and the moral entropy of a spiritually disinherited mankind."[69] Krasiński's work pursued a totally different direction than Mickiewicz or Słowacki: instead of analysing the condition of a colonized nation, "he created a dystopian story about a revolution and the historical consequences of its triumph," the first of its kind in the history of Polish literature, thus anticipating the characteristics and consequences of the great supranational social conflicts of the twentieth century.[70] With great foresight, he presented "the false soteriology of revolution," whereby the "test of collective salvation of mankind" is carried out through "negation of the spiritual dimension of humanity and neo-pagan sacralisation of the body" and the "sanctification of killing."[71] Krasiński's insights about the quasi-religious nature of revolution turned out to be relevant to the diverse projections of the "brave new world" promised to humanity by twentieth-century regimes. In conjunction with its suggestive rhetoric and its vivid characters, the message of Krasiński's play is thoroughly universal.

In his introduction to the English translation of *The Undivine Comedy*, G.K. Chesterton, who was aware of the impact of the Bolshevik Revolution, pointed to the work's prophetic potential.[72] But he could not have known that the vision presented in the play would soon turn into ghastly reality in all Central and Eastern European countries as well as in other parts of the world due to the expansion of Soviet communism. Nevertheless, Krasiński's diagnosis would never tread the world's intellectual stage, even though his "successors, Fyodor Dostoyevsky and Friedrich Nietzsche, coped with the same questions in their works, and earned fame in the process of doing so."[73] Yet "the grand verbal duel between Henry and Pancras [the two competing protagonists – D.S.] is worth anthologizing in the same way in which Dostoyevsky's Grand Inquisitor scene has been anthologized."[74] Moreover, the central problem posed by Krasiński's play – the vision of the revolution's leader, Pancras, confronted with the vision of the Galilean (Christ) – is a harbinger of the never-ending conflict between the Marxist "historical inevitability" playing out in human history, with all its social and moral consequences, and the transcendental order of eschatological reality. Krasiński reveals that this conflict, which cannot be solved in the earthly realm, can only lead to a catastrophe in the social order, since it is impossible to create a social utopia while eliminating metaphysics from it.

This diagnosis acquires fascinating new currency from the perspective of contemporary debates about post-secular society.

The *Lausanne lyrics*, written in 1839 and 1840 during Mickiewicz's stay in that city and unpublished during his lifetime, amount to no more than a handful of poems. Though brief, they are considered the pinnacle of Polish lyrical poetry – works "of rare perfection," according to Miłosz.[75] The unparalleled artistry in these "lyrical notes" flows from the depth of reflection on the condition of man faced with the Inexpressible – with the mystery of nature and existence – combined with extraordinarily simple and condensed yet melodious wording. The form of these poems is pure and subdued, stripped of all ornamentation, so that an undisturbed harmony between thought and word is achieved. Some of these poems are lyrical descriptions several stanzas long, such as "[Nad wodą wielką i czystą ...]" ([Above Water Vast and Pure ...]); others are mere fragments.

The couplet "[Uciec z duszą na listek...]" ([To flee with One's Soul onto a Leaf ...]) has the latter form. This perfectly concise work – "like a poetic sigh liberated spontaneously in a scrap of a poem"[76] – not only expresses the subject's tender affection for all creation, but under the cover of this emotion evokes a metaphysical longing to preserve fleeting human existence in an undefined but familiar and desired infinity:

> To flee with one's soul onto a leaf and like a butterfly search
> There for a small home and a little nest –

The Lausanne lyrics are free of Romantic rebellion against the world. Instead, they express an internal peace reached due to a subtly implied *metanoia*, an internal transformation.[77] With the lyrical subject aware of the need for this transformation, the metamorphosis allows him to transcend the limits of time through a mystical experience of space, which constitutes the central theme of the Lausanne lyrics. In contrast to *The Undivine Comedy*, access to the depth of meaning enclosed in Mickiewicz's final poetic cycle is possible only in the original language. Miłosz described these poems as "untranslatable masterpieces of metaphysical meditation" and "examples of that pure poetry which verges on silence."[78]

Many of Norwid's poetic works are also untranslatable due to their refined linguistic transformations and etymological and semantic play. They require the reader's careful study, with emphasis placed on extracting the important meanings of words from below their surface meanings (meaning those in current circulation and distrusted by the poet). Norwid was a rebel, but not in the spirit of Romantic individualism. Rather, he was rebelling against all surface forms, which he saw as a petrifications of human thought:

> In the whole of Norwid's writing, we find the spirit of protest and struggle: in relation to everything which is stamped with the hallmark of mechanical tradition, empty convention, fascination with externals, passive compliance with conventions, and in relation to social or national structures that bear the stigma of parochialism. Norwid's work constitutes a great "*non possumus*" in the face of everything that limits growth and development, and enslaves man.[79]

In Norwid's difficult oeuvre, which varies in quality, the most universal message comes across in his aphorisms, short fragments of lyrics and prose, and his letters. These reflections contain perspectives that are still relevant to twenty-first-century readers.

Often presented as paradoxes, Norwid's observations pertain to various, frequently intertwined aspects of individual and social life: religion and ethics, politics and economics, epistemology and art. For example, in expressing his opinion on the shock value of ugliness in art, he simultaneously posed the problem of the relation between art and the truth that it should pursue: "I have seen carrots and turnips in a beautifully cooked broth, the carrots and turnips cut into the most elegant patterns: stars and numbers, burning hearts, crosses even ...! All the same, the carrots and turnips were still carrots and turnips."[80] Truth was an important subject for Norwid. As a Christian, a humanist, and a moralist, he emphasized the need for unity between declared ideals and human actions: "Truth is not just knowledge, it is life itself." In a similar spirit, he warned against the separation of action from the ethical order: "No virtue is so rare and splendid that it cannot be misused."

Tradition held a significant place in Norwid's conceptualization of man and culture. He saw it as the cultural foundation of society's existence –metaphorically, as a "spring" that had to be respected and that had the power to transform culture and imbue life with value: "You can drink from a carafe if you grip its neck and press it to your lips, but if you wish to drink from a spring, you must go on your knees and bow your head." In his social analyses, Norwid often went outside the Polish context. Even when he touched on the subject of patriotism, he did so in a universal way, free of idolatrous adoration of his own nation. His writings express a sense of belonging to a European community, although not at the price of betraying the ties with his own nation. He opposed equally forms of extreme individualism and totalitarian social currents, predicting that their consequences for humanity would be deplorable. He was terrified by the spectre of despotism and social utopias, for violence would be necessary to realize either. The cult of technology was foreign to him; he saw it as a threat to humanistic values. Norwid looked upon the crisis of European civilization and culture from a Christian and biblical point of view, and his diagnoses of the human condition resound with the same pessimism that, several decades later, would be given voice in T.S. Eliot's *The Waste Land* and *The Hollow Men.*

Romanticism Today

The reception of Polish Romanticism by Poles was from the outset characterized by respect for the *opus vitae* of the great poets, whose proliferation in a single era was exceptional. However, respect for their work did not mean uncritical acceptance of their ideas. To the contrary, Romanticism has long been the subject of multiple rereadings and passionate discussions. In terms of the discourse of Polish identity, two readings of Romanticism, both from the beginning of the twentieth century, have left an imprint: those of Stanisław Wyspiański (1869–1907) – a poet, playwright, and painter – and Stanisław Brzozowski (1878–1911) – a writer and a self-taught cultural philosopher. Wyspiański conducted an incisive and rhetorically expansive critique of Romantic exaltation and the Romantic myth, especially in his dramas *Wesele* (The Wedding, 1901) and *Wyzwolenie* (Deliverance, 1903).[81] He saw the myth of an uprising led by an extraordinary, alienated individual, a poet-prophet and spiritual guide, as an instrument for enslaving the collective consciousness. That is why, in the end, such a myth could not liberate a nation. As for exaltation, he viewed it as an impediment to realistic approaches to "hard" political and social realities. Brzozowski, in turn, lamented in *Legenda Młodej Polski* (The Legend of Young Poland, 1909) that Polish Romanticism glorified action that consisted of "martyr-like and heroic self-immolation rather than construction and elevation. Hence the terrible discrepancy between the *methods* of thought and action that lead to lasting results in *the historical world* and forms of emotional thinking, binding us to national tradition."[82] For Brzozowski, the Romantics' exalted approach to reality together with their subjectivism and cult of feeling, and combined with their absolutization of the idea of beauty, demanded that his contemporaries treat Romanticism with scepticism as a source of ideological inspiration.

Brzozowski's critique of Romanticism was hardly an outlier in Europe at the time. Similar accusations were levelled at it in France (by Pierre Lasserre and Ernest Seillière), where Romanticism was blamed for the defeat of 1871, for irrationalism in social and political thought, and for pathological egotism. But at the turn of nineteenth and twentieth centuries, the Polish discussion of Romanticism included a factor that was absent in similar discussions in France or Germany. This factor was the inferiority complex of the colonized. Fascinated by the British version of Romantic thought, Brzozowski criticized Polish Romanticism for being only "a superficial means of escaping the discomforts of given local reality," whereas "British Romanticism – from Blake, through Byron to Lamb – participates in the universal world of burgeoning modernity."[83] The trauma of long-term subjugation, among its many consequences, implies a search for a "surrogate hegemon"[84] – in other words, for a foreign authority, which the colonized wish for when the actual hegemon (in this case, Russia) is perceived as undeserving of respect. In the Polish context, this meant that the interrogation of the Romantic legacy involved both revisions and the settling of accounts with the past, and interventions in the present aimed at social and political transformation. However, while this interrogation aspired to examine the cultural foundations of social existence and the possibilities of its critical self-awareness, its own foundations were not free of the mental repercussions of colonization.

Due to the role that Romanticism played in shaping Polish discourse of identity, the works of the Romantics have been especially susceptible to popular schematic readings. Hence, polemics against Romanticism have not been limited to discussions of its texts and ideas; they have also involved interpretive clichés and stereotypes and have viewed both literary heroes and their deeds – as well as writers and their lives – through their prism. A classic example of this sort of demythologizing is found in the works of the literary critic and translator Tadeusz "Boy" Żeleński, who in his essays *Ludzie żywi* (Living People, 1929) and *Brązownicy* (The Gilders, 1930) insisted on "bringing down the monument" of Mickiewicz created by literary historians in order to restore the poet's "human" dimensions.

In the second half of the twentieth century, the most renowned Polish writers, including Witold Gombrowicz (1904–69), Tadeusz Różewicz (1921–2014), and Sławomir Mrożek (1930–2013), began closely analysing the language and ideas of Romanticism, especially as they had been crystallized in Romantic drama. Indeed, Harold Segel speaks of "the antipathy of most post-World War II Polish drama to the myths and ideals bequeathed by the Romantic past," which he notes "expresses itself in ironic association … or in parody of Romantic characters and plays." The "pastiche of recognizable Romantic themes" in the works of these authors is there for humorous effect, but it also has an ideological purpose: "to demonstrate the harmfulness of inculcating school children with Romantic values through the traditional teaching of Romanticism in Polish schools," to depict the "traditional value systems and cultures as irrelevant, indeed meaningless in the light of the events of World War II," and "to portray the metamorphosis of a wartime Romantic hero into the postwar antihero who is uncertain of his own identity."[85]

The Romantic model of nation-centric patriotism was sometimes the target of communist criticism, and Romanticism itself was treated instrumentally by communist propagandists; thus, many readers responded cautiously to the kinds of parody and pastiche employed by Mrożek in the 1960s, as well Tadeusz Konwicki (1926–2015) and others, for reasons of their political and moral ambiguity. On the one hand, such works were praised for their brave polemic against national stereotypes; on the other, they were seen as attacks on national tradition that oddly harmonized with the official cultural-political line. This was particularly true of Mrożek's *Śmierć porucznika* (Death of the Lieutenant, 1963), a play that mercilessly mocks "the obsession with doomed heroism" and "the halo that surrounds Romantic stereotypes in the national value system."[86] The play became part of the discussion about the currency of the Romantic tradition that broke out around a highly debated book by Zbigniew Załuski (1926–78) titled *Siedem polskich grzechów głównych* (Seven Polish Deadly Sins, 1962). Konwicki's work, saturated with a polemic against Romanticism – especially its cult of sacrifice – simultaneously and paradoxically constituted an argument for the durability of Romantic articulations and Romantic imagery.

The subversive strategies of contemporary literature with regard to Romantic tradition proved to be ineffective, however, in demolishing the Romantic myth, even if they succeeded in distancing the public from some Romantic ideals and rhetoric. When facing decisive moments of its history, Polish society does not turn to ironic readings of the Romantic inheritance, after all. When it adopts the Romantic idiom, it does so not to parody it, but rather as a means to interpret present-day experience in a way that integrates it into the national mythology, the continuity of which – as has generally been believed – should be upheld rather than broken. This was the case in 1968, when a production of Mickiewicz's *Forefathers' Eve* under the direction of Kazimierz Dejmek at the Polish Theatre in Warsaw served as a powerful riposte to the strengthening of the communist regime and the kowtowing of Polish politicians to the Soviet Union. This was also the case under martial law (1982–3) and afterwards, when under conditions of increasing oppression and in an atmosphere of social frustration and stagnation, attitudes of Romantic provenance – non-conformism and rebellion, as well as humility and martyrdom, most poignantly personified by the protagonists of *Forefathers' Eve, Part III* – once again became models of social behaviour.

Interesting interpretations of these attitudes can be found in two feature films: Agnieszka Holland's *Zabić księdza* (To Kill a Priest, USA–France, 1989), and Rafał Wieczyński's *Popiełuszko. Wolność jest w nas* (Popiełuszko: Freedom Is within Us, Poland, 2009). These two films tell the story, each in a different way, of the most infamous political murder in the history of communist Poland – that of the Catholic priest Jerzy Popiełuszko, perpetrated in 1983 on the orders of the secret service. In Holland's film, the hero is reminiscent of Konrad in Mickiewicz's *Forefathers' Eve*: a lone warrior, mentally and physically strong but misunderstood by those around him. Wieczyński's protagonist, by contrast, is decidedly "soft" and gentle – qualities that situate him much closer to the play's humble priest Peter.

Despite the ongoing debate over Romanticism in Polish literature and culture – a debate that now spans more than 150 years – Romantic ideas and the allegories, symbols, and extensive rhetorical figures through which they are articulated have lost neither their vitality nor their resonance. This is largely because Romanticism provided Poles with another model of patriotism besides Sarmatian republicanism.[87] Like the latter, it faced the communists' criticism and both subtle and blunt manipulation. During the communist dictatorship, "the vision of Polish artistic traditions was highly restrictive, and favoured so-called progressive and realistic modes ... and they ... left limited space for Romanticism, not only for Krasiński and Norwid, but also for many of Mickiewicz's and Słowacki's works."[88] Admittedly, the regime loosened its grip over time, but not much changed in terms of its appraisal of Romantic ideology. Romanticism was criticized for its national character and religious and spiritual inclinations and it was blamed for the tragedy of the Warsaw Uprising (1944), which was interpreted as an inevitable result of the Romantic mentality as it had been passed down to the younger generations. In its propagandistic and curricular versions, Polish Romanticism was manipulated so thoroughly that it had little in common with its historical "original." Its international and revolutionary dimensions were cast as supposedly consistent with Marxist and Leninist doctrine, while aspects at odds with this ideological matrix were eliminated. Mickiewicz's and Norwid's notions of progress, democracy, work for the good of the collective, and the brotherhood of nations were taken out of context, whereas passages in which the poets pointed to the Christian roots of these ideas were omitted. Krasiński, the intractable enemy of revolution as a means of social change, was passed over in silence, as if he had never existed. All of these manoeuvres had one aim: to construct Romanticism as an era that anticipated the happy, classless, international, secular society of the Polish People's Republic. Such was the "necessary fiction" of communism – a grand narrative produced by the official discourse of authorities who had subordinated themselves to Soviet hegemony.

It is ever more apparent today that the "twilight" of the Romantic paradigm did not arrive in 1989, as Maria Janion, a renowned scholar of that era, contended in the early 1990s. According to Janion, since "the Romantic ideals lost their power of persuasion, even if it had been superficial and consisting of platitudes," the time had come to look for other values – for instance, existential ones – to take the place of the supposedly exhausted model of patriotic literature.[89] The matter turned out to be more complicated, however. On the one hand, new methodological approaches have been revealing previously unnoticed horizons of Romantic poetry and are making us aware of the importance of rereading Romanticism for the hermeneutics of Polish identity discourse. On the other hand, in this time of geopolitical pressures ("clash of civilizations") and efforts to forge European political unity, thinking in Romantic categories is in no danger of extinction.

Mickiewicz, Słowacki, Krasiński, and Norwid created a language that became the universal paradigm of communication in Polish culture– its "degree zero," in Barthes's terms. With its natural effects and specific ideational models, this language embedded in Polish society a lasting approach to grasping reality, especially where that reality intersected with (geo)political and social analysis and ethics. These writers' precise and rhetorically powerful, and thus extremely persuasive, symbolic images became canonized, and to this day those images serve as common currency in public discourse. Whenever the elites have been exposed for their opportunism and for their disconnection from the rest of society, their behaviour has been interpreted through the prism of the "Warsaw salon" and the Senator's ball scenes from *Forefathers' Eve, Part III*, in which Mickiewicz showed how the colonized had been polarized into two camps: sensitive patriots, or indifferent *compradores*. And whenever a warning against the detrimental effects of uncritical acceptance of foreign ways was required, Słowacki's words from "Grób Agamemnona" (Agamemnon's Tomb) would be invoked:

> Poland! You are still deceived with baubles;
> You were the nations' peacock and parrot,
> Now you are a handmaid of other peoples.[90]

The Romantics's rhetoric was not only the "degree zero" of social communication but also, it seems, an object of ideological manipulation. Such is the fate that befell Norwid's famous dictum, from which the communists sourced only a fragment for their slogan during the martial law period: "Ojczyzna jest to *wielki-zbiorowy-Obowiązek*" (Homeland is a *great-collective-Responsibility*). They passed over in silence the fact that, further down in the text, Norwid added that this responsibility "separates into, or rather consists of, in the nature of things, two: the responsibility of the Homeland towards the human being, and responsibility of the human being towards the Homeland."[91] In communist Poland, texts by Norwid and others that could be endorsed as progressive, revolutionary, and thus "proto-communistic" were privileged. Such deliberate appropriations of Romanticism by the hegemonic communist discourse spoke to the unceasing authority of the Romantic poets in Poland, even in the second half of the twentieth century. Mickiewicz was by far the most popular poet and was granted the highest respect, not only on account of the fundamental significance of his works for Polish identity discourse, but also because he exemplified the synthesis of "word" and "action" (in exile, he had been an active political organizer). Thus he functions in Polish history as a national "warrior-priest." For that reason, his position became only more problematic, for it earned him the status of an absolute, unquestionable authority: "He was (and still is) construed as the national patriarch, as the patron saint of Polish cultural legitimacy, even superiority, indeed as Poland itself."[92]

Since the 1980s, Norwid has played a different role in social consciousness than Mickiewicz. Referring to Norwid as the "fourth bard" in an 1987 address to artists, John Paul II re-evaluated the Romantic legacy in light of the ongoing political challenge posed by Polish society's mental and cultural losses incurred with the decay of the communist system.[93] Indeed, during both the highs of "Solidarity" and the lows of martial law, Norwid's work proved essential as a means to interpret the Polish experience and as a source of wise reflections and warnings for the future. Many anthologies of his poems and aphorisms published at the time instantly disappeared from bookstores to enter the space of social communication. Norwid's oeuvre was recognized as an especially pertinent intellectual project and a profound ethical reflection free of trivialities and easy solutions. Norwid's personalism – that is, his conviction that every human being possesses indefatigable subjecthood and dignity, which forbids the instrumental treatment of a person – had particular significance for readers at the end of the twentieth century, in the context of the communist experience. In the waning years of communism, his work, although difficult and demanding, provided – with the help of its Christian elements – a fertile ground for the replanting of Polish culture. During the years of post-communist transformation, even outside Catholic circles, it was *his* oeuvre that had the greatest impact on discussions of the ethos of the Polish intelligentsia.[94]

The Polish intelligentsia still communicate in the language of Romanticism, mainly through the language of its four greatest poets. Not only artists but also politicians, journalists, and "average citizens" reach for the Romantic dictionary when seeking words to express the most important current collective experiences. Such was the case during the "Solidarity" strikes of 1980, when "through its mythical contents the Romantic Messianic poetry could evoke in the shipyard workers the feeling that they fulfilled a mission begun by their ancestors. It could also give them hope in victory by implanting the belief that God has a special plan for Poland and that suffering in the struggle for a just cause must be rewarded."[95] This was again the case during the bleak years under martial law, declared on 13 December 1981, when the churches – the only independent spaces at the time – were filled with Catholic as well as Romantic and Messianic symbols, such as crosses, gallows, funeral sashes, coffins, and empty tombs.

And it was also the case after the crash of the presidential plane near Smolensk on 10 April 2010, which the nationalist press referred to as, among other things, "treason," a "crime," and another "partition of Poland." In so doing, they gestured towards the question posed by Mickiewicz in the poem "Pomnik Piotra Wielkiego" (Monument of Peter the Great), included in *Forefathers' Eve, Part III*: "What will happen to the waterfall of tyranny?"[96] This question invited other questions that were aligned with the Romantic proclivity to seek the ethical and transcendental sense of political events: "Why did Poland's president perish? And dozens of people along with him, the elite of our country? Why did we have to live through something like Katyn again? Why has Poland once again, at the threshold of the third millennium of Christianity, become the object of such unthinkable aggression?"[97]

Such rhetoric, borrowed from Romanticism, operates at high registers and is characterized by a high degree of emotionality. It often makes it difficult for those who employ it to transition to a sober evaluation of reality and to create a long-term program of action. It also conceals their anger, frustration, and sense of powerlessness in the face of "historical fatalism" or "the will of providence," for it is in terms of such categories that Poles interpret their experience of national community. At the same time, under conditions of oppression, by evoking the Romantic era of sacrifice, rebellion, and moral victory in the face of defeat, this rhetoric provides those who utilize it with a sense of a continuum of national existence.

The logic of Romantic historiosophy is rarely heard in the speeches of national dignitaries, especially those of a liberal and leftist orientation. It can be detected in other corners of public discourse, however. It is given voice in young people's literature – for example, in the poetry of Wojciech Wencel (collection *De profundis*, 2010), who uses it as a metaphor for recent Polish history, or in the work of Przemysław Dakowicz, for whom the Romantic understanding of the historical role of national community constitutes an ethical imperative for contemporary poetry (as in the volume *Teoria wiersza polskiego* [Theory of the Polish Poem, 2013], and in the essays in *Obcowanie. Manifesty i eseje* [Interaction: Manifestos and Essays, 2014).

Romanticism also resonates in pop culture. A Romantic attitude characterizes the heroes of Andrzej Wajda's films,[98] starting with *Popiół i diament* (Ashes and Diamonds, 1958) and *Katyń* (2007). The Romantic ethos has also inspired some young directors who are fascinated by the Warsaw Uprising, such as Irek Dobrowolski (*Sierpniowe niebo. 63 dni chwały* [August Sky: 63 Days of Glory, 2013]) and Jan Komasa (*Miasto 44* [City 44, 2014]). Kordian Piwowarski has recovered the biographies of young Home Army soldiers in his film *Baczyński* (2013), which presents the figure of the young poet Krzysztof Kamil Baczyński (1921–44) – referred to as the second Słowacki because of his talent and sources of inspiration – who perished as a soldier during the Warsaw Uprising. Romantic ideals come to the fore in the songs of "Panny Wyklęte" ("Doomed Girls"), which make contemporary the model of behaviour of young people from Poland's underground resistance during and after the Second World War.

"Cursed soldiers," or "doomed soldiers" ("Żołnierze wyklęci") is a term borrowed from the official discourse of communist propaganda to identify soldiers from underground resistance movements, numbering from 120,000 to 180,000, who refused to give up their arms after the end of the Second World War and carried on a partisan war against the communist regime's security forces. Many of them were murdered during round-ups, or they were captured, tortured, executed, and buried in unknown graves. Their existence was to be permanently erased from collective memory, and even in the post-communist Poland, some leftists have described them as as criminals. Not until 2001 was a national holiday declared – Narodowy Dzień Żołnierzy Wyklętych (National Day of Remembrance of the Doomed Soldiers) – thus restoring their lost dignity. "Doomed Girls" is a project of the Polish music scene, realized by the Foundation of Independence and inspired by the history of the "doomed soldiers." Part of that project involves seeking an idiom attractive to younger generations that will allow them to express patriotic themes in a contemporary way. That idiom often contains references to the language of Romanticism and to the values it communicates, such as the imperative to defend one's homeland, belief in the final victory of the just cause however hopeless the fight or solitary the fighter, and, finally, faith in divine protection. All of these have their sources in the Romantic imagination.

For much of Polish society – especially for those who identify with patriotic, national, and Catholic traditions – Romanticism remains an accepted code of communication. In extreme cases this code is appropriated – mainly by those circles that cast themselves as national or Catholic – or it is harshly criticized by leftist intellectuals or (interestingly) by those whose ideological sympathies suggest they are potential allies of proponents of Romanticism's "long duration." Finally, the legacy of Romanticism is evoked by patriotic circles of the secular right, who by definition are distanced from the Catholic tradition. Clearly, current debates about Romanticism do not completely overlap with the main political divisions in Polish public debate.

Hence, not only affirmation but also various shades of negation, from sharp criticism and total rejection through mockery to selective distancing from some elements of Romanticism, have ensured that Romantic ideas and symbols continue to circulate in Polish culture, polarizing public debate in the process. Romanticism remains a central discourse that Poles spontaneously reach for when diagnosing their situation, defining their threats and goals, and building their identity accordingly. The transformational approach to the Romantic legacy ensures its position as "a living paradigm," productive for contemporary culture, as distinct from Romanticism understood as a "total paradigm" (one that makes compulsory the full duplication of Romantic ideas), or as "archival paradigm" (wherein Romanticism amounts to a museum exhibit).[99] Not just culture is at stake here, however. Currently, Polish identity – which many view as being at a crossroads – is also defined in the context of Romanticism:

> Poles may be the last nation in Europe to maintain its age-old republican and theologically-political character. It would seem that it has to get rid of it now. We can still reasonably doubt, however, whether the only alternative is the simple liberalism of an endlessly open, global society of insatiable consumers, although this conclusion was unfortunately reached in Central and Eastern Europe after the fall of communism. It is this conclusion, and not only the obvious need of modernization, that is behind the desire to reject the legacy of Romanticism.[100]

As we can see, even today in post-communist Poland, attitudes towards the Romantic legacy remain pertinent to the public debate; they define and serve as measures of actual political positions. This will likely change in the near future. As the contemporary historian and literary critic Jan Prokop puts it, "after all, we have played with the same deck of cards for two hundred years!"[101]

Paradoxically, the Romantic dream that Poland's liberation would lead other subjugated nations of Europe to freedom came true in 1989 with the "revolutions" that erupted in Eastern Europe. This is a kind of posthumous victory for Romanticism. Yet there is something ironic in that victory, since the fall of communism is symbolized today by the fall of the Berlin Wall rather than Polish "Solidarity" on the global stage. Poles do not appreciate their own role in this victory either, for they, as Boris Buden puts it, have too easily believed in their immaturity and in their need to "learn from" the West. Both these notions were impressed on them by the hegemonic discourse of the Western world, and as a consequence they quickly forgot that by overthrowing the communist regime, they had proved something opposite: their maturity and responsibility.[102]

Dariusz Skórczewski
The John Paul II Catholic University of Lublin
Translated by Agnieszka Polakowska

NOTES

1 Davies, *God's Playground* [1982], 9.
2 Smith, *The Ethnic Origins of Nations*, 93.
3 "In Poland and Ireland, the priesthood has become almost the guardian of a political community and identity in the face of both internal challenges and external pressures." Ibid., 159.
4 Filipowicz, "Mickiewicz: 'East' and 'West,'" 607.
5 See Assmann, *Politische Theologie zwischen Ägypten und Israel*, 114.
6 The term comes from Walicki, *Philosophy and Romantic Nationalism*, 83.
7 Zajewski, "Europe and the Polish Issue in the 19th Century," 115.
8 Hoffmeister, *Deutsche und europäische Romantik*, 210.
9 Zamoyski, *The Polish Way*, 295.
10 Janion and Żmigrodzka, *Romantyzm i historia*, 155, 156.
11 Mickiewicz, "Księgi narodu polskiego," 16–17. See also Weintraub, "Three Myths of America," 280–95.

12 Created in 1579 by King Stefan Batory, Vilnius University was closed in 1832 by Tsar Nicholas I as part of the repressions after the November Uprising.
13 Stefanowska, *Próba zdrowego rozumu*, 176.
14 Mickiewicz, "Do Józefa Jeżowskiego," 144.
15 See Nandy, *The Intimate Enemy*, 1983.
16 Sawicki, "Ethos polskiej literatury," 19–31.
17 On this subject, see Krysowski, "'Zamęt, skąd światło wybłysło," 11–36.
18 See Kępiński, *Mickiewicz hermetyczny*; Cieśla-Korytowska, *Romantyczna poezja mistyczna*, 1989.
19 This is the subject of the unfortunately ideologically biased book by Maria Janion, *Niesamowita Słowiańszczyzna*, 2006. The author presents Polish Romanticism as a period of eruptions of anti-Catholic attitudes and interprets the Christianization of Polish lands during the Middle Ages in terms of colonial conquest. For a polemic about the book, see Skórczewski, "'Słowiańskie' kłopoty z tożsamością," 407–25.
20 Bronisław Baczko as quoted in Walicki, *Philosophy and Romantic Nationalism*, 89.
21 See Saganiak, *Człowiek i doświadczenie wewnętrzne*, 292–344.
22 Jedlicki, *Jakiej cywilizacji Polacy potrzebują*, 63.
23 Nandy, *The Intimate Enemy*, xi.
24 Buddensieg, "Goethe und Polen," 1–30. See also Henryk Serejski, *Europa a rozbiory Polski*, 223.
25 See Hegel, *Vorlesungen*, 499–500. Theodor Adorno was uncritically repeating Hegel's theories even in the 1950s, which indicates the longevity of the epistemological politics of paternalistic exclusion, reflected in the Western European (and more specifically German) humanistic discourse towards non-Germanic Central and Eastern Europe. See Gall, "Słowacki postkolonialny," 155.
26 Nicoll and Wilmurt, *World Drama*, 368.
27 Kowalczykowa, *Słowacki*, 173.
28 Situations where fascination with Poland translated into an interest in its Romantic literature were rare in Europe during the nineteenth and twentieth centuries. German empathy brought on a wave of compassion for the victims of Russian repression during the November Uprising (1830–31). This bore fruit in the form of *Polenlieder* – lyrics dedicated by German poets to Poles, the Romantic rebels. Much more recent books such as Lednicki, ed., *Adam Mickiewicz in World Literature*, and Roman Koropeckyj, *Adam Mickiewicz* (2008), are exceptions that confirm the rule.
29 Grabowski, "Polish Theater," 214–20.
30 Sobczak, "Próba polsko-rosyjskiego pojednania," 158.
31 Zamoyski, *The Polish Way*, 293.
32 Ibid., 293.
33 Ostrowski, [untitled], 374.
34 Nowak, *Ofiary*, 24.
35 Nowak, *Od Imperium do Imperium*, 123.
36 Zamoyski, *The Polish Way*, 297.
37 Jedlicki, "Narodowość a cywilizacja," 22.
38 The popularity of Henryk Sienkiewicz's novels in the United States at the turn of the nineteenth and twentieth centuries was the exception, but he did not belong to the Romantic tradition.
39 Zgorzelski, *Romantyzm w Polsce*, 30.

40 For example, the *Oxford Companion to English Literature*, edited by Paul Harvey ([1932] 1958), contains an article on Pushkin (645) but no mention of Mickiewicz. The case is similar in Maunder's *Encyclopedia of Literary Romanticism* (2010), where no Polish writer is listed.
41 Davies, *God's Playground*, vol. 1, 401.
42 Mochnacki, "Niektóre uwagi nad poezją romantyczną," 65.
43 Zamoyski, *The Polish Way*, 295.
44 Bachórz, *Jak pachnie na Litwie Mickiewicza*, 206.
45 Jedlicki, *Jakiej cywilizacji Polacy potrzebują*, 52–3.
46 Mochnacki, "O literaturze polskiej," 234.
47 Pieróg, *Maurycy Mochnacki*, 156.
48 Norwid, "Promethidion," 134.
49 A telling example is the inclusion in 1981 of a citation from Czesław Miłosz's poem "Który skrzywdziłeś" (You Who Wronged) on a monument in Gdańsk dedicated by shipyard workers to the victims of the communist regime in 1970. This gesture once again weaves poetry into the life of Poles, providing them with an idiom to grasp their historical experience; it also manifests the symbolic elevation of the poet – the 1980 Noble Prize laureate – by the workers to the position of contemporary "prophet," as modelled on the Romantic bard.
50 In contrast to, for example, the ethnosymbolic conceptualization of Anthony Smith. See Łuczewski, *Odwieczny naród*, 64ff.
51 Norwid, "Do J.B. Zaleskiego," 144.
52 Żmigrodzka, "Antynomie mistycznego mesjanizmu Słowackiego," 154.
53 Davies, *God's Playground*, vol. 1 [2005], 401.
54 Dmowski, *Niemcy, Rosja i kwestia polska*, 212.
55 Krasnodębski, "Adam Mickiewicz' politische Theologie," 40–56.
56 See Talmon, *Politischer Messianismus*, 466–7.
57 Mickiewicz's Messianism and its precepts were subjects of polemic for, among others, Norwid. See Walicki, "Cyprian Norwid," 447–91.
58 Norwid, "Do Augusta Cieszkowskiego," 275.
59 Słowacki, "Do Emigracji o potrzebie idei," 315.
60 See Magdziak-Miszewska et al., eds., *Polacy i Rosjanie*, 6.
61 Bocheński, "Rusyfikacja Polski współczesnej," 27.
62 Mickiewicz, *Digression*, 362.
63 Duk, "Mickiewicz, Krasiński and Russia," 41.
64 See Trojanowiczowa, *Sybir romantyków*; Dworak, *Obrazy Rosjan*.
65 Krasiński, "Memoriał do Piusa IX," 514–15.
66 Nowak, *Ofiary*, 40.
67 Said, *Orientalism*, 328.
68 Norwid, "Co to jest ojczyzna," 50.
69 Fiećko, *Krasiński przeciw Mickiewiczowi*, 33.
70 Ibid., 31.
71 Waśko, *Zygmunt Krasiński*, 162, 163.
72 Krasiński, *Undivine Comedy*, 1924.
73 Thompson, "On Zygmunt Krasiński's *Undivine Comedy*," 495.
74 Ibid., 498.
75 Miłosz, *The History of Polish Literature*, 229.
76 Zgorzelski, "Elegijna poezja Mickiewicza," 190.

77 On the need for *metanoia* in one of the cycle's poems, see Sawicki, "'Wiersz-płacz'?," 159.
78 Miłosz, *The History of Polish Literature*, 230.
79 Sawicki, "Norwid's Struggle with Form," 43.
80 Czerniawski, *Cyprian Kamil Norwid*, 101, 103. All further citations of Norwid's thoughts come from this source.
81 Segel, "Polish Romantic Drama in Perspective," 268.
82 Brzozowski, *Eseje i studia o literaturze*, 1042.
83 Bielik-Robson, "Syndrom romantyczny," 56, 57.
84 Ewa Thompson's term. See "Whose Discourse? Telling the Story in Post-Communist Poland."
85 Segel, "Polish Romantic Drama in Perspective," 270.
86 Stephan, *Mrożek*, 127.
87 See Walicki, *The Three Traditions in Polish Patriotism*, 1988.
88 Głowiński, "Październik 1956," 42.
89 Janion, "Zmierzch paradygmatu," 14, 22.
90 Translated by Michael Mikoś in *Polish Romantic Literature*, 84.
91 Norwid, "Memoriał o Młodej Emigracji," 109, 113.
92 Filipowicz, "Mickiewicz: 'East' and 'West,'" 608.
93 John Paul II, "Do środowisk twórczych," 91.
94 See special issue of *Ethos* on Norwid – *Ethos* 20 (1992).
95 Törnquist Plewa, *The Wheel of Polish Fortune*, 71.
96 In Miłosz's translation – Miłosz, *The History of Polish Literature*, 224.
97 Polak-Pałkiewicz, "'I cóż się stanie z kaskadą tyraństwa?"
98 See Wnuk, "Wajda romantyczny," 291–8; Nurczyńska-Fidelska, "Historia i romantyzm," 10.
99 These are the terms used by Jarosław Ławski in an important article, "Symplifikat," 325–84. For more on Romantic continuations in contemporary Polish literature, see Bagłajewski, *Obecność romantyzmu.*
100 Krasnodębski, "Teologia polityczna Adama Mickiewicza," 242.
101 Prokop, *Universum polskie. Literatura, wyobraźnia zbiorowa, mity polityczne,* 16.
102 Buden, *Zone des Übergangs.*

WORKS CITED

Assmann, Jan. *Politische Theologie zwischen Ägypten und Israel.* München: Carl Friedrich von Siemens Stiftung, 1992.

Bachórz, Józef, *Jak pachnie na Litwie Mickiewicza i inne studia o romantyzmie.* Gdańsk: słowo/obraz terytoria, 2003.

Bagłajewski, Arkadiusz. *Obecność romantyzmu.* Lublin: UMCS, 2015.

Bielik-Robson, Agata. "Syndrom romantyczny. Stanisław Brzozowski i rewizja romantyzmu." *Słupskie Prace Filologiczne*, 2007.

Bocheński, Adolf. "Rusyfikacja Polski współczesnej." *Problemy*, 15 December 1934; repr. in *Teologia Polityczna Co Miesiąc* 10 (2014): 26–33.

Brzozowski, Stanisław. *Eseje i studia o literaturze.* Selected and edited by Henryk Markiewicz. Wrocław: Ossolineum, 1990.

Buddensieg, Herman. "Goethe und Polen." In *Mickiewicz-Blätter*, 13 (1968): 1–30.

Buden, Boris. *Zone des Übergangs. Vom Ende des Postkommunismus.* Frankfurt am Main: Suhrkamp, 2009.

Cieśla-Korytowska, Maria. *Romantyczna poezja mistyczna. Ballanche, Novalis, Słowacki.* Kraków: Znak, 1989.

Czerniawski, Adam. *Cyprian Kamil Norwid. Poezje/Poems*. Kraków: Wydawnictwo Literackie, 1986.

Davies, Norman. *God's Playground: A History of Poland*, vol. 2. Oxford: Clarendon Press, 1982.

– *God's Playground: A History of Poland in Two Volumes*. Oxford: Oxford University Press, 2005.

Dmowski, Roman. *Niemcy, Rosja i kwestia polska*. Lwów: Towarzystwo Wydawnicze H. Altenberg, 1908.

Duk, Anne-Marie. "Mickiewicz, Krasiński and Russia." In *Muza Domowa: A Celebration of Donald Pirie's Contribution to Polish Studies*. Edited by Rosemary Hunt and Ursula Phillips. 37–48. Nottingham: Astra Press, 1995.

Dworak, Anna Marta. *Obrazy Rosjan w pamiętnikach z lat 1825–1835*. Lublin: Wydawnictwo KUL, 2014.

Fiećko, Jerzy. *Krasiński przeciw Mickiewiczowi. Najważniejszy spór romantyków*. Poznań: Wydawnictwo Poznańskie, 2011.

Filipowicz, Halina. "Mickiewicz: 'East' and 'West.'" *Slavic and East European Journal* 45, no. 4 (2001): 606–23.

Gall, Alfred. "Słowacki postkolonialny. Próba usytuowania tekstów genezyjskich. *Król-Duch, Ksiądz Marek, Sen srebrny Salomei, Samuel Zborowski* w perspektywie postkolonialnej." In *Słowacki postkolonialny.* Edited by Michał Kuziak. 145–83. Bydgoszcz: Teatr Polski, 2012.

Głowiński, Michał. "Październik 1956. Wielkie otwieranie." In *Realia, dyskursy, portrety. Studia i szkice*. 39–50. Kraków: Universitas, 2011.

Grabowski, Artur. "Polish Theater." In *Western Drama through the Ages: A Student Reference Guide*. Edited by Kimball King. 209–38. Westport: Greenwood, 2007.

Harvey, Paul, ed. *Oxford Companion to English Literature* [1932]. Oxford: Clarendon Press, 1958.

Hegel, Georg Wilhelm Friedrich. *Vorlesungen über die Philosophie der Geschichte*. In *Werke im 20 Bänden*, vol. 12. Frankfurt am Main: Suhrkamp, 1970.

Hoffmeister, Gerhart. *Deutsche und europäische Romantik.* Stuttgart: Metzler, 1990.

Janion, Maria. "Zmierzch paradygmatu." In *Czy będziesz wiedział, co przeżyłeś*. 5–23. Warszawa: Sic!, 1996.

– *Niesamowita Słowiańszczyzna. Fantazmaty literatury*. Kraków: Wydawnictwo Literackie, 2006.

Janion, Maria, and Maria Żmigrodzka. *Romantyzm i historia.* Gdańsk: słowo/obraz terytoria, 2001.

Jedlicki, Jerzy, *Jakiej cywilizacji Polacy potrzebują. Studia z dziejów idei i wyobraźni XIX wieku.* Warszawa: PWN, 1988.

– "Narodowość a cywilizacja." In *Uniwersalizm i swoistość kultury polskiej*, vol 2. Edited by Jerzy Kłoczowski. Lublin: RW KUL, 1990.

John Paul II. "Do środowisk twórczych." *Więź* 10–12 (1987): 89–93.

Kępiński, Zdzisław. *Mickiewicz hermetyczny*. Warszawa: PIW, 1980.

Koropeckyj, Roman. *Adam Mickiewicz: The Life of a Romantic.* Ithaca: Cornell University Press, 2008.

Kowalczykowa, Alina. *Słowacki*. Warszawa: PWN, 1994.

Krasiński, Zygmunt. "Do Moskali." In *Pisma*, vol. 3: *Drobne utwory poetyczne (1833–1859).* Edited by Tadeusz Pini. 75. Lwów: B. Połoniecki, 1904.

– "Memoriał do Piusa IX" [1 January 1848]. In *Pisma Zygmunta Krasińskiego*, vol. 7. Edited by Jan Czubek. Kraków: Gebethner i Wolff, 1912.

– *Undivine Comedy*. Translated by H.E. Kennedy and Z. Umińska. London: 1924.

Krasnodębski, Zdzisław. "Adam Mickiewicz' politische Theologie." In *Sendung und Dichtung. Adam Mickiewicz in Europa*. Edited by Zdzisław Krasnodębski and Stanisław Garsztecki. Hamburg: Reinhold Krämer Verlag, 2002.

– "Teologia polityczna Adama Mickiewicza." Translated by Marta Bucholc. *Teologia Polityczna* 4 (2006–7). 230-42.

Krysowski, Olaf. "'Zamęt, skąd światło wybłysło.' Gnostycki mit początku w twórczości Zygmunta Krasińskiego." In *Zygmunt Krasiński w świetle i cieniu myśli romantycznej*. Edited by Mirosław Strzyżewski. 11–36. Toruń: Wyd. Naukowe UMK, 2014.

Ławski, Jarosław. "Symplifikat. Kartka z dziejów Mickiewiczowskiego mesjanizmu." In *Romantyzm i nowoczesność*. Edited by Michał Kuziak. 325–83. Kraków: Universitas, 2009.

Lednicki, Wacław, ed. *Adam Mickiewicz in World Literature: A Symposium*. Berkeley: University of California Press, 1956.

Łuczewski, Michał. *Odwieczny naród. Polak i katolik w Żmiącej*. Toruń: UMK, 2012.

Magdziak-Miszewska, Agnieszka, et al., eds. *Polacy i Rosjanie. 100 kluczowych pojęć*. Warszawa: Biblioteka "Więzi," 2002.

Maunder, Andrew. *Encyclopedia of Literary Romanticism*. New York: Facts on File, 2010.

Mickiewicz, Adam. *Digression*. Translated by Marjorie Beatrice Peacock. In *The Poems of Adam Mickiewicz*. Edited by George Rapall Noyes. 337–68. New York: PIASA, 1944.

– [Uciec z duszą na listek …]. In *Dzieła*, vol. 1: *Wiersze*. Edited by Czesław Zgorzelski. 414. Warszawa: Czytelnik, 1993.

– "Do Józefa Jeżowskiego [30 September–12 October 1820]." In *Dzieła*, vol. 14: *Listy. Część pierwsza 1815– 1829*. Edited by Maria Dernałowicz et al. 143–5. Warszawa: Czytelnik, 1998.

– "Księgi narodu polskiego i pielgrzymstwa polskiego." In *Dzieła*, vol. 5: *Proza artystyczna i pisma krytyczne*. Edited by Zygmunt Dokurno et al. 9–62. Warszawa: Czytelnik, 1996.

Miłosz, Czesław. *The History of Polish Literature*. Berkeley: University of California Press, 1983.

Mochnacki, Maurycy "O literaturze polskiej w wieku dziewiętnastym." In *Rozprawy Literackie*. Edited by Mirosław Strzyżewski. 191–381. Wrocław: Ossolineum, 2004.

– "Niektóre uwagi nad poezją romantyczną z powodu rozprawy Jana Śniadeckiego *O pismach klasycznych i romantycznych*." In *Rozprawy literackie*. Edited by Mirosław Strzyżewski. 60–101. Wrocław: Ossolineum, 2004.

Nandy, Ashis. *The Intimate Enemy: Loss and Recovery of Self under Colonialism*. Delhi: Oxford University Press, 1983.

Nicoll, Allardyce, and Arthur Wilmurt. *World Drama: From Aeschylus to Anouilh*. Paris: Harrap, 1976.

Norwid, Cyprian. "Do wroga." In *Pisma wszystkie*, vol. 1: *Wiersze 1*. Edited by Juliusz Wiktor Gomulicki. 373–4. Warszawa: PIW, 1971.

– "Memoriał o Młodej Emigracji." In *Pisma wszystkie*, vol. 7: *Proza 1*. Edited by Juliusz Wiktor Gomulicki. 107–14. Warszawa: PIW, 1973.

– "Co to jest ojczyzna" [inc. "Żeby zapytał kto Jana III-go …"] In *Pisma wszystkie*, vol. 7: *Proza 1*. Edited by Juliusz Wiktor Gomulicki. 50. Warszawa: PIW, 1973.

– "Do J.B. Zaleskiego." In *Dzieła wszystkie*, vol. 10: *Listy 1: 1839–1854*. Edited by Jadwiga Rudnicka. 143–6. Lublin: TN KUL, 2008.

– "Do Augusta Cieszkowskiego." In *Dzieła wszystkie*, vol. 10: *Listy 1: 1839–1854*. Edited by Jadwiga Rudnicka. 275–80. Lublin: TN KUL, 2008.

– "Promethidion." In *Dzieła wszystkie*, vol. 4: *Poematy 2*. Edited by Stefan Sawicki and Piotr Chlebowski. 93–140. Lublin: TN KUL, 2011.
Nowak, Andrzej. *Od Imperium do Imperium. Spojrzenia na historię Europy Wschodniej*. Kraków: Arcana, 2004.
– *Ofiary, imperia i historycy. Studia przypadków (od XVIII do XXI wieku)*. Kraków: Arcana, 2009.
Nurczyńska-Fidelska, Ewelina."Historia i romantyzm. Szkic o twórczości Andrzeja Wajdy." In *Kino polskie w trzynastu sekwencjach*. Edited by Ewelina Nurczyńska-Fidelska. 9-20. Kraków: Rabid, 2005.
Ostrowski, Józefat Bolesław. [untitled]. *Kurier Polski*. 1830. 28 Dec. 1830.
Pieróg, Stanisław. *Maurycy Mochnacki. Studium romantycznej świadomości*. Warszawa: PIW, 1982.
Polak-Pałkiewicz, Ewa. "'I cóż się stanie z kaskadą tyraństwa?" http://ewapolak-palkiewicz.pl/i-coz-sie-stanie-z-kaskada-tyranstwa.
Prokop, Jan. *Universum polskie. Literatura, wyobraźnia zbiorowa, mity polityczne*. Kraków: Universitas, 1993.
Saganiak, Magdalena. *Człowiek i doświadczenie wewnętrzne. Późna twórczość Mickiewicza i Słowackiego*. Warszawa: Wydawnictwo UKSW, 2009.
Said, Edward W. *Orientalism*. New York: Vintage, 1994.
Sawicki, Stefan. "Ethos polskiej literatury." In *Wartość – sacrum – Norwid. Studia i szkice aksjologicznoliterackie*. 19–31. Lublin: RW KUL, 1994.
– "Norwid's Struggle with Form." In *From Norwid to Kantor: Essays on Polish Modernism Dedicated to Professor G.M. Hyde*. Edited by Grażyna Bystydzieńska and Emma Harris. 37–49. Warszawa: Wydawnictwa Uniwersytetu Warszawskiego, 1999.
– "'Wiersz-płacz?'" In *Wartość – sacrum – Norwid. Studia i szkice aksjologicznoliterackie*. 149–62. Lublin: RW KUL, 1994.
Segel, Harold B., "Polish Romantic Drama in Perspective." In *Romantic Drama*. Edited by Gerald Gillespie. 259–72. Amsterdam: Jan Benjamins, 1993.
Serejski, Henryk. *Europa a rozbiory Polski. Studium historiograficzne*. Warszawa: Wydawnictwo Naukowe PWN, 2009.
Skórczewski, Dariusz. "'Słowiańskie' kłopoty z tożsamością. Na marginesie *Niesamowitej Słowiańszczyzny*." In *Teoria – literatura – dyskurs. Pejzaż postkolonialny*. 407–25. Lublin: KUL, 2013.
Słowacki, Juliusz. *Dzieła wszystkie*. 17 vols. Edited by Juliusz Kleiner. Wrocław: Ossolineum, 1952–75.
– "Do Emigracji o potrzebie idei." In *Dzieła wszystkie,* vol. 7. Edited by Juliusz Kleiner. Wrocław: Ossolineum, 1956.
– "Hymn (Bogarodzico! Dziewico!)" In *Dzieła wybrane*, vol. 1: *Liryki i powieści poetyckie*. Edited by Julian Krzyżanowski. 7. Wrocław: Ossolineum, 1989.
– "Grób Agamemnona." Translated by Michael Mikoś. In *Polish Romantic Literature: An Anthology*. Edited by Michael Mikoś. Bloomington: Slavica, 2003.
Smith, Anthony D. *The Ethnic Origins of Nations*. Malden: Blackwell, 1988.
Sobczak, Jan. "Próba polsko-rosyjskiego pojednania u schyłku XIX stulecia." In *Między irredentą a kolaboracją. Postawy społeczeństwa polskiego wobec zaborców*. Edited by Sławomir Kalembka and Norbert Kasparek. 150–66. Olsztyn: UWM, 1999.
Stephan, Halina. *Mrożek*. Kraków: Wydawnictwo Literackie, 1996.
Stefanowska, Zofia. *Próba zdrowego rozumu. Studia o Mickiewiczu*. Warszawa: PIW, 1976.

Talmon, Jakob. *Politischer Messianismus. Die romantische Phase*. Köln: Opladen, 1963.

Thompson, Ewa M. "On Zygmunt Krasiński's *Undivine Comedy*." *Chesterton Review* 27, no. 4 (2001): 495–501.

– "Whose Discourse? Telling the Story in Post-Communist Poland." *The Other Shore* 1, no. 1 (2010): 1–15.

Törnquist Plewa, Barbara. *The Wheel of Polish Fortune: Myths in Polish Collective Consciousness during the First Years of Solidarity*. Lund: Lund University, 1992.

Trojanowiczowa, Zofia. *Sybir romantyków*. Poznań: W Drodze, 1993.

Walicki, Andrzej, "Cyprian Norwid. Trzy wątki myśli." In *Prace wybrane*, vol. 2: *Filozofia polskiego romantyzmu*. 447–91. Kraków: Universitas, 2009.

– *Philosophy and Romantic Nationalism: The Case of Poland*. Notre Dame: University of Notre Dame Press, 1994.

– *The Three Traditions in Polish Patriotism and Their Contemporary Rrelevance*. Bloomington: Polish Studies Center, 1988.

Waśko, Andrzej. *Zygmunt Krasiński. Oblicza poety*. Kraków: Arcana, 2001.

Weintraub, Wiktor. "Three Myths of America in Polish Romantic Literature." In *Studies in Polish Civilization*. Edited by Damian S. Wandycz. 280–95. New York: Columbia University Press and PIASA, 1971.

Wnuk, Agnieszka. "Wajda romantyczny. Kreacja bohatera w twórczości filmowej Andrzeja Wajdy." In *Kody kultury. Interakcja – transformacja – synergia*. Edited by Halina Kubicka and Olga Taranek. 291–9. Wrocław: Sutoris, 2009.

Zajewski, Władysław. "Europe and the Polish Issue in the 19th Century." In *Nation – Church – Culture: Essays on Polish History*, vol. 2. Edited by Adam Chruszczewski et al. 109–33. Lublin: RW KUL, 1990.

Zamoyski, Adam. *The Polish Way: A Thousand-Year History of Poles and Their Culture*. New York: Hippocrene Books, 2004.

Zgorzelski, Czesław. "Elegijna poezja Mickiewicza." In *Zarysy i szkice literackie*. 153–73. Warszawa: PIW, 1988.

– *Romantyzm w Polsce*. Lublin: TN KUL, 1957.

Żmigrodzka, Maria. "Antynomie mistycznego mesjanizmu Słowackiego." In *Przez wieki idąca powieść. Wybór pism o literaturze XIX i XX wieku*. 254–64. Warszawa: IBL, 2002.

A Concise Companion to Polish Modernism

1. The Meaning of the Term

All eras and artistic currents known in Western literary studies have their analogies in Polish scholarship. Yet despite the identical names of, for example, the Enlightenment, Romanticism, Realism, Classicism, and the avant-garde, the scope and significance of the phenomena indicated by them are different even today in Western and Eastern European literary studies. This is particularly true for the term "modernism." From the time it first appeared in Poland towards the end of the nineteenth century until the beginning of the twenty-first century, modernism was a collective name for various new directions in art at the turn of the nineteenth and twentieth centuries, such as Decadence, Parnassism, Expressionism, and especially Symbolism. The year 1918 is seen as the end of modernism as thus understood; in Poland, it also marked two beginnings: the post–First World War resurrection of the Polish state (which had ceased to exist in 1795), and the beginning of the avant-garde in art – the most important artistic current in Polish twentieth-century culture. A new, contemporary meaning of modernism started to become popular only at the beginning of the twentieth-first century in connection with the need to compare Polish (Central European) and Western literary phenomena. In its broad understanding, used ever more frequently but not yet stabilized in Poland, "modernism" refers to literary and artistic ideas that define the nature of "modernity," meaning contemporaneity and the present. Putting it differently, literary modernism is a collection of answers to the problems of modernity, as provided by artists in literature (and art) since the end of the nineteenth century.

Modernity emerged in the nineteenth century due to civilizational developments such as the capitalist system, the Industrial Revolution, the pursuit of economic progress, the shaping of parliamentary democracy and of free market principles, and the scientific revolution in mathematics, physics, chemistry, and social studies, among them ethnology, linguistics, and psychology. These nineteenth-century revolutions also brought rapid changes in the understanding of history and social processes; these changes were accompanied by new concepts for understanding forms of culture and the functioning of human consciousness (for instance, the workings of memory, mental processes, and perception). Thus understood, modernism appeared as an artistic movement in Europe and the United States in the mid-nineteenth century and developed during the first half of the twentieth. According to Western scholars, it reached its apogee during the 1930s and had disappeared by the mid-1960s (in the United States, by the 1950s), replaced by postmodernism/postmodernity. From today's perspective, however, it is apparent that modernism is not a single current, idea, or program, but rather many different ones – a dense network of relations created by opposite and often mutually exclusive answers to questions about the consequences of modernity. In this sense, modernism is the analysis and criticism of modernity, a multiplicity of oppositional ideas, programs, and values as well as their realizations. Accounting for historical and cultural differentiations is therefore essential to describing historical forms of modernism. In other words, from its very beginnings, modernism developed entirely differently not only in North America and Europe, but also – first and foremost – in individual countries. This is especially true for Central and Eastern Europe and, in this instance, Poland. In the context of this discussion, differentiating between Western and Eastern European modernism is a fundamental methodological task.

2. Eastern European Modernism

Like every cultural phenomenon, Eastern European modernism arose and developed within specific social, historical, and cultural as well as political and religious traditions. For this reason, modernism in Central and Eastern Europe (here: Poland) differed fundamentally from, for example, Anglo-Saxon modernism in its many variants. Although modernism was admittedly an international phenomenon (European and American), its local indicators, problems, and interpretations were determined by national traditions (cultural, linguistic, and artistic) and historical experiences as well as their transnational, regional, and multicultural contexts. The best case in point is the Vienna Secession, which radiated north and east to Kiev, Saint Petersburg, and Moscow and south towards Ljubljana, Zagreb, and Trieste.

What does "national" mean, exactly, in the context of modernism? Polish modernism at the end of the nineteenth century existed in an entirely different cultural, geographical, state, and ethnic reality than it did after the First and Second World Wars or at the beginning of the twenty-first century. It is important to remember that the notion of nationality in Polish literature has been historically "multi-national," multi-denominational, and multi-cultural (the hero of the Polish national anthem, Jan Henryk Dąbrowski, was German and did not speak Polish very well). Also, when classifying writers, the language they wrote in is the only criterion of their nationality. For example, among writers born on the territories of the historical Poland (which in the nineteenth century already did not exist), Izaac Bashevis Singer is considered to be a Jewish and Bruno Schulz a Polish writer; Joseph Conrad is a part of the English and Wacław Berent of the Polish literary canon; and Horst Bienek is a German writer while Aleksander Wat is a Polish one. Ethnic categories do not overlap with linguistic ones here. Such polarization of identities is characteristic of Eastern European modernism and indicative of its authors' complicated lineages, of the osmosis of cultures and languages, and of multiplied identities. This was one of the more important themes of modernism – an answer to the twentieth century's forced migrations, conversions, assimilations, deportations, emigrations, and (in its final decades) e-migrations.

3. Modernism and Modernity

There was no single modernism in world literature because different writers understood and defined modernity differently. Moreover, modernism in literature is not only a matter of literary conventions, manifestos, or artistic theories, but also a collection of diverse phenomena of an entire culture and social life, at least since the mid-nineteenth century (and, in a broader perspective, since the Renaissance). This essay does not cover all aspects of literary modernism – it bypasses, for instance, the modernism of popular literature. Yet it should be noted that the broad field of "literature for kitchen maids," as Witold Gombrowicz called it, was not only an integral element of modernism in Poland (and in all literatures) but also a decisive component of modern culture. Modern culture's ambition, after all, has been to reach a mass audience with the help of new media such as film, popular press, advertising, comics, television, pageants, and spectacles, including the theatralization of public life. In this sense, modernism was a collection of answers to the accelerated processes of democratization that became the intellectual, artistic, and existential experience of many artists and intellectuals. This tells us why both Western and Eastern European modernism was a much broader phenomenon, not limited to literature and art. It was an all-encompassing, multidirectional phenomenon of twentieth-century civilization that – by constantly reiterating questions about the consequences of modernity – turned out to be the most lasting, cross-generational experience of the most important artists and thinkers in Europe and America. The same is true for Poland, even though the Polish state did not exist when modernism first appeared at the turn of the nineteenth and twentieth centuries.

Twentieth-century literature articulates diverse conceptualizations of modernity, and Polish literature is no different in this regard from other European literatures. Yet notions of modernism in Poland (indeed, in all of Central and Eastern Europe) were much more dependent on the time and place of their formulation than was the case in most Western European countries. This is because in Poland such conceptualizations were contingent not just on world view and artistic ideas, but first and foremost on historical events that determined how modernization evolved. For Poles, the principal event was not the Scientific Revolution of the seventeenth century, as was the case in Western Europe, but rather the Enlightenment, followed by the reforms of the First Commonwealth undertaken towards the end of the eighteenth century.[1] The following factors were also at play: (1) the non-existence of the Polish state between 1795 and 1918, which subordinated the problems of modernization to the pursuit of independence and the fight to preserve national identity; (2) the modernizing processes in Poland during between 1919 and 1939 and that nation's position between the totalitarian states of the Soviet Union and the Third Reich; (3) the German and Soviet occupations of Poland during the Second World War; and (4) the communist system in Poland between 1944 and 1989, which evolved from totalitarian Stalinism to military communism in the 1980s. These historical factors need to be outlined more precisely before starting a discussion of specifically literary issues.

A number of different dates have been given as the beginning of Polish modern literature. Some predictably point to the turn of the nineteenth and twentieth centuries, others to the year 1918, but there are also those who move the date to 1945 and even 1956. Each date has its justification and all are tied to a completely different understanding of modernity. The oldest notion of modernism in Polish literature, by contrast, is not linked to specific dates but rather to artistic ideas. For close to two hundred years, scholars have concurred in pointing to Romanticism as its fountainhead, and it seems difficult to argue with this notion.[2] The dominance of Romantic symbolics in the Polish collective imaginarium is an obvious fact – its props are the stable orientation points not only of Polish culture but also of Polish public life. For the past two centuries, all of Polish literature – prose, poetry, and drama – as well as art – music, fine arts, film, and theatre – has been in constant dialogue with the Romantic tradition, the best-known examples of which are the works of Adam Mickiewicz (1798–1855) and Frederick Chopin (1810–49). It is precisely their names that are the most recognizable signs of the continuity of the Polish cultural tradition, and they can be found not only in high art (literature, theatre, and music) but also in mass culture (in the labels of vodka, candy, and countless gadgets). The paradox is that Polish Romantic literature was created entirely outside of Poland – indeed, when Poland as a state no longer existed – and mainly in France.

There are thus two distinct streams that questions about the sources, determinants, and definitions of modernism and modernity in Polish literature can follow. The first includes historical and civilizational issues, and the second, literary (artistic) ones. Accordingly, the main thematic current in the first instance is that of modernity as a model of the state and of its culture, while in the second, it is art's response to modernity and its artistic languages that take centre stage. The first theme appears in Poland towards the end of the eighteenth century, during the Enlightenment, and the second at the end of the nineteenth century, when it marks the beginning of modernism.

The sources of literature are not internal to it; rather, they are a function of changes taking place in culture, science, and customs – in a word, all aspects of social life – but especially in history. Despite the legend that continues to this day, it was not the culture of Romanticism that marked the onset of modernity in Polish literature. Polish Romanticism was not an answer to the problems of modernity, for it had not encountered modernity. Polish Romantics commented on those problems, of course, but only as unacceptable civilizational processes in Western Europe. Many such signals can be found in the exilic work of Adam Mickiewicz, Juliusz Słowacki (1809–49), and Cyprian Norwid (1821–83), all of whom spent their final years in Paris. Paradoxically, however, the sceptical attitude of Polish Romantics towards Western civilization significantly affected how modernity came to be understood in Poland, albeit much later, at the turn of the nineteenth and twentieth centuries. Romanticism initiated revolutionary artistic changes in Polish literature, especially in drama and poetry (tellingly, early modernism was sometimes called neo-Romanticism in Poland), becoming the most important reference point for all subsequent generations of writers.[3] First and foremost, however, it pointed to differences in the understanding of civilizational processes in Western and East-Central Europe. That being said, modernity in Poland began not during Romanticism, but a generation earlier – at exactly the same time as in Western Europe and in the United States, namely, the eighteenth century. It also touched on the same issues, although the scope, development, and determinants of modernity, and especially the consequences of modernizing actions undertaken in Poland, had a distinct genesis and progressed entirely differently than in the West.

To begin with a few comparisons: in the second half of the eighteenth century, rapid social and political processes referred to as "revolutions" took place in the United States, Poland, and France. They brought forth the constitutions that continue to serve as the foundations of all modern states: the United States Constitution of 1787, the Polish Constitution of 3 May 1791, and the French Constitution adopted later that same year. All of these constitutions derived from Enlightenment ideas. They aimed to strengthen and unify the state, to grow its army for defence purposes, and to act for the benefit of the entire nation, which was understood as all citizens regardless of background and social status. Moreover, and importantly so, they tried to enhance personal freedoms and to defend civil rights. All three rested on identical values, although the concrete institutional changes written therein emerged from entirely separate socio-political conditions and traditions. As Stanisław Małachowski (1736–1809), the Speaker of the Sejm (the Polish parliament), declared when the May 3 Constitution was passed: "In this age we have two most eminent republican governments: one British and the other American, which corrected the flaws of the first. But this one, which today (May 3, 1791) we have established, will be the most perfect, because combined in it can be found the finest aspects of both, ones that most appropriately suit our purposes."[4]

What were these conditions? The First Commonwealth was a willing union of two countries – Poland and Lithuania – which is why it is also called the Commonwealth of Both Nations. In reality, though, it was a multi-national, multi-denominational, and multicultural elective monarchy. During the eighteenth century, Poland, like France, was still a feudal country. In terms of social structure, Poland consisted of three main estates, one of which – the *szlachta* (gentry), comprising 10 per cent of the population – had benefited from the principles of a developed democracy since the sixteenth century. The remaining estates (burghers and peasants) were excluded from the privileges of the nobility, although the burghers did have their own rights. The peasants, for their part, were treated as the gentry's workforce, which is why historians of feudalism have referred to the Polish village as "the internal colony" of the state. The need to change the feudal structure of society and to expand civil rights to all social estates was a perennial theme of writers, who demanded fundamental reforms to the state. The realization of this demand was not easy, however. Poland in the eighteenth century was no longer a sovereign state, but the object of aggressive colonization efforts – primarily by Russia, but also Austria and Prussia. Russia, which had stationed troops on Commonwealth lands since 1717, formally guaranteed Poland's borders and political system in 1767. This meant that the King of Poland did not have the right to implement any institutional changes without Russia's consent. To protest this law, some of the nobility organized an armed insurgency, the Bar Confederation (1768–72), which is now considered the first Polish uprising. In retaliation, Russia, Austria, and Prussia effectuated the Commonwealth's first partition (1772), as a result of which Poland lost 211,000 square kilometres of its territory and 4.5 million of its people. (The United States, in turn, gained a national hero, Kazimierz Pułaski (1745–79), who had to flee the revenge of Poland and Russia for having participated in the Bar Confederation and thus became one of the first Polish political émigrés.)

The institutional principles of Poland at that time, colloquially referred to as "golden liberty," testified to a developed democracy that was distinct from the enlightened absolutism of countries such as England and France. In Europe at that time, enlightened absolutism was seen as a determinant of a modern state, whereas the Polish model of democracy, which drastically limited the king's power in favour of the nobility's privileges, was considered an example of backwardness. Two principles served as the basis of the First Commonwealth. The first was the principle of *liberum veto* (in operation today at the United Nations Security Council), which allowed for the objection of one parliamentary member to nullify any legislation that was passed by all other members. The second was an elective monarchy, meaning that the king of Poland was chosen through "general elections" – which here meant by the entire nobility. Both these principles worked against Poland's interests in the eighteenth century. Russia, Prussia, and Austria not only bribed members of the Sejm, but also employed their own agents. As a result, any modernization plans developed by the Commonwealth immediately activated internal opposition of that part of the aristocracy that did not want to lose the privileges (and property) guaranteed by Russia – a phenomenon well known in the history of colonialism. The proponents of Poland's modernization aimed to extend civil liberties to all social estates, as well as to strengthen the state and protect it from foreign interference. Modernization's opponents, for their part, understood freedom as the status quo, whose purpose was to secure their own unlimited political privileges and economic interests.

The American constitution was the symbolic capstone of the War of Independence (1775–83). Following the Treaty of Paris (1783), the United Stated ceased to be a British colony and formed a sovereign, republican state. The Polish constitution established a constitutional monarchy, one that limited the colonizing expansion of Russia and Prussia, while the French constitution initially transformed its absolute monarchy into a constitutional one and then into a republic (in 1792). The American and French constitutions set in motion powerful social, political, scientific, and industrial forces that soon made possible the dynamic development of all areas of social life in Europe and America known as modernization and that led to the creation of modern democratic states. Unfortunately, Poland's history took an entirely different course – the Polish constitution became the reason why neighbouring empires liquidated the Polish state.

The 3 May Constitution was the culmination of the state's modernizing movement, which lasted more than a dozen years and opened the same avenues of change for Poland as the American and French constitutions did for those countries. To counteract the interference of neighbouring powers in Poland's elections, the Polish constitution introduced a hereditary monarchy (such as is still in place in the United Kingdom and other European constitutional monarchies, for example, Sweden, Spain, Holland, Belgium, and Norway). Poland's transformation into a strong and sovereign democratic state threatened Russia's and Prussia's interests enough to propel them to take instant and aggressive counteractions.

In 1792, in agreement with Prussia, Russia brought about the abolishment of the 3 May Constitution. After a short and savage war,[5] both states enacted Poland's second partition (1793). At this time, Poland lost another 308,000 square kilometres of its territory and 4 million of its people. Two years later, in 1795, in response to a second uprising in defence of Polish independence organized in 1794 by Tadeusz Kościuszko (another American hero), the three empires of Russia, Prussia, and Austria carried out the complete liquidation of the Polish state. As a result of the three partitions, Russia annexed 462,000 square kilometres of Poland's territories and 5.5 million of its people, while Prussia took 141,000 square kilometres and approximately 2.6 million people, and Austria 130,000 square kilometres and about 4.2 million people. Poland had disappeared from the world map, and according to the plans of the three empires, it was to never appear on it again.

4. The History and Modernity of Literature

The events described above had a fundamental significance for conceptualizations of modernity in Polish art, in that they served as its constant subject for decades to come. At the end of the eighteenth century, a branch of literature blossomed that commented on ongoing political events; due to its journalistic character, it is still called "occasional" writing. Such literature created a tradition of political engagement for future generations, especially in the twentieth century, using to this end all literary forms and genres, including poetry, drama, satire, journalism, and short- and long-form fiction. These works were often anonymous or written under a pseudonym, but some were signed by their authors.

The most important social phenomenon that arose from the eighteenth-century liquidation of the Polish state was emigration, which continued in waves until the 1990s, with the final ones having been prompted by the abolishment of "Solidarity" and the introduction of martial law in Poland in 1981. This emigration – spanning close to 250 years and the largest in Central Europe – has determined the shape of Polish culture right up to the present day. The Polish national anthem was written in Italy in 1797 as a song of the émigrés, with its main theme being their return to a free Poland. Admittedly, freedom is a motif in the anthems of many countries, including the United States, France, and Canada.[6] Yet only the Polish anthem speaks of a state that no longer exists, or rather exists solely in the memory of its former citizens and in their hope that its independence will be restored: "Poland has not yet perished / So long as we still live."

The most important works of nineteenth-century Polish literature were written in exile. French literature has its "poètes maudits" – rebels "accursed" for lifestyle and artistic reasons. Polish literature also has its "poètes maudits" – émigrés "accursed" by the partitioning powers for political reasons, who were at the same time the objects of a national cult. One such "accursed" émigré was Adam Mickiewicz, the greatest among a group that included Fredrick Chopin, Juliusz Słowacki, and Cyprian Kamil Norwid. This had long-term consequences for Polish culture, since the literature of émigrés took up historical and current subjects that were prohibited on Poland's former territories, which at the time were held by the partitioning powers. It also created a reservoir of allusions, "winged words," cultural signs and codes that are still in use among Poles today. Remembering a no longer existing state – sometimes with nostalgia, other times with trauma – became the main theme of Polish literature at the end of the eighteenth century. This was accompanied by reflection on the passing of states and nations and on the inevitable destruction of the legacy of many generations in the course of historical events such as wars and uprisings. This reflection initiated a very characteristic – in Polish literature – current of catastrophism, the pessimism of which is identical across the eighteenth, nineteenth, and twentieth centuries.

The partition of the Commonwealth, the successive failed uprisings and repressions, and especially the confiscation of Polish landowners' properties by the Russian authorities, activated a westward emigration of Poles that has continued into the present day. The partitions also initiated one of the most important leitmotifs in Polish literature and art – the exodus from one's birthplace. Modern European literature, centred on the psychology and memory of the individual, is well characterized by the title of Marcel Proust's *In Search of Lost Time* (1913–27); in modern Polish literature, by contrast, the most resilient theme has been the physical search for a "lost homeland" – in other words, the experience of exile.[7] The lack of their own state and the anti-Polish politics of the partitioning powers, whose main goal was denationalization, made the struggle for the survival of national identity the fundamental problem of Poles during the nineteenth century. Polish society, confronted with intense Germanization and Russification, had to fight for its identity instead of investing in modern administrative structures, the law, and institutions of public life. Indeed, such was the experience of most Eastern European nations. In the Polish context, it was not only national uprisings (in 1830 and 1863) that served as instruments of this fight, but also – indeed, primarily – culture and language (speaking Polish had been forbidden by the occupying powers in the eighteenth, nineteenth, and twentieth centuries). This helps explain the Polish veneration of various media of collective memory, such as museums, books, maps, artworks, objects, and national heroes.

When describing the indicators of modernity in Polish culture, one must remember that from the dissolution of the Commonwealth in 1795 up until the establishment of the Third Republic in 1989–90 – in other words, for two whole centuries – Poland was a sovereign nation for only twenty years, during the period of the Second Republic (1919–39). In Western Europe and America, the last two centuries were a time of the dynamic formation of modern political, social, and economic systems, and of the development of public institutions, education, industry, technology, and sciences. Polish society was almost entirely excluded from this civilizational acceleration. In 1918, when a sovereign Poland was created as a result of US President Woodrow Wilson's fourteen points in 1918, Western Europe and United States were already advanced, modern, and industrialized. Meanwhile, as a new state on the European map, Poland was with difficulty emerging from three separate geographical areas and from the distinct social, political, and cultural systems of the Russian, Austrio-Hungarian, and Prussian empires. At that time, Poland was an impoverished state, burdened by a multitude of economic and social problems and having to contend with a significant group of ethnic minorities that comprised around 30 per cent of its total population. The scale of this last challenge can be more easily grasped in the context of the internal, often violent conflicts that beset many European nations today, whose populations are around 10 per cent ethnic minorities (three times less than in Interwar Poland). It is also important to note that these conflicts are taking place within liberal and democratic frameworks, whereas a nation-state model was dominant in Europe before the Second World War.

Interestingly, the Polish women's movement received a boost from Poland's situation at that time. Since it was men who participated in the fight for national independence and who were often imprisoned and/or deported for their activities, the burdens of quotidian life rested on the shoulders of women. Unlike in the West, however, women's struggle for emancipation within a patriarchal society was viewed through the lens of their right to participate with men in the struggle for the freedom and sovereignty of their country. As a result, Polish women received voting rights in 1918, far sooner than women in many other countries.[8]

The politics of the partitioning powers transformed over time, although their assumptions were similar. They evolved from the concept of denationalization and a ban on speaking Polish in the Russian and Prussian annexed lands, to relative tolerance at the turn of the nineteenth and twentieth centuries under the Austrian partition. Despite the censorship in all three partitions, Polish writers participated in the European exchange of artistic ideas, which were absorbed by Polish literature and art with only slight delays. An intense artistic life developed in the key cultural centres of each partition (Poznań in Prussia, Cracow and Lviv in Austria, Warsaw and Vilnius in Russia), including publications, exhibitions, and concerts. This does not alter the fact, however, that the conditions in which literature developed and the directions of its evolution were fundamentally different than they were for Western artists. Polish literature of early modernism was created by writers whose first language was not infrequently Russian, German, or Yiddish and who had been raised in various cultural milieux. Ethnic and national minority artists flourished in Poland after 1918, with Warsaw becoming a centre of the Yiddish avant-garde. Multiculturalism and multilingualism would characterize Polish modernist literature until 1939.

Realism, understood as diverse techniques for representing modern reality, was a hallmark of nineteenth- and twentieth-century European literature. But realism – and especially its most important genre, the novel – was the weakest element in Polish nineteenth-century literature. In the first half of the nineteenth century, poetry and historical dramas flourished in Poland but the novel was almost non-existent. Rapid development of Polish prose would occur only in the second half of the century, with the work of authors such as Bolesław Prus (1847–1912), Eliza Orzeszkowa (1841–1910), Henryk Sienkiewicz (1846–1916), Stefan Żeromski (1864–1925), Władysław Reymont (1867–1925), and Wacław Berent (1878–1940). It was severely deformed, however, by censorship as well as by the dominance of the social and historical problematic. Indeed, the historical aspect of Polish nineteenth-century prose amounted to a disguise for contemporary themes that could not be represented directly for reasons of censorship.

At the turn of the nineteenth and twentieth centuries, a rapid generational change took place in literature and art, accompanied by new artistic ideas that radically altered all European art. Although Polish culture at that time still functioned within three different states, the artistic and intellectual fervour of Vienna, Prague, Berlin, Saint Petersburg, Kiev, and Moscow quickly found its parallels in Warsaw, Lviv, and Cracow. Polish writers and artists, moving with relative ease between cultural centres of that time, were quite familiar with the principal assumptions of the new art, which was already being called modernism. As a result, many works by Scandinavian, German, French, Italian, and Russian authors were quickly translated into Polish. The diversity and richness of early modernism in Poland stemmed from the interweaving of, and sharp dialogue between, very different artistic concepts, poetics, and ideological assumptions, which had as their common thread the contestation of the principles of mimetic art. Thanks to this diversification, literary modernism in Poland soon blossomed with expressive artistic proposals that led to the formation of several (artistic and ideological) currents and that propelled the output of individual artists who worked on their sidelines.

Among the most important currents of modernism, which lasted throughout the entire twentieth century in Poland, were Decadence, Parnassism, Classicism, Symbolism, Expressionism, Futurism, Catastrophism, and the avant-garde. The first four of these formed towards the end of the nineteenth century, the remaining four in subsequent decades, but their continuations can be found even at the turn of the twentieth and twenty-first centuries. Notably, neither Decadence, nor Parnassism, nor Classicism, nor Catastrophism belonged to the twentieth-century paradigm of the avant-garde, for they did not absorb the idea of "modernity" – meaning the idea of newness and the cult of technology and progress – into their programmatic platforms. Taken together, however, with all of their oppositions, categorical polemics, and irresolvable artistic conflicts, they gave rise to a common phenomenon known today as "modernism in Poland."[9]

The intellectual climate at the end of the nineteenth century, influenced by developments in psychology, took more interest in issues of the individual than in descriptions of social reality. Together, these different factors led to the crystallization of two interpenetrating tendencies in Polish modernist literature: subjectivity and subjectivism. Subjectivity here refers to the focus on the individual, along with his or her burden of fate, experiences, feelings, emotions, and language. Subjectivism, in turn, refers to the subordination of the representation of the world in literature to human perception and consciousness. For this reason, authorial narration (in which the figures of author, narrator, and protagonist overlap) became one of the key determinants in Polish literature from the beginning of modernism. This led to an ever greater role for autobiographical elements in Polish literary works, as exemplified by the writing of Jarosław Iwaszkiewicz (1894–1980), Stanisław Ignacy Witkiewicz, also known as Witkacy (1885–1939), Bruno Schulz (1892–1942), Witold Gombrowicz (1904–69), Czesław Miłosz (1911–2004), Tadeusz Różewicz (1921–2014), and Zbigniew Herbert (1924–98), to name only a few.

Despite colloquial interpretations, it was not the rejection of realism but the transformation of its model – its modernization, enrichment, and adaptation to the new paradigm of knowledge about human beings – that constituted the aim of modern (modernist) literature. The literary representation of reality – faithful, precise, true, and new – was the ideal of modernists. Modernism thus arose from the rejection of past literary conventions, especially linguistic ones, which – according to modernists – had falsified and deformed reality or failed to notice its newest or most significant aspects. Many contrary conventions permeate realism in modernist literature; within it, naturalism encounters myth, literalism meets poeticism,[10] realism holds hands with science fiction, to say nothing about other aesthetics and poetics. At its onset, modernism in Poland was a crucible of very different concepts of modernity in literature, which, however, shared a rejection of unequivocal art that "faithfully describes" a chosen fragment of reality (mimesis). For example, in the Symbolist paradigm, modernity was defined as the presence of transcendental values, while in the paradigm of the avant-garde, modernity meant the artistic realization of new ideas of everyday life, as expressed in Tadeusz Peiper's (1891–1969) manifesto "Miasto. Masa. Maszyna" (City, Mass, Machine, 1922).

During the first phase of Polish modernist literature, a key role in the realm of poetics was played by loose composition and narrative digressions, which helped combine the most important ingredients of the "new art." According to the understanding of modernity at that time, art's most important task was to replace literalism of meaning with multiplicity and inconclusiveness. The meaning of a modernist literary (artistic) work ceased to be concrete, precise, and graspable. The work became a collection of suggestions meant to evoke a mood and to stir emotions without resolving anything. Although the main ingredients of early, turn-of-the-century modernism were the tenets of Impressionism and Symbolism, its actual beginnings in Polish art were already present in the ideas of Naturalism. These included the defalsification of reality (e.g., through the violation of social taboos), precision and brutalization of descriptions, and high regard for craftsmanship that preceded the strictly modernist conceptualization of art's autonomy and autotelism. The loosening of poetics and the subjectification of methods for representing reality that were a part of early modernism in Poland between 1895 and 1918 (Young Poland) prepared the way for Polish modernism and the avant-garde of the 1920s.

But realism was not the most innovative determinant of the literary poetics of modernism between 1895 and 1939. That honour goes instead to linguistic experiments and to the grotesque, which – along with the phenomena of narrative poeticism that accompanied them – became the most important signals of the destruction of mimetic representations of reality, as seen, for example, in the work of Juliusz Kaden-Bandrowski (1885–1944), Berent, Witkacy, Gombrowicz, and Schulz. In this regard, the popularity of the linguistic grotesque and Witkacy's conceptualization of the novel as anti-art were of particular significance. Witkacy used the attributes of modern prose poetics later recognized as markers of High Modernism, including discursive narration, contrasts between opposing conventions and aesthetics (styles, genres, and themes), the critique of social stereotypes in language, and the carnivalization of language (linguistic grotesque).

5. Main Determinants of Literary Modernism in Poland

Polish modernism developed dynamically from the end of nineteenth century until the outbreak of the Second World War. Initially, it grew out of the anti-Positivist turn, with the first generation of Polish modernist writers and artists adapting the main artistic and philosophical ideas of the West and the East to their context. Among other things, these ideas included art's autonomy; the ties between literature and knowledge about human beings (philosophy, psychology, ethnology); the transnational and transcultural character of artistic motifs and means (Secession); and – first and foremost – the polysemy of artworks. The earliest Polish modernists called attention to the conventional qualities of artistic creation and the social nature of its forms. They also diagnosed the crisis of mimesis and the impact of language on its consequences, and they explored ludic sources of art (such as cabaret and parody). By the early years of modernism, the idea that modern art is an analysis, an unmasking, and an abandonment of ready-made forms for representing reality had crystallized; the aim of the "new art" was to arrive at a synthesis of its elements – to condense, simplify, and model them. Turn-of-the-century modernists thus left behind the notion of art as a representation of "life" and as an "ethnographic document." Form became art's departure point, and the shaping of form revealed the themes and meanings of the artwork. It was obvious to all modernists that art does not mean copying reality, but rather constructing it.

The rules of this construction could be radically different, encompassing for instance the Naturalist and Symbolist idea of "an artist's temperament," the hat of the Dadaists, hybrid works that Witkacy called "sacks," montage, "single use" types of expression, play with stereotypes, and literary "readymades." This idea would continue throughout the twentieth century in all types of modernism in Poland, embodied in various means, aesthetics, and values. It led to the sanctioning of the pluralism of literary media (types, genres, styles, conventions, and themes), providing the impulse towards a permanent transgression of literary boundaries. Between 1919 and 1939, people no longer saw this idea as new or challenging – it was now simply the alphabet of modern art used to create literature.

Given that the first phase of Polish modernism coincided with a non-existent Polish state, it was only during the Second Republic that modernism acquired a more institutional character. After 1918, the individual artists typical of early Polish modernism gave way to new literary groups, such as Skamander, Futurists, Formists, the Kraków avant-garde, Reflector, and Żagary. The hermit-artist had been replaced by the "artistic collective." While characteristic of Polish modernism of the 1920s and 1930s, the strategy of group debuts, manifestos, and public announcements is still practised today. After 1918, the first formation of modernists met with radical opposition. The understanding of art as a metaphysical absolute disappeared; the concept of "art for art's sake" (*l'art pour l'art*) fell out of date. These were replaced by new literary catchphrases: the signals of modernity (the everyday, colloquialism, the city) and of modernism (experiment, play, deformation, construction, parody, technique, form). This systemic change from early to later modernism completely transformed the understanding of art's social function and its relation with society. Concepts that placed art and artists in opposition to society were replaced by concepts (and their practice) that assigned to art the task of direct intervention in reality. The early modernist (and post-Romantic) concept of the extraordinary (and "accursed") artist transformed into that of the artist as an artisan, an everyman, and even the creator of social reality.

Ideas originating in various avant-gardes (Cubism, Futurism, Dadaism) gave rise to a radical transformation of language, poetics, and genres in literature. It was not only the notion of an author, but also that of the reader, that had shifted. Avant-garde modernism, which radiated also in other directions, had as its ambition – putting it most literally – to inject modernity into all aspects of everyday life, including technology, urbanization, mass society, and rapidly accelerating communications. New artistic media were to become the equivalents of changes in social life. In the realm of narrative genres, reportage came to be seen as exemplifying modern literature, while juxtaposition – rapid montage based on contrasts of meanings and styles – exemplified it on the level of composition. A fundamental shift took place in conceptualizations of the structure of artworks. As was the case with the Symbolists, Expressionists, and Classicists before them, the avant-gardists, Futurists, Cubists, and Surrealists inferred that art was an autonomous entity based on the new ways of representing reality. At the centre of this concept of art's autonomy were such indicators of a modernist work as construction, montage, collage, simultaneity, and deformation, as well as artistic scandal and provocation – and, in particular, surprising and shocking the reader, spectator, or listener.

A relation between literature and fine arts was typical for all phases of twentieth-century modernism, especially within the output of a single artist, as was true in Poland for Stanisław Wyspiański (1869–1907), Witkacy, Schulz, and Herbert. The avant-gardists reached for a key innovation of early modernist culture, namely the visualization of the text, which was to be both read and watched. The visualization of the modernist text tied together all of Polish twentieth-century modernism – it links the typography of the Secession, and the avant-garde and post–avant-garde practices of the interwar years, with present-day issues of visualization within new media and digital recording.

The key indicators of modernism included experiments with the means of literary expression – language, conventions, genres, and themes – along with the rejection of mimesis and verisimilitude in art. At the same time, however, modernism was constituted also by ideas not derived from literary poetics. Among them were the transgression of all types of taboos – sexual, familial, national, and political; the treatment of subjectivity as an endangered value in the twentieth century; corporeality as a basic component of human identity (the rejection of mind–body dualism); provocations and scandals; and the engagement of artists in political parties and social movements. The modern artist became an intellectual for whom the signals of modernity included not only newness and experimentation, but also values such as truth, freedom, independence, and political activism.

From the beginning of twentieth century, the paradigm of modernity thus included issues that were identical across all of European literatures, as well as those that were completely different in specific countries. The problems of modernity also varied in their intensity and included issues both artistic and non-artistic. To put it more concisely: modernity was an all-encompassing and long-term revision of the nineteenth-century model of the world – an attempt to radically change it while preserving its legacy. As a defence of culture against new threats, modernism was also a thorough hermeneutics of cultural legacy. At its centre, therefore, were social, philosophical, anthropological, religious, and ethical questions, as well as issues of customs (sexual, for instance), which modernist literature in its own way expressed, diagnosed, or simply discovered prior to their entrance into specialized fields of knowledge. The artistic output of the most remarkable Polish twentieth-century writers[11] speaks clearly to the issues of modern literary poetics. But since these writers were also modernist thinkers, questions about what literature should *be* were subordinated in their work, not so much to the analysis of artistic language but rather to the philosophy of human beings, concepts of society and culture, and the anthropological sense of twentieth century's historical experiences.

The *non-artistic issues* that served as indicators of modernity in twentieth-century Poland included the following: the scientific revolution and its consequences, such as the undermining of a one-dimensional, stable image of the world; psychoanalysis and the new psychology; the role of eroticism, corporeality, and sexuality in human life; gender in culture, the social status of women (emancipation), and various feminist issues; multiculturalism; the discovery of every kind of difference and otherness (including cultural) as new realms of experience; the forms and content of totalitarianism (communist and Nazi); the confrontation between liberalism and totalitarianism, and nationalism and universalism (cosmopolitanism); individual, historical, and social memory; various forms of genocide, including the Holocaust; issues of ethnology, history, religion, ideology, and philosophical anthropology; a new understanding of language and the place of verbal systems in culture; issues of the commercialization of culture; the mutual relations of "low" and "high" values; the place of the recipient in art; stereotypes about the image of the world as constructed by media and propaganda; art forms as distinct semiotic systems; problems of expression, communication, and representation of the world; and censorship as a source of taboo and of the deformation of public discourses.

Taking the long view, modernism was the consequence of industrialization; but in art itself, it was largely an expression of world views, a multifaceted theory of culture, and a study of modernity's impact on the understanding of human beings. That is why, in the history of Polish modernism, terms such as "newness," "modernity," "modernism," and "modernization" were not synonymous. Newness did not automatically mean modernity, and vice versa – paradoxically – the program of "modernity" did not have to be based on the concept of newness. In turn, relations between modernization as a civilizational process and modernity in art were never as direct as the etymology of these terms suggests. For example, the Secession (Art Nouveau), both as a style and as an artistic movement, was an attempt to create a new and modern art understood as both a negation of and a challenge to the styleless nineteenth-century industrial modernization aesthetic. In short, artistic conceptualizations of modernity were not merely the effects of modernization processes. Indeed, the artistic pursuits of Polish modernist writers, with the exception of the avant-garde, rarely evoked slogans of modernization. These writers also looked for other sources of literary modernity – for example, in tradition, mythology, history, knowledge of human psychology, and problems of individual and social identity. Most important to this differentiation, however, is the fact that "modernity" was understood also as a *radical polemic against modernization, and even – paradoxically – against modernity*. I labelled this stance "anti-modern modernity" many years ago in characterizing Gombrowicz's *Ferdydurke*, the flagship novel of modern Polish literature.[12]

This formula describes the greatest paradox of the artistic output of the most important Polish high modernist writers. The conflict between "modernity" and "newness" is the primary theme in the works of Witkacy, Gombrowicz, Schulz, Miłosz, Herbert, Kantor, Wisława Szymborska (1923–2012), and Jarosław Marek Rymkiewicz (b. 1935), to name just a few. Many artists and thinkers saw twentieth-century modernization as a threat to culture (art) and to individual sensitivity and personality. From its onset, modernism in Poland was a rebellion against the aesthetics of the industrial epoch, as exemplified by Berent's novel *Fachowiec* (The Specialist, 1895). It was also – indeed, primarily – a means to defend human beings against the dangers that would soon materialize precisely as a result of industrialization and its consequences (e.g., the processes of democratization). The civilization of modernity was a *promised land* only for the Futurists; for other artists it most often signified "twilight," "the end," "degeneration," "regress," "the heart of darkness," or "the wasteland." Miłosz called the ideals of the moderns "legends" and the epoch of modernity "the dark times"; similarly, in the context of totalitarianism, Herling-Grudziński repeatedly wrote about "the cursed twentieth century."[13] Reymont's most famous novel *Ziemia obiecana* (The Promised Land, 1898) typifies this attitude. Set in the city of Łódź (sometimes called the "Polish Manchester"), it tells of Poland's greatest industrial success, yet its main message relates to its vision of a "city-monster" that forces a man to give up his humanity for the illusion of progress. The sharp clash between modernity and its negative consequences fuelled the popularity of so-called anti-utopias in the literature of the first half of the twentieth century; this is one of the most interesting indicators of literary modernism in Poland (with Witkacy's oeuvre being its clearest example).

6. The Second World War and Polish Modernisms

The Second World War was a total civilizational catastrophe for Poland, bringing with it the loss of national sovereignty, the death of millions of its citizens, and immeasurable material losses. In 1939, Poland was attacked first by Nazi Germany on 1 September and then again, on 17 September, by the Soviet Union. Despite treaties with Great Britain and France, Poland did not receive any military reinforcements, and after thirty-six days of fighting, the Polish forces capitulated. One consequence of the German/Soviet aggression was the fourth partition of Poland, which had been decided on in a secret treaty between Stalin and Hitler dated 23 August 1939 and aimed to once again erase Poland from the world map and to exterminate Polish citizens, especially Jews. The Third Reich considered Jews to be non-human and condemned them to total extermination as per the so-called *Endlösung* – "the Final Solution to the Jewish Question." Slavs, too, were treated as subhuman (*Untermenschen*). Both the Third Reich and the Soviet Union aimed to exterminate Polish society, especially its most educated classes; their plan was to turn the former Polish state into a reservoir of cheap slave labour. Thus, the Germans deported Poles to the Third Reich for use as forced labour, and the Russians deported them to the Gulag, their own organized system of slave labour. For the nations of Eastern Europe, the Second World War was a fight not simply for independence, but first and foremost for biological survival. More than six million Polish citizens died during the war, with Jews accounting for 2.7 to 3 million of that number. Around half a million Jews died in ghettos and work camps; 200,000 more were murdered by German *Einsatzgruppen* (SS death squads), and somewhere between 1.4 to 1.8 million were murdered in extermination camps (most of them at Treblinka, Auschwitz, Chełmno, Sobibór, Bełżec, and Majdanek).[14]

Poland's national wealth suffered apocalyptic losses as a result of the German occupation, collapsing to 38 per cent of prewar (1939) levels. Overall, the Germans plundered 43 per cent of Poland's cultural goods. Losses to library collections alone stood at approximately 66 per cent, with 22 million books destroyed. All in all, the German occupiers stole from Poland around 516,000 individual artworks and destroyed its entire civilizational infrastructure, including universities, schools, and research institutes. The health care system accrued losses of 56 per cent; industry, 64.5 per cent; and transportation infrastructure, 50 per cent. Poland's total losses as a result of the German occupation are calculated at between 650 and 700 billion US dollars (at 2004 exchange rates). The Soviet Union's annexation of Poland's eastern territories in 1939 was accepted by the Allies during the Tehran Conference in 1943 and the Yalta Conference in 1945. Under pressure from the United States and Great Britain, Poland was forced to concede 48 per cent of its lands to the Soviet Union, losing around 178,000 square kilometres in the east and receiving in exchange – at Germany's cost – around 101,000 square kilometres in the west. The huge material losses that Poland incurred as a result of Red Army actions between 1939 and 1945 were never assessed after the war, nor in subsequent years, when technological equipment and even entire factories, as well as cultural goods, were moved from Poland to the Soviet Union.[15]

The German and Soviet occupations of 1939–45 destroyed Poland's legacy, including the institutions and social structures established in the Second Republic. Most of its educated classes, including artists, either were murdered during the war or died by other means. Most of the first generation of Polish modernists met the same fate, while those who survived were forced into exile. The war also claimed the lives of many of Poland's youngest writers (among them Krzysztof Kamil Baczyński [1921–44], Tadeusz Gajcy [1922–44], and Andrzej Trzebiński [1922–43]), whose work foreshadowed a great generational change in Polish literature, in terms of both artistry and world view.

After Poland's sovereignty was restored in 1918, Poles had returned to their homeland in great waves from all over the world, mainly from the former Russian and Austrian empires. The energy and patriotism of these people, the diversity of their life experiences, and their education and knowledge of languages and of other civilizations, including non-European ones, had a huge impact on the vitality of the young nation, and especially on the richness and dynamism of Polish culture. Precisely the opposite was true in 1939 and after 1945. First because of the war and later due the communist repression that followed it, a large portion of the prewar social elites remained in exile, while tens of thousands of those who remained in Poland fell victim to either Nazi or Soviet policies of extermination. After 1945, Poland was swallowed by the totalitarian system of Soviet communism, which made its economic development impossible, especially since Polish communists, acting on Soviet orders, had rejected the Marshall Plan, which would eventually restore the economy of Western Europe. Poland's association with Soviet Russia also impeded technological progress, obstructed the development of social institutions that modern states need in order to function, restricted participation in the flourishing Western culture, and precluded activities that were independent of the state of both individuals and professional groups. Finally – stating the obvious, perhaps – it placed Poland within an organized system of repression, discrimination, and violence.

Polish émigré literature (1939–89): the literary life and literature produced outside of Poland's borders as a result of the Second World War and geopolitical changes that either forced or inclined writers to leave their homeland and (often) remain abroad. At its onset and during the Second World War (1939–45), those able to leave Poland ended up mostly in the United States, France, and Great Britain. It was within the cultural hubs of these countries (New York, Paris, and London, respectively) that the main centres of Polish émigré cultural life were established after the war (1945–51), although not to the exclusion of other places (for instance, Munich, Geneva, and Montreal). By 1952 the significance of these émigré centres had grown with the founding of various book series, literary prizes, and publications. Their position remained stable until 1981, when a new wave of emigration, prompted by the suppression of "Solidarity" and the introduction of martial law in Poland, led to a symbolic "changing of the guard." Some established émigré publications ceased (*Wiadomości* in 1981; *Oficyna Poetów* in 1980) as new ones, such as *Zeszyty Literackie* (1983 in Paris; from 1990 in Warsaw); *Puls* (established in 1977 in Łódź, from 1982 published in London, and between 1991 and 1993 in Warsaw), commenced operations (often moving abroad from Poland), with Berlin and other German cities growing in significance. Signs of the coming political transformation, and of the changing role of Polish émigré culture, were also perceptible in Poland. The 1980 Nobel Prize for Literature awarded to Miłosz, for instance, prompted the official publication of some of his works (with the telling exception of *Zniewolony umysł* (The Captive Mind, 1953) and of other essays that were still considered too anti-systemic to be published in Poland). In turn, a thriving independent publishing movement, the so-called *drugi obieg* (second circulation), made accessible many forbidden works, both Polish and otherwise. The impact of postwar émigré contributions to Polish culture is evidenced by the fact that its literary output was comparable to that of medium-sized European countries such as Portugal and Switzerland.

Literature written during the war in Poland as well as outside its new borders (and also after the war) was a natural continuation of interwar modernism. In the Polish People's Republic after 1945, however, after a three-year transitional period during which the writing of previous decades was still referenced, the continuity of literature (its ties to the ideas, themes, and techniques of modernism) was severed when socialist realism was declared the only legitimate art. Socialist realism was Stalinism's tool of brutal political propaganda; its purpose was to Sovietize culture.[16] In these circumstances, the émigré literature that was developing mainly in Paris and London after the Second World War served as the continuation of Polish interwar literature. The majority of émigré writers had debuted in Poland in the 1930s and now continued their activities in exile. Émigré literature ensured the continuity of modernist literature, but it also took up themes of civilizational significance that would be fully appreciated only at the turn of the twentieth and twenty-first centuries. The differences between literature written in exile and literature written in Poland were among the most salient characteristics of Polish modernism in the second half of the twentieth century. During that period, literature in communist Poland functioned within a system of state censorship. Except for the short period of socialist realism (1949–56), it was subject not to absolute mandates, but rather to absolute prohibitions. These concerned primarily matters of Polish–Russian relations after 1917 as well as those of everyday life under a communist system, and, indirectly, all comparisons of living conditions between the communist state and the West.

For Polish émigré literature, it was the 1930s that served as a reference point, while for literature written at home, the avant-garde of the 1920s played that role. The fact that the avant-garde was the most popular and strongly endorsed artistic tradition in communist Poland was a paradox of modernist literature of that time. Except for the period of strict Stalinism when the communist authorities stigmatized it as "formalism," the avant-garde was generally considered the most important component of the Polish twentieth-century literary tradition. The term "avant-garde" was, in fact, understood in a very broad way. After 1956, with the end of Stalinism and the beginning of the so-called thaw in public life, when the doors were reopened to previously prohibited Polish cultural traditions, the avant-garde was seen as including both the historical prewar avant-garde and the works of Witkacy, Gombrowicz, and Schulz – indeed, even the Baroque tradition. The paradoxes of the avant-garde illustrate well this variant of Polish postwar modernism. The 1920s avant-garde appealed to a mass society, but avant-garde literature was actually addressed to the few. It countered the Symbolist conceptualization of poetry, but in reality it continued to embrace the fundamental assumption of Symbolism – namely, the radical separation of the languages of poetry and prose. It declared "an embrace of the present," but its interpretation of contemporaneity was actually very narrow and idealized. Looking at reality through the lens of a leftist utopia of unceasing progress made it impossible for the avant-gardists to grasp the dangers of Soviet totalitarianism. Avant-garde aesthetics were to reflect the "new skin of the world," yet the writers who debuted over the next decade (Miłosz, Gombrowicz) saw its program as manifesting complete isolation from reality – an aesthetic enclosed in a proverbial "ivory tower."

In the 1930s, only the idea of the avant-garde remained of the avant-garde program. Avant-gardism became an inspiration for new artistic and philosophical explorations in the realm of fine arts and new media, preceding phenomena that would appear in Polish art after 1956. The avant-garde of the 1920s and 1930s revolutionized the understanding and function of semiotics in modernist art (in terms of words, sound, image, montage, etc.). During the Second World War, however, the avant-garde was not an attractive idea for literature, and afterwards, during the period of socialist realism, it was entirely forbidden as antithetical to Marxist aesthetics. It was revived in poetry only after 1956, in the work of Stanisław Młodożeniec (1895–1959), Anatol Stern (1899–1968), Adam Ważyk (1905–82), and Aleksander Wat (1900–67). The concept of the avant-garde was instrumental in the shaping of linguistic prose and poetry in Polish twentieth-century literature, creating the most enduring artistic tradition of Polish modernism from the 1920s until the end of the century.

The acceptance of avant-garde traditions in a communist country was tied to the fact that most prewar avant-gardists who had survived the war had leftist convictions and belonged to the artistic establishment at that time. Their interest in formal issues in art suited the communist authorities, which censored only political and historical subjects. This led to another paradox of Polish modernism. After 1945, realistic literature that raised prohibited themes touching on the realities of life under communism turned out to be the most censored. Realist writers – for example, Marek Hłasko (1934–69), Marek Nowakowski (1935–2014), and Kazimierz Orłoś (b. 1935) – thus had to publish their works abroad through émigré publishing houses. Avant-garde writers, meanwhile, were able to publish their works in communist Poland without the slightest of obstacles.

After 1956, writers residing in Poland were gradually released from communist censorial and intellectual restrictions. At that point they discovered new areas of social experience, the most important of which was language. In émigré literature, language was something to be preserved, part of the memory of a lost homeland; in Poland, it became the object of suspicion and various deformations. This stance – called *lingwizm* (linguistic literature) in Poland – stemmed from the avant-garde tradition of a ludic and analytical attitude towards language. Its historical source was the denuding of social linguistic conventions in early modernism and during the 1920s. Owing to those sources, high modernism in Poland (of the 1960s and 1970s) was characterized by a programmatic wariness of language as a system and of its artistic and social uses.

Polish postwar émigré and domestic literature began interpenetrating selectively after 1956, and more noticeably after 1976, when an alternative – uncensored – (self)publishing movement was established. The apogee of this process came after the fall of communism, in the 1990s, with modernist works of émigré literature written several decades earlier partnering, paradoxically, with the newest works of Polish literature and becoming the main object of critical interest. During that decade, as the division between émigré and domestic literature ceased to exist, two variants of Polish modernism joined forces. The differences between émigré modernist literature and its home-grown variant were fundamental. Most evidently, literature written in communist Poland had been censored, while that written abroad enjoyed freedom of speech. Moreover, socialist realism, which turned all art into a tool of Stalinist propaganda, had been a key experience for writers in the Polish People's Republic. Participation in this propaganda, which had been the choice of most authors and artists, subsequently became a shameful, even traumatic subject for them. For reasons of censorship, this was not addressed directly, which is why contemporary experiences such as the Stalinist terror were dressed up in a costume of distant history, often that of the Catholic Church, with the Inquisition serving as an allegory for the Stalinist purges. The same was true for other themes with hidden functions. Thus, interest in the Baroque and Symbolist traditions was a response to the earlier, socialist-realist sterilization of language and imagination, while psychological themes and translations of French and American literature (existentialism in the former case, and Hemingway and Faulkner in the latter) reconnected Polish literature with its severed prewar traditions, joining it also to the most current artistic phenomena.

The third notable difference between émigré and domestic Polish literature concerns the issue of institutional affiliation: the literary system in communist Poland had been subjugated to the politics of the ruling party, while for émigré literature all institutional ties, decisions, and judgments were freely chosen by either individuals or groups. Of most significance for émigré literary activity were the monthly *Kultura* (Culture) in Paris, edited by Jerzy Giedroyć (1906–2000), and the weekly *Wiadomości* (News) in London, edited by Mieczysław Grydzewski (1894–1970). Yet another difference concerns choice of thematics: at home, the Nazi occupation served as a primary theme of literature, whereas émigré writers focused on the experience of Soviet deportations and the Gulag. The martyrology of Polish Jews and the Holocaust, in turn, had become a subject unto itself. Moreover, where the émigré context fostered the development of realistic novels and individualistic genres such as essays, journals, and autobiographies (as exemplified by Gombrowicz, Herling-Grudziński, Wat, and Miłosz), the greatest successes in the literature of communist Poland came through formal experiments with prose, poetry (Julian Przyboś [1901–70], Miron Białoszewski [1922–83], The New Wave), and drama

(Różewicz). A related yet separate distinction is connected to the ambitions of both literatures: where émigré authors aimed to preserve the memory of the multicultural and multinational Poland of the interwar period (for instance, by choosing Jewish, Ukrainian, Lithuanian, Russian, or German themes), writers at home presented the society and reality of a communist country. Until 1968, in a negative reaction to the Stalinist destruction of literature, writers in Poland looked to the traditions of Mediterranean culture, mythology, and formal aesthetics instead.

POLISH ÉMIGRÉ CULTURE AND LITERATURE AFTER 1989

After Poland's transition to democracy, in tandem with the abolishment of censorship, the role of émigré culture underwent transformation. While it was included in new historical and literary syntheses, it was no longer of service as a counterpoint and/or motivation for literary life in Poland, and it disappeared in its previous form. Over the course of the 1990s, a number of émigré literary publications and prizes ceased to exist. Instead, the symbolic capital of Polish émigré life was taken over by research institutions in Poland, which established their own centres for the study of émigré culture (for instance, in Toruń, Katowice, Lublin, Warsaw, and Poznań) along with new literary publications and prizes. Selected works of Polish émigré writers are today included in high school curricula. Emigration itself continues, however. Since Poland joined the European Union, close to two million people have left, among them a number of writers (for example, Natasza Goerke, Manuela Gretkowska, and Izabela Filipiak). They do not necessarily identify themselves with emigration, however, opting for terms such as post-emigration or migration. Moreover, "émigré" literature must now also account for bilingual writers who, while of Polish descent, publish works in more than one language (for instance, the German-based Magdalena Parys, Dariusz Muszer, and Brygida Helbig).

Attitudes towards language, conventions of expression (such as irony, parody, and the grotesque), and the literary – mainly Romantic – tradition, mark another point of fundamental disparity between the two variants of Polish literature. Émigré writers cultivated the traditions, literary language, and multilingualism of Poland's former eastern borderlands, which had been annexed by the Soviet Union in 1939, forming a current of borderland literature. In the literature of communist Poland, meanwhile, more playful approaches to tradition, both ludic and cognitive (Mrożek, Różewicz, Białoszewski, Lem), flourished. There was considerable growth in interest in various functions of language – as a mechanism of communication and of political propaganda, and as the carrier of philosophical meanings (Szymborska) – and in the language of people from the so-called social margins. Linguistic interests first bore fruit in parodies of communist newspeak seen in the poetry of the New Wave (also called Generation '68), and shortly thereafter became part of the shared literary legacy of the Polish People's Republic. Finally, while émigré literature was relatively unknown in communist Poland, notable exceptions existed in the form of Gombrowicz's narrative works and Miłosz's poetry, both of which had a significant impact on domestic literature.

7. The Long Duration of Late Modernism

Despite the systemic and generational changes taking place at the time, the final decades of Polish twentieth-century literature were vitalized by inspirations that were introduced to its milieu by postwar modernist formations, specifically the generations of '56 and '68. Subjects typical of the interwar period were reactivated at this time, although in entirely different configurations. The place of Symbolism was taken by Vitalism, Poeticism, and Conventionalism. While the real end of communist Poland's literary system came with the abolition of censorship (in 1990), this did not mark the end of modernism's superordinate place in Polish twentieth-century literature. Perhaps incongruously, the revitalization of modernist ideas was accompanied by efforts to move beyond the modernist tradition, as evidenced by postmodern readings of the most original works of Polish modernism and especially by the adaptation of postmodern idiom to contemporary culture. Here examples include the deconstruction of aesthetic and ideological canons; the ennoblement and canonization of mass culture; notions about the exhaustion of language and the death of the novel; and ideas about the programmatic creation of texts from literary stereotypes, about anti-literature, about "spoilage" and "banalization;" as well as the aesthetization of economic mechanisms and their incorporation into the poetics of texts.

Postmodernism was being explored in Poland almost at the same time that communism was being abolished. The political system was changing, as was the role of literature and art, and a new generation of writers and artists was entering the public forum. Some critics linked these two changes – political and aesthetic – so tightly that they automatically associated post-communism with postmodernism. Since Polish literature published after 1989 had no postmodernist works, critics reached for examples from the past; in doing so they unthinkingly chose the most remarkable of Polish modernist authors, such as Witkacy, Schulz, and Gombrowicz. During the 1990s the term "modernism" was still identified exclusively with the short period of 1895 to 1918 – in other words, in today's terminology, with early modernism. This confusion over the significance and scope of the term modernism, however, soon bore fruit in the shape of two fundamental theses. The first held that Polish modernism differed from Western European modernism with regard to its periodization as well as its content – namely, by virtue of its own, Eastern European traditions and contexts. The other thesis maintained that the indicators of postmodern literature in its Anglo-Saxon understanding belonged to the original components of European, including Polish, modernism, if only because of the key role played by Futurism and Surrealism, which were absent from Anglo-Saxon modernism. These phenomena shared in the diagnosis of the crisis of representation and the contestation of the rules of realism. These rules had been formulated during early modernism and are best exemplified in the Polish context by *Pałuba* (The Hag, 1903), a novel by Karol Irzykowski (1873–1944). From this transpires that toying with the realistic tradition so as to undermine illusion, and the use of metafiction, parody, and intertextuality, was an original finding of early modernism in Poland that continued through all of its subsequent phases. Central to this process were the linguistic grotesque, both non-parodic and parodic (where language was the subject of parody in a given work), and the discovery that literature does not convey neutral meanings, but rather creates them through its use of conventions. Among the earliest discoveries of Polish modernism was thus the fact that literature can serve as its own subject.

Modernist traditions are still very strong in the works of the Polish writers who debuted after 1989. Indeed, they have been bolstered over the last decade of the twentieth century by the most important achievements of Western modernism, such as the works of Carl Jung, Friedrich Nietzsche, Bronisław Malinowski, James George Frazer, José Ortega y Gasset, Erich Fromm, Hermann Broch, T.S. Eliot, Samuel Beckett, Franz Kafka, and Jorge Luis Borges, to mention only a few from among the many. During the 1980s and 1990s, literary criticism made a number of attempts to move beyond these traditions by adapting the main ideas of postmodernism (among them feminism and queer studies) and post-structuralism (postcolonial theory). Yet it is difficult to ascertain today whether these phenomena are a transgression of modernism's boundaries, or – as is more likely – merely another version of its themes, variants, ideas, and modes. In any case, the qualities of Polish modernist literature outlined thus far in this discussion can now be summarized under the rubrics of periodization, themes, and achievements.

Periodization

Three different phases can be distinguished in the now more than a century long history of Polish modernist literature:

I. The period of early modernism (roughly 1895 to 1918), when the Polish state did not exist and Symbolism was the main artistic mode of modernism.
II. The period of high modernism (1919 to 1939/1945), when Poland was reborn as a sovereign state and the avant-garde was the main mode of modernism in art.
III. The period of split modernism (1939/1945–89), when modernist literature forked into two streams. One was émigré literature (1939–89), which continued the work of high modernism, with realism and recent historical themes (such as loss of independence) as its dominant modes. The other was literature written at home – first in the Polish People's Republic (1945–89), and later in the Third Republic (from 1989–90 on). Literature written in Poland also continued with high modernism, initially through the tradition of the prewar avant-garde, via experiments with form, the use of grotesque and parody, and especially linguistic poetry and prose. After 1956, in turn, modernist practice involved an increasingly complete synthesis of all its variants, with a key point of reference being the Second World War and the experience of communist Poland (the Holocaust, Stalinism, censorship, and the communist regime with its repressions and stifling of freedom). It is an open question when the continuation of high modernism transformed into late modernism; at fault here are Polish literature's constant returns to traditions severed by history. In this context, one can point to phenomena from the 1960s and 1970s just as well as to those from the 1990s, depending on the choice of methodology.

Themes

The very close relation between modernism and Poland's political history resulted in many traits that differentiate Polish literary modernism from its Western counterpart. The slow liquidation of the Polish state in eighteenth century (partitions of 1772, 1793, and 1795), its subsequent absence from nineteenth-century world maps, the double-erasure of its sovereignty during the twentieth century (1939 and 1945), and the experience of Stalinism and of socialist realism meant that history became the paramount subject and reference point for all phases of Polish modernism. That history was understood as both a collective and an individual experience, and in terms of collective memory and the reconstruction of sources. As a result, the radical opposition between the past and the present (future) – between tradition and progress – does not exist in Polish modernism. Indeed, the opposite is the case: history as a theme (in the form of interpretation, reconstruction, and new documentation, or even parable or allegory of the present) has been a constant element in every phase of Polish literary modernism. In the context of the eighteenth and nineteenth centuries, its themes relate to the dissolution of the Polish state and its consequences; for twentieth-century history, the spotlight falls on the simultaneous experience of two occupations (German and Soviet), mass genocide (the Holocaust, the extermination of both groups and individuals), and everyday life under the oppressive communist system.

These events are also behind two central categories of Polish literary modernism – those of memory, and those of historical experience. Although the issue of memory was already recognized in modernism's early phase, it flourished in the 1930s along with the development of psychological literature. Historical experience, in turn, became a primary category as a result of the Second World War and provided a means of approach to extreme experiences such as the German and Soviet concentration camps, the Holocaust, and the murderous actions of the communist state. These two categories, which have grown more popular in discussions of modernism over the last few decades, have completely altered previous assessments of the avant-garde's significance. Seen as a synonym for modern art for many decades in Poland, the avant-garde as an artistic proposal turned out to be useless for describing the Eastern European historical experience. The language of the avant-garde could not express the experiences of tens of millions of people, and the complete defeat of the avant-garde's social utopias did not help. In high and late Polish modernism, the place of the avant-garde was thus taken up by documentarism, realism, and historicism.

The resulting return to literature's cognitive function accounts for the triumph of realism in the literary output of high modernism. The escape from realism into various kinds of fictions typical of early modernism (Symbolism) was systematically replaced after 1945 with literature based on the reliable narrator and his truthful testimony. This did not affect, however, the strong popularity of fantasy and science fiction writing in mass culture. The modernist ambition to separate the work from the artist, present in both early and avant-garde modernism, was negated by the 1930s in Poland, in significant measure due to Gombrowicz's influence. Authorial narration – and especially genres such as autobiography and reportage – turned out to be the most popular form of expression in the literature of high and late Polish modernism. Western European modernism connected the modernity of prose to the internal monologue, stream-of-consciousness writing, and even impersonal narration leading to narrative pointillism. Polish modernist prose, meanwhile, from the start specialized in authorial narration.

Achievements

In Polish modernism, the repeated disruptions of literature's continuity and the powerfully felt need to overcome them created a syndrome of civilizational delay in relation to the West, evidenced by a compulsion to make up for lost ground and catch up to it, and – consequently – by the derivativeness of Polish literature and art. This thesis was formulated most strongly by Karol Irzykowski and Witold Gombrowicz, having already been put forward by the Romantics. Many artistic phenomena appeared in Poland at least a decade after they emerged in Western modernism, but for reasons clear by now, few of them constituted the specific characteristics and accomplishments of Polish modernism. Of these, virtually all were linked to the names of specific authors.

Karol Irzykowski's fascination with late-nineteenth-century German humanism generated the first and most extraordinary meta-novel of European modernism: *The Hag*, written in 1899 and published four years later. Independently of his radically original artistic solutions pertaining to narrative technique, composition, and genre structure, Irzykowski anticipated many ideas from the realms of psychoanalysis, social and cognitive psychology, and linguistics. His novel introduced auto-thematic narrative techniques to Polish literary modernism, which became popular only in the 1960s, during modernism's late phase. For Zofia Nałkowska, it was the literature of the French Enlightenment that proved inspirational. During early modernism, she introduced to Polish literature a narrative mini-genre called "characters" (modelled on French "les caractères"). From today's perspective, her most important work – besides her diary and her novels, which were of great significance to Polish feminist literature – was the micro-novel *Choucas* (1925). In it, she presented for the first time the problems of the Armenian genocide and of nationalist stereotypes; twenty years later, in the micro-stories in *Medaliony* (Medallions, 1946) she returned to these problems by focusing on the Holocaust. Witold Gombrowicz was also fascinated by French and German humanism, and in the 1930s he formulated the concept of anthropology of form, with form understood as the universal product of social relations that deform human subjectivity. Gombrowicz's radical anthropocentrism became one of the most important identifying marks of high modernism and is present in all of his works, especially in his *Dziennik* (Diary).

An entirely different variant of high modernism can be traced to Bruno Schulz, who – by combining Greek, Jewish, and Christian intellectual traditions, and (in an aesthetic sense) Symbolism with the avant-garde – worked out perhaps the most original conceptualization of high modernist literature in Poland – namely, the mythification of reality. Schulz understood the mythification of reality differently than early modernists, not as the use of mythical figures and plots, but rather as a metaphorization of language, an art he mastered to perfection. Czesław Miłosz, like Schulz, also renewed the links between Symbolist and avant-garde traditions. Alongside the catastrophism of his representation of history that was typical of Polish modernism, he ushered the intellectual tractatus and essayistic discourse into Polish poetry. The most internationally known of his works, however, is the typically modernist anti-utopia *The Captive Mind*, which references Witkacy's conceptualizations and exposes – in an essayistic form – the mental mechanisms of self-subjugation among intellectuals living under communism. Witkacy was a central figure of high modernism in Poland. His concept of the novel as an anti-art preceded by half a century John Barth's notion of "the literature of exhaustion," while his conceptualization of drama impacted the ideas of theatre reform in Poland during late modernism. The theatre work of Tadeusz Kantor, Jerzy Grotowski (1933–99), Tadeusz Różewicz, and many other artists turned out to be the biggest "interdisciplinary" success of Polish modernism.

The above-mentioned authors are among the most recognized writers of the early phase of high modernism in Poland, and their work serves as a consistent point of reference for all other writers of late modernism, including Gustaw Herling-Grudziński, Miron Białoszewski, Zbigniew Herbert, Wisława Szymborska, Sławomir Mrożek, and Stanisław Lem. From the perspective of the beginning of the twenty-first century, their work is not only a continuation of the Polish modernists' discussion with twentieth-century realizations of the idea of modernity, but – first and foremost – an original contribution to contemporary literature. While the inclusion of these writers in modernist literature does not raise any objections today, a similar inclusion of the writers who debuted after 1989 is contested. All debutants, after all, see themselves as soloists, with their place in the choir becoming clear only with time. The temporal distance separating critics from current literary events is too slight for us to use terms that belong to the history of literature. Nevertheless, it is possible to point out some general and typical phenomena in post-1989 literature that already speak to modernism's *longue durée*.

The basic attitude of young writers in the 1990s involved rejecting historical and social themes, which were seen as the "ballast" of literary tradition. Personal subjects that bore on the individual – for instance, familial, sexual, or lifestyle taboos – served as identifying marks of the new literature. Its determinants included corporeality, eroticism, psychological and gender differences, and the oppression of family life, as well as antipathy towards predominant value systems and towards social institutions (for instance, religion and education). Inspired by countercultural currents – for example, feminism – the works of these young writers opened new horizons and have attracted a large readership. From the perspective of modernism's history, however, the newness of this literature is paradoxical, since it repeats – under an entirely different set of conditions, of course – the gestures of the first modernists, who called for the liberation of individuals and of their subjectivities from domination by social discourses. After all, the intellectual masters of the '90s generation – such as Freud, Heidegger, Lacan, Gadamer, and Baudrillard – are among the great names of European modernism. Another characteristic of the newest literature is that its natural context has been that of a great wave of world literature translations for a number of decades now, and – since Poland's inclusion in the Schengen area – of the frequent travels of the young authors. The new literature is also distinguished by a freedom of experimentation not limited to language and artistic forms, but extending to changes in the media of literary communication. A significant portion of the new literature, along with its readers and critics, has moved onto the Internet.

Finally, among the other characteristics that can help define new Polish literature, one is of particular interest for revealing its relationship with modernist tradition in an unexpected way. The greatest works of modernism were anti-systemic, disturbing the dominant aesthetic order and world view. Their authors – despite their successes – were actually outsiders, rebels against the mainstream of their day. The best example here is Gombrowicz, a writer as modern as could be, who bucked the current of prevailing tastes with each of his works. Indeed, in his novel *Ferdydurke* (1937), he relentlessly mocked the mainstream, referring to its representatives as fledglings (Młodziaki). The best-known and most highly praised works of the newest Polish literature, meanwhile, are part of today's mainstream. This literature does not oppose that mainstream, but rather creates it. Its subjects, artistic techniques, experiments, even scandals, as well as its overall reception, do not signal individual or social rebellion, but rather membership in the cultural establishment.

This thought-provoking reversal of meanings, the transformation of modernist art's position in public life, is undoubtedly a consequence of the triumph of the marketplace and of the commercialization of literature. These phenomena were recognized as part of modernity very early on and they were subject to the modernists' constant critique throughout both early and high modernism. Modernism at the turn of the nineteenth and twentieth centuries made the "city-monster" into a symbol of the dangers that modernity posed to the individual and to culture. High modernism, especially the avant-garde, tamed this "monster" and even turned it into a cult object. The modernism from the turn of the twentieth and twenty-first centuries added a new experience to this mix – of the "marketplace-monster" that must consume fresh meat every morning, as it would in myth. The only difference is that today such sacrifice is made willingly.

Włodzimierz Bolecki
The Institute of Literary Research of the Polish
Academy of Sciences, Warsaw
Translated by Agnieszka Polakowska

NOTES

1 The First Commonwealth refers to the Polish–Lithuanian Commonwealth that existed from the sixteenth century until its third partition in 1795.

2 The Romantic period in Poland lasted, approximately, from 1822 to 1864.

3 Characteristically, young Polish poets defined their modernity as a continuation of Romanticism even in the 1960s and 1970s (for example, Stanisław Barańczak).

4 The Stanisław Małachowski speech, delivered on 3 May 1791, can be found in Siarczynski's *The Third of May, 1791*, 73. This source is also cited in Libiszowska, *Opinia polska wobec rewolucji amerykańskiej*, 136.

5 On 4 November 1794, in the course of a single day, more than 20,000 civilian residents of Praga, a district of Warsaw on the right bank of the Vistula, were massacred by Russian troops in the Battle of Praga (in Polish, the Praga Massacre).

6 American National Anthem (1814): "And the star-spangled banner in triumph shall wave / O'er the land of the free and the home of the brave!" French National Anthem (1792): "Allons enfants de la Patrie, / Le jour de gloire est arrivé. / Contre nous de la tyrannie / L'étendard sanglant est levé." Canadian National Anthem (1880): "From far and wide, O Canada, / We stand on guard for thee. / God keep our land glorious and free! / O Canada, we stand on guard for thee."

7 The title of Czesław Miłosz's book *Szukanie ojczyzny* (Looking for a Homeland; 1992), which gathers all of the themes present in his work, is telling in this context.

8 To compare, in the United States and Czechoslovakia (now the Czech Republic and Slovakia), women were granted the right to vote in 1920; in Sweden, 1921; in Great Britain and Northern Ireland, 1928; in Portugal and Spain, 1931; in France, 1944; in Yugoslavia, 1945; in India, Japan, and Mexico, 1947; in Switzerland, 1971; and in Liechtenstein, 1984.

9 This is the title of a book series published by Universitas in Kraków since 2004, and dedicated to modernism in Polish culture.

10 The term "poeticism" is used here in the Russian Formalists' sense, namely, as signalling an orientation towards the sign and its autotelicity, rather than towards connotation and cognitive function. In a typological sense, the poeticism of narration is a negation of realistic narration.

11 To name only Gombrowicz, Miłosz, Aleksander Wat (1900–67), Tadeusz Kantor (1915–90), Stanisław Lem (1921–2006), Gustaw Herling-Grudziński (1919–2000), and Herbert.

12 See Bolecki, *Modalności modernizmu*, 434–41.
13 See Miłosz, *Legendy nowoczesności*, and Herling-Grudziński, *Dziennik pisany nocą*, vol. 3 (for example, the entry from 5 May 1998).
14 Around half a million Jews survived the war, but only 100,000 under German occupation. According to historians, 220 out of every 1,000 citizens died during the Second World War in Poland. In comparison, Russia lost 116 people per every 1,000; Holland, 22; France, 15, the United Kingdom, 8; Belgium, 7; and the United States, 2.9. Among the educated classes, as a result of planned extermination actions by both the Soviet Union and the Third Reich (such as Intelligenzaktion, AB-Aktion, and the Katyn massacre), Poland lost 39 per cent of its doctors, 33 per cent of its teachers, 30 per cent of its scientists and post-secondary instructors (including 700 professors), 28 per cent of its clergy, and 26 per cent of its lawyers. The data pertaining to this subject are still being compiled. Among the most important sources are: Raul Hilberg, *The Destruction of the European Jews* (New Haven: Yale University Press, 2003); Jacek Leociak, "Liczba ofiar jako metafora w dyskursie publicznym o Zagładzie," in *Polska 1939–1945. Straty osobowe i ofiary represji pod dwiema okupacjami*, ed. Wojciech Materski and Tomasz Szarota (Warszawa: Instytut Pamięci Narodowej – Komisja Ścigania Zbrodni przeciwko Narodowi Polskiemu, 2009); Albert Stankowski and Piotr Weiser, "Demograficzne skutki Holokaustu," in *Następstwa zagłady Żydów. Polska 1944–2010*, ed. Feliks Tych and Monika Adamczyk-Garbowska (Lublin: Wydawn. Uniwersytet Marii Curie-Skłodowskiej: Żydowski Instytut Historyczny im. Emanuela Ringelbluma, 2011), 15–39; Krzysztof Persak, "Introduction," in *Zarys krajobrazu. Wieś polska wobec zagłady Żydów 1942–1945*, ed. Barbara Engelking and Jan Grabowski (Warszawa: Stowarzyszenie Centrum Badań nad Zagładą Żydów, 2011), 25–8; *German Crimes in Poland* by Central Commission for Investigation of German Crimes in Poland, 2007; *Polska 1939–1945. Straty osobowe i ofiary represji*, ed. Wojciech Materski, Tomasz Szarota (Warszawa: Instytut Pamięci Narodowej – Komisja Ścigania Zbrodni przeciwko Narodowi Polskiemu, 2009); Timothy Snyder, *Bloodlands: Europe between Hitler and Stalin* (New York: Basic Books, 2010); and Snyder, *Black Earth: The Holocaust as History and Warning* (New York: Tim Duggan Books, 2015). For an additional bibliography, see also https://en.wikipedia.org/wiki/Nazi_crimes_against_the_Polish_nation and https://en.wikipedia.org/wiki/World_War_II_casualties_of_Poland.
15 The data concerning these issues are still incomplete. See *Sprawozdanie w przedmiocie strat i szkód wojennych Polski w latach 1939–1945* (Warszawa: Biuro Odszkodowań Wojennych, 1947); *Problem reparacji, odszkodowań i świadczeń w stosunkach polsko-niemieckich*, ed. S. Dębski (Warszawa: Polski Instytut Spraw Międzynarodowych, 2004); and Włodzimierz Kalicki and Monika Kuhnke, *Sztuka zagrabiona: uprowadzenie Madonny* (Warszawa: Agora S.A., 2014). See also https://en.wikipedia.org/wiki/World_War_II_looting_of_Poland; https://pl.wikipedia.org/wiki/Grabież_polskich_dóbr_kultury_w_czasie_II_wojny_światowej; and https://pl.wikipedia.org/wiki/Straty_materialne_Polski_w_czasie_II_wojny_światowej.
16 The Stalinization of Polish culture had begun in 1939 in Lviv and in 1941 in Vilnius, after their occupation by the Soviet Union.

WORKS CITED

Bolecki, Włodzimierz. *Modalności modernizmu. Studia, Analizy, Interpretacje*. Warszawa: IBL, 2012.

Herling-Grudziński, Gustaw. *Dziennik pisany nocą*, vol. 3. Kraków: Wydawnictwo Literackie, 2012.
Libiszowska, Zofia. *Opinia polska wobec rewolucji amerykańskiej w XVIII wieku*. Wrocław: Zakład Narodowy im. Ossolińskich, 1962.
Miłosz, Czesław. *Legendy nowoczesności: eseje okupacyjne*. Kraków: Wydawnictwo Literackie, 1996.
– *Szukanie ojczyzny*. Kraków: Znak, 1992.
Siarczyński, Antoni, ed. *The Third of May, 1791*. Warszawa: Gröll Publishing, 1791.

The Modernist Formation of Polish Literature

Points of Departure: Geopolitics, Memory, Identity

Inquiries into modernism face the fundamental difficulty of identifying what this term denotes in a manner that not only secures the agreement of the majority of scholars interested in the modernist problematics, but also encompasses its basic – diverse, often contradictory, and sometimes mutually exclusive – artistic and ideological variants. These variants become apparent within the parameters of specific national literatures, as well as (and all the more so) in the realm of European or Western literature, as soon as one attempts a comparative study of modernism. In my estimation, facts speak in favour of approaching this difficulty not as something that needs to be overcome or neutralized (for this is impossible), but rather as a discursive characteristic of modernist literature.

No two modernisms are alike among different national literatures, and even in their multiplicity, if not in each of them individually, modernism is fuelled (forms itself and evolves) by a process of permanent exclusion and differentiation, through oppositions and contradictions that arise both from the specifics of its general, formational character and from local traditions and conditions. If there is an aspect of commensurability to be sought under these circumstances, it is on the same principle as was followed by scholars of (at first) folklore and (later) intertextuality and discourse in their search for an arche-text (i.e., an archetypal text). In all likelihood, its characteristics do not correspond to any concrete variant of a text, but rather encompass a "prototypical" – characterized by empirically grounded invariables – set of such variants.

The term "modernist formation" is widespread today and understood in a relatively agreed upon way; given its paramount position in this discussion, however, it demands at least a short historical commentary. The concept of modernism maintains here its hybrid nature, characterized by the persistent interaction of three notions: *modernity* (in a philosophical/cultural sense), *modernization* (in a civilizational/technological sense), and *modernism* (in an artistic/literary sense that, one might add, has many historical and geographical variants and an extremely complex conceptual semantic). In turn, the idea of a formation (discursive, intellectual, and literary) owes its fundamental ideological and semantic content to Michael Foucault's conceptualization of it. Inspiration is also drawn from sources that utilize this category in the Polish critical tradition, however, and in particular the legacy of Stanisław Brzozowski. His original conception of the specific rhetorics and poetics of culture, outlined at the beginning of twentieth century, posits them as a historical process of self-constituting and successively changing "cultural formations" (which he sometimes refers to as "spiritual formations"). Simplifying the matter, a modernist formation viewed from this perspective would be a way of conceptually grasping the whole of a culture, wherein the very manner in which the subject perceives itself and the world – meaning its key problematics and its means of conceptual/linguistic articulation, repertoire of social roles, behavioural scripts, and principles for constructing knowledge and world view assumptions (whether ontological, epistemological, or axiological) – is regulated and sanctioned through specific historical – in this case precisely modernist – constellations of discursive institutions.

In the case of Polish literature, the geopolitical background of the modernist formation is more than a set of its external contexts and cannot be excluded from its characterization. Suffice it to say that the constituting process of the modernist formation in Polish literature took place during the last decade of the nineteenth century and the first two decades of the twentieth, and thus during a period of political enslavement, when Polish lands and their inhabitants (including both writers and their audiences) were subject to the rule of three neighbouring countries (Austria, Prussia, and Russia). Consequently, they were subordinated to differing strategies of centre/periphery correlations, and to different models according to which knowledge and authority functioned, as well as to many variants (in form, intensity, and methods of instilling) of the idea of modernity, of modernizing progress, and of conceptualizing the very understanding of modernism in literature and art.

This geopolitical background affects a concrete (for instance, the initial) moment of a historico-literary process, besides constituting an inherent component of both the ideological and formal profile of modernist literature, and of its interpretive and experiential understanding. Two facts need to be kept in mind here. First, for some seventy years of the twentieth century (until 1918 and again from 1939 to 1989), Polish literature was written, published, and received in the absence of national, and consequently also individual and communal, independence. Second, the shift in Poland's state borders that took place as a result of the Second World War drastically altered its prewar territory and ethnic composition, which dramatically affected the situation of Polish writers and readers. Given that literature and especially modern literature not only articulates but also shapes human experience, these facts had many significant consequences.

I will point out four phenomena that are, in my view, of fundamental importance. The first is the community and nation-building function that the novel in particular played after the restoration of Poland's independence in 1918 (which had its extensions or mutations after the Second World War). The non-existence of a Polish state impeded the process of forming a modern national consciousness, which had begun at the turn of the twentieth century.[1] It also affected the role the novel played at that time in "inventing traditions" of the nation. The restoration of independence in 1918 brought with it an intense acceleration of this process, in which literature (the novel in particular, but also reportage and journalism) would play a more significant part. Simply put, the historical value and rank of the novel and prose of the 1920s (and to some extent the 1930s as well) was determined precisely by its function of forming an imagined national community.[2]

The second phenomenon is the deep division of Polish literature into national and emigrant streams (1939–89), obsolescent for the past two decades but still to this day a considerable challenge for literary historians.[3] Their positions were not symmetrical (emigrant literature defined itself in relation to the national one, but not vice versa); they had for several decades distinct publishing houses, channels of communication, and spheres of cultural life, as well as separate canonical writers and circles of readers.[4] The geopolitical changes of 1989 made this division historical, thus annulling – as befits the mobile contemporary world – the political charge of one's chosen place of residence.

The third phenomenon is the eruption of diverse literature thematically oriented towards working through the losses and legitimizing the gains of Poland's twentieth-century history. Most recently, this literature has been seeking a formula to describe the ongoing processes of hybridization and the palimpsestic layering of cultural memories, including those pertaining to ethnicity, territory, and identity. At stake here is literature of the "borderlands," which activates the memory of the lost eastern territories of the Second Polish Republic, as well as literature of "small homelands," anticipated by the myth of the harmonious coexistence of individuals and communities in a multi-ethnic Austrio-Hungarian Empire.[5] Also at issue is the literature of the "Recovered Territories" (in the northern and western regions of Poland following the Second World War), where official memory politics were invested in constructing an image of homogenous Polishness founded on the myth of the return of ancient Piast lands to the homeland. With increasing intensity, these politics are being confronted with images of the palimpsestically interwoven multi-ethnic and multi-cultural past and present of these lands. Finally, Holocaust writing is also under consideration here, along with the interest it generates in Polish-Jewish literature and its traditions and, more generally, in narrations about relations between the dominant (Polish) community and other ethnic minorities.

The fourth phenomenon is the significant role of political censorship, especially up until 1918 and during the postwar period of 1945–90.[6] Its role constitutes strong proof of the invasive effect of politics on national literature; at the same time, it testifies to the influence of political censorship on the character and social status of literature, the conventions of literature's reception and understanding, and the position of the writer. Generally speaking, such censorial oppression gave literature high social rank as a discourse contesting the heavily rationed freedom of speech in the public realm; it also bestowed on the writer the missionary role of standing for the "non-literary" values of freedom, truth, and justice. It inclined the reader, moreover, to an "Aesopian" mode of reading, one that was sensitive to all manner of uncensored meanings that could be derived from the text through the process of allegorical or allusive interpretation.

Putting it briefly, the significance of these geopolitical factors stems from the fact that they are actual components of this literature's poetics, since they influence both choices relating to form, genre, rhetoric, and style, and preferences relating to thematics, ideology, aesthetics, and world view. Moreover, they allow us to understand the reasons behind the dominance of memory and identity problematics in contemporary Polish literature, in part because the question of identity – in its simplest and most popular form – is a question of where one belongs. To the question of "Who am I?" (Who are you?), the hero, narrator, or author attempts to provide an answer that is actually responding to a different question: "Where am I from?" (Where are you from?). From which nation, culture, class, profession, and family do I/you descend? With which community, cultural traditions and values, traumatic or great experiences, and symbolic imaginarium am I/are you bound up to an extent that proves decisive in its impact on our way of living, thinking, and acting? In this process of arriving at self-knowledge, the categories of memory and identity prove to be tangled together. The question of identity activates the work of memory, which unearths the layers of traumatic experiences, choices, and genealogical traces that are supressed in the course of daily life. The opposite is also true, however: brooding on the past actualizes the problem of identity (individual and communal) and inclines us to question our identity anew.

Yet this does not mean that this background of geopolitics, memory, and identity confines the significance and influence of Polish literature to the hermetic, local circle of a community that shares in these types of experiences. As is the case with other literatures, this specificity has at least three dimensions. The first is idiosyncratic, to which access is gained through communal experience (as was known already to Goethe, who wrote that if one wishes to understand an author, it is necessary to travel to his country). The second is comparative and marries a given local literature to transcultural currents of world literature (created under conditions of political oppression and the Holocaust experience; characterized as exilic, migrational, and hybrid in its identity). Whereas the third is "glocal": a dimension both global and local, in which a universal problematic realizes itself in a concrete, local form within a network of real, historical conditions. Hence the following theoretical conclusion: historical, cultural poetics should also become the poetics of geopolitics.

Models of Culture

Modern literature formed and transformed itself in a realm of broader historical processes, transcultural transformations, and models of progress. To simplify the matter, these processes can be subordinated to three main models of culture, which determine – even today, albeit to differing degrees – its status and substantive characteristics and functions. The classic model of culture during the time of Polish modernity, which began to lose its central position before mid-twentieth century and is gradually becoming historical today, can be called the literary model. Within its scope, it was the literary text and canon that determined the paradigmatic model of symbolic culture, giving shape to and ensuring the stability of the cultural imaginarium (binding for individuals and communities), and installing at its centre producers and advocates of its values: critics, scholars, and intellectuals.

The next cultural model – audiovisual – developed at an accelerated pace during the first half of the twentieth century, when two earlier inventions – the printing press (fifteenth century) and photographic film (nineteenth century) – were quickly joined by film, magnetic tape, gramophone records, and video. One of the most important characteristics they all share is the emphasis placed on the specificity of the medium,[7] which determines their disciplinary distinctiveness and the range and limitations of their delivery, as well as their accessibility and the appropriate reception of their transmission – in other words, the conditions for registering, preserving, reproducing, and disseminating on a mass scale what seems to be antecedent to and independent of these media: events that transpire in the realm of sensory experience (in real time and space).

It is perhaps this aspect that distinguishes the last model – cyberculture – from the preceding ones: digitalization constitutes a common language for transmissions previously differentiated through their media, thus marginalizing the specific conditions of the medium. Records of narrations, images, and sounds can be created as a result of recording and processing real events in the physical realm as much as they can be the effect of electronic production. This world, it seems, is less a world of media than a world of mediation, with its specific ontological status. Here, mediation is no longer (if it ever really was) a neutral environment for the transmission of something that is antecedent and independent of it; rather, mediation develops what it mediates, shaping the characteristics and forms of contrasting or oppositional elements.[8]

Without delving into the details of this complex situation, I can merely note here that each of these models assigns a different place and role to literature. Simply put, the dynamics of modernism's development are determined by a rivalry between the literary/humanistic model of culture and the audiovisual/specialized one. The key to understanding the audiovisual/specialized model is the differentiating significance of the medium's specificity, which offers a privileged (and perhaps the sole) point of access to the content of a transmission. From this is derived the belief in the autonomous status of a literary text (meaning its independence from genesis, context, authorial intention, and readerly stance) and its essentially fictive quality, along with the (related to it) suspension of its referentiality and perhaps even its cognitive function. Both will become the leading assumptions of the autonomous model of literature and art. Its development takes place as the model of modern audiovisual culture is being formed, wherein it is precisely the specificity of the medium – "the languages of art" – that decide on the identity and distinctiveness of the disciplines of cultural creation. The first, literary/humanistic model, in turn, takes on a new form within the parameters of the modernist formation, becoming a model of engaged literature (art) first as a rival of the autonomous model, and then as its partner, if not its frame of reference, yet all the while maintaining the status of a compass of literary and cultural transformations.

The third model (cybercultural) has only recently begun to make its presence known, and its holistic, not to say totalizing, character certainly engenders diverse and significant consequences that are, however, still difficult to predict. Its main characteristics relate to authorship, changes in the function of the author and forms of publication and circulation, the disappearance of some genres and the emergence of others, and a transformed understanding of the literary text as merely a component of a hybrid, multi-medium product – an open record that is susceptible to change and produced also by its readers. This last characteristic calls into question the tenets of a theory of interpretation that builds its conceptualizations and methodological procedures with reference to a closed and final text-as-object, leading also to changes in the role of the textual recipient.

Models of Literature

Another problem to consider in our inquiries into modernism is posed by the very scope of modernist literature, even in its most basic understanding. Has the concept of literature that functioned during the twentieth century exhausted itself in the traditional understanding of *belles-lettres* – "fine" literature – particularly in the sense of autonomous, artistic fiction? Going further: Was the scope of this concept constant? And if it did undergo revision in line with the transformations of modern literature, does not the grasping of this evolution in a historical perspective require us to consider these corrections and dislocations from the very beginning of the process, meaning also the time when it still had the character of nascent, hardly visible tendencies? Finally: Is this meaning not equally and substantively impacted by the changing methods of understanding, interpreting, and reading literature? And if this is difficult to deny, is it not necessary to agree that this understanding of literature is part of literature itself? This line of questioning, in turn, leads to the realization that knowledge and study of literature (and thus also the writing of the history of literature) is a never-ending activity. This does not mean, however, that it is arbitrary.

Without engaging in a detailed discussion of this crucial and complex issue, I nevertheless want to signal the trajectory of its argument, which has as its point of departure the recognition that mediated understanding is characteristic of the humanities in general. We have direct access neither to the past, nor to that which precedes conceptualization, nor to that which is singular. This means that the tools of humanistic inquiry (models, theories, conceptual frameworks, methods and techniques of discursive organization of data, ways of reading) play the function of mediators of knowledge. Cultural reality is written, so to speak – Adorno *dixit* – on the instruments of knowledge; it is accessible only in a shape formed and profiled by mediating procedures of inquiry.[9]

Likewise with literature: from the perspective of our actual knowledge of the subject and the preferred network of critical concepts and situational and contextual frameworks that condition our ways of reading, we activate a meaning that is retroactively assigned to the studied text. New methods of reading bring with them new vocabularies, which allow us to formulate different questions and to obtain different answers regarding the text. For this reason, a comprehensive, all-encompassing, and final interpretation does not (and cannot) exist. Each such interpretation is perspectival; each makes the subject accessible while forming it in accordance with accepted categories and contextual frameworks. In the final analysis, each occupies a place in a retrospectively constructed typography of interpretations.[10]

History of literature seen from this point of view, therefore, is always also a history of its interpretations, constantly written anew while actualizing and providing insight into ever-changing historical constellations of contextual relations that establish meanings, choices, hierarchies, and connections among its various elements. This is tellingly exemplified by the invasion of new theories, methods, and critical orientations since 1989 (including feminist criticism, gender studies, memory studies, cultural studies, and postcolonial studies). It has led to significant changes in the image of twentieth-century Polish literature – including its characteristics and meanings, and the hierarchies between its movements and creators – and consequently also to a shift in understanding of what this literature, its specificity and its modernism, was about.

My reading of Polish twentieth-century literature, from the threshold of the second decade of the twenty-first century, considers the consequences of such a position. One of the most challenging of these is the dissonance between the historicity of current events at the time they occurred and our retrospective grasp of their their logic and hierarchy. Both these historicities belong to the history of literature and have their own place and specificity within that history. The first one, the historicity of the process, creates a realm of potentialities (things initiated but not accomplished) that can nevertheless change their status – for instance, when cast in the role of a precursory accomplishment, from the perspective of a future literary evolution and new ways of reading (when, as Borges has noted, a great author will appear who will create his own precursors). The second historicity, of cultural products, does not have a secured position in the historico-literary order for the same reasons; a future artistic and interpretive constellation can lead to their marginalization and even exclusion from a new canon of the history of literature.

It is impossible, in any case, to grasp these two processes simultaneously. Likewise, it is impossible to describe or explain "it all": all of the adjusted borders, nuanced dislocations, local or temporal divergences or diversifications in the evolutionary process ...

Given this situation, I propose that we look at Polish literature of the twentieth century using literary and (subsequently) discursive models, which laid out together will serve as a "road map," so to speak. They are meant to ensure the identification of main, causal factors (rules, institutional orders of discourse) that can aid our orientation in this challenging terrain; and to allow us to grasp singular or locally unique characteristics in typical, perhaps even universal categories. Clearly, this approach is not free of simplifications and schematizations; to the contrary, it assumes them to be necessary to the process. In the name of a representative model, it sacrifices idiomatic and unique characteristics of works and the complexities of particular oeuvres, movements, and tendencies. By delineating an inner space of possibility, however, it allows us to consider parts of these "potentialities" and to grasp the changing dynamic of a historico-literary process.

From this idealized perspective, let us assume that modern literature was evolving through a process of differentiation – in other words, in the course of creating and eliminating successive oppositions that initially allowed for its demarcation and distinctiveness and that were subsequently assimilated and internalized by it. Both the most significant and the most general among these oppositions concerned the very concept of literature – its specificity, position, and function. This is the case, first and foremost, with the binary pairs of elite and popular (mass) literature and of autonomous and engaged (instrumental) literature.[11] By setting the parameters within which modern understanding of literature as an institution is constituted, both of these binary oppositions are crucial as categories of its analysis.

This constituting process took place on the cusp of the nineteenth and twentieth centuries, which is to say at a moment when modern variants of literature – autonomous on the one hand, and popular on the other – were crystallizing and becoming independent from each other. Both variants were components of literature's key aesthetic and ideological alternatives that were up until then "missing" from the Polish literary tradition, since it had previously functioned within the framework of an elite and engaged model. Considered together, these two oppositional orders determined both the scope of diversification of artistic forms and the internal stratification of literary discourses, in effect allowing us to identify the basic types of literary models (as well as styles of criticism and forms of communication networks).

Given the object of this discussion, my examples and systematizing propositions are limited to modern Polish literature in terms of the content and scope of this concept, as well as its historical exemplifications. That being said, I believe that my conclusions have a broader application and can be related to the status and specificity of literary modernism as it functions in the realm of European cultural traditions. The already mentioned key binary conceptualizations of literature as autonomous versus engaged and elite versus popular influenced the formation of the following four models of modern Polish literature during the first decades of the twentieth century. Their exemplification here is purely illustrative.

A. The Elite and Autonomous Model

Its examples include the work of authors of "high modernism," such as Bolesław Leśmian, Stanisław Ignacy Witkiewicz, Bruno Schulz, Witold Gombrowicz, Czesław Miłosz, Gustaw Herling-Grudziński, Zbigniew Herbert, and Wisława Szymborska; the ideologically non-instrumental work of avant-garde artists such as Julian Przyboś, Adam Ważyk, Józef

Czechowicz, Bogdan Czaykowski, Miron Białoszewski, Sławomir Mrożek, and Tadeusz Różewicz; the experimental psychological prose of Zofia Nałkowska, Maria Kuncewiczowa, Leopold Buczkowski, Andrzej Kuśniewicz, Kazimierz Brandys, and Włodzimierz Odojewski; the hermetic current in the work of the Skamander group poets, among them Kazimierz Wierzyński, Julian Tuwim, and Jarosław Iwaszkiewicz; and the criticism of Karol Irzykowski, Jerzy Kwiatkowski, and Jan Błoński.

B. The Elite and Engaged Model

This category encompasses, among others, the avant-garde's programmatic, engaged work by Tadeusz Peiper, Brunon Jasieński, and Aleksander Wat; the critical and socially engaged prose of Andrzej Strug, Tadeusz Borowski, Józef Mackiewicz, Jerzy Andrzejewski, and Tadeusz Konwicki; the work of the "Generation '68" poets such as Stanisław Barańczak, Ryszard Krynicki, and Adam Zagajewski; and the criticism of Stanisław Brzozowski, Kazimierz Wyka, and Artur Sandauer.

C. The Popular and Engaged Model (Instrumental)

Here belong literary forms of the interwar period such as the traditional, artistically conventional poetry of left-wing sympathizers (Władysław Broniewski) and/or right-wing sympathizers (Konstanty I. Gałczyński); the literary work of ideologues from both sides of the political spectrum; and the criticism of Stanisław Baczyński (on the "leftist" hand) and of Zygmunt Wasilewski (on the right-wing side). This model also encompasses the larger part of national literature created under the communist regime.

D. The Popular and Autonomous Model

This category includes phenomena such as the popular–ludic poetic work of the Skamander group; the postwar poetry of Konstanty I. Gałczyński; the prewar popular sensationalist novels of manners by Ferdynand Ossendowski, Sergiusz Piasecki, and Tadeusz Dołęga Mostowicz; Leopold Tyrmand's postwar *Zły* (The Man with the White Eyes, 1955); the science fiction writing of Stanisław Lem; and the literary criticism of Tadeusz Boy-Żeleński. Popular literature has been developing especially dynamically since the 1960s.

It should be emphasized that the position of dominance among these models, using a yardstick of aesthetic and artistic measure, was eventually attained by the first (elite and autonomous) model, after a prolonged rivalry for this position with the elite and engaged model (this rivalry is usually discussed as a duel between modernist Classicism and the modernist avant-garde). The remaining two models were not yet sufficiently well crystallized and did not produce (according to each model's accepted canons) worthwhile literary phenomena; throughout the first decades of the twentieth century, therefore, they served only as the background of the rivalry between the elite (autonomous versus engaged) models. It is only since the 1960s that the popular models have begun to attain positions parallel to those of the first two elite models. This stratification of literary practices and programs has gradually been blurring as a result of the geopolitical, civilizational, and cultural transformations that took place after 1989. It has not been replaced, however, by new models of writing. It is thus difficult to characterize literary phenomena of the past two decades using these four models of practising and understanding literature; nevertheless, they serve as an important framework for characterizing current literary developments.

It is for this reason that one of these models – elite/autonomous – functions in the following discussion as an actual and historical point of reference for the concept of modernist literature. It is precisely this model that served as the prototype for modernist literature and as the main frame of reference for introducing literary changes. Consequently, such "modernized" understanding of modernism has, in the final analysis, a double-meaning: the broader meaning of an overarching concept of a literary, artistic, and cultural formation, and a narrower meaning of a configuration of prototypical qualities of modernist literature, as exemplified by the elite/autonomous model of modern literature.

Models of Literary Discourses: Introductory Remarks

My opening hypothesis is that modern literature (as specified earlier) was exposed to the increasing influence of diverse forms and genres of non-fictional prose almost from the onset of the twentieth century. Among those forms and genres, three types of non-fictional writing were foundational: intimate-autobiographical prose, journalistic-documentary prose, and essays. Admittedly, this writing was initially situated "outside" of literature (in its standard, traditional understanding), but with the passage of time it gained both in artistic merit and in popularity among readers.

One of the most problematic issues in this context concerns the genre status of these types of writing. Their unquestionable impact on literature (especially on the novel), in conjunction with their rising aesthetic and intellectual status, has inspired in-depth studies devoted exclusively to particular types of this writing and produced new definitions of contemporary literary genres (fictional and non-fictional), using characteristics that are often a clear departure from the traditional genre categorizations of *belles-lettres* literature.[12]

A consideration of the century-long evolution of these (currently considered literary) forms and of the history of their relations will allow us to form hypotheses that are more far-reaching and that will reverse our initial assumptions about these relations. For it can be said from the perspective adopted here that the evolution of modern literature had three phases:

a. *The first phase*: the determination of the specificity of the dominant discourse of modern literature as that of autonomous fiction of "high artistic merit" and the emergence of three types of non-fictional writing (with the status of fictionality being tied more to the discursive characteristics of elite/autonomous literature than to its genre markers, as is shown below);
b. *The second phase*: the differentiation of these four discourses as relatively autonomous types of (literary and non-literary) writing and the transformations that each underwent as a result of their interplay; and
c. *The third (late or postmodern) phase*: the redefinition of literature as an institutionalized discursive discipline with characteristics co-determined by the properties of the four discourses and the results of their evolutionary changes and interactions.

Having discussed the autonomous discourse of "high literature" as the prototypical variant of modern literature, it is now time to consider examples as well as the breadth of non-fictional discourses in Polish twentieth-century literature. To start, each type of non-fictional writing derives its genealogy from the oldest of traditions – documentary forms from travel journals, autobiographic forms from ancient autobiographical genres, essayistic forms from the heritage of rhetoric and meditation. It goes without saying, however, that the turn of the twentieth century brought new initiatives within each of these fields that inaugurated substantially different and precisely modern forms of such writing, which were legitimated as such by the institutions of literature.

To anchor this in concrete examples, the documentary current of writing in its main variant – modern reportage – was inaugurated in Polish literature by Władysław S. Reymont's *Pielgrzymka do Jasnej Góry* (Pilgrimage to Jasna Góra, 1895). This was a peculiar inauguration, for there was no shortage of significant antecedents during the nineteenth century (from Kraszewski to Prus). The beginning of the twentieth century was an opportune time for the development of reportage due to the influence of the new mass press, with the period of the First World War providing numerous and interesting materials of the journalistic and documentary variety. The interwar period, in turn, witnessed the flourishing of this type of writing in the works of Konrad Wrzos and Wanda Melcer, and especially of Ksawery Pruszyński and Melchior Wańkowicz. Finally, the Second World War furthered this development, which during the postwar period (on the cusp of the 1960s and 1970s) raised this type of writing to the status of literature, mainly as a result of the outstanding achievements of Kazimierz Moczarski, Ryszard Kapuściński, Hanna Krall, and Henryk Grynberg.

The second current of autobiographic writing, in its key variant – the modern, intimate diary – begins with Stefan Żeromski's *Dzienniki* (Diaries, 1882) and continues with those of Karol Irzykowski (from 1891), Zofia Nałkowska (from 1899), Henryk Elzenberg (from 1907), Bronisław Malinowski (from 1908) and Stanisław Brzozowski (from 1913). Many of these authors kept a diary right up until their death, sometimes over decades – until the 1940s for Irzykowski, the 1950s for Nałkowska's, the 1960s for Elzenberg. With the passage of time, the same diaristic activity would be taken up in different formats by the authors and intellectuals of younger generations (including Maria Dąbrowska, Jan Lechoń, Witold Gombrowicz, Czesław Miłosz, Adolf Rudnicki, Jerzy Andrzejewski, Andrzej Bobkowski, Gustaw Herling-Grudziński, Sławomir Mrożek, and Miron Białoszewski). This process intensified and took on new forms after the 1950s, when – with the publication of Gombrowicz's *Diary* – the taboo of privacy precluding the publication of this type of writing while its author or characters are still alive was broken.

If the typical modern prose writer practises both fiction and diary writing (sometimes erasing the distinction between them), then this process is only now coming to an end as far as publishing is concerned, with the posthumous appearance of intimate diaries by writers of earlier generations. Among the more recent generations of writers, however, the diary has lacked appeal in a structural sense; within the framework of contemporary cyberculture, maintaining a blog or a Facebook page has become the equivalent of the earlier form, even though its unique characteristics cannot be compared with the former practice and demand an entirely different critical vocabulary.

The third current – of essayistic writing undertaken with awareness of practising a separate type of modern intellectual/literary discourse – commenced with the texts of Stanisław Przybyszewski (*Zur Psychologie des Individuums. I. Chopin und* Nietzsche, 1892), Stanisław Brzozowski (*My młodzi* [*We, the Young*], 1902), and Karol Irzykowski (*Pałuba* [*The Hag*], 1903). The 1920s were a time of the "invasion of the essay" – a period of growth and outstanding achievements in this genre, as exemplified by the works of Jerzy Stempowski and Bolesław Miciński. Since then, the popularity and literary status of the essay form has been rising steadily, as exemplified by the writing of Józef Wittlin, Stanisław Vincenz, Józef Czapski, and Leszek Kołakowski; it has been treated on par with fictional literary texts since the turn of the 1960s and 1970s, as exemplified by the works of Czesław Miłosz, Zbigniew Herbert, Jan Kott, Andrzej Dobosz, Włodzimierz Paźniewski, and Adam Zagajewski.

The above brief historical typology signals the scale, abundance, and significance of these non-fictional modes of writing, which were the closest neighbour of (fictional) literature at the beginning of the twentieth century. During the period of late modernism (1930–1950s/60s), non-fictional literary practices interacted both with high literature and with one another. This process transformed their genre indicators and in later years permeated, so to speak, the zone of fictional literature, thus transforming its traits, status, and definition. It goes without saying that each of these types of writing is marked by great internal diversification and evolutionary dynamism, which unfortunately I have to put aside here.[13] I also cannot pay sufficient attention to the fact that each of them has its equivalents in other national literatures; within their scope, the period of modernity and postmodernity has been characterized by significant kinship of the tendencies discussed here, even though they are realized differently in each case. In the face of this kinship, assessing the theoretical consequences of such shared tendencies is an intriguing undertaking as well as an important one.

Four Discourses of Modern Literature (Thesis I)

What I have proposed so far is meant to buttress a summary justification of three general and a few more detailed theses. Within the framework of each model that I have discussed (elite/autonomous; elite/engaged; popular/autonomous; and popular/engaged), modern literature is characterized by the interplay of four kinds of discourses. Due to its prototypical character in the process of forming the specific traits of literature as an institution in the period of modernity (and to a certain degree postmodernity), subsequent remarks are limited to the elite/autonomous model. The first general thesis is that modern literature forms and transforms its traits from within in the process of interaction of four discourses: fictional, documentary, autobiographical, and essayistic. I call these types of writing discourses because: they constitute forms of socially institutionalized types of practice with culturally specific rules and conditions; are more than genre-specific (since, according to the traditional classification, each of them contains a cluster of various genres); and are marked by a situational and articulational specificity.

Fictional discourse is a modern discourse of literature as an autonomous institution that is characterized by (a) the separation of textual references from the pre-textual sphere of reality, and thus the suspension of the utterance's referentiality (intransitivity); (b) the separation of the empirical author from the source of (textual) utterance (depersonalization); (c) the separation of authorial intention and cognitive conceptualization from textual meaning – the fusion of the medium with the message makes the semantic content of the text untranslatable and inarticulable in another language, including the functional one (unparaphrasability), for which reason the text loses its usual cognitive character.

Documentary discourse (journalistic, testimonial) has as its key characteristic the phenomenon of displaced or reversed referentiality, which involves transferring the burden of making and legitimating a reference from the object to the subject. The reference of the text to reality and the relationship of the work to the world is accomplished here due to the text's status as subjective testimony: not through symbolic (sign-based) representation, but through indexical participation; not due to the correspondence between, or representation of, objects of utterance and objects in the world of everyday life, but through the participation of the subject in both realms – through the subject's act of witnessing, which authenticates what is said with the truth of its own (point of) view.

Autobiographical discourse (intimistic, memoiristic): I regard the undermining of the traditional, essentializing conceptualization of the subject as its most significant characteristic. Modern autobiographical discourse testifies to the fact that the articulation of truth about a subject and its status reveals the processual nature of subjective identity as well as its co-constitution through language (discursive practice). The subject's self-knowledge of its own identity is not a matter of verbal declaration of a hidden (but determined in advance and in another place) essence of its personality, or of externalizing the internal truth about its own distinctiveness and integrity, which is pre-existent and independent of articulation. Rather, it is first and foremost the result of self-creation in the art of narration. The essence of the subject is revealed to be a narrativization of an individual's existential experiences and the effect of negotiation of its self-perception in midst of social interactions with others, which are mediated by signs.

Essayistic discourse: In my view, its main characteristic is the thorough transformation of the relation between an idea and a word, between thought and language. My thesis is that the modern essay is born together with the notion – inspired in part by the philosophical writings of Nietzsche and Bergson – that thought is not something that precedes and is independent of language, and that literary means of articulation are not simply an additional, rhetorically "ornamental" way of recording thought. In modern essayistic discourse, the thought process is revealed to be inseparable from the process of linguistic articulation. Thinking is, so to speak, an internalized act of speaking; knowledge is interpretation; truth is a process, a search.

Consequences: Redefinition Traditional Understanding of Literature (Thesis II)

Viewed from this perspective, the redefinition of the *belles-lettres* concept of literature is most easily grasped with reference to the early modernist framing of literature as autonomous fiction of high artistic merit, since each of the three listed aspects of this modern understanding of literature changes its characteristics under the influence of one of the non-fictional discourses (Thesis II):

- The trait of suspended referentiality is weakened as a result of the penetration of the literary text by the characteristics of documentary discourse and by the display of a subject-based bond between the text and the world (which earlier usually remained hidden behind the curtain of artistic representation). We are dealing here with a shifted or "testimonial" referentiality;
- The trait of depersonalization of a text and withdrawal of the authorial subject is transformed through interaction with conventions and strategies of the

autobiographical discourse. As a consequence, both the forms of presentation of the textual subject in modern literature and the dominant conceptualizations of human subjectivity change. We are dealing here with an acknowledgment of the social, cultural, and thus also linguistic and discursive nature of the human being, who has always partaken in both the physical and the discursive aspects of his or her existence. The distinctiveness and integrity of such a being are formed by a process of dialogically acquired self-knowledge and the concept of "narrative identity";
- The trait of extreme idiosyncrasy (impossibility of paraphrasing) of the literary text and of its semantic autonomy changed to some extent under the influence of the essayistic discourse. This discourse impacted and supplemented the (separate) fictional discourse; it also transformed the character of literature as a whole as a result of restoring literary discourse to the status of a legitimate medium of knowledge. This pertains especially to those aspects of cultural reality that are overlooked, stifled, or marginalized by non-literary discourses. We are dealing here, on the one hand, with the recognition of literature's figurative language as an experimental cognitive device (rather than a supplementary ornament), and on the other hand, with understanding the development of a literary discourse in terms of an inventive process of intellectual inquiry (rather than just a verbal description of prelinguistically produced knowledge).

Accepting that the semantic range of modern literature encompasses four fundamental discourses (one fictional and three non-fictional) that became more closely interwoven over the course of the twentieth century, which transformed their existing traits and genre characteristics, does not mean we are contending with some new, monolithic, and homogenous strategy of literary writing. On the contrary, inner hybridization is taking place within each of these discourses. Moreover and just as importantly, it is clear that in its own distinct way each of them is becoming the carrier/mediator – sometimes as an engaged promoter, sometimes as an emancipatory, critical, or even subversive explorer – of the memory and identity problematics raised at the outset of this discussion.

Generally speaking, modern literature as a cultural and discursive institution was born (much the same way as art) under the programmatic banner of differentiation. Such differentiation was oriented towards eliminating foreign elements from specific (essential?) characteristics of the discipline at hand (poetry aimed to be "pure poetry"; fine art, "pure art"; music, "pure music"), and excluding anything "impure." In the subsequent phase, modern literature developed through the process of inclusive absorption, internalization, and assimilation of what previously had been considered external, foreign, and impure. In the third phase, modern literature not only acquiesced to the progressive hybridization of its own techniques and practices, but also discovered that the purity to which it had aspired was no more than a doctrinal utopia or a nostalgically recalled myth. Paraphrasing Bruno Latour, it could be said that in this postmodern (or late modern) period, modern literature became aware that it was never really modern.

Points of Arrival: Modernity at the Core (as the "Kernel") of Postmodernity (Thesis III)

I contend that postmodern literature is a consequence of the evolution of the discourses of literary modernity, which constitute less its constant frame of reference than an indispensible component of its inner character. The specific manner of modern literature's development, wherein successive external oppositions were transformed into internal differentiations (from "either/or" to "also/as well as"), has led to the assimilation of traits characterizing competing forms of writing, and especially of significant characteristics of the engaged and popular literature models. The point of view adopted here has limited the scope of inquiry essentially to "high" or elite/autonomous literature. This is justified to the extent that modern literature (in its narrow meaning) has defined itself through oppositions, in other words through that which it wanted to be distinguished from. In this case, it has defined its identity through a conscious opposition to popular or mass culture on the one hand, and, on the other, to literature that is engaged, or instrumentalized through ideology and power, as well as through traditional justifications of literary calling that are often specific to a given ethnocultural community. Recall here, however, that this was inadequate insofar as literature's autonomy vis-à-vis mass culture as well as its politicization (or "politicality") were revealed over time to be forms of internal opposition that – in being built and subsequently overcome – affected the evolution of all of modern literature (in its broad understanding). It was, moreover, the breakdown of this very opposition that became one of the clearest symptoms of modernity's crisis (and of the development of postmodern poetics).

This process replaced the rule of exclusiveness – of defining distinctiveness through exclusion and differentiation – with the rule of inclusiveness, whereby specificity is defined through coexistence and the interweaving of heterogeneous rules, competing traditions, and alternative poetics. Among other things, this means that the characteristics of modern literature constitute the "kernel" – the most deeply internalized part – of the creative output of postmodernity (Thesis III).

To conclude, a note on the three general tendencies that resulted from the evolution of twentieth-century literature is in order. First, the ontological status of literature changed over the course of the twentieth century, and along with it the scope and semantic content of *belles-lettres*, which is no longer defined through immanent characteristics that constitute the essence of an exemplary literary work of art, an essence understood ahistorically and aculturally, but rather through stable – within the framework of a given historical and cultural formation – institutional criteria for attaining the status of "literariness." Let us remember that the opposition between essentialist and institutional ways of defining literature was present from the onset of the twentieth century (the latter, for example, in the notion of "canonization" as conceptualized by Yury Tynyanov and Viktor Shklovsky). The evolution of twentieth-century literature involved a transition from its essentialist to its institutional conceptualization; whereas the former conceptualization assigned a marginal, eccentric character to the idea of institutionalization, the latter, in becoming dominant, now sometimes defines its essentialist counterpart as the substantialization of institutionalization.

The second change that must be noted concerns the status of literature as an object of literary study. It is no longer treated like a linguistic system – as a normative system of genres and types of speech, a specific system of linguistic and aesthetic rules – but rather as a field of linguistic discourse, a practice that is socially or culturally codified. Discourse is defined here in the most general way as an institutionalized – within the framework of a given historical and cultural/literary community, discipline of knowledge, political structure, and so on – social means of using language, and thus as a specific type of utterance rather than a concrete discursive practice. The opposition between literature as language and literature as discourse also appeared on the threshold of the twentieth century, in the guise of the emblematic opposition between poetry as a "language within a language" (a systematic construction) and poetry as a linguistic heterology (a colloquial/conversational constellation). Moreover, its evolution also culminated in a reversal of hierarchy – from the primacy of an autotelic construction to the primacy of a polyphonic heterology arising from and based in the universe of discourse.

Third, the pragmatic status of literature underwent profound changes within the scope of literature's pre- and extra-literary environments and the realm of its object, subject, and "situational" references. As a consequence, socio-psychological, historico-political, and cultural contexts ceased to be treated as areas extrinsic to the closed and autonomous field of literature. Instead they became its necessary, intrinsic dimension and a legitimate component of the discursive discipline of literature. The history of the oppositional categories of autonomy and engagement, which appeared in various incarnations throughout the twentieth century and set the pattern of antagonistic forces within the main current of literary transformations, makes tangible this transformation. Paradoxically, although these forces were oppositional, they both assumed that literature is situated vis-à-vis reality, from which they could isolate themselves or towards which they could strive, and which they could represent, counter, or reflect.

With time, this position was rendered susceptible to rapid corrosion or even implosion within the contemporary sociocultural reality subjected to the rule of mass media and global communication. As a result, it transformed into a position in which literature was a mediated (and media-dominated) discursive discipline that belonged to or was affiliated with the discursive universe of cultural reality. Some will see this as proof of literature's intransitivity – its lack of access to the "other side"; others will consider it a human form of contact with reality, a means of forming and accessing it; others still will look at it as a form of truth (understood not as a reflection but as the *property* of literature) and as an articulation of contemporary experience. This experience is based in the sensation of constant oscillation between belonging and disorientation – simultaneous rootedness and estrangement – arising from immersion in the non-transparent realm of alien, incomprehensible, and palimpstistically interpenetrative communal "worlds." None of these worlds constitutes (or leads to) a centre, a unifying foundation,[14] but perhaps even in this way they reveal the "underbelly" of what had been taken for the centre or the foundation up until now.

Supplementary Remarks: The Example of Tadeusz Różewicz's Writing

By way of an ending, let us consider a concrete example of actual manifestations of these tendencies in contemporary Polish literature. The work of writers such as Dorota Masłowska, Olga Tokarczuk, Piotr Sommer, or Andrzej Stasiuk would all be fitting, but it is the oeuvre of Tadeusz Różewicz that delivers its truly prototypical instance. Różewicz's body of work has been accumulating for more than seventy years now, and all of the key contradictions and experiences of modern art have been inscribed upon it as if on a palimpsest. It is a body of work in which modern art's maturation and transformation has been made permanent; in which the entire literary history of modernity and (Polish) postmodernity is perceptible and graspable in a concrete discursive instance.

To begin with, Różewicz's oeuvre was from the start engaged in an uninterrupted dialogue with competing models of modern literature, beginning with the conflict and ending with the feedback between the opposing elite and mass models of literature, as well as the autonomous and engaged ones. Second, because his body of work was imprinted early on with the traumatic traces of artistically, existentially, and ideologically compelling attempts to articulate the key experiences of modernity (as much in their local, Polish contexts as in Western or universal ones). Among them are the experiences of the Holocaust, with Różewicz's poetry rising to the challenge of Adorno's warning; the experiences of war that decimate values and expose the true nature of the "human zoo"; and the experiences of civilizational crisis in the domains of principles, autonomous subjectivity, stable (individual and communal) identity, spatial situatedness in one's "own" place, and the rational organization of time subjugated to the logic of "predictability."

Third, because this body of work – also very early on – became subject to changes ensuing from the equality of all four discourses within the exemplary heterology of Różewicz's text. The stylistic and genre characteristics of his works testify to a decisive questioning of the genre "purity" of literature as a system and constitute a practice of literary heterology that is open to all registers and varieties of discourse. Fourth, because Różewicz's poetic, prose, and dramatic texts are distinguished by significant ontological instability. The appearance (publication) of successive versions of manuscripts and constant changes in new editions of works written thus far consequently put into question the "inviolable" status of the artistic object. It is impossible to identify the "original" text – neither its first nor its final version.[15]

The fifth and final reason is that Różewicz's literary output ostentatiously discards the modern rules of autonomous art, which isolates itself from the "disorder" of life through artificial, in this case artistic, rules and a hermetic language, and equally openly speaks in favour of basing the work of literature on the principle of its creator's and his art's belonging to the world. This body of work in no way recalls a precious vessel that hermetically seals off inexhaustible deposits of sense from the invasive influence of foreign, "external" factors (Keat's "well wrought urn"). Rather, it brings to mind a singular if inconspicuous knot, woven from discursive threads of human experience, the pattern of which inventively assumes and confers the shape of our contemporary self-knowledge.

Ryszard Nycz
Jagiellonian University, Cracow
Translated by Agnieszka Polakowska

NOTES

1 See Hobsbawn and Ranger, *The Invention of Tradition*; Anderson, *Imagined Communities*; Anderson, *The Spectre of Comparison*; and Culler, "The Novel and the Nation."
2 See, for example, the works of Stefan Żeromski, Wacław Berent, Juliusz Kaden-Bandrowski, and Andrzej Strug.
3 These dilemmas are efficiently summed up by the title of Jan Błoński's article "Jedna, dwie czy jedna w drugiej?" (One, Two, or One in the Other?).
4 Only a relatively small and privileged group of writers and readers in Communist Poland would have had access to both national and emigrant streams of literature.
5 In Polish, this myth is referred to as *cekania*. The term is an abbreviation of the two titles held by the Austro-Hungarian monarch, who was the *cesarz* (emperor) of Austria and the *król* (king) of Hungary. In German this concept was referred to as k.u.k: *kaiserlich und königlich*.

6 The Main Office of Control of Press, Publications and Shows was closed down in 1990.
7 See Hopfinger, *Literatura i media po 1989 roku.*
8 See Debray, *Wprowadzenie do mediologii.*
9 See Nycz, "Lekcja Adorna."
10 For more on this subject, see Nycz, "Literatura," 2012b.
11 See Nycz, *Język modernizmu*, 1997.
12 See Balbus, "Zagłada gatunków"; Balcerzan, "W stronę genologii multimedialnej"; Grochowski, *Tekstowe hybrydy.*
13 See Ziątek, *Wiek dokumentu*; Czermińska, *Autobiograficzny trójkąt*; Zawadzki, *Nowoczesna eseistyka filozoficzna*; Sendyka, *Nowoczesny esej.*
14 See Vattimo, *The Transparent Society.*
15 See Skrendo, *Tadeusz Różewicz i granice literatury.*

WORKS CITED

Anderson, Benedict. *Imagined Communities: Reflections on the Origin and Spread of Nationalism.* London: Verso, 1991.

– *The Spectre of Comparison: Nationalism, Southeast Asia, and the World.* London: Verso, 1998.

Balbus, Stanisław. "Zagłada gatunków." In *Genologia Dzisiaj.* Edited by Włodzimierz Bolecki and Ireneusz Opacki. 19–32. Warszawa: Instytut Badań Literackich, 2000.

Balcerzan, Edward. "W stronę genologii multimedialnej." In *Genologia dzisiaj.* Edited by Włodzimierz Bolecki and Ireneusz Opacki. 86–101. Warszawa: Instytut Badań Literackich, 2000.

Błoński, Jan. "Jedna, dwie czy jedna w drugiej?" *Teksty Drugie* 4 (1994): 61–70.

Culler, Jonathan. "The Novel and the Nation." In *The Literary in Theory.* 43–72. Stanford: Stanford University Press, 2007.

Czermińska, Małgorzata. *Autobiograficzny trójkąt. Świadectwo, wyznanie i wyzwanie.* Kraków: Universitas, 2000.

Debray, Regis. *Wprowadzenie do mediologii.* Translated by Alina Kapciak. Warszawa: Oficyna Naukowa, 2010.

Grochowski, Grzegorz. *Tekstowe hybrydy. Literackość i jej pogranicza.* Wrocław: Fundacja na Rzecz Nauki Polskiej, 2000.

Hobsbawm, Eric, and Terence Ranger, eds. *The Invention of Tradition.* Cambridge: Cambridge University Press, 1992.

Hopfinger, Maryla. *Literatura i media po 1989 roku.* Warszawa: Oficyna Naukowa, 2010.

Nycz, Ryszard. *Język modernizmu. Prolegomena historycznoliterackie.* Wrocław: Fundacja na Rzecz Nauki Polskiej, 1997.

– "Lekcja Adorna. Tekst jako sposób poznania, albo o kulturze jako palimpseście." *Teksty Drugie* 3 (2012): 34–50.

– "Literatura: Litery lektura. O tekście, interpretacji, doświadczeniu rozumienia i doświadczeniu lektury." In *Teoria, literatura, życie. Praktykowanie teorii w humanistyce współczesnej.* Edited by Anna Legeżyńska and Ryszard Nycz. 63–93. Warszawa: Instytut Badań Literackich PAN, 2012.

Sendyka, Roma. *Nowoczesny esej. Studium historycznej świadomości gatunku.* Kraków: Universitas, 2006.

Skrendo, Andrzej. *Tadeusz Różewicz i granice literatury. Poetyka i etyka transgresji*. Kraków: Universitas, 2002.

Vattimo, Gianni. *The Transparent Society*. Translated by David Webb. Baltimore: Johns Hopkins University Press, 1992.

Zawadzki, Andrzej. *Nowoczesna eseistyka filozoficzna w piśmiennictwie polskim pierwszej połowy XX wieku*. Kraków: Universitas, 2000.

Ziątek, Zygmunt. *Wiek dokumentu. Inspiracje dokumentarne w polskiej prozie współczesnej*. Warszawa: Instytut Badań Literackich, 1999.

PART II

Strategies

Requiem for a Canon? The Peculiar Case of the Transatlantic Canon

The question of "what to teach" underpins many considerations of the canon, giving rise not only to anxiety but also to pedagogical practices and experiments, both individual and collective. This consideration of a specific canon – that is, of the Polish literary canon in North America – begins with a foundational observation that in American educational practices instructors do not deal with its simple transplantation, but with a different and more complex phenomenon. I will call it a transatlantic canon. At the onset of my discussion I would like to emphasize that this transatlantic canon is not a shortened, condensed, or imported *in toto* version of the literary canon as it has been taught, discussed, and controlled in Poland. To put it succinctly, the transatlantic canon is construed as functioning within a different linguistic and cultural environment and as engaging in a discursive field centred on the Western canon. It is a somewhat freer adaptation of the more stringent, original canon, its skeletal younger brother that came into being largely through negotiations with educational traditions in American academe. One of its characteristic features, therefore, is its perennial belatedness in relation to the "main" canon taught in Polish schools. Whether caused by problems of accessibility, which have become less acute over the past two decades due to the Internet, or by the arduous processes of translating and publishing old and new literary works, this belatedness is a fact of life for Polish studies abroad and for their curricular demands.

New translations, which frequently and necessarily modify the transatlantic canon, shed a critical light on translations already in circulation and can call into question the success of earlier renditions. Also, in acting as transmitters of canonical texts, translators rise to a more elevated position, as their work serves to fill serious gaps. Paradoxically, the translator's labour does not tend to canonize the translation itself, since no translation can entirely restore the meaning encompassed by the original canonical work. The translated text lacks the fixed meaning of the canonical original; thus, the translation pulls the conveyed meaning into the realm of a negotiated reinscription. As such, it goes against the grain of the canon, whose mission is to make texts permanent. The shadow of untranslatability and the processes of rearticulation make the divide between the Polish canon and its transatlantic reinscription paradoxically unbridgeable. For the transatlantic canon as it currently stands is an ever-changing field, plagued with all of the absurdities that inevitably arise when two different cultural and linguistic formations are forced into a dialogic setting dominated by only one of them.

Thinking about a canon and its formation quickly metamorphoses into a seemingly wider consideration of control or ideology. Approached from the point of view of textual authority, the notion of a canon in the sphere of literature comes close to that of dogma in religion, although they do not overlap completely. The origin of this slight disparity begins in the age of secularism. The act of elevating a literary work to the status of a canonical text is grounded in the recognition of a literary work's importance. Unlike in dogmatic writing, where religious value is the primary determinant of a work's canonical status, the assessment of the literary value of a work depends on a constellation of aesthetic, cognitive, and other values, among which cultural originality ranks high. Quite poignantly, the semantics of regulation and control that come to the fore in canonical reading lists are already present in the origin of the word canon, as the Greek word *kanõn* means both a rod and a measuring stick.[1] If we follow the Greek etymology further still, *kanõn* derives from the word *kanna,* which denotes a reed or any long-stemmed plant such as sugar cane. Thus the word signifies a measuring or a protective stick, as well as a stick endowed with nurturing qualities, like sugar cane. Far from exhausting this lexical capacity, a cane is also understood as an instrument of corporal punishment known as a school cane, or a judicial cane. Thus the concept of power and authority appears at the etymological foundation of the discourse on the canon.

As we see, the ancient etymology encompasses a range of cognitive, dietary, and punitive rules. Within this register, a measuring rod, invoked in two separate instances in the Old Testament, is endowed with a meaning close to the contemporary discourse on the canon. For both the prophet Ezekiel, who sizes the imaginary temple using a cane (Ezekiel 40:3), and John the Apostle, who uses the tool to assess the size of New Jerusalem in his Revelation, a cane serves as a yardstick for prophetic imagination, an instrument that turns a vision and its imaginary content into something more concrete, of measurable value. While one can ascribe these qualities to the semantics inherent in canonical literature, the regulatory and restrictive authority carried by a literary text (and used as such in composing canonical lists) seems to come to the foreground more strongly than other prescriptive determinants of the canon.

By definition, canonical literature should seldom undergo revisions. It is meant to be untouchable, like the sacred writings of various religions. This resistance to change enhances the peculiar, occasionally undesirable power of the canonical text to participate in the circulation of normative ideas. Throughout the ages, the Christian churches, and particularly the Catholic Church, have resisted changes to their canonical corpus. In the past, in a gesture pointing to a literary canon, the Catholic Church produced its own, almost perfect opposite: the infamous papal institution of *Index Librorum Prohibitorum,* an anti-canon, if you will, whose controlling authority remained strong for ages in largely Catholic countries such as Poland.[2] This curious instrument of suppression and stagnancy was designed by the Church to limit undesirable developments in the domains of both knowledge and literature. Through the *Index*, the Church aimed to stop the publication and dissemination of literary and scientific texts because of the ideologies or morals espoused therein. However, canonical texts and censorial erasure were not always mutually exclusive; the prohibitive *Index* often incited curiosity about "forbidden fruits," and the scandalous aura that surrounded such works helped heighten readers' awareness of them.[3] Ultimately, this form of censorship did not succeed, as many works of literature listed in the *Index* have become central to national literary canons and still inform the core of the now-crumbling edifice of the Western canon.

Canonicity and canon formation are connected with domination and control in more than one way. In the West, during the last decades of the previous century, a revisionary process triggered by movements such as the pluralistic turn, multiculturalism, and postcolonialism destabilized the discourse on the literary canon from the outside. The canon itself became subject to questioning, fragmentation, and numerous revisions. For example, several slave narratives have been incorporated into the American literary canon.[4] At the same time, Harriet Beecher Stowe's *Uncle Tom's Cabin*, once a very popular anti-slavery narrative, has been greatly limited in its pedagogical and aesthetic application and is often viewed as a symbol of a bygone era because of its many striking insensitivities. Changes to the canon were further fortified by the impact of feminism and feminist literary criticism, which targeted such giants of patriarchalism in American literature as Ernest Hemingway and John Steinbeck. These relativizing intellectual forces have revised and undermined the concept of a canon and its cultural relevance, although not the curriculum's need for one.

In the present environment, only a handful of critics would admit to believing in a singular canon for all, yet nostalgia for the Western canon's lost unity lingers on.[5] Some twenty years ago, Paul Lauter, one of the canon's nostalgic defendants, succinctly divided American educational practices into two schools or approaches in his book *Canons and Contexts*:

> The two forms of literary study I wish to distinguish here are, first, the various formalist or speculative criticisms, heavily indebted to Continental philosophy, deeply concerned with questions of epistemology, and practiced primarily at a set of graduate institutions in the United States, France, and elsewhere on the European continent; and, second, what I shall term "canonical" criticism, focused on how we construct our syllabi and anthologies, on the roots of our systems of valuation, and on how we decide what is important for us to teach and for our students to learn, or at least to read.[6]

Regardless of Lauter's conceptual weakness in describing the cultural setting as solely Western, a discussion of syllabi, anthologies, and reading lists is not an innocent preoccupation. As Lauter admits, such activities assert themselves on the present in order to shape the future of North American literary studies as a field:

> I think that this distinction ... is the most recent version of an old contention between what might be called aesthetic (formalist, interpretive) and moral and thus evaluative or what I will call "canonical" approaches to texts ... I believe that understanding the history of these differing forms of literary study in the past three decades is crucial to perceiving where literary study is now and where one might want it to go.[7]

In the case of an influential champion of canonical criticism, Harold Bloom, the temptation to shape the future took a different turn, one not grounded in moral values. Bloom clings to the concept of the canon more from a desire to inject some sense of order into our cultural values than out of desperation caused by the loss of a dominant canon; he envisions, measures, and shapes the canon in a mode reminiscent of the ancient prophets. In his resistance to the canon's stasis, Bloom attempts to reinstate the lost paradisal wholeness that once marked Western literature, centred, according to him, on William Shakespeare's oeuvre. His rebuilding of the dismantled canon has had some positive repercussions. Obviously, the critic does not see in the canonical/classical texts an embodiment of didactic or conservative ideals, but "a mode of originality that either cannot be assimilated or that so assimilates us that we cease to see it as strange."[8] Thus defended and redefined, the canon may regain its weakened values and authority, and may even be projected onto the future, not the least because Bloom, despite employing the yardstick of originality on the somewhat overlapping notions of the canon and the classic, takes a decidedly inclusive approach to other literatures. Despite his "hard core" view of some aspects of the canon, Bloom is the critic who tested and reformed the canonical. It is worthy to note that several contemporary Polish poets, among them Czesław Miłosz (1911–2004) and Adam Zagajewski (b. 1945), made Bloom's list along with literary masters from other national literatures.[9] For my discussion, the significance of this recognition is minimal, as it illustrates only the point where the canonical mainstream coincides with the transatlantic canon without impacting the latter.[10]

Perhaps in the eyes of Western critics, Bloom's inclusion of several names from the Polish canon speaks to its present porousness, which allows for such an act of cultural absorption. I believe, however, that the critic's gesture is not so much a diagnosis of the Polish canon's growing relevance, but rather an obligatory, indeed politically correct recognition of those poets whose contribution to American and world poetry has been nothing less than substantial. This change prompts the question of the Polish canon discourse within and outside Poland: one could advance the argument that, in the American pedagogical practice and heuristics related to Polish literature, we are dealing with a different evaluation of authors than in Poland, where the young generation of readers, poets, and critics fails to appreciate and even rejects Miłosz's poetry despite its canonical status. But this requires a quick look at the Polish canon in Poland, where its evolution, often caused by broader, external changes, has not affected its central role in Polish culture. Arguably, one reason for the canon's strength there is that the Polish canon is more pertinent to primary and secondary education and thus influences a wider population of students, while in America the transatlantic canon functions on the post-secondary level of the college and university educational system.

Since the canon represents a more or less fixed constellation of literary masterpieces, the canonical text, unlike the classic one, does not stand alone, but rather belongs to a larger system of texts, evaluated and selected for its relevance to the canon. The classic is, according to Ankhi Mukherjee, "a singular act of literature," whereas the canonical text requires a list of other canonical texts.[11] By its definition, the canonical text signals a synchronic organization of the corpus of national literature across ages, and as such implies a degree of interconnectivity and collectivity derived from a linguistic unity, cultural tradition and its dominant themes, a nation's history, and other determinants. The canon's *ur*-texts indicate a linear direction, a sense of continuous growth of the Polish language and of the Christian values usually espoused by them. These intertwined Christian values and intertextual connections between older and newer literary works used to warrant the continuity of the canon.

Such continuity is not inherited; it must be invented. According to T.S. Eliot's famous essay "Tradition and the Individual Talent," a modern poem must include an awareness of older literature among its literary values.[12] Indeed, in the Polish scenario, the status of the canonical list is informed and guarded by the authority of textbooks and educational curricula, which develop and strengthen the already perceived artistic, linguistic, and religious connections among, for example, such texts as the hymn "Bogurodzica" (Mother of God), Jan Długosz's *Annals*,[13] and Henryk Sienkiewicz's *Krzyżacy* (Teutonic Knights, 1900).[14] Długosz's references to "Mother of God," Sienkiewicz's use of Jan Długosz, and the fact that Poland's oldest literary masterpiece's singular authority was evoked even on a battlefield and further disseminated through Aleksander Ford's cinematic adaptation of *Teutonic Knights*, permeate and bring coherence to our contemporary understanding of the hymn.[15]

While educators believe that the canon is a necessary construct, John Guillory, in an opposite gesture, claims that a canon results from ideology, implying that it is not a necessary proposition unless one assumes that ideology is always an unavoidable necessity. In postwar Polish history, revisions to the existing canon and the imposition of a socialist-realist aesthetic on literature provide evidence that, within a given political framework, a literary canon is a useful tool for reversing values in areas such as religion, taste, tradition, and national identity. Official censorship, be it papal, governmental, or otherwise, has often intervened in canonical evolution as a regulatory agent, shaping the canon to control politically undesirable literary texts, just as it did in postwar Poland, where the communist regime carefully emulated Soviet norms in programming both education and the literary canon.[16] Due to the consistent institutional approaches and practices of control-from-above, Polish literary masterpieces were eliminated from or "pushed to the margins"[17] of educational programs and textbooks, to be replaced by Polish and Russian socialist-realist literary works.[18] The general tendency was to remove everything that belonged to more recent experimental literature, hence the erasure of avant-garde literary production from the canon at this point in Poland's history.

Claims of governmental authority, when backed by the executive power of a totalitarian state, usually have an immediate negative impact on the pedagogy of literature. But even in post-communist Poland's political environment, the construction of the canon has occasionally turned into its dismantling. Political interventions in school curricula, exercised by both conservative and liberal politicians, resurrect the old, certainly not exclusively Polish spectre of extrinsic, dogmatic control; when the state implements an ideological *doxa* in society and its educational institutions through (deservingly or not) canonized works, thus endowing them with a regulatory power, such works are in danger of being reduced to mere didactic and ideological instruments.

The beginning of our canon is determined by texts that survived through the ages and that are known as the oldest extant texts, whereas the beginnings of canon formation – and of modern awareness of the canon – date back to the nineteenth century. Therefore, I would like to take a brief look at the ideological workings of the Polish canon in one of the better known textbooks of old Polish literature – namely, Ignacy Chrzanowski's *Historia literatury niepodległej Polski (965–1795)* (The History of Literature in the Independent Poland).[19] Chrzanowski posits Romantic literature as the pinnacle of Polish literary achievement – as a national treasure that transcends previous literary periods – and interprets other national canons, in particular the Russian one, as driven purely by politics. Indeed, at the time, canon formation was so tightly interlocked with the grand narrative of Polish national identity and independence that they overlapped. As Chrzanowski writes:

> The greatness of our literature comes only later in the post-partition times: this greatness would be given to her only by Mickiewicz. The literature of independent Poland is rich, beautiful and sensible, morally pure, but it cannot be called *great* despite Kochanowski, Krasicki, Skarga and Modrzewski. But when the ship sank, our literature soared to heights that never were reached during the times of independence, and played in the nation's life a role so great as at no other time in the world.[20]

In other words, the more troublesome the nation's situation, the better its literary creation(!). This implies that at least during two historic changes, after 1918 and especially after 1989, with the collapse of the national narrative, Polish literature should have experienced a decline, but this is not at all the case. More importantly, Chrzanowski's verdict regarding Kochanowski, Krasicki, and Modrzewski illustrates not only the weakness of the patriotic dogma but also a destabilization of the foundational belief in literary values as inherent in the canon. Despite the network of the associated patriotic and patriarchal ideas that generate the canon's interconnectivity, the canon itself remains within the domain of controllable, even institutionalized changes. There have been, however, certain surprising occurrences and uncontrolled processes over the ages. One could argue that Sarmatism continues to be such a subversive (although incrementally weakening) force, subjected to dissemination and opposed to the centralizing type of thinking from which a canon evolves. The canon cannot exist without a centripetal, unifying, integrative energy; contrary to this, the effects of the centrifugal dynamic of dissemination are usually counter-canonical, for they push canonical works to the periphery. Ultimately, to paraphrase Cyprian Kamil Norwid's poetic remark, so well-entrenched in Polish culture, the future is an eternal corrector of the canon.

The case of the literary canon in Polish culture and tradition is not exceptional, in that the corpus of canonical writings has not defied changes, in particular the recent ones arising from suspicion of a single, monadic world view and its reflection in literature. Rather, by absorbing some of these changes, the body of our "cultural capital" has become more porous and less rigid. This said, the belief in literature's centrality and in the single system of values espoused by its canon lingers in the debate about the Polish canon.[21] In particular, the impact of the politics of representation, delimited by the language of political correctness and by the postcolonial blues spurred by discourse abroad, has found its way into the canonical corpus to destabilize certain well-entrenched works of fiction. A 2008 conference organized in Warsaw by the Collegium Artes Liberales under the telling title "Whose Africa? On Sienkiewicz's *In the Desert and Wilderness*" attests to a growing awareness of the seemingly "threatened" Polish literary canon. The conference organizers chose Sienkiewicz's novel for children, which was published in 1911 and almost instantly became very popular, to contest its main assumptions about the Polish national identity and the superiority of white men's civilization. The issues at stake for this conference were determined by postcolonial discourse, one of the main factors in considering the Polish canon's porousness.

In the necessary shift to the other shore of the Atlantic, one may discern the inception and mechanics of the transatlantic canon by examining English-language textbooks designed to teach the history of Polish literature. In doing so, I follow the direction established by Andrea Lanoux in her book *Od narodu do kanonu* (From the Nation to the Canon).[22] How do academic textbooks written for a foreign, American audience translate Polish cultural identity, and how do they sort out the canonical texts? In other words, how do they inform and present the transatlantic canon? To begin with, there are only a handful of academic textbooks dedicated to the history of Polish literature, namely (in chronological order) Manfred Kridl's *A Survey of Polish Literature and Culture*, Czesław Miłosz's *The History of Polish Literature*, and Julian Krzyżanowski's *A History of Polish Literature*. All three were published for American students – an audience that two of the authors (Kridl and Miłosz) knew from their extensive pedagogical experience.[23]

Published in Poland, Krzyżanowski's *A History of Polish Literature* is very informative, thorough, and devoid of factual errors.[24] Its sheer volume, however, makes the textbook difficult to use in a one-semester or even two-semester survey of Polish literature. Another problem stems from Krzyżanowski's initial design; his *History* was intended for Polish university students, who do not have to rely on translations and can read, for example, seventeenth-century poetry in the original. For an American student who has only recently started to learn the Polish language, reading and absorbing this textbook's factual information is a formidable task. However, it is the absence of any counter-narrative, or even the slightest critical gesture towards the grand narrative of Polish martyrdom, that prevents this textbook from contributing to a future canon (re)formation. Krzyżanowski follows the long-established status quo by elaborating on "the existing order" while including more historical detail than other authors before him. Thinking about the challenge that foreign readers may face in consuming his *opus*, I quote Miłosz's unequivocally negative valuation as a warning: "Krzyżanowski's Polish Romantic Literature … is a collection of every banality which is supposed to confirm for ever the image la Pologne martyre."[25]

Kridl's *A Survey of Polish Literature and Culture* resulted from his 1945 publication *Literatura polska na tle rozwoju kultury* (Polish Literature in the Context of Cultural Development) and was part of his broader pedagogical design, which demonstrated an astute understanding of the specific needs of American students. This was made evident by his adding *An Anthology of Polish Literature* to *A Survey*.[26] Its appearance in the 1950s, along with Olga Scherer-Virski's anthology *The Modern Polish Short Story*, marks a milestone in the development of what I call the transatlantic canon. In the preface to his textbook, in a gesture characteristic of his formalist training, Kridl claims that he approaches literary works from the literary point of view and selects his authors on the basis of "their significance and achievements."[27] Certainly, it would be difficult to find a more non-ideological declaration than Kridl's. Miłosz in his textbook engages with this approach with much less caution.

Undoubtedly, in this small constellation, Miłosz's *The History of Polish Literature* stands out for more than one reason.[28] To begin with, the author infuses the historical record with his personal point of view, thereby augmenting several aspects of his narrative. By his own admission, his narration of the history of Polish literature is devoid of formalized and scholarly style while emulating the traditional scheme of periodization. Having lived through and witnessed almost the entire twentieth century, Miłosz intervenes in the canon's formation, using his vast knowledge and formidable pedagogical experience to make a lasting impact on American Polish literary studies. The textbook is still in use and continues to play a role despite its outdated scope and some factual errors. Described on the dust jacket in exaggerated terms as a "magisterial, authoritative, comprehensive survey of Polish literature from the earliest times down to the last quarter of the twentieth century," Miłosz's narrative contains two compelling counter-narratives emerging from his treatment of both the Polish Reformation and émigré literature. One of them is an ideological assertion that refutes the common perception that Polishness is completely identified with Catholicism and that culminates in a fascinating chapter on the Polish Reformation and Protestantism;[29] the other defies the official notion of literature under communism. Miłosz's counter-narratives facilitate an argument that the concept of canonicity should contain within itself a subversive force that can disturb its stability.

Because the canonical construct in its transatlantic variation is so strongly identified with academic teaching, it is important to note which writers are either not taught or taught less often on this side of the pond. In this respect, much depends on translation and its predictable and unavoidable alterations of the original, on being able to contend with the perennial insufficiency of already translated works, and, more importantly, on the task of filling in the blank spaces left by texts yet to be translated. Thus far, the most painful absence is that of nineteenth- and twentieth-century authors, especially since that absence has been determined largely by the mechanics and politics of translation, and less so by the difficulty of the originals. This is best illustrated by the lack of translations of a host of psychological novels of extraordinary quality, such as Zofia Nałkowska's (1884–1954) *Niedobra miłość* (Bad Love, 1928), Helena Boguszewska's (1886–1978) *Całe życie Sabiny* (The Whole Life of Sabina, 1934), and Tadeusz Breza's (1905–70) *Adam Grywałd* (1936). Evidently inferior translations also pose a problem, becoming unusable in a post-secondary environment if marred by a translator's inadequate language skills or insufficient cultural knowledge of Poland. Henryk Sienkiewicz (1846–1916), who was once the most popular Polish writer in America, falls into this category.[30] Although a handful of Eliza Orzeszkowa's (1841–1910) short stories have been translated (along with the totally unreadable *Meir Ezofowicz*), the absence of English renditions of her major novels constitutes a gap within the transatlantic canon. Bolesław Leśmian's (1877–1937) masterful poetry remains virtually unknown because of inadequate attempts to translate it into English; it represents one of the greatest challenges for a Polish poetry translator and is believed by some to be untranslatable.

The trust the reader bestows on the translator as a decision maker, as someone who knows not only the Polish language but also the literature written in it, is in danger when the value of a translation is in question. Thankfully, there are now around a dozen accomplished Polish-to-English translators producing work of highest quality, without which one could not teach Polish literature in North American universities. Their skills, knowledge, and taste are contributing to what Walter Benjamin referred to as "the dignity of this literary mode" – that is, to the cultural position of translations.[31] The translator has emerged today as the "unacknowledged legislator" of the transatlantic canon.[32] Each new work that receives acclaim on the Polish literary stage – in particular through the Nike Award Committee's decisions and critics' reviews – can enter the sphere of American Polonists' pedagogy through translation, and several prize venues are handing out awards for the most successful renditions.

To return to pedagogical practices, I would reiterate that the teaching of canonical texts in Poland takes place in a different discursive setting than the teaching of the transatlantic canon in North America, where the Polish canon has no impact on the broader mass culture.[33] One aspect of the transatlantic canon that needs to be emphasized, therefore, is that it is an adaptation of the Polish canon – achieved through translations – to a different language, culture, people, and educational system. There are other reasons why the transatlantic canon should not be seen as a shortened, simplified, or derivative version of the Polish canon. The two are set apart, for instance, by an emerging cultural phenomenon of literature written by Polish Americans authors. This sub-canon, which has been added successfully to some Polish studies curricula in recent years, offers one more reason for maintaining a distinction between the Polish and transatlantic canons. And just as the literature of Polish American authors is of diminished relevance in Poland, so are some aspects of the Polish canon on this side of the Atlantic. Such is the case with the postwar trajectory of the canon, for instance: socialist-realist works are included in the Polish canon because they articulate the nation's political environment and culture, but they are usually omitted from the transatlantic canon, where they play no such role.

Furthermore, the transatlantic canon is part and parcel of the Polonists' academic pedagogy and a response to the American and Canadian university systems as they are lived and structured. Regarding this particular dislocation, one point of view is worth invoking, for it gives a sense of how stereotyped Polish literature is – and, by extension, Polish identity. To put it briefly, the Polish literary canon in its transatlantic version is perceived by some American Slavists as permeated with a sense of historical tragedy and loss, filled with doom and brooding. Polish literature is no fun; in contrast, the Czech canon is perceived as offering pleasure to readers, as laced with jovial humour (and a discreetly shed tear). This suggests the presence of a a competition among the various Slavic literatures and, more importantly, another hierarchical reading list. Indeed, laughter has an incredible cleansing energy that destabilizes formalized hierarchies of values, and it does have an established presence in the Czech culture. As any reader of Vladislav Vančura, Božena Němcová, or Karel Hynek Mácha would confirm, however, Czech literature does not revolve around the aesthetic principle of laughter. Meanwhile, Jan Kochanowski's (1530–84) epigrams, Adam Mickiewicz's (1798–1855) *Pan Tadeusz* (Sir Thaddeus, 1834), Aleksander Fredro's (1793–1876) comedies, Bolesław Prus's (1847–1912) short stories, Witold Gombrowicz's (1904–69) novels and plays, and more recently Jerzy Pilch's (b. 1952) and Tomasz Różycki's (b. 1970) works defy the notion that Polish literature is inherently dark. The writings of these authors, and many others, clearly demonstrate how to laugh through and survive national misfortunes.

One could argue that the transatlantic canon serves mainly as a matrix or a template onto which academic instructors can project their own approaches to teaching Polish literature in translation. Being somewhat flexible, that framework has this additional aspect: it allows an individualized representation of Polish literature. But when used in this manner it cannot adequately represent the Polish literary canon, which ends up looking deformed. The transatlantic canon, twice removed from its origins, acquires under these circumstances by necessity a stronger *telos*; there are works that *must* be translated and writers who *must* be introduced. Although not dependent on politicians and administrators, it is subject to continuous reinscription by translators and academic instructors, who reduce the canon's repeatability through continuous expansion and change. In fact, the transatlantic canon is itself a complex reinscription.

Bożena Shallcross
University of Chicago

NOTES

1 *Webster's Third New International Dictionary*, vol. 1, 328.

2 The date when the Roman Office of the Inquisition launched the publication varies; according to some scholars it was 1559. Pope Paul VI abolished the publication of the *ILP* in 1966.

3 The list included works by Michel Montaigne, Francois Rabelais, Jean de La Fontaine, Jean-Jacques Rousseau, Henri Stendhal, Victor Hugo, and James Joyce, to mention only a few. Abolishing the Index did not have much immediate impact; for example, the

twentieth-century Polish mystic Mother Maria Faustyna Kowalska's meditations remained on the *Index Librorum Prohibitorum* until she was canonized in 2000. Only then did her diary receive *nihil obstat* for an official publication.

4 Some of them are commonly taught today in American schools, with the autobiography *The Interesting Narrative of the Life of Olaudah Equiano* deserving special mention.

5 The story of the dismantling of the Western canon, its fading importance, and its co-existence with a growing number of fragmented minor canons or – sub-canons, if you will – has a plot somewhat reminiscent of the Tower of Babel. Once the linguistic unity secured by the language of Paradise was destroyed, mankind became divided by its linguistic diversity (which we see threatened today) and by the lack of other means of communication, such as a pre-verbal language, sign language, or translation. The usefulness of this parallel in canon discourse, however, can go only so far.

6 Lauter, *Canons and Contexts*, 134.

7 Ibid., 135.

8 Bloom, *The Western Canon*, 3.

9 Another collateral phenomenon in canon discourse is constituted by numerous emerging minor canons, or sub-canons. One notable instance is Robert Drake's canonization of gay writing in his anthology *The Gay Canon*. Drake aptly illustrates the process of pluralistic fragmentation of the once monumental and indivisible Western canon, yet one could argue that he was guided by the old ordering and prescriptive spirit of a canon, and merely replaced a reading list for the Great Books course with one for the Great Queer Books course.

10 Although the opposite can be true: Bruno Schulz's impact on several important American authors, especially Cynthia Ozick, Jonathan Safran Foer, and Nicole Krauss, is one example.

11 Mukherjee, "'What Is a Classic?,' 1026–42.

12 "In a peculiar sense [an artist or poet] ... must inevitably be judged by the standards of the past." See Eliot, "Tradition and the Individual Talent." Following Eliot, J.M. Coetzee defines the classic as shaped by criticism: "Rather than being the foe of the classic, criticism, and indeed criticism of the most skeptical kind, may be what the classic uses to define itself and ensure its survival. See Coetzee, "What Is a Classic?," 19.

13 Although Długosz's *Annals* stop in 1480, the year of his death, the work was first printed in 1701–3.

14 Interestingly, the English translation appeared in the same year as the original; its speed augured nothing good.

15 Jan Długosz mentions that "Bogurodzica" was sung by the Polish knights before the first Battle of Tannenberg (Grunwald, 1410).

16 The organizers of the 1951 Congress of Polish Sciences and Letters decided to fundamentally revise Polish knowledge according to the Marxist-Leninist doctrine, with a particular emphasis on the humanities. For example, some textbooks, most notably history textbooks, were mere translations of Soviet history textbooks.

17 Michał Glowiński's phrase relates to the marginalized position of Zygmunt Krasiński and Cyprian Kamil Norwid in Polish socialist-realist canon; see Michał Głowiński, "Kanon literacki," 92.

18 The politics of translation regarding Soviet literature were based on publishing numerous editions; for example, Dimitri Furmanov's *Chapayev* had six editions between 1949 and 1955. See Smulski, "Przekłady z literatury krajów socjalistycznych," 232.

19 Taking a closer look at this work is more than warranted by the multiple editions (over a dozen) that have been issued since its first publication in 1908.

20 Chrzanowski, *Historia literatury niepodległej Polski (965–1795)*, 837.
21 The question seemed paramount during the first decade of this century as several publications re-evaluated the state of the Polish literary canon. For example, see Głowiński, "Kanony literackie. Od socrealizmu do pluralizmu"; Iwasiów and Czerska, *Kanon i obrzeża*; and Czermińska et al., *Polonistyka w przebudowie*, which includes several articles devoted to the subject of the canon.
22 Andrea Lanoux, *Od narodu do kanonu*.
23 In the case of Krzyżanowski, his wide pedagogical practice included teaching in London, but not (to my knowledge) in North America.
24 Krzyżanowski, *A History of Polish Literature*. The original title, *Dzieje literatury polskiej od początków do czasów najnowszych* (A History of Polish literature from Its Beginnings to the most recent times), ambitiously promised more than the book could deliver during the Polish People's Republic, since it could not include the "most recent" émigré literature.
25 Miłosz, "O historii polskiej literatury, wolnomyślicielach i masonach" in *Prywatne obowiązki*, 115.
26 Kridl, ed., *An Anthology of Polish Literature*. Other anthologies followed, contributing to the development of the transatlantic canon. Most notable among these were Carpenter, *Monumenta Polonica*; and several volumes translated by Michael J. Mikos, including, most recently, *Polish Literature from 1864 to 1918: An Anthology*.
27 Kridl, *A History of Polish Literature and Culture*, 1. Kridl was an expert in Polish nineteenth-century literature, which explains his emphasis on Romanticism.
28 Miłosz's *The History of Polish Literature* was first published in 1973 by Macmillan in New York. Since his textbook originated in his lecture notes, it offers a unique form of testimony to Miłosz's transformation from a poet to a historian of literature. For more on this topic, see Teresa Walas, "Czesław Miłosz jako historyk literatury polskiej."
29 According to Miłosz's students, one of his favourite themes was Arianism. For more on the poet's pedagogical strategies, see Franaszek, *Miłosz. Biografia*, esp. the chapter "Dwustronne porachunki," 588–601.
30 Michael J. Mikos vividly portrays this in his book on Sienkiewicz's American translator Jeremiah Curtin. See Mikos, *W pogoni za Sienkiewiczem*.
31 Benjamin, "The Task of the Translator," 258.
32 The expression was coined by Percy Bysshe Shelley in "A Defence of Poetry," in *English Essays from Sir Philip Sidney to Macaulay*, 377.
33 This is the case, of course, with all Slavic literatures. The notable exception is Lev (Leo) Tolstoy, whose novel *Anna Karenina* features in Oprah Winfrey's Book Club, an entry that has earned it the widest possible circulation for a canonical Russian work. A handful of other works have had a modicum of impact in North America – for instance, Sienkiewicz's *Quo Vadis* in both the literary version and its cinematic adaptation.

WORKS CITED

Benjamin, Walter. "The Task of the Translator." In *Selected Writings,* vol. 1: *1913–1926*. Edited by Marcus Bullock and Michael W. Jennings. 253–63. Cambridge, MA: Harvard University Press, 2002.

Bloom, Harold. *The Western Canon: The Books and Schools of the Ages*. New York: Riverhead, 1994.

Carpenter, Bogdana. *Monumenta Polonica: The First Four Centuries of Polish Poetry: A Bilingual Anthology*. Ann Arbor: University of Michigan / Michigan Slavic, 1989.
Chrzanowski, Ignacy. *Historia literatury niepodległej Polski (965–1795)*. Warszawa: Państwowy Instytut Wydawniczy, 1971.
Coetzee, John Maxwell. "What Is a Classic?" In *Stranger Shores: Essays, 1986–1999*. 1–16. London: Vintage Press, 2002.
Czermińska, Małgorzata et al. *Polonistyka w przebudowie. Literaturoznawstwo – wiedza o języku – wiedza o kulturze – edukacja*. Kraków: Universitas, 2005.
Drake, Robert. *The Gay Canon: Great Books Every Gay Man Should Read*. New York: Doubleday, 1998.
Eliot, T.S. "Tradition and the Individual Talent." In *The Sacred Wood: Essays on Poetry and Criticism* [1921]. London: Dodo Press, 2009. http://www.bartleby.com/200/sw4.html.
Franaszek, Andrzej. *Miłosz. Biografia*. Kraków: Znak, 2011.
Głowiński, Michał. "Kanon literacki." In *Dictionary of Socialist Realism* (*Słownik realizmu socjalistycznego*). Edited by Zdzisław Łapiński and Wojciech Tomasik. 91–3. Kraków: Universitas, 2004.
– "Kanony literackie. Od socrealizmu do pluralizmu." In *Dzień Ulissesa i inne szkica na tematy nie mitologiczne*. 51–69. Kraków: Wydawnictwo Literackie, 2000.
Iwasiów, Inga, and Tatiana Czerska. *Kanon i obrzeża*. Kraków: Universitas, 2005.
Kridl, Manfred, ed. *An Anthology of Polish Literature*. New York: Columbia University Press, 1957.
– *A History of Polish Literature and Culture*. Translated by Olga Scherer-Virski. The Hague: Mouton, 1956.
Krzyżanowski, Julian. *A History of Polish Literature*. Translated by Doris Ronowicz, revised by Maria Bokszczanin and Halina Geber. Warszawa: PWN-Polish Scientific Publishers, 1978.
Lanoux, Andrea. *Od narodu do kanonu*. Warszawa: Wydawnictwo IBL PAN, 2003.
Lauter, Paul. *Canons and Contexts*. New York: Oxford University Press, 1991.
Maurice, Michael, ed. *The Annals of Jan Długosz: An English Abridgement. Długosz, Jan, 1415–1480*. Charlton: IM Publications, 1997.
Mikos, Michael J. *W pogoni za Sienkiewiczem. Z odnalezionych dzienników Almy Curtin*. Warszawa: Wydawnictwo Constans, 1994.
– ed. *Polish Literature from 1864 to 1918: Realism and Young Poland: An Anthology*. Bloomington: Slavica Publishers, 2006.
Miłosz, Czesław. "O historii polskiej literatury, wolnomyślicielach i masonach." In *Prywatne obowiązki*. 113–36. Paryż: Instytut Literacki, 1972.
Mukherjee, Ankhi. "'What Is a Classic?': International Literary Criticism and the Classic Question." *PMLA* 125, no. 4 (2010): 1026–42.
Shelley, Percy Bysshe. "A Defence of Poetry." In *English Essays from Sir Philip Sidney to Macaulay*. Harvard Classics, vol. 27. New York: P.F. Collier and Son, 1910.
Smulski, Jerzy. "Przekłady z literatury krajów socjalistycznych." In *Dictionary of Socialist Realism* (*Słownik realizmu socjalistycznego*). Edited by Zdzisław Łapiński and Wojciech Tomasik. 230–4. Kraków: Universitas, 2004.
Walas, Teresa. "Czesław Miłosz jako historyk literatury polskiej." *Dekada Literacka* 11, no. 1 (1994): 8–10.
Webster's Third New International Dictionary. vol. 1. Chicago: Encyclopedia Britannica, 1981.

Polish Modernist Literature: Emancipative Strategies in Prose

I understand emancipative strategies of Polish prose as undertakings that support "new" social groups in empowering their subjectivity through access to culture, or – in weaker versions – through public negotiation of the conditions and rules of such access. Emancipation thus understood is sourced in the nineteenth century, and especially its second half, which marks the threshold of modernity for Poland. The emancipative strategies conceived at that time did not easily exhaust their potential, remaining current into the twentieth century. At this time, the previously established strategies of mainly social emancipation are joined by a strategy that had earlier been undertaken only marginally – namely, that of liberating the subject from obligations towards its environment, ideology, family, collective responsibilities, and fatherland. This approach was realized in two basic variants. The first – Witold Gombrowicz's – was narcissistic, in that its energy, including libidinal, was directed entirely at the speaking subject. The second – Czesław Miłosz's – was post-Hegelian and stemmed from distrust of nature (also social) and the temptation to escape its laws by establishing the closest possible contact with a divine and spiritual "second space."

Other phenomena related to the above-mentioned strategies are noteworthy for linking the nineteenth and twentieth centuries. I have in mind here, first, the strategy of rising to the demands of history (or, in the language of Stanisław Brzozowski, reaching "historic maturity"). This particular variant of emancipation requires a strong, determined subject capable of taking responsibility and of meeting challenges not in the name of its own happiness, freedom, ambition, and success, but in the name and for the benefit of others. Included here is the work of modernist writers with a historiosophic and socially engaged bent, such as Stefan Żeromski and Maria Dąbrowska. Second, the subversive freedom to perceive and interpret reality that is written into some emancipative strategies can be attained also in another way – through an intellectual tension that allows our species to attain self-awareness. This type of knowledge about the world is mediated through the body, biology, and biographical experiences and examined with anatomical precision. The notion of a human organism can be extended, in some sense, also to history and society; the way of life of this organism also stems from basic elements: corporeality, deprivation, hunger, desire, and the need to inflict pain and to feel bliss, as well as the need for love and intellectual and artistic satisfaction.

Zofia Nałkowska (1884–1954) was a master of this sort of diagnosis. Her analysis of the mechanisms of war and the birth of Nazism stemmed from an in-depth awareness of the human species and from female experience, for the female subject is always (or usually) situated in a weaker position and at risk of psychic and physical violence. Due to their relative physical weakness, the challenges of motherhood, and their need for love, women experience suffering perhaps more often and more deeply than men, and they can more easily grasp how a world that is rooted in violence functions: the subordination they experience in their individual development is mirrored in historical developments. Various ideologies and attitudes impose subordination: the temptation to become superhuman; a belief in cultural, gender, or racial superiority; the desire to act out power, cruelty, and ruthlessness. This emancipative strategy does not allow for any form of liberation or for complete satisfaction. What *is* possible is the attainment of awareness of the rules and mechanisms of human action. It is precisely a clear recognition (knowledge) of human nature, stripped of both ornamentation and consolation, and secured through unceasing intellectual effort under extreme conditions, that serves as source of strength and dignity. Even when threatened by the terrors of occupation, Nałkowska insisted in her *Dzienniki* (Diaries): this is my fate and I would not exchange it.

The map of emancipative strategies in Polish modernist literature is thus formed, so to speak, by multi-storeyed tectonic plates and faults that overlap one another to some extent. Among them are ever-diversifying social interests, addressed on a wide scale during the nineteenth century and resonating throughout the subsequent age for at least two reasons: the strength of the subject reinforced by Nietzschean and other philosophical inspirations (e.g., in the works of Narcyza Żmichowska (1819–76) and Stanisław Brzozowski), and postwar social mechanisms (in proletarian and peasant prose, for example). The twentieth-century variants of freedom "from" (in Gombrowicz and Miłosz) also feature on this map. Between these emancipatory "plates" we encounter uplifts characterized by the reinforced subjectivity of socially engaged individuals. Nałkowska's strategy presents a different kind of transition from nineteenth-century social emancipation to the negative freedom that constitutes the object of aspiration for twentieth-century. It is immersed both in naturalism and in empirico-critical theories of experience, as well as in Brzozowski's culturalism – that is, the conviction that human beings create the world that surrounds them through their own efforts. Nałkowska discards religion and metaphysics along with other conceptualizations of goodness inherent in human nature, but she does not negate human bonds with the world; no one is self-contained, she contends. To accept what one knows about the world, to avoid easy consolations, and to hold on to one's ethical code and standards of intellectual discipline and solidarity with others – such is the task for the times.

The strategies presented here are not entirely separable. Miłosz references Brzozowski in his late essays, and Gombrowicz, despite his declared reservations regarding his older colleague, reveals in his works a kinship with Nałkowska. All of these writers, though belonging to different generations, often reference their nineteenth-century predecessors. The map of emancipative tropes thus sketched out coalesces into a network of linked paths. The emancipative projects of the authors mentioned here and in what follows are integral to this map. They serve as orientation points in a web of mutual relations and as means to measure the distances between specific strategies: social emancipation (of peasants, proletariat, and Jews); the emancipation of women (with reservations regarding its success); and the emancipation of the subject through the search for negative freedom – that is, freedom "from" social obligations as well as from family, civil, or group responsibilities.

I. Different Variants of Social Emancipation: Liminal Strategies

Background: Nineteenth Century

During the 1840s, an intellectual movement arose in Poland's partitioned territories (as of 1795, Poland had disappeared from Europe's map, having been between Russia, Prussia, and Austria-Hungary). That movement revived after a period of repression that followed the defeat of the November Uprising and a war with Russia in 1830–1. During this period, the persistent desire for national sovereignty became ever more closely bound up with the conviction that the restoration of political freedom would require changes in social structure: the abolition of serfdom in rural areas, the modernization of society, the expansion of both capital and education, the participation of women in the public sphere, an improved standard of living, and greater social trust.

> Note that with some exceptions (Żmichowska), nineteenth-century emancipative strategies did not presuppose the strengthening of the subject's position, and that striving for negative freedom – freedom "from" – during the twentieth century was not directly linked to a social context. This was not the case for the turns of these centuries, when the two issues – the strength of subjectivity, and social awareness (of Brzozowski, Żeromski and Nałkowska) – went hand in hand.

During the decades between the failed November Uprising of 1830–1 and the failed January Uprising of 1863–4, a group of women recorded in Polish history as Entuzjastki (Enthusiasts) began engaging in charitable work as well as in illegal conspiratorial work. Their uniqueness, however – and in particular the uniqueness of their leader, Narcyza Żmichowska – was evident in their emphasis on self-knowledge, in their reflections on female subjectivity and on the status of literature, and in their a critical attitude towards the Romantic cult of the artist and towards conspiratorial activities – this despite their own participation in conspiratorial organizations, which was often compelled by their feelings of solidarity with victims of persecution.

Żmichowska, the author of the notable psychological (and crypto-biographical) novel *Poganka* (Heathen, 1846) and of a brilliant correspondence conducted within familial and social circles, countered the fever of Romanticism with a different model of existence. She based that model in the recognition of (intellectual, artistic, sexual) predispositions of the subject, in the courage of self-realization, and in the strength of the bonds of love and friendship, which – as in the doctrine of Saint-Simonism – she viewed as the true source of social energies. Two other issues must be mentioned here. First, Żmichowska's world – comparable to that of George Sand and George Eliot – reserved a special place for the female subject. The cultural "younger-ness" of women allowed them, according to Żmichowska, to occupy a place "on the margins," at a distance from the generally acceptable choices that often absolved one from thinking – for instance, from the imperative to lay a sacrifice on the altar of the fatherland. Such a position allowed, as she put it, "writing in parentheses," by which she meant inserting between the lines – whether openly or secretly – observations on the subject of (for example) non-normative, homoerotic sexuality, which seems to have been her experience. Second, Żmichowska's unwavering confidence in herself, as a talented teacher blessed with personal charisma and a controversial figure according to both conservative and clerical circles, stemmed not from arrogance but from her unconventional faith in Christianity as a religion of love and freedom rather than a doctrine that enforced restrictions and suffering.

Paying this much attention to Żmichowska, a seemingly anachronistic figure, is warranted by her intellectual independence. Inspired by the work of philosophers of the previous epoch (such as Henri de Saint-Simon, Barthélemy Enfantic, Pierre Leroux, and, among German theologians and philosophers, Ferdinand Baur as well as possibly Friedrich Schleiermacher and Arthur Schopenhauer), she fostered this independence not by cultivating solitude and her own uniqueness, but rather by developing ties – however unreliable, unfulfilled, and prone to snap under pressure – with her surroundings.

Żmichowska embraced the imperative of personal freedom – to be paid for with sacrifice and realized with determination under conditions of political enslavement, censorship, and persecutions. She was also convinced that individual sovereignty was a precondition for the restoration of state independence. Her return to popularity during the interwar years is therefore not surprising. It was towards the end of the 1920s that Tadeusz Boy-Żeleński (1874–1941), the son of Żmichowska's friend, Wanda Grabowska-Żeleńska, and an excellent critic and translator of French literature into Polish, republished several of her works, preceding them with enthusiastic biographical sketches. Boy-Żeleński, who launched a campaign for women's rights, including reproductive rights and the right to divorce, recognized and appreciated Żmichowska; although she obviously had not written about issues pertaining directly to sexuality, her position in relation to her own generation was no less shocking than that of her late "grandson," who was in equal measure admired for his various talents and ridiculed for his interest in subjects viewed as "low," shameful, and inappropriate for a literary critic.

Speaking of Boy-Żeleński, in a brief departure from strict chronology, a mention is due to his friend Irena Krzywicka (1899–1994), a writer and notable journalist who engaged with similar issues. On the pages of the most prominent literary weekly of the interwar years, *Wiadomości Literackie* (Literary News), and in its supplement *Życie Świadome* (Conscious Life), she published excellent articles about sexual education, the causes and consequences of venereal diseases, the double-morality tolerated in the behaviour of men, prostitution as a social disease, the fate of children, cruelty towards animals, family violence, and many other issues that remain current today. One of her pieces – "Rozmowa kobiet o Narcyzie Żmichowskiej" (Women Talking about Narcyza Żmichowska, 1929) – approached its subject using the dialogue form that was favoured by nineteenth-century writers. In a fictitious conversation, Krzywicka formulated inconclusive opinions about her predecessor and her work; the essay's poetics followed the same rules of dialogism and polyphonic narration as practised by the author of *Heathen*.

In in the second half of the nineteenth century, Eliza Orzeszkowa (1841–1910) embraced an all-encompassing emancipative strategy that addressed multiple subordinate social subjects. In her journalism and novels, she focused on women, Jews, and peasants. She advocated education for women and the granting of all civil rights to Jews and the rural proletariat (in the second half of the nineteenth century, the working class of the Polish Kingdom – the area annexed to Russian in the partition – was not yet numerous enough to have drawn the attention of writers as much as its peasantry). Orzeszkowa spoke in favour of emancipative equilibrium, by which she meant a balance between rights and responsibilities, with the former arising from the process of becoming equal citizens, and the latter from taking on more prominent social positions. This balance, once struck, would guarantee social utility, which would flow from new human resources acquired for the civilizational project.

Orzeszkowa believed (or *wanted* to believe) in harmonious, safe, and controlled emancipation. She argued that the emancipation of women was an expression of the modern form of trust and respect shown to the fair sex in Polish noble culture. She also maintained that women had become mature enough to merit that trust and respect and would not turn their acquired abilities and rights against their brothers, who had been so gravely affected by history. She linked the emancipation of the Jews to the option of assimilation; lacking regard for traditional Jewish religiosity, she did not notice the violence inherent in the project of adapting minorities to models delineated by the majority. Simultaneously – in a rare gesture at the time – she broached the ethical, brotherly, and humanitarian aspects of friendship between Poles and Jews. In her novella *Ogniwa* (Links, 1895), the bond that unites two elders, a Polish count and a Jewish watchmaker, each with one foot in the grave, takes the form of moral anxiety and a concern that Levinas would later express with the question "Am I my brother's keeper?" Yes, she answers, we bear responsibility for the fate of others that stems from the fundamental principle of coexistence as well as from empathy, similar experiences, the internalized expectations of the Other, and a pained conscience.

In describing village life, Orzeszkowa sidestepped or sanitized the antagonism between the manor and the *folwark*. Indeed, she did not often broach the topic of the rural proletariat, preferring to juxtapose the ethos of the manor with that of the freeholders, meaning peasants descended from impoverished nobility, with their strong sense of dignity. Here, she tied emancipation to the reawakening of historical memory and to the tradition of amity (whether in fact or fiction) between nobles and peasants from the times of the January Uprising.

Her belief in peaceful emancipation notwithstanding, Orzeszkowa could not help but notice some of its dangers. In both her journalistic writing and her narrative texts (such as *Widma* [Specters, 1880]), she warned against socialist and communist indoctrination and the radicalism of ambiguously defined (without the use of titles or names) Russian political and social thought. She did not think that Zionist ideas had a chance of becoming reality; and separatist ideas – for example, those expounded by Theodor Herzl – filled her with disappointment (*O nacjonalizmie żydowskim* [On Jewish Nationalism, 1911]). This was not how Polish-Jewish history was supposed to look! Yet she identified with her own Polish world to an ever lesser extent. The emancipating masses were adopting not only noble patriotism from their spiritual leaders, but also nationalistic ideas that were foreign to her and based in a national egoism that agitated for violence towards others. The vision of society reaching a higher level of knowledge and ethics in partial consequence of emancipation appeared to be illusory.

It is worth mentioning here Bolesław Prus (1847–1912), a strong proponent of the acquisition of knowledge and cultural awareness by the lowest social strata, including Jews. He maintained a considerable distance only towards the emancipation of women, out of his concern for the future of families and children. As an observer of daily life who was interested not only in the world's materiality but also in the principles of practical reason and the philosophy of the everyday, Prus focused his attention on raising the standard of daily existence (citing examples from Western countries, primarily England) and on the mechanisms that embroil people in dramatic situations, that is, on our illogical – albeit consistent with human psychology – struggles against fate. He perceived the problem of emancipation in this way: one can acquire appropriate knowledge without knowing how to use it. This is precisely what characterizes Wokulski, the protagonist of *Lalka* (The Doll, 1887–9), Prus's strongest work and, according to many, the greatest Polish novel. Wokulski is an emancipated capitalist who discards naive faith in youthful dreams (he participated in an uprising and was deported to Siberia) and who sets out to establish a career and make a fortune. Some see him as a *nouveau riche*, and others curry favour with the rich man; he himself is contemptuous of the aristocratic world and finds the extreme poverty of Warsaw's suburbs repugnant. There is no place where he feels comfortable or at home. He knows his own value, but he wastes it by romancing a conventional, though beautiful and well-born, woman. It is easier to make a civilizational leap than it is to eliminate one's proclivity for bad choices and inexplicable behaviours. Life is evidently something other than a theory of action, a project, or a calculation, which applies also to emancipation.

Phenomenon of Life – Historicity – Radicalism

Prus valued life, a phenomenon that was decisive in all matters, the basis of action and the test of ideas. None of its forms, not even a mushroom colony, was simple enough to ignore. So it is not surprising that the author of *The Doll* was so well received by Stanisław Brzozowski (1878–1911), an outstanding critic and journalist of the new generation, and a thinker prone to radicalism and ideological turnarounds. He was incredibly demanding and oriented towards a social and cultural reality, believing that – once it was experienced, understood, and conquered – it would open the way to a new phase of historicity. The similarities between the two writers did not, of course, erase the differences between them. Prus was fascinated by the phenomenon of life itself, while Brzozowski paid attention to humans' efforts to create social reality and to liberate themselves from nature, historical circumstances, chance, and ignorance.

In the Polish context, Brzozowski was the greatest and most consistent advocate of emancipation understood as a process of liberating humanity from the conditions created by nature and economics. Referring to the masters of his later creative phase (after a period of fascination with Nietzsche and Stirner), he wrote in *Kultura i życie* (Culture and Life, 1907): "I state without hesitation that all of modern thought up to Marx is a mental process of solving problems delineated from Kant's point-of-view. Marx can only be understood in relation to Kant; those who understand him differently understand him badly ... The world has as much meaning for human beings as they are able to extract from it."[1] Brzozowski concluded that the appropriate field of human activity is not nature (existence), but history understood as a realm "of human responsibility and his action."[2] He viewed this approach as marking the principal difference between the old philosophy of being and a modern, critical philosophy. The former has epistemological aims, adapting its thought and concepts to the object of investigation, while the latter has the task of building a "new history" and social reality, in which human beings will be the true creators, makers, and subjects of action. If the belief in the power of human beings is not to be co-opted by "blasé columnists," it must, according to Brzozowski, refer to an actual human ability to harness nature, to the functionality of tools at human disposal, and to the strength of human hands. Thought that frees the mind from the authority of rules – for instance, moral rules – becomes truly radical when it leads to the simultaneous liberation of labour: "It follows that liberation and intensification of labour is an essential goal, and that every new advance made by the working class is of more significance to culture than impressing the principles of Voltairism on thousands of shopkeepers."[3]

Brzozowski's radicalism focused on a bold critique of Polish culture that is perhaps best articulated in *Legenda Młodej Polski* (Legend of the Young Poland, 1910). He assessed negatively, though not always unequivocally, Polish Romanticism ("the rebellion of flowers against roots")[4] and Positivism (for its almost complete provincialism), as well as Young Poland (for its isolation from "everything in the world").[5] He called his native culture infantile, and he excoriated its traditional values, which he described as tied to Catholicism, the ethos of the gentry, and the cult of the family (in this, the philosopher's biographical experiences undoubtedly carried some weight). Instead, he assigned the creative function in culture to the proletariat that was aware of its own historical position. This did not mean that he favoured socially defined literature, however. He located the imperative of continuous activity and self-agency in difficult, ambitious, and open-ended projects that revealed the subject's struggle on multiple planes (here he referenced the English writings of John H. Newman, Robert Browning, and George Meredith, which were then especially esteemed).

Brzozowski carried out his emancipative strategy also as a literary critic and visionary. He wrote about, among others, Stefan Żeromski (1864–1925), although without always seeing him as an ally – that is, as someone who responded to Poland's civilizational delay with similar zeal. He remained ambivalent towards the author of *Ludzie bezdomni* (Homeless People, 1899), as did many authors among his contemporaries. For example, he criticized Żeromski's lyricism while lauding the overwhelming sense of responsibility felt by his protagonists. For Brzozowski, responsibility for the state of the world was the calling card of Żeromski's prose. The same could be said of Żeromski's emotional demonstrativeness, exhibited through the intensity of represented emotions, dramatic imagery, and a rich linguistic register. What specifically did Żeromski's emancipative strategies consist of? In the first place, he showed the failure of social emancipation. This failure extended to feudal relations that still ruled the countryside, where, just as in feudal times, peasants were abused by their masters for the slightest trespasses and unimaginable poverty suppressed all rebellion or protest, as well as to factory work that was ruinous to health without securing sustenance. Second, he showed the process of ideological maturation of the proletariat that had been accelerating since 1918 and that threatened to turn into a social revolution akin to the one in Soviet Russia. Żeromski warned against the rise in sympathy for communist ideology. Last but not least, the protagonists in his novels who represented the intelligentsia stepped outside of their professional roles to take responsibility for the fate of those who had been deprived of a voice. One can speak, therefore, of their liberation from professional roles and from the predictable ethos of professionalism. Such metamorphosis – for example, that of a doctor into a social activist who now demanded sacrifice not only from himself but also from his colleagues – brought Żeromski's heroes into conflict with their surroundings and exposed the author himself to charges of social radicalism. His heroes were also vulnerable to censure on account of their unbridled sexuality, elemental eroticism, emotional intensity, and hunger for women. Żeromski's revelatory diaries (written between 1882 and 1891 and published for the first time between 1953 and 1956 after considerable censorship) reveal strong links between the behaviour of his male heroes and experiences from their author's life.

Maria Dąbrowska (1889–1965) belongs somewhere between Prus and Żeromski. With the old master, she shared an interest in the phenomenon of life and the meaning of the everyday. With the author of *Przedwiośnie* (The Coming Spring, 1925), in turn, she shared an ear for language and a sensitivity to dialects (e.g., in *Ludzie stamtąd* [People from There], 1926). This sensitivity is juxtaposed in her roman-flueve *Noce i Dnie* (Nights and Days, 1932–4) with the speech of the narrator, which is typical of the intelligentsia: restrained, carefully polished, and seemingly "transparent." Dąbrowska's prose strikes much the same note as Joseph Conrad's, as was true also for Prus: for all three writers, life was, in its way, an ethical phenomenon. We make mistakes in living that we can likewise – that is, through spontaneously undertaken effort – correct. Dąbrowska's protagonists, especially her folk characters, are sexual beings. Much like Żeromski's, Dąbrowska's diaries, which caused a sensation after their posthumous publication, reveal how important a role erotic activity played in her life. Can eroticism be a form of liberation?

Femininity and Violence

That question becomes relevant also in the case of Zofia Nałkowska, who came from a family of intellectuals (her father was a well-known geographer and journalist of the Young Poland period, her mother a teacher and author of geography textbooks). Her early works were rooted in autobiography and posed questions about the nature of women and love. She wondered whether satisfying relations between the two sexes are possible, for example in *Kobiety* (Women, 1906). For Nałkowska, who always strongly emphasized her own gender identity ("I am first a woman, and then a human being," she declared), these were not marginal themes. They were not secondary to more important, universal, social, or philosophical issues; indeed, they were at the very centre of her intellectual investigations, which she always conducted by experiencing the world, its stimuli, and its corporeality. It was impossible for her to bracket off these determinants. She saw the body as a container in which the work of consciousness takes place, thought (including technological and military) arises, and masterworks are created. The body does not limit the spirit; it is the carrier of culture, the place where it is born, in both its variants: the first creative and humanistic, the other murderous.

Nałkowska's anthropology and ethics were shaped by two fundamental observations. First, humans desire to be cruel. The most human element, the one that distinguishes us from other species, is the pleasure of causing pain, rather than goodness and beauty. Second, there is no qualitative difference between the cruelty of war and, for instance, the killings that take place every day among people, in families, behind closed doors, between parents and children and women and men. In every situation, cruelty is ruled by the same disinterested thirst for destruction, debasement, and hurt, often combined with a perverse satisfaction, a form of sexual satiation. War does not make people bad; rather, people's bad instincts drive the world towards war, in which they find a particularly favourable field for inculpable cruelty. Joining these two insights into one formula, Nałkowska arrives at a conclusion that is so categorical as to be paralysing: the cruelty of history does not constitute the negation of humanity – it is its quintessence.

Much of Nałkowska's work writes war and the spectre of revolution into the order of existence, mimicking their structure. Such is the case with her earlier novels *Hrabia Emil* (Count Emil, 1920), *Romans Teresy Hennert* (The Romance of Teresa Hennert, 1924), *Choucas* (1926), and *Granica* (The Frontier, 1935), as well as in her journals from the time of the occupation, *Dzienniki czasów wojny* (Wartime Journals, 1970; Nałkowska kept a diary from 1899 until her death). The same is also true for *Medaliony* (Medallions, 1946). In these works, the rhythms of nature, hunting, tournaments, cruelty to animals, and competition – including, perhaps primarily, competition in love – follow the pattern of a game, with war being one of its forms. If something needs to be improved, it is life itself, but this would entail shifting onto different tracks and adopting different rules of existence. Since Nałkowska was bound to firm anthropological models, she recognized that humans are incapable of a systemic correction. If such a correction does sometimes occur, it is through the female experience of love as a sacrifice. Her female protagonists accept their fate with hopeless determination – they are defenceless and mute, and images of their suffering often correspond with frequently evoked scenes of animal slaughter.

Is there a place here for emancipative thought? From the perspective of women, emancipation is not attainable; from that of underprivileged social groups, it is difficult to say the least. Women, liberated from economic and judicial dependence, will continue to be victimized, since their need for love will embroil them in subjugation and reconcile them to violence. "Poor folk" will be forced into humility and compromise by poverty and lack of social backing. What remains? Nałkowska suggests a strategy that is less than perfect yet still impressive: intellectual discipline that will allow a subject to understand its own position as well as the violence-based mechanism by which the world functions. She employs this strategy herself: her prose, sparse in words, aphoristic, elliptical, and developed with precision, provides an excellent example of the condensation of thought that in its conclusions reaches far beyond the direct object of experience. Is this a paradox, or an objectification of the subjective, or a liberation through art?

Postwar Social Prose: Proletariat and Peasants

Social emancipation, which had been taken up in the nineteenth century, returned to literature after each of the world wars. It took the form of social prose aimed at diagnosing the situation of the urban and rural proletariat. The literary group "Przedmieście" (The Suburb), founded in 1933 and active until 1937 (and for a brief period reactivated in 1958) was its most interesting initiative. Among its members were Helena Boguszewska (1886–1978), Jerzy Kornacki (1908–81), Halina Górska (1898–1942), Halina Krahelska (1886–1945), Bruno Schulz (1892–1942), Sydor Rey, or more accurately Izydor Reiss (1908–79), and Nałkowska. The group underscored the need to develop a new type of prose capable of documenting the situation of the proletariat, ethnic minorities, and children born in poverty. In the introduction to the collective work *Przedmieście* (The Suburb, 1934), Halina Krahelska wrote:

> Our methodological assumptions differentiate us quite clearly from middle-class literature, however rich in talent. One key difference is that only people who feel psychologically driven to actively engage with the working man in his historic struggle for the right to a life and for changes to the social and economic system can belong to our group. Only this emotional,

> mental engagement guarantees an appropriate approach to the life issues and psychology of the proletariat.[6]

In theory, this group's postulates should have appeared in postwar socialist-realist prose. The Soviet authorities, however, supported honest observation of the working world only in their pronouncements; for as long as they imposed their ideology on literature from above, there would be no room in it for observation, honest debate, and the emancipation of a proletarian protagonist.

The founders of the "Przedmieście" literary group pointed out that the name of their initiative was to be understood metaphorically – it was not just the industrial suburbs that were at stake; so were the marginalized suburbs of Polish culture. They insisted that their program left room for descriptions of rural poverty as well. Even so, the short literary works that emerged from this group's collective experiments – located on the borderlands of reportage and narrative, such as Górska's *Ślepe tory* (Blind Tracks, 1937) – dealt primarily with the city. The current of so-called peasant prose, which has as its central subject the social advancement of people born and raised in the countryside amid poverty and without educational opportunities, developed independently and bore more literary fruit. In the interwar years, the situation in the countryside was explored by, among others, Jalu Kurek (1904–83), Stanisław Piętak (1909–64), Jan Wiktor (1890–1967), Leon Kruczkowski (1900–62), and Józef Morton (1911–64). Bruno Jasieński (1901–38), in his narrative poem *Słowo o Jakubie Szeli* (A Word about Jakub Szela, 1926), chose as his protagonist the nineteenth-century peasant insurgent who, in 1846, led a savage slaughter of landowners in Galicia (a realm under Austrian partition at the time). The event shocked the Polish landowning class and reverberated for many years. Rural issues are also key to the authors of *Pamiętniki chłopów* (Peasant Diaries, 1935–6), who submitted their writings to a contest held by the Institute of Social Economy, a well-meaning organization founded in 1920 for the purpose of diagnosing and solving the new state's social problems. The novels of Kurek (primarily *Grypa szaleje w Napra*wie [Influenza Rages in Naprawo, 1934]) and of Piętak (*Młodość Jasia Kunefała* [Jaś Kunefał's Adolescence, 1938]) established a particular model of writing about village life, one characterized by brutal descriptions of a simple but impoverished way of life. These descriptions did not, however, undercut the lyrical qualities of these works, which focused on the aspirations of young peasants who overcame educational barriers with the help of their family, or despite their wishes. After the Second World War, this manner of writing infused the prose of Tadeusz Nowak (1930–91) and Marian Pilot (b. 1936). In turn, the novels *Tańczący jastrząb* (The Dancing Hawk, 1964) and *Pałac* (Palace, 1970), written by Julian Kawalec (1916–2014) and Wiesław Myśliwski (b. 1932), respectively, present the psychological consequences of peasants' advancement to new social roles as creators and inheritors of national culture. Myśliwski, a great storyteller of the lives of Polish peasantry born, like the author himself, before the war, and who had experienced all of the historical and systemic ailments that were the lot of Polish society between 1939 and 1989, is one of the outstanding Polish prose writers of the past fifty years.

Myśliwski's every novel could play an emblematic role in relation to the twentieth-century fate of Polish peasants. This is especially true of *Kamień na kamieniu* (Stone upon Stone, 1984), a saga of the Pietruszka family that brilliantly presents the difficulty of restoring the peasant ethos that had been shaken by both the war and the socialist transformation that followed. An even more drastic variant of emancipation is found in another work – Marian Pilot's *Pióropusz* (War Bonnet, 2010). Various genre traditions intersect in this work – the conventions of a *Bildungsroman* and of an emancipative novel, the elements of a novel about childhood and fragments of a family saga, autobiographical and fictional frameworks – only to immediately take flight into elemental yet refined, erratic and pained, plain yet impressive verbal fireworks. The author's lexical inventiveness is inversely proportional to the status of his characters. The family presented in this quasi-autobiography belongs to a rural *Lumpenproletariat*, a world of poverty outside the law, the reality of which is debased, marginalized, disrespected, and larcenous. From this seemingly worthless shambles, however, a writer is born who, perceiving the poverty of his family home, notices also its subversive greatness, in Agamben's terms – its holiness and profanity, rebelliousness, dignity, and heroism.

Until 1989, and thus for almost two hundred years, **the freedom of the subject** in Poland was limited in two ways: by the political situation and, equally onerously, by social expectations, which burdened writers with the responsibility to participate in a common fate – that of a citizen of a country trying to extricate itself from political non-existence and of a co-creator of a peripheral culture focused on its secondary status. In the period of early modernism (the turn of the nineteenth and twentieth centuries), the variant of subjective liberty derived from philosophy (of Kant, Nietzsche, or Stirner) and the aspect of activism proclaimed (in their own fashion) by Sorel and Marx, was deemed sufficient. Around the mid-twentieth century the situation allowed for more radical solutions – for a complete break with social expectations, a departure from well-worn paths, and a sidestepping of both the ethos of domestic intelligentsia fighting against censorship, and that of the émigré artist consigned to the Polish diaspora scattered across the Western countries. This form of radical freedom and emancipation was available only to the greatest of the great, those who were most aware of their situation. These individuals were simultaneously the weakest (most prone to temptation) and the strongest (most prepared to deal with loneliness and the hardship of rejection).

II. Freedom of the Subject: Two Variants

Starting at the end of the eighteenth century, Polish culture vested writers with responsibilities that extended far beyond the generally accepted repertoire of artist's roles. This was largely the result of a disadvantageous political situation, the loss of sovereignty, the lack of public institutions, and censorship. After the failure of the November Uprising (1831), Polish culture circulated on two levels: the national, which was limited by censorship, and the exilic, which was free of these restrictions but burdened with duties of another kind, such as the need to represent a non-existent nation and a people deprived of their voice. The restoration of independence in 1918 did not release writers from their obligations as they engaged with the building of a democratic state. After 1939 they once again lived under occupation, either German or Soviet. After the Second World War, when Poland found itself within the Russian (this time Soviet) sphere of influence, its writers once again had to define themselves and make vital life choices under adverse circumstances.

Gombrowicz: Polish Form, Self-Form, and the Horror of Existence

Witold Gombrowicz's (1904–69) struggle for his own independence as well as that of Polish culture is widely acknowledged. He gained the former only at a distance from his family, his close friends, and his homeland, having chosen to remain in Argentina when the war began in 1939. Far from his compatriots, he pointed out their provincialism, insincerity, and superficiality. He thought that "a Pole does not know how to act toward Poland, it confuses him and makes him mannered. It inhibits the Pole to such a degree that nothing really 'works' for him. Poland forces him into a cramped state – he wants to help it too much, he wants to elevate it too much."[7] More was at stake here than Poles' irrepressible desire to reassure themselves and the world that they belonged to it; as Gombrowicz noted ironically in the first volume of his *Diaries* (1957), after all Poles have Mickiewicz, Słowacki, Chopin, Maria Curie-Skłodowska, and the Constitution of the 3rd of May. The real issue was that, in hiding behind sources of authority, "life and modern minds were being sacrificed to the deceased."[8] A similar, although differently motivated need to escape from historical circumstances – "from Poland, from graves, from misfortunes, from constant futile efforts" – was expressed by Andrzej Bobkowski (1913–61) in *Szkice piórkiem* (Pen Sketches, 1957), a wartime journal (France 1940–4) written from the perspective of a subject enjoying an inner freedom and seeking the right to happiness.[9]

Gombrowicz argued that real life is conditional on the ability to shrug off esteemed "giants," from whom one must become independent; and on the ability to circumvent form or, alternatively, to create one's own form, without imitating anything given by either the East or the West (such as, respectively, communist ideology and the cult of community that suppresses the individual, or liberalism, middle-class values, and the adoration of art). Without these abilities, existence becomes an imitation of life, a "Great Masquerade," something that only seems like a life. Commenting on the literary world of prewar Poland, Gombrowicz underscores its artificiality and the posturing of artists as the ideologues of great causes, poking fun at Jerzy Andrzejewski's pretend (in his opinion) Catholicism and Konstanty Ildefons Gałczyński's alcohol-infused nationalism. He asserts that these mystifications were apparent and obvious to him even then. Consequently, he saw the postwar metamorphoses of Polish intellectuals, which he read about, for example, in Miłosz's *Zniewolony umysł* (Captive Mind, 1953), as a natural consequence of their prewar games of appearances.

The position that Gombrowicz reserved for himself (and perhaps partly for Miłosz) was difficult, and not just on the biographical, material level of a homeless, uncertain life on the edge of poverty. His criticism of prewar Poland and the post-gentry mentality notwithstanding, he felt a sense of belonging to this world. He saw himself as someone who – having specific historical experiences – could not place excessive trust in the phenomena and values treated so seriously in the West, such as art. When Westerners "see a man kneeling before Bach's music, I see people who force each other to genuflect and feel delight and admiration."[10] It is relatively easy to discard or at least deride the past, for instance, one's familial past; with a bit of luck and determination, it is possible to escape the pressure of "Great Ideology" (communism) and negate art ("I do not believe in art, I do not believe in music," Gombrowicz provocatively declared). But where was one to go from there – what could one admire and where could one seek refuge?

In some ways, Gombrowicz's intelligence, hyper-awareness, and iron determination and logic, posed a problem. Since he considered form – imposed by nation, family, tradition, and other people – as something that threatened the individual, and since he took it to be an irreducible, inescapable means of social interaction, he had to accept – at least theoretically – his dependence on the formulated principle. His freedom became, in a sense, a hostage to his thought. At best, he could dream of a limited emancipation. Yet he was also capable of something that was beyond the reach of mere mortals: he could play with form and determine his own form, which he created in various interactions. The status given to the "inter-human" was precisely what made Gombrowicz's philosophy so original.

Creativity provided Gombrowicz with space for experimentation. In his diary, he established an intimate, an once honest and artificial contact with the reader, forcing his perception upon him, seducing him and demanding admiration, intimidating him with his intelligence and awareness of the game being played, the rules of which he shamelessly exposed in his entries. He revealed the desire to "travel as far as possible into the virgin territory of culture, into its still half-wild, and so indecent, places, while exciting you to extremes, to excite even myself."[11] He was playing a game and knew he was playing it; he entangled the reader and felt entangled himself. Having embroiled himself in a net of tensions, he maintained the semblance of control over the situation. He used ambiguities: the subject position in the charades he constructed was not completely determined; it was both internal and external to the rules of the game, at once dominant and subservient, as elusive as a figure reflected in multiple mirrors. His famous statement: "Monday – I, Tuesday – I, Wednesday – I, Thursday – I" had to have an audience, a spectator who, in being allowed to see behind the curtain of Gombrowicz's art of life, forced the author to descend ever further into the depths of his self.[12]

On liberating himself from various obligations dictated by culture and tradition, Gombrowicz felt the pressure of primal forces – virginal and, as he wrote, half-wild. What was this archaic force? With what can we identify it? With the horror of being? With Lacan's the Real, as Michał P. Markowski writes in his monograph about Gombrowicz (*Czarny nurt* [Black Current], 2004)? With the pressure of erotic desires, a lust that is relentless, treacherous, harmful to health and perhaps even to life (venereal diseases together with their consequences)? The author's intimate journal *Kronos* (Chronos, 2013), published after years of gossip and conjecture and made up of factographic micro-entries, throws some light on these issues. His annual summaries consist of four points, akin to headings of popular horoscopes: notes about health (ever worse, ever more fallible: infections, liver, teeth, eczema, allergies, difficulties with breathing, asthma, digestive problems); the state of finances (changeable, with a propensity to increase in proportion to successive translations); professional successes or failures (as above), and the intensity of erotic life (diminishing along with weakening physical condition). They offer no distractions, no rapture, and no effusiveness, only a somber recitation, a cold calculation, and a strict account. This is the intransgressible framework that held Gombrowicz within its iron grip.

MIŁOSZ: SAILING ONWARD

In thinking about Czesław Miłosz (1911–2004), I am reminded of the ending of a certain poem by Adam Mickiewicz (1798–1855), the greatest of Polish Romantic poets, who after numerous exploits was able to mislead tsarist officials and emigrate to the West, where he spent the remainder of his life as the spiritual leader of what is known today as the Great Emigration. In "Żeglarz" (The Sailor, in *Odessa Sonnets*, 1826), the poet – accused, among other things, of too close a relation with Russian elites – writes:

"In wishing to judge me, you must be not with me, but in me / I'm flowing onward, you be homeward bound."[13] Miłosz's biography and artistic accomplishments amount to a similar sequence of choices, which either anticipated coming events (such as the catastrophism he proclaimed long before the war, his critique of communist ideology realized at the very apogee of its rule, and his distance from the French intellectual left at a time when its influence was rising), or exposed the poet to accusations cast from both sides of the barricade dividing the postwar world. Miłosz was censured in exile for access to the communist establishment (he was an employee of the Polish diplomatic service in Paris and New York from 1945 to 1950), and when he asked for political asylum in France in 1951, he was accused of treason by the communists, derogated by professional colleagues in Poland, and erased from Polish literary circulation and the memory of its readers. He was also mistrusted by émigré circles, especially by countrymen tied to London's weekly *Wiadomości*, and distanced from their activities; for many years he remained in difficult material and life circumstances, isolated and reliant on the goodwill of those close to him, and on his talent, which in the end took him as far as anyone can go.

Miłosz's unorthodox behaviour was not limited to issues related to Poland's postwar system. His relationship to the war and to the moral responsibilities emerging therefrom was similarly complicated. During the first years of the German occupation, he participated in underground literary life, feeling a bond with much younger poets, and he became susceptible to the patriotic idiom. In the introduction to the collection of his correspondence with Polish writers from 1945 to 1950 (*Zaraz po wojnie* [Immediately after the War], 1998), Miłosz wrote:

> The sudden liberation, breakthrough, seeming replacement of fatherland with "sonland," à la Gombrowicz, occurred in my case in 1943 and has had a measurable effect on my poetry ever since, as well as on my actions, for at stake here was clearly the act of political choice, without which I would not be able to conquer the demands of virtue. This act of choosing meant no more than openness to an unknown fate, but it clearly countered Polish orthodoxy. It was a joyous emancipation from the compulsion of responsibility.[14]

This mental break was immediately noticed, treated with suspicion, and held against the author for many years as an evasion of the risk that accompanied conspiracy and participation in the Warsaw Uprising (1944). For Miłosz, however, it was a condition for writing poetry. In his case, the search for an individual poetic idiom went hand in hand with the attempt to reconcile the attained tone (voice) with his conscience. In the same work the author concluded:

> Among the author's many internal contradictions, a mention is due, I think, to the syndrome of a good boy who very much tries, in his eyes, to be good, but, since he does not really succeed in this, constantly suffers from pangs of conscience. I can treat this duality of sin and self-chastisement acquired in a Catholic school humorously, but it nevertheless explains much in my poetry.[15]

Making choices that aligned with his internal convictions and announcing them to the world – even though this was often mistaken for egotism and megalomania – constituted for him part of a mental and ethical mechanism that was at times incredibly uncomfortable, yet necessary as a condition of writing.

Miłosz's relationship to Polishness was very complex. Born near Kaunas, a city now part of Lithuania, on the lands of the former Grand Duchy of Lithuania, which had been tied to the Commonwealth since the sixteenth century, but which maintained its mental and cultural separateness, he saw himself as a Lithuanian who spoke Polish. This self-identification – scandalous for many Poles – expressed the poet's sentiment for the land of his youth, immortalized in *Dolina Issy* (The Issa Valley, 1955) and in numerous poems, narrative and otherwise. But it also conveyed his criticism of prewar (and to some extent also postwar and Romantic) Polish patriotism, which denied other nations the right to similar sentiments if they collided with Poles' emotions and expectations, or the historical status quo. His sensitivity to the "Lithuanian question" was due in part to the influence of his cousin Oskar Miłosz (1877–1939), a Lithuanian poet writing in French, who was unusually severe in his judgment of interwar Polish politics with regard to the eastern regions of the Commonwealth, tracing them back to post-Romantic messianism. Oskar Miłosz wrote: "Speaking in favour of independent Lithuania, which Poles considered to be the 'rebellious Kingdom of Kaunas,' I speak as an opponent of Polish expansion in the East."[16]

The author of *The Issa Valley* upheld and expanded on these reservations, subjecting interwar Poland to a crushing appraisal in *Wyprawa w Dwudziestolecie* (Excursion through the Twenties and Thirties, 1999), a selection of literary and journalistic fragments from works written between 1918 and 1939 and accompanied by his commentary. In that book, Miłosz showed the poverty of villages and cities as well as the consequences of the Great Depression, anti-Semitism, and attitudes towards citizens of different nationalities and ethnicities. He recognized that his vision of the "Sanation" Poland was not objective:

> Of course, my position is of a particular kind, determined perhaps by the fact that I was born in Lithuania, not in Poland, and that I looked on its issues from Vilnius, or from a Vilnian perspective. This means that the Poland of Warsaw, Cracow and Poznan was, so to speak, outside of my first impressions and experiences. Nevertheless, I do not deserve to be called a "borderland" man; even the term irritates me. I never heard this word applied to us in our family. To the contrary: we were from here, namely the former Grand Duchy of Lithuania, with the main cities of our region being Vilnius and Riga.[17]

A number of gestures underscore Miłosz's permanent position outside of any kind of a community: his choice of a life path – a difficult and risky decision, even though advantageous and successful in the end; his subversion of sanctified dogmas (of patriotism, Polishness, national heroism), which was decisive and provocative, if always open to polemics and the exchange of ideas, and which he undertook to attest to his own distinctiveness; his search for ever-new idioms and poetic languages – from the visuality of catastrophism to the asceticism of haikus, from a translation of the Bible to *silva rerum*, from a stylized chronicle to a refined or prosaic correspondence. His status as an outsider applied regardless of whether the community in question referred to a national sphere, a specific style or poetic group, or his circle of friends or family. Yet the author, who was strongly inclined to congeniality and who admitted that for him, "energy in alcohol consumption … sexual energy, and … creative energy were linked,"[18] nevertheless disappeared behind the doors of his study and there – in isolation and solitude – created art.

The instance when autobiographical events are transformed into an artefact, memories and impressions become a poetic phrase, and a multiplicity of experiences is turned into a literary construct, deserves particular attention in Miłosz's case. The poet dedicated the essay "O wygnaniu" ("On Exile") in *Searching for Homeland* to this problem, revealing the tragedy of emigration and the émigré's loneliness in attempting to restore under new conditions – in a foreign city, amid an unknown landscape – a sense of familiarity and home. Such escape beyond oneself usually fails, exposing the subject to sufferings and frustrations that cannot be attended to, since they are the lot of too many people with too many different, alienating experiences. At the same time, however, Miłosz notices something that complements and transforms his situation. In the contemporary world, mobility assumes the necessity of communication and mutual contact between people with different experiences, histories, and languages, and the feelings of discomfort and otherness he describes create space for communication: "Perhaps a loss of harmony with the surrounding space, the inability to feel at home in the world, so oppressive to an expatriate, a refugee, an immigrant, however we call him, paradoxically integrates him in contemporary society and makes him, if he is an artist, understood by all. Even more, to express the existential situation of modern man, one must live in exile of some sort."[19]

A poet in exile, facing the test of inner freedom, becomes a kind of medium for the essence of the contemporary world. He takes on the role of a translator, an intermediary, and a *trickster*, mediating between people and their cultures. He brings them closer together, gets them used to one another, encourages them to take another step, to taste and to touch, like a merchant displaying his exotic wares in bygone times. Yet the most paradoxical consequence of exile is the return to the land of one's childhood that takes place at some point. This return does not have to be literal. Rather, a mental return is at stake and a more sympathetic outlook on the homeland, which is not always a product of gnawing nostalgia. Miłosz also enacted such a return, both metaphorically and literally. In the 1990s, he lived in Cracow in a residence on Bogusławska Street offered to him by the city, having previously already lived on both sides of the Atlantic, dividing his time between Poland and United States. Even more interesting, however, is his ideological "come back." Miłosz makes a spiritual return, teeming with a never before revealed fascination for the idiom of Polishness, for Romanticism and messianism, including the version expounded by Andrzej Towiański (the leader of a messianic sect that believed in Poland's resurrection and that governed the spirit of the Polish emigrant community in Paris of the 1840s, to which Adam Mickiewicz for a time belonged). Essays published during 2002 in Cracow's *Tygodnik Powszechny* testify to this thought-provoking metanoia. Aware of his transformation, Miłosz tried to mitigate it, treating his new interests as the presentation of a problem rather than the resolution of an issue. He asked, for instance, whether Polishness is expressed in some specific historical form and what made the phenomenon of Towiański possible. Nevertheless, it is clear that Miłosz came full circle. His biography is an exemplary case of the defector who, having conquered the world, triumphantly (and at the same time humbly) returns to his homeland. Polishness given as a fate was unacceptable to him, but Polishness as a choice became precisely his fate.

III. Difficult Freedom

The above heading is not a citation from Levinas, but a reflection on the position of the subject during a time of political freedom in Poland after 1989. The much-yearned-for freedom turned out to be a difficult experience, one that deprived Polish writers of a long-lived source of activity that the struggle for independence (one's own and national) provided and that knocked them off the pedestal onto which they had been raised over the previous centuries. The writer became simply a man of letters, an element of democratic culture, a literary professional earning a living by writing. Young artists who debuted after 1989 actually complained of a biographical void, the lack of a generational experience. Their experience was centred precisely on a lack of historical experiences, other-than-economic necessities, and social obligations.

Freedom, a trecherous gift that demands maturity and self-discipline, had to be carefully considered, adjusted, and managed. From the perspective of the past twenty-five years, it is possible to speak of two emancipative strategies that are an important element of contemporary literary reality and that would have been impossible to realize under previous (and not only political) conditions. They are the emancipation of memory, and the emancipation of non-normative sexuality that precipitated the proverbial "coming out" of many Polish writers.

The emancipation of memory meant a return to historical events (such as the Second World War, the Warsaw Uprising, and the Holocaust) that was denuded of opportunistic omissions, courageous, and always painful, as well as the presentation of these events within a framework of personal (sometimes autobiographic) narration that focused on aspects and perspectives absent from official historiographic accounts. Works that countered textbook and ideologized knowledge had been created earlier as well, of course, as was the case with *Do piachu ...* (Bite the Dust ..., 1979), a play by Tadeusz Różewicz (1921–2014) that painted a non-heroic portrait of the Polish partisan forces during the Second World War. Such publications were a quickly marginalized exception, however. After 1989, a wave of works that presented a different view of the war swept in, bringing back memories of Polish Jews and the Holocaust.

Henryk Grynberg (b. 1936) continued his Jewish odyssey in documentary prose, first with emigrant and later also with Polish publishers, with works such as *Dziedzictwo* (Heritage, 1993), *Pamiętnik Marii Koper* (Memoir of Maria Koper, 1993), and *Dzieci Syjonu* (Children of Zion, 1994), as well as in novels, poems, and short stories. Hanna Krall (b. 1935) also dedicated herself to Jewish subject matter; among other works, she is the author of the short story collections *Hipnoza* (Hypnosis, 1989), *Dowody na istnienie* (Evidence for Existence, 2000), *Tam już nie ma żadnej rzeki* (There Is No River There Anymore, 2001), *Taniec na cudzym weselu* (Dancing at Someone Else's Wedding, 2002), and *Król kier znów na wylocie* (Chasing the King of Hearts, 2006). The experiences of children of the Holocaust have been described by, among others, Marek Edelman (1922–2009), the last leader of the Warsaw Ghetto Uprising, in numerous books and interviews, most notably that given to Hanna Krall and related in *Zdążyć przed Panem Bogiem* (Shielding the Flame, 1977); Jerzy Ficowski (1924–2006) in *Czekanie na sen psa* (Waiting for the Dog to Sleep, 1973; English trans. 2006); Michał Głowiński (b. 1934) in *Czarne sezony* (The Black Seasons, 1999), *Historia jednej topoli* (The Story of One Poplar, 2003), and *Kręgi obcości* (Spheres of Strangeness, 2010); Roma Ligocka (b. 1938) in *Dziewczynka w czerwonym płaszczyku* (The Girl in the Red Coat: A Memoir, 2002);

Irit Amiel (b. 1931) in *Osmaleni* (Scorched, 1999) and *Wdychać głęboko* (Inhale Deeply, 2002); Janina Bauman (1926–2009) in *Zima o poranku. Opowieść dziewczynki z warszawskiego getta* (Winter in the Morning: A Young Girl's Life in the Warsaw Ghetto and Beyond, 1939–45, 1999); Icchak Cukierman (1915–81) in *Nadmiar pamięci. Wspomnienia 1939–1946* (A Surplus of Memory: Chronicle of the Warsaw Ghetto Uprising, 2000; English trans. 1993); and Ida Fink (1921–2011) in *Podróż* (The Journey, 1990) and *Odpływający ogród* (The Garden Floating Away, 2002).

The listed authors exemplify only a few ways in which the aforementioned emancipative strategy was realized. The phenomenon is much broader and extends to academic studies conducted by a number of Polish institutions (including the Polish Centre for Holocaust Research, affiliated with the Institute of Philosophy and Sociology of the Polish Academy of Sciences in Warsaw), numerous publications, and the scholarly and essayistic works of Jan Grabowski, Jan Tomasz Gross, Irena Grudzińska-Gross, Barbara Engelking, Jacek Leociak, Joanna Tokarsa-Bakir, Alina Cała, Helena Datner, Paweł Śpiewak, Jolanta Żyndul, and Sławomir Buryła. Again, this is only a partial list that by no means exhausts the possibilities. The scholars mentioned here are those whose essayistic writing enters into social rather than strictly academic debates about Polish and Jewish identity, Polish complicity in the Holocaust, and anti-Semitic attitudes. The problem itself – of the sources of anti-Semitism, our shared responsibility for the Holocaust, and current attitudes towards Jews – remains unresolved and perhaps never will be resolved. Yet the fact that the debate is taking place on various levels of social discourse, that its participants do not hide their descent, that we publicly honour the memory of Jews and consider their work – indeed, their presence – to be an irreplaceable element of Polish cultural capital, is one of the more valuable gains that have resulted from the difficult freedom experienced by Poles since 1989.

Even though it is most visible there, the settling of past accounts applies not only to the "Jewish question" and complicates the view of Polish history in general. Non-standard interpretations of Polish history are appearing with increasing frequency. They do not always reinterpret historical events, as happens in *Stankiewicz. Powrót* (Stankiewicz: The Return, 1984), a diptych by Eustachy Rylski (b. 1944), or in his later novel *Warunek* (Condition, 2005), in which key Polish themes of patriotism and national identity acquire surprising meanings and contexts. Narratives often sidestep "Great History" in order to recall the personal experience of the narrator, as is the case with the novels of Andrzej Czcibor-Piotrowski (1931–2014), such as *Rzeczy nienasycone* (Insatiable Things, 1999) and *Cud w Esfahanie* (Miracle in Esfahan, 2001), in which a childhood spent in exile in Kazakhstan and Iran is tied primarily to his strong, sensual feelings of love for his mother. Sometimes the idiom of Polishness is constructed in a seemingly traditional manner, but with the use of forms that arouse certain anxieties – either by being too ambiguous or too overdrawn, or with their application of artistic licence to historical sources. The essays of Jarosław Marek Rymkiewicz (b. 1928) offer one example; his collections include *Wieszanie* (Hanging, 2007), *Kinderszenen* (Childhood Scenes, 2008), *Samuel Zborowski* (2010), and *Reytan. Upadek Polski* (Reytan: The Fall of Poland, 2013). Historical fantasy offers another model of "playing with" history in its building of alternative plot lines, as seen in *Lód* (Ice, 2007) by Jacek Dukaj (b. 1974). In some ways, the past has been made more familiar by the authors of popular literature and crime novels set, for example, before the Second World War, with the books of Marek Krajewski, Marcin Wroński, and Tadeusz Cegielski providing a few examples.

Narrations that both reconstruct and reinterpret the past appear less frequently. One such "total" narration is Jacek Dehnel's (b. 1980) *Matka Makryna* (Mother Makryna, 2014), the story of a woman who pretended to be the abbess of a Uniate Basilian convent, an order that was persecuted by the tsarist authorities and forced to convert to the Eastern Orthodoxy during the nineteenth century. The false Mother Makryna arrived in Paris in 1845 with the aura of a martyr and later travelled on to Rome. Despite many suspicions, she was never unmasked; it seems that no one wanted her to be denounced. Playing the victim (perhaps primarily of Russian violence) was one of the roles of the Polish patriot; other roles were much more difficult. Dehnel's narration runs along two tracks: mystification collides with a true story of martyrdom of a different kind – that of a woman abused by her husband.

A complex and detailed portrait of German occupation during the Second World War is presented by Szczepan Twardoch (b. 1979) in the novel *Morfina* (Morphine, 2013). Its protagonist, part German, part Polish, becomes embroiled in conspiratorial, erotic, and adventurous activities while setting aside questions of identity, heroism, or historical justice. For war had also this side: private, intimate, and separated from Great History by a curtain woven from other human tragedies and unfulfilled dreams. Kazimierz Brandys (1916–2000) and Andrzej Szczypiorski (1928–2000) had already used this perspective. In Brandys's *Jak być kochaną?* (How to Be Loved?, 1960), the unreciprocated, hidden love of the heroine for her actor-friend overshadows everything else, including the horrors of war; in Szczypiorski's *Początek* (The Beginning, 1986), the ethical systems and actions of the protagonists deviate from readerly expectations. Half a century ago, Brandys's work – which was grippingly filmed by the outstanding director Wojciech Has – merely supplemented the national martyrology, while Szczypiorski's novel did not find a publisher in Poland. Today, Twardoch's narration and other unconventional perspectives mark the generally accepted way of writing about Polish history.

The issue of sexual freedom and the right to non-normative erotic practices may seem unequal in weight to the task of disarming the patriotic and martyrological image of Polish history and culture. Despite appearances, however, the literary "coming out" of gays and lesbians constitutes a missing element of the same transformational process, which is aimed at the modernization of Polish society, the reconstruction of mindsets, the democratization of social life, and the fostering of tolerance and of respect for fundamental rights. Of course, homosexual themes have always been present in modern Polish literature. In the past, however, the thread of homosexual desire was spun covertly, with artistic prose and figurative speech providing unlimited possibilities for indirect communication. The homoerotic experience can be expressed directly by today's writers, as exemplified by Grzegorz Musiał (b. 1952) in *Czeska biżuteria* (Czech Jewellery, 1993) and *Al fine* (1997); Michał Witkowski (b. 1975) in his famous novel *Lubiewo* (2005); Bartosz Żurawiecki (b. 1971) in *Trzech panów w łóżku, nie licząc kota* (Three Men in Bed, Not Counting the Cat, 2005); and the plays and novels of Marcin Szczygielski (b. 1972) and Ewa Schilling (b. 1971), who has written a number of novels and collections of stories, including *Lustro* (Mirror, 1998) and *Akacja* (*Acacia*, 2001). Homosexual motifs are also present in the work of Izabela Filipiak (b. 1961) and Inga Iwasiów (b. 1963).

These literary accomplishments are supported by historical and literary investigations that have uncovered homoerotic motifs in the works of many Polish writers who were not linked to this source of sensibility before – for instance, Jarosław Iwaszkiewicz (1894–1980) and Jerzy Andrzejewski (1909–83). To this one might add works that hypothesize the homosexuality of notable Polish women writers such as Narcyza Żmichowska, Maria Konopnicka (1842–1910), Maria Dąbrowska, and Anna Kowalska (1903–69).

IV. Summary

The emancipative strategies in Polish literature of the last 150 years concerned social issues, such as equal opportunity for underprivileged social groups (peasants, workers, women, and Jews), as well as individual ones – freedom from various obligations towards the collective, freedom of sexual preferences, or freedom to choose where to live without being accused of running away or looking for an "easy" life. Two observations are in order. First, the two types of emancipative strategies are not completely separate; one could even say that their most interesting examples combine a concrete social message with a developed subjectivity that refers to original philosophical assumptions, life experiences, sensibility, and ethics. Second, it is not only the strategies that deserve description and reflection, but also the individual means of their realization. There are always more variants than there are principal trajectories (strategies) of emancipation. Since literature and writers are at stake in this discussion, one cannot omit emancipation's narrative, artistic, linguistic, and biographical contexts, for they too impact its form. For this reason, the most important individual projects belong to these two types of emancipation – social and individual. This dual framework allows us to grasp both their ideological and literary aspects; the theme survives without effacing the artistic idiom.

Grażyna Borkowska
The Institute of Literary Research of the Polish Academy of Sciences
Translated by Agnieszka Polakowska

NOTES

1 Brzozowski, *Kultura i życie*, 390.
2 Ibid., 392.
3 Ibid., 400.
4 Brzozowski, *Legenda Młodej Polski*, 34.
5 Ibid., 51.
6 Krahelska, *Przedmieście*, VIII.
7 Gombrowicz, *Diary*, vol. 1, 7.
8 Ibid., 7.
9 Bobkowski, *Szkice piórkiem*, 526.
10 Gombrowicz, *Diary*, vol. 1, 25.
11 Ibid., 43.
12 Ibid., 3.
13 Mickiewicz, "Żeglarz," https://wolnelektury.pl/katalog/lektura/sonety-odeskie-zeglarz.html.
14 Miłosz, *Zaraz po wojnie: Korespondencja z pisarzami 1945–1950*, 10–11.
15 Ibid., 11.
16 Miłosz, *Szukanie Ojczyzny*, 8.
17 Miłosz, *Wyprawa w Dwudziestolecie*, 9.

18 Miłosz, *A Year of the Hunter*, 222.

19 Miłosz in Koudelka and Miłosz, *Exiles* (unpaginated). Online: http://www.americansuburbx.com/2009/06/theory-czeslaw-milosz-on-josef.html.

WORKS CITED

Bobkowski, Andrzej. *Szkice piórkiem*. Warszawa: PoMOST, 1995.

Brzozowski, Stanisław. *Kultura i życie*. Lwów: Ksiegarnia B. Polanieckiego, 1907.

– *Legenda Młodej Polski. Studia o strukturze duszy kulturalnej*. Lwów: Nakład Księgarni Polskiej, 1910.

Gombrowicz, Witold. *Diary*, vol. 1. Translated by Lillian Vallee. New Haven: Yale University Press, 2012.

Koudelka, Josef, and Czesław Miłosz. *Exiles*. New York: Aperture, 2014.

Krahelska, Halina. *Przedmieście*. Edited by H. Boguszewska and J. Kornacki. Warszawa: Rój, 1934.

Miłosz, Czesław. *Szukanie Ojczyzny*. Kraków: Znak, 1992.

– *A Year of the Hunter*. Translated by Madeline G. Levine. New York: Farrar, Straus and Giroux, 1994.

– *Wyprawa w Dwudziestolecie*. Kraków: Wydawnictwo Literackie, 1999.

– *Zaraz po wojnie: Korespondencja z pisarzami 1945–1950*. Edited by Jerzy Illg. Znak: Kraków, 1998.

Delectatio furiosa, or, the Modes of Cultural Transgression

I. The Central Concept

Transgression articulates, interrogates, challenges, and redraws the limits of the prohibited, the unrecognized, the displaced, the disowned, or the denied. Its domains are the axiological, the sacred, the extreme, the excessive, the bodily, the sexual, and the erotic. It traverses value judgments, respect, desire, fear, and disgust. It moves freely between rationality and irrationality (as Foucault proves when rethinking the Nietzschean discussion of the Apollonian and Dionysian drives)[1] and between Eros and Thanatos (as in Bataille's theories of eroticism and Freud's of death drives). As a psychological imperative, it can be identified with our craving, akin to spiritual transcendence, for individual expansion beyond physical, psychological, and cultural boundaries, and for the creation of the new. As such, it both defies and defines our experience and understanding of the world and of our position in it, always pointing to where we are not – yet.

> John Jervis usefully defines the transgressive as "reflexive, questioning both its own role and that of the culture that has defined it in its otherness. It is not simply a reversal, a mechanical inversion of an existing order it opposes. Transgression, unlike opposition or reversal, involves hybridization, the mixing of categories and the questioning of the boundaries that separate categories. It is not, in itself, subversion; it is not an overt and deliberate challenge to the status quo. What it does do, though, is implicitly interrogate the law, pointing not just to the specific, and frequently arbitrary, mechanisms of power on which it rests – despite its universalizing pretensions – but also to its complicity, its involvement in what it prohibits."
>
> – Jervis, *Transgressing the Modern: Explorations in the Western Experience of Otherness*, 4

> Transgressive behavior therefore does not deny limits or boundaries; rather it exceeds them and thus completes them. Every rule, limit, boundary or edge carries with it its own fracture, penetration or impulse to disobey. The transgression is a component of the rule.
>
> – Jenks, *Transgression*, 7

As a self-reflexive philosophical, aesthetic, psychological, and sociological concept, transgression involves crossing boundaries while keeping a close eye on what is being transgressed. It also assesses the profits from the existence of what is exceeded and invites close scrutiny of cultural processes and their defence mechanisms. Its usefulness as a critical concept lies partly in its inconclusiveness. Unlike revolutions, rebellions, and countercultures, transgression does not try to erase limits; it probes and completes them, allowing for careful examination of what was challenged but not destroyed. Transgression is also time, space, and context specific, depending as much on the act as on its reception. This critical and contextual positioning makes the category particularly useful for cultural analysis.

II. The Crucial Contexts

The scope and intensity of Poland's share in the traumas of twentieth-century world history is nothing short of extraordinary, whatever its parallels with the experiences of other nations. In 1918, the war to end all wars brought Poland independence after 123 years of partitions, but only after decimating its population and devastating its territory and economy. It is rarely remembered that it took six more wars and uprisings to secure the Polish borders before the Second World War dissolved them once again in the autumn of 1939, subjugating Polish citizens to the terror of the German and Soviet occupations and the Holocaust. The more than forty years of postwar communism that Józef Mackiewicz (1902–85), not without reason, called "the greatest danger to threaten the world,"[2] completed Poland's traumatic ordeals. In terms of human experience on a collective scale, the tectonic shifts in Poland's twentieth-century physical, political, and social map, amplified by repeated war terror and unprecedented human and material losses, annihilated all of its previously imagined cultural boundaries and taboos. Life *in extremis* was turned into a mass experience. The conviction that these experiences left an ineradicable imprint on European civilization served as the starting point for the playwrights and theatre directors of particular interest here: they are, chronologically, Stanisław Ignacy Witkiewicz (pen name Witkacy, 1885–1939), Witold Gombrowicz (1904–69), Tadeusz Kantor (1915–90), Tadeusz Różewicz (1921–2014), and Jerzy Grotowski (1933–99).

Of equal importance to history, or simply indivisible from it, in the Polish context at least, is the paradigm of Christianity with its religious imaginarium and cultural impact. This is certainly true for all the artists discussed in this essay. Their work evokes the transgressive figure of a suffering Christ sacrificed for the deliverance of humanity, most often subversively, in recognition of the fundamental and still vital role of Jesus's story in the shaping of European civilization. In this they come close to Leszek Kołakowski's sentiment, as put forth in his posthumously published essay *Jezus ośmieszony* (Jesus Mocked):

> A religious reformer from a small, unenlightened tribe, which was despised by the great and the learned and existed on the peripheries of the Roman Empire, became the spiritual symbol par excellence of the greatest and most creative (not necessarily the most virtuous) civilization of the world, and it is still, after two thousand years, the light of this civilization and, in a moral sense at least, its identifying mark – no one has convinced me that a simple explanation for this is possible, even though I am familiar with proposed explanations … The fact that a new universe emerged from the weak, unadorned hands of a Galilean Jew is incomprehensible if we are trying to look at it from the perspective of His epoch.[3]

As they confront their intimate worlds, civilizational changes, and historical experiences with Christ's cultural archetype, the artists embed their works in doubled gestures of exaltation and degradation, *sacrum* and *profanum*. The first, only invoked on stage, is immediately undercut by the latter – by outright mockery, physical crudeness, linguistic profanities, cruelty, and violence. The fortitude of these means testifies to the lasting authority of what is being challenged. The audience's reception and the artists' self-sacrificial impulses become crucial elements in this transgressive strategy.

III. The Protagonists

The artists discussed in this essay – Witkacy, Kantor, Grotowski, Gombrowicz, and Różewicz, in order of their appearance here – represent three generations. All are strong artistic personalities, as indeed one would expect given the subject of transgression. Their search for "a language for the thought of the limit,"[4] and their experiments with transgression's "affirmative negation" and "negative affirmation,"[5] are historically and axiologically embedded. They have no doubts that transgression is art's *raison d'être*; even so, they probe the values foundational to this conviction.[6] For them, the sacred and the profane, whether seen as antithetic or otherwise, are still of great cultural importance. Metaphysics may be suspect but it still has a hold on their vision of art and its mission of crossing boundaries, confronting us with the void, and touching the mystery with a tremor. Their artistic projects are not just aesthetic experiments, or ways of cultivating their creative desires. Rather, they are practices of existence, the only spaces in which their subjectivities can manifest themselves. In all of their cases, art is the vessel of living: transgression in one deeply touches the other. The stakes are personal and are higher for it. Culturally, they take us from the apogee of Polish modernism, with its incipient (and dreaded) threat of mass society, to the centre of its postmodern formation, with its global networks and liquid incarnations.[7] Together, their lives trace in art the long path from the *belle* to the post-Holocaust *époque*.

Witkacy had assumed his pen name by 1912, but he was born as an artist a few years later, in Russia, during the continental agony of the First World War and the February and October Revolutions of 1917. His experience of these events could only be guessed at until recently.[8] A Russian subject at the time, he was an officer in the prestigious (but also decadent) tsarist Pavlovsky Regiment; he served on the front lines, was seriously wounded, and was decorated for valour. Unlike his talented friend, Tadeusz Miciński (1873–1918), Witkacy did not become a victim of nascent Soviet communism. While the lessons of his earlier life were formative to his ideas about the metaphysical dimension of art and life, it was those derived from the experience of war and revolution that fuelled much of his catastrophic historiosophy. It is this historiosophy that, as will become clear later, incapacitates the recurring transgressive gestures of his plays.

Gombrowicz came of age in interwar Poland but he was spared a direct encounter with Europe's totalitarian madness. He escaped it unknowingly when he boarded the cruise ship *Chrobry* on 29 July 1939 for its maiden voyage to Argentina; he remained there after the war broke out and would end up living there for the next twenty-four years. His share in the quintessentially modern experience of exile was atypical in that it had a liberating rather than a traumatic impact on him. Yet perhaps not surprisingly, Gombrowicz repeatedly engaged with two themes frequently evoked in national grand narratives: war (in

Pornografia, *Historia*, and *Ślub*), and revolution (in *Operetka*). In particular, it was the liminality of these experiences that was of most interest to the author.

Both Kantor and Różewicz experienced the Second World War directly and were, interchangeably, relentless and reluctant as post–avant-garde explorers of the abyss it opened; the war, the Holocaust, and Stalinism all left pronounced marks on their work.[9] Różewicz served as a soldier, but also as a writer, in the underground Polish Home Army during the war. His clandestine volume *Echa leśne* (Forest Echoes) was compiled in 1944 under his army codename "Satyr."[10] Kantor's Teatr Niezależny (Independent Theatre) in Kraków had commenced its underground activities the year before, in 1943. Since artistic activity was punishable by death in German-occupied Poland, Kantor's note on the door of the room in which his 1944 performance of Stanisław Wyspiański's *Powrót Odysa* (The Return of Odysseus, 1907) took place was meant also literally: "One does not enter the theatre with impunity."[11] Kantor's and Różewicz's close encounters with death and with war trauma are stamped on their work and define their understanding of transgressive practice.

Like many artists of his generation (I will mention only the playwrights Sławomir Mrożek [1930–2013] and Ireneusz Iredyński [1939–85], and Jerzy Grzegorzewski [1939–2005] and Konrad Swinarski [1929–75] from among theatre directors), Grotowski remained deeply affected during Stalinist times by his wartime childhood and adolescence. Chronic health problems also played an important part in his life choices. His formative experiences, however, came during the 1960s, a time of great cultural and social shifts in Poland, when some of the ideals that had fuelled postwar reconstruction efforts underwent fundamental revision. Among his Polish contemporaries, Grotowski was the epitome of such efforts. Unlike those undertaken by his peers, Grotowski's resonated not only in Poland but also abroad. This resonance was nurtured by Grotowski's theatre, para-theatre, and research work, and by the tensions between its domestic and foreign reception, as well as by its lasting legacy, which continues through the Grotowski Institute in Wrocław (established as Ośrodek Badań Twórczości Jerzego Grotowskiego i Poszukiwań Teatralno-Kulturowych in 1989) and the Work Center of Jerzy Grotowski and Thomas Richards in Pontedera, Italy (founded in 1986).

The artistic projects of these artists exemplify the particularly intense intersections of *bios* – the individual, the personal, and the intimate – with *logos* and *mythos* – the cultural and the historical, respectively.[12] This essay probes the transgressive charge of the junctures created through these artists' incessant efforts to move beyond their own boundaries in life and in art (as embodied in the prominent figure of the artist in their work). It also redefines the horizon against which such efforts are undertaken by focusing specifically on how they approached the idea of sacrifice. The latter emerges from, to begin with, the eccentric (if not scandalous) paradigms of Catholicism and Romanticism in Polish culture,[13] as well as from art's role in contending with the existential dimension of human life. Sacrifice also evokes the ancient Greek idea of the *pharmakon* – a drug that is both a remedy and a poison.[14]

This last point informs our understanding of the place of discursive violence in Polish theatre, directing us to the actual *pharmakos*: the scapegoat, which is the third possible understanding of *pharmakon*. Present in the work of all the artists discussed here, this figure becomes essential to our understanding of relationships between the individual and the community, and of the social and cultural rituals at the core of Polish theatre's transgressive tradition. Such a lens also allows us to perceive the discussed artists as *pharmakeis* – simultaneously healers, apothecaries, and poisoners, wizards, magicians, and sorcerers: transgressors by definition – and the risks, often taken by them, of also becoming *pharmakoi* –scapegoats. Finally, the scapegoat highlights the ambiguities of *anamnesis* – a calling to remembrance, a memorial sacrifice – as it functions at the crossroads of Plato's epistemology (wherein our immortal souls have learned everything and in each reincarnation allow us to recollect that knowledge), the knowledge collected throughout medical history, and the Eucharistic "reminiscence" of Christ's sacrificial passion, resurrection, and ascension.

Notably – with the exception of Różewicz, who stands apart in more than one way, as will soon become clear – the subjects of this discussion see themselves, or are perceived by others, as *potwory* (monsters). Everyone who knew Witkacy mentioned his psychotic behaviour, including Gombrowicz, who famously wrote, indicting also himself:

> From the first moment, Witkacy fatigued me and bored me. He was never at rest, always highly strung, tormenting himself and others with his perpetual playacting, his craving to shock and to draw attention to himself, forever cruelly and painfully playing with people. All of these shortcomings, which I shared, I now observed as in a distorting mirror, turned monstrous and inflated to apocalyptic proportions.[15]

Kantor's despotic working methods and violent outbursts are likewise the stuff of legend. Grotowski, "a cruel genius … fascinated by power,"[16] still incites conflicting sentiments of admiration and disdain for his guru-like approach to collaborators, who were the main means of achieving his artistic goals but whom he often abandoned when moving on to other projects.

These artists' transgressive "monstrosity" went hand in hand with their eccentric individualism, their hubris and egotism, and their charisma, which acted like a magnetic field on their faithful and long-term collaborators and which still attracts critics, readers, and audiences. Appearing in various guises – as madmen, prophets, gurus, shamans, demiurges, and witnesses – these performers of the self constantly challenged the reality around them, and they still do so through their work. It is here that one finds the roots of Witkacy's insistence on his separateness as *l'artiste maudit*, an accursed outsider, and of his historiosophic aspirations; of Kantor's decision to create his own, private (in more than one sense) theatre with existential ambitions; of Gombrowicz's new anthropology and his liberating immersion in exilic indeterminacy; and of Grotowski's departure, in the midst of his booming career, from the theatre (and later from Poland) in a continuous search for iconoclastic redemption. Even Różewicz, the odd man out in this collective portrait in terms of personality, saw himself as an outlier.[17]

All of these artists were consumed by their work, obsessed with the tensions between its discipline and its spontaneity, precision and improvisation, rationality and irrationality, order and chaos. All were further linked through their shared cultural heritage of Polish Romanticism and modernism and through their mutual fascination with one another (for instance, Kantor's with Witkacy and Gombrowicz, and Grotowski's with Gombrowicz). This sometimes took the form of dislike (e.g., Różewicz's for Witkacy and Gombrowicz, or the reciprocal disdain of Kantor and Grotowski).

Each in his own way, and certainly as a group, they embodied the existential paradox of transgression, which opens strong personalities to the idea of their unlimited potential, fuelling the imperative to transgress, yet with the same gesture encloses them in their individual egos. Aware of both this trap and of their separateness and exceptionality, they often viewed their sense of uniqueness with suspicion, irony, and anxiety. Hence transgression, which hinges on the particularly intense need for individual autonomy and for freedom from cultural conventions and personal limitations, breeds insatiability and may lead to torturous desire, the (ultimately futile) intensification of transgressive means (e.g., through excess, repetition, obsession), or even self-destruction. The lives and works of the artists discussed here allow us to look directly at the various tensions produced by this paradox.

Three particular areas of these artists' practice comprise the specificity of transgression in twentieth-century Polish drama and theatre: their conceptualization of a subject; their atheistic metaphysics; and the simultaneously sacred and profame aesthetics of their dramatic worlds. They all share philosophical and artistic allergies to societal pressures, mass culture, and civilization, to collective affects and affective compensations, and to cultural stereotypes and automatisms; rightly, they discern in them forces of violent coercion, intellectual and otherwise. They without a doubt share such anti-modern impulses with other European artists, but they are also reacting to a culturally specific emphasis on collectivity, including its worship by communist ideology. They do not, however, aspire to unbridled individualism, recognizing that it can result in dangerous aberrations and that a reckless imagination can have violent consequences. In the uneasy interplay of the sacred and the profane, and of Apollonian and Dionysian forces – of reason and unreason, control and chaos, restriction and flux – they constantly transgress the limits drawn by the first, while recognizing the perils of the boundlessness of the latter.

IV. Transgression and Excess

Witkacy: Excess and the Impossibility of Transgression

Let's start with the obvious, and repeat after countless scholars that what was at stake for Witkacy was metaphysics. He saw the artist and the world as being on a collision course. Since the internal and the external constitute an opposition, the artist's mission was to project the intensified unity of his own personality onto the outside world through the formal unity of his works. This projected unity, according to Witkacy, is the metaphysical feeling. Thus, for the metaphysically inclined, art is the last resort against existential dread – the banal, the egalitarian, and the mechanized. It serves in the artist's creative battle with the world and allows him to transgress his individual existence. The egocentrism of this gesture is ameliorated by the projected ability of the reader and viewer (both in life and art) to have a similarly transgressive experience.

> Witkiewicz's ontology is his metaphysics … There can be no Nothingness because it is "inconceivable." The fundamental thread of Witkiewicz's metaphysical thought was the search for the necessary structural features of being … The seeking of the unity in multiplicity thus points to what is indispensable to and at the same time final for being.
>
> – Witkacy, *Psychoholizm*, 44

Such interlocking of the personal and the artistic is paradoxical considering their categorical separation in Witkacy's aesthetic theories. It also has many incarnations and far-reaching ramifications. Witkacy's outbursts of creativity, particularly given the limited resonance of his works, which remained mostly unpublished during his lifetime, point to his powerful imperative to create. Between 1919 and 1924, for example, he wrote his three main aesthetic theses[18] and more than thirty plays; of the latter, however, only five were published. This outpouring makes evident Witkacy's permanent dissatisfaction with what transpired from the creative imperative and with his inability to fully "exude his extraordinary dynamism" and activate "his enormous energetic potential, which was locked in his personality."[19]

This excess of the self, which yearns to transgress its boundaries in a creative gesture of singularity, but can neither measure up to this task nor secure the desired experience of the Mystery of Existence, made performance Witkacy's only means of negotiating and unifying the acts of living and creation. He was known for his love of disguises and role-playing, for staging unexpected social encounters, for provoking uncomfortable situations and creating tense relationships, because he performed his life and lived his art, equally lonely in both. There is possibly no better example of the proximity between his life and art "projects" than his obsession with faces, including his own, which he explored in photographs and paintings. By experimenting with multiple reflections, mirror images, doubles, and mystifications, Witkacy repeatedly scrutinized the strangeness and uniqueness of individual existence. Such repeated intensification and excessive efforts at amplifying oneself ("natężania siebie"), however, in the end annihilate both the experience and its transgressiveness. Excessive concentration ends not in the breach of law, but in dissolution into chaos – or the dreaded boredom – with no further borders to transgress.

Witkacy's most "unsavoury" play, *Matka* (The Mother, 1924) is a good example of such ineffective concentration of the most obvious form of transgression – that of norms. The play's eponymous mother betrays her husband, a criminal who ends up on the gallows; her son Leon is battening on his mother's income from knitting for the benefit of his philosophical writings, as well as prostituting himself along with his wife, and selling state secrets under the influence of alcohol and cocaine. This charged amalgamation leads to increasingly outrageous dramatic events and to the characters' problems with metaphysical experience. How so? The relationship between the mother and the son entangles them in a double-bind of sacrifice and victimization, simultaneously parodying Gothic vampirism, Freudian psychoanalysis, the sacrificial maternal figure (from its universal Christian incarnation to its Polish Romantic version), and the cursed (sacrificial) modernist artist – *l'artist maudit*. The playwright also turns parody's edge against himself, since Leon's diagnosis of the world and his ideas about possible remedies for its condition reflect Witkacy's beliefs and disclose his own metaphysical and historiosophic outlook.

The Mother is excessive on all counts. It "exceeds" in its iconoclastic attitude towards familial relations, sexual extravagance, and drug-induced orgies of imagination; in its aesthetic hybridity, parodies, disguises, and masks; in its inclination towards the grotesque, the strange, and the outrageous; in the intensive recycling and transcoding of ideas; and in Witkacy's use of language, which is frenetically innovative in its dark humour and stylistic playfulness as well as famous for its ingenious neologisms, linguistic eccentricities, and language games.[20] This linguistic excess has as much to do with Witkacy's approach to intellectual problems as with his historiosophy. The temporal framework of his transgressive projects stretches between two catastrophes: of his once-lived revolutionary past, and of the projected mechanized future. The present – the ultimate time of dramatic action (but also of life) – dissipates in both meanings of the word: it is scattered and squandered. For Witkacy's dramatic art, the temporal dimension is accursed for being shared with life (for which he had nothing but contempt) and for provoking the terror of existence. To provide an escape from life – to transgress life successfully – art should avoid the present tense. Hence, most of Witkacy's characters do not live in the present and instead inhabit a timeless zone of their own discourse, or, as in *The Mother*'s epilogue, are thrown into a timeless space of Pure Form – in this instance, their subconscious.

To put it differently, Witkacy's view of the unavoidable demise of the world, the essence of his historiosophy, counteracts and annuls the transgressive potential of Pure Form, which he identifies as the only aesthetic means to achieve metaphysical feeling that enables the experience of the Mystery of Existence. In Witkacy's case, these interconnections among history, form, and metaphysics are absolute, and in being absolute, they are not sufficiently dynamic to allow his thought to be of – and at – the limit. Since transgression requires individual effort, and Witkacy's catastrophic historiosophy insists on the eventual destruction of the individual through the process of social mechanization, his work constantly moves the limit to be transgressed just beyond reach.

The problems with temporality are one of the reasons why the two most important elements of dramatic structure – the action of the play and the characters in it – are of secondary importance in Witkiewicz's theatre. Words do not do things in it, no matter how outrageous the plot. They describe or recall what has already been done – somewhere else. The heteroglossic exuberance of the characters goes hand in hand with the paresis of their will and deed, notwithstanding the revolutionary changes around them. Witkacy's transgression oscillates between excess and exhaustion. Many scholars have commented on certain recurring character types in Witkacy's theatre.[21] Konstanty Puzyna (1929–89), the greatest theatre critic of his generation and the editor of Witkacy's plays, identified some of these characters as, for example, "a titanic leader, a tyrant, an artist or a scientist, a perverse *hetaira* from an upper class, a sweet girlie with a naughty expression on her face."[22] Kantor's intuition to use mannequins when staging Witkacy's *Kurka wodna* (Water Hen, 1967) and *Szewcy* (The Shoemakers, 1970) was right on point. Indeed, there is something already dead in Witkacy's dramatic world, which presents itself in madness and convulsions of excess.

"Śmierć z rozpasania" (death from licentiousness),[23] as Błoński calls it, pervades not only the play's particular elements and its final outcome, but also the transgressive experience itself, which dies of the same disease. Bataille, who was fascinated with the potlatch, a gift-giving ritual held by the Indigenous peoples of the North America's Pacific Northwest, conceived of excess (waste) as a necessary condition for transgression.[24] He proposed that the "accursed share," the luxurious excess of economy, should be spent in the arts, eroticism, and spectacles to prevent it from catastrophic outpourings in wars and revolutions. Witkacy's excess, however, could neither be accommodated by cultural norms nor spent lavishly and without gain. Witkacy both counted on and discounted the gains from spent energy: his own, that of his characters and of the actors performing them, and that of the audience implicated in the spectacle, not to mention society at large, for it too figured prominently in his economy of excess.

It may well be that Witkacy's ultimate victory came when death – so excessively and ineffectively multiplied in his theatre – took its real toll on 18 September 1939, when, after learning of the Soviet invasion of Poland while trying to escape the German invasion from the West, he committed suicide by overdose. A suicide is the ultimate transgression in its unrepeatable probing of the final boundary. Witkacy had toyed with it throughout his life, starting with the formative, traumatic experience of his fiancée's suicide. Jadwiga Janczewska's death in 1914 followed from the transgressive blurring of borders between reality and mystification so characteristic of Witkacy's social life at the time. He also tested life's limits in war and revolution – history's transgressors. In the end, it was in his dramatic suicide that life and art played their final hand.

V. Transgression and Presence

Tadeusz Kantor: Morbidity of Presence

Although thirty years younger, Kantor acknowledged his sense of connection to Witkacy both directly and in his work. He experimented with the European and Polish avant-garde and Witkacy's plays for more than twenty years, sharing in the latter's catastrophic world view and marking each stage of his career with increasingly radical experiments with Witkacy's texts and ideas. It was the highly acclaimed production of *Umarła klasa* (The Dead Class, 1975), however, that brought Kantor international fame and initiated the last phase of his artistic activity, morbidly named the "Teatr Śmierci" (Theatre of Death; later renamed "Teatr Miłości i Śmierci" [The Theatre of Love and Death], following the favoured modernist pairing of ancient Eros and Thanatos). All of his subsequent work – *Wielopole, Wielopole* (1980), *Niech sczerną artyści* (Let the Artists Die, 1985), *Nigdy tu już nie powrócę* (I Shall Never Return, 1988), and the unfinished, due to the artist's death, *Dziś są moje urodziny* (Today Is My Birthday, 1990)[25] – is infused with Judeo-Christian, mostly Christ-centric references, which broaden the historical context and cultural intertexts of Kantor's productions and heighten his personal stakes in them. In this, Kantor relies not on Witkacy, but on his predecessors: Adam Mickiewicz (1798–1855), the bard of Polish Romantic messianism, and the multi-talented, Symbolist polemicist Stanisław Wyspiański (1869–1907). Kantor's artistic genealogy thus spans the distance between Romanticism and high modernism, which were transgressive in their aesthetics and metaphysics, and the avant-garde tradition, which transgressed ideas of art along with artistic and social conventions.

> The fact that Kantor made Witkiewicz's plays into the literary foundation of his theatre does not mean that the ideas of Kantor's theatre are a realization of Witkiewicz's postulates. Kantor's spiritual stance belongs to Witkiewicz's time; he is bound to "this time" by his youth – "stormy," risky, and uncompromising. Yet, when Witkiewicz was committing suicide, Kantor was already stepping into war time. The war discarded all aesthetic and philosophical principles. He was left alone and had to look reality – and death – in the eye."
>
> – Tadeusz Kantor, "Mówić o sobie w trzeciej osobie," 433

Kantor's interest in the Polish Romantics and Wyspiański was tied to their thanatological imagination, which contrasted sharply with that of religious orthodoxy while maintaining a deep spiritual link with its eschatological perspective.[26] Both in Mickiewicz's

Dziady (Forefathers' Eve; Parts I, II, and IV, 1820–3; Part III, 1832) and in Wyspiański's plays, the world of the dead is within reach and can be evoked, summoned, and brought back to effectively confront the living, to secure their assistance, communicate some wisdom, and consolidate their community. Once the dead accomplish their mission, however, they disappear into the beyond. In the case of Kantor's "séances" – as he sometimes called the performances of the "Theatre of Death" – their presence is both more concrete and more illusory than that of any of their predecessors in Polish theatre. Here, the dead are summoned from the "photographic plates" of the artist's personal memory as well as from cultural and historical contexts, but they appear with no other purpose than to die again in a repeated yet always unsuccessful process of coming back to life on stage. For Kantor, their reappearance from the recesses of memory is synonymous with the act of artistic creation, with the latter relying on the practices of disreputable substitution. Such substitution brings to life a fragile and dubious presence of helpless, ridiculous, and pretentious characters caught between deadly clichés, stereotypes, and automatisms of their past lives, and art's archaic and useless illusion.

While these practices reached their pinnacle in the "Theatre of Death," Kantor's artistic path reveals their earlier traces. Already in the 1944 production of Wyspiański's *Return of Odysseus*, Kantor substituted the original phantom character with a historical spectre of a dead German soldier returning from the battle of Stalingrad. By the time he created *The Dead Class*, the perplexing presence of his dead is much more layered. They appear in their adult, decrepit bodies, yet they belong – together with their mannequins, the fraudulent, twice-uncanny doubles – to the time of their mischievous childhood. In *Wielopole, Wielopole*, in turn, they are the insidious copies of Kantor's family members. Finally, in *Today Is My Birthday*, it is Tadeusz Kantor who comes back, posthumously, both as a recorded voice and – fittingly in the context of his own practice – embodied by an actor. This trajectory points to Kantor's increasingly more prominent, autobiographical, or rather auto-thanatological, presence on stage, and speaks to the intensifying internalization and self-reflexivity of his "Theatre of Death." Kantor replicated and re-edited his creative gestures from one production to the next, organizing them into spiral, intertextual, and repetitive patterns.[27] This obsession with returns and repetitions played a self-analytical and therapeutic function for the artist, and an affective one for his audience.[28] The performances thus became momentary counteractions to death – their own and that of their participants.

While *The Dead Class* initiated the "Theatre of Death," *Wielopole, Wielopole* marked a decisive shift in Kantor's work. Not only did it forsake the literary material that was still present, albeit residually, in *The Dead Class*, but it also, for the first time, openly and subversively engaged Christian imagery. In *Wielopole, Wielopole*, Kantor resurrects the remnants of his family story to associate them with the rite of Christ's Passion – sacred for Christianity and central for the sacrificial trope in Polish culture. By confronting these remnants with the religious and cultural archetype on the one hand, and with twentieth-century history on the other, he profanes the rite with physical crudeness, linguistic obscenities, and executions and rapes while trying to sanctify the shabby reality of his traumatized memory and repressed anxieties with an aleatoric enactment of the Passion's components: the last supper, the flogging and the scorning, the way of the cross, and the crucifixion.

Through what Kantor calls his "Poor Little Room of the Imagination" flow the past's badly damaged fragments, faint echoes, and misleading traces: of the metaphysical order that once provided a cohesive, transcendental frame of reference and maintained the totality of the world; of Wielopole's multi-ethnic community; of the First World War from which Kantor's father never returned, despite surviving its atrocities; and of the Second World War, in which most of the Jewish population of Wielopole as well as his father perished.[29] All of this past is resuscitated through images – violent, degraded, lyrical, and symbolic all at once – rather than in words, which Kantor limits to a few repetitious incantations, fragments of sclerotic family conversations, and defective biblical quotations.[30]

This deformed family drama unfolds in a room in a vicarage in Wielopole, where Kantor spent his early childhood.[31] The dark and decrepit room is empty but for a few sticks of furniture, along with some mounds and crosses invoking the burial places of memory and history. The overall impression is reinforced by the presence of First World World War infantry soldiers, Kantor's father Marian among them, posing for a photograph in the corner of the room. In an ironically self-reflexive gesture, Kantor makes the twin uncles clownishly restore the room's order only to announce, at the end of their efforts, that they were never part of that story to begin with. Their ambivalent operations on the space evoke similar operations of the subconscious.[32] Making the past present associates remembering with creation. Kantor signals such temporal intersections through the physical degradation of his characters (they appear shoddy, or repulsively corpse-like) and by their indeterminate existence. His "dear departed" are merely suspicious substitutes for his family, not only because they appear embodied by actors (even though Kantor's theatre deplored illusion) but also because in his theatre, creation becomes part of the process of decomposition. Some of these departed are less mechanical than others, but all could be effectively replaced with mannequins, as happens with Uncle Józef, the priest, and Mother Helka. Kantor, the ultimate demiurge, who is actively present on stage throughout the performance, does not recall, resurrect, or re-create the past, but rather makes the stage a channel through which the already disintegrated past flows. It finds its surrogates in "poor," "discarded," "useless," but "real" matter,[33] which as early as 1961 he sanctified as the "Reality of the Lowest Rank." In Kantor's works, as in Witkacy's, ontology equates with metaphysics.

Two opposing yet intertwined strategies are at work in *Wielopole, Wielopole*. The first – of exaltation – involves continuous attempts to elevate the haunting triviality of family squabbles and tensions by sanctifying the familial history through the sacrificial myth of Christ's Passion, just as the Romantics had done with national history a century earlier. The other strategy – of degradation – diminishes the grandeur of this gesture by inflicting on familial relations the cruelty and violence of history. This is the dynamic at work when Father Marian carries off the newly-wed Mother Helka as if she had been crucified. Her subsequent elevation on a chair bearing the name Golgotha – a poor, sacrilegious substitute for both the cross and the "place of the skull" – sharpens this association, anticipates her violation by the soldiers, and foreshadows the peculiar Pietà when Marian lifts her battered mannequin from the ground. Other crucifixions – of Uncle-Priest Józef, his mannequin, and cousin Adaś, a young recruit – all play a similar part in Kantor's transgressive mass: a profanatory, empty, and yet deeply affective offering.

Such double-bind of degradation and exaltation in Kantor's production echoes, as does Jerzy Grotowski's "dialectic of derision and apotheosis,"[34] a similar interplay pervading the image of crucified Christ; it also reflects the violent dynamic of dying and returning, of forgetting and remembering. In *Wielopole, Wielopole*, however, the references to Christ's Passion and Christian funereal rituals and commemorations do not affirm the hope of either individual or collective redemption and resurrection. Instead, they test the lasting cultural and affective impact of the sacred and the profane on the creative process and its reception. Kantor's decision to make his family an object of such a test freed the transgressive potential of the mnemonic strategy of surrogacy and required him to claim personal responsibility for its artistic and affective consequences, which he did by remaining actively on stage throughout the performance.

Whereas the Romantics still believed in the importance of perfection for their transgressive spirituality, Kantor, like Grotowski and Różewicz, understood that in the twentieth century, the sacred can instead be encountered in degradation, in the experience of the exhausted, tortured human body. It is out of the realness of the momentary and the surrogate, of the impossible yet yearned for, that affect is born. This opens the possibility that transgression, even if successful only for a moment, can engage the eschatological and existential anxieties by testing the tensions of the sacred and the profane at the intersections of the individual, cultural, and historical experience of the world. It is also possible that, paradoxically, such an act still has real consequences in the theatre, precisely because it dies every time it is completed before living again in a creative gesture. In Kantor's performances, every time the dead come back to life only to keep dying again with no promise of a new life for them, the audience is given a glimpse of art's redemptive power.

Jerzy Grotowski: Gravitas of Presence

Nowhere in the Polish twentieth-century theatre is sacrifice as foundational a trope as in Grotowski's "Teatr przedstawień" (Theatre of Productions), a phase of his career that included his work with the "Teatr 13 Rzędów" (Theatre of 13 Rows, 1959–64) in Opole[35] and the "Teatr Laboratorium" (Laboratory Theatre, 1965–9) in Wrocław,[36] both of which he ran with considerable help from Ludwik Flaszen (b. 1930), his literary adviser and a brilliant critic. Like Kantor, Grotowski was obsessed with the cultural repercussions of the story of Christ's sacrificial mission, contemplating their impact on Polish collective identity and their implications for the modern world. Not surprisingly, his sources of inspiration were similar to Kantor's: the heretical and paradigmatic works of the Polish Romantics, specifically Adam Mickiewicz and Juliusz Słowacki (1809–49), and Wyspiański's modernist criticism of them. Grotowski dramaturgically reworked the concepts of sacrificial offering prevalent in Polish Romanticism and brought its mistrust of the religious institutionalization of redemption to a new level. His transgressive gestures are directed against the most cherished of Polish cultural traditions, which grew out of once-revolutionary Romantic ideas yet turned into dreary clichés in their popular afterlife. These were not gestures of destruction, denunciation, or even denigration of these traditions, since Grotowski counted on their strength in his productions. Rather, they served to confront entrenched social and cultural expectations with their contemporary relevance.[37]

The main Romantic textual source for Grotowski's thinking about theatre, as many scholars have pointed out (and as was true also for Kantor), was Mickiewicz's *Forefathers' Eve*. This grand Romantic drama shaped a whole paradigm in Polish culture. It has been called the "queen bee's cell"[38] by Dariusz Kosiński for its distinct contribution to European twentieth-century theatre, which he terms the "Polish theatre of transformation" and identifies with individual spiritual transformation on the one hand, and with theatre's transformative project in relation to history, culture, and society on the other. Unlike Kantor, who did not stage Mickiewicz's masterpiece though he thought about doing so many times,[39] Grotowski undertook the task in 1961, in the "first attempt at playing out the 'return of Christ' in the theatre, something which in later performances [acquired] the status of a model situation."[40]

> **Theatre of transformation** belongs to a broad family of very diverse phenomena and practices ... Many of these practices have multiple performative aspects ... None of them highlights theatricality and performativity as vehicles of transformation as decisively as the discussed Polish tradition.
>
> – Kosiński, *Teatra polskie. Historie*, 125

> The poster for Grotowski's production of *Forefathers' Eve* featured a citation from Part IV of the play: "It's full of witchcraft, and this blasphemous rite / Our folk in their coarse ignorance confirms; / Whence all strange tales, and myriad alarms, / And superstitions by the hundred score, / Of midnight ghosts, of spirits, and of charms.
>
> – Mickiewicz, *Forefathers*, 97

The autobiographical and historical frameworks of Mickiewicz's play include his youthful traumas of imprisonment and exile. In its deep eschatological structure, the play also calls on diverse cultural tropes, such as the Dionysian myth, pagan death rituals, initiation mysteries, and trance ceremonies. Its main character, Konrad, is simultaneously a poet, a performer, a blasphemer, an initiated seer-priest, and a suffering, living sacrifice laid at the altar of freedom – a *pharmakon*, *pharmakos*, and a Christ-centric "cultural model of personality."[41] In his ritual-focused staging of *Forefathers' Eve* (1961), Grotowski distilled its Part III (the most revered part, for its ideas of national messianism) down to the Great Improvisation – Konrad's central monologue and sacrilegious rebellion against God. In an inspired outburst of poetic genius and extravagant hubris, Konrad imagines himself to be an incarnation of the entire nation, and in its name he desires to successfully compete with the Creator.

Heretical already as a literary character, Konrad acquired an additional, demonic and spectral dimension in Grotowski's production. By alluding to Catholic rites, their soundscape and iconography, Grotowski translated Konrad's phantasmagorical provenance, his rebellion, humiliation, and suffering, as well as his preposterousness, into "a black mass of jingoism," unmasking the utopian and heretical underpinnings of the Romantic deification of the nation.[42] Grotowski's production of *Forefathers' Eve* counterpointed the eponymous pagan ritual of communicating with dead ancestors with ordinary objects, with grotesque and sometimes eroticized costumes, and with at times playful, at times ostentatiously affected, histrionic behaviours: in short, the sacred with the profane.

> Kosiński usefully captures the dynamics of Grotowski's *Kordian*: "The playful first part drew in the spectators, who were in subsequent parts subtly yet decisively attacked with precisely the aggrandized image of themselves as members of a national community that they came to love. This process involved first presenting these ideas mockingly as anachronistic and affected, which distanced the spectators from them, followed by a twisted apotheosis of what had been jeered at, separated from, and abandoned by the community."
>
> – Kosiński, *Grotowski. Profanacje*, 91

In turn, in his staging of *Kordian* (1962), Słowacki's 1833 response to Mickiewicz's messianic ideas, Grotowski extended the concept of one of its scenes into the interpretive framework of the whole production. He construed the ineffective revolutionary plans of the satanically inspired rebel, who saw himself as the sacrificial saviour of his nation and its freedom, as the at once noble and ridiculous nightmares and delusions of inmates in a mental asylum, of which the audience also became a part. By depriving Kordian's world of its metaphysical dimension and moving it into the sphere of phantasms instead, Grotowski was asking his audience to confront the foundations of their own collective identities.

Even more provocative than *Kordian*, however, were Grotowski's choices for his multiple versions of Wyspiański's visionary play, *Akropolis* (1962–7). In it, Grotowski replaced the Wawel Cathedral in Kraków – Poland's venerated religious, cultural, and historical site, as well as the play's setting (and a certain model of interpreting the world)[43] – with a concentration camp.[44] This shocking substitution had far reaching consequences. Wyspiański's poetic imagination brought to life various cultural artefacts from the cathedral, including sculptures on its tombs, mythical and biblical figures from its Renaissance tapestries, and carvings from the church's choir, and engaged these long-lasting and cherished manifestations of European civilization in a visionary discussion about new modes of individual and national self-creation and resurrection. Grotowski, by contrast, in a double-act of blasphemous "resurrection," first brings to life and then, in the final scene, annihilates the spectres of the murdered inmates, erasing their futile efforts and their defiled desires and longings. They are his testimony to the totalitarian civilization of the twentieth-century "cemetery of the tribes."[45] His *Studium o Hamlecie* (Hamlet Study, 1964), in turn, reworks Wyspiański's innovative reading of the Shakespearian character. By making Hamlet a Jewish intellectual exhumed by the Gravedigger, Grotowski tackles the wartime attitudes of a rural community vis-à-vis the military and heroic paradigm of Polish culture, a topic that will reappear in Polish theatre only a few decades later.

At the very centre of Grotowski's experiments with the Romantic paradigm stand quintessentially modernist dualisms: the individual and the collective, matter and soul, body and spirit, reason and intuition. In order to explore them artistically, Grotowski consulted diverse sources, from the Gospels and Christian mystics and theologians[46] to their heretical, blasphemous competitors: Gnosticism, occultism, and esotericism.[47] His artistic project fed off an acute modern hunger for transcendence and for the fragmented subject's renewed unity in the face of a disenchanted, collapsing world. While this project grew from the apocalyptic aspect of Christianity, it found its artistic expression in the scrutiny of cultural contradictions, antinomies, and antagonisms reminiscent of Brecht's theatre. The small scale and marginal existence of Grotowski's Theatre of Productions (both spatially and audience-wise, particularly in Opole), and its limited group of core devotees, ascetic training and performance discipline of actors, as well as esoteric language, indicate that the projected resolution of the mentioned dualisms was aimed not at the collective, but at the individual, both on stage and in the audience. Leszek Kolankiewicz identified this goal as *metanoia* – a change in the inner man.[48] Such change is connected to the experience of the mystery and the sacred. Grotowski wanted to bring to life new, individual, iconoclastic variants of the sacred by confronting its old forms with the experience of the contemporary world and by filtering them through his own psyche. He located the site of such possibility in the transgressive idea of the "violation of a living organism."[49] Just as it was for Kantor, the act of creation and the reconstitution of the world were also at stake for Grotowski.

> The drama [*The Constant Prince*] focuses on the martyr's fate of the Portuguese Infante Don Fernando (1402–43) who having found himself imprisoned refused to agree to being freed in exchange for ceding the strategic port of Ceuta to the Moors. As a result, he died of exhaustion, considering it a voluntary death, which sanctified his sacrifice. Written in 1843, the Polish version of the drama is faithful to the original, yet at the same time it went deeper and was supplemented by elements exploring spiritual transformation linked to the readiness for the complete sacrifice of anything sensual and corporeal for supernatural values. According to Słowacki's own testimony, in creating his own version he filtered the experience of Don Fernando through himself in a manner resembling the theatrical experiencing of a protagonist's fate.
>
> – http://www.grotowski.net/en/encyclopedia/constant-prince-ksiaze-niezlomny

It only *seems* paradoxical that Grotowski saw theatre as an appropriate channel for this process, and this despite it in the end proving insufficient for the task. In its traditional understanding, theatre is a collective and mediatory art, but it also demands *doing* – a concrete, disciplined, bodily praxis – in the here and now, and it carries out that praxis through a singular psycho-physical organism.[50] Once opened to the idea of *kenosis*, the emptying of one's will (most spectacularly exemplified by Christ) and the elimination of all physical and psychological barriers in its actor, theatre can become a forum for a genuinely transformative, unmediated encounter with the carnal and spiritual mystery of creation.

For Grotowski, the living organism of his actor became the conduit for the pursuit of his own obsessions. During an act of a total (engaging his whole being), authentic (not acted but lived), and pure (selfless) sacrifice, his actor could attain the unity of body and soul, the carnal and the spiritual, the erotic and the mystical, the excessive and the ascetic. Ryszard Cieślak (1937–90) in his role of the Constant Prince (1965)[51] has entered the history of the European theatre as the main example of such a "total act."[52] Many detailed descriptions and analyses of this production are readily available.[53] For our purposes, suffice it to say that its main conceptual framework arose from sharply defined antinomies and contrasts between the collective of the court and the Prince. The set design placed the latter on a small platform, which served as both his altar and his tomb, and the choreography positioned the court in menacing, circular movements around him. Cloaked in black robes, they stood in stark contrast to the almost naked body of the Prince, who, like Christ on the Golgotha, wore only a loincloth. Cieślak's and the court's performances referenced directly the religious iconography of Christ's Passion (including whipping, the crown of thorns, crucifixion, and the Pietà), as well as Catholic devotions (the confession and litanies) and the most sacred of sacraments: the Holy Communion. Infused with such visual references, created mostly by the actors' bodies and their movements, the production transformed the Prince into a living Christ figure, thus already transgressing the suggestions of the original text. Cieślak's performance shifted this association from the realm of mimesis into experiential reality by replacing the imitation of Christ's sacrifice with the sacrificial act of his body on stage in the hope of a transgressive, earthly self-redemption.

Polish culture knows such heretic measures very well. As already mentioned, in *Forefathers' Eve, Part III*, Mickiewicz corrects God's plans for humanity. He projects Christian soteriology onto the stage of history and proposes a messianic idea of collective, earthly salvation to bring justice, equality, and most of all freedom to the enslaved Europeans at the cost of a bloody sacrifice of one (Polish) nation. Grotowski follows a similarly transgressive route, but he translates Mickiewicz's idea of a nation's self-purification through its act of self-sacrifice into an individual act of self-redemption through the internal work of the actor. In the production, the mastered body and the emptied, sublimated self of the actor give the actor's presence its gravitas and turn it into a vessel of "Eros and Caritas" in one.[54]

Starting with *Kordian* in 1962, Grotowski created a self-ironic figure of a director/charlatan/magician in each of his productions, as Kosiński insightfully observes. This figure, in turn, designs "a cruel game that is motivated by dark and dangerous psychological forces that combine sadomasochistic desires with erotic fascination, often of a homosexual character."[55] In the process, as befits a *pharmakos* in his dual role of healer and poisoner, of wizard and magician, Grotowski changed from a theatre director into a "midwife" of the "total act," hoping that its creative and redemptive power would deliver the actor, the audience, and himself from existential dread and from fear of death.

His new function, however, can also be viewed differently. In his desire to create the world anew and secure its salvation, he became a new god offering up the sacrifice of his actor-son to the audience, but also to himself.

> Ludwik Flaszen mentions the persistence of the Faustian motif in Grotowski's life. He recalls that during Grotowski's work on Christopher Marlowe's *The Tragical History of the Life and Death of Doctor Faustus* his friend mentioned signing a pact with the devil: "He understood – after Thomas Mann – that behind a vocation in art there is something that may conventionally be called 'demonism.'" Flaszen (only half-jokingly) describes the smell of sulphur in the air, a violet-blue-grey glow emanating from people during that production: "A professional exorcist would have probably stated that we have felt there the close presence of an Evil Spirit."
>
> – Flaszen, *Grotowski & Company*, 286

This is a truly transgressive act: demonic in nature – who, if not Satan, copies God's gestures in the hope of acquiring their power? – and Faustian in execution.[56] Such an act acknowledges both the existence and the ultimate authority of the sacred, of what is simultaneously desirable and forbidden, attractive and dangerous. Grotowski referred to his theatre as a *mysterium tremendum et fascinans* (mystery of terror and fascination) – words that describe the direct experience of *sacrum*. Transgressing the sacred leads to genuine existential tremor and once again stirs up the desire to cross its taboos. In Grotowski's theatre, this is never done with impunity.

Grotowski's last production, *Apocalypsis cum figuris*,[57] weaved together all of his hopes and obsessions and ultimately proved deadly for his theatre. This production, which officially premiered on 11 February 1969, became a "black mass" revolving around the second, but unwanted, coming of Christ. The first seeds of this idea were present already in his *Forefathers' Eve* and ripened in *The Constant Prince*. Unlike these productions, however, *Apocalypsis* was not based on a single dramatic text; rather, it was composed from fragments of the Gospels, Dostoyevski's *The Brothers Karamazov,* and texts by T.S. Eliot and Simone Weil. Despite multiple revisions, its form could not contain Grotowski's project. The presence of the actor could not turn into an unmediated experience for the audience, and thus the transfer from representation to presence could be sustained. This happened partly because "pushing his actors towards a 'total act' produced an excess of sincerity," as Lisa Wolford usefully observes.[58] While philosophical excess impeded Witkacy's transgressive gestures, rendering them impotent, the excess of programmatic authenticity annulled Grotowski's theatre project. Once sincerity takes over the site of performance, performance is no more. Once successfully transgressed, the theatre proves immaterial.

VI. Transgression and Existence

Gombrowicz: The Abyss of Chaos

Known mainly as a prose writer, Witold Gombrowicz was also a playwright, albeit not much of a theatregoer. In contrast to the ultra-prolific Witkacy, he completed only three plays, leaving a fourth one unfinished. Yet like Witkacy, he left a lasting imprint on the imagination and practice of three generations of theatre directors, first and foremost Kantor and Grotowski, but also Jerzy Jarocki (1929–2012), Jerzy Grzegorzewski (1939–2005), and Grzegorz Jarzyna (b. 1968). His first play, *Iwona, księżniczka Burgunda* (Ivona, Princess of Burgundia, 1938), enjoyed some popularity outside of Poland. Concise and amusing, with the bewilderingly silent eponymous heroine and her uncanny impact on the royal court at its centre, it is also the easiest of Gombrowicz's plays to stage. The same cannot be said about *Ślub* (The Marriage, 1953),[59] a philosophically complex, theatrically demanding, oneiric, and heavily intertextual work that calls for basic familiarity with not only Dante, Goethe, and Shakespeare, but also Mickiewicz, Zygmunt Krasiński (1812–59), and Wyspiański. His final play, *Operetka* (Operetta, 1966), offers a carnivalesque version of Gombrowicz's historiosophy in an ironically rendered, amusingly outdated musical form.[60]

Gombrowicz, like all the other artists discussed here, unashamedly projects his most deeply personal issues (*bios*) onto the historical stage (*mythos*), with his unfinished fourth play *Historia* (History, 1973) offering the most transparent evidence of this practice. He opens the play with his family, bearing their real names and peculiarities, sitting "as if in an old photograph"[61] – indeed, sitting as Kantor's family does in his theatre. Witold, an adolescent social rebel, incites all kinds of anxieties in his middle-class family by walking barefoot in the company of a caretaker's son; he unsettles them just like Ivona's silence disturbs the members of the royal court in Gombrowicz's first, prewar play. His "barefoot revolutionary psyche"[62] awakens his Mother's germophobia, his Father's social apprehensions, and his brother James's fascination with male violence. Although Witold claims that his "bare foot is defenseless against History,"[63] his mission becomes to forestall the First and later the Second World War by advising Tsar Nicholas and Kaiser Wilhelm, as well as the Polish Marshal Józef Piłsudski, to take off their shoes and "escape from themselves,"[64] and thus from their social and historical roles.

It is this need for escape that is behind Gombrowicz's transgressive impulses both in his own life (as attested by his thoughts on the advantages of exile) and in his art. These impulses work on two planes: one is horizontal, or in Gombrowicz's terms "interhuman"; the other is vertical, personal. The first, propelled by Gombrowicz's unrelenting scepticism, unmasks the mechanisms of social and cultural conventions, stereotypes, usurpations, and roles and finds its aesthetic expression in playful deformations and degradations, and in the grotesque and the carnivalesque. Gombrowicz is merciless in baring the pretences of Polish social and cultural formations, cutting through both the façades of his own social background (middle class, with landed-gentry origins) and prevalent traditions of Catholicism, Sarmatism, and Romanticism. The other, vertical trajectory, traces the transformations of Gombrowicz's "private pathology" into "a universal mission."[65] It is the results of these two trajectories crossing paths that are of most interest here.

> HENRY: I reject every order, every concept / I distrust every abstraction, every doctrine / I don't believe in God or in Reason! / Enough of these gods! Give me man! / May he be like me, troubled and immature / Confused and incomplete, dark and obscure / So I can dance with him! Play with him! Fight with him!
>
> Pretend to him! Ingratiate myself with him! / And rape him, love him and forge myself / Anew from him, so I can grow through him, and in that way / celebrate my marriage in the sacred human church!
>
> – Gombrowicz, *The Marriage*, 182

In Gombrowicz's plays, *bios*, *logos*, and *mythos* are intricately interwoven and share philosophical premises. At their heart is the desperate individual effort at self-articulation, made despite the unceasing pressures of human relations and betrayals of language and in the name of endowing the terrifying chaos of the internal and external world with sense and meaning, however tentative.[66] This is what Gombrowicz means when he claims that his task is "to force the way through Non-Reality to Reality" – a postulate shared also by Kantor.[67] The latter searched for such reality among the lowest ranks of what had already been used and discarded, whereas Gombrowicz finds his way to it on the sclerotic heights of social relations, after shredding their pretences and unveiling their violence. Like Witkacy, Kantor, and Grotowski, he locates his individual self at the centre of his artistic project and populates his plays with his *Doppelgänger*. This decision is not narcissistic, however, but rather grounded in his understanding of the precariousness of his existential situation within a mysterious, incomprehensible, and unpredictable world. It also stems from his awareness of the ultimately demonic chaos lurking over the precipice of reason, and the simultaneous realization that the latter is capable of preposterous usurpations.

Nowhere in Gombrowicz's theatre is this understanding more profoundly explored than in *The Marriage*, which without question is his masterpiece. In it, another Polish Odysseus, Henry, a traumatized soldier fighting in France, tries to return home. His oneiric journey takes him through tortuous anxieties and shameful desires. They materialize on the theatrical landscape of a ruined church and in the desert of shattered transcendence left by its desecration, and in a family home degraded into a disreputable inn[68] imitating a royal court, in the end becoming a prison of Henry's own making. During the war, time is truly "out of joint"; the home and the social and metaphysical order it once signified are no more, and the prodigal son's return takes preposterous forms. The rupture of the old world opens freedom's exciting spaces while also exposing its terrifying abyss.

Henry's first, half-willed response to the obscure world of his dream is compensatory: by intensifying the lost dignity of his family, he unexpectedly elevates them to royal standing. Having discovered the potential of such creative gestures and their interhuman mechanisms, however, he dethrones his father and becomes a tyrant himself. Hoping to exercise an absolute authority, Henry plans to marry his disgraced fiancée, Molly, by a rite of his own making. In this way he will force his world to recognize the constitutive power of such authority. Henry underestimates the pressure of repressed chaos and his own desires, however. When his *Doppelgänger*, the Drunkard, implicates Henry's army buddy and alter ego, Johnny, as Molly's lover, Henry tests his power by demanding that Johnny commit suicide. When he is obeyed, his world – the "interhuman church" he was building – collapses.

This bizarre dramatic action, full of page-long monologues, musical orchestrations, and stylistic experiments, exposes more than just Henry's violent, bisexual "history of desire" for Molly and Johnny.[69] It also lets loose the disturbing, magical automatisms of language, which betray the subconscious impulses of the characters in their encounters with one another. The play performs the oppressive outcome of such uncontrollable automatisms as they react to the other side of language: the demonic incomprehensibility of silence and the power of repression. In other words, the play's perplexing twists rest on the same foundation as every transgressive act, namely the dynamics of reason and instinct, fear and excitement – another instance of *mysterium tremendum et fascinas*, known to us also from the works of Grotowski. Gombrowicz both fears and is fascinated by the unpredictable, often inhuman consequences of words acting in the interhuman realm (in social relations, cognition, communication, etc.). In his work, a single utterance can be omnipotent; contrast this with Witkacy, whose words remain impotent despite their constant creative proliferation. In *The Marriage*, it is thus possible for single words (such as "finger" or "to touch") to open up an endless network of associations and wreak havoc in the dramatic world. At the same time, fear and fascination drive Gombrowicz's exploration of the impenetrable and inexpressible unreason of repression and silence, with its direct theatrical manifestation found in *Ivona, Princess of Burgundia*.

> I am very afraid of the devil. A strange confession from the lips of an unbeliever … What good are the police, rights, all guarantees and means of solicitude if a Monster strolls freely among us and nothing protects us from him, nothing, nothing, there is no barrier between him and us. His hand is free among us, the most free of the free! What separates the bliss of the casual stroller from the underground wailing of the voices of the tormented? Absolutely nothing, only empty space … The earth upon which we walk is so covered with pain, we wade in it up to our knees – and this is today's, yesterday's, the day before yesterday's pain, the pain from a thousand years ago – for one should not be deluded, pain does not dissolve in time and the cry of a child from thirty centuries ago is no less of a cry than the one that resounded three days ago. This is the pain of all generations and all beings – not just of man.
>
> – Gombrowicz, *Diary*, vol. 2, 437

Fear and excitement, and repulsion and awe, dominate the affective landscape of Gombrowicz's dramas. They are clearly anchored, as Michał Markowski shows, in Freud's idea of the uncanny (*Das Unheimliche*, 1919) – of the desirable, threatening, and unknown all at once.[70] They also spring from the diabolical horror of pain and the absolute incomprehensibility of evil. They rely on Gombrowicz's fundamental metaphysical pessimism, which is helpless in the face of the inscrutability of other human beings and our inescapable (and potentially violent) relationality. This pessimism also does not stand up when confronted with the impenetrability of our psyches and the desires buried at their depths; or when encountering the demonic chaos and nothingness lurking from beyond the oppressive form. For Gombrowicz, who called himself an "avant-garde conservatist,"[71] transgression is born not from excessive courage towards existence, but rather out of the pervasive fear of it.

Caught between the prison of language and reason, and the chaos of silence and unreason, Gombrowicz's individual must struggle for a taste of freedom in between. *The Marriage* stages the difficulty of attaining such freedom and the impossibility of making it last. Henry's discovery of the exciting, unbridled potentiality of interhuman relations goes hand in hand with his fear of its engulfing anarchy and violence. The play thus treads the Foucaultian sexual borderline between Apollonian and Dionysian forces.

In its oneiric poetics, *The Marriage* is a testing ground for what Gombrowicz imagined the transgressive, expected *jouissance* of the interhuman realm to be. It also performs the Freudian prohibitive *Umwelt*, which is the last line of defence and an alibi against the certain disappointment of a realized *jouissance*. In *The Marriage*, the civilizational order, or the God that used to perform the function of such an alibi, is replaced by the interhuman church – the experimental surrogate for the past alibi. Henry, fully aware that the actualized *jouissance* will always be "not it," assumes the role of the father (king, God), sacrificing Johnny on the altar of his expected *jouissance* in order to prevent its actualization. Transgression is thus most possible when *jouissance* does not happen.

VII. Transgression and the Traumatic

Różewicz: The Abject

Tadeusz Różewicz's artistic project is, in some respects, the most radical of those discussed in this essay. A survivor of the Second World War, he was caught between a strongly felt moral responsibility to bear witness to that civilizational cataclysm, and a conviction that art, along with God and man, had perished in it.[72] The search for a language and a form with which to express this experience and its aftermath became his main goal and his challenge. Not surprisingly, he found both in the irreconcilable inconsistencies, non-dialectical contradictions, and impasses – in short, in aporias – that best corresponded to the postwar human condition. Różewicz became their sharp analyst, embodying what he explored. As "one of the great European poets of the 20th century,"[73] he was both an heir to the Polish and European avant-garde and its harsh critic, an early classic who disputed the legitimacy of writing poetry in the post-Holocaust era,[74] and a reluctant postmodernist *avant la lettre* who disparaged this formation when it became popular in Poland in the 1990s.

Różewicz transgressed the boundaries of all the genres he practised. His poems, plays, prose, film scripts, diary notes, and essays are all subject to constant intrusion by other genres: the poems are prosaic (Różewicz created a new, distinct type of Polish verse), the plays and prose have a poetic structure (he was interested in creating realistic-poetic drama), and all of his writing bears its author's distinct signature. This is true despite Różewicz's once-stated aspiration to write like "an anonym," in the unremarkable voice of a nameless, disinherited, and disenchanted man, who would in fact become the unheroic hero of his first published play, now a recognized masterpiece, *Kartoteka* (The Card Index, 1960). Różewicz complicated diachronic investigations of his work by working on some pieces for decades; he also rewrote others repeatedly throughout his life, placing them in new contexts in his subsequent volumes. The title of his short dramatic experiments and commentaries, *Teatr niekonsekwencji* (Theatre of Inconsistences, 1970), could be easily applied to all of his writing, which paradoxically turns Różewicz into one of the most consistent artists in Polish postwar literature.

The writer was also an avid reader, and his readerly fascinations left a strong imprint on his own work. He looked for rescue from anxiety and despair in European literature,[75] and searched for the "sainthood in a man of art" among the memoires and letters of his favourite artists, whom he often saw as ambiguous sacrificial figures.[76] He located the pulse of his contemporaneity in newspapers and often travelled with the Bible, which he knew well and used as a frame of reference, particularly when writing – obsessively, just like Gombrowicz – about the incomprehensibility of suffering. In both his poems and his plays, Christ-the-Man stands squarely at the centre of this preoccupation.[77] He wrote close to forty plays – seventeen of them full-length – mostly in the 1960s and 1970s, discontinuing his interest in the theatre with an almost symbolic gesture: the collective work *Kartoteka rozrzucona* (The Card Index Scattered, 1993) – a rewrite of his first play.[78]

The focus of this discussion is *Do piachu ...* (Bite the Dust ..., 1979),[79] one of Różewicz's most controversial plays, and one that raises incomprehensible, profane suffering to the level of tragic, secular sainthood. This play exemplifies particularly well the transgressiveness of the sacrificial trope when *bios*, *logos*, and *mythos* intersect, not only in Różewicz's work, but also in Polish postwar culture. Its Rilkian subtitle, "The Song about the Love and Death of Private Waluś,"[80] foretells a tale of a soldier's death, yet its hero stands at quite a distance from Rilke's. Waluś is a plebeian partisan, a brutish simpleton who, while curious about culture and liturgically literate, is not habituated to dignifying conventions even for his base physiological needs. Hopelessly lost in the turmoil of a total war, he dies a disgraceful death, defecating on his own grave while praying before being ruthlessly killed by fellow soldiers in a botched execution following his court martial. His "love song" is the charge of having raped an old woman during a burglary at a rectory. His death is bloody, useless, and most probably unjust.

The play challenges more than its famous literary intertext. It cuts deep into some of the most cherished Polish cultural imaginings of the war, and it does so with a double-edged sword. Its one edge is demythologizing – anti-heroic.[81] The underground Home Army in *Bite the Dust* ... is not the competent military formation composed of urban intelligentsia that it was often imagined to be in postwar communicative memory.[82] Such a perception was an effort to counterbalance the ruthless persecution of the Home Army soldiers and the aggressive rewriting of history by the communist authorities; their skilful appropriations of selective traditions and compressions of historical details and distinctions called for counteraction. This mode of remembrance turned the heroic ethos of the underground soldiers into an alternative cultural memory and a cherished national mythos.

Informed by Różewicz's wartime experiences, *Bite the Dust* ... engages and transgresses the multiple levels of this memory and of *mythos*, most obviously by presenting the Home Army as an inept rural unit of socially and politically challenged officers and bickering peasants, whose dilemmas are mostly physiological, born between the kitchen and the latrine. This deheroizing aspect of *Bite the Dust* ... also aligns – albeit largely through irony and satire – with the communist disavowal of the National Armed Forces (NSZ), an important underground military formation during the Second World War that was ruthlessly persecuted afterwards. As a consequence, the play met with a hostile reception, though often for conflicting reasons, whether historical, social, or political. It also did not escape the official censorship. Not surprisingly, the exasperated playwright forbade its translation and almost to the end of his life withheld his permission to stage it.

The other edge of Różewicz's approach is anti-aesthetic and existential. This is how the historical and existential "stations" of Waluś's journey through war's brutality and incomprehensibility, social prejudice and injustice, and human cruelty and indifference acquire a tragic dimension, turning his story into an exquisite and haunting work of art.[83] The play's extreme means of expression – its obscene language and brutal physiology (vomiting, sitting in a latrine, relieving oneself moments before death) – were once considered highly objectionable. They may be seen as less offensive today, given the focus of contemporary theatre and performance on the aesthetics of the body, with all its functions, shapes, and (dis)abilities. In *Bite the Dust* ..., it is the convulsions of a dying body that affect the audience directly, burdening it with the search for sense in Waluś's suffering and sacrifice.

The intersections of Różewicz's own biography, Polish memories of the war, and the realities of the partisan fighting, can be read differently in this play, however, when Waluś is seen as their main locus. From the perspective of *bios*, he becomes a *homo sacer* – set apart from his community and killed. From the cultural perspective, he resembles the Athenian *pharmakoi* who, on the first day of the Thargelia, a festival of Apollo, were first well-fed and then taken outside the city walls to be killed as an exercise in ritual purification. In both readings, the killing of Waluś heightens rather than remedies the wrongs of his deeply flawed community, in part because of the challenges of administering legal justice in times of lawlessness, and in part because of the absurdity of making death a payback for transgressions during a bloodbath. Finally, his historical dimension in the twentieth century echoes that of the historical Christ-the-Man, since Waluś is entangled in powerful forces, betrayed by his fellow soldiers, and unjustly condemned to death for their trespasses. Forsaken by his comrades, mocked and disparaged, fed in a gesture of empathy similar to Veronica's wiping of Christ's bloodied face, he dies, like Christ, an offensive death.

Yet Waluś is no "scatological Christ," a dying piece of meat stuffed with a hearty goulash made of the pig's carcass that for most of the play hangs centre stage as if "crucified."[84] The "anthropology of mere carnality" is not the play's sole horizon.[85] If it were, the audience would feel nothing but horror and disgust. Instead, along with repulsion, the spectator feels empathy for Waluś and an obligation to remember him. His inconsequentiality thus acquires the non-carnal body of a central character, while other, better-developed *dramatis personae* fade into the background. This is the saving power of Różewicz's art, both for the audience and for the poet-playwright: "So many years had to pass before I understood that the writer-poet does not have the right to scorn, that his only right from the moment God abandoned the human being is to love."[86]

VIII. Conclusion

The transgressive projects of Witkacy, Kantor, Grotowski, Gombrowicz, and Różewicz all stem from their aesthetic, philosophical, and ethical investment in experimenting with the intersections of *bios*, *logos*, and *mythos*. In all three areas, they probe the borderline experiences of violence, suffering, and death and engage the sacrificial *topos* in order to do so. Such interest testifies to their physical fragilities or psychological neuroses, their personal issues with familial relations and social structures, and their shared anxieties in the face of the terror of existence and history. Their own selves are central to their works and remain the ultimate lens through which they view the world and assess its limits. With regard to sexual prohibitions and social inhibitions, their transgressions were indicated only in their works' complex systems of symbolic signification, or were restricted to their private lives. The broader contexts of their transgressive strategies have more to do with dominant Polish cultural paradigms, the artists' historical experiences, and their philosophical pessimism.

In the Polish theatre of transgression, the subject challenges the constrictions of the Apollonian forces while withstanding the enchantment of the Dionysian ones. Unfortunately, in Witkacy's plays, he loses on both counts. The subject's excessive individuality dissipates in ultimately fruitless exercises of repeatedly intensified transgressions; its search for metaphysical experience proves ineffective for both itself and the audience. In Gombrowicz's world, the subject's struggle for momentary autonomy allows him to transgress the ever-changing boundaries of the interhuman form but also prompts him to seek refuge from the incommunicable, demonic chaos of indeterminacy in precisely that form. In Grotowski's productions, the subject is overexposed in his "all too human" physical and psychological vulnerability and excess of authenticity, and ends up transgressing the boundaries of performance too efficiently. In Kantor's séances, the subject is imprisoned within a degraded, post-apocalyptic materiality and becomes an objectified and pitiful substitute for a human – a post- or non-human subject. Finally, in Różewicz's plays, individual transgressions do not affirm the subject's singularity but make him a victim of collective historicity. The level of effectiveness of these writers' transgressive strategies varies from the perilously unsuccessful (Witkacy), through the precariously persuasive (Gombrowicz and Kantor) and the reluctantly acceptable (Różewicz), to the successfully suicidal (Grotowski) – the last similar to the (un)happy merging of art with life in the avant-garde's project.

Time and again, all five writers confronted the subjects of their works with the horror of pain, suffering, and evil. Despite their heavy reliance on Christian sacrificial tropes, none of them considered the religious explanation of the meaning of this experience to be viable anymore. Yet in offering up such pain and suffering to the audience, they embraced the sacrifice's core implications. Horrified by pain's incomprehensibility, they explored its limits by performing subconscious anxieties and desires, including their own, by grappling with biological constraints and the absurdity of life's finality and by examining religious, cultural, and sexual prohibitions, as well as historical manifestations of evil. Their metaphysical pessimism was well-founded. In asking the question *unde malum* ("Where does evil come from?"), these spiritual atheists and agnostics looked the diabolical straight in the eye. Witkacy, Kantor, Grotowski, Gombrowicz, and Różewicz observed the world while it was coming undone, and thus most of their transgressive activity revolved around testing the possibilities of creating it anew, even if only momentarily and from second-rate or second-hand materials. They tested that potential fully aware of the scandalous nature of their usurpations and of the spectral character of their creations. The same went for their ambition to create a non-religious sacredness; the realm of the sacred and the profane, of good and evil, whether conceived dualistically or otherwise, was of fundamental importance to their experience of the world.

Their demiurgic activity manifested itself mostly in philosophical and ethical concepts, but it also materialized in new aesthetics. The works of the artists discussed here are imprinted with their distinct aesthetic signatures while also sharing a few important characteristics. Regardless of the area their material belongs to – be it *bios*, *logos*, or *mythos* – it is organized by the violent dynamics of repulsion and awe, fear and excitement, prohibition and permissiveness, brutalization and sublimation, degradation and exaltation, exhaustion and intensification. All three areas are murky, heavy, deformed, cruel, and violent, but they also burst into the mockable, the grotesque, the comical, and the canivalesque. These artists paid their dues for the freedom of imagination (the Dionysian element) with the currency of artistic form and discipline (the Apollonian element). This process is reversed for the audience. In the theatre of Kantor, Grotowski, Gombrowicz, and Różewicz, the audience pays with the currency of affect and emotion (including disgust) for the appreciation of their creations' formal inventiveness and precision. Witkacy imagined his theatre as such, but made the underrated currency of the Mystery of Existence its price.

For Witkacy, Kantor, Grotowski, Gombrowicz, and Różewicz, art was a way of making sense of human existence; for them, it gave the disappearing subjectivity a recognizable albeit momentary shape and provided the language with which it could express its experience of the world. For Gombrowicz, art was also a way of coping with the incomprehensible terror and pain of being that had proved insufficient in the end for Witkacy. The Theatre of Death lessened Kantor's anxieties about the passing of his own life, while Grotowski's performances convinced him of the ultimate superiority of direct human encounters over theatre productions. Różewicz's exit from the theatre marked the limits (artistic and philosophical) of his complex idea of recycling. These metaphysical and therapeutic functions were personal by-products of the artists' public aspirations, however. It was only when their innermost desires, neuroses, anxieties, and hopes traversed the culturally resonant memory of the generations and its historical particularities that their transgressive strategy – the self-sacrifice of the artist himself – acquired its full culture-altering potential.

Tamara Trojanowska
University of Toronto

NOTES

1 See, for example, Walker, "Seizing Power."
2 Mackiewicz, *The Triumph of Provocation*, 200.
3 Kołakowski, *Jezus ośmieszony*, 78–9.
4 Foucault, "A Preface to Transgression," 40.
5 See Skrendo, *Tadeusz Różewicz i granice literatury*, 66.
6 In 1990, Kantor declared: "In art there is only sacrilege, only rebellion, there is only protest, only acceptance of evil; the acknowledgment of Satan as one of the prime movers in art. Not goodness … goodness is very sentimental." Quoted from Osiński, "Tadeusz Kantor i Jerzy Grotowski wobec romantyzmu," 165.
7 The concept has been popularized by Zygmunt Bauman's series of books about seemingly endless variations of "liquid" phenomena (starting with *Liquid Modernity* in 2000 to *Liquid Evil* in 2016). The overuse of the term has erased its analytical currency, but it remains a useful capsule to convey the diagnosis.
8 We owe the unravelling of many secrets connected to this decisive period of Witkacy's life to Krzysztof Dubiński's recent book, *Wojna Witkacego, czyli kumboł w galifetach.*
9 In both cases, these explorations extended to the First World War, an event that had been neglected in Polish cultural memory for decades.
10 It appeared in print only in 1985.
11 In Polish the phrase read: "Do teatru nie wchodzi się bezkarnie." In this context, the inclusion of Kantor's late 1950s and 1960s stagings of Witkacy's plays (alongside his better known "Theatre of Death") in Grzegorz Niziołek's book *Polski teatr Zagłady* (Polish Holocaust Theatre, 2013) should not surprise. Niziołek's book also calls attention to the rarely discussed historical underpinnings of Grotowski's aesthetics and ethics by giving a prominent place both to his memorable *Acropolis* (1962) and to the less obvious choice of *The Constant Prince* (1965). Kantor and Grotowski as directors of theatre concerned with the Holocaust are the subjects of Magda Romańska's book, *The Post-Traumatic Theatre of Grotowski and Kantor*.
12 For an understanding of history as *mythos* (active cultural memory), see Assmann, *Religion and Cultural Memory*.
13 I am referring here to the primary understanding of *scandalon*, meaning a stumbling block. From the perspective of Western European cultural development, the traditions of both Catholicism and Polish Romanticism – particularly with their messianic underpinnings and the Dionysian dimension of the latter – are scandalous; they are stumbling blocks to Western rationality.
14 For a discussion of the indeterminate meaning of *pharmakon* and writing, see Derrida's "Plato's Pharmacy." For a discussion of *pharmakon* and violence, see Girard's *Violence and the Sacred*.
15 Gombrowicz, *Polish Memoirs*, 118.
16 Flaszen and Kolankiewicz, "A Word about Poor Theatre," 30.
17 His sense of being an outlier is clear from his conversation with Kazimierz Braun, as related in Braun and Różewicz, *Języki teatru*.
18 The theses include *Nowe formy w malarstwie i wynikające stąd nieporozumienia* (New Forms in Painting and the Misunderstandings Arising Therefrom, 1919); *Szkice estetyczne* (Aesthetic Essays, 1922); and *Teatr* (Theatre, 1923).
19 Teodor Birula-Białynicki, *Fragmenty wspomnień o St. Ign. Witkiewiczu*, as quoted in Potocka, ed., *Witkacy. Psychoholizm*, 43.

20 Witkacy's titles exemplify his playfulness well, to reference only *Metaphysics of a Two-Headed Calf*, *Tumor Brainowicz*, *The Madman and the Nun*, *The Crazy Locomotive*, and *The Belzebub Sonata*. His first philosophical treatise, "Marzenia improduktywa: dywagacja metafizyczna" (Inproductive Dreams or Philosophical Divagations), written when he was eighteen, also testifies to his penetrating self-awareness, distancing self-irony, and doubt, which mark all his creative endeavours.

21 See, in particular, Ziomek, "Personalne dossier dramatów Witkacego."

22 Puzyna, "Wstęp," 31.

23 Błoński, *Witkacy*, 106.

24 During a potlatch, wealth is not only distributed but also sometimes destroyed or wasted. For this reason the ceremony was outlawed in both Canada and the United States in the nineteenth century. "For Bataille human sovereignty is assured not through the accumulation of profit but through the form of consumption that creates no use-value, the consumption of excess, the generation of waste and loss." Jenks, *Transgression*, 113.

25 For more information about Kantor's life and art, visit http://www.cricoteka.pl/pl/en/.

26 In both Judaism and Christianity, the summoning of the dead by the living, particularly through necromancers, is strictly forbidden. It is blasphemous because it contradicts faith in, and love of, God. Even the exemptions, wherein spirits of the dead contact the living, confirm the spiritual reasons for the prohibition. One of those reasons is the possibility of demonic possession of those displaying *spiritus pythonis.*

27 His cricotages from the mid-1980s renewed his youthful fascination with Constructivism, Surrealism, Bauhaus, and Dada. He also quoted his wartime performance of Wyspiański in *I Shall Never Return*, and cited images from the first two performances of the Theatre of Death in its later incarnations.

28 For an excellent discussion of Kantor's theatre in terms of trauma theory, see Gluhovic, *Performing European Memories*, 101–70.

29 See Kantor, "The Real 'I' 1988," in *A Journey through Other Spaces*, 164. Kantor stages the return to his home in much the same way as Gombrowicz in *The Marriage*, using the oneiric poetics of a subjective drama.

30 The incantations include the plebeian wailing of the royal and messianic Psalm 110, and the insolent use of the most popular of the Polish First World War military songs, "The Grey Infantry" ("Szara piechota"). For a thorough analysis of these two elements, see Trojanowska, "Transgression and Eschatology."

31 The association with the vicarage was reinforced by the production's poster, which included an image of the actual church in Kantor's birthplace. He rehearsed the production in the desecrated church in Florence. The connection to the opening scene in Gombrowicz's *The Marriage* will become clear in the course of my discussion.

32 The link between the two was well established by Bachelard's *Poetics of Space*.

33 Kantor, "Annexed Reality 1963," in *A Journey through Other Spaces*, 71–6.

34 The phrase was coined by Tadeusz Kudliński in his review of Grotowski's production of *The Forefathers' Eve*, and later adopted by the director in his writings. See Kudliński, "*Dziady* w 13 rzędach."

35 Since 1962 known as Theatre Laboratory of 13 Rows.

36 The closing date of 1969 marks the official premier of *Apocalypsis cum Figuris*. For details about the history of the production and the existence and then dissolution of the Laboratory Theatre, visit http://www.grotowski.net/en/encyclopedia/laboratory-theatre.

37 Throughout his career, Grotowski was out of step with what was *en vogue* at the time in Polish culture. He studied Slanislavsky seriously even though the Russian director had fallen

out of favour with theatre artists, primarily because socialist realism strongly approved of his system (see Osiński, "Tadeusz Kantor i Jerzy Grotowski," 147–84). He was dissecting Polish Romantics when the Western avant-garde triumphantly took over Polish stages in the 1960s, and he abandoned the Romantics when they came to dominate Polish theatre in the 1970s (Dziewulska, *Artyści i pielgrzymi*, 130–1).

38 Kosiński, *Teatra polskie*, 117.

39 See Pleśniarowicz, "Polski teatr śmierci," 17–18.

40 http://www.grotowski.net/en/encyclopedia/dziady-forefathers-eve.

41 Masłowski, *Gest, symbol i rytuały polskiego teatru romantycznego*, 71 (quoted here from Kosiński, *Polski teatr przemiany*, 46).

42 Kosiński, *Grotowski. Profanacje*, 87.

43 For an erudite essay on the meaning of the cathedral for European civilization, see Pasierb, *Katedra, symbol Europy*, in which he claims "[that] a cathedral symbolizes the whole Christian and European historical universe" (19).

44 The most notorious one, Auschwitz, was located about 60 kilometres west of Kraków.

45 Flaszen, "Wyspiański's *Akropolis*," 64.

46 He borrowed his main concept of acting – *via negativa* – from the apophatic theology of Pseudo-Dionysius the Areopagite, and his concept of *ogołocenie* (emptying) from a Spanish mystic, St John of the Cross. He took interest in Hans Urs von Balthasar and his theological dramatic theory.

47 From Thomas Mann, through Blavatsky's Theosophy, to George Ivanovich Gurdijeff and others. His interests also included ideoplasty, telepathy, hypnosis, radiation, and shamanism, not to mention his often-discussed fascination with Hinduism and Buddhism.

48 See Kolankiewicz and Flaszen, "Dostojewski – Wielki Inkwizytor."

49 Grotowski, "Towards a Poor Theatre," 35.

50 For a discussion of this understanding of theatre and performance, see Auslander, "Against Ontology"; and Phelan, "The Ontology of Performance."

51 The eponymous hero of the 1629 play by the Spanish playwright and poet Pedro Calderón de la Barca (1600–81), which was translated (and paraphrased) into Polish by Juliusz Słowacki in 1843.

52 To prepare for it, Grotowski and Cieślak worked separately from the rest of the company, reading, among other works, St John of the Cross's *Spiritual Canticle*. Written during the saint's imprisonment in Toledo, the work relates his excruciating bodily trials and mystical experiences. See Flaszen and Jarocki, "Goście Starego Teatru," 8.

53 A good starting point is http://www.grotowski.net/en/encyclopedia/constant-prince-ksiaze-niezlomny, which provides a basic bibliography, and Serge Ouaknine's *Książę Niezłomny* (available also in its French 1970 original).

54 Grotowski wrote: "This defiance of taboo, this transgression, provides the shock which rips off the mask, enabling us to give ourselves nakedly to something which is impossible to define but which contains Eros and Caritas." "Towards a Poor Theatre," 34.

55 Kosiński, *Grotowski. Profanacje*, 125.

56 Not surprisingly, Grotowski also staged Marlowe's *Doctor Faustus*.

57 The title of *Apocalypsis cum figuris* originated from the series of fifteen woodblock prints by Albrecht Dürer (1498), with whose art Thomas Mann was greatly taken and which influenced Grotowski's interest in the demonic.

58 Lisa Wolford, *Grotowski's Objective Drama Research*, 5.

59 The play was finished in 1947, published first in its Spanish translation in 1948, and in its original only in 1953.

60 For analysis of the Bakhtinian understanding of the carnivalesque in *Operetta*, see Danek, "Oblicze. Gombrowicz i śmierć." For analysis of its theatrical form, see Trojanowska, "Teatralne konsekwencje operetki w *Operetce*."

61 Gombrowicz, *History (an Operetta)*, 100.

62 Ibid., 107.

63 Ibid., 109.

64 Ibid., 117.

65 Jeleński, "Od bosości do nagości," 350. Much more is now known about the sources and forms of such "pathology" from Gombrowicz's private diary *Kronos* (2013) – a testimony to his powerful need to keep a peculiar account of his life story.

66 Thus Gombrowicz's individuals cause cataclysmic historical events, but also interpret history as happening in direct relation to their own needs and desires (Gombrowicz saw the war as happening to liberate him from himself and Poland).

67 Gombrowicz, *A Kind of Testament*, 10.

68 A gesture repeated by Grotowski in his production *Hamlet Study*.

69 No other critic did as good a job of analysing the psychoanalytical ramifications of Gombrowicz's play as Jan Błoński in "*Ślub* jako tragedia psychoanalityczna."

70 See Markowski, *Czarny nurt*, 61–188.

71 Gombrowicz, *A Kind of Testament*, 152.

72 "I considered the war to be a catastrophe of European civilization equal to Biblical flood – till today this crisis, contrary to many opinions, has not been overcome," says Różewicz in "Ufajcie obcemu przechodniowi," 191.

73 These words of Seamus Heaney endorse the English translation of Różewicz's volume *Matka odchodzi* (Mother Departs, 1999).

74 The publication of his *Poezje zebrane* (Collected Poems, 1957) at the age of thirty-six was a spectacular achievement for a still young writer, and the first step towards securing his exalted future status.

75 He was a loyal interlocutor of Dostoyevsky, Thomas Mann, Franz Kafka, Joseph Conrad, T.S. Eliot, Ezra Pound, and Samuel Beckett, as well as of Friedrich Hölderlin, Rainer Maria Rilke, Ludwig Wittgenstein, Anton Chekhov, James Joyce, Adam Mickiewicz, and Cyprian Kamil Norwid, to name just a few of Różewicz's most frequent rereadings.

76 Stolarczyk, *Wbrew sobie*, 115.

77 See Żukowski, *Obrazy Chrystusa w twórczości Aleksandra Wata i Tadeusza Różewicza*.

78 Różewicz worked on it with a group of actors in 1992 at the Polish Theatre in Wrocław during a cycle of open rehearsals.

79 Różewicz started writing it as early as 1948, first as a work of fiction, and by 1955 as a play. Completed in 1972, it did not see the light of day in print or on stage because of communist censorship until 1979.

80 See Rilke's famous epic poem *Weise von Liebe und Tod des Cornets Christoph Rilke* (The Lay of the Love and Death of Christopher Cornet Rilke, 1912).

81 Różewicz was not the only artist in Polish culture to present such a non-heroic side of the war, and *Bite the Dust ...* is not his first text about it. There have been other prominent revaluations both in literature (to mention only Miron Białoszewski's *Pamiętnik z Powstania Warszawskiego* [Memoir of the Warsaw Uprising, 1970]) and in film (for example, Andrzej Wajda's *Kanał* [Canal, 1956] and Andrzej Munk's *Zezowate szczęście* [Crossed-eyed Luck, 1960]).

82 This cultural means of remembrance actualized the nineteenth-century Romantic ideal of camaraderie known from the famous prison scene in Mickiewicz's *The Forefathers' Eve, Part III*.

83 For example, its 2003 premiere at the Teatr Provisorium i Kompania Teatr in Lublin (dir. Janusz Opryński and Witold Mazurkiewicz), disposed of all political references and presented the play as "the way of the cross" of a historical man caught in a war.

84 In his interpretation, Tomasz Żukowski sees a parallel between Waluś's last meal and the Communion, *Agnus Dei*, also prayed by him in the preceding scene, and concludes that "At the end, this 'Lord's Supper' ends as excrement in a pit into which Waluś's body is shoved right after." Żukowski, *Obrazy Chrystusa w twórczości Aleksandra Wata i Tadeusza Różewicza*, 283.

85 Ibid., 288.

86 Różewicz, "Sobowtór," 427.

WORKS CITED

Assmann, Jan. *Religion and Cultural Memory: Ten Studies*. Translated by Rodney Livingstone. Stanford: Stanford University Press, 2006.

Auslander, Philip. "Against Ontology." In *Liveness: Performance in a Mediatized Culture*. 38–53. New York: Routledge, 1999.

Bachelard, Gaston. *The Poetics of Space*. Translated by Maria Jolas. New York: Orion Press, 1964.

Bataille, George. *The Accursed Share – an Essay on General Economy*. Translated by Robert Hurley. New York: Zone Books, 1988–c1991.

Błoński, Jan. "*Ślub* jako tragedia psychoanalityczna." In *Forma, śmiech i rzeczy ostateczne: studia o Gombrowiczu*. 113–39. Kraków: Znak, 1994.

– *Od Stasia do Witkacego*. Kraków: Wydawnictwo Literackie, 1997.

– *Witkacy*. Kraków: Wydawnictwo Literackie, 2000.

Braun, Kazimierz, and Tadeusz Różewicz. *Języki teatru*. Wrocław: Wydawnictwo Dolnośląskie, 1989.

Danek, Danuta. "Oblicze. Gombrowicz i śmierć." In *Gombrowicz i krytycy*. Edited by Zdzisław Łapiński. 707–41. Kraków: Wydawnictwo Literackie, 1984.

Derrida, Jacques. "Plato's Pharmacy." In *Dissemination*. Translated by Barbara Johnson. 61–72. London: Athlone Press, 1981.

Dubiński, Krzysztof. *Wojna Witkacego czyli kumboł w galifetach*. Warszawa: Iskry, 2015.

Dziewulska, Małgorzata. *Artyści i pielgrzymi*. Wrocław: Wydawnictwo Dolnośląskie, 1995.

Flaszen, Ludwik. *Grotowski & Company*. Translated by Andrzej Wojtasik with Paul Allain. Edited by Paul Allain. Holstebro: Icarus, 2010.

– "Wyspiański's *Akropolis*." In *Grotowski Sourcebook*. Edited by Lisa Wolford and Richard Schechner. 64–72. New York: Routledge, 2001.

Flaszen, Ludwik, and Jerzy Jarocki. "Goście Starego Teatru. Spotkanie dziesiąte: z Ludwikiem Flaszenem rozmawia Jerzy Jarocki. 13 lutego 1994." *Teatr* 10 (1994): 4–10.

Flaszen, Ludwik, and Leszek Kolankiewicz. "A Word about Poor Theatre." In *Voices from Within: Grotowski's Polish Collaborators*. Edited by Paul Allain and Grzegorz Ziółkowski. 17–35. London: Polish Theatre Perspectives, 2015.

Foucault, Michel. "A Preface to Transgression." In *Language, Counter-Memory, Practice: Selected Essays and Interviews*. Edited by Donald F. Bouchard, translated by Donald F. Bouchard and Sherry Simon. 29–52. Ithaca: Cornell University Press, 1977.

Girard, René. *Violence and the Sacred*. Translated by Patrick Gregory. Baltimore: Johns Hopkins University Press, 1977.

Gluhovic, Milija. *Performing European Memories: Trauma, Ethics, Politics*. New York: Palgrave Macmillan, 2013.

Gombrowicz, Witold. *Diary*, vol. 2. Translated by Lillian Vallee. New Haven: Yale University Press, 2012.

– *History (an Operetta)*. Translated by Allen Kuharski and Dariusz Bukowski. *Performing Arts Journal* (PAJ) 20, no. 1 (1998): 99–117.

– *A Kind of Testament*. Edited by Dominique de Roux; translated by Alastair Hamilton. London: Dalkey Archive Press, 2007.

– *Kronos*. Kraków: Wydawnictwo Literackie, 2013.

– *Polish Memoirs*. Translated by Bill Johnston. New Haven: Yale University Press, 2004.

– *Three Plays*. Translated by Krystyna Griffith-Jones, Catherine Robins, and Louis Iribarne. London and New York: Marion Boyars, 1998.

Grotowski, Jerzy. "Towards a Poor Theatre." In *Grotowski Sourcebook*. Edited by Lisa Wolford and Richard Schechner. 28–37. New York: Routledge, 2001.

Jeleński, Konstanty. "Od bosości do nagości. O nieznanej sztuce Witolda Gombrowicza." In Witold Gombrowicz, *Iwona, księżniczka Burgunda, Ślub, Operetka, Historia*. 333–69. Kraków: Wydawnictwo Literackie, 1995.

Jenks, Chris. *Transgression*. New York: Routledge, 2003.

Jervis, John. *Transgressing the Modern: Explorations in the Western Experience of Otherness*. Oxford: Blackwell Publishers, 1999.

Kantor, Tadeusz. *A Journey through Other Spaces: Essays and Manifestos, 1944–1990*. Edited and translated by Michal Kobialka. Berkeley: University of California Press, 1993.

– "Mówić o sobie w trzeciej osobie." In *Pisma. Teatr Śmierci. Teksty z lat 1975–1984*, vol. 2. Edited by Krzysztof Pleśniarowicz. 433–67. Kraków: Wydawnictwo Literackie, 2004.

Kołakowski. Leszek. *Jezus ośmieszony. Esej apologetyczny i sceptyczny*. Translated by Dorota Zańko. Kraków: Znak, 2014.

Kolankiewicz, Leszek, and Ludwik Flaszen. "Wielki Inkwizytor." *Didaskalia – Gazeta Teatralna* 95 (February 2010): 113–19. http://www.e-teatr.pl/pl/artykuly/101508,druk.html.

Kosiński, Dariusz. *Grotowski. Profanacje*. Wrocław: Instytut im. Jerzego Grotowskiego, 2015.

– *Polski teatr przemiany*. Wrocław: Instytut im. Jerzego Grotowskiego, 2007.

– *Teatra polskie. Historie*. Warszawa: Wydawnictwo Naukowe PWN, 2010.

Kudliński, Tadeusz. *"Dziady* w 13 Rzędach, czyli krakowiacy w Opolu." *Dziennik Polski* 159 (1961): 3. Reprinted in *Misterium zgrozy i urzeczenia. Przedstawienia Jerzego Grotowskiego i Teatru Laboratorium*. Edited by. Janusz Degler and Grzegorza Ziółkowski. 139–40. Wrocław: Instytut im. Jerzego Grotowskiego, 2006.

Mackiewicz, Józef. *The Triumph of Provocation*. Translated by Jerzy Hauptmann, S.D. Lukac, and Martin Dewhirst. New Haven: Yale University Press, c2009.

Markowski, Michał Paweł. *Czarny nurt. Gombrowicz, świat, literatura*. Kraków: Wydawnictwo Literackie, 2004.

Masłowski, Michał. *Gest, symbol i rytuały polskiego teatru romantycznego*. Warszawa: PWN, 1998.

Mickiewicz, Adam. *Forefathers*. Translated by Count Potocki of Montalk. London: Polish Cultural Foundation, 1968.

Niziołek, Grzegorz. *Polski teatr Zagłady*. Warszawa: Instytut Teatralny im. Zbigniewa Raszewskiego, Wydawnictwo Krytyki Politycznej, 2013.

Osiński, Zbigniew. "Tadeusz Kantor i Jerzy Grotowski wobec romantyzmu." In *Tradycja romantyczna w teatrze polskim*. Edited by Dariusz Kosiński. 157–86. Kraków: Towarzystwo Naukowe Societas Vistulana, 2007.

Ouaknine, Serge. *Książę Niezłomny. Studium i rekonstrukcja spektaklu Jerzego Grotowskiego i Teatru Laboratorium.* Wrocław: Instytut im. Jerzego Grotowskiego, 2011.

Pasierb, Janusz. *Katedra, symbol Europy. La Cathédrale Europe.* Pelplin: Bernardinum, 2003.

Phelan, Peggy. "The Ontology of Performance: Representation without Reproduction." In *Unmarked: The Politics of Performance.* 146–66. New York: Routledge, 1993.

Pleśniarowicz, Krzysztof. "Polski teatr śmierci: Mickiewicz, Wyspiański, Kantor." *Teatr* 12 (1993): 17–19.

Potocka, Maria Anna, ed. *Witkacy. Psychoholizm.* Kraków: Bunkier sztuki, 2009.

Puzyna, Konstatnty. "Wstęp." In Stanisław Ignacy Witkiewicz, *Dramaty*, vol. 1. iii–cxi. Warszawa: PIW, 1962.

Romańska, Magda. *The Post-Traumatic Theatre of Grotowski and Kantor: History and Holocaust in "Akropolis" and "Dead Class."* London: Anthem Press, 2012.

Różewicz, Tadeusz. "Sobowtór." In *Proza*, vol. 3. 411–30. Wrocław: Wydawnictwo Dolnośląskie, 2004.

– "Ufajcie obcemu przechodniowi." An interview by Richard Chetwynd. In *Wbrew sobie. Rozmowy z Tadeuszem Różewiczem.* Edited by Jan Stolarczyk. 187–99. Wrocław: Biuro Literackie, 2011.

Skrendo, Andrzej. *Tadeusz Różewicz i granice literatury. Poetyka i etyka transgresji.* Kraków: Universitas, 2002.

Stolarczyk, Jan, ed. *Wbrew sobie. Rozmowy z Tadeuszem Różewiczem.* Wrocław: Biuro Literackie, 2011.

Trojanowska, Tamara. "Teatralne konsekwencje operetki w *Operetce.*" *Dialog* 5–6 (1986): 168–74.

– "Transgression and Eschatology in the Works of Tadeusz Kantor." In *The Theatre of Tadeusz Kantor.* Edited by Magda Romańska and Cathleen Cioffi. Evanston: Northwestern University Press, 2017.

Walker, John V. "Seizing Power: Decadence and Transgression in Foucault and Paglia." *Postmodern Culture* 5, no. 1 (September 1994): 8. http://pmc.iath.virginia.edu/text-only/issue.994/walker.994.

Wolford, Lisa. *Grotowski's Objective Drama Research.* Mississippi: University Press of Mississippi, 1996.

Ziomek, Jerzy. "Personalne dossier dramatów Witkacego." In *Studia o Stanisławie Ignacym Witkiewiczu.* Edited by Michał Głowiński and Janusz Sławiński. Wrocław: Zakład Narodowy im. Ossolińskich 1972.

Żukowski, Tomasz. *Obrazy Chrystusa w twórczości Aleksandra Wata i Tadeusza Różewicza.* Warszawa: Stowarzyszenie Pro Cultura Litteraria: Instytut Badań Literackich PAN Wydawnictwo, 2013.

Delectatio morosa, or, the Modes of Affective Compensation in Polish Memory Culture

PART ONE: SYMBOLIC CONSTELLATIONS

The Warsaw Rising Museum opened in Warsaw in 2004 on the sixtieth anniversary of the outbreak of the uprising and it has since then beaten records for attendance and popularity. Stylistically coherent from the moment visitors enter the permanent exhibition to the moment they exit through the gift shop, it is one of the most technologically advanced and interactive museums in Poland. At its centre stands a steel wall – called the Monument – marred by bullets and shrapnel. When visitors put their ears to the wall, they can hear the sounds of the uprising – a fusion of documentary recordings from the uprising's radio station, Warsaw's popular melodies, and songs of the uprising. They can also feel the monument gently pulsate, with the pulsations (exactly sixty-three per minute, the same as the number of days in the uprising) symbolizing the "bijące serce walczącej Warszawy" (beating heart of fighting Warsaw). Every twenty minutes, the soundscape of the entire space is dominated by the recorded noise of air raids intertwined with the pulsating rhythm of the beating heart. The exhibition combines visual and sound effects with strategies orchestrated to engage the visitor's entire body. For instance, to re-enact the experience of moving through the sewers (which were used during the uprising as evacuation paths), the visitor is invited to enter a reconstructed sewer. While travelling through the several-metres-long sewer built to a historically accurate height and width, visitors must stoop and hold on to the walls to maintain their balance. The guides, to intensify the effect, often turn off the lights to allow people to grope in darkness through the claustrophobic space. The museum succeeds in the production of affect *par excellence* – the emotions may be hard to name, but they are felt intensely.

It is a much-needed museum, and some of its many initiatives are meaningful tools for understanding and preserving the memory of this iconic historical event. This is the case, for example, with the "Archiwum historii mówionej" (oral history archive), which gathers testimonies of the uprising's participants. The museum also manages, however, to circumvent painful questions about the uprising's *raison d'être*: Was it worth the price of so many lives and the total destruction of the capital? Would the history of postwar Poland be different if the uprising had never happened? These questions touch the very core of Polish postwar history. Yet the museum sublates them into the sphere of affective subscription to the uprising's myth. In its effective use of media and technology, it asks visitors to suspend their "here and now" and to enter the sphere of the simulacrum to enact solidarity with the dead. The museum acknowledges that its core mission is to disseminate the Uprising's heroic interpretation, which is configured as the patriotic approach to

Polish history. However, its unacknowledged mission seems to be more about re-enacting the event and institutionalizing its affect than it is about the uprising's commemoration.

Post-1989 Transformations

As the popularity of the museum indicates, the affective – rather than critical – approach to history still holds power over Polish society regardless of the substantial transformations of collective memory since the fall of communism in 1989. The opening of archives, the absence of censorship, and new democratic ways of circulating information generated a flood of memories in post-1989 Poland. Most symptomatic of the country's democratization was the striking diversification of those memories and the pluralization of their modes of circulation. From national memory through regional memory (with the East and West Kresy – "borderlands" – as a prime example of regional diversity), from collective to personal, or individual, memory (which often clashes with or at least complicates national or collective modes of identification) – the cultural hunger to connect to the past has been palpable in Poland, manifesting itself in all channels of cultural production and societal communication.

The range of conduits for the past grew exponentionally: from state-governed institutions (monuments, museums, school curricula); to officially sanctioned collective rituals and memories (as in, say, official speeches of the president or the prime minister); to the mass media, which became a platform for national public debates about controversial events in the Polish past and the main venue for popularizing (predominantly national) memory, as represented in popular films and TV series. They also extended to art and literature (a more limited audience) and, finally, to the personal accounts, both written and oral, transmitted in micro-collectives such as the family.

Clearly, all these different types of memory existed during the communist era; but the democratization of culture that has enabled a different flow of information and the simultaneous circulation of knowledge from multiple sources had the effect of decentralizing national memory – something that according to sociologists is typical of democracies.[1] In other words, the transformations of memory have been paradigmatic;[2] they have not been solely a matter of erasing blank spots or advancing historical awareness, although the cumulative effect of these two factors was considerable. Rather, these new developments have shifted the very structure of relations to the past. The categories of nation and state have been receding, for example, while other categories, such as the experiences of ethnic and regional groups, have moved to the fore. Questions and dilemmas that were percolating under the surface long before the collapse of communism have acquired a sense of cultural urgency, and Polish society has thrown itself into reassessing its past and its future: What has been erased from or sanitized in the Polish past? What do we acknowledge, and what do we repress? Where are the blank spots and the grey zones? How do we speak about agency and victimization? How can we relate to the past so that we attest to it while also moving forward?

The feeling that Poland was standing at a crossroads was tangible after 1989, and a debate about how its society should reaffirm or reshape its cultural traditions, symbolic paradigms, and discursive networks became fundamental to its future. There was a cultural awareness that the framework of Polish culture in place for the past two centuries, and inextricably linked to the country's traumatic past and periods of subjugation, might not serve the interests of its future sovereignty. A quarter-century later, it is clear that the old framework has once again proved, as it did in the past, its great adaptability to

Poland's changing political and cultural circumstances. The question from the beginning of the 1990s of how to reorient the culture's main points of reference, meanwhile, waits for an adequate answer.

As many cultural critics and sociologists have noted, Polish culture orients itself in relation to the traumatic and shapes its symbolic dimension through interpretation and reinterpretation of the traumatic. Insofar as the traumatic has been historically a principal frame for the Polish collective identity, the human, material, and cultural losses associated with such events as the Nazi occupation, the Yalta Agreement, and the Warsaw Uprising continue to play a central role in how Poles relate to their collective identity and memory today. In other words, these traumatic events have been and remain the organizers of the Polish cultural imagination despite the temporal distance between these events and the "postmemorial" generations.

POSTMEMORY

This term was coined by Marianne Hirsch to denote a type of memory that does not arise from personal experience but that belongs to later generations who know the past either from cultural representations or through transgenerational transmission. Postmemory can be highly affective because the time gap and the impossibility of accessing the past directly forces it to depend on mediated accounts (photographs, diaries, monuments, film, comics, etc.) and to replace what cannot be experienced with what can be imagined. Hence, postmemory depends on mental projection and on the imaginary re-creation of the past. This re-creation often imbues postmemory with a haunting, obsessive quality and may even lead to a secondary traumatization (i.e., the traumatization that results from identification with the victim). The term postmemory is usually applied in relation to the transmission of traumatic experiences. Hirsch claims that "postmemory is not a movement, method, or idea; I see it, rather, as a structure of inter- and trans-generational transmission of traumatic knowledge and experience."

– Hirsch, "The Generation of Postmemory" 106

During long periods of lacking or limited sovereignty (i.e., the times of partitions, occupations, and communism), Polish culture was forced to develop a mechanism that would enable it to absorb and process an avalanche of traumatic events. This mechanism has proved powerful enough to persist even after the country regained independence in 1989 and the circumstances of subjugation that gave rise to it no longer held sway. The democratization process in the last quarter of the century has affected the way collective memories have been generated and distributed, yet many events in the public sphere of contemporary Poland convey the impression that Polish culture is entrenched in anachronistic cultural patterns. I propose the term "affective compensation" to discuss the kind of accommodation of the traumatic that is deeply rooted in Polish cultural imagination.

Compensation

By affective compensation I mean a symbolic economy of collective affect. A legal analogy may be useful here. In the legal understanding, compensation is an exchange of two incomparable things, for instance, the award of financial reparations for a lost limb. It is not intended to repair the damage in the sense of replacing the thing that was lost, which is an impossible task, but rather to repair the projected loss of life's pleasures resulting from that loss (so-called hedonic compensation). Through the exchange of two things that belong to different orders, financial reparation is meant to bind negative feelings of loss, that is, to bar their potential spillover resulting from unacknowledged losses. There is an understanding that although one thing cannot replace the other, the very act of compensation is a mode of societal recognition of loss, a symbolic exchange to counter the potential unrest that could emerge if those who experienced losses felt alienated from the society because their losses were unacknowledged.

Collective affective compensation also recognizes loss. Every culture develops ways to deal with the traumatic and to compensate for their members' losses. On a structural level many cultural rituals for responding to loss are similar across cultures (just as rituals of mourning often reveal structural similarities). At the same time, however, each culture manifests its relationship to trauma and loss uniquely and in ways that are deeply embedded in a given collective's symbolic repository and contextualized by this collective's historical experience and political environment.

What Is Affect?

In the context of this essay, affect does not indicate the emotions experienced by an individual and interiorized subject, but rather a type of intensity that charges the field of cultural communication and social practices.[3] Affect in the most basic sense is a mode of social mimicry, one that characterizes our bodily existence in time and space; from the evolutionary perspective, we share affect with primates from the earliest stages of our development (one example of such mimicry is that of a mother engaged in the exchange of smiles with her infant). The capacity to affect others and to be affected through social mimicry is a biological tool that enables social communication and bonding and that ultimately secures collective survival. In Spinoza's description, through affect "the body's power of acting is increased or diminished, aided or restrained."[4] Collective affect and the affective relationship between the individual and the collective signify something much less specific than emotions, but also something much more fundamental. Affective dynamics precede emotions, which emerge from them. On the individual level (biologically and preconsciously) and on the level of collective communication, affect varies in intensity and thereby creates different contexts for the articulation of emotions, which are specific, nameable, and symbolizable. Emotions and cognition are the endpoints of the field of affect, which signifies the potential for various degrees of intensity "to move and be moved" (Spinoza) – to reach and be reached.

If affect means the potential for reachability, then this potential can be politically and culturally harnessed for various needs and articulated under a range of ideological and emotional labels. This intensity of affect can help us understand the compensatory reaction to oppression, but its function is not reserved for the oppressed alone. Affect can have its own politics, and it can be enrolled in the service of a range of normativizing powers and discursive regimes, in Foucauldian terms. In other words, affect is enrolled in the creation and sustenance of a social hierarchy when it comes to forms of representations, systems of values, and configurations of cultural identities that constitute the life of the collective and particularly its public space.

Many transformative events in Polish history show how affect can be socially and politically mobilized. In its most intense form we can observe affect in moments of collective effervescence, to use the Durkheimian notion, of which the so-called *wypadki sierpniowe* (literally "August events") of 1980 serve as a good example. This was the workers' strike at the Gdańsk shipyard, which quickly snowballed into civic unrest on a national scale, leading in turn to the birth of the Solidarity movement. It began as a direct response to yet another hardship for workers – an increase in food prices – but ended with a list of demands (the creation of the independent labour union foremost among them) that addressed major transgressions of human and civil rights by the communist regime. In its initial phase, the Solidarity movement crystallized the will of the people; the fact that they would no longer be satisfied with limited concessions from the regime was largely connected to the movement's affective power.

That the shipyard workers set aside their own immediate interests and joined "in solidarity" with other workers striking across the city and ultimately across the country was undoubtedly the most affective moment of the dissident movement.[5] The many accounts and the documentary footage of the August 1980 strikes show how affect-laden they were. One can point here, for example, to the communal singing and praying with which the strikers kept up their spirits and dampened political disagreements. What can be discursively formulated as Solidarity's political agenda was not the only reason for its realization; the transmission of affect contributed greatly to the domino effect of the movement and its ultimate success.

Not surprisingly, in the dark decade following the imposition of martial law in December 1981, places of performative intensity, such as churches and theatres, in which the political and the bodily – literally sensory (gestures, singing, the tactile sensation of being part of the crowd) – were inseparable, provided what official institutional culture could not. These affective spaces became places of cultural and political dissent from the official mainstream. The fact that mass demonstrations often began in churches had more to do with the heightened affect of the communal ritual than with the religiosity of the participants. Such settings reinforced a sense of liminal *communitas,* to use Victor Turner's potent anthropological term, a powerful unstructured community united by shared experience – in this case, the experience of social unrest.[6]

Affective Compensation: The Affect of the Romantic Paradigm and Its Transmission

Affect holds a central position in the most persistent paradigm of Polish culture – the so-called *paradygmat romantyczny* (Romantic paradigm).[7] In contemporary Poland, this formative meta-narrative (in the Lyotardian sense of a narrative that organizes communal imagination and reinforces the community's self-image) is a fusion of the Romantic period's legacy with what this legacy had become through the long process of cultural transmission. For centuries, its main function has been to provide symbolic and affective compensation for staggering historical, political, and cultural losses.

The Romantic paradigm refers back to the Romantic period in Polish culture (roughly 1822–63, with the trauma of the bloody January Uprising against Russia marking its end), yet its affective and compensatory power did not emerge directly from the complex, hyper-self-aware cultural formation of Romanticism. Rather, it emerged from Romanticism's "popular" blueprint, the simplified posthumous transmission of Romanticism proper, that is, the kind of transmission that discounted the complexities and paradoxes of the seminal Romantic texts it disseminated in the first place.

The main difference between these seminal texts and their popular reception corresponds to the difference between critique and compensation. Romanticism as a cultural formation emerged in Poland in the wake of the loss of independence, and the qualities it shared with European Romanticism in general thus became integrated with intense political engagement for the cause of independence.[8] Universal revolutionary ideas and desire for the material and spiritual transformation of the world were often combined in the writings of Polish Romantics with a biting social, political, existential, and theological critique of not only pre-partitioned Poland and its society but also of the order of things as such. Polish Romanticism was simultaneously deeply national and universal; even the messianic ideas conveyed by Mickiewicz's use of the expression "Poland the Christ of Nations" spoke less of national hubris and more of the desire to recast Poland's suffering as a tool of universal redemption.

Yet in the popular dissemination, the painful assessments of social inequalities in Polish society, the heretical nature of the Romantic inquiries into *unde malum* (contained in iconic texts taught in every Polish school), and the radical nature of messianism as a transnational political theology, have all lost their teeth, having been reduced to a repository of symbols, phrases, motives, and affects. Romantic poets were elevated to the status of spiritual leaders of the stateless nation, and their texts served as symbolic substitutions of significance that had been lost in the political realm. Romanticism in its transgenerational transmission became a national mythology that elevated suffering and sacrifice and that eliminated the radicality of Romantic thinking together with its potential to inspire political and existential transformation. This transmission of "Romanticism without the text"[9] intensified the compensatory drive of the Romantic formation at the price of excluding what the finest Romantic "texts" (whether literary, visual, or musical) actually encoded: radical political, ethical, existential, and social critique. In sum, what could not easily fit into the compensatory narrative was ignored, and this ultimately thinned Romanticism's complexities and critical potential.

The Romantic meta-narrative has been crucial for Polish culture because it was born of a prolonged traumatization triggered by Poland's loss of independence at the end of the eighteenth century and by the partitions that followed. In the nineteenth century it was shaped by oppression and by two bloody uprisings against Russia, and in the twentieth century by two world wars, including the horrors of the Nazi and Soviet occupations, the Holocaust, and the near-annihilation of the nation's material and cultural heritage. The Romantic paradigm became the cultural paradigm for coping with the long-term impact of these losses. It organized Polish literary and public language as a set of communally recognizable *topoi,* and it has remained central because it was remarkably adaptable to various needs to compensate for historical traumas and political failures.

In its most simplistic and most persistent form, the Romantic paradigm fetishized suffering, elevated the Polish fate to the status of martyrology (and history to the status of fate), and often promoted self-congratulatory patriotism. It heightened the position of the victim as epistemologically privileged: as having access to the kind of knowing that others were not entitled to experience. Messianism's universalism and its philosophical dimension became overshadowed by the perception of suffering as a source of national identity and moral superiority. According to the abridged Romantic blueprints, the traumatic opened up onto the extraordinary. This elevation of suffering and martyrdom to the level of the sublime became manifested in the aestheticization of death: the myth of the "beautiful death," sacralized death, sacrificial death, heroic death, death as a spectacle of revenge on an indifferent world (Słowacki's "let us be seen – as we die!"),[10] as a fetish and a necrophilic obsession – *delectatio morosa,* a communal perverse pleasure, so brutally mocked by Czesław Miłosz (1911–2004).[11]

The Romantic Paradigm and Its Critics

The Romantic paradigm has received its fair share of criticism from the most formative minds in Polish culture, beginning with the Romantics themselves: Cyprian Kamil Norwid (1821–83), a late Romantic, chastised Poland's symbolic self-elevation as a nation and its deficiencies as a society. The early modernist Stanisław Brzozowski (1878–1911) rebuked Polish Romanticism as a mode of escape from real social and intellectual engagement in the life of local collectives, while the later Witold Gombrowicz (1904–69) repeatedly expressed his distaste for the the Polish collective's Romantic predilection for either heroism or nihilism. He also criticized Polish writers for their inability to write about the world and the war from an ordinary perspective. However, the ironic self-awareness of Romanticism's trap is most stunning and shattering in its most tragic practitioners – the poets of the lost Second World War generation: Krzysztof Kamil Baczyński (1921–44), Tadeusz Gajcy (1922–44), and Stanisław Trzebiński (1922–43), the first two of whom were killed in the Warsaw Uprising. While willingly submitting to Romanticism's power, they bitterly despaired over its legacy: the "mocking laughter of future generations."[12]

Czesław Miłosz had an allergic reaction to the Romantic paradigm for almost the entire length of his long career. He perceived Polish culture as fixated on Poland's traumatic past and on the notion of sacrifice, without which it could not function. In his uncompromising rhetoric, he diagnosed the tendency towards conflation in Polish collective memory as generating "some kind of collective psychosis" by "keeping memory alive at any price and in such a way that even distant events seemed current, as if they happened just yesterday".[13] In Miłosz's view, this "psychosis" was intertwined with Polish culture's tendency towards unsurpassable collectivity. He emphasized the "abundance of (Polish) literature focusing on the suffering of the collective hero in WWII."[14] Not surprisingly, Poland's collective heroes were *national* ones; individual heroes rarely overlap with national meta-narratives.

In summary, the Romantic paradigm was debated, rejected, mocked, and ironized in gestures of cultural self-reflexivity. It stimulated counter-narratives, yet it remains the ever-present reference point for Polish national and cultural identity. Poland's first years of sovereignty – the early 1990s – were marked by renewed debates about the paradigm's supposed twilight, which was famously declared (and later renounced) by a renowned scholar of Polish Romanticism, Maria Janion.[15] In the context of the growing heterogeneity of Polish post-communist society, she had initially claimed that the "Romantico-symbolic" culture based on the Romantic ethos of values shared by the entire community (fatherland, independence, freedom, etc.) had been exhausted. Poland was entering normalcy, and the old narrative was to disappear. It was with regard to the mode of its disappearance that the post-1989 transformation of the culture was seen as either revolutionary or evolutionary.

Regardless of the criticisms levelled against it, the Romantic paradigm consistently proved its usefulness and confirmed its force as *the* meta-narrative in times of historical and social upheaval. Thus, for instance, both the Warsaw Uprising of 1944 and the Solidarity movement of 1980 were inserted into the tradition of patriotism (Walicki) understood in relation to nineteenth-century Romantic uprisings; and more recent events – such as the tragic crash of the presidential plane in April 2010 – were also inscribed onto the blueprints of this sacrificial, martyrological, and heroic narrative.[16] Such inscription often signals cultural inertia – instead of searching for new idioms to address its losses, Polish culture regardless of circumstances reaches towards the *spécialité de la maison*: the language of Romantic affect and compensation.

Conflation

This kind of inscription conflates difference into sameness. It collapses different historical and political events and their incomparable contexts into the repetition of the familiar same. It presupposes an obliteration of the boundaries between past and present, which in turn leads to a redemptive view of Polish history, in which we find a fixation on the general "Polish experience" instead of specific "events" (i.e., units of experience localizable in time). In this light, experience never belongs to the past because it is continually and compulsively re-enacted. Hence, loss cannot be recognized as loss because it conditions redemptive narratives, that is, narratives that retroactively assume that the traumatic experience serves some goal. The retroactive logic at work in such narratives posits that the traumatic has to happen for something good to emerge from it. In some sense, these redemptive narratives bind despair, preventing its uncontrollable spillover by configuring often unimaginable losses and traumas as teleological: as leading to a certain end – *telos* – and hence as meaningful. After the Smolensk crash of the presidential plane, for instance, the initial response of the media was to conflate this catastrophe with what had happened in Katyn during the Second World War. It was called, for instance, "the second Katyn," which symbolically shortened the gap between past and present and transformed the tragic accident into a traumatic repetition of the Polish fate. If nothing else, such reactions point to an automatic recourse to the familiar pattern of affective compensation. The proximity of the crash to the traumatically loaded site of Katyn and the goal of the trip – to celebrate the Katyn massacre's anniversary – together were potent enough to trigger Romantic rhetoric promoting the return of the past in another repetition of sameness.

In Polish culture, affect long ago established itself as a force for and carrier of the transgenerational transmission of "conflated memory." Resorting to conflated memory impeded the development of a sufficiently specific and diverse vocabulary (both cognitive and emotional) to address the range of historical events and subject positions. Polish public discourse is often characterized by resistance to acknowledging the "grey zones" within the range of subject positions occupied by members of Polish society, particularly in relation to events of the Second World War. The notion of sacrificial or heroic victimhood still reigns as the strongest collective narrative of the past, and attachment to it has hampered the binding of affect and its redirection towards definable emotions and discursive articulations. Hence, it inhibits the working-through of the past.

MOURNING AND MELANCHOLIA

The distinction between *mourning* and *melancholia* was established by Freud in his essay "Mourning and Melancholia" (1917). Both mourning and melancholia are triggered by real loss (whether this loss means the death of a loved one or the undoing of an ideal). According to the psychoanalyst, the difference between them relates to how this loss is absorbed ("worked through") by the ego. In mourning there is a clear relation between the lost object and the affect related to loss; mourning works towards resolution and closure, understood as the mourner's acceptance of the loss and his or her healthy functioning. Hence, mourning is future-oriented. Melancholia is a type of excessive and frustrated mourning, in which the loss is never accepted and its referential status becomes unclear. At a certain point, "one cannot see clearly what it is that has been lost" ("Mourning and Melancholia," 245). This leads to a fixation on the past, repetitions of the same symptoms, and a lack of desire to move forward ("acting out"). As Freud defines it, "the complex of melancholia behaves like an open wound" (253).

– Freud, "Mourning and Melancholia"

Historically, such a mechanism makes perfect sense. Polish culture was long unable to mourn its numerous losses properly (i.e., to mourn in the public sphere and through institutionalized practices). It responded to this serious limitation by substituting mourning with the acting out and reinforcement of its cultural repository of victimhood. Let me clarify here that when I refer to "mourning," I think of it as equivalent to "working through" loss (in Polish, *praca żałoby*), thus echoing the long-established Freudian binary of "mourning" and "melancholia." In the psychoanalytical vocabulary, these terms have equivalents in "working through" and "acting out," respectively, with these equivalents now broadly used by sociologists, historians, and cultural critics. While "working through" points to a reflective relation with the past often identified with narrative memory, "acting out" stresses the return of the symptom, a repeated manifestation of traumas not yet worked through, which in radical form can become a paralysing fixation, a traumatic memory, an inability to distinguish between what happened in the past and what is happening in the present.

Hence, affective compensation, in contrast to its legal variant, has a paradoxical function. Whereas legal compensation keeps a sense of injustice from spilling over by symbolically substituting what is lost with something belonging to a different order, affective compensation needs the traumatic to repeat and relies on the wound remaining open. The repetition of the traumatic becomes and allows for the collective's consistent narration about itself. Such consistency does not belong to the sphere of historical experience, which is rarely consistent and homogenous (beginning with the fact that every collective experiences an event from diverse subject positions). Such consistency is possible, however, in the sphere of meta-narratives, and the will for consistency has driven the transmission of the Romantic meta-narrative from its onset. The adaptability of the Romantic paradigm, its affective force, and what it produces in terms of compensation and consistency, helps us understand the persistence of the same mechanism for two centuries up until the present.

Sanitization of Memory during the Communist Period as Reinforcement of the Romantic Paradigm: Affective Compensation "from Above" and "from Below"

Cultural inertia is not the only reason for the conflation of diverse historical events into one "Polish experience." If one remedy for the conflation of and automatic recourse to the Romantic paradigm is historical awareness (i.e., the awareness of the multilayered nature of historical events), then note must be taken of the decades of repression and sanitization of collective memory under communism, which devastated this awareness across Polish society. The same affective force that facilitated mass participation in the Warsaw Uprising and in Solidarity also facilitated the communist government's creation of a selective Polish history. Conflation of historical events was one of the strategies that the new authorities in postwar Poland used to legitimize their position. The affect accumulated around transmission of Polish history as heroic and sacrificial was conveniently on hand to create a sense of continuity between different political orders and to conceal what had been ruptured at the level of the state. The censorship and erasure of historical particularities surrounding events that were politically unsuitable made it possible to fit them into a larger symbolic trajectory.

While the Warsaw Rising Museum serves as a prime example of the vitality of the Romantic paradigm, the sanitization of the memory of the historical event of the Warsaw Uprising represents how affective compensation was harnessed and manipulated to serve politically opposing forces. From the new communist regime's perspective, such sanitization was necessary since the uprising's political goals could not be openly admitted. While the military aim of the Polish underground resistance was to liberate the capital from the Nazi occupying forces, the political one was to do it before the Red Army reached the capital (Soviet forces were already approaching from the east and proclaiming communism in Poland's eastern territories). The anti-Soviet sentiment behind the Warsaw Uprising made it into a forbidden topic in the public sphere until the end of the Stalinist period, and made its participants into targets for persecution by the new regime.[17] The memory of the event shared by the population of the capital could not be easily suppressed, however, and the government, especially after the "thaw" of 1956, had to find ways of incorporating it into its official historical and ideological narrative. As a result, for most of the postwar period, the memory of the uprising was adapted in ways that blurred the event's political specificity and conflated it in official public memory with other wartime events. This involved, for instance, adjoining commemoration of the uprising to official commemorative practices shaped by the well-established sacrificial rhetoric of "the heroism of the Polish solider."[18] Hence, the official and institutional memory promoted integration and homogenization of the past according to the blueprints for the heroic and martyrological Romantic paradigm. The historical and political particularities were left opaque in order to undermine, when needed, the distinctions between specific historical agents and to facilitate the incorporation of inconvenient historical events into the official rhetoric.

With its anti-Soviet profile silenced, the uprising could be presented together with such ideologically unobjectionable events as the participation of Polish troops alongside the Red Army in the battle for Berlin. Both events fit under the heroic umbrella of the "struggle against Nazism". As an anti-Soviet event organized by the prewar Polish government, the uprising was always a subject of censorship; it was only a matter of whether that censorship was heavy or light, and this depended on the particular political circumstances in the Polish People's Republic. This censorship actually strengthened martyrological impulses: the more the authorities tried to restrict the memory of the uprising, the more elevated its status in collective memory became.

As a counterforce to the sanitization and appropriation of the uprising by the authorities, there arose a new type of censorship and erasure – "from below." In a Catholic culture, with its powerfully rooted imperative of proper mourning, the lack of official recognition and institutional commemoration of the fallen insurrectionists led to a powerful current of collective affect. For years, until the thaw of 1956, no official permission had been issued to allow survivors and the families of insurrectionists to celebrate the uprising's anniversary, so the affect only intensified. When celebrating was finally permitted, it was to coincide with historical events befitting the new regime. But even before 1956, the insurrectionists' graves, marked only with birch crosses, had become places of spontaneous annual commemoration for the people of Warsaw, which took place behind the regime's back. In the absence of any state-supported commemorations of the uprising, it became paramount to distinguish the insurrectionists' graves from those of other war victims; marking the graves with the names of insurrectionists and their military units thus became another stage of the battle for memory. Finally, the permission to group these graves in the same quarter of the Powązki cemetery in Warsaw created a collective of the dead, which silently pointed to the political division among the living.

This "necropolitics" of the uprising exemplify how an unacknowledged loss in the public sphere generated a need for symbolic compensation. The state's aggressive attempts to control the memory of the uprising led to a paradox: the simultaneous politicization and depoliticization of the event. Since the memory of the uprising was inextricably linked to the prewar republic and the Home Army, to commemorate the uprising meant the delegitimization of the postwar Soviet order along with its attempts to erase the uprising's memory and its mission. In this sense, the memory of the uprising was emphatically political. Yet at the same time, the restrictions placed on public mourning of the insurrectionists and the state's denunciation of the uprising's goals made any kind of political critique of the rationale behind the uprising seem like an act of disloyalty to the dead. The collective memory of the uprising thus became depoliticized: to counteract the censorship "from above," the censorship "from below" tried to guard the allegiance to the dead and their deed. To mourn the insurrectionists in the hostile environment of the new regime meant setting aside political questions and sober assessments regarding the uprising's political *raison d'être*.[19] This mourning and guarding manifested itself in the persistent heroicization of the uprising, an attitude that in itself, in another twist, created a powerful politics of the collective. The uprising thus became an iconic event of sacrificial patriotism and remains so to this day.[20]

This suppression from above and elevation from below of the memory of the event became a form of, to use Tomasz Łubieński's phrase, "double censorship."[21] The mechanism of double-censorship further limited the symbolic imaginarium of the uprising. Instead of being reduced and bound to facilitate the process of "working through," the affect of the event intensified and thus proliferated.[22] Once the uprising could be publicly acknowledged, however censored, its memorialization aimed at the production of affect. This affect, which accumulated around unprocessed – or selectively processed – collective traumatic memories, itself functioned as a compensatory mechanism. In other words, the affect manifested itself with elation and exaltation, which was the compensation itself.

Such elation and exaltation has features of a religious experience, especially since – as in the case of the memory of the uprising – the affect is related to the notion of sacrifice that is so central to the Catholic tradition and so deeply rooted in Polish culture. When experienced on the collective level, in the crowd during public celebrations of the uprising's anniversaries, for instance, affect intensifies the collective effervescence and bonding, which adds a religious dimension to the experience.

In the context of changing political conditions, the memory of the Warsaw Uprising acquired its own complex history. What is consistent throughout that history is the mechanism of regenerating the affect of traumatic intensity through constant reiteration of the event's sacrificial character. The mechanism of affective compensation, reinforced by officially sanitized memory, boosted the affect accumulated around unprocessed – or selectively processed – collective traumatic memories. Sanitized institutional memory promoted the integration and homogenization of the past by blurring the outlines of the particular experiences of particular groups, rather than differentiating them and emphasizing their specificity, which would facilitate the process of "working through." Compensation depended on the production of ever more affect; the past was to remain an open wound. Being loyal to this wound and ensuring that it did not heal became part of the Polish ethos.

In sum, the communists' sanitization of Polish history married Romantic rhetoric with the ideological goals of the new regime. It looked to homogenize the past so that the historical events that did not fit the historical propaganda could be, if not suppressed, at the very least obfuscated. Collective affect and Romantic rhetorical *topoi* were the readymade tools at the regime's disposal. As the history of the collective memory of the Warsaw Uprising indicates, the affect used by the regime generated the counter-affect of the collective. Ironically, in both cases the price of this affect was historical awareness and a critical approach to the past.

Return to the Museum

This reiteration and proliferation of affect is visible not just in the perspective of the generation that experienced the uprising first-hand and that witnessed the manipulation of its memory during the communist period; we see the same tendency in the recent institutionalization of the uprising's memory designed primarily for the postmemorial generations, such as the Warsaw Rising Museum described at the onset of this discussion. The museum has institutionalized the affect and ethos of the uprising for young generations of Poles.

With this production of affect, the museum refuses to locate the uprising in historical time or to contain it within temporal boundaries. From among the uprising's fatalities, the insurrectionists are privileged over civilian losses, which were ten times greater.[23] This hierarchy is necessary to sustain the economy of sacrifice – the heroism of the insurrectionists is redemptive, whereas the suffering of the civilians, if not purposeless, is at best only complementary to what really counts.[24] The museum does not delve into the historical context or the consequences of the uprising for Poland's postwar history. Within the museum's framework, the agonizing question for so many – Was it worth it? – dissipates from the start, answered in advance of being asked by the central motto over the exhibit pertaining to the Nazi occupation: "you had to live through it all to understand that Warsaw could not but fight" ("trzeba było to wszystko przeżyć, żeby zrozumieć, że

Warszawa nie mogła się nie bić"). The museum institutionalizes not so much the memory of the uprising as the affect of its memory, and its focus on affect may be problematic in its effect.

After all, affect can have its own politics, and in the affective transmission of the uprising's myth, history is taught and the formulation of future Polish identities is given direction. Again, focusing on affect creates an illusion of consistency in the reception of the painful past, which otherwise would need to be encountered critically, with an understanding that loyalty to the dead might not necessarily entail loyalty to the event itself. Affect shields the museum's visitors from having to confront the uprising's losses vis-à-vis its political complexities. It discourages a difficult reflection on history and invites visitors only to feel. This affect also compensates for the museum's deficiencies, making its short-sighted approach – encouraging visitors to suspend critical thinking for the pleasure of feeling – appear as a virtue. The patriotism the museum wants to inspire presupposes an acting out of the trauma of history, perhaps even a retraumatization, rather than a working through of the past.

The museum exhibits the Romantic paradigm and its compensatory value by showcasing an affective exchange. The insurrectionists' *bios* – life as such – is now available for cultural circulation: *non omnis moriar* (I shall not wholly die), *semper fideles* (always faithful), *dulce et decorum est pro patria mori* (it is sweet and noble to die for the fatherland), and, most Polish of all, *gloria victis* (glory to the defeated). The museum compensates for the insurrectionists' deaths by elevating a community of traumatic solidarity, a community of insurrectionists among themselves and the community of the dead with the living, that is, the visitors. In this community of traumatic solidarity, past and present are conflated in a field of affect that welcomes all who are willing to feel. To experience the museum the way it asks to be experienced – that is, affectively – means to leave one's critical thinking about history at its threshold. It means allowing questions about the historical consequences of the uprising to be silenced by the proliferation of affect. To be loyal to the uprising means to fall under the spell of its traumatic sublime. In contrast to legal compensation, which aims at binding affect and working through the traumatic, the compensatory mechanism of the museum is affect itself. The mechanism the subjugated Polish culture kept activating for the past two hundred years whenever Polish society needed a vocabulary for addressing its losses has become institutionalized in the museum as the way to read history.

PART TWO: CRITICAL CONSIDERATIONS

Empathy: Recognition and Assessment

In discussing the Romantic legacy, it is crucial to distinguish between the societal behaviours and cultural patterns transmitted through the Romantic paradigm and the reasons that generated it in the first place. While the transmitted paradigm now comes with an oversimplified compensatory mechanism, the need for it arose from Poland's traumatic history, and dismissing the existence of this need – or at the very least, the lasting power of its imprint – will not further our understanding of Poland's cultural dynamics. What interests me is precisely how the affect of Romantic simplification accommodates this need, how the Romantic paradigm perpetuates itself in the form of cultural inertia, and, ultimately, how to redirect the course that this paradigm has taken in Polish culture. It is important, however, to distinguish here between the language of analysis and the language of judgment, between the recognition of the need to fill the void left by real losses and the assessment of the cultural manifestations this need assumes. In other words, explorations of memory require empathy.

Dominick LaCapra proposes a compelling attitude of "empathic unsettlement" as a productive and ethical position for the critic to take.[25] Empathic unsettlement entails resisting harmonizing narratives and presupposes mediation between a critical attitude and a recognition of the real historic, cultural, and simply human needs behind fixations and compensations, even if this compensation is often problematic and self-indulgent. As a society still dealing with traumas, both past and recent, that have yet to be worked through, the Polish collective needs to find ways to recognize its past beyond the affective, the compensatory, and the redemptive. The strategy of producing primarily affective memory about certain historical events can create an unproductive public culture in thrall to the endlessly frustrated mourning of losses. Yet it is not productive simply to dismiss these affective strategies as inadequate. Postmemorial generations require affect in order to connect to the past, but it must also be possible for them to be led by this affect to critical thinking about historical traumas and dilemmas. The balance between the two is critical for a nation's negotiation of its place in the constellation of other collective memories in global memory culture.

Globalization, Affective Compensation, and the Enlightenment Rhetoric after 1989

Globalization creates new points of reference for collective memories, shifting the point of gravity from the nation-state to "the world" – the global community. Deterritorialized, the collective memories of various groups circulate simultaneously in shared cultural spaces – whether physical or cyber – competing for attention from different audiences. In a globalizing culture, rarely does a given collective have full control over its own narrative. Rather, the global tendency in memory culture is to commemorate transnationally and cross-culturally (e.g., D-Day in France, the Victory Day parade in Moscow, the outbreak of the war at Westerplatte). Physical sites become shared by multiple communities and inscribed with multiple meanings (as with, for instance, Holocaust memory tourism).

In other words, places, events, and experiences in a globalizing world become nexuses of multi-cultural meanings in which memories of different collectives – national, ethnic, cultural, religious, or otherwise – are intertwined, entangled, and hybridized yet often still compete for the privileged place of the "main narrative" for global audiences. Global culture "should be thought of as both the processes by which individuals become interconnected and the ways these global interconnections are understood."[26] Globalization makes memories circulate quickly and multi-directionally among different collectives, and this transcultural circulation affects the ways in which local collectives shape their politics of memory in relation to their place on the memorial map of the world – often, with foreign cameras rolling.[27]

Poland's historical predicament makes it an interesting case study for the process of memory's globalization. After all, Poland presents the complex case of a country whose relatively recently regained sovereignty and consequent attempts to reinvent a national tradition have been affected simultaneously by the internationalization and globalization of memory culture. Thus, the post-1989 period has been characterized by two pulls. Poles' collective memory has been undergoing extensive historical reconstruction, fuelled by access to archives and exhilarated by the absence of censorship. Decentralization, democratization, regionalization, and the privatization of memory have been revolutionizing the system for producing and disseminating collective narratives. Simultaneously, these domestic developments have been overlapping with the accelerated inscription of Polish memory onto global collective memories, especially since Poland joined the European Union in 2004, which has required it to respond to the EU's supra-national memorial agenda.[28] To a great extent we can talk about post-1989 memorial transformations in Poland as particularly intense because the internal paradigmatic changes coincided with rapid cultural internationalization and globalization, visible in such phenomena as world celebrations of various anniversaries meant to universalize approaches to memory (e.g., D-Day in France, the Victory Day parade in Moscow, and the outbreak of the Second War War at Westerplatte).[29]

The universalization of approaches to memory is also evident in the numerous international media events organized around the culture of public apology and reconciliation.[30] However, none of these apologies have had the impact of the German chancellor Willy Brandt's famous kneeling at the monument to the Ghetto Heroes in 1970. That they are now expected, and then performed with a familiar rhetoric, is sometimes perceived as an empty gesture and as reconciliation kitsch.[31] Yet cultural and moral legitimacy in global media requires that nation-states play by the rules of global rhetoric; globalization has produced a sense of being "seen" and always potentially judged by others. The results of such sensitivity to exposure may vary, but global visibility always transforms the "local" into something else.

In sum, simultaneously gifted and burdened with its new status and international visibility, Poland has had to reinvent its own sovereign post-communist identity and formulate the rhetoric, politics, and ethics of its self-narrative with global positioning in mind. Participating in the global media distribution of memory has meant learning to export national tradition to the international scene; this has affected the way Poland now perceives its place on the memorial map of Europe, and this in turn has shaped its culture of, and debate about, memory.[32] It has also meant "working through" Poland's unacknowledged, repressed, and sanitized past under the world's watchful eye. Of the four mentioned main patterns of transformation of memory in post-1989 Poland, it is deheroicization,[33] which questions the dominant paradigm of Polish collective victimhood, that most reflects globalizing and internationalizing tendencies.

THE JEDWABNE DEBATE

The most intense debate about the deheroicization of the post-communist period in Poland was triggered by the publication of Jan Gross's *Sąsiedzi* (Neighbors, 2000), an account of a pogrom of Jews by their Polish neighbours in the village of Jedwabne in 1941. During the communist period, Polish–Jewish relations were an area in which conflation as a strategy of homogenization was particularly striking. The Holocaust was commemorated and taught to young generations of Poles not as ethnically specific but rather as part of the story of "universal" Polish victimhood. Historians were raising the question of pogroms as early as the 1970s, and relations between Poles and Jews during the Second World War were a topic of influential debate among intellectuals in 1987, when Jan Błoński published his article "Poor Poles look at the Ghetto," but only after 1989 did the topic reach a broad national forum. The exposure of the Jedwabne pogrom was a great shock for Polish society, and the debate that followed was of unprecedented proportions, intensified by media and international attention. It opened up many questions about the nature of Polish–Jewish relations and their history and about Poland's meta-narratives. Issues previously considered taboo were raised, such as the presence of anti-Semitism in Polish society and the accusation against Polish Jews that they harboured pro-Soviet sympathies. The Jedwabne debate undoubtedly represented the most striking and painful clash between the heroic Romantic paradigm and the revisionary mode. For a range of perspectives on the debate, see Antony Polonsky and Joanna Michlic's *The Neighbors Respond: The Controversy over the Jedwabne Massacre in Poland* (2003).

The revisionary debates at the turn of the millennium on wartime transgressions and grey zones in Polish history showed Poles to be entangled in historically complex power relationships, sometimes in the position of perpetrators or inhabiting the so-called grey zone.[34] The most notable of these debates, about the pogrom of Jews by Poles in the village of Jedwabne in 1941, took place in the harsh glare of international attention (it could hardly have been otherwise). The fact that these debates were exported to the world before they could be processed by the local culture through local means triggered in some sectors of Polish society a sense of shame that less-than-heroic aspects of Polish history had been exposed internationally. According to some historians, it was this sense of exposure and shame that led to a political backlash characterized by "affirmative memory" (as Traba calls it)[35] – that is, to a reheroicization of the Polish past as consistently propagated by Poland's conservative party.

One reason for such backlash was referred to as "Enlightenment rhetoric" by Bartosz Korzeniewski in his analysis of the then President Kwaśniewski's public apology at Jedwabne in 2001. In that speech, Kwaśniewski created a binary between those who were enlightened and who understood the need to ask for forgiveness and those who clung in a reactionary way to the national mode of innocent victimhood; between those who owned the deed and the shame and those who did not; between those who were courageous enough to recognize the past ("spójrzmy prawdzie w oczy") and those who cleaved to the heroic martyrology out of cowardice. Kwaśniewski's words were well intentioned, and they met the expectations of international observers (as well as a large portion of Polish society), but according to Korzeniewski, they were not as productive domestically as they could have been. Although in official post-1989 rhetoric the revisionary view of Polish history has been configured as a condition for Poland to move towards a brighter European future, this kind of Enlightenment idiom did not address the problem of the collective need for a meta-narrative, or its need for an expanded symbolic vocabulary that would allow Poles to assume a variety of subject positions without fear of locating themselves outside of national history (which so far is still deeply embedded in the Romantic paradigm). Such an expanded vocabulary is particularly crucial when it comes to better understanding the relationship between trauma, victimhood, and innocence. After all, how the traumatic is positioned in the collective imagination directly pertains to the markers of national identity.

Fantasy

In general, public discourse and the media lack the language needed to redirect the affect accumulated around the fantasy of Polish experience and identity. The notion of fantasy is invaluable for the discussion of Polish collective memory, for both trauma and fantasy generate compensation and affect. I share Renata Salecl's understanding of fantasy, which she describes in *Spoils of Freedom* (15) as "the way people structure their desire around some traumatic element that cannot be symbolized. Fantasy gives consistency to what we call 'reality.'"

If fantasy gives consistency to what we call "reality," then fantasy always has a compensatory function. Fantasy compensates for that which history delivers as erratic, conflicting, and resistant to consistent narration. It is a scenario that cultures bring into play to conceal the ultimate inconsistency of historical experience. If the Romantic paradigm simplified cultural interpretation of the traumatic historical experience, it did so because it operated according to the compensatory rules of fantasy. It offered a steady narration for what otherwise would have been a chaotically traumatic history. Indeed, we could say that the Romantic paradigm has served as the principle fantasy of Polish culture.

Every culture strives for consistency in its meta-narratives and compensates for its lack with fantasy. Yet to say that every collective compensates does not mean that every collective compensates in the same way. There is a difference between compensation in cultures that are sovereign and compensation in cultures that are – or have been – subjugated and that have limited tools at their disposal to symbolize traumatic events in the public sphere. In the Polish case, the amazing career of the Romantic paradigm can be attributed to an insufficient "working through" in the public sphere. The problem of the contemporary Polish culture is that in spite of its new political circumstances and the country's sovereignty, no new fantasy has evolved to adequately reflect Poland's present circumstances and aspirations; the Romantic paradigm, anachronistic on the one hand, and susceptible to political manipulation on the other, thus survives.

Fantasy, to be effective and to provide the symbolic consistency craved by the collective, needs to carry affect. Only by carrying affect can fantasy be productive in a Foucauldian sense – simultaneously generating and limiting a sense of collective identity. In this sense, Poland's Romantic fantasy has been highly productive. No equivalent or modification of that fantasy – that is, no modification that would respond to the symbolic demands of today's Poland – has yet emerged. The old paradigm still holds a good deal of cultural and political capital and is still contributing to the already intense polarization in Polish society. Between the performative lament over the loss of Polish identity and the disappearance of traditional virtues such as patriotism on the one hand (e.g., forgetting about the motto *God, Honour, Fatherland*), and – on the other – the celebration of Poland's post-1989 "return to Europe" (which has put the Romantic paradigm's contemporary efficacy into question), no adequate symbolic vocabulary of self-identification has been developed thus far to accommodate Poland's past and its current geopolitical position and to embrace its future possibilities.[36]

Affective Enclaves

Whether meta-narratives are needed or even possible in globalizing democracies is a broader question. Dispensing with them is certainly not easy, especially in a culture like Poland's, which has developed a tradition of identifying itself through traumatic loss and its symbolic compensation and has consequently depended on the experience of collective affect. Serguei Oushakine, an anthropologist writing on post-Soviet Russia who has studied how the fall of communism affected the way communities deal with traumas – especially traumas that remain institutionally unacknowledged – emphasizes in his book *The Patriotism of Despair* the need for "affective enclaves." Such enclaves are spaces in which often spontaneously formed communities (for instance, communities of mothers whose sons were killed while serving in the Soviet army) create alternative forms of social kinship that are based on a commonality of loss and then use these forms of kinship to communicate with the outside world. For "communities of loss that found themselves in a radically changing environment without any accommodating tools or navigating charts," these forms of social kinship become a strategy for surviving symbolic disorientation.[37]

Although it would be hard to compare the situation in Poland with the cultural disorientation in remote areas of the former Soviet Union, a considerable portion of Polish society tends to seek symbolic language of the affective enclave and to crave the fantasy of consistency. The need to generate this kind of language can be found, for instance, in the long-term responses to the Smolensk catastrophe of 2010.[38] The initial response to the catastrophe bonded society through rituals of collective mourning deeply rooted in Polish culture. Soon after, however, the catastrophe became a source of societal and political polarization. At stake was not only the truth of the event (whether the crash was an accident or a crime orchestrated by Russia to eliminate Polish elites, mirroring the Katyn massacre) but also the meta-narrative of Polish history.

Depending on how the event was interpreted, Polish history acquired radically different trajectories. If Poland had again been violated by its old oppressor, then Polish history remained in the realm of endless repetition of the same pattern of martyrology and innocent victimhood. Such a pattern fulfilled Poles' yearning to sacralize their history; the alternative, after all, was to view that history as a profane playground of contingencies, chances, and tragic randomness (which it would have been if the crash were the result of human error). The resistance that a considerable portion of the society has shown towards the official results of the investigation (which concluded that the crash was indeed an accident) manifests a resistance to abandoning the Romantic grand narrative and to entering the profane by seeking an explanation on the human level only. According to the Romantic grand narrative, trusting the profane would mean "the end of history."[39]

The Smolensk catastrophe divided Polish society into "conservatives" supporting conspiracy theories, in which Russia had undertaken another attack on Polish elites, and "progressives/liberals," who viewed that same event through the lens of Enlightenment rhetoric. The tools of polarization ranged from public debates about where to bury the presidential couple and what monument should commemorate them, to Poland's position in Europe and its relations with Russia.[40] The crash activated all dormant postcolonial anxieties – if they were ever dormant – as well as Polish society's ambivalent relationship with its own international aspirations. If Russia had conspired against Poland and if "the West" had allowed this conspiracy to remain buried, then Poland's most fundamental issues – including its position in the EU, perceived by some as threatening Polish national values with cultural colonization – needed to be re-examined. The traumatic offers a road back to the familiar affect of martyrology, creating an illusion of affective enclave.

The need to view the Smolensk catastrophe as the repetition of the martyrological "Polish fate" may be symptomatic of Poles' need for a fantasy capable of unifying their society. Such a fantasy – in Salecl's sense – is fundamentally a need for the sacred to validate the profane. It can also be an expression of real yearning for a sense of affective belonging to the collective by those who – after decades of functioning in the socialist state – now feel alienated by the post-1989 political, economic, and cultural transformations.

Only the Traumatic Unites

In light of these divisions and anxieties, the Smolensk crash and the Warsaw Uprising seem to occupy a similar place in the collective memory. The crash is a relatively recent event; the uprising is growing more popular over time. At least since 2004 – when on its sixtieth anniversary the uprising was first celebrated on a truly international scale – and possibly earlier, the event has been elevated from a local (Warsaw) to the national level.[41] The uprising has never been *just* a local event,[42] but institutional efforts over the past dozen years or so indicate that the memory of the uprising is intended to help establish an all-national "affective" Polish identity.[43]

Poles today seem eager to unite over the uprising (or, to be precise, around the affect of its memory) rather than over the memory of events that probably should or at least potentially could – but did not – become foundational myths of an independent Poland, such as the events of 1980 and 1989.[44] Arguably, we could say that the affect of 1989 has not yet crystalized, whereas the affect of the uprising has clearly been established, both institutionally and collectively. The uprising is a closed event; 1989, by contrast, still signifies the symbolic beginning of an open-ended process, not only because this fateful year saw a series of revolutionary transformations, but also because their repercussions – both good and bad – continue to reverberate.

It is easier to unite around the Warsaw Uprising because its affective fantasy, centred on heroism and sacrifice, allows for consistency in national self-narration. The year 1989 cannot offer such a fantasy, if only because it created a set of complicated identities and because those identities bear directly on the current, highly polarized political situation. It is possible that celebration of the uprising has become a form of affective enclave, collective therapy, communal ritual, and bonding over elated mourning. Perhaps the memory of the uprising has become a home in which Poles desire to rest their tired and perturbed Polish identities. Of course, any historical assessment of the uprising is difficult and multifaceted, but how the event functions in the space of collective memory and consciousness has little to do with its historical realities. The great career of the Warsaw Rising Museum has gone hand in hand with the growing popularity of the uprising in popular culture.[45] Both the institutional memory of the event and its popular representations rely on affect. The uprising in its multiple embodiments remains a vehicle for affective national identification, a fantasy of consistent national identity.

When Warsaw residents gather together on the uprising's anniversary (with the rest of Poland in front of the television) to sing the "forbidden songs" of wartime, they bond in a fantasy of the nation that embraces the dead and the living in a powerful albeit momentary *communitas*. In the participatory collective re-enactment of loyalty to the dead – specifically the dead who fit the sacrificial economy – the community bonds over something that it conjures through its communal affect but that it cannot quite symbolize. As Salecl tells us, "in the fantasy structure of the homeland, the nation (in the sense of national identification) is the element that cannot be symbolized. The nation is an element in us that is more than ourselves, something that defines us, but at the same time is undefinable; we cannot specify what it means nor can we erase it. We may even say that the nation is linked to the place of the Real in the symbolic network."[46]

Polish collective memory fixates on the past. Yet to state this baldly is not so much inaccurate as reductive and at times unproductive. It suggests that the collective remains immobilized in its fixation, obsessively returning to the one and the same, and that there is little to be learned from these returns. But fixations do not have rigid boundaries; affective returns to the traumatic (or, in psychoanalytic terms, "acting out"), and reflective efforts to move forward (or, in psychoanalytic terms, "work through") are intertwined, and rarely does one or the other manifest itself in a pure form.

To recognize and acknowledge their complex dynamics and to see how these transform over time under changing social, political, and cultural circumstances, we must understand what makes any given community "tick." Without such recognition we alienate ourselves from a real understanding of the collective imagination and miss a chance for our voices to mediate creatively between the past, the present, and the future. This is what often happens in Polish public and political discourse: the participants trap themselves in long-entrenched positions of affective self-indulgence in Poland's traumas, or in discursive self-separation from these positions, which is often expressed in the rhetoric of the Enlightenment.

There is much to be recuperated by scholarship and works of criticism from collective memories sanitized and repressed under communism, and much has to be done politically to unhook the Polish psyche from its Romantic self-entrenchment. That said, a lot has already been done in the realm of fiction and imagination. Art and literature can help us to imagine different trajectories for our collective memories and to rethink various possibilities and subjectivities embedded in each historical event. Many artists and writers do just that. The post-1989 period yielded an onslaught of works – literary and others, such as performance and visual works – that returned to traumatic experiences, particularly wartime experiences, through the use of the imaginary and the fantastic. This time, by "fantastic" I mean the kind of representation that, according to Todorov, destabilizes the reader's understanding of what really happened.[47] Why was the last quarter of the twentieth century characterized by what I call "traumatic fantasies" created by writers and artists belonging to the postmemorial generation? Clearly, some new cultural symptoms, desires, and needs are now manifesting themselves in today's Polish prose, which is full of ghosts that cannot abandon their earthly domains, fetuses that narrate *in utero*, and Jewish children with supernatural abilities. These fantasies (very different from the understanding of fantasy that Salecl offers) invite us to conduct empathic criticism; they help us envision new patterns of thinking about our own history and identity. These patterns are anti-realist, but that is precisely why they allow one to conceive of a connection between the past and the present that does not need to assert the continuity between them and that does not require one to identify with wartime trauma in order to secure an identity in the present. They show us that there is more to the recuperation of history than historical accuracy or discursive criticism and that there is more to loyalty to the dead than succumbing to the siren call of traumatic affect. Perhaps Polish culture, often self-limiting in its reliance on affective compensation, has already begun to learn – in the Aristotelian spirit of the pedagogical supremacy of fiction over historical particularities – that what it needs is the work of imagination. If we reimagine our relationship to the past, we may be able to reimagine – and construct – a sustainable future for our cultural identities.

Joanna Niżyńska
Indiana University, Bloomington

NOTES

1 Korzeniewski, *Transformacja pamięci*, 118, 160.
2 Ibid., 113.
3 Theories of affect have been an important part of various theoretical and cultural debates, and although "affect theory" has been emerging only since the mid-1990s (as a sign of exhaustion with the "linguistic turn"), affect in its philosophical, physiological, psychological, cultural, and political manifestations has always been part of cultural theories and discourses (to recall only the Aristotelian notion of "phylia" – social bond).
4 Spinoza, "Of the Origin and Nature of the Affects," 154.
5 The shipyard strike was not the beginning of the dissident movement but rather a culminating moment that brought to fruition the dissident work of the 1970s and particularly the type of work that united Polish workers and intelligentsia. It is sufficient to mention the activities of the Komitet Obrony Robotników (Workers' Defence Committee – KOR) formed in 1976 to legally defend workers and alleviate the hardships of their daily lives (following the government repressions after the workers' unrest in 1976).
6 At the same time, the heightened affect characterizing *communitas* also neutralized a sense of historical and social specificity of the moment and the place as well as the political heterogeneity of the participants. This kind of community is by definition temporary, and the sense of affective bonds cannot be sustained when the collective evolves into a social system. Hence, there were plenty of moments in the history of the dissident movement that pointed to a sense of *communitas*, whereas the period of 1989, instead of celebrating regained independence, was marked by political discord. Political heterogeneity, which was in a sense overlooked during the period of oppression, became pronounced once there were no conditions to generate a sense of *communitas*. Consequently, the post-1989 period in Poland has been characterized by nostalgia for the periods of social unrest and "real solidarity."
7 Another term, used less often, is *paradygmat romantyczno-symboliczny* (the Romantico-symbolic paradigm).
8 For a detailed discussion of this tension, see Dariusz Skórczewski's "Romanticism" (in this volume).
9 "Romantyzm bez tekstu," as German Ritz aptly called it (private conversation).
10 Słowacki, "The Funeral of Captain Meyzner."
11 Miłosz, "Prywatne obowiązki wobec literatury polskiej," 117.
12 Tadeusz Borowski, "Pieśń." The poem ends with the lines "zostanie po nas złom żelazny / i głuchy, drwiący śmiech pokoleń", which in English translate to: "We'll leave behind us scrap metal / And the dull mocking laughter of generations."
13 Miłosz, "Prywatne obowiązki wobec literatury polskiej," 115. In the Polish: "Podtrzymywanie pamięci za wszelką cenę, tak żeby odległe wypadki były ciągle żywe, jakby zdarzyły się wczoraj, może łatwo prowadzić do czegoś w rodzaju zbiorowej psychozy."

14 Ibid., 115. In the Polish: "zalew literatury na temat 'cierpień bohatera kolektywnego' w czasie WWII."
15 Janion, "Zmierzch paradygmatu," 12.
16 I write about this inscription in "The Politics of Mourning," 467–79. See also Dariusz Kosiński, *Teatra polskie*.
17 The persecutions of the insurrectionists included false accusations, imprisonment, show trials, and frequent executions. See Davies, *Rising '44*, 507–617.
18 For instance, commemorations of the uprising were encouraged on dates that overlapped with Communist holidays such as the establishment of Communist authority in Poland on 22 July. The issue of the place of burial of the insurrectionists was also important. In the wake of mass exhumations during the rebuilding of Warsaw, the authorities initially prohibited the reburials of the insurrectionists in the same quarter to prevent giving the graves a distinct identification with the Home Army. See Davies, *Rising '44*.
19 In this type of heroic memorialization, the Home Army – a complex organization with multiple political factions and leaders with different visions for independent Poland – was treated as monolithic and homogenous. To a large extent, this view still persists.
20 Sixty years after the uprising, 45 per cent of Poles still saw it as a crucial event in Polish history; 30 per cent claimed that their lives had been affected by it. See *Główny Urząd Statystyczny*, 2004; https://stat.gov.pl/obszary-tematyczne/roczniki-statystyczne/.
21 Łubieński, *Ani tryumf ani zgon*, 50.
22 This is particularly visible in numerous literary representations of the uprising. A few works written before the end of communism contradict the heroic imaginarium – for example, Anna Świrszczyńska's *Budowałam barykadę* (Building the Barricade, 1974), Miron Białoszewski's *Pamiętnik z powstania warszawskiego* (A Memoir of the Warsaw Uprising, 1970), and Aleksander Ścibor-Rylski's *Pierścionek z końskiego włosia* (The Horsehair Ring, 1991). All three authors were survivors of the uprising.
23 Ironically, whether the censorship came from above or below, it bracketed off civilian experience. Generations of Warsaw residents were raised on stories about those who survived the uprising, but the institutionalized memory stayed within the boundaries drawn on Romantic – and martyrological – blueprints. Oral testimonies, family stories, and civilian witnessing have been the stuff of the uprising's cultural memory, but they did not enter the culture of commemoration or commemorative practices the way the heroic version of the uprising did.
24 Although civilians are treated marginally in the museum's main exhibition, the institution began new and commendable initiatives regarding the civilian population. It is important to mention the efforts to collect the names and other details about the Warsaw inhabitants who died in the uprising, as well as the march commemorating the civilians who died (Marsz Pamięci Ofiar Cywilnych, 2015) and the two open-air exhibitions "Zachowajmy ich w pamięci" (Let's Preserve Their Memory) about the civilians in the uprising (2015, 2016). See http://www.1944.pl/artykul/marsz-pamieci-i-otwarcie-wystawy-zachowajmy-ic,4331.html.
25 LaCapra, *Writing History, Writing Trauma*, 78.
26 Kendall R. Phillips and G. Mitchell Reyes, "Surveying Global Memoryscapes: The Shifting Terrain of Public Memory Studies," 7.
27 See Rothberg, *Multidirectional Memory*.
28 The European Union's reconciliatory approach to memory has had a great impact on memory culture in Poland. The EU cannot afford to contest memories among its members, and it is committed to the reconciliatory model of a pan-European history. It has direct influence on the

German–Polish memorial relationship, but it has also shifted the way Polish culture relates to the role of Russia during the Second World War.

29 Emphasized by Korzeniewski, *Transformacja pamięci*, 57–8.

30 An example is the meeting of Polish president Aleksander Kwaśniewski and Ukrainian president Viktor Yushchenko at the Eaglets Cemetery in Lviv in 2005, configured as a Polish–Ukrainian reconciliation. In 1995, on the fiftieth anniversary of the end of the Second World War, foreign minister Władysław Bartoszewski (1922–2015) apologized to German expellees for Polish transgressions during the period of expulsions, and Poles in turn received public apologies from German chancellor Angela Merkel at the Westerplatte during a ceremony celebrating the seventieth anniversary of the outbreak of the war.

31 The term "reconciliation kitsch" was coined by Klaus Bachmann. See *Die Tageszeitung*, 6 April 1994.

32 The creation of institutions such as the European Network Remembrance and Solidarity (ENRS) during Poland's presidency of the EU Council in 2011 is an example of Poland's commitment to shaping the discussion on memory and history in Europe.

33 Korzeniewski, who proposes the four patterns, uses the popular Polish expression "odbrązowianie" for deheroicization. *Transformacja pamięci*, 108.

34 These deheroicizing revisionist accounts often exposed the mechanism of compensation as conveniently selective; oppressed Poles felt entitled to a superior position by virtue of their collective suffering, yet they denied the same to those whom they had oppressed, colonized, and victimized.

35 Robert Traba, "Procesy zbiorowego pamiętania i zapominania," 386.

36 The resurgence of Sarmatism in 1970s Communist Poland might have reflected nostalgia for the pre-Romantic paradigm. Poland's self-sculpting during the hosting of the European soccer championship in 2012 as "Polska jest fajna" (Poland is fun!) – symptomatic of a limited vocabulary of self-identification – was a point of political contention as well.

37 Oushakine, *The Patriotism of Despair*, 129.

38 On 10 April 2010, a plane carrying Polish President Lech Kaczyński and his wife, the country's top officials, as well as representatives of civic organizations crashed near Smolensk, Russia. There were no survivors. The delegation was on its way to commemorate the anniversary of the Katyn massacre of 1940. Although the official investigation of the catastrophe concluded that it had been caused by pilot error and poor weather, the crash led to a surge of conspiracy theories involving Russia – theories that symbolically paralleled the decapitation of the Polish intelligentsia in the Katyn massacre. The *katastrofa smoleńska* (Smolensk catastrophe), as it became known, was the most polarizing event in Poland's post-1989 history.

39 Kosiński expresses a similar view in *Teatra polskie*.

40 In a symbolic gesture that raised death above political efficacy, the president and his wife were bestowed the highest honours of burial in the Wawel Royal Castle, the place of burial for Polish kings and the greatest historical figures. The funeral ceremonies were perhaps the most spectacular displays of state grandeur in post-1989 Poland.

41 The museum opened in 2004 on the sixtieth anniversary of the uprising, but in a ceremony meant to reinforce the internationalization of the uprising's memory. Led by the then mayor of Warsaw, Lech Kaczyński, and attended by the country's most prominent political and cultural figures, the event was held just three months after Poland joined the EU. The former German chancellor Gerhard Schröder attended, as did Colin Powell, the US Secretary of State at the time, as well as John Prescott, then deputy prime minister of Great Britain. These events were

designed both to reassure Poles who feared that joining the EU would weaken their national identity and to emphasize Poland's standing in the international community.

42 At the same time, however important the uprising was for the entire country, it also remains local in quite specific ways, reflecting how memory circulates in popular culture. For instance, the rivalry between the two main Warsaw soccer clubs, Legia Warszawa and Polonia Warszawa, manifests itself, among other ways, in how the clubs express their loyalty to the city by tapping into the memory of the uprising. The uprising often resurfaces in the identity narration of the clubs' fans; the clubs mark their presence on the anniversary of the uprising with candles and flowers in their respective colors and with demarcating placards. Moreover, the Polonia stadium is famously decorated with murals representing scenes from the uprising.

43 One such vehicle has been the increasingly popular sing-along concerts on Piłsudski Square, where, on the anniversary of the outbreak of the uprising, thousands of Warsaw residents gather. These concerts are broadcast on public television. Even if only a fraction of the Polish population can fully participate in the event, the entire country has claimed full ownership of it in an unprecedented manner. Participation in singing the uprising songs, if only while watching a broadcast of the concert, unites the collective under the totem of heroism and sacrifice.

44 Andrea Bohlam in her analysis of commemorations of the twenty-fifth anniversary of 1989 compares these "failed" celebrations to the highly successful annual celebrations of the uprising. She focuses on the role of music in each celebration and on its performative and participatory quality (with the later, especially with regard to the Warsaw uprising celebration). The differences between these two celebrations indicate society's unease with its collective identity in relation to the country's recent past. Unpublished manuscript.

45 The uprising has become a crowd-pleasing theme for numerous works in popular culture. It is explored in all genres, for example, in such diverse works as the film *Miasto 44* (City 44, dir. Paweł Komasa, 2014); the music album *Powstanie warszawskie* (The Warsaw Uprising, 2005) by the crossover band Lao Che; the popular comics for children *Tytus, Romek i A'Tomek jako warszawscy powstańcy* (Tytus, Romek, and A'Tomek as the Insurrectionists) by Henryk Jerzy Chmielewski (2009); and the still unrealized animated film *Hardkor 44* by Tomasz Bagiński. Interestingly, the subject of the uprising has become popular with several foreign bands, for example, the metal rock band Sabaton (Swedish), the Heaven Shall Burn (German), and the Hail of Bullets (Dutch).

46 Salecl, *Spoils of Freedom*, 15.

47 Tzvetan Todorov defined fantastic representation as the kind of representation that does not allow the reader to decide whether what happens in the narration is real or not. "The fantastic occupies the duration of this uncertainty … The fantastic is that hesitation experienced by a person who knows only the laws of nature, confronting an apparently supernatural event." Todorov, *The Fantastic*, 25.

WORKS CITED

Borowski, Tadeusz. "Pieśń." In *Wspomnienia, wiersze, opowiadania*. 29–30. Warszawa: Państwowy Instytut Wydawniczy, 1974.

Błoński, Jan. "Biedni Polacy patrzą na ghetto." *Tygodnik Powszechny* 2 (1987): 1, 4.

Davies, Norman. *Rising '44: The Battle for Warsaw*. New York: Viking Books, 2004.

Freud, Sigmund. "Mourning and Melancholia." In *The Standard Edition of the Complete Psychological Works of Sigmund Freud,* vol. 14. Translated by James Strachey. London: Hogarth, 1953–74.

Gross, Jan T. *Neighbors: The Destruction of the Jewish Community in Jedwabne, Poland.* Princeton: Princeton University Press, 2001.

Hirsch, Marianne. "The Generation of Postmemory." *Poetics Today* 29, no. 1 (2008): 103–28.

Janion, Maria. "Zmierzch paradygmatu." In *Czy będziesz wiedział co przeżyłeś?* 5–23. Warszawa: Wydawnictwo SIC!, 1996.

Korzeniewski, Bartosz. *Transformacja pamięci. Przewartościowanie pamięci przeszłości a wybrane aspekty funkcjonowania dyskursu publicznego o przeszłości w Polsce po 1989 roku.* Poznań: Wydawnictwo Poznańskiego Towarzystwa Przyjaciół Nauk, 2010.

Kosiński, Dariusz. *Teatra polskie, Rok katastrofy.* Kraków: Społeczny Instytut Wydawniczy Znak, 2013.

LaCapra, Dominick. *Writing History, Writing Trauma.* Baltimore: Johns Hopkins University Press, 2000.

Łubieński, Tomasz. *Ani tryumf ani zgon. Szkice o powstaniu warszawskim.* Warszawa: Wydawnictwo Nowy Świat, 2004.

Mark, James. *The Unfinished Revolution: Making Sense of the Communist Past in Central-Eastern Europe.* New Haven: Yale University Press, 2010.

Miłosz, Czesław. "Prywatne obowiązki wobec literatury polskiej." In *Prywatne obowiązki.* 95–135. Kraków: Wydawnictwo Literackie, 2001.

Niżyńska, Joanna. "The Politics of Mourning and the Crisis of Poland's Symbolic Language after April 10, 2010." *East European Politics and Societies*, 24, no. 4 (2010): 467–79.

Oushakine, Serguei Alex. *The Patriotism of Despair: Nation, War, and Loss in Russia.* Ithaca: Cornell University Press, 2009.

Phillips, Kendall R., and G Mitchell Reyes. "Surveying Global Memoryscapes: The Shifting Terrain of Public Memory Studies." In *Global Memoryscapes: Contesting Remembrance in a Transnational Age.* 1–26. Tuscaloosa: University of Alabama Press, 2011.

Polonsky, Antony, and Joanna Michlic. *The Neighbors Respond: The Controversy over the Jedwabne Massacre in Poland.* Princeton: Princeton University Press, 2004.

Rothberg, Michael. *Multidirectional Memory: Remembering the Holocaust in the Age of Decolonization.* Stanford: Stanford University Press, 2009.

Salecl, Renata, *The Spoils of Freedom: Psychoanalysis and Feminism after the Fall of Socialism.* New York: Routledge, 1994.

Słowacki, Juliusz. "The Funeral of Captain Meyzner." Translated by Walter Whipple. http://www.mission.net/poland/warsaw/literature/poems/meyzner.htm.

Spinoza, Benedict de. "Of the Origin and Nature of the Affects." In *A Spinoza Reader: The* Ethics *and Other Works.* Translated by Edwin Curley. 152–96. Princeton: Princeton University Press, 1994.

Todorov, Tzvetan. *The Fantastic: A Structural Approach to a Literary Genre.* Translated by Richard Howard. Ithaca: Cornell University Press, 1975.

Traba, Robert. "Procesy zbiorowego pamiętania i zapominania." In *Pamięć i afekty.* 367–94. Warszawa: Wydawnictwo Instytut Badań Literackich, 2014.

PART III

Transmissions

IMMIGRANT/ÉMIGRÉ, MIGRANT, AND TRANSNATIONAL LITERATURE AND CULTURE

Emigration and Its Cultural Legacy in Twentieth-Century Polish Intellectual History

Refugees and Deportees: 1939–45

Soon after Nazi Germany invaded Poland from the west on 1 September 1939, and the Soviet Union from the east on 17 September, Poland lost its sovereignty and found itself under occupation once again. The September campaign and Poland's fall prompted a wave of migration, with the government of the Second Polish Republic along with soldiers and civilians – around 150,000 people altogether – fleeing to Romania, Hungary, Lithuania, and Latvia. Prisoners of war held by the Soviets, as well as civilians in the occupied eastern territories (about one million Poles), were deported to the interior of the Soviet Union, where they were imprisoned, often in Gulag camps. On their arrival, either they were shot (as happened to more than 10,000 Polish officers in the Katyn forest, who were murdered by the NKVD), or they died from disease, cold, and hunger (it is estimated that around one in four deportees died in the Soviet Union).[1] Another 1.3 million Poles were deported to Germany to be used as forced labour in agriculture and industry.

Many refugees tried to reach France, and those who succeeded immediately began to rebuild the structures of government, culture, and education. They did so despite their dispersion, a lack of funds and organization, the challenges of building new lives, and the rising fear of war. After Romania interned Poland's highest officials, a Polish government-in-exile was formed in Paris in June 1940 with General Władysław Sikorski (1881–1943) as prime minister. Six months before that, in December 1939, the Polish University Abroad had been established in the French capital, and in March 1940, also in Paris, Mieczysław Grydzewski (1894–1970) relaunched the most popular interwar Polish weekly, *Wiadomości Literackie* (Literary News) under the new title *Wiadomości Polskie, Polityczne i Literackie* (Polish Political and Literary News). Meanwhile, the Polish Army began to re-form itself; by the time Nazi Germany invaded France, it could count 90,000 soldiers there. Less than one-third of them made their way to Great Britain after France capitulated in June 1940; others sought refuge in, for instance, the United States or Switzerland. The Polish government-in-exile and President Władysław Raczkiewicz took refuge in London, where they resumed their activities.

The deportees who ended up in the Gulag camps, many of them located above the Arctic Circle, were given the hope of freedom only in July 1941, when – after the Nazis invaded the Soviet Union – the Sikorski–Mayski Agreement was signed. This allowed General Władysław Anders to begin recruiting soldiers for the Polish Armed Forces in the east, who were to join in the fight against Nazi Germany. Those who were able to reach the gathering point (around 78,000 of them) left the Soviet Union in mid-1942, forming the core of the Polish II Corps of the Polish Armed Forces. In coming years, its divisions would fight in North Africa and Western Europe.

The Polish refugee/deportee armies on the Western Front were a significant fighting force, but Stalin intentionally undermined them in the international arena. Under his pressure, the Allied forces diminished the achievements of the Polish forces and did not treat the Polish government-in-exile as an equal partner. This ostracism was evident in February 1944, when the British withdrew the paper allowance from the then London-based *Polish Political and Literary News* after it openly criticized the Soviet Union and the submissiveness of Western countries. This led to the closure of that publication. It was also evident in the pointed exclusion of Polish forces from the London Victory Celebrations on 8 May 1946.

The agreement struck by the leaders of the United States, Great Britain, and the Soviet Union at the Tehran Conference in 1943, confirmed in February 1945 in Yalta, deprived Poland of one-third of its prewar territory and placed the country within the Soviet sphere of influence. Poles still in Western Europe bitterly resented this. When the Provisional Government of National Unity, a Soviet puppet, assumed power in Poland in June 1945, and was then recognized by the governments of Western Europe, which withdrew their support for the government-in-exile (July 1945), Polish refugees and deportees alike felt betrayed. Yalta became a symbol for them, the moment when they transformed into a new formation – emigration.

> It is no longer the balance in Europe that is at stake, but its very existence as a civilizational model and link. Today, the borderline runs no longer through Poland, or through the Western border of Soviet occupation, but is extended far beyond them, spanning the entire globe. Moreover, the division line does not mark only the ground, or the present time, but demarcates two worlds of culture, two notions of life, two ideas of the human being. They can be called by their name: the Western and the Eastern world, the Christian and the anti-Christian notion of life, the liberal and democratic, and the totalitarian and slavish idea of the human being ... Emigration lives as long as it fights. In order to live, we too must fight.
>
> – Tymon Terlecki, "Emigracja walki," *Wiadomości* 2 (1946): 2

Remaining abroad thus became a political decision, and the activities of those who made that choice, starting in 1945, had as their foremost aim the release of Poland from Soviet influence and its restoration to full sovereignty. Adam Pragier (1886–1976), a minister of the Polish government-in-exile, asserted that emigration had "the duty to fight for independence that no one else can fulfill."[2] In this context, all activities – including literary and artistic work – were viewed as forms of political engagement. This situation reawakened the tradition of the Great Emigration of the first half of the nineteenth century, which had been a response to the failure of the November Uprising (1830–1). At that time, Polish exiles – including, among others, Adam Mickiewicz (1798–1855), Juliusz Słowacki (1809–49), and Fryderyk Chopin (1810–49) – also sought the freedom of their homeland. This is why the 1945 emigration is typically referred to as the Second Great Emigration and is remembered, somewhat simplistically, for its pursuit of national independence.

Writers of such stature as Witold Gombrowicz (1904–69), Andrzej Bobkowski (1913–61), Marian Pankowski (1919–2011), Stefan Themerson (1910–88), and Czesław Miłosz (1911–2004) escape this easy classification, and their work – an expression of both individual talent and artistic maturity – escapes the boundaries of simple definitions and approaches. Moreover, such artists underscored their distinctiveness by not viewing exile in terms of personal and national defeat, as was typical of the émigré community. Instead, they saw their time in the West as an opportunity to develop and enrich their work by exploring previously unseen horizons.

The Great Emigration encompassed two forms of cultural activity. The first of these was publishing. Overcoming the limitations imposed by war, it printed editions of Polish literary classics, the poets of the Great Emigration among them, as well as the poetry of soldiers, mostly in highly popular anthologies (*Poezja Karpacka* [*Carpathian Poetry*]; *Nasze granice w Monte Cassino* [Our Borders at Monte Cassino]). The second form of cultural activity was the press. Besides the already mentioned *Polish Political and Literary News* (Paris/London), one finds titles such as *Polska Walcząca* (Fighting Poland, France), *Ku Wolnej Polsce* (Towards Free Poland, Palestine), *Polak w Indiach* (A Pole in India), *Przy Kierownicy w Tobruku* (At the Wheel in Tobruk, Libya), *Orzeł Biały* (White Eagle, USSR–Iran–Iraq–Palestine–Italy–Belgium), *Tygodniowy Serwis Literacki Koła Pisarzy z Polski–Tygodnik Polski* (Weekly Literary Review of the Polish Writers' Circle–Polish Weekly, New York), *Skrzydła* (Wings, Great Britain), and *Dziennik Polski i Dziennik Żołnierza* (The Polish Daily and Soldiers' Daily, London). Both forms of activity by these refugee poets, publishers, and editors served to build national bonds and to stimulate patriotism, as well as to formulate the émigré political program.

Emigration 1945–89

In 1945, Europe was divided by the Iron Curtain, as Winston Churchill had named it. The number of Polish emigrants who decided to remain on its Western side fluctuated constantly between 1945 and 1989. At its peak, there were around 1.5 million of them. A significant number settled in Great Britain, the home of Polish government-in-exile until 1990 and the headquarters of the Polish Armed Forces in the West during the Second World War; others chose the United States, France, Germany, Canada, Australia, Belgium, and various South American countries. Not everyone decided to stay abroad after the war, however; some chose to return to Poland. The governments of Western countries were relieved at this, for it reduced the costs of aid for the DPs. The communist authorities in Poland also welcomed these returnees, for it could use them for propaganda and thereby persuade the rest of the world that the socialist system had no equal and was to be envied. But the reality these returnees faced was very different. Those who were former Home Army soldiers, participants in the Warsaw Uprising, active members of independence and émigré organizations, or soldiers in Anders' Army were viewed as "enemy elements" by the Polish authorities and often persecuted and – in the best-case scenario – imprisoned upon their return. Between 1945 to 1948 – "a period of relocation and dispersion,"[3] in the words of Bolesław Klimaszewski – the wave of returnees to Poland was accompanied by a movement in the opposite direction. The writers who returned to Poland at this time included Julian Tuwim (1894–1953), Tadeusz Borowski (1922–51), Władysław Broniewski (1897–1962), Gustaw Morcinek (1891–1963), and Arkady Fiedler (1894–1985). Simultaneously, some writers came to view remaining in a socialist Poland as dangerous, and crossed the border illegally, heading for Western Europe; among them were the prose writers Wiesław Wohnout (1902–88) and Stanisława Kuszelewska (1894–1966), the latter of whom had fought in the Warsaw Uprising, as well as Ferdynand Goetel (1890–1960), a member of the Polish delegation to investigate the Katyn massacre.

> The decidedly anti-communist and anti-Soviet *Daily* delivered an image of the world that corresponded with readers' expectations, serving during the post-war period as the most influential source of information abroad about events in Poland and the world ... Until the mid-1950s, *News* was the first, meaning the most influential, opinion-forming, and popular periodical in émigré circles, aware of its significance and position.
>
> – Rafał Habielski, *Życie społeczne i kulturalne emigracji*, 141, 145

Throughout these years, the émigré community was refining its political program and intensifying its cultural activities. The end of the war allowed for the establishment of a number of institutions that in subsequent years would participate in the shaping of Polish attitudes abroad. Two events deserve a separate mention here. In the fall of 1945, the Association of Polish Writers in Exile was formed in London, and in April 1946, the *Polish Political and Literary News* were relaunched there as the now "non-adjectival" – Tymon Terlecki's term – *Wiadomości* (News).[4] From the start, Mieczysław Grydzewski's weekly, along with the *Polish Daily* and the *Soldier's Daily*, took an anti-Soviet position and exerted considerable influence on the émigré program. Journalists like Tymon Terlecki (1905–2000), Zygmunt Nowakowski (1891–1963), and Józef Mackiewicz (1902–85) set the tone of its discussion, calling for the restitution of Poland's sovereignty, the return of lands annexed by the Soviet Union in the east, free elections, and the end of Soviet authority over Poland. Confronted with rising pressure to leave Great Britain and return to their homeland, and with measures taken by Poland's communist authorities, the émigré circles associated with these newspapers adopted an "unbowed and unbending" stance, rejecting any form of cooperation with the "Warsaw regime," as they called it.[5]

> We are in favour of complete liberation, sovereignty, and true democracy, but we do not reject half-way measures, such as, for instance, neutralism. We do not reject partial freedom in the name of complete freedom on behalf of those who for the last sixteen years have been deprived of freedom altogether.
>
> – Juliusz Mieroszewski, "Karty na stół," 8

One expression of this stance was a resolution tabled by the Association of Polish Writers in Exile (1947) that called on Polish writers abroad to refrain from publishing their work in Poland. Those who decided to return to the homeland, or even simply to visit it, were viewed with suspicion. For this reason, the reportage of Aleksander Janta-Połczyński

(1908–74) in *Wracam z Polski 1948* (I'm Coming Back from Poland 1948), in which he related his two-month visit to the homeland, met with vehement criticism. The author was accused of presenting only the positive aspects of the transformations taking place in the new Polish state (rebuilding, economic development, reforms) and excluding the negative ones (persecutions of "enemies of the state"). The unbending stance of the émigré circles in London, which was becoming the centre of Polish emigration, was bolstered by their conviction that the Polish question would continue to have an important impact on relations between Western Europe and the Soviet Union.

A second, less radical attitude, however, slowly began to emerge as a result of Jerzy Giedroyć's (1906–2000) monthly *Kultura* (Culture). Based in Paris and thus referred to as Parisian, *Culture* from the start adopted a more open stance on contacts with Poland. It allowed for the possibility of negotiation and cooperation with the government authorities and other organizations in Poland, and it counted them as part of its target audience. As Juliusz Mieroszewski (1906–76) wrote in "Karty na stół" (Cards on the Table): "In our understanding 'politics for Poland' is a broader term than 'politics of independence.'"[6] The difference between the London and Paris circles was clearly demarcated when, after Stalin's death in 1953, a political change that came to be known as "the thaw" (1955–6) began to take place in Poland. *Culture*, noting the process of de-Stalinization and liberalization of life in Poland, decided to extend some trust towards the new government, now headed by Władysław Gomułka (1905–82). The Association of Polish Writers in Exile answered this with another resolution that rejected the possibility of cooperation between émigré writers and Polish publishers. A considerable part of the emigrant community did not receive that resolution well. Among those who spoke against it were writers associated with *Culture* and of such stature as Witold Gombrowicz, Gustaw Herling-Grudziński (1919–2000), Józef Wittlin (1896–1976), and Czesław Miłosz. Although those responsible for shaping the political position of *Culture*, including Juliusz Mieroszewski, were soon disappointed, seeing how the political transformations in Poland turned out to be temporary, the line drawn between the Paris and London emigrations was never to be erased.

Another difference between Paris's *Culture* and London's *News* concerned the presence of the Polish issue in the international arena and the proposed actions stemming therefrom. During the early postwar years, the émigré community in London expected – indeed, awaited – an outbreak of a third world war. It was convinced that the Soviet Union would be destroyed in such a war and that a free Poland would be reborn on its ruins. The fact that this did not happen, and that each passing year made such a war less and less likely, did not erode in the slightest their conviction that they were right. *Culture*, by contrast, gazed into the future and argued against pipe dreams of a rapid and thorough change of political powers in Europe, proposing instead that Poland work on building and maintaining good relations with its closest neighbours, including those that remained in the Soviet sphere of influence, such as Ukraine, Belarus, and Lithuania.

The third divisive issue between *Culture* and *News* concerned their attitude towards Polish borders. The London circles viewed Poland's recovered territories in the west as compensation for its wartime sacrifice that should not be linked in any way with the country's loss of the eastern borderlands, the return of which was seen as beyond any argument. *Culture*, for its part, proposed the acceptance of Poland's postwar borders, having concluded that the current balance of power in Europe was not going to change much. The Polish government-in-exile began to loosen its stance, reluctantly accepting

Poland's eastern border and limiting its proposals to the withdrawal of Soviet troops from Poland and the holding of free elections. By the 1960s, however, it was *Culture* that was playing a dominant role in shaping the political and cultural aspects of Polish emigration.

The pages of *Culture* offered political analyses, sociological and economic coverage, and historical articles. It aimed to reach readers in Poland, where such content had been stifled by censorship. Giedroyć saw a need for that outreach even before he established the monthly, as the director of the Instytut Literacki (Literary Institute, 1946–2000). Many of the books published by the institute reached Poland through illegal channels (for instance, they were smuggled across the Czech border, over the Tatra Mountains) and shaped the thinking of the oppositional elites in the homeland. From among more than five hundred titles, separate mention is due to Leszek Kołakowski's (1927–2009) *Główne nurty marksizmu* (Main Currents of Marxism, 1976–8), the books of *Culture*'s most prominent journalist Juliusz Mieroszewski, Wiktor Sukiennicki's (1901–83) *Kolumbowy błąd* (The Colombuses' Error, 1959), the historical works of Paweł Zaremba (1915–79), and the books of oppositionists still in Poland such as Adam Michnik (b. 1946), Jacek Kuroń (1934–2004), and Władysław Bieńkowski (1906–91). In addition, the Literary Institute published the important analyses and significant opinions of anti-Soviet foreign writers, among them Aleksandr Solzhenitsyn, Andrei Sakharov, Borys Lewytzkyj, Michel Garder, and Milovan Djilas.

The third crucial centre of émigré activity was Radio Free Europe. Established in 1949 and financed by the US Congress, it disseminated democratic ideas and kept the citizens of countries within the Soviet sphere of influence informed about the actual state of local and global politics and economy. In May 1952, the Polish bureau of Radio Free Europe was established, with Jan Nowak-Jeziorański (1914–2005) as its director. It focused on informational and opinion-shaping programs and was the most popular Western radio broadcaster in Poland, as well as the most suppressed and fought against by the communist authorities. Radio Free Europe played a significant role during the subsequent upheavals and political changes in Poland (1968, 1970, 1980), mainly due to the speed of its commentary. When oppositionists were arrested or otherwise persecuted in Poland, the station broadcast the news within a few hours. It also delivered much valuable information about the actual – whether social, economic, or educational – situation in Poland, presenting the facts, which were at odds with the official propaganda of the Polish Peoples' Republic.

As the influence of *Culture* and Radio Free Europe grew stronger, that of the London emigration grew weaker. As the years passed, emigrants who had become detached from Polish reality slowly lost relevance, with émigré institutions (such as the Polish government-in-exile) becoming purely symbolic. This was a consequence of the censorship that made it much more difficult to reach people in Poland, as well as the London circles' refusal to acknowledge the changes transpiring there. The "unbending" members of the emigration believed that all of Polish society was against the imposed socialist system. They thought that the Polish nation was entirely against the communist regime and that a mere spark would be enough to bring about its explosion. This was not the case, however. This erroneous conviction was accompanied by a distrust of visitors who arrived, albeit infrequently, from Poland; because these people had received permission to travel abroad from officials of the Polish People's Republic, they were viewed as collaborators. This reluctance was even extended to the realm of culture emerging from Poland; some in the "unbowed" emigrant community were inclined to read only Polish novels about the past, believing that all works that dealt with the present had to have been infected by the socialist virus.

Emigrés arriving from Poland in later years, including Czesław Miłosz, were unable to change this mindset. Miłosz's decision to remain in the West in 1951 echoed powerfully throughout the émigré world. He was well-received by the *Culture* circles but not by the "unbowed, unbending" part of the emigration, who continued to distrust him – as the former cultural attaché in Paris, he was a former employee of the Polish communist authorities. Following in his footsteps, after the thaw of 1956, Sławomir Mrożek (1930–2013), Marek Hłasko (1934–69), Leopold Tyrmand (1920–85), and Aleksander Wat (1900–67), to name only a few other writers, also chose exile. This wave of departures went hand in hand with a wave of returns, which also undermined the uncompromising position of the émigrés. The year that Miłosz decided to stay in France, Antoni Słonimski (1895–1976) decided to return to Poland, and between 1956 and 1967, other writers followed him, including Zofia Kossak-Szczucka (1889–1968), Melchior Wańkowicz (1892–1974), Jerzy Stanisław Sito (1934–2011), and Teodor Parnicki (1908–88). But it was Stanisław "Cat" Mackiewicz's (1896–1966) decision to return to Poland that disappointed the émigré community most strongly, since he was their favourite *News* writer as well as the prime minister of the Polish government-in-exile between 1954 and 1955.

Subsequent arrivals from Poland met with diverse reactions. Not all of them headed for London – those who were educated, well known, and of high social or official rank often took up posts at universities. This was the case in the latter half of the 1960s and the beginning of the 1970s with, among others, Leszek Kołakowski, Zygmunt Bauman (1925–2017), Jan Kott (1914–2001), and Roman Karst (1911–88), who either left Poland or decided not to return there after residencies abroad. The writers Henryk Grynberg (b. 1936) and Włodzimierz Odojewski (1930–2016) emigrated in similar circumstances around this time. The growing social unrest initiated by the bloody events of December 1970, when workers' strikes in Gdańsk and Gdynia were brutally suppressed, and fuelled by the worsening economic situation (starting in 1976), led to a wave of strikes in 1980 and – by way of response – to the introduction of martial law on 13 December 1981. These events prompted close to one million Poles to emigrate. This time, though, the emigrants headed mainly for the United States, Australia, Canada, South Africa, and what was then West Germany. This largest of all Polish postwar emigration waves included, among others, Stanisław Barańczak (1946–2014), Janusz Głowacki (1938–2017), Adam Zagajewski (b. 1945), Kazimierz Brandys (1916–2000), and Wojciech Karpiński (b. 1943).

The émigrés from the 1970s and 1980s had experience in political opposition, most significantly with the samizdat publishing movement, established in the mid-1970s, which they had helped organize and which printed and distributed illegal publications and books, including reprints of the most important works written in exile. Having a different perspective on issues in Poland and Eastern Europe, they chose to only partly integrate with the wartime emigration, often deciding to speak in their own voice. New publications and publishing houses were thus created, such as the quarterly *Aneks* (The Annex), founded in 1973 in London and joined by a homonymous publishing house two years later, and the quarterly *Puls* (The Pulse), a continuation of a quarterly underground publication in Poland that began appearing in London in 1982.

Back in Poland, economic difficulties that steadily grew worse throughout the 1980s and accompanying waves of social protest led to the commencement of talks between the government and the opposition in 1989. As a result of the Round Table negotiations

(February–April 1989), the first partly free elections in the history of postwar Poland were called; they were won by the democratic opposition represented by Lech Wałęsa (b. 1943). After Wałęsa was chosen as the president of the Republic of Poland in December 1990, and Soviet troops were withdrawn from that country in 1993, the Polish emigration could declare that it had achieved its objectives. On 22 December 1990, Ryszard Kaczorowski (1919–2010), the president of the government-in-exile, gave Wałęsa the presidential insignia that had been removed from Poland by Ignacy Mościcki (1867–1946) when he escaped from the Nazis in 1939. The gesture signalled the end of the Second Great Emigration.

The significance of this date is only symbolic, of course. Émigré institutions and publishers continued to function – in Paris, for example, *Culture* would continue to come out until Giedroyć's death in 2000 – and some are active to this day. Well-known artists and writers, who were now able to visit Poland freely or to choose to return permanently, continued their work, to mention only Czesław Miłosz, Sławomir Mrożek, and Gustaw Herling-Grudziński. Moreover, the opening of borders symbolically confirmed by the fall of the Berlin Wall in November 1989, and the possibility of unrestricted travel and relocation to other parts of the world that followed, prompted yet another wave of emigration from Poland at the beginning of the 1990s. This time, however, unlike in past years, Poles were leaving their homeland for purely economic reasons, although their destinations remained the same. After Poland's admission to the European Union (2004) and the Schengen Area (2007), Poles left *en masse* for England, Germany, Ireland, the Netherlands, and other Western countries. It is estimated that more than two million Poles have chosen to emigrate since their country joined the EU. They too form cultural institutions and publish magazines, but the influence of these ventures on Polish society is undoubtedly slight.

The Émigré Cultural Legacy and Its Significance

The Second Great Emigration left an indelible legacy, primarily cultural though also political and scientific. This legacy shaped the attitudes and opinions of the Polish intelligentsia, who – not without difficulties, and often under the threat of persecution – studied and absorbed its lessons. Its influence was possible because the Iron Curtain was never completely impermeable. Radio Free Europe reached across it most broadly and easily; the printed word encountered more difficulties. Émigré works were stashed in luggage, hidden between alternative covers, surreptitiously smuggled and secretly handed over, then passed from one set of hands to the next once in Poland. Borrowed for a few hours at a time, they were read for the knowledge and information they provided that was forbidden in Poland. The prominent currents of émigré literature were largely determined by historical and political conditions.

Even while still participating in the Second World War, Polish emigrants tried to record testimonies to its horrors and to analyse its causes and consequences. Among those who reached for a pen were politicians (Adam Pragier, Adam Ciołkosz [1902–78], Stanisław Stroński [1882–1955], Stanisław Kot [1885–1975]), military leaders (including generals Władysław Anders [1892–1970], Tadeusz Bór-Komorowski [1895–1966], Stanisław Maczek [1892–1984], Stanisław Sosabowski [1892–1967], and Józef Haller [1873–1960]), regular soldiers (Janusz Kowalewski [1910–96], Jan Bielatowicz [1913–65], Karol Zbyszewski [1904–90], Czesław Jeśman [1912–87]), and journalists (Melchior

Wańkowicz, Ksawery Pruszyński [1907–50], Janusz Meissner [1901–78]). They presented the history of the Polish armed forces, which was entirely unknown in Poland and often also in the West, starting with the defensive war in September 1939 against Germany and Russia and ending with the battles in Africa and Western Europe. Among the countless books dedicated to this subject, of special note are a memoir by General Anders, *Bez ostatniego rozdziału* (An Army in Exile, 1950); Melchior Wańkowicz's reportage, *Bitwa o Monte Cassino* (Battle for Monte Cassino, 1947); and the most popular émigré novel during the war period, Arkady Fiedler's *Dywizjon 303* (Squadron 303, 1942), which centres on the heroic Polish pilots who participated in the Battle of Britain.

Another extremely important theme was war crimes. In postwar Poland there was an effort to document Nazi crimes, reveal the cruelty of the German occupiers, and testify to the German concentration camps. The emigration, for its part, focused on Soviet war crimes, a subject that had been silenced in Poland. The Katyn massacre occupied a prominent place in this context. It gained publicity in the West as a result of Józef Mackiewicz's book *Zbrodnia katyńska w świetle dokumentów* (The Crime of Katyn: Facts and Documents). Published in 1948, it caused a considerable stir, as did Gustaw Herling-Grudziński's memoir *Inny świat. Zapiski sowieckie* (A World Apart, 1951). Initially published in English translation and with an introduction by Bertrand Russell, *A World Apart* appeared in Polish – abroad – two years later, but had to wait for its first official Polish edition until 1988. Although Herling-Grudziński's book was not the first work of Gulag literature, having been preceded by, among others, Józef Czapski's (1896–1993) *Wspomnienia starobielskie* (Memoirs from Starobilsk, 1944) and *Na nieludzkiej ziemi* (In Inhuman Lands, 1949), Anatol Krakowiecki's (1901–50) *Książka o Kołymie* (A Book about Kolyma, 1950), and Wacław Grubiński's (1883–1973) *Między młotem a sierpem* (Between the Hammer and the Sickle, 1948), it echoed the farthest across the Western world.

The documentation of the Second World War also took on an institutional aspect in exile. Research studies appeared alongside memoirs and analyses, conducted under the auspices of organizations such as the Józef Piłsudski Institute for Research in Modern History of Poland in New York, the Polish Historical Society in Great Britain (the quarterly *Historical Portfolios* was one of its branches), the Polish Institute and Sikorski Museum in London, and the Polish Underground Movement Study Trust, also in London. The monumental six-volume *Armia Krajowa w dokumentach 1939–1945* (Home Army: Documents 1939–1945) stands out in this context along with the work of such historians as Marian Kukiel (1885–1973), Wacław Jędrzejewicz (1893–1993), and Władysław Pobóg-Malinowski (1899–1962).

Another important place in the émigré literary consciousness was taken up by interwar Poland. Most émigré artists had spent their youth in a free Poland, and this gave rise to an understandable sentiment for the interwar years and the lost homeland. In literature this resulted in a significant wave of nostalgic memoirs, diaries, and essays published both in book form and in periodicals. The same theme was prominent in many stories and novels. Indeed, its literary effect was at times remarkable. It is sufficient to mention here the anthology of authors' reminiscences edited by Mieczysław Grydzewski during the war, *Kraj lat dziecinnych* (The Country of Childhood Years, 1942), as well as such enduring works as Czesław Miłosz's *Dolina Issy* (The Issa Valley, 1955) and *Rodzinna Europa* (Native Realm: A Search for Self-Definition, 1959); Stanisław Vincenz's (1888–1971) *Na wysokiej połoninie* (On the High Uplands, 1955); Tadeusz Nowakowski's (1917–96) *Obóz*

Wszystkich Świętych (Camp of All Saints, 1957), Józef Wittlin's *Mój Lwów* (My Lviv, 1946), Maria Czapska's (1894–1981) *Europa w rodzinie* (A Family of Central Europe, 1970), and Zygmunt Haupt's (1907–95) *Pierścień z papieru* (The Paper Ring, 1963).

It was fairly quickly noticed that this constant looking back to the past, these descriptions of "small homelands," and this preservation in print of images held in memory, did not attract many Western readers; even the émigré community was lukewarm to it. Thus two important propositions emerged: the first, clearly present in the work of Tymon Terlecki, among others, was that ties with European and world cultures should be encouraged and maintained; the second was that steps must be taken to prevent the denationalization of émigré communities, especially of their youngest members, including children born abroad.

A number of writers contributed to the realization of the first proposal with works that, translated into numerous languages, secured them a noteworthy place on the world's literary stage. Among them were Witold Gombrowicz, Sławomir Mrożek, Gustaw Herling-Grudziński, and Józef Wittlin. Another group of authors, taking up Joseph Conrad's legacy, wrote in English and found readers in English-speaking countries, as was the case with Jerzy Pietrkiewicz (1916–2007) and Jerzy Kosiński (1933–91). Worth remembering also are those writers who took up the task of translation, thus rendering the achievements of Polish literature accessible to Western readers, and vice versa. This group includes Stanisław Barańczak, Jan Kott, Adam Czerniawski (b. 1934), Bolesław Taborski (1927–2010), Florian Śmieja (b. 1925), and Jan Winczakiewicz (1921–2012). Meanwhile, Polish professors working at Western universities made important contributions to contemporary philosophical, sociological, literary, and historical research. Exemplary in this regard are Leszek Kołakowski (Oxford) and Zygmunt Bauman (University of Leeds), as well as Piotr Wandycz (1923–2017; Yale), Józef Maria Bocheński (1902–95; Université de Fribourg), Wiktor Weintraub (1908–88; Harvard), and Oskar Halecki (1891–1973; Columbia).

All of the above-mentioned groups found a representative in the most renowned of Polish émigré authors – the poet, essayist, novelist, translator, and professor Czesław Miłosz, who published the most important of his works abroad. Alongside his poetry, of particular significance are *Zniewolony umysł* (The Captive Mind, 1953), which analyses the attitudes of Polish intellectuals towards communism, and *Zdobycie władzy* (The Seizure of Power, 1955), which revealed the mechanisms of the functioning of socialist states. Of greatest importance for his reception both in Poland and abroad, however, was the Nobel Prize in Literature that he received for the totality of his literary achievement in 1980.

The second proposition – to prevent the denationalization of younger generations of Polish emigrants – has not been realized to a satisfactory degree. The problem was a central one for émigré culture as early as the 1950s. Appeals were made to undertake activities to nurture Polish identity among younger generations and to maintain their connections with Polish culture and language, yet when the younger generations responded with initiatives, their efforts met with distrust. The alienated poetic group "Kontynenty" (Continents) is one example. Its founders, including Florian Śmieja, Adam Czerniawski, Bogdan Czaykowski (1932–2007), Zygmunt Ławrynowicz (1925–87), Bolesław Taborski, Jan Darowski (1926–2008), Jerzy Stanisław Sito, and Janusz Ihnatowicz (b. 1929), left Poland during the Second World War as children or teenagers and finished their studies at British universities during the 1940s and 1950s. At this time, they made decisions regarding their future, including literary pursuits. Though they were tempted to switch from Polish to either English or Spanish, for reasons of profitability, all of them chose their native tongue as their means of creative expression. The title of Bogdan Czaykowski's debut *Trzciny Czcionek* (Cane's Font, 1957), with its consonant clusters that are so hard for English speakers to pronounce, is telling here. At the same time, having been educated in the West, they willingly drew on Western culture and – like the Paris-based journal *Culture* – were much more open to contacts with Poland than the older generation of emigrants. This, along with personal decisions (a number of members of this group moved to the United States and Canada, and one returned to Poland), led to the eventual disbanding of the group. Its members continued to write in Polish, and indeed those who are still alive still do. But younger Poles, born abroad, have by and large chosen the language and culture of the country where their parents settled.

A few other phenomena in émigré literary culture are worth pointing out. Poets from different generations and formations, from the "Skamander" and "Żagary" groups up to the "New Wave" (viz. Czesław Miłosz, Kazimierz Wierzyński [1894–1969], Stanisław Barańczak, Marian Czuchnowski [1909–91], Jerzy Pietrkiewicz, Wacław Iwaniuk [1912–2001], Bogdan Czaykowski, Adam Czerniawski, Józef Łobodowski [1909–88], Adam Zagajewski), aligned with prose writers in tackling political, military, sociocultural, and existential themes (Witold Gombrowicz, Czesław Straszewicz [1904–63], Stefan Themerson, Józef Mackiewicz, Leopold Tyrmand, Zofia Romanowiczowa [1922–2010], Tadeusz Nowakowski, Zygmunt Haupt, Stanisław Vincenz, Gustaw Herling-Grudziński, Janusz Jasieńczyk [1907–96], Leo Lipski [1917–97]). This was also true for cultural and philosophical writers as well as memoirists and political and cultural journalists (the first represented by Jerzy Stempowski [1893–1969], Józef Wittlin, Tymon Terlecki, and Bolesław Miciński [1911–43], the second by Andrzej Bobkowski, Stefania Zahorska [1890–1961], Wacław A. Zbyszewski [1903–85], Aleksander Wat, Stefania Kossowska [1909–2003], Jan Lechoń [1899–1956], Herminia Naglerowa [1890–1957], Stanisław Cat Mackiewicz, and Ignacy Wieniewski [1896–1986]). Historico-philosophical and socio-existential drama, in turn, was sometimes aided by literary criticism, whether anecdotal and descriptive or formal and academic (with Marian Hemar [1901–72], Marian Pankowski, and Bronisław Przyłuski [1905–80] representing drama, and Michał Chmielowiec [1918–74], Wit Tarnawski [1894–1988], Jan Bielatowicz, Juliusz Sakowski [1905–77], Maria Danilewicz Zielińska [1907–2003], and Wojciech Karpiński representing criticism).

All of the above-mentioned figures were known in Poland to only a few at various points between 1945 and 1990. The government of the Polish Peoples' Republic was aware that it could not fully control either publishing or reading, of course, and it gradually allowed into print those books by émigré authors that met their specific requirements. As Bolesław Klimaszewski has shown, almost five hundred books by émigrés reached the local market through national publishing houses in Poland. The works that were allowed into print were by writers who had decided to return to the homeland, or by deceased authors who no longer posed a threat (Jan Lechoń, Aleksander Janta Połczyński [1908–74]), or by artists who did not openly manifest their political positions or thematize them in their work (Stefan Themerson, Sławomir Mrożek, Zygmunt Ławrynowicz, Tadeusz Sułkowski [1907–60]). The remaining émigré writers were precluded from publishing. This situation began to change when samizdat publishing became a reality; another five hundred titles were published by this means between 1978 and 1990.

> Our planet that gets smaller every year, with its fantastic proliferation of mass media, is witnessing a process that escapes definition, characterized by a refusal to remember. Certainly, the illiterates of past centuries, then an enormous majority of mankind, knew little of the history of their respective countries and of their civilization. In the minds of modern illiterates, however, who know how to read and write and even teach in schools and at universities, history is present but blurred, in a state of strange confusion; Molière becomes a contemporary of Napoleon, Voltaire, a contemporary of Lenin. Also, events of the last decades, of such primary importance that knowledge or ignorance of them will be decisive for the future of mankind, move away, grow pale, lose all consistency as if Frederic Nietzsche's prediction of European nihilism found a literal fulfillment.
>
> – Czesław Miłosz, Nobel Lecture (http://www.nobelprize.org/nobel_prizes/literature/laureates/1980/milosz-lecture.html)

A radical change took place with the fall of the Polish Peoples' Republic, which brought in a golden age for the cultural legacy of the Polish émigré community. Small and large publishing houses established at that time tried to make up for a forty-five-year-long backlog by reprinting both well-known and more obscure books that had been written in exile. Another wave of émigré publications made its way to Poland, this time through legal channels. After a period of rapid absorption of emigrant writing (1990–5), however, to the surprise of some communities both abroad and in Poland, the interest in the emigrant legacy began to fade. Józef Mackiewicz's prediction that "the beginning of publishing in Poland will be an end of émigré writing"[7] gained new resonance at that time. A number of factors contributed to the situation.

The first was the development of a free market economy, in which literature gained a number of new competitors, including videos, computer games, and – starting in 1994 – the Internet. Craving world entertainment, Poles began to look for new experiences and emotions, not infrequently reaching for popular culture in the process. The second factor stemmed from a characteristic exhaustion of the attractiveness of emigration. The forbidden fruit of its culture was no longer tempting; the émigré community that had previously fought for Poland's sovereignty had achieved its aim and was unable to describe the new, dynamically changing democratic and capitalist reality. The increasing distance between the emigration and Poland was yet another factor, with distance understood not literally but in terms of differences in mindsets, attitudes towards fundamental issues, and, finally, language. Emigrants who were out of touch with their country and who focused on preserving an image of prewar Poland in their memory, discarding for the most part the changes that had occurred there, lost their significance as partners in a dialogue. Finally, the fourth factor, addressed by Miłosz in his Nobel lecture: the growing process of "a refusal to remember." Having lost the sense of being endangered by an external, foreign enemy, namely the Soviet Union, Poles consigned to oblivion the times of the Polish Peoples' Republic.

Fortunately, this tendency has not become mandatory. The work to remember the émigré legacy and to return it to Polish culture continues. When the initial infatuation with émigré literature passed, the time came for other arts. Presently, various centres in Poland are showcasing the accomplished work of artists and musicians. Among the musicians, one finds such renowned names as Roman Palester (1907–89), Szymon Laks (1901–83), and Andrzej Panufnik (1914–91), while the artists include Jan Lebeinstein (1930–99), Feliks Topolski (1907–89), August Zamoyski (1893–1970), Marek Żuławski (1908–85), Stanisław Frenkel (1918–2001), and Józef Czapski, along with many others.

Political emigration has come to an end. For many years it had raised Polish spirits, given people hope, encouraged them to persevere, informed them about silenced issues and phenomena, corrected the image of the world that socialism had corrupted, and persisted in loyalty to the objectives it had set for itself. Although its activities took on an ever more symbolic form and its ranks were diminished by the inevitable passage of time, and despite the ridicule and accusations of being out of touch with changing realities that had been levelled against it, it is nevertheless difficult to imagine Poland's twentieth-century history appearing as it now does without the participation and engagement of its emigration.

Rafał Moczkodan
Nicolaus Copernicus University, Toruń
Translated by Agnieszka Polakowska

NOTES

1 http://katyn.ipn.gov.pl.
2 Pragier, "Dziś i jutro emigracji," 2.
3 Klimaszewski, *Wstępna periodyzacja polskiego*, 57.
4 Terlecki, "O *Wiadomościach* bezprzymiotnikowych."
5 See Habielski, *Niezłomni, nieprzejednani.*
6 Mieroszewski, "Karty na stół," 3.
7 Mackiewicz, opinion in a survey conducted by *Culture*, "Literatura emigracyjna a Kraj (dok.)," 85.

WORKS CITED

Habielski, Rafał. *Niezłomni, nieprzejednani. Emigracyjne „Wiadomości" i ich krąg 1940–1981.* Warszawa: PIW, 1991.

– *Życie społeczne i kulturalne emigracji.* Warszawa: Biblioteka "Więzi," 1999.

Klimaszewski, Bolesław. "Wstępna periodyzacja polskiego życia literackiego na obczyźnie 1939–1980." *Ruch Literacki* 1 (1989): 49–65.

Mackiewicz, Józef. "Wypowiedź w ankiecie 'Literatura emigracyjna a Kraj (dok.)'" *Kultura* 1–2 (1957): 84–5.

Miłosz, Czesław. Nobel Lecture. http://www.nobelprize.org/nobel_prizes/literature/laureates/1980/milosz-lecture.html.

Mieroszewski, Juliusz. "Karty na stół." *Kultura* 1 (1956): 3–11.

Pragier, Adam. "Dziś i jutro emigracji." *Dziennik Polski i Dziennik Żołnierza* 86 (1946): 2.

Terlecki, Tymon. "Emigracja walki." *Wiadomości* 2 (1946): 2.

– "O *Wiadomościach* bezprzymiotnikowych." In *XXX-lecie Wiadomości*. 47–55. London: Oficyna Poetów i Malarzy, 1957.

IMMIGRANT/ÉMIGRÉ, MIGRANT, AND TRANSNATIONAL LITERATURE AND CULTURE

The Polish-Language Cabaret Song: Its Multi-Ethnic Pedigree and Transnational Adventures, 1919–1968

In 1959, fourteen years after the end of the Second World War and sixteen years after the Warsaw Ghetto Uprising, showman Jerzy Jurandot (1911–79) published *Dzieje śmiechu* (A History of Laughter), his memoir of Warsaw's interwar Polish-language literary cabaret. *A History of Laughter* focuses primarily on *Qui Pro Quo,* the 514-seat theatre that flourished for more than a decade (1919–32) on Senatorska Street, and, more generally, the five successor-cabarets that *Qui Pro Quo* inspired.[1] Jurandot's was a lifelong love affair; he remembers how hard he fell for cabaret artists and shows in the early years, watching from his cheap back-row seat: "I know how intensely I lived through each program of *Qui Pro Quo* because I still remember them all verbatim after seeing them just once ... Even today I know by heart all the songs sung by Krukowski, Ordonka, and Rentgen, Lawiński's monologues, sketches – entire programs ... It was marvelous, a great era of Polish song."[2] By the mid-1930s, Jurandot had graduated from avid cabaret fan to writing cabaret songs, sketches, and occasionally entire shows.[3]

What were the songs of this great era? What made them so memorable? Why did Jurandot and other reminiscing cabaret artists consider this entertainment worth resurrecting, contextualizing, and celebrating after the horrors of the Holocaust and the war? I have singled out Jurandot's memoir here not only because his career demonstrates the popularity of the cabaret song from the 1920s through the 1950s, but also because his text directs us to what I consider to be the songs' most distinctive, important features – their flourishing during the decades of Poland's national independence, their multifaceted form, their co-creation by a diverse set of artists, and their fascinating psychosocial impact on Varsovians and, subsequently, on Poles beyond the nation's borders. Following the trails blazed by Jurandot and others, I want to show how the cabaret song delighted affluent Warsaw audiences on sundry levels and integrated them into a diverse urban community, and to trace how its creators adapted this eminently portable art form to buoy up and comfort Poles who had been scattered by the war or who were adjusting to post-war life in an ideologically regulated People's Republic of Poland.

The Pedigree of the Interwar Cabaret Song

Jurandot locates the golden era of the cabaret song in the interwar period, when he came under its spell. Historians of the Polish theatre might disagree, since they date the birth of the Polish cabaret to 1905, when artists and academics in Kraków created texts for "a spontaneous exclusive party" at *Zielony Balonik* (The Green Balloon), the name of a local coffeehouse. Explicitly commercial and less artistically experimental cabarets were launched elsewhere in partitioned Poland before and during the First World War.[4] The interwar cabaret and the songs and sketches it generated then forged a new sort of *high-brow* popular entertainment that had never existed before on Polish territory. The interwar cabaret song was produced in a rapidly modernizing city by local artists eager to appropriate the latest in global culture.

During those years, Warsaw, Poland's largest city, at last existed as a national European capital. The declaration of Polish independence in 1918 liberated writers, painters, composers, and performers from serving the cause of an oppressed, martyred fatherland. Independence encouraged Varsovians of different classes and ethnicities to pursue their own interests and, in some cases, to cross class and ethnic boundaries in creating and consuming new forms of art and leisure. Remembering the early years of *Qui Pro Quo*, comedian Kazimierz Krukowski (1901–84), one of Jurandot's favourites, declared that this new kind of cabaret formed "a pact of eternal friendship" with Warsaw audiences: "Onstage you could say what you liked and sing what you liked. The public wanted to laugh, to enjoy a new life and savor the greatest treasure they had ever received – freedom … Warsaw wanted to laugh at what had been taboo for many, many years."[5]

The Polish-language literary cabarets, along with *Morskie Oko* (Eye of the Sea), a larger revue theatre that stayed afloat from 1925 to 1933, were designed as upscale entertainment, avoiding the tawdry ambience, crude repertoire, and scantily clothed female performers of tingel tangel shows (a popular conception of the cabaret featured in such films as *The Blue Angel* [1930] and *Cabaret* [1972]).[6] In contrast to New York cabaret, these Warsaw establishments ceded the casual combination of dining, dancing, and floorshow to fancy restaurants such as the Oaza or the Adria.[7] Like Berlin cabaret in the first two decades of the twentieth century, Warsaw cabaret revelled in political satire and cultivated an intense synesthetic theatricality, though its humour was far less acidic and its atmosphere unshadowed by the horrors of war.[8] The Polish-language literary cabaret rose on a wave of urbane nationalism even while the cabaret of the Weimar Republic was foundering on national defeat and economic crisis. *Qui Pro Quo* and similar theatres rendered the bohemian accessible and affable; they aimed to engage liberals and progressives with their witty, original, infectious play. Indeed, Polish-language literary cabarets invested in high-quality numbers performed on a traditional stage before a modest to sizeable house (from 130 to 1,200 seats). They competed with serious theatre, the opera, and the ballet for affluent, educated Polish-speaking audiences, usually made up of liberal Christians and acculturated Jews.[9] We must bear in mind that the capital of Poland doubled as a great Jewish metropolis, where an impressive one-third of its residents identified themselves as Jews or "of Jewish background."[10]

Acculturated Jews played a fundamental role in producing as well as patronizing the Polish-language literary cabaret. As luck had it, the establishment of the cabaret after 1918 coincided with the global spread of American popular song via records and radio broadcasts. The creators of ragtime, jazz, and syncopated music for such new dances as the foxtrot, the turkey trot, the Charleston, and the black bottom were African American, to be sure, yet it was American Jews, particularly the children of recent immigrants from Eastern Europe, who proved to be its most adept white appropriators, playing with and popularizing these new musical styles through shows and recordings.[11]

With their big city access to imported records and continental radio broadcasts, young Jewish musicians in Warsaw were bowled over by the intoxicating rhythms, vitality, and spontaneity of American popular music. What they lacked in direct contact with the American musical scene, they made up for with their excellent professional training and middle-class privileges. Unlike American Jewish popular composers, most of these young men were the children of classical musicians who were well-established in the capital or in other Polish cities. Such composers as Zygmunt Karasiński (1898–1973), Szymon Kataszek (1898–1943), Zygmunt Wiehler (1890–1977), Jerzy Petersburski (1895–1979), the brothers Artur (1897–1943) and Henryk (1902–77) Gold, and Henryk Wars (1902–77) did not perceive writing and performing for the cabaret, revue, radio, recording studio, or film as a sociocultural descent, as their parents certainly did. Jurandot names these "excellent maestros" as the reliable generators of Polish-language *szlagiery* (hits).[12] As they blended different ethnic motifs and modalities with modern American rhythms, these young Jewish artists were not lowering their standards, but striving to break into a "bigtime" of at once elemental and sophisticated world music. Even as right-wing Catholic groups wielded the term *zażydzenie* (Judaization) to demonize "some sort of new Jewish-Polish culture" that was perverting "true Poland" from within, the songs and dance tunes composed by these gifted Jewish musicians asserted *Poland's* place on an enormously popular international music scene.[13]

The Polish-language literary cabaret's "pact of eternal friendship" with Warsaw audiences promised not only the most modern music but also deftly written original lyrics and sketches. This guarantee of high-quality verbal art tended to distinguish the cabaret from the more visually spectacular revue of *Morskie Oko* (Eye of the Sea), which offered what Jurandot describes as a parade of "half-dressed show girls on a gigantic staircase," and from impresario Andrzej Włast's (1885–1942 or 1943) programs copied from the *Folies Bergère* and *Casino de Paris*.[14] A few poets from the Skamander movement – mainly Julian Tuwim (1894–1953) and, to a more limited extent, Antoni Słonimski (1895–1976) – wrote for the literary cabaret. Besides these Skamandrites, other writers who regularly contributed to Poland's leading liberal journal, *Wiadomości literackie* (Literary News), particularly the translator and social and cultural critic Tadeusz Boy-Żeleński (1874–1941) and the writer Irena Krzywicka (1899–1994), promoted the cabaret's excellence through reviews and occasional essays. Some histories of Polish literature even cede an aside about the involvement of the canonically great in cabaret. For example, Czesław Miłosz (1911–2004) observes in writing about Tuwim: "He produced numerous texts for light theatrical revues and cabarets, which earned him a good deal of money and, thus, left him time for more serious pursuits."[15]

Claiming the poetic pedigree of the Polish-language literary cabaret – an endorsement that Boy-Żeleński liked to reiterate in reviews – may have assuaged feelings of ambivalence for Tuwim and his chief partner in cabaret writing, Marian Hemar (1901–72).[16] Tuwim scholar Tomasz Stępień describes the famous poet as "the most Skamandrite of Skamandrites" in his conflicting literary and social ambitions – a middle-class Jew who managed the great leap from provincial, middle-class Łódź to the Parnassus of Warsaw even as he sought to play the anti-establishment jester through his cabaret satires and songs.[17] Hemar, born Jan Maria Hescheles in Lwów at the beginning of the century, was a powerhouse of cabaret production, composing lyrics for more than 3,000 songs and at least 1,000 sketches. He was obsessively involved in the cabaret's day-to-day operations as a writer and occasional composer. At the same time, he was an acculturated Jew steeped in Polish literature and, very likely in consequence, a Skamandrite wannabe, a cabaret genius who longed to be a great Polish poet.[18]

Despite Tuwim's prominence and Hemar's ambition, this notion of the cabaret's poetic pedigree is inaccurate; it dismisses the exciting changes actually taking place in early-twentieth-century Polish theatre and entertainment. It is time that we identify and evaluate what excellent cabaret writing really entailed. Producing material for a new show every month threw all the artists into the pressure-cooker working conditions of a theatre delivering topical coverage. Their audiences both relished and depended on their processing of serious news into digestible satire and their comic spin on the latest fads and fashions.[19] To make matters tougher, the show's producers insisted on a witty, coherent show complete with hilarious sketches and monologues, sophisticated love songs, and character songs built on ingenious wordplay that included foreign-language phrases (both accurate and not). No one writing for the Polish-language literary cabaret could dash off their numbers and then enjoy copious spare time for "serious pursuits," as Miłosz implies.

The cabaret management quickly realized that, instead of recruiting established poets willing to slum, it would have to forge its own first-rate professional lyricists, who would need to resemble more closely the gifted creators of the classic American songbook – artists such as Irving Berlin, Ira Gershwin, Lorenzo Hart, and Cole Porter.[20] Before 1918, writers Konrad Tom (Runowiecki; 1887–1957), Jerzy Boczkowski (1882–1953), and a more disciplined Andrzej Włast had led the way, and Boczkowski, as Jurandot attests, established a rigorous school for writers at *Qui Pro Quo* that even Hemar had to pass – he laboured for several months before he began producing work that could be used in a show.[21] Almost all of the graduates of this school were acculturated middle-class Jews who had gravitated to the Polish-language literary cabaret because it welcomed talented, cosmopolitan, thoroughly modern young people, whatever their ethnicity and social connections. This group included Bronisław Horowicz (1910–2005), Światopełk Karpiński (1909–40), Andrzej Nowicki (1909–86), Janusz Minkiewicz (1914–81), Emanuel Szlechter (1904–43), Ludwik Starski (1903–84), Tadeusz Wittlin (1909–98), Władysław Szlengiel (1912 or 1914–43), Emanuel Schlechter (1904–43), and, of course, Jerzy Jurandot.[22] Jurandot, whose given surname was Glejgewicht, had emerged as the heir apparent to Tuwim and Hemar by the late 1930s, yet he never lost his reverence for the cabaret as a marvellous synthesis of words, music, and performance; his was a new generation that did not disdain professionalized creativity. Thus, both the music and the words for this high-quality popular entertainment were created by Jews who saw themselves as modern metropolitan Polish artists, equal citizens in a multi-ethnic independent nation.[23]

By the mid-1920s, both sets of artists, especially the lyricists, were working closely with the vocalists who would be singing their songs. Krukowski credits Hemar and Boczkowski with this performer-specific orientation: "Authors knew WHAT to write, and actors knew HOW to perform what was written. Boczkowski, who warned writers he would and could not match actors to already composed songs, monologues, and sketches, used to say, 'Adapt your texts for the troupe we have.'"[24] Writers and performers could not form exclusive pairs – the ratio of authors to actors was abysmal – but clear temperamental affinities arose between those who excelled at composing pure nonsense or linguistically complex songs (Tuwim, Hemar) and quick-witted comedians who could handle the rapid-fire tongue-twisting lyrics these men dished out, performers such as Adolf Dymsza (1900–75), Mira Zimińska (1901–97), and Krukowski. As certain actors blossomed into audience favourites and metropolitan stars, the need to play to those stars' specialties and to cultivate their established *dramatis personae* became more acute. The most successful lyricists combined the skills of poet, dramatist, and comic; if they did not, critics faulted them for wasting the *stars'* talents.[25] Over the course of Warsaw's roaring twenties, the Polish-language literary cabaret evolved into an actors' theatre.

Cabaret performers were much more diverse than composers and lyricists in gender, class, and ethnicity; almost all of them had trained on the job. The troupes encompassed young, good-looking, sexually emancipated, mainly Christian women from the working class (or from families employed in provincial theatres); young men who were Christian and working-class; young, acculturated Jewish men who were renegades from middle-class upwardly mobile families; and a handful of older Christian men already established on the pre-cabaret popular stage for their stock characters as messengers, teamsters, and street vendors. Most of these performers proved to be skilled impersonators eager to parody different social types and even one another. In their constantly morphing diversity, they developed a broad, uncensored, specifically Varsovian *commedia dell'arte*, whose stock characters ranged from officer-bureaucrats to pseudo-intellectual tramps, from snooty society ladies to ebullient flappers and careworn dancers for hire, from local Jewish shopkeepers with ambitious dreams to visiting bumpkins awed by the big city. To a great extent, the Polish-language literary cabaret reflected the diverse characters of their hometown, with contributions from the actors' own experiences. Given the camaraderie that developed between certain writers and performers, some budding stars occasionally dared to request a song based on their own ideas. According to the comedienne Zimińska, her entreaty to a tired "Julek" (Tuwim) for a ballad about a city girl mourning her caddish lover netted her her favourite song, "Pokoik na Hożej" (A Little Room on Hoża Street).[26]

What Jurandot heralds as the "great era of Polish song" resulted from a number of happy coincidences: Polish independence, which opened the door culturally, if not always politically, to multi-ethnic empowerment; a group of poets, critics, and politicians joined (at least in the 1920s) in the project of liberalizing and modernizing this new nation; the emergence of urban audiences and entrepreneurs ready for lively, original entertainment that reflected their particular time and place; and the coming of age and coming together of young artists (men and women, working-class and middle-class, Jewish and Christian) who were eager to play together. As Krukowski asserts, "the most important ingredient for *Qui Pro Quo's* success and popularity was young people and more young people."[27] Cabaret songs were written and performed by a new nation's brand-new stars.

How the Cabaret Song Was Made

My survey of the different artists who created the cabaret song shows contextually what cabaret scholar Wolfgang Ruttkowski argues typologically: the cabaret song represented neither literary nor musical genre, but best approximated "a certain style of performance."[28] Even its component parts eluded strict definition. Its text might qualify as a love lyric or a satirical couplet. Its music could be a dance tune (slow fox, tango) or a melody deliberately interrupted by spoken passages for greater dramatic effect.[29] The creators of the cabaret song agree, however, that its success depended on the coherence between music, text, and performance. In his commentary on songwriting, Hemar resisted privileging lyrics and lyricists: "A song's worth is determined by its ephemeral popular success. Attention paid to the beauty of the original text and music attests to the private ability of the author[s], but has no bearing on the song's success. In a good song, neither the text nor the music is most important. What decides its worth is the harmony between music and text."[30] Quite often, Hemar handily solved the problem of achieving such harmony by writing his lyrics to existing songs in another language ("Manolla" [1933] to a tune by Andres Segovia) or by writing the melody himself ("Upić się warto" [Getting Drunk Is Worth It, 1934]).

The talented, prolific composer Henryk Wars appreciated the challenge for both composer and lyricist, as he reflected in a postwar interview: "Writing music for a given text is a little harder for the composer because he already knows that the song will be performed by a woman or a man. This means he has to choose the right key and limit the melody's scale to fit what the singer can manage. But if the melody is all ready to go, then the lyricist has problems." (Jurandot likewise points out the efforts of composers to match the range of their melody to that of the singer.)[31] It is not clear how many of Wars's cabaret songs originated as melodies, but his biographer Ryszard Wołański surmises that Wars usually ceded Tuwim's texts first place, composing for the poet's completed lyrics.[32]

Jurandot, who had been schooled rigorously by Boczkowski at *Qui Pro Quo,* provides more illuminating detail about how "theatrical songs" were made. His prescriptions for theatrical songs anticipate what Ruttkowski observes; he treated them as condensed performances "for the actor's interpretation": "In a theatrical song (or stage song, eventually a cabaret song – what you will), the words are just as important and often more important than the music. These songs are designed for the actor's interpretation, they are songs with a plot, songs in which something happens, something takes root, develops and moves towards a *pointe* (or even each stanza contains its own content and *pointe,* as in couplets) … Their literary value is certainly higher, but neither before nor after the war did they become widely sung 'hits'; they are too complicated, too difficult to remember."[33]

Though Jurandot warns us that reading lyrics as if they were poems "does the greatest disservice to the author," I propose a closer analysis of one song text that became famous for elaborating the world view of the Polish-language literary cabaret's most beloved persona, the sympathetic Jewish shopkeeper Lopek, who was incarnated by Krukowski. Konrad Tom wrote the lyrics for "Jak się nie ma, co się lubi, to się lubi, co się ma" (If You Don't Have What You Like, Then You Like What You Have); Boczkowski composed the music; and Krukowski performed it first in the May 1930 *Qui Pro Quo* show "Budżet wiosenny" (Spring budget) and many times thereafter. Lopek, who debuted onstage in 1926, proved to be an exceptional cabaret character, developed by writers Hemar, Tom, and Włast into a harried family man (with wife Malcia, son Hipek, and daughter Mincia) and a wry, home-grown philosopher.[34] Though his songs include the occasional grammatical mistakes and malapropisms of a semi-acculturated Jew, his language never devolves into *żydlaczenie,* a Polish "broken by Yiddish" that was often used for anti-Semitic caricature. Instead, as Jurandot vividly remembers, Lopek became an audience favourite, a new kind of Varsovian everyman, whose appearance onstage usually elicited "three or four encores" during which his fans begged him to sing the songs he had made popular in previous shows.[35] "Jak się nie ma, co się lubi …" was one of his signature pieces:

"Jak się nie ma, co się lubi, to się lubi, co się ma"
Spartańska skromność dla mężczyzy jest ozdobą
Filozof Schopenfeld tak rzekł, czy któryś tam
Więc jak czasami zastanawiam się nad sobą
To ja podziwiam, jaki skromny jestem sam

Ja się nie drapię, ja się nie wspinam nad poziomu
Ja nie zazdraszczam się z innymi, co by mieć.
Niech inny prosię i łososie żre w swym domu.
A mnie wystarczy trochę farfy łachy śledź.
Ja może tyż bym lubił pić, podpuszczać pasa
Od braci Hirschfeld jeść sałatkę z ananasa.
No ale trudno, trza to życie brać
Żeby wiedzieć, czy mnie stać.
Jak się nie ma co się lubi
To się lubi, co się ma.
Z te zasadę spać się kładę
Co się tyczy moje ja
Może nawet bardzo lubię
Jadać stek w Myśliwskim Klubie
Ale chętniej jem potrawy,
Które Malcia we mnie pcha.
Wiem, że lepsza pieczeń z wieprza
Dobra gąska nie jest zła
Jest potrawa, już podawa
Wszystko jedno ta, czy ta
Czy sędziwa trochę rybka
Czy to klops z gęsiego pipka
Jak się nie ma, co się lubi,
To się lubi, co się ma.
Nie jestem Wenus, Jerzy Marr czy inny Brodzisz
Przeciętny człowiek, bez pretensji co do płeć,
Ale przypuśćmy, że pan sobie chodzisz,
Pan widzisz kobiet, pan masz chęci, co do mieć.
I Sokołowska, Pogorzelska, Ordonówna
Te nóżki, buźki, pan zachwyca się co krok.
A w domu Malcia, jak pan w myśli je porówna
Z tą moją Malcią, moim wrogom taki rok.
Ja może tyż bym chciał romansik mieć na boku,
Być Dulcynejem, Desdemonem, ujdę w tłoku.
No ale trudno, tak to życie trzeba brać
Żeby wiedzieć, czy mnie stać.
Jak się nie ma, co się lubi
To się lubi, co się ma.
Z te zasadę spać się kładę
Przy mnie leży Malcia ma.
Może, w gruncie rzeczy, wolę
Gretę Garbo, Negri Polę,
Ale biorę o tę porę
Nawet to, co Malcia da.
Wiem, to nie jest amecyje
Nie jest to, co ja bym pragł.
Już nie mówię, co do ilość,

Wręcz przeciwnie, co do smak.
Co mam zrobić, chociaż widzę
Jeszcze sobie sam obrzydzę.
Jak się nie ma, co się lubi
To się lubi, co się ma.

"If you don't have what you want, then you want what you have"[36]
Spartan modesty becomes a man,
So Schopenfeld or someone else once said.
And when I sometimes think about myself,
I'm amazed of what modesty I'm made.
I don't try to climb above my station.
I don't envy others who have more.
So what if they pig out on ham and salmon,
And I make do with herring as before.
Perhaps I'd like to drink and stuff myself
With pineapple salad from Hirschfelds.
Yes, it's tough, but life is hard.
You know what you can afford.
If you don't have what you wanted,
Then you want just what you've got.
It's my motto when I go to bed.
It will always be my lot.
Though I might like to dine at the Hunter's Club
And feast on their juicy steaks,
I'd rather shovel in the dishes
That my Malcia always makes.
I know roast pork is better
And a good goose is hard to beat.
But if there's food that's on the table,
There's no difference what I eat.
Be it fish of second freshness
Or minced meat from a goose's ass,
If you don't have what you wanted,
Then you want whatever will pass.
I'm no Venus, Jerzy Marr, or other Hunklieb,
A normal guy, with no reasons to complain.
But let's say that you're out walking,
You see some women, you feel a pain.
And Sokołowska, Pogorzelska, Ordonówna –
Their legs, their lips weaken you in the knees.
At home is Malcia, and that option
I'd only wish on my enemies.
Maybe I'd have liked a little romance,
A Dulcineum or Desdemonem.
Yes, it's tough, but life is hard.
You know what you can afford

If you don't have what you wanted,
Then you want what you can keep.
It's my motto when I go to bed,
Where my Malcia's fast asleep.
Truth to tell, I'd rather be with
Greta Garbo or Pola Negri,
But at bedtime I will settle
For whatever Malcia gives me.
I know this is no great bargain,
It's not something I might have chased.
I'm not even talking numbers,
But a simple matter of taste.
What can I do, although I see this?
I'm disgusted with myself.
If you don't have what you wanted,
Then you want what's on the shelf.

Though Krukowski himself came from an upper-middle-class Jewish family, had trained as a classical tenor and had earned the reputation of a big city *bon vivante* (fine diner, fancy dresser, owner of racehorses), he instantly evoked Lopek and his milieu onstage through his costume (bowler hat, rumpled gabardine coat, greasepaint mustache), his beleaguered or bemused expression, and the low-pitched, nasal voice with which he sang his shopkeeper's songs. Lopek approached the audience as friends in whom he could confide or before whom he could vent his frustrations; his appearance simply resumed an ongoing conversation. In the one recording of this song that I have been able to access, Krukowski talks through the three-stanza verse and then sings the four-stanza refrain in a sprightly, knowing way, as if Lopek is gamely resigned to his fate.

"Jak się nie ma, co się lubi, to się lubi, co się ma" does bear linguistic and cultural markers of Lopek's semi-acculturated Jewishness, as do other *szmonces* songs, which were written to articulate the opinions and impressions of lower-middle-class Jewish Varsovians.[37] Tom inserts occasional grammatical mistakes in his character's Polish (e.g., incorrectly conjugated verbs, verbs followed by direct or indirect objects incorrectly declined, the mispronunication of *też* as *tyż*). Also, Lopek signals his confusion over high-culture references when he attributes a maxim about male modesty to the nonexistent philosopher "Schopenfeld" and mixes up genders in comparing *himself* to Venus, Dulcinea, and Desdemona (the last two are affixed with incorrect masculine endings). He garbles the French term "parfait au lait" as "farfy łachy," using this froufrou term to describe herring in sour cream, and he cites one Yiddish word, "metziah," rendered here as "amecyje," which refers to a great bargain or "a steal."

But unlike other *szmonces* songs intended to showcase the nonsensical social ambitions of the Jewish *petit bourgeoisie*, "Jak się nie ma, co się lubi, to się lubi, co się ma" demonstrates Lopek's clear understanding of the big-city luxuries that he desires but cannot afford. In this regard, Tom's lyrics exemplify the more nuanced, sympathetic handling of *szmonces* characters by the Jewish writers for the Polish-language literary cabaret. Lopek's dilemma stems not from his Jewishness but from his more general predicament as a down-at-heels Varsovian, an aspiring modern man who simply does not have the means to enjoy the latest, best goods advertised in the capital. It is important to note that the same character who waxes vague about Venus can list the correct names of Warsaw's current establishments (the Hirschfeld Brothers, the Hunter's Club) and Polish and foreign movie stars. Lopek is a fully literate student of the city. Moreover, though Krukowski sings the song as written, grammatical mistakes and all, his Polish diction is impeccable. The relationship between singer and song here is tricky: only Krukowski could play Lopek, but Lopek was inevitably filtered through the audience's familiarity with Krukowski's wit, self-awareness, and showmanship. Lopek, like Pikuś, a dandyish, voluble cabaret persona incarnated by Józef Ursteinin (1884–1923) in the early 1920s, was a Jewish character with whom the entire audience could identify.

Lopek's city-literate philosophy is, predictably enough, about the gap between his desires and his real choices as a consumer of food and sex. Religion and politics are conspicuously absent. In both verses Lopek proves to his urbane audience that he can specify what is on offer – be it salmon, steak, and pineapples or (Zula) Pogorzelska, Greta Garbo, and Pola Negri. The lyrics lead the listeners by the nose, first encouraging their sense of superiority to (and pity for) Lopek with regard to food, then reminding them of the universal pitfalls of consumer desire. In the second verse, Lopek presumes greater familiarity with the men in the audience, asking them to imagine the female stars who drive them wild: "Pan widzisz kobiet, pan masz chęci, co do mieć." It is the business of capitalism to sell stage shows and films via sexual fantasies that can never be realized, only re-viewed. The references to female cabaret bombshells transform this verse into meta-commentary and an implicit tease, with the male patrons restricted to seats in the house while Lopek/Krukowski enjoys more intimate proximity to Pogorzelska and Ordonówna. By the third repetition of the song's title, its axiom serves as a perfect ending *pointe*, demonstrating that Lopek's make-do world view holds true for all.

The Cabaret Song on the Road

In interwar Warsaw, cabaret songs fused "world-class" popular music with sophisticated lyrics for interpretation by talented singer/actors. The song and its singer existed in a fascinating symbiosis. A great song could transform its interpreter into a star; stars, in turn, could mark a song with their imprint, as a condensed comedy/drama about their character's experience, lifestyle, or philosophy. The cabaret song as performance or character illustration fulfilled multiple functions in such theatres as *Qui Pro Quo*: it entertained the audience, informed them about the latest news and fashions, introduced them to the diverse *commedia dell'arte* of the city, and cultivated an informal camaraderie between performers and patrons. Bedazzled by their intimacy with the stars, the audience interacted with a multi-ethnic, cross-class, thoroughly emancipated metropolis – a metropolis that persisted onstage until the German–Soviet invasion in September 1939.

Near the end of *A History of Laughter*, Jurandot writes that interwar cabaret songs did not disappear with their engendering context. After the Second World War, Jurandot learned that a 1938 collection of his songs titled *Niedobrze, Panie Bobrze* (after one of his hits) travelled with Polish prisoners into Nazi Germany:

> Individual copies made their way into the West as well as the Far East. They cropped up in soldiers' barracks, prisoner of war camps, and even concentration camps. The young actor Włodzimierz Skoczylas (1923–93) told me about their first sad Christmas Eve in Buchenwald. Desperate to shake off their mood of gloom and despair, Skoczylas tried reciting the

funniest texts in the collection. "And it worked, you see. For a short time we forgot where we were and even laughed … It was then I understood what power there is in words, and I decided to become an actor."[38]

Skoczylas's testimony, echoed by many others, demonstrates how the cabaret song endured and had an enormous impact on its listeners, even as a verbal text outside an actual cabaret. The texts alone were sufficient to evoke the cabaret's atmosphere and to connect those listeners who remembered the melodies with a playful, comical show. Equally important was the survival of dozens of cabaret artists. Though the vast majority of Jewish actors and musicians were murdered by the Nazis in the ghettos and concentration camps, other artists (both Jewish and Gentile) managed to flee east into Soviet occupied territory – among them, Henryk Wars, Jerzy Petersburski, Henryk Gold, Konrad Tom, Kazimierz Krukowski, Ludwik Lawiński (1887–1971), Hanka Ordonówna (1902–50), and Zofia Terné (1909–87). These refugees were recruited into the theatre revue units embedded in the Polish II Corps (also known as the Anders Army), which formed in the Soviet Union in 1941 and trekked through Iran, Iraq, Syria, Mandate Palestine, and Egypt before joining the 1944 Allied invasion of Italy.

The shows performed by these wartime units benefited immensely from the participation of these experienced professionals, who had to deal with makeshift stages, lack of costumes and sets, and often minimal musical accompaniment. Stars like Krukowski/Lopek, whom a mass public might know from films, were national celebrities who impressed both military and civilian, Polish and foreign viewers with their stage *savoir faire* and improvisational skills. New songs, co-created like their interwar counterparts, carried out similar functions with more sincerity than insouciance – apprising soldiers of recent news of war (usually through broad caricatures), venting comically about local discomforts (sandstorms, desert heat, vermin, army rations), and deciphering such modern phenomena as women in uniform (civilians who had joined the Polish Women's Auxiliary).

These artists made a different impact, however, when they reprised prewar songs about the capital. The theatre revue units were performing for a distinctly *un*cosmopolitan public – for young men who had been deported from the towns and villages of eastern Poland. Most of these enlisted men likely had never set foot in Warsaw, let alone a Warsaw cabaret. In lieu of reassembling the city's rambunctious cast of characters, from emancipated shopgirls to acculturating Jewish shopkeepers, the Warsaw artists chose material that gave the soldiers a sentimental Warsaw education, invoking a capital filled with beautiful or glamorous sites (the Saxon Gardens, Łazienki Palace, the fashionable streets of Nowy Świat and Marszałkowska) and tempting amenities (cafés, cabarets, flower vendors). During the war, prewar cabaret songs, as well as new songs embellishing on the artists' homesickness for their city, taught soldier audiences to cherish their capital symbolically and to savour it materially, rendering it as a kind of earthly paradise (one that would soon be destroyed by Nazi vengeance and Soviet collusion). I note here that these nostalgic songs sanitized the city even as they beautified it, admitting none of Warsaw's dark realities – the desperate poverty of many of its residents, the rising fascism, and the anti-Semitic attacks and boycotts that targeted Jews almost everywhere *but* in the cabaret.

After the war, cabaret artists continued to write and perform songs, though their location vis-à-vis the Iron Curtain determined what they wrote and for whom. Many of those connected with the II Corps' theatre units were marooned in Great Britain, denied citizenship in the new Polish People's Republic, and thus relegated to performing for their fellow refugees. Their situation worsened when Britain's theatre unions, feeling the pinch of the postwar economy, prohibited the Poles' use of available venues.[39] Polish London could not become a surrogate Warsaw, and Polish refugees were not reliable patrons, preoccupied as they were with finding homes and jobs. The one artist who cobbled together a long-term career on the Polonian stage in Britain was Hemar. He had evacuated to London in 1941, well before the II Corps' arrival, and from 1942 until the late 1960s he regularly produced shows that featured sharp political satire and employed other gifted cabaret artists in exile, perhaps most notably the Lwów singing star Włada Majewska (1911–2011). Hemar succeeded because he was a first-rate lyricist, a good composer, and a natural polemicist. His shows for Polonia accurately gauged and played to his audiences' changing life interests. In the meantime, in his one-man "Cabaret of Marian Hemar," a fifteen-minute weekly feature broadcast on Radio Free Europe, the satirist entertained listeners in Poland as he skewered the Polish government with his biting versified commentaries. Hemar did not truck in nostalgia, but in politics and the present.

In contrast, Feliks Konarski (1907–91), the lyricist best known as "Ref-Ren," pledged his loyalty and talent to past patrons who had become friends. Konarski and his wife, the comedienne Nina Oleńska (1903–83), had only moderate success as performing artists before the war, but they soon became the favourites of the II Corps' rank and file. This kindly, modest lyricist often produced songs by personal request, as his memoirs reiterate; he wrote quickly and with genuine sentiment, clear sympathy for the homesick and frustrated enlisted man, and few stylistic surprises.[40] Oleńska, in turn, played the hapless, overwhelmed, funny, and sharp-tongued "Volunteer Helenka," a character she had developed with her husband. Volunteer Helenka boosted the morale of soldiers and female volunteers with songs complaining about army red tape or pondering her inadequate love life. Settling in London after the war, Konarski and Oleńska immediately began touring Polish military bases and, eventually, towns where II Corps veterans had settled, always ready to reminisce and comfort. By the 1950s their tours had expanded to include big cities in the United States and Canada.

In 1965 the couple relocated to Chicago, where there was a huge Polish American community, at the invitation of local poet Zbigniew Chałko (1921–94). Besides performing on the road, Konarski, like Hemar, ventured into radio, with the primary goal of remembering and entertaining rather than launching brilliant political polemics. Konarski's weekly show, titled "Czerwone maki na Monte Cassino" (Red Poppies on Monte Cassino) after the enormously popular war anthem that he and composer Alfred Schuetz had written in 1944, functioned for twenty-five years as an oasis of Polish-language nostalgia and good popular music for several generations of Polish Americans. Ref-Ren composed new numbers for his performers about everyday topics and new fads. As poet and reviewer Tamara Karren (1913–97) correctly observes, he and his wife entrenched themselves "as a kind of institution": "For us, the older, so-called wartime generation, Ref-Ren is both a symbol and a living link connecting our get-togethers with our memories, both good and bad."[41]

Though most of the members of this wartime generation would not witness it, Warsaw's heritage as a generator of cabaret song – particularly about itself and its residents – persisted through the first two decades after the war. Those who had survived the war in Poland, artists such as Jurandot and his wife, the writer and dancer Stefania Grodzieńska (1914–2010), returned to the decimated capital as soon as its rebuilding allowed them to do so. *Teatr Syrena* (The Siren Theatre), which these survivors provisionally created in

Łódź, moved to Warsaw in 1948, with the optimistic intent to continue the *Qui Pro Quo* tradition despite a drastically changing political climate. By the latter half of the 1950s, after the Polish October, such important players as Krukowski and Petersburski were permitted and willing to repatriate. *Syrena* reunited the remaining stars of the prewar constellation and encouraged their performances of prewar signature songs, as long as these did not explicitly support the prewar regime. *Syrena*'s writers, composers, and performers focused their repertoire mainly on light satire about Varsovians' daily lives – their desires, challenges, and increasing cultural contacts with the world at large. Of course, any songs written about the capital's destruction and slow restoration carefully avoided mention of the Home Army, the particulars of the 1944 uprising, and ideological clashes between the forces competing to liberate the city.

As evidenced by the publication of Jurandot and Krukowski's memoirs in the late 1950s, the song-performances developed in the prewar Polish-language literary cabaret had become a treasured national art form and a productive model for future variations. The cabaret song's synthesis of deft lyrics, enhancing music, and often understated, emotionally trenchant delivery had been adapted with great success for very different stages under very different sociopolitical circumstances. The stage could be a truck bed or a parish hall; what mattered most was the singer's dramatic ability and intensely engaged, improvisational relationship with the audience. As many artists discovered during and after the war, one could take the song out of the physical cabaret, but one could never remove the cabaret's performing ethos from the song.

Beth Holmgren
Duke University

NOTES

1 These last were *Banda* (The Band, 1931–3), *Cyganeria* (Bohemia, 1933–4), *Stara Banda* (The Old Band, 1934), *Cyrulik Warszawski* (The Barber of Warsaw, 1935–9), and *Mały Qui Pro Quo* (Little Qui Pro Quo, 1937–9). Tomasz Stępień lists this line-up in his study *Kabaret Juliana Tuwima*, 6. Fox, in *Kabarety i rewie*, 214, provides this information about the seating in *Qui Pro Quo*, counting 136 rows and 10 loggias.
2 Jurandot, *Dzieje śmiechu*, 10–11.
3 See Tadeusz Boy-Żeleński's rave review of one of Jurandot's shows in *1001 Noc Teatru. Wrażeń teatralnych seria osiemnasta* (Warsaw: Państwowy Instytut Wydawniczy, 1975), 561. The original review appeared in *Kurier Poranny*, 31 May 1938.
4 Fox, *Kabarety i rewie*, 13; Segel, *Turn-of-the-Century Cabaret*, 225–50.
5 Krukowski, *Moja Warszawka*, 65.
6 Peter Jelavich locates Tingeltangel shows at the bottom of the urban entertainment hierarchy – "with its risque songs and women wandering through the audience selling naughty postcards or making assignations." Jelavich, *Berlin Cabaret*, 21.
7 On the New York cabarets of this period, see Erenberg, *Steppin' Out*, 122–6.
8 Jelavich, *Berlin Cabaret*, 81–3, 143–5.
9 Groński, *Jak w przedwojennym kabarecie*, 40; Fox, *Kabarety i rewie*, 51.
10 See, especially, the introduction to Dynner and Guesnet, eds., *Warsaw: The Jewish Metropolis*, 1–16. For Yiddish-speaking Jews, the most innovative Yiddish-language

kleynkunst theatre, Ararat, was based in Łódź; Yiddish cabaret arrived later in the capital, when director/actor Dovid Herman opened the cabaret Azazel. Sandrow, *Vagabond Stars*, 323–4, 325–8; Gross, "Mordechai Gebirtig," 109.

11 Hamm, *Yesterdays*, 329, 332, 345–6.
12 Jurandot, *Dzieje śmiechu*, 19.
13 Modras, "The Interwar Polish Catholic Press on the Jewish Question," 182.
14 Jurandot, *Dzieje śmiechu*, 18.
15 Czesław Miłosz, *The History of Polish Literature*, 387.
16 See, for example, Boy-Żeleński's review of *Qui Pro Quo*'s premiere; *Flirt z Melpomeną*, 607–8. The original text appeared in *Kurier codzienny*, 18 September 1926.
17 Stępień, *Kabaret Julian Tuwima*, 12, 274–5.
18 Mieszkowska, *Ja kabareciarz*, 21, 28, 32, 33, 60.
19 Groński, *Jak w przedwojennym kabarecie,* 8–9.
20 See Furia, *The Poets of Tin Pan Alley*.
21 Jurandot, *Dzieje śmiechu*, 14.
22 Groński, *Jak w przedwojennym kabarecie,* 67.
23 Backlash against the Polish-language literary cabaret's "Jewishness" was predictable. Fox reports that the right-wing nationalist publication *Merkeriusz polski* damned cabaret writers as a "mafia" that excluded Gentiles. *Kabarety i rewie*, 197.
24 Krukowski, *Moja Warszawka,* 80–1.
25 Fox, *Kabarety i rewie,* 199–200.
26 Zimińska-Sygietyńska, *Nie żyłam samotnie*, 87.
27 Krukowski, *Moja Warszawka,* 93.
28 Ruttkowski, "Cabaret Songs," 3–4, 25, 45.
29 Ibid., 47, 50.
30 Mieszkowska, *Ja kabareciarz,* 40.
31 Jurandot, *Dzieje śmiechu,* 25.
32 Wołański, *Już nie zapomnisz mnie*, 76.
33 Jurandot, *Dzieje śmiechu,* 23.
34 Krukowski, *Moja Warszawska,* 81, 73.
35 Jurandot, *Dzieje śmiechu,* 9–10.
36 My very imperfect English translation, with the expert help of Madeline Levine.
37 For more on what constitutes *szmonces,* see Uścińska, "Elegia Starozakonna." See also Fox, *Kabarety i rewie,*168, 170–4; and Groński, *Jak w przedwojennym kabarecie,* 44–6.
38 Jurandot, *Dzieje śmiechu,* 143.
39 Krukowski, *Z Melpomeną na emigracyj*, 96.
40 Konarski, *Piosenki z plecaka Helenki.*
41 Tamara Karren, "Ref-Ren – piosenkarz i kronikarz naszego losu," *Tydzień polski,* 20 lipca 1985.

WORKS CITED

Boy-Żeleński, Tadeusz. *Flirt z Mełpomeną. Wieczór siódmy i ósmy.* In *Pisma,* vol. 22. 607–8. Warszawa: Państwowy Instytut Wydawniczy, 1965.

– *1001 Noc Teatru. Wrażeń teatralnych seria osiemnasta*. 561. Warszawa: Państwowy Instytut Wydawniczy, 1975.

Dynner, Glenn, and François Guesnet, eds. *Warsaw: The Jewish Metropolis: Essays in Honor of the 75th Birth of Professor Antony Polonsky.* Leiden: Brill, 2015.
Erenberg, Lewis A. *Steppin' Out: New York Nightlife and the Transformation of American Culture, 1890–1930.* Westport: Greenwood Press, 1981.
Fox, Dorota. *Kabarety i rewie międzywojennej Warszawy.* Katowice: Wydawnictwo Śląsk, 2007.
Furia, Philip. *The Poets of Tin Pan Alley: A History of America's Great Lyricists.* Oxford: Oxford University Press, 1990.
Hamm, Charles. *Yesterdays: Popular Song in America.* New York: W.W. Norton, 1979.
Jelavich, Peter. *Berlin Cabaret.* Cambridge, MA: Harvard University Press, 1993.
Jurandot, Jerzy. *Dzieje śmiechu.* Warszawa: Iskra, 1959.
Groński, Ryszard Marek. *Jak w przedwojennym kabarecie. Kabaret warszawski, 1918–1939.* Warszawa: Warszawskie Wydawnictwo Artystyczne i Filmowe, 1978.
Gross, Natan. "Mordechai Gebirtig: The Folk Song and the Cabaret Song." *POLIN* 16 (109). 107–17.
Karren, Tamara. "Ref-Ren – piosenkarz i kronikarz naszego losu." *Tydzień polski,* 20 July 1985.
Konarski, Feliks. *Piosenki z plecaka Helenki (z nutami).* Rzym: Nakladem Autora, 1946.
Krukowski, Kazimierz. *Moja Warszawka.* Warszawa: Filmowa Agencja Wydawnicza, 1957.
– *Z Melpomeną na emigracji.* Warszawa: Czytelnik, 1987.
Mieszkowska, Anna. *Ja kabareciarz. Marian Hemar od Lwowa do Londynu.* Warszawa: Warszawskie Wydawnictwo Literackie MUZA, 2006.
Miłosz, Czesław. *The History of Polish Literature.* New York: Macmillan, 1969.
Modras, Ronald. "The Interwar Polish Catholic Press on the Jewish Question." *Annals of the American Academy of Political and Social Sciences* 548 (1996): 182.
Ruttkowski, Wolfgang. "Cabaret Songs" *Popular Music and Society* 25, nos. 3–4 (2001): 45.
Sandrow, Nahma. *Vagabond Stars: A World History of Yiddish Theater.* New York: Harper & Row, 1977.
Segel, Harold B. *Turn-of-the-Century Cabaret. Paris, Barcelona, Berlin, Munich, Vienna, Cracow, Moscow, St. Petersburg, Zurich.* New York: Columbia University Press, 1987.
Stephan, Halina. *Mrożek.* Kraków: Wydawnictwo Literackie, 1996.
Stępień, Tomasz. *Kabaret Juliana Tuwima.* Katowice: Wydawnictwo Śląsk, 1989.
Uścińska, Agnieszka. "Elegia Starozakonna, czyli szmonces w kulturze polskiej jako żart z pogranicza kultur." In *Jaki Jest Kabaret.* Edited by Dorota Fox and Jacek Mikołajczyk. Katowice: Oficyna Wydawnicza, Uniwersytet Śląski, 2012.
Wołański, Ryszard. *Już nie zapomnisz mnie. Opowieść o Henryku Warsie.* Warszawa: Wydawnictwo Literackie MUZA SA, 2010.
Zimińska-Sygietyńska, Mira. *Nie żyłam samotnie.* Edited by Mieczysław Sroka. Warszawa: Wydawnictwa Artystyczne i Filmowe, 1985.

LITERATURE IN LANGUAGES OTHER THAN POLISH

Polish Literature and Its Languages

Let us begin with a question: To what extent has Polish literature been multicultural?

Compared to multilingual and multicultural world literatures, the status of Polish literature seems relatively simple: it is written in one language and mostly in one country, and it is usually called Polish without special reservations. For successive generations of writers and poets, the Polish language was a singular tool in their struggle to maintain their cultural identity during the years of Poland's political non-existence. In the Slavonic group of languages, Polish is somewhat unique in that it has been continuously used in literature since the fifteenth century. However, there have been many important exceptions to this rule over the ages that are worth presenting and examining, both to bring together what is usually discussed apart and to try to situate individual cases in broader contexts. While bilingualism is not common among Polish writers, some literary works have been composed in a different language by authors writing mainly in Polish. Also, Poland has always had bicultural writers who used Polish along with another language, or even two, in their work. These exceptions are worth noting for two other reasons: to introduce foreigners to a "minor" literature that was at times originally composed in their own "major" language (such as French, English, German, Russian, and Spanish, not to mention the once universal Latin), and to obtain a different perspective on Poland's supposedly univocal national literature, whose languages are as diverse as Polish, Yiddish, and Lithuanian.

I. The Latin Universum

Historically, the first eminent example of biculturalism in Polish literature came with the so-called Polish-Latin poets, who established a universal language culture that enabled unrestricted literary communication between Poland and Europe and that created a common cultural code that lasted for centuries. These poets, some of them foreigners residing in Poland, initially wrote only in Latin (from the twelfth to the fifteenth century), and later also in Polish (from the fifteenth to the seventeenth century). The Latin language enabled all European writers to belong to a single cultural centre, in which some Polish-Latin authors were especially successful: the title *poëta laureatus* was awarded in Rome to, for instance, Jan Dantyszek (Dantiscus, 1485–1548), Klemens Janicki (Janicius, 1516–43), and Maciej Kazimierz Sarbiewski (Sarbievius, 1595–1640). Since they used a universal language, their aims were different from those of later Polish authors. Polish-Latin poets were not motivated by the need to introduce their texts to the European mainstream, for they were present there without translation. Rather, they were acting on a growing need to create their own cultural centre with its own literary language.

One could say, with some irony and mostly in jest, that Polish literature's dilemma of how to function in the world was born from the great effort of the bilingual Jan Kochanowski (1530–84), Poland's leading Renaissance poet. Kochanowski strove to establish and shape Polish as a literary language. He began his career in Latin as the author of *odae*, *elegiae*, and *foricoenia*, and he took his cue to adapt Polish to the needs of sophisticated literary usage from Polish-Latin poets who wrote in both languages – for example, Władysław from Gielniów (ca. 1440–1505) – and from the first writer to use only Polish in his work: Mikołaj Rej (1505–69). It was in great measure his success in the endeavour that set Polish literature on its own track, for better and for worse. He must have been aware of the role that Pierre Ronsard, the leader of the French "La Pléiade," played at that time in promoting the "enrichment" of the French language, and thus in laying the foundations for the World Republic of Literature operating in French, as Pascal Casanova claims.[1] It was on his way back from Italy that Kochanowski jotted down "Ronsardum vidi," a curious and remarkable note – the only one of its kind among Kochanowski's Italian–French travel jottings. There can be no doubt, at any rate, that Kochanowski was deeply engaged in promoting the Polish language, given that he created some of the founding works of Polish literature both in poetry and in drama. Polish literature's problems with marketing are due not only to the shift to a national language but also to its inability to create a sustainable cultural centre for itself.

In the discourse on Polish literary culture, which is understandably focused on writing in Polish, the significance of Latin as one of Poland's literary languages is all too easily forgotten. Yet Latin for a long time was an important part of Poland's European cultural heritage. Sarbiewski, the above-mentioned seventeenth-century star of European poetry and poetics, composed only one sermon in Polish, which suggests that he belonged to the Latin European culture more than to his native one. Yet he functioned in both centres – the papal court as well as the royal court in Poland – and thus played a crucial role in the Polish as well as the European literary system. His books of Latin lyrics were widely disseminated, published in Köln, Vilnius, and Antwerp (the latter, published in 1632, was adorned with graphics by Peter Paul Rubens), and they were commented on both in Poland and abroad. His role in the educational system of the Polish–Lithuanian Commonwealth also cannot be overestimated: Sarbiewski was a professor of theology and rhetoric at the Vilnius Academy. One of the names he acquired during his long career – Horatius Sarmaticus – seems to acknowledge his bicultural competencies.

Starting in the late fifteenth century, Polish-Latin authors began to function more regularly in two languages and thus in two cultural spheres: the peripheral Polish and the central Latin. Szymon Szymonowic (1558–1629), for instance, was known mostly for his pastoral idylls – *sielanka* – to which he gave the still current name (with roots in Ruthenian), and which he endowed with a realistic tone unprecedented in the genre's earlier Polish examples. Szymonowic (Simonides) was also known, however, as Pindarus Polonus: the author of eminent Latin poems published by a prestigious publishing house in Leyden in 1619, and of *Ioel Propheta*, which was awarded a poetical laurel wreath by Pope Clement VIII.

It is crucial to bear in mind here that Latin was a living language for generations of Polish writers up to the second half of the twentieth century. Commonly taught at schools and universities, it was a basic tool for acquiring essential philological and cultural competencies and for entering Polish literary life. For example, Henryk Sienkiewicz (1846–1916), the 1905 Nobel Prize laureate known for his historical and realist novels, which have been translated into many languages, himself translated Horace into Polish, a fact not widely known. The same can be said about Poland's famous twentieth-century poet Julian Tuwim (1894–1953), who is mostly known as a translator from modern European languages rather than from "dead" Latin. Tuwim would at times include Latin phrases in his Polish poems, sometimes jokingly, as in the poem "Lekcja" (Lesson), and sometimes more seriously, as in the poem "Nad Cezarem" (On Caesar), but always with strong feeling for the language of classical literature and philosophy.

Czesław Miłosz (1911–2004) is yet another example of the importance of Latin for modern Polish poets. By way of education, it was Latin rather than French or English that became the 1980 Nobel Prize laureate's first foreign language, and it was translations from Latin that shaped his sensibilities as a translator and teacher. As he admitted in conversations with Ewa Czarnecka, he based his educational ideas on his own Latin lessons. He always emphasized the significance of Latin for his humanistic education and literary tastes.[2] Like Tuwim (and many other Polish poets, Zbigniew Herbert among them), Miłosz included Latin phrases in his poems. An Epicurean epitaph, "non fui, fui, non sum, non desidero" (I was not, I was, I am not, I do not desire), plays an important role in his long cycle *Gdzie wschodzi słońce i kędy zapada* (From the Rising of the Sun, 1974).[3] That cycle points to the importance of Latin for Miłosz and also to his longing for Lithuanian. In part VII, "Bells in Winter," Miłosz introduces the choirmaster who:

Wchodząc na stopnie, śpiewa: Introibo ad altare Dei.	Ascending the stairs sings: Introibo ad altare Dei.
Ad Deum qui laetificat iuventutem meam.	Ad Deam qui laetificat jouventuem meam
Prie Dievo, kurs linksmina mano jaunystė	Prie Dievo kurs linksmina mano jaunystė.
Mano jaunystė.	Mano janustė.
Moja młodość.	My youth.
Jak długo w obrzędzie	As long as I perform the rite
Chwieję kadzielnicą i wzbija się dym	And sway the censer and the smoke of my words
Tych moich słów.	Rises here.
(Miłosz, Gdzie wschodzi słońce i kędy zapada, 71)	(Miłosz, New and Collected Poems 1931–2001, 329–330)

The words come from the opening prayer of the Latin Tridentine Mass: "I will go up to the altar of God, to God who is the joy of my youth," with the second part of the line repeated in Lithuanian. They express Miłosz's sense of being at home as a poet in both the universal (Latin) and the bicultural (Polish-Lithuanian) Christian world.

II. Literary Languages of the Minorities and the Polish Cultural Centre

Another of Miłosz's poems provides some insight into the complicated language situation of the Polish–Lithuanian Commonwealth, which is one more factor to consider when discussing linguistic and multicultural aspects of Polish literature. In his "Filologia" (Philology), Miłosz evokes a seventeenth-century Jesuit, Konstatny Szyrwid (Širvydas, ca. 1579–1631), who was the author of the first Lithuanian–Latin–Polish dictionary. Latin functions in the poem as a much needed medium between Lithuanian and Polish for Polish poets, who did not usually know Lithuanian. While Miłosz liked to present himself as a Lithuanian, he never wrote in Lithuanian and had little command of the language, though some of his fellow world poets and interpreters believed his self-identification was also linguistic. The case was similar with Adam Mickiewicz (1798–1855), who opened Poland's national Romantic epos *Pan Tadeusz* (Sir Thaddeus, 1834) with the famous invocation to "Lithuania, My Country!" There was no false note in such gestures, since Lithuania was a natural part of the Res Publica of Two Nations, as the Polish–Lithuanian Commonwealth was also called. After the eighteenth-century partitions of Poland, the sentiment for Lithuania continued to be cherished, and only intensified after Poland was subjected to Soviet rule after the Second World War. Miłosz's "Philology" references other Polish writers with roots in Lithuania – "Mr. Norwid" and "Mr. Gombrowicz, both from Samogitia" (Żmudż in Polish, Žemaitija in Lithuanian) – and also acknowledges that "No one among the bards returned to the speech of the ancestors."[4]

Lithuanian writers not only usually shared the two cultures but also used both languages. Again, we could ask what the label "Lithuanian writer" means, and again, the instinctive answer is that it indicates someone who writes in Lithuanian and/or who regards himself/herself as a Lithuanian author. Thus Miłosz could call himself a Lithuanian but not a Lithuanian poet, since he did not create in Lithuanian. It is noteworthy that Polish functioned in Lithuania as a literary language until at least the twentieth century. The already mentioned Szyrwid, for instance, published a bilingual Polish–Lithuanian edition of sermons. The list of authors who wrote in both languages also includes the Romantic man of letters Dionizy Paszkiewicz (Dionizas Poška, 1757–1830), mentioned by Mickiewicz in his epics, as well as the Romantic poets Antoni Klement (Antanas Klementas, 1756–1823) and Sylwester Walenowicz (Silvestras Valiūnas, 1789–1831),[5] and "the creator of Lithuanian expressionism" Józef Albin Herbaczewski (Juozapas Albinas Herbačiauskas, 1876–1944).[6] Sometimes Polish was the primary literary language of Lithuanian writers. The elder Iwanowska sister– Zofia – would translate the Polish poems and short stories of her younger sister Maria into Lithuanian (later, Maria began to create and publish in Lithuanian too). Karolina Proniewska (Karolina Praniauskaitė, 1828–59), who is called "the first Lithuanian poetess," composed her poems in Polish (*Piosneczki*, 1858) and translated them from Polish into Lithuanian. Some of her translations are said to have had an unprecedented impact on Lithuanian culture as fundamental works of Lithuanian high art.[7] In some sense, then, the Polish language, while peripheral from a broad European perspective, at times played the role of a cultural centre from a specifically *Eastern* European perspective.

This was the case not only for Lithuanian poets and writers but also for Ukrainian ones. As late as the end of the nineteenth century, the leading Ukrainian writer and poet Ivan Franko (1856–1916) published two novels in Polish: *Lelum i Polelum* (Lelum and Polelum, 1888) and *Dla ogniska domowego* (For the Hearth and Home, 1892). Polish also became the literary language of some minorities, for example the Tatars (who sometimes used Arabic as the language of religious practice, particularly in set phrases).[8] Some Tatar poets use Polish to this day, Selim Chazbijewicz and Musa Czachorowski being two prominent examples. The mostly oral Roma literature also found an avenue for expression in Polish when Jerzy Ficowski recorded and then translated poems by Papusza (Bronisława Wajs, 1910–87), who is now regarded as the greatest Roma poetess. Before he published them in the early 1950s, her poems existed only in oral form and in her notes (in both Roma and Polish). The first transcriptions and translations were far from faithful to the original with regard to verse rules, wording, and phrasing, as modern interpreters point out in an effort to "correct" culturally different texts. Nevertheless, these transcriptions and translations are preserving work that otherwise might have been completely lost.[9]

Polish Jews had established a tradition of writing in Hebrew and Yiddish by the mid-nineteenth century. Until 1939, Jewish literature, especially in Yiddish, proliferated more on Polish territories than anywhere else in the world. This was due in part to Poland's large Jewish population (3,500,000 before the Second World War) and in part to the Jewish community's success in overcoming discriminatory language rules introduced by the partitioning powers of Russia, Prussia, and Austria-Hungary. The Russian Empire was especially strict in forbidding Yiddish and Hebrew in education, publishing, and theatre.[10] The tradition of Jewish writing dates back to the Haskalah, the Jewish Enlightenment, a movement that developed in Eastern Europe in the mid-nineteenth century. Hebrew magazines began to be published, and Hebrew secular literature bloomed. Among its many authors were Josua Höschel Schorr (considered the Galician Voltaire, 1814–95) and the short story writer Mordechaj Dawid Brandstaetter (1844–1928), the grandfather of Roman Brandstaetter (1906–87), an eminent twentieth-century Polish writer of Jewish origin. The next generation of Jewish writers, connected to the Sifrut Ha'thija, wrote mostly in Hebrew. In the nineteenth century, Yiddish was regarded as a vernacular language; over time, however, it would become the most popular language of Jewish literature in Poland, and Yiddish-language works both by relatively unknown writers and by future stars of world literature – such as Sholem Asch (1880–1957), Israel Joshua Singer (1893–1944), and his brother Isaac Bashevis Singer (1902–91) – would be published by both Jewish and Polish publishers. For instance, Israel Joshua Singer's famous novel *Josie Kałb*, much appreciated by Polish writers, was first published in 1932 in Warsaw by the Jewish "Aroysgegebn durkh'n mehaberin," and later (in 1934, in Singer's self-translation) by a leading mainstream literary publisher, "Rój."

During the interwar years, Jewish writers in Poland had their own Writers' Union and their own branch of the PEN Club, along with numerous literary magazines, libraries, and publishing houses.[11] The literary debut of Nobel laureate Isaac Bashevis Singer, *A Satan from Goraj* ("De‘r śatan ‘iyn Go‘rayy"), was published by the Bibljoteka Pen-Klubu Żydowskiego (Library of the Jewish Pen Club) in 1935. Many Jewish writers also wrote in Polish. Eugenia Prokop-Janiec, in line with the criteria of the interwar epoch, defines Polish-Jewish literature as literature written in Polish but dealing with Jewish themes (thematic criterion), and literature produced by authors who identified themselves as Jewish and who manifested their connections with Jewish literature (biographical and cultural criterion).[12] A special place in the Polish-Jewish writing tradition belongs to poetical prayers that include Polish paraphrases of lines from Hebrew prayers.[13] Hebrew lines often appeared also in the titles of Polish-Jewish poems, and Jehovah's names were incorporated into poetic prayers written in Polish.[14]

From a bicultural perspective, Polish-Jewish authors who used both Polish and Yiddish (or Hebrew) in their writing, and who functioned in both Polish and Yiddish (Hebrew) literary circles, which were usually separate, are of particular interest. This was the case with Rubin (Reuwen) Feldszuh (pen names: Ben-Szem, Benshem, 1900–60), a prose writer, journalist, publisher, political activist, and teacher, who contributed to the German, Hebrew, Yiddish, and Polish-Jewish press. He published prose works in Polish (e.g., *Czerwone dusze* [Red Souls, Warszawa: "Perły," 1932]) and essays and social criticism in Yiddish, as well as memoirs, mostly in Hebrew and Yiddish, which were published in Tel-Aviv and Buenos Aires after the Second World War. Hersz Awrohem Fenster (1908–42) was another poet, prose writer, and translator who contributed to the Polish, Jewish, and Yiddish press. He published in both Polish and Yiddish: first a Polish collection of poetry *O tem, co opuszczam* (All I Am Leaving Behind [Warszawa: Dom Książki Polskiej, 1932]), then a volume of poetry in Yiddish, *Di levone gejt unter: lider* (The Moon Sets: Poems; Warshe, "Literarishe Bleter": gezect "Ejrope," 1938). Riwka (Regina) Gufrein (1908–83), a writer, journalist, teacher, literary critic, and translator (as well as a diplomatic representative of Israel in the Polish People's Republic from 1948 to 1951), made her debut in Polish in 1925 in the literary magazine *Chwila*, and published also in Hebrew in newspapers after 1934. Among her translations of Polish literary works into Hebrew were Julian Stryjkowski's novels and the poetry of Anna Kamieńska.[15] Maurycy (Mosze) Szymel (also Schimmel, Schimel, 1903–42), whose bicultural literary achievements have recently attracted scholarly attention,[16] was another poet, prose writer, translator, critic, and publicist (as well as a member of the poetic group associated with *Chwila*); he contributed to Polish, Polish-Jewish, and Yiddish papers (*Gazeta Warszawska, Ster, Hajnt, Globus, Szriftn*). In 1932 he published two collections of poetry in Polish – *Wieczór liryczny* (Lyrical Evening) and *Skrzypce przedmieścia* (The Outskirts' Violin) – and in 1937, a collection of poetry in Yiddish, *Mir iz umetik* (I am sad). He was also the author of a novel in Polish, *Gdzie jesteś Ewo?* (Where Are You Eve?), which was published in instalments in the magazine *Nowy Głos* (New Voice, 1938, nos. 44–76), and of Yiddish wartime poems that came out in 1951 in the anthology *Lid dos iz geblibn. Lider fun jidisze dichter in Pojln umgekumene bejs der hitleriszer okupacje* (The Poems of Jewish Poets Who Died in Poland during the Nazi Occupation).[17] Debora Vogel (Dvoyre Fogel, 1902–42) was yet another bicultural Jewish-Polish writer and critic, who is better known to the general Polish public due to her connections with famous artists and writers of the epoch, including Stanisław Ignacy Witkiewicz (1885–1939) and Bruno Schulz (1892–1942). Vogel was not only a literary and art critic who wrote both in Polish and Yiddish, but also the author of two Yiddish poetry collections and a collection of poetic prose that first appeared in Yiddish (*Akacjes Blien*, 1935), then in Polish self-translation as *Akacje kwitną. Montaże* (Thorn Trees Are Blooming: Montages, 1936), with illustrations by Henryk Streng (Maciej Włodarski, [1903–60], who was a student of Fernard Léger and an eminent Polish avant-garde painter of Jewish origin.[18]

III. Between Modern Languages and New Cultural Centres

Many Polish men of letters of Jewish origin, among them some of the best poets and writers of Polish literature – Bolesław Leśmian (1877–1937), Julian Tuwim, and Bruno Schulz – never wrote in Yiddish or Hebrew. This does not mean, however, that they never used other languages in their work. For instance, Bolesław Leśmian, who was born in Warsaw and spent his youth in a Russian-speaking milieu in Kiev, is famous for his youthful *Piesni Wasylisy Priemudroj* (Songs of Wasilissa the Wise, 1906–7). These poems are seen as exceptional examples of Russian-language use that is indicative of two languages and cultures without being easily reduced to either.[19] The case is only more interesting for being singular: despite this initial, aesthetically motivated creative foray into the Russian language, Leśmian later composed his poems and prose only in Polish. A leading Polish revolutionary poet, Władysław Broniewski (1897–1962), also composed some poems in Russian, although in his case the motivation was political; written in a Soviet prison, his simple, bitter poems were directed against the Soviet terror.[20]

A different political motivation was important for Bruno Jasieński (1901–38), the most eminent of Polish-Russian prose writers. His novel *I Burn Paris* appeared first in Russia[21] (as *Ja žgu Pariž*, 1928) and in France (as *Je brûle Paris*), with the Polish version (*Palę Paryż*) appearing only a year later. A polemic against Paul Morand's *Je brûle Moscou*, Jasieński's novel offered harsh social commentary and predicted a proletarian revolution that would destroy the bourgeois social order. No wonder it proved a great success in the Soviet Union, especially after Jasieński prepared a revised version in 1934 that "subordinated the material of *I Burn Paris* to the Marxist interpretation of class struggle."[22] According to legend, Jasieńki was welcomed in Leningrad by enthusiastic crowds after being expelled from France. Notably, his further writing in Russian was completely different from his previous work in Polish and in French (with much help from a translator, no doubt).[23] In Polish, Jasieński was a revolutionary Futurist poet, famous for his manifestos and experiments with language. The French and Polish versions of *I Burn Paris* (and the first Russian ones) use many interesting stylistic devices, including metaphorical descriptions of reality in the Futurist tradition. In Russia, Jasieński became more and more a political writer, producing novels that embraced the tenets of socialist realism. One of his novels, *Chelovek meniaet kozhu* (Man Changes His Skin, 1932–3), even made the school curriculum in the Tadzhik Socialist Republic, for whose sovietization Jasieński fought hard before becoming a victim of Stalin's terror. He was sentenced to death in 1938 and shot the same year.

Jasieński was not the only Polish author to publish a work initially in a language other than Polish. Two others were Gustaw Herling-Grudziński (1919–2000) and Czesław Miłosz. Herling-Grudziński's *Inny świat. Zapiski sowieckie* (A World Apart: A Memoir of the Gulag), known also for its short preface by Bertrand Russell, was first published in English translation in London in 1951; Miłosz's *Zdobycie władzy* (La prise du pouvoir), in turn, which brought its author the Prix Littéraire Européen, first came out in French translation in Paris in 1953. While these works were translated or co-translated, there are also novels by Polish authors that, for various reasons, were originally written in French or another Western language. When writers adopted Russian, it was typically for political reasons (conversely, some students refused to write in Russian, the oppressor's language, when it was enforced in schools). Writing in a *Western* language, especially French and English, was linked mostly to a desire to participate in modern cultural centres and their literary discourses. The beginning of this phenomenon can be traced back to the turn of the eighteenth century, when French was the recognized language of European culture. There we find *Manuscrit trouvé à Saragosse* (The Manuscript Found in Saragossa), a masterpiece of narrative writing by Count Jan Potocki (1761–1815), a graduate of schools in Lausanne and Geneva who spent most of his life in Poland or Europe or on exotic travels (he was supposedly the first Pole to fly in a balloon). His novel appeared at the beginning of the nineteenth century in both Saint Petersburg and Paris, which makes it an international work of the Enlightenment.

Exceptionally, while Potocki was a Pole and played an active role at the Polish court and in the early parliamentary system (and, after the partitions, also in tsarist institutions), he wrote only in French. His choice of language was motivated not only by his education but also by the idea of a common Europe with a common language (and French seemed to be the one for the epoch) sharing its many cultural experiences. Still, Potocki's novel is not an ideological work, nor is it explicitly connected to either French or Polish culture. First and foremost, it is a highly sophisticated adventure narrative that relates the travels in Spain of a certain Alfons van Worden, who meets unusual people of various cultural backgrounds on his way to Madrid and has strange, often supernatural, experiences. The people he meets narrate their stories, and the heroes of their stories tell their own, and so on, making the novel a fine example of the "story within a story" technique, typical of the *Arabian Nights* tales. Its peculiar nature – it was written in French by a Pole – meant that it was consigned largely to the peripheries of Polish culture, at least until it was adapted for the cinema by the famous Polish film director Wojciech Has in the mid-1960s. Indeed, interest in the novel has revived since then. Its modern critical editions and new scholarly interpretations are based on new findings in French, Polish, Spanish, and Russian libraries and have been published in France, while its first unabridged translation by Anna Wasilewska appeared in Poland in 2015 (as *Rękopis znaleziony w Saragossie*), as did its first Web adaptation.[24] That this once forgotten text is having a second chance is fitting: Potocki's novel is a fine introduction to European Enlightenment culture, with its search for universality and a transnational narrative. It can also be read, as French biographers and interpreters of Potocki put it, as "le dernier grand roman des Lumières européennes" (the last great novel of the European Enlightenment).[25] With Has's masterful film adaptation of *The Saragossa Manuscript* now digitally remastered under the auspices of Martin Scorsese and available in many languages, this intriguing example of international Polish writing may find new life in the changing cultural environment of a united Europe.

Potocki's case is quite different from that of Józef Korzeniowski, better known to the world as Joseph Conrad (1857–1924), whose English writing made him a master of English language and literature. Potocki was a Polish author who chose French for his writing, which enabled him to reach both Polish and European readers at the time. Conrad was an English author of Polish origins, whose writing, due to its exclusively English language and circulation and the author's position in British society, belongs to the English-language canon. His Polish background and intertextual references play an important role in his work, of course: one example of the former could be Conrad's use of a Polish gentry tale (*gawęda*) as a narrative model. Also, Conrad's sensitivity to the incomprehensibility of "minor" languages within the dominant linguistic centre is well exemplified in his short story "Amy Foster" (1901). In it, the hero is a Polish highlander named Yanko Goorall, who after a fraught journey arrives in England and establishes a family there. While in the grip of a high fever at his own home, he cries out for water in Polish and dies because no one understands him. His English wife is scared half to death by his wild cries. Notably, the original English text denotes Yanko's cries for water in … English. Instead of *Wody! Daj mi wody!*, as you would expect in Polish, we find: "Water! Give me water!," along with a narrator's explanation that "he may have thought he was speaking in English."[26] There is a difference between writers like Conrad, who, though born in Poland, chose to make his home elsewhere and switched entirely to a foreign language, thus ceasing his unmediated linguistic connection to his literary culture of birth,[27] and those like Potocki, who never stopped being a part of his country's literary culture, even when he chose a different language for his writing. Although Potocki wrote only in French, he continued to function in his home culture, where French was then in fact a widely understood literary language. Testifying to this fact is, for example, the *comedia dell'arte* play titled *Recueil des Parades* (1792) that Potocki wrote for his cousin Princess Izabela Lubomirska's theatre in Łańcut.

Many eminent Polish authors were strongly influenced by French culture, albeit in various historical and cultural contexts. In the nineteenth century, Adam Mickiewicz's work most obviously springs to mind. In the early 1840s, while a professor of Slavonic Literatures at the Collège de France in Paris and a political exile, Poland's leading Romantic poet lectured in French to an international audience not only on Slavonic literatures, and on political and mystical issues (for which he was later expelled from his position), but also on a wide range of academic interests that included world literature and philosophy. For example, he gave lectures about the American philosopher Ralph Waldo Emerson, whose essays were completely unknown in Continental Europe at the time. Two of these lectures – "History" and "Man the Reformer" – later appeared separately in the magazine *La Tribune des Peuples*, which Mickiewicz edited. His versions of these essays are intriguing for the author's daring attempt to find his voice among three cultures: American, French, and Polish.[28] His lectures, which also included many of his translations from Polish and other Slavonic literatures, were likewise later published in French and Polish translations, from versions produced by copyists present during the lectures and later revised by Mickiewicz himself. For those who do not read Polish, the French versions of Mickiewicz's lectures offer a still fascinating introduction to Slavonic literary cultures.

In the later historical context of Poland's post-1918 independence, Polish writers would sometimes choose the French language for the sake of being read and perceived from within a cultural centre and to participate in the European cultural exchange on equal basis. The Polish–French magazine *L'Art Contemporain* was founded in 1929 as a means to present Polish and French modern literature and art. Each of the magazine's three issues included an introductory article titled *Kilométrage* by Jan Brzękowski (1903–83), in both French and Polish. This bilingual practice was applied to other content as well, such as essays on art and Polish and French poetry.[29] This short-lived magazine's attempt to enter the European cultural stage was symptomatic of Polish writers' conscious efforts to join the European art and literature exchange. Out of the *L'Art Contemporain* circle, only Jan Brzękowski continued to write in French, becoming a rare example of a Polish bilingual poet. He published, among others, such volumes of poetry as *Spectacle métallique* (1937), *Les Murs du silence* (1958), and *Déplacement du paysage* (1973), and he was proud that the critical response they evoked was comparable to what any native French poet could have got.[30] In the French-language context, it is worth mentioning that Marian Pankowski (1919–2011), a Polish émigré in Brussels in the second half of the twentieth century known mostly for his Polish-language novels, dramas, and poems, was also the author of two poetry volumes published in French. According to Dorota Walczak-Delanois, the translator who is now preparing their bilingual edition, these poems are an intriguing example of Pankowski's rewriting practices and, sometimes, of self-censorship.[31]

Since French was the language of the cultural centre that the Polish intelligentsia knew best, at least until the mid-twentieth century, there are many examples of Polish writers adopting it for various reasons. Other Romance languages, however, were at times represented in Polish literary culture in connection with particular historical contexts. The most interesting example is Witold Gombrowicz (1904–69), a pre-eminent figure in Polish modernist literature. After spending much of his adult life in Argentina, where he landed just before the outbreak of the Second World War, Gombrowicz began to write in Spanish. He prepared the Spanish-language editions of some of his works, including his *Dziennik* (Diary), which differs greatly from the Polish version. Most significantly, *Diario argentino* is supplemented by new entries on Argentina; this creates a kind of heterotopia, a place where many cultures and spaces exist at the same time. Silvana Mandolessi carefully interprets this phenomenon, wondering whether Gombrowicz became part of Argentinian literature.[32] He certainly became an unusual member of Argentinian literary and artistic circles. Some details on this situation are provided in his Spanish correspondence with his friend Goma (Juan Carlos Gómez), for example. Gombrowicz also became a hypertext for Argentinian writers. He appeared, for instance, in Ricardo Piglia's *Respiracion artificial* and Luis Martin's *Las cartas profanes* as a European intellectual – *ecrivan estranjero* – a partner in ongoing discussions about Argentina and the world.[33]

German was the more typically chosen foreign language for Polish prose writers, despite the fraught history between the two countries. Under the Prussian partition, the German language was the only one allowed in the educational system, with the rule being applied especially strictly in the Silesian and Pomeranian regions. The best-known example of a Polish writer writing in both German and Polish at that time is Stanisław Przybyszewski (1868–1927), the *enfant terrible* of the Young Poland period. Having graduated from a German *Gymnasium* (advanced high school) in Toruń (Thorn), he went on to Berlin to study architecture. There he engaged with Nietzsche's philosophy, Satanism, and the bohemian life, and began his literary career, publishing both psychological essays and literary works.[34] Przybyszewski also prepared the Polish editions of his works, sometimes depending on fellow writers-translators, and composed long prose-poems and dramas in Polish. One of his most famous works, the trilogy *Homo Sapiens,* was first published in Germany (1895–6), where it was well-received. Its Polish version was then published in Lviv at the turn of the nineteenth century, and translated into English within a decade.[35] Przybyszewski's bilingualism has been analysed in a monograph, whose author claims that his original German texts are more interesting than the Polish versions, since they are driven by a spirit of real creativity, while the latter are more like "re-creations."[36] These works were also characterized by Przybyszewski's passionate struggle with language, a struggle in which his friend, the German poet Richard Dehmel, played a helping hand.[37] There is certainly more to explore in Przybyszewski's vast oeuvre. The same is true of the bilingual writing of Tadeusz Rittner (1873–1921), a playwright and literary critic from the same generation who has not been studied in depth yet. The son of a Polonised Austrian family from Lviv, Rittner chose Polish citizenship after the First World War and kept writing in both Polish and German throughout his life. One of his plays, *W małym domku* (In a Small House, 1904), became a key text in Polish realistic theatre, while the German versions of Rittner's plays have been almost completely forgotten.[38]

The tradition of Polish-German writing continued with emigrant writers during the 1980s, albeit on quite a different basis. Having found political asylum and economical support, they began writing in a new language to tell their life stories, which could not be published in communist Poland for political reasons. This was the case for Christian Skrzyposzek (1943–99), the author of *Freie Tribune* (Free Tribune), which appeared in German translation by Olaf Kuhn in 1983, then in Berlin in the original Polish version as *Wolna Trybuna* (1985), and finally in Warsaw in 1999. Skrzyposzek's bilingual work (he wrote a now lost autobiography and published a play in the theatre magazine *Dialog* in Poland in the 1960s, and worked on preparing Polish versions of his German texts) was in the end dominated by German writings. His final novel, *Die Annonce* (2005), which was edited and published after his death in Germany, became part of German literature as naturally as the works of Radek Knapp and Artur Becker, for instance, do nowadays. Dariusz Muszer (b. 1959) presents a different case, in that he has consistently translated his novels into Polish. The best-known examples – *Die Freiheit riecht nach Vanille* (*Wolność pachnie wanilią* [Freedom Smells of Vanilla], 1999/2008) and *Gottes homepage* (*Homepage Boga* [God's Homepage], 2003/2013) – were written in German and first published in Germany. Muszer fills the Polish versions of his novels with various hybrid language forms: creative translations of phrases and idioms, and provoking language calques, as well as various alienation effects. His Polish version of *Freedom Smells of Vanilla* includes meta-language commentary, for instance: "Głupio pobiegło, jak to mawiają w Niemczech, gdy chcą powiedzieć, że głupio wyszło"" (It ran silly, as they say in Germany, when they want to say that something went wrong).[39] The author also includes German words in the Polish lexical system, and vice versa. This conscious play on languages is characteristic of his bilingual writing.[40]

Another interesting Polish-German writer, this time defined by a borderland context, is Piotr (Peter) Lachmann, a poet, essayist, playwright, translator, and theatre director who was born to a German family before the Second World War in Gleiwitz, which became Gliwice, and part of Poland, after the war. Glewitz/Gliwice always had a bicultural character, and Lachmann, who attended Polish schools there, continued to write in two languages even after leaving for Germany, where he spent most of his life. According to Przemysław Chojnowski, who is currently working on a monograph about his "liminal" writing, Lachmann is a model example of a language and culture man of a borderland.[41]

Working in two languages and translating oneself are characteristic of Polish–German authors. Both are also typical of Polish–English authors, especially since 1950, possibly because English has become a global language. Stefan Themerson (1910–88), a writer, poet, philosopher, photographer, filmmaker, and composer, was one of the most important and widely known Polish writers. Having launched his brilliant career in Poland before the Second World War, he continued it successfully after the war in the free world (Britain). Besides Polish and English, he wrote occasionally in French, and translated some of his Polish works into English. His best-known work, the philosophical satire *Professor Mmaa's Lecture*, was written in Polish in the 1940s, then self-translated into English and published in London in 1953 (with a foreword by Bertrand Russell). This novel enjoyed an international career both for its unusual idea (a professor gives a lecture on *Homo sapiens* to an audience of termites) and for its linguistic and philosophical complexity.[42] Among today's authors, Ewa Kuryluk (b. 1946) – an artist, art historian, and writer – has translated her English texts into Polish (*Grand Hotel Oriental*, 1997) while continuing to write in English and, increasingly, in Polish.

Czesław Miłosz was probably the most prestigious of Polish self-translators into English, although it is difficult to ascertain the authorship of his English poems, which were almost always written first in Polish (with a few exceptions, such as "To Raja Rao") and translated in cooperation with a native English speaker, most often Robert Hass. What seems more important to Miłosz's bicultural case, however, is his strong participation in the life of English, and especially American, literary and cultural circles. Miłosz met English readers and poets, conducted seminars on poetry, and wrote essays on literature in English; he also compiled an anthology of world poetry, *A Book of Luminous Things* (which included Polish poems and had a Polish, slightly different version: *Wypisy z ksiąg użytecznych*). With its publication, Miłosz became the first Polish author to try to shape the world canon of poetry, or at least the first to play a leading role in such an endeavour. So far, even when bilingual and/or bicultural, Polish authors have not functioned in this manner in the World Republic of Letters. That republic's language is no longer French, but English, something that Pascal Casanova's *La République mondiale des Lettres* hardly admits but that Miłosz fully recognized.

Miłosz's activities and English publications made him one of the most influential foreign poets in America, to the point that he came to serve as a sort of hypertext for many American poets (in a parallel to Gombrowicz). For instance, in Robert Cording's poem "Czeslaw Milosz's Glasses," a masterly portrait of a great moral poet, Miłosz becomes a sort of a paragon for a generation of poets. By contrast, in Poland, Miłosz was attacked by poets of the same generation for being too traditional and too moralistic. In America, Miłosz was often a poet with whom others carried on a profound intertextual dialogue on morality and ethics. Edward Hirsch's poem "A Partial History of My Stupidity," which begins with the first line of Miłosz's poem "Rachunek" (Account, 1980) in its English version – "The history of my stupidity would fill many volumes" (Dzieje mojej głupoty wypełniłyby wiele tomów) – is a good example of such dialogue. Miłosz the international poet, however, was slightly different from his Polish version. He was a bit less complicated linguistically, and in consequence semantically, and he was more present in his other literary activities and thus able to sustain his English-language audience – an uncommon achievement among Polish poets in the English-speaking world.

The path followed by Miłosz differed significantly from those taken by Polish émigré poets who left just after the end of the Second World War. The members of "Kontynenty" (Continents), a group of poets active in London between 1959 and 1964, would write almost exclusively in Polish. In time, they also produced interesting translations, self-translations, and, quite uniquely, mutual translations of one another's works. Andrzej Busza (b. 1938) and Bogdan Czaykowski (1932–2007) are a good example of the latter practice.[43] Wacław Iwaniuk (1912–2001), a Polish poet who lived in Canada and wrote and published in Polish, also published an original volume of poetry in English after many years of living in exile, titled *Evenings on Lake Ontario: From My Canadian Diary* (1981). Instances of poets who once wrote and published in Polish beginning to publish in English are more frequent now. Among them is Joanna Kurowska, initially known for poems published in the Paris *Kultura,* a prominent émigré Polish-language literary magazine, who has now composed three volumes of poetry in English. In her last volume, *The Butterfly's Choice* (2014), she presents coming to the United States mostly as a linguistic experience: "Coming here was a plunge in language."[44] The conclusion of her poem "The Day I Became an American," which celebrates her new identity in a slightly ironic, Whitmanesque manner, reads: "Today I am *telling* you, / I am one of you," making the act of telling constitutive of a shared experience with others who also "came here," among them Latino construction workers and maids from Eastern Europe.[45]

IV. New Transcultural Writing

It must be noted that despite the dominance of English in the globalized world, bilingual writing today is changing its forms. It is no longer about writing in two languages, self-translations, or self-adaptations, or even about the switch to a new, double-coded language. Elwira Grossman points to a new trend in Polish–Scottish drama of using both languages on stage, as exemplified by *Cherry Blossom* (2008), a play by Catherine Grosvenor (b. 1978) that was written collaboratively and staged by the Traverse Theatre in Edinburgh. Forty per cent of the script devoted to two different Polish immigrant stories was spoken in Polish during performances both in Scotland and in Poland, with a translation projected onto the stage. As Grossman put it, "the point was to reinforce the confusion experienced by migrants … who do not know the language of the host country."[46] Another example is the trilingual performance of *This Is Why We Live*, based on Szymborska's poetry and developed by a multilingual and transnational ensemble of artists, which was presented in Polish, English, and French, and without subtitles.[47] Perhaps, as Grossman suggests, these productions are a case of a new, transnational writing for the stage that makes language central to human experience. Works of this kind might be able to overcome a long-standing language trap: What language can a subaltern speak in literature to be able to articulate what (s)he wants to say as well as to be heard in the new culture? This is the dilemma observed in Conrad's Yanko Goorall, who was made to speak English in an English text even though, within the narrative, he was unable to do so and died as a result.

V. Conclusions

To call Polish literature monolithic is clearly an oversimplification. Over the ages, Poland has produced numerous writers who used other languages in their work, for different reasons and in different cultural and historical contexts. These literary attempts to enter into dialogue with regional and world literatures through the medium of a different language deserve further study. There are many possible angles from which to view literature created by Polish and bicultural writers who used Polish: in a context of a universal/global language (such as Latin once, and English today); as examples of language use determined by a dominant cultural centre (besides Latin and English, French and Polish fall in this category); or from the perspective of playing with languages of the (im)migration centres. Apart from general reasons, there are also many individual reasons why Polish writers adopted or used a foreign language: mostly political (Bruno Jasieński), purely artistic (Bolesław Leśmian), more pragmatic and market-directed (Witold Gombrowicz and Czesław Miłosz), or – as the newest examples show – socially oriented, where the focus is on producing a language mix that gives true voice to those who could not be heard otherwise. Differences aside, all multilingual writing is a gesture of invitation made by a "minor" literature to the wider world. It is also an attempt to provide this world with direct access to another culture. After all, as Mickiewicz claimed in his Paris lectures, which he delivered in French and infused with his Emersonian intuition and English quotations: the term Słowianie (Slavs) comes from the word *słowo*, meaning "word."

Marta Skwara
University of Szczecin

NOTES

1 Casanova, *La République mondiale des Lettres*, 90–107.

2 Miłosz, *Conversations*, 185.

3 Unfortunately, the Latin inscription, which in Polish editions is quoted in Polish with the original Latin version given in the footnote, almost disappears from the English version of the poem as a result of having been moved to the endnotes. See Miłosz, *New and Collected Poems 1931–2001*, 315.

4 Ibid., 306.
5 Among many others. For further details, see Bukowiec, *Dwujęzyczne początki nowoczesnej literatury litewskiej.*
6 Narusiene, *Józef Albin Herbaczewski*, 90.
7 Bojtár, *Foreword to the Past*, 243.
8 For a comprehensive overview of Tatar literature and its languages, see Czerwiński and Konopacki, eds., *Estetyczne aspekty literatury*, 2015.
9 Kledzik, "Recording an Oral Message," 207–34.
10 Fuks, "Żydowska literatura," 1054.
11 Fuks, "Żydowska literatura w Polsce XX wieku," 1247.
12 Prokop-Janiec, *Polish-Jewish Literature in the Interwar Years*, 5.
13 A good example of such practice is Natan Füllenbaum's poem "Aszer Jacar" ("Asher Yatzar"). See ibid., 119.
14 Jakób Lewittes's poem "Prayer" ("Modlitwa") from his collection *Posthumous* (*Posthumus*), published in Warsaw by "Rój" in 1930, is a good example of the latter.
15 Prokop-Janiec, *Polish-Jewish Literature in the Interwar Years*, 243–5.
16 See Antosik-Piela and Prokop-Janiec, *Twarzą ku nocy*, 2015.
17 Prokop-Janiec, *Polish-Jewish Literature in the Interwar Years*, 255.
18 For more on Debora Vogel's work, see Szymaniak, *Być agentem wiecznej idei.*
19 For its analysis in the context of Russian Symbolist poetry, see Brzostowska-Tereszkiewicz, "Sofia zaklęta w baśniową carewnę."
20 Broniewski, "Czełowiek – eto zwuczit gordo."
21 Jaworski, *Bruno Jasieński w Paryżu,* 137.
22 Kolesnikoff, *Bruno Jasieński*, 84.
23 Jaworski, *Bruno Jasieński w Paryżu,* 138.
24 http://haart.e-kei.pl/rekopis/00_intro.html.
25 Rosset and Triaire, *Jean Potocki*, 335.
26 Conrad, *Amy Foster*, 140.
27 This is the case not only of Conrad, but also of modern writers active in Germany (Radek Knapp, Artur Becker), Sweden (Rita Tonborg, Zbigniew Kuklarz), the United States (Eva Hoffman), and Canada (Ewa Stachniak).
28 See Skwara, *Krąg transcendentalistów amerykańskich*, 121–45.
29 We may only assume, since no names of translators appear, that it was Brzękowski and Czyżewski who were behind the French translations. The latter was a translator from French and the author of the 1914 poem "Medium," which appeared in French in the first issue of the magazine.
30 Brzękowski, *W Krakowie i w Paryżu*, 286–95. For analyses of Brzekowski's poetry in French, see Walczak-Delanois, "L'image et 'l'imagination libérée' dans la poésie polonaise et française de Jan Brzękowski: ('Zaciśnięte dookoła ust' 1936, 'Spectacle métallique' 1937)" and Sak-Grzelczak, "O francuskojęzycznych wierszach Jana Brzękowskiego."
31 Dorota Walczak-Delanois (personal communication, 13 October 2016). For her early research of Pankowski's writing, see *"Sztuka poetycka Mariana Pankowskiego."*
32 Mandolesi, "Heterotopia i literatura narodowa," 245–61.
33 Gendaj, "Gombrowicz polityczny?," 224–9.
34 An example of the former is Zur Psychologie des Individuums. I. Chopin und Nietzsche. II. Ola Hansson, 1892. Whereas the latter is represented by Totenmess, 1853; De Profundis, 1895; Vigilien, 1895; *Homo Sapiens*, 1895–1896; and Satanskinder, 1897, to name only a few.

35 Its last translator, Thomas Seltzer, noted on the editorial page that he was translating from Polish. It was published in New York by A.A. Knopf in 1915, but found "obscene" and so did not take hold in the United States. Indeed, the trilogy deals with both deviance and sexuality, and its hero, an émigré from partitioned Poland, bears some resemblance to the author in his struggles with eroticism and alcoholism in bohemian Berlin. One could say that Przybyszewski arrived in New York half a century too early.

36 Łuczyński, *Dwujęzyczna twórczość Stanisława Przybyszewskiego*, 71–2.

37 Ibid., 70–2.

38 The use of German by Polish intellectuals living in Galicia during the Austrian partition extends beyond literature. Roman Ingarden, who wrote philosophy in both German and Polish, should be recalled here, as well as the versatile artist and philosopher Stanisław Ignacy Witkiewicz (Witkacy), who corresponded in German with Hans Cornelius. As far as Witkacy's grotesque dramas were concerned, the author prepared French versions of some of them together with his wife.

39 Muszer, *Wolność pachnie wanilią*, 29.

40 For further analysis, see Makarska, "Między Polską a Niemcami," 2013.

41 Chojnowski, *Liminalność i bycie pomiędzy w twórczości Petera / Piotra Lachmanna. Studium literacko-kulturowe*.

42 For more information about Themerson's bi-lingualism, see Kraskowska, *Twórczość Stefana Themersona.*

43 See their co-authored volume *Pełnia i przesilenie = Full moon and summer solstice*.

44 Kurowska, *The Butterfly's Choice*, 12.

45 Ibid., 27.

46 Grossman, "Transnational or Bi-cultural?," 242.

47 This co-production by Open Heart Surgery, Tara Arts (UK), and Théâtre de L'Enfumeraie (Le Mans, France) was performed in Toronto in October 2016. I thank Tamara Trojanowska for pointing me to this example.

WORKS CITED

Antosik-Piela, Maria and Eugenia Prokop-Janiec, eds. *Twarzą ku nocy. Twórczość literacka Maurycego Szymla*. Kraków: Wydawnictwo Uniwersytetu Jagiellońskiego, 2015.

Bojtár, Endre. *Foreword to the Past: A Cultural History of the Baltic People.* Budapest: Central European University Press, 2000.

Broniewski, Władysław. "Czełowiek – eto zwuczit gordo" [1940]. *Polonistyka* 8 (1990): 403.

Brzękowski, Jan. *W Krakowie i w Paryżu. Wspomnienia i szkice.* Warszawa: Państwowy Instytut Wydawniczy, 1968.

Brzostowska-Tereszkiewicz, Tamara. "Sofia zaklęta w baśniową carewnę: 'Pieśni Wasilisy Priemudroj' Bolesława Leśmiana wobec rosyjskiej poezji symbolistycznej." *Pamiętnik Literacki* 3 (2003): 27–49.

Bukowiec, Paweł. *Dwujęzyczne początki nowoczesnej literatury litewskiej. Rzecz z pogranicza polonistyki*. Kraków: TAiWPN Universitas, 2008.

Busza, Andrzej, and Bogdan Czaykowski. *Pełnia i przesilenie = Full moon and summer solstice*. Toronto: Polski Fundusz Wydawniczy w Kanadzie, Rzeszów: Stowarzyszenie Literacko-Artystyczne "Fraza," 2008.

Casanova, Pascale. *La République mondiale des Lettres*. Paris: Éditions du Seuil, 1999.

Chojnowski, *Liminalność i bycie pomiędzy w twórczości Petera / Piotra Lachmanna. Studium literacko-kulturowe*. Kraków: Universitas TAiWPN, in press.
Conrad, Joseph. "Amy Foster." In *Typhoon and Other Stories*. 105–42. Garden City: Doubleday, Page & Company. 1925.
Czerwiński, Grzegorz, and Artur Konopacki, eds. *Estetyczne aspekty literatury polskich, białoruskich i litewskich tatarów (od XVI do XXI wieku)*. Białystok: Alter Studio, 2015.
Fuks, Marian. "Żydowska literature." In *Słownik literatury polskiej XIX wieku*. Edited by Alina Kowalczykowa and Józef Bachórz. 1054–7. Wrocław: Zakład Narodowy Im. Ossolińskich. Wydawnictwo, 1991
– "Żydowska literatura w Polsce XX wieku." In *Słownik literatury polskiej XX wieku*. Edited by Alina Brodzka er al. 1247–52. Wrocław: Zakład Narodowy Im. Ossolińskich. Wydawnictwo, 1992.
Gendaj, Natalia. "Gombrowicz polityczny? Miejsce pisarza w literaturze argentyńskiej." In *Literatura polska w świecie*, vol. 4: *Oblicza światowości*. Edited by Roman Cudak. Katowice: Uniwersytet Śląski: Wydawnictwo Gnome, 2012.
Grossman, Elwira M. "Transnational or Bi-cultural? Challenges in Reading post-1989 Drama 'Written Outside the Nation.'" In *Polish Literature in Transformation*. Edited by Ursula Phillips with Knut Andreas Grimstad and Kris Van Heuckelom. Zurich, Berlin: LIT Verlag, 2013.
Jaworski, Krzysztof. *Bruno Jasieński w Paryżu (1925–1928)*. Kielce: Wydawnictwo Akademii Świętokrzyskiej, 2003.
Kledzik, Emilia. "Recording an Oral Message: Jerzy Ficowski and Papusza's Poetic Project in the Postcolonial Perspective." *Rocznik Komparatystyczny* 4 (2013): 207–34.
Kolesnikoff, Nina. *Bruno Jasieński: His Evolution from Futurism to Socialist Realism*. Waterloo: Wilfrid Laurier University Press, 1982.
Kraskowska, Ewa. *Twórczość Stefana Themersona. Dwujęzyczność a literatura*. Wrocław: Zakład Narodowy im. Ossolińskich, 1989.
Kurowska, Joanna. *The Butterfly's Choice*. Frankfort: Broadstone Books, 2014.
Łuczyński, Krzysztof. *Dwujęzyczna twórczość Stanisława Przybyszewskiego 1892–1900*. Kielce: Wydawnictwo Wyższej Szkoły Pedagogicznej w Kielcach, 1982.
Makarska, Renata. "Między Polską a Niemcami, między językami. Skrzyposzek, Niewrzęda, Muszer." In *Między językami, kulturami, literaturami. Polska literatura (e)migracyjna w Berlinie i Sztokholmie po roku 1981*. Edited by Teodorowicz-Hellman Ewa and Gesche Janina. 330–57. Stockholm: Stockholms Universytet. Slaviska Institutionen 2013.
Mandolesi, Silvana. *Heterotopia i literatura narodowa w* Dzienniku argentyńskim *Witolda Gombrowicza*. Translated by Natalia Gendaj. *Rocznik Komparatystyczny* 2 (2011): 245–61.
Miłosz, Czesław. *Conversations*. Edited by Cynthia L. Haven. Jackson: University Press of Mississippi, 2006.
– *Gdzie wschodzi słońce i kędy zapada*. Gdańsk: Słowo/Obraz Terytoria, 2004.
– *New and Collected Poems 1931–2001*. New York: Ecco Press, 2001.
– *Wypisy z ksiąg użytecznych*. Kraków: Znak, 1994.
– ed. *A Book of Luminous Things: An International Anthology of Poetry*. New York: Harcourt Brace, 1996.
Muszer, Dawid. *Wolność pachnie wanilią*. Szczecin: Wydawnictwo Forma. Stowarzyszenie Literackie Forma, 2008.
Narusiene, Vaiva. *Józef Albin Herbaczewski. Pisarz polsko-litewski*. Kraków: TAiWPN Universitas, 2007.

Potocki, Jan. *Rękopis znaleziony w Saragossie*. Translated by Anna Wasilewska, edited by François Rosset and Dominique Triaire. Kraków: Wydawnictwo Literackie, 2015.
Prokop-Janiec, Eugenia. "Living in Languages: Jewish Multilingualism as Reflected in the Polish and Polish-Jewish Literature of the 20th century." *Studia Judaica: Biuletyn Polskiego Towarzystwa Studiów Żydowskich* 1 (2002): 109–17.
– *Polish-Jewish Literature in the Interwar Years*. Translated by Abe Shenitzer. Syracuse: Syracuse University Press, 2003.
Rosset, François, and Dominique Triaire. *Jean Potocki. Biographie*. Paris: Édition Flammarion, 2004.
Sak-Grzelczak, Ewa. "O francuskojęzycznych wierszach Jana Brzękowskiego." *Zeszyty Naukowe Uniwersytetu Rzeszowskiego*. Seria Filologiczna. *Historia Literatury* 3 (2008) 208–21.
Skwara, Marta. *Krąg transcendentalistów amerykańskich w literaturze polskiej XIX i XX wieku. Dzieje recepcji, idei i powinowactw z wyboru*. Szczecin: Wydawnictwo Uniwersytetu Szczecińskiego, 2004.
Szymaniak, Karolina. *Być agentem wiecznej idei. Przemiany poglądów estetycznych Debory Vogel*. Kraków: Universitas TAiWPN, 2006.
Walczak-Delanois, Dorota. "L'image et 'l'imagination libérée' dans la poésie polonaise et française de Jan Brzękowski: ('Zaciśnięte dookoła ust' 1936, 'Spectacle métallique' 1937)." *Romanica Cracoviensia* 3 (2003): 161–70.
– "Sztuka poetycka Mariana Pankowskiego. Między żywiołem polskim i frankofońskim." *Prace Polonistyczne* 70 (2015): 233–59.

Translation as Comparison

1. Discipline and Modernization

When it entered the academy in the first half of the nineteenth century, comparative literature seemed to its advocates to be a chance to modernize ossified historical literary practices. Founded on a powerful desire to organize knowledge about the literary world by means of a precisely formulated method, it matched the natural sciences of the time in its scholarly ambitions. It enviously looked towards the procedures formulated in fields like anatomy (Georges Cuvier), physiology (Henri M. de Blainville), and embryology (Jean J.M.C. Coste), thus partaking in the great drive towards scholarly credibility that pervaded areas described today as the humanities and social sciences from the first works of Joseph M. Degérando and Jean F. Sobry up to the times of Edward A. Freeman.

This drive would bear fruit in the twentieth century with the birth of literary theory, whose roots go back to the first comparative projects, as Rodolphe Gasché demonstrated when interpreting the output of the Jena Romantics.[1] Newly reformed philology, exemplified by the work of scholars like François Raynouard and Jean J. Ampère, would become the staunchest ally of the budding discipline. Both philology and comparative literature systematically searched for a common basis of the linguistic diversity from which national literatures, which were then trying to strengthen, demarcate, or – in the case of the Polish literature – save their own boundaries, derived their richness. Comparative literature was a specific cognitive project that not only manifested a yearning for accurate classification of cultural phenomena but was also the answer of national republics of letters to changing conditions of international communication and new possibilities experienced in "the era of the railroad" characterized by "a tendency of people to seek rapprochement and contact," as Adam Mickiewicz (1798–1855) has put it.[2] Together with the havoc resulting from the historical upheavals of the Napoleonic era, it was the constitutive factors of this prehistory of globalization that inspired Goethe to formulate the concept of *Weltliteratur* (World literature), which, like the idea of *Bildung* that supported it, was rooted in Hegelian philosophy. A peculiar interpretation – or perhaps overinterpretation – of this concept, which emphasized the need to form a stable library of masterpieces rather than the urge to observe the mechanisms of a developing "trade" in culture, would lead to discussions about the object of comparative literature and to attempts to laboriously build the *corpus* of the discipline.

The twentieth-century history of comparative studies is erected on two building blocks: first, on the modernizing discourse emerging from the rationalism of the Enlightenment – an epistemological project that aimed to embrace the diversity of the literary world through attempts to find its universal laws; and second, on the Romantic ontological project growing out of the spirit of Hegelianism, focused on the idea of *Bildung* and aimed at self-mastery of the individual and the community through confrontation with cultural otherness. The assumptions of both projects, however, would be significantly modified by twentieth-century history, and particularly by the Second World War. The experience of traumatic displacement, both psychological and physical, that emerged from the ruins of the war-torn world, together with a subsequent crisis of language and its cognitive potential, culminated in the dissemination of the idea of incommensurability, which would transform the foundations of comparative discourse and delineate the institutionalization of comparative literature in the middle of the twentieth century. Some eminent European humanists exiled from their own homes by the onslaught of fascist ideology found shelter in the United States as chairs of Comparative Literature departments. The twentieth-century lesson delivered by the Second World War would gradually undermine the universalist ambitions of the discipline's founders and, more importantly, sharpen the intensity of its criticism. Since the 1940s and 1950s it has been clear that relations between aesthetics and politics, capable of raising burning questions about war and peace, have grown into an important area of comparative studies.

The assumptions of a discipline founded – for the second time, one might say – on the heritage of dislocation unfold three perspectives before us: first, they expose the role of translation in the development of knowledge about intercultural dialogue; second, they allow for the identification of Polish comparative literature's specificity; and third, they capture the conditions of modern Polish literature's development.

It is worth noting here that the Chair of Comparative Literature founded in 1818 at the University of Warsaw was, according to available historical data, the first position of its kind in the world. It was created barely two years after the publication of the anthology by François J.M. Noël and François de la Place – *Leçons françaises de littérature et de morale*, subtitled *Cours de littérature compare* – that was of key importance for the discipline's beginnings. Moreover, the first appointee to that chair, Professor Ludwik Osiński (1775–1838), conducted classes there long before the influential lectures of Abel F. Villemain, Philarète Chasles, and Jean J. Ampère. However, Poland did not exist on maps of Europe at the time. Polish literary and artistic activities developed primarily in exile, and the task of literature was to foster the spirit of the national community, to search for a language capable of expressing the situation of homelessness and an already permanent sense of loss, to maintain bonds with the past, and to fight for national independence. This was the climate in which Polish comparative literature evolved and attempted to establish an institutional basis; from the time of its promising beginnings, its discontinuous history was driven by certain acts rather than by a stable course of development. As far as its foundational texts are concerned, for many years the most important role was played by Adam Mickiewicz's Paris lectures, which were devoted to Slavic literatures and which he delivered while holding the Chair of Slavic Languages and Literature at the Collège de France between 1840 and 1844. One dimension of Mickiewicz's broad comparative project that deserves emphasis is his awareness of new ways of speaking about literature and its history, an awareness that informed his delineation both of the developmental threads of various literary traditions and of the influences and borrowings important for understanding Polish literature. In earlier lectures conducted in Lausanne (1839–40), Mickiewicz asserted that "the French have created comparative literature, and in this way they have broadened the field of vision by introducing a new object for comparison, that is modern literature."[3] This awareness of the appearance of a new entity in literary discourse, along with an echo of the ambitions that brought it forth, could be heard in his inaugural lecture in Paris, where Mickiewicz spoke of the various functions and tasks fulfilled by ancient and modern languages, which were reflected in the internal, dialectal differentiation of Slavic speech. He compared the discovery of this linguistic panorama, "unusual and unique" in its own way, to an imagined "discovery of the anatomist" ("un anatomiste") of "an organic entity" that, "traversing through all of the lower stages of life, preserved together within itself vegetable, animal and human forms of life, and each of them evolved to its fullness and wholeness."[4] It is worth underscoring here that Mickiewicz placed the task he had undertaken in a particular historical context, describing the situation of Polish literature at that time and the legacy it would pass on to the twentieth century: "I am a foreigner. I must speak a language that has nothing to do with the language that usually serves as the tool for my thoughts; nothing in common with its origin, neither in form nor in flow. This pertains not only to the translation of my thoughts and emotions into a foreign tongue here before you; I will have to transform each thought, each emotion entirely and extemporaneously."[5] It is thus translation and transformation in a situation of exile that underpins the most important foundational texts of Polish comparative literature.

The fate of Mickiewicz and other Polish Romantic writers resembles the situation of intellectuals a century later, as described by George Steiner: "The masterpiece of modern comparative literature, Auerbach's *Mimesis* was written in Turkey by a refugee deprived, overnight, of his livelihood, first language and library."[6] The exile experience, which would continue to be a common one for modern Polish literature and its interpreters for most of the twentieth century, mainly due to the spread of fascism and Stalinism, provided a powerful if painful lesson on the subject of interlinguistic and intercultural interference. It also became part of the twentieth-century reconfiguration of comparative literature.

If we extract from the Latin word *transfero* (*translatum*) the underlying potential for dislocation and transferral from place to place, then this loss of home may also be perceived as a kind of *translatio*. Alongside attempts to construct a powerful edifice of universal theory (inherited from nineteenth century), the need to observe border areas and scrutinize what could not come into existence within dominant discourses was gradually gaining recognition as part of the discipline. This was due to historical traumas, but also to the result of the developing processes of "globalization, democratization and decolonization," to use Mary Louise Pratt's formula.[7] Having grown into the most important task of comparative literature, this focus on the peripheries cast the problem of translation in a new light and accentuated the importance of personal testimony.[8]

2. Dislocation and Translation

A dynamic image of existence on the margins, in translation and in exile, emerges from one of the most important personal testimonies in modern Polish literature – the writings of Czesław Miłosz (1911–2004). Miłosz's place in twentieth-century comparative literature parallels that of Mickiewicz's in the nineteenth. Indeed, Miłosz consciously took up the intellectual and cultural heritage of his predecessor to propose an expansive project for building an aesthetic and intellectual framework for modern Polish literature in the richer context of world literature. His project is especially worthy of attention for combining the highest order of poetic practice with the work of a translator and of an astute scholar of literature and culture.

Born, like Mickiewicz, in Lithuania, Miłosz grew up in a world whose multi-ethnic, multicultural, and multi-linguistic character no longer exists. The tyranny of twentieth-century totalitarianisms irrevocably altered the image of Vilnius, an important city in Polish culture over the previous two centuries, which Miłosz remembered as a "Polish-Jewish island surrounded by a Lithuanian and Belarusian ethnic area."[9] The disintegration of this unique space, which contemporary comparative literature might define as a "translation zone,"[10] formed the beginning of Miłosz's own extensive wanderings between languages and cultures, which brought him to Paris, the United States, and later, in the twilight of his life, to Kraków. This peculiar personal *translatio* shaped his particular "autobiogeography," dictating a certain bi- or multi-focal perspective on individual and communal experiences, as well as multiple affiliations with various regions and traditions, which he repeatedly described in his writings. Miłosz's autobiogeography also determined the special role that translation between languages and cultures would play in his work.

At the same time, the scope and prestige of Miłosz's influence ensured that his work as a translator, along with related transformations of his own poetics and politics as a writer, accelerated and consolidated the turn of modern Polish poetry towards English literature. This turn occurred first of all within his choices as a translator. In the interwar period, Miłosz produced occasional translations from French (Charles Baudelaire, Patrice de La Tour du Pin, Oscar Miłosz), as well as collaborative translations from Lithuanian (poems by Kazys Boruta, co-translated with Pranas Ancevicius). During the war, he clearly shifted interest towards English-language authors, translating Eliot's *The Waste Land* and Shakespeare's *As You Like It*. The second half of the 1940s was a fertile period of intense translation activity, which he characterized as a form of missionary work involving the introduction of fruits gathered from around the world into the Polish language. Working in Washington and New York, he published his translations and critical discussions in the Polish literary press, familiarizing his compatriots with the poetic achievements of celebrated figures, including the work of various African American poets (Negro spirituals). His fascination with English-language poetry did not diminish even when he moved to France and began to work for *Kultura*, a Paris-based journal of great significance to the Polish emigrant community.

In the 1960s and 1970s, as he settled into the Californian university milieu as a professor at UC Berkeley, Miłosz produced translations of Walt Whitman, whom he had long admired, Robinson Jeffers, whom he had recently discovered, William Blake and Thomas Traherne, whom he had translated before, and Thomas Merton, with whom he had corresponded. He also translated Constantine Cavafy and Kabir from their English versions. This period would see a deepening of Miłosz's spiritual conflict with American civilization, as well as attempts to introduce Americans to Polish poetry through Zbigniew Herbert (1924–88), Aleksander Wat (1900–67), Anna Świrszczyńska (pen-name Anna Swir; 1909–84), and other authors included in his repeatedly republished compilation, *Postwar Polish Poetry* (1st ed. 1965, reprinted 1970 and 1983).

Miłosz would continue his translation work well into his later years. In the 1990s he published the *Haiku* collection, a selection of Denise Levertov's poems, and an extensive anthology of his poetic obsessions as a poet and translator (*A Book of Luminous Things*, 1996). Though the influence of English literature on Miłosz was exceptionally strong, his output as a translator remained diverse. In the 1940 and 1950s he published translations of authors as various as Jacques Maritain, Raymond Aron, Jeanne Hersch, Daniel Bell, and Simone Weil. In the 1980s he surprised readers with a whole series of translations from the Bible (the Book of Job, the Gospel of Saint Mark, the Revelation, the Five Scrolls (the Megillot), and the Book of Wisdom).

The rich collection of translations in Miłosz's poetic volumes, essay collections, anthologies, and press publications, and his extensive paratexts – including commentaries, notes, footnotes, and introductions – reveal a powerful constellation of work with multiple aims and functions. On the one hand, these aims include the (re)introduction of world literature's rich output into Polish literary circulation, along with the renewal and reorientation of poetic language. On the other hand, Miłosz also worked on inserting his native tradition into the broader context of world literature. Moreover, his translation activity, including self-translations, fundamentally shaped his own creative work in both its Polish and its English-language versions.

The interpretive possibilities of Miłosz's poetics and world view expand significantly when we consider the poets he chose to translate. They included his poetic or philosophical allies (Walt Whitman, T.S. Eliot) as well as those who served as contrasting points of reference (Wallace Stevens, Robinson Jeffers). A good example here would be his fascination with Eliot, who helped him resist the excessive aestheticism of the Young Poland movement from the nineteenth and early twentieth centuries; it was also Eliot who guarded Miłosz against the susceptibility to emotive and rhythmic excesses typical of the interwar Skamander group poets, who were influenced by Romanticism and French Symbolism. The poetics of *The Waste Land*, which Miłosz would recall as formative and canonical towards the end of his life along with Yeats's "Sailing to Byzantium" and "The Tower,"[11] allowed him to move towards colloquial speech while simultaneously striving to express the most difficult intellectual dilemmas. Miłosz also showed an affinity for the religious underpinnings of this anti-avant-garde innovator, especially with his turn towards conceptions of Christian society as an antidote to the progressive disintegration of Western civilization.

Miłosz saw **the Bible** as the yardstick for poetry and a source of inspiration for his own forms of expression. He believed that its retranslation was a chance to reinvigorate the Polish language that had become impoverished through communist propaganda. Studying ancient languages and numerous translations of the Scripture, he sought to create a biblical language that would be stately but not excessively refined, rooted in the past yet comprehensible, and in accordance with modern sensitivities. This language was to reveal the sacred power of the word and it was to shape contemporary Polish language much as medieval and Renaissance translations had shaped it in the past.

The cultural significance and scope of Miłosz's constellation of translations and accompanying paratexts reveals itself most clearly against the background of other projects of a similar nature, both earlier and later. A closer look at the history of translation in Poland, which accompanies the evolution of Polish language and literature, reveals that it dates back to a fifteenth-century treatise on orthography written by Jakub Parkoszowic (1440). This history has now passed through three principal stages of development – the Old Polish, Romantic, and modern eras; over time, the mutual infiltration of translated works with native ones that was characteristic of old literature has declined, which has led to reflections on the boundaries of autonomy between a translation and the original text.

During the Enlightenment, a number of diverse conceptions in translation studies were formed on Polish soil by Stanisław Staszic (1755–1826), Ignacy Krasicki (1735–1801), Franciszek Bohomolec (1720–84), and others, mainly under the influence of ancient and French authors (e.g., Jean le Rond d'Alambert). Romanticism did not develop this tradition significantly. It added to it the criticism of native dependence on foreign models of writing, which treated translation as a lazy enemy of original and creative literary activities, as Maurycy Mochnacki (1803–34) claimed;[12] it also underscored the negative results of the dominance of the school of imitators and translators of the French style. Simultaneously, however, new achievements in the art of translation were being made by, among others, Mickiewicz, Juliusz Słowacki, Julian Ursyn Niemcewicz (1758–1841), and Cyprian Kamil Norwid (1821–83). The failure of the January Uprising in 1863, which sapped hopes of another attempt at independence, brought a wave of "organic" translations of books that would contribute to the development of social and economic life, and to the re-creation of free state structures and institutions, rather than encourage the Poles to fight. It was precisely at this time that the canon of Polish translations of Shakespeare was established in the form of editions published by Stanisław Egbert Koźmian (1811–85), Leon Urlich (1811–85), and Józef Paszkowski (1817–61). The significance of these works for the future development of Polish literature and the art of translation was enormous. It is Paszkowski's Shakespeare, though, that has had the most enduring impact on the Polish language, and it remains to this day a point of reference for successive generations of translators and the reading public.

The turn of the twentieth century witnessed a flourishing of the art of translation, which was to open more widely Poland's window onto Europe, according to Zenon Przesmycki, pen name Miriam (1861–1944). Its fruit was found in selected texts and anthologies, as well as in the columns of periodicals such as *Świat* (World, 1888–95) and *Chimera* (1901–7), which propagated the philosophies of Arthur Schopenhauer, Frederick Nietzsche, and Henri Bergson, and new works by Henrik Ibsen, August Strindberg, Stefan George, Maurice Maeterlinck, Gabriele D'Annunzio, Leo Tolstoy, Fyodor Dostoevsky, Anton Chekhov, and others. Abundant translations of French Symbolists and English Romantics followed soon after, along with those of medieval and Renaissance poets and the writers and philosophers of antiquity (the translation of works from antiquity was continued by numerous classical philologists in the interwar period). The view of English poetry was enriched for Poles also by Jan Kasprowicz (1860–1926), who translated both Christopher Marlowe and William Butler Yeats. The translation output of this poet and professor of comparative literature at the University of Lviv reveals the deep influence of the linguistic idiom of the Young Poland movement, generally considered outdated today; his translations contain a multitude of poetic exaggerations, mannerisms, and folk stylizations characteristic of the Galician intelligentsia's fascination with local peasantry (so-called chłopomania – "peasant-mania").

Some interesting bilingual artists also appeared on the literary map of Young Poland, including Stanisław Przybyszewski (1868–1927) and Tadeusz Rittner (1873–1921). Also developing were the talents of translators such as Edward Porębowicz (1862–1937) and Tadeusz Boy-Żeleński (1874–1941); the first published numerous comparative studies and translated from English, French, Spanish, and Italian (among other languages), while the latter established the Polish canon of French literature with the famous "Boy's Library," which included over one hundred influential volumes.

The Boy Library (1915–1935) was created by Tadeusz Żeleński (pen name Boy), a writer, theatre and literature critic, columnist, satirist, and rationalist who revised norms of society and custom. A doctor by training, he combined medical service in the Austrian army with lively translation work, which was intended to mollify the nightmare of the First World War. His aim was to modernize Polish culture by incorporating the canon of French literature: from *The Song of Roland* and Villon through the works of Montaigne, Pascal, Rabelais, Diderot, Voltaire, Chateaubriand, the collected works of Molière, and almost the entire *Comédie Humaine* by Balzac, to Stendhal, Proust, Gide, and Jarry. These translations, initially published at his own expense, were accompanied by valuable critical texts and, later, monographs: *Molier* (1924) and *Balzac* (1934).

The pinnacle of his translation work, like that of Edward Porębowicz and Leopold Staff (1878–1957), came during the interwar period of regained independence, when translations from different language areas (e.g., Scandinavian, French, Italian, Russian, Spanish), often addressed to a broad group of readers, came in great abundance. Boy's translations remain relevant and enjoy unflagging admiration to this day. Polish literary language owes a valuable broadening of its range to the titanic work of this translator, whose intention was to turn French writers into Polish classics. His output – together with his stylistic invention, sense of rhythm, and lexical virtuosity – has drawn comparisons with Stanisław Barańczak (1946–2014), whose talents would renew and significantly reinforce the influence of English literature in the second half of the twentieth century.

The aforementioned translators of Young Poland both completed and revised their translations, looking for new linguistic possibilities, as was the case with Staff's indirect translations of Chinese poetry and Rabindranath Tagore. The interwar period produced many new outstanding disciples of the art of translation, including Julian Tuwim (1894–1953) and Władysław Broniewski (1897–1962) (Russian works), Jarosław Iwaszkiewicz (1894–1980) (mostly French, English, and Russian literature), Wacław Berent (1878–1940) and Maria Dąbrowska (1889–1965) (Scandinavian literature), Stefan Napierski (1899–1940) (American and German lyric poetry), Florian Sobieniowski (1881–1964) and Stanisław Helsztyński (1891–1986) (English literature), Aniela Zagórska (1881–1943) (Joseph Conrad's works), Franciszek Mirandola (1871–1930), and Edward Boyé (1897–1943), an outstanding talent who translated from Italian and Spanish but who passed away too early to compete with Boy's achievements. The translation of Franz Kafka's *The Trial* (1936), whose attribution to Bruno Schulz (1892–1942) is questionable, to say the least, is considered to be a literary gem of the era. All evidence suggests that the text was actually translated by Józefina Szelińska (1905–91), Schulz's fiancée. As a woman unknown in the literary milieu at the time, she stood little chance that her translation project would find a publisher and bring her success. Indeed, her name was omitted in many later re-editions of the book. It only appeared in 2007, and two years later Jakub Ekier proposed a new translation based on a fuller, critical-historical source enriched by previously absent fragments.

The custom of noting the translator's name was introduced in reviews of numerous translations published in the interwar period, manifesting the rise in prestige of translation work. The creative enthusiasm of those years (1918–39) was suppressed by the Second World War, and the collapse of the publishing market forced translators to set aside their work until better times. Contrary to expectations, the expected improvement did not arrive after the war ended: the period of Soviet influence resulted in the subordination of translation work to a centralized publishing policy that was implemented by major state institutions. Thus, the period between 1945 and 1989 saw the stabilization of the translator's work within large publishing houses. At the same time, theoretical and critical reflections on the problems of translation continued to evolve, and some fascinating debates between writers still took place. One such debate was the famous feud between Adam Ważyk (1905–82) and Julian Tuwim about the translation of Pushkin. It only seemingly concerned the literary choices such as metre, rhyming structure, character, and the number of verses in the translations of Pushkin's *Eugene Onegin*. In essence, the critique of Tuwim's translation presented by Ważyk in 1949 was ideologically motivated: some of Tuwim's aesthetic decisions were accused of reflecting the poet's own class origin and bourgeois culture, which was hostile to socialism. When Ważyk published his own version of the same work in 1953, Tuwim wittily got back at him with a stinging critique.

The Polish People's Republic will go down in history as an era of censorship. Its purview covered not only works inconvenient for the government (for instance, by George Orwell and Arthur Koestler), and translators who remonstrated against the system, but also various "morally indecent" passages, most often erotic scenes, which were classified as obscene; a considerable part of Henry Miller's output could not appear on the Polish market for this reason. The aesthetic censorship of the Stalinist years (1950–5) eliminated avant-garde and elitist works from the translation market, which was instead dominated by socialist-realist Soviet literature and some progressive Western writers (of the Éluard or Aragon type). Some excellent publications were nevertheless produced during this time, for instance, *Antologia współczesnej poezji francuskiej* (Anthology of Contemporary French Poetry, edited by Adam Ważyk), Samuel Pepys' *Dziennik* (The Diary, translated by Maria Dąbrowska), Tolstoy's *Anna Karenina* (translated by Kazimiera Iłłakowiczówna), and the works of Pablo Neruda (in Jarosław Iwaszkiewicz's translation). Many classical writers offered shelter from the oppressive system for their translators and readers before the so-called thaw in 1956, a broader social phenomenon that followed Stalin's death in 1953 and involved a considerable relaxation of socialist-realist rigour, including in the translation market. At that point, however, the backlog caused by the communist regime attracted scant interest and the attention of numerous excellent translators turned to contemporary works and figures like Ernest Hemingway, William Faulkner, Jean-Paul Sartre, Albert Camus, and Thomas Mann, among many others.

Literatura na Świecie (World Literature) – published since 1971, a monthly journal focused on the most important events in world literature, the reception of Polish literature abroad, and foreign literature in Poland. The choice of material was initially based on linguistic and national criteria, with later focus on selected writers (Joyce, Brodsky, Proust, Pessoa, Cavafy), specific themes (the erotic, death, artificial intelligence), and spheres of culture (Scandinavia, the Maghreb, New York). Apart from translations of brand-new, modern, or old literature (poetry, prose, essays, drama), including classic and avant-garde texts, the journal has been publishing comparative studies as well as literary and translation criticism. Between 1990 and 2006 it co-published books by Ashbery, Perec, Paz, and others.

The Polish thaw was followed by a decade-long "small stabilization." Among many ambitious undertakings of the time were great surveys of the anthology and guide type (e.g., of French, English, or Russian poetry), as well as *Ulysses* in Maciej Słomczyński's (1920–98) translation, which became a great success. This atmosphere lasted until the appearance of underground press publications at the end of the 1970s. Despite the repressions of martial law (1981–3), which affected many authors and translators, the 1980s abounded in excellent translation projects and saw some successes in the fight against censorship, such as the special issue devoted to the erotic trend in Miller's works, published by *Literatura na Świecie* in 1988. Such successes were a harbinger of the freedoms that followed the breakthrough of 1989, when the publishing and translation market opened onto the West. Interest in the literary output of Poland's eastern neighbours diminished at this time, with the exception of outstanding authors previously regarded as politically inconvenient, such as Joseph Brodsky, Osip Mandelstam, Andrei Platonov, Mikhail Zoshchenko, and Viktor Erofeyev, along with interesting representatives of contemporary Russian literature. The number of works published in translation increased significantly.

One measure of the new freedom was the appearance of a stream of exquisite translations by Stanisław Barańczak, to whom we owe a library of English-language writers. Much like Miłosz, Barańczak chose to translate eminent or canonical poets, who often complemented and inspired his own poetic work, based on his revelatory experiences as a reader, as indicated by his early fascinations with Joseph Brodsky, Osip Mandelstam, and Dylan Thomas. In the case of his translations of Brodsky, we find not only a fascination with his poetry, but also a set of shared poetic interests stretching back to the Baroque era, metaphysical poetry, and John Donne. Barańczak complemented his translation and poetic work with theoretical reflections on translation,[13] which allowed him to situate his work in relation to the earlier achievements of such translators as Adam Czerniawski (b. 1934), Ludmiła Marjańska (1923–2005), Kazimiera Iłłakowiczówna (1888 or 1892–1983), Jerzy Stanisław Sito (1934–2011), Roman Klewin (1917–2004), Józef Waczków (1933–2004), and Adam Pomorski (b. 1956).

Barańczak has translated from Russian (among others, Anna Akhmatova, Marina Tsvetaeva, and Boris Pasternak), German (Paul Celan, Rainer Maria Rilke, Bertold Brecht), Lithuanian (Tomas Venclova), Spanish (Saint John of the Cross), Italian (Dante, various opera libretti), Hungarian (József Berda, István Vos, László Benjámin), and Croatian (Ivan Slaming, Luko Paljetak). His pre-eminent achievements, however, are primarily works that renewed and reinforced the canon of English-language literature as it exists in Polish modern literature, as the titles of his most representative publications make apparent: *Antologia angielskiej poezji metafizycznej XVII stulecia* (Anthology of Seventeenth-Century English Metaphysical Poetry); *Z Tobą, więc ze wszystkim: 222 arcydzieła angielskiej i amerykańskiej liryki religijnej* (With You, So with Everything: 222 Masterpieces of the English and American Religious Lyric); *Miłość jest wszystkim, co istnieje: 300 najsławniejszych angielskich i amerykańskich wierszy miłosnych* (Love Is All There Is: 300 of the Most Famous English and American Love Poems); *Od Chaucera do Larkina: 400 nieśmiertelnych wierszy 125 poetów anglojęzycznych z 8 stuleci* (From Chaucer to Larkin: 400 Immortal Poems by 125 English-Language Poets over Eight Centuries).

With great persistence and panache, he also produced successive volumes of the "Library of English Language Poets," along with a collection of his translations of Shakespeare's plays, which stand out for their dynamic syntax in linguistic registers that are more attractive to younger generations of readers and better suited to the aesthetic preferences and needs of the contemporary Polish theatre. Wisława Szymborska (1923–2012) described Barańczak as the "English-language equivalent of Boy," while Miłosz regarded him as the heir to the work first started by himself and Józef Czechowicz (1903–39), a translatorial genius of the sort who comes along once every few hundred years. According to Jan Kott (1914–2001), a man of the theatre, Barańczak had perfect linguistic pitch and a magical gift for rhyme. His translations have delighted actors, theatre experts, opera enthusiasts, and scholars. Some have even seen in him a talent without precedent in the history of Polish poetry. Others, though, have expressed various reservations about Barańczak's achievements (the same was true in Boy's case), accusing him of excessive use of metaphors, of poeticizing his translations, of adding elements that did not exist in the original, and of imposing his poetic voice on diverse poetic languages.

Beside Barańczak's work, there were many other significant achievements in translation after 1989. Zygmunt Kubiak (1929–2004) further familiarized readers with ancient and English literature. Krzysztof Lisowski (b. 1954) published successive volumes of an outstanding *Antologia poezji francuskiej* (Anthology of French Poetry), endeavouring to maintain the representative nature of the texts while also uncovering works he regarded as unfairly forgotten; taken together, the four volumes compiled over a period of forty years present a complete image of twelve centuries of French poetry and its Polish reception. Krzysztof Boczkowski (b. 1936) prepared his own canon of T.S. Eliot readings. Krystyna Rodowska (b. 1937) translated Latin American poetry, as well as Marcel Proust and Jean Genet. Carlos Marrodan Casas (b. 1948) successfully brought various works by masters of magic realism into the Polish language. Leszek Engelking (b. 1955), a well-known translator of Ezra Pound, among others, produced a masterful translation of *Ada* by Vladimir Nabokov, which was also translated by Robert Stiller (1928—2016) and Michał Kłobukowski (b. 1951). Adam Szymanowski (1938–2001) and Krzysztof Żaboklicki (b. 1934) worked on the novels of Umberto Eco.

Various collaborative translations also appeared, including works by Artur Międzyrzecki (1922–96) and Julia Hartwig (1921–2017). Sławomir Błaut (1930–2014) has translated more than a dozen German and Austrian writers, including the almost complete prose works of Günter Grass. Among countless translations by Sława Lisiecka (b. 1947) are various works by Thomas Bernhard and Elfriede Jelinek, while Małgorzata Łukasiewicz (b. 1948) has masterfully exploited Polish-language possibilities in her translations of Hermann Hesse, Patrick Süskind, and Heinrich Böl. Antoni Libera (b. 1949) has translated and edited the works of Samuel Beckett, attempting to convey his characteristic poetics of silence in the Polish language. In recent years, Piotr Kamiński (b. 1949) has joined the ranks of outstanding Shakespeare translators, while a seemingly impossible translation of Joyce's *Finnegans Wake* by Krzysztof Bartnicki (b. 1971) became one of the literary events of 2012. This period has also seen intensive work from Ireneusz Kania (b. 1940), a polyglot whose range as a translator, like Barańczak's, is breathtaking. Apart from countless translations from ancient and multiple modern European languages, he has introduced Polish readers to important works from various Asian cultures.

This overview provides little more than a modest sample of the extensive range of significant translation achievements in the new political and cultural climate. These works have shaped the relationship between native literature and broader literary phenomena that have influenced transformations in the world literary canon. On the subject of the canon, it is worth pointing out that the achievements of the last two decades have not been restricted to filling in the gaps in the library of classics, or to fresh reception of previously translated works. We have also seen a consolidation of work by poet-translators who, like Barańczak or Słomczyński before them, are not satisfied by becoming mere ambassadors for important foreign authors. Instead, they have set for themselves the goal of creating their own canon according to their personal predilections.

Piotr Sommer (b. 1948) – a poet who has translated, among others, Brian Patten, John Ashbery, Charles Reznikoff, Douglas Dunn, Derek Mahon, and Seamus Heaney – favours poetic language that opposes the high speech that has dominated Polish poetry, shifting it towards everyday language. At the same time, he promotes an image of a poet whose most important obligation is to be faithful to language itself, rather than bound to community roles of a spiritual leader, moral authority, or historical witness, as proscribed by the Romantic tradition that dominated for much of the twentieth century. In this Sommer is part of an important current in Polish poetry, represented also by Bohdan Zadura (b. 1945) and Andrzej Sosnowski (b. 1959), which developed alongside of a new, personal strategy of poetic translation. This strategy speaks to an intergenerational dispute that has both aesthetic and ethical dimensions, expressing itself also in a critical attitude towards the selection of texts in Julia Hartwig and Artur Międzyrzecki's well-known anthology of American poetry, *Opiewam nowoczesnego człowieka* (The Modern Man I Sing, 1992). The anthologies proposed by Sommer and Zadura make no claims to representative breadth and are instead "programmatically unrepresentative" (Zadura), provoking a debate on the possibilities and limitations of existing poetic discourses.

Modern Polish translation theory dates back the work of anthropologist Bronisław Malinowski (1884–1942) and phenomenologist Roman Ingarden (1893–1970). The former focused on language research, while the latter developed an original theory of literary work. The field as a whole has developed in the last seventy years, strongly influenced by structuralism and its critics. Contributors to this tradition have included Olgierd Wojtasiewicz, Zenon Klemensiewicz, Stefania Skwarczyńska, Edward Balcerzan, Jerzy Ziomek, Stanisław Barańczak, Jerzy Święch, Anna Legeżyńska, Ewa Kraskowska, Seweryna Wysłouch, Roman Lewicki, Tadeusz Sławek, and younger generations of scholars. Two linguists, Anna Wierzbicka (e.g., *Semantics, Culture, and Cognition: Universal Human Concepts in Culture-Specific Configurations* [New York: Oxford University Press, 1992]) and Elżbieta Tabakowska (e.g., *Cognitive Linguistics and Poetics of Translation* [Tübingen: Gunter Narr Verlag, 1993]), deserve special mention for their impact on translation and literature studies.

From a somewhat broader historical perspective, all of the phenomena outlined above suggest that the time for catching up on the backlog caused by the communist regime has come. After 1989, Polish comparative literature was institutionally reborn and research on the theory and practice of translation began to develop in new directions and with new vitality.[14] The tools at its disposal today, combined with gender or postcolonial perspectives, allow for more subtle historical-literary analyses, renewing the interpretative modes that have fossilized over time.

3. Between Comparative Literature and Translation Studies

In the last two decades, after the fall of the Berlin Wall and the end of the Cold War, comparative literature has turned more readily towards Central Europe in order to include the historical experience of this part of the world in its discursive framework. This interest encounters a condition peculiar to Polish comparative literature, which – having been shaped for many years in the context of foreign domination – particularly intensely supports the process of redefining the national community and its public discourses in the aftermath of systemic change. At present, its development could be perceived in reference to the intellectual and artistic heritage of two modern Polish writers. On the one hand, it looks to the literary output of Czesław Miłosz with its clear Romantic underpinnings, as well as his efforts to build (via translations and academic work) a broad world context for reading Polish literature, including his own works. On the other, it reaches for Witold Gombrowicz (1904–69), a representative of critical modernity who wrote in his diaries about the (im)possibility of comparing what is one's own with what is foreign: "To compare Mickiewicz to Dante or to Shakespeare is to compare fruit to preserves, a natural product to a processed one; a meadow, field or village to a cathedral or city, an idyllic soul to an urban one."[15] This quotation may be used as a motto for comparative literature that is based on deconstruction, demystification, and decanonization. Such a strategy would be much different from Miłosz's seeking to overcome the incommensurability of cultural systems through his constant effort to place Polish literature alongside other literary traditions, enabling its observation in another pattern.

Knowledge about interlingual and intercultural translation, indispensable to such observation, has come a long way from the margins to the centre of comparative literature, much as the discipline itself has moved into the academy. Its history, which I can only signal here, goes back to the 1970s and has accompanied the development of translation studies, a field that has experienced uncommon popularity over the last two decades.[16] During this period, as never before, various attempts[17] have been made to show that comparative literature can be described, following Steiner's formula, "as an art of understanding centered in the eventuality and defeats of translation."[18]

In fact, the complex bilateral relations between comparative literature and translation studies have found a separate platform for conducting intellectual disputes and struggles for influence, thus concluding an era when translation was regarded as an additional, secondary element of the comparatist's work, who would ideally move freely between original texts. Taken together, these disciplines have significantly refreshed the language for describing linguistic and cultural transfer mechanisms based on the binary and hierarchical "original to translation/copy/duplicate/reproduction" relation, which combines linguistic, textocentric observations based on contrastive linguistics with analysis of the work of various social mechanisms. The rich landscape of the most recent studies in translation and comparative literature – disciplines that have become more and more closely connected not only in Europe, but also in the United States – stretches from macro- and micro-political postcolonial perspectives to the feminist exploration of intimacy, although the former is no stranger to intimacy, and the latter to political questions.

The scale of the impact of the renewed language of both formations is reflected in two turns that have already been widely described: the cultural turn that has taken place within translation studies, and the translation turn[19] that has occurred within cultural studies. It is possible to add a third one as well, namely, the translation turn in comparative literature. One of its "manifestos" comes in the form of a book by Emily Apter that approaches the idea of traumatic neighbourhood, which is based on the proximity of violence and love and the meeting of intimacy and politics in the spheres of contact: borderlands or metropolises inhabited by various ethnic, linguistic, religious, or social groups. Her vision of comparative literature, which she calls *translatio*, attempts to abolish the stigma of subordination inherent in the figure of the Creole and to detach both the discipline and language from simplifications resulting from easy national segregation. In her book, inspired to a large extent by the philological projects of Leo Spitzer and Edward Said, Apter grapples with the challenge of the incommensurability of cultural experience, which is closely related to the eternal paradox of translation based on the lack and unattainability of compensation.

As the driving engine of translation, this paradox is broadly commented on by, among others, Paul Ricoeur in his late collection of essays titled *Sur la traduction*,[20] in which he considers the problem of translation in the context of the dual sense that Freud gives to the word "work" when, in one text, he writes about the work of remembrance and, in another, about the work of mourning. That dual meaning reveals the logic of functioning specific to translation, which on the one hand depends on striving to rescue and to preserve and on the other demands reconciliation with loss. In both cases it is about coping with the experience of leaving and dying, preserved in the famous Benjaminian category of *Überleben*, *afterlife*, or *sur-vivre*. In the activity described here we confront a particular paradox: the simultaneous appearance of the need for hospitality, assimilation, and domestication and the continually accompanying sense of resistance, foreignness, or defence. This paradox is at the basis of the ontological status of dual affiliation of translation, of the politics and economics that are specific to it and that generate two key phantasms. On the one hand, there is the conviction that two originals cannot exist. This leads to emphasis on the derivative, secondary, and subordinate character of the copy, whose only property is that it approaches its prototype with more or less skill. On the other hand, there is the dream of a second original, which is faithful and perfect.

The contradictory aims of translation, described by many metaphors and critical languages of modernity – from Schleiermacher through Rosenzweig to the most recent statements by Apter – are also displayed by Ricoeur, who brings two incompatible discourses into direct confrontation: the analytic philosophy of Quine, and the language of psychoanalysis where the drive to translate coexists with resistance, which appears within it. The latter derives, of course, from the incommensurability of languages, from the reserves of untranslatability that reside within them:

> Not only are the semantic fields not superimposed on one another, but the syntaxes are not equivalent, the turns of phrase do not serve as a vehicle for the same cultural legacies; and what is to be said about the half-silent connotations, which alter the best-defined denotations of the original vocabulary, and which drift, as it were, between the signs, the sentences, the sequences whether short or long. It is to this heterogeneity that the foreign texts owes its resistance to translation and, in this sense, its intermittent untranslatability.[21]

The impossible stabilization of the translation within an unchanging semiotic field, and the lack of an absolute *tertium comparationis* – a third text whose status would be like "that of the third man in Plato's *Parmenides*, a third party between the idea of man and the human examples that are thought to participate in the real and true idea"[22] – fuels both the resistance "against" and the drive "to" translation. The character of the work of the translator who confronts the paradox of equivalence without adequacy is agonic; it leaves him in a state of dissatisfaction, it forces him into serving two masters whose interests overlap only partly. On the one hand, the translator sculpts the identity-related sensitivity of the language called the mother tongue or the father tongue; on the other, he attempts to overcome the fear of transposition and mediation, he confronts the resistance, which the endless yet culturally conditioned process of semiosis poses before all attempts to transpose certain accepted rules of representation.

It is exactly this law of double-affiliation, which is also a law of double-alienation, that causes the translator's work to take place on two fronts and that makes the dialectic of remembrance and mourning present in this work. What is at stake, however, Ricoeur asks, in this dramatic moment when the work of mourning finds its equivalent in translation studies? The answer is brief: "the ideal of the perfect translation."[23] Only one's resignation from it

> makes it possible to live, as agreed deficiency, the impossibility, articulated a short while ago, of serving two masters: the author and the reader. This mourning also makes it possible to take one the two supposedly conflicting tasks of "bringing the author to the reader" and "bringing the reader to the author." In brief, the courage to take on the well-known problem of faithfulness and betrayal: vow/suspicion. But with which perfect translation is this renunciation, this work of mourning, concerned? Lacoue-Labarthe and Jean Luc-Nancy provided a really good account of it in the German Romantics under the heading, "the literary absolute." This absolute governs an approximation enterprise, which has taken different names, "regeneration" of the target language in Goethe, "potentiating" the source language in Novalis, convergence of the two-part process of *Bildung* with work on both sides in von Humboldt.[24]

Among various forms that express longing for the ideal translation, Ricoeur singles out two in particular. On the one hand, he points to the dream of creating a total library that derives from the milieu of the *Aufklärung* – that is, the idea of a book collection that is an endless network of translation of all works into all languages, a network that eliminates untranslatability as a function of cultural conditions and communal restrictions. On the other hand, he points to the teleological vision of pure language, which every translation carries within itself as its messianic echo. Both forms, omni-translation and the expected arrival of the saving reign of *Reine Sprache*, are equivalent to the longing that translation be a gain – a lossless gain. Mourning should concern precisely this gain without loss and lead to the reconciliation with the impassable difference between what is one's own and what is foreign. Parting from the ideal translation, and working through this loss, carries within it hope and promise:

> And it is this mourning for the absolute translation that produces the happiness associated with translating. The happiness associated with translating is a gain when, tied to the loss of the linguistic absolute, it acknowledges the difference between adequacy and equivalence, equivalence without adequacy. There is its happiness. When the translator acknowledges and assumes the irreducibility of the pair, the peculiar and the foreign, he finds his reward in the recognition of the impassable status of the dialogicality of the act of translating as the reasonable horizon of the desire to translate. In spite of the agonistics that make a drama of the translator's task, he can find his happiness in what I would like to call *linguistic hospitality*.[25]

This work of recollection and mourning, combined with the challenge of linguistic hospitality, is also one of the tasks of the new comparative literature. Comparative literature aims to scrutinize the existing policy of translation in the sphere of contact, to investigate the reasons for the formation and the ways of transcending the life impasse – meaning the attempt to maintain balance between the awareness of failure inherent in the broadly understood translation, stemming from the differently located systems of communication, and the necessity to accept a constant need or even an obligation to translate.

The lesson about the necessities of the discipline proposed by Apter leads along the routes of the modern exodus, which comparative literature accepts as its own condition in line with the logic of border crossing and ongoing interrogation, by creating itself as a result of sending oneself into exile. The desire to accumulate data in the hope of discovering universal laws of the literary world, following Wilhelm von Humboldt's vision of education as based on Hegelian anthropological foundations with their postulate of the unity of knowledge and the subject, undergoes a considerable displacement during the postwar period, and especially in most recent comparative studies. Language constructed as a result of tension between the particular and the universal frequently yields to discourse formed by tension between politics and intimacy. The communitarian aspect often gives way to the individual one, while the reductive morphologism and the desire for sterile description give way to the richness and opacity of life experience. Instead of doing justice to the precise demarcation of its boundaries, positivist in spirit and method, the comparatist transposition of the world into the domain of comparison is inclined to understand the discipline as a kind of a critical mode, or an art, of reading.

This does not mean that the concept of theory is itself relegated to the ash heap of history, but rather that it is seen to have limits, opening the way for new approaches towards comparative studies. Negotiations conducted on the theoretical ground between "the singular" and "the universal" lead us again towards the paradoxes of translation conceptualized to be as impossible as it is necessary (Apter) – something that both opens and closes the space of communication and understanding. One of the main tasks of comparative literature is to maintain a balance between the contradictory demands of translation. Although – as Haun Saussy says[26] – the dreams of a pantoscopic, all-embracing discipline based on scientific models have diminished, another nineteenth-century desire was reborn. Namely, the desire for self-mastery inherent in the idea of the *Bildung* – on transcending one's own boundaries – and thus on **ex**istence in the strict sense of the word (going beyond oneself). Comparative literature that adds value to its significance becomes an existential project through and through.

The concept of comparative literature as an art of interpretation focused on translation and border zones, which takes on particular significance in a world in which people and capital move from place to place with increasing rapidity, echoes strongly with the experiences of modern Polish literature, shaped to a large extent by exile. For many of its representatives, including Miłosz, life in translation became an often painful necessity. This phenomenon is accompanied by a growing awareness that linguistic and cultural transfer – the tension between what is one's own and other, the translatable and the untranslatable – shapes the development of a given language and culture both from within and without. Consequently, languages are never complete formations, given in advance; rather, they emerge in the play of internal and external differences. This process, subject to various unifying procedures, reveals its ideological, political, ethical, and aesthetic dimensions when achievements of translation are examined.

The above overview emphasizes crucial points in the relation between translation and modern Polish literature, situating them within established conventions for describing the dynamics and specific characteristics of processes within literary history. It also goes beyond these conventions to underscore the significance of outstanding translators whose work does not fit within the narrow framework of the established divisions. Here we find the specific intertwining of the poet's role with that of a translator, burdened with multiple responsibilities: the formation of social and cultural bonds; the struggle for freedom of speech, thought, and association; the consolidation of the community's independence; the development of its original voice; and the confirmation of its belonging to the rich tradition of world literature. In the Polish literary and cultural landscape, in which translations continue to appear in great numbers, we find a fertile ground for asking numerous questions: What is the strength and condition of native literary production, and to what extent is it independent from models borrowed elsewhere? What is the role of foreign canons in the stabilization and destabilization of discourses functioning within the public sphere (translations during the era of the partitions, the influence of translation politics subjugated to censorship during the communist period)? What are the limits of domesticating otherness (as in the stylizations of Young Poland translations), and the possibilities for renewing language and building a sense of belonging to the main current of Western civilizational development – that is, the tools for intellectual and aesthetic modernization (Boy, Miłosz, Barańczak)? From a broad perspective even seemingly innocent disputes over the poetics of translation (for instance, between Julian Tuwim and Adam Ważyk) can be viewed in the context of political and ideological class struggles. By the same token, Miłosz's work draws attention both to the personal and to the social dimensions of the translator's activity. On a personal level, it played a role in the formation of his own poetics and as self-therapy during the war; on a social level, his translations of the Bible renewed religious language, while those of the English-language modernists offered new interpretations of the modern subject's transformations. Much has happened in modern Polish literature thanks to translation, and much still remains to be explored.

Tomasz Bilczewski
Jagiellonian University

NOTES

1 Gasché, "Comparatively Theoretical," 169–87.
2 Mickiewicz, "Adam Mickiewicz's First Lecture," 1477.
3 Mickiewicz, "Pisma historyczne," 191.
4 Mickiewicz, "Adam Mickiewicz's First Lecture," 1478.
5 Ibid., 1476.
6 Steiner, *No Passion Spent*, 148.
7 Pratt, "Comparative Literature and Global Citizenship," 58–65.
8 Spariosu, "Exile, Play, and Intellectual Autobiography"; Bernheimer, "Introduction," 12.
9 Miłosz, *Zaczynając od moich ulic*, 205.
10 Apter, *The Translation Zone*, 2006.
11 Eliot, *Ziemia jałowa / The Waste Land*; Yeats, *Odjazd do Bizancjum. Wieża / Sailing to Byzantium. The Tower*, 2004.

12 Mochnacki, "Thoughts," 2007.
13 See Barańczak, *Ocalone w tłumaczeniu*, 1992.
14 For an overview of modern translation theory in Poland, see de Bończa Bukowski and Heydel, eds., *Polska myśl przekładoznawcza.*
15 Gombrowicz, *Diary*, vol. 1, 4–5.
16 Berman, "Teaching in – and about – Translation," 82–90.
17 See Spivak, *Death of a Discipline*; Apter, *The Translation Zone*; Corngold, *Comparative Literature.*
18 Steiner, *No Passion Spent*, 151.
19 See: Basnett, "The Translation Turn in Cultural Studies," 23–140.
20 Ricoeur, *On Translation*, 2006.
21 Ibid., 6.
22 Ibid., 7.
23 Ibid., 8.
24 Ibid., 7–8.
25 Ibid., 10.
26 Saussy, "Exquisite Cadavers Stitched from Fresh Nightmares," 3–42.

WORKS CITED

Apter, Emily. *The Translation Zone: A New Comparative Literature*. Princeton: Princeton University Press, 2006.

Basnett, Susan. "The Translation Turn in Cultural Studies." In *Constructing Cultures*. Edited by Susan Basnett and André Lefevere. Clevedon: Multilingual Matters, 1998.

Barańczak, Stanisław. *Ocalone w tłumaczeniu. Szkice o warsztacie tłumacza poezji z dołączeniem małej antologii przekładów*. Poznań: Wydawn. a5, 1992.

Berman, Sandra. "Teaching in – and about – Translation," *Profession* (2010): 82–90.

Bernheimer, Charles, ed. "Introduction." In *Comparative Literature in the Age of Multiculturalism*. Baltimore: Johns Hopkins University Press, 1995.

Corngold, Stanley. *Comparative Literature: The Delay in Translation.* In *Nation, Language and the Ethics of Translation.* Edited by Sandra Berman and Michael Wood. Princeton: Princeton University Press, 2006.

de Bończa Bukowski, Piotr, and Magda Heydel, eds. *Polska myśl przekładoznawcza. Antologia.* Kraków: Wydawnictwo Uniwersytetu Jagiellońskiego, 2013.

Eliot, T.S. *Ziemia jałowa / The Waste Land.* Translated by Czesław Miłosz. Kraków: Wydawnictwo Literackie, 2004.

Gasché, Rodolphe. "Comparatively Theoretical." In *The Honor of Thinking: Critique, Theory, Philosophy*. 169-87. Stanford: Stanford University Press, 2007.

Gombrowicz, Witold. *Diary*, vol. 1. Translated by Lillian Vallee. Evanston: Northwestern University Press, 1988.

Mickiewicz Adam. "Adam Mickiewicz's First Lecture in Collège de France 1840–1844. Translated by Bożena Shallcross. *Sarmatian Review* 2 (2009): 1476–80.

– "Pisma historyczne. Wykłady lozańskie." In *Dzieła.* 167–252. Warszawa: Czytelnik, 1999.

Miłosz, Czesław. *Zaczynając od moich ulic*. Paryż: Instytut Literacki, 1985.

Mochnacki, Maurycy. "Thoughts on How the Translation of Foreign Belles-Lettres Influences Polish Literature." Translated by Zuzanna Ładyga. In *National Romanticism: The Formation of*

National Movements: Discourses of Collective Identity in Central and Southeast Europe 1770–1945, vol. II. Edited by Balázs Trencsényi and Michal Kopeček. New York: Central European University Press, 2007.

Pratt, Mary Louis. "Comparative Literature and Global Citizenship." In *Comparative Literature in the Age of Multiculturalism*. Edited by Charles Bernheimer. Baltimore: Johns Hopkins University Press, 1995.

Ricoeur, Paul. *On Translation*. Translated by Eileen Brennan. London and New York: Routledge, 2006.

Saussy, Haun. "Exquisite Cadavers Stitched from Fresh Nightmares: Of Memes, Hives, and Selfish Genes." In *Comparative Literature in an Age of Globalization*. Edited by Saussy. Baltimore: Johns Hopkins University Press 2006.

Spariosu, Mihai. "Exile, Play, and Intellectual Autobiography." In *Building a Profession: Autobiographical Perspectives on the History of Comparative Literature in the United States*. Edited by Lionel Gossman and Mihai Spariosu. Albany: SUNY Press, 1994.

Spivak, Gayatri Chakravorty. *Death of a Discipline*. New York: Columbia University Press, 2003.

Steiner, George. *No Passion Spent: Essays 1978–1995*. London: Faber & Faber, 2010.

Yeats, William Butler. *Odjazd do Bizancjum. Wieża / Sailing to Byzantium: The Tower*. Translated by Czesław Miłosz. Kraków: Wydawnictwo Literackie, 2004.

Translated from the Polish: The Fates, Feats, and Foibles of Polish Literature in English

The day before I began writing this article, I found myself at a reception talking to Peter, the chair of the English department at my university. When he learned that my principal role in my own department is as a translator of Polish literature, he immediately said: "Oh I love Polish literature!" Most instructive for the present purpose were the names he adduced to lend his claim some weight. "Herbert, Zagajewski; and Szymborska's Polish, right? Also, I'm a huge fan of Gombrowicz. You know, *Ferdydurke*, *Pornografia*, *Cosmos* – in those Grove editions …"

I mention this encounter because Peter's perspective on Polish literature in translation is in fact rather typical of the ways in which the American reading public perceives Polish writing. The twentieth-century poetry of Zbigniew Herbert (1924–98), Wisława Szymborska (1923–2012), and Adam Zagajewski (b. 1945), along with the novels of Witold Gombrowicz (1904–69), are among the most widely known Polish texts in North America. The major names missing from Peter's list are Czesław Miłosz (1911–2004) and Bruno Schulz (1892–1942), both of whom are familiar to many Americans who have an interest in non-American literature but otherwise know little or nothing of the Polish tradition. A few may have come across Herbert and Szymborska's contemporary Tadeusz Różewicz (1921–2014), and perhaps the early-twentieth-century writer Stanisław Ignacy Witkiewicz (1885–1939), known commonly as Witkacy; but one rarely hears the names of other Polish authors mentioned by what we might term the general readership – which is to say, those whose reading habits are not driven by academic purposes but rather spring from an enjoyment of, and interest in, the world of writing for its own sake.

In the rest of this essay I will survey what has been translated from Polish, consider whether it has been successful and why, and examine how Polish writing is seen from a North American perspective. When I was originally invited to write this piece, one interesting question the editors suggested I address was: "What is it about the institutional process that is worth knowing for your readers when they consume the product of your translatorial skills and creativity?" At the end of the essay I will return to this question and offer at least a partial answer.

The Classics

The Polish classics – whether the early-nineteenth-century Romantic *wieszcze* or "bards" (Adam Mickiewicz [1798–1855], Juliusz Słowacki [1809–49], Zygmunt Krasiński [1812–59], and the somewhat later Cyprian Kamil Norwid [1821–83]), the great late-nineteenth-century novelists (Bolesław Prus [1847–1912], Eliza Orzeszkowa

[1841–1910], Henryk Sienkiewicz [1846–1916]), or even earlier figures like Ignacy Krasicki (1735–1801) from the late eighteenth century and Jan Kochanowski (1530–84) from the sixteenth – have attracted English-language translators for well over a century. In the 1890s Jeremiah Curtin (1835–1906), a colourful character and self-taught reader of Polish, published translations of Sienkiewicz and, later, Prus. Despite Curtin's manifold limitations as a translator,[1] his rendering of Sienkiewicz's *Quo Vadis* (in 1897) was highly popular, and indeed is still widely available (in some cases in unattributed editions). Sienkiewicz's novels have since been retranslated more than once, perhaps most notably by W.S. Kuniczak (1930–2000). Prus's major works, too – *Lalka* (The Doll, 1887–9), *Faraon* (Pharaoh, 1895–6), and most recently *Emancypantki* (Emancipated Women, 1890–3) – are available in more modern translations. As for the Romantic tradition, Adam Mickiewicz's long narrative poem *Pan Tadeusz* (Sir Thaddeus, 1833) commonly regarded as the Polish national epic, was first translated by Maude Ashurst Biggs in 1885; several other translations have appeared over the years, including renderings by Kenneth Mackenzie (1964) and Watson Kirkconnell (1962) that are still used today in university classes, and, in the case of Mackenzie's version, read by general readers. To a lesser extent, there have also been English translations of other Romantic poets. The former include the poetry of Norwid in translations by Adam Czerniawski (b. 1934) from 2004, and Danuta Borchardt from 2011; a recent collection of Słowacki's work (2009) translated by various hands; and a widely used anthology of Romantic drama translated by Harold Segel (1930–2016) from 1977. There still exist huge gaps, though, including many of the plays of Krasiński and Słowacki. Such lacunae also exist in nineteenth-century prose. Amazon has started offering e-versions of pre-1923[2] translations, often unattributed and of uncertain quality, of some works by writers such as Józef Ignacy Kraszewski (1812–87). But it remains the case that, for instance, the major novels of Eliza Orzeszkowa, including *Nad Niemnem* (On the Banks of the Niemen, 1888), remain unavailable in any version in English. This points to the regrettable fact that women writers have been even less visible than their male counterparts, not just in the early literature but in that of the last century too – an erasure in which the home culture too is complicit.[3]

Even when translations have appeared, distribution is often minimal or non-existent, meaning that titles rarely reach the eyes of large numbers of potential readers. The books are often published either in Poland or elsewhere in Europe (e.g., by the Central European University Press in Budapest, Hungary), virtually assuring a lack of visibility in the United States; or by university presses; or finally by small publishing houses such as Hippocrene that are likely to have a primarily ethnic (i.e., Polish immigrant) audience. Not coincidentally, the classics of Polish literature are hardly ever encountered in the broader intellectual discourse. Few public intellectuals in North America ever mention Mickiewicz or Prus the way one might commonly refer, say, to Baudelaire or Tolstoy. This produces certain effects in the way Polish writing is perceived in "the West," especially in English-speaking countries. First, the impression is created that Polish culture did not participate in the general development of "European" writing from the Renaissance up till the twentieth century. Second, it means that in the case of those Polish writers who *are* well known in English – for example, Miłosz or Gombrowicz – the Western readership is largely or completely unaware of the rich tradition that shaped these writers in crucial ways. In other words, the ways in which such authors are understood in anglophone settings are significantly different from their reception in their native culture.

At one level, one is tempted to complain about the lack of appreciation of, for example, the novels of Prus. If American readers can appreciate Dostoevsky or Tolstoy, why can someone as great as Prus not be one of that number? Yet the truth is, many "minor" literatures suffer the same fate. Few of our general North American readers could name any nineteenth-century author writing in Dutch, Swedish, Czech, Portuguese, or Yiddish, however great those traditions might be. Such a fact seems to have much more to do with cultural hegemony: hegemonic cultures such as British and American seem interested primarily or exclusively in other heavyweights like themselves. In any case, the marginalization of Polish writing is not exceptional. Add to this imbalance outdated and often inadequate translations that are more likely to deter readers than entice them, and the problem is compounded. In fact, it is extremely hard to find North American publishers for nineteenth-century fiction (let alone other genres like verse drama or poetry). Novels that are long (and thus much more expensive to produce) and that do not promise a wide readership are not an attractive proposition for a publishing house, even in many cases for academic houses not driven primarily by profit.

All in all, while it is crucial that Polish classics continue to be published in English – and of course, that the translations be actually good – it remains true that, with the occasional exception, such translations are going to appeal primarily to two constituencies: the academic world, where they often appear on course reading lists; and those of Polish descent who yearn to reconnect with their cultural heritage. These constituencies are certainly not negligible; it is simply to be expected that translations of the Polish classics remain unlikely to find a wider audience in North America.

The Twentieth Century

As suggested above, and in contrast to the standing of the Polish classics, much Polish literature of the twentieth century has fared rather well in the English-speaking world, even though the names fall mostly within a fairly delimited time period from the 1930s to the 1990s. Yet of course the picture is somewhat more complex than this simple and optimistic diagnosis suggests. The present section will look at what has been most popular in translation and why; what has been published in translation yet not received recognition; and what major gaps need to be filled.

From an American perspective, Polish prose above all means two names: Bruno Schulz and Witold Gombrowicz. Schulz's stories were first published in English in 1963, in the translation by Celina Wieniawska that is still the only one available.[4] It is not a perfect translation in many ways, but conveys enough of Schulz's style and content (and one might argue that for Schulz, style *is* content) to give English-language readers a sense of his work. The case of Gombrowicz is less straightforward. His major novels were brought out in the 1960s by Grove Press, but in problematic translations made indirectly from the French. It was not till the 2000s that Yale University Press published most of the novels in new, fuller, and more accurate translations made directly from the Polish by Danuta Borchardt. As of now both versions of the books are in circulation: Grove is no doubt unwilling to withdraw from the market a group of titles that have proved popular (and thus profitable) over several decades. As a result, the two versions sit rather uneasily side by side on bookstore shelves.[5] The situation is reminiscent of that of Kafka: The early, imperfect but very popular and influential Muir translations of his works, including the major novels, are still available alongside newer and closer renderings. It would seem in both cases that particular affection or attention is lavished on the first translations and that subsequent ones may not get all the attention they deserve from readers. Similar issues arose in 2008 when Alissa Valles published the *Collected Poems* of Zbigniew Herbert, thereby upsetting many North American readers used to the "standard" – that is, first – translations by John and Bogdana Carpenter.

The poetry landscape has been similarly dominated by a handful of names: Herbert, Miłosz, Szymborska, Zagajewski, and, for some better-informed readers, Tadeusz Różewicz. In the case of these poets, though (with the exception of Herbert), the work has been translated by various hands and the association of writer with translator has often been less strong.

What has not "made it" in, or into, English? The list is of course quite long. It starts at the very beginning of the century with Wyspiański's *Wesele* (The Wedding, 1901), a play whose hermetic subject matter and (just as important) tight metrical form make it all but inaccessible in translation (translations have been published but have not been widely read or, all the more, performed). Much of the best formal poetry of the twentieth century, from Bolesław Leśmian (1877–1937) through Julian Tuwim (1894–1953) to Krzysztof Kamil Baczyński (1921–44), probably cannot be fully appreciated by English-language readers – my own small book of Baczyński translations remains read mostly by Poles, while I am unaware of any collection of poems by either Leśmian or Tuwim available in English. Translators face formidable – indeed, perhaps insurmountable – challenges with these poets because of their work's complexity of content and intricacy of form, which may not carry across linguistic boundaries.

Yet among the texts that have not (yet) made the crossing are a number of modernist novels that might in fact have a chance of garnering some readership here. As far back as 1988 a group of Polish literature scholars – Stanisław Barańczak (1946–2014), Bogdana Carpenter, and Madeline Levine – compiled a list of what they called "essential [pre-1945] works that are or should be available in English translation."[6] A surprising number of these works remain untranslated today, including the major novels of Wacław Berent (1878–1940), Karol Irzykowski (1873–1944), Maria Dąbrowska (1889–1965), Zofia Nałkowska (1884–1954), and others, though a few translators are in fact working on some of these projects at present, and two Nałkowska novels appeared in English in 2014. Last, a number of writers situated on the margins of the Polish tradition, often though not always in a geographical sense, also remain unknown in English: for instance, Andrzej Bobkowski (1913–61) who after the Second World War lived in exile in Guatemala, Zygmunt Haupt (1907–95), another postwar exile who settled in the United States, and others. Several such writers have been rediscovered in post-1989 Poland, having been marginalized during the communist period. Such writers too could appeal to English-language readers, precisely because they often represent a cosmopolitan perspective that is less rooted in Polish realia and thus more accessible, and perhaps more interesting, to readers outside the country.

As concerns Polish drama, the major twentieth-century playwrights are represented somewhat unevenly. Many of Witkacy's best-known plays have been published in English, translated mainly by Daniel Gerould (1928–2012). The dramas of Gombrowicz and Różewicz are also available, though only in dated translations from the 1960s. Similarly, most of Sławomir Mrożek's (1930–2013) major plays are available in English, but only in translations from the 1950s and 1960s. Of course, printed drama texts occupy a liminal space between literature and theatre, and it is an open question whether one can talk of the "reception" of plays in book form. At the same time, it must be recognized that very few works in translation from any language are staged in the United States, with the exception of the established repertoire (the Greeks, Moliere, Chekhov, Ibsen, Brecht, maybe a couple more). It is also true that the work of the dramatists mentioned above is stylistically at odds with the essentially realist and naturalist preferences in contemporary American drama (it is instructive that even well-known playwrights in the absurdist tradition like Beckett and Ionesco are relatively infrequently staged in North America). While many in the theatre world know the work of the four Polish dramatists listed above, and while their plays are occasionally produced in English, the theatre-going public cannot be said to be familiar with this theatre.

After 1989

For several years after the end of communism, American presses were leery of taking on any of the new generation of authors who had emerged in the late 1980s and early 1990s. My own impression, as I tried unsuccessfully in the mid- and late 1990s to interest editors in authors such as Magdalena Tulli (b. 1955) and Jerzy Pilch (b. 1952), was that without the point of reference of communism and the political struggle against it, American publishers were unsure how to approach Polish books, what to think of them, or how to evaluate them. With a couple of exceptions, few new authors appeared in English and even fewer attracted critical attention. Publishing houses preferred to stick to more or less familiar names: Miłosz, Szymborska, Zagajewski, and some lesser writers such as Andrzej Szczypiorski (1928–2000). Things really started to change around the turn of the millennium. An influential anthology of new Polish writing in the *Chicago Review* in 2000, put together by Bill Martin, led the way for issues of other journals devoted to new Polish literature. Gradually, more and more novels and other prose work began to appear by writers like Andrzej Stasiuk (b. 1960), Jerzy Pilch, Stefan Chwin (b. 1949), Olga Tokarczuk (b. 1962), Magdalena Tulli, Dorota Masłowska (b. 1983), Paweł Huelle (b. 1957), and Michał Witkowski (b. 1975). As this list suggests, as of the present moment – late 2015 – Polish prose is in rather good shape in North America. This is undoubtedly due in large measure to the emergence of a new generation of highly competent and discerning translators such as Antonia Lloyd-Jones, Philip Boehm, and Margarita Nafpaktitis.

The same cannot truly be said of recent poetry. Poetry from Poland is still highly regarded by American readers. But for the overwhelming majority of these readers, "Polish poetry" means the older authors mentioned above. Other highly gifted poets of Zagajewski's generation – one thinks of Stanisław Barańczak, Ewa Lipska (b. 1945), and Piotr Sommer (b. 1948), though of course any list of names is invidious – and many younger ones are not in any real sense present in the American awareness. The work of younger poets has appeared in a few anthologies; Zephyr Press's single-author series of Polish poets has included volumes by Marzanna Kielar (b. 1963), Tomasz Różycki (b. 1970), Eugeniusz Tkaczyszyn-Dycki (b. 1962), Tadeusz Dąbrowski b. 1979), and MLB (the pen name of Miłosz Biedrzycki, b. 1967), with more to follow. Also published elsewhere are Andrzej Sosnowski, Janusz Szuber (b. 1947), and others. Yet none of these books has been widely reviewed. The only poet of the younger generation who seems to be making a mark in the United States at the moment is Tomasz Różycki, whose lyric poetry has been translated by Mira Rosenthal. It may simply be the case that, while a lot of prose travels fairly well and can be appreciated whether or not the author is present, the greater intimacy and difficulty of poetry means that face-to-face encounters at readings and other cultural events play a greater role. It is also the case that in the United States at least, the poetry world tends with very few exceptions to be inward-looking, and there is a great deal of competition for attention among poets writing in this country; both these tendencies militate against an openness to poetry from elsewhere. The new Polish poetry, though it has been made available in English in capable translations, has not as yet crossed the cultural divide into widespread North American awareness.

As far as drama is concerned, there is even less to tell. As noted above, translated drama is notoriously difficult to stage in the United States. Polish theatre companies visit the United States with some frequency, and some, like Theatre Provisorium (Teatr Provisorium-Kompania Teatr), and Theater of the Eighth Day (Teatr Ósmego Dnia), have performed their work in English renderings. But translations of contemporary plays have been few and far between, and productions of these translations even rarer. Present-day Polish drama has yet to make an impression on the English-speaking world.

What Is Success and How Is It Achieved?

At this point, it is worth pausing a moment and reflecting on what is meant by "success" in terms of literary translation.

In fact, the literary marketplace in the United States is such a huge and busy place that it becomes rather hard to know what counts as success. In the mid-1990s, when I was starting out as a translator, Andrzej Szczypiorski's novels were a "hit," selling well and being reviewed in the *New York Times*, the *Washington Post*, and elsewhere. Now, fifteen years later, they are largely forgotten. At the time they seemed to fill a need among American readers for accessible narratives with clear, comprehensible political and historical messages. Now that this need has gone with the fading of communism in the popular imaginarium, such novels are no longer of interest. Other than the few names that do in fact seem well-established in the American literary consciousness (Gombrowicz, Schulz, Miłosz, Szymborska), it is very hard to judge which authors and which books can be said to have staying power.

What are the indicators of success here? Literary prizes are certainly a major factor, especially the Nobel Prize. Miłosz was little-known here, especially as a poet, till he won the Nobel in 1980; the same goes for Wisława Szymborska before 1996. Now Szymborska, and to a slightly lesser extent Miłosz too, are widely read by the general public (an event celebrating the centenary of Miłosz's birth drew a crowd of hundreds in New York). All credit, by the way, to the translators who championed these two poets before their rise to fame. Other literary prizes, while less prestigious – the IMPAC DUBLIN award, the Neustadt Prize, won by Adam Zagajewski in 2004, or the US National Book Critics Circle Awards, for instance – can all help cement an author's reputation.

Reviews are also crucial, especially in certain periodicals. Back in 1999 I published a translation of Stefan Żeromski's novel *Wierna rzeka* (The Faithful River, 1912) with Northwestern University Press. A tiny five-line review, really little more than a positive mention, appeared in the Briefly Noted column of *The New Yorker* – and sales spiked dramatically. The same happened in 2007 with Andrzej Stasiuk's *Dziewięć* (Nine, 1999) when it was reviewed by the novelist Irvine Welsh in the *New York Times Book Review*. The point, of course, is not numbers of sales, but the attention such reviews bring to

Polish literature. My sense is that precisely because the book marketplace is so vast, American readers are grateful for direction, and reviews in a small handful of publications – those mentioned, plus the *New York Review of Books* and maybe one or two others – can be extremely influential. By the same token, when a translation is brought out a good publisher will go to considerable lengths to encourage these and other newspapers and magazines to review it.

There are also any number of other, less tangible ways in which Polish writers can establish a reputation in English. Course adoptions in university classes are a key element of sales for many small-run books and can promote familiarity with a writer. While I do not have extensive statistics, it might be worth mentioning that a typical print run for a translated Polish book with an independent publisher might be between 2,000 and 5,000 copies. Sales figures over 2,000 are considered good. *The Faithful River* did well in this manner, finding its way onto reading lists for courses not just in Polish literature but also, for example, in nineteenth-century European history. The physical presence of writers in the United States in general, and especially at major literary events like the PEN World Voices Festival, the annual conference of the AWP (Association of Writers and Writing Programs), and major book fairs, can be a big help, especially if the writer is able to function in English. Inclusion in major international anthologies, such as the Dalkey Archive's annual *Best European Fiction* series, is another way for a reputation to be solidified. None of these methods alone is enough, but taken together they enhance the writer's presence on the North American literary scene. Lastly, while it may seem simplistic to point this out, it is definitely the case that some authors are much easier to appreciate than others – the prevalent free-verse, plain-spoken tradition of Herbert and Szymborska, for example, is much more accessible than that of more hermetic or formally complex writers. Recall that even in the case of Miłosz, major rhymed poems from the early period like the *Traktat moralny* (Moral Treatise) remain untranslated into English. The same goes for prose: the relatively accessible novels of, say, Paweł Huelle are easier to approach than those of, for example, Magdalena Tulli.[7]

Book publishers vary considerably as to the amount of promotion of new titles they engage in. In this regard, Archipelago Books has been exemplary – the press has aggressively organized book launches, readings, and other events related to the Polish titles they sell. This work helps generate much wider awareness of new books and authors being published; it also puts a human face on the enterprise. As well as affecting sales, readings and other encounters with authors and translators offer a key venue for North American reading audiences to get to know Polish writers and writing.

In this regard, it is crucial to acknowledge the vital work being done by the Polish Book Institute (Instytut Książki) in Kraków, and by the Polish Cultural Institute in New York and its sister institute in London. The Book Institute, whose origins lie in an institution set up when Poland was guest of honour at the Frankfurt Book Fair in 2000, has over the last decade made immense strides in professionalizing the presentation of new Polish books to potential publishers outside the country. Above all, the Book Institute offers small but important financial support for the publication of Polish books. A biannual catalogue with short extracts and reviews is now translated into English by experienced translators. The institute has provided further support through translation fellowships in Poland for experienced and beginning translators. Three international conferences have been organized for translators of Polish writing around the world, all held in Kraków (in 2005, 2009, and 2013). Also, funding has been made available for the production of samples to send to publishers, which, as pointed out above, is a crucial dimension of the promotion of Polish literature in North America.

The Polish Cultural Institute in turn has worked hard to promote Polish writing in the United States, arranging writers' tours, readings, and other events. For example, the PCI has successfully included Polish novels in the readings of the European Book Club in New York, thus ensuring a readership for certain contemporary novels and more broadly, an awareness of new Polish writing; it has also striven to include Polish writers in PEN events such as the PEN World Voices Festival, which in recent years has featured Polish authors such as Dorota Masłowska, Andrzej Stasiuk, and Piotr Sommer. Readings by other contemporary writers are increasingly frequently organized and supported by the PCI.

To conclude this discussion of success, it is important to consider two writers who have not previously been mentioned, yet who have achieved far greater renown than any thus far considered. The first of these is Ryszard Kapuściński (1932–2007). Kapuściński's books are greatly popular among the reading public in English-speaking countries. His brand of literary travel writing falls rather neatly into the category of "creative non-fiction" that has become a staple of American and other English-language literary creativity. This sort of literate journalism, of course, stems from a long tradition in Polish writing. Kapuściński's global subject matter, his accessible yet writerly style, and (in the pre-1989 period at least) the evident political dimension of works such as *Cesarz* (The Emperor, 1978), all contributed to a popularity that had not waned at the time of his death in 2007.

The second Polish writer who has been hugely successful in translation is Stanisław Lem (1921–2006). Lem's 1960 science fiction novel *Solaris* is a classic of its genre and is extremely widely known in the English-speaking world. Many other novels by Lem are available in English, and interest in his work has not been pinned to political or historical factors – indeed, it has been pointed out that in the only print version of *Solaris* currently available, there is no mention of the fact that Lem is Polish or that the book was originally written in Polish. It is also true that Lem's writing appeals to a somewhat different constituency of readers than mainstream fiction. In any case, it seems that Lem's philosophically infused narratives are among the few bodies of writing that have effectively sidestepped or transcended "Polishness" and its attendant marginalizations in the anglophone world.[8]

Quo Vademus?

What conclusions can be drawn from the last hundred-plus years of Polish literature in translation? Where do we stand now, and where should we go? And finally, to return to the question mentioned at the beginning of this essay, what should consumers of Polish literature in translation know about the production of such texts?

It will always be an uphill struggle to find a publisher for a Polish novel or volume of poems. As an experienced translator, I still regularly have difficulty placing books, especially those by writers hitherto unknown in English. Polish is and will almost certainly always remain a "minority literature" from the point of view of North America and the English-speaking world. While this situation may be regrettable, it is not irreversible. Publishing Polish books in translation is not easy, but as the record of the last fifteen years shows, it can be done successfully.

In considering such efforts, it is worth remembering that in the great majority of cases, translators of Polish literature are also promoters of that literature. Unlike American writers, Polish writers usually do not have an agent in the United States. This means that a huge amount of work is put in by translators preparing and sending samples, cover letters, and other material aimed at finding publishers for Polish writing. In such efforts, the helpfulness of the Book Institute and the practical assistance it provides is invaluable – the institute has done a great deal to establish and maintain contacts between Polish and North American publishers, for example. But a large part of the "entrepreneurial" work is done by translators.

One moral that is not too hard to extract from the picture painted above is that Polish writers and presses need to be careful about the contracts they enter into with American publishers. One example will have to suffice. In the case of Stanisław Lem's *Solaris*, an unfavourable contract signed several decades ago has led to a situation where not only is an imperfect translation (made from the French) the only one available in print, but it has also proved extremely difficult for the author's estate to have a new translation published in book form. In several other cases (though by no means the majority), American publishing companies have ridden roughshod over the best interests of Polish writers, altering their work, preventing or delaying publication, and otherwise hindering the production and distribution of quality translations. By and large, Polish publishers today are much more savvy than their predecessors of past decades. But Polish culture, as many others, remains a minor phenomenon in the United States, and as a result its producers will always be vulnerable here.

It also needs to be said that the quality of those translations that do get published remains uneven. This problem – which had dogged Polish writing in English from the early days – has often led to a failure to recognize outstanding talents. Some literature can survive bad translation, emerging maimed but still recognizable: this is true of the early translations of Gombrowicz and some of Lem's work, and also of Miłosz's translations of his own work, which were not as good as later renderings by other translators. But other equally outstanding writers did not survive inelegant or inaccurate translations because such translations effectively destroyed their chances with readers. (I prefer not to give examples, given the small world of Polish translation.) Conversely, many writers who *have* earned recognition in the United States have been blessed with good translators – I am thinking of Clare Cavanagh's translations of Adam Zagajewski and, with Stanisław Barańczak, of Wisława Szymborska; Antonia Lloyd-Jones's translations of Paweł Huelle and Olga Tokarczuk; and the work of Czesław Miłosz as rendered by translators such as Robert Pinsky and Robert Hass, in collaboration with the author. Obvious as it may sound, it is worth reiterating that good translators need to be trained and treasured.

As the transformative year of 1989 recedes and with it the reading public's expectations for particular subject matter (primarily the struggle against communism), Polish books are increasingly judged by the same criteria as other international literature: Is it well written? In fiction, do we find an engaging and carefully constructed plot, compelling characters, clever observations? At this stage, it is unclear whether there exists a particular set of expectations about Polish literature in terms of its being specifically *Polish* – mostly because American publishers and their readership still do not have a proper grasp of what that means. (Though truth be told, are those of us who toil at these things every day any better placed in this regard? As for myself, I find it increasingly hard to say what is "Polish" about Polish literature, other than the most blindingly obvious facts of language and literary heritage.) What is expected, however, is that it be *different* – from its American counterpart, that is. I think this is why Andrzej Stasiuk, for instance, is increasingly popular here. Americans are by and large unable to appreciate Stasiuk in the context of Polish literature, not having the points of reference that any Polish reader will recognize instantly. But Stasiuk is also different from American writers, and from other international authors who are widely read here. It is this distinctness, not his distinctness in the context of the Polish tradition, that determines his success in English.

Where do we stand today? It is fair to say that the situation of Polish literature in English translation is quite healthy. First, it remains the case for recent books that of all the so-called Central and East European literatures – including, surprisingly enough, Russian – recent Polish literature in English is one of the most widely available. Thanks both to competent translators and to willing publishers, most of the major post-1989 authors are available in English. There will always be a problem with the classics – nineteenth-century literature and before – but such issues are not peculiar to Polish, nor are they likely to be solved in the foreseeable future. This should not stop translators from publishing good translations of the classics – these are needed by the constituencies mentioned above. And who knows? Perhaps there will come a time when names like Słowacki and Orzeszkowa will in fact have some kind of resonance for English-language readers.

The situation for poetry and drama is less clear. In the case of poetry, though existing translations are often quite good, few Polish poets write in a way that is immediately accessible to a US readership. In the United States, creative writing programs have unwittingly formed a rather limited set of preferences and expectations for poetry, with a tendency towards the personal and confessional, the demotic, and the playful. Many good Polish poets – an example close to my heart is Eugeniusz Tkaczyszyn-Dycki (b. 1962) – do not fall into this mode, so even where they have been translated they have not garnered much attention. Once again this should not deter translators, only give them realistic expectations with regard to the reception of their work.

Similar limitations exist in theatre translation. As theatre translator Catherine Grosvenor put it at a recent conference, English-speaking audiences "like their fourth wall" – that is, they prefer rather traditional dramas in the realist mode. It is much harder to generate wide interest in the alternative theatrical traditions so strongly represented by Poland – the legacy of Jerzy Grotowski (1933–99), Tadeusz Kantor (1915–90), and their ilk is amply taken up by companies such as Theatre of the Eighth Day, Theatre Provisorium, and Gardzienice, but such work, though it is often well received in the United States and elsewhere (e.g., at the Edinburgh Festival), is hard to convert into anything that might be thought of as mainstream success. Yet again, translators should not feel discouraged – this is merely a question of what can be expected and why.

More positively, there are signs of interest in other genres. Literary journalism is still alive and well in Poland after Kapuściński, and contemporary journalistic writing such as the work of Wojciech Jagielski (b. 1960), Mariusz Szczygieł (b. 1966), and Jacek Hugo-Bader (b. 1957) is beginning to appear in English. There is also a rising interest in detective fiction. The English-speaking world seems at present to have an insatiable hunger for crime writing from other countries, and translations of writers such as Marek Krajewski (b. 1966) and Zygmunt Miłoszewski (b. 1976) are starting to appear.

For the moment, though, the most "successful" Polish writers in English remain those mentioned earlier: Miłosz, Herbert, and Szymborska; Schulz and Gombrowicz; Kapuściński and Lem. It is interesting that a quarter-century after the fall of the communist system in Poland, none of the writers to have emerged since that historical juncture have assumed positions of comparable prominence in the anglophone literary imagination. Literary tastes are of course notoriously fickle, and literary fashions often ephemeral.

It is impossible to know which of today's Polish writers will still be read and enjoyed fifty years hence – or indeed, which authors of previous times will be "discovered" by English-language readers. Translators' discernment when it comes to selecting and promoting particular works and authors offers the best hope for Polish literature in English. I would like to end with a personal story that gives me hope for the future of Polish literature in translation. Many years ago, in the late 1980s, I bought a book in a used bookstore in Poland titled *Kamień na kamieniu* (Stone Upon Stone, 1984) by Wiesław Myśliwski (b. 1932). The book blew me away from its opening paragraph, and all in all left a deeper impression on me than almost anything else I had ever read before in Polish. A few years after that, I began translating Polish literature for publication in the United States. In the back of my mind I nursed a vague ambition to translate Myśliwski's book. Yet the more I learned about the world of publishing, the less likely it seemed that such a translation would ever see the light of day. As I already mentioned, publishers prefer shorter novels to longer ones, which are more expensive to produce – a crucial consideration when the financial reward is likely to be meagre. Americans prefer books with a straightforward narrative (unlike the complex embeddings of Myśliwski's novel). And they like authors they have already heard of. All of these facts militated against *Stone Upon Stone*, which is more than five hundred pages in length, has a non-linear narrative, and is by an author almost unknown in the English-speaking world.[9]

Yet a few years ago my publisher at Archipelago Books, Jill Schoolman, heard about Myśliwski in connection with a new book he had brought out titled *Traktat o łuskaniu fasoli* (A Treatise on Shelling Beans, 2006). She asked me about the author; I immediately told her about *Stone Upon Stone*. She asked for a sample, which I prepared in trepidation. She liked it, and agreed to publish the book. When it came out it was carefully marketed, and readings were arranged in several cities (unfortunately the author was unable to travel, so the translator took on the task). It was also reviewed widely, including a crucial short couple of paragraphs in *The New Yorker* and a review in the *Times Literary Supplement* in Britain. In a word, a long and *prima facie* difficult novel by an unknown Polish writer had gotten some serious attention from English-speaking readers.

Literary translation is a crucial endeavour. The number of people who appreciate Polish writing will always exceed the number of those who can read it in the original – even readers with a reasonable grasp of the language often prefer to read in English. While it is always gratifying when the authors one translates, or indeed one's own translations, win awards and prizes, I personally gain a much deeper pleasure from e-mails and conversations in which strangers tell me how much they have enjoyed a particular book that I translated. While with Polish literature the numbers of readers are usually quite small, they are not negligible, and interest is enduring. I salute my fellow-translators and encourage them to persevere in their difficult but important endeavours.

Bill Johnston
Indiana University, Bloomington

NOTES

1 See Segel, "Sienkiewicz's First Translator, Jeremiah Curtin," 189–214.

2 In American law, anything published before 1923 is considered to be in the public domain and therefore copyright considerations do not apply.

3 See Borkowska, *Alienated Women.*
4 At the time of writing, Madeline Levine was preparing a retranslation of Schulz's stories, to be published in March 2018 with Northwestern University Press under the title *Collected Stories: Bruno Schulz.*
5 Of course, one could argue that the existence of more than one translation is not a problem – English-language readers will commonly find multiple translations of any major early work of literature, for example. The issue here, though, is that there are only two options, one of which is not a proper translation made directly from the original language, but what is termed a "relay translation" – a regrettable phenomenon that nevertheless is encountered with some frequency in many minor literatures.
6 The list was published somewhat later, in the now defunct journal *2B*, in 1995.
7 This discussion brings to mind the character in Tadeusz Konwicki's novel *Mała Apokalipsa* (A Minor Apocalypse, 1979) who writes novels in Polish in such a way as to make them easily translatable into Western languages. One wonders whether contemporary writers are ever moved by such considerations.
8 Two pieces of anecdotal evidence may serve to indicate the popularity of these two authors in the United States. In the early 2000s I nominated Ryszard Kapuściński for a prestigious lectureship at Indiana University. The application was supported by a dozen enthusiastic letters from colleagues in a wide range of units who, to the best of my knowledge, had little or no connection with Polish Studies; these included scholars from African Studies, Latin American Studies, Journalism, English, and Creative Writing. As for Lem, on the Internet-based bookstore amazon.com most Polish novels garner three or four customer reviews at best. When my translation of Lem's *Solaris* appeared in 2011, within days there were more than forty reviews.
9 Myśliwski's novel *Pałac* (The Palace, 1970) had been published in 1990 in an English translation by Ursula Phillips, but had received little attention.

WORKS CITED

Barańczak, Stanisław, Bogdana Carpenter, and Madeline Levine. *2B* 5–6 (1995): 88–90.

Borkowska, Grażyna. *Alienated Women: A Study on Polish Women's Fiction 1845–1918.* Translated by Ursula Phillips. Budapest: Central European University Press, 2001.

Segel, Harold B. "Sienkiewicz's First Translator, Jeremiah Curtin." *Slavic Review* 24, no. 2 (1965): 189–214.

SELECTED LITERARY TRANSLATIONS SINCE 1989

Poetry

Biedrzycki, Miłosz. *69.* Translated by Frank L. Vigoda. Brookline: Zephyr Press, 2010.

– *Massachusetts.* Translated by Frank L. Vigoda. Riverside: University of California–Riverside, 2010.

Carnivorous Boy, Carnivorous Bird: Poetry from Poland. Translated by Anna Scucińska and Elżbieta Wójcik-Leese, edited by Marcin Baran. Brookline: Zephyr Press, 2004.

Dąbrowski, Tadeusz. *Black Square.* Translated by Antonia Lloyd-Jones. Brookline: Zephyr Press, 2011.

Herbert, Zbigniew. *Mr. Cogito*. Translated by John Carpenter and Bogdana Carpenter. New York: Ecco Press, 1995.
– *The Collected Poems, 1956–1998*. Translated by Alissa Valles. New York: Ecco Press, 2007.
– *Elegy for the Departure and Other Poems*. Translated by John Carpenter and Bogdana Carpenter. New York: Ecco Press, 1999.Kielar, Marzanna Bogumiła. *Salt Monody*. Translated by Elżbieta Wójcik-Leese. Brookline: Zephyr Press, 2006.
Kapuściński, Ryszard. *Wrote Stone: The Selected Poetry of Ryszard Kapuściński*. Translated by Diana Kuprel and Marek Kusiba. Windsor: Biblioasis, 2007.
Kochanowski, Jan. *The Envoys*. Translated by Bill Johnston. Kraków: Księgarnia Akademicka, 2007.
– *Laments: A Bilingual Edition*. Translated by Stanisław Barańczak and Seamus Heaney. New York: Noonday Press, 1995.
– *Treny. Laments*. Translated by Michael Mikoś. 2nd ed. Lublin: Norbertinum, 1998.
– *Treny: The Laments of Kochanowski*. Translated by Adam Czerniawski. Rev. ed. Oxford: Legenda, 2001.
Miłosz, Czesław. *Facing the River: New Poems*. Translated by Czesław Miłosz and Robert Hass. Hopewell: Ecco Press, 1995.
– *New and Collected Poems 1931–2001*. Translated by Czesław Miłosz and Robert Hass, Robert Pinsky, Dale Scott, et al. New York: Ecco Press, 2001.
– *Provinces: Poems 1987–1991*. Translated by Czesław Miłosz and Robert Hass. New York: Ecco Press, 1991.
– *Road-side Dog*. Translated by Czesław Miłosz and Robert Hass. New York: Farrar, Straus and Giroux, 1998.
– *Second Space: New Poems*. Translated by Czesław Miłosz and Robert Hass. New York: Ecco Press, 2004.
– *Selected Poems, 1931–2004*. Translated by Czesław Miłosz and Robert Hass. New York: Ecco Press, 2006.
– *The Separate Notebooks*. Translated by Robert Hass, Robert Pinsky, and Renata Gorczyński. New York: Ecco Press, 1984.
– *A Treatise on Poetry*. Translated by Czesław Miłosz and Robert Hass. New York: Ecco Press, 2001.
Norwid, Cyprian Kamil. *Selected Poems*. Translated by Danuta Borchardt. Brooklyn: Archipelago Books, 2011.
– *Selected Poems*. Translated by Adam Czerniawski. London: Anvil Press, 2004.
Różewicz, Tadeusz. *Sobbing Superpower: Selected Poems of Tadeusz Różewicz*. Translated by Joanna Trzeciak. New York: W.W. Norton, 2011.
– *Tadeusz Różewicz: New Poems*. Translated by Bill Johnston. New York: Archipelago Books, 2007.
– *They Came to See a Poet*. Translated by Adam Czerniawski. London: Anvil Press Poetry, 2004.
Różycki, Tomasz. *Colonies*. Translated by Mira Rosenthal. Brookline: Zephyr Press, 2013.
– *The Forgotten Keys*. Translated by Mira Rosenthal. Brookline: Zephyr Press, 2007.
– *Twelve Stations*. Translated by Bill Johnston. Brookline: Zephyr Press, 2015.
Scattering the Dark: an Anthology of Polish Women Poets. Edited by Karen Kovacik. Buffalo: White Pine Press, 2016.
Six Polish Poets. Edited by Jacek Dehnel. Todmorden: Arc, 2008.
Słowacki, Juliusz. *This Fateful Power*. Lublin, Norbertinum, 1999.
Spoiling Cannibals' Fun: Polish Poetry of the Last Two Decades of Communist Rule. Edited by Stanisław Barańczak and Clara Cavanagh. Evanston: Northwestern University Press, 1991.

Szymborska, Wisława. *Here.* Translated by Clare Cavanagh and Stanisław Barańczak. Boston: Houghton Mifflin Harcourt, 2010.

– *Map: Collected and Last Poems.* Translated by Clare Cavanagh and Stanisław Barańczak. Boston: Houghton Mifflin Harcourt, 2015.

– *Miracle Fair: Selected Poems of Wislawa Szymborska.* Translated by Joanna Trzeciak. New York: Norton, 2001.

– *Monologue of a Dog: New Poems.* Translated by Clare Cavanagh and Stanisław Barańczak. Orlando: Harcourt, 2006.

– *Nothing Twice: Selected Poems.* Translated by Clare Cavanagh and Stanisław Barańczak. Kraków: Wydawnictwo Literackie, 1997.

– *People on a Bridge: Poems.* Translated by Adam Czerniawski. London, Boston: Forest Books, 1990.

– *Poems, New and Collected, 1957–1997.* Translated by Stanisław Barańczak and Clare Cavanagh. New York: Harcourt Brace and Co., 1998.

– *View with a Grain of Sand: Selected Poems.* Translated by Stanisław Barańczak and Clare Cavanagh. New York: Harcourt Brace and Co., 1995.

Tkaczyszyn-Dycki, Eugeniusz. *Peregrinary.* Translated by Bill Johnston. Brookline: Zephyr Press, 2008.

Zagajewski, Adam. *Eternal Enemies.* Translated by Clare Cavanagh. New York: Farrar, Straus and Giroux, 2008.

– *Mysticism for Beginnners.* Translated by Clare Cavanagh. New York: Farrar, Straus and Giroux, 1997.

– *Unseen Hand.* Translated by Clare Cavanagh. New York: Farrar, Straus and Giroux, 2011.

– *Without End: New and Selected Poems.* Translated by Clare Cavanagh. New York: Farrar, Straus and Giroux, 2002.

Young Poets of a New Poland: An Anthology. Edited by Krystyna Lars and Donald Pirie. London and Lincoln Center: Forest Books, 1993.

Drama

Loose Screws: Nine New Plays from Poland. Translated by Bill Johnston, Benjamin Paloff, Philip Boehm, Margarita Nafpaktitis, and Mira Rosenthal, edited by Dominika Laster. London, New York, and Calcutta: Seagull Books, 2015.

Masłowska, Dorota. *A Couple of Poor, Polish-Speaking Romanians.* Translated by Lisa Goldman and Paul Sirett. England: Oberon Books, 2008.

Rożewicz, Tadeusz. *Reading the Apocalypse in Bed: Selected Plays and Short Pieces.* Translated by Adam Czerniawski, Barbara Plebanek, and Tony Howard. London: Marion Boyars, 1998.

Słowacki, Juliusz. *Balladina.* Translated by Bill Johnston. Newcastle upon Tyne: Cambridge Scholars Publishing, [n.d.].

– *Poland's Angry Romantic: Two Poems and a Play by Juliusz Słowacki.* Edited and translated by Peter Cochran. Newcastle upon Tyne: Cambridge Scholars Publishing, 2009.

Witkiewicz, Stanisław Ignacy. *Witkiewicz Reader.* Translated and edited by Daniel Gerould. Evanston: Northwestern University Press, 1992.

Prose

Białoszewski, Miron. *A Memoir of the Warsaw Uprising.* Translated by Madeline Levine. Ann Arbor: Ardis, 2015.

Chwin, Stefan. *Death in Danzig.* Translated by Philip Boehm. Orlando: Harcourt, 2005.

Gombrowicz, Witold. *Bacacay.* Translated by Bill Johnston. New York: Archipelago Books, 2004.
– *Cosmos.* Translated by Danuta Borchardt. New Haven: Yale University Press, 2005.
– *Ferdydurke.* Translated by Danuta Borchardt. New Haven: Yale University Press, 2000.
– *Pornografia.* Translated by Danuta Borchardt. New York: Grove Press, 2009.
– *Trans-Atlantyk: An Alternate Translation.* Translated by Danuta Borchardt. New Haven: Yale University Press, 2014.
Herling-Grudziński, Gustaw. *The Noonday Cemetery and Other Stories.* Translated by Bill Johnston. New York: New Directions, 2003.
Huelle, Paweł. *Castorp.* Translated by Antonia Lloyd-Jones. London: Serpent's Tail, 2007.
– *Cold Sea Stories.* Translated by Antonia Lloyd-Jones. Manchester: Comma, 2012.
– *The Last Supper.* Translated by Antonia Lloyd-Jones. London: Serpent's Tail, 2008.
– *Mercedes-Benz: From Letters to Hrabal.* Translated by Antonia Lloyd-Jones. London: Serpent's Tail, 2005.
– *Who Was David Weiser?* Translated by Michael Kandel. New York: Harcourt Brace Jovanovich, 1992.
Iwaszkiewicz, Jarosław. *The Birch Grove and Other Stories.* Translated by Antonia Lloyd-Jones. Budapest: Central European University Press, 2002.
Krall, Hanna. *Chasing the King of Hearts.* Translated by Philip Boehm. London: Peirene, 2013.
Lem, Stanisław. *The Invincible.* Translated by Bill Johnston. Kraków: Pro Auctore Wojciech Zemek, 2014.
– *Solaris.* Translated by Bill Johnston. Newark: Audible.com (audiobook), 2011.
Libera, Antoni. *Madame.* Translated by Agnieszka Kołakowska. New York: Farrar, Straus and Giroux, 2000.
Masłowska, Dorota. *Snow White and Russian Red.* Translated by Benjamin Paloff. With illustrations by Krysztof Ostrowski. New York: Black Cat, 2005.
Myśliwski, Wiesław. *The Palace.* Translated by Ursula Phillips. London: Owen, 1990.
– *Stone upon Stone.* Translated by Bill Johnston. Brooklyn: Archipelago Books, 2010.
– *A Treatise on Shelling Beans.* Translated by Bill Johnston. New York: Archipelago Books, 2013.
Nałkowska, Zofia. *Boundary.* Translated by Ursula Phillips. DeKalb: Northern Illinois University Press, 2016.
– *Choucas: An International Novel.* Translated by Ursula Phillips. DeKalb: Northern Illinois University Press, 2014.
– *Medallions.* Translated by Diana Kuprel. Evanston: Northwestern University Press, 2000.
Pilch, Jerzy. *His Current Woman.* Translated by Bill Johnston. Evanston: Northwestern University Press, 2002.
– *The Mighty Angel.* Translated by Bill Johnston. Rochester: Open Letter, 2009.
– *My First Suicide.* Translated by David A. Frick. Rochester: Open Letter, 2012.
– *A Thousand Peaceful Cities.* Translated by David A. Frick. Rochester: Open Letter, 2010.
Plebanek, Grażyna. *Illegal Liaisons.* Translated by Danusia Stok. Williamstown: New Europe Books, 2013.
A Polish Book of Monsters: Five Dark Tales from Contemporary Poland. Translated by Michael Kandel. New York: PIASA Books, 2010.
Prus, Bołeslaw. *The Sins of Childhood and Other Stories.* Translated by Bill Johnston. Evanston: Northwestern University Press, 1996.
Szczypiorski, Andrzej. *The Beautiful Mrs Seidenman.* Translated by Klara Główczewska. New York: Grove Press, 1990.

– *A Mass for Arras.* Translated by Richard Lourie. London: Weidenfeld and Nicolson, 1993.
– *Self-Portrait with Woman.* Translated by Bill Johnston. New York: Grove Press, 1995.
– *The Shadow Catcher: A Novel.* Translated by Bill Johnston. New York: Grove Press, 1997.
Stasiuk, Andrzej. *Dukla.* Translated by Bill Johnston. Champaign: Dalkey Archive Press, 2011.
– *Fado.* Translated by Bill Johnston. Champaign: Dalkey Archive Press, 2009.
– *Nine.* Translated by Bill Johnston. Orlando: Harcourt, 2007.
– *On the Road to Babadag: Travels in the Other Europe.* Translated by Michael Kandel. Boston: Houghton Mifflin Harcourt, 2011.
– *Tales of Galicia.* Translated by Margarita Nafpaktitis. Prague: Twisted Spoon Press, 2003.
Tokarczuk, Olga. *House of Day, House of Night.* Translated by Antonia Lloyd-Jones. Evanston: Northwestern University Press, 2003.
– *Primeval and Other Times.* Translated by Antonia Lloyd-Jones. Prague: Twisted Spoon Press, 2010.
Tulli, Magdalena. *Dreams and Stones.* Translated by Bill Johnston. New York: Archipelago Books, 2004.
– *Flaw.* Translated by Bill Johnston. Brooklyn: Archipelago Books, 2007.
– *Moving Parts.* Translated by Bill Johnston. Brooklyn: Archipelago Books, 2005.
– *In Red.* Translated by Bill Johnston. Brooklyn: Archipelago Books, 2011.
Witkowski, Michał. *Lovetown.* Translated by William Martin. London: Portobello Books, 2011.
Wojdowski, Bogdan. *Bread for the Departed.* Translated by Madeline Levine. Evanston: Northwestern University Press, 1997.
Żeromski, Stefan. *The Coming Spring.* Translated by Bill Johnston. Budapest: Central European University Press, 2007.
– *The Faithful River.* Translated by Bill Johnston. Evanston: Northwestern University Press, 1999.

Popular Fiction

Krajewski, Marek. *The Minotaur's Head.* Translated by Danusia Stok. London: MacLehose Press/ Quercus, 2012.
Miłoszewski, Zygmunt. *Entanglement.* Translated by Antonia Lloyd Jones. London: Bitter Lemongrass Press, 2010.
– *A Grain of Truth.* Translated by Antonia Lloyd-Jones. Wydawnictwo W.A.B., 2011.
– *Rage.* Translated by Antonia Lloyd-Jones. Seattle: AmazonCrossing, 2016.

Essays

Herbert, Zbigniew. *The King of the Ants.* Translation by John Carpenter and Bogdana Carpenter. New York: Ecco Press, 1999.
– *Still Life with a Bridle: Essays and Apocryphas.* Translation by John Carpenter and Bogdana Carpenter. New York: Ecco Press, 1993.
Janion, Maria. *Hero, Conspiracy, and Death: The Jewish Lectures.* Translated by Alex Shannon. Frankfurt am Main: Peter Lang GmbH, 2014.
Michnik, Adam. *In Search of Lost Meaning: The New Eastern Europe.* Translated by Roman S. Czarny, edited by Irena Grudzińska Gross. Berkeley: University of California Press, 2011.
– *The Trouble with History: Morality, Revolution, and Counterrevolution.* Translated by Elżbieta Matynia, Agnieszka Marczyk, and Roman Czarny, edited by Irena Grudzinska Gross. New Haven: Yale University Press, 2014.

Miłosz, Czesław. *To Begin Where I Am: Selected Essays.* Translated by Bogdana Carpenter and Madeline Levine. London: Macmillan, 2001.

– *Beginning with My Streets: Essays and Recollections.* Translated by Madeline Levine. New York: Farrar, Straus and Giroux, 1991.

Zagajewski, Adam. *A Defense of Ardor.* Translated by Clare Cavanagh. New York: Farrar, Straus and Giroux, c2004.

Reportage

Grynberg, Michał. *Words to Outlive Us: Voices from the Warsaw Ghetto.* Translated by Philip Boehm. New York: Metropolitan Books, 2002.

Hugo-Bader, Jacek. *Kolyma Diaries: A Journey into Russia's Haunted Hinterland.* Translated by Antonia Lloyd-Jones. London: Portobello Books, 2014.

– *White Fever: A Journey Into the Heart of Siberia.* Translated by Antonia Lloyd-Jones. Berkeley: Counterpoint, 2012.

Jagielski, Wojciech. *Burning the Grass: At the Heart of Change in South Africa, 1990–2011.* Translated by Antonia Lloyd-Jones. New York: Seven Stories Press, 2015.

– *The Night Wanderers: Uganda's Children and the Lord's Resistance Army.* Translated by Antonia Lloyd-Jones. New York: Seven Stories Press, 2012.

– *Towers of Stone: the Battle of Wills in Chechnya.* Translated by Soren A. Gauger. New York: Seven Stories Press, 2009.

Kapuściński, Ryszard. *Imperium.* Translated by Klara Główczewska. New York: A.A. Knopf, 1994.

– *My Morning Walk.* Warsaw: Agora Publishing House, 2009.

– *The Other.* Translated by Antonia Lloyd-Jones. London; New York: Verso, 2008.

– *Our Responsibilities in a Multicultural World.* Translated by Michael Jacobs. Kraków: The Judaica Foundation, Center for Jewish Culture, 2002.

– *The Shadow of the Sun.* Translated by Klara Główczewska. New York: A.A. Knopf, 2001.

– *Travels with Herodotus.* Translated by Nicolas Coster. New York: A.A. Knopf, 2007.

Szczygieł, Mariusz. *Gottland: Mostly True Stories from Half of Czechoslovakia.* Translated by Antonia Lloyd-Jones. Brooklyn: Melville House, 2014.

Tochman, Wojciech. *Like Eating a Stone: Surviving the Past in Bosnia.* Translated by Antonia Lloyd-Jones. New York: Atlas, 2008.

History, Biography, and Autobiography

Dichter, Wilhelm. *God's Horse and the Atheists' School.* Translated by Madeline G. Levine. Evanston: Northwestern University Press, 2012.

Domosławski, Artur. *Ryszard Kapuściński: A Life.* Translated by Antonia Lloyd-Jones. London and New York: Verso, 2012.

Hen, Józef. *Nowolipie Street.* Translated by Krystyna Boron. Bethesday: DL Books LLC, 2012.

Krall, Hanna. *The Woman from Hamburg and Other True Stories.* New York: Other Press, 2006.

Miłosz, Czesław. *A Year of the Hunter.* Translated by Madeline G. Levine. New York: Farrar, Straus and Giroux, 1994.

Olczak-Ronikier, Joanna. *In the Garden of Memory: A Family Memoir.* Translated by Antonia Lloyd-Jones. London: Weidenfeld and Nicolson, 2004.

Popular Science

Szczeklik, Andrzej. *Catharsis: On the Art of Medicine.* Translated by Antonia Lloyd-Jones. Chicago: University of Chicago Press, 2005.

– *Kore: On Sickness, the Sick, and the Search for the Soul of Medicine.* Translated by Antonia Lloyd-Jones. Berkeley: Counterpoint, 2012.

Philosophy

Karłowicz, Dariusz. *The Archparadox of Death: Martyrdom as a Philosophical Category.* New York: Peter Lang, 2016.

Kołakowski, Leszek. *Freedom, Fame, Lying, and Betrayal: Essays on Everyday Life.* Translated by Agnieszka Kołakowska. London: Penguin Books, 1999.

– *God Owes Us Nothing: A Brief Remark on Pascal's Religion and on the Spirit of Jansenism.* Chicago: University of Chicago Press, 1995.

– *Is God Happy? Selected Essays.* London: Penguin Books, 2012.

– *Modernity on Endless Trial.* Translated by Stefan Czerniawski, Wolfgang Freis, and Agnieszka Kolakowska. Chicago: University of Chicago Press, 1990.

– *My Correct Views on Everything.* Edited by Zbigniew Janowski. South Bend: St Augustine's Press, 2005.

– *The Presence of Myth.* Translated by Adam Czerniawski. Chicago: University of Chicago Press, 1989.

– *The Two Eyes of Spinoza and Other Essays on Philosophers.* Translated by Agnieszka Kołakowska and Frederic Fransen, edited by Zbigniew Janowski. South Bend: St. Augustine's Press, 2004.

– *Why Is There Something Rather Than Nothing? 23 Questions from Great Philosophers.* Translated by Agnieszka Kołakowska. London: Allen Lane, 2007.

Michalski, Krzysztof. *Logic and Time: An Essay on Husserl's Theory of Meaning.* Translated by Adam Czerniawski. Dordrecht and Boston: Kluver Academic, 1997.

Tischner, Józef, J.M. Życiński, and George F. McLean, eds. *The Philosophy of Person: Solidarity and Cultural Creativity.* Washington: Paideia Press: Council for Research in Values and Philosophy, 1994.

Special anthologies:

Slavica anthologies of the excerpts from Polish literature translated by Michael Mikoś: *Polish Renaissance Literature*, 1994; *Polish Baroque and Enlightenment Literature*, 1995; *Polish Romantic Literature*, 2002; *Polish Literature from 1864 to 1918. Realism and Young Poland*, 2006; *Polish Literature from 1918 to 2000*, 2008.

Compiled by Bethany Braley
Indiana University, Bloomington

PART IV

Genres and Their Discontents

Interwar Prose

The widely accepted term for works of high modernism by Polish authors is "interwar literature." The idea of modernism, as it is currently understood, did not exist in Poland for many decades and was associated, as Kazimierz Wyka suggested, with the first ten years of Young Poland (Młoda Polska) at the end of the nineteenth century. There was no one term for the poetics and philosophy of creativity of the interwar period. At the same time, literature in these two decades was strongly influenced by historical events, which imposed a thematic framework on them and led to their periodization. I will therefore take a relatively traditional approach to the prose of this period, connecting developments in politics with those in literature, even though prose was less beholden than poetry to historical developments.

It was Polish poetry, particularly its avant-garde variety, that established itself after the First World War as the new voice of a society reclaiming its independence following 123 years of subjugation. In some sense, poetry really was beginning anew, breaking for the most part with literary tradition. Moreover, the authors associated with these various poetic groups – Expressionists, Futurists, the Kraków avant-garde, and even Skamander, which was relatively conservative in matters of literary form – were just arriving on the literary scene. Prose, by contrast, enjoyed a greater degree of continuity, since most of the important novelists and short story writers were already established by the time of the First World War. Stefan Żeromski (1864–1925), Wacław Sieroszewski (1858–1945), Andrzej Strug (1871–1937), Zofia Nałkowska (1884–1954), Juliusz Kaden-Bandrowski (1885–1944), Stanisław Ignacy Witkiewicz (pen name Witkacy; 1885–1939), and Roman Jaworski (1883–1944) were all seasoned writers by 1918, different as their prose was in terms of its thematics and poetics.

Without the drive to seek out entirely new forms or means of expression, the most important prose works published after 1918 were written in a relatively traditional style, although the first innovative Polish novel of the twentieth century, Karol Irzykowski's *Pałuba* (The Hag), appeared in 1903. The influence of *The Hag* on Polish literature – in particular, its relentless analyses (reminiscent of Freudian depth psychology) of its characters', narrator's, and even author's thought processes – became apparent only several decades later, when young writers became familiar with psychoanalysis and established a fashion for psychological novels. Prose was thus already exhibiting avant-garde tendencies before the war, while the avant-garde's predilection for the fantastic and the grotesque can easily be found in early works by Witkacy, Jaworski, and Strug.

War, Revolution, and Literature

In Western Europe, the most important event of 1918 was the end of the First World War; for Poles, by contrast, it was the restoration of independence after more than a century of partitions. For this reason, the atrocities of war – though they by no means bypassed Polish soil – did not become a major literary theme after the peace accords were signed. Furthermore, because Poland had been partitioned among the major warring powers, the war had pitted Poles against one another. For Poles, war did not really end in 1918. Even after the First World War had officially ended, uprisings against German occupying forces continued to flare in the Prussian Partition; there were also clashes with Ukrainians over Lviv and with Lithuanians over Vilnius; and, most significantly, there was a devastating conflict between the newly formed Polish army and the Soviet army to the East, a conflict that grew into an full-out Polish–Bolshevik war, which culminated in a Polish victory at Warsaw in August 1920.

These military efforts on various fronts were celebrated in only a small number of books. Andrzej Strug wrote *Odznaki za wierną służbę* (Badges for Faithful Service, 1921), a slim first-person account of the military exploits of a young soldier in Piłsudski's legions. After taking part in a raid from Austrian Kraków on the Russian partition, he is disillusioned to find that the Poles living there view the struggle for independence differently and that they hardly treat Piłsudski's soldiers as liberators. Juliusz Kaden-Bandrowski portrayed several notable legionnaires in his book *Piłsudczycy* (The Piłsudski Legions, 1915). More interesting, however, is his long novel *Łuk* (The Bow, 1919), which is set in Kraków during the First World War. Its heroine, Marysia, a young woman with a son just a few years old, is left to face the hardships of wartime alone when her husband volunteers for the Austrian army. In these conditions, Kaden's heroine comes into her own; she gradually sheds her role as an obedient wife, learns to fend for herself, and pursues her sexual desires. At the end of the book, Marysia emerges as a woman stripped of illusions, perhaps even ruthless, but at the same time steeled for her confrontation with life. In *The Bow*, the war itself is pushed to the margins of the plot, and today it can be read as one of Poland's first feminist novels.

The Bow suggests that in Poland after 1918, the struggle for independence lost the central place it had occupied in the literature of the nineteenth and early twentieth centuries, leaving a void that would have to be filled by new themes. War was one of these new themes, of course, but it was treated as part of the human condition and not as an aspect of the Polish struggle for independence. Moreover, war became a fully fledged theme in Polish novels somewhat later than in the West, and even after it did, it was treated in connection with the idea of pacifism, or with the psychology of the soldier. Józef Wittlin (1896–1976) explored pacifist ideas in the novel *Sól ziemi* (Salt of the Earth, 1936). Wittlin's novel is about an ordinary, kind-hearted boy from the Hutsul countryside who is completely ignorant of international conflict until, at the start of the First World War, he is drafted into the Austrian army. There he undergoes the compulsory education that, in soldiers around the world, inculcates hatred for the enemy. *Salt of the Earth* was intended as the first volume of a projected cycle of novels, which was to include also *Powieść o cierpliwym piechurze* (Novel about the Patient Infantryman). While the cycle was never completed, *Salt of the Earth* met with a great deal of popularity and was translated into numerous languages.

Less popular was Andrzej Strug's three-volume *Żółty krzyż* (Yellow Cross, 1932–3), a sensationalist novel about wartime espionage. "Yellow cross" was the name given to the deadly gas whose chemical formula Entente intelligence operatives attempted to extract from the Germans. In the novel, these efforts cost the life of the beautiful Ewa Evard, an actress-turned-spy whose cover is blown by German counter-intelligence. Her death before a firing squad is held up as proof of the senselessness and enormity of war. Pacifist novels such as this can be compared to works by American, French, and German authors who took the absurdity of war as one of their themes: Ernest Hemingway's *A Farewell to Arms* (1929), Henri Barbusse's *Under Fire* (1916), Erich Maria Remarque's *All Quiet on the Western Front* (1928), and Arnold Zweig's *The Case of Sergeant Grisha* (1927). In Poland, however, this theme was decidedly less popular than in the West.

For Poles, the First World War, though it brought unprecedented destruction and carnage, was not, strictly speaking, senseless; after all, it led to Poland's independence. The Bolshevik Revolution, by contrast, was a very real threat and led to a number of bloody, mainly Polish–Ukrainian conflicts of a social-national character, as well as the destruction of the culture associated with the Polish gentry in the former eastern territories. The revolution in Ukrainian lands was taken up in literature by, among others, Maria Dunin-Kozicka (1877–1948) in *Burza od Wschodu* (Storm from the East, 1918–20) and Zofia Kossak (1889–1968) in *Pożoga* (Conflagration, 1922). Ferdynand Goetel in *Przez płonący wschód* (Across the Burning East, 1922) and *Pątnik Karapeta* (The Pilgrim of the Karapet, 1923), as well as Ferdynand Ossendowski (1876–1945) in *Cień ponurego Wschodu. Za kulisami życia rosyjskiego* (The Shadow of the Gloomy East: Russian Life behind the Scenes, 1923) and in *Przez kraj ludzi, bogów i zwierząt* (Beasts, Men, and Gods, 1923), described their travels through the Central Asian provinces of the former Russian Empire, in the midst of revolution and civil war. Eugeniusz Małaczewski (1895–1922), who unfortunately died young, dealt with the horrors of the revolution in his stories *Koń na wzgórzu* (Horse on the Hill, 1921). The most important book about the Polish–Soviet War of 1920, *W polu* (In the Field) by Stanisław Rembek (1901–85), was published only in 1937. It is a psychological narrative about a small Polish army division that loses almost all of its soldiers in a prolonged retreat from an enemy offensive; the surviving soldiers experience the defeat as a psychotic breakdown. Rembek never showed interest in depicting heroic exploits; he even overlooked that the Polish army eventually triumphed over the Soviets. Still, no one has done a better job describing the "magical thinking" of a soldier, or showing the role that an inconspicuous pebble in a soldier's boot might play during a battle. Rembek also tackles the delicate question of pro-communist sympathies among the Polish forces. This last question was particularly important for the new Polish state and was featured in several novels, whose purpose was to foment debates over how the new Poland ought to look.

Literature, Politics, and the Problems of the New State

After the First World War, Poland realized *a different variant of modernization* than neighbouring states. The Soviet Union collectivized the village and developed heavy industry. Nazi Germany socialized the village and based progress on heavy industry and arms manufacturing. The Polish variant involved gradual agricultural reforms, such as the subdivision of large estates and the allotment of land to landless peasants and smallholders. It also involved modernizing projects aimed at balancing the ratio between agricultural and industrial production. Its greatest undertakings included the construction of a railway linking the Upper

Silesian coal basin with the port of Gdynia (1926–33), itself the product of modernization: construction of the Gdynia port began in 1920, and by 1936 it was the biggest and most modern of Baltic ports, the tenth in Europe in terms of trade, with annual transshipments of 8.7 billion tons in 1938. Most famous, perhaps, was the construction of the Central Industrial Region (Centralny Okręg Przemysłowy, or COP), which covered 60,000 square kilometres and was home to 5.6 million people. The region was divided into three zones, with the first dedicated to the extraction of raw materials and the second to the production of food, while the third served as an energy base where petroleum, natural gas, and electricity were developed and distributed. Total investments in the COP region reached 1.9 billion Polish *złoty*. The accelerated modernization of an agrarian state produced results: the percentage of GDP derived from industry increased from 32 per cent in 1929 to 50 per cent in 1939.

The most important work in this regard was *Przedwiośnie* (The Coming Spring, 1924), by Stefan Żeromski. It caused a good deal of controversy but at the same time was taken very seriously. Its author was a figure of great authority; during the partitions he was among the writers whose works had anticipated Poland's independence and had speculated about what the new, free Poland might look like. Żeromski was a leftist, but he rejected the idea of a Bolshevik-style revolution; the entire first part of his novel, which is set in Baku, expresses his loathing for the revolutionary style of thought and action and his conviction that revolution means economic ruin and prodigality, as well as – on an ethical level – the universal extinction of values. In the next two parts of his novel the hero, a young revolutionary named Cezary Baryka, makes his way to Poland, where he is temporarily cured of his communist sympathies, only to be faced with the most conservative model of "Polishness" – the country estate, with all the laziness and class-selfishness of its inhabitants. Baryka finally ends up at a university in Warsaw, but even there he is unable to settle on a social and political ideology. He is tempted by various sides advocating reasonable, gradual reforms, as well as (once again) by communism. His decision is suspended until the second part of the novel – *Wiosna* (Spring) – which never appeared due to the untimely death of its author.

The Coming Spring skilfully depicts the fundamental ideological conflict with which Poles were contending at the time. Leftist ideology was very popular but carried with it the threat of Soviet rule. Nationalist right-wing views held some attraction as well, particularly among the lower middle classes. These views, however, with their anti-Semitism and programmatic aggression towards national minorities, could never rely on popular support. Faced with this choice, Żeromski – in a famous political pamphlet titled *Snobizm i postęp* (Snobbism and Progress, 1923) – opted for a "third way," one that was socially progressive and leftist while rejecting revolution as a course of action. This mythical "third way" was never realized: heated political passions led to the assassination of Gabriel Narutowicz (1865–1922), the first Polish president chosen in a general election, who was viewed as a leftist and was supported by, among others, Poland's national minorities. Immediately after his inauguration, in December 1922, he was assassinated by a fanatical member of the nationalist right.

The organization of the newly formed Polish state became an important literary theme of the 1920s. The mythical images of a free and happy Poland that proliferated during the partitions could now be juxtaposed with a rather unappealing reality. The classic image of a "dream" Poland can be found in Żeromski's *The Coming Spring*, in the "glass house" narrative that Cezar Baryka's father tells on his deathbed. This mythical tale is based on the conviction that political freedom would bring about a spiritual transformation in the Polish people. In the story, a brilliant engineer designs a new civilization, one built on nothing more than water and sand – materials that seemed universally accessible at the time. The constructive force in this tale is not "almighty capital," but the unfettered Polish imagination. The civilization of glass houses runs on creative power that generates a society of socio-economic equals, who are also morally (and physically) pure citizens. Never mind that this tale turned out to be an idle fantasy and that real life in the Poland of AD 1918 was marked by poverty and degradation. Żeromski seized on something that Poles had been secretly hoping for: that freedom would automatically grant them moral perfection, purging them of the occupying powers' demoralizing influence. At the same time, Żeromski showed how Poland's social legacy, in the form of class-selfishness on the one hand, and poverty and degradation on the other, ensured that these hopes did not stand a chance at quick realization.

Another novelist who explored this theme was Juliusz Kaden-Bandrowski, as seen in *General Barcz* (1923), a political *roman-à-clef* whose eponymous hero bears a striking resemblance to Piłsudski. Barcz's inner circle is rife with intrigue and brutal power struggles, which the author describes with a certain amount of insider knowledge (he had belonged to a faction that backed Piłsudski), and in a highly emotional Expressionist style. Kaden-Bandrowski's two subsequent novels, *Czarne skrzydła* (Black Wings, 1925) and *Mateusz Bigda* (1932), also reflect his disillusionment with politics and politicians: *Black Wings* takes aim at the socialist party, while *Mateusz Bigda* attacks the leaders of the peasant parties that played a major role between the wars, when Poland was an agrarian state. One classic work that takes a critical view of Poland's political situation is Andrzej Strug's *Pokolenie Marka Świdy* (Mark Świda's Generation, 1925). The novel's protagonist, Świda, returns from the Polish–Soviet War to find he has no place in the new social reality – a prominent literary theme of that time. The heroes of Zofia Nałkowska's *Romans Teresy Hennert* (The Romance of Teresa Hennert, 1924) are for the most part badly paid officers, unable to find their footing in postwar Poland. Soldiers who had formerly fought for Poland's independence shamelessly take part in financial schemes while women attempt to make their way in the world by exploiting their own sexuality and the networks they develop through sexual means. The novel's eponymous "love affair" ends tragically, with the love of the selfless and uncompromising lovers a form of protest against the utilitarianism that now pervades every aspect of human relations.

Several novels about the injustices that greeted former independence-fighters in the new Poland were published only after the Second World War. Among them is Sergiusz Piasecki's (1901–64) *Żywot człowieka rozbrojonego* (The Life of a Disarmed Man), published in 1962, though a first draft had been written in 1935. Another example is Florian Czarnyszewicz's (1900–64) *Losy pasierbów* (Fates of the Foster-Sons), which came out in 1958 in Argentina, where a number of Poles – facing unemployment at home – had ended up, even before the war. Many of them had fought to preserve the Polish way of life in the gentry farmsteads in Babruysk, in the farthest reaches of Belarus. Even several decades after Poland gained its independence, therefore, writers continued to view the indifference with which the heroes of this struggle were met at home as a grave sin on the part of the government and the politicians. The protagonists of the aforementioned novels are comparable to America's "Lost Generation"; however, in the Polish case, this generation was also responsible for building the newly formed nation, and was deeply committed to its social and political life.

The Formation of the New Society in the Mirror of Prose

Another important literary theme that emerged at this time was the creation of a modern Polish society. Independent Poland was made up of three distinct communities, coming from three different partitions, each at a different level of economic development and with its own set of traditions. Most importantly, these communities were underdeveloped in terms of education, social institutions, and customs – in other words, everything that determines civic participation in the life of the community. The outstanding representative of the new socially conscious literature in interwar Poland was Maria Dąbrowska (1889–1965). She was the author of the multi-volume family saga *Noce i dnie* (Nights and Days, 1932–4), which covers the decades from the failed January Uprising of 1864 to the outbreak of the First World War. Her principal characters are members of the impoverished gentry, who lost their standing as a result of tsarist policies against Poles involved in the national uprising. Through hard work, the protagonists rebuild their lives, at the same time coming into contact with new ideas. One of the main characters, Agnieszka Niechcic (Dąbrowska's alter ego), goes to Western Europe as a student and becomes involved in the socialist movement. Dąbrowska herself was committed to working for the common good and inculcating prosocial behaviour through cooperatives. This would require education on a grand scale, but it could begin at the level of small social organizations, such as the family or the country estate.

Dąbrowska's book is set in the decades following the January Uprising, a time of national mourning yet also one of the rare periods of lasting peace and relative prosperity in Europe. The code of chivalry that has been prized for so long among the Polish nobles is giving way to other virtues better suited to peacetime and to a new type of society, whose creation Dąbrowska presents in her novel. These virtues include industriousness, integrity, responsibility for oneself and others, willingness to cooperate for a common good, and openness to useful innovation. People who show these virtues are to become the backbone of the new Polish state. Dąbrowska is not preachy; on the contrary, she is sympathetic to her characters' human weaknesses and idiosyncrasies – she makes them seem like real people rather than schematic figures illustrating her theories. This is exemplified by the novel's heroes, Bogumił and Barbara Niechcic, who torment each other but stay together through thick and thin despite their many differences.

The poet Julian Przyboś (1901–70) admired Maria Dąbrowska for creating an exemplary Polish style in *Nights and Days* – simple, cogent, and transparent. This could not be said of all social-minded prose. Literature had to contend with a complex, heterogeneous society that was transforming itself politically and was subject to social upheaval. Such a society produced a language characterized by dialects, jargon, and milieu-specific idioms. Dąbrowska's early collection of short stories, *Ludzie stamtąd* (People from Over There, 1926), which depicts the lives of farmhands, is marked by a fascination with people who live close to the landed gentry yet are greatly different from that milieu, in which the author herself was raised.

In 1933, Helena Boguszewska (1886–1978) and Jerzy Kornacki (1908–81) founded the literary group "Przedmieście" (Suburb), which set out to describe the changes taking place in communities on the outskirts of cities. Most of the people in these communities were migrants from the countryside, who had been uprooted from their old traditions and customs but were still not accustomed to urban culture. The neo-naturalist novels produced by the Suburb circle might not have been highbrow literature, but they fulfilled an essential social role, especially in a country like Poland, where industrialization was steadily pulling people from the countryside into the cities. The most popular author of novels about "ordinary people," though not a member of Suburb, was Pola Gojawiczyńska (1896–1963), who wrote *Dziewczęta z Nowolipek* (The Girls from Nowolipki, 1935). This tale about the loves and ambitions of young women from a working-class neighbourhood in Warsaw was reissued several times and adapted for the screen both before and after the Second World War (by dir. Józef Lejtes in 1937 and dir. Barbara Sass in 1985).

Another novel about the lives of young women that was turned into a film – in this case one of higher calibre and directed by Eugeniusz Cękalski the same year that the novel was published – was Maria Ukniewska's (1907–62) *Strachy* (Fears, 1938). The author herself was a former chorus girl, and her novel portrays the dramatic fates of girls in her profession during an economic crisis. Ukniewska escaped that world, marrying a young, prosperous landowner and diplomat, Andrzej Kuśniewicz (1904–93), who made his career as a writer after the Second World War. Her friends, however, were subjected to countless indignities and were completely at the mercy of their bosses and lovers. *Fears* belongs to a sub-genre of naturalism – the "powieść środowiskowa" (milieu novel), whose authors come from the social environments they describe. A number of such novels were written around this time; the most important of them were *Zaklęte rewiry* (Enchanted Quarters, 1936) by Henryk Worcell (1909–82) and two novels by Sergiusz Piasecki: *Kochanek Wielkiej Niedźwiedzicy* (The Lover of the Great Bear, 1937) and *Bogom nocy równi* (Equal to the Gods of Night, 1939). Worcell's novel is set in the world of waiters at an elegant restaurant; Piasecki's books take place among smugglers and low-level spies operating along the eastern border separating Poland from the Soviet Union. Piasecki himself was a convicted felon who had served a term in prison (where he had written his first novels). Thanks to the efforts of the prominent writer Melchior Wańkowicz (1892–1974) and others, he was released early, after which he dedicated his life to literature. Worcell, too, switched professions and became a full-time writer. Neither of them had a gift comparable to Jean Genet's, but their close observations of the worlds in which they moved still fascinate readers thanks to their accurate depictions of specific people, events, dialects, and value systems from social strata that were typically inaccessible to the world of the intelligentsia.

Literary Visions of the "Great Transformation of the World"

More interesting from a literary perspective are the novels and short stories that responded to civilizational upheaval in the aftermath of war and revolution. The world, which had once appeared so stable, suddenly seemed anything but. This is strikingly expressed in the prose of the futurist poets Bruno Jasieński (1901–38) and Aleksander Wat (1900–67). The former was the author of a short, deeply grotesque work, which he called a "novel," in keeping with his belief that the novels of his times must be maximally condensed. In *Nogi Izoldy Morgan* (Izolda Morgan's Legs, 1923), Jasieński incorporates fantastical events – such as a tram severing a girl's legs in such a manner that the legs remain "alive" – into a story about revolutionary workers protesting the encroachment of technology into everyday life. Jasieński's sojourn in France resulted in the novel *Palę Paryż* (I Burn Paris, 1929), for which he was expelled from the country. In it, Jasieński imagines a future Paris whose population has been decimated by an epidemic caused by sabotage. The physically sturdy proletarians have better chances of surviving the plague and they come to rule the city, which has been isolated from the rest of the world. Jasieński's novel offered one of many visions of a workers' revolution that – as authors on the far left believed – would soon change the world. Jasieński later moved to the Soviet Union and made a successful career as an official Soviet writer. But he soon fell victim to the Stalinist purges and was executed in a Moscow prison – a fate shared by countless other Soviet writers.

Wat's short stories, collected in *Bezrobotny Lucyfer* (Lucifer Unemployed, 1927), depict versions of the future in which everything is the inverse of what we know. In "Królowie na wygnaniu" (Kings in Exile), the Caucasian race gradually loses its dominant position, giving way to people of colour; meanwhile, the aristocrats of the world, crammed together on a desert island, abandon their cultural inheritance and descend to the level of cavemen. In the title story, Lucifer finds that he has nothing more to offer, since civilization itself has become satanic. "Żyd wieczny tułacz" (The Wandering Jew), in turn, shows that Jews and Christians could conceivably switch places in the future in terms of social and racial relations.

The most interesting work of this kind, from a literary standpoint, is *Wesele hrabiego Orgaza* (The Wedding of Count Orgaz, 1925), a fantastical vision of the future by Roman Jaworski (1883–1944), in which two rival billionaires decide to rescue humanity from their postwar degeneration. One of them buys up all of the world's art, thereby forcing people to new heights of creativity; the other leads people to a religious and metaphysical reawakening. All of this is accomplished through the organization of a "super-cabaret" titled "The Death-Agony Dance," the centrepiece of which is a staging of "The Wedding of Count Orgaz" – a reference to El Greco's famous painting, "The Burial of Count Orgaz." The novel is a dazzling whirlwind of ideas, allusions to Polish and world literature, and linguistic and stylistic innovations. Many of its artistic techniques anticipate Witkacy and Witold Gombrowicz (1904–69), while the use of verbal collage and intertextuality is reminiscent of John Dos Passos.

The most famous author working in this vein of speculative science fiction was Stanisław Ignacy Witkiewicz, who published two novels between the wars: *Pożegnanie jesieni* (Farewell to Autumn, 1927) and *Nienasycenie* (Insatiability, 1930). In both, the protagonist is a young man who undergoes numerous initiations – erotic, artistic, philosophical, political, and so on – only to find that the world that thereby opens up before him is on the verge of collapse. Witkacy was a catastrophist: he believed that contemporary culture was going to the dogs. He saw a threat in democratization and the mass diffusion of everything he felt should be the concern of a chosen few – be it the ability to experience the mysteries of existence on a metaphysical level (a necessary precursor to religious experience and the creation of philosophical systems and values), or art itself, which he felt should be completely unconcerned with utility. According to Witkacy, the declining Old World culture would pass through political and military death throes before finally transforming itself – as in *Farewell to Autumn* – into a Soviet-style totalitarian system (Witkacy had personally witnessed the October Revolution). Such a system would be held together by a monstrous bureaucratic apparatus and by the subjugation of the individual to the state. Social equality would be ensured by providing equal access to material goods while wiping out individual creativity and intellectual freedom. In *Insatiability*, the new sociopolitical order comes to Poland on the heels of a vast Chinese army, which achieves military victory through pharmacology: whoever takes the "Murti-Bing pill" meekly accepts his or her fate, along with whatever world view the Chinese impose. After the Second World War, Czesław Miłosz references the Murti-Bing pills in *Zniewolony Umysł* (The Captive Mind, 1953), using them as a metaphor for the role of Stalinist ideology in the degradation of Polish culture.

The prose of Jasieński, Wat, Jaworski, and Witkacy coincided with the realization that the world was capable of changing radically and with astonishing speed. Hence their passion for experimentation and the pursuit of an image of reality that could be moulded according to the author's wishes and subjected to various thought experiments. Antoni Słonimski's *Torpeda czasu* (The Torpedo of Time, 1927) was written around this time. In this fantastical novel, the main characters travel back in time to the French Revolution in order to change the course of history; however, Słonimski shows that no matter how we try to alter the past, everything will turn out exactly the same. Here, the idea of manipulation and experimentation also remains in force.

This idea influenced the historical novel as well. The most important works of this genre in interwar Poland departed from the nineteenth-century model promulgated by Henryk Sienkiewicz (1846–1916) – a model that aimed to satisfy national pride with colourful setpieces and to leave the reader with a moralizing message. In its place there now appeared novels that treated history as an object of investigation, that raised difficult questions about the human condition, and that juxtaposed the past with the present in an attempt at historical synthesis. Examples of this new kind of historical novel include *Żywe kamienie* (Living Stones, 1918) by Wacław Berent (1878–1940), which views the Late Middle Ages – a time of tremendous upheaval – through the lens of its art, and *Czerwone tarcze* (Red Shields, 1934) by Jarosław Iwaszkiewicz (1894–1980), which creates and analyses a complex spiritual portrait of Prince Henryk Sandomierski (ca. 1131–66). Another work that deserves mention is Zofia Kossak's trilogy: *Krzyżowcy* (The Crusaders, 1935), *Król trędowaty* (The Leper King, 1936), and *Bez oręża* (Blessed Are the Meek, 1937). These works present a multifaceted view of Europe at the time of the Crusades, depicting it as a period of crisis in Christian institutions and of religious revival spurred by the ideas of St Francis of Assisi. Finally, there is *Żelazna korona* (Iron Crown, 1936) by the young writer Hanna Malewska (1911–83), set during the reign of Charles V.

The most important and original of the Polish historical novelists, Teodor Parnicki (1908–88), debuted in the interwar period as well, although most of his works were written after the Second World War. Set in a variety of eras and cultures, Parnicki's novels "interrogate" these cultures with remarkably difficult and searching questions and demand tremendous effort on the reader's part to follow the extraordinarily complex connections among people, events, and cultural phenomena. In 1937, Parnicki published his novel *Aecjusz, ostatni Rzymianin* (Aetius, the Last Roman), which depicts Ancient Rome in the waning years of the empire. The most popular author of historical prose at the time – besides Zofia Kossak – was Jan Parandowski (1895–1978), who wrote a number of novels set in the ancient world, including *Dysk olimpijski* (The Olympic Discus, 1933), which was awarded the bronze medal in literature at the sixth Olympic Art Competitions – regrettably, at the infamous 1936 Summer Olympics in Berlin.

The Psychological Novel

PSYCHOANALYTICAL INSPIRATIONS IN TWENTIETH-CENTURY PROSE

Psychology asserts that people are defined by key childhood experiences. It follows that an individual's biography does not unfold linearly, but rather in a spiral, through constant returns to those experiences and through efforts to transform them. Twentieth-century prose used this assertion to abandon the linear plot in favour of experimental disruptions of chronology and temporal systems that run in time with the individual clock of the unconscious. Marcel Proust's *In Search of Lost Time* (1871–1922) is one famous example from world literature, while Maria Kuncewiczowa's *Cudzoziemka* (The Stranger, 1936) represents this tendency in the Polish canon.

In the 1920s and 1930s, literature turned increasingly to issues of psychology, and psychological prose made tremendous headway as a genre. It often merged with other novelistic forms, as in the case of Iwaszkiewicz's *Red Shields*, or Dąbrowska's *Nights and Days*, which combined social themes with fine psychological analyses of the characters. Similarly, Zofia Nałkowska – perhaps the most highly regarded female author of the interwar decades – integrated psychological analysis with political, sociological, and ethical motifs. The year 1935 saw the publication of *Granica* (Boundary), considered one of the finest Polish novels of the twentieth century. The protagonist, Zenon Ziembiewicz, the son of a tenant on a gentry estate, having watched his father (a man of dubious morals) betray his mother with the village girls, vows to be different. He moves to the city to pursue a career, studies in Paris with financial help from an aristocratic patron, and plans to marry a woman from a good family. By chance he meets Justyna, a village girl from his own district whom he had courted in his youth, when her boldness and intelligence had set her apart from other girls her age. Both of them feel lonely and uprooted in the city, and they rekindle their relationship. Ziembiewicz, who wants to be "better" than his father, makes a show of his feelings for her and gives her hope for a life together, only to force her to abort their unborn child while he marries someone else. Meanwhile, with help from his aristocratic sponsor, he launches a career as a politician; to that end, he tries to cut Justyna out of his life. The story ends badly: as a politician, Ziembiewicz becomes a puppet of his sponsor and is implicated in the decision to open fire on a workers' demonstration, which signals the corruption of his youthful ideals. Justyna, crazed with grief and outrage, gets rid of her child and then throws acid in Zenon's face. Zenon commits suicide. Nałkowska, deliberately casting her plot as a dime novel romance, begins the novel by instructing readers to judge Zenon according to the simple rules of "human decency." She then sets in motion a whole complex machinery of psychological analysis, which she uses to interpret her characters' actions. In the end, she demonstrates that, in spite of everything, the rules of ethics remain unshakeable and that her initial judgment of her hero remains valid. In the final dialogue between Zenon and his wife, the author poses yet another question: Are our personalities determined by our circumstances and relationships with others, or do we become the people we imagine ourselves to be, according to whatever ideals we adopt as our own? This question will be taken up again in the work of Gombrowicz.

Boundary is a classic example of the psychological novel as practised by Nałkowska. In describing events, it considers not only psychological motivations but social and political ones as well. The novel's secondary characters are as fleshed out as the protagonists. There is the splendid figure of Mrs Kolichowska, for instance, who lives at the mercy of her husband when she is young and finds herself without prospects later, when she is widowed and has "aged badly" (i.e., lost her looks). Like many of Nałkowska's female characters, Mrs Kolichowska embodies the basic tenets of feminist criticism. Her hardships and personal defeats result from the social position of women at that time (there are more similarities between Mrs Kolichowska and the author than meet the eye).

Nałkowska published a number of important books in the 1920s and 1930s, including *Choucas* (1927), which resembles Thomas Mann's *The Magic Mountain* in miniature. Its action, however, is moved to the period right after the First World War, when unprecedented atrocities revealed a new, demonic aspect of human nature (the Armenian genocide plays an important role in the novel). Nałkowska's other books of note include *Niedobra miłość* (Bad Love, 1928), *Niecierpliwi* (Anxious, 1938), and the aforementioned *The Romance of Teresa Hennert*. Her trademark is to focus on her characters' private lives and emotional experiences, from which she draws conclusions about human nature.

The works of Maria Kuncewiczowa (1895–1989) come closer to the classic psychological novel. Her *Przymierze z dzieckiem* (Covenant with a Child, 1927) is a highly original and unsentimental analysis of the bond between a mother and her infant. However, it was *Cudzoziemka* (The Stranger, 1936) that brought Kuncewiczowa renown. This novel tells the story of a woman whose hopes for love and a career as a violinist are crushed by the men in her life. One man leaves her, and another – a music teacher – instructs her how to cheat in art. Róża's whole life becomes marked by disappointment and unfulfilment; in response, she subconsciously tries to take revenge on her milieu and torments those closest to her. Then in her old age she finds a doctor who is able to identify her psychological complex, allowing her – on her deathbed – to break free of her curse. The novel has the structure of a psychoanalytic session and is narrated retrospectively.

Kuncewiczowa debuted in 1927. Several years later, in the early 1930s, an entire generation of talented prose writers – many of whom would write psychological novels – launched their careers. Among them was Michał Choromański (1904–72), who published his most famous book, *Zazdrość i medycyna* (Jealousy and Medicine), in 1933. Choromański's novel analyses the psyche of a jealous husband who tries unsuccessfully to prove that his wife, Rebeka, has been unfaithful. The wife, perhaps because she is emotionally cold and impenetrable (which according to the author forms the basis for the "feminine mystique"), never gets caught. The novel employs an unusual narrative technique; while the narrator is, to all appearances, "omniscient," the author limits this omniscience in interesting ways. For example, we never know for certain the nature of the operation that the surgeon (Rebeka's lover) performs on her (though most likely it is for an ectopic pregnancy), because the narrative voice is "located" behind the doctor's shoulders, which effectively blocks the view of the operation. This becomes an incisive metaphor for the limits of cognition, which prevent us from "knowing everything" about anyone, even those closest to us.

Psychology also sees the human being as a combination of universal drives and individual problems. Consequently, everyone must develop means of communication that will lead to self-understanding and serve as means of communicating with the self. In literature, this resulted in an expansion of monologue-based forms, and of internal monologues in particular. The latter were a means of representing both thought processes and internal life; they were also a manifestation of this life and a means to express the most intimate, not yet rationally processed, psychic content. Monologue forms dominate James Joyce's *Ulysses* (1918–20; 1922), William Faulkner's *The Sound and the Fury* (1929), and Hermann Broch's *The Death of Virgil* (1945) on the world stage; as well as Karol Irzykowski's *Pałuba* (The Hag, 1903) in Poland. The Polish stream-of-consciousness novel crystallized only after 1956, especially in the work of Jerzy Andrzejewski and his *Bramy raju* (Gates of Paradise, 1960), Władysław Odojewski's *Zasypie wszystko, zawieje ...* (Everything Will Be Covered by the Snow, 1973), Wilhelm Mach's *Góry nad czarny morzem* (Mountains over a Black Sea, 1961), and Leopold Buczkowski's *Kamień w pieluszkach* (A Stone in Diapers, 1978).

Another talented author who debuted in the 1930s was Tadeusz Breza (1905–70), who is best-known for the novel *Adam Grywałd* (1936). The book's hero tries to start an affair with the brother of a woman who had rejected his advances; but what begins as retaliation ultimately entangles the hero in a complex web of emotional dependency. Homosexuality as a literary theme only began to appear in Polish prose in the 1920s and 1930s and was often heavily disguised and censored. We can therefore speak of Breza as being in the vanguard of queer literature in Poland.

Polish literature in the 1930s was dominated by psychological prose. Its popularity was so great that when the Second World War broke out, writers responded with yet more psychological novels. Stefan Otwinowski (1910–76), Stanisław Rembek, Maria Kuncewiczowa, and Herminia Naglerowa (1890–1957) all focus on their characters' psychological reactions to war and its repercussions. The genre fell out of use shortly after the war, only to resurface once more in the literature of the 1960s and 1970s.

Catastrophism and Mythology

According to *psychoanalysis*, a person is a mystery to him or her self. This mystery can never be fully solved, although we can search our psyche for an answer as to what created it. Twentieth-century prose conveys this process of self-analysis through investigations typically conducted within the framework of detective narratives, as happens in Tadeusz Breza's *Adam Grywałd* (1936) and Michał Choromański's *Zazdrość i medycyna* (Jealousy and Medicine, 1932).

The rise of totalitarianism in the countries bordering Poland, the economic crisis, and the threat of imminent war all contributed to the catastrophic outlook of the 1930s. This brand of catastrophism was different from Witkacy's; where his had been carefully contrived and rationally justified (as something inevitable), the catastrophism of the 1930s was more emotional, at times dark and amorphous, and bound up in the contemporary crisis of faith and values. It found its highest expression in poetry rather than prose; however, it figures in several novels of the time as well. Some of them describe the poverty of the countryside and the corrupt policies being carried out there, as is the case with *Grypa szaleje w Naprawie* (Influenza Rages in Naprawa, 1934) by Jalu Kurek (1904–83), and *Cynk* (Lead, 1937) and *Pieniądz* (Money, 1938) by Marian Czuchnowski (1909–91). Others, such as Zbigniew Uniłowski's (1909–37) well-known autobiographical novel *Wspólny pokój* (Shared Room, 1932), focus on the tragic experiences of young writers. Still other works featured generational catastrophism, for instance Marian Ruth-Buczkowski's (1910–89) *Tragiczne pokolenie* (The Tragic Generation, 1936). The ultimate expression of existential tragedy, however, can be found in the most famous of the novels mentioned here – *Ład serca* (Heart's Harmony, 1938) by Jerzy Andrzejewski (1909–83).

The world portrayed in these novels is generally grim and hostile towards its characters, and their plots never lead to happy resolution. Even for Andrzejewski, whose works are modelled on the Catholic novels of François Mauriac (*Le Désert de l'amour, Le Nœud de vipères*) and Georges Bernanos (*Journal d'un curé de campagne*), evil can sometimes appear more powerful than divine providence. How was one to come to terms with this wave of pessimism? The remedy, as it turned out, was the belief in a mythological order, in the idea that the world – through stripped of higher values and threatened by evil and anomie – could occasionally, and without warning, reveal some higher, metaphysical order. Without a doubt, the outstanding Polish writer working in this mythological vein was Bruno Schulz (1892–1942), an unassuming Jew who taught drawing and crafts in the small provincial town of Drohobycz.

In his two short story collections, *Sklepy cynamonowe* (Cinnamon Shops, 1933) and *Sanatorium pod klepsydrą* (Sanatorium under the Sign of the Hourglass, 1937), Schulz seems merely to sketch scenes from the everyday life of his characters – who are remarkably similar to Schulz's own family – in a small town exactly like Drohobycz. Beneath the surface, however, Schulz's stories are iterations of a universal cosmogonic myth. The town – a hermetic *theatrum mundi* – reflects in itself other structures, such as home, psyche, and cosmos; while at night, in dreams or reveries, it transforms into a kind of labyrinth crowded on all sides by mythical symbols. Schulz's sky, too, is highly symbolic, covered as it is with the signs of the zodiac, while his concept of time is rigorously structured. Schulz's great clock measures cyclical time, and each cycle has its own measure: a single day, a year, a lifespan, the succession of historical epochs. Each thing that occurs in Schulz's prose occupies a narrowly defined place within these cycles. Death, too, has its place there, although in Schulz's universe it is never an end. Jakub, the protagonist's aging father, dies several times, but never for good. The town's solemn old shops give way to modern commercialism (Drohobycz had a period of great prosperity at the turn of the twentieth century owing to the petroleum boom), but the old way of life never disappears entirely; the "dead season" is always followed by the "Great Season," just as winter is succeeded by spring and summer.

Schulz's Jakub is a funny old man, to be sure, but he is also a great conjurer, an artist working in mixed media, a thinker, and a priest. True, as an artist he is rather provincial, and accustomed to disappointment, but the same could probably be said for all artists, even those working in Paris or New York. The artist's condition is always marked by irony; his works are always a bit shoddy and fall short of the intention. But always and everywhere – even on the world's periphery – we await sudden fulfilment. We await the coming of the Messiah, who could turn out to be anyone, even the small-town thief, Szloma, just released from prison this spring. In Schulz's work, the figure of the artist-as-creator is especially potent, because his material is the word, and each word in human language refers to the original, divine Word that contains all things in itself. This original Word – which is simultaneously the entire Cosmos, and God-as-performative utterance – shattered into a thousand word-shards. The poet arranges these shards, working backwards, and, in seeking out the connections between them, creates long and complex metaphorical chains. For this reason, metaphor and other tropes are never merely ornamental for Schulz; rather, they are the adhesive of the world, which is always trying to find its way back to unity and metaphysical sanction. The symbol for this is the Book, which represents the idea of universal order.

Few authors are capable of using mythology to find true consolation in the face of catastrophic dread, for it requires tremendous intellectual and artistic maturity. In Polish literature, Schulz stands alone. He is sometimes compared to Kafka, but the similarities between them are rather superficial: Schulz strove to cure himself and mankind of dread, while Kafka is darker and far more grim in his outlook.

Existentialism and the New Concept of Man

The last years of the nineteenth century saw a radical shift in the concept of the individual. Man had long been seen as an essentially rational being; now, thanks to writers such as Dostoevsky, he began to be perceived as an enigmatic "self," whose motivations were often obscure. Philosophy, anthropology, and economics were gradually being dominated by the three "masters of suspicion": Nietzsche, Marx, and Freud. But an alternative intellectual line developed in the twentieth century as well: existentialism.

The existentialist concept of man, broadly formulated between the wars, became extremely popular in the 1940s during the postwar European crisis of consciousness, because it promoted the belief that the individual was ultimately neither the product of various social and psychological determinants, nor a passive object, putty in the hands of politicians and ideologues. The narrow space of personal freedom that existentialism granted the individual became an opportunity to restore human dignity. Man, as envisioned by the writers associated with existentialism, could be appalling at times – like the soulless murderer Mersault in Camus's *The Stranger* (1942) – but he could not be denied his subjective existence or the right to shape his own destiny.

By granting man his long-desired freedom from determination, existentialism simultaneously confronted him with a series of unsolvable problems. The individual, according to existentialism, is always alone and ignorant of life's meaning; he is tormented by the seeming absurdity of existence and by the fear of death. These anxieties often made their way into Polish literature, particularly in the 1930s. They found their ultimate expression in the prose of Jarosław Iwaszkiewicz, particularly in his stories "Brzezina" (The Birch Grove) and "Panny z Wilka" (The Wilko Girls), published in one volume in 1933, and "Młyn nad Utratą" (The Mill on the Utrata River, 1936); and in the novels *Red Shields* and *Pasje błędomierskie* (Błędomierz passions, 1938). Iwaszkiewicz's characters struggle with the senselessness of existence and with a painful awareness of life's evanescence and its termination in the mystery of death. Joy – as in "The Birch Grove" – can be attained only through love and union with nature, which renews itself endlessly. One cannot grasp it by way of reason or deliberation. There are existentialist motifs in the prewar works of Jerzy Andrzejewski as well, particularly in his famous novel of the 1930s, *Heart's Harmony*. The hero, Father Siecheń, wants to atone for his sins and strives for redemption and sanctity, but quickly discovers how daunting a task he has set himself, how ambiguous and uncertain the ethical ramifications of one's actions can be. Every victory he achieves in one area (such as converting the felon Morawiec) is matched by defeat in another: he is plagued by guilt for his part in the unhappiness of a woman he left some time ago and is devastated when his ward, Michaś, leaves the Church. Andrzejewski's novel features a number of existentialist motifs, including solitude in the face of moral dilemma, the burden of freedom that comes with absolute responsibility, and the tragedy of individual existence.

The greatest exponent of existentialism in Polish literature, Witold Gombrowicz, was worlds apart in his prose from both Iwaszkiewicz and Andrzejewski. His poetics are unlike anyone else's. The world he created in his works is a grotesque and fantastical variation on reality, and his style parodies several literary traditions at once. His creative stance was rebellious and mocking from the start – his hero, instead of contending with his suffering alone, bravely puts up a fight with a world intent on tormenting him. Gombrowicz has been grouped with other writers – Witkacy and Schulz, Adolf Rudnicki (1912–90) and Michał Choromański – on the basis of shared stylistic features (they all contributed to the "grotesque current" in Polish prose). His manner of working through philosophical problems, however, aligns him more with authors such as Fyodor Dostoevsky, André Gide, and Thomas Mann.

Gombrowicz launched his career with a short story collection titled *Pamiętnik z okresu dojrzewania* (Memoirs from the Time of Immaturity, 1933; re-released in 1957 as Bakakaj [Bacacay]). The characters in his stories are troubled by their own identities, by sex, and by processes of acculturation. At the time, critics read these stories as examples of psychological prose or as accounts of bizarre psychological "incidents" rather than as serious analyses of the problems that arise on the border between the individual and society, presented in the guise of the grotesque. Gombrowicz was so stung by these reviews that he decided to take revenge on the critics and wrote his next book, *Ferdydurke* (1937), with them in mind. But in that novel, Gombrowicz's mockery of the critics quickly gives way to far more universal problems.

Ferdydurke has a highly original structure; it has three parts that are separated by two short narratives with no connection to the main plot and that can in fact be read as parodies of the novelistic form. Each narrative is preceded by a preface; the first can be read as the author's literary manifesto, while the second is a parody of prefaces as such, done in the style of Rabelais. The three parts of *Ferdydurke* depict three different worlds: of the school, of the home (of the engineer Młodziak and his wife, the devotees of the modern and new, and of relaxed mores), and of an old-fashioned Polish country estate. The novel's hero, Józio, has just turned thirty when he is visited by the teacher Pimko, who deems that his education is lacking and sends him back to school. He later finds lodgings, first with the Młodziaks and after that at the country estate. These three social spheres operate by strict but very different rules, with which Józio is forced to comply. In each sphere, the hero struggles to preserve his authenticity and sovereignty against the distorting interference of others. This is typically played out through highly complicated operations on the symbolic order proper to each of these realities. As the operations plunge each world into chaos and destruction, the hero escapes to the next world, where the whole process is repeated.

Ferdydurke is acknowledged as one of the most important Polish novels of the twentieth century. Its vision of man locked in a struggle for his own integrity and unable to break free was a potent metaphor for the plight of the individual in relation to culture, as well as to oppressive political regimes. It was also a manifesto on the Polish variety of existentialism, which differed from Sartre's in that Gombrowicz placed significantly more emphasis on the theme of "immaturity"; in his world, man is never equal to his own intellectual demands and is always coming off as slightly infantile. At the same time, he secretly admires the child in himself and in others.

Non-Fiction

The interwar period saw interesting developments in the genre of reportage. The masters of this genre were Melchior Wańkowicz, Ksawery Pruszyński (1907–50), and Aleksander Janta-Połczyński (1908–74). Wańkowicz began his career writing books that boosted national morale during the Polish–Bolshevik War. After that, he tried writing books for children, but soon came to be known as a reporter specializing in dangerous and controversial topics. In *Opierzona rewolucja* (The Full-Fledged Revolution, 1934), he described the Soviet Union a dozen or so years after the Bolshevik victory. Shortly after, he published his most famous work from the interwar period, *Na tropach Smętka* (Tracking Smętek, 1936), which describes his journey, by car and kayak, through eastern Prussia, and the Poles he encountered there. For this book he was to be arrested immediately following the German invasion, but luckily he managed to escape to Romania. This allowed him to write his now-classic wartime reportage, including the monumental *Bitwa o Monte Cassino* (Battle of Monte Cassino, 1945–7). Wańkowicz was a rare bird: a reporter and feature writer who was broad-minded but who also had clear political ideas. Another such example was Ksawery Pruszyński. In 1932 he published his first collection of reportage, in which he predicted the exact location where the Second World War would begin, and that it would begin in the 1930s (*Sarajewo 1914, Szanghaj 1932, Gdańsk 193?*). Prior to the Second World War he also found time to write books about Palestine and the civil war in Spain (*W czerwonej Hiszpanii* [*In Red Spain*, 1939]). During the war he became first an important and influential feature writer, and later a diplomat; in 1941–2 he served as press attaché to the Polish embassy in the Soviet Union. Pruszyński's books and Wańkowicz's share a characteristic that would later become widespread in Polish reportage – namely, genre-mixing, that is, combining reportage with elements of literary fiction. Of the three masters of reportage from the interwar period, the most traditional "flying reporter" was Aleksander Janta-Połczyński, who travelled across four continents and authored numerous books and columns in which he dazzled readers with an endless variety of landscapes and cultures.

Another non-fiction genre that flourished around this time was travel literature. This was largely due to historical upheavals that had driven many Poles abroad. In some cases these were journeys east, so often immortalized by Siberian exiles. These travellers to the East modelled themselves on Wacław Sieroszewski (1858–1945), who had been publishing his works since the turn of the century. An ethnographer and prose writer, Sieroszewski relied on first-hand knowledge about the peoples of Siberia, Japan, and Korea for his many books. War and revolution drove Ferdynand Goetel (1890–1960) and Ferdynand Ossendowski east as well. Other Poles, mostly political émigrés, went west and settled in Europe. But it was the more daring ventures, to Africa and the Americas, that resulted in travel literature and reportage. Mieczysław Lepecki (1897–1969) – a former adjutant of Marshal Piłsudski – and Arkady Fiedler (1894–1985) both drew on their expeditions across South America for their many travel narratives; and Kazimierz Nowak (1897–1937) immortalized his remarkable travels through Africa in numerous reportage columns, which have only recently been compiled by Łukasz Wierzbicki (*Rowerem i pieszo przez Czarny Ląd. Listy z podróży afrykańskiej z lat 1931–1936* [By Bicycle and on Foot across the Dark Continent: Letters from the African Travels of 1931–1936, 2000]).

Just as Polish reporters readily incorporated fictional elements into their reportage, many fiction writers were willing to blur the line between fiction and non-fiction – for example, Kuncewiczowa, who wrote a book about her travels through Palestine (*Miasto Heroda. Notatki palestyńskie* [The City of Herod: Notes on Palestine, 1939]). The most interesting example of this kind of writing was the work of Zbigniew Uniłowski, who travelled to South America on a grant from the Ministry of Foreign Affairs in order to study the lives of Polish immigrants managing farms in Brazil. His travels resulted in two books of reportage: *Żyto w dżungli* (Rye in the Jungle, 1936) and *Pamiętnik morski* (Diary of a Sea Voyager, 1937). The former is especially interesting, for it deliberately violates the conventions of reportage, which is usually expected to be generous towards one's fellow countrymen as they familiarize themselves with strange foreign places. But Uniłowski's tropics are oppressive and, frankly, boring; and furthermore, his Poles are a quarrelsome lot, given to crooked dealings and too amenable to the influence of the Church, whose role the author holds in low regard. Thus, everything in Uniłowski's book flies in the face of conventional reportage.

Conclusion

The reputation of Polish prose from the twenty-year interwar period has undergone numerous shifts up until our time. In the 1920s and 1930s, the pecking order looked entirely different than it does today. Back then, the greatest Polish prose writers according to public opinion were – first and foremost – Sefan Żeromski, Andrzej Strug, Władysław Stanisław Reymont, and Wacław Berent; and one rung below them, Juliusz Kaden-Bandrowski, Zofia Nałkowska, and Maria Dąbrowska. Today this hierarchy is no longer valid; the first four writers (with the possible exception of Strug) are generally written off as belonging to the nineteenth century, while the three latter authors are held in high esteem, though none are as admired – in Poland or around the world – as Stanisław Ignacy Witkiewicz, Bruno Schulz, and Witold Gombrowicz, all of whom were considered eccentrics in the 1920s and 1930s. This radical shift in reputation owes a great deal to the Second World War. Each of these three prewar writers tried, in his own way, to respond to the kinds of questions about humanity and the world that became fundamental after the war. Their work was therefore much more interesting for generations living in the second half of the twentieth century than for the critics and readers of the interwar period.

Another unique aspect of Polish literature between the wars is its multiculturalism. As Czesław Miłosz emphasized, it is difficult to give an account of Polish literature between the wars without acknowledging the role played by Jewish authors – both those who were completely assimilated and who contributed directly to Polish culture (such as Schulz, Wat, Jasieński, Słonimski, and Rudnicki), and those who operated on the border between cultures, writing in Polish and Yiddish by turns, like Debora Vogel (1900–42). There was also an entire body of literature written in Yiddish, a language not typically understood by Poles, though it existed side by side with their culture. From this milieu came the Nobel laureate Isaac Bashevis Singer (ca. 1902–91). A smaller, though still essential, role was played by Ukrainian, Belarusian, and Lithuanian writers, some of whom contributed directly to Polish literature as well.

The literature of the 1920s and 1930s is characterized by its diversity. It is full of conservative elements and stylistic anachronisms alluding to the bygone age of Young Poland, but at the same time it boldly generated currents that would continue to develop long after the Second World War: catastrophism, existentialist literature, literary feminism (which in the 1930s went through several more or less radical incarnations, beginning with Nałkowska and Irena Krzywicka (1899–1994) and ending with Maria Komornicka (1876–1949), a true martyr of her feminine condition). The legacy of the 1920s and 1930s was suppressed during the Stalinist years, and its influence on subsequent Polish literature was therefore belated, but it is now enormously influential. In addition to Witkacy, Schulz, and Gombrowicz – all of them well known both in Poland and abroad – there are numerous other writers from the 1920s and 1930s who have either become classics in their own right or are just now being rediscovered.

Żeromski – to take one example – invented a unique model for discussing the newly liberated state in *The Coming Spring*, even if it is a negative point of reference for prose published after 1989, which has sought in vain to create its own *Coming Spring*. Dąbrowska has also remained a classic on the strength of *Nights and Days*. (Both novels have been turned into popular films: Filip Bajon directed *The Coming Spring* in 2001, while Jerzy Antczak's *Nights and Days* came out in 1975.) The development of feminist criticism has led to new ways of reading prose by women, especially Nałkowska, Kuncewiczowa, and Krzywicka, and has helped uncover aspects of their prose that had previously been ignored. Wat's *Lucifer Unemployed* is growing in estimation, as is the reputation of its author, who is now considered one of the most important Polish writers of the twentieth century. Finally, another writer who deserves mention here is Roman Jaworski as the author of *The Wedding of Count Orgaz*, a book that was not reissued in the Polish People's Republic, despite being groundbreaking and highly original. The book's fate was sealed by the harmless jokes it contained at the expense of the Soviet Union, though their presence in the book is self-explanatory, given that the novel is a send-up of world culture as a whole. Jaworski's novel, which was finally rediscovered and adapted for the stage in Kraków, is awaiting its rightful place in the estimation of critics and readers.

Jerzy Jarzębski
Jagiellonian University, Kraków
Translated by Philip Redko

Modern Midrash: A Poetics of Exegesis, Empathy and Encounter (Bruno Schulz)

"Within Polish letters, Schulz is utterly unique: a singular revelation of Jewish genius. Strange and original, with a power bordering on the ecstatic."

– Rachel Auerbach, "*Nisht-oysgeshpunene fedem*," 1964[1]

The poetic prose of Galician Jewish writer and graphic artist Bruno Schulz (1892–1942) burst onto the literary scene of independent Poland in 1934 in the form of a small volume of short stories titled *Sklepy Cynamonowe* (Cinnamon Shops), published by Warsaw's Rój publishing house. The stories featured a first-person narrator, the author's own alter ego, whose memories of childhood in a small town unfolded in a dense and sensuous prose rich with allegorical potential. Strongly influenced by Schulz's training as a graphic artist, the stories in *Cinnamon Shops* pulsed with an organic vitality that suggested a bold experiment in late or neo-Secessionist art, with words transferred to the page but hardly containable within the columns of text. They took shape around constellations of imagery: the "heavenly geography" of the sky; the riotous ebullience of backyards; the alluring interiors of the "cinnamon shops" filled with the "aroma of distant countries and rare commodities"[2] and the tawdriness of the commercial world; the winking eyes of peacock feathers and wallpaper flourishes; sexually charged household scenes; and the powerful and explosive figure of the protagonist's father, fashioned as a "metaphysical conjurer," "defending the lost cause of poetry" – and a second alter ego for the author himself. He appeared in many of the stories, adopting successive roles as an Old Testament prophet in whose shop bolts of cloth unfurled into a Canaanite Biblical landscape; as a poet, "Heresiarch" and theorist of form and creation; as a man shaken by illness, suffering and mad; even transformed, in a nod to Franz Kafka, whom Schulz greatly admired, into a cockroach and a taxidermied bird.

Setting aside the loose continuity provided by portrayals of the protagonist's father, the fluid dynamism of these stories was fuelled less by plot development than by the author's drive to experiment with a new form of modernist prose writing, one that could express "deep transformations taking place in the depths of the collective consciousness"[3] by transforming and adapting the spiritual heritage of Jewish theological and hermeneutic tradition to a modern, secular form of expression that could transcend national boundaries. The prose moved downward and inward more often than forward, opening up and giving expression to states of perception, and plumbing everyday objects and events to discover the mystical and mythical resonances within them. Combining expressionist, fin-de-siècle neo-Romantic and neo-Hasidic elements with aspects of the oral tale and of memoir, the stories explored, according to Schulz, the region in which individual biography merges with timeless and primordial myth. "All poetry is mythologizing," he wrote, "and strives to restore myths to the world."[4] He saved in his own work a special place for Jewish myth and tradition, with which his own generation of secularizing and "deracinated" Jewish intellectuals was negotiating both spiritual and artistic relationships. Like the physical objects within them, Schulz's stories also transformed at times into philosophical and aesthetic divagations, in which the author developed and articulated his modernist poetics and his conception of the mutability and the irony of form.

BRUNO SCHULZ ON EPHRAIM MOSES LILIEN

Political nationalism did not discard the deep and mystical strengths, the subterranean reserves that made it a popular movement … It tried to salvage them, and to transpose them … onto its new, Europeanized ideology. This historical process also had to play itself out within the domain of art. Political programs are only the rationalized surface, the external expression of deep transformations taking place in the depths of the collective consciousness. These transformations cannot complete themselves within the categories of political thought alone, but must ferment in the mythical depths, out of which are born longings, rapture, ideals, and the forms of the collective imagination.

– Schulz, "E.M. Lilien," 71:2

Cinnamon Shops was followed two years later by *Sanatorium pod Klepsydrą* (Sanatorium under the Sign of the Hourglass),[5] which featured illustrations by Schulz himself. By this time, the writer had already gained independent recognition as a graphic artist with, most notably, a portfolio of erotically and masochistically themed prints titled *Xięga Bałwochwalcza* (Book of Idolatry). *Sanatorium* included a number of the author's earlier, unpublished short stories, several of them character sketches of outcast or lonely figures ("Dodo," "Edzio," "Emeryt" [The Old Age Pensioner], "Samotność" [Loneliness]). It opened, however, with a striking new series of thematically connected stories, "Księga" (The Book), "Genialna epoka" (The Age of Genius), and "Wiosna" (Spring). Featuring Schulz's now-familiar narrator Joseph as the child protagonist, these stories drew on popularly recognizable kabbalistic and Hasidic themes – including imagery and language connected with messianic anticipation, with the concept of repair or *tikkun*, and with the search to liberate the *Shekinah* or divine spirit in the material world – grafting those themes onto the aesthetic project and onto the contemporary reality of the secular, modern artist.

Schulz would further solidify his public role on the Polish literary scene in an interview with the playwright and painter Stanisław Ignacy Witkiewicz (Witkacy), a friend and supporter of Schulz's, that appeared in the Warsaw magazine *Tygodnik Ilustrowany* in 1935. He also engaged in an open exchange of letters with author Witold Gombrowicz in the monthly *Studio* in 1936. In these letters, as in his manifesto-style essay "The Mythicization of Reality" and several short and penetrating studies of writers and artists whom he admired (including Franz Kafka, Witold Gombrowicz, Moses Ephraim Lilien, Zofia Nałkowska, and Debora Vogel), Schulz would continually revisit and elaborate on his own maturing aesthetic philosophy. He often used metaphorical figures that invite unpacking by critics of his own work. He wrote of Kafka, for example, and at the same time of himself: "Kafka sees the realistic surface of existence with unusual precision … but these to him are but a loose epidermis without roots, which he lifts off like a delicate membrane and fits onto his transcendental world, grafts onto his reality. His attitude to reality is radically ironic, treacherous, profoundly ill-intentioned – the relationship of a prestidigitator to his raw material."[6]

Speaking of the Galician Jewish graphic artist Moses Ephraim Lilien, also a native of Drohobycz, who created a distinctly Zionist embodiment of the *Jugendstil* style in art, he wrote that as an artist Lilien represented "a transition from religious, mythic, messianic Jewish nationalism to a nationalism that is modern and realistic."[7] Schulz's use of the term "realistic" echoes much stronger critiques of political Zionism expressed among many in his generation, critiques that he clearly shared – and points to his own decision to seek a continuation of the Jewish messianic tradition not in political programs, but through the medium of art, which has access to the spiritual depths of the individual and the collective: through a continuation of the "mythologizing" urge common to all peoples.

The limited but captivating body of Bruno Schulz's written work that appeared in the mid-1930s has entered into, transformed, and enriched Polish, Jewish, and Central European modernisms, stretching the boundaries of how each of these modern literatures is understood. It has also earned a place, together with Schulz's graphic works, in the field of Holocaust studies. Bruno Schulz died during the Holocaust, murdered in 1942 by Gestapo officer Karl Günther during the wartime occupation of Drohobycz, even as Aryan papers and plans for his escape had been prepared. The final works of art that he would produce before his death were fairy-tale-themed frescoes that he painted on the walls of a child's bedroom in the Drohobycz home of SS Commander Felix Landau, who had taken him under his protection.[8] The frescoes, discovered sixty years later in 2002, were partly removed to the Yad Vashem museum in Israel, where Schulz is memorialized as a Jewish artist and Holocaust victim.

At the same time, Schulz's work flamboyantly resists incorporation into any one national, ethnic, political, or cultural alignment. Indeed, Schulz's poetics, which highlight with relish the transience and "irony" of form, together with the vitality, mutability, and infinite potentiality of matter, highlight for the contemporary reader the limitations of national paradigms for framing and speaking about culture. They also point to the special power of peripheral literary modernisms to destabilize political and social categories. Emerging, in Auerbach's[9] words, like a "singular revelation" within a post–First World War, post-Imperial Galician environment of rising nationalisms, Schulz's artistic and spiritual vision (for they were inseparable) resisted both Jewish and Polish nationalisms – in favour of the individual, the universal, and a powerful aesthetics both of and from the margins. "Where is truth [lit: the excommunicated or exiled one] to shelter," Schulz's narrator asks in the story "Spring," "where is it to find asylum if not in a place where nobody is looking for it: in fairground calendars and almanacs, in the canticles of beggars and tramps …?"[10] The gesture of longing for asylum and escape glimpsed in this line would remain a constant in Schulz's work and lend a sense of urgency to what we may read today as a quietly revolutionary poetics of empathy and encounter.

"MYTH" AND JEWISH TRADITION IN SCHULZ

It is only now we realize what the soil is on which Spring thrives ... Here are graves that are still warm, the litter, and the rot. Age-old tales ... Here are columbaria, the drawers for the dead, in which they lie dessicated, blackened like roots, awaiting their moment.

– Bruno Schulz, *The Street of Crocodiles and Other Stories*, 161

Schulz's specific form of deracinated, dehistoricized myth reflects an unexpected reaffirmation and recuperation of Jewish identification; a vital sublimation of Jewish content, and of Jewish genealogy. In negotiating this relationship with tradition, Schulz can be seen to engage in a storyteller's sleight-of-hand – producing a storytelling mechanism not unlike the chess-playing puppet in Walter Benjamin's *Theses on History*. For Benjamin the successful chess player, who represents historical materialism, is triumphant only because he "enlists the services of theology, which today, as we know, is wizened and has to keep out of sight." In Schulz's literary performance, Jewishness functions much like the hunchback theology in Benjamin's parable. Thus in Schulz's work we confront both the subtle identification of Jewishness with death and dying, marginality and misshapenness, *and* the constant recuperation precisely of that which is marginal – of the scrapheap or the shards – and of that which is dead, abandoned, or decayed, lying in the catacomb or grotto awaiting its own "Spring" – namely, waiting for the living poet to make it part of his present aesthetic project: a modernist/Jewish renaissance.

As a Jewish artist writing in the Polish language in Drohobycz, a provincial Galician city within newly independent Poland, Schulz's position was doubly or triply peripheral: he was writing from a marginal, minority position within Polish culture, which was itself peripheral to the centres of European culture. And within the Central and Eastern European Jewish world in which he lived, he certainly represented a minority position: during a period of growing nationalism and, for Jews, disillusionment with the promise of assimilation, emphasis within the Jewish intelligentsia had turned towards the cultivation of modern Jewish literatures in Yiddish and Hebrew and the affirmation of a distinct national Jewish culture.[11] A Jewish writer who chose to write in Polish could be seen at the time to have turned his back on, and even to be irrelevant to, the cultural project of his nation. Nevertheless, like his exact contemporary Walter Benjamin within German-language letters, and like Franz Kafka a decade before him, Schulz would develop a distinctly Jewish modernist aesthetic, shaped by and drawing upon the world of Eastern European Jewish literary, hermeneutic, and folk traditions, while at the same time choosing to actively encrypt, downplay, or universalize that Jewish content, thus producing a narrative space of transnational and world literature, as well as an imagined textual homeland – his own universally accessible "Republic of Dreams." In Schulz's story by that name ("Republika Marzeń," 1936), the countryside of his narrator's childhood, or of his dreams, becomes "no man's land, or God's land": "In those far-off days our gang of boys hit on the outlandish and impossible notion of straying even further, beyond that inn, into no man's or God's land, of patrolling borders both neutral and disputed, where boundary-lines petered out and the compass role of the winds skittered erratically under a high-arching sky."[12] Reminiscent of the children's republic that Schulz's contemporary, the educator and pediatrician Janusz Korczak (Henryk Goldszmit, 1878 or 1879–1942), strove to create in his orphanages, Schulz's republic of dreams was a place that accorded dignity to the individual, and to the marginalized.

In a description of *Cinnamon Shops* that Schulz sent to a German publisher, in hopes of reaching a readership outside the bounds of the Polish language,[13] he wrote of himself: "The author has the impression that the deepest bottom of biography, the final shape of fate, cannot be reached either through the description of one's external biography, or through psychological analysis, no matter how deeply it may penetrate. The ultimate data of a human life lie rather in an entirely different spiritual dimension, not in the category of facts but in their spiritual meaning."[14] Not based on historical events, and not seeking to reflect the experience of a specific community, nation, or social milieu, Schulz's narrative landscape – and indeed his philosophy of art, perception, and interpretation – honours and gives expression to the unique spiritual and imaginative world that is the province of the individual.

To describe that unique and also "authentic" world, Schulz proposed the term "mythicized reality" or "mythologized realty." Here he was using the term *myth* in an idiosyncratic way that pried it loose from national and communal stories. Myth for Schulz is simultaneously universal and individual. His evocation of a foundational matrix, and of subterranean warehouses and silos that contain the mythic detritus of all cultures and all ages – an abyss into which the artist sinks his probe – represents at the same time a plea for the removal of the boundaries that bind matter, and also individuals, into the forms and shapes into which history would squeeze them. "Weep, ladies, over your own fate," pronounces the father figure in "Traktat o Manekinach" (Treatise on Tailors' Dummies), "when you see the misery of imprisoned matter, of tortured matter which does not know what it is and why it is, nor where the gesture may lead that has been imposed on it forever."[15]

Here again, a quality of empathy comes to the fore in Schulz's writing: a sensitivity to what he calls the "terrible sadness of all jesting golems."[16] Schulz's reflections on the nature of matter and form also draw attention to the painful fate of the individual – the individual trapped in historical time, not yet redeemed, however momentarily, by poetry or criticism – who is subjected to the roles, stereotypes, and political and social complexes that the dominant languages and power structures of her day would impose upon her. In this way his modernist literary project fashions itself as a celebratory and revolutionary plot to liberate all things, and all beings, from the prisons within which they are restrained. "It is then that the revelation took place," proclaims the narrator of "Spring," Joseph, upon encountering the stamp album that serves as one of several metonymies in Schulz's stories for his own texts: "the secret message of good tidings, the special announcement of the limitless possibilities of being. Bright, fierce, and breathtaking horizons opened wide, the world trembled and shook in its joints, leaning dangerously, threatening to break out from its rules and habits."[17]

Throughout Schulz's stories, the model for that individual not yet trapped in the prison of "real" history and of contemporary ideologies was the child – his protagonist and alter ego Joseph: the child as interpreter and "exegete" of the fragmented and disposable modern world; reader of the streets and cityscapes through which he or she wanders as through the pages of a text or stamp album, lying open and promiscuously available to his interpretation. "That's the best way to read," wrote Schulz to his close friend Romana Halpern:

> – reading oneself, one's own book, between the lines. This is how we used to read in childhood, and that is why the same books, once so rich and full of pith, are like trees stripped bare of leaves when read in adulthood – stripped, that is of the commentary we used to putty over the gaps … Whoever still has in him the memory and marrow of childhood should rewrite these books as he experienced them.[18]

And this is precisely the project that Schulz himself had undertaken. His literary experiments in this vein began as extended postscripts in private letters written to the poet and literary critic Debora Vogel (1900–42),[19] with whom he carried on intensely formative discussions on aesthetics during their visits in Lwów in 1930. As the pioneer of his own genre of modern midrash, which he described as a "neverending exegesis," Schulz sought precisely a textual form adequate to capture and evoke the alchemy, the seemingly magical transformation of reality, or "mythicization of reality," that takes place as the individual *encounters* the material world of form – reading it, interpreting it, filling it with portent and meaning, with flights of fancy, connecting what he or she encounters in the cityscape or in the text with mythic intuitions inherited "in the dawn of childhood." "The kind of art I care about is precisely a regression, childhood revisited," Schulz wrote in a letter to the literary critic Andrzej Pleśniewicz (1909–45) on 4 March 1936: "If it were possible to reverse development, to attain the state of childhood again, to have its abundance and limitlessness once more, that 'age of genius', those 'messianic times' promised and sworn to us by all mythologies, would come to pass."[20]

Thus in Schulz's work, the utopian and liberatory potential of literature is envisioned most frequently as a return to or recovery of the imaginative and spiritual reality of the child, with the attendant freedom, the transgression or obviation of social, linguistic, and perceptual boundaries, the state of immunity from history and law that that implies.

The central constellation of "encounter" at the heart of Schulz's work includes not only the encounter of the child exegete with the material and textual world, but also the encounter of the modern, secular artist with Jewish tradition, towards which he situates himself in a line of inheritance. "Ah, when writing down these tales, revising the stories about my father on the used margins of its text," muses the narrator in "Noc wielkiego sezonu" (Night of the Great Season), "don't I, too, surrender to the secret hope that they will merge imperceptibly with the yellowing pages of that most splendid, moldering book, that they will sink into the gentle rustle of its pages and become absorbed there?"[21] And finally, but crucially, that constellation includes the encounter of the *storyteller* with his *listener*: the highly charged moment of connection in which the individual seeks to convey his or her "authentic" reality to another. That moment of encounter fascinated Schulz himself, and he sought it throughout his life. Some of the most characteristic and non-traditional aspects of his narrative style represent an attempt to capture in writing the experience of live storytelling, of storytelling that takes place in the present moment – a form of art that dissipates as soon as it has taken shape. "What accounts for the strange fascination exerted by the living individuality, for the amazing charm of communicating with it?" wrote Schulz to his acquaintance Stefan Szuman in 1932. "I am not satisfied with the crystallizations of the spirit or intellect, objectivized intellectual constructs contained in systems, in books."[22]

In a sense, those expressions of Schulz's vision that did crystallize into written form – including in pieces of personal correspondence that were painstakingly sought out and collected by Schulz's devoted biographer, Jerzy Ficowski (1924–2006) – can be seen not only as the small but brilliant output of a Jewish artist whose life and artistic vision were cut short by the Second World War. We may also view Schulz's published writings as a trace of and signpost for a much larger body of work that the artist produced in his lifetime: for Schulz was also an oral storyteller. Uncharted territories of his imaginative landscape emerged in the form of oral tales told to his friends and lovers, and to students of the Drohobycz *Gymnasium*, where he taught shop and drawing to support his family after the death of his wealthy brother and sponsor, Izydor Schulz. "I remember drawing classes that Schulz would sometimes fill with stories of extraordinary invention – for example, of interplanetary travel," recalled Emil Górski, a student of Schulz's who later became a close friend: "While spinning these tales – and these were improvised, naturally – he would draw magnificent illustrations on the chalkboard in different colors, which in the course of the plot he would erase and replace with new ones … We all sat so fascinated that the school bell signaling the lesson's end would wake us as if from a beautiful dream."[23] According to Górski, Schulz remained a storyteller throughout his life, even in his final years in the Drohobycz ghetto during the German occupation: "He liked to spin for us, whenever it was possible, long stories about a miraculous Citadel … a fantastic product of his imagination … mighty and safe, unconquerable to the enemy … We all were to shelter ourselves there."[24] His account evokes the enduring element of escape from the political realities of his environment – an element that had played a role in shaping Schulz's nostalgic and also utopian poetics.

Knowledge of Schulz as an oral storyteller – a biographical detail that recurs with persistence in the recollections of all who knew him – provides a prism through which to illuminate defining elements of his extraordinarily original narrative experiments. Indeed, accounts like Górski's represent only traces of the "authentic books" or spontaneous "commentaries" – Schulz's oral genre of modern midrash – that his written works sought to emulate. The works themselves and the private spiritual world to which they gave expression dissipated, leaving traces in the lives of the individuals who experienced them. "There are things that cannot ever entirely, and completely, occur," says the narrator of "The Book," in another of Schulz's metatextual reflections on his own narrative project:

> They are only trying to happen, checking whether the ground of reality can carry them. And quickly they withdraw, fearing to lose their integrity in the frailty of realization. And if they break into their capital, lose a thing or two in these attempts at incarnation, then soon, jealously, they retrieve their possessions, call them in, reintegrate: as a result, white spots appear in our biography – scented stigmata, the faded silvery imprints of the bare feet of angels, scattered footmarks on our nights and days.[25]

Schulz's poetics of empathy and encounter, his quiet revolution from the margins, was founded on more than one paradox. Perhaps chief among them was its attempt to give linguistic form, within nature-history, to that which must necessarily escape form; its attempt to capture in writing an intimation of that infinitely renewed and renewable potentiality that is the source of "mythicized reality" – the living moment of engagement between the human spirit and the material world.

Karen Underhill
University of Illinois at Chicago

NOTES

1 Auerbach [Oyerbakh], "Nisht-oysgeshpunene fedem," *Di goldene keyt* 50 (1964): 137.
2 Schulz, *The Street of Crocodiles and Other Stories*, 56.
3 Schulz, "E.M. Lilien," 71–2.
4 Schulz, *Letters and Drawings*, 116.
5 For the critical edition of Schulz's collected works, with a scholarly introduction by Jerzy Jarzębski, see the Biblioteka Narodowa volume: *Opowiadania, wybór esejów i listów*.
6 Schulz, *The Collected Works of Bruno Schulz,* 349.
7 Schulz, "E.M. Lilien," 71–2.
8 For a detailed discussion of the controversy surrounding the discovery and removal of Schulz's frescoes from the walls of the former Landau residence in 2001, and the debate surrounding ownership of and responsibility for Schulz's artistic legacy in Poland, Israel, and Ukraine, see Paloff, "Who Owns Bruno Schulz?"
9 Rachel Auerbach [Rokhl Oyerbakh] (1903–76) was a writer and essayist in Yiddish and Polish, a native of the Lwów region of Galicia, and founding editor of *Tsushtayer*, a journal of Galician Yiddish culture, in which Bruno Schulz's graphic works were featured in 1930. Auerbach was close friends with Debora Vogel during the period when Schulz wrote letters to Vogel that would develop into the stories in *Cinnamon Shops*. She would devote her life to documenting the Warsaw Ghetto, which she survived, in her own diaries, in articles, and through the collection of survivor testimonials.
10 Schulz, *The Street of Crocodiles and Other Stories*, 184.
11 For a study of what Benjamin Harshav has called the "Modern Jewish Revolution," and the choices made by Jewish writers in post–First World War Central and Eastern Europe, see, for example, Benjamin Harshav, *Language in Time of Revolution* (1993); Mikhail Krutikov, *Yiddish Fiction and the Crisis of Modernity 1905–1914* (2001); Joshua Shanes, *Diaspora Nationalism and Jewish Identity in Hapsburg Galicia* (2012); and Kenneth Moss, *Jewish Renaissance in the Russian Revolution* (2009).
12 Schulz, *The Street of Crocodiles and Other Stories*, 318.
13 "I'd very much like to capture that prize [the prestigious *Wiadomości Literackie* award]," he wrote to Romana Halpern, "chiefly because it is the stepping-stone by which to break through the boundaries of the Polish language." Letter to RH, 21 February 1938, *The Collected Works,* 430.
14 Schulz, "Exposé o książce Brunona Schulza *Sklepy cynamonowe*," 177.
15 Schulz, *The Street of Crocodiles and Other Stories*, 35.
16 Ibid., 35.
17 Ibid., 150.
18 Schulz, *The Collected Works*, 402.
19 Debora Vogel was a writer, art critic, and philosopher, and the author of poetry (the volumes *Tog-figurn* [Day Figures, 1930] and *Manekinen* [Mannequins, 1934]), prose (*Akatsies blien.*

Montazhn [The Acacias Are Blooming. Montages, 1935]), and critical essays in Polish and Yiddish, as well as a founding editor with Rachel Auerbach of the journal of Yiddish culture *Tsushtayer* in Lwów. She made Schulz's acquaintance through S.I. Witkiewicz and the two developed a deep friendship and a mutually influential intellectual and artistic bond. Their plans for marriage, which Vogel's mother did not approve, were never realized.

20 Schulz, *The Collected Works*, 385.

21 Schulz, *The Street of Crocodiles and Other Stories*, 84.

22 Schulz, *The Collected Works*, 305.

23 Ficowski, *Bruno Schulz*, 69–70.

24 Ibid., 70.

25 Schulz, *The Collected Works*, 138.

WORKS CITED

Auerbach, Rachel [Rokhl Oyerbakh]. "Nisht-oysgeshpunene fedem." *Di goldene keyt* 50 (1964): 131–43.

Ficowski, Jerzy, ed. *Bruno Schulz. Listy, fragmenty, wspomnienia o pisarzu.* Wrocław: Wydawnictwo Literackie, 1984.

Lipszyc, Adam. "Schulz na szaro, Schulz przed prawem." In *Schulz. Przewodnik krytyki politycznej.* 35–53. Warszawa: Wydawnictwo KP, 2012.

Paloff, Benjamin. "Who Owns Bruno Schulz?" *Boston Review* 29, no. 6 (December 2004–January 2005): 22–5.

Schulz, Bruno. *The Collected Works of Bruno Schulz*. Edited by Jerzy Ficowski. London: Picador, 1998.

– "E.M. Lilien." *Przegląd Podkarpacia* 71 (1937): 2.

– "Exposé o książce *Sklepy cynamonowe*." In *Księga listów.* Edited by Jerzy Ficowski. 175–8. Kraków: Wydawnictwo Literackie, 1975.

– *Letters and Drawings of Bruno Schulz with Selected Prose*. Translated by Walter Arndt with Victoria Nelson, edited by Jerzy Ficowski. New York: Harper and Row, 1988.

– *Opowiadania, wybór esejów i listów*. Edited by Jerzy Jarzębski. Wrocław: Zakład Narodowy im. Ossolińskich, 1989.

– *The Street of Crocodiles and Other Stories*. Translated by Celina Wieniawska. New York: Penguin, 2008.

Iconoclasm and Nation Building (Witold Gombrowicz)

Witold Gombrowicz (1904–69) is a modernist novelist and playwright, a provocateur whose work is fuelled by antinomy and paradox. For instance, he conceived his literary work as a means of "liberating the Pole from his nation" to help him become a "human being in the world."[1] Yet, he revolutionized Polish literature by unmasking one of its fundamental themes – the discourse on historical forms of Polishness – as a set of pathological dependencies, which his writing managed to transpose, perhaps for the first time in the nation's literary history, into new cultural, exilic contexts. Similarly, Gombrowicz pined for worldwide fame and financial recognition. Yet he persisted in writing in exile (in Argentina, West Germany, and France, in that order) almost exclusively *in* Polish. Over the span of three decades he produced two plays, three novels, and a three-volume literary *cum* spiritual autobiography, *Dziennik* (The Diary), which stands as perhaps the defining work of twentieth-century Polish literature, but which was not available in translation in its entirety until years after his death.

Gombrowicz was born to a gentry family, albeit one reduced in means by the dawning of the twentieth century. The exaggeration of class distinctions in interwar Polish society – a strategy employed by Marxists, progressives, and nationalists alike – did not escape Gombrowicz's keen satirical eye. Initially, however, he too was stuck in its mire. His solution to this predicament involved a radical assertion of autonomy. Contrary to family expectations, Gombrowicz would not commit to a career as an attorney and instead spent much of the later 1920s and early 1930s honing his critical wits and style in the grand bohemian cafés of Warsaw.

"Ziemiańska" is one of the most famous cafés in Polish cultural and social life. Established in 1918 on Mazowiecka Street in Warsaw, its name was inspired by the neighbouring Landed Gentry Credit Society (Towarzystwo Kredytowe Ziemskie). The café became a meeting place for the new élite – more democratic than the aristocratic salons, it was still hierarchical, with membership dependent on connections and achievements. As a platform for meetings among artists, professors, officers, diplomats, and publishers (among them Julian Tuwim, Jan Lechoń, Jarosław Iwaszkiewicz, Antoni Słonimski, and Bolesław Wieniawa-Długoszewski), the café aided in the formation of social networks, admission to "society," and artistic recognition, as well as in the formation of opinions on fashionable artistic phenomena.

His name is now part of the legend of the Ziemiańska Café, a fabled meeting place for various cliques of the Polish avant-garde. Yet little in his early biography – that of an upper-class bohemian – points towards his later incarnation as a great iconoclast of Polish national myths, one paradoxically devoted to the renewal and modernization of Polish literature.[2] This was not apparent in his debut collection of stories, *Pamiętnik z okresu dojrzewania* (Memoir from the Time of Immaturity, 1933)[3], which is written in a generic cosmopolitan style, common at the time among his contemporaries.[4]

Two defining events would soon change this state of affairs. The first was the 1937 publication of his novel *Ferdydurke*, which established him as a literary figure to watch in Poland. Best described as a picaresque novel with elements of vanguardist manifesto (calling especially for autonomy from *form*), surrealist nightmare, and playful eroticism, the work also served as a grand funeral pyre for traditional Polish grandstanding gestures, patriotic *pronunciamentos*, and similar anachronisms, which were about to be annihilated by a new cultural vanguard. The second event initiated Gombrowicz's three-decade long exile: in August 1939, he joined a transatlantic voyage as part of a Polish cultural delegation to Argentina aboard the ship MS *Chrobry*. When the Second World War broke out, he decided not to return to Europe. In his first novel written in exile, *Trans-Atlantyk* (1953), he delineates and mythologizes his reasons for staying behind, presenting exile as both a blessing (for his identity formation) and a curse (shared with generations of Poles separated from their native land for various reasons). Along with *The Diary* and its belated accompaniment *Kronos*, the novels he wrote in exile include *Pornografia* (Pornography) and *Kosmos* (Cosmos), both published in Polish by a Paris-based émigré press, the Instytut Literacki, in 1960 and 1965, respectively.

As his writing reveals, however, Gombrowicz never actually left Poland. His creative forces as well as his demons were sustained by the interwar Poland (1919–39) that he had physically left behind – by what was at least in his eyes the freakish land of his youth, the "monster" that, according to *Trans-Atlantyk*, for centuries had refused to *be born* – that is, to take on form and definition – a half-baked entity that constantly demanded blood sacrifice from the body of the nation.

Gombrowicz's Poland was a strange creature indeed, difficult to evaluate with a cool head and even harder to warm-heartedly love. The Second Republic was a political assemblage in a state of permanent tension. Forged in the foundry of the First World War by the Treaty of Versailles, it was a hybrid project, at once deeply desired and profoundly conflicted. The lands from which the Second Republic were carved out had once been part of the Polish–Lithuanian Commonwealth, but they had undergone dramatic social and ethnic changes during the 123 years of partitions. The state's dilemma – How was it to forge a uniform Polishness from disparate constituents and drastically varied regions? – is closely observed in *Ferdydurke*. This is particularly evident in the picaresque sections that describe the protagonists' flight from ultramodern trappings and discourses in the capital towards the pastoral *dwór* (manor house), a prime recursive symbol and ostensible repository of deep authentic values, a Polish version of *la France profonde*. It is at the familial (and all too familiar) country estate that Gombrowicz brings the antinomian discourse of social and class formation and deformation – *Ferdydurke*'s leitmotif – to an unexpected climax. To the extent that the manor house signified a certain inalienable right of Polishness, a mode of being, it simultaneously betokened deformations: the nation had been twisted under the pressure of its own mannerisms into a surrealist grotesque: in short, a pose.

Who are the antagonists against whom the *szlachta* (gentry) parade their class privilege with such deadly seriousness? *Ferdydurke's* narrator and protagonist, Józio (a thinly veiled Gombrowicz), who in some ways is "housed" in the routines of the proper and the familiar, but who is an outsider nonetheless, is correct to dread his well-born relatives and their coterie. For it is through a mixture of unspoken menace and real violence that *form* is regimented and class consciousness of the *ancien régime* becomes instilled in the social body. The protracted episode of sadistic "domestic" violence committed by house masters against their servants that erupts at the end of *Ferdydurke* mirrors the real collision between vastly opposed, if not irreconcilable, visions of the future shape of the world, or more precisely of the nation to come.

> *Landed gentry*: a social group that was part of the feudal system, consisting of members of the landowning class. Their estates were usually passed down through inheritance and based on an agricultural economy; their profitability depended on the free labour of serfs. From the mid-nineteenth century, the landed gentry included owners of estates of more than fifty hectares. A significant number of small landowners lost their estates and status as a result of the nineteenth-century Industrial Revolution, the abolition of serfdom (in 1848 in the Austrian, and 1864 in the Russian partition), and the repressions that followed the January Uprising of 1861. They either joined the intelligentsia, became administrators of other estates, or fell into the proletariat. The March Constitution of 1921 abolished birth and class privileges; however, the poorly implemented law regarding the division of estates, as well as the poverty of peasants in eastern Poland, sustained post-feudal relations in rural areas. The end of the landed gentry as a social class came in the aftermath of the Second World War, when Poland lost its eastern Borderlands (vast areas of today's Belarus and Ukraine) and communist agricultural reforms appropriated estates of more than fifty hectares from the landowners.

The book's dénouement sees Gombrowicz launching an assault on his own people and roots – the *szlachta*, which at one time had encompassed the idea of the nation and the state conceived as a Commonwealth of Nobles. This makes for a nearly Marxist conclusion: the revolution to come – in this case through reification of class miscegenation – must sweep away both the pedagogical actions of the state[5] and the privileges of the landed gentry, who in the semi-feudal conditions of interwar Poland occupied the top social echelon.[6] Gombrowicz stops short of sanctioning a full-blown seizure of power, however. He does not allow the proto-proletariat, which has the upper hand in terms of the substance of their grievances, their numbers, and the putative logic of "history" *qua* inexorable class conflict, to codify their supremacy against their oppressors.

Instead, *Ferdydurke* stages a carnivalesque inversion. The scene of "fraternization" between Józio's upper-caste friend and a servant working in the manor is synecdochal of Poland's class relations and culminates in a spontaneous attack on the manor house – and attack that evokes a revolution. It devolves instead, however, into a playful mayhem of bodies, tumbling around and transforming into a mass corporeality in a manner reminiscent of setpieces by Gombrowicz's contemporary Stanisław Ignacy Witkiewicz (Witkacy,

1885–1939). Any gains achieved thereby are destined to be temporary: this proletariat is disorganized and is merely expressing the force of its collective id through rioting, in effect enacting (yet) another peasant (rather than proletarian) revolt. The novel's narrator does not stick around to witness the unavoidable return of the status quo ante. Rather, his personal (or only) solution is to escape via the language of surrealist dream logic.

Along with Zosia, a *szlachta* debutante whom Józio persuades to elope with him, the narrator is caught up in a flight towards a longed-for freedom, all the while aware that such freedom must be temporary. Another recursion of form and convention is always just around the corner, foregrounded in *Ferdydurke* by language that here mocks the conventions of Romantic writing. The innocent Zosia, however, deeply ensnared in form's trappings, sincerely believes their escape will make self-realization possible. *Ferdydurke* is Gombrowicz's first enactment of an identity position that will become his literary hallmark. Seeking autonomy through indictment of the social body and escape from its trappings, while also yearning for a sense of "connectedness" (though ever-vigilant about its potential snares), Gombrowicz takes the position of a universal moralist, an envoy of "younger," still unsettled cultures, tirelessly defining for himself the role of the Other.

In the context of his subsequent works, written in exile, the argument of *Ferdydurke* seems flawed despite its accurate characterization of victims of form and its sharp satire on reborn Poland's missteps. Its principal weakness is, paradoxically, that it relies too heavily on the *discourse* of form. For all the narratological acrobatics, the form/deformation dialectic of the book is stuck at the storyboard stage. The dynamite charge laid in support of a *new path* – a kind of Ninety-Five Theses of Polish vanguardism – is partly neutralized by the author's insistence on absurdist humour at the expense of both those who are putatively de-formed (including Zosia and other denizens of the manor house) and those who uncritically submit to form (both peasants and those enchanted by modernity). In the end, they all lack authentic agency in equal measure.

THE MODERN NOVEL (FROM THE AVANT-GARDE TO CRITICISM)

The modern novel is the product of the revolution in prose that culminated during the interwar period and is represented by (among others) Franz Kafka, Virginia Woolf, André Gide, John Dos Passos, William Faulkner, James Joyce, Marcel Proust, Bruno Schulz, Stanisław Ignacy Witkiewicz, Witold Gombrowicz, and Jean-Paul Sartre. Its important characteristics include the negation of realism and naturalism and – more broadly speaking – the questioning of the mimetic abilities of prose, which led to experiments with technique and an expansion of auto-thematic commentary. The experiments (for instance, the point-of-view method, simultaneity, and stream-of-consciousness writing) were meant to represent the most unformed aspects of human reality, while the commentary broke through illusion, exposed the artificiality of all artistic forms, and burdened the reader with permanent doubt. The modern novel is also marked by the questioning of commonsensical explanations of human experiences. This is expressed through the undermining of individualism, the emphasis on the repeatability and schematic nature of experience; at the same time, it suggests that a surplus of significance is present in even the most trivial biographies. The modern novel is also characterized by doubt as to whether human identity is stable and whether it really depends on internal forces such as will and reason. Thus, all identities are presented as social constructs and as the effects of the play of inter-human forms. In the framework of the novel, social relations are a domain of artificiality and arbitrariness, but the novelistic exposé of the law of various forms does not lead to proposals of harmony and naturalness.

In *Ferdydurke*, Gombrowicz proffers a viable formula for a vanguardist charge against the rule of form but does not succeed in catalysing it. He relaxes the offensive until it is nothing more than a celebration of alterity as a proposed mode of opposition. Reduced to a choice between absurdities, the work fizzles out at its conclusion, and the thrust of its outraged protest dissipates. While Gombrowicz remained committed to undermining cultural paradigms through a skilful deployment of dialectical discourse, with trenchant parody as his principal weapon, it was the experience of exile, with all its dislocation and pain, that provided the necessary liberation for him personally – also from his own historically conditioned blind spots. The cataclysmic juggernaut that doomed his homeland along with the entire order of Versailles Europe paradoxically caused Gombrowicz to be reborn as a European writer – indeed, a universal one.

George Gasyna
University of Illinois at Urbana–Champaign

NOTES

1 See Gombrowicz, *Dziennik II*, 22; for more on the idea, see also 23–4.
2 By the mid-1950s, Gombrowicz would freely admit to having become a cultural terrorist, smuggling "contraband" aimed at destroying various national myths and sanctities. See, for instance, his second preface to *Trans-Altantyk* ("Przedmowa do Trans-Atlantyku, 1957"), in *Trans-Atlantyk*, 2000, 6; cf. Miłosz's thoughts on the subject in "Podzwonne," 428–30.
3 Gombrowicz, *Pamiętnik z okresu dojrzewania* (Warszawa: Towarzystwo Wydawnicze "Rój," 1933).
4 Gombrowicz, *Polish Memories*, 92–3.
5 Such as patriotic education crews touring the outlying provinces throughout the 1920s and 1930s, or the Polish Academy of Literature, founded in 1933 and modelled on the Académie française – both loosely parodied in the book.
6 In the context of a mostly agrarian, semi-developed country, their position was analogous to that of the mostly urban high bourgeoisie in more advanced societies. See Marx, "Manifesto of the Communist Party," 204–12, 218–22.

WORKS CITED

Gombrowicz, Witold. *Dziennik I: 1953–1956*. Kraków: Wydawnictwo Literackie, 2000.
– *Dziennik II: 1957–1961*. Kraków: Wydawnictwo Literackie, 2000.
– *Dziennik III: 1961–1967*. Kraków: Wydawnictwo Literackie, 2000.
– *Ferdydurke* [1937]. Kraków: Wydawnictwo Literackie, 2000.

– *Ferdydurke*. Translated by Danuta Borchardt. New Haven and London: Yale University Press, 2000.
– *Pamiętnik z okresu dojrzewania* [Memoirs from a Time of Immaturity]. Warszawa: Towarzystwo Wydawnicze "Rój", 1933.
– *Polish Memories*. Translated by Bill Johnston. New Haven: Yale University Press, 2004.
– *Trans-Atlantyk* [1953]. Kraków: Wydawnictwo Literackie, 2000.
– *Trans-Atlantyk.* Translated by Carolyn French and Nina Karsov. New Haven: Yale University Press, 1994.
Marx, Karl. "Manifesto of the Communist Party." In *The Portable Karl Marx*. Edited by Eugene Kamenka. 203–28. London: Penguin, 1983.
Miłosz, Czesław. *The History of Polish Literature*, 2nd ed. Berkeley: University of California Press, 1983.
– "Podzwonne." In Miłosz, *Zaczynając od moich ulic* [Beginning with My Streets]. 423–30. Kraków: Znak, 2006.
Paczkowski, Andrzej. *The Spring Will Be Ours: Poland and the Poles from Occupation to Freedom.* Translated by Jane Cave. University Park: Pennsylvania State University Press, 2003.
Peterkiewicz, Jerzy, "The Fork and the Fear: Remembering Gombrowicz." *Encounter*, March 1971, 57–60.
Shore, Marci. *Caviar and Ashes: A Warsaw Generation's Life and Death in Marxism, 1918–1968.* New Haven: Yale University Press, 2009.

Politics and Ethics of Human Relations (Zofia Nałkowska)

A well-known figure of the modernist milieu, a daughter of the acclaimed scholar and critic Wacław Nałkowski (1851–1911), an admirer of the controversial literary critic and philosopher Stanisław Brzozowski (1878–1911), Zofia Nałkowska (1884–1954) developed her distinctive literary style, including an innovative approach to the novel form, starting in the early 1900s and continuing throughout the interwar years of Poland's political independence (1919–39).

Her most celebrated interwar novels, such as *Romans Teresy Hennert* (The Romance of Teresa Hennert, 1924), *Niedobra miłość* (Bad Love, 1928), and *Granica* (Boundary, 1935), evaluate social and ethical aspects of Poland's transition to independence by focusing on the behaviours of provincial officials and ex-military personnel adjusting to civil governance and economic change in uncharted political conditions. Although she places her characters in the provinces, she sees Polish public life in the wider context of the post–First World War international situation.

Nałkowska also wrote about women's sexuality and emotional lives; this was the main focus of her pre-1914 prose. Novels such as *Kobiety* (Women, 1906), *Książę* (The Prince, 1907), *Rówieśnice* (Contemporaries, 1909), *Narcyza* (1910), and *Węże i róże* (Snakes and Roses, 1915), and the short story collections *Koteczka czyli białe tulipany* (Little Kitten, or White Tulips, 1909) and *Lustra* (Mirrors, 1913), have prompted feminist critics to treat her as a "woman writer" concerned primarily with women's private experiences. On its own, however, neither a sociopolitical nor a feminist perspective does justice to Nałkowska's writing. In her work, the public and the private spheres are indivisible: the private (including the erotic) is political, just as the political can be private. In *Niecierpliwi* (The Impatient, 1939), Nałkowska extends the existential position identified with female experience in her earlier works to include also that of men. What was previously brought about by "bad love" – confinement in the domestic sphere, "family nausea," the fatal links between eroticism, madness, and suicide – now translates into the experience of both genders, with all characters being driven by "impatience" – that is, by the impulse to self-annihilation.[1] At the same time, Nałkowska never renounced her modernist conception of the incompatibility of the sexes.

Nałkowska's debut, a trilogy with the collective title *Women*, was published when she was only twenty-two and offers an account of a young woman's search for personal identity and sexual fulfilment (for "the whole of life"). In its concerns, it parallels the ethical issues raised by Nałkowska in her 1907 speech to the Polish Women's Congress, where she called for an end to the double-standard that allowed men sexual freedom while denying it to women. The main character of *Women*, Janka, after experiencing several intimate relationships, opts to return to her "ice fields" (the apt title of

Part One of the trilogy) – namely, to a scholarly and professional life without sexual involvement – in an attempt to protect herself from further emotional injury. In her choices and dilemmas, Nałkowska's first female protagonist anticipates other women in her prose, all of whom struggle with aspects of the female experience. Whereas the experiences of Janka in *Women* and Ernestina in *Snakes and Roses* probe the perils of intimate relationships, those of other female characters in these works express negative attitudes towards maternity, as is (respectively) the case with the virtuous Marta, in her suffering and madness, which is triggered by her inability to cope either with male infidelity or with motherhood, and with Marusia, who murders her handicapped daughter before committing suicide. In *Contemporaries*, the dualism – or antagonism – between the "ice fields" and the search for happiness in love involves the additional dimension of social responsibility. One of its protagonists, Małgorzata, works for a living and, like Narcyza, denies herself love for the sake of independence. It should be added here that all the novels of Nałkowska's early phase are marked by two tendencies: one towards Nietzschean individualism, characteristic of the New Women who responded to its vitalism and will to power but who seemed to ignore its misogynist overtones, and the other towards what Grażyna Borkowska has called a "feminization" of culture.[2] Meanwhile the emphasis on aesthetic considerations in her early work and its narcissistic character have raised doubts as to her "feminism," in the sense of whether her work speaks for or provides a model for other women.

A fundamental shift of emphasis took place in Nałkowska's consciousness around 1914–15, prompted by the outbreak of the First World War, when her individual self ceased to be the focus of her literary deliberations and her gaze shifted towards other people and the sufferings of the world around her. At about this time, she became associated with the Piłsudski circle, acquiring first-hand knowledge of the legions aiming to restore Poland's independence. In 1922 she married Jan Jur-Gorzechowski, who soon after became a commander of the military police in Grodno, the city that provides the vital background for Nałkowska's later, "social criticism" novels. Nałkowska quickly became disillusioned with the behaviour of government officials and their social acolytes, and especially with their attitudes towards ethnic minorities and political opponents. She expresses some of these reservations in *Bad Love* through the character of the half-American wife of a landowner and diplomat – a model of modern womanhood that Nałkowska does not develop anywhere else.[3]

First World War experiences are the subject of Nałkowska's collection of short stories *Tajemnice krwi* (Secrets of the Blood, 1917) and the novel *Hrabia Emil* (Count Emil, 1920). The important point to note in this context is that these works focus on the human cost of war rather than on the struggle to realize a specific political agenda. In her assessment of human nature, Nałkowska saw war merely as an intensification, if not a simplification, of "normal" peacetime behaviours; for her, war was not qualitatively different from peace. Emil's story is marked by the antagonism between fin-de-siècle narcissistic aestheticism and the need for personal engagement in society, a tension that Nałkowska had already addressed in her second novel *The Prince*. Emil's commitment to the legion requires the artificial suppression of all his former instincts and intellectual doubts. He does not die self-sacrificially on the battlefield, however, but in his own bed, after a drawn-out "natural" illness that mirrors the novel's opening scenes of his father's disintegration from venereal disease. By creating this parallel, Nałkowska reinforces some of the more permanent themes of her work – of bodily suffering and decay, inherited illnesses and character traits, and obsessive relationships between men and women.

BIOLOGISM

A striking aspect of Nałkowska's style is her attention to fleshly details, their connections with human or animal bodily suffering, and their power to evoke the empathy that forms the cornerstone of her consciousness and ethics. Carefully selected for maximum shocking impact, whether it be the abject decay of old women's bodies, the grotesque insectile abdomen of a woman who has experienced multiple births, wounded fish writhing at the bottom of a boat, or a live fish stripped of its skin, such imagery symbolizes a perception of life, of emotions and psychological motivations, as being deeply affected and even determined by physical existence, including the dark workings of sexual desire.

Her most famous novel, *Boundary*, charts the rise and fall of a young official, Zenon Ziembiewicz, in the political and social context of a provincial town and its environs in the immediate post-independence era. Again, the private life of the main protagonist is shown to parallel his behaviour in the public arena, with events – such as his failure to deal humanely with a strike at a local factory – happening seemingly outside his control. It is not Zenon's actions in the public sphere, however, but in the private one that surface to ensure his public embarrassment, physical disfigurement, and suicide. Both his former lover Justyna and his wife Elżbieta become victims of his "bad love." It is rarely noted that *Boundary* is also a novel about the psychological and emotional consequences of abortion; it is Justyna's decision to abort Zenon's child that triggers her eccentric and obsessive behaviour, the loss of her job, and her isolation and eventual attack on Zenon, and that serves as the motor of the plot in the second half of the novel.

NARRATION AND PERSPECTIVE

Nałkowska's novels and stories are mostly third person narratives, yet her post–First World War fiction rarely features an all-knowing narrator imposing a dominant perspective. Rather, the perspective shifts as each character struggles with the world from her or his distinct but limited psychological point of view. Like a moving camera recording evidence, the narrator is present as a form of consciousness observing but refraining from direct speculation; judgments are left to her characters, none of whom is the author's exclusive *porte-parole*. Art thus dominates over any partisan position yet remains committed to the author's deep humanitarianism and solidarity with the suffering world.

Relatively underestimated yet crucially important is Nałkowska's "international" novel *Choucas* (1927), which reveals the moral position she had reached by the mid-1920s after witnessing the first years of Polish self-governance, as well as her prophetic intuitions about where European society was heading. Sometimes described as the Polish "Magic Mountain," the novel is set in a Swiss sanatorium where representatives of different nationalities, including three survivors of the Armenian genocide (1915–16), discuss the international situation after the war. The novel is one of the rare testimonies to the psychological impact of that atrocity. Discussions within the novel hinge on perceptions of national identity; negative attitudes towards nations other than one's own are shown to be based on emotional reactions to mechanically internalized stereotypes rather than on any consistent ideology. The novel endorses the pacifist humanitarian claim that people all over the world are fundamentally the same; "one nation should not oppress another," says one of the Armenian women. This "modern" sensibility is matched by a new style of narration, characterized by a detached, fact-based commentary: when we read *Medaliony* (Medallions, 1946), Nałkowska's collection of Holocaust stories, we should remember *Choucas*.[4]

Nałkowska was emotionally prepared for what she was to witness during the Second World War: the Nazi crimes, however shocking, merely confirmed her pessimistic assessment of human nature – hence the motto to *Medallions:* "People dealt this fate to people."[5] Both *Choucas* and *Medallions* confirm that, in the final analysis, Nałkowska's position is not one of moral relativism, as is sometimes suggested due to the fact that she did not adhere to any religion, or to a clear and consistent ideological standpoint, or even to a belief in an objective truth. On the contrary, these works prove that her supreme legacy is her deep, humanitarian empathy with the suffering of other living creatures, where the ultimate source of knowledge or morality appears to be only human consciousness itself. Likewise, if it is possible at all to make any final judgment about her feminism, then we should note that she only arrived at the above position through experiencing and exposing the sexual inequality of women with men, and the public as well as private (in fact, inseparable) consequences stemming from it.

Ursula Phillips
University College London, School of Slavonic
and East European Studies

NOTES

1 Ewa Kraskowska explains "bad love" as a recurring syndrome, whereby a woman submits to a man's passion only to be betrayed by his subsequent and repeated unfaithfulness; she then internalizes this experience of rejection and suffers in ways that men do not. With time, Nałkowska came to regard "bad love" as symptomatic of all human relationships. See Kraskowska, *Piórem niewieścim. Z problemów prozy kobiecej dwudziestolecia międzywojennego*, 47–55.
2 Borkowska, *Alienated Women*, 255. Her term refers to what she perceives as the "imposition of the category of gender on neutral (from the point of view of sex) cultural situations."
3 Smoleń, "Płeć i śmierć," 225–6.
4 Bolecki, "Ludobójstwo i początki prozy nowoczesnej," 49.
5 Nałkowska, *Medallions*.

WORKS CITED

Bolecki, Włodzimierz. "Ludobójstwo i początki prozy nowoczesnej (*Choucas* Zofii Nałkowskiej)." *Arkusz* 5 (2003): 49.

Borkowska, Grażyna. *Alienated Women: A Study on Polish Women's Fiction 1845–1918*. Translated by Ursula Phillips. Budapest: Central European University Press, 2001.

Kraskowska, Ewa. *Piórem niewieścim. Z problemów prozy kobiecej dwudziestolecia międzywojennego*. Poznań: Wyd. Naukowe Uniwersytetu Adama Mickiewicza, 1999.

Nałkowska. Zofia. *Medallions*. Translated by Diana Kuprel. Evanston: Northwestern University Press, 2000.

Smoleń, Barbara. "Płeć i śmierć. Tanatyczna wyobraźnia Zofii Nałkowskiej." In *Ciało, płeć, literatura. Prace ofiarowane Profesorowi Germanowi Ritzowi w pięćdziesiątą rocznicę urodzin*. Edited by Magdalena Hornung, Marcin Jędrzejczak, and Tadeusz Korsak. 197–233. Warszawa: Wiedza Powszechna, 2001.

Troubled Modernism (Jarosław Iwaszkiewicz)

The term "modernist" is frequently invoked to categorize twentieth-century authors who have little in common by way of literary style, time and place of literary activity, or affiliation with a group or movement. But even within a single author's career, the work tends to resist categorization along such lines; this is even truer if the career is a long one. In the case of Jarosław Iwaszkiewicz (1894–1980), whose life spanned nearly a century of aesthetic and political changes, the term "modernist" is simply too vague and temporally unbounded to do the writer any justice.

Iwaszkiewicz's work defies classification according to the categories favoured by literary historians. He debuted as a member of the Skamander group, the most influential literary movement in the newly independent Second Polish Republic. Like other avant-garde movements in Eastern Europe, Skamander began under the influence of Futurism, but its members soon abandoned their radical notions and positioned themselves at the centre of Poland's flourishing literary scene, while at the same time downplaying their opposition to the political status quo. During the programmatic first phase of Skamander, Iwaszkiewicz remained on the movement's fringes. This peripherality later allowed him to circumvent the dominant literary conventions of the 1920s with greater ease than could other members of Skamander, such as Julian Tuwim (1894–1953) and Jan Lechoń (1899–1956), and helped him develop his own distinct voice. Iwaszkiewicz reached his creative maturity in early 1930s. In the five subsequent decades, marked by fascism and socialism, he maintained the sovereignty of his voice despite the threats to individual expression posed by these political regimes.

Iwaszkiewicz's ability to remain aesthetically and, to a large extent, ideologically true to himself had less to do with his take on aesthetic modernism, which was less radical than that of Witold Gombrowicz (1904–69) or Bruno Schulz (1892–1942), than with the sheer breadth of his oeuvre, which is divided evenly between poetry and prose. In Polish modernism, dominated by poetry from the early 1920s, Iwaszkiewicz staked out a unique position by achieving mastery in both genres. His lyrical cycle *Powrót do Europy* (Return to Europe, 1931) and his short stories "Panny z Wilka" (The Wilko Girls, 1933) and "Brzezina" (The Birch Grove, 1933) – which remain classics to this day – were written almost simultaneously in the early 1930s. This ability to work in both genres side by side, allowing ideas and impulses to flow between them, would remain a staple of his working method for years to come. Poets such as Czesław Miłosz (1911–2004) lauded him first and foremost as a poet, and this was how Iwaszkiewicz identified himself as well. It is his prose, however – lyrical in its own right, yet constituting a unique and autonomous genre – that has earned him international fame. In the long run, his short stories have proved more lasting than his novels. This is particularly true of his novels of the 1920s and 1930s, such as *Księżyc wschodzi* (The Moon Is Rising, 1925), *Czerwone tarcze* (Red Shields, 1934), and *Zmowa mężczyzn* (Conspiracy of Men, 1930). The latter two are presented as a historical and a social novel, respectively, although both are highly autobiographical, as is always the case with Iwaszkiewicz's writings. This dual talent, in poetry and prose, distinguishes him from other Polish poets. Perhaps the only other exception is Tadeusz Różewicz (1921–2014), whose postwar output covers multiple genres – poetry, drama, and prose; however, his experiments in prose were more of a phase than a lifelong commitment. Miron Białoszewski (1922–83) also comes to mind, but for Białoszewski poetry and prose were hardly two separate genres.

Geopoetics: a performative term that attributes to space a processual character similar to a text. Space understood as text yields to both writing and reading and is unready in a double-sense. Firstly, the means of perception (types of representation or narrations) decide on the methods of shaping space. For example, an industrial approach results in space being treated as a world to be subjugated, while a scientific one leads to its systematization. Second, descriptions of spaces can change social means of perception and, consequently, attitudes towards space. While classic geography considers a map to be a means to trace a terrain, geopoetics – to the contrary – see it as a means to shape space. From a methodological perspective, geopoetics focus on the aspect of agency in the relation between culture and space.

When Poland regained its independence in 1918, Warsaw became the centre of a national literary revival. However, many Polish writers of the time were not from Warsaw, but rather from the eastern part of Poland known as the Borderlands. Iwaszkiewicz was from Ukraine, and in his writings this place of origin became a kind of *ur*-space, a nexus connecting many of his other themes and ideas. For Iwaszkiewicz, geographical space took on a geopoetic significance. In this respect, he placed himself in the tradition of the Ukrainian School, a nineteenth-century Polish literary movement that romanticized Ukrainian landscapes, peoples, and customs; this, in turn, suggested a particularly strong bond with Juliusz Słowacki (1809–49), that school's best-known representative. Unlike the Romantics, however, Iwaszkiewicz did not imagine Ukraine as the utopian homestead of a new and liberated Poland, but rather as a lost homeland that lived in memory only. In the 1920s he had even planned to write a "great Ukrainian novel," but this work never materialized. His political ties may explain why. The young Iwaszkiewicz aligned himself with Józef Piłsudski's political regime. The vision of Ukraine in the planned work would have been at odds with Piłsudski's eastern politics, and the writer was not prepared at the time to take an oppositional stance to it.

"Ukrainian School": this term encompasses several Polish Romantic writers from the first half of the nineteenth century whose work deals with Ukrainian themes. The most important of these works are Antoni Malczewski's poetic novel *Maria* (1824), Seweryn Goszczyński's

narrative poem *Zamek kaniowski* (Kaniv Castle, 1828), Michał Czajkowski's poetic prose *Powiści kozackie* (Cossack Tales, 1837), and Juliusz Słowacki's digressive narrative poem *Beniowski* (1841), as well as his play *Sen Srebrny Salomei* (The Silver Dream of Salome, 1843). The image of Ukraine emerging from these works is comparable to that of Scotland as presented in the work of the English Lake Poets. It is saturated with history and at the same time fairy-tale-like, on the one hand giving rise to melancholy and on the other primevally wild. These characteristics of Ukraine were represented by the figure of a Cossack – wild, hot-tempered, audacious, and valuing freedom over life – who became the preferred hero of this literature. The image of Ukraine evolved from a view that was notably idealized and Polonized (Malczewski), through one that revealed Polish–Ukrainian conflicts (Goszczyński), up to a tragic perspective in which the Polish–Ukrainian union led to mutual destruction that necessitated the creation of two separate nations (Słowacki).

In the literature of post-partition nineteenth-century Poland, the Ukrainian trope was frequently coupled with the idea of Europe. Iwaszkiewicz remained true to this tradition. His childhood images of Ukraine resonate with later images of Italy, and even more of Sicily. Iwaszkiewicz's literary orientation towards Europe, which continued even after 1945, was always rooted in Ukraine. His passionate interest in the aestheticism of Belle Époque Europe, particularly Oscar Wilde's version of it, can be traced from his youth; later on, this aestheticism would find an echo in Ukrainian and, even more strongly, Russian modernist trends. Finally, it was in Ukraine that Iwaszkiewicz first encountered tsarist and then revolutionary Russia. He never harboured any illusions about Russia's politics but nevertheless was irresistibly attracted to its cultural vibrancy. Iwaszkiewicz's Europe was pan-European; in this, it differed from the local and limited idea of Europe shared by many of his Central European contemporaries. He oriented his Europe along both the east–west axis (emphasizing Poland's unique relationship with Russia and historical orientation towards France), and also along the north–south axis, so as to include both his personal fascination with Italy on the one hand and Poland's relationship with Scandinavia on the other. Furthermore, Iwaszkiewicz assigned two centres to this extensive mapping of Europe: Polish–Ukrainian and, perhaps suprisingly, German. Germany's central role in the articulation of a European aesthetic ideal was, of course, upended in the 1930s, when that ideal was placed in the service of a coercive political agenda that would eventually tear Europe apart. It is worth bearing in mind that Iwaszkiewicz, both as a traveller and as a reader, constructed his idea of Europe in the shadow of rising nationalism.

Iwaszkiewicz knew an impressive number of languages and often used his polyglottic skills to explore a range of foreign writings in order to inspire his own. These explorations were more important for his prose than for his poetry. Outside of Polish literature, he turned mainly to French and German authors such as Proust, Gide, and Mann, all crucial influences on his conception of the modern novel. This orientation towards Continental literature may account for the apparent lack of influence by Anglo-American authors on Iwaszkiewicz's work; his indifference towards English-language literature, in turn, may account for the tepid anglophone reception of Iwaszkiewicz's works – in stark contrast to their vibrant reception in Continental Europe. In the Polish literary context, Iwaszkiewicz did not follow in the footsteps of earlier innovators like Wacław Berent (1878–1940) and Karol Irzykowski (1873–1944); nor did he attempt to match the experiments of his contemporaries, such as Witkacy (1885–1939), Schulz, and Gombrowicz. His closest literary predecessor was Stefan Żeromski (1864–1925), an exemplar of Polish high modernism. What drew Iwaszkiewicz to Żeromski was not only the old master's sensualism, his investigation of Eros, but also Żeromski's later realism, with its focus on mimesis and dramatic narrative. Iwaszkiewicz's approach to modern narrative was directed towards the reader; he sought communicative exchange and avoided narration for its own sake. Iwaszkiewicz was a storyteller whose subject was modernism – that is, the modern anthropological condition – rather than a modernist storyteller. His reservations about the literary avant-garde can be compared to those of Czesław Miłosz, whose road to modernism was similarly long, particularly during Miłosz's American years.

In both poetry and prose, Iwaszkiewicz gravitated towards themes of human existence in the twentieth century. Rather than create typological characters of the sort demanded by realism and, later on, by socialist realism, he portrayed idiosyncratic individuals. The authenticity and intimacy of his characterizations is linked to the autobiographical quality of his work. An increasing number of Iwaszkiewicz's autobiographical writings published in recent years – including diaries and letters to intimate acquaintances, such as his wife, daughters, and fellow writers – show that Iwaszkiewicz was deeply concerned with finding a language for intimacy. For a number of reasons both political and cultural, Polish literature had tended to shy away from articulations of intimate feeling, but in his private confessions Iwaszkiewicz managed to hit on just such a language. However, a comparison of these strictly autobiographical materials with Iwaszkiewicz's fiction, especially such famous short stories as "The Wilko Girls" and "Kochankowie z Marony" (Lovers from Marona, 1961), confirms that he separated his intimate language (drawn from life, but then abstracted and used in the service of imaginary content) from intimate experience. For example, Iwaszkiewicz always refrains from using simplistic clichés of sublimation, such as those related to his hidden homosexuality.

In Iwaszkiewicz's fiction, intimacy is always grounded in a historical and social context and is never disengaged from the world at large. Iwaszkiewicz does not lose sight of external reality, even in his most introspective writings. This often produces an ironic tension in his narratives. Large-scale historical frameworks and sociopolitical contexts never overdetermine the individual fate of his characters. This is a particular strength of Iwaszkiewicz's stories, but it contains a paradox. Iwaszkiewicz's strategy of portraying concrete political details without committing to their political implications is an expression of his lifelong historical pessimism, a pessimism that can ultimately be traced back to the Ukrainian School of Polish Romanticism. In the twentieth century, such pessimism allowed both the author and his characters to hold on to their inner independence and protected them against ideological seduction. At the same time, however, it prevented their open resistance. In his readers' perception, Iwaszkiewicz's public image contrasted unfavourably with the political independence of his characters. After 1949 and, paradoxically, even more so after the "thaw" of 1956, the writer's entanglement with the communist regime could not be reconciled with his writing. Having chosen to play a leading role in the official literary establishment, Iwaszkiewicz excluded himself from the milieu of dissenters against communism at home and abroad. During those decades, public figures were expected to commit to a political stance and the demand for resistance steadily grew. The nineteenth-century ideal of artistic sovereignty, to which Iwaszkiewicz was always committed, needed a much stronger political than artistic confirmation in the twentieth century, in both the East and the West, but particularly in the East. This was a matter not of individual choice but of public opinion. Iwaszkiewicz struggled with this paradox for half his creative life and was never able to resolve it successfully.

Iwaszkiewicz began his career as an admirer of aestheticism and artistic elitism but was gradually transformed into a national writer, much like Żeromski a few decades earlier and like Miłosz later on, albeit in a quite different manner. This public role grew out of a combination of his moderate version of modernist poetics and his engagement with typically Polish themes. However, recent developments in the reception of Iwaszkiewicz's work in Poland and beyond have once again relieved him of this role. Current interpretations of his work have returned to the initial position of his aestheticism, which originally derived from the modernism of the nineteenth century but now encompass an anthropologically understood modernism of the twentieth century. Short stories and poetry dominate this current trend in his reception, while his novels, including his grand attempt at a contemporary trilogy, *Sława i Chwała* (Fame and Glory, 1956–62), have for now taken a back seat. It is a testament to Iwaszkiewicz's unique creative and intellectual gifts that he was able to maintain his idiosyncratic style for more than half a century while at the same time embracing the great themes of twentieth-century art.

German Ritz
University of Zurich
Translated by Edith Krannich

Shifting Sands: History of Polish Prose, 1945–2015

The legacy of mass death and the demands of a new life – these were the two parameters of the situation of Polish society after the end of the Second World War. Death spoke through emptiness and absence: six million Poles died during the war, including three million Polish Jews; one-third of its social elite disappeared, including 39 per cent of doctors, 33 per cent of teachers, 30 per cent of scientists and academics, 28 per cent of the clergy, and 26 per cent of lawyers. Poland lost 38 per cent of its national wealth (to compare: France lost 1.5 per cent, and Great Britain 0.8 per cent), 43 per cent of its cultural property, 55 per cent of its health services infrastructure (hospitals, equipment, clinics), and over 50 per cent of its transport and communication infrastructure.

The language of death, expressed in quantifiable losses and damages, commingled with the language of new life. Forced changes to territory, national demographics, and the class structure and political system were the most important indicators of the new situation. The society that emerged on the postwar scene was displaced and incomplete, "out of place" and "not in full force." These shifts had taken place on four levels:

1. *Geographical/cultural*, through the resettlement of former Borderland inhabitants in Poland's western regions and through emigration from Poland;
2. *Class/cultural*, through the transfer of land to peasants, the elimination of the landowning class, and the migration of impoverished rural and small-town residents to industrial centres;
3. *Ideological/institutional*, through changes at the centre – that is, in the ruling ideology and means of governance – tied to the shift from a capitalist system to a communist one;
4. *Ethnic/ethical*: Poles had become the *sole* instead of the majority nationality as a result of the Holocaust and the loss of the multi-ethnic Borderlands.

1. THE MOST IMPORTANT WORKS OF POLISH ÉMIGRÉ LITERATURE:

1. *Works about the Second World War*: Melchior Wańkowicz's *Bitwa o Monte Casino* (The Battle of Monte Cassino, 1945); Beata Obertyńska's *Z domu niewoli* (In the House of Slavery, 1946); Maria Kuncewiczowa's *Zmowa nieobecnych* (The Conspiracy of the Absent, 1946); Józef Mackiewicz's *Zbrodnia katyńska w świetle dokumentów* (The Katyn Crime in the Light of Documents, 1948); Józef Czapski's *Na nieludzkiej ziemi* (The Inhuman Land,

1949); Gustaw Herling-Grudziński's *Inny świat* (A World Apart: The Journal of a Gulag Survivor, 1951).

2. *Works establishing the significance of émigré life for the independent exchange of ideas and as a source of new poetics*: Czesław Miłosz's *Zniewolony Umysł* (The Captive Mind, 1953); Witold Gombrowicz's *Trans-Atlantyk* (1953) and *Dziennik* (Diary; published on an on-going basis in *Kultura* between 1953–69); Czesław Straszewicz's *Turyści z bocianich gniazd* (Tourists from Stork Nests, 1953); Mackiewicz's *Droga donikąd* (Road to Nowhere, 1955) and *Kontra* (1957); Herling-Grudziński's *Dziennik pisany nocą* (Journal Written at Night, published in *Kultura* starting in 1971 [after Gombrowicz's death] and in English as *Volcano and Miracle: A Selection of Fiction and Nonfiction from the Journal Written at Night*).

3. *Works from the 1970s and 1980s*: Władysław Odojewski's *Zasypie wszystko, zawieje…* (And the Snow Will Cover Everything, 1973); Leszek Kołakowski's *Główne nurty marksizmu* (Main Currents of Marxism: The Founders, the Golden Age, and the Breakdown, 1976–8); Miłosz's *Ziemia Ulro* (The Land of Urlo, 1977), *Ogród nauk* (Garden of Knowledge, 1979) and *Świadectwo poezji* (The Witness of Poetry, 1983); Aleksander Wat's *Mój wiek* (My Century: The Odyssey of a Polish Intellectual, 1977); Maria Danilewicz-Zielińska's *Szkice o literaturze emigracyjnej* (Essays on Émigré Literature, 1978); Jerzy Ficowski's *Odczytywanie popiołów* (A Reading of Ashes: Poems, 1979); Stanisław Barańczak's *Etyka i poetyka* (Ethics and Poetry, 1979) and *Czytelnik ubezwłasnowolniony* (Incapacitated Reader, 1983); Marian Pankowski's *Rudolf* (1980); Leopold Tyrmand's *Dziennik 1954* (Diary 1954, 1980); Ewa Czarnecka's *Podróżny świata. Rozmowy z Czesławem Miłoszem* (World Traveller: Conversations with Czesław Miłosz, 1983); Henryk Grynberg's *Prawda nieartystyczna* (Inartistic Truth, 1984); Chrystian Skrzyposzek's *Wolna Trybuna* (Free Tribune, 1985); Teresa Torańska's *Oni* ("Them": Stalin's Polish Puppets, 1985); Adam Zagajewski's *Solidarność i samotność* (Solidarity, Solitude: Essays, 1986); Ida Fink's *Skrawek czasu* (A Scrap of Time and Other Stories, 1987) and *Podróż* (The Journey, 1990); Zygmunt Haupt's *Szpica* (The Vangarde, 1989).

The experience of being "not in full force" and "out of place" consituted the most important challenge in postwar literature, which faced the task of working out a new symbolic order. To describe the fate of this order, it is necessary to traverse the entire period from its beginning to its end more than once.

I. First Shift: From Geopolitics to Geopoetics

Borderlands – the Construction of a Myth

Towards the end of the 1940s, a current appeared in Polish prose that grounded its symbolic order in a transformed image of the Borderlands. The books of this current constitute one of the most important traditions in Polish twentieth-century literature – the prose of "small homelands." The significance of this current stemmed primarily from Poland's loss of the territories it had held between 1918 and 1939 in Lithuania, Belarus, and Ukraine as a result of the Yalta agreements of February 1945. Changes to the nation's administrative map brought with them the compulsory resettlement of approximately two million Poles from the east to the west of the country. This was more than simply a resettlement; it also meant a sudden end to the four-hundred-year-old multicultural Commonwealth. Since the sixteenth century, Poland had been a multi-ethnic, multilingual, and multi-denominational country. During the interwar period, 31 per cent of Poles belonged to a minority (over 5 million Ukrainians, almost 3.5 million Jews, over a million Belarusians, and over 700,000 Germans). Postwar transformations of the political map led to a wholesale change in Poland's ethnic structure; it became a country with a single ethnicity, language, and faith.

The first to undertake the reorganization of the Polish imagination were authors of emigrant literature, writing during the war or shortly afterwards. In 1942, Florian Czarnyszewicz (1900–64), residing in Argentina since 1924, published *Nadberezyńcy* (Berezina People). This *gawęda* (epic tale) is one of the greatest stories about Polish daily life in the Belarusian Borderlands. Józef Wittlin (1896–1976) created a literary portrait of his hometown in *Mój Lwów* (My Lviv, 1946) while in New York, and Czesław Miłosz (1911–2004) wrote *Dolina Issy* (The Issa Valley, 1955) in Paris. Zygmunt Haupt (1907–75) was living in Winchester, Virginia, when he published *Pierścień z papieru* (The Paper Ring, 1963), a short story collection made from tender memory, original talent, and unbridled linguistic invention. *Atlantyda* (Atlantis) by Andrzej Chciuk (1920–78) – "the best émigré book by a writer of Polish descent published in 1969" according to London's *News* (Wiadomości) – was written in Australia. The monumental Hutsulian epic *Na wysokiej połoninie* (On a High Pasture), the life's work of Stanisław Vincenz (1888–1971), is to this day considered a reliable source of ethnographic knowledge; he began writing it while still in Poland (vol. 1 in 1936), and finished it in the south of France; it was published posthumously (1974, 1979).

These works – to which one may add works by Marian Hemar, Józef Łobodowski, Julian Wołoszynowski, Sergiusz Piasecki (1901–64), and Kazimierz Wierzyński (1894–1969) – changed the earlier model of writing about the Borderlands. During the nineteenth century, mainly due to the influence of Henryk Sienkiewicz's (1846–1916) novels, these regions had been looked upon as in need of conquest and the gift of civilization, as places where primeval beauty confronted cultural order. Postwar novels introduced a radical shift in this perspective, mainly in terms of the rules of social coexistence.

The first of these new rules stated that collectively, the Borderlands were greater than the sum of all the differences between distinct Borderland communities. And there were many such differences, for the Borderlands were inhabited by Poles, Lithuanians, Belarusians, Ukrainians, Russians, Germans, Jews, and Tatars. Such identies were not ethnic or religious, however, but regional. Accordingly, a resident of Vilnius would answer the question "Who are you?" not by saying "a Pole/German/Jew," but rather "a Vilnian." The small homeland was not just a region but the basis of identification. Vincenz's Hutsul region, Stempowski's Dniester Valley, Wittlin's Lviv, Haupt's Galicia, Chciuk's Drochobych, and Miłosz's Lithuania marked the characteristic margins of modernity – territories where the rules of coexistence had not yet been defined by nationalism and state.

> Vincenz knows that people today long for homeland, and instead are granted only a state. Homeland is organic, grown into the past, never too large, warming to the heart, close as one's own body. A state is mechanical.
>
> – Miłosz, "La Combe," 34

Second, complementing this identity, nature (land, water, animals) was treated as an integral part of the homeland. Human beings were not so much users as integral inhabitants of this world, and their humanity was shaped by constant experience of that fact. Everything within the small homeland was in its place, and thus to be "here" was to inhabit a world imbued with sense in each of its parts. The third rule of coexistence – after the commonality of differences and coexistence with nature – was that small homelands had no hegemons. Their inhabitants had pre-democratic customs and institutions at their disposal – such as the assembly, *veche*, or conference – that allowed them to resolve conflicts without violating principles of equality.

> The myth of the Borderlands is radically anti-totalitarian and cannot be reconciled with any dominant ideology – of class or of nation – since its essence is tolerance toward difference and reserve toward all ideas that, abstractly and from above, order social reality.
>
> – Jarzębski, "Exodus (ewolucja obrazu kresów po wojnie)," 146

Taken together, these characteristics – diversity, commonality, coexistence with nature, and equality – comprised the magical realism of the Borderlands (similar to what we find in Latin American prose). It is not the spells, local beliefs, magicians, whisperers, and medicine men we encounter in books and films (such as *The Issa Valley* adaptation, directed by Konwicki in 1980) that constitute this magical realism, but the fact that small homelands create an alternative to modernity. Small homelands resist pragmatism, nationalism, and secularization. In this sense, émigré novels – and a little later, also those written in Poland – took on the qualities of both regressive and progressive utopias (much as we find in Latin American prose). In a world wounded by nationalism, they were a proposal of coexistence. The essence of the proposition was that Europe was a continent of small homelands.

Borderlands: The Reversal of the Myth

The Borderlands: an arcadia of tolerance, a homeland of agreeable differences, a space of harmony on Europe's margins, a victim of modernity – this was the myth created by émigré literature. Writers at home also contributed to this narration, among them Tadeusz Konwicki (1926–2015) with *Dziura w niebie* (Hole in the Sky, 1959), *Zwierzoczłekoupiór* (The Anthropos-Spectre-Beast, 1969), and *Kronika wypadków miłosnych* (A Chronicle of Amorous Accidents, 1974); Julian Stryjkowski (1905–96) with *Głosy w ciemności* (Voices in the Darkness, 1956), *Austeria* (1966), *Sen Azrila* (Azril's Dream, 1975), and *Echo* (1988); and Andrzej Kuśniewicz (1904–93) with *Król Obojga Sycylii* (King of the Two Sicilies, 1970), *Strefy* (Zones, 1971), *Lekcja martwego języka* (Extinct Language Lesson, 1977), *Mieszaniny obyczajowe* (Mishmash of Manners, 1985), and *Nawrócenie* (The Conversion, 1987); as well as Melchior Wańkowicz (1892–1974), Jarosław Iwaszkiewicz (1894–1980), and Artur Sandauer (1913–89).

Another version of the Borderlands myth appeared in the 1970s. If the myth's earlier version can be called bright, then its later one deserves to be called gloomy. Key to creating this version of the myth was Włodzimierz Odojewski (1930–2016), author of the Podolian cycle consisting of *Kwarantanna* (Quarantine, 1960), *Zmierzch świata* (The

Dying Day, 1962; trans. 1964), *Wyspa ocalenia* (No Island of Salvation, 1964; trans. 1965), and *Zasypie wszystko, zawieje ...* (Snow Will Cover Everything ..., 1973). This cycle, and in particular its final novel, a masterpiece of Polish literature, narrates the lives of two half-brothers, the Pole Piotr Czerestwieński, the offspring of a legal union, and the Ukrainian Semen Gawryluk, the fruit of a romance with a Ukrainian woman. The relationship between the brothers becomes metonymical of the relations between the two nationalities. Ukrainians are the rightful inhabitants but have been colonized, debased, and reduced to an undifferentiated peasant mass; Poles are the colonizers who wield the power and block efforts to achieve social equality. When the Second World War begins, violence becomes a means of levelling the playing field.

If the bright myth presents the Borderlands as a paradise, Odojewski exposes its hellish aspect. While the "bright" stories move at a languid pace, following the seasons and matchmakers' labours, Odojewski pulls the reader into a whirlwind of history that is in constant "absurd motion without moving forward."[1] Whereas the "bright" Borderlands paint a picture of people coexisting with nature, Odojewski's version leaves accursed the beauty of the land. The "bright" version of the Borderlands envisions society as a system of separate families, while Odojewski presents it as an extended family founded against the will of its members and woven from both legitimate and shameful strands, the latter masking its founding violence and continuing injustice. Thus presented, Ukraine is the murky underbelly of the Borderlands, its dark side, an anti-paradise concealing a colonial reality and its consequences. It is what nostalgia has tried to erase.

The Borderlands: The Transfer of the Myth

The Borderlands returned to literature for the third time at the turn of the 1980s and 1990s by means of a second generation of writers, meaning those who had spent their early childhood in the Borderlands and had been expatriated together with their parents after the Second World War. They had spent their lives in postwar Poland, yet their postmemory was defined by the traumatic experience of losing the Borderlands arcadia. So as adult writers, they faced the challenge of having to confront both places.

Two approaches to this challenge can be found in the works of Adam Zagajewski (b. 1945), Zbigniew Żakiewicz (1932–2010), Aleksander Jurewicz (b. 1952), and Anna Bolecka (b. 1951). The first approach, taken by Zagajewski in *Jechać do Lwowa* (To Go to Lviv, 1985) and *W cudzym pięknie* (Another Beauty, 1998), and by Żakiewicz in *Saga wileńska* (Vilnian Saga, 1992) and *Ujrzane, w czasie zatrzymane* (Seen, Stopped in Time, 1996), involves creating a narrative of reconciliation centred on discovering similarities between the Borderlands and postwar Poland conducive to the domestication of the foreign space. The second approach, exemplified by Jurewicz in *Lida* (1994) and *Pan Bóg nie słyszy głuchych* (*God Does Not Hear the Deaf*, 1995), is characterized by a double-estrangement – towards communist Poland and towards the Borderlands. In Jurewicz's stories, the otherness of the Borderlands stems from that region having been narrated by the Other. This does not, however, invalidate nostalgia for it. The poetics of the first approach brings the two realities together, while in the second case a breach develops that cannot be overcome. In both variants, the symbolic order – even when open-ended – has been created by the phantom presence of the Borderlands. The desire to be free of the Borderlands becomes noticeable when the places of settlement are considered, which, in the books discussed here, refer primarily to the so-called Regained (or Recovered) Territories.

Recovered Territories (initially also the Western, Stipulated, or Returning Lands): a term used after the Second World War to refer to the western and northern regions of contemporary Poland (Silesia, West Pomerania, Warmia, and Masuria) that were placed under Polish jurisdiction as per the Potsdam Conference resolutions (1945). The term "recovered territories" implies that these regions were formerly Polish; this was expressed also by the phrasing "the return of northern and western lands to the motherland."

Works dedicated to the subject of (re)settlement were being written right after the war, albeit infrequently – for example, Eugeniusz Paukszta's (1916–79) *Trud ziemi nowej* (The Toil of New Land, 1948). The politics of the time, however, required that emphasis be placed on the new system's successes and the national unity of Poles rather than on specific regional challenges and the difficulties faced by the settlers. It was only during the 1960s that the issue of the Recovered Territories returned in a more complex though still censored form.[2] These books showed the creation of the new society: as the initial isolation of various groups (German, Cassubian, and Silesian, both indigenous and newcomers) gradually dissipates due to shared work and problems, a limited cultural commonality emerges. This is accompanied by the controlling function of state structures; thus, "settlement" novels constitute a record of the birth of socialist modernity, during which the Borderlands culture retreats to the domestic sphere.

The Polish historical novel was similar in its aims though incomparably more ambitious. It is represented by the five-volume cycle *Bolesław Chrobry* (1947–74) by Antoni Gołubiew (1907–79); by the Piast and Jagiełło novels of Karol Bunsch (1898–1987), starting with *Dzikowy skarb* (Dzik's Treasure, 1945) and continuing through to *Warna 1444* (Varna 1444, 1971); and by the novels of Hanna Malewska (1911–83), such as *Listy staropolskie z epoki Wazów* (Old Polish Letters from the Vasa Epoch, 1959) and *Panowie Leszczyńscy* (Gentlemen Leszczyńscy, 1961); as well as by the works of Zofia Kossak-Szczucka (1889–1968) and Jan Dobraczyński (1910–94). In various ways, all of these works are rooted in the Polish society of the past and – when dealing with this subject – reveal the historical complications that beset the Recovered Territories.

Stanisław Srokowski's excellent novel *Repatriates* (1988) [is] a synthesis of a collective fate and a history of particular individuals ... A train, one of many at that time as might be guessed, traverses the depopulated by war and ethic purges Ukraine, Poland, and finally former Germany [the Recovered Territories] ... Locked inside it is an entire village repatriated from Podolia, mainly Polish, although Ukrainians and Jews escaping to the west also join the train community. This Polish–Ukrainian–Jewish organism hurries into the unknown through a terrifyingly barren, slaughtered world. The speed is one of escape driven by both fear of the horrific ethnic purges in the Borderlands, and by desire for a possibly better life. This train encompasses an entire world. ... People are born and die on the train amid neighbourly quarrels. It stops only to drop off the dead and clean itself of dirt. Everyone dreams about a return, but the new land on which they are one day dropped off immediately requires work.

– Bakuła, "Między wygnaniem a kolonizacją. O kilku odmianach polskiej powieści migracyjnej w XX wieku (na skromnym tle porównawczym)," 168

Expanded knowledge served to balance the scales between the Borderlands and Poland's other regions. A characteristic purging of Borderland symbols can be found in the novels written towards the end of the 1980s by Stanisław Srokowski (b. 1936), who spent his early childhood in the eastern Borderlands (Podhajec) and was resettled to Mieszkowice near the German border along with his parents in 1945.

The literature of the 1990s proposed yet another symbolic order, one that did not forgo the semantics of the Borderlands but instead transfered their myth according to a new set of rules.[3] In the prose of the 1960s, narration had been driven by the desire to impose a uniform identity on the Recovered Territories; during the 1990s, authors sought a poetics that could express a plural and open identity. Writers began to discover that their cities were palimpsests comprising layers of a concealed past. These layers were national and ethnic (German, Cassubian, and Jewish), religious (Evangelical, Eastern Orthodox, and Judaic), and class-based (primarily true for the middle class). When this palimpsest was viewed through the Borderland myth, it showed that the present-day cities of the Recovered Territories – Szczecin, Gdańsk, Elbląg, Olsztyn, Wrocław – were themselves phantom Borderlands. The Western Lands were no longer inhabited by an ethnically diverse society, and thus narrated representations of former lives could not be used to describe their present day. As a result, these novels are melancholic: discovered traces of former cultures – Jewish, German, Cassubian – turn their narrators into obsessive explorers of the past and situate them on the margins of the present.

Central and Eastern Europe: Reorientation of the Map

A different approach to the creation of a symbolic order is found in literature that situates Polish culture within a Central European framework. In 1984, Milan Kundera's essay "The Tragedy of Central Europe" appeared almost simultaneously on the pages of the *New York Review of Books* (26 April) and in the fifth issue of the Polish émigré journal *Zeszyty Literackie* (Literary Notebooks). It presented the dramatic situation of Poles, Czechs, Slovaks, and Hungarians who, as a result of the Yalta Conference, one day found themselves politically transferred to the East and thrown into a foreign history. Rejecting their separation from Western Europe, they rose up in (bloodily suppressed) rebellions – in 1956 (Hungary and Poland), 1968 (Poland and Czechoslovakia), and in 1970 and 1980 (Poland).

From Kundera's perspective, Central Europe – Poland, Czechoslovakia, and Hungary – was the epicentre of nonconformity with communism. The reason for their postwar rebellions was the rift between their own cultural legacy and the new political order. That legacy was defined by a wealth of nationalities, cultures, faiths, and languages. According to Kundera, Central Europe had no experience with forceful solutions to conflicts, since it practised the life principle of "the greatest variety within the smallest space," while the Russian principle was "the smallest variety within the greatest space."[4] Extrapolating Central Europe from a generalized Eastern Europe, Kundera accomplished an extraordinary task: he transformed geopolitics into geopoetics. The postwar division of Europe had followed from a recognition that borders are inviolable – and, consequently, that so is the map. Kundera's essay defied a map thus drawn, and showed that the division could be derived from narration, not force.

His ideas fell on fertile ground. The formula of "smallest space, greatest variety," together with an emphasized role for culture, was well suited to the phantasmal geography of the Borderlands. In Polish literature during the 1990s, one can thus see the map being reoriented – that is, the gradual expansion of the realm in which Polish culture is rooted and a transition from the imaginarium of the Borderlands to the one of Central Europe. The differences between the Borderland and Central European maps are quite clear. The Borderlands had turned Polish culture towards the East and made it exceptional; now, the conceptualization of Central Europe was "shifting" history towards the West, and Polish culture's exceptionality was being disavowed for reasons having to do with its similarities to Czech, Slovak, and Hungarian cultures. The Borderlands imply thinking in categories of European civilization's farthest reaches, while the idea of Central Europe signals geographic proximity to Western Europe. Joining the pro-European orientation of the idea of the "Centre" with the victim status suggested by Kundera produced an image as inspiring as it was dangerous, since it led to thinking in unequivocal terms. Literature was able to maintain its independence, and this undermined both the Central European myth and the myth of the unification of the Centre with the West.

Half of this task was accomplished by novels that evoke the notion of Central Europe in order to undermine platitudes of unification. Their authors – Stefan Chwin (*Esther* [1999] and *Dolina radości* [The Valley of Joy, 2006]), and Paweł Huelle (*Inne historie* [Other Stories, 1999], *Mercedes-Benz* [2001], and *Castorp* [2004]) – proposed a model for contesting the present and the forces prevailing in it from the perspective of Central Europe. They invoked Central Europe from the turn of the nineteenth and twentieth centuries in a form provided by Kundera: bourgeois, fair, not ideologized, practising a fluid identity opposed to nationalisms and violence. This was a Europe of societies and cities, not states and nations; capitalist, but exchanging money for art; technologically advanced, but using innovation to enjoy life's pleasures. This Europe was to be a counterweight to present-day Europe, which in the novels of Chwin and Huelle appears as a continent that is globalizing, disrespectful of local differences, consumerist, and threatened by fundamentalism and nihilism. For present-day Europe, Central Europe from a hundred years ago was meant to be a lesson in a different culture, useful in staving off postmodern dangers.

The writer who undermined both the myth of Central Europe and myths of unification was Andrzej Stasiuk. Together with Jurii Andrukhovych, he published a book titled *Moja Europa* (My Europe).[5] In the essay "Dziennik okrętowy" (Logbook) included therein, Stasiuk describes the creation of his own territory: "There is a piece of Belarus inside, quite a lot of Ukraine, respectable and comparable expanses of Romania and Hungary, almost all of Slovakia and a patch of the Czech Republic. And about a third of the homeland. There is no Germany or Russia, which I accept with some surprise, but also with discrete relief."[6]

His private map brought a significant correction in transferring the centre downward. Stasiuk undermined the earlier positioning of the Centre with a simple question: Where is one to fit Romania, Bulgaria, and Albania – in other words, regions of poverty and backwardness? If Central Europe does not include them, then it is not truly Europe, and if it does acknowledge them, then it ceases to be an idealized, bourgeois arcadia. Stasiuk's geopoetics radically reversed the 1980s tendency to orient the map towards the West, and against the East (Russia), in an attempt to join Poland with Western Europe. The discourse he proposed established a realm different from both the West and the East. The Central European discourse proposed by Stasiuk in *My Europe* and developed in his subsequent books (*Zima* [Winter, 2001]; *Jadąc do Babadag* [On the Way to Babadag,

2004]; *Fado* [2006]; *Dojczland* [2007]) constitutes a language of double-distinctiveness rather than assimilation.

Stasiuk is an anti-Kundera. While the Czech author occidentalizes Central Europe, Stasiuk orientalizes it. Kundera argues that the West has betrayed Mitteleuropa, while for Stasiuk it is its elegant conceptualization that has undermined Central Europe. Kundera (along with Chwin and Huelle) sees Central Europe as a reservoir of beautiful historical treasures, while Stasiuk sees it as a rusted storehouse of socialist industry and as a market stall stocked with imitations of Western products. Whereas György Konrád, Czesław Miłosz, and Danilo Kiš consider it primarily a bourgeois product, for Stasiuk it constitutes a plebeian map. While proponents of integration speak of Central Europe as an intermediate phase, Stasiuk treats it as a permanent condition. Moreover, in Stasiuk's conceptualization, Central Europe is a distorting mirror of the West: its inhabitants will never reach Western civilizational levels, and all they can offer the West is a parody of postmodernity. The Centre parrots the West because it has unwittingly embraced the civilizational mission of the West as its legitimizing myth, and Central Europe as precisely the realm in which this mission reveals its ineffectiveness.

Through Stasiuk's travel essays, a new cycle began in the great epic about the formation of a symbolic order under post-Yalta conditions. The epic that began with a nostalgic conjuring of the eastern Borderlands as an alternative to nationalistic Europe ended with the expansion of the Centre as an alternative to a postmodern Europe. It transpires from this shift, however, that in order to set roots in one's own space, its map must first be narrated.

II. Second Shift: Playing Class

Returning once again to the end of the war and the change in the political system: on 22 July 1944 the Polish Committee of National Liberation put out a proclamation to the nation known since then as the July Manifesto. Approved by Stalin in Moscow, the proclamation denied legitimacy to the London-based Second Polish Republic, which the Allies had recognized, and declared the PKWN to be the only legal power; it then outlined new national borders (which encompassed former eastern Prussia and Silesia but not the Borderlands) and declared the nationalization of properties over 50 hectares and the handover of land to peasants. However, the way in which the July Manifesto was implemented did not match its promises. Contrary to the law, not only agricultural lands but also estates that had nothing to do with agricultural production were parcelled out. Peasants did receive land assignments, but shortly afterwards, compulsory crop quotas were set amid attempts to convince everyone to collectivize their fields into *kolkhozy*. For the peasant class, the change in proprietary relations combined with the transformation of the social structure was without precedent and meant that a modern peasant culture had to be developed.

The significance of this challenge emerges fully in the context of the double-shift in peasant culture after the war. The first shift was tied to the allotment of land to peasants and their social advancement, since the alliance between the working and peasant classes was to be the basis for national economic development. The second shift flowed from the state's emphasis on industrialization (between 1945 and 1970, several million people left rural life and entered a new – working, white-collar, or intelligentsia – class). The first of these processes bolstered peasant culture by giving it a nominally equal place among others. The second signalled the modernization of rural life and radical changes to its culture. Peasant culture thus found itself having to simultaneously aggregate and transgress its traditions. This created a European-scale phenomenon – a waxing *and* waning of class consciousness – that would be articulated in exceptional literary works.[7]

Three basic models of cultural description emerged from the extraordinary eruption of peasant prose during the 1960s. The first of these, founded by Tadeusz Nowak (1930–91), can be called *autarkic*. Nowak's key idea was to present peasant culture as a self-sufficient cosmos in which a human being can find all of the symbols necessary to understand the world and can feel all the emotions necessary to experience the fullness of humanity. His novels thus undermine the belief that peasant culture is poorer than urban culture; in them, the peasant world takes the form of a fantastic fairy tale, told in a magical mode.

The second, more predictable model can be called *alienational* and is founded on the expectation of conflict between traditional peasant culture and classless modernity. That encounter cannot end in an alliance: the introduction of universal education, electrification, health services, and mass media to the village activates an irreversible process in which the peasant culture gradually disappears, along with its beliefs, myths, rituals, and regional differentiations, replaced by rationalism and cultural standardization. The most important works that follow this model, therefore, call attention to the conflicted nature of the process taking place in Polish history and diagnose the extent of this conflict. They do this either seriously, as in *Tańczący jastrząb* (The Dancing Hawk, 1962) by Julian Kawalec (1916–2014), or in the grotesque manner of Edward Redliński (b. 1940) in *Konopielka* (1973). Once activated, the process of alienation continues: when peasant children leave the village and take up work as engineers or doctors, no modern culture in which to plant their roots awaits them. Displaced to the city, the peasant ceases to be a peasant but does not become a member of the middle-class or the intelligentsia, since the distinct culture of the urban classes has become blurred after the war. Peasant children are aspiring to a class that, as a result of the advancement of peasants, has become obsolescent.

The process does not end here, however. In *Awans* (Promotion, 1973), Redliński shows an amusing reverse side of the peasant class's alienation, manifested in their longing for rural life. This longing transforms the village into a peculiar museum of simplicity: urban dwellers, who themselves have family roots in the village, return to that life in order to "immerse [themselves] in nature," and this forces the village inhabitants to play the role of simple peasants. As a result, a class of pseudo-urbanites and pseudo-peasants forms. All of them have experienced alienation, but no one is able to imagine a future form of "native" society. In this alienational model – articulated through melancholy, pathos, or irony – progress is a cultural catastrophe, masked by laughter. The first breach of cultural stasis – the stable system of differences – has activated an unstoppable process as a result of which no one can restore their sense of cultural rootedness.

Between the autarkic and alienational models we find the work of Wiesław Myśliwski (b. 1932). His novels bring to the surface the auto-transgressive potential that exists in peasant culture. In *Nagi sad* (The Barren Orchard, 1967), for example, the author reveals the progressive impulse born of parental imagination that prepares children for entry into modernization. In this way, Myśliwski moves beyond a conflict-based view of relations between modernity and tradition. Unlike most writers of the peasant literary current, he does see modernity in traditional peasant culture – not in the form of rationalistic thought, but in the form of invention that prepares the younger generation to choose change.

Myśliwski deepens the portrait of auto-transgression in *Pałac* (Palace, 1970), a masterpiece of Polish literature that shows a peasant's contravention of class when he enters the world of gentry forms and becomes the master of a gentry manor. Instead of showing a conflict between modernity and tradition, the author outlines a situation that abolishes the opposition between Shepherd and Master. If the Shepherd were to storm the palace and begin to rob it, he would not be able to master the Master's culture. Jakub, however, passes the test of the Master (in a Hegelian sense of the term): in a palace set ablaze, in one of the most astonishing scenes in Polish literature, he sits down at a piano and welcomes death while playing music. At the instant of sacrificing his life for a culture that is foreign to him, he becomes its rightful owner. The right to inhabit the palace is thus granted to him not by revolution, but by the ability to transcend the limits of his own culture, which is independent of social origins and which he has found within himself.

In order to convey such a complex vision of peasant culture, Myśliwski created his own form of monologue. When assessed from a formal and linguistic perspective, peasant prose reveals interesting differences. Nowak styled his novels as fairy tales; their incantational syntax and use of dialects, and the naivety of their narrators, confirmed the self-sufficiency and self-enclosed nature of peasant culture. In the alienational variant, a clash of two languages – peasant dialect and the language of white-collar workers or intelligentsia – dominated. This conflict represented the impossibility of both mutual understanding and a shared language. Myśliwski, for his part, created a multivocal monologue: in this form, the character delivering the monologue – by means of reminiscence, imitation, mimicry, or fabrication – internally generates the utterances and styles of other people. For the author, monologue is a means to make the spoken word present – to translate living speech into literature; for his protagonists, it is a means to acquire self-knowledge and to replicate the world, to hone their communication skills and their self-creative abilities. As a result, the monologue – the most univocal of forms – becomes polyphonic in Myśliwski's hands.

The third transgression – paradoxical and final – is articulated by Myśliwski in *Kamień na kamieniu* (Stone upon Stone, 1984), which critics uniformly view as the end point of the peasant current. This transgression consists in expressing an awareness of the end of culture through a protagonist who belongs to it. The cause of peasant culture's evanescence is thus rendered understandable. In *Palace*, the author makes it clear that after the departure of the landowner and possessor of higher culture, the peasant – in his former incarnation – must die. If his descendants are to feel alive, they must create a new culture, one that encompasses tradition *and* modernity. In the context of this historical challenge, *Stone upon Stone* is a diagnosis of failure: creating a new form capable of preserving living speech proves impossible, and as a result we end up reading an epic.

This sheds light on the subsequent fate of peasant prose. During the 1960s and 1970s writers sought to synthesize peasant culture; during the 1980s they created a synthesis of its disappearance. In *Wniebogłosy* (At the Top of One's Lungs, 1982), for example, Tadeusz Nowak re-created the history of the postwar terror that stifled peasant self-sufficiency. Displacement offered another point of departure. In *Widnokrąg* (Horizon, 1996), Myśliwski offered an alternative solution by moving its action to a small town and placing hope in the preservation of living speech in its community. Moved by similar interests, in *Nikiformy* (1982) Redliński turned to the exploitation of urban language, revealing it, however, to be a disorderly tangle of styles and impersonal forms.

In more recent years, peasant culture has returned to literature sporadically, gaining in significance only when previous knowledge and myths are undergoing revision. For example, Ewa Ostrowska (1938–2012) in *Owoc żywota twego* (Fruit of Thy Womb, 2004) presents rural life from the perspective of a woman, revealing the depths of hatred, contempt, and cruelty that permeate male-centred peasant culture. Marian Pilot (b. 1936), in *Pióropusz* (War Bonnet, 2011), highlights the strangers within peasant culture itself, who occupy the lowest rung in the social hierarchy. Both Pilot and Ostrowska describe the margins of a culture previously presented as monolithic. The protagonist of *War Bonnet*, a resident of the margins, leaves the village motivated not by poverty but by the unfulfilled desire for equality. Pilot's novel – a litany of insults and abuses, a record of pervasive deceit and betrayal – is an act of linguistic revenge taken by someone who has never and nowhere felt at home.

Pilot's unexpectedly picaresque novel began a new chapter in the history of peasant culture in Poland. The 1960s made it apparent that plebeian society needed to work out a new – mixed, hybrid rather than synthetic – symbolic order. Peasant culture, however, was never taken into consideration in such an order, due to its social inferiority and the stereotype of peasant submissiveness. In the twenty-first century the peasant legacy is returning as a tradition of anger. It is not by accident that Pilot's novel, which describes vengeance fantasies, coincided in time with Paweł Demirski and Monika Strzępka's production *W imię Jakuba S.* (In the Name of Jakub S., 2011).

The titular Jakub S. refers to Jakub Szela, the peasant leader of the 1846 massacre of the gentry. In their comments about the show, Demirski and Strzępka wrote:

> The majority of Polish society has its roots in the village … Present-day middle class and those who aspire to it are Jakub Szela's descendants. The question is: are we capable of accepting other tropes of identity than those taught in schools, where Szela is a vengeful primitive and a traitor, and his uprising no more than a murder, provoked by the Austrian administration, of the best sons of the Polish nation? Is it possible to say today without shame that we are Europeans because we were once capable of murder? Can we construct anew our story, our history, and the history of our/not our land?[8]

This controversial question, in linking European identity to a peasant uprising and the act of murder, shows that rebellion is the desirable element of the peasant legacy. Such a rebellion can entwine peasant roots with today's middle class, and past uprisings with European aspirations. Jakub Szela has returned, because his peasant biography holds the potential of uncompromising rebellion against a social order built on capitalism and concealed identities. In this sense, the game of class has been renewed.

III. Third Shift: the Moving Centre

In 1945, the centre – understood as a symbolic language used to describe reality and as political power – shifted. It consisted of leftist ideas of historical justice and equality and a totalitarian source of power. The authorities had an army at their disposal as well as an apparatus of coercion, in that they oversaw the Prosecutor's Office and censorship policies. They also had a political program, and they aimed to take control of public communication. In this regard, the new centre needed literature that would translate the language of doctrine into poems and novels. Writers were thus presented with a dangerous opportunity: to speak in the language of power.

APART, or Where Literature Wished to Be (1944–9)

The writers' first answer was negative. It was expressed by a poetics that Kazimierz Wyka (1910–75) termed "the literature of reckonings of the intelligentsia." His reading list included *Mury Jerycha* (The Walls of Jericho, 1946) by Tadeusz Breza (1905–70), *Jezioro Bodeńskie* (Lake Constance, 1946) and *Pożegnania* (Farewells, 1948) by Stanisław Dygat (1914–78), *Drewniany koń* (Wooden Horse, 1946) by Kazimierz Brandys (1916–2000), *Sedan* (1948) by Paweł Hertz (1918–2001), and *Sprzysiężenie* (*Conspiracy*, 1947) by Stefan Kisielewski (1911–91). An excellent critic and historian of Polish twentieth-century literature, Wyka concluded that these novels signalled the end of an epoch in the history of the Polish intelligentsia. That end manifested itself in the intelligentsia's sense of alienation from social life and their impulse to correct everything on their own.

Other critics added to this list *Śmierć liberała* (The Death of a Liberal, 1947) by Artur Sandauer, *Węzły życia* (Knots of Life, 1948) by Zofia Nałkowska (1884–1954), and *Popiół i diament* (Ashes and Diamonds, 1948) by Jerzy Andrzejewski (1909–83), as well as *Rojsty* (1948; publ. 1956) by Tadeusz Konwicki. All of these works feature a narrator-protagonist who cannot find a single lasting value under various social masks. These novels' criticism encompassed social reality, ideology, and the personality of their narrators; it was tantamount to a declaration of disengagement from the language of power and the search for separateness.

TOGETHER, or the Pyrrhic Victory of the Avant-Garde (1949–56)

In January 1949, a new literary program was decreed. The terror was out in the open by now, so artists knew they would not be able to practise their craft outside of the state-sanctioned framework. Many writers acquiesced to the new program despite knowing it was a recipe for bad art; they believed, or wanted to believe, that its simplistic literary formula was based on a useful ideological program that would lead to universal justice. To be outside of this historical current was to be outside of history altogether – somewhere on the garbage heap of history. For this reason, very few decided to write "for the desk drawer," as Zbigniew Herbert (1924–98) and Leopold Tyrmand (1920–85) did; the majority, including even well-known and respected authors, accepted the new program.

Following the formula adopted earlier in the Soviet Union, the new poetics was called socialist realism, with realism understood as "agreeable to the socialist interpretation of history." From the moment the new program was imposed, the state – which had all means of literary distribution at its disposal (i.e., publishing houses, wholesalers, bookstores, radio, press, and cultural clubs) – was able to control every text and, indeed, to steer the process of writing itself. Literature was expected to be conventional, didactic, and aligned with the party – in other words, it was to be part of the process of building a new system *and* wielding totalitarian power.[9] As a result, the border between literature and reality began to blur: literature became a part of politics even while politics took on the qualities of a changeable literary text, one that gradually absorbed reality. It was precisely as a result of this overlap that an alliance between socialist-realist novels and the European avant-garde tradition unexpectedly emerged. Leaving aside its diversified esthetics, the avant-garde aimed to negate the bourgeois function of art, to transgress the boundary between art and reality, to project a history for the future and join in its creation through artistic activity. These goals were met by socialist realism, which became a totalitarian avant-garde.

> *Socialist realism* (like Nazi art, for example) finds itself in the position to which the avant-garde originally aspired – outside the museums and art history and set apart from traditional and socially established cultural norms … Stalinist culture brought out into the open the myth of the demiurge, the transformer of society and the universe, which, although it was presumed by the avant-garde, was not explicitly expressed in avant-garde artistic practice, and it set this myth in the center of its entire social and artistic life. Like the avant-garde, Stalinist culture continues to be oriented toward the future; it is projective rather than mimetic, a visualization of the collective dream of the new world and the new humanity rather than the product of an individual artist's temperament; it does not retire to the museum, but aspires to exert an active influence upon life. In brief, it cannot simply be regarded as "regressive" or pre-avant-garde.
>
> – Groys, *The Total Art of Stalinism: Avant-Garde, Aesthetic Dictatorship, and Beyond*, 7, 113

The defeat of socialist realism – which was quite quickly sealed with Stalin's death, Khrushchev's speech about the "cult of the individual," and a series of critical texts – was far-reaching. It impacted tendentious art and the social engagement of the artist, as well as the programmatic subject matter of social advancement through work, the collective, and gender equality. Art was able to renew itself quickly and to restore the public's trust, and some socialist-realist subjects – especially the value of collective work – never really returned to Polish literature. Art's attempt to speak in the language of power thus ended in failure, leading to the hasty separation of the two.

Languages of Distance: Leaving Stalinism Behind

After 1955, having lost the public's trust, writers had to address in their work questions about the nature of Stalinism, the reasons for their own involvement in it, and the conditions for defending the autonomy of literature. There were basically three approaches to this task. The first – the parodic – involved mocking the language of authority, as Sławomir Mrożek (1930–2013) did in *Słoń* (The Elephant, 1957) and *Wesele w Atomicach* (Ugupu Bird, 1959). The parodic strategy relied on subversion: narration encroached on the language of authority but contrasted it with the mundane everyday. It was thus demystifying in its effects; by mocking the authorities it stripped them of charisma and the ability to incite fear.

> The director of the Zoological Gardens has shown himself to be an upstart. He regarded his animals simply as stepping stones on the road of his career. He was indifferent to the educational importance of his establishment. In his Zoo the giraffe had a short neck, the badger had no burrow and the whistlers, having lost all interest, whistled rarely and with some reluctance.
>
> The Zoo was in a provincial town, and it was short of some of the most important animals, among them the elephant … The Zoo was notified that it had at long last been allocated an elephant. [However] the director had sent a letter to Warsaw, renouncing the allocation and putting forward a plan for obtaining an elephant by more economic means.
>
> – Mrożek, *The Elephant*, 16

The second solution involved the use of palinodes. A palinode – a literary work aimed at reversing previously stated views – met the three main goals of writers at that time: to define Stalinism, clarify the author's position towards the regime, and propose a language of resistance to it. In these regards, it set a norm of behaviour for writers and became a model for establishing contact with the reader. The best-known poetic work of 1955, "Poemat dla dorosłych" (Poem for Adults) by Adam Ważyk (1905–82), was a palinode of the poet's socialist-realist, urban-bucolic "Lud wejdzie do śródmieścia" (The People Will Enter Downtown). The most popular prose publication of this turning point was a short story collection by Marek Hłasko (1934–69) titled *Pierwszy krok w chmurach* (The First Step in the Clouds, 1956). It cancelled out the author's debut works, namely the novel *Sonata marymoncka* (Marymoncka Street Sonata, 1954) and his short story "Baza Sokołowska" (Sokołowska Base, 1954), both of which presented stories about a young man's entry into a work collective that aligned with the socialist-realist model. Kazimierz Brandys's *Obrona "Grenady"* (The Defence of "Grenada," 1956) and *Matka królów* (Sons and Comrades, 1957)[10] were rebuttals of his socialist-realist novel *Obywatele* (Citizens, 1954). The novella *Człowiek z marmuru* (Man of Marble, 1963) by Aleksander Ścibor-Rylski (1928–83) revoked the author's earlier production novel *Węgiel* (Coal, 1950); it also became, in 1976, the basis for one of the best-known Polish films by Andrzej Wajda (1926–2016). Jerzy Andrzejewski's *Ciemności kryją ziemię* (The Inquisitors, 1957), in turn, repealed his political writings, including *Partia i twórczość pisarza* (*The Party and the Writer's Craft*, 1952).

Both the parody and the palinode subverted Stalinist language through repetition; both also abandoned the centre, which was ruled by the discourse of authority. Having abandoned that centre as the foundation of literature, they sought a properly literary poetics that would enable them to analyse the praxis of power. A solution was found in the parable. Prose thus reached for images of absolute rule from the times of Ancient Greece and Rome and the Inquisition. In *Zdobycie władzy* (The Seizure of Power, Paris 1952), Czesław Miłosz referenced *The History of the Peloponnesian War* by Thucydides; while in her short story collection *Sir Tomasz More odmawia* (Sir Thomas More Declines, 1956), Hanna Malewska (1911–83) presented a confrontation between the Renaissance philosopher and an absolute monarch. In *The Inquisitors*, Andrzejewski used the figure of the Grand Inquisitor Torquemada, an embodiment of the cruelty and omnipotence of the Holy Office, to suggest that totalitarianism is founded on personal authority – that is, on a person who exempts others from doubt. Jacek Bocheński (b. 1926), in turn, recalled the biography of Julius Caesar in his phenomenal novel *Boski Juliusz* (Divine Julius, 1961), narrating it as a guide through ancient history and presenting Caesar as the archetype of a ruler who enters onto the path of an insane search for divinity.

Parody, palinode, and parable – literature was being reborn through literature. Reaching for diverse traditions, it signalled the construction of a new symbolic centre.

The Budding Hegemon: 1960s and 1970s

During the 1960s, Poland was no longer a totalitarian state, although it was still ruled by a regime in which the censors effectively controlled all books, films, and theatre productions. A new hegemon appeared during this period, however, in the form of mass culture. From this perspective, the end of Stalinism was marked not by the stories in Hłasko's *The First Step in the Clouds*, but by the spectacular success of Leopold Tyrmand's *Zły* (The Man with the White Eyes, 1955). The novel is set in the ruins of postwar Warsaw, which was teeming with criminals as well as ordinary, intimidated people. Within this setting, Tyrmand played out a well-known scenario: a dark streetfighter-knight single-handedly goes after gangs, rescues normal people, and avenges wrongs done to him and them. *The Man with the White Eyes* thus articulated dreams about the return of justice to the city's streets and the restoration of self-agency to the Polish citizenry. By borrowing stylistic conventions from reportage and the crime novel, from the tradition of the brooding Romantic hero, and from Varsovian folklore, and by exposing the censored yet plain fact that organized crime existed, Tyrmand ensured that his novel would enter the history of Polish postwar literature as the first work to connect with both elite and mass readership.

Writers sensitized to the relationship between the authorities and mass communication began to notice a new type of reader during the 1960s. As Kazimierz Brandys wrote in *Listy do Pani Z.* (Letters to Mrs. Z, 1957):

> This mid-person, non-proletarian and non-capitalist works and earns, has middling good will, middling good looks and social feelings, is a middling buyer and thinker – is, in sum, impressive not in quality but in quantity, in the mass. Civilization equips this representative, garbs it in serially-produced clothes, arms it with tools, feeds it with vitamins and entertains and forces life styles on it with films, press, sport, and TV. It offers it something less than culture and more than society, a shape that is not a model, a borderland of fact and consciousness, movement and direction.[11]

The appearance of this new type of reader attracted some classic complaints; Adolf Rudnicki (1912–90), Tadeusz Różewicz (1921–2014), and Stanisław Dygat saw the new reader as a consumer of sensations who did not distinguish between beauty and attractiveness, and who willingly absorbed both masterworks and kitsch. At the same time, the interpretation that mass culture did not, after all, reject high modernism also came into view.

This was exemplified by Jerzy Andrzejewski's *Idzie skacząc po górach* (A Sitter for a Satyr, 1963; English trans. 1965), a novel stunning in its cynicism. The author presents the great artist Ortiz, who strongly resembles Picasso, as he achieves spectacular success after a period of absence. The victory of originality over mass appeal is illusory, however. In reality, what we are witnessing is the injection of high modernist art into market circulation: avant-garde work is being exchanged for news releases, news releases for notoriety, and notoriety for prestige and money. Ortiz is thus simultaneously an independent artist, since he does not conform to anyone's tastes, and a subservient one, for at the centre of the spectacle is no longer the work but the spectacle itself. The work and the artist become encircled by distributors of value who ensure that the work receives publicity – without them, it would be a mute gift without a recipient. The media that guarantee the circulation of excitement turn out to be both an ally and an all-consuming hegemon.

The Pulpified Centre: 1970s

The new, murky centre, fostered by a confluence of faded traditions, weakening socialist ideology, and an ever-strengthening mass culture, became the object of critical attention in prose during the 1970s. Novels that distrusted both authority and social opinion appeared, among them Jerzy Andrzejewski's *Miazga* (The Pulp; 1970, 1st samizdat ed. 1979), Marek Nowakowski's *Wesele jeszcze raz* (The Wedding Once Again!, 1973; 1st samizdat ed. 1981), and Kazimierz Brandys' *Nierzeczywistość* (Unreality, 1975; 1st samizdat ed. 1977), as well as Tadeusz Konwicki's *Kompleks polski* (The Polish Complex, 1977) and *Mała Apokalipsa* (A Minor Apocalypse, 1979). All of these books shared a similar fate: submitted to official publishing houses (*The Pulp* and *The Wedding Once Again!*), they were either shelved or rejected by censorship; they appeared only after an independent publishing system was established in Poland.

Other common features of these books included a sharp critique of the political system and simultaneous pessimism about society; they asked whether Polish postwar society was creating a culture adequate to the process of modernization and helpful to the process of acquiring self-awareness. Their answers to that question were profoundly bleak: society was undergoing a great systemic and class transformation, but without creating any clear, home-grown forms. This was clear from the metaphors their authors used to name the state of society: Andrzejewski's "pulp," Brandys' "unreality," Konwicki's "dishevelment" (*rozmamłanie*), and Nowakowski's "putrescence" (*zgojenie*). Such terms pointed to a state of social deformation that created a false image of the world (unreality) and rendered it susceptible to manipulation. Similar images appeared in other novels. Kazimierz Orłoś (b. 1935) wrote about self-contamination by lies in *Trzecie kłamstwo* (The Third Lie, 1980), while Bogdan Madej (1934–2002) showed the slow descent of Polish life into petty wheeling and dealing in *Maść na szczury* (Rat Ointment, 1977). Jan Komolka (b. 1947) focused on the social proclivity for repressing all forms of otherness in *Ucieczka do nieba* (Escape to Heaven, 1975; publ. 1980), whereas the impressive trilogy *Obłęd* (Madness, 1979) by Jerzy Krzysztoń (1931–82) showed the insanity born of the Polish Romantic tradition, which strongly impacted Polish perceptions of reality and lacked a counterweight in Polish culture.

In the novels from the second half of the 1970s, therefore, social self-awareness and political vocabularies were presented in a critical light: national and Romantic traditions and the cultural legacy of peasants, workers, and the intelligentsia were neither absorbed nor transformed, so they played no part in shaping contemporaneity. The ever more rampant mass culture – be it domestic or imported – confronted a native culture that was largely an anachronistic holdover. As a consequence, the members of the collective were at once relocated and unable to define their own place. No one possessed the power necessary to shape modern Polishness. The centre – pulpified, dishevelled, unreal – was ruled by inertia.

The Exchange of the Centre: 1981–5

Polish prose, viewed from the perspective of novels written in the 1970s, could have progressed towards weighty questions about collective identity, since prose writers had worked out a position independent of both the language of authority and social languages. History, however, entered onto the stage. The birth of "Solidarity" in 1980 – the first independent trade union in the Eastern Bloc – heralded the rebirth of collective, consolidating myths. At this time, though diagnosed as having been pulpified, Polish society turned out to be capable of defining collective values (such as Polishness, Catholicism, and individual dignity) and of reconciling them with modernity (solidarity, social property).

> In the novels of Brandys, Konwicki, and Krzysztoń there is no room for striking shipyard workers who kneel to receive communion in August of 1980. For this was not some "crowd" or "the plebs," but a new working class derived primarily from villages and small towns, and cemented by traditional Catholicism ... This image is to some extent a collective portrait of the new Polish society – uprooted and simultaneously calling on the most lasting and elementary parts of the national tradition in moments of danger.
>
> – Fiut, "Socjalizm realny – co to za zwierz?," 24

The introduction of martial law on 13 December 1981 and the accompanying repressions stalled the critical functions of prose. The years 1981 to 1985 were a time of unequal duelling between the armed authorities and a society seeking reform. Literature faced the need to engage on society's side. A stalemate ensued: on the one hand, prose was treated as a source of social self-knowledge; on the other, it was expected to confirm social platitudes and stereotypes. Moreover, while literature enjoyed an exalted place in the hierarchy of independent sources of truth, it was also believed that truth resided in petty critiques of the regime. As literature's role rose sharply in importance, critical realism was replaced by tendentious realism. The historical form of this tendency can be termed "anti-socialist realism." This literary strategy exposed socialism as a murderous system that is based in deceit and violence and prone to mismanagement and that results in a repulsive, prison-like world.[12] The poetics of these works had two extremes: "patriotic kitsch" and "anti-communist agit-prop." The first evoked tearful sadness, while the latter legitimized indignation and anger. Between these two extremes were a handful of texts whose authors (Konwicki, Anderman, Rymkiewicz) resorted to self-irony to suggest that they were representing states of social consciousness rather than the state of reality. Also, these authors included themselves in their plots to signal that they too, like most Poles, found themselves trapped in history that trumped the autonomy of art with the imperative of social engagement.

The prose from the turn of the 1970s and 1980s did not produce any masterpieces, but it did bring about a significant shift, in that it reclaimed elements of various traditions that had been co-opted by the authorities and placed them back in the hands of society. By presenting the regime as pro-Soviet, it situated it outside of European culture; by introducing members of "Solidarity" as the heirs to national insurrection, it cut off the regime's access to national tradition; by showing opposition members to be the heirs to socialist movements, it divested the regime of its leftist values. Literature thus sealed the most important victory over the regime – the cultural victory – leaving the ruling powers with only bare violence, stripped of any legitimacy. The symbolic centre controlled by the authorities had been hollowed out and could once again be filled by literature. There was a problem with the new centre, however: it was constituted by an excessively unified language.

The Multiplied Centre: 1985–95

Halfway through the 1980s, as the prose of anti-socialist realism was reaching its apogee, an entirely new current appeared in Polish literature, one that revealed excessive unification as a problem and proposed a solution to it. To explain: in the mid-1980s, before the Round Table talks in Poland and the fall of the Berlin Wall, Polish literature had already imagined a new society. The goal was not to create a utopia, but a proposal that would retain its roots in Polish culture yet move beyond the no longer sufficient anti-communist stance. The new symbolic language was organized by the idea of multiplicity. This was expressed in literature by a *poetics of proper names*, present in numerous texts of the period, including *Sublokatorka* (The Subtenant, 1985) by Hanna Krall (b. 1935); *Początek* (The Beginning, 1986) by Andrzej Szczypiorski (1928–2000); *Bohiń* (Bohin Manor, 1987) by Tadeusz Konwicki; *Zagłada* (Annihilation, 1987) by Piotr Szewc (b. 1961); *Umschlagplatz* (The Collection Point, 1987) by Jarosław Marek Rymkiewicz (b. 1935); *Weiser Dawidek* (Who Was David Weiser?, 1987) by Paweł Huelle; *W ptaszarni* (In the Aviary, 1989) by Grzegorz Musiał (b. 1952); and *Kronika z Mazur* (The Masurian Chronicle, 1989) by Erwin Kruk (b. 1941). Paradoxically, it is *ghosts* that are the most real content of these novels; they represent what 1980s Poland was missing the most – namely, social difference. At a time when communism was waning in Poland, Polish culture was in danger of becoming excessively undifferentiated; these novels called on the ghosts of past differences for help.

In these novels, the narration developed around an initial emptiness, one that alluded to the disappearance of Poland's former inhabitants. Monologues came close to articulating absence, but had no chance of actually speaking its name; the language of the inexpressible became the guardian of singularity. A key role in evoking absence was played by Jewish ghosts, but other differences also returned, indicative of the former richness of nationalities and ethnicities in interwar Poland. Among those summoned were Masurians (Erwin Kruk), the Romani (Jerzy Ficowski in *Cyganie w Polsce. Dzieje i obyczaje* [The Roma in Poland: History and Customs, 1989], and Lithuanians (Konwicki), as well as Belarusians and Ukrainians (Jacek Bocheński in *Stan po zapaści* [The State after Collapse, 1986]). Since wartime and postwar history was marked by the disappearance of these communities in Poland, their representatives in these novels could appear only as ghosts. These authors were presenting histories of the disappearance of nations and groups in order to shed light on the fundamental mechanism of modernity, whereby differences are removed through either assimilation or extermination. The biographies of apparitions from the past signalled how to begin history anew. The idea for a new beginning relied on creating a different collective identity – one open to Otherness, protective of its differences, and free of violence.

A Cultural War: Late 1990s and Early Twenty-First Century

The search for proper names in prose, along with the accompanying ethic of forgoing violence, faced no competition until the mid-1990s. *Absolutna amnezja* (Absolute Amnesia) by Izabela Filipiak (b. 1961) and *Hanemann* by Stefan Chwin, both published in 1995, were the last strong chords struck by this tendency. Like the earlier *Who Was David Weiser?*, both of these novels end with the mysterious disappearance of their protagonists. A different perspective began to crystallize in Polish prose only around 1995. It was necessary, since emancipative literature had begun situating itself dangerously close to the dominant discourse. Within this discourse, the key terms "pluralism" and "tolerance" had little to say about shared narrations.

An early version of the new approach can be found in Andrzej Stasiuk's *Biały kruk* (White Raven, 1995), a novel that expresses provocative praise of the freedom of life in socialist Poland and a youthful rebellion against capitalism. From this perspective, the socialist state is no longer the only representative of violence. Liberal capitalism has turned out to be its new embodiment, and it is presented in the novel as a complex system of exclusions that functions differently but just as effectively. This idea appears in numerous works, including the well-known film *Dług* (Debt) by Krzysztof Krauze (1953–2014) and various novels and short stories, among them Marek Nowakowski's *Prawo prerii* (Law of the Prairies, 1999), Edward Redliński's *Krfotok* (1998), and *Transformejszen* (2002), Mariusz Sieniewicz's *Czwarte niebo* (The Fourth Heaven, 2003), Dawid Bieńkowski's *Nic* (Nothing, 2005), Sławomir Shuty's *Zwał* (The Heap, 2004), Agnieszka Drotkiewicz's *Paris London Dachau* (2004), Eustachy Rylski's *Człowiek w cieniu* (Man in the Shadow, 2004), and Rafał Ziemkiewicz's *Ciało obce* (Foreign Body, 2005). This form of systemic violence creates a new victim profile: collective subjects are its target, starting with family, through social (and especially working) class and the religious community, right up to the nation. On this basis, this current could be called the "prose of collective names."

Whereas the prose of proper names shows the destructive effects of violence, the prose of collective names insists that violence is the only means of defence against the new oppression. The earlier current was signalled by the poetics of inexpressibility and the ethic of dignity that the poetics co-created. Between 1995 and 2005, in turn, the conflict between market oppression and disappearing collective subjects was explained through a clash of two styles: liberal newspeak and obscenity. The language of capitalism is a tool of subordination – its terms, logic, and argumentation create a monopolistic interpretation of reality. Opposite to it stands frustrating logorrhea – a verbal blast, an explosion of language that is neither able nor willing to name the world. A verbal blast is an emotional weapon rather than a rhetorical one; its function is to find, offend, humiliate, and annihilate its target. On a linguistic plane, therefore, it parallels acts of violence: it is a phantasmal assassination meant to destroy the world. This sort of prose thus became a part of the cultural war; its significance, however, stemmed from pointing out the deficits of collective expression.

The Reprieve: Turn of the First and Second Decades of the Twenty-First Century

During the twenty-first century the conflict between the two attitudes acquired a ritual character. Breaking this ritual involved staging a conflict within a novel. The task was taken up with bravado by Dorota Masłowska (b. 1983) in her novel *Wojna polsko-ruska pod flagą biało-czerwoną* (Snow White and Russian Red, 2002), the biggest literary event of this century's first decade in Poland. The novel was mistakenly taken for a portrait of a lout, a representative of the social margins. The protagonist, Andrzej Robakowski, aka Silny (Nails), a young man with a high school education and no job, but with a considerable appetite for life, is a representative of the majority. This is indicated by his aversions (misogyny, homophobia, anti-Russian, anti-German, and anti-capitalist sentiments), his dreams (of a woman, riches, and respect), as well as his peculiar incoherence. Silny is at once progressive and regressive, revolutionary and reactionary, internationalist and nationalist. He functions like a waste disposal plant that processes everything indiscriminately into a pulp of frustration. Once all-encompassing concepts – the welfare state, emancipation of the individual, the free market – are unceremoniously mixed and transformed into grounds of entitlement. Silny thus ridicules all sides of the conflicts of late modernity. Masłowska's victory in this regard relates to her use of literature as a shredder of discourses – a critical tool of distancing from all public languages.

Other novels offered a similar presentation yet different solutions to this conflict. Among them are Olga Tokarczuk's *Prowadź swój pług przez kości umarłych* (Lead Your Plow through the Bones of the Dead, 2009), Mariusz Sieniewicz's *Rebelia* (Insurgency, 2007), Bartosz Żurawiecki's *Nieobecni* (The Absent Ones, 2011), Sylwia Chutnik's *Cwaniary* (Cunning Girls, 2012), Joanna Bator's *Ciemno, prawie noc* (Dark, Almost Night, 2012), and Igor Ostachowicz's *Noc żywych Żydów* (The Night of Living Jews, 2012). This list can be further expanded with Jarosław Marek Rymkiewicz's essayistic trilogy *Wieszanie* (Hanging, 2007), *Kinderszenen* (Scenes from Childhood, 2008), and *Samuel Zborowski* (2010), and Paweł Demirski's play *Śmierć podatnika* (The Death of the Taxpayer, 2008). These writers represent an entire spectrum of political options. They are linked by a focus on the process of social reconfiguration that leads to the creation of an interim collective with a mixed identity. Furthermore, this collective comes together when it uses violence to demonstrate a readiness to defend its key value. This violence, in turn, fulfils its function not when it removes someone from the world but when it brings history to a standstill. It is precisely this moment – of suspending previous divisions – that requires the greatest literary invention. During late modernity – given the dematerialization of capital and the disappearance of stable institutions – there are no existing ideologies or traditions capable of creating a symbolic language to describe reality. This becomes the task of literature.

IV. The Fourth Shift: Disappearing Certainty

We return to the end of the Second World War one last time. Among its consequences was the radical doubt cast on the fundamentals of the human world – on previous concepts of the subject, on modernity as progress, and on language as a tool of communication. The Holocaust, the war, the Soviet Gulag and postwar terror, all revealed that there is nothing that cannot be done – not only to an individual, but also to millions of people at a time. If everything is movable then nothing is fixed in its place.

Previous sections of this discussion addressed literature that responded to postwar shifts by searching for available forms of support. It is now time to look at literature that saw radical doubt as the proper answer to that situation.

Holocaust Literature: The Laboratory of Human Annihilation

> I am mobile herein the Danger that I can be moved from place to place pulled out of landscapes replanted from street to street I am mobile I and my contemporaries The First condition of future life is thus to come to a standstill.
>
> – Różewicz, "Tarcza z pajęczyny," 251–2

In 1946, three remarkable books were written in Poland: *Czarny Potok* (Black Torrent, publ. 1956) by Leopold Buczkowski (1905–89), Zofia Nałkowska's *Medaliony* (Medallions, 1946), and *Pożegnanie z Marią i inne opowiadania* (This Way for the Gas, Ladies and Gentlemen, 1946) by Tadeusz Borowski (1922–51). Like three embodiments of antimatter, these books consumed the energy of humanism in different ways, without giving much if anything in return.

Zofia Nałkowka, a member of the Central Commission for Investigation of German Crimes in Poland, collected the materials for *Medallions* while speaking with former prisoners and interrogating prison camp functionaries. The result is modest in size – eight stories and a total of sixty pages – yet harrowing in its effect. Its desert-like prose is amassed from separate grains, arid, limitless, with every difference adding to the monotony of death. Nałkowska was not aiming to prepare a full description of camp reality, but to establish an external perspective that would make it possible to understand and judge Auschwitz. Such external axiology would enable the differentiation of peace from war. Hence her narration conveys a clear expectation that prisoners and executioners alike will morally assess their experiences. Wartime experiences, however, appear to be enclosed in a separate, as if non-human, reality; they are either inexpressible or incomprehensible. This threatens to situate the camps outside of the human domain and to create a morality singular to them. To prevent this, the author precedes her stories with the famous motto *Ludzie ludziom zgotowali ten los* ("People dealt this fate to people"). This exposed a radical contradiction, however: the camp was of human design, yet one can neither understand it nor separate it from postwar reality nor establish an axiology external to it. As long as such outside perspective does not exist, the camp sits in judgment of the world. The open-endedness of the search for an outside-the-camp reality and humanism's defeat in the face of the Holocaust – this is the proper content of *Medallions*. It is only when faced with the failure of the search that the author writes about the "criminals, murderers, thieves"[13] who made up the Nazi ranks. This allows readers to believe that Nazism and the camps were a deviation from the main course of European culture. The works of Seweryna Szmaglewska (1916–92), Zofia Kossak-Szczucka (1889–1968), and Gustaw Morcinek (1891–1963) deliver more explicit judgments, made without any reservations.

Tadeusz Borowski opposed such external axiology. Imprisoned in Auschwitz in 1943, he wrote a cycle of short stories that consistently maintain the internal perspective of the camp. From this perspective, the world of the camp appears as a universal civilization of slavery, one that has existed since antiquity and has slowly been perfected: "The Egyptian pyramids, the temples, and Greek statues – what a hideous crime they were!"[14] Auschwitz is the pinnacle of this civilization – a perfect, totalitarian world that erases the boundaries between perpetrator and victim. The camp could be survived only at someone else's cost, which meant that the previous – humanistic – form of man was exterminated in the camps. In contrast to Nałkowska, therefore, Borowski argues that the camp cannot be understood from the outside. The author does not invalidate all moral concepts, but he shows, in a narrative analysis unique in world literature, the way in which the camp machine disassembled traditional morality, replacing its values with totalitarian principles. The camp he describes is a factory that pulls everyone – guards and prisoners alike – into the process of producing naked life, as Giorgio Agamben would put it – in other words, into the process of transforming a human being into matter susceptible to being formed at will. After the epoch of camps, we know that a human being is always the product of external conditions.

> We should learn from Nałkowska and Borowski how to write the truth, but not how to generalize it. They both saw the truth in close up, but perhaps from too close up. From the distance of several decades it is more clearly apparent that Holocaust was a unique phenomenon, without precedence, the consequence of a great mistake of the ages, without which Auschwitz would have been at most a concentration camp [and not a Jewish extermination camp].
>
> – Grynberg, "Holocaust w literaturze polskiej," 160

Nałkowska and Borowski afflicted their readers with a pervasive sense of doubt even though she concluded that rational culture had to be rebuilt, and he, by engaging with communism, determined that the human being must be created anew. Both were convinced that the camps' industry of death had a universal character. For this reason, both used the term "people" – Nałkowska in the memorable motto, and Borowski in the title of the short story "Ludzie, którzy szli" (The People Who Walked On). This generalization stemmed from the belief that there was no difference between Poles and Jews in the internally uniform world of the camp. In trying to universalize the victims of the death industry, they overshadowed the Holocaust.

The novel that brought readers into a world of an infinitely differentiated interior was Leopold Buczkowski's *Black Torrent.* A gloomy masterpiece of disintegration, the novel is the most far-reaching experiment in Polish literature in finding equivalence between the Holocaust and an art form: its degree of compositional and linguistic instability corresponds with the destruction of the human world. It is set in Podolia (present-day western Ukraine) during the fall of 1943; at this time, Germans and Ukrainians are hunting down Jews throughout the area and taking aim at Poles as well. A handful of Jews resist: hunted down like animals, they defend themselves with the little strength they have left – against the enemy, betrayal, and savagery. The characters' identities are unclear. The stories told by the different narrators are incoherent, and no one has a grasp of the whole. All are aware that "it was barely possible to fasten this picture to the rest."[15] The continuity of the narrative is broken since everything disintegrates in front of our eyes: it is no longer possible to answer the simplest of questions – "What's this?"[16] – and so human reality disappears, becoming a part of nature. It is a time of "the disappearance of a human face,"[17] and so the human subject disintegrates; no language can express the horror "continually without measure,"[18] and so culture crumbles.

In his bleak epiphany, Borowski saw the slavery perfected in concentration camps spreading throughout the world. The reverse process is visible in Buczkowski's work, where a constant implosion of the human world exposes "the black depths of all possibility."[19] "We walked on in silence – with us there came a voice that judged us without words,"[20] says one of the narrators, and this statement, as if taken from Beckett, makes it clear that the heroes of Buczkowski's novel took part in an apocalypse that will not be followed by salvation.

These three positions set three different courses for literature. *Medallions* set an example for literature that tries to rebuild rational humanity and thus treats the Holocaust as an aberration. *This Way for the Gas, Ladies and Gentlemen* marks the onset of literature that treats concentration camps as a source of knowledge about society and the rules of its functioning. *Black Torrent*, in turn, initiates those works that frame the Holocaust as a disintegration that has permanently saturated the human subject, language, and modernity. The Holocaust viewed as an aberration, as the norm, and as the end that lasts until this day – these are the three living traditions developed by Polish literature right after the war.

Mixed Traditions

Holocaust testimonies that approximated the poetics worked out by Nałkowska were written quite often. This poetics conceals two dangers, however: the introduction of an internal judgment that rescues from despair but can close off understanding; and the generalization of victims, or, more precisely, omission of the fact that the Nazi machine aimed first and foremost to exterminate the Jews. For this reason, the most important texts of the 1960s and the first half of the 1970s – by Henryk Grynberg (b. 1936), Bogdan Wojdowski (1930–94), Julian Stryjkowski, and Stanisław Wygodzki (1907–92) – speak from within the Holocaust experience. They highlight the fact that during the Holocaust death was endlessly multiplied and varied, taking place in camps, in ghettos, on city streets, and in forests, and moreover, that the Holocaust – like a catastrophe without an expiry date – continues to this day.

The Auschwitz virus had penetrated the lives of the saved, infecting language and nesting within postwar conceptualizations of the social order. These works countered the erasure of Jews from collective memory, which dominated the 1960s up to the mid-1970s, primarily through active memory that undermined the platitudes of postwar life. In the context of this process of recalling the Holocaust, a key event was the publication of a short book by Hanna Krall titled *Zdążyć przed Panem Bogiem* (Shielding the Flame, 1977) – a record of the author's conversation with Marek Edelman, the last living leader of the Warsaw Ghetto Uprising of 1943. The book came as a shock. Its key statement – "We are not writing history, after all. We are writing about remembering"[21] – gets to the crux of the matter, namely, the double-disappearance of Jews from Polish life – first as a result of the Holocaust, and then due to their erasure from memory.

Krall's book was quickly included in secondary school curricula, and it made possible the inclusion of the Warsaw Ghetto Uprising in Polish factography after a hiatus of twenty years, in this way broadening the historical horizon. It also deepened the problem, however; the renewed memory induced an impulse in Polish culture that transformed itself into a multi-generational alliance and multi-dimensional investigation. Its first act began halfway through the 1980s, with the broadcast of a shortened version of Claude Lanzmann's film *Shoah* (1985) and the publication of Jan Błoński's essay "Biedny chrześcijanin patrzy na getto" (A Poor Christian Looks at the Ghetto, 1987). In his essay, the literary critic called for an admission of guilt born of the failure to help the Jews and acquiescence to the German-perpetrated mass murder.

> If only we had behaved more humanely in the past, had been wiser, more generous, then genocide would perhaps have been "less imaginable," would probably have been considerably more difficult to carry out, and almost certainly would have met with much greater resistance than it did. To put it differently, it would not have met with the indifference and moral turpitude of the society in whose full view it took place.
>
> – Błoński, " A Poor Christian Looks at the Ghetto," 46

Shortly thereafter, a large number of books appeared that restored Jews to collective memory.[22] They produced a cross-generational and postmemory bond with the dead Jews, in the latter case through debuting writers. These books guaranteed that the subject of the Holocaust and of the Jewish presence in Polish history would not disappear, even after the last witnesses departed. This outside perspective placed these books at risk, however: their lament pointed to a historical injustice that had taken place on Polish lands and equally impacted both Jews and Poles. The evil became apparent, the judgment unequivocal.

A break in this tendency came with a book by Piotr Matywiecki (b. 1943) titled *Kamień graniczny* (The Border Stone, 1994), an apophatic life study of a person born after the destruction of the ghetto. Its author discursively points to Leopold Buczkowski's negative ontology. An excellent poet and scholar of Polish literature, Matywiecki uses his *silva rerum*–styled essay as an attempt to define his own existence in the context of the death contrived by the Holocaust – the death of Jewish community and identity, and the destruction of the place and the disappearance of the language of positive ontology. In Polish literature, no one before him had conducted so incisive an analysis of this incursion of nothingness into post-Holocaust existence. *The Border Stone* is very consistent in this regard: its narration is directed at apparitions and conducted in a language that no longer represents reality. During this period, Borowski's tradition also returned to Polish literature in a particular form, with narrations that turned away from mourning the dead and towards reconstruction of the prewar everyday, understood as the norms constitutive of modern society and contributory to the Holocaust.

This process culminated in two books – the novel *Tworki* (1999) by Marek Bieńczyk (b. 1956), and a sociological study by Jan T. Gross (b. 1947) titled *Sąsiedzi. Historia zagłady żydowskiego miasteczka* (Neighbours: Destruction of the Jewish Community in Jedwabne, Poland, 2000; Eng. 2001). The first drew upon Buczkowski's tradition, the second, on Borowski's. *Tworki* is a novel about language and culture as a matrix of perception of reality. Its protagonist finds work in 1942 in a hospital for the mentally ill in the Tworki district (near Warsaw), where Jews are hiding among the administration. He cannot comprehend their disappearance – in other words, the Holocaust happening right in front of everyone's eyes – since his cultural competence does not extend to the heroism of Jewish death. An example of a blind eyewitness, the protagonist grew up in a culture built on Kant's conceptualization of the human being as having inherent value, on belief in transcendence, and on faith in the relationship between word and reality. A patient with the significant name of Antiplato tries in vain to convince him that theirs is a world "lacking a universal referent" and with an "uprooted axis of the earth."[23] In this way, *Tworki* renews reflection about the Holocaust as a still current semiotic and anthropological catastrophe that led to the death of Platonic ideals and the disappearance of the Kantian human being. At the end of the novel, the narrator calls on readers to create their own narrations in order to tie their individual existence to the absence of Jews and to better understand their own everyday language.

Tworki is a prelude to *Neighbours*. While dedicated to the murder of several hundred Jews by their Polish neighbours, Gross's book – the most important publication about the Holocaust in Polish writing of late modernity – is actually a study of ordinariness. It shows that everyday structures, both prewar and during the occupation, segregated, subjugated, and excluded Jews, with age-old traditions rendering such structures invisible. Ordinariness normalized the dehumanizing exclusion, which went unnoticed both in provincial life (Gross) and among the liberal intelligentsia (Bieńczyk). During the postwar period, as Gross analysed in *Strach* (Fear, 2003), such structures worked to strip Jews of their historical subjectivity, in other words to erase the people, their material traces, and their memories.

Polish writers retained their critical awareness – indeed, they were among the few in European culture to do so. Their works make us aware that every representation of the Holocaust, if it wants to say something honest about the dead, has to cross over into the sphere of death, where fallen myths of modernity, remnants of language, and the former subject's remains rest.

Gulag Literature: Laboratory of the Transformation of Mankind

While the Holocaust confronted literature with the phenomenon of modern extermination, the labour camps in Russia exposed a modernity of exploitation. The Polish epic of exile and imprisonment from the territories of the Soviet Union consists of hundreds of books, published mostly in exile or after 1989. Among them one finds detailed descriptions of interrogations, specific prisons, deportations, and camp labour (respectively, in Wacław Grubiński's *Między młotem i sierpem* [Between the Hammer and the Sickle, 1948]; Aleksander Wat's *Świat na haku i pod kluczem* [World on the Hook and Under Lock and Key, 1985]; Jan T. Gross and Irena Grudzińska-Gross's *W czterdziestym nas matko na Sibir zesłali* [They Shipped Us, Mother, to Siberia in 1940, 1983]; and Anatol Krakowiecki's *Książka o Kolymie* [Book about Kolyma, 1950]). They include experiences of soldiers and civilians, and of men and women (Herminia Naglerowa's *Kazachstańskie noce* [Kazakhstan Nights, 1958] and *Ludzie sponiewierani* [Battered People, 1945]; Beata Obertyńska's *W domu niewoli* [In the House of Slavery, 1946]), as well as of children and adults (Hanka Ordonówna's *Tułacze dzieci* [Vagabond Children, 1948]), and they record both long-term exile and heroic escapes (Maria Byrska's *Ucieczka z zesłania* [Escape from Exile, 1985]).

Human suffering does not fit into paradigms. Its expression, however, which exist in Polish literature in immediate accounts as well as in recollections written down after many years, have taken the form of a specific typological triad. At its centre stands *Inny Świat* (A World Apart, 1951), a canonical work by Gustaw Herling-Grudziński (1919–2000) based on his imprisonment at a labour camp in Yertsevo (1940–2). This memoir analyses the Gulag experience from the perspective of someone who resisted enslavement of both the body and the mind. The dichotomy of body and mind demarcated by the author allowed him to carry on a defensive struggle on two fronts. The first was ethical and intellectual: Herling-Grudziński acted as an ethnographer calmly observing a foreign world. He embodied a scientist in order to maintain a distance from the camp and uncover the mystery of its functioning. He thus discovered that the system of forced labour was aimed not to "punish the criminal" as much as "to exploit him economically and transform him psychologically."[24] This total transformation, namely the "disintegration of his individual personality" and full subordination, occurred when the prisoner disavowed a reality that was external to the camp and gave himself over to the camp's disposal. At such a point, the camp became a complete world – "a world apart" became the entire world.

Only those who maintained their previous moral criteria could resist the camp, and they did so with the only weapon that was still theirs – their body. Freedom was retained by those who chose willing suffering over the camp system. Herling-Grudziński arrived at this argument while observing with awe a prisoner who put his hand into the fire every day in order not to be sent to work; in this way, he retained control over his body. Many months later, the author would act in kind by taking up a desperate hunger strike to enforce the leave from camp that was due to him as a result of a 1941 agreement between the Polish government and the Soviet Union to create a Polish Army, which had asked for an amnesty for Poles – an amnesty the Russians did not want to honour. Herling-Grudziński decided to launch a hunger strike despite food rations that kept prisoners "at the lowest level of humanity."[25] He succeeded.

Remarkable on a literary level, Herling-Grudziński's book, which referenced Dostoevsky's *House of the Dead*, established a canonical conceptualization of the camps, the position of their prisoners, and the role of literature. The author's tendency to universalize his observations served this cause at the cost of eliding historical and human differences. To understand these differences, it is worth comparing *A World Apart* with two other books – *Po wyzwoleniu* (After Liberation, 1985) by Barbara Skarga (1919–2009), and a collection of short stories, *Dzień i noc* (Day and Night, 1957) by Leo Lipski (1917–97). Skarga spent ten years in camps and in exile (1945–55). From her perspective, camp reality was differentiated with reference to history and gender. Historical contingency stemmed from the fact that, after Yalta, Poland found itself within the sphere of Soviet domination, which meant that the prisoners could no longer call on legal European conventions. Skarga's understanding of the gendered reality of the camp is noticeably different from Herling-Grudziński's. He casts a man in the role of the independent body, but presents women as incapable of such physical resilience. In *A World Apart*, sanctity in the camp is accessible only to the male body and a woman must seek male protection within it. Skarga, on the other hand – like Naglerowa, Obertyńska, and Byrska – reveals a different form of resistance to the human disintegration in the camp, arguing that it was enabled by female domestic skills (sewing, cooking, and caring for the aesthetics of the everyday) and that female solidarity could be much more durable and frequent than solidarity among men.

Where Skarga asks the reader to pay attention to history and gender, Lipski directs it towards a more careful observation of the body. In Herling-Grudziński's book, the body has a singular name, while in Lipski's work it is nameless, collective, and divided into parts; whereas in *A World Apart* the camp invades the inside of human beings through their consciousness, in *Day and Night* it does so through the skin and bodily cavities. Herling-Grudziński's narration concerns the exceptional body that transgresses camp limits through voluntary suffering; the prisoner is supported by a consciousness of the existence of a morality that is alternative to that of the camp. Lipski describes the massive body of the camp, enclosed within its own boundaries and denied the possibility of transgression. His narration begins with a blasphemous greeting "Praise be to Citizen Jesus Christ," which indicates that the camps have swallowed up the external, Christian reality and formed their own transcendence; in other words, they have become a complete world, now without an exterior.

The difference in their presentation of human relations is also evident. Herling-Grudziński draws hope from observed acts of sacrifice or solidarity, while Lipski writes, "Perhaps you too will find something that you will have to look at,"[26] meaning that his narrator's gaze and memory encompass masses of prisoners who were humiliated in front of others. Herling-Grudziński separates himself from the camp with his text; Lipski writes about experiences that cannot be sublimated and from which the prisoner's body will never break free after leaving the camp. According to Herling-Grudziński, literature should cleanse human beings of the totalitarian experience, rooting them once again in European culture. For Lipski, however, a return to the former paradigm is impossible. Instead, new literature should take into account an entirely corporeal human being – "a squelchy sack, stuffed with tripe, soft and moist. Many holes from which it pours, drips, and which stink."[27] Lipski wants to describe this human being with the poetics of *a reversed carnival*. If the carnival, as Bakhtin proposes, is a reversal of the official order, a time and space of celebrating life and its dynamics that erases all hierarchies and divisions, then the camp from Lipski's perspective turns out to be a cruel *reversal of the reversal*. His prose is corporeal, but stripped of vitality; it displays human orifices, but doubts fertility; it is faecal, but without joyful gluttony and unbridled consumption; it is anti-official, but does not point to any alternative human community. Within Lipski's framework, human beings – or more properly, post-human beings – could be redeemed if the Golgotha happened in a latrine. The relation between Lipski and Herling-Grudziński finds a parallel in that of Shalamov and Solzhenitsyn, or Buczkowski and Nałkowska: Lipski (as Shalamov and Buczkowski) is situated in opposition to hopes held until now, from the perspective of a boundless interior, and on the side of the body.

These are the three panels of a triptych, as contradictory as they are complementary: an icon of a masculine path to self-purification in the centre, with a historical and gender perspective on one side, and a corporeal and non-individuated one on the other. They do not exhaust literature's riches but rather lead in the direction of infinite pluralism of narrations, with each one giving rise to another difference.

The Laboratory of Uncertainty

The search for form as an answer to a fundamental doubt and to the loss of certainty does not have to be linked to a concrete experience of war, or camps, or the Holocaust. Memory and postmemory became sufficiently strong media of consciousness after 1945 to make the first-handedness of experience unnecessary. It is possible to demarcate in Polish literature an axis that connects very different writers and books. They do not belong to a single generation or group, and they do not pursue a common theme or use similar poetics. Rather, the similarities among them have a character of shared obsessions – they all drill into reality in search of a foothold and accept that such a foothold will not be found. This most extraordinary group is made up of authors who are singular, eccentric, and rebellious: Witold Gombrowicz (1904–69), Teodor Parnicki (1908–88), Mieczysław Piotrowski (1910–77), Stanisław Lem (1921–2006), Tadeusz Różewicz, Miron Białoszewski (1922–83), Stanisław Czycz (1929–96), and Edward Stachura (1937–79). From time to time they drew on one another for inspiration, sometimes also competing with one another. They shared an approach to literature, which they treated like a creative and cognitive laboratory. For them, literature was not a reservoir of forms but a means for creating them. They were further characterized by a similar approach to reality; they considered social *doxa* as a departure point in the narrative process of dismantling. This process did not exhaust itself in breaking down collective notions; it aimed further – at answering the question of whether truth about reality can be known and expressed.

The epistemological experiment conducted by these artists turns their texts into an expedition towards that which is unconcealed – a makeshift method of arriving at *aletheia*. We encounter such expeditions in Lem's *Solaris* (1961) as well as his later works *Doskonała próżnia* (A Perfect Vacuum, 1971; Eng. 1979) and *Wielkość urojona* (Imaginary Magnitude, 1973; Eng. 1984). They also figure in Gombrowicz's *Kosmos* (Cosmos, 1965); in Białoszewski's *Pamiętnik z powstania warszawskiego* (A Memoir of the Warsaw Uprising, 1970); in Edward Stachura's *Cała jaskrawość* (All the Brightness, 1969) and *Siekierezada* (Axiliad, 1971); in Czycz's stories "Ajol" (1967) and "And" (1967); and in Różewicz's *Przerwany egzamin* (The Interrupted Examination, 1960) and the *silva rerum*–styled *Przygotowanie do wieczoru autorskiego* (Preparation for an Author's Evening, 1971).

This is a very odd set of works, yet despite all the differences that separate them and their writers, it is difficult to dismiss the multiple convergences of their method. The mentioned pursuit of *aletheia* appears in the guise of a cognitive adventure that oscillates between play and nightmare. It can begin, as it does in *Cosmos*, with weariness with the truisms about the world and the first surprise at the sight of a hung bird; or, in Różewicz's case, with the sensation that everyone alive after the great wartime killing is dead. In *Solaris*, in turn, the adventure begins with a vision of a mysterious ocean capable of materializing the contents of the human subconscious; in Stachura's stories, with a chance encounter with a tourist who tells the story of how he attained divine consciousness; or, as happens in Białoszewski's *Memoir*, with the sight of the city after bombardment, where "everything was all jumbled together and perforated by the shells"[28] – shapeless, turned inside out, its underpinnings exposed. These differentiated, even innocent opening scenarios gradually lead to the suspension of all interpretive practices and beliefs about reality. The world loses its clarity, and language detaches itself from things until the protagonists confront the thing in itself – a de-formed reality.

What reveals itself to them, what is indeed unconcealed, is not a truth that can be discursively expressed. It is more matter than form, a process rather than a state. Białoszewski called it "living, but not alive."[29] The question of how to grasp it sets the compositional challenge. The unformed reality cannot be grasped by the mechanism of a particular convention; required instead is the process of constant forming and de-forming. The narration thus strives towards some resolution and then congeals, comes to a standstill, turns in a circle, and again proceeds forward. Each of the mentioned texts has some kind of a plot line; none of them lead to a concrete closure. Their inconclusiveness signals that enduring cognizance is impossible and that the model plot progression of "beginning – middle – end" is only a social contract – a contract about the order of reality.

The motifs of cognizance and autothematics are thus intertwined. Literature is a process: since writing unfolds truth, all commentary that bears on cognizance becomes a commentary on literature and its aspects. When Białoszewski writes about "holding on to the grand design,"[30] he means both the chronology of reminiscing and the composition of the text; when Gombrowicz's narrator concludes that the significance of an event can be declared only after the fact, he immediately adds: "Can nothing be ever truly expressed, rendered in its anonymous becoming, can no one ever render the babbling of the nascent moment, how is it that, born out of chaos, we can never encounter it again, no sooner do we look than order … and form ... are born under our very eyes?"[31] Within this sentence, the issue of discovering reality is mixed with that of finding a novelistic expression of this discovery.

To the two questions that are intertwined with each other in both of these Möbiusoid texts – "What is reality?" and "How to express it?" – a third one is added: "Who am I?" Who is the person investigating and trying to grasp reality in words? In this way, the narrators discover the fictive nature of "I": if the human world becomes blurred, the definitiveness of subjectivity also disappears. In reaching the non-human facet of reality, they discover the accidental nature of their own identity: "I wasn't present. Isn't it true (I thought), that one is almost never present,"[32] the narrator of *Cosmos* asserts; "I am not longer I,"[33] states the narrator of Czycz's "Ajol"; "I have died several times and it is worthwhile to tell those still living about it,"[34] Różewicz's narrator confesses. "I" exists due to relations – with the world and with other people. "I" is created through linguistic acts of naming both oneself and external reality. If even one corner of this triangle falls away, the entire construction descends into chaos. The breakdown of language will prevent the naming of the world, thus making impossible the naming of oneself and the formation of relationships. The tracing of the appearance and disappearance of human reality constitutes the proper content of these novels.

In the framework of literary history, the discussed configuration of texts is a culmination of Polish post–avant-garde prose. It no longer has the avant-garde's faith in progress, nor the conviction about the leading role of artists, nor does it search for a meta-language to explain the process of artistic creation. Its authors do not give up on reproducing reality, however, even though they also expose the literary process of its production. They thus question the mimetic capabilities of prose, undermining the close adherence of language to the world as well as the stability of the subject. For this reason, their narrations simultaneously speak about a fragment of a world and about its textuality – about the processes of its investigation and signification, about the arbitrary nature of defining relations between things, and about the discovery of shapelessness underneath the surface of form. The thematics of particular authors emerged from the specificity of their experiences and interests. Różewicz wrote about life searching for values after its own monstrous death, Białoszewski about reality seen as constant communication, Parnicki about the past viewed as a tangle of messages, and Stachura about the pursuit of writing that could equal life. Whatever they wrote about, however, their practice concurrently involved the representation of a theme, commentary on the literary techniques accompanying such representation, and the questioning of the immutability and stability of the subject. For this reason, their texts are at once the gloomiest and the most ecstatic of works in Polish postwar literature, revealing the world as an infinite void that is being filled with signs.

The first heirs of this idiosyncratic group of writers arrived with the so-called linguistic revolution in prose. Among them are artists such as Janusz Anderman (b. 1949), Jan Komolka (b. 1947), Ryszard Schubert (b.1949), Janusz Głowacki (1938–2017), and Tomasz Łubieński (b.1938), all of whom reach for the languages of social communication and reveal their vitality.[35] Their prose led to the conclusion that most styles have undergone a process of pulpification similar to that of social bonds – that the ties between these languages and the roots of living (rural and urban) speech are ever weaker, devastated, and infected by propaganda. Within social communication, they turn into either gibberish or a sociolect of obedience, and ever more rarely serve as a tool of understanding, a means of achieving accord, and a way of constructing an image of reality that counters mass media and the political centre.

The second significant referencing of the post–avant-garde legacy came in the 1990s, in the works of Magdalena Tulli (b. 1955), Natasza Goerke (b. 1962), Marek Bieńczyk (b. 1956), and Zbigniew Kruszyński (b. 1957). While post–avant-garde works exemplify the crisis of modernism, the texts of the 1990s reveal the horizons of postmodernity. Here, discourses and languages are the basis of reality and the system of its organization. Whereas in earlier post–avant-garde prose, mystery derives from the lack of form, in the prose of the 1990s it stems from its excessive longevity. The metaphors of Bieńczyk and Tulli and the stylistic devices of Goerke and Kruszyński are not purely artistic measures, but also, perhaps more so, operations performed on social communication and the linguistic structures of communal life. Accordingly, their multitude of intertextual references and liberal use of pastiche are not part of disinterested literary play, but interventions into social life that reveal discursive networks to be the networks of social life. Post–avant-garde prose writers saw their originality in the creation of a one-time, makeshift form used to reveal the process of the world's textual production. In the understanding of their younger successors, originality is not about creating one's own form, but about the exploratory combination of social communication forms. The position of the artist is thus different in their case, as is the society of their recipients, who are ever more accustomed to the unsteadiness of foundations, the shifting of boundaries, and the dependence of the world's outline on linguistic metaphors.

Polish postwar prose started with the creation of an orientation system for a world in which a forcible shift of all set points had taken place. Today's prose exists in a world in which such systems continuously multiply and all are suspect. As a result, contemporary literature is becoming a system of suspicion in an uncertain world.

> [People] never come into the world or die, except in connection with the circumstances that precede these events and then follow them; they are utterly bound by rules determined by the relations between words. Nothing will occur that cannot be named, and everything that can be named will sooner or later occur.
>
> – Tulli, *Dreams and Stones,* 91

Przemysław Czapliński
Adam Mickiewicz University, Poznań
Translated by Agnieszka Polakowska

NOTES

1 Odojewski, *Zasypie wszystko, zawieje ...*, 730.

2 The most important books about Recovered Territories in Polish 1960s prose include: Romuald Cabaj (1921–68), *Pierwszy rozdział* (First Chapter, 1962); Józef Hen (b. 1923), *Krzyż walecznych* (Cross of Valour, 1964); Anna Kowalska (1903–69), *Uliczka klasztorna* (Convent Alley, 1949); Henryk Panas (1912–1985), *Bóg, wilki, ludzie* (God, Wolves, People, 1960), *Cierpki owoc* (Bitter Fruit, 1962), *Grzesznicy* (Sinners, 1966); Eugeniusz Paukszta, *Przejaśnia się niebo* (The Sky Is Clearing Up, 1967), *Wrastanie* (Taking Root, 1964), *Po burzy jest pogoda* (The Calm After the Storm, 1966); Zygmunt Trziszka (1935–2000), *Dom pod białą skarpą* (House under White Escarpment, 1965); Henryk Worcell (1909–82), *Parafianie* (Parishioners, 1960), *Najtrudniejszy język świata* (Most Difficult Language in the World, 1965); and Wojciech Żukrowski (1916–2000), *Skąpani w ogniu* (Bathed in Fire, 1961).

3 The most important books of the 1990s that set this order include: Stefan Chwin (b. 1949), *Krótka historia pewnego żartu* (The Short History of a Certain Joke, 1991), *Hanemann* (Death in Danzig, 1995); Paweł Huelle (b. 1957), *Opowiadania na czas przeprowadzki* (Moving House and Other Stories, 1991); Andrzej Stasiuk (b. 1960), *Opowieści galicyjskie* (Tales of Galicia, 1995); Kazimierz Brakoniecki (b. 1952), *Światowanie* (Globalation, 1999); Artur Daniel Liskowacki (b. 1956), *Ulice Szczecina* (The Streets of Szczecin, 1997), *Cukiernica panny Kirsch* (Miss Kirsch's Confectionary, 1997), *Eine kleine* (2000); Olga Tokarczuk (b. 1962), *E.E.* (1995) and *Dom dzienny, dom nocny* (House of Day, House of Night, 1998); and Mariusz Sieniewicz (b. 1972), *Prababka* (Great-Grandmother, 1999).

4 Kundera, "The Tragedy of Central Europe," 33.

5 Andrukhovych and Stasiuk, *Moja Europa*.

6 Ibid., 77–8.

7 The most important authors and novels of the peasant current during the 1960s and 1970s include Józef Morton, *Mój drugi ożenek* (My Second Marriage, 1961), *Ucieczka z raju* (Escape from Paradise, 1969), and *Appasionata* (1976); Tadeusz Nowak, *Przebudzenie* (Awakening, 1962), *Obcoplemienna ballada* (A Foreign Tribe's Ballad, 1963), *W puchu alleluja* (In the Down of Allelujah, 1965), *Takie większe wesele* (A Bigger Wedding, 1966), *A jak królem, a jak katem będziesz* (And If You Were a King, and If You Were an Executioner, 1968), *Diabły* (Devils, 1971), and *Dwunastu* (The Twelve, 1974); Julian Kawalec, *Ziemi przypisany* (Assigned to the Earth, 1962), *W słońcu* (In the Sun, 1963), *Tańczący jastrząb* (The Dancing Hawk, 1964), *Wezwanie* (Summons, 1968), *Szukam domu* (Wanted: Home, 1968), *Przepłyniesz rzekę* (You Will Cross a River, 1973), *Szara aureola* (The Grey Halo, 1973), and *Wielki festyn* (The Great Festival, 1974); Stanisław Piętak, *Matnia* (Noose, 1962), *Plama* (Stain, 1963), and *Odmieniec* (Misfit, 1964); Marian Pilot, *Panny szczerbate* (Gap-toothed Ladies, 1962), *Sień* (Foyer, 1965), *Opowieści świętojańskie* (St John's Tales, 1966), *Majdan* (Courtyard, 1969), *Pantałyk* (1970), and *Zakaz zwałki* (1974); Jan Bolesław Ożóg, *Bracia* (Brothers, 1969); Zygmunt Trziszka, *Wielkie świniobicie* (1965); Wiesław Myśliwski, *Nagi sad* (Naked Orchard, 1967) and *Pałac* (Palace, 1970); Józef Ozga-Michalski, *Sowizdrzał świętokrzyski* (1971); and Edward Redliński, *Awans* (1973) and *Konopielka* (1973).

8 Paweł Demirski – introduction to his production. http://teatrdramatyczny.pl/index.php?option=com_content&view=article&id=1694&Itemid=618.

9 The most important socialist realist novels in Polish literature include Kazimierz Brandys, *Początek opowieści* (The Beginning of the Story, 1951) and *Obywatele* (Citizens, 1954);

Andrzej Braun, *Lewanty,* vols. 1–2 (Freighters, 1952); Tadeusz Breza, *Uczta Baltazara* (Balthazar's Feast, 1952); Bogusław Hamera, *Na przykład Plewa* (For Example, Plewa, 1950); Jarosław Iwaszkiewicz, *Podróż do Sandomierza. Powieść dla młodzieży* (A Trip to Sandomierz: A Novel for Youth, 1953); Tadeusz Konwicki, *Przy budowie* (Construction Site, 1950) and *Władza* (Power, 1954); Mirosław Kowalewski, *Kampania znaczy walka* (Campaign Means Struggle, 1950); Józef Morton, *Zapomniana wieś* (The Forgotten Village, 1952); Igor Newerly, *Archipelag ludzi zapomnianych. Opowieść historyczna z roku 1948* (The Archipelago of Forgotten People: A Historical Novel from 1948, 1950); Edmund Niziurski, *Gorące dni* (Hot Days, 1951); Jerzy Pytlakowski, *Fundamenty* (Fundaments, 1950); Aleksander Ścibor-Rylski, *Węgiel* (Coal, 1950); Jan Wilczek, *Nr 16 produkuje* (Number 16 Produces, 1949); and Witold Zalewski, *Traktory zdobędą wiosnę* (Tractors will Conquer Spring, 1950).
10 Translated by David J Welsh in 1960.
11 Brandys, *Letters to Mrs Z*, 20.
12 See, for instance, Marek Nowakowski, *Raport o stanie wojennym* (A Report on Martial Law, 1982) and *Notatki z codzienności* (Notes from the Everyday, 1983); Janusz Głowacki, *Moc truchleje* (Great Powers Tremble, 1981); Tadeusz Konwicki, *Rzeka podziemna, podziemne ptaki* (Underground River, Underground Birds, 1984); Kazimierz Orłoś, *Cudowna melina* (A Wonderful Drinkery, 1973), *Trzecie kłamstwo* (The Third Lie, 1980), *Pustynia Gobi* (The Gobi Desert, 1983), and *Przechowalnia* (Storage Room, 1985); Janusz Anderman, *Brak tchu* (Shortness of Breath, 1983); Marian Miszalski, *Wysokie progi* (High Thresholds, 1984); Krzysztof Czabański, *ABC* (1985); Andrzej Mandalian, *Operacja: Kartagina!* (Operation Carthage!, 1985); Aleksy Dalcz, *Umierający i zmartwychwstali. Apokryf współczesny* (The Dying and the Ressurected: A Contemporary Apocrypha, 1985); Sławomir Mrożek, *Alfa* (1984); and Jarosław Marek Rymkiewicz, *Rozmowy polskie latem 1983* (Polish Conversations in Spring 1983, 1984).
13 Nałkowska, *Medallions*, 48.
14 Borowski, "Auschwitz, Our Home (A Letter)," 131.
15 Buczkowski, *Black Torrent*, 178.
16 Ibid., 52.
17 Ibid., 33.
18 Ibid., 166.
19 Ibid., 33.
20 Ibid., 187.
21 Krall, *To Outwit God*, 198.
22 Among them: Hanna Krall, *Sublokatorka* (Subtenant, 1985); Andrzej Szczypiorski, *Początek* (The Beginning, 1986); Tadeusz Konwicki, *Bohiń* (Bohyn Manor, 1987); Piotr Szewc, *Zagłada* (Annihilation, 1987); Jarosław Marek Rymkiewicz, *Umschlagplatz* (1987); Paweł Huelle, *Weiser Dawidek* (Who Was Dawid Weiser?, 1987); and Adolf Rudnicki, *Teatr zawsze grany* (*The Always Open Theatre*, 1987).
23 Bieńczyk, *Tworki,* 40.
24 Herling-Grudzinski, *A World Apart*, 65.
25 Ibid., 68.
26 Lipski, "Dzień i noc," 7.
27 Ibid., 111.
28 Białoszewski, *A Memoir of the Warsaw Uprising*, 67.
29 Ibid., 64.

30 Ibid., 67.
31 Gombrowicz, *Cosmos,* 25.
32 Ibid., 102.
33 Czycz, "Ajol." In *Ajol i Laor,* 28.
34 Różewicz, "*Nowa szkoła filozoficzna,*" 117–18.
35 See Galant, *Polska proza lingwistyczna.*

WORKS CITED

Andrukhovych, Yuri, and Andrzej Stasiuk, *Moja Europa. Dwa eseje o Europie zwanej Środkową.* Kołowiec: Wydawnictwo Czarne, 2000.

Bakuła, Bogusław. "Między wygnaniem a kolonizacją. O kilku odmianach polskiej powieści migracyjnej w XX wieku (na skromnym tle porównawczym)." In *Narracje migracyjne w literaturze polskiej XX i XXI wieku.* Edited by Hanna Gosk. 161–91. Kraków: Universitas, 2012.

Białoszewski, Miron. *A Memoir of the Warsaw Uprising.* Translated and edited by Madeline Levine. Evanston: Northwestern University Press, 1991.

Bieńczyk, Marek. *Tworki.* Translated by Benjamin Paloff. Evanston: Northwestern University Press, 2008.

Błoński, Jan. "A Poor Christian Looks at the Ghetto." In *'My Brother's Keeper?': Recent Polish Debates on the Holocaust.* Edited by Antony Polonsky. 34–52. London: Routledge in association with Institute for Polish-Jewish Studies, 1990.

Borowski, Tadeusz. "Auschwitz, Our Home (A Letter)." In *This Way for the Gas, Ladies and Gentleman.* Selected and translated by Barbara Vedder. 98–142. New York: Penguin Books, 1976.

Brandys, Kazimierz. *Letters to Mrs Z.* Translated by Morris Edelson. Highland Park: December Press, 1987.

Buczkowski, Leopold. *Black Torrent.* Translated by David Welsh. Cambridge, MA: MIT Press, 1969.

Czycz, Stanisław. "Ajol." In *Ajol i Laor.* 17–87. Kraków: Wydawnictwo Literackie, 1996.

Fiut, Aleksander. "Socjalizm realny – co to za zwierz?" *Tytuł,* 1 (1997): 5–26.

Galant, Jan. *Polska proza lingwistyczna. Debiuty lat siedemdziesiątych.* Poznań: Wydawnictwo "Poznańskie Studia Polonistyczne", 1999.

Gombrowicz, Witold. *Cosmos.* Translated by Danuta Borchardt. New Haven: Yale University Press, 2005.

Groys, Boris. *The Total Art of Stalinism: Avant-Garde, Aesthetic Dictatorship, and Beyond.* Translated by Charles Rougle. Princeton: Princeton University Press, 1992.

Grynberg, Henryk. "Holocaust w literaturze polskiej." In *Prawda nieartystyczna.* 139–79. Warszawa: PIW, 1994.

Herling-Grudziński, Gustaw. *A World Apart.* Translated by Joseph Marek. New York: Roy, 1951.

Jarzębski, Jerzy. "Exodus (ewolucja obrazu kresów po wojnie)." In *W Polsce, czyli wszędzie. Szkice o polskiej prozie współczesnej.* 129–47. Warszawa: Wyd. PEN, 1992.

Krall, Hanna. "To Outwit God." Translated by Joanna Stasinska Weschler and Lawrence Weschler. In *The Subtenant. To Outwit God.* 129–251. Evanston: Northwestern University Press, 1992.

Kundera, Milan. "The Tragedy of Central Europe." *New York Review of Books,* 26 April 1984, 33–8.

Lipski, Leo. “Dzień i noc.” In *Piotruś.* 59–145. Olsztyn: ODN, 1995.
Miłosz, Czesław. “La Combe.” *Kultura* 10 (1958): 26–38.
Mrożek, Slawomir. “The Elephant.” In *The Elephant.* Translated by Konrad Syrop. 16–20. Westport: Greenwood Press, 1975.
Nałkowska, Zofia. *Medallions*. Translated by Diana Kuprel. Evanston: Northwestern University Press, 2000.
Odojewski, Włodzimierz. *Zasypie wszystko, zawieje ...* Warszawa: Twój Styl, 2001.
Różewicz, Tadeusz. “Nowa szkoła filozoficzna.” In *Proza,* vol. 1. 109–29. Kraków: Wydawnictwo Literackie, 1990.
– “Tarcza z pajęczyny.” In *Proza*, vol. 1. 243–71. Kraków: Wydawnictwo Literackie, 1990.
Tulli, Magdalena. *Dreams and Stones*. Translated by Bill Johnston. New York: Archipelago Books, 2004.

Post-Traumatic Outsider (Leopold Buczkowski)

Leopold Buczkowski (1905–89) was an outstanding Polish writer of the twentieth century yet at the same time one of the least-known outside of Poland. This is partly due to the structural complexity of his works as well as their distinctive language, which does not lend itself readily to translation.

Leopold Buczkowski – novelist, poet, painter, sculptor, graphic designer, composer; a man of numerous interests and talents. Fearing the Ukrainian nationalists, he fled Podolia in 1944 and settled in Konstancin, near Warsaw. Thereafter he could revisit his homeland only by way of his books.

His works in prose are:

1947 – *Wertepy* (Rough Terrain)
1954 – *Czarny Potok* (Black Torrent)
1957 – *Dorycki krużganek* (The Doric Cloister)
1960 – *Młody poeta w zamku* (The Young Poet in the Castle)
1966 – *Pierwsza świetność* (First Splendor)
1970 – *Uroda na czasie* (Trendy Beauty)
1974 – *Kąpiele w Lucca* (The Baths at Lucca)
1975 – *Oficer na nieszporach* (An Officer at Vespers)
1978 – *Kamień w pieluszkach* (A Stone in Diapers)
2001 – *Dziennik wojenny* (War Diary)

With these can be included three volumes of his conversations with Zygmunt Trziszka: *Wszystko jest dialogiem* (Everything Is Dialogue, 1984); *Proza żywa* (*Living Prose*, 1986); and *Żywe dialogi* (*Living Dialogues*, 1989).

In *Wertepy* (Rough Terrain) and *Czarny potok* (Black Torrent), the author uses obsolete linguistic registers and words that cannot be found even in the most specialized dictionaries, since their meanings have disappeared with the deaths of those who last spoke them. It is the language of the Borderlands (Kresy) – a language that, reflecting as it does the dense concentration of peoples and ethnic groups in Podolia, presents difficulties even for Polish readers. Buczkowski's early work (1937–66), from *Rough Terrain* to *Pierwsza świetność* [First Splendor] by way of *Dziennik wojenny* [War Diary], is characterized by an unusual sensitivity to the richness and beauty of language.

Buczkowski's first published work was the novel *Rough Terrain*, written before the Second World War but only published ten years later. Its appearance was delayed by the censors, who found its portrayal of village life and of ethnic relations in the Borderlands too shocking, not to mention disparaging of the Polish administrators in that region. In *Rough Terrain*, rural communal life is determined by one's survival instincts. Cruelty and ruthlessness are basic existential principles. The characters struggle to adapt to the harsh rules of survival. At the same time, the book portrays village life in a manner rarely found in Polish literature. Buczkowski combines descriptions of brutality with touching and lyrical images of nature. He uses a similar technique in *Black Torrent*, in which the portrayed cruelty is even greater yet embedded in equally evocative descriptions of the landscape (dominated by black and grey tones). In *Rough Terrain*, and even more so in *Black Torrent*, the abundance and interpenetration of motifs, the use of parallel and simultaneous narratives, the slowing down of time, and the violation of chronology lead inevitably to a relaxation of the classical novel's strictures.

The Eastern Borderlands lie in present-day Western Ukraine. Prior to the Second World War, these territories were part of Poland, having been conquered and colonized by the Polish nobility in the seventeenth century. Over several centuries they became home to a mosaic of peoples, cultures, creeds, and languages. The Borderlands witnessed a multitude of bloody events and mass killings, with Poles, Jews, and Ukrainians among their many victims. Poles remember the atrocities committed by Ukrainian nationalists during the Second World War against the Polish inhabitants of these lands. Ukrainians remember the persecutions following the war, in particular "Operation Vistula" (the resettlement of Ukrainian populations from the southeastern reaches of Poland). Jews remember the killings and pogroms carried out by Ukrainian Cossacks during the Chmielnicki Uprising in the seventeenth century as well as the atrocities committed by Nazi *Einsatzgruppen* in 1941–42. Podolia and its environs provide the backdrop for several of Buczkowski's early novels, which depict the fascinating cultural richness of the Borderlands and contain shocking examples of cruelty. From the start, Buczkowski's works have been concerned with the preservation of Podolia's multicultural collective memory.

Black Torrent is Buczkowski's best-known, most frequently reprinted, and most remarkable work. While *Rough Terrain* still shows traits of the classical novel, *Black Torrent* marks a clear shift towards experimentation. There is no single unifying authorial perspective. No one character stands in for the author. None of them can be said to represent his beliefs or his point of view. Its plot breaks down into smaller units, each of which could exist on its own. The method for combining individual scenes in *Black Torrent* resembles montage. The novel's episodic structure – the fact that no single event is privileged over any other – has made its reception still more problematic, since it can create the impression of haphazard composition.

Despite its challenging character, *Black Torrent* is the greatest Polish novel about the Holocaust and one of the most remarkable novels ever written about the extermination of the Jews. It is a poignant critique of the European culture that led to the dramatic events of the twentieth century. Buczkowski similarly indicts European art and civilization in *Dorycki krużganek* (The Doric Cloister), *Młody poeta w zamku* (The Young Poet in the Castle), *Proza żywa* (Living Prose), and *Wszystko jest dialogiem* (Everything Is Dialogue). The disordered plot of *Black Torrent* mirrors the chaos of wartime existence in the Borderlands. Buczkowski believed that after the Holocaust the world could no longer be described using conventional artistic methods. Like Theodor Adorno, he regarded dissonance as the fundamental means of artistic expression for art after Auschwitz. In *The Doric Cloister*, to show the incomprehensibility of war, he uses the technique of multiple points of view, presenting one event from different perspectives. Each of the individual narrators, whom the reader usually cannot identify, presents his own version of events.

In addition to dissonance and the juxtaposition of antithetical qualities, Buczkowski was one of the first authors to use poetic fragments to express the tragedy of war and the Holocaust. Buczkowski's gaze reaches back before the Holocaust and the Second World War to encompass the entire *idea* of the past, which we receive in fragments that rarely arrange themselves into a neat whole. Indeed, the composite fragments no longer make up a whole. Even on repeated readings, *Black Torrent* does not lend itself to reconstruction as a coherent story. There are always lingering question marks. We can never be absolutely sure who is speaking, to whom, when, and in what place. There are only a few instances in the novel when this is possible.

The Doric Cloister and *First Splendor* unfold in the same world as *Black Torrent*. They too are accounts of the slaughter of Poles and Jews in the Borderlands. We do, however, acquire a new epistemological perspective. Whereas *Black Torrent* depicts a state of disintegration, *The Doric Cloister* and *First Splendor* are attempts to reconstruct the world after catastrophe. Buczkowski questions whether, and in what fashion, one can re-create a destroyed reality. Attempts to portray horror often lead to a schematic rather than accurate knowledge of events. Only the novel-document allows one to avoid cognitive and artistic simplifications. In this respect, Buczkowski's prose – as Agnieszka Karpowicz points out – is a kind of archive, comprising "documents assembled from numerous texts, recollections, investigations, inquiries, scenarios and accounts presented as an aggregate of reported speech."[1] The archive is a key element in the Museum of the Imagination. The Museum of the Imagination is Buczkowski's answer to the crisis of civilization brought on by the war: art can no longer simply imitate, but must actively construct reality. It must create rather than describe.

Buczkowski's diary, in which he recorded his experiences between 1943 and 1945, was published after his death. It is one of the most unusual autobiographical wartime accounts in existence, and the manner in which it describes the tragedy that falls on Poles and Jews is unprecedented. Its prose style recalls the traumatic narration of *Black Torrent*. Buczkowski breaks with typical diaristic narration, with its internal logic and tendency towards clarity of exposition; instead, he attempts to re-create the chaos of wartime through language and narrative structure. To do this, he invents a unique prose style with its own rules of syntax and punctuation. The Warsaw Uprising is depicted here – as in Białoszewski's *A Memoir of the Warsaw Uprising* – through the prism of civilian tragedy. Buczkowski's reluctance to aestheticize reality is obvious. In the works he wrote between the war diary and *First Splendor*, death is always inhumane and abhorrent, imbued with more shame than pathos. This author's portrayals of death are characteristically antiheroic.

Buczkowski's late works (beginning with *Uroda na czasie* [Trendy Beauty]) are extremely difficult, both for general readers and for literary experts. They are among the most complex literary works in the Polish language. Buczkowski no longer embeds his heroes in a specific historical time frame, but rather among the great *topoi* of European culture, so that myths, legends, and creatures of the author's imagination mingle with actual people. In *Trendy Beauty*, *Oficer an nieszporach* (An Officer at Vespers), *Kąpiele w Lucca* (The Baths at Lucca), *Kamień w pieluszkach* (A Stone in Diapers), and the unfinished novel *Bagules*, one cannot speak of such categories as "hero," "plot," or "action." We are left with words and individual sentences that cannot be combined into a meaningful whole, since meaning breaks down already on the level of the sentence, to say nothing of the paragraph or the chapter.

In *Polowanie na postmodernistów* (Hunting for Postmodernists, 1999), Włodzimierz Bolecki includes Buczkowski among the small number of postmodernist authors in Poland.[2] If one can call Buczkowski a postmodernist, it is thanks to his late works, in which pastiche, parody, paraphrase, allusion, and citations (sometimes quasi- or crypto-quotes) play a key role. Along with allusions to other authors and cultural phenomena, we find intertextual references to his own works. The author further complicates matters by doggedly covering his tracks, modifying and altering his self-quotations and other intertextual references. In *The Baths at Lucca* and *A Stone in Diapers*, reality attains the status of text and thus a key component of Buczkowski's earliest novels – the relation to actual historical reality – is lost. This change is all the more significant when we consider that the author of *Black Torrent* frequently emphasized the importance of personal experience in shaping the artist's psyche. In *Living Prose,* we read the following: "Experiences, are of the greatest importance in writing."[3] The sources of literature spring from the richness of experience coupled with a talent for observation. Buczkowski's admiration for the narrative gifts of ordinary people is telling in this respect.

In addition to his extraordinary literary texts, Buczkowski left behind numerous drawings, paintings, and photographs, often depicting his homeland in Podolia or documenting the horrors of war. Taped recordings of Buczkowski's musical compositions have survived as well. Alongside traditional Ukrainian, Polish, and Jewish songs, they include dodecaphonic compositions reminiscent of John Cage's experiments.

Buczkowski was an outsider and a revolutionary who would not submit to prevailing artistic conventions. He sometimes spoke of his diverse creative output as of a single work, in which music, painting, literature, sculpture, photography, illustration, and graphic design formed a complementary whole. He longed to keep this totality "open" instead of locking himself into a technique or a way of seeing the world particular to one type of art. This may also explain why it is so difficult to place him within any one trend in Polish art.

The reception of Buczkowski's works (particularly his late works) attests both to the helplessness of critics encountering his ideas and works, and to the staying power of these texts. Interest in his work has been growing for some time, particularly among younger scholars and students. Perhaps one reason for this is their desire to finally unlock Buczkowski's prose. Recent methodological angles can provide new access points into his work. In the past, he has been read through a structuralist lens, or using methods derived from linguistics; readers today have other tools at their disposal, including geopoetics, trauma studies, art history (particularly studies of collage), and chaos theory. Each of these methodologies is useful in analysing a particular facet of his work, but for now a comprehensive reading of Buczkowski's oeuvre continues to elude us.

Sławomir Buryła
Warmian-Masurian University, Olsztyn
Translated by Phil Redko

NOTES

1 Karpowicz, *Kolaż*, 179.
2 See Bolecki, *Polowanie na postmodernistów*.
3 Buczkowski, *Proza żywa*, 67.

WORKS CITED

Bolecki, Włodzimierz. *Polowanie na postmodernistów (w Polsce) i inne szkice*. Kraków: Wydawnictwo Literackie, 1999.
Buczkowski, Leopold. *Proza żywa*. Bydgoszcz: Pomorze, 1986.
Karpowicz, Agnieszka. *Kolaż. Awangardowy gest kreacji. Themerson, Buczkowski, Białoszewski.* Warszawa: Wydawnictwa Uniwersytetu Warszawskiego, 2007. 7.

Futurological Philosophy (Stanisław Lem)

"Good books tell the truth, even when they're about things that never have been and never will be. They're truthful in a different way." So states Pirx the Pilot, one of Stanisław Lem's most iconic literary characters.[1] Lem's voluminous oeuvre of narratives and essays offers such truthfulness in the guise of science fiction fantasy, satiric fables, ironic parables, and philosophical speculation. Best-known as an innovative science fiction writer who also wrote non-fiction, Lem (1921–2006) can equally well be seen as a philosophical writer whose essays are complemented by science fiction narratives that embody his ideas on the development of science and technology, their impact on society, and the relationship of humans to the non-human world.

Lem's privileged childhood could not protect him from the horrors of twentieth-century Eastern Europe. He lived through war, occupation, and dispossession: through the Nazi and Soviet occupations of his home town of Lwów (now Lviv in Ukraine) during the Second World War and exodus to Kraków in communist Poland, through various political upheavals, including the rise of Solidarity and voluntary exile in Vienna during martial law in Poland, to the fall of communism in Eastern Europe, when he returned to Kraków. These experiences revealed to him the unpredictability of life and the role of chance – recurrent themes in his writings. Lem's growing national and international popularity, including critical acclaim and numerous awards, reached its peak in Poland with the 2005 publication of his *Collected Works* in no less than thirty volumes.

Despite its great potential as speculative literature, science fiction is considered a formulaic popular genre. This makes it difficult for its practitioners to break into the mainstream, though such distinguished writers as Nabokov, Vonnegut, Pynchon, and Calvino have broached science fiction topics in their works. Although Lem's use of hybrid literary forms and his fluctuations between fictional and discursive narratives have made him difficult to categorize, such important critics as Darko Suvin, Fredric Jameson, and Istvan Csicsery-Ronay, and such eminent sci-fi practitioners as Samuel Delany and Ursula Le Guin, consider Lem one of the genre's greatest writers. At the same time, Lem is a unique literary figure, due to the sheer volume of his output, the exalted yet marginal position he occupies in Polish letters, and the fact that he is an Eastern European who has influenced science fiction worldwide.

Lem, who was trained as a physician, offers readers a penetrating, sceptical analysis of the human condition, the cognitive and ethical implications of developments in science and technology, and the dangers of human hubris. He tackles existential questions through the *topoi* of intergalactic travels, robotic worlds, and encounters with alien life, employing these in an astonishing variety of forms, all the while playing with various combinations of multiple genres – adventure, fantasy, philosophical speculation, cybernetic fairytales, and satirical parables. His works stem in part from the eighteenth-century satires of Swift, from Voltaire's and Diderot's *contes philosophiques*, as well as from the modernist fantasies of such Polish writers as Bruno Schulz (1892–1942), Stanisław Ignacy Witkiewicz (1885–1939), and Witold Gombrowicz (1904–69). An avid reader, Lem also fell under the spell of Kafka and Borges.

Lem's best-known novel, *Solaris* (1961), has inspired two critically acclaimed film adaptations, one Soviet (directed by Andrei Tarkovsky in 1972), the other American (directed by Steven Soderbergh in 2002). The first adaptation testifies to Lem's considerable following in the Soviet Union. This should come as no surprise, since science fiction, with its focus on distant worlds in a distant future, served to camouflage contemporary concerns and hence could flourish even in the heavily censored Eastern Bloc. Furthermore, the Cold War space race that engaged the world's two superpowers made the genre popular in both East and West. *Solaris* is a good example of how Lem eluded communist censorship and at the same time created narratives with international appeal. The world of his novel is that of an advanced global civilization, which has colonized other planets and whose spaceships roam the galaxies. Neither wars nor nation-states are mentioned, nor is capitalism; Earth appears to be under a global government, and penetration of the universe by humans is subject to UN conventions. This setting allows Lem to concentrate on universal philosophical questions while bringing a new and exciting genre to Polish literature.

Conte philosophique – a genre of prose fiction that first appeared in France in the eighteenth century. It allowed authors to critique social, political, and religious aspects of society, philosophical schools, and human foibles. Witty, inventive, morally instructive, and critical of the status quo, the *conte philosophique* was able to elude strong government censorship by casting itself as a fairy tale or fantasy. Voltaire's *Zadig* (1747) and *Candide* (1759) are the best-known, though Diderot, La Fontaine, and Perrault also employed the genre.

The narrator of *Solaris*, psychologist Kris Kelvin, arrives at the space station hovering above the jelly-like ocean of the planet Solaris, to find the place in disarray, the head of the mission dead, and the other two scientists in hiding. The automated machines on the space station work perfectly, but the humans have fallen apart – one of them has committed suicide – and are haunted by mysterious and unshakeable "visitors": responding to the humans' increasingly aggressive probing of the enigmatic planet, the ocean, apparently a powerful sentient entity, penetrates the psyches of the men in their sleep and produces indestructible, life-like, three-dimensional images of their innermost guilts and desires. Kelvin soon receives his own "guest" in the guise of a living, breathing copy of his former lover, who had committed suicide when he rejected her ten years earlier. This new Harey[2] conjures up all of Kelvin's guilt, but also love, desire, exasperation, and acceptance. She is not human, yet she becomes more human-like as they stay together, even to the extent of pondering her own existence and realizing that she is only a tool in the ocean's experiment. This realization prompts her to consider another romantic suicide;

thus, paradoxically, history is allowed to repeat itself, perhaps once again reflecting Kelvin's subconscious desire to rid himself of an engrossing relationship.

Solaris functions on several multivalent levels. It is an inventive narrative of space exploration and of the inability to effect real, meaningful contact with a truly alien Other. Lem's main concern in *Solaris*, as in much of his mature fiction, is the total impossibility of such contact and the inevitable use of human paradigms to grapple with the non-human Other. Trapped in human consciousness, we are unable to move outside it. The astronauts in the novel do not battle monsters or discover galactic civilizations, but are forced to confront their innermost selves. *Solaris* is also a potent horror story, played out on a desolate space station surrounded by infinite space, and overshadowed by an inscrutable, monstrous presence outside, a kind of cosmic Moby Dick haunting its human aggressors. It is also an unusual and affecting love story, in which the protagonist must grapple with feelings for his dead earthly lover and the alien who closely mirrors her. Cumulatively it becomes a profound philosophical meditation on the essence of human selfhood and the human quest for transcendent meaning.

In his extended descriptions of the planet and the various strange and enormous forms created by the sentient ocean, Lem's language and imagination come close to the exuberant surrealism of Bruno Schulz. He evokes classical mythology and Judeo-Christian allusions in Kelvin's discussions of the ocean with his colleague Snaut[3] – discussions that lead to their tentative theory of an imperfect, evolving god and that emphasize the impenetrability of any motives that could be ascribed to the ocean's probing of the humans. The astronauts have seen themselves as "Knights of the Holy Contact," to use Snaut's witty phrase, but their quest leads them to an unknowable Grail, and their epiphany is that it is impossible to interpret the nature and actions of an alien presence. Lem's summary of the scholarly field of Solaristics in the novel is both a superb pastiche of the development of a scientific field and a powerful cautionary tale of scholarly futility.

Lem's innovative, multilayered science fiction is both philosophical and speculative, deploying tropes of mirrors, masks, palimpsests, and codes. Its ambiguity resists interpretation. His inventive and witty language, which intertwines scientific and philosophical discourse with the colloquial and the poetic, parallels a remarkable range of topics, reflecting his intensive reading of scientific literature and consummate grasp of the current state of techno-science. His fiction reveals an almost manic proliferation and exuberance of approaches, from serious science fiction narratives, such as *Solaris*, *Powrót z gwiazd* (*Return from the Stars*, 1961), *Niezwyciężony* (The Invincible, 1964), and *Głos Pana* (His Master's Voice, 1968), to the hilariously hallucinatory *Kongres futurologiczny* (Futurological Congress, 1971); from the philosophical pseudo-detective stories of *Śledztwo* (The Investigation, 1959) and *Katar* (The Chain of Chance, 1976) and the Kafkaesque spy thriller *Pamiętnik znaleziony w wannie* (Memoirs Found in a Bathtub, 1961) to the faux-naive robotic fairytales and mordant satires in *Bajki robotów* (Mortal Engines, 1964) and *Cyberiada* (The Cyberiad: Fables for the Cybernetic Age, 1965).

Parable – a short allegorical tale with a strong moral message. The best-known parables are found in the New Testament, such as the story of the Good Samaritan, and have exerted an important influence on Western literature. John Steinbeck's *The Pearl* (1948) is a parable in the form of a novella. Many of Lem's stories in the *Cyberiad* can be considered parables.

Lem's fiction is paralleled and complemented by a variety of philosophical essays, articles, memoirs, and interviews. *Summa Technologiae* (1964; rev. 1967 and 1974; Eng. trans. 2013) is an astonishingly prescient volume of essays about the influence of science and technology on human evolution, in which Lem posits such later developments as artificial intelligence and virtual reality, as well as "cyborgization." In his two-volume *Fantastyka i futurologia* (1971), translated into English in part as *Microworlds: Writings on Science Fiction and Fantasy* (1984), Lem shows himself an astute and combative literary theorist and critic, with some bitter reflections on the simplistic narratives of most English-language science fiction. His own writing moved towards innovative hybrid forms in the 1970s, as is most notably apparent in his reviews of imaginary books collected in *Doskonała próżnia* (A Perfect Vacuum, 1971), and in *Wielkość urojona* (Imaginary Magnitude, 1973), a collection of introductions to non-existent books. These non-narrative fictional forms allowed Lem to engage in more flexible and playful discursive practices. In *A Perfect Vacuum*, for example, he offers plots of possible novels, comic sci-fi ideas, satiric literary criticism, and serious reflections on the nature of the universe, all summarized in the book's opening review, that of *A Perfect Vacuum* itself.

After the fall of communism and the end of censorship, Lem stopped writing science fiction. In his capacity as "Grand Old Man" of Polish letters, he now devoted himself wholeheartedly to directly addressing the condition of humanity in his times. His essays, articles, newspaper columns, and interviews are collected in such volumes as *Tajemnica chińskiego pokoju* (The Mystery of the Chinese Room, 1996), *Bomba megabitowa* (The Megabyte Bomb, 1999), and *Rasa drapieżców* (Race of Predators, 2006). Provocative, witty, and ironic, they provide acutely perceptive commentaries on such developing aspects of science and technology as contemporary genetics, information technology, and robotics, and on global trends, consumerism, politics, literature, and culture, rounding out an already astonishingly broad literary oeuvre. With his penetrating insights into the uses of science and his vivid inventions of distant worlds that mirror humankind's universal dilemmas, Stanislaw Lem remains unique and far-reaching in his vision, and astounding and provocative in his effect on readers, not unlike the sentient ocean of Solaris.

Elżbieta Foeller-Pituch
Northwestern University, Evanston

NOTES

1 Stanisław Lem, "Pirx's Tale," in *More Tales of Prix the Pilot*, 3.

2 The character is renamed Rheya in the 2002 English translation by Joanna Kilmartin and Steve Cox.

3 Renamed Snow in the English translation.

WORKS CITED AND CONSULTED

Jarzebski, Jerzy. *Wszechswiat Lema*. Kraków: Wydawnictwo Literackie, 2002.

Lem, Stanisław. Official website: http://www.lem.pl.

– *More Tales of Pirx the Pilot.* Translated by Louis Iribarane with Magdalena Majcherczyk. London: Mandarin Paperbacks, 1983.

Madison, Davis. *Stanislaw Lem*. Mercer Island: Starmont House, 1990.
Swirski, Peter, ed. *A Stanislaw Lem Reader*. Evanston: Northwestern University Press, 1997.
– *The Art and Science of Stanislaw Lem*. Montreal and Kingston: McGill–Queen's University Press, 2006.
– *Between Literature and Science: Poe, Lem, and Explorations in Aesthetics, Cognitive Science, and Literary Knowledge.* Montreal and Kingston: McGill–Queen's University Press, 2000.
Tighe, Carl. "Stanislaw Lem." *The Politics of Literature: Poland 1945–1989*. 158–76. Cardiff: University of Wales Press, 1999.
Ziegfeld, Richard E. *Stanislaw Lem*. New York: Ungar, 1985.

Mythical Subversions (Olga Tokarczuk)

Over the course of her literary career, critics have seen Olga Tokarczuk (b. 1962) as a regional writer, an author of women's literature, a representative of magic realism, and – more recently – a representative of ecological and historical writing. While the question of her place in Polish literature remains open, her literary oeuvre is a clear indication that this contemporary woman writer is unique in her literary vision, language, and achievements. Many of the authors who debuted right after the fall of the communist regime in Poland brought the specificity of their native regions and cultures into national literature. Consequently, Tokarczuk's interest in Silesia initially gave critics cause to view her as a regional writer, as was also the case with Stefan Chwin (b. 1942), Paweł Huelle (b. 1957), and Inga Iwasiów (b. 1963). Categorizing Tokarczuk as a regional author, however, does not do justice to the scope of her literary interests. Thankfully, and in part due to the writing of the above-mentioned authors, traditional thinking about culture in terms of administratively constructed centres and peripheries has evolved since 1989.

Born in 1962 in the small town of Sulechów (near Zielona Góra), Tokarczuk studied psychology at the University of Warsaw and worked as a therapist in Wrocław before embarking on a career as a professional writer. She debuted in 1989 with the poetry collection *Miasta w lustrach* (Cities in Mirrors), and published her first novel, *Podróż ludzi księgi* (The Journey of the Book-People), in 1993.

Tokarczuk's literary works are characterized by a rejection of the entire system of cultural binaries and of the constraints they impose on language. This rejection may be seen as a consequence of her own "marginalized" position, in terms of both gender and region. Tokarczuk's interrogation of the limitations of symbolic cultural orders makes the popularity of her books an interesting phenomenon. Though her literary texts differ considerably from one another, there is something systematic and consistent in the way she creates and posits new views of the world with each new work.

Tokarczuk consistently introduces readers to new ways of looking at reality. The system of values to which she has continued to refer in her later work was already established in her first book, *The Journey of the Book-People*. Besides the themes of time and space, which are fundamental to Tokarczuk's prose in general, this fictional travelogue foregrounds the importance of language. Gauche, a mute orphan raised by nuns in eighteenth-century France, thinks that "by pronouncing words we have power over an object. When we put words in relations to other words, we create new relations between things – we create a world."[1] It is this thought that underpins Tokarczuk's literary worlds.

Through characters like Gauche, Tokarczuk familiarizes her readers with the principles that govern the world, beginning with the concept and essence of time (which is "always going around in circles"): "Gauche quickly understood the essence of time, and he thus did not feel the need to push forward, as other people did. He stayed in his time, as in a secure shell, growing up slowly, and slowly assimilating its hardly noticeable rhythm."[2] This observation also applies to many of Tokarczuk's later characters, who generally do not struggle with time, but rather wait for the right moment to come. Though she reclaims and reconfigures the quotidian (thus giving cause for comparisons of her prose to magic realism), she also usually picks up her characters just as they break out of ordinary life, and leaves them just as they go back to circular time and a foreseeable future. Moreover, for Tokarczuk and her characters time is not only temporal but spatial as well; time and space are dependent on each other, which is why Anna in *Anna In w grobowcach świata* (Anna In and the Tombs of the World, 2006) searches for the entrance to the underworld using its picture as her guide. Since time has an impact on space, she has to wait patiently on the street until a red mailbox appears and makes her view of the place identical with the picture. Only then does the entrance become accessible to her – only then can her journey begin.

The theme of travelling allows Tokarczuk to incorporate various stories, perspectives, and voices into the narratives of her consecutive books. Her belief in the spatial attributes of time may also explain why life, as she presents it, becomes especially interesting when people travel, through time and space; indeed, constant movement is the central theme of *Bieguni* (Runners), the novel that earned Tokarczuk the prestigious NIKE literary award for best Polish book published in 2007. Gauche also learns as he travels after leaving the convent. One of his lessons, which is imparted also to Tokarczuk's readers, is that, as the author puts it, people carry their time within themselves, and that all people who carry fragmented time are identical, however different they look from the outside. While gaining a better understanding of the idea of time, Gauche also starts to realize the meaning of difference, and he later discovers that binary oppositions and the culturally imposed evaluations inscribed on them are misleading. When he sees what is presented to him as the perfect human body, for instance, he recognizes that it is different from the bodies he sees around him, partly because it is neither male nor female. For Tokarczuk the body, just like time and space, is yet another construct. Some of her characters are able to overcome their bodily limitations, as exemplified by the man who breastfeeds a newborn child in *Gra na wielu bębenkach* (Playing on Many Drums, 2001), or by Kumernis, the saint depicted by Paschalis (another character with a conflicted body) in *Dom dzienny, dom nocny* (House of Day, House of Night, 1998). For Kumeris, the transformation of a woman into a man is a gift from God and a sign of her sainthood. As Tokarczuk's readers learn in *The Journey of the Book-People*, the body's limitations and imperfections lay in its origin. Members of a secret society searching for the book believe that "in the beginning God created the universe from a broken letter. Out of a broken word the body spilled out, like blood. *Body* is an imperfect word."[3]

Tokarczuk's interest in language is reflected in her extraordinary sensitivity to singular words and her intricate phrasing. Her quest for a perspective that is not conditioned by a gendered position manifests itself in narrators who escape binary oppositions. Her *House of Day, House of Night* begins as follows:

> The first night I had a dream. I dreamed I was pure sight, without a body or a name. I was suspended high above a valley at some undefined point from which I could see everything. I could move around my field of vision, yet remain in the same place … I could see a valley with a house standing in the middle of it, but it wasn't my house, or my valley, because nothing belonged to me. I didn't even belong to myself. There was no such thing as "I."[4]

In *Anna In and the Tombs of the World*, a contemporary version of the myth of the Sumerian goddess Inanna, Tokarczuk once again constructs a narrator without a body or a name. She confronts her readers with the issue of time here as well, although the question is now more clearly tied to linguistic expression. As she points out, the words future (*przyszłość*) and past (*przeszłość*) are almost identical in Polish: "In the language in which I write the future and the past differ only by one vowel. E transforms into Y and this sounds like a calling."[5] Tokarczuk also understands, however, that we can only speak within the constraints of the language available to us and that the basic structures of language align most valued concepts with the male.

Acknowledging that the female is repressed in language and that "there is a lack of words for the most important things,"[6] Tokarczuk reveals the flaws that exist within language and attempts to fill these linguistic gaps with new structures that validate female positions and experiences. She articulates this most clearly when she writes:

> I thought about words which are unjust perhaps because they originate in an unequal, sloppily divided world. How can you say to a woman: "be a man," "take it like a man"? "Be a woman," "take it like a woman"?! How can you describe in a woman that unnamed virtue?[7]

Superiority of the symbolic over the semiotic, to use Julia Kristeva's terminology, explains other aspects of the exclusion of women from language that emerge in Tokarczuk's novels. The psychological dimension of her literary texts, which is easily linked to her fascination with Carl Jung, helps her develop her own style of *écriture féminine.* In *House of Day, House of Night*, she illustrates the issue of creating a suitable language to express non-patriarchal approaches to reality through the character of Paschalis. In an endeavour to write about Kumernis, the legendary woman saint, Tokarczuk's narrator notes:

> It seemed to him that it would not only be important to write about what happened and to name the entire configuration of events and deeds. It would be equally important, and maybe even more important to leave a place and space for that which never was, that which never actually occurred, but only could have occurred – it was enough that it was imagined.[8]

The narration in *Anna In and the Tombs of the World* resembles a form of incantation, with short recurring sentences like "I, every woman, a storyteller," "I, every man, a storyteller" interspersed throughout the narrative. In other words, Tokarczuk employs various attributes of prosody such as tone, stress, and rhythm – that is, modes characteristic of what Kristeva calls the semiotic. In a similar vein, *Ostatnie historie* (The Last Stories,

2004) is comprised of three narrations, all delivered by women and all revolving around a central theme of the impossibility of conveying the experience of death. Their fragmented narrations are filled with gaps, silences, and omissions.

Like other Polish women writers of her generation, such as Izabela Filipiak (b. 1961), Manuela Gretkowska (b. 1964), Inga Iwasiów, Natasza Goerke (b. 1960), and Joanna Bator (b. 1968), Tokarczuk broke with what German Ritz described as the traditional, limited spectrum of female roles in Polish literature, and has created a variety of female characters.[9] Though she does not openly push a political feminist agenda (as Manuela Gretkowska does, for example), she is constantly opposing what is symbolically marked as male – the centre, the public realm, reason, knowledge, and progress – with what is symbolically considered female – the margins, the private realm, intuition, imagination, and circular time. In fact, Tokarczuk tries to escape traditional categorizations altogether; the place inhabited by her characters always serves as the centre of the world. At the beginning of *Prawiek i inne czasy* (Primeval and Other Times, 1996), the narrator states simply that "Primeval is a place located in the center of the universe."[10] As the reader learns through Tokarczuk's other novels, however, the centre is a fluid concept that changes location as people migrate, travel, move houses, and grow old. *House of Day, House of Night*, in turn, challenges another ingrained binary idea – namely, that of gendered private and public spaces. First, Tokarczuk substitutes them with another binary by pointing out differences between the real and virtual (television) worlds. "When you don't watch TV, the whole world ... seems to be completely feminine," observes her narrator, immediately adding:

> Women sell food in stores, organize meetings, shop with their children, fill the buses to Nowa Ruda and back, cut hair, arrange evening get-togethers, kiss on both cheeks, smell nice, try on clothes in stores, sell phone cards at the post office, deliver letters written by women which are read by other women.[11]

What begins as an enumeration of activities becomes a stream of fragments that sum up the everyday lives of women in the little town of Nowa Ruda. Constructing her own *écriture féminine*, Tokarczuk departs from the linear and orderly characteristics of traditional discourse in her observations and descriptions, building a different mode of narration; she breaks with the symbolically male logic, replacing it with what appears on the surface to be various fragmented and disorganized observations.

Kinga Dunin writes about *Księgi Jakubowe* (The Books of Jacob): "The protagonist of Olga Tokarczuk's magnificent new novel, Jacob Frank, was a real historical figure, though all but forgotten. Yet Frank was a fascinating and enigmatic man whose fortunes are connected with many places in Europe and beyond. It's hard to believe that lots of novels haven't been written about him, or lots of films made – but the reality is that Jacob Frank is known only to a few scholars. He lived in the eighteenth century, when history began to speed up, as the French Revolution approached, and the currents of the Enlightenment were on the rise. The mystical religiosity of this Jewish heretic, considered the last Messiah, while it may seem particular to its day, also contributed to the demolition of the old structures and divisions between Jews and practitioners of other religions. In the mid-eighteenth century several

thousand of his followers, under the auspices of the Polish king and nobility, converted to Catholicism. It was not their first conversion: they had already become Muslim, too."
http://www.bookinstitute.pl/ksiazki-detal,literatura-polska,9926,the-books-of-jacob.html

By presenting the illusive nature of all socially and culturally constructed boundaries in her consecutive collections of short stories, essays, and novels – including the recently published *Księgi Jakubowe* (The Books of Jacob, 2014), for which she received the prestigious literary NIKE award once again, in 2015 – Tokarczuk draws the reader's attention to the ultimate arbitrariness and fluidity of social constructs. She validates perspectives and problems that have traditionally been relegated to the margins, all the while evading thematic or identity-based critical categories. Moreover, her writing has contributed to the gradual erosion of those categories and to their waning use in critical discourses in Poland today. The mythical tone of Tokarczuk's writing and her ability to escape classifications while achieving both ongoing critical acclaim and commercial success are yet further reasons why she is considered one of Poland's most interesting and important contemporary authors.

Bożena Karwowska
University of British Columbia

NOTES

1 Tokarczuk, *Podróż ludzi księgi*, 8. Translation mine.
2 Ibid.
3 Ibid.
4 Tokarczuk, *House of Day, House of Night*, 1.
5 Tokarczuk, *Anna In w grobowcach świata*, 7. "Nie obchodzi mnie czas, tyle razy wywiódł nas w pole. W języku, w którym piszę, przeszłość i przyszłość różnią się tylko jedną samogłoską. E przechodzi w Y i brzmi to jak zawołanie." Translation mine.
6 Tokarczuk, *House of Day, House of Night,* 259–60.
7 Translation from Paleczek, "Olga Tokarczuk's *House of Day, House of Night,*" 55. Tokarczuk, *Dom dzienny, dom nocny*, 104.
8 Translation from Paleczek, "Olga Tokarczuk's *House of Day, House of Night,*" 50. Quotation from Tokarczuk, *Dom dzienny, dom nocny*, 114.
9 See Ritz, "Dyskurs płci w ujęciu porównawczym."
10 Tokarczuk, *Primeval and Other Times*, 9.
11 Translation from Paleczek, "Olga Tokarczuk's *House of Day, House of Night,*" 49–50. Quotation from Tokarczuk, *Dom dzienny, dom nocny*, 103–4.

WORKS CITED

Paleczek, Urszula. "Olga Tokarczuk's *House of Day, House of Night*: Gendered Language in Feminist Translation." *Canadian Slavonic Papers* 52, nos. 1–2 (March–June 2010): 47–57.

Ritz, German. "Dyskurs płci w ujęciu porównawczym." Translated by Małgorzata Łukasiewicz. *Teksty Drugie* 4 (1999): 117–23.

Tokarczuk, Olga. *Anna In w grobowcach świata.* Kraków: Znak, 2006.

– *Dom dzienny, dom nocny.* Wałbrzych: Ruta, 1998.

– *House of Day, House of Night.* Translated by Antonia Lloyd-Jones. Evanston: Northwestern University Press, 2003.

– *Podróż ludzi księgi.* Warszawa: Przedświt, 1993.

– *Primeval and Other Times.* Translated by Antonia Lloyd-Jones. Prague: Twisted Spoon Press, 2010.

Alternative Cartographies (Andrzej Stasiuk)

Andrzej Stasiuk (b. 1960) is one of the most interesting Polish authors among those who debuted after the political watershed of 1989. His characteristic style of prose, which oscillates around three main themes – masculine identity, travel, and Central European space – makes his writing easily recognizable after only a few sentences. At the same time, his work is representative of a generation of Polish writers who came of age in the waning phase of postwar socialism. These writers stood at a distance from both the one-time communist regime and its patriotic opposition, and – during the period of democratic transformation – were critical of neoliberal capitalism's victorious march through the former Eastern Bloc countries. Stasiuk's first book, a collection of prison tales titled *Mury Hebronu* (Walls of Hebron, 1992), attracted the attention of critics not only because of its subject matter, but also due to its literary language, which combines stark descriptions of prison existence with refined epigrams and poetic irony. The title of Stasiuk's debut volume refers to his personal experience: at the beginning of the 1980s, still during the time of the Polish People's Republic, he had spent a year and a half in prison for desertion from the army. In 1986 he left his hometown of Warsaw and settled in the Beskids, a mountainous province along Poland's southeastern boundary, close to the border with Slovakia and Ukraine. The author's biographical trials and tribulations, his decision to settle far from the centres of literary life, and his unceasing travels have all inscribed themselves onto his literary self-creation as a rebel, an outsider, and an alcohol-inclined author of strong, masculine prose. In *Jak zostałem pisarzem (próba biografii intelektualnej)* (How I Became a Writer [An Attempt at an Intellectual Biography, 1998]), Stasiuk approached both the genre of literary autobiography and his own authorial myth with irony, denuding it of all heroism. The quality and uniqueness of Stasiuk's prose arises from contrasting and often unexpected connections. Among the characteristics of his style are the combination of bold themes with subtle, poetic language; the merger of exposition that verges on gender or ethnic stereotypes with self-ironic reflection and melancholic sensitivity; and the blending of programmatic repetition of themes and motifs (among them male friendship and travelling through the same landscapes) with a richness of observation and sophisticated means of description.

Stasiuk's output oscillates between literary fiction (such as the novel *Dziewięć* [Nine, 1999], a story about a mafia-entangled small-time entrepreneur set in Warsaw of the 1990s); autobiographically tinged narrations (such as the Beskids-based short story collection *Dukla* [1997]); and travel essays (including *Jadąc do Babadag* [On the Road to Babadag, 2004]). His narratives, which are always rooted in concrete realities and true topographies and contain links to the author's own life story even when they are not openly autobiographic, nevertheless go beyond a realistic mode of representation. They incorporate lyrical descriptions, poetic shorthand, and metaphors that sometimes transform themselves into hallucinatory phantasmagoria, or even fantasy (such as the ghost of the murderer wandering through the village in *Opowieści galicyjskie* [Tales of Galicia, 1995]). Fantastical motifs appear also in his plays – yet another mode of the author's artistic expression – as seen in *Noc czyli słowiańsko-germańska tragifarsa medyczna* (Night, or a Slavo-Germanic Medical Tragifarse, 2005). Extraordinarily sensual and suggestive descriptions of space, especially of the topography of the East-Central European provinces, are an identifying mark of Stasiuk's prose. His inventive metaphors for sensory perception have revitalized landscape description in Polish literature. His melancholic geography rests on description of the perceptible and is realized in essayistic travel narrations:

> The day after, I had to be in Baia Mare, which once was called Nagybánya. I had to sniff out that incessant *once*, which, where I live, is the present, because tomorrow never arrives; it remains in distant countries. Our tomorrow is seduced by their allure, bribed, or possibly just tired. Whatever is to come never gets here; it gets used up en route, flickers out like the light from a lantern too far away. A perpetual decline reigns here, and children are born exhausted … Men stand on street corners staring at the emptiness of the day. They spit on the sidewalk and smoke cigarettes. That's the present. That's how it is in the town of Sabinov, in the town of Gorlice, Gönc, Caransebeş, in the whole region between the Black Sea and the Baltic. They stand and count the cigarettes in the packs and the change in their pockets. Time, approaching from afar, is like the air that someone else has already breathed.[1]

Gender According to Men

Stasiuk's prose, especially in his books from the 1990s – *The Walls of Hebron*, *Biały kruk* (White Raven, 1995) *Przez rzekę* (Across the River, 1996), and *Dukla* – is considered to be exceptionally masculine, somewhat reminiscent of the atmosphere of Charles Bukowski's fiction. Its protagonists – often social outsiders – value the freedom of travel, male friendships, and alcoholic excess. There are only a few female characters in his writing, and they function primarily as objects of male desire. Male immaturity is another theme in Stasiuk's work. In *Dukla*, for example, memories of cigarette butts tossed by adult men and smoked by young boys serve as a particular kind of initiation into masculinity: "Our spit mingled with the spit of men. It may well have acted like a vaccine, as a kind of existential homeopathy, protecting us from a too abrupt fall into adulthood."[2] Stasiuk's narrations are always presented from a gendered, masculine, and heterosexual perspective, albeit one that is not infrequently underpinned by homoeroticism in the intense, also physical closeness of male protagonists. Thus his prose rides the 1990s wave of Polish literature concerned with sexual identity, a wave most visible in feminist writing – for example, that of Izabela Filipiak (b. 1961) or Manuela Gretkowska (b. 1964). Stasiuk's narration appears to be the masculine equivalent of the feminine narrations that were explicitly articulated in the 1990s and that explored the problematic of sexuality and gender identity, often resorting to the grotesque. This masculine version of literature fascinated by gender and experimenting with its literary representation tips over through excess towards deconstruction both in Stasiuk's prose and in the work of the mentioned feminist authors. For example, in *Across the River*, Stasiuk condenses codified literary clichés and almost archaic *topoi* of heterosexual masculinity to the point that they break down into two symptomatic, delirious fantasies: one of a homosexual encounter in a state of alcoholic intoxication, and the other of the narrator's fight with a woman in a pub cellar. This hyperbolization and exaggeration of masculinity also exposes gender performance. Stasiuk is aware of cultural gender clichés, and his heroes cannot necessarily be counted among the literary macho men – they experience their masculinity too intensely and without triumphalism. Moreover, the images of stereotypical masculinity are too closely followed by ones of pitiful, even ridiculous masculinity. The theme of sexuality subsides in Stasiuk's prose towards the end of the 1990s, although sensitivity to gender and to the masculine point of view remains an identifying mark. It is displaced by new, obsessively recurring and intertwined themes: of travel and of the East-Central European space during the time of the post-communist transformation.

Travelling and Writing: Geography Replacing History

Travel is the principal means of existence for the heroes of Stasiuk's prose, but theirs are not far-reaching journeys to unknown destinations. To the contrary: the protagonists of Stasiuk's prose – like the author himself – are constantly moving (driving, roaming) through terrains known to them, around Warsaw, the Beskid Mountains, and the East-Central European provinces. Travelling in Stasiuk's books is on principle a wandering and a circling about, a constant returning to the same places. His accounts of it, therefore, also depart from linear narration and continuity, becoming entangled in returns and repetitions. It is in this manner that a group of friends wander through the Beskids in *White Raven*, and it is in this manner that the author himself travels around, avoiding large cities, when describing the East-Central European provinces in "Dziennik okrętowy" (Logbook, 2000), in *On the Road to Babadag*, and in *Dziennik pisany później* (Journal Written Later, 2010). Stasiuk does not write his travel accounts as they happen; his essayistic books are journeys from memory. Recalling and contemplating images from his travels sets the rhythm of narration. His ways of storytelling are derived not only from his ways of travelling, but also from the way memory functions as the images and events it registers break free from chronology and logical sequence.

The debate about Central Europe: During the 1980s, "Eastern Bloc" émigré writers carried on a discussion about the cultural belonging of countries that became Soviet satellite states after the Second World War, such as Poland, Czechoslovakia, and Hungary.

This debate was initiated by the 1983 essay "Un Occident kidnappé" (A Kidnapped West) by the Czech writer Milan Kundera, published in the French periodical *Le débat*. Kundera underlined the historical ties between Central Europe and the West, as well as the cultural specificity of Central Europe, which was cut off from the West by the Cold War political border. Other important participants in this debate included Györgi Konrád (Hungary), Danilo Kiš (former Yugoslavia), and Czesław Miłosz (Poland).

Interestingly, Stasiuk links his way of travelling as well as of writing directly to the nature of the spaces through which he journeys: to the topography of East-Central Europe, which, according to him, is synonymous with disorder, decay, and stagnation. This is conveyed in numerous suggestive descriptions, such as the above-cited passage from the collection of essayist travels *On the Road to Babadag*. According to Stasiuk, the space he describes is resistant to historical discourse and diachronic inspection: "Neglect is the essence of this region. History, deeds, consequences, ideas, and plans dissolve into the landscape … A long narrative about the spirit of the times … seems a project as pathetic as it is pretentious, like a novel written from the point of view of God."[3] Stasiuk's passion is thus geography rather than history. More than that: geography allows him to break free of history, which the author sees as the curse of the twentieth century. His topography of the East-Central European provinces presents a landscape of stillness and duration – the antithesis of modernity's historical thought, which is oriented to the future, towards development and progress. Stasiuk's literary topography inscribes itself onto the Eastern European version of literary postmodernism shaped in reaction to the political turning point of 1989. The dissolution of the Eastern Bloc and of the binary order of global politics was received in this part of Europe as "the end of history" primarily in the sense of it being an end of a modernity that had been depraved by totalitarianism and authoritarianism. The turn towards geography and the parting with history, and the related poetics of non-linear, fragmentary travelogue in Stasiuk's prose, constitute one of the clearest conceptualizations of literary postmodernism in Polish literature.

Stasiuk as a Cartographer of the *Other* Europe

Stasiuk's essayistic journeys can be included in a new – not only Polish – current of literary topography that is inspired by real geographical space and that underscores the performative character of its own literary creation, balancing on the border of autobiography, factography, and poetic invention. It is not an accident that this prose appeared in East-Central European literatures after 1989, with the freedom of travel and voluntary migrations and with changes to Europe's political geography (the dissolution of the Soviet Union and expansion of the European Union) that rapidly transformed the map of the continent. In his essays, Stasiuk creates a very suggestive vision of the regions between Russia and Germany, which encompass countries that prior to the political watershed were satellites of the Soviet Union. Stasiuk's literary cartography is a project of an *other* Europe – a transnational region that is different from Western Europe in sharing the collective experience of the communist experiment. As the cartographer of the *other Europe*, Stasiuk assigns clear borders to its territories – boundaries that are primarily mental, independent of both limitations to and freedom of movement in this part of the continent. In "Logbook," the author used a compass to demarcate the sphere of his "private" Europe, with a radius of 300 kilometres from his place of residence in the Beskids, which includes parts of Poland, Ukraine, Slovakia, and Hungary. In the essays in *On the Road to Babadag*, Stasiuk expanded "his" territory to include Romania, Moldavia, the former Yugoslavia, and Albania. His looped travels territorialize this space, assigning its virtual but mentally impregnable borders in the East (Russia) as well as in the West (Germany). The book dedicated to Stasiuk's travels to Germany, *Dojczland* (Deutschland, 2007), only confirms his construction of a "private" Europe. In it, the author provocatively presents himself as a literary *Gastarbeiter* who travels to Germany for purely economic reasons, while the country itself appears as a cold, soulless *non lieu* (not place) that resists poetic description. Stasiuk counterposes East-Central and Western Europe following the relation between a periphery and a centre. He calls it an "international wasteland,"[4] since it processes goods and ideas already used up in the West; in this way, he relates it to the centre through parodist mimicry. At the same time, the East's otherness is threatened by the spread of Western norms. Stasiuk's literary construction is thus, on the one hand, a nostalgic vision of obsolescent landscapes of old (non-modern) Europe, and on the other, an attempt to grasp this Europe's hybrid status as revealed in its specific sourcing and processing of Western models during a period of transformation. The background of Stasiuk's project of the *other* Europe echoes the discussions about the positioning of Central Europe held by Eastern European political emigrants during the 1980s. These debates reminded Western Europe of its affiliations with sovietized Central European countries. Today, Stasiuk contrarily opposes these regions to not only Russia, but also Western Europe, underscoring their distinctiveness, which is visible not only in their economic dependence on Western Europe, but also in a certain refractory quality of their cultures. From the standpoint of postcolonial theories, Stasiuk effectuates a specific self-orientalization of East-Central Europe as a post-imperial (post-Soviet) province subjected to the dominance of a Western European centre. Reaching even deeper into the past, one can hear in Stasiuk's prose echoes of the Old Polish, Sarmatian vision of the cultural separateness of this part of Europe, grasped in the Baroque concept of *Western Easternness and Eastern Westernness.*

Magdalena Marszałek
University of Potsdam
Translated by Agnieszka Polakowska

NOTES

1 Stasiuk, *On the Road to Babadag*, 67.
2 Stasiuk, *Dukla*, 95.
3 Stasiuk, *On the Road to Babadag*, 44–5.
4 Ibid., 205.

WORKS CITED

Stasiuk, Andrzej. *Mury Hebronu*. Warszawa: Wydawnictwo Głodnych Duchów, 1992.
– *Biały kruk*. Poznań: Biblioteka Czasu Kultury, 1994.
– *Opowieści galicyjskie*. Kraków: Znak, 1995.
– *Przez rzekę*. Gładyszów: Czarne, 1996.
– *Jak zostałem pisarzem (próba biografii intelektualnej)*. Gładyszów: Czarne, 1998.
– *Dziewięć*. Gładyszów: Czarne, 1999.
– *Noc, czyli słowiańsko-germańska tragifarsa medyczna*. Wołowiec: Czarne, 2005.
– *Dojczland*. Wołowiec: Czarne, 2007.
– *Dziennik pisany później*. Wołowic: Czarne, 2010.
– *On the Road to Babadag*. Translated by Michael Kandel. Boston and New York: Houghton Mifflin Harcourt, 2011.
– *Dukla*. Translated by Bill Johnston. Champaign: Dalkey Archive Press, 2011.
Stasiuk, Andrzej, and Jurij Andruchowycz. "Dziennik okrętowy." In *Moja Europa. Dwa eseje o Europie zwanej Środkową*. 75–140. Wołowiec: Czarne, 2000.

INTERWAR, WAR, POSTWAR, AND POST-1989 POETRY

Polish Twentieth-Century Poetry

Marjorie Perloff in the introduction to one of her best-known books writes that early-twentieth-century literature still has much to tell us at the beginning of the twenty-first. Her words can also serve as an introduction to this brief history of twentieth-century Polish poetry:

> Now that the long twentieth century is finally behind us, perhaps we can begin to see this embryonic phase with new eyes. Far from being irrelevant and obsolete, the aesthetic of early modernism has provided the seeds of the materialist poetic which is increasingly our own – a poetic that seems much more attuned to the readymades, the "delays" in glass and verbal enigmas of Marcel Duchamp, to the non-generic, non-representational texts of Gertrude Stein, and to the sound and visual poems, the poem-manifestos and artist's books of Velimir Khlebnikov than to the authenticity model – the "true voice of feeling" or "natural speech" paradigm – so dominant in the sixties and seventies.[1]

Today, Polish critics speak of ("late") modernism more willingly than of postmodernism, and young poets still draw on the early avant-garde, both in their linguistic experiments and in their social engagement. From their perspective, doing so has several significant advantages: in looking towards the avant-garde tradition, they cannot be accused of traditionalism; they can escape the dominance of feeling and empathy while indulging their passion for demystification; they can argue that poetry is useful and still insist of art's autonomy; and they can link their poems to contemporary political discourses on their own terms. As a consequence, tradition ceases to be a matter of nostalgia or resentment and becomes worthy of attention once again.

In discussions about poetic traditions, it is the term "tradition" that causes the most problems. Its meaning is not clear either to those who view poetry as the mouthpiece and guardian of "imponderabilities," or to those who see the poem mainly as "an event in language." The first group of artists includes Jarosław Iwaszkiewicz (1894–1980), Czesław Miłosz (1911–2004), Zbigniew Herbert (1924–98), and Adam Zagajewski (b. 1945) – poets who still long for a culture in which poetry is either a collectively experienced ideal, or a means to share the author's intimate experience, or a way to transform the world back into a home. The second group, which includes Julian Przyboś (1901–70), Miron Białoszewski (1922–83), Krystyna Miłobędzka (b. 1932), and Piotr Sommer (b. 1948), approaches the poem as a distinct space that need not be part of a discourse and need not directly influence reality. Both groups have a strong sense that the ground on which they have based their respective positions is shifting. In this context, a retro–avant-gardist "poem-object," which is constructed from the substance of words or critically reproduces the spectacle of the contemporary world, seems more modern and less pretentious than a poem seen as the voice of God or of a nation, or even as the poet's inner voice.

Yet it would be a gross oversimplification to conclude that the twentieth-century history of Polish poetry is simply about a conflict between the avant-garde and traditionalism. The avant-garde provided a strong impulse and remains an important point of reference for Polish poetry, but in the final analysis, the role it played and continues to play is a form of insurance against aesthetic straightforwardness rather than a constant horizon of inquiry and a guarantee of artistic autonomy. Polish poetry drew its authority from its capacity to answer the challenges of history and to inure the time-pressed human being to a symbolic homelessness. Its linguistic and autotelic aspects, its search for and creation of languages of modernity, and its utopism and engagement in the future, functioned paradoxically, acting both as a harness for an (over)simplified metaphysics and as a stimulus for reflection about the nature and expressions of poeticism. The avant-garde never disowned tradition and was itself several times renounced for extended periods of time. Yet it is difficult to imagine the poetry of Czesław Miłosz without studying Józef Czechowicz (1903–39), or that of Tadeusz Różewicz (1921–2014) and Zbigniew Herbert without looking at Julian Przyboś, or Wisława Szymborska's (1923–2012) and Krystyna Miłobędzka's poetic practive without a lesson on constructivism, or that of Ryszard Krynicki (b. 1943) without Tadeusz Peiper's work.

To attain a coherent view of Polish twentieth-century poetry, one must consider a number of fundamental issues (along with their arbitrariness), including (1) the most important ideological and aesthetic formations; (2) attitude towards community – solidarity versus solitude; (3) strong and independent poets; (4) breakthroughs and crises; and (5) the canon, continuity, and discontinuity. These themes provide the canvas of this essay.

Without delving too deeply into the countless debates and controversies surrounding the definition of modernity, it is enough to state here that in the Polish context that definition rests on three pillars – the avant-garde, Romanticism, and Classicism. In this configuration, the avant-garde is a new force, while twentieth-century Classicism and Romanticism reference the great Old Polish and Romantic traditions of the past. Obviously, the latter are not continuations of Romanticism or (even more so) of some hidden form of nineteenth-century Classicism. Rather, they are the result of choices made among values preserved in cultural memory, the manifestations of a differently understood subjectivity of the artist, and a different means of putting creative freedom to good use. In this sense, the twentieth century begins for Polish poetry around 1910, a time when the artistic current of Young Poland – a result of the overlapping of Romanticism and naturalism, to explain it most simply – performed an analysis of its own aims and achievements through the works of Stanisław Brzozowski (1878–1911) and Karol Irzykowski (1873–1944).

Some of Young Poland's representatives, of course, for instance Leopold Staff (1878–1957) and Bolesław Leśmian (1877–1937), continued to play a prominent role after the current had run its course. Leśmian in particular is still considered to be one of the greatest poets in the history of the Polish language; he is admired for his craft, imagination, linguistic invention, extreme idiomaticity, creative independence and uniqueness, and philosophical originality, as well as for his discovery and articulation of non-being and his fusion of high and popular (folk) culture. According to some scholars, it was he who, along with Bruno Schulz (1892–1944) and Stanisław Ignacy Witkiewicz (1885–1939), brought about a revolutionary change in Polish literature, ushering it permanently into modernity.[2] The key issue for Leśmian was no longer poeticism, the daughter of emotion, nor was it realism – the congruence of language and the world – nor was it ethicism – the monitoring of the relation between the everyday and the authoritative word, or between the word and something supposedly immutable and antecedent to it. For him, the core concern was all that extended beyond the world, beyond life, beyond law and all that is visible, capable of being experienced, given, and imagined. This is evident in "Pierwsza schadzka" (First Rendezvous), for instance, a remarkable poem that describes a meeting between ghosts that still bear traces of their previous forms but are already profoundly different, incomprehensible, and for this reason lonely:

> Our first tryst beyond the grave. Nothing bars the entrance.
> Find your footing carefully … Kiss the wayside vine.
> Is that – you? – already changed, and still – no difference?
> My eyes are dim … Give me hold! … Your hand, as for a sign!
>
> There are no signs! They've long since scattered past their meaning!
> No holds left to hold onto – no one believes in yours or mine ...
> The laughter has faded into dark; they're finished with their keening.
> Cobwebs in the corners make a cozy nest – for time …
>
> Part the way – to moths and blossoms! ... Turn from fancy distances …
> Perhaps the realest thing is this – hay before us strewn …
> Why do you cry? – To those immersed in their existences,
> Our pain – amounts to less than shimmering bands of moon.[3]

I. The Avant-garde and Neighbouring Areas

The avant-garde and modernism have been identified with or separated from each other to various degrees at various times. Faced as we are with a surplus of ways to order the history of literature, and the difficulties each way brings, a categorical approach is necessary. Accordingly, in the context of this discussion the terms *modernism* and *avant-garde* are related, with the first having a superordinate status and the latter actualizing a large part of modernism's basic determinants:

> A prominent feature of modernism is the phenomenon called the avant-garde … that is, a small, self-conscious group of artists and authors who deliberately undertake, in Ezra Pound's phrase, to "make it new." By violating the accepted conventions and proprieties, not only of art but of social discourse, they set out to create ever-new artistic forms and styles and to introduce hitherto neglected, and sometimes forbidden, subject matter.[4]

The Polish avant-garde, for all of its internal diversification and conflicts, branches into two main currents: anarchical (Futurism) and constructivist (the circle of the Kraków periodical *Zwrotnica* [The Switch]). Futurism was a subject of interest in Poland almost as soon as it appeared in Italy (on Filippo Marinetti's initiative) and, soon after that, in other countries, first and foremost Russia. The conditions that were necessary for its full emergence in Poland developed only after the First World War and the restoration of Poland's sovereignty, however. It became a symptom of the same euphoria that swept over Poland's young generation (and not only them) at this time, regardless of political or artistic world view. It was finally possible to step out of the shadow cast by the hero of Adam Mickiewicz's great drama, *Dziady* (Forefathers' Eve), and to throw off "Konrad's coat," as Antoni Słonimski put it in the poem "Czarna wiosna" (Black Spring, 1919). It was now possible to stop prioritizing national matters over artistic ones; to engage in literature as literature; to provide readers with experiences either previously unknown or viewed as secondary, such as the simple pleasure of reading; and, finally, to take up themes that previously had been either absent or dismissed (such as civilization, the city, the everyday, and the average human being). This euphoria was experienced in common, although the languages it spoke were diverse.

According to Bruno Jasieński, poetry's standard conventions had been depleted, an opinion he illustrates in "But w butonierce" (Shoe in a Buttonhole, 1921), a poem with an ego-futuristic provenance. From Jasieński's perspective, it was simply too easy to write in the manner of the Young Poland poets (e.g., Kazimierz Tetmajer and Leopold Staff), or as the Romantics once did, and as those who followed old conventions still did. It was easy to show off one's fluency of versification, to multiply often used schemata, and to join the ranks of writers whose relationship with readers could be described as mutually unproductive. Jasieński thus mocked the existing literary hierarchy and the tendency to treat poetry as an object for girls' to swoon over. He also mocked respect for a past that did not understand the present and he proclaimed the coming of new authors, social and poetic climates, as well as lyrical and lifestyle customs. He devalued the principles of traditional poetry, replacing them with the rule of unexpected, suprising associations, as exemplified by the "shoe in the buttonhole" (the word play is more apparent in Polish, where the word for shoe is "but," which is actually "found" in the "**but**onierka" – and, indeed, in the "buttonhole"). In addition to all this, verbal and situational nonsense became permissible, and voice was given to reality that had something new to say rather than to stagnant literature.

Polish Futurism developed around two centres: Kraków, which from the beginning approached programmatic tasks with seriousness; and Warsaw, where the initial aim was simply to pull down the garish decorations that concealed what art should directly reveal – vital and ludic values. The Kraków formation, represented mainly by Jasieński, Tytus Czyżewski (1880–1945), and Stanisław Młodożeniec (1895–1959), grew out of the "Formists," a group of painters, philosophers, mathematicians, and literary figures founded in 1917–18 by Andrzej and Zbigniew Pronaszko (respectively: 1888–1961 and 1885–1958), Leon Chwistek (1884–1944), Jacek Mierzejewski (1883–1925), and Stanisław Ignacy Witkiewicz, among others. They shared an aversion to naturalistic representation, a belief in the artist's right to unbridled imagination, and a preoccupation with the issue of form. This last preoccupation led to various results, from Wikiewicz's theory of "pure form" to Chwistek's theory of "the plurality of realities." The "poeticism" of Young Poland's poetry was also abandoned: "The discursive principle, descriptiveness, along with symbolic imagination and the evocation of moods – were discarded … The model Formist work was an arbitrary arrangement of diverse fragments of reality, similarly to how a painting was a division of the world into different, mutually interpenetrating planes."[5]

All of this is apparent in Czyżewski's famous "Hymn do maszyny mego ciała" (Hymn to the Machine of My Body ,1920). The poem's graphic layout poses a surprising dilemma for the recipient – should the work be read, or should it be looked at? Or should it perhaps be solved, like a riddle or a mathematical puzzle? The poet is aiming to disorient readers, and most of all to surprise them, by deaesthetisizing and demythologizing the body, by reducing its sacred "essence" – the spiritual "mystery" it supposedly encloses – to an internalized logic of engineering, biology, and chemistry, and by employing an exalted form to express a dynamic content. Notably, this work simultaneously directs us *outward*, towards the negated tradition of poetry that sentimentally poses questions of identity, and *inward*, towards oneself as something that does not necessarily only "mean" but also independently "is." It is a material, graphic, and phonic object, a construction raised on some chosen *a priori* principle.

While Czyżewski was drawn to the idea of making poems more like paintings, Aleksander Wat (1900–67) – who belonged to the Warsaw contingent along with Anatol Stern (1899–1968) and Adam Ważyk (1905–82) – explored the acoustic qualities of language. His "Namopanik Barwistanu" (1920) is characterized by a far-reaching destruction of words in such a way that the reader's (listener's?) attention focuses on their phonetic aspect instead of on what they signify. They are so greatly transformed, however, that they can be treated as allusions to words in the forms in which we use them, first of all, and, second, to something that precedes language as we know it – the mother-speech of contemporary Slavic languages. The poem carries out a liberation from the bondage of logic and syntax – a liberation postulated by the Futurists. It does not, however, lead to movement beyond language; indeed, to the contrary, it leads to a descent into proto-Slavic depths. It is worth noting here, moreover, another trace of the futuristic splitting into two directions – on the one hand urban, civilizational, marked by fascination with mass, speed, and competition, and on the other primitivistic, leaning towards the low (folk, magical, pagan) roots of culture.

The first summary of the Futurists' activities came very quickly; in 1923, Bruno Jasieński published "Futuryzm polski (bilans)" (Polish Futurism [Balance Sheet]). This short essay begins with the assertion that "Futurism is a form of collective consciousness that must be overcome. I am no longer a Futurist, meanwhile all of you are Futurists." The author further emphasizes the specific (so he believed) achievement of the movement he had led – an organic approach to the machine. For Jasieński the machine is not, as it was in the case of the Italian Futurists, a fetishized model and examplar, nor is it – as it was in the Russian version – only "the product and servant of man"; rather, it becomes a "new organ" of a human being. As Jasieński wrote, "Polish Futurism taught the modern man to see in the objects produced by civilization the beauty of our own enhanced body."[6] In articulating this opinion, he came close to Tadeusz Peiper (1891–1969), who summarized and analysed the Futurists' program and poetics in the same issue of *The Switch*, although much more critically. There, Peiper lists some of the characteristics of Futurism – its active, destructive attitude towards the past ("fight with the museum"), its materialism ("a poetics of molecules and electrons"), its demolition of syntax and logic, and its dynamism. In characterizing Marinetti's approach to the machine, he polemically underscores that it is not the material side of technology that is of interest, but the human being – its maker and user.

AXIOLOGY OF INNOVATION

Pure negation of the "old" can be considered as an axiological quality of innovation, of course. Taking this stance depends on the negative assessment of everything that is past, traditional, and forgone ... Such an assumption accompanies many Avant-garde currents that, as a matter of fact, often quickly "burn out," as shown through the examples of Dadaism and Futurism ... "Newness" – as wrote Paul Valery – "is one of those stimulating poisons that in the end become more necessary than all nourishment; ever since the poison took hold of us, the doses must be increased and made deadly under the threat of death."

– Stróżewski, *Dialektyka twórczości*, 337

Spectacle, performance, event, definitions of the poet as a social actor, and avant-garde poetry have become permanently fused. The *poet faber* is not simply a craftsman scrupulously working to destroy syntax or (conversely) to construct a poem in accordance with more or less generalized instructions contained in manifestos and programs, applying the unwritten rules of the artistic circle to which he belongs. The term *poet faber* points to that of *homo faber* – the human being as the creator of tools and the subject of civilization – and even to *Deus Faber*, the labouring God. Yet this creative craftsman, who has set serious artistic and social goals, and who has a sense of mission in both art and life, reveals above-average ludic leanings – this person is playing the role of an artist who shocks the bourgeois audience and – in his playfulness – has at his disposal a weapon against the indifference of the crowd and the bitter antagonism of sworn traditionalists.

Literary life in the 1920s had acquired the previously unknown character of a spectacle. It was commonplace to stylize these poets as bohemians, provocateurs, and outsiders. They could be seen in the Warsaw café "Pod Pikadorem," which began hosting evenings for young poets on 29 November 1918. The authors of the Skamander group dominated there – initially the popular Jan Lechoń, Julian Tuwim (1894–1953), and Antoni Słonimski, and later also Jarosław Iwaszkiewicz and Kazimierz Wierzyński (1894–1969). Although they were much more broadly accepted than the Futurists – Wat, Stern, and Jerzy Jankowski (1887–1941) – the latter performed at their side for a two-month period (from February and until the club's closing) on almost equal terms. Their alliance was all the more fitting since the Skamander poets viewed themselves – and were seen at the time – as subverters, destroyers of the Young Poland model, disciples of lightness, jest, and irony. They used methods of self-promotion similar to those utilized by the avant-garde – they put up posters with their poems, provoked the public, and promoted a literary lifestyle that stripped the poet of all bard-like insignia but also released him from the burden of national responsibilities. This transformation was evident in the price list for poetic services enforced at "Pod Pikadorem" (in marks): "a) normal conversation (3–5 min. long) with the right to shake hands: 50 M; b) receipt of a read poem: 75 M; c) receipt of a manuscript – without dedication: 150 M; with dedication: 500 M. Note: addition of the words 'to my beloved' – 100 M. Marriage proposals: only on Thursdays. Note 1: the poet Tuwim does not accept applications. Note 2: the remaining poets will only receive offers from interested parties with more than 75 000 M in dowry (regardless of gender, nationality, and religion)."

In provoking public opinion, the Futurists went significantly further, as is clear from, among other things, their legal difficulties. Anatol Stern was arrested in December 1919, transferred from Warsaw to Vilnius, and subsequently sentenced to a year in prison, all as a result of a few words in the poem "Uśmiech Primavery" (The Smile of Primavera), for which he was charged with blasphemy. In the end, Stern did not go to prison, but the case carried on for a very long time. The judicial system at the time was not known for its tolerance and sense of humour, and the same was true of Polish censors, who in February 1921 confiscated the almanac *Gga* published by the Stern–Wat duo late in 1920. The poetry was accused of indecency. A folded-in-half page, published by the same poetic duo in the spring of 1921 under the grandiose title "Nieśmiertelny tom futuryzm" (Immortal Volume of Futurisms), met an identical fate.

The no less colourful Niezalegalizowany Klub Futurystów Pod Katarynką (The Non-Legalized Futurists' Club under the Barrel Organ) was active in Kraków. Young poets organized numerous events there, also making incursions into Warsaw, Łódź, and other cities, and publishing almanacs and pamphlets, such as the 1921 *Jedniodniówka futurystów* (Futurists' Pamphlet) and *Nuż w bżuhu* (Nive in a Stomak). Kraków was also the home base of *The Switch*. The journal was headed by Tadeusz Peiper, the author of meticulously thought-out poetic practice models as well as a poet. According to some scholars, the avant-garde in its proper (i.e., narrow and precise) meaning was constituted by the editorial circle of *The Switch*. It is that circle that is commonly referred to now as the "Kraków Avant-garde," and its activities and the output of its members are now seen as the most intellectually mature and artistically valuable outcome of the experiments of that time.

The first series of *The Switch*, consisting of six issues, came out from May 1922 until October 1923. Since Peiper was yet to finish the outline of his poetic proposal and the journal regularly printed the work of Futurists, *The Switch* was seen as simply the innovators' forum. Its sixth issue, however, revealed its critical distance from the Futurists and presented a crystallized version of its chief editor's views. After *The Switch* folded, Peiper printed both his programmatic and poetic texts, and his young adherents – Julian Przyboś, Jan Brzękowski (1903–83), Jalu Kurek (1904–83), and Adam Ważyk – published their first volumes of poetry. By the time the next six issues of the revamped *The Switch* came out between May 1926 and December 1927, the group had been fully formed, united by its mentor's ideas, and was proud of the achievements of its individual members. When the publication folded definitively, this relatively unified formation began to disintegrate and its more recent members began to crystallize their own authorial poetics. Peiperists were transforming themselves into anti-Peiperists, defining their position in confrontation and competition with the master's conceptualizations, and this despite a degree of their continued dependence on him (although his engagement with them grew ever weaker). This factor was decisive to their sense of belonging to a single group. It can be seen in the journal *Linia* (Line), edited by Jalu Kurek from 1931 to 1933 with the help of the authors who once wrote for *The Switch*, and in Brzękowski's and Przyboś's work with the group "a.r.," which brought together painters as renowned as Władysław Strzemiński (1893–1952) and Katarzyna Kobro (1898–1951). Generally speaking, the Kraków avant-gardists, and in particular Przyboś, "carried" their ideas with them through the war and into the first postwar decade, "returning" them to Polish literature after the political and censorial thaw of 1956.

The *Switch* circle could be just as biting and hot-headed as the Futurists, as exemplified by Przyboś's controversial article "Chamuły poezji" (The Boordles of Poetry, *Zwrotnica* 7), in which he spoke against the widely respected Young Poland poet Jan Kasprowicz. The zeal of the Kraków avant-garde was different in tone, more intellectual and more seriously polemical, than that of the Futurists. It had a constructivist character, and conceived of the demand to create as "a moral task, joined to the desire of transforming reality through art, and an active concept of personality and of the role of a writer in the creative process. The place of passivity … was to be taken up by the creative will, and the uncontrolled transmission of experiences replaced by their selection."[7] It is enough to recall Peiper's often analysed poem "Noga" (Leg, 1924). From its first words, it is clear that this work must be read differently than the works of Futurists, even though the latter were not always exemplars of joyful anarchism. Language returns as a material but also as an object of adoration – it becomes a type of admired machine. It is complex, inherently modern, fertile with meaning, and creative. The poet who writes "This hymn made of silk above cruelty made of sugar" – the poem's first line – does not want to disassemble or expose language; rather, he is using its grammatical and lexical potentialities to rouse linguistic imagination into action. By developing a sentence that constantly grows more complex, he arrives at the flowering of successive connotations motivated either by the (not necessarily primary) meanings of words or by the logic of rhetorical figures (panegyric hyperboles). This outgrowth of associations from the meanings, rather than from the sounds or appearances of words, is what prevents the poem from becoming an accidental or perhaps aleatoric utterance, and also from being too literal. Admittedly, the recipient's participation is strongly assumed. But this does not equate with unlimited licence; the reader is the work's co-constructor, who in the process of "working" encounters a multiplicity of periphrases and circumlocutory terms for objects that testify to the joyous inventiveness of the poem's author.

Tadeusz Peiper was older by a few years than the other avant-garde artists and decidedly more experienced. Before the First World War, he studied in Kraków, Berlin, and Paris, spending a few years in Spain in an international company of people devoted to philosophy and art. On his return to Kraków in 1920, he sought out collaborators while presiding in cafés, in the tradition of Madrid artists. The world view of the resulting poetic school was based on several assertions. First, that culture was superior to nature – a stance at odds with the sentimental belief that primeval innocence had been despoiled by civilization, the city, and industry, and with the almost universally held view that the ideal of beauty is a work of nature. Peiper insisted that the contemporary human being is formed by civilization, on which he depends, rather than by nature, for which he naively and insincerely longs. Second, that history is evolutionary and progressive in character – an extension of positivistic and of leftist notions (which were close to the poet) about gradual emancipation being tied to the development of science and technology, as well as to improved social organization. *Yes*, then, to evolution, progress, work, and *no* to revolution, catastrophe, chaos. Third, that the increasing differentiation of the roles an individual must play in contemporary society led to ever tighter and ever more complicated social relations, and that processes of massification inevitably led to homogenization. And finally fourth, that there was a structural parallel between art and the world, and that art had a transformative impact on reality. Thus art was not a reflection of something external to it, a realistic illustration, a mirror carried along the road, but rather a means to develop a stronger bond founded on analogy between art's own complexity and the rules ordering the world.

> A new epoch begins: the epoch of an embrace with the present.
>
> Obedient to life's instinct, transforming instinct into an idea, today's man sets off on a path to reconciliation and fraternization with this new edition of the world, which he had long since began to create but to which he has not yet grown accustomed. He nods in agreement with life's modern scene, and so the city becomes his magical island of great affect. He nods in agreement with modern forms of human coexistence, and so the masses become his sought for collaborator of the new beauty. He nods in agreement with the modern tools of life, and so the machine becomes the poetic enchantress of his fiery dreams.
>
> – Peiper, "Tędy," 5–6

Several points add up to Peiper's theory of poetry. The first and most important is the conviction that poetry is a form of language – "speech transformed," intense and organized in an extraordinary way. The Futurists' idea of "words at freedom" is opposed here by the idea that poetry is the construction of beautiful sentences – captivating combinations of terms and associations of images in which a significant role is played by metaphor, which serves as the means of both transforming reality and making the utterance concise. The concept of a beautiful sentence gives rise to the "blooming composition" (*układ rozkwitania*) – a means of composing a poem in which the initial emergence of an object (episode or event) is subsequently enriched by its uncommon characteristics. Of even greater importance is the rule of equivalence and the method of pseudonymization, meaning the replacement of a word that is directly referential with one of its lyrical equivalents. As Pieper wrote: "Prose names, and poetry pseudonymizes … The development of poetry is rooted in the verbal equivalent's increasing distance from the name [of] a thing."[8]

> The outbreak of the Second World War on 1 September 1939 scattered Polish poets around the world. The Skamander poets ended up in exile: Jan Lechoń, Julian Tuwim, and Kazimierz Wierzyński initially took refuge in France; soon after, faced with its fall, they reached New York through Portugal and Brazil. Meanwhile, Antoni Słonimski settled in London.
>
> Kazimiera Iłłakowiczówna spent the war in Romania. Aleksander Wat, Adam Ważyk, Tadeusz Peiper, and Władysław Broniewski first lived in Soviet-occupied Lviv; after their arrest in 1940 by the NKVD and time spent in various Soviet prisons, Broniewski and Wat were deported to Kazakhstan.
>
> After the war, some of them decided to return to Poland (Broniewski in 1945, Tuwim in 1946, Iłłakowiczówna in 1947, Słonimski in 1951), while others chose to remain abroad. Their choice was dictated as much by personal reasons as by ethical ones. The factors here

were their individual attitudes towards communism, which took hold of Poland in 1948, and the related restrictions on Polish independence and on the publication of their work.

Sadly, Maria Pawlikowski-Jasnorzewska died prematurely in London (1945), and Lechoń committed suicide by jumping from the twelfth floor of a New York hotel in 1956.

Of the group that formed around *The Switch*, Julian Przyboś is considered the most distinguished. He had the greatest lyrical talent and, after Peiper, the most theoretical inventiveness. It was to him that the task of bridging prewar and postwar times fell. He also appealed to readers, which was not the case with all notable avant-gardists. He wrote many remarkable poems that propagated the possibilities enclosed in the aesthetics he postulated. To this one may add that he sought posterity's approval; he lived and created with a masterpiece in mind, read the great Romantics, and believed in "the revenge of a mortal hand," in the words of Wisława Szymborska.[9]

Civilizational exaltation was present in Przyboś's first two, dogmatically Peiperist volumes – *Śruby* (Screws, 1925) and *Oburącz* (With Both Hands, 1926) – but it left his work soon afterward. An evident affirmation of clarity and rigour remained. This is perhaps what Miłosz had in mind when he wrote about Przyboś's certain lack of feelings, or perhaps his propriety – a shame surrounding emotions stemming from the dominant position of the intellect. The rational creator is, after all, extremely ambitious for trying to achieve all that is possible, or, at any rate, for holding the opinion that everything is possible. This suggests that with each poem, the poet intends to initiate a new history of poetry, and even to create a world, each time from scratch:

> Przyboś' human being is a *homo faber*. The essence of humanity and simultaneously the bond that joins him with nature is the practice of productive activity. Here the peasant son meets with Marx. Przyboś immediately identifies activity with linguistic invention, however. The poet becomes the highest among all of those who are active, the most ideal of workers. Here Marx would likely grimace, though surely indulgently … The human being is thus defined by its activity, but it is working in language that is the fullest form of activity. This is the core of Przyboś' world view and – at the same time – the reason for numerous misunderstandings.[10]

The result is a never-weakening motion of thoughts and images, or – as Zbigniew Bieńkowski (1913–94), one of Przyboś's successors, put it – an "unceasing reformation, revision, a constant impulse of opposition" towards both his own work and contemporary poetry. This in turn means that Przyboś's work served as a touchstone of possibilities for poems that appeared later. As Bieńkowski noted: "as happened during Tuwim's rule, or the rule of Ildefons Gałczyński, or that of Tadeusz Różewicz, one seeks criteria and anticriteria in Przyboś and his poetics. He is still the threshold of sensitivity, the boundary of imagination, which one must cross to find himself on this or the other side."[11]

In the swarm of the Kraków avant-garde
Only Przyboś merits our surprise.
Nations and countries crumbled to dust,

> To ashes, and Przyboś remained Przyboś.
> No madness ate at his heart, which is human,
> And thus intelligible. What was his secret?
> In Shakespeare's time they called it euphuism.
> A style composed of metaphor entirely.
> Przyboś was a rationalist deep down.
> He felt what a reasonale social person
> Was supposed to feel, thought what they thought.
> He wanted to put motion into static images.
>
> And the avant-garde made the usual mistake.
> They renovated an old Krakóvian rite:
> Ascribing to language more importance
> Than it could, without ridicule, sustain.
>
> – Miłosz, "A Treatise on Poetry," 121

Przyboś's work was characterized by rationalism, rigour, clarity, and existential optimism, yet he was not an advocate of univocity. To the contrary – he was familiar with darkness and eschatologically inclined; he both attracted and confronted oppositions as a result of his fascination with the realm that stretches between them. Tellingly, his own work has the interword as its brand – a reservoir of meanings that arises as a consequence of using some words and not others and that cannot be reduced to the sum of their meanings. The creation of this effect is aided by ellipsis and metaphor, which extract maximal deposits of meanings and images from the minimum number of words.

Since the end of the 1970s, Przyboś's ideas have not fared well, having been overshadowed by the triumph of History – the explosion of liberational aspirations, the choice of a Pole for a Pope, the rise of Solidarity, and the introduction of martial law. In terms of literature, this triumph has meant the privileging of metaphysical, political, and ethical themes and attitudes. After 1989 and the fall of communism, there were many indicators of a forthcoming postmodernist formation, with its mocking approach towards avant-gardist dreams of greatness. In fact, however, postmodernism was barely able to break through and its proponents were unable to articulate the mockery.

The legacy of *The Switch* circle crowns the history of the Polish avant-garde. Since then, the term has indicated more and more strongly a foundation (a reference system, language, tradition) without which the specific shape of poetry in the years immediately preceding the Second World War, of poetry after 1956, and even of some present-day phenomena could be neither imagined nor understood. Let us recall those elements that help identify the multiple phenomena transpiring over the 1920s and 1930s – two decades that are closely related notwithstanding some spectacular differences. These elements include the imperative of inventiveness; a critical attitude towards art as a hierarchical and mythologized institution based in the authority of the past; anti-traditionalism; an inclination towards self-theorization, manifestos, and programophilia; the inclusion of one's own work in the broader project of deep transformation of the contemporary world; and, finally, collectivity and the organized nature of artistic endeavours, which are not, however, at odds with the goal of attaining individual distinctiveness.

The Avant-Garde as a Tradition

The post-mortem life of the avant-garde had begun by the 1930s. This was not because groups had stopped forming, or because journals, programs, and manifestos were no longer being produced – indeed, they were constantly being produced. Nor was it a matter of diminished creative output by the leaders and members of the avant-garde's diverse movements, since most of them did not cease their activities – indeed, some had their greatest accomplishments still ahead of them. Rather, it was the innovative impetus of the previous two decades that had come to an end – many plans and hopes had either come to fruition or reached a dead end. A time for taking stock had come, and for making some of its elements part of the literary tradition.

Those who write about the poetic wave that arrived during the 1930s – the second avant-garde – usually emphasize the difficulty of placing it in relation to its predecessors. This relation was as programmatic (in its continuations, transformations, and evolutions) as it was situational. Its situational aspect was characterized by opposition to the cultural centre, identified with the Skamander hub at café Ziemiańska and the journal *Wiadomości Literackie* (Literary News); by critical views on contemporary cultural and political subjects; and by predilections for group activities and socially based literary activities. Also significant was that the artists of the 1930s considered themselves part of the avant-garde formation, as evidenced by the evening of 10 May 1934, when the avant-garde Invasion of Warsaw took place. At that time, the avant-garde representatives of four cities met in the hall of the Hygine Association at Karowa Street 31, among them: the organizer Józef Czechowicz and Józef Łobodowski (from Lublin); Teodor Bujnicki, Czesław Miłosz, Jerzy Putrament, and Jerzy Zagórski (from Vilnius), Brzękowski, Kurek, and Przyboś (from Kraków), and Adam Ważyk (from Warsaw). They succeeded in their plan to express community solidarity and the unity of some of their convictions, but unexpectedly, the evening also revealed a number of previously unnoticed differences among these various avant-garde centres and generations. The avant-garde had always been sharply differentiated; now it appeared to consist *almost entirely* of differences. If anything still bound it together and gave it an identity and a direction to its sensitivities, perhaps it was innovation, the still untarnished sign of the avant-garde formation.

THE AVANT-GARDE ARTIST

More than a rejection or dissolution of the past, avant-garde originality is conceived as a literal origin, a beginning from ground zero, a birth. Marinetti, thrown from his automobile one evening in 1909 into a factory ditch filled with water, emerges as if from amniotic fluid to be born – without ancestors – a futurist. The parable of absolute self-creation that begins the first *Futurist Menifesto* functions as a model for what is meant by originality among the early twentieth-century avant-garde. For originality becomes an organicist metaphor referring not so much to formal invention as to sources of life.

– Krauss, "The Originality of the Avant-Garde," 157

There is at least one more reason to speak about the "second avant-garde" as something relatively coherent: the catastrophic world view held by the majority of its members, albeit in their own specific ways. This catastrophism had a literary lineage, having descended from a pessimistic philosophy of history (Miguel de Unamuno, Oswald Spengler, Florian Znaniecki), a sociological reflection on culture (Ortega y Gasset), and Freudism. It was also tied to life experience, however. The First World War had struck a blow against faith in human rationality, and even in humanity's survival, and the victory of fascism in Italy underscored that modern democracy had its limits. Meanwhile, the great crisis begat by the Wall Street crash of 1929 depleted trust in the capitalist world order, and the truth about Stalinism (where it could be accessed) had corroded hope in the alternative offered by true socialism. Simultaneously, to the West, Hitlerism was beginning to reveal its monstrous nature. In these circumstances, it seemed reasonable to anticipate the apocalypse, as evidenced by Miłosz's poem "O książce" (About a Book) from the volume *Trzy zimy* (Three Winters, 1936).[12]

ROMANTIC SOURCES OF AVANT-GARDISM

Before Przyboś, the Żagary poets studied – and experienced – Mickiewicz, who remained constantly present in Miłosz's work, in any case. From Romanticism is born the faith in imagination along with the belief in the prophetic abilities of the poet, who is elevated above the blind, unseeing crowd, which is sometimes treated with pitying disdain ("Ptaki" [Birds]). This disdain, however, stirs up qualms of conscience, since poetry has been vested – again, in line with Romantic tradition – with the responsibility of spiritual leadership, of rescuing "the ignorant people," which probably predisposed one toward surprising political oscillations ... What is also striking – from the onset – is the framing of one's own and society's experience in terms that are not always religious, perhaps, but that are certainly eschatological and metaphysical. The mystery of existence, a fear and a fascination with the incomprehensible, and finally – a sense of guilt and moral responsibility ... or in the most general terms, the sense of the sacred – have rarely spoken with greater power in contemporary lyrical poetry.

– Błoński, "Patos, romantyzm, proroctwo," 32–3

The expressive force of this poem is remarkable, as is the rhetorical impact of the first person plural of the poetic subject, the audacity of its civilizational diagnosis (the dusk of the book), its sense of existential tragedy, and its intoxication with terror. But where has its avant-gardism gone? It has not disappeared as much as it has been absorbed – into language and a bold style that are sourced in the tradition of prophetic literature, and unafraid of crossing its boundaries and of moving in the direction of a dark future, perceptible not only in the sphere of enigmatic premonitions but also in more concrete, political signs. Avant-gardism becomes, at any rate, one of the many characteristics of Miłosz's poetry, albeit a weakening one, dominated by both Romanticism – as Jan Błoński asserts – and later also Classicism.

The situation with Józef Czechowicz was similar. Czechowicz was older than Miłosz and one of his masters – a remarkable poet who proved important to many, including

Tadeusz Różewicz. His poems are muted, intimate, delicate, and devoid of the characteristic arrogance of the early avant-gardists. Many of them "take place" in rural landscapes that are idealized, pastoral, and stylized after the fashion of the Secession. Sometimes it takes focused attention to notice the moment when the Catastrophe sneaks into this Arcadia. This catastrophe does not deafen with the "clamour of metals," as it does in Miłosz's work; rather, it stirs up sadness and strikes an elegiac note that demands reflection on mortality. This – unlike death, which is a violence and a scandal – creates something like an atmosphere around us, one that breathes through us, and absorbs and upends us. As Różewicz notes, "Czechowicz is fully of the provinces, made in his entirety from dreams, music, silence, and enthrallment. And from weakness. He is neither rural nor urban, but a poet of the borderland. He is like a suburban meadow, richly scented with herbs, flowers and grasses, yet within reach of city sounds; like clouds mixing with factory smoke."[13]

The Retreat and the Return

The avant-garde muse was silent throughout the war, humiliated by civilization's use of all its powers for self-destruction. Immediately after the war, when it again wished to speak, it was denied a voice. The victorious ideology of socialism in its Stalinist variant viewed the avant-garde as a hostile phenomenon, rooted in bourgeois excesses, despite the mostly leftist and often even communist sympathies of the avant-gardists. Its return proved possible only after the October Thaw of 1956, when Stalinist repression began to weaken and numerous avant-garde attributes were reborn. A group of young and talented poets had arrived on the scene, to mention only Miron Białoszewski (*Obroty rzeczy* [Revolutions of Things, 1956]) and Zbigniew Herbert (*Struna światła* [String of Light, 1956]). The basic ethos of the avant-garde – with its emphasis on working on language, searching for new means of expression, resisting worn patterns of literary communication, and reacting critically to the conditions of reality – regained its currency. Its echo was carried by the work of language poets such as Białoszewski, Zbigniew Bieńkowski, Tymoteusz Karpowicz (1921–2005), and Witold Wirpsza (1918–85) – resonating most strongly in their conflict with language as a system. Expressionism was heard in the poems of Stanisław Grochowiak (1934–76), and Surrealism in the work of Jerzy Harasymowicz (1933–99).

Within this group, Miron Białoszewski was an exceptional personality. The core of his poetry, starting with *Revolutions of Things*, can be grasped in a few key qualities. One of them is the central position of the subject surprised by its own existence, and the conditions of life and of language ("I gape astonished / and I astonish myself / and comment on the lives of things around me [...] / pull the ropes of clotheslines / and the bells of boots, / for the carnival of poetry, / for a solemn unceasing amazement").[14] Another is an attitude towards freedom and authenticity that is characteristic of existentialism. A third concerns the poet's deconstructive approach to language as a self-steering system marked by permanent performativity, and his denotation of speech acts, operations on phraseology, and exposure of "the grammar of the word." The final key characteristic of Białoszewski's poetry stems from his anti-institutionalism and from his aesthetic choosiness, which is combined with an interest in secondariness, peripherality, and inferiority.

Another strong echo of the avant-garde can be heard in the work of the Generation '68 poets, among them figures as notable as Stanisław Barańczak (1946–2014), Ryszard Krynicki, Adam Zagajewski, and Julian Kornhauser (b. 1946). Their work is linked by their experience of violence, both physical and rhetorical, stemming from the brutal pacification of the March 1968 student protests. They take up social themes, a prominent one being the devastating impact of newspeak (language intended to manipulate public opinion) on interpersonal relations. Barańczak is the most dynamic of this group. As a writer, he is both rebellious and structuralist; he opposes the limitations imposed by all intellectual and social orders, and he almost instinctively seeks to catch the diversity of phenomena in a tightly woven net of definitions and typology. Sometimes he engrosses us with a straightforward "no," other times with a riveting concept. From his perspective, "artificiality" is a poem's natural state. The artificiality of ink and the naturalness of blood mix in his poetry, just as they did in one of his more famous early texts, "Pismo" (Writing), from his volume *Korekta twarzy* (Facial Correction, 1968):

> Want everything: force yourself into these tight, spiked dog collars, pierce right through the pages fused into a block, aiming at what is most darkly hidden in the tunnels of letters, but forever lacing together the pages with a thin and conjunctive mesh; and so fettered by its openings, by one's own eyes, but yet free, deep within and outside incandescent like a star with the rays of wrists and neck shackled in black pillories. Through here, through rows of uneven rings, flies the arrow of you, a streak still unclear to you, until it veers, thrown off course. Then it will explode you toward you, turned face to face.
>
> And in the light of this sharpness you will notice the inlets of rivers drying on paper and understand: this is how fast in the whiteness of this snow black and living blood congeals.[15]

Over time, Barańczak's virtuosity and ethics opened onto metaphysics, to which he was very close already in *Widokówka z tego świata* (Postcard from This World, 1988) – and closest perhaps in its titular poem and in the villanelle "Co mam powiedzieć" (What Can I Say). The titular poem is a dialogue with God, but one in which God and man are of equal standing and equally mysterious to each other; the villanelle, in turn, calls forth the motif of a desert while asking whose voice and what words can be heard there. Unfortunately, the present-day desert is no longer the seat of even the Devil and thus it cannot be the place where John, Christ, Elijah, Paul, and Anthony encountered their own selves and internally fortified them. The desert is the desert, having no specific use, and in its undefined realm nothing has any significance.

Here one could reference, on the one hand, everything that Barańczak has said about twentieth-century totalitarianisms and the torment of the everyday, and on the other, the faith that there exists some superior, Divine (?) account that deals with the truth and that this account will be settled in the end. In this case, however, the following supposition will suffice – that the Kantian alliance between reason and ethic so admired by Barańczak must constitute the reverse of a cavernous melancholy. "Escape from the desert," as it is understood here, is an offshoot of the impossibility of "escape into the desert."

The Avant-Garde Today?

It is possible to insist that the conditions necessary to see the triumph of postmodernism as complete have not yet been met in Poland. It is possible to trace Futuristic elements in the activities of the Orange Alternative and of the early *Brulion* (*Rough Draft*) – two milieux that have subverted mainstream Polish culture through the use of irony, satire, parody, and the grotesque. Not without reason, it is possible to ascribe to Andrzej Sosnowski (b.

1959) avant-garde predecessors – for example, Peiper, Brzękowski, Ezra Pound, and the Surrealists; likewise, it is possible to grant the status of a new generation of language poets to Joanna Mueller (b. 1979) and a few of her peers. It is possible, but is it necessary? No reasonable person insists now that the avant-garde has disappeared without a trace or that it can be erased from the living memory of literature; it is equally unlikely that anyone at this point believes its ideal must be unconditionally upheld. According to Zygmunt Bauman,

> In today's postmodern world, speaking about the avant-garde is a misunderstanding – even if this or that artist can take a position remembered from the times of "storm and stress"; it will be more a pose than a position, however – stripped of former sense, empty, with nothing to foretell and no ensuing obligations, a manifestation of nostalgia rather than of spirit, and certainly not of the strength of spirit. The term "postmodern avant-garde" is a *contradictio in adiecto* [contradiction in terms].[16]

It is difficult to argue with this opinion, even though many artists as well as readers find it hard to agree with the reality Bauman describes. Can this rejection of "art without ethos" become the beginning of a new avant-garde?

Sosnowski, an influential poet and author of insightful essays about poetry who debuted at the beginning of the 1990s, has stated that "the issue [sanction of literature and literature itself – PŚ] is not yet lost, as long as attention does not entirely turn away from language, from its possibilities and ways of coping with life and the world, which clearly badly wants to be 'postliterary,' even 'postverbal' already. And so there is no sanction, beside writing itself."[17]

His words renounce the traditional grounds and rules of creativity. In Sosnowski's work the reader encounters writing as writing – the poem condemned to its own nature – and a particular self-sufficiency – an existence independent of the world. In many of Sosnowski's poems, their beauty communicates only itself, without delivering a lesson, a message, or any wisdom. The world is as it is – concurrent, diverse, and crowded. So it appears through the window of the poem: a window rather than a prism or a distorting mirror, for the main characteristic of Sosnowski's mode of perception is the lack of hierarchy among observed phenomena. Each one can turn into an impulse for the subject. The result is a poem both extremely objective and extremely subjective; chaotic and precise; thought out to the last detail and simultaneously aleatoric, accidental, its final shape established by the recipient. The meanings of words (often secondary, unnoticed) initiate chain poetic reactions, in which participate two forces at odds through the history of Polish postwar poetry: imagination, imagery, and visuality on the one side, and "word craft" (*słowiarstwo*) and the idolatry of the text on the other. As a result, Sosnowski's work packs a truly explosive punch. Rather than exploding, however, his poems implode. They attract ever more sense-like elements from all sides and absorb them, growing denser and larger – like black holes.

After Sosnowski, the thought of searching for a proper avant-garde, rather than just its staffage, can seem utopian. Yet recent years indicate a growing hunger for utopias. Poets born in the 1970s have discovered for themselves Wirpsza, Karpowicz, and especially Krystyna Miłobędzka, who successfully mixes the element of language experiment (an experiment with the minimal use of words, almost with silence) with the element of philosophical meditation over micro-existence, which takes place in the everyday, in the space of the home, the garden, among one's nearest. At the beginning of the second decade of the twenty-first century, twenty-something and younger poets are also fascinated by Bruno Jasieński – like he did, they want a new language for a new world, and a new world to replace the existing one.

II. In the Long Shadow of Romanticism

Romanticism is constantly present in twentieth-century Polish poetry. Maria Janion, a renowned scholar of nineteenth- and twentieth-century literature, sees it as a constitutive factor for all of Polish culture starting in the first half of the nineteenth century until 1989, when the Romantic and Symbolic paradigm gave way to liberal and democratic culture. Its stubborn recurrence can be variously explained: with recourse to the memory of the great literature of Polish Romanticism, or to the currency of messianic (redemptive) ideas under conditions of the absence or endangerment of national freedom, or, finally – in the most complex instances – as an expression of awareness, or at least premonition, that its collection of values is both modern and able to protect against disenchantment with the world and from threats to subjectivity. While the ties between Romanticism and modernity are sometimes overblown or negated, there can be no doubt that Polish poetry regularly nullifies the issue of how to deal with the Romantic legacy, capitulating in the face of its monumental complexity and treating it as a phenomenon as natural as air.

The poetry that Jan Lechoń wrote during the interwar period provides an excellent illustration of powerlessness in relation to Romanticism. This is particularly true for his engaging and well-received debut volume *Karmazynowy poemat* (The Crimson Poem, 1920), in which we find one of the most infamous programmatic poems of that time, the still often referenced "Herostrates": "Should he ever rear his head in the Old Town / And that Kilinski fasten his green eyes upon you. / Kill him! – And drag his body to one side, / And only bring me the news of that happy event."[18] The blasphemous mockery with which Lechoń tries to unmask Romanticism in its vulgarized version, reduced to simplified emotions and cheap martyrological symbolism, breaks down in the final stanza. The famous verse – "and in spring let me see spring, not Poland" – turns out to be a provocation, an instrument to shake up and wake up the recipient – it is the creation of a poet who, as in the popularized version of Romanticism, is at the service of an idea called "Poland."[19]

It is not the numerous dialogues with the canonical poets of Polish Romanticism – Adam Mickiewicz (1798–1855), Juliusz Słowacki (1809–49), and Cyprian Kamil Norwid (1821–83) – that signal alignment with their tradition, but rather the difficult-to-describe case of history's imagination. Romanticism speaks more forcefully whenever historicism – that is, the understanding and experience of history as a living force, one that determines both individual and collective fates and that necessitates the effort of defining both individual and collective identities – intensifies. During the 1930s, a period referred to as either the second avant-garde or catastrophism, the intensification of historicism strongly impacted a variety of artists. Among poets, critics saw its mark on the poems of Józef Czechowicz, in Miłosz's first two volumes, and in the work of other poets in the Vilnius Żagary group (Teodor Bujnicki and Jerzy Zagórski). It was perceptible also in the work of Skamander poets of that time, especially in Julian Tuwim's narrative poem "Bal w operze" (The Ball at the Opera, 1936), a passionately engaged and mercilessly critical portrait of the social elite, one that delivers an incisive and surprisingly current analysis of the mechanisms of disorientation and propaganda. The poet is both alienated and committed, and his poem is vested with the right to unmask wrongs and with the power to lead others out of darkness, or to wake them from apathy.

Now is the moment without a name:
the door swelled out and was extinguished.
In the tumult, loud as a burning flame,
and in the shadows, faces you cannot distinguish.

Then a short cry from next door;
then a thud like a rock falling down
and as from a wound the darkness flows
and in the clattering cart a body is thrown.

Now is the moment without a name
branded in time as in an anthem. It spells out,
with a filament of blood like a string,
its name on the flagstones behind the cart.

15 November 1941
– Baczyński, "Without a Name," 67

The talented poets who debuted around the time of the Nazi occupation, such as Krzysztof Kamil Baczyński (1921–44), Tadeusz Gajcy (1922–44), Zdzisław Stroiński (1921–44), and Tadeusz Borowski (1922–51), drew on an even richer arsenal of devices with catastrophic and Romantic provenance. Their poems translated the reality of the poets' experience into the language of the great tragedies of the past. History is the protagonist of their poems, while poetry seems defective, in the sense that it is alienating and unable to turn back the decrees of time. Despite being infected by the awareness of near defeat, however, the figure of the poet is vested with prophetic attributes – the ability to see through the mysteries of fate. An antinomy of word and action takes central place in this poetry, along with messianic motifs, signs of Romantic religiosity, and even borrowings from the repertoire of Romantic genres (such as the ballad, elegy, tale, or narrative poem). The originality of Poland's war generation poets arises from a collision between the literature that inspired them in their work and the experience that forced them to transgress the limits of that inspiration. Even though these poets repeat after the Romantics a series of dramatic gestures – like them oscillating between a sense of belonging to a victimized collective, and a sense of their own fate's inalienable singularity – they nevertheless appear entirely unique.

Why "nevertheless"? For the simple reason that war exposes and even denigrates existing forms of expression. This has been noted by, among others, Czesław Miłosz, who in the chapter "Ruins and Poetry" discusses Herbert's "Nothing in Prospero's Cloak":

> Poems of this kind seem to fulfill a surrogate function, that is, they direct a global accusation at human speech, history and even the very fabric of life in society, instead of pointing out

> the concrete reasons for the anger and disgust. That probably happens because, as was the case in Poland during war, reality eludes the means of language and is the source of deep traumas, including the natural trauma of a country betrayed by its Allies. The reality of the war years is a great subject, but a great subject is not enough and it even makes inadequacies in workmanship all the more visible. There is another element which shows art in an ambiguous light. Noble intentions should be rewarded and a literary text so conceived should acquire a durable existence, but most often the reverse is true: some detachment, some coldness, is necessary to elaborate a form. People thrown into the middle of events that tear cries of pain from their mouths have difficulty in finding the distance necessary to transform the material artistically.[20]

Yet the quality of Baczyński's poetic achievement undercuts Miłosz's statements. He wrote independently and quickly freed himself from the determinants of the Romantic tradition. Stanisław Stabro puts it as follows:

> The individual human being is the source of all values in Baczyński's poetry. No ideal, command, or coersion has the right to strip this individual of its conscience and the right to doubt. In this sense, Baczyński's world is a world devoid of traditionally understood moral sanctions. For this poet, reality is graspable only in the state of "in statu nascendi," which is opposite to a static vision … It is thus a Romanticism completely aware of its traps and pitfalls.[21]

Like many other poets of his generation, Baczyński died fighting during the Warsaw Uprising of 1944. His short life quickly became the stuff of legends, made up of talent remarked upon by the greatest literary critics (including Kazimierz Wyka), of love that was the source of many stirring poems, of engagement in the struggle against the occupier, and finally of death – exalted and full of pathos.

After the war, the communists used Romanticism instrumentally, sometimes as a model of social engagement, but more often as a bulwark for their materialistic philosophy and political opportunism. In any case, it consistently remained the subject of critical and literary debates, as well as a component of poetic programs (e.g., Jerzy Kwiatkowski, Stanisław Barańczak). It exploded anew after the rise of Solidarity in August 1980 and was fully reborn after the introduction of martial law in December 1981.

The first literary institutions abroad were established relatively quickly. In London, the periodical *Wiadomości* (News) was launched in 1946, with Mieczysław Grydzewski as its editor, and in 1947 the first issue of the monthly *Kultura* (Culture) appeared in Rome, moving soon afterwards to Maisons-Laffitte near Paris. The charismatic Jerzy Giedroyć (1906–2000) was its editor for several decades.

News became a pillar for older poets (who in the Skamander group included Lechoń, Wierzyński, and Stanisław Baliński), while the younger, second avant-garde poets (Józef Łobodowski, Marian Pankowski, and finally – after 1951 – Czesław Miłosz) were drawn towards *Kultura*.

Between 1950 and 1992, the publishing house Oficyna Poetów i Malarzy (Poets' and Painters' Press) and its associated journal *Oficyna Poetów* (Poets' Press, 1966–80) were active in London, headed by Krystyna and Czesław Bednarczyk.

From 1959 to 1964, the journal *Kontynenty–Nowy Merkuriusz* (Continents–The New Mercury) was published in London. The first part of its title became the name of the "Continents" literary group, whose members included Bogdan Czaykowski (1932–2007), Florian Śmieja (b. 1925), Adam Czerniawski (b. 1934), and Janusz Artur Ihnatowicz (b. 1929). The first two poets later moved to Canada, which was already home to Wacław Iwaniuk (1912–2001).

After another great wave of emigration spurred by the introduction of martial law in Poland in 1981, the quarterly *Literary Notebooks* was launched in Paris, with a focus on poetry and essays. Barbara Toruńczyk was its first editor-in-chieft, and leading poets of Generation '68 were among its other editors and staff, who included Stanisław Barańczak and Adam Zagajewski. In Toronto, the Polish-Canadian Publishing Fund was founded in 1977 and over the years promoted many Polish émigré poets of different generations, including Florian Śmieja, Wacław Iwaniuk, Bogdan Czaykowski, Andrzej Busza (b. 1938), Roman Chojnacki (b. 1954), Jerzy Gizella (b. 1949), Aleksander Rybczyński, Grażyna Zambrzycka (b. 1956), and Edward Zyman (b. 1943).

Martial law was seen as proof that there existed a historical script for Poland. One of the most symptomatic poems aimed at the decoding of Polish fate is Jan Polkowski's (b. 1953) "Przesłanie Pana X" (The Envoy of Mr. X) from the volume *To nie jest poezja* (This Is Not Poetry, 1980).[22] The poem references Zbigniew Herbert's "Przesłanie Pana Cogito" (The Envoy of Mr. Cogito), consciously reducing its maximalism and universalism to material, anti-transcendental, and claustrophobic experiences. It is rich in signs of confinement, limitation, and imprisonment; and of deep sleep, suffocation, dying, and finality. Polkowski replaces Herbert's lofty irony with the bitter irony of powerlessness. There is pathos in Polkowski's poem as well, of course, but in a different way. In Herbert, there is only one exit from the situation: a tragic, lonely, and condemned to misunderstanding, but nevertheless certain greatness. Polkowski transforms it into a point of no return. Mr X, born "into the people chosen / for extermination," testifies to his undeserved yet unavoidable defeat. The ultimate sign of this is his namelessness.

Romanticism, including in its popular, pedestrian form, manifested itself in various ways. It expressed itself most clearly as a framing of history as an independent force with its own rules and aims, capable of laying claim to entire nations and of repeating its decrees and presenting them as objective necessities. This determinism, derived from Hegel, which had inspired both the Romantics and Marx, was highly troubling for poets:

After two hundred years,
Lech Wałęsa,
After two hundred years
Of liberty regained and lost again
You became the the Polish people's chief
And just like the one before
You are going up against world powers [...][23]

The influence of Romanticism was also signalled by the unconditional precedence of freedom. No other value equalled it, not even truth, although the need for truth was often discussed. Freedom, defined in generalities, emerged as the hallmark of opposition to the system. It was equivalent to life, of which the authorities (communists, Soviets) had robbed the nation. It was the yearning for freedom for everyone, and not just for an individual, that after some years gave rise to these words by Marcin Świetlicki (b. 1961):

> How easy then for the slave to travel the monstrously
> long and practically impossible road
> from the alphabet to God, it lasts only a moment,
> like spitting – in the poetry of slaves.[24]

Finally, echoes of Romanticism can be heard in the strong emphasis placed on identity at this time. Identity, rootedness, Polishness, tradition: these were the values that differentiated a nation from a formless, pliant, submissive mass lacking awareness and pride – a mass that was seen as the goal of the communists. The restoration or preservation of identity came to be seen as the basic task of poetry as well as other cultural domains. It provided the common moral denominator for both strong poems and weak ones; it connected Stanisław Barańczak – the author of *Atlantyda* (Atlantis, 1986) and *A Postcard from This World* – with anonymous voices set to rhyme under the influence of momentary impulses.

Where is Romanticism today? It survives in the "poetry of circumstance," fuelled by extraordinary events, such as the Smolensk plane crash in 2010 that claimed the lives of Poland's president Lech Kaczyński and close to a hundred other prominent people. In some instances, it co-creates phenomena of particular interest. The poetry of Marcin Świetlicki is one such case. The most remarkable of the "barbarians" – a group of poets who arrived on the literary scene in the early 1990s – Świetlicki is a superb artist who enjoys considerable popularity. He is a (post)modern arch-poet. He is, on one hand, free from the rule of some earlier prohibitions. For instance, he participates in the realm of mass culture by performing with a rock group. On the other hand, his awareness that the place of poetry in society has changed does not lead to or justify self-limitation, nor does it make him cynical. Świetlicki's poems are tough, rough, prickly, sour, and ironic, although they can also be tender and it is not difficult to find a rivulet of humour in them. Humour and horror, to be precise. Świetlicki does not drift towards the borders of Formalism, a poetry where language either masks or replaces the world, nor does he give in to a manic-depressive intertextuality. He also does not mimic the adherents of mediation – of the *de facto* inaccessibility and inexpressibility of the world – who are enthralled with the work of John Ashbery and, in the Polish context, of Andrzej Sosnowski. Świetlicki wants to be a poet on a grand scale. He is seemingly well-established in a contemporary context, yet he continuously breaks out of that framework. The present is, after all, a drama: at every moment it becomes the past, and as it passes we too pass along with it, in all manner of systematic and sudden ways. He is an ironic existentialist who continuously but not compulsively speaks about death.

The present is a drama all the more for not wishing to see its own drama. It is empty in a peculiar way, despite being furnished with various rituals, institutions of social life, precepts, prohibitions, intellectual and political correctness, and useful deceptions. Such is Świetlicki – a moralist, a poet of resistance against the rule of institutions and discourses, opposing all that thinks in our stead, that makes us stand at attention, that hinders communication with another person, and that turns us into ghosts or zombies. Such is

Świetlicki – the existentialist who testifies to an impossible love, unexpressed, rough, and closely related to solitude. In this way, the Romantic aspect of this postmodernist modern poet produces the effect of an arch-poet, a witness to the age, a sensor, someone who looks for a place but cannot find a home there, and who desires to offer something to the world despite being at odds with it.

The Romantic artist is characterized, according to one expert on the epoch, by "a talent disclosed from the earliest years of his life, an unusual appearance that speaks to a psychological difference, a lonely path to fame, lack of understanding from one's nearest, life failures that strengthen the artist internally, and bad luck in love."[25] Avoiding unnecessary commentary on Świetlicki's appearance and personal life, the facts that he started to write while young and is famous for his "unjoinability" still strike a chord with this description. The man we encounter through his poems seems simultaneously deeply humble and thoroughly egoistic, difficult, conflicted, and unpredictable – a figure that evades unequivocalness.

Classicism *contra* Crisis

Arguments persist about whether twentieth-century Classicism exists. Is this possible? And if it is, is the sense of this possibility moral or aesthetic? The impossibility of Classicism is tied to the interpretation of Classicism *sensu stricto*. Scholars of the Classicist formation emphasize the opposition between its twentieth-century manifestations and notions that were fundamental to it at its origins. Henri Peyre contends that the Neoclassicism of the nineteenth and twentieth centuries was driven by completely different ideals than its supposed seventeenth-century prototype:

> Seventeenth-century classicism assumed … an acceptance of one's time and milieu. This is a rare phenomenon among writers and artists since the victory of democracy and the birth of great media forced upon them the opposition toward the public, or proud and painful solitude. The neoclassicists of our century certainly did not feel this kind of acceptance. Glorifying classicism, as they had done, meant, first and foremost, protesting against the present.[26]

The scholar notes at least two other characteristics that deserve attention. He points first to the loss of a universal aspect of Neoclassicism and its nationalization during the twentieth century, and second, to the occurence of something that can be called elemental Classicism. This latter type is less a derivative of a program than an expression of deeply internalized cultural predispositions. In the case of French literature, this immanent, unconscious inclination is expressed, Peyre writes, through the "love of the concrete, of the object, almost of matter,"[27] an effort to organize, control, and order sensations, as well as the reduction of "excess," which in time is replaced in ever greater measure by an in-depth exploration of one's own experiences.

The theses concerning the "second nature" of French writing have been painted here with a broad brush. It is all the more tempting to formulate another hypothesis on their basis, namely, that in broadly understood contemporary literature there are some writers with the gift of a Classicist personality, so to speak. Peyre notes that

> [if] the deep classicism of French literature and art did not lead to sterilization and conservative stagnation – with the exception of academicism's ephemeral victories, quickly eliminated

by the protesting youth – it is because it is more the (transitory) achievement of individuals than a collective product or the result of historical and social circumstances.[28]

To this he adds that Classical balance is, for these individuals, a state of temporary harmony "between the abilities to feel and to understand," rather than "an eclecticism or a compromise."[29]

Classicism *after* Classicism is thus actualized through the work of a certain kind of individuality rather than in specific programs and declarations. It is individual achievements that fortify it and that allow us to track its existence. What is more, immanent Classicism is often in conflict – frequently noted and perhaps inevitable – with thematized Classicism. Paradoxically, it is the former Classicism that is genuine, while the latter is simulated. The former grows into the tissue of its time, while the latter tries to refute its contemporaneity. Finally, while the former Classicism (proper, not anachronistic and not instrumental) remains hidden, the latter overarticulates itself. The former manifests itself in idioms, the latter through rhetoric:

The common denominator of all twentieth-century classicisms is a conscious regressivism, and thereby traditionalism. In literature, this means an affirmative attitude toward the past treated syncretically, for – tellingly – the systematic selection of tradition is suspended … The classicist program is an attempt to sneak through a narrow opening between Scylla of progress and Charybdis of the consciousness of crisis. It is thus an answer to a crisis, one of many.[30]

This crisis is worth a closer look. Paul Ricoeur identifies the following signs of this crisis: the divergence of individualism and liberalism (Louis Dumont); the unfulfilled promises of *Aufklärung* (Frankfurt School philosophers); the annihilation of fundamental values; "disenchantment" of the world as the price of rationalism's triumph; and the "death of God" and the fall of agnostic humanism, in other words the "death of man" (Friedrich Nietzsche and Max Weber). As he sums up, "what seems common to these diverse interpretations of the contemporary crisis is the idea of the superimposing of two crises, that of traditional society under the pressure of modern society and that of modern society itself insofar as it appears as an aborted offspring of traditional society."[31]

Ricoeur himself shifts the emphasis to the lack of consensus and engagement in modern societies, with the latter being a result of the collapse of the significance of the sacred. Tellingly, without either denying the gravity of the crisis, or hiding the anxiety over its possible longevity, or refuting the death of Christianity, Ricoeur underscores the possibility of renewing the legacy of the past through a return to and reinterpretation of its sources. At stake is not the expansion of the sacred but the deepening of its substance. Following the famous hermeneutician, one could say that modernity – both the daughter and the mother of crisis – creates antibodies, or counterforces, that seek to alleviate the suffering caused by its basal conflicts and uncertainties.

This crisis is a common problem for all types of modernism, a phenomenon so multinominal as to elude any satisfying summary. Richard Sheppard lists a series of shared characteristics that different critics have remarked on:

These have included an "uncompromising intellectuality," a preoccupation with nihilism, a "discontinuity," an attraction to the Dionysiac, a "formalism, an "attitude of detachment," the use of myth as "an arbitrary means of ordering art" and a "reflexivism," an "antidemocratic"

> cast of mind, an "emphasis on subjectivity," a "feeling of alienation and loneliness," the sense of the "ever-present threat of chaos ... in conjunction with the sense of search" and "the experience of panic terror," a particular form of irony that derives from "the rift between the self and world," "consciousness, observation, and detachment," a commitment to metaphor as "the very essence of poetry itself."[32]

The contradictions within this set of characteristics attest to the difficulty of explaining modernism, but the list also contains some leitmotifs: anxiety, disorientation within a changed world, and experience of the dramatic singularity of time. In addition, following Fredric Jameson, Sheppard considers modernist art and literature to be as much a reflection of a crisis as an answer to it. He lists nine such answers. The first is nihilistic, the second ecstatic, and the third mystical (here the author points to, among others, T.S. Eliot and the ending of *The Waste Land*). The fourth answer is aesthetic, the fifth is escapist. Here, Sheppard first recalls Rilke and Yeats, who responded to the Great War with a "flight out of time," and then Eliot and Pound, who "both moved backwards in time to associate themselves with the pre-modern consciousness and system of beliefs which ... were free from uncertainties, instability and sense of meaninglessness which marked the modern age."[33]

The hieratic conservatism exemplified by Eliot and Pound found its reverse in progressivistic engagement, which was oriented towards a future shaped by a leftist, even Bolshevik revolution (Kandinsky, Mayakovsky, Alexander Blok, Ernst Toller, Johannes Becher). According to Sheppard, "both groups of modernists were marked by a deep yearning after a total, centered world in which the New Man under socialism or the redeemed humanity under God could rediscover a secure identity and transcendent sense of purpose."[34] The sixth answer is primitive, and the seventh modernolatric (as in Futurism). The eighth – Constructivism and "new objectivism" – links the avant-garde with Classicism. Finally, the ninth answer portends the postmodernist condition, or "an acceptance *of an anarchic landscape of worlds in the plural*," with recognizable antinomy, the attitude of duality, the simultaneousness of "acceptance and renunciation."[35]

Consideration of both Ricoeur's and Sheppard's outlined ideas leads to a rather surprising question: Is there anything that can be pointed to in Classicism that cannot be found in modernism? Sheppard's list helps us understand that escape from contemporaneity, or the desire to transgress its boundaries, is not a sufficient premise for distinguishing Neoclassicism from modernism and cannot constitute proof of its strong, separate existence. Classicism thus becomes part of the modernistic chaos; it is more often evidenced by the Classicist intentions of authors than by works deserving of the label. An extreme hypothesis emerges, namely, that only a work that testifies to the defeat or at least ineffectiveness of the Classicist program can be considered a notable work of Classicism. Such works establish a meaningful relation between poetry and God – the word and the thing, the living and the dead – from within the modernist crisis and not from beyond its undefinable borders; they sincerely desire to escape the power of the unbearable epoch and are defeated in a singular and convincing way.

Michał Paweł Markowski distinguishes two basic aesthetic traditions within modernity. The first is hermetic (the Kantian "dream of the asemantic ideal of pure beauty and its disinterested contemplation"); the other is hermeneutic (the Hegelian "dream of the spirit's recognition in the work of art").[36] It is not by accident that we are intrigued by the Romantic Eliot, or by the late Leopold Staff when he is struck by the thought that he was a person who "Did not seek the flat hands of applause, / Admired mornings and evenings / Wrote down his poems in the sand/ And did not use metaphor" ("Klęska" [Defeat]).[37] The same is true for Jarosław Iwaszkiewicz in the context of the collision between the "culturedness" of his poems and his real, approaching death; and for the "dark" Miłosz of the poem "To" (This); and for Herbert in poems where the wounded author peeks through a bulwark of high values. The same also holds for Stanisław Barańczak, who was known to use form as a shield; and for Adam Zagajewski as a poet unknown to himself, desperately entreating emptiness; and for Bohdan Zadura (b. 1945) who has no delusions about the ability of entreaties to perform miracles and once again enchant the world. For it is the desert that constitutes modernism's only shared experience.

The wasteland, the domain of nihilism, and perhaps also the effect of being burned out by the Black Sun (Freud and successors) or the Black Enlightenment (Adorno and Horkheimer), appears also in the guise of emptiness, desolation, winter, snow, snowy plains, or limitless transparency distorted by totalism. The desert presented by Borges in the short story "The Two Kings and the Two Labyrinths" is perhaps most famous; it is a labyrinth without an exit since it consists exclusively of exits. "The desert is expanding" – says Nietzsche. For Derrida, the desert is a metaphor – the "code name" for negativity, in the words of Agata Bielik-Robson:

> *Bemidbar* ... is a condition in which a human being is uprooted from natural harmony, expelled into the emptiness of its primal negativity, and is suspended between different, equally possible options: he can wade further through the limitless sands, led by desire for a messianic life; he can settle in the desert, in the state of permanent suspension between life and death; and he can also always return, like the prodigal son of nature, to her "house of fatty slavery."[38]

The desert thus understood is a synonym of ambivalence, suspension, indecision, irresolution, and imprisonment in an excess of possibilities – an aporia.

This definition of modernity signals the lines of opposition to it. Classicism as an anti-modernism, which has no possibility of breaking away from the object of its negation, seems to have been the first of modernism's inner rebellions. At stake in it, in the first place, was the renewal of the notion of culture as a reservoir of values directed at ordering, hierarchizing, and fulfilling the tasks of the Great Code, with the power to transform a collective into a community.[39] This was the task of, among others, Jarosław Marek Rymkiewicz (b. 1935), who aimed to establish or reactivate the foundational myths of the Polish national culture most evidently in his essays, but also in his poetry. Defending the literary centre, the invariable canon, and, so to speak, the past and present choices of the majority, was part of the aim. Another of its parts – and here Rymkiewicz can serve as an example again, although Miłosz's poetry is an even clearer instance – was the vindication of an object, or simply of a reality that had ceased to be accessible to language. Miłosz spoke of poetry in terms of a stubborn chase after reality. According to some notable critics, Miłosz is primarily a mimetic artist, who represents reality and draws hope and moral consolation from its existence. The opposite is true of Rymkiewicz. He is a poet subjected to the pull of two opposite poles; he wants to return to the pre-modern state in which one did not have to rationalize the writing of poetry while also wanting to include in poems (pastiche) a sign of recognition that the traditions invoked by his poetry are not his own. His poems both call on community and establish their own distinctiveness; they speak literally and point to a "different realm"; they describe matter and search for transcendence.

The vindication extended also towards culture – its pure forms, the attuned voices of the past and the present, the legible message of masterworks, and seriousness. Adam Zagajewski has been a recent and great defender of seriousness, exorcising irony (for instance, in the essay collection *W cudzym pięknie* [Another Beauty, 1999]) and seeking a place for beauty and traditionally understood exaltation, as well as for elevated style and the ceremonial aspect of poetic language. He has not lacked precedessors, however, to mention only Jan Polkowski, Julia Hartwig (b. 1921), Artur Międzyrzecki (1922–96), Paweł Hertz (1918–2001), Mieczysław Jastrun (1903–83), and Leopold Staff. Finally, the vindication aimed also at life, which deserves no less attention than death. After the war, the occupation, and the Holocaust, life ceased to be an apparent value. It became uncertain, and even – in the face of the mass-scale death of innocents – morally suspect. Here Miłosz makes an appearance again, with Tadeusz Różewicz at his side.

According to both authors, the authentic life, anchored in surviving values and in alliance with God, and which in itself in the guarantee of creativity, should not be a counterfeit or an illusion, a poor substitute, a bluff, or a compromise with the memory of horrific crimes. The consequences of this stance in their work, however, turn out to be different. Miłosz seeks an exit out of the darkness. If nothingness (*Nichtung*) destroys, he seems to think, then life fertilizes. He thus bets on attentiveness. A careful look allows him to discover the beauty of the body, the pleasure of existence, love, and lust, the detailed beauty of nature, and finally the mysterious, deeper order whose traces have not yet been totally erased. Różewicz, for his part, is disgruntled: he is sickened by how a human being pretends that he is still Human, that the ideas of God, humanism, art, and poetry are not bankrupt, and that it is possible to live after the Holocaust as if something irreversible had not happened.

Różewicz is a moralist who does not give the reader even a moment's respite from humanity's fall into the abyss of evil. His work delineated a path of pessimism and expiation that runs through Polish poetry to this day, starting with his first volumes (*Niepokój* [Anxiety, 1947] and *Czerwona rękawiczka* [The Red Glove, 1948]). Różewicz's path cuts across territories of memory of the people who were murdered (also in Jerzy Ficowski, Henryk Grynberg, Irit Amiel, Piotr Matywiecki, Piotr Sommer, Piotr Szewc, Krystyna Dąbrowska), philosophical realms where death is represented as the superordinate element in relation to life (in Rymkiewicz and Dariusz Suska), and spaces of intimate contemplation of the passing of life (in the late poems of Jarosław Iwaszkiewicz, dispersed across Szymborska's entire ouevre, in Stanisław Barańczak's final volumes, and in Marcin Świetlicki's entire body of work). Death is a grand theme in Polish poetry, and one that is present also in Classicism, which can likewise be understood as an attempt to counterpoint death – to infuse the landscape with vital elements, to oppose pessimism with enduring elements (of tradition, art, or faith), and to do justice to the visible world that does not, after all, give rise only to horror or guilt. Classicism was simultaneously an *answer* to a crisis and the *language* of a crisis, a rebellion against its own impossibility. While the defeated, adversarial Classicism is of most interest here, from Eliot to Krzysztof Koehler (b. 1963), the current took root – or seemed to – in a reductive consciousness, not so much simplified as aimed at simplification. It sought to substitute polyvalence and ambivalence with dichotomy, with the strong-sounding, simple difference articulated by Herbert in "A Knocker": "I strike the board / it answers me / yes – yes / no – no [...] I thump on the board / and it prompts me / with the moralist's dry poem / yes – yes / no – no."[40]

Herbert deserves closer attention. He is one of the best-known Polish poets in the world and the author of one of the most famous Polish poems, "The Envoy of Mr. Cogito":

Go where those others went to the dark boundary
for the golden fleece of nothingness your last prize

go upright among those who are on their knees
among those with their backs turned and those toppled in the dust

you were saved not in order to live
you have little time you must give testimony

be courageous when the mind deceives you be courageous
in the final account only this is important

and let your helpless Anger be like the sea
whenever you hear the voice of the insulted and beaten

let your sister Scorn not leave you
for the informers executioners cowards – they will win
they will go to your funeral and with relief will throw a lump of earth
the woodborer will write your smoothed-over biography

and do not forgive truly it is not in your power
to forgive in the name of those betrayed at dawn

beware however of unnecessary pride
keep looking at your clown's face in the mirror
repeat: I was called – weren't there better ones than I

beware of dryness of heart love the morning spring
the bird with an unknown name the winter oak
light on a wall the splendour of the sky
they don't need your warm breath
they are there to say: no one will console you

be vigilant – when the light on the mountains gives the sign – arise and go
as long as blood turns in the breast your dark star
repeat old incantations of humanity fables and legends
because this is how you will attain the good you will not attain
repeat great words repeat them stubbornly
like those crossing the desert who perished in the sand

and they will reward you with what they have at hand
with the whip of laughter with murder on a garbage heap
go because only in this way will you be admitted to the company of cold skulls
to the company of your ancestors: Gilgamesh Hector Roland

the defenders of the kingdom without limit and the city of ashes
Be faithful Go[41]

Almost from the beginning, an array of qualities were ascribed to Herbert's world view, including intransigence, definitiveness, imperativeness, and moral implacability. These characteristics were seen as the source of his cohesive poetics and his loyalty to basic ethical principles. The following opinion comes from one of the first analyses of his poetry: "he arrived in the world wearing the armour of double classicism: that of Antiquity, and that of the avant-garde and Różewicz. He is an artist of uncommon intellect and erudition, a learned poet with philosophical ambitions and, at the same time, with the charm of an excellent ironist."[42] In *Struna światła* (String of Light, 1956), Herbert indeed appeared in armour, but it was from the outset cracked and faulty, penetrable and misshapen. His later work can be understood, in turns, as an intentional sealing and an inadvertent loosening of a construction aimed at providing poetry with a form resistant to the paralysing influence of nothingness during a time of crisis. The desire for integration was his steady companion, and it was to be fulfilled through performative conclusions and, it seems, irony. Yet many of his excellent works were born out of – or thanks to – defeat, when the will of form and the will of distance (irony) either failed or turned on each other. Putting it succinctly, when armour neither arms nor guards, existence makes an appearance, weak yet – *nolens volens* – alluring. The poet-authority becomes a fellow human being when he stops disguising himself and when tragedy is interchangeable with comedy, weakness seems the offshoot of strength, and the difference between "yes" and "no" ceases to be irrefutable, or – in the spirit of Stanisław Brzozowski – when thought is allowed to pass through the body and is derived from or turns into experience.

From the beginning, Herbert's interpreters noticed that ancient themes, history, and literary portraits of art masterpieces as well as ekphrases do not serve as consolation in his work, or – if they do – then only as a type of retrospective utopia, a mirror in which the present should reflect (on) itself. Over the past two decades, this tendency has fuelled the need to discover in Herbert's work values that are existential, individual, and marked by awareness of the role played by chance, incident, the body, or illness. The character of the poet's final volumes aided this tendency. From this new perspective, the encounter with history is important for making apparent the discontinuity and fragility that emerge from human experiences, rather than the duty and mission arising from individual decisions. In line with such a reading, siding with the weak – the heroes and victims excluded from commemoration – does not protect against one's own weakness. Moralism appears in the end as merely a means to rhetorically order the world and to place chaos and diversity under a spell. In a word, much is being done to move Herbert into the realm of so-called weak thought, which has as its domain infirmity, the trace, the remnant, and the event: – all that, in pointing at the whole, can no longer reclaim or reconstruct it. Herbert's "Awakening" provides one example of a "weak poem":

When the horror subsided the floodlights went out
we discovered that we were on a rubbish-heap in very strange
poses
some with outretched necks
others with open mouths from which still trickled my native
land

still others with fists pressed to eyes
cramped emphatically pathetically taut
in our hands we held pieces of sheet iron and bones
(the floodlights had transformed them into symbols)
but now they were no more than sheet iron and bones

We had nowhere to go we stayed on the rubbish-heap
We tidied things up
the bones and iron sheets we deposited in an archive

We listened to the chirping of streetcars to a swallow-like
voices of factories
and a new life was rolling at our feet[43]

This poem skilfully combines a sense of bankruptcy of sacrifice-worthy idealistic notions with disturbed poetic conventions, becoming a highly unsubordinate or, better put, defective sonnet. Its fourteen verses express disappointment, with the coda – in the form of a simple indication of signs of "new life" – masterfully reflecting the atmosphere of powerlessness that prevails once high emotions settle and hope is lost. In its first part, attention is drawn by the artificiality and theatricality of behaviours and the thespian pedigree of "strange poses." It is as if reality in a state of exceptionality, pregnant with historicity and saturated with lofty "horror," was the work of some demiurge or director, who has at his disposal a blinding light that makes it impossible for the heroes of burgeoning history to see actors within themselves. The awakening in a different world, in a different light or in the shadows, exposes the almost kitsch-like nature of patriotic fever. Such a reading is aided by scattered rhymes, colloquiality, and ellipticity of representation. "Awakening" is also an epiphany of triviality: the instability of meaning is revealed with a certainty that almost stifles the complaint. The grand gesture is only a gesture, and sense is the product of circumstance (again in parentheses, now almost cynical: "the floodlights had transformed them into symbols"), while weapons – "bones and sheet iron" – become archival artefacts.

The bitterness of this poem is unparalleled. If we were to relate it to March 1968 – the rebellion of intellectuals and students against restrictions on freedom of speech – it would be difficult to find a better, more restrained, or more painful recapitulation. If it is seen as a commentary on history, then pessimism moves – yet again in Herbert's poetry – to centre stage. Here history, with power as its domain, comands culture, the domain of principles: it steers it according to its needs, stages it, makes it into a spectacle, flooding the stage with blinding light, and taking away the right to illusion. The figures in the poem, awakened from a dream of heroism, are not asked to remain faithful to this dream. The new life, unrolling underfoot, chirping and swallow-like, does not deserve to be believed in, which means that the awakened people will not cling to it unconditionally. This will surely lead to a split existence, spent in part on remembrance of illusions and in part on longing after them. They may try to realize their dreams once more, but these are mere suppositions, for the poet does not demand that they – or he, given the pronoun "we" – deny their experience.

To return for a moment to "The Envoy of Mr. Cogito": by not formulatinging a message of loyalty to "the defenders of the kingdom," the poet offers solidarity with powerlessness instead of consolation. By stopping short of a conclusive "envoy," even though the circumstances outlined in the poem open up a space for such a message, he counts himself among the "insulted and beaten." He does not decide to stand with them, nor does he elevate himself above them; he simply *is* one of many. Irony does not work here either as an instrument of cognition or as an indicator of abomination; it does not help to separate oneself from what was revealed after the floodlights went out. Rather, by creating a movement of thought in a realm of rapidly materialized emptiness, it turns this emptiness into a place, an object, something that is as human as possible. The poet's interplace, identical to the space of indeterminacy, has a lava-like tendency to spread out in all directions and to swallow everything it comes across. It is reminiscent of a monster made up solely of a maw:

Lucky Saint George
from his knight's saddle
could exactly evaluate
the strength and movements of the dragon

the first principle of strategy
is to assess the enemy accurately

Mr. Cogito
is in a worse position

he sits in the low
saddle of a valley
covered with thick fog
through fog it is impossible to perceive
fiery eyes
greedy claws
jaws

through fog
one sees only
the shimmering of nothingness

the monster of Mr. Cogito
has no measurements

it is difficult to describe
escapes definition

it is like an immense depression
spread out over the country

it can't be pierced
with a pen
with an argument
or spear

were it not for its suffocating weight
and the death it sends down
one would think
it is the hallucination
of a sick imagination (…)[44]

What is the difference between Herbert's fog and Różewicz's "nothing"? The fog is perhaps even more omnipresent and takes possession also of nature. What is its difference in relation to Borges's desert? And finally, how is it different from his own "kingdom without limit"? This answer is obvious: the kingdom is a place where fundamental values reside, whereas the fog (the monster, the dragon) consumes all differences between these values until we lose the opportunity, the ability, and the will to fight for them.

How does one not become lost in the fog on the way to a kingdom without limit, and thus also without any border markers? At the core, this is an issue of form. For Herbert, impetuosity indicates not only outbursts of emotion but also the fraying of simple form. Herbert strove for a simple, impenetrable form. It emerges from the process of filtering diversity into a monolith, an axiom, an entreaty. When no longer in need of consolation or fortification by heroes as they once were, and when in more need of conversation and intimacy than of drama and dialogue, readers look to Herbert's poetry for a voice that falters and is muted, and a form that is broken. This prompts the risky conclusion that, in this poetry, life is an error of verse. Looking at it philosophically, one could say that it is a perspective error of the only truth – namely, death. This could pertain to Różewicz: a dark and outspoken poet but not a depressive one. Herbert, however, is a depressive poet; he holds on to rationalism and abstract authority with an ever firmer grip, attempting to counter the truth of contemporary times with a universal truth, with "error," in his case, being an inadvertent effect – and all the more interesting for it.

In the 1980s, Stanisław Barańczak did not view himself as an émigré artist (an exile, a pilgrim, or the guardian of the national spirit). After 1989, the concept of an émigré artist lost its original meaning. Many Polish poets of the middle and younger generations resided and still reside abroad, however. Czesław Miłosz, Tymoteusz Karpowicz, and Stanisław Barańczak all lived in the United States, and Maciej Niemiec in Paris; all of them are now deceased. Artur Szlosarek and Krzysztof Niewrzęda still reside in Berlin; Grzegorz Wróblewski is in Copenhagen, while Wioletta Grzegorzewska is in England. London and Berlin, which are home to large communities of Poles, continue to function as places of literary exchange between Poland and the poets and readers who live abroad.

The situation of poetry after 1989 changed noticeably. Setting aside the question whether that year constitutes a strong, deep caesura for literature, or is simply one of those shifts in values that occur from time to time, the widely held belief in its significance among poets and readers cannot be denied. While critics expected important new literature to emerge, the poets were convinced that was truly new about their work was its insignificance.

They called themselves “barbarians,” by which they meant strangers in the contemporary world. In the poem “Akslop” (Poland spelled backwards), Miłosz Biedrzycki (b. 1967) writes about “Diwron” and “Cziweżór” (Norwid and Różewicz, respectively), the “local curiosities” meant to astound the tourists. In “Wiersz wspólny (półfinałowy)” (Joint Poem [Semi-Finals]), the three famous Marcins of the quarterly *rough draft* (Baran, Sendecki, and Świetlicki) declare emphatically that “out the window there is dick all of an idea.”[45] Older by a generation, Bohdan Zadura has on many occasions pointed out the social uselessness of poetry; he has also self-ironically confessed to having lost the certainty that writing a good poem “brings greater pleasure / than the sight of svelte buttocks.”[46] This disavowal of poetry by poets was somewhat of a tease in the early 1990s; yet it did not weaken in subsequent years; indeed, faced with the strong dominance of mass culture, it evolved into an inevitable and bitter irony, one that extended also to artists of other generations, such as Szymborska and Różewicz.

Awareness that the former splendour of the lyric was nearing its end – despite its central location in Polish culture, at the intersection of various strands of national ambitions, where pride is rooted in tradition – was expressed in diverse ways. Besides the language of blasphemy, mockery, and grandstanding (used by Biedrzycki and Świetlicki, for example), there were others – nostalgic, catastrophic, or mythopoetic. A common feature of these diverse attitudes was the conviction that they constituted an adequate reaction to the conditions created for literature by reality and that they expressed a realistic stance towards the influences shaping their readers' position in the here and now.

This attitude provoked some objections, for instance, from Jarosław Marek Rymkiewicz:

> It is a very interesting problem: why in literature such as ours, in literature where the greatest works (almost all) were written in a high tone (Kochanowski's *Laments*, the poems of Sęp-Szarzyński, Mickiewicz's *Forefathers' Eve, Part III*, Słowacki's *Anhelli*), this high tone has now become unseeming. This does not mean that I do not value things said in an ambiguous tone, or said ironically. Yet it is worth pausing on why writers in Poland are for many years now rewarded for snickering. And the more ridiculous the snickering, the higher the prize.[47]

Rymkiewicz noted an especially large amount of such snickering among young poets. So did Adam Zagajewski, who returned at the end of the twentieth century to tendencies he had shown at the beginning of his poetic journey. At that time, his inclinations had been muted by the sense that poetry had an obligation to intervene, but they reawoke in the 1980s and were again in full cry by the end of the 1990s. Words from Zagajewski's very early poem – “tell the truth that's what you serve” – could easily serve as the touchstone for his decidedly mature works.[48] Speaking the truth means, after all, turning against ambiguity, uncertainty, and secrecy. It means letting go of distance, quotation marks, play, and pose and conquering one's fear of language's power to express things directly. It means taking a break from one's daily scene and giving voice to an internal necessity. Zagajewski wrote:

> Surely, we don't go to poetry for sarcasm or irony, for critical distance, learned dialectics or clever jokes. These worthy qualities and forms perform splendidly in their proper place – in an essay, a scholarly tract, a broadside in an opposition newspaper. In poetry, though, we seek the vision, the fire, the flame that accompanies spiritual revelation. In short, from poetry we expect poetry.[49]

Of course, it was not poetry without substance – and more specifically, poetry without substance that referred the reader beyond the poem – that concerned Zagajewski. Rather, at stake for the poet was poetry with a substance that cannot be reduced without detriment or translated into non-poetic languages; his concern was for the pre-discursive experience tied to "discovery" or epiphany, to a sense of mystery and the permanent, inexpressible yet impossible-to-avoid sensation of the majesty of being. Zagajewski was right to inquire into the other, overlooked possibilities of poetry. A poem does not have to remain bound up with everyday experience, nor does it have to avoid emotion at all costs. When irony triumphs, it can only be because we misunderstand its essence. The reader, who has not changed as much as various theories claim, still treats the poet as a venerable messenger. It would not be difficult to add other arguments to this line of reasoning, although this would not lessen the essential issue – namely, the seizure of pathos by mass culture.

To summarize: the critical stance towards reality in the poetry of the past two decades has placed the "barbarians" and the Neoclassicists on the same side. It is the side of otherness – of irreconcilability with the world. At the same time, these poets differ, intentionally and objectively, from artists who consider reality to be a phantom. Their attitude towards language – contrasted with that of poets like Tymoteusz Karpowicz and Andrzej Sosnowski – also brings the "barbarians" and Neoclassicists closer together. Admittedly, the former strive for a more colloquial style, eliminating as much as possible the artificiality of the utterance, while the latter emphasize and try to make use of this artificiality, also for the benefit of tradition. Both sides care about the communicativeness and semantic effectiveness of the poem, however. They consider notions of aporia and poetry's apophatic nature, which point to language as the characteristic, perhaps the sole *perpetuum mobile*, to be the equivalent of the play of empty signifiers.

In this sense, both Neoclassicists and "barbarians" are part of modernism's continuation, whereas Sosnowski – preceded by a few artists, such as Witold Wirpsza and Tymoteusz Karpowicz – actually moves beyond modernism. By extension, both associations with the Classicism of the 1990s do not describe Classicism, but rather testify equally to the will of an aesthetic and world-view *agon*, as well as the need to rejuvenate critical language. The space of conflict is the space of life. It is difficult to imagine speaking of poetry without speaking of Classicism. For this reason, the true end of Polish Classicism is not possible.

Solidarity and Solitude

Borrowed from an important collection of essays by Adam Zagajewski, *Solidarność i samotność* (Solidarity, Solitude: Essays, 1986), the pairing of solidarity and solitude accurately signals the challenges of being a Polish poet, who is doubly predestined. On the one hand, being sentenced to solitude and separateness turns one into a poet, while on the other being condemned to Polishness secures one's place in a community and imprisons one within it. As Edward Hirsch, an American scholar of Polish poetry, admits:

> The best Polish poets are determined to speak in their own voices. They have mounted in their work a witty and tireless defense of individual subjectivity against collectivist thinking … I admire postwar Polish poetry for its unfashionable clarity, its democratic ethos, its commitment to an idiosyncratic individuality, its suspicion of absolutes and rejection of

tyranny. I admire its humane values, its eminent sanity, its deep humility before the plenitude of the world. Each of these Polish poets has struggled to find an individual way to replace the nihilism that engulfed civilization after the end of the war. Miłosz has sought a ground for transcendence; Różewicz endorses what has been called a "qualified humanism"; Herbert stubbornly maintains an allegiance to "uncertain clarity"; Szymborska rejoices in what she calls "commonplace miracles" and the gaiety of art; Zagajewski becomes a rapturous skeptic, an ecstatic ironist. These poets try to tell the truth about human suffering, but they also seek to make meaning out of that suffering. Hence Miłosz's brave claim: "Human reason is beautiful and invincible." Here is a poetry that takes history into account even as it seeks to transcend history, to find the stability of truth.[50]

What does an "own voice" mean, however? Reflecting on this question leads to a surprising conclusion: the Polish poet desires, first and foremost, to be unshackled from his fate. He wants *not* to be a Romantic, *not* to propagate Classicism, and *not* to sign up to an avant-garde program; he wants the right *not* to affiliate, and he wants both non-partisan criticism and immoderate praise. All of this would mean achieving independence from the time in which one lives – *not* experiencing the crisis of the human being, culture, language, *not* encountering any of the anxieties that nourished and poisoned modernism. As far as we know, no one like this has appeared in Polish poetry of the past hundred years. We also know that the poems of the most important Polish poets were not dictated by any of the above-mentioned currents. Was Miłosz really a Classicist? Did Herbert actually depart from the avant-garde? Was Tadeusz Różewicz not the greatest of the Romantics, after all? This is why their names have appeared at various points in this discussion, undermining its proposed order.

Różewicz at the End of the Century

The last phase of Różewicz's work injected an unexpected momentum into Polish poetry of the past two decades. This is somewhat surpising, for a display of new energy was not expected of this poet, who in the 1980s was clearly moving towards silence and the closure of his body of work. It seemed equally unlikely that his voice would be heard under the changed circumstances; it was difficult to imagine that a world born in 1989 (by its own understanding) would listen to an aged poet who was so closely linked to the postwar decades. What did Różewicz have to offer the 1990s, when it was too early for the new world to become disheartened with itself, and too late for the poet to radically transform himself and counter the associations ascribed to him throughout the communist years?

He had three assets at his disposal. First, his poetic *modus vivendi* was suitable for tearing down traditional models, which had become pregnant with pathos over the previous decade. He appeared rather as a "counter-poet" who sabotaged conventional self-creations and validations of lyrical poetry. He was situated by others as closer to reality and for this was rewarded with trust – unlike Miłosz. Różewicz's greatness was not turned against him, for his work connoted anti-heroization, a blend of terror and mockery, the knocking down of pedestals, sensitivity to the temptations of hubris, a veridical rather than a know-it-all character, a non-permissive stance towards the state of satisfaction, a harshness and even a cantankerousness. Second, his diatribes against mass society overlapped with the experience of the first half of the 1990s, steered in large measure by an inherited even if up until this point mostly subjectless distrust. The "object" that emerged from the systemic transformation – a world at once endlessly sensual and mediatized – appealed to literature only incidentally and for a short time; soon after, this world revealed the domineering and homogenizing effect of its unchecked proliferation.

Third, Różewicz was a master of contemporary poetry's most important theme – death – which, in the absence of immediately noteworthy new ideas, has come to be viewed as literature's strongest motif. Death had not departed with the old world; on the contrary, it now presented itself on a monumental scale along with its acolytes – sickness, old age, and chance. It was all the more prominent for having as its backdrop a now barren stage, vacated by communism, Solidarity, the Soviet Union, history, and the fatherland. Różewicz's voice resonates most in drastic descriptions of objectification ("Walentynki" [Valentine's Day]; "Recykling"), in piercing laments ("Matka Odchodzi" [Mother Departs]), in self-portraits ("Poet Emeritus," "Czego byłoby żal" [What Would Be Regretted]), and in sombre portraits of both people and humanity.

After the publication of *Płaskorzeźba* (Bas-Relief, 1991), Różewicz underscored some of his predispositions (theological, countercultural, and pessimistic); then later – starting with *Szara strefa* (The Grey Zone, 2002) – he dissolved, dispersed, and even parodied what he had tried for decades to build. This has given rise to the opinion that the Różewicz of the past two decades is a poet significantly different from the earlier Różewicz. It is easy to notice that, in addition to poems that condense meanings as they did before, there are more works based in enumeration, which – differently than before – tend towards logorrhea. Aleatoric constructions and dysconstructions play an increasingly important part. Aleatoricism assumes the participation of the recipient, and dysconstructions constitute a type of annulment of themselves and of the events they could become within a social space – they set communication in motion and then immediately block it. I am thinking here of numerous poems that leave the reader feeling powerless, situated outside any sort of value system – indeed, outside poetry understood as a sphere of communication and exchange. These irresponsible texts, like spitefully stuck-out tongues, transport poems from the domain of poetry to the realm of gestures. They belie proper, normalized, perhaps even normal poetry by activating and subsequently severing associations with its previous forms. At the same time, Różewicz does not allow everything that is presented as poetry to be treated as such. At stake, then, is not the expansion of the territory of poetry, but the transgression of its boundaries, or, more precisely, their repeated transgression until the point of their dissolution, when all certainty disappears as to whether something – a newspaper excerpt, the sound of a television, logorrhea, or an antic – can be considered poetry.

Różewicz's "Kuchnia wasza nać" from *To i owo* (This and That, 2012) is an excellent example of an outrageous poem that nevertheless lends itself to characterization in terms of both poetics and ethics.[51] Regarding poetics, it can be seen as a persiflage, an example of formal mimesis, a vulgar song, or a phraseological operation (its title alludes to a strong and common profanity). Regarding ethics, it is a parody of fashionable behaviour and a mockery of thoughtlessness, seen as a condition for staying on the right side of currently dominant lifestyle trends. It is not enough to stop at these statements, however – it must be added that the poem is irritating: manifestly slapdash, generalizing, unqualified, annoying, and petty. It destroys in equal measure the diagnosis, the message, and the subject. How to explain this? It is possible to think of Różewicz as a tragic idealist, in other words a poet who, in denying poetry as it exists the right to the truth, acts in the name of an impossible poetry, a certain ideal that cannot be known since it cannot be reached. Paradoxically, therefore, the truth demands that it not be spoken of, subjectivity calls for its self-destruction, and the advantages derived from fame and respect command their ridicule. Różewicz's "I" is thus ambivalent; it is loyal to faith in value that deserves sacrifice, yet it is also loyal to the void that alone can testify to this value. As a result, his "I" must question itself repeatedly, and not through declarations, which would constitute only a more complex form of narcissism, but through the radical transformation and destruction of its message.

To End and Begin With

The most distinctive poet in Polish poetry of recent years is, in my opinion, Eugeniusz Tkaczyszyn-Dycki (b. 1962), whose poems penetrate irreconcilable antinomies. The Baroque, death, sensuality, and a piercing yet hidden irony emerge on first reading. The trouble is that most often, on subsequent readings, nothing is revealed beyond what was visible to start with. Dycki's poems resist inquiry and interpretive concepts. Moreover, they do not appear to change over time – it seems that Dycki's poetic project was born in a form almost entirely mature and virtually complete. So it is not its linear transformations, and especially not its maturing, that one must address, but rather the co-presence of forms and the play of variants within it. Dycki's poetry is constructed of elements such as diversity and simultaneousness, repetitiveness and singularity, non-identical identity, and contradiction.

As an artist, Dycki brought the attributes of his style to the point of obsession and mannerism almost without a moment's delay, to some extent by his second poem. That is why what appears in one instance as an expression of existential horror, in another instance (or in another's view) seems like a joke or part of a thought-out strategy. The order of his lyrical world, experienced through a return to the same images, motifs, terms, and figures, becomes an illusion, an unsteady ground for the reader to tread. Where am I – the reader asks – in the reality of another's life that could also be mine, or in a text that can be absorbed only through an aesthetic interaction? Where does the melancholy stem from – from empathy, the blurring of boundaries between "I" and "not-I"? Where does the pleasure come from – from the distance that protects me from dissolving into the realm of another's sensuality?

Someone who encounters for the first time this author's nearly stock phrase – "Autumn already, O Lord, and I haven't got a home" – has every right to feel naively concerned about the plight of a homeless person during the rainy season that foretells of the arrival of merciless winter.[52] Lack of refuge from the cold, with its accompanying sensations of permanent danger, dispensability, and exclusion, as well as bitterness and emptiness, is the most painful of life's experiences. For the lack of a home, still understood almost literally, is a lack of a future that is born, after all, of hope. But the home is not, of course, only a physical value, although it is this value – endangered or lost – that underpins all other values. Desires and fears of a higher order, whether psychological or spiritual, are understood with reference to primary desires and fears. The homelessness of the protagonist of Tkaczyszyn-Dycki's poems has this bodily, physical aspect. It is tied to constant movement, the wandering between cities, as well as to the loss of people who personalized the home, and especially the mother.

When we read the mentioned phrase once again, we conclude that this homelessness is both literal and symbolic. It concerns the world and its order, or rather disorder. Not having a home means doubting the wholeness, centrality, and sense of the universe. The prayer-like, supplicatory timbre of the evoked words brings out their somewhat self-ironic, bitter taste and also directs the reader beyond the realm of senses – towards God, or some other fundamental text. It demands that we ask what is a home versus what is its non-existence. Tkaczyszyn-Dycki thus describes a spiritual homelessness, which initially calls to mind being lost in contemporaneity as a result of the ineffectiveness of culture, but which is also universal, stemming from the human condition. At the same time, the poet avoids the monophonic lament, hiding his *tremendum* behind a shield of convention and stylization, and unmasking his own writing in various ways. In effect, the reservoir of readerly reactions cannot be exhausted either on compassion or on aesthetic aristocraticism; the pleasure of encountering a cultured and predictable text is interrupted time and time again, although the reverse also occurs: Dycki's paroxysms are smoothed out and straightened, and language regains its form, while thoughts expressed in the poem cease to irritate or hurt. Reading, we move between text and life – between a poem that points to itself as a poem and a poem that points somewhere beyond itself – into a darkness.

In this manner, the age that began with Leśmian and is rich with the poetry of several great masters, in the first place that of the intentionally luminous Miłosz and of the *nolens volens* dark Różewicz, ends with the writing of no less remarkable successors, led by Świetlicki, Sosnowski, and Tkaczyszyn-Dycki. A century has come to an end, but not poetry. The directives that, in various forms, are shared by the traditions discussed in this essay remain current. The most important among these is the principle of responsibility for the social world, for remembering what is eternal to human beings, for defining the new human being who creates new communicative possibilities and resides in virtual spaces, for rejuvenating language that shrinks under pressure from narrowly pragmatic values, for recalling ideas that sensitize us to history's harms and sins, and for words and emotions that should not be erased from the future's dictionary. Although the poem's voice does not ring loudly today, it contains – like the black box of the Malaysian plane that disappeared in 2014 and has yet to be found – a truth that is hard to do without.[53]

Piotr Śliwiński
Adam Mickiewicz University, Poland
Translated by Agnieszka Polakowska

NOTES

1 Marjorie Perloff, *21st-Century Modernism: The "New" Poetics*, 3.

2 See, for example, Michał Paweł Markowski, *Polska literatura nowoczesna: Leśmian, Schulz, Witkacy*.

3 Benjamin Paloff's unpublished translation of Leśmian's "Pierwsza schadzka" from *Napój cierniste* (1936):

Pierwsza schadzka za grobem! Rozwalona brama.
Stąpaj pilnie!... Ucałuj ten po drodze krzak.
Czy to - ty? - Już zmieniona, a jeszcze - ta sama?
Upewnij!... Wzrok mi słabnie... Podaj dłonią znak!

Nie ma znaków! Od dawna już w nic się rozwiały!
Nie ma żadnych upewnień! Nikt nie wierzy w nas! ...

Zmilkły śmiechy w ciemnościach i płacze ustały.
W pajęczynie po kątach zagnieździł się - czas...

Zejdź z drogi - ćmom i kwiatom!... Postroń się złudzeniom!...
Chyba najrzeczywistszy jest ten - siana stóg...
Czemu płaczesz? - Dla ludzi, oddanych istnieniom,
Ból nasz - ledwo jest dreszczem księżycowych smug.

4 M.H. Abrams, *A Glossary of Literary Terms*, 168.
5 Helena Zaworska, *O Nową Sztukę. Polskie programy artystyczne lat 1917–1922*, 86.
6 Bruno Jasieński, "Futuryzm polski (bilans)," 4.
7 Stanisław Jaworski, "Wstęp," in Tadeusz Peiper, *Pisma wybrane*, xxi.
8 As quoted in Sławiński, *Koncepcja języka poetyckiego Awangardy Krakowskiej*, 81.
9 Wisława Szymborska, "Joy of Writing," 128.
10 Jan Błoński, "Bieguny poezji" in *Wszystko co literackie*, 174–5.
11 Zbigniew Bieńkowski, *Przyszłość przeszłości*, 137.
12 Czesław Miłosz, "O Książce":

Gdzież jest miejsce dla ciebie w tym wieku zamętu,
książko mądra, spokojna, stopie elementów,
pogodzonych na wieki spojrzeniem artysty?
[...]
My niespokojni, ślepi i epoce wierni,
gdzieś daleko idziemy [...]
Wawrzyn jest niedostępny nam, świadomym kary,
jaką czas tym wyznacza, którzy pokochali
doczesność, ogłuszoną łoskotem metali.
Więc sławę nam znaczono stworzyć – bezimienną,
Jak okrzyk pożegnalny odchodzących – w ciemność

13 Tadeusz Różewicz, "Z umarłych rąk Czechowicza," 7.
14 Białoszewski, "Of My Hermitage With Calling," 10: "Dziwię się / i dziwię siebie / i komentuje wciąż żywoty otoczenia / pociągające za sznury od bielizny / i za dzwony od butów na odpust poezji / na nieustanne uroczyste zdziwienie."
15 Barańczak, "Pismo," 10.
16 Bauman, "Ponowoczesność, czyli o niemożliwości awangardy," 176.
17 Sosnowski, "Czy jesteś w takim razie poetą postmodernistycznym?", 56.
18 Keane, *Skamander: The Poets and their Poetry 1918–1929,* 65. "Jeżeli gdzieś na Starym pokaże się Mieście / I utkwi w was Kiliński swe oczy zielone. / Zabijcie go! – A trupa zawleczcie na stronę / I tylko wieść mi o tym radosną przynieście." Jan Lechoń, "Herostrates."
19 As quoted in Miłosz, *The History of Polish Literature*, 385.
20 Miłosz, *Witness of Poetry*, 83.
21 Stabro, *Chwila bez imienia*, 314.
22 Jan Polkowski, "The Envoy of Mr. X", 79.
23 Miłosz, "Do Lecha Wałęsy":

Po dwustu latach,
Lechu Wałęso,
Po dwustu latach

Odzyskiwanej i znów traconej wolności
Zostałeś naczelnikiem polskiego ludu
I tak jak tamten
masz przeciw sobie mocarstwa [...]

24 Świetlicki, "For Jan Polkowski." Translated by William Martin, 278. The poem was written in 1988, delivered during a "NaGłos" event in 1989, and first published in Polish in 1992 in the volume *Cold Countries*.
25 Waldemar Okoń, *Słownik literatury polskiej XIX wieku*, 42–3.
26 Peyre, *Co to jest klasycyzm?* Translated by Maciej Żurowski, 254–5.
27 Ibid., 277.
28 Ibid., 29.
29 Ibid., 279.
30 Abramowska, "Czy to jest klasycyzm?," 269.
31 Ricoeur, "Is the Present Crisis a Specifically Modern Phenomenon?" 145.
32 Sheppard, "The Problematics of European Modernism," 4.
33 Ibid., 36.
34 Ibid., 37.
35 Ibid., 40.
36 Markowski, "Poetry and Modernity," 85.
37 Staff, *Wiersze Wybrane*, 343: "Nie szukał płaskich rąk oklasku, / Podziwiał ranki i wieczory, / Spisywał wiersze swe na piasku / I nie używał metafory."
38 Bielik-Robson, "Na pustyni," *Kryptoteologie późnej nowoczesności*, 14–15.
39 See Frye, *The Great Code*.
40 Herbert, "A Knocker," 78.
41 Herbert, "The Envoy of Mr. Cogito," 95–7.
42 Kwiatkowski, "Wizja przeciw równaniu," 1.
43 Herbert, "Awakening," in *Selected Poems*, 132.
44 Herbert, "The Monster of Mr. Cogito."
45 Baran, Sendecki, and Świetlicki, "Wiersz wspólny (półfinałowy)": "tak, za oknem ni chuja idei."
46 Zadura, "Z czego wyrosłem": "z przekonania / że dobry wiersz / daje większą przyjemność / niż widok zgrabnych pośladków."
47 Rymkiewicz, "Terror szyderców," 170.
48 Zagajewski, "Truth," 4.
49 Zagajewski, "The Shabby and the Sublime," 31.
50 Hirsch, *How to Read a Poem*, 179, 190–1.
51 kuchnia wasza mać!
sponsorzy szmiry i zdziry
kuchnia włoska kuchnia grecka
kuchnia staropolska
kuchnia kuchnia kuchnia
kuchnia wasza mać
kuchnia jak u ludzi
kuchnia jak u mamy
kuchnia jak u cioci
kuchnia domowa

grochówka wojskowa
kurwa wasza mać
kuchnia chińska
kuchnia rosyjska
kuchnia francuska
kuchnia niemiecka
kuchnia australijska (?)
kuchnia amerykańska (coś takiego!)
[...]
jajka przepiórcze
na płetwie rekina
strusie na rożnie
z pędów bambusa
jądra koguta
w gniazdkach bocianich
gruszki na wierzbie
w kiszkach baranich

52 In Polish, the phrase reads "jesień już Panie a ja nie mam domu." Its prevalence is signaled by the title of a collection of critical commentaries on the author, edited by Grzegorz Jankowicz, *Jesień już Panie a ja nie mam domu. Eugeniusz Tkaczyszyn-Dycki i krytycy.*

53 The comparison between poetry and the black box of a plane is borrowed from Andrzej Sosnowski's talk given at a Silesius Poetic Workshop in Wrocław on 16 May 2014.

WORKS CITED

Abramowska, Janina. "Czy to jest klasycyzm?" In *Przez znaki do człowieka*. Edited by Barbara Sienkiewicz. 269–77. Poznań: WiS, 1997.

Abrams, Meyer Howard. *A Glossary of Literary Terms*. 7th ed. Forth Worth: Harcourt Brace, 1999.

Baczyński, Krzysztof Kamil. "Without a Name." In *White Magic and Other Poems*. Translated by Bill Johnston. 67. Los Angeles: Green Integer, 2005.

Baran, Marcin, Marcin Sendecki, and Marcin Świetlicki. "Wiersz wspólny (połfinałowy)." http://e-poezja.pl/forum/814_wiersz_wspolny_polfinalowy_marcin_baran_sendecki_i_swietlicki.html.

Barańczak, Stranisław. *Widokówka z tego świata i inne rymy z lat 1986–1988*. Paryż: Zeszyty Literackie, 1988.

– "Pismo." In *159 wierszy*. 10. Kraków: Znak, 1993.

Bauman, Zygmunt. "Ponowoczesność, czyli o niemożliwości awangardy." *Teksty Drugie* 5–6: 1994: 171–9.

Bielik-Robson, Agata. *"Na pustyni." Kryptoteologie późnej nowoczesności*. Kraków: Towarzystwo Autorów i Wydawców Prac Naukowych Universitas, 2008.

Białoszewski, Miron. "Of My Hermitage with Calling." In *The Revolutions of Things: Selected Poems of Miron Bialoszewski*. Translated by Andrzej Busza and Bogdan Czaykowski. 10–11. Washington: Charioteer Press, 1974.

Bieńkowski, Zbigniew. *Przyszłość przeszłości*. Wrocław: Wydawnictwo Dolnośląskie, 1996.

Błoński, Jan. "Bieguny poezji." In *Wszystko co literackie*. Edited by Jerzy Jarzębski. 178–83. Kraków: Wydawnictwo Literackie, 2001.
– "Patos, romantyzm, proroctwo." In *Miłosz jak świat*. Kraków: Wydawnictwo Literackie, 1998.
Frye, Northrop. *The Great Code: The Bible and Literature*. Edited by Alvin A. Lee. Toronto: University of Toronto Press, 2006.
Herbert, Zbigniew. "Awakening." Translated by Czesław Miłosz and Peter Dale Scott. In *Selected Poems of Zbigniew Herbert*. 132. Harmondsworth, Middlesex, England: Penguin, 1968.
– "The Envoy of Mr. Cogito." Translated by Bogdana and John Carpenter. In *Selected Poems*. 95–7. Kraków: Wydawnictwo Literackie, 2000.
– "A Knocker." Translated by Czesław Miłosz and Peter Dale Scott. In *Selected Poems of Zbigniew Herbert*. 78. New York: Ecco Press, 1985.
– "The Monster of Mr Cogito." Translated by Bogdana and John Carpenter. http://dungtientran3.blogspot.ca/2006/11/zbigniew-herbert.html.
Hirsch, Edward. "Poetry and History: Polish Poetry after the End of the World." In *How to Read a Poem (and Fall in Love with Poetry)*. 172–91. San Diego, New York, and London: Harcourt, 1999.
Jankowicz, Grzegorz, ed. *Jesień już Panie a ja nie mam domu. Eugeniusz Tkaczyszyn-Dycki i krytycy*. Kraków: ha!art, 2001.
Jasieński, Bruno. "Futuryzm polski (bilans)." *Zwrotnica* 6 (1923): 177–84.
Jaworski, Stanisław, ed. "Wstęp." In Tadeusz Peiper, *Pisma wybrane*. iii–lxxvi. Wrocław: Zakład Narodowy im. Ossolińskich, 1979.
Keane, Barry. *Skamander: The Poets and Their Poetry 1918–1929*. Warszawa: Agade, 2004.
Krauss, Rosalind. E. "The Originality of the Avant-Garde." In *The Originality of the Avant-garde and Other Modernist Myths*. 151–70. Cambridge, MA: MIT Press, 1986.
Kwiatkowski, Jerzy. "Wizja przeciw równaniu. Nowa walka romantyków z klasykami." *Życie Literackie* 3 (1958): 1, 6–8.
Lechoń, Jan. "Herostrates." In *A Story of Poland in Sixty Poems*. Vol. 2. Edited by Anita Debska. 23. Toruń: Attick Press, 2010.
Leśmian, Bolesław. "Pierwsza schadzka." *Napój cierniosty*. 9. Warszawa: J. Mortkowicz, 1936.
Markowski, Michał Paweł. "Poetry and Modernity: An Incomplete Project." In *Identity and Interpretation*. 73–97. Stockholm: Department of Slavic Languages and Literatures, 2003.
– *Polska literatura nowoczesna. Leśmian, Schulz, Witkacy*. Kraków: Universitas, 2007.
Miłosz, Czesław. "Do Lecha Wałesy." *Przegląd Polski* 76 (1982).
– *The History of Polish Literature*. Berkeley: University of California Press, 1983.
– "A Treatise on Poetry." In *New and Collected Poems 1931–2001*. 107–52. New York: Ecco, 2003.
– *Witness of Poetry*. Cambridge, MA: Harvard University Press, 1983.
Okoń, Waldemar. *Słownik literatury polskiej XIX wieku*. Wrocław: Zakład Narodowy im. Ossolińskich, 1991.
Peiper, Tadeusz. "Tędy." In *Pisma wybrane*. Edited by S. Jaworski. 3–204. Wrocław: Zakład Narodowy im. Ossolińskich, 1979.
Perloff, Marjorie. *21st-Century Modernism: The "New" Poetics*. Malden: Blackwell, 2002.
Peyre, Henri. *Co to jest klasycyzm?* Translated by Maciej Żurowski. Warszawa: Państwowe Wydawnictwo Naukowe, 1985.
Polkowski, Jan. "The Envoy of Mr. X." In *Young Poets of a New Poland*. Translated by Donald Pirie. Edited by Krystyna Lars. 79–80. London: Forest Books, 1993.

Ricoeur, Paul. "Is the Present Crisis a Specifically Modern Phenomenon?" In *The Ancients and the Moderns*. Edited by Reginald Lilly. 130–47. Bloomington: Indiana University Press, 1996.

Różewicz, Tadeusz. *To i owo*. Kołobrzeg: Biuro Literackie, 2012.

– "Z umarłych rąk Czechowicza." Introduction to Józef Czechowicz, *Wiersze wybrane*. 5–14. Warszawa: Państwowy Instytut Wydawniczy, 1987.

Rymkiewicz, Jarosław Marek. "'Terror szyderców,' z poetą rozmawiali: T. Majeran i D. Suska." *Fronda* 6 (1996): 170–8. http://pismofronda.pl/wp-content/uploads/Fronda06.pdf.

Sheppard, Richard. "The Problematics of European Modernism." In *Theorizing Modernism: Essays in Critical Theory*. Edited by Steve Giles. 1–51. London: Routledge, 1993.

Sławiński, Janusz. *Koncepcja języka poetyckiego Awangardy Krakowskiej*. Kraków: Towarzystwo Autorów i Wydawców Prac Naukowych "Universitas," 1998.

Sosnowski, Andrzej. "Czy jesteś w takim razie poetą postmodernistycznym?" Interview by Michał Paweł Markowski. Edited by Grzegorz Jankowicz. *Nowy Wiek* 7–8 (2001–2): 53–61.

Stabro, Stanisław. *Chwila bez imienia. O poezji Krzysztofa Kamila Baczyńskiego*. Kraków: Towarzystwo Autorów i Wydawców Prac Naukowych "Universitas," 2003.

Staff, Leopold. *Wiersze wybrane*. Warszawa: PWN, 1973.

Stróżewski, Władysław. *Dialektyka twórczości*. Kraków: Polskie Wydawnictwo Muzyczne, 1983.

Świetlicki, Marcin. "For Jan Polkowski." Translated by Willian Martin. *Chicago Review* 46, nos. 3–4 (2000): 278–9.

Szymborska, Wisława. "Joy of Writing." In *Miracle Fair: Selected Poems of Wisława Szymborska*. Translated by Joanna Trzeciak. 127–8. New York: W.W. Norton, 2001.

Vattimo, Gianni. *Oltre interpretazione. Il significato dell'hermeneutica per la filosofia*. Roma: Laterza, 1995.

Zadura, Bogdan. "Z czego wyrosłem." http://www.akcentpismo.pl/pliki/nr1.08/zadura.html.

Zagajewski, Adam. "The Shabby and the Sublime." In *A Defense of Ardor*. Translated by Clare Cavanagh. 25–50. New York: Farrar, Straus and Giroux, 2004.

– *Solidarity, Solitude: Essays*. Translated by Lillian Vallee. New York: Ecco Press, c1990.

– "Truth." In *Selected Poems*. Translated by Clare Cavanagh, Renata Gorczynski, Benjamin Ivry and C.K. Williams. 4. London: Faber and Faber, 2004.

Zaworska, Helena. *O Nową Sztukę. Polskie programy artystyczne lat 1917–1922*. Warszawa: Państwowy Instytut Wydawniczy, 1963.

INTERWAR, WAR, POSTWAR, AND POST-1989 POETRY

Matter, Spirit, and Linguistic Metamorphoses (Bolesław Leśmian)

Young Poland: Lasting roughly from 1890 until Polish independence in 1918, Young Poland was a loose aesthetic movement, analogous to similar movements elsewhere in Europe (notably Young Vienna and Young Scandinavia) in its rejection of naturalism and realism, which had dominated art and literature throughout the second half of the nineteenth century. Writers and artists of Young Poland sought to revive older Romantic values, such as spiritualism and intuitionism. They also distrusted material reality and showed an interest in nature as well as in peasant culture (as distinct from the realists' preoccupation with the city). Its major proponents included the playwright and artist Stanisław Wyspiański (1869–1907) and the poet Leopold Staff (1878–1957).

Little-known in the West, Bolesław Leśmian (1877?–1937) was a poet of subtle thought and exceedingly challenging language. Czesław Miłosz noted that he was regarded "as the most accomplished Polish poet of the twentieth century."[1] He was comparable in style and intellect to major European poets of his day – notably to William Butler Yeats (1865–1939), with whom he shared an abiding interest in folklore and traditional song. His relative obscurity can be attributed to his dense wordplay and his complex philosophical concerns.[2] His work is typical of the Young Poland movement in that it reflects neo-Romantic dichotomies between the material and the spiritual, harmony and chaos, urban modernity and rural traditionalism. Even among artistic cohorts engaged with philosophical problems, Leśmian's metaphysics stands out for its depth and rigour. Drawn especially to the ideas of the French philosopher Henri Bergson (1859–1941), Leśmian constructed the lyric poem as a platform for enacting and animating paradoxes, both conceptual and linguistic. It is no wonder, then, that he has come to be recognized as something of a "poet's poet."

Following Bergson, Leśmian asserts that all of material reality is suffused with an undifferentiated essence, a ground tone akin to Bergson's *élan vital.* Confronted with this universal energy – which Leśmian sometimes characterizes as "a song without words" – the poet's task is to unveil the fundamental link between form and formlessness, between the visible and the invisible. In an early theoretical exposition, "Przemiany rzeczywistości" (Metamorphoses of Reality, 1910–11), Leśmian explains how the poet projects his mind into the higher, invisible reality and then looks back on the material world, describing how it appears from the level of spirit. In this way, Leśmian presents poetry as a tool, one that raises our consciousness of this higher reality: "Man seen as a song without words eludes our definitions. He knows, however, that in order to become real, he has to find his tone, he has to draw out his song without words. It is his only, his truest reality."[3]

> **Henri Bergson:** A French philosopher of Jewish origin, Bergson was the world's leading voice on the nature of time before his views were largely supplanted by Einstein's theories. Influential throughout Europe and North America – William James was an enthusiastic correspondent and advocate for his ideas – Bergson emphasized intuition as a tool for understanding the world; memory as the accumulation of time in things; and *élan vital,* the life-force that drives change *in* living things (as evolution) and *through* living things (creativity). In Bergson, writers like Bolesław Leśmian found a philosophical explication of their own investigation of how spirit and matter interact.

This paradox – of the concrete reconstituted through the ethereal, of the universal constructed collaboratively by individuals – repeats itself throughout Leśmian's oeuvre, including in a poem bearing the unlikely title "Słowa do pieśni bez słów" (Words to a Song without Words, 1936). Formally, too, Leśmian's poems exhibit a tension between fastidiously observed form (typically syllabic quatrains and couplets) and idiosyncratic punctuation. But this tension is most evident in Leśmian's signature neologisms – his so-called Leśmianisms (*leśmianizmy*) – which employ prefixes and suffixes to create abstractions of concrete nouns or to concretize a concept. Whereas other poets of Young Poland adorn their pastoral imagery with "blossom" (*kwiecie*) – "These dark leaves and white blossom," Julian Tuwim (1894–1953) writes in an early poem, marking a typical contrast – Leśmian's wordplay imagines a "terrible nonblossom" (*straszne bezkwiecie*). Where other poets might "see the peaceful, blinking stars" (Tuwim again), Leśmian envisions "the sky a-shiver from the blinkery of stars" (*niebo w dreszczach od gwiazd mrugawicy*).[4]

A strong example of all of these forces at work is the posthumous lyric "Tu jestem – w mrokach ziemi" (I'm here – in earthly darkness):

I'm here – in earthly darkness, and am – as yet afar,
Where I am lodged in holy mists and in the rush of stars,
Where, orally atremble, air tells me dreams in song,
And those are dreams I know well, for I am far beyond.
I come from all around me; I find myself there, waiting;
Singingly I rush here, and there – perform breath-bating;
And I go on like prayer, beyond my inborn grief,
Which doesn't seek fulfillment, but wants to be itself.[5]

This poem specifically addresses the problem of the subject's duality, his being split between the here of "earthly darkness" and the ethereal plane of "holy mists," "dream," and "song." The speaker is simultaneously omnipresent and grounded, actively moving and passively waiting. Carried along the traditional thirteen-syllable line with caesura (7+6), whose melodiousness in Leśmian bears distinct echoes of folk song, the reader is likely to trip on dense alliterations or puzzle over such Leśmianisms as "orally atremble" (*drżąc ustnie*) and "singingly I rush here" (*tu się spieszę dośpiewnie*). The point, as the poem itself lays bare in the closing couplet, is not to reconcile these opposites but rather to recognize paradox as a fundamental aspect of human existence.

Leśmian's biography is itself rife with paradox. Born in Warsaw to a family of Jewish intelligentsia – different sources provide 1877, 1878, and 1879 as the year of his birth – he was raised in Kiev, where he was at one point arrested and spent some months in prison, possibly for reciting the politically subversive "Great Improvisation" from Mickiewicz's *Dziady* (Forefathers' Eve, Part III). Leśmian was, in fact, not Leśmian at all, but Lesman, the name that appears in his personal correspondence and business papers. Leśmian is his polonized *nom de plume,* which he most likely assumed at the suggestion of his uncle, the poet Antoni Lange (1863–1929).

"Great Improvisation" – the infamous monologue spoken by Konrad in the second scene of Adam Mickiewicz's 1832 verse drama *Dziady* (Forefather's Eve, Part III). The "Great Improvisation" quickly came to be seen as emblematic of the Polish Romantic ethos, expressing both the individual spiritual struggle to move beyond good and evil and the national struggle to cast off oppression by a foreign power. The text was explicitly subversive of religious and political authority – Konrad's effort to usurp God culminates in the Devil shouting "The Tsar!" Performing it could easily lead to arrest in the Congress Kingdom.

Younger than the Symbolist aesthetes of Young Poland, Leśmian had little use for the Parnassianism and decadent tendencies of Stanisław Przybyszewski (1868–1927) or Zenon Przesmycki (pen name Miriam, 1861–1944), though the latter published many of Leśmian's early poems in his journal *Chimera* and played a key role in bringing his first collection, *Sad rozstajny* (Divergent Orchard, 1912), to print. Nearly two decades older than the poets connected with the influential interwar journal *Skamander,* Leśmian shared their fondness for antiquities and traditional forms, and he mentored the young Tuwim, another Jewish poet forging a career in Polish letters.

Some of the earliest poems in Leśmian's thirty-year career were composed not in Polish but in Russian, appearing in 1906 and 1907 in *Zolotoe Runo* and *Vesy,* both journals associated with the Moscow Symbolists, with whom the young Leśmian had become acquainted in Paris. It was also during his first extended stay in Paris, from 1903 to 1906, that Leśmian likely wrote his only dramatic work in Russian, the non-extant *Vasilii Buslaev*, while also cultivating his appreciation for Bergson. Though he had developed a reputation as a writer's writer, Leśmian maintained a measured distance from the cultural spotlight. After *Divergent Orchard,* he published only two more collections before his death in 1937: *Łąka* (Meadow, 1920) and *Napój cienisty* (Draught of Shadows, 1936). A fourth, posthumous collection, *Dziejba leśna* (Forest Happenings, 1938), appeared the following year. After 1918 he lived in Hrubieszów, a largely Jewish provincial town in southeastern Poland, near the present-day border with Ukraine. There he made his living as a civil law notary, a practice he continued in nearby Zamość from 1923 until his death. In 1929, during one of Leśmian's frequent trips to Warsaw and abroad, his assistant defrauded the firm of a vast sum, for which the poet himself became liable. The financial and psychological toll this episode took would weigh on Leśmian for the rest of his life and at least partly accounts for the dark, fatalistic tone of much of his later writing.

Indeed, Leśmian sees tragedy less in our having to cope with contradiction than in our quixotic attempts to overcome it. In one of his most celebrated poems, the ballad "Dziewczyna" (Girl, 1924), he delivers an allegory of how the struggle for contact with the Absolute leads to self-annihilation. As the poem opens, twelve brothers "who believed in dreams" take up hammers against a wall, beyond which they hear the cries of a young girl. In a driving rhythm that imitates their hammering – the poem's couplets in the original are composed in long, seventeen-syllable lines (8+9) – Leśmian relays the brothers' obsessive labour, long after their own corporeality has disintegrated:

And echoing a thousand times, the wall collapsed and shook the hills.
But there was nothing past the wall, no living soul, nor any Girl.

And no one's eyes, nor any mouth, and wreathed in flowers, no one's fate.
For it was voice and only voice – a voice that does not carry weight.

But nothing – than lament and grief and dark and the unknown and loss.
Such is the world, the hostile world. Why must we have a world like this?

Despite the dreams that were a lie, despite the way that wonders fade,
The heavy hammers came to rest, arranged to mark the work they'd made.

And there was sudden, silent horror – emptiness in airy blue.
So why deride this emptiness? The emptiness won't sneer at you.[6]

As the poem's ending demonstrates, for Leśmian the separation between matter and spirit is there to be recognized, not transcended, and there is plenty in his work to suggest that what the poet calls "the world" consists specifically in this tension, which produces a discomfort that must simply be endured. This is not merely the poet's orientation towards what surrounds him, but an expression of how the individual and the Absolute are mutually dependent. Thus Leśmian says, in an interview from 1934, that he does not know how to express this metaphysics, but that "when I am speaking about nature I regard it as something I not only long for, but that longs for me as well."[7]

Benjamin Paloff
University of Michigan, Ann Arbor

NOTES

1 Miłosz, *The History of Polish Literature,* 347.
2 The affinity between Leśmian and Yeats was championed in the postwar period by Miłosz and Jerzy Pietrkiewicz. See Jolanta Dudek, "The Reception of Yeat's Work in Poland (1898–2004)," in *The Reception of W.B. Yeats in Europe*, 127–8.

3 Leśmian, "Metamorphoses of Reality," 4.

4 Tuwim's poems are "Akacje" ("Acacias") and "Wieczorem" ("In the Evening"), respectively. The Leśmianisms are drawn from "Rok nieistnienia" ("The Year of Nonexistence") and "Gwiazdy" ("Stars"), respectively. All translations of poetry are mine.

5 Tu jestem – w mrokach ziemi i jestem – tam jeszcze
W szumie gwiazd, gdzie niecały w mgle bożej się mieszczę,
Gdzie powietrze, drżąc ustnie, sny mówi i gra mi,
I jestem jeszcze dalej poza tymi snami.
Zewsząd idę ku sobie; wszędzie na się czekam,
Tu się spieszę dośpiewnie, tam – docisznie zwlekam
I trwam, niby modlitwa, poza swą żałobą,
Ta, co spełnić się nie chce, bo woli być sobą.

6 I runął mur, tysiącem ech wstrząsając wzgórza i doliny!
Lecz poza murem – nic i nic! Ni żywej duszy, ni Dziewczyny!

Niczyich oczu ani ust! I niczyjego w kwiatach losu!
Bo to był głos i tylko – głos, i nic nie było, oprócz głosu!

Nic – tylko płacz i żal i mrok i niewiadomość i zatrata!
Takiż to świat! Niedobry świat! Czemuż innego nie ma świata?

Wobec kłamliwych jawnie snów, wobec zmarniałych w nicość cudów,
Potężne młoty legły w rząd na znak spełnionych godnie trudów.

I była zgroza nagłych cisz! I była próżnia w całym niebie!
A ty z tej próżni czemu drwisz, kiedy ta próżnia nie drwi z ciebie?

7 Leśmian, *Szkice literackie,* vol. 2, 545.

WORKS CITED

Dudek, Jolanta. "The Reception of Yeat's Work in Poland (1898–2004)." In *The Reception of W.B. Yeats in Europe*. Edited by Klaus Peter Jochum. 127–8. London: Continuum, 2006.

Leśmian, Bolesław. "Metamorphoses of Reality." Translated by Alissa Valles. In *Polish Writers on Writing.* Edited by Adam Zagajewski. 2–6. San Antonio: Trinity University Press, 2007.

– *Szkice literackie.* Edited by Jacek Trznadel. *Dzieła wszystkie*. Vol. 2. Warszawa: Państwowy Instytut Wydawniczy, 2011.

Miłosz, Czesław. *The History of Polish Literature,* 2nd ed. Berkeley: University of California Press, 1983.

INTERWAR, WAR, POSTWAR, AND POST-1989 POETRY

Metaphor, Vision, and Poetic Construction (Julian Przyboś)

Julian Przyboś (1901–70) was unquestionably the foremost Polish avant-garde poet of the interwar years; no poet embraced the tenets of the Kraków avant-garde more successfully – and more imaginatively – than Przyboś. In contrast to most Western avant-garde movements, the Kraków avant-garde, the most important such group in Poland, known also by the name of its magazine *Zwrotnica* (The Switch), was constructivist and intellectual. It promoted concepts of order, rigour, structure, and logic. Resisting the syntactic slackness characteristic of Western avant-garde movements, the Kraków avant-garde made syntax a cornerstone of its poetic program. It declared poetry to be the "art of beautiful sentences" and maintained that without syntax a poem can at best "offer an inventory of the world but not its life."[1] While it shared the Italian Futurists' enthusiasm for modernity, it did not view their founder's Marinetti's "words at freedom" as a means to incorporate modern technology into the fibre of poetic language. Like the French Surrealists, Polish poets made the metaphor the cornerstone of their poetic language, but they based that language on conceptual relationships rather than on free association.

Julian Przyboś's first two volumes of poetry, *Śruby* (Screws, 1925) and *Oburącz* (With Both Hands, 1926), are paeans to modernity as represented by the masses, the metropolis, and the machine – the three "M's" of the Kraków avant-garde's manifesto. Assaulting the reader with verbs, adjectives, and nouns in rapid succession, Przyboś's poems are tense and dramatic. Reality becomes a dynamic interplay of geometrical figures set in frantic motion. Blocks, tubes, cones, cylinders, and spheres turn, strike, wriggle, vibrate, gallop, and peal in a *perpetuum mobile*, as the title of one of the poems indicates.

The avant-garde nature of Przyboś's first two volumes is a function of their subject matter; his next three – *Sponad* (From Above, 1930), *W głąb las* (In the Depth a Forest, 1932) and *Równanie serca* (Equation of the Heart, 1938) – realize a concept of poetic language that is an original variant of the Kraków avant-garde poetics. The title of Przyboś's collection of essays *Linia i gwar* (Line and Buzz, 1959) intimates the new polarity of his poetic endeavour: the rigour of the line together with the chaos of buzz. In a departure from orthodox constructivist theory, experience – both sensory and emotional – occupies a prominent place in Przyboś's poetry of the 1930s, and his poems are "situated" in time as well as in space. Although Przyboś continued to view metaphors as the essential trait of poetry, his own metaphors shifted away from the abstract game of concepts towards images rooted in a concrete, visual experience. He strived for metaphors that were authentic and verifiable, and visual experience was one of the ways in which he remained close to his object. The result is a distinct, original poetic vision.

The visuality of Przyboś's metaphors is of a special kind. Although firmly rooted in visual reality, his images create an effect that is unrealistic and that borders on the fantastic – an effect that can be called optical illusion. His extensive use of movement and light – the two most natural agents of optical distortion – allowed him to change the relationships between objects and to alter reality in accordance with his poetic vision. We see this, for instance, in the poem "Pochód" (Demonstration), in which the optical illusion of "jumping windows" is a result of the quick pace of the marchers: "The windows jumped out of the walls / into stretched-out pairs of hands" (*Okna wyskoczyły z murów / w wyciągnięte ramiona par*). The speaker in Przyboś's poems is almost never a detached observer but someone immersed in the experience, which he simultaneously undergoes and actively creates. He is both subject and object of the poem's events. One critic has described Przyboś's "creationist attitude," and his treatment of the world as a "projection of human individuality."[2]

Przyboś's "creationist" attitude is also connected to a particular kind of vision. He once defined the ultimate poetic moment as the "between-words" (or interwords): "sparks shooting from the creative juxtapositions of words and phrases."[3] Although he was a master of purely verbal games and linguistic fireworks, the most striking effects of "between-words" in his poetry relate to his visual metaphors, particularly in "double" images in which different, often distant images overlap. The following poem from *Equation of the Heart* is a good example of Przyboś's art, for it incorporates most of his characteristic devices: the centrality of the speaker, the importance of movement, tight organization, and extensive use of double-images and associations:

DEEPER

A traffic jam blared out by cars, the policeman turns fast on his heel, faster
and faster – the loud square unfurled like a flag – and went silent.
It subsided.
I am waiting, nameless and distant.
The carts carved a rut around, they furrowed a rut around, and beyond a crowd
   passed forever, cemetery of silence.
Ridge after ridge the plow heaves aside this pack of people and the horse at the
   whiffletree turns back.
Underneath, deeper, from under geological layers, from drifts, black forests of
   ferns and horsetails a movable malachite bottom rises up, the
   darkness bubbles like boiling water, the powerful blackness shines
and greenness freezes motionless under my feet.
Over the graying furrow of the street
I am waiting
silent, pensive and living from the dead.[4]

The poem simultaneously follows two axes, spatial and temporal. Spatially, from the street scene in a foreign country to a rural scene in the speaker's native village, and from there "deeper" into the dark magma of the earth's core. Temporally, from the present moment to the speaker's childhood, and from there to an immemorial past beyond human memory. The descent from light into darkness, from noise into silence, from movement to stasis, from a palpable reality into an imaginary vision, and from life to death, has a personal as well as a cosmic dimension. But both movements are projections of the speaker's mind, the result of his emotional and intellectual reaction to an alien and alienating urban environment. The feeling of estrangement when watching traffic in a foreign city triggers a defensive mnemonic mechanism allowing a return to the reassuring familiarity of the past; at the same time, it leads to an intellectual reflection on the meaning of time and death. Double-images (square–flag, street–furrow, ridges–people), including synaesthetic double-images (traffic jam blared out by the cars, the noisy square unfurled like a flag), echo and visualize the speaker's dual perspective – he is caught "between" the present and the past, the urban and the rural scapes, the sense of strangeness and the feeling of familiarity. Moreover, these double-images function as structural supports and justify the chain of associations that would otherwise appear fortuitous.

The poem also illustrates the evolution in Przyboś's attitude towards modernity, from the enthusiastic openness of his early youthful poems to his reserved distance in poems written in the 1930s. A surprising number of these poems involve a nostalgic return to childhood, an evocation of the poet's "deeper" rural past. In them, ploughs and horses, sycamores and oak trees, orioles and crowing cocks, his mother's voice and his father's sickle, replace factories, cities, radio towers, cars, cogs, and wheels. These changes in scenery and vocabulary do not, however, produce a corresponding change in Przyboś's unique and inventive poetic diction, which combines the rigorous structure and logic of constructivist poetics with associationism and a reliance on the visual that brought him closer to the practice of French Surrealist poets. However, a brief comparison between him and the Surrealists reveals a distance that is greater and deeper than the apparent similarities. The Surrealists valued visuality and associationism because these things enabled them to reveal the subconscious; for Przyboś, associations and metaphors were tools to be manipulated for specific effects he wanted to achieve. Faithful to the principles of Polish constructivism, he treated the poem as a structure and the play of associations as a means to organize the reader's emotions, not as a means of direct expression. His poems show the absolute control of a writer who is conscious of the effect of his art, and they solidify his position as an iconic poet of the Polish avant-garde.

Bogdana Carpenter
University of Michigan, Ann Arbor

NOTES

1 Peiper, *Nowe usta* (1925); reprinted in his *Tędy. Nowe usta*, 154. All translations in this text are my own and can be found in Carpenter, *The Poetic Avant-Garde in Poland 1918–1939*.

2 Sandauer, *Poeci czterech pokoleń*, 158.

3 Przyboś, *Linia i gwar. Szkice*, 182.

4 *GŁĘBIEJ*

Zator roztrąbiony przez auta, policjant okręca się na pięcie,
  szybciej, coraz szybciej – głośny plac rozwinął się jak flaga – i ucichł.
Opadł.
Czekam, bezimienny i daleki.
Dookoła wozy wyjeździły koleinę, dookoła wybruździły koleinę, za którą tłum
  przeszły na zawsze, cmentarz ciszy.

Pług skiba za skibą odwala tę przebrzmiałą czeredę i odwraca się koń u orczyka.
Spod nich, głębiej, spod złoży geologicznych, spod sztolni, z czarnych borów
 paproci i skrzypów podnosi się ruchome dno z malachitu, bulgoce
 mrok jak wrzątek, potężna czerń świeci
i zieleń nieruchomieje pod moimi stopami.
Nad poszarzałą bruzdą jezdni
czekam
zamilkły z zadumy i żywy z umarłych.

WORKS CITED

Carpenter, Bogdana. *The Poetic Avant-garde in Poland 1918-1939*. Seattle: University of Washington Press, 1983.

Peiper, Tadeusz. *Tędy. Nowe usta*. Kraków: Wydawnictwo Literackie, 1972.

Przyboś, Julian. *Linia i gwar. Szkice*, vol. 2. Kraków: Wydawnictwo Literackie, 1959.

Sandauer, Artur. *Poeci czterech pokoleń*. Kraków: Wydawnictwo Literackie, 1977.

INTERWAR, WAR, POSTWAR, AND POST-1989 POETRY

Depth of Doubt (Tadeusz Różewicz)

Tadeusz Różewicz (1921–2014) was a poet, a playwright, a prose writer, an essayist, and a screenwriter, and he left behind masterpieces in each of these genres. According to a study by the Polish Book Institute, his work has been translated into almost fifty languages, superseding in this regard the Nobel Prize recipients Czesław Miłosz (1911–2004) and Wisława Szymborska (1923–2012). His *Utwory zebrane* (Collected Works, 2003–6) have filled twelve volumes so far and are still not complete, since Różewicz continued to publish new works in his final years. In Poland as well as internationally, he is seen as one of the twentieth century's most important and accomplished writers.

Situating Różewicz on the literary map of the twentieth century is not easy, since (among other reasons) he enters into dialogue with so many other authors. These interactions are usually polemic in nature, which also means they are difficult to evaluate. Artists writing in German appear to be the most important: Franz Kafka, Rainer Maria Rilke, Gottfried Benn, Paul Celan, and, among earlier figures, Friedrich Hölderlin and Johann Wolfgang Goethe. Among Anglo-Saxon authors, the standouts are T.S. Eliot, Ezra Pound, and Samuel Beckett. Overall, Kafka and Beckett seem to be the most significant. Różewicz's multiple references to Kafka confirm and simultaneously discredit the distinguished position of that artist in contemporary culture. His references to Beckett are less apparent but equally important. Among the shared starting assumptions of Różewicz and Beckett are these: existence means guilt; being an artist means losing, and losing as no one else does; and "there is nothing to express, nothing with which to express, nothing from which to express, no power to express, no desire to express, together with the obligation to express."[1] In "Miłość do popiołów" (Love for Ashes) from *Na powierzchni poematu i w środku* (On the Surface of a Poem and in Its Middle, 1983), Różewicz writes that he adores Beckett "for breathing so peacefully / in expectation of the end of the world," ending with: "but even he begins to bore."[2]

The volume of poetry titled *Niepokój* (Anxiety, 1947) is considered to be Różewicz's debut. Together with *Czerwona rękawiczka* (The Red Glove), published a year later, it constitutes the foundation of his poetics. Nowadays, however, the book *Echa leśne* (Forest Echoes, 1944) is often considered his proper debut. It was written while the author was fighting with a partisan unit against the German forces occupying Poland but appeared in print only in 1985; it was not included in his *Collected Works.* It is likely that the author saw it as a youthful and immature work. Yet it is significant for initiating a key motif in Różewicz's oeuvre – the annihilation of values caused by the Second World War – as well as for showing the author's dependence on the Polish Romantic tradition, from which he would later distance himself.

In 1949, the period of socialist realism began in Poland, during which state authorities tried to turn literature into a tool of communist propaganda. Różewicz wrote a great deal during this period, which lasted until 1956. He would omit some of these texts from later editions of his work, but not most of them, thus underscoring both the continuity of his oeuvre and his strong independence from the rules imposed by the authorities. Whether this was actually the case is arguable today; it is generally thought that Różewicz was able to maintain relative creative autonomy, although the poems written during this period are the weakest among his work.

With the publication of the volume *Poemat otwarty* (An Open Poem, 1956), Różewicz returned to the foundations of his poetics and broadened his themes. He became, as is often emphasized, the youngest classic poet in contemporary Polish literature. On the one hand, his poetics are often imitated; on the other, they provoke controversy, especially because of his stubbornly repeated declaration of his lack of faith in the value of art. The 1970s and 1980s were a period of creative crisis for him, caused by both external and internal factors. With regard to the former, these factors were primarily political: Różewicz positioned himself outside of both the official cultural politics of the party and the nascent oppositional culture. With regard to the latter, they were philosophical: silence understood as the result of belief in art's death became Różewicz's most important theme. The volume of Różewicz's conversations with the theatre director Kazimierz Braun, *Języki teatru* (The Languages of Theatre, 1989), offers the best evidence of this crisis. It testifies to the poet's poignant feeling of being lost and unappreciated. Irritating at times, the book is nonetheless important for our understanding of Różewicz.

The publication of the volume of poetry *Płaskorzeźba* (Bas-Relief, 1991) marked "the return of Różewicz." In a country liberated from the communist regime, he became one of the most influential, imitated, and esteemed writers. Różewicz documented his position with a whole series of new works, especially poetic ones, such as *Zawsze fragment. Recycling* (Always a Fragment: Recycling, 1998), *Nożyk profesora* (The Professor's Knife, 2001), *Szara strefa* (The Grey Zone, 2002), and *Wyjście* (Exit, 2004).

The chronology of Różewicz's oeuvre can be thus presented as follows: the early period (his first two books), his socialist realist years (until 1956), the period of mature creativity (up to the publication of *Bas-Relief*), and the late period. His poetry maintains its distinct identity throughout each of these phases, however, which the author makes use of and highlights by publishing volumes that cut across the distinction between new and previous works. The best example of this is *Matka odchodzi* (The Mother Departs, 1999), which contains works that span half a century – both well-known ones, and others published for the first time – and features both prose and poetry. Moreover, Różewicz juxtaposes his own work here with his mother Stefania's reminiscences, as well as with texts by his two brothers (Janusz, a talented poet murdered by the Gestapo, and Stanisław, a well-known film director). These diverse elements create a cohesive whole that is nevertheless difficult to classify.

The Modern *Silva Rerum* – a twentieth-century literary practice that departs from specific forms or conventions and contributes to the self-knowledge of literature by questioning all of its definitions. The term, which was proposed by Ryszard Nycz in *Sylwa współczesna. Problem konstrukcji tekstu* (The Contemporary Silva Rerum: The Problem of Textual

Construction, 1984), references the Polish nobility's practice of keeping home chronicles, called *silva rerum* (from Latin: "forest of things"). Common between the sixteenth and eighteenth centuries, this form of writing is a mixture of notes about practical and everyday matters (such as recipes for health and cooking, maxims, quotes, receipts, descriptions of visits and familial gatherings). The modern *silva* does not refer to the Old Polish form directly. It emerged from the negative diagnoses of modernist authors and their experiences of alienation – professional (the writer is less a human being than a producer of works), formal (with all texts turning into forms), and communicative (with published texts rendered defenceless against the interpretation of readers). The *silva rerum* form aims to escape these alienations and is characterized by its valuation of the writing process as more important than the finished product (i.e., a completed work); by the lack of shared aesthetic categories that would impart an emotionally coherent character to the writing; and by the lack of a clear compositional and thematic design (inclusion of loose fragments, notes, sketches, ideas, and essays). Some of its modern examples are Witold Gombrowicz's *Dziennik* (Diary, 1957–61; 1961–6), Różewicz's own *Przygotowania do wieczoru autorskiego* (Preparations for a Poetry Evening, 1971), Tadeusz Konwicki's *Kalendarz i klepsydra* (The Calendar and the Hour-Glass, 1976), Leopold Buczkowski's *Pierwsza świetność* (First Splendor, 1966), Kazimierz Brandys' *Miesiące* (A Warsaw Diary, 1981), and Edward Stachura's *Fabula Rasa. Rzecz o egoizmie* (Fabula Rasa: On Egoism, 1979)

Różewicz wanted his texts to remain in constant flux. He not only composed his books from new and old texts but also rewrote his own poems. The volume that opens his *Collected Works*, titled *Anxiety*, differs significantly from its first 1947 edition as well as from the versions included in his earlier collections. By no means are these "corrections" – what is happening here is the conscious development of an artistic strategy. This approach makes the periodization of particular works more challenging, and what is more important, it demands a new way of reading. It suggests that poems do not have a finite form; that the meaning of a work changes radically according to circumstances; and even that the poet's texts do not possess a stable meaning, but only the meaning they acquire by moving through ever-changing contexts. As a result, Różewicz's texts share some features with translations, in that they appear in many commensurate versions.

As a poet, Różewicz is seen as the legislator of a new style in Polish postwar literature – a style turned against both the dominant Polish tradition of Romanticism and the avant-garde tradition, which is native to him. Różewicz's thesis about "the death of poetry," formulated during the 1960s, serves as the calling card for this new style, which expresses the key dilemmas of his oeuvre: the inevitable defeat of representation and a desire for referentiality; the inescapable designification of language; the conviction that traditional forms of speaking are powerless; and a dependence on the inheritance of Mediterranean culture. Różewicz's work is thus propelled by a sequence of contradictions. The most significant of these is that he writes his poems in the belief that language has, so to speak, become "disjoined" from reality; in writing, he aims to renew the ties between the two even while remaining convinced that the task is doomed to failure. Yet this does not happen. In fact, the most outstanding of Różewicz's poems speak about "the death of poetry."

The main themes explored by Różewicz are the war and the Holocaust, the critique of contemporary civilization, fine arts, and religious tradition. The first of these is perhaps the most important. In Różewicz's understanding, the Second World War was an event comparable to the biblical flood: it divided history into two incommensurable parts, marked the end of the great tradition of European culture, and undermined all axiological hierarchies. Tellingly, Różewicz's position is similar to that formulated by Theodor Adorno in *Minima moralia* (1951). Adorno's statement that the disinherited are the only true heirs of culture perfectly expresses Różewicz's stance. On the one hand, the poet attacks those who hurriedly tried to reconstruct the destroyed edifice of culture; on the other, he fights against those who joyfully welcomed the demise of values as a kind of liberation. Różewicz seems to have believed – following Heidegger – that the war destroyed the very ground on which culture could have been rebuilt and that the poet's primary duty was to experience this loss in all its depth. Indeed, Heidegger – as a great philosopher who became intoxicated by Nazism – became a key figure for the later Różewicz. He represented what was most important to Różewicz: the great European tradition and its auto-destruction. Friedrich Nietzsche was of no lesser importance to him as a harbinger of the twentieth-century crisis of religion, a sage who resigned an academic chair in the name of loyalty to his intellectual calling, as well as a helpless and lonely human being struggling with illness and physical weakness.

The poems from Różewicz's first two collections express his conviction that one should not speak of the annihilation of values brought about by the war in an ornate way – for example, by using an Expressionist poetics – but rather with language that is stripped down, humble, and focused on events. His poetic program is thus minimalist, insofar as it examines what survived the inferno of war, as well as maximalist, rooted in the assumption that only poetry able to express the experience of war and the Holocaust has a right to exist. Throughout his artistic career, Różewicz attempted to create a new poetic language. Of particular significance are three of his later poems: "Dezerterzy" (Deserters, in *Collected Works*, vol. 9); and "Recycling" and "Professor's Knife" (from *Always a Fragment: Recycling*). The incorporation of a picture of a naked woman into the last of the just-mentioned collections – with the volume title and the author's name superimposed on it – is particularly meaningful. The photograph can easily be taken for an artistic nude, but in fact it shows the body of a dead concentration camp prisoner, as the reader learns at the back of the book. This gesture reveals that the horror of the Holocaust is too easy to aestheticize, as well as that horror resists language, and that overcoming that resistance is the strongest justification for writing poetry. The most recent studies of Różewicz's oeuvre, which follow certain biographical traces and suggestions sowed by the author in some of his texts, read his work as the testimony of a Jewish survivor of the Holocaust.

By the 1960s, Różewicz was critiquing contemporary civilization. In books such as *Rozmowa z księciem* (Conversation with a Prince, 1960), *Nic w płaszczu Prospera* (Nothing in Prospero's Coat, 1963), *Twarz trzecia* (The Third Face, 1968), and *Regio* (1969), one finds groundbreaking diagnoses, in the Polish context, of post-industrial civilization as well as of consumerist and multimedia culture. For this reason, some critics have started to call Różewicz the patron saint of postmodernism. He developed this critical perspective further in works published after 1989. In effect, he was a postmodernist before anyone else noticed the phenomenon, and – by the time others had noticed it – he had already moved on to something else entirely.

The dramatic acts of faithlessness expressed in such masterpieces of Polish poetry as "cierń" (thorn, from *Regio*), "bez" (without, from *Bas-relief*), and "widziałem Go"

(I saw Him, from *Always a Fragment: Recycling*) can be misleading. It is possible to view Różewicz as a poet of affirmation rather than negation. The subject he affirms is to be understood not as radiant completeness, or as art as salvation, but as a disappearing substance, hollowed of its content, with the human seen as a dependent and accidental being, and art as the deepest kind of experience of our existential and epistemic poverty. The absence of justification encompasses everything. Różewicz seeks it and his hunger for justice is not satiated by its counterfeits. This is perhaps at the core of his religiosity, for the desire for justice is a deeply religious desire.

Różewicz's dialogue with visual arts, and especially painting, is meant to restore – as the author himself admits – the demolished temple of culture. This is why, right after the war, he chose to study art history rather than philology. He sometimes suggested, especially in letters to the eminent painter Jerzy Nowosielski, that the painter performs well in places where the poet's word is helpless, in other words, that the sacral constitution of the world is more easily grasped with an image rather than a poem.[3] Perhaps the most important of Różewicz's poems about painting, however, seems to prove otherwise. In "Francis Bacon czyli Diego Velázquez na fotelu dentystycznym" (Francis Bacon, or Diego Velázquez in the Dentist Chair, from *Always Fragment*), Różewicz's accomplishment, in his own eyes, is equal to that of Bacon. They both show "the destruction and disintegration of the world, but also, strangely, as if paradoxically ... a synthesis of this disintegration, perhaps the most inquisitive one, the most dramatic and full of expression."[4] Besides Bacon, Różewicz's favourite contemporary painters include Lucien Freud; among the most important of earlier figures are Vermeer, Bosch, Breugel, Rembrandt, Rubens, Hals, and Klee.

To end with, a note about genre classifications. Różewicz divided his *Collected Works* according to tradition into poetry, drama, and prose, but this division is a matter of convention. Różewicz was primarily a poet, as he often rightly stressed, and as is evidenced by his frequent practice of referring to his dramas as poems, and vice versa. The line between prose and poetry is likewise provisional. Różewicz's best prose work, somewhat paradoxically, is the vast and structurally quite traditional short story "Śmierć w starych dekoracjach" (Death among Old Decorations, 1970). It takes after Goethe in its motif of a trip to Italy. Its hero, an average resident of Central Europe, dies at the end in a storehouse of old decorations. It is unclear whether this symbolic scene signifies salvation or the utter loss of desire for a return to origins. Różewicz's most noteworthy stories – "Przerwany egzamin" (Interrupted Exam), "Próba rekonstrukcji" (Attempt at Reconstruction), and "Tarcza z pajęczyny" (Spider-Web Shield) – contain strong poetic elements – more precisely, they are subjected to other rules of cohesion than those of prose. Similar in this regard is *Preparations for a Poetry Reading*, 1971. This work is of key significance to understanding Różewicz's creative outlook. It contains programmatic statements, essays, sketches, notes, commentaries, memoirs, and so on. It reveals yet another boundary that is blurred in Różewicz's work: between literary creation and commentary on it. In fact, Różewicz did not like to otherwise comment on his work. He looked on scholars of his oeuvre with distrust and usually found their various evaluations of it to be either premature or partial.

Andrzej Skrendo
University of Szczecin
Translated by Agnieszka Polakowska

NOTES

1 Samuel Beckett and Georges Duthuit, *Three Dialogues*, 103.
2 Tadeusz Różewicz, *Na powierzchni poematu i w środku*, 159.
3 See Różewicz and Zofia and Jerzy Nowosielscy, *Korespondencja*.
4 See the interview with Różewicz titled "O implozji poezji" in Stolarczyk, ed. *Wbrew sobie*, 169.

WORKS CITED AND CONSULTED

Beckett, Samuel, and Georges Duthuit. *Three Dialogues*. London: J. Calder, 1965.

Braun, Kazimierz, and Tadeusz Różewicz. *Języki teatru*. Wrocław: Wydawnictwo Dolnośląskie, 1989.

Nycz, Ryszard. *Sylwy współczesne. Problem konstrukcji tekstu.* Wrocław: Zakład Narodowy im. Ossolińskich, 1984.

Różewicz, Tadeusz. *Na powierzchni poematu i w środku. Nowy wybór wierszy*. Warszawa: Czytelnik, 1983.

– *Utwory zebrane*. Vols 1–12. Wrocław: Wydawnictwo Dolnośląskie, 2003–6.

Różewicz, Tadeusz, and Zofia and Jerzy Nowosielscy. *Korespondencja*. Kraków: Wydawnictwo Literackie, 2009.

Stolarczyk, Jan, ed. "O implozji poezji." In *Wbrew sobie. Rozmowy z Tadeuszem Różewiczem*. 169–72. Wrocław: Biuro Literackie, 2011.

Against Dualities with Life-Writing (Miron Białoszewski)

Miron Białoszewski (1922–83) was only seventeen when the Second World War began, and the trauma of its experience left a permanent mark on his psyche. After the war, his literary debut was delayed by Stalinism and the enforced poetics of socialist realism, and appeared only in 1956. He published four volumes of poetry between 1956 and 1965: *Obroty rzeczy* (Revolutions of Things, 1956), *Rachunek zachciankowy* (Calculus of Whims, 1959), *Mylne wzruszenia* (Misdirected Sentiments, 1961), and *Było i było* (There Was and There Was, 1965), and with each publication he became both more established and more controversial. Białoszewski revolutionized poetry in postwar Poland through his unique ideas about the relationship between poetry and life. His poetic experiments deal with three of the major problems of modernity: the comprehensibility and accessibility of the real, the possibilities and limitations of language, and the philosophical stability of the self.[1] These experiments led Białoszewski to a radical conclusion – that reality, language, and the self are contingent, unpredictable, and accidental yet at the same time interconnected and interdependent.[2]

After *There Was and There Was*, Białoszewski wrote exclusively in prose until 1978. In 1970 he published his seminal work, *Pamiętnik z powstania warszawskiego* (A Memoir of the Warsaw Uprising), in which he describes daily life during this harrowing historical ordeal. In 1971 a volume of his writings on theatre appeared, titled *Teatr Osobny, 1955–1963* (The Separate Theatre, 1955–1963). *Donosy rzeczywistości* (Reality Reports, 1973) and *Szumy, zlepy, ciągi* (Hums, Lumps and Currents, 1977) are collections of short narratives written in innovative and idiosyncratic prose; these stories have come to be called "minor narrations." The year 1977 also saw the publication of *Zawał* (The Heart Attack), a diary-like account of his heart attack and convalescence in a sanatorium.

> Had Białoszewski lived in Paris or New York, where he felt as at home as "in Sieradz" during a visit to collect his Alfred Jurzykowski Award in 1982, no one would have asked him who he slept with, when he woke up, and how he dressed. But he lived the lifestyle of a French Surrealist or a New York beatnik in communist Warsaw, in a state-alloted bachelor apartment. This was his natural mode, comfortable, in some sense indulgent, where everything that serviced the practicalities of life was reduced to the bare minimum (just like the rubbish, which he simply swept under the wardrobe before a doctor's home visit).
>
> – Sobolewski, *Człowiek Miron*, 68–9

By the time Białoszewski returned to poetry in *Odczepić się* (To Detach Oneself, 1978), his poetics and world view were fully developed. Here and in subsequent volumes he maintains the pragmatic attitude of a researcher investigating life in all its manifestations. His position is not that of a detached observer of reality, but that of an involved participant in life. Thus it is life and the quotidian, rather than abstract reality, that holds his attention in his later work, starting with *To Detach Oneself* and continuing in *Wiersze wybrane i dobrane* (Selected and Added Poems, 1980), *Rozkurz* (Jumble, 1980), *Stara proza, nowe wiersze* (Old Prose, New Poems, 1984), *Oho* (A-ha, 1985) and *Obmapywanie Europy. AAAmeryka. Ostatnie wiersze* (Mapping Europe: AAAmerica: Last Poems, 1988). After Białoszewski's death in 1983, his *Collected Works* appeared in eleven volumes. In accordance with his will, his *Tajny dziennik* (Secret Diary) was released in 2012.

Białoszewski's creative arc can be traced from his early tests of epistemological and ontological assumptions about the stability of reality, language, and the self, to his far-reaching conclusions about the inherent instability of these categories and the contingency of life in general. He recognized these latter uncertainties and absorbed them into his world view; in his late poetry, his artistic, existential, and ethical aim was to "write everything" and to merge life and art completely. His creative evolution was gradual, free of sudden ruptures and extreme changes of position. His approach was that of a pragmatic scientist who tests his philosophical premises without expectations about possible outcomes and who consistently draws conclusions from his experiments. Białoszewski was a process-oriented writer who realized that he could never expect completion or closure to the unfolding of his "life-writing."

> The greatest challenge in reading Białoszewski is thus to avoid two extremes. One is to avoid biographical mimetism by looking at Białoszewski's writing in a bio-chronological way and for a source of information on his life. At one end of the spectrum is, hence, the intentional fallacy, the idea of authorial intention controlling the meaning of the work. On the other end, we have a post-structuralist discussion of the tropological character of literature, in which the constant doubling of subject/object; creating/being created; "I"/"not I"; and the permeability of binaries of writing/living and written/lived (à la de Man and Derrida) dismisses the very possibility of biography. Neither of these extremes present an adequate way to read Białoszewski's work.
>
> – Niżyńska, *The Kingdom of Insignificance: Miron Białoszewski and the Quotidian, the Queer, and the Traumatic*, 16

The poet's originality rests on his poetic articulations of the contingency of language. In this, his approach to language differed from that of his contemporaries. For other poets of that period, including Czesław Miłosz (1911–2004), Zbigniew Herbert (1924–98), and Wisława Szymborska (1923–2012), language could be mysterious, uncontrollable, and imperfect but rarely if ever contingent. Tadeusz Różewicz (1921–2014) seems much closer to Białoszewski in his position on language, but though they began with a similar premise, the two poets arrived at very different conclusions. Różewicz saw the contingency of language as a problem limiting our ability to communicate and comprehend one another and the world; Białoszewski saw it as a source of new possibilities.

The focus on processes, contexts, and new connections (already present in *There Was and There Was*), rather than on objects, concepts, and ideas, places Białoszewski in a unique location on the Polish literary map. Where Herbert, Miłosz, and Szymborska try to control the chaos of the world, and Różewicz examines the impossibility of such control, Białoszewski takes a much more interactive approach. Rather than struggling to assert control over chaos, his poetic persona explores the processuality of life in various interactions with its unpredictability and contingency. To put it another way, instead of imposing an intellectual and poetic order of his own devising onto reality, he adopts strategies that allow him to cope with life's "facticity" and gain something from this experience. His poetic "I" is wilfully ignorant of its boundaries and maintains a readiness to forge new connections and interactions in a continuously changing context. His poetic subjectivity is constantly evolving.

Facticity[3]
won't even blink

so I say something to it
and I grunt

still nothing

so I substantialize
via immobility

it grunted
and then I
- you pig

Facticity[4]
sits and looks in the window

I do nothing

it couldn't take it
and makes faces

so I think hard what to tell it
and I say
- y
together with it

How many times do I fit[5]
into this quantificatory
into my space?

A good one time

And not even 'cause time after time
I stick out

with my looking outs
with my anxieties
with my raptures

Though they share a title, the two poems called "Facticity" are different in their conceit and execution. Both enact an exchange between speaker and reality – reality conceived as facts rooted in the here and now – but while the speaker in the first poem is active and engaged, in the second the active role is played by reality, while the speaker is somewhat subdued. Thus, the relationship between speaker and reality is bidirectional; both act and both react to each other's actions and provocations. The enacted situations do not extend beyond the immediate encounter. At times the speaker is in conflict with reality, and then his attitude is negative and critical; at other times he is amazed by it, and his attitude is affirmative and celebratory. In both cases his interactions are bidirectional and open, and they always take their cues from a particular context.

However, these acts of communication are predominently non-verbal. The participants make faces, grunt, and sound out vowels (the Polish "y"), but despite being anthropomorphized, reality does not speak. It is impossible to translate something non-linguistic into a linguistic expression, to translate "from facticity / into expressibility."[6] The only spoken phrase is a humorous "you pig," designating a creature that does not use language. The world presented in the poems is anti-logocentric: words are not rooted in reality, and they do not possess an essential connection with the objects to which they refer. Instead, words *influence* reality – they play an unpredictable role and have an unexpected impact on the context in which they appear. Moreover, Białoszewski's insistence on the contingency of language puts him at odds with the traditional philosophical split between subject and object. The subject can be neither defined nor confined; it always "spills over." On the one hand, the subject cannot be separated from language, and on the other, the object cannot be separated from its description. These descriptions help subjects interact with one another and the world, but they are not universally valid. Their usefulness varies with the context, and they do not come with fixed definitions or identifiers. The knowledge gained from these interactions is indefinite and approximate and verifiable only in its particular context.

Białoszewski's poetic interactions with reality traverse essential dualisms – traverse rather than overcome, as he leaves us no way to reconcile, translate, or explain one aspect of reality in the terms of another. The poet does not judge; to do so, he would have to remove himself from the situation in order to observe and evaluate it objectively. Białoszewski, however, has no recourse to such objectivity because he sees himself as a participant who is inseparable from his context. In the dualisms he explores there are no privileged partners or universal hierarchies. All hierarchies and dependencies are temporary, contextual, and mutable.

The poet's radical project does not rely on any fixed methodology, but consistently realizes and propagates a certain attitude towards life, language, and reality. For Białoszewski, as for Wittgenstein, language is rooted not in reality but in life, "a life of action and activities – a rootedness which takes the form of a two-way relationship."[7] Hence the subject is neither fully controlled by language, nor fully in control of it. Instead, both subject and language constantly affect and influence each other. Deleuze has described this kind of relationship as "a complex unity: one step for life, one step for thought. Modes of life inspire ways of thinking; modes of thinking create ways of living. Life *activates* thought, and thought in turn *affirms* life."[8] Consequently, the poet is invested in the relations of causation and justification but not in the relations of representation. He "copes" with reality instead of "representing" it. "Coping" means that the subject is interested less in what is going on than in what to do next to more fully satisfy his own desires and beliefs and to grow from the experience. Coping is not representation because its aim is not to produce ultimate and immutable descriptions, but rather to remain in a state of openness to future events and new possibilities. Whereas representation always extends beyond its immediate context, coping never exceeds the bounds of its occurrence.

Białoszewski's subject can never decide where to draw the line between himself and the outside world, as is evident in the poem "How Many Times Do I Fit." It is impossible for him to universalize any context and to close himself off from reality. Life itself safeguards the bidirectionality of interactions between self and reality. Moreover, in order to be able to conceptualize its life, to think it, the subject must enter into language. Every term in the subject–language–reality continuum is involved with, and dependent on, every other. This continuum cannot be divided into its constituent parts, and consequently the distinction between subject and object is abolished. With his poetic language, Białoszewski radically blurs and traverses subject–object dualism. His poems attest to the functionality and modifiability of all "natural" divisions. They are descriptions, and all descriptions can be redescribed. The same can be said of the dualism between art and life, because for Białoszewski "writing and life go hand in hand. And sometimes they are the same."[9]

Artur Płaczkiewicz
Independent Scholar, Canada

NOTES

1 All translations are my own. See also Brzozowski, *O wierszach Mirona Białoszewskiego*, 1993.
2 For a detailed analysis, see my book *Miron Białoszewski: Radical Quest beyond Dualisms*, 2012.
3 Białoszewski, *Utwory zebrane*, vol. 10, 127.
4 Ibid., vol. 10, 87–8.
5 Ibid., vol. 7, 72–3.
6 Ibid., vol. 10, 120.
7 Dilman, *Wittgenstein's Copernican Revolution*, 8.
8 Deleuze, *Pure Immanence*, 66.
9 Białoszewski, cited in Burkot, *Miron Białoszewski*, 143.

WORKS CITED

Białoszewski, Miron. *Utwory zebrane*, vols. 1–10. Warszawa: PIW, 1987–2000.
Brzozowski, Jacek, ed. *O wierszach Mirona Białoszewskiego*. Łódź: Oficyna Bibliofilów, 1993.
Burkot, Stanisław. *Miron Białoszewski*. Warszawa: Wydawnictwa Szkolne i Pedagogiczne, 1992.
Deleuze, Gilles. *Pure Immanence: Essays on a Life*. New York: Zone Books, 2001.
Dilman, Ilham. *Wittgenstein's Copernican Revolution: The Question of Linguistic Idealism*. Houndmills: Palgrave, 2002.
Niżyńska, Joanna. *The Kingdom of Insignificance: Miron Białoszewski and the Quotidian, the Queer, and the Traumatic*. Evanston: Northwestern University Press, 2013.
Płaczkiewicz, Artur. *Miron Białoszewski: Radical Quest beyond Dualisms*. Frankfurt am Main: Peter Lang, 2012.
Sobolewski, Tadeusz. *Człowiek Miron*. Kraków: Wydawnictwo Znak, 2012.

INTERWAR, WAR, POSTWAR, AND POST-1989 POETRY

Euphoria of the Ordinary (Anna Świrszczyńska)

Anna Świrszczyńska (1909–84) was one of the most original and socially progressive Polish poets of the twentieth century, with a creative output of ten volumes of poetry and prose poems published between 1936 and 1985. She also produced a large body of writing for children drawn from Polish history and Slavic folklore, as well as plays, essays, journalism, and autobiographical writings. As a poet, Świrszczyńska is known for her laconic style and her writings about women, war, and love. She published her most acclaimed volumes of poetry in the 1970s and 1980s, including the groundbreaking collections *Jestem baba* (I Am a Woman, 1972) and *Budowałam barykadę* (Building the Barricade, 1974).[1] Much of her poetry was ahead of its time and radical in the context of Polish letters, as was the case with her collection of stylized verse inspired by African poetry, *Czarne słowa* (Black Words, 1967); as a result, it was underestimated by contemporary critics and readers.

Born in Warsaw on 7 February 1909 to the painter Jan Świerczyński and Stanisława z Bojarskich, Świrszczyńska received her last name as the result of a misspelling on her birth certificate. She kept it until the end of her life, adopting the pen name Świr ("freak") during the Second World War; she would use the name Swir years later in order to simplify her surname for the English readers of her work.[2] The only child of an impoverished artist, she would later recall her family's perpetual financial troubles, as well as the visual richness of her father's home studio. From 1927 to 1932 she studied Polish literature at Warsaw University; she began publishing while still a student, with her first poem "Śnieg" (Snow, 1930) appearing in the illustrated children's weekly, *Płomyk* (Little Flame). Świrszczyńska remained in Warsaw during the war, contributing to underground literary publications and working various jobs as a clerk and waitress. During the Warsaw Uprising of 1944, she served as a Home Army nurse in a makeshift hospital "without water and without medicine."[3] After the war she moved to Kraków, where she married actor Jan Adamski (whom she would divorce two decades later), and gave birth to a daughter in 1946. From 1946 to 1950, she was the literary director at the Państwowy Teatr Młodego Widza (State Theatre of the Young Viewer, now the Bagatela Theatre), and from 1951 onward she supported herself by her pen, writing for the theatre, newspapers, and radio, as well as authoring children's books. She remained outside the literary mainstream in Kraków and was an early adherent of vegetarianism, yoga, and jogging, all practices she maintained until her death on 30 September 1984.

Świrszczyńska published her first book, *Wiersze i proza* (Poems and Prose), in 1936. Years later, Czesław Miłosz (1911–2004), a staunch advocate and promoter of her work, called it a "dazzling debut."[4] During the war, she published "Rok 1941" (The Year 1941) in an underground anthology, earning acclaim in clandestine literary circles both for this poem and for her drama, *Orfeusz* (Orpheus, 1943). In postwar Kraków, she published dozens of works for children, mostly collections of poetry and plays, some of which appeared in multiple editions and in foreign translation. Her second volume of verse, *Liryki zebrane* (Collected Poems), appeared in 1958, more than two decades after her first. Between 1967 and 1985, Świrszczyńska published eight volumes of poetry, all with a characteristic intensity and minimalist style. In her mature poems, she renders her favourite themes – suffering and love – as tragic or euphoric experiences of ordinary people, often in relation to liminal moments of death and birth. Her fascination with the human body as something distinct from the spirit, and frequently alien to the conscious self, led Miłosz to call her one of Poland's greatest metaphysical poets since the Baroque poet Mikołaj Sęp-Szarzyński (1550?–81?).[5]

Although it is possible to trace an evolution in Świrszczyńska's oeuvre from the historical narratives and Classical motifs of her earliest period (such as her play *Orpheus*, first performed in 1946) to the terse poems of her creative maturity in the 1970s and 1980s, her work also exhibits a number of thematic and stylistic constants that endured throughout her career. Her deep interest in the physicality of existence (whether conceived as human life or as a life force in nature) and in such extreme states as suffering, pain, and ecstasy, are always present in her work. When writing of human existence, she conveys vitality through screams, shouts, tears, laughter, and sex, just as wind, waves, and fire express elemental life forces in nature. She often uses repetition to underscore heightened or anguished emotional states or to deepen moments of spiritual reflection ("kneeling on knees of worship," "darkness darkens like the inside of a massive brain," and "a center also has its center / I want to reach the center of that center").[6] Critics have identified a sense of detachment and rebelliousness among the hallmarks of her poetry; also evident is a stylistic preference for conciseness, immediacy, and intensity, as well as a fascination with biological functions, the grotesque, and the lives of women.[7]

Among Świrszczyńska's favourite genres is the poetic miniature, a brief (usually three- to fifteen-line) depiction of an individual in an extreme state or in the process of experiencing a life-changing moment. Her frequent use of this form has been attributed to her extensive exposure to visual art as a child: her lyric persona is that of a consummate observer, even when she is depicting herself.[8] *Building the Barricade*, a volume about the Warsaw Uprising published thirty years after the event, consists of dispassionate sketches of everyday occurrences and reflects Świrszczyńska's lifelong interest in suffering, love, and death. Unlike the heroic depictions of the uprising that became canonical after the war, Świrszczyńska's poetic miniatures chronicle the experiences of ordinary Warsaw citizens – "the barman, the jeweler's lover, the hairdresser" – as they struggle to survive each day's violence, at times becoming reluctant defenders of the city. Similarly, her portrayals of the soldiers and teenage girls and boys who fought and survived, or who perished from violence or hunger, strike a subversive tone in their persistent refusal to obscure the scale of suffering. In its unremitting focus on the human cost of war, *Building the Barricade* is highly unusual among Polish literary accounts of the uprising; in this regard it can be compared to Miron Białoszewski's *Pamiętnik z powstania warszawskiego* (Memoir of the Warsaw Uprising, 1970), another belated testimony of the event.[9]

In a parallel with Tadeusz Różewicz (1921–2014), Świrszczyńska continually reworked and revised her poems, hence their latest published versions are often very different from earlier renditions; "The Year 1941" is a striking case in point.[10] As a result, one can follow her development as a poet through the changes she made to individual poems over time – a feature that imbues her oeuvre with a sense of openness and vitality. She rarely expressed her views on writing, and such statements that do exist tend to be brief, as in the poem "Jak to jest z pisaniem" (How It Is with Writing): "When there is too much of me / I lay / an egg of a poem."[11] Here, poetic expression is conceived as a function of excess: the process itself is a kind of birth, thus echoing Świrszczyńska's views on the materiality of life force, while also displaying her affinity for the low, the animal, and the earthy. Her theory of style, as formulated in her introduction to *Poezje wybrane* (Selected Poems, 1973), offers a radical vision of poetic expression: "Style is the enemy of the poet, and its nonexistence is its highest merit. One could say, in paradoxical summation, that the writer has two tasks: the first is to create one's own style; the second is to destroy one's style. The second is more difficult and takes more time."[12] This view of form is echoed by the thematic content of her work, which becomes increasingly sceptical of identifying the human body with a person's essence, even as the body remains the only instrument through which existence can be experienced. An extension of this problem is Świrszczyńska's interest in the aging body, which she lovingly chronicles up to its imminent, inevitable demise.

Świrszczyńska's late poetry written between 1978 to 1985 is "condensed" (to use one of her favourite words) to an absolute minimum. Often only a few lines long, these poems convey the same intensity of human experience as the early work, only now mundane activities are her focus – doing laundry, sleeping, bathing, eating – or, as in a 1985 poem, running: "I run on the beach. / People are surprised. / 'A grey-haired hag and she runs.' / I run on the beach / with a brazen look. / People laugh. / 'Grey-haired and brazen.' / They like that."[13] This shift from the extraordinary to the ordinary gives rise to a new theme – the transformative power of small pleasures – as in her 1978 poem, "Skąd wziąć złoty aksamit" (Where Can I Get Some Gold Velvet): "When I eat strawberries, / my tragic vision of the world / is annihilated by the delight / that I am eating strawberries."[14] Her late poetry often focuses on relationships of all kinds (with men, children, parents), but also on the solitary individual attuned to the joy and pain of being; it is concerned with the remarkable aspects of everyday experiences and with self-discovery, both through engagement with others and in thoughtful solitude.

A good deal has been written about Świrszczyńska's feminism: *I Am a Woman* can be read as an exposition of crimes committed daily against women in the form of domestic violence, sexual assault, incest, and public humiliation. The collection includes her famous poetic cycle, *Trzy poematy. Miłość Felicji, Antoniny, i Stefani* (Three Poems: Loves of Felicia, Antonina, and Stephanie), which epitomizes her fascination with the lives of women. The cycle depicts three women at different life stages and their respective views of love. In these poems, Świrszczyńska pays close attention to the speakers' sense of embodiment, conveying their alienation and their desire to separate from their bodily selves: "I want to walk away from my hand, / from the two eyes that look at me in the mirror. / From my left leg / from my right leg / from the rest. / I categorically desire to be someplace else. / I ecstatically desire another way of being. / I want to make myself anew / by myself to make myself anew. / I don't need to live, / but I must make myself / anew."[15]

Several prominent critics have interpreted Świrszczyńska's feminist stance in *I Am a Woman* as a call for social justice (Miłosz), or as an egalitarian Marxist impulse (Kwiatkowski), rather than as an indictment of systemic male chauvinism or an emphatic assertion of women's voices.[16] The debate over Świrszczyńska's status as a feminist writer has been a rallying point for critics: many of Świrszczyńska's admirers, including Renata Stawowy, Renata Ingbrant, Anna Wysocka, and Małgorzata Baranowska, have pointed to a spirited female voice in much of her work, while Miłosz repeatedly emphasized her position as a "universal" (rather than a "woman") writer. Her lyric voice in *I Am a Woman* is so undeniably powerful, and her treatment of gendered situations (such as the experience of a gynecological exam) so unique in Polish letters, as to sway the critical reception of her work towards feminist interpretations.

Świrszczyńska is one of the few Polish woman writers, along with Wisława Szymborska (1923–2012), to gain international recognition for her highly original poetry. Much of her work published in English translation has appeared in anthologies of literature about the Second World War and in collections of women's writing.[17] Świrszczyńska's highly original treatments of form, gender, and historical calamity – the central problems of twentieth-century art – make her a compelling voice in Polish literature, one that is still being discovered.

Andrea Lanoux
Connecticut College, New London

NOTES

1 The title *Jestem baba* (reprinted in 1973, 1975, and 1985) has suffered more in English translation than other titles of her work; the term *baba* (a derogatory term for woman) has been rendered in English variously as "hag," "broad," or simply "woman." The collection first appeared in English translation as *I'm the Old Woman* (Canterbury: Baba Books, 1985), translated by Margaret Marshment and Grażyna Baran.

2 Ingbrant, *From Her Point of View*, 71.

3 "Nosiłam baseny" (I Carried Basins), in Świrszczyńska, *Poezja*, 267. All translations from the Polish are mine.

4 Miłosz, "Przedmowa," in Świrszczyńska, *Poezja*.

5 Ibid., 10.

6 Świrszczyńska's use of repetition as an intensifying device increased in her mature work from 1970 onward, beginning with the collection *Wiatr* (Wind, 1970): "Klęczący na klęczkach uwielbienia"; "Ciemność ciemna jak wnętrze olbrzymiego mozgu"; "Środek też ma swój środek / chcę dojść do środka tego środka." Świrszczyńska, *Poezja*, 139, 140, 159.

7 For an account of Świrszczyńska's critical reception, see Ingbrant, *From Her Point of View*, 47–67.

8 Miłosz, "Przedmowa," 14.

9 Along with the work of Miron Białoszewski and Tadeusz Różewicz, Miłosz cites *Building the Barricade* as one of the most staggering documents of war in Polish literature. Miłosz, "Przedmowa," 7–8.

10 Świrszczyńska, *Poezje*, 75–80.

11 "Kiedy jest mnie za dużo / znoszę / jajko wiersza." "Jak to jest z pisaniem" (1978), in ibid., 310.

12 Ibid., 24.

13 "Biegam po plaży" (1985), in ibid., 379.

14 "Skąd wziąć złoty aksamit" (1978), in ibid., 305.

15 "Na nowo," in ibid., 212.

16 Miłosz, "Przedmowa," 8; Ingbrant, *From Her Point of View*, 57.
17 See, for example, Schiff, ed., *Holocaust Poetry*; Teichman and Leider, eds., *Truth and Lamentation*; Weissbort, *The Poetry of Survival*; and Arnold et al., eds., *A Chorus for Peace*.

WORKS CITED

Arnold, Marilyn, et al., eds. *A Chorus for Peace: A Global Anthology of Poetry by Women*. Iowa City: University of Iowa Press, 2002.

Ingbrant, Renata. *From Her Point of View: Woman's Anti-World in the Poetry of Anna Świrszczyńska*. Stockholm: Stolkholm University, 2007.

Miłosz, Czesław. "Przedmowa." In Anna Świrszczyńska, *Poezja*. 5–16. Warszawa: Państwowy Instytut Wydawniczy, 1997.

Schiff, Hilda, ed. *Holocaust Poetry*. New York: St Martin's Press, 1995.

Świrszczyńska, Anna. *Poezja*. Warszawa: Państwowy Instytut Wydawniczy, 1997.

Teichman, Milton, and Sharon Leider, eds. *Truth and Lamentation: Stories and Poems of the Holocaust*. Urbana: University of Illinois Press, 1994.

Weissbort, Daniel. *The Poetry of Survival: Post-War Poets of Central and Eastern Europe*. London: Penguin Books, 1993.

Drama of the Interwar Period (1918–1939)

In assessing the re-emergence of interwar drama in the aftermath of the Second World War, one Polish scholar of the period has enumerated: "At least a hundred works of thirty authors of that time [returning] onto our stages."[1] Czesław Miłosz (1911–2004), in turn, in his *History of Polish Literature* (1969) distinguished from among many interwar theatre artists just Leon Schiller and from its playwrights only Stanisław Ignacy Witkiewicz, better known as Witkacy. To account for its multiplicity without losing sight of its greatest achievements – that is the task of this short guide through interwar drama. The order of this guide is determined by three simultaneously applied parameters: the function of drama, its key types, and its themes.

Restored Freedom: Social Duty and Avant-Garde Projects

The path taken by drama during the interwar period, a time of heated artistic explorations, was by no means straight. The restoration of Poland's independence in 1918 brought two different attitudes: one turned towards historical and social matters, while the other intensively reworked the notion of art itself. In fact, both approaches had a similar aim – the construction of a new society. The first, however, articulated the problem more directly, while the second, seemingly focused entirely on new art forms, introduced avant-garde principles to drama in the belief that they would bring about desired transformation.

> The first film séances took place in Poland toward the end of nineteenth century. In 1914, in all the partitioned lands, a network of cinemas already existed; there were several and even several dozen of cinemas for every permanent theatre. The first soccer match took place in Warsaw in 1907. These events were to change the world of spectacle with passage of time, and their consequences were made fully apparent only after 1914. Until the war broke out, the old world of spectacle endured, in which theatre aroused greatest interest.
>
> – Raszewski, *Krótka historia teatru polskiego*, 188

Stefan Żeromski (1864–1925) represents the first attitude. The author placed an unusually strong emphasis on problems tied to national self-determination, and along with these on political and especially social issues, which had not been solved automatically with the restoration of state sovereignty. Żeromski was an artist of considerable significance even before the First World War, primarily on the basis of his short stories and novels, so the year 1918 did not mark a sudden change in optics or style for him; rather, he began to deepen his search for the "moral sanction" of the nation's now independent existence. His early postwar dramatic works, which include *Ponad śnieg bielszym się stanę* (I Shall be Whiter Than Snow, 1919), *Biała rękawiczka* (White Glove, 1920), and *Turoń* (Turon, 1923), present a few possible paths that society might take in the new situation. This was an author who spoke out loudly about necessary social reforms, related mainly to the rural population, and his heroes usually represent the remnants of the aristocracy and gentry and thus exemplify the anachronistic elements of the new reality. They are the ones who should pay off old debts, if not by transferring their fortunes and forgoing their privileges, then at least by redeeming their own sins against their former serfs. In these texts, besides settling accounts with history, Żeromski is recalling recent dangers (such as the 1905 and the Bolshevik revolutions) as well as pointing out present threats.

During the interwar period, however, only one play by Żeromski – his last – enjoyed true fame: *Uciekła mi przepióreczka* (My Little Quail Has Gone, 1924). In it, the author abandoned the tragedy and pathos of his previous works, turning quite unexpectedly towards comedy, which he used to deliver a subversive lesson about appearances. The play's protagonist does not hesitate to become public anathema in the name of his maximalist understanding of loyalty and personal honour (it is here that one finds the famous lines: "I trampled upon my fame for such is my custom").[2] This unexpected work (for Żeromski) did not advance a firm social thesis, although it illustrated well his conviction that civic action was necessary, especially among the educated and privileged social strata. The play's popularity was significantly enhanced by its staging at Teatr Reduta (Redoubt Theatre), where Juliusz Osterwa (1885–1947), an excellent actor and that theatre's founder, gave a performance that would define Żeromski's protagonist, Przełęcki, for decades. Osterwa made use of his masculine charisma to underscore the peculiar game played by the hero, who remains unfathomable to other characters, who accept his buffoonish airs for "truth." The play's dramatic effect is thus rooted in situational irony, that is, in a conscious discrepancy between representation and reality. So it is not completely clear whether Przełęcki – thrilling and charming, but also an actor playing the great role of a noble romantic for whom no one has any more use – is not simply another of Żeromski's anachronistic heroes, this time transplanted into contemporary times.

The pressing need for new dramatic forms was more clearly articulated by avant-garde artists in their manifestos, journals, and happenings. The first half of the interwar period belonged to them. In the deluge of manifestos, however, one would look in vain for those of new drama – at stake was mainly new theatre, with the old proscenium theatre becoming the primary target of attacks, along with everything else that was taken for an ossified bourgeois convention of nineteenth-century provenance. The influence of Western theatrical reforms needs to be accounted for as well: the idea that theatre should be treated as a separate art form was crystallizing, and Edward Gordon Craig's concept of the "theatre artist" called for sweeping reonsideration of theatrical art. Interesting experimental plays were created by members of the Kraków avant-garde, a largely poetic group. In creating these works, they were concerned precisely with providing projects for a new but not yet existent theatre, composing avant-garde plays in ways that would impose the desired form of their performance.

> Contemporary drama is bankrupt, revealing its substantial lack of substance, its illusory dread, theatrical artificiality, falsity and hypocrisy. Death to it! Death to this theatrical soulless routine ... We demand whirlwind in the theatre, a fundamental reform of contemporary drama, and we forsake "pictures from life," photographed through the keyhole of a palace or a tenement."
>
> – Czosnowski, "Herezje teatralne," 88

The leader of the Kraków avant-garde, Tadeusz Peiper (1891–1969), who was also called "the pope" of the avant-garde, proposed unprecedented solutions bearing on almost every theatre element in his play *Szósta! Szósta!* (Six! Six!, 1925). The plot itself – of an older writer who tries to trick a younger writer into not publishing a book – is not as important as the precise design of the work, which aimed at the synthetic presentation of the possibilities of new theatre. The play is meant to function primarily through its formal qualities and disciplined construction, hence its rejection of realism and of the direct expression of emotions. Its temporal scheme is its most obvious device: the second part of the play returns to an episode that takes place before the first part ends and in a way that develops what was signalled earlier. This composition was compared to the "order of gradual flowering" (*układ rozkwitania*) – the poetic technique Peiper described in theory and realized in practice and that was defined by the fact that "some image or event ... [is] presented by the poet in several developments, where each development contains the entirety of that image … but in a form more lush and richer than the preceding one."[3]

Peiper believed that theatre does not "mirror" anything, but creates its own rules. In Peiper's conceptualization, therefore, theatre time respects neither chronology nor the temporal sequences encoded in realistic plays, but instead is visibly constructed. In the first part of *Six! Six!*, the author still employs well-known and fairly traditional comedic and melodramatic schemata – a romance, a fight over a woman, a manly competition for dominance – albeit already somewhat transformed, for example through the use of the simultaneous technique. Some of these schemata are sensational in nature, in that the older rival maliciously convinces his fiancé to visit the young writer in order to disrupt his creative work and later hires thugs to accost and kidnap him. Neither of these schemes succeeds: the young writer's book appears in print, and it is to this publication that the second part of the play is dedicated. A gigantic book appears on the stage, from which emerge the figures described by its author (and the play's hero), including all of those who participated in the intrigue. The writer overcomes all of his rivals by "imprisoning" them in his book and thus turns all his life experiences into a work of art.

This part of the play is a pure display of avant-garde theatre in at least four ways. First, it introduces a repository of modernity, and its dynamics invert the calmness of the first part. It takes place in a huge printing house filled with noisy presses and ventilators, and workers who move rhythmically. Second, the workers' movement is choreographed as a kind of ballet, offering an insight into the "relations between people, and even a few twists and little dramas."[4] It thus reveals an important – for Peiper – idea about the possibility of shaping events on stage without the use of words, with recourse only to gesture. He also uses a motif of considerable inspiration to the avant-garde: the creation of choreography out of physical labour in combination with the rhythm of machines, which aimed to illustrate the beauty of an entirely man-made modernity. Third, the play provides an opportunity for the director to co-create it by intentionally leaving blank spaces that can be filled out by an inventive theatre artist. Fourth, the figure of the writer shows the modern artist as a creator of new order, courageously transforming reality into a work of art. Finally, the play employs several tactics of disillusionment, calling attention in a self-reflective way to the creation of a fully autonomous world in art, but one that nevertheless remains in constant "embrace with the present."[5]

Other poets from the Kraków avant-garde group – Julian Przyboś (1901–70), Jan Brzękowski (1903–83), and Jalu Kurek (1904–83) – used similarly formal constructions. All of their plays projected a radically anti-traditional theatre that would reject realistic motivations and that would be capable of developing a new language for modern society in accordance with avant-garde views. In the works of other innovators of the 1920s there was less gravity and seemingly more playfulness, conveyed through carefree experiments with form and even cabaret-style buffoonery. However, as can be seen in the early 1920s dramatic miniatures of Tytus Czyżewski (1880–1945), a Futurist–Formist painter and writer, despite their surface playfulness, these works reveal dynamic contradictions and explorations of the new epoch. For instance, Czyżewski's grotesque *Wąż, Orfeusz i Eurydyka* (The Snake, Orpheus, and Eurydice, 1922) does not offer a new version of the ancient myth. To the contrary, it is the destruction of that myth that is enacted in the play through a few synthetic images: Orpheus's harp breaks and is replaced with the sound of a factory siren and of other noises that make up the music of civilization (the ring of a telephone, a locomotive whistle, gramophone speaker, hum of a fan). The bodies of the lovers, faded and hardened into marble statues, are drowned in the lake as a sign of annihilation of love's old form. The phallus remains as the main symbol of love, but it is an electric phallus, transformed into a giant light bulb that is given a new name – dynamofallos – by the God Pluto, who emerges from the underground like a coal miner from a mine, an image that vividly presents the relation between coal and electricity.

A fascination with emblems of modernity expressed in concise and vivid scenes in Czyżewski's dramatic miniatures speaks to his affinity with Italian synthetic theatre. *Transcendentalne Panopticum* (Transcendental Panopticon, 1920) is a good example of his particular fascination with electricity that powers machines and even people. In this miniature, electricity galvanizes the corpses of great poets from the past and keeps them active as long as it flows. New inventions such as cinema, the automobile, and the aeroplane play a significant role in his other pieces. In *Elektryczne wizje* (Electric Visions, 1920), for example, Dante travels through the hell of civilization by plane. Synthetic theatre has to be chiselled out of a minimum of words, and with the use of props rarely seen in the "old" theatre, in ways that bring it closer to fine arts, which can express diverse content in a condensed form. Yet the author is not unconditionally enthusiastic for the technological innovations that are changing the face of the world and its people; indeed, his grotesques speak also to fear of destructive technologization, expressed by a gigantic, mechanistic arsenal that swallows up humanity.

Like other avant-gardists, Czyżewski also reached for lower genres, following the concept of "re-theatricalization of theatre" that was well known in Poland as a result of its earlier theoretical explication by Leon Schiller (1887–1954). His seminal text, *Nowy kierunek badań teatrologicznych* (The New Direction of Theatre Studies), explored the idea of theatre's retheatricalization already in 1913. Schiller saw "the crisis of theatre" as having been caused by the domination of literature and by the influence of actors who desired applause for conventional performances. He saw a chance for the rebirth of high art in the return to the forgotten traditions of the theatre of the past, in other words, to forms that took shape before the reign of literature. Furthermore, he saw this opportunity in making the stage space autonomous, in its dynamization through movement, and finally in a drastic departure from literariness. Following Shiller, Czyżewski thus references pageantic, burlesque, and carnivalesque elements. According to his definition, *Osioł i słońce w metamorfozie* (The Donkey and the Sun in Metamorphosis, 1922) is a "formo-satirico-buffoonery."[6] Following the order set by this definition, the play is, first, a work of "new form"; second, a satire aimed both at critics hostile to the avant-garde and at the bourgeois audience that refuses to understand the new art; and third, a staging of a world upside down, steeped in playfulness and near in spirit to the circus or cabaret, which allows the artist to create an unexpected and separate reality in the theatre, one that plays with spectators' expectations. Peiper saw a chance for retheatralization also in a return to the still practised traditional folk spectacles. Theatre forms of old had yet another characteristic of great importance to the avant-garde – they were mass spectacles. In their new incarnation, they freed both actors and audiences from the traditional theatre building and let them inhabit new spaces. This practice was also linked to the need to find new ways of connecting with audiences.

Witold Wandurski (1891–1934) also experimented with stylized folk theatre, especially in his early but best-known play *Śmierć na gruszy* (Death on a Pear Tree, 1923). Wandurski's rejuvenation of plebeian theatre, however, was aimed at a different audience: as a communist avant-gardist, he addressed his work to the proletariat, which had been uprooted from its rural past as a result of migration to the cities and factory work. He founded the Workers' Theatre in Łódź, which he directed from 1925 to 1927, inspired primarily by the achievements of the Russian avant-garde, among them Vsevolod Meyerhold and Nikolai Evreinov. He fully realized that his audience did not need psychological and literary theatre, but instead ideologically simple and easily understood spectacles that would be simultaneously festive and grandiose, lively and engaging. He aimed to provoke heated and emotional reactions in his audience and in this manner, as happens at a fairground theatre, to actively influence the actors' performance. Indeed, Wandurski incorporated the probable remarks of spectators engaging in dialogue with the characters on stage into his play, making it into an expansive and detailed performance script for the spectacle.

In *Death on a Pear Tree*, the author utilized an old folk tale about the crafty entrapment of Death in a tree, as a result of which people stopped dying. Since they did not stop aging, however, in due course, exhausted by life, they desired nothing more than Death's return. Wandurski went beyond fairy-tale magic and spectacle, however, to reflect the primarily political aims of his theatre. His play included grotesque and horrifying war scenes, such as a march of the disabled and the images of dismembered yet still living battle victims, who – unable to die – circle about helplessly in search of their heads, arms, and legs. The play was also a satire on agitators and leaders from the intelligentsia "who know better" what is good for the people. Wandurski developed the play in a way that allowed the people to make their own decisions as they attempted, in a quasi-revolutionary march, to bring Death down from the pear tree and restore life's normal course. Thanks to a multitude of meta-theatrical measures – the inclusion of commentaries about art, contemporary theatre, the play's construction, acting, and audience participation in the script, as well as the use of the "theatre within a theatre" device and of folk stylization – *Death in the Pear Tree* is both a political play and a clear display of modern proletarian theatre.

Bruno Jasieński (1901–38) shared with Wandurski not only leftist views about the tasks of art, but also his fate; both artists were executed by firing squad in the Soviet Union during the 1930s, to which they had independently immigrated as ideological communists (their plays were found and published only towards the end of the 1950s). Jasieński was one the leading Polish Futurists, an author of poems and manifestos, and the organizer of many "poetro-concerts" (*poezokoncerty*) and poetic "recitals," which frequently ended with scandal and even police intervention. He wrote his most famous play, *Bal manekinów* (The Mannequins' Ball, 1931) in Paris, where he spent several years and co-founded the Polish workers' stage. Paris provides the setting of his play, which is a political satire that attacks the world of great capital (much like in Wandurski's *Gra o Herodzie* [Play About Herod, 1926]). The plot involves revitalized mannequins (a frequent motif of avant-garde art) from a chic fashion house, who organize an evening soirée while the humans, whom they consider to be mere copies of themselves, are not around. When a Human in a coat, the leader of a socialist workers' party, wanders in from the street, he must die for having discovered the mannequins' secret. The Male Mannequin then attaches his severed head to himself and attends a real human ball, where – taken for the party leader – he finds himself embroiled in various deceitful manoeuvres: between factory owners, who try to bribe him with considerable sums; between factions of workers, with some calling for a strike and others trying to prevent it; and finally between the attendees at a pretentious high society party at a factory owner's house. When the actual headless leader appears at a critical moment, the Mannequin – in a demonstration of his disgust at the stupidity, flagrant self-interest, and deceptions of people – hurriedly gives him back his head and runs away. Jasieński's play is primarily a grotesque condemnation of party opportunism, with politics – in its worst, most despicable manifestation – as the object of its critique. This type of political radicalism of avant-garde drama is most visible in Jasieński's and Wandurski's works, but it is also present in Peiper's late play *Skoro go nie ma* (Since He's Not Here, 1933), about the revolutionary riots of workers in Kraków.

> The feeling of liberation from the realm of national and martyrological problems, imposed by the [earlier] situation of partitions, was conducive to the expansion of new forms in art. The most sensitive of artists were soon, in fact, consumed by the no less difficult and painful realm of social issues, but the sense of being citizens of a sovereign nation begat in them a desire for integration with contemporary European art, favoured universalistic tendencies, and enabled contacts.
>
> – Marczak-Oborski, "Awangardowa wielość rzeczywistości," 6

The darkness of Czyżewski's miniatures and the grotesque nature of Jasieński's mannequins are somewhat reminiscent of the undoubtedly most remarkable (though underappreciated by his contemporaries) interwar artist, Stanisław Ignacy Witkiewicz, known also as Witkacy (1885–1939). He does not belong in an avant-garde framework, for although he was an innovator of form and leaned towards theoretical declarations, he questioned the idea of progress that is so key to the avant-garde formation. Witkacy was a fully autonomous and individual artist. One can certainly identify Formist, Expressionist, and Surrealist influences in his work, yet all of the "isms" typical of the epoch cannot account for the originality of his work. As Stanisław Marczak-Oborski writes, Witkacy "created a new genre: the catastrophic philosophical farce" and pointed the way towards the Theatre of the Absurd of the 1950s.[7] Yet another acclaimed critic of Polish postwar theatre, Konstanty Puzyna, calls Witkacy's innovative form "a furious expressionistic socio-political grotesque."[8] Witkacy's plays are certainly a curious and explosive mixture of terrifyingly uncanny figures (also of corpses) and circumstances (also of torture). Nothing in them happens according to known dramatic "norms"; instead, everything follows the author's idiosyncratic rules. Yet it is life itself that is at stake in his works.

> If we want to talk about the similarities between Witkacy and Ionesco, then their surrealist humour is less important than their identical view of contemporary alienation; the triple-nosed Roberta of the author of *Chairs* is less important than the "last individualist" Bérenger and the ideal, terrifying, modern city from *The Killer Without Cause*, and the uniformization of society spreading like fire through *Rhinoceros*. And if we want to compare Witkacy to Beckett, then again Beckett's pessimism will be an insignificant detail, with the much more important matter being the great dramatic study of isolation and *boredom*. It is precisely these frustrating feelings that permeate the entirety of Witkacy's work.
>
> – Puzyna, "Wstęp," 41

In his theory of pure form, Witkacy explained that the aim of art is to induce "metaphysical feelings" in the audience – in other words, to create the experience of contact with mystery, which only art can generate in the contemporary world.[9] This is possible, however, only through the formal composition of a work. In the theatre, according to Witkacy, such composition should rely on unusual combinations of actions and utterances, having no references to a non-artistic reality. Putting it differently, practical, realistic, or psychological approaches no longer have any effect on contemporary audiences, which are in need of cognitive and aesthetic shock therapy. This theory was not fully reflected in Witkacy's theatre, since the panopticon of his horrific, clownish, and often distasteful characters also points to pertinent social and philosophical issues that touch the core of real life. This is particularly true of Witkacy's central obsession – namely, his catastrophic vision of humanity's collapse as a result of the disappearance of individuality and the degradation of unique individuals, who will be replaced by a human mass that is unified and deprived of all higher feelings – happy as cattle.[10] Witkacy's characters are thus often the last representatives of the dying world: artists (be they "true" or entirely jaded and degenerated), thinkers, and former aristocrats – "ex-people," as he described them – in search of metaphysical experience.[11] What stands in their way are upheavals and revolutions (which are inevitable, according to their furious leaders) that lead to the creation of a mechanized society; or "natural" inter-human bonds, since family and love relationships pose a significant challenge to the "life creativity" of Witkacy's protagonists. Under the cover of clowning, parody, pastiche and a grotesque "buffo" tone, Witkacy's work conceals a serious diagnosis of the world's disintegration and reveals a ghastly portrait of a transitional epoch rocked by successive revolutions and leading inexorably to the birth of totalitarianisms.

What History Is For

While Witkacy analysed ongoing historical processes in terms of their universality, works that were strictly historical (written before the First World War) often served as veiled statements about contemporary times, or to foster the spirit of Polish independence. This was no longer necessary in an independent country; even so, historical subjects were still highly regarded in the literary hierarchy and the tradition of tapping historical "example" when addressing the current situation was still alive, including in drama. The national past was sometimes glorified – for instance, in *Hetman Stanisław Żółkiewski* (1925) by Kazimierz Brończyk (1888–1967) – but it was more often used for critical reflection. Such is the case in *Samuel Zborowski* (1929), a play by Ferdynand Goetel (1890–1960) about a conflict between King Stefan Batory and the rebellious knight Zborowski, which the king ultimately wins, thus demonstrating the rule of a (disturbingly) powerful hand. This work alluded to the then ongoing political conflicts (particularly within the parliament), with the author standing clearly on the side of strong national rule over anarchy and rebellious opposition. Maria Dąbrowska (1889–1965) took a similar approach in her only play, *Geniusz sierocy* (The Orphan Genius, 1939), in which she portrayed the rule of King Władysław IV in the first half of seventeenth century, primarily as an analogy to the interwar situation of Poland, which was splintered by political conflicts.

> There were two main problematic and thematic spheres in realistic historical drama of the interwar period: the first, more extensive, concentrated around revolution, the second ... around issues of Polish national interests and dilemmas arising from them, such as: "Realpolitik" vs. "romantic" politics, and the ideal of strong, state-building governance vs. the ideal of individual civic freedom.
>
> – Kwiatkowski, *Literatura dwudziestolecia*, 358

The most important historical playwright of the time, Adolf Nowaczyński (1876–1944), undermined dominant historical concepts and argued that "it is erroneous to think that during the seven centuries of our national existence we have been a conglomerate of only robust Catholic hords" and that "beside the Poland that got drunk, brawled, and later beat its chests in confessionals ... there also existed a minority Poland, powerful in its intellect, ideas, and character, and impressive with the lofty flight of free thought – a non-Catholic Poland, a humanistic Poland, an Arianian Poland."[12] In *Cezar i człowiek* (Caesar and the Man, 1937), Nowaczyński thus narrates a meeting between Nicholas Copernicus and Cesare Borgia that takes place in 1500, in the middle of the Renaissance. Copernicus represents spiritual values and Borgia the criminal tyranny that threatens them, although for audiences at that time is was more important to read this as a warning against the destructive force of fascism. Yet in this – purely spiritual – conflict, it is still the man, and not Caesar, who emerges victorious. This play, like all of Nowaczyński's work, is a panoramic chronicle with an epic reach that encompasses masses of secondary characters. His best-known play of the interwar period, *Wiosna Narodów. W cichym zakątku* (Spring of Nations: In a Quiet Corner, 1929), has a different character. It is a perverse portrait (in the sense of being written as if to counter its chosen subject, the tempestuous 1848 Spring of Nations), in which the Kraków Republic is presented as a multinational but provincial "corner" that cares little about the ongoing revolution.

Another strong current of historical dramas focused on the creation of a new theatrical portrait of a single individual. Many of them were great leaders, revolutionaries, or other figures recorded in the annals of history, who were either demythologized – or "debronzed," in Boy-Żelenski's idiom – or, alternatively, valorized. But these central characters were also often artists. The plays of Jarosław Iwaszkiewicz (1894–1980) – *Lato w Nohant* (Summer in Nohant, 1936) and *Maskarada* (Masquerade, 1938) – are *vies romancées* revolving around two Romantic artists: Chopin and Pushkin, respectively. By presenting them in everyday situations and implicating them in mundane conflicts, Iwaszkiewicz shows the damaging effect of quotidian life on artists. *Summer in Nohant* is more than a biographical and historical play, however, since it also problematizes Polish and French cultural differences and the artistic attitudes tied to them, as represented by Chopin and George Sand. Towards the end of the interwar period, Ludwik Hieronim Morstin (1886–1966) wrote a notable play titled *Obrona Ksantypy* (The Defence of Xanthippe, 1939). A devotee of and an expert in antiquity, Morstin dedicated his dramatic tetralogy to ancient female figures, freely reinterpreting their cultural images. *Penelopa* (Penelope, 1943), written during the war, actualizes the theme of marital fidelity, while the postwar *Kleopatra* (Cleopatra, 1960) rehabilitates the Egyptian queen by underscoring her political acuity. *The Defence of Xanthippe* reserves a central place for the wife of Socrates, and – instead of her classic faults (proverbial quarrelsomeness and spite) – highlights her resourcefulness and solitary efforts to oversee the health and domestic affairs of her husband, who is completely detached from life. Today, the "defence" fails to convince: Xanthippe stops fighting with her husband about their poverty and his lack of interest in her and the children once she realizes how much respect his Athenian friends have for him. The unbearable shrew transforms herself under Morstin's direction into a heroine who sacrifices her own needs to a great intellect.

The most interesting representative of historical drama from today's perspective is undoubtedly Stanisława Przybyszewska (1901–35), who was almost entirely unknown during the interwar period. She is the author of three plays on the subject of the French Revolution, all written between 1924 and 1929: the one-act play *Dziewięćdziesiąty trzeci* (Ninety-Third), the sprawling *Sprawa Dantona* (The Danton Case), and the unfinished *Thermidor*. The French Revolution, which Przybyszewska was obsessed with all her life (which was short and bleak: she died in extreme poverty as a result of illnesses and drug-related emaciation at the age of thirty-four), was linked for her with other great political and social upheavals of the time, including the October Revolution in Russia. Przybyszewska tried to uncover the basic laws of these upheavals, with the French Revolution serving as their model. This is particularly noticeable in *The Danton Case*, a chronicle of several tense, revolutionary weeks in 1794. Przybyszewska based her play on a conflict between two prominent revolutionary leaders, Robespierre and Danton, although over the course of multiple edits, the play became largely a portrait of Robespierre. She sought to present his reasoning, in defiance of historians' evaluations, as the arguments of a visionary and a strategist, a genius who through the "cumulative" power of his greatness brought about a necessary social change: necessary indeed, although bloody. The tragedy of Robespierre is rooted in his prescience: he acts with awareness of a historical mission, rejecting all emotions and appearing almost as "the brain of revolution" embodied, although he is also painfully aware of the many consequences of repairing the world through terror. Every revolution depends on this paradox. As Saint-Just, one of the characters, states: "Even if it is so ... one must go on. Let there be what must be. Even then it is worth dying for that faith."[13]

For all of her admiration for the historical Robespierre, and given her goal of undermining the myth of Danton's purity – she portrays him as a traitor and a demagogue – Przybyszewska wrote an incisive drama about the mechanisms of revolutionary terror that in the end destroys those who created it. The two interwar theatre productions of *The Danton Case* (the first of which took place due to Leon Schiller's involvement) passed without much notice. It was only during the postwar years that the play was rescued from oblivion. Its world fame came with Andrzej Wajda's screen adaptation (1982), with Wojciech Pszoniak and Gerard Depardieu in the roles of Robespierre and Danton, respectively. It must be added here that Wajda's interpretation, marked by the then ongoing Polish "revolution" – namely, the rise of Solidarity in 1980 and its brutal pacification a year and a half later – significantly changed the substance of Przybyszewska's play. In particular, it greatly simplified the complicated political motivations as she had represented them, as well as the terrifying mass madness that Robespierre notes when he doubts in the end whether people had "really been created for freedom."[14]

Dramatized history thus served not only ongoing discourses (political, consolatory, and ethical), but also the study of historical mechanisms, articulated perhaps most clearly by Witkacy and Przybyszewska.

The Potential of Comedy

> Beside traditional comedic proposals à la Krzywoszewski or Kiedrzyński, the interwar period also produced works in which the term comedy no longer names a genre. Authorial qualifications included with the text are misleading, may foretell of a coming parody, signal an act of literary provocation, make genre designation into a philosophical term, a kind of statement of worldview ... Fossilized and automated models are revived in a net of new works, signifying anew. Themselves a sign, they participate in the creation of new literary matter, making a new text."
>
> – Krajewska, *Komedia polska XX-lecia międzywojennego. Tradycjonaliści i nowatorzy*, 157

Separate heed should be paid to the torrent of comedies and farces – the "popular plays" written by professionally efficient producers – that were staged throughout the interwar period. Some of their authors departed from stock formulas – for instance, the conventional "happy ending," and didacticism and moralizing. Excoriations of trashy comedies were also intensifying. In 1918 the members of the poetic group "Pro Arte" (which later evolved into the poetic formation Skamander) caused a scandal during a performance of Stefan Krzywoszewski's *Mrs Chorążyna* at Arnold Szyfman's Polish Theatre in Warsaw, a modern facility that was considered a "national theatre" of sorts. Pamphlets protesting the lowering of artistic standards were thrown from the balcony, the stage was stormed, a proclamation was read out, and amid all the chaos, whistles, and shouting, the performance was halted. The audience did not join in the protest and instead tried to throw the provocateurs out and see the play through to the end.

New comedies were lauded for addressing postwar social changes, although otherwise they remained utterly conventional. Here excelled, among others, Stefan Kiedrzyński (1888–1943), Adam Grzymała-Siedlecki (1876–1967), Wacław Grubiński (1883–1973), and Włodzimierz Perzyński (1877–1930). They were preoccupied with the problems of marriage, love, and money, usually between representatives of two social strata – landowners, intelligentsia, and the fallen aristocrats on the one hand, and the rapidly ascending nouveau riche on the other. *Dzieje salonu* (The History of a Salon, 1921) by Kazimierz Wroczyński (1883–1957) served as their model; it displayed the acute tensions between customs originating in the postwar social mingling. These were succinctly expressed in the famous line "Scram, boors!," given in response to a marriage proposal from the family of a rich "boor," Józek, to an impoverished but well-born maiden. Many comedies produced at that time focused on financial inequalities, anachronistic class pretensions, and their accompanying resentments. Maria Morozowicz-Szczepkowska (1885–1968) returned to this theme towards the end of the interwar period with *Walący się dom* (The Dilapidated House, 1937), in which she showed the absurdly strong sentimental attachment to gentry traditions, even when they flew in the face of common sense, modern customs, and the possibility of social advancement.

Comedy dominated the interwar period and was perhaps the most creatively transformed genre, especially when taken up by writers looking to tap comedic formulas for new purposes. Creators of "scientific comedies" like Antoni Cwojdziński (1896–1972) and Bruno Winawer (1883–1944) thought that science, due to its rising significance, should be incorporated into art. Cwojdziński was more consistent in expressing his belief that science could rejuvenate comedy; he did not so much "popularize" known theories in his plays as present them "in action" – that is, as influencing their protagonists. He did it in such a way as to render them understandable to the layperson. An easily understandable summary of the theory of relativity is folded into *Teoria Einsteina* (Einstein's Theory, 1934); psychoanalysis appears in the comedy *Freuda teoria snów* (Freud's Theory of Dreams, 1937); and Ernst Kretschmer's typology linking physical and psychological traits in *Temperamenty* (Temperaments, 1938). Winawer's plays were closer to cabaret sketches; he had an ear for puns and a proclivity for paradoxes and jokes. He used the figure of a scientist more often than scientific theories *per se* (or he used the latter in a form that approached science fiction, as in *Promienie FF* [FF Rays, 1921]). In his works, the scientist was usually poor but brilliant, and he had been wronged by some crooks and was helpless to defend himself. Following the genre's conventions, however, Winawer indulged in compensatory "happy endings," in which the protagonist reclaimed his dignity, the appreciation of others, and sometimes even his beloved (as happens in *Roztwór Profesora Pytla* [Professor Pytel's Solution, 1919] and *Księga Hioba* [Book of Job, 1921]).

Another means of refreshing the genre of comedy was by lyricizing it. Two of the most important authors in this current – Jerzy Szaniawski (1886–1970) and Maria Pawlikowska-Jasnorzewska (1891–1945) – wrote works that only in some respects embraced comedic conventions. The eleven plays that Szaniawski wrote in the interwar period had a highly recognizable style. They were often staged by excellent directors and starred equally excellent actors; this brought the author both fame and respect. Szaniawski was not interested in politics or history. His plays are set mainly in small towns, though never specific ones. His settings are simply representative of typical small towns, and come with standard features such a town hall, a church, and a town council, as well as a resident doctor, pharmacist, and lawyer, with all its residents living in peace and according to their own customs. The tranquility of these settings is then disturbed by something out of the ordinary; in the case of *Ptak* (Bird, 1923), for example, it is caused by the appearance of a young man who plans to release a "great golden bird" into the sky, to the displeasure of the town councillors, who believe that "bird" is actually a dangerous codeword for something else. The student, however, actually does release a bird, and for no other reason than "to make things pretty."[15] In so doing, he awakens longings and dreams in the town residents that incline them towards change. Saturated with a poetic, almost fairy-tale like atmosphere, and humorous in its playful dialogues between geriatric city councillors, the play does not lend itself to rational explication. It does not pursue any kind of a moral, nor does it lead to a concrete denouement; it remains a sketch about the contrast between the inertia of conventions and the liberating, joyful imagination capable of breaking with them.

In Szaniawski's other comedies, the protagonist has to resolve a more clearly outlined inner conflict. In *Żeglarz* (Sailor, 1925), one of the most popular plays of the interwar years, the town residents raise a monument to their legendary hero as they prepare to celebrate the fiftieth anniversary of his death, not knowing that Captain Nut did not actually perish and was not at all heroic. Why has the truth about the captain not come out into the open? Is it because the legend has allowed the residents of a dull town to dream of something loftier and to believe that heroes can be born in their midst? Szaniawski's play does not offer an answer, leaving the problem of truth and lies unresolved. The interpretation of *Sailor* during the interwar years was hotly debated in Poland. This is not surprising, for the play raised questions close to the heart of Polish national identity in focusing on people's tendency to accept manipulated legends uncritically, as well as on the need for the existence of myth "as a different truth about the past" and "the expression of deep needs of the collective psyche."[16] The term "comedy" in this case refers not so much to the genre as to this "manufacture of delusion," calling attention to differences in experiencing and understanding the world, and to the existence of something that always remains outside of the order of things. It must be added that Szaniawski's later plays shed the comedic classification. If Żeromski's path led from tragedy to comedy, Szaniawski took the opposite road. His works become darker and darker, and their action moves from towns to desolate hinterlands, where the protagonists face threats from both their environment and the depths of their own natures (*Most* [Bridge, 1933]). Even these plays, however, retain Szaniawski's unique lyricism, which is perceptible in understatements, ambiguity, and an emphasis on the obscurity of events.

Attempts to renew the genre of tragedy were also made in the interwar period, albeit infrequently. The work of Karol Hubert Rostworowski (1877–1938), who was highly renowned at the time, serves as one example. In *Niespodzianka* (The Surprise, 1929), he tried to revive the genre of tragedy by setting the action of the play in a village, where he thought he might discover an earlier type of religiosity and intensity of passions. He was not alone in thinking this; "village plays" (*wiejskie dramaty*) were quite abundant at this time and represented also by Leopold Staff and Emil Zegadłowicz. *The Surprise* is a tragedy about a mother who, desperate to provide for her two children, murders a foreigner from America with an axe and steals his money. Afterwards, she realizes that the foreigner was in fact her oldest son, who had emigrated in search of a better life a long time before and had just returned home, unrecognized. This play grew into a trilogy, with the next two parts presenting the fate of the middle son. His education in the city is funded by the money stolen by his mother, and he unceasingly struggles with the weight of her crime, although in the end he does become a successful scientist. Rostworowski is strangely reticent about this advancement of a peasant child: the trilogy in its entirety suggests that it would have been better for the social order had he not been removed from his birthplace. This went unnoticed by critics at the time, who praised the authenticity of its dialogue (*The Surprise* was written in dialect) and its strong structure.

The comedies of Maria Pawlikowska-Jasnorzewska are also a separate category. The author described them variously as fantasy, tragicomedy, farce, and grotesquery. Jasnorzewska, who is known mainly from her remarkable love poetry, carries this theme over to her dramatic work. These are not "plays about love," despite borrowing from the rather schematic cast of characters of classical comedy: lovers, modern successful women, cuckolded or unfaithful husbands, grouchy in-laws, and bubbly servants. Instead, they are dramas about the *struggle* for love: seemingly light and humorous and set usually in high society, they function as intellectual and social provocations. The author places her female protagonists in positions that both call for and enable them to decide about their own emotional involvement, most often against social norms. In *Egipska pszenica* (The Egyptian Wheat, 1932), Jasnorzewska bravely questions the institution of marriage, positing it as a union that damages love instead of nurturing it, and portraying the inequality of men and women within marital relationships. What is more, she poses "tactless" questions about the "proper" age of partners and specifically the right of a mature woman to happiness and self-realization at the side of a significantly younger lover.

Regarding Pawlikowska's other comedies, Antoni Słonimski, the sharpest of Polish feuilletonists in the interwar period, wrote that "her Highness, the Princess of the Polish Lyric was able to match wit with poetry in an unmatched manner."[17] He did not think as highly of *The Egyptian Wheat*, but he did appreciate its representation of love that "was not middle-class, slovenly and sleepy, but predatory in its fight for every moment, every beat of the heart."[18] Even in works decidedly more saturated with lyricism, Pawlikowska transgressed social taboos, creating configurations of love in which fulfilment was achieved against social norms and always out of a strong need for love and passion. She did not stay away from sensual associations – her heroines are self-aware as women – and for this reason she is sometimes compared to the older-by-a-generation author Gabriela Zapolska (1857–1921), who was the first to transgress the limits of "what is left unspoken" in women's drama.[19]

The playwriting of women caused quite a stir at the time because female writers were starting not only to write about women but also to strongly emphasize the female perspective and the specific problems women faced. A particularly strong example of this approach is *Dom kobiet* (The House of Women, 1930) by Zofia Nałkowska (1884–1954). This play was a literary sensation not just for being the dramatic debut of a superb novelist, but also, indeed primarily, for its entirely female cast of characters. It represents eight women of different generations, all living in the same house. These women speak about men, however, who are either absent or recently deceased (one of the main characters is the newly widowed Joanna), and in the course of their conversations they discover that they lived with someone whom they did not know at all, who was "somebody else" (the widow's husband led a double-life and had children with another woman). These returns – of almost Ibsenian ghosts – prompt the women to reconsider their present situation and emotions, which shifts their judgments of former "facts" and transforms their memories; put another way, it is not so much their present that suddenly and radically changes, but their past ("everything is different," as the Grandmother says).[20] The play was a strong entry into the Polish psychological drama. Authors of feminist orientation criticized Nałkowska for missing the target – all of the women admittedly live exclusively through the problems of their (sometimes already deceased) men – but the play can also be read as an accusation levelled at a culture that continues to bind women while allowing men to live freely.

Maria Morozowicz-Szczepkowska was undoubtedly more radical in her approach. She based *Sprawa Moniki* (The Case of Monica, 1932) on a similar idea: the play presents three women wronged by one man, who does not appear on the stage at all. Yet *The Case of Monica* stands in a polemical relation to *The House of Women*, which Morozowicz-Szczepkowska considered "a gallery of squawking hags."[21] Her own charge of male irresponsibility and betrayal is more heated and direct. The main character is portrayed as an independent professional woman who makes her own decisions and is responsible for her own life. *The Case of Monica* was "an address to women to have the ambition to become full-fledged human beings, and not only love-struck mates," as its author wrote.[22] American audiences may know this work in a greatly altered version: the play made it to Broadway and was later reworked into a screenplay for *Doctor Monica* (1934), a Warner Brothers film with Kay Francis in the title role.

To return to Pawlikowska-Jasnorzewska: her best-known play today is without a doubt the tragicomedy *Baba-dziwo* (A Woman of Wonder 1938). While still a witty comedy, the tone of *A Woman of Wonder* is decidedly different for also being a cutting anti-fascist grotesque. The play features a monstrous, and always uniformed, woman-chief Valida Vrana, who establishes totalitarian rule in her country and announces the conscription of young women into the army, as well as orders that they bear a child with a man chosen by the state for the glory of the fatherland. The state propaganda slogan reads "procreate and work," a paraphrase of the Benedictine motto "pray and work."[23] Terror rules the country, intensified by mass media controlled by the dictator, as marked by huge speakers in the streets. In its grotesque aspect, the tragicomedy is reminiscent of Witkacy's work; in fact, he and Jasnorzewska co-wrote a play titled *Koniec świata* (The End of the World), which unfortunately has been lost. The similarity is visible in the figure of the monstrous "womaton" from Witkacy's plays, or that of the degraded individual who, in a totalitarian state, is deprived not only of freedom but also of personality. In an ironic twist of history, the Warsaw premiere of *The Woman of Wonder* took place on 1 September 1939, the day the Germans invaded Poland and the Second World War began.

The anti-totalitarian current in Polish interwar drama was strongest among its comedies. Before *A Woman of Wonder*, Antoni Słonimski (1895–1976) ridiculed the totalitarian system without striking directly at it through portraits of its representatives in *Rodzina* (Family, 1933). He also introduced the theme of (in)authenticity, which was important also to Witkacy and – first and foremost – to Witold Gombrowicz. In *Family*, two guests – a Soviet commissar and a young Nazi from Bavaria, both born in that region – arrive at a manor turned guest house owned by the slightly unhinged Count Lekcicki. The first wants to visit his mother, a poor peasant; the latter is there in order to confirm his purely Aryan and aristocratic ancestry. In the end, the commissar learns that he is actually the son of Count Lekcicki, having been conceived out of wedlock, and the Nazi discovers that he is the son of a poor Jew, Rosenberg. Both extremes are mocked mercilessly, almost cabaret-style. The *bon mot* conceived by Słonimski in the process – Poland is a "revolving bulwark" (threatened by Bolshevism on one side, fascism on the other) – entered and for a long time remained part of colloquial speech.[24] *Family* beat theatre records for popularity not only because it was a comedy (on a serious and dangerous theme) written by a "rebellious scoffer," but also because it was seen as an important voice in support of the right to personal freedom and a safe existence.[25]

A few years later, in 1936, another anti-fascist comedy (or rather vaudeville, for it included songs) was staged at the cabaret Cyrulik Warszawski (Varsovian Barber). *Kariera Alfa Omegi* (The Career of Alpha Omega) was written by Marian Hemar (1901–72) and Julian Tuwim (1894–1953), and presented a portrait of a "leader" that emphasized his road to "leadership," which is today vividly reminiscent of Brecht's later *The Resistible Rise of Arturo Ui*. The comedy made clear biographical allusions to the most famous Polish tenor of the time, the internationally known Jan Kiepura (1902–66). It is the story of a poor "boy from Birchtown" (Kiepura came from Sosnowiec – "Pinetown") who develops his singing talent, conquers the world, and "reaches the heights of fame and at this height becomes dizzy" (as Kazimierz Wierzyński wrote in a review), for he becomes convinced that his electrifying voice "is the best instrument for ruling a country."[26] The analogy to the German *Führer* may seem quite surprising, given that Kiepura is remembered first and foremost as a great singer. In 1936, however, rumours about his political ambitions abounded, and he had just been celebrated at the Berlin Olympic Games. Crowds of many thousands adored him wherever he appeared, and the artist took every opportunity to speak from balconies, windows, or even the roof of a car. Sometimes these speeches were about the "everlasting fatherland" and concluded with the collective singing of the national anthem.[27] The amusing and not yet dangerous career of the dynamic, ambitious, and sympathetic Alpha Omega turns darker only at the end, when he is visited by the representatives of youth associations. They ensure him of their loyalty, after which they agree on a common outfit (shirts in a specific colour) and on their motto and identifying gesture ("Our greeting will be ... hand up! Which one? Both. Why should we skimp."); they also define their enemies ("Out with the freckled! No one who has had freckles in the family, up to three generations back, can belong to us") as they ecstatically prepare for action.[28] The satire aims not only at the figure of the leader, who believes in his uniqueness and historical mission, but also at the irrational readiness of the masses to follow absurd ideas (a significant part was played by the "voice" of the leader itself). This vaudeville was successfully performed in the capital for a long time; however, its performances outside Warsaw were sometimes halted or boycotted, and the right-wing press wrote about it with indignation – a sign that Tuwim's and Hemar's mockery had hit its target.

A new understanding of comedy and its possible uses can serve as a lens for examining the work of not only Witkacy, but also the "early" Witold Gombrowicz (1904–69). His play *Iwona, księżniczka Burgunda* (Ivona, Princess of Burgundia) was first published in 1938 in the journal *Skamander* but staged only during the post-October thaw in 1957, only then becoming noticeably present in cultural circulation. It generously drew on the rules of the farce and the grotesque, in the process transforming itself into an absurd "fatalistic tragedy."[29] In his commentaries, Gombrowicz called it interchangeably a "tragicomedy" and a "comedy." In terms of genre and textual associations, it can be read as a parody of Shakespearian drama, among other forms. The play's eponymous heroine, an unattractive, awkward, and timid girl, appears at the royal court and through her sheer existence causes others around her to discover their own, numerous defects and deeply shameful desires, and to recover memories of their own criminal acts. Her apathy and formlessness give rise to the sense that one can do anything to her, yet Ivona does not yield to the court's attempts to shape her. Indeed, those who undertake such attempts discover within themselves dark forces and aggressive instincts, tamed until now by court customs and ceremony. The play ends with Ivona's carefully prepared, royal-style murder, committed from a distance with a help of a fish bone, which the heroine chokes on during dinner.

> When it comes to "form," it means not only a custom, convention, or social habitus, as it was initially understood. It also means a necessary way of grasping reality by the experiencing subject, or perhaps even – who knows – the power residing in being itself. You can speak of form when – in the encounter between people – the dominant norm of feeling and behaviour arises. But also at times when – in the face of all that is unclear, incomprehensible, and unfulfilled – the human mind tries to smooth and sort it all out into comprehensible entities. Finally, also when we discover that a constant struggle – or exchange – between chaos (youth, energy) and form (order, maturity) takes place in being ... and moreover, that this exchange *is* being. In a word, Gombrowicz's form can be interpreted in sociological or epistemological terms, or even those of cosmogony: depending on where the accent is placed, it means either an inter-human relation, an epistemological tool, or the principle of being.
>
> – Błoński, "Historia i operetka, 261–2

The play of form characteristic of Gombrowicz is exercised in *Ivona* on two levels. On the level of genre, the farce is modified by the characters themselves as they try to escape their given patterns to "play" other roles, even though their efforts amount only to grotesquery. On the second, inter-human level, the force of ritual behaviours practised up until now, which keeps the heroes in check, is knocked off kilter and replaced by a destructive, savage force of instinct suddenly awakened in the face of something radically different. *Ivona* is thus a form of psychoanalysis conducted on a collective that reveals its low, shameful, and undesirable traits – linked mostly to desire, non-normative sexuality, and male–female tensions – which previously had been hidden under the armour of culture. All of the court's ambitions are contained precisely in forms delineating the framework of inter-human coexistence. Inevitably, they are restored immediately after Ivona's death – a period of mourning is declared and appropriate gestures are made – which only makes the profound crisis of the portrayed world more apparent.

~

Polish interwar drama can be viewed in light of the reforms in Western theatre and of the transformations within playwriting at the turn of the nineteenth and twentieth centuries. There are clear changes to its understanding of theatre's function, with the director/

theatre artist becoming the proper "author" of a work. Plays also undergo change, often as a result of new ways of expression worked out by Ibsen, Strindberg, and Shaw, who revolutionized realism in theatre. At the same time, Polish drama can be seen as staying in a continuous dialogue with the Polish vision of theatre, particularly that of the Romantics and Stanisław Wyspiański (1869–1907). It was they who turned drama into a vehicle for outlining their distinct theatrical vision, which necessitates its own, specific performances; and it was also they who elevated drama to the rank of artistic expression, anchored in drama's multivocality, its ways of making problems emerge through dialogue, and its precise imagery. It is true that the "popular plays" that theatres relied on to stay in business comprised an enormous part of interwar drama. But it is also true that a few strong interwar currents – the grotesque (also in its anti-totalitarian version), as well as poetic and avant-garde plays – significantly impacted the later shape of Polish drama tradition.

Ewa Guderian-Czaplińska
Adam Mickiewicz University, Poznań
Translated by Agnieszka Polakowska

NOTES

1 Marczak-Oborski, "Uwagi o dramaturgii polskiej," 104.
2 Żeromski, "Uciekła mi przepióreczka," 99.
3 Peiper, "Nowe usta," 349.
4 Peiper, "Szósta! Szósta!," 265.
5 Peiper, "Punkt wyjścia," *Zwrotnica* 1 (May 1922), 3–4. "A new epoch is beginning: an epoch of embracing the present ... The city, mass, machine and its derivatives: speed, innovation, newness, the power of human being and the epoch, a wrestling match with heaven, flight on steel wings, a bath in the day's freshest vodka, a leap into the now – they are becoming for us the subject of unknown rapture." Translated from Peiper, *Tędy. Nowe usta*, 27–8.
6 Czyżewski, "Osioł i słońce w metamorfozie," 121.
7 Marczak-Oborski, "Uwagi o dramaturgii polskiej," 101.
8 Puzyna, "Wstęp," 27.
9 See Witkiewicz, "Metaphysical Feelings."
10 Witkiewicz, *Nienasycenie*, 66.
11 The figure of the "ex-people" is discussed, for example, by Konstanty Puzyna in "Witkacy i rewolucja," 161–5.
12 Nowaczyński, "O dramacie z przeszłości," 53.
13 Przybyszewska, *The Danton Case*, 199.
14 Ibid., 199.
15 Szaniawski, *Ptak*, 120–4.
16 Kwiatkowski, *Literatura dwudziestolecia*, 338.
17 Słonimski, *Egipska pszenica*, 192.
18 Słonimski, *Niebiescy zalotnicy*, 142.
19 *O czym się nie mówi* (What Is Left Unspoken, 1909) is the title of Gabriela Zapolska's novel that tackles such problems as prostitution and STDs.
20 Nałkowska, *Dom kobiet*, 126.

21 Morozowicz-Szczepkowska, *Z lotu ptaka*, 277.
22 Ibid., 282.
23 Pawlikowska-Jasnorzewska, *Baba-Dziwo*, 291.
24 Słonimski, *Rodzina*, 12.
25 Gosk, "Niepokorny szyderca," 39.
26 Sieradzki, *Burza wokół Alfa Omegi*, 125.
27 Ibid., 126.
28 Tuwim and Hemar, "Kariera Alfa Omegi," 82.
29 Jastrzębski, "O pojęciu groteski," 103.

WORKS CITED

Błoński, Jan. "Historia i operetka." In *Gombrowicz i krytycy*. Edited by Zdzisław Łapiński. 257–82. Kraków: Wydawnictwo Literackie, 1984.

Czosnowski, Stanisław. "Herezje teatralne." In *Myśl teatralna polskiej awangardy 1919–1939. Antologia*. Edited by Stanisław Marczak-Oborski. 85–8. Warszawa: Wydawnictwa Artystyczne i Filmowe, 1973.

Czyżewski, Tytus. "Osioł i słońce w metamorfozie." In *Poezje i próby dramatyczne*. Edited by Alicja Baluch. 120–37. Wrocław: Zakład Narodowy im. Ossolińskich, 1992.

Gosk, Hanna. "Niepokorny szyderca." *Nowe Książki* 11 (1996): 39.

Jastrzębski, Zdzisław. "O pojęciu groteski i niektórych jej aspektach w dramacie polskim doby obecnej." *Dialog* 11, no. 11 (1966): 94–108.

Krajewska, Anna. *Komedia polska XX-lecia międzywojennego. Tradycjonaliści i nowatorzy.* Wrocław: Wydawnictwo Wiedza o Kulturze, 1989.

Kwiatkowski, Jerzy. *Literatura dwudziestolecia.* Warszawa: Państwowe Wydawnictwo Naukowe, 1990.

Marczak-Oborski, Stanisław. "Awangardowa wielość rzeczywistości." In *Myśl teatralna polskiej awangardy. Antologia.* 5–37. Warszawa: Wydawnictwa Artystyczne i Filmowe, 1973.

– "Uwagi o dramaturgii polskiej 1918–1939." *Dialog* 24, no. 4 (1979): 101–4.

Morozowicz-Szczepkowska, Maria. *Z lotu ptaka. Wspomnienia.* Warszawa: Państwowy Instytut Wydawniczy, 1968.

Nałkowska, Zofia. "Dom kobiet." In *Dzieła. Utwory dramatyczne*, vol. 3. Warszawa: Czytelnik, 1990.

Nowaczyński, Adolf. "O dramacie z przeszłości." In *Porachunki i projekty. Teksty o teatrze z lat 1900–1938*. Edited by Henryk Izydor Rogacki. 50–7. Wrocław: Wydawnictwo Wiedza o Kulturze, 1993.

Pawlikowska-Jasnorzewska, Maria. "Baba-Dziwo." In *Dramaty*, vol. 2. Edited by Anna Bolecka, Warszawa: Czytelnik, 1986.

Peiper, Tadeusz. "Nowe usta. Odczyt o poezji." In *Tędy: Nowe usta*. 329–67. Kraków: Wydawnictwo Literackie, 1972.

– "Punkt wyjścia." In *Tędy: Nowe usta*. 27–8. Kraków: Wydawnictwo Literackie, 1972.

– "Szósta! Szósta!" In *Poematy i utwory teatralne*. 239–84. Edited by Andrzej K. Waśkiewicz. Kraków: Wydawnictwo Literackie, 1979.

Przybyszewska, Stanisława. *The Danton Case; Thermidor: Two Plays*. Translated by Bolesław Taborski. Evanston: Northwestern University Press, 1989.

Puzyna, Konstanty. "Witkacy i rewolucja." In *Witkacy*. Edited by Janusz Degler. 161–5. Warszawa: Errata, 1999.

– "Wstęp." In Stanisław Ignacy Witkiewicz, *Dramaty*, vol. 1. Edited by Konstanty Puzyna. 5–46. Warszawa: Państwowy Instytut Wydawniczy, 1972.

Raszewski, Zbigniew. *Krótka historia teatru polskiego*. Warszawa: PIW, 1978.

Sieradzki, Jacek. "Burza wokół Alfa Omegi." *Dialog* 23, no. 11 (1978): 124–9.

Słonimski, Antoni. "Egipska pszenica." In *Gwałt na Melpomenie*, vol. 2. 192–4. Warszawa: Wydawnictwo Czytelnik, 1959.

– "Niebiescy zalotnicy." In *Gwałt na Melpomenie*, vol. 2. 141–143. Warszawa: Wydawnictwo Czytelnik, 1959.

– "Rodzina." *Wiadomości Literackie* 11 (1934): 6–15.

Szaniawski, Jerzy. "Ptak." In *Dramaty wybrane*. 83–148. Kraków: Wydawnictwo Literackie, 1973.

Tuwim, Julian, and Marian Hemar. "Kariera Alfa Omegi." *Dialog* 11 (1978): 44–83.

Witkiewicz, Stanisław Ignacy. "Metaphysical Feelings." In *The Witkiewicz Reader*. Translated and edited by Daniel Gerould. 285–6. Evanston: Northwestern University Press, 1992.

– *Nienasycenie*. Warszawa: PIW, 1982.

Żeromski, Stefan. "Uciekła mi przepióreczka …" In *Antologia dramatu polskiego 1918–1978*, vol. 1. Edited by Stanisław Witold Balicki and Stanisław Marczak-Oborski. 15–100. Warszawa: PIW, 1981.

Apocalyptic Fears; Aesthetic Daring (Stanisław Ignacy Witkiewicz)

Playwright, painter, photographer, novelist, and philosopher, Stanisław Ignacy Witkiewicz (pen name Witkacy, 1885–1939) was an idiosyncratic and multitalented artistic personality who, although unrecognized in his own lifetime, has emerged as a seminal figure of the interwar avant-garde. He brought to the theatre extraordinary visual sensibility, seismographic apprehension of the tremors of social change, and an intuitive grasp of the impact of scientific revolutions on the new century.

Endowed with a powerful scenic imagination, Witkacy created a dramatic universe full of hyperbolic characters, surprising configurations of events, inventive *coups de théâtre*, and spectacular stage effects. His predilection was for a cosmopolitan world featuring a large cast of characters with bizarrely comic polyglot names, striking facial profiles, and flamboyant costumes. Many of his plays (he wrote more than thirty of them) are set in far-flung places: in the exotic Far East (*Mr. Price, czyli Bzik tropikalny* [Mr Price, or Tropical Madness, 1920]), a mythical South Sea kingdom (*Niepodległość trójkątów* [The Independence of Triangles, 1921]), or a fabulous Middle Europe (*Kurka wodna* [The Water Hen, 1921]). In other works, such as *Mątwa* (The Cuttlefish, or The Hyrcanian World View, 1922), there is an artificially constructed stage space, a purely theatrical arrangement of coordinates where past, present, and future intersect. At these crossroads, the representatives of different cultures and civilizations – expatriate Poles, Hassidic Jews, Russian cavalry officers, British mathematicians, Aboriginal royalty, American millionaires, Asian houseboys, and Romanian *femmes fatales* – confront one another with disdain, and modern science is measured against ancient magical practices.

The world in Witkacy's plays has lost its bearings. National, ethnic, and personal identities have eroded; class allegiances no longer hold; everything and everyone has grown hybrid, *ersatz*, and makeshift. Political positions are so interbred that it is no longer possible to tell right from left or up from down. In Witkacy's dramatic universe, in this pandemic mishmash lacking any centre or ideological coherence, Poland and Polish issues – an obsession of Witkacy's predecessors in Polish theatre, to mention only Adam Mickiewicz (1798–1855) and Stanisław Wyspiański (1869–1907) – are not of primary importance. Characterized by grotesque humour, drug-induced dream logic, and psychedelic colours, Witkacy's world is instead a breeding ground for the existential anguish of human loneliness and for apocalyptic fears of loss of metaphysical feelings and of the extinction of art in the coming anthill civilization. Endangered creativity is the major theme of Witkacy's dystopian vision of a nightmarish future. His protagonists are painters, poets, and musicians as well as scientists, thinkers, and social activists pushed up against the metaphysical wall. At odds with the universe, with their society, and with themselves, these self-tormented pseudo-geniuses are filled with rage or despair and rendered absurdly helpless by their own unruly creative impulses. They must battle against state control, mass culture, self-doubt, and the theft of their work and identity by their sinister doubles.

The mechanization of society is one of their main enemies. The machine used by modern tyranny is a regulator implanted in humankind's brain, and the enslavement that Witkacy envisages is a very personal one: the tyranny of society and of the many over the individual. Accordingly, he explores, as the crux of mechanization, issues that had not yet attained currency in the early 1920s: psychiatric incarceration, thought control, confession to crimes not committed, social regimentation and indoctrination, and rule by secret government (*Oni* [They, 1920]). A perceptive analyst of the arbitrary workings of power both within the family and the state, Witkacy made conspiracy theory a driving force in many of his plays. Society is always masked; its true power structures remain hidden; those who truly hold the reins lurk concealed in the background. No one knows who is actually running the whole show from behind the scenes, as bizarre cults and psychotic gurus unpredictably replace one another (*Gyubal Wahazar*, 1921; *Bezimienne dzieło* [The Anonymous Work, 1921]).

Zakopane is a small town at the foot of the majestic Tatra Mountains. When Stanisław Witkiewicz settled his family there in 1890, it was a cultural and, at one point, also a political centre, buzzing with creative and social life, political conspiracies, and the erotic conquests of Polish intellectual and artistic élites. It was frequented by the likes of count Władysław Zamoyski (1853–1924), one of the most noble Polish social and business activists; the Nobel Prize–winning novelist Henryk Sienkiewicz (1846–1916); Stefan Żeromski (1864–1925), known as "the conscience of Polish literature"; Tadeusz Miciński (1873–1918), a Mannichean "worshipper of mysteries"; Mieczysław Karłowicz (1876–1909), a composer, mountaineer, skier, and photographer; famous painters such as Leon Wyczółkowski (1852–1936) and Jacek Malczewski (1854–1929); Helena Modrzejewska (1840–1909), an international star of nineteenth-century Polish and American theatre (known in America as Modjeska) and an old love interest of Witkiewicz *père*, as well as Witkacy's godmother; and, last but not least, Józef Piłsudski (1867–1935), Witkiewicz's cousin and the future chief of state and Marshal of Poland, who conspired with his Polish Socialist Party in Zakopane before the First World War. After the war, Zakopane lost much of its aura and was referred to as "the most stinky, musty, parochial … stupid, thoughtless, and cretin-like point in Poland" (Adolf Nowaczyński as quoted by Michał Paweł Markowski, 281).

The sources of inspiration for Witkacy's imagination were many. He did not adhere to the rules of realistic representation in his plays; however, he drew heavily on his observations, memories, and readings related to his travels (often closely linked, as in his reading of *Lord Jim* on the voyage to Ceylon – later reflected in *Metafizyka dwugłowego cielęcia* [Metaphysics of a Two-Headed Calf, 1921]). He was also creatively stimulated by his father and friends in fin-de-siècle Zakopane, and by his torrid liaison with the modernist actress Irena Solska – the demonic woman who reappears in *They* and other works. Photography was also central to Witkacy's sensibility. From early childhood, he was encouraged by his father to play before the camera and adopt amusing poses. Taking pictures of himself and his circle served to revolutionize his perceptions of space and time, deepen his penetration of the unconscious, and provide mediation between self and world.

Witkacy was eight years old when intense perusal of an illustrated edition of Shakespeare led him to playwriting. By parodying Shakespeare, he was able to create his own theatre built on centuries of dramatic traditions and stage conventions. Deeply ingrained as a fundamental cast of his mind, parody became for Witkacy a spur to creativity and a mode of criticism, a method of conducting a dialogue with the past and of fashioning new structures out of the ruins of old ones.

Witkacy's plays continue to fascinate not only because of their hyper-vivid characters, striking events, and exotic settings, but also because of their rich profusion of new forms. For example, within a year the playwright wrote a sprawling account of the last days of Saint Petersburg in *Maciej Korbowa i Bellatrix* (Maciej Korbowa and Bellatrix, 1918), which had a cast of nineteen named characters and twenty-one extras (playing roving revolutionaries), and the intensely introspective and tightly designed *Pragmatyści* (Pragmatists, 1919), which had five named characters and two episodic "end-game" policemen. Witkacy constantly experimented with the size and shape of his dramas and chose to remain unbound to any single formula. He approached theatrical composition like a painter sizing up a canvas, assessing his available resources and gauging what effects could be produced by what combinations of line and colour. Instead of telling a story about psychologically conceived characters, he constructed his plays out of the formal elements themselves. His materials were the dimensions and proportions of drama, the dynamic interrelations of component parts, and the weight and density of varying numbers of figures, considered as bodies making entrances and exits on stage (the forty Mandelbaums in *Nadobnisie i koczkodany, czyli Zielona pigułka* [Dainty Shapes and Hairy Apes, or The Green Pill, 1922]). This last insight was appropriated later on by the Polish theatre artist Tadeusz Kantor (1915–90).

Witkacy's luxuriant and fertile imagination, fed by recurrent dreams and stimulated by drugs and alcohol, was not completely in his own control; he wrote rapidly, as if possessed. Yet he also strived to place his theatre within a complete philosophical system and to explain his own artistic practice theoretically, in accord with his *Teatr. Wstęp do teorii Czystej Formy w teatrze* (Theatre: Introduction to the Theory of Pure Form in the Theatre, 1923). He had formulated his ideas before composing his plays.

With a sharp eye and an alert ear for dramatic styles and modes, Witkacy played the game of parody in many different registers, deploying parodic versions of particular works as well as of authors, genres and movements, conventions and traditions, and, in general, all the paraphernalia, rituals, and resources of the theatre. Each of his plays is intrinsically meta-theatrical. Even when the original author and play has been largely forgotten, the style or genre is recognizable. For instance, his play *W małym dworku* (Country House, 1921) parodies Tadeusz Rittner's turn-of-the-century realistic drama *W małym domku* (In a Little House, 1904). Parody was not the goal, however, but the method. Witkacy inhabited and appropriated both stage and film genres, such as the ghost story, the spy thriller, and the South Sea romance. He constantly displaced, rearranged, and recombined elements of theatrical syntax to create new forms and shapes as he forged his own autonomous, rather than mimetic, scenic language composed of sound, gesture, and image.

> Witkacy was the first in Polish literature to appropriate graphomania. He especially loved to encrust his plays with fragments of idiotic poems, imbecile sayings, silly rhymes ... The imagination of Witkacy constantly oscillates between laughter and horror ... The laughter of Witkacy is one of cynicism, anarchism, and destruction.
>
> – Błoński, *Witkacy*, 118–19

Witkacy maintained that the wrong people were writing for the stage. He argued that children and painters, and not professional men of the theatre, should become playwrights. Through the theory and practice of pure form, the concept he developed in his theoretical writings about theatre, he hoped to restore to the stage the magical perceptions of childhood and the modern painter's sense of colour and dynamic shapes. Like his contemporary Antonin Artaud, Witkacy wanted the theatre to fulfil the function that magic and ritual once had had.

A major component of Witkacy's new scenic language was his own unique voice. Throughout his career he embraced a wide range of artistic and intellectual pursuits that made him exceptional among playwrights. By 1920, in both his theory and his practice of theatre, Witkacy had become actively engaged with Freud's psychology, Picasso's Cubism, Einstein's relativity, and Malinowski's anthropology, all of which inform his dramas. Because he rejected high-art solemnity for an irreverent mocking personal tone that was both self-assertive and self-depreciatory, his originality was not recognized or taken seriously (except by a tiny minority) until some thirty years later.

Intensely personal even when most parodic, Witkacy's semi-confessional plays call up, like ghosts at a séance, the author's own primal fears, dream-like memories, and personal obsessions. A subgenre invented by Witkacy is the "comedy with corpses," featuring his characteristic and innovative device of the returning "risen corpse," who comes back quite naturally as though alive (*Wariat i zakonnica* [The Madman and the Nun, 1923]). This contact with the other world and evocation of the dead places Witkacy in the great tradition of world theatre and makes him the direct precursor of Tadeusz Kantor's "Theatre of Death."

Daniel Gerould
City University of New York

WORKS CITED

Błoński, Jan. *Witkacy*. Kraków: Wydawnictwo Literackie, 2000.

Markowski, Michał Paweł. *Polska literatura nowoczesna. Leśmian, Schulz, Witkacy.* Kraków: Universitas, 2007.

Witkiewicz, Stanisław Witkacy. *Damaty*. 2nd ed. Edited by Konstanty Puzyna. Warszawa: Państwowy Instytut Wydawniczy, 1983.

Revolution as the Psychic Condition of the Twentieth Century (Stanisława Przybyszewska)[1]

Sprawa Dantona (The Danton Case, 1929), a chronicle of the French Revolution, is the only dramatic work written in Polish by the Polish-born Stanisława Przybyszewska (1901–35). It echoes the tension Przybyszewska felt between her Polish heritage and the French literary history with which she had come to most identify. In *The Danton Case*, she created a masterfully organized dramatic distillation of the chaotic events of the French Revolution during the Reign of Terror. In a series of desperate letters to one of the most influential leaders of the French Revolution, Maximilien Robespierre (1758–94), which she wrote in tandem with the play, she painted an anguished self-portrait of her own mental and physical breakdown while living in solitude in a one-room garret in Danzig. Yet she was no victim of circumstances; she was the architect of her own destiny and had chosen to be a martyr to her art.

Przybyszewska was born the illegitimate daughter of Stanisław Przyszewski (1868–1927), a famous modernist writer, critic, and thinker who was also an irresponsible father; for many years he refused to acknowledge his daughter and viewed her as merely one more illegitimate child. As a result, Przybyszewska was permanently estranged from both patrilineal family relations and her home country of Poland. This abandonment had a profound impact on her personal and literary development: she rejected the notion of paternity as well as assigned gender roles. She also claimed, paradoxically, that she had inherited from her father her feminine intuitiveness and her surrender to inspiration, as well as her dependence on drugs. She was determined to oppose the disorder of her father's life through extreme discipline and dedication to her own writing. Her biographers, Jadwiga Kosicka and Daniel Gerould, note that "it was not what her father gave Przybyszewska, but what he denied her that made her into a playwright."[2]

Przybyszewska saw her mother, Aniela Pająk (1864–1912), who was an Impressionist painter, as the source of her own artistic abilities, bold masculine traits, and logical thinking. Together, they moved from place to place in Poland, Austria, and France and lived with relatives; in the process, Przybyszewska received a cosmopolitan and polyglot education. Lacking any strong sense of national identity, she embraced her marginalized position and stressed that she did not have and did not want a fatherland. Danzig (now Gdańsk) – a city of ambiguous status and divided national identity – suited her perfectly, and she refused to consider leaving it even as the Nazis threat grew more apparent.

Without a fatherland with which to identify, Przybyszewska was free to trace her literary heritage to those who inspired her most – French and English authors, such as Pierre Corneille (1606–84) and Bernard Shaw (1856–1950) – rather than to the Polish Romantic tradition of Adam Mickiewicz (1798–1855), Zygmunt Krasiński (1812–59), and Juliusz Słowacki (1809–49). She became a Polish author who did not write about Poland and who did not make its history and culture the focus of her attention. Instead she found the key to her own times in the momentous events that unfolded in Paris after the fall of the Bastille on 14 July 1789. *The Danton Case* (supplemented by *Thermidor*, an unfinished play written earlier in German) is a major contribution to the dramatic literature on the French Revolution, worthy of a place alongside Georg Büchner's *Danton's Death* (1835), which was also an inspiration for Przybyszewska's work.

Her great accomplishment in *The Danton Case* is that she breathed life into the heroes of the French Revolution by capturing their fierce ambition and strong hunger for life. She bridged the gulf between her own age and the distant past by imaginatively living with the revolutionary heroes, by arguing with them, and by joining their impassioned debates. The characters and events of 1793 seemed more real and closer to her mind and heart than her neighbours on the streets of Danzig. Her fascination with the French Revolution began with a visit to the Musée Carnavalet as a youth in Paris and was bolstered by her week-long imprisonment in Poznań in 1922, where she was placed on suspicion of subversive activities because of her work at a communist bookstore in Warsaw. It was through this experience that she developed her long-lasting obsession with those who, like Robespierre, had been wrongfully imprisoned. Her extensive research on the subject revealed to her a "sense of order and purpose that the present could never supply."[3] Not at home in her own age, she took refuge in another century: she began dating her letters using the revolutionary calendar and spoke of Danton and Robespierre as her contemporaries.

Przybyszewska was the first playwright to rehabilitate Robespierre, who had long been portrayed as the sinister villain responsible for the Reign of Terror. Immersing herself in the latest research on the subject, she based *The Danton Case* on the new historiography of the French socialist Albert Mathiez, who was the first to radically reinterpret Robespierre as a brilliant politician and tactician. *The Danton Case* is a carefully crafted rejoinder to Büchner's *Danton's Death*, which Przybyszewska had read eleven times and greatly admired for its revolutionary zeal and authentic atmosphere, but which she deplored for its glorification of the nihilistic sensualist Danton. Przybyszewska broke with the long-entrenched and highly negative consensus about Robespierre and redressed the imbalance between him and Danton that had been so glaring in Büchner, who had dropped Robespierre halfway through his play, in Act II.

In a 1929 "Self-Interview," which she called a "thinking dialogue of solitude," Przybyszewska discusses her two heroes as the archetype for two contrasting revolutionary leaders. The idealistic, ascetic Robespierre was determined to transform natural man into a higher political being, whereas the cynical, corrupt Danton was ready to make whatever compromises were necessary to profit himself. By subordinating creative thinking to natural will, Danton had betrayed his own calling. Przybyszewska struggled her whole life against nature in all its malevolent manifestations, which for her included the random and senseless propagation of the species, the physiological necessities of existence, and the base animal side of the human psyche. Genius must oppose that "fiendish little beast Nature" – or "executioner Nature" – and improve on its blunders and shortcomings, which she identified as having caused Danton's downfall. In her writings, she declared Danton to be a genius who, like her father, had squandered his talents. She herself aimed to emulate Robespierre, the moral opposite of both Danton and her father, viewing him as a strong but complicated man who strived to overcome human egotism and cowardice.[4] She placed her faith in exceptional individuals capable of sacrificing their private lives to a higher cause: Shaw's Saint Joan and Caesar offered her such examples. Full of love for Robespierre and admiration for his heroic mind, she portrayed him not as a rigid fanatic but as incorruptible, a sick and lonely genius like herself. Fashioned partly in her own image, her Robespierre is an asexual and suprapersonal individuality striving to live in the realm of pure thought, whose absolute devotion to reason causes his downfall.

Her admiration for Robespierre, best expressed at the play's turning point in Act IV, stemmed from the courage he showed in launching the Terror, which he knew would lead to a dictatorship and ultimately to his political and personal defeat. Przybyszewska believed, just as her hero did, that "the masses are essentially passive and dependent on active individuals, [that] they gradually slip into indifference and passivity" and forsake the pursuit of liberty once they have been provided with sufficient food, water and shelter, "and [that] the only method of safeguarding would be a mutual controlling of the rulers and ruled as a way of neutralizing the fatal impulses of human nature."[5] Robespierre realized that to save the revolution, he would have to destroy it, and because he was prepared to do so, he became the moral compass that Przybyszewska could find nowhere else in her time.

Reading the French Revolution through the lens of her own times – most specifically, the Russian Revolution – Przybyszewska conceived "revolution as the psychic condition of the twentieth century."[6] In the play, she gives her characters a modern sensibility and has them speak a provocative up-to-date language whose verbal anachronisms and Soviet-style revolutionary jargon and acronyms underscore the continuity between 1789 and 1917. The dialogue moves from racy colloquialisms to heightened rhetorical eloquence, while the subtext is psychologically nuanced, rich in dark undercurrents and hidden erotic resonances. She sees the revolutionary tribunals as manifestations of mass culture and politics as a form of spectator sport, manipulated by journalists and reflecting the demagogue's grip on the bloodthirsty mob. She captures the atmosphere of the mass rallies of the late 1920s and early 1930s, the rise of dictatorships, and the era's fascination with tyranny. Deeply concerned with the form of her drama, she gave *The Danton Case* a musical structure, paying close attention to the rhythm of contrasting scenes, alternating tempestuous public gatherings on the street and at the tribunals with introspective tableaux of private life.

Przybyszewska rejected the metaphoric style and open form of Büchner's *Danton's Death* and distanced herself from the compositional traditions of Polish Romantic drama. Looking to the latest trends in the West for her dramaturgical idiom, she adopted the sober principles of the New Objectivity (*Neue Sachlichkeit*) that were developed in Germany in the 1920s in response to the lyrical excesses of Expressionism, which Büchner had both anticipated and influenced and to which her father had contributed. Reportage, observation, documentation, facts, clarity, and hard-edged contours took the place of uncontrolled outbursts of poetic frenzy. Her precise, highly visual, and often cinematographic stage directions indicating gestures and facial expressions were addressed as much to readers as to theatre practitioners. The synthesis of these literary and visual elements demonstrates how – throughout history and into the present day – the inevitability of power consolidating in one man's hands reveals "the radical evil of the revolutionary mechanism."[7] By examining and reanimating Robespierre and the French Revolution, Przybyszewska hoped to discover "what in the past could be of use to the present."[8]

Interest in **Przybyszewska** has grown in Poland over the past three decades. Its pinnacle came in 2015 in the city of Gdańsk, where she lived for the last twelve of her thirty-four years, with the commemoration of the eightieth anniversary of her death. A debate about Przybyszewska's oeuvre was organized by the Instytut Kultury Miejskiej (Institute of Urban Culture) in cooperation with the feminist group She-Metropolitan (Metropolitanka: http://metropolitanka.ikm.gda.pl/o-nas). This coincided with the launch of a collection of her rediscovered short stories, *Cyrograf na własnej skórze i inne opowiadania* (A Pact with the Devil on My Own Skin, and Other Stories, 2015). Opera Gedanensis premiered a commissioned work about Stanisława Przybyszewska, *Olimpia z Gdańska* (Olympia from Gdańsk), in which her life runs parallel to that of Olimpia de Gouges, Robespierre's mistress. Also of note is the graphic novel that accompanied the opera's premiere, which was the first of its kind in the context of Polish opera adaptations. Finally, one of Gdańsk's streetcars was named after Przybyszewska, as part of a patronage program organized by the city to commemorate significant figures of its past.

The Danton Case has enjoyed repeated success in Polish theatre since 1967 (when it was rediscovered), most notably in Andrzej Wajda's austere, unadorned staging in 1975, which turned the audience into participants in the performance. Wajda's acclaimed French–Polish film version of the play, *Danton* (1983), made during the martial law period in Poland (1981–3), reversed Przybyszewska's rehabilitation of Robespierre, however, and rendered Danton the appealing hero. This interpretative reversal both revealed the strength of the author's dramaturgy and betrayed her intellectual viewpoint.

Daniel Gerould, New York

NOTES

1 The writing of this article was interrupted by the author's death. The editors adapted it to the needs of this volume by using the published edition of Przybyszewska's work with an Introduction by Daniel Gerould.
2 Kosicka and Gerould, *A Life of Solitude,* 3.
3 Ibid., 32.
4 Ibid., 44.
5 Ibid., 43.
6 Przybyszewska, *The Danton Case*; *Thermidor*, 14.
7 Gerould, "Stanisława Przybyszewska," 12.
8 Kosicka and Gerould, *A Life of Solitude,* 42.

WORKS CITED

Gerould, Daniel. "Stanisława Przybyszewska and the Mechanism of Revolution: *The Danton Case* and *Thermidor.*" In *The Danton Case; Thermidor: Two Plays.* Translated by Bolesław Taborski. 1–18. Evanston: Northwestern University Press, 1989.

Kosicka, Jadwiga, and Daniel Gerould, ed. and trans. *A Life of Solitude: Stanisława Przybyszewska, a Biographical Study with Selected Letters.* Evanston: Northwestern University Press, 1986.

Przybyszewska, Stanisława. *The Danton Case; Thermidor: Two Plays.* Translated by Bolesław Taborski. Evanston, IL: Northwestern University Press, 1989.

– *Cyrograf na własnej skórze i inne opowiadania.* Edited by Dagmara Binkowska et al. Gdańsk: Fundacja Terytoria Książki, 2015.

The Power of Spectacle (Leon Schiller)

During the interwar period there were two major directors working in Polish theatre: Leon Schiller (1887–1954) and Juliusz Osterwa (1885–1947). It was they who were responsible for two distinct, and radically different, directions pursued in theatre at that time. The renowned theatre historian Zbigniew Raszewski spells out the key differences between them in *Krótka historia teatru polskiego* (A Short History of the Polish Theatre, 1977), where he labels Osterwa's theatre a "director's theatre" and Schiller's a "staging theatre." Osterwa worked primarily at the Teatr Reduta (Redoubt Theatre) that he himself had founded; Schiller, except for a brief period between 1924 and 1926 (when he was artistic director of the Bogusławski Theatre), never had a stage or a crew of his own, though he directed many acclaimed productions at the Teatr Polski (Polish Theatre) in Warsaw and at the Teatr Wielki (Grand Theatre) in Lviv. Osterwa's intimate "chamber" theatre was a laboratory set up to arrive at the truth (theatrical and otherwise) through arduous actor-to-actor work. It was directly opposed in this respect to the monumental, visionary, and total spectacles of Schiller, which were often based on exquisite dramatic texts that united all participants in a shared theatrical experience.

Although Schiller's and Osterwa's paths diverged sharply, the beginnings of their careers had a lot in common. Both sought a specifically Polish type of theatre rooted in the Old Polish theatre. Both drew on the ideas of the most influential artists in recent tradition – Adam Mickiewicz (1798–1855) and Stanisław Wyspiański (1869–1907) – combining it with modern European theatrical ideas and practices. Even this early on, however, the distinctiveness of Schiller's principles and passions was becoming apparent. It was awakened perhaps by his coming-of-age in Kraków, the modernist hotbed of the Young Poland movement (although Osterwa was also born and raised there). At the turn of the twentieth century, Kraków itself was a theatre – thanks to the intense presence of Wyspiański, its cabarets (where Schiller would sing as a high school student), its traditional folk spectacles, and its atmosphere of bourgeois and national celebration on the one hand and of artistic rebellion on the other. Equally important for Schiller's development were his travels in Europe. In Paris in 1909, after a lengthy correspondence, he met Edward Gordon Craig, who had published Schiller's important texts on Wyspiański in his journal *The Mask*. In Vienna in 1916, in turn, the future director undertook individual studies of music.

Schiller was an obsessive collector of antique Polish musical documents, music scores, and old songs. He amassed a large library, beginning with Kolberg's editions, which included drama and theatre artifacts, Old Polish mystery plays, and forgotten vaudevilles. He approached these materials like a true scholar; his knowledge of music and theatre history was immense. On the basis of these texts, he staged two remarkable mystery plays at the Redoubt Theatre: *Pastorałka* (Pastorale, 1922) and *Wielkanoc* (Easter, 1923). The latter included *Historyja o Chwalebnym Zmartwychwstaniu Pańskim* (History of the Glorious Ressurection of the Lord), a resurrection mystery arranged by the monk Mikołaj of Wilkowiecko in the sixteenth century. Schiller's was the first twentieth-century staging of this mystery. Following the rules of the genre, he embellished the original text with topical interludes that he had written.

Though Schiller looked back fondly to the forgotten Polish tradition of mystery plays, it was not his plan to create religious theatre. He embodied a particular blend of affects: a "religious disposition" on the one hand, and Romantic social radicalism on the other. He was open about his leftist views, and the later productions of his career, created after leaving the Redoubt Theatre, even earned him the label of a communist. The right-wing press launched a series of ideological attacks against him, and he was arrested in Lwów after signing an antiwar manifesto promulgated by the Communist Party of Western Ukraine, which was active in the Kresy regions (Borderlands). His productions of Brecht's *Threepenny Opera*, Wolf's *Cyankali*, Żeromski's *Story of Sin*, and Tretyakov's *Roar China!* ended in brawls; sometimes, as happened in Lwów, these resulted in Schiller having to leave both the theatre and the city. For all that, his staging of Mickiewicz's *Dziady* (Forefathers' Eve) in Lwów in 1932 – in which he emphasized the play's visual drama and its elements of mystery theatre – was the most remarkable, acclaimed, and admired of this play's twentieth-century stagings, and is studied to this day. He also staged innovative productions of Shakespeare – using a live jazz band in *As You Like It*, for instance. He animated theatre life by writing, teaching, and directing (in many different theatres), as well as collaborated on radio and film projects.

Schiller's phenomenal creative energy was brought to bear on diverse – but always theatrical – activities. He was equally impressive in monumental spectacles and in charming, unpretentious vaudevilles. His belief in proper training for theatre artists led to the opening of the Department of Directing Art at the National Academy of Dramatic Art in Warsaw in 1933, with himself as its chair. In 1952 he launched the prestigious academic journal *Pamiętnik Teatralny* (The Theatre Memoir), which is published to this day. Finally, he was responsible for many new directions in theatre studies.[1]

Schiller was both a communist and a lay monk. During the Second World War he was sent to Auschwitz, but was released in 1941 thanks to an enormous bribe. After his return from the camp, he became a Benedictine oblate and lived and worked in Henryków, near Warsaw, where the Sisters of the Good Samaritan ran a home for girls. There, with the girls as actors, he staged his moving wartime production of *Pastorale*, among other plays. After the war, however, he promptly sided with the new government and joined in the Communist Party. He fulfilled state functions (serving as a member of parliament) and held important posts. He was in charge of the most important theatres, including Teatr Wojska Polskiego (Polish Army Theatre) and the Polish Theatre in Warsaw, and he served as chancellor of the Academy for the Dramatic Arts and as chairman of the Society of Polish Theatre and Film Artists (SPATiF). In 1950, after falling out of favour with the communist authorities, he was fired from most of these posts and blocked from further directing opportunities. As he famously and sarcastically put it: "We have conducted land reform, we have nationalized industry, we have kicked me out of the theatre."

> Schiller had something titanic about him, not in a figurative, but a very literal sense. He could cope with almost superhuman demands … The idea of moderation was foreign to him. Every large-scale spectacle that he planned exceeded all material, technical, production, and even human capabilities. This man, possessed by the stage, haunted by an obsession with enormity, could not be confined to the stages of our time, perhaps not to any stage in this world. It was a source of his clearly Romantic, truly promethean anguish.
>
> – Terlecki, "Leon Schiller," 269–70

Monumental Theatre

Following Schiller's own lead, we can distinguish three important strands in his body of work: (1) works exemplifying the idea of "monumental theatre"; (2) a group of productions characteristic of *Zeittheater* (today's theatre, current theatre, the theatre of its time); and (3) "song-plays" (*obrazki śpiewające* – thematically staged montages of old songs, folk songs and rituals, and musical performances).

The first of these has become irrevocably linked with Schiller. It was he who first conceived of and defined Polish monumental theatre. To be sure, the ideas of Craig and other turn-of-the-century reformers of Western theatre had an impact. Like them, Schiller evidently considered himself a new type of "theatre artist," one who could raise theatre to the level of art. He derived the underpinnings of his approach from Polish concepts, however, noting that the "outlines of Polish Monumental Theatre" were latent in the playwriting of the Romantic triad (Mickiewicz, Słowacki, Krasiński) as well as of Norwid and Wyspiański.

Monumental theatre – and more precisely, Polish monumental theatre, as an original concept within the mainstream of European theatre reforms – is as much a metaphor as a concrete undertaking. It is a metaphor insofar as it aimed to express, first and foremost, the grandeur of ideas conveyed by the Polish arch-dramas. In this, its roots can be traced back to Adam Mickiewicz's vision of a "Slavic theatre," outlined in his Parisian lectures in 1840,[2] and to the "immense theatre" (*teatr ogromny*), which was the dream of Stanisław Wyspiański (as expressed in his poem "I ciągle widzę ich twarze" [And I Still See Their Faces][3] and elaborated in his *Studium o Hamlecie* [Study of Hamlet, 1905]).[4] It was also a concrete undertaking in that it entailed basic transformations in architectonics and set design, a break with the bourgeois proscenium stage, and the discovery of suitable means for staging previously unperformed texts – means capable of carrying the vision contained in the dramatic work. Its very name evokes the "monument" as something exalted, elevated over and above mediocrity, grand in both a symbolic and a physical sense, and existing in an open space (indeed, it was also Wyspiański's dream to build a Greek-style theatre on the slopes of Wawel Hill in Kraków). Furthermore, the notion of a monument alludes to "commemoration" and "remembering," signalling the intent to bring forth ideas deposited in plays, transpose them in time (and even against time), and rediscover, reanimate, and experience them anew in an original, ecstatic form.

Both meanings of monumental theatre – metaphoric and concrete – had a significant impact on the types of plays Schiller directed. His personal canon consisted of mostly

Romantic and modernist works that were characterized by an open structure and by a musical rhythm of both speech and scene composition (such as Mickiewicz's *Forefathers' Eve*); plays that were densely symbolic yet at the same time reflected a unique historical, or cosmic vision, in which man wrestles with divine and infernal powers that are locked in perpetual crisis.

The monumental theatre would not have been possible without the collaboration of outstanding set designers, most of them drawn from Cubist (or, as they were known in Poland, Formist) circles. Since the dream of a theatre of "vast aerial spaces" could not be realized for purely practical reasons (with the exception of a few outdoor productions), their goal was not a literal exodus from the theatre but rather its striking transformation. Schiller and his set designers – in particular the brothers Andrzej (1888–1961) and Zbigniew (1885–1958) Pronaszko, as well as Wincenty Drabik (1881–1933) – created synthetic spectacles by using platforms and structures with dominant architectural accents, and by manipulating stage lights to produce an effect of unusual depth and shifting contrasts.

The finest example of monumental theatre by far was Schiller's production of *Forefathers' Eve*, which he adapted and staged with Andrzej Pronaszko. On the darkened stage, multiple platforms were piled up to form flat terraces leading to the top of a hill crowned with three large crosses. Among the many symbolic meanings of these crosses, besides the biblical, was an allusion to the Hill of Three Crosses in Vilnius, the city of Mickiewicz's youth and the setting for parts of the play. Behind the crosses, a horizon opened onto a wide cosmic space; scene changes were signalled by little more than architectural contours, the arch of a doorway or a grille, which would vanish at the end of a scene. This gave the stage the character of a medieval mystery or – as Schiller put it – a synchronic look. The spirits were endowed with voices but not bodies. They were represented by pillars of light, sometimes clear (spirits of children), and other times crimson (the spectre of an evil master). Their presence could also be inferred from the expressive reactions of the crowd onstage. In the play's Warsaw salon scene, Schiller demonstrated his renowned ability "to direct a crowd": while the young people were engaged in heated discussions on the proscenium, they were contrasted with the automatic movements of the government elite on the platforms above them. The main characters stood apart, against the menacing backdrop with its raised crosses. In Schiller's production of *Forefathers' Eve*, all of the most important features of monumental theatre came together: a great drama about the collective destiny of a nation was staged by a theatre artist as both a grand spectacle and a mysterious communion with the audience, using modern theatrical means, including the rhythmic synthesis of space, set design, movement, light, and music.

Schiller used similar methods in his *Zeittheater* productions. He often spoke of a "mass theatre," a popular theatre aimed at a general public that would at the same time be a modern theatre raising important social issues. He realized this ambition at the Bogusławski Theatre in Warsaw. The project proved too radical, however: instead of the promised "theatre for the masses," Schiller in reality produced there an avant-garde, high-quality theatre, successfully expanding the repertoire to include works that were generally considered "unstageable" – such as Stanisław Wyspiański's *Achilleis* (1903), Stefan Żeromski's *Róża* (Rose, 1909), and Tadeusz Miciński's *Kniaź Patiomkin* (Prince Patiomkin, 1906) – and updating them so as to bridge their historical distance. In his staging of Krasiński's *Nie-boska komedia* (Un-divine Comedy, 1835), for example, the revolutionaries wore Bolshevik uniforms, while the police brutality in his staging of *Rose* was a clear allusion to contemporary police practices. The theatre closed after two seasons, but Schiller continued to pursue his mission at other theatres with an even greater incisiveness. He adapted for the stage Żeromski's novel *Dzieje grzechu* (Story of Sin) in 1926 and staged Wolf's *Cyankali* (1930). In both works, what interested him was not the drama of social mores, or the sensational aspects of seductions, abortions, infanticide, and prostitution – though these were burning social issues and fodder for contemporary journalists – but the "idea of sin" and the "moral content" of the works. His explanations were in vain, however; the performances triggered scandal and protests by conservative audiences and critics.

Finally, one can discern elements of monumental theatre also in Schiller's "song-plays," particularly at the beginning and at the end of his interwar period work. These elements seem more pronounced at the end of that period, since the director put on several spectacular shows outdoors and engaged large casts of singers and dancers in them. At the beginning these elements existed as potentialities, since in drawing on Polish folk traditions and rituals Schiller saw a path to the renewal or (as he put it in his early articles) the "retheatricalization" of the Polish theatre (with works such as Wojciech Bogusławski's *Krakowiacy i Górale* [Krakovians and Highlanders, 1794] also having the added value of social rebellion, which was so important to Schiller).

Why did **Monumental Theatre** not outlast the Second World War? As Kosiński writes:

"It was a theatre of synthesis, of that which is perceived from a distance, from the vantage point of the sublime, where one can make out the rising "edifice of the future" but not the bodies of workers crushed into its foundations. The image of a monumentalized revolution aroused the enthusiasm of leftist intellectuals and artists, because it confirmed the essentially optimistic vision of the world in which they tried so hard to believe. The reverence surrounding Leon Schiller can be explained by the fact that he put their dreams onstage, while at the same time using the theatre to shelter himself from the contradictions that ran rife in his psyche, his biography, and his intellectual bent ... The world once more became intelligible because it could be considered as a cosmic monumental theatre. Unfortunately this was only an illusion, which the year 1939 ruthlessly shattered – with dire consequences."

– Kosiński, *Teatra polskie*, 446

Monumental theatre, though it boasted brilliant practitioners besides Schiller, most notably Wilam Horzyca (1889–1959), began and ended with the twenty-year interwar period. It was a historical phenomenon, and it is from this perspective that its achievements are viewed today. Nevertheless, Schiller's vision of theatre and the goals he established for theatre scholarship and pedagogy – his other life's work, to which he devoted himself as fervently as to directing – are part of the founding legacy of Polish theatre studies to this day.

Ewa Guderian-Czaplińska
Adam Mickiewicz University, Poznań
Translated by Philip Redko

NOTES

1 Schiller's writings, compiled and edited by Jerzy Timoszewicz of the Institute of Art at the Polish Academy of Sciences, were published in five thick volumes between 1978 and 2004.
2 Mickiewicz, "Lesson XVI," 91–7.
3 Wyspiański, "I ciągle widzę ich twarze."
4 See Wyspiański, "Hamlet," in *Dzieła Zebrane*, vol. 13. Kraków: Wydawnictwo Literackie, 1961.

WORKS CITED AND CONSULTED

Duniec, Krystyna. *Kaprysy Prospera. Szekspirowskie inscenizacje Leona Schillera*. Warszawa: Oficyna Wydawnicza Errata, 1998.

Kosiński, Dariusz. *Teatra polskie. Historie*. Warszawa: Wydawnictwo Naukowe PWN: Instytut Teatralny im. Zbigniewa Raszewskiego, 2010.

Mickiewicz Adam. *Forefathers*. Translated by Count Geoffrey Potocki de Montalk. London: Polish Cultural Foundation, 1968.

– "Lesson XVI." In Daniel Gerould, "From Adam Mickiewicz's *Lectures on Slavic Drama*." *Drama Review* 30, no. 3 (1986): 91–7.

Raszewski, Zbigniew. *Krótka historia teatru polskiego*. Warszawa: Państwowy Instytut Wydawniczy, 1977.

Schiller, Leon. *Teatr ogromny*. Edited by Zbigniew Raszewski. Warszawa: Czytelnik, 1961.

Skwarczyńska, Stefania, *Leona Schillera trzy opracowania 'Nie-boskiej komedii' w dziejach jej inscenizacji w Polsce*. Warszawa: Pax, 1959.

Szczublewski, Józef. *Artyści i urzędnicy, czyli szaleństwa Leona Schillera*. Warszawa: Państwowy Instytut Wydawniczy, 1961.

Terlecki, Tymon. "Leon Schiller." In *Spotkania ze swoimi*. 268–94. Wrocław: Wydawnictwo Uniwersytetu Wrocławskiego, 1999.

Timoszewicz, Jerzy "*Dziady" w inscenizacji Leona Schillera*. Warszawa: Państwowy Instytut Wydawniczy, 1970.

Wyspiański, Stanisław. "I ciągle widzę ich twarze." In *Dzieła Zebrane*, vol. 11. 160–1. Kraków: Wydawnictwo Literackie, 1961. http://literat.ug.edu.pl/wyswier/017.htm.

– "Hamlet." In *Dzieła Zebrane*, vol. 13. 5–195. Kraków: Wydawnictwo Literackie, 1961.

The Theatre of Truth (Juliusz Osterwa)

Juliusz Osterwa (1885–1947) is a towering figure in the history of Polish theatre – a talented actor, director, pedagogue, and manager as well as a visionary theatre reformer. In his acting and directing, he liked to fuse seemingly irreconcilable genres, styles, and approaches: realism and lyricism, for example, or psychological insight and Romantic symbolism. His favourite genres were realistic dramas with a poetic touch (e.g., the plays of Tadeusz Rittner and Stefan Żeromski) and universal works with contemporary relevance (Juliusz Słowacki and Stanisław Wyspiański). His approach to his own roles and to the productions he directed emphasized interaction between the performers and the audience. As a director, a leader of theatre companies, and a pedagogue, he taught a method that was both personal and interactional. He managed two large theatres in his time – Teatr Narodowy (The National Theatre) in Warsaw and the Słowacki Theatre in Kraków – as well as his own theatre, the Reduta (Redoubt Theatre), first in Warsaw and later in Wilno. He also ran two acting schools, one at the Redoubt Theatre, the other in Kraków. As a theatre reformer, he theorized and practised a communal and interactive approach to the work process, theatre production, and the functioning of a theatre in its cultural, social, national, and political contexts.

Born into a poor family in Kraków, Osterwa was orphaned at an early age and became a self-made man of sorts. He made his acting debut in 1904, thus beginning an apprenticeship to older and more experienced actors in the theatres of Kraków, Poznań, Wilno, and, after 1912, at the Teatr Rozmaitości (Variety Theatre) in Warsaw – the leading Polish stage at that time.[1] Just as important for Osterwa's apprenticeship in the theatre were his extensive travels abroad, where he observed such actors as Albert Basserman, Franz Kainz, and Sandro Moissi and became acquainted with Konstantin Stanislavsky and his Moscow Art Theatre. A thoughtful man by nature, Osterwa studied the newest theatre trends and theories of acting, kept notes on his observations, and analysed both his own performances and the performances of others. This analytical predisposition helped shape his major achievements.

As a handsome young actor with a melodious voice, great personal charm, and versatility, Osterwa was first drawn to comedy and farce. In his maturity, he turned to tragedy and contemporary psychological realist drama. He usually played the lead in productions he directed. In the process of his professional growth, he switched his acting method from "character acting" (as practised and taught by Stanislavsky, Richard Boleslavsky, and Lee Strasberg) to what Osterwa himself termed "personality acting" – a method of his own invention that drew on elements of poetic universality. Character acting is based on the transformation of an actor into a character; Osterwa's method was to endow a character with the actor's personal characteristics, thereby revealing profound layers of his own personality – memories, emotions, experiences, and imagination – while at the same time illuminating the universal and archetypal aspects of the character. The best examples of Osterwa's method were his own roles as Prince Fernand in Słowacki's version of Calderon's *The Constant Prince* (in which the prince chooses martyrdom rather than betray his faith for profit), and as the artist and the revolutionary Konrad from Wyspiański's *Wyzwolenie* (The Deliverance, 1903).

> Osterwa sought out the reasons for what he considered to be the society's contemptuous opinions about the theatre community. The painful memory of his own family's disapproval [of his career choice] and perhaps other personal life experiences as well, meant that the entirety of his artistic life was subordinated to the attempts to dignify theatre arts, as well as the professions of acting and directing. He always placed strong emphasis on actors' work ethic. His artistic activities were driven by a desire to secure lasting social favour for theatre professions and theatre arts.
>
> (http://teatrpolski.waw.pl/pl/aktualnosci/100_lat_teatru__fotohistory/?id_act=656)

In Osterwa's view, the foundation of theatre was truth, in both a theatrical and a moral sense. He saw acting as a process whereby a character's truth is revealed through the simultaneous unveiling of the actor's own truth as a human being. In this, his approach was similar to those of Stanislavsky in Russia, Eleonora Duse in Italy, Charles Dullin in France, and Stefan Jaracz in Poland, among others. But Osterwa went further: for him, acting was an "act of sacrifice" on the part of the actor, whose aim was to bring about an "act of redemption" on the part of the spectators. The performance itself was thus a "sacerdotal sacrifice for the congregation." Osterwa's goal was to achieve "communion" between the actors/priests and the public/congregation; his ideal was the figure of the actor/saint. He used this approach in his own productions, both as an actor and as a director, besides teaching it to his acting students.

In Poland this method was known as "redoubt acting" (*aktorstwo redutowe*). It took its name from the Redoubt Theatre, a theatrical laboratory for new acting, directing, and playwriting that Osterwa founded in Warsaw in 1919. The theatre's name, with its military connotations (a redoubt is a type of fortification), reflected Osterwa's professionally and ethically rigorous approach to the art of the theatre. In 1922 he opened the Redoubt Institute, an acting school whose demanding program was designed to train actors in the context of communal living and service to the nation. The Redoubt's first incarnation was in Warsaw (1919–25), where it served as both a theatre and an acting school; it then relocated to Vilnius (1925–31) as a resident and touring company, before returning to Warsaw (1931–9). The acting method developed by Osterwa at the Redoubt was characterized by profound self-analysis, rigorous mental discipline, vocal and physical training, interaction with fellow performers and spectators, and an emphasis on the spiritual, social, and political dimensions of theatre, whether in rehearsals, productions, or any other interactions with the theatre community. Osterwa also taught that a character's inherent poetry could only be uncovered through an investigation of its ethics. Redoubt acting was thus an amalgam of personal, artistic, communal, and moral aims. This method reached its highest expression in Osterwa's productions of Słowacki's *Kordian* (four stagings between 1916 and 1933), *The Constant Prince* (1918 and four subsequent stagings), and *Fantazy* (five stagings between 1916 and 1946), Wyspiański's *The Deliverance* (several stagings from 1918 to 1935), and Żeromski's *Ponad śnieg bielszym sie stanę* (I Shall Be Whiter Than Snow, 1919) and *Uciekła mi przepióreczka* (My Little Quail Has Gone, 1924).

At the outbreak of the First World War, Osterwa, who held an Austrian citizenship (as the Polish state did not exist at the time), was arrested by the Russians in Warsaw and interned within the Russian Empire. There, he organized performances for his fellow Polish fellow internees and for Poles living in Russia. His aim was to serve his fellow countrymen and help them survive the harsh conditions of life in exile and in wartime. The experience of sharing his audience's fate awakened in him a profound sense of community as well as a desire to share with his audiences more than just thought, emotion, and poetry, but also – indeed, above all – communal, patriotic, and spiritual values. He began to treat shows not as "performances" before a public but as living "communal processes" of exchange between actors and spectators, even to the point of involving spectators in the action of the play and using productions as platforms for addressing burning national issues. Thus, Osterwa began to see the theatre as the centre of a large community with three overlapping zones: the actors onstage, the congregation of actors and spectators inside the theatre, and the nation at large.

In his approach to theatre, Osterwa carried on a long-standing Polish tradition of the "civic theatre," in other words theatre that is embedded and actively involved in the nation's political, social, cultural, and spiritual life. This idea of a theatre dedicated to national service, to the promulgation of shared values, and to playing an active role in contemporary politics, combined a striving for aesthetic perfection with a strong emphasis on ethical values. This tradition goes back to the Polish Renaissance; its first example was Jan Kochanowski's (1530–84) *Odprawa posłów greckich* (The Dismissal of the Greek Envoys, written and staged for the first time in 1578). It was then passed on to Wojciech Bogusławski (1757–1829), sometimes called the father of the Polish national theatre, who used his thespian, dramaturgical, and managerial talents to mobilize the "civic theatre" in the defence of Poland's cultural independence and identity during the partitions (1795–1918). The tradition continued among theatre companies and playwrights throughout the nineteenth century, until Poland regained its independence in 1918. It then resurfaced during the Second World War (1939–45), when many artists from the Polish theatre, Osterwa included, took part in the national resistance movement against first German and then Soviet occupation. Their resistance took the form of a unique kind of production, held secretly in private homes or monasteries, and punishable by death. The "civic theatre" tradition was brought back under martial law (1981–3) and continued until the fall of the communist regime in 1989.

Osterwa's approach to theatre was evident both in the way he staged his productions and in their larger political, social, and cultural contexts. In terms of staging, Osterwa's goal was to establish a unified community of actors and spectators. The process would be set in motion by actors (through interactions among the characters onstage, and between actors and spectators) and facilitated through an innovative use of space. In the Warsaw and Vilnius incarnations of the Redoubt Theatre, Osterwa abolished the proscenium frame; his preference was for outdoor performances in natural or urban settings. For example, in 1932 he set Sutton Vane's play *Outward Bound* on a riverboat, and *The Constant Prince* amid actual Renaissance architecture.

To build stronger ties both inside the theatre and in the community at large, Osterwa organized community-building activities – such as lectures, meetings with audience members, and workshops for amateurs – around his productions. While on tour he also used extras as performers as well as musicians from the local community. He treated theatre as a communal effort, involving the theatregoing public directly in the process of theatre-making. As part of his initiative to make theatre the centre of cultural life in the community, Osterwa was particularly interested in sponsoring new playwriting and in commissioning, producing, and directing new works for the stage. Through these efforts, he contributed significantly to the development of Polish drama in the twentieth century. A roll call of authors produced by the Redoubt includes the best of the 1920s and 1930s: Tadeusz Rittner, Jerzy Szaniawski, and Stefan Żeromski, to name just three. Żeromski's masterpiece, *My Little Quail Has Gone*, was written especially for Osterwa, who also played the lead. This production was a high point of Osterwa's career.

Another significant achievement of that career was his experimental theatre, which he developed over a number of years. Early on, Osterwa used traditional methods based on the school of psychological realism, but the poetic demands of the Polish Classical repertoire soon radically broadened his directorial imagination. This broadening manifested itself in his reinterpretations of the canon. A prime example of this new approach was Wyspiański's *The Deliverance*, performed, as the author had intended, on a bare stage. In one scene, the actors rose from their seats in the auditorium with the houselights still on, as though they were spectators, before launching into a dialogue with Konrad, the main character (played by Osterwa). Osterwa's 1926 staging of *The Constant Prince* was an open-air spectacle. It toured the country and was staged in old courtyards – such as that of Wawel Castle in Kraków – as well as in marketplaces and in front of churches. These productions used both electricity and open flame (torches and large bonfires) for lighting. *The Constant Prince* drew thousands of spectators to each performance.

In another effort to break down the barriers between actors and spectators, in 1932 Osterwa staged *Outward Bound* by Sutton Vane, a play in which the action is set on a boat, on a real riverboat sailing down the Vistula. At various locations throughout the boat, actors mingled with spectators, who were free to move around between deck, lounge, staircase, and cabin. That year also marked the twenty-fifth anniversary of Wyspiański's death. To commemorate this, Osterwa staged an unusual performance at the medieval Church of Franciscan Friars in Kraków, whose enormous stained glass windows had been designed by Wyspiański. Osterwa dimmed the lights inside the church and lit Wyspiański's windows from outside, making them explode with colour. Two choirs hidden in the darkness sang, while Osterwa, standing at the pulpit surrounded by dozens of candles, delivered soliloquies from Wyspiański's plays. It was a powerful manifestation of Osterwa's style and of his approach to theatre that showed his commitment to Polish tradition in all the arts. It also testified to his strong belief in the community-building role and communion-like nature of theatrical experience.

Jerzy Grotowski considered Osterwa one of his masters and explained the relationship between Reduta (Redoubt Theatre) and his Theatre Laboratory in terms of their symbolic representation: "The loop of Reduta had the letter "R' written in the center – we took it over without a change, writing in an 'L' for 'Laboratory.' The idea [of taking over the emblem] came first of all from my irritation with the lack of respect theatre people often have when they speak about the monastery style and naïve ideas of Reduta. In my opinion Reduta was the most important theatre phenomenon during the interwar period, mainly because of their attempt at long-term research on the actor's craft and because of their ethical proclamations, which may sound naïve today, but which made perfect sense, because they were an attempt at cleansing theatre of the influences of the artistic demimonde. Craft, and a vocation through craft – I think there is no way to create theatrical work without confronting these two notions. Reduta was an attempt at that confrontation. Our research on techniques in the art of the actor differ, but our understanding of the purpose of this work seems parallel, at least, we would like it to be. We consider Reduta a great tradition of Polish theatre, and we would feel proud if our work were recognized as a continuation [of theirs]. And this is the second reason for our taking up Reduta's emblem. [...] In our aspirations, Reduta provides us with a moral heritage.

– quoted after Osiński, "Returning to the Subject," 52–3

Osterwa lost his job during the Second World War, when the German occupiers closed Polish theatres along with other cultural and educational institutions. He became involved in clandestine theatrical activities, creating two "theatrical orders" that he called *Dal* (Faraway) and *Bractwo św. Genezjusza* (*Genezja*) (The Fraternity of St Genesius [Genezja]). These groups combined artistry with religion and were based on the ideal of the actor-monk, whose virtues and mission reflected Osterwa's previous ideal of the actor-saint, namely, to serve the people through art, social work, and prayer.

Osterwa's influence on Polish theatre was already strong during his lifetime. He was a celebrated actor, a director of large-scale productions attended by thousands, a manager of the best theatres, an indisputable authority on acting pedagogy, a visionary reformer, and a moralist who believed that theatres had a duty and responsibility beyond aesthetic gratification. His creative temperament was partly a reflection of his faith; he remained a practising Roman Catholic his entire life. This, too, contributed to his widespread acceptance in Poland.

After Osterwa's death from cancer in 1947, the postwar, Soviet-imposed regime tried to erase his contributions from the annals of Polish theatre. From a hardline communist, Marxist, and atheist viewpoint, Osterwa – a patriotic Catholic idealist with strong anti-communist leanings – was unacceptable. Yet his teachings and ideas, as well as the memory of his works, have survived – largely through the efforts of theatre historians – and they have continued to inspire actors, directors, and other artists of the stage to this day.

Kazimierz Braun
University at Buffalo

NOTE

1 The Variety, originally called the Polish National Theatre, was renamed in the nineteenth century by the Russian ruling class. In independent Poland its original name was restored.

WORKS CITED AND CONSULTED

Braun, Kazimierz. "Juliusz Osterwa: osobowa formacja człowieka teatru." 127–37. In *Wielka Reforma Teatru w Europie*. Wrocław: Ossolineum, 1984.

– "Juliusz Osterwa – Polish Theatre Reformer". *Balagan: Slavisches Drama, Theater und Kino* 1, no. 2 (1995): 49–59.

– *A History of Polish Theatre, 1939–1989: Spheres of Captivity and Freedom.* 136–7 passim. Westport: Greenwood Press, 1996.

– *A Concise History of Polish Theatre from the Eleventh to the Twentieth Centuries.* 158–70 passim. Lewiston: Edwin Mellen Press, 2003.

Guszpit, Ireneusz. *Przez teatr poza teatr.* Wrocław: Els, 1989.

Limanowski, Mieczysław, and Juliusz Osterwa. *Listy.* Edited by Zbigniew Osiński. Warszawa: Państwowy Instytut Wydawniczy, 1987.

Osiński, Zbigniew. "Returning to the Subject: The Heritage of Reduta in Grotowski's Laboratory Theatre." Translated and edited by Kris Salata. *TDR: The Drama Review* 52, no. 2 (2008): 52–74.

Osterwa, Juliusz. *Listy Juliusza Osterwy.* Edited by Elżbieta Osterwianka. Warszawa: Państwowy Instytut Wydawniczy, 1968.

– *O Zespole Reduty wspomnienia 1919–1939.* Warszawa: Czytelnik, 1970.

– *Reduta i teatr.* Edited by Zbigniew Osiński and Teresa G. Zabłocka. Wrocław: Wiedza o Kulturze, 1990.

– *Z zapisków.* Edited by Ireneusz Guszpit. Wrocław: Wiedza o Kulturze, 1991.

Śmigielski, Bogdan. *Reduta w Wilnie.* Warszawa: Pax, 1989.

Szczublewski, Józef. *Pierwsza Reduta Osterwy.* Warszawa: Państwowy Instytut Wydawniczy, 1965.

– *Żywot Osterwy.* Warszawa: Państwowy Instytut Wydawniczy, 1971.

Drama as a Manifold Portrait: Polish Drama after the Second World War

A famous black-and-white photograph from the beginning of twentieth century, in which future Polish playwright Stanisław Ignacy Witkiewicz (1885–1939) captured himself in a military uniform, provides a fitting entry point to the following discussion of Polish postwar drama. The photograph dates back to the First World War, in which the later author of *Szewcy* (The Shoemakers, 1948) participated as an officer in the Russian Army. At the time, Poland was still partitioned among the now warring powers of Russia, Prussia, and Austria, which meant that Polish soldiers of different armies were killing one another in fratricidal battle. The photograph is titled "A Manifold Self-Portrait," for Witkacy took it of himself at an atelier in Saint Petersburg using a popular at that time trick with two mirrors: placed at a ninety-degree angle to each other, they show the man standing in front of them from four sides, thus creating the illusion that five officers are staring intently at one another.

This startling self-portrait has been carefully directed and staged. The main hero of this drama stands with his back to the lens, entirely concealing his face and thus contradicting the very essence of portraiture. At the same time, he captures on camera his multiple reflections, creating as a result not one but four different portraits, which are, however, only a reflection of the original. It is easy to image the photo as a frame from a suddenly stopped film; then, an old-fashioned projector restarts with a rattle and the hero with his back to us begins to speak and make expressive gestures, initiating a discussion among the people staring at one another. Through the use of more modern technology, we can multiply perspectives, takes, and sets, creating an ever more refined illusion of this multivocal debate, with the discreetly turned-away author still its instigator.

Witkacy's "Multiple Self-Portrait" can serve as a suggestive metaphor for modern drama, with its complicated artistic structure still betraying the presence of an authorial "I" – invisible, but clearly showing through the characters, their mannerisms, thoughts, and actions. It can also serve as metaphor for the modern human condition, with individual subjectivity losing its cohesion and breaking up like the splintered image in the mirror. Moreover, it speaks to the hero's ever more limited ability – in a situation of disappearing subjectivity – to encounter and communicate with other people. Finally, it provokes reflection about the problems of artistic representation in an epoch that uses drama to explore the complicated consciousness of modern human beings and their struggles, both internal and external.

A Tool of Inquiry and a Mirror of Social Conflicts

Evoking Witkacy's old photograph at the beginning of a narrative about Polish postwar drama is justified by the fact that this narrative really begins earlier, at the beginning of the twentieth century, when the structure typical of this literary genre, which enacts human behaviour with the aid of character's speech acts, began to serve refined artistic aims. Like the avant-garde poets and Cubist painters, playwrights used their work to expose diverse aspects of individual and collective life and to explore multiple layers of human consciousness. They were dissatisfied with one-dimensional representations of individual and group experience, shown in some selected aspect: psychological, social, political, ethical, or religious. So instead, they sought a synthesis of these aspects, convinced that they are dependent on one another and together constitute a multidimensional, essentially Cubist composition of the modern human personality. The dramatic hero, they explained, is bound by the rules that govern this synthesis, but also constitutes and later uses them, staging his life in the manner of Witkacy in the "Manifold Self-Portrait." By speaking, thinking, feeling, discovering, dreaming, acting, and entering into interhuman interactions, the hero constitutes himself in a constant, conscious and unconscious act of self-creation. Many mirrors reflect his consciousness. A human being is gifted, after all, with memory, imagination, and language, lives in a concrete place, acts in a given historical moment, and draws on a specific value system. The perspective of his existence crosses beyond the threshold of his contemporaneity. By thinking, speaking, and acting the hero draws on collective knowledge and shared mythology, which precede the historical moment of his life and exceed the geographical boundaries of his existence. Universal within a framework of a specific cultural formation, both are also changeable in being inconsistently and selectively invoked.

In order to present human life as a manifold, multi-dimensional, and dynamic portrait, the modern playwright constructs multiple, interpenetrating semantic and stylistic planes. Dramatic action, treated as a tool of inquiry, progresses or builds up on several planes at once and in multiple ways. The action of characters is both literal and metaphorical, or symbolic; common human behaviour acquires the shape of meaningful, necessary, and forced actions, reminiscent of a mysterious ritual. Individual experiences are a consequence of other people's earlier actions and take root in collective mythologies. This layered, contemporary or historical "here and now" of the hero can also serve as an allusion to external events or situations experienced by a given collective: a society, a nation, a fellowship of nations, or humanity. The image of the world and of people is given directly or mediated through references to other works or languages, either imitated or parodied.

Depending on the plane that dominates the represented world, new drama comes close to a given convention, but does not attain it, since in doing so it would lose access to other layers of reality. It thus constantly balances between fundamentally different categories of realism and fantasy, naturalism and symbolism, impressionism and expressionism. Drama can also present itself as a literary and theatrical work, building in this way yet another dimension of the description of reality, or exposing yet another aspect of its existence.

The multiplicity of human life's perspectives is presented more often as dissonant rather than harmonious. Harmony is an expression of a single idea that conjoins human inquiry and experience and that arises from a scientific, philosophical, religious, and even an artistic ground. Dissonance speaks to the impossibility of accomodating different frameworks of reality within one system, which usually leads to the fragmentation of the hero's consciousness. The internal incoherence of dramatic characters is sometimes projected onto the shattered world they inhabit. In extreme cases such a world is graspable only in categories of the grotesque, which sometimes disclaims the work itself. Not surprisingly, the grotesque turned out to be the most adequate of aesthetic categories when faced with the evolutionary and revolutionary transformations of the hero's consciousness in twentieth-century drama. It was during the Renaissance, which marked the beginning of modernity, that European drama had lost the coherence between the hero's consciousness, the motivation behind his actions, and the condition of the world in which he acts. Subsequent epochs only deepened the gulf between these three categories, with the development of a scientific world view having the greatest influence on this process. The twentieth century's wars and revolutions, unprecedented in terms of their atrocities and destruction, rapidly sped up the decomposition of consciousness and the world. The first great wave of avant-garde art arose on the eve of the First World War and swelled after it ended, giving expression to the violent fracture of culture's philosophical foundations. The Second World War destroyed these foundations altogether; drama would express this in a form that belied its basic categories of hero and action, becoming an anti-drama as a result. It nevertheless persisted in its ambition to encompass the entirety of human experience, which now means primarily catastrophe.

During the first half of the twentieth century, Polish writers resorted to three dramatic poetics tied to three theatrical styles: realism, the grotesque, and the poetic drama. These three currents constitute a key tradition for postwar drama, while frequently themselves undergoing parodic reorganization. This does not diminish the status of drama itself, which has occupied a unique place in Polish culture since Romanticism, as a venue that makes possible the recognition and experience of the most important (though often hidden) social problems and conflicts, which are activated performatively in the text. According to Victor Turner, artistic drama is a polymorphic mirror of social drama, and it is precisely from this perspective that I want to consider the postwar history of the genre in Poland.[1] The dramatic hero is always at the centre of my discussion, since his multiplied portrait most fully reflects the consciousness of modern man. In mapping postwar Polish drama, therefore, we will be constantly observing the transformations of the hero of our times.

Historical Context of Postwar Drama

Polish postwar drama was shaped by the experience of two totalitarianisms: Nazi Germany and Stalinist Russia. Six years of Nazi occupation determined the thematic of Polish drama for many years and had a fundamental impact on the condition of both the hero and the represented world. Poland's political situation in the aftermath of the Second World War is the second most important consideration in the context of this discussion, for it dictated both what Polish drama was permitted to say, impelled by authoritarian power, and what it was *not* allowed to say, in that it was gagged by that same power and its institutions, including the state censors. The resolutions reached by leaders of the United States, Great Britain, and the Soviet Union placed Poland within the sphere of Stalin's communist empire, greatly limiting its sovereignty for forty-five years. Quite quickly, many writers began to cooperate with the new regime for opportunistic or ideological reasons, while a scant group of artists remained independent and paid for their stance with publication bans, exclusion from creative associations, and a difficult material situation.[2]

This division was most sharply in place during the so-called Stalinist years, from 1949 to 1955, during which the communist regime brutally disposed of its real and imagined opposition. That campaign eased somewhat afterwards, only to intensify again during the period of democratic opposition in Poland – at the turn of the 1970s and 1980s, when some writers refused to publish with national presses altogether, resorting to samizdat publication instead (outside the reach of censorship, in home-made journals and books, and at risk of persecution by the authorities). Writers who collaborated with the authorities during the Stalinist period completely subordinated their artistic freedom to communist propaganda. As a result, the field of drama yielded plays written in the style of socialist realism, which presented a falsified image of the social situation in postwar Poland, one that reflected communist ideology and propaganda. The schematic and manipulative social realist dramas produced in numerous Polish theatres at the order of the authorities do not really deserve to be called works of art. The same cannot be said about the few works that were written right after the war, when the communist regime did not yet dominate the entire space of public life and social realism was not yet the requisite literary and artistic doctrine. These works, while they expressed the artist's ideological commitment to communism, were meant to engage in a genuine discussion of politics and world views rather than propaganda.

Realism and Values: Leon Kruczkowski's *Germans*

Among the most interesting of these plays is *Niemcy* (Germans) by Leon Kruczkowski (1900–62), published and staged in 1949, but written a little earlier. It is a realistic work in that the sense and composition of its story are subordinate to its aim of testing the morality of its heroes, the titular Germans – specifically, the family of Walter Sonnebruch, a biology professor, which gathers in Göttingen in 1943 to celebrate his jubilee. This family represents German society during the Nazi dictatorship. While Walter Sonnebruch does not engage with Hitler's politics, neither does he stop conducting his research, which serves the German state. His son Willi is a Gestapo officer in Norway, where he supresses the anti-German underground, while his daughter Ruth is a pianist who does not sympathize with the Nazis but who willingly exploits opportunities to perform in Occupied Europe. Also among the guests is a former janitor Hoppe, now a policeman in the German-occupied General Governorate, who obediently carries out death sentences even on children. The jubilee is disturbed by the arrival of the professor's former colleague, Joachim Peters, a communist who has escaped from a concentration camp and is now seeking shelter in Sonnerbruch's house. Only Ruth is willing to help the escapee, for which she pays with her freedom when she is arrested.

Four years after the war, Kruczkowski crafted a collective hero out of the perpetrators of a historically unprecedented genocide, which was conducted in an industrial manner in extermination camps. It was not his aim, however, to create an account of war crimes. Rather, he was attempting to morally evaluate Germans presented as Europe's intellectual and cultural elite rather than as a collective possessed by a murderous ideology and subordinated to one madman. It was not madness but rather their *conformism* that paved the way to genocide (which Kruczkowski intentionally did not represent in the play). What gives Kruczkowski's drama a universal perspective is that the Sonnenbruchs are not monsters – to the contrary, they are people who may be seen as impressive, and even serve as an example to those who too easily submit to the authorities. What made the play useful in communist Poland was the character of the honest and persecuted communist Peters. The moral victory in Kruczkowski's play belongs solely to the follower of the communist ideology on which the Stalinist regime was founded. *Germans* can be read ironically, however, as a morality test for all social élites that secure life's comforts by breaking moral principles and yielding to a dictatorship – including that of Stalin, although Kruczkowski did not make this claim. Indeed, in his later work he aligned himself with the strictures of socialist realism.

Realism and Vision: Szaniawski's *Two Theatres*

At the time that Kruczkowski was writing *Germans*, the new authorities in Poland were still battling remnants of the underground independence movement using police and the military, and were imprisoning wartime heroes – officers of the Home Army. Their tragic fate did not become the theme of any postwar drama, however, since this would have been too politically risky. In turning to the years of the Nazi occupation, dramatists were making an important attempt to come to terms with the ethical problems of its participants – the perpetrators, victims, and witnesses of its crimes. Yet in doing so, they were turning their backs on the Poland's postwar reality, which presented equally thorny ethical dilemmas; addressing them, however, was forbidden. This is why the allusions to the Warsaw Uprising in the most interesting play written right after the war, Jerzy Szaniawski's (1886–1970) *Dwa teatry* (Two Theatres, 1946), turned out to be so important. In one of that play's monologues, Szaniawski creates a catastrophic image of a city that alludes to the Warsaw Uprising, when many thousands of Poles rose up against the German occupier and did so out of fear of the fast-approaching Soviet Army. The liberation of Polish territories by the Soviet forces led to their immediate subordination. Since communist propaganda claimed that Poles were deeply happy to be included in the so-called Eastern Bloc (of socialist nations under Soviet control), the resistance of the Warsaw insurgents was a forbidden topic in postwar Poland. The uprising itself was subjected to a sharp official critique despite the widely held sentiments of Poles. In these circumstances, writers began addressing issues and events of importance to the nation – the ones that the censors and propagandists were attempting to bury – in veiled ways, using metaphors and historical allusions. In this regard, Szaniawski was a forerunner.

This said, the principal theme of Szaniawski's work is art, not history. Its characters are all theatre artists: a playwright, a director, actors, and even technical workers. The fundamental question formulated by the author relates to how accurately theatrical conventions can represent reality. The play centres on a discussion about the purpose of theatre art, with the debate focusing on two different types of theatre, expressed through two metaphors: of a mirror, and of a dream. The mirror signifies realistic theatre that references experiences known by audiences from daily life; the dream signifies poetic theatre, which tries to render unusual situations and grasp elusive inner states through metaphors and symbols. Although the Director is privately a collector of dreams, which he writes down in a journal, he stands on guard for realism in art and does not agree to the Author's suggestion that he stage a play about the destruction of a city. He also refuses to allow the poet, whom he calls "Rain Boy" (chłopiec z deszczu), to work on a wordless drama titled "Children's Crusade" (Krucjata dziecięca), which presents child soldiers in helmets on their way to extermination. Instead, the Director produces realistic, one-act plays about people facing morally difficult choices. It takes the experience of war to change his perspective on theatre. Thereafter, the theatre becomes a place in which real-life situations can be accompanied by images from the imagination. The imagination of the Author and Rain Boy had anticipated reality, which turned into a wartime nightmare. *Two Theatres* also creates a collective hero out of the artists summoned to reflect upon the world and to express its rules. The violent ethical crisis engendered by the war forces them to drastically revise their aesthetic ideas. In the final analysis, Szaniawski's play lauds art as the domain of both realism and poetic vision, a belief that finds its clear reflection in postwar drama.

Political "Thaw": The Heyday of Drama

The year 1956 brought a political "thaw" to Poland. The social realist doctrine was set aside, and drama and theatre quickly began to make up for lost time. New plays, many of which had been written earlier but not permitted in print, appeared in journals, especially in *Dialog* (Dialogue), a monthly that had been established specifically to publish them. Polish stages started to produce new Polish drama and also returned to prewar plays; translations and premieres of Western works followed shortly thereafter. The works of Sartre, Camus, Durrenmatt, Brecht, Miller, and Williams, as well as by the creators of the Theatre of the Absurd (Genet, Beckett, Ionesco), enjoyed a lively reception. After being suppressed in Stalinist Poland, poetic drama (Stanisław Wyspiański; Karol Hubert Rostworowski) and avant-garde theatre (Stanisław Ignacy Witkiewicz; the Futurists) returned to the stage. The years 1956 to 1969 were a heyday for Polish theatre, radio, and television dramas. Initially, these plays tried to settle accounts with Stalinism, which was possible only indirectly, by means of historical analogies and references to foreign contexts. For the purpose of exposing the lethal mechanisms of brute political power, playwrights set their works in Ancient Greece, Rome, or Spain during the Inquisition. The most interesting work of this current is the poetic *Jaskinia filozofów* (The Cave of Philosophers, 1956) by Zbigniew Herbert (1924–98), which was seen to allude to Stalinist prisons.

POETRY IN MODERN DRAMA

Zbigniew Herbert, one of the greatest twentieth-century Polish poets, created his own type of modern poetic drama by experimenting with the radio play form at the turn of the 1950s and 1960s. In writing plays, Herbert questions the value of poetry as a means to express human suffering and the meaning of life. Traditional dramatic action does not play a central role in his works. His heroes are not a part of a specific conflict, and their relations are not defined by a clear plot aimed at changing their current situation or realizing their goals. Herbert is most interested in the state of human consciousness when confronted by fear, loneliness, exclusion, pain, and death. He sees as dramatic the moment when a victim tries to name the essence of his experience; indeed, this is the fount of all his theatre work. In this regard, he comes close to the twentieth-century existentialists, who based their dramatic situations on the liminal experience, turning it into the parable of human life, and who made the dialogue between characters a vehicle for philosophical concerns. It is not by accident that Socrates is the hero of Herbert's first play, *The Cave of Philosophers*. Yet the author shows a non-canonical – for being poetic – side of the Greek thinker. Herbert believed that the most effective form of human cognition is not the rationalized discourse of philosophers, but the discourse of poets, which is based in metaphor, saturated with symbolism, and organically tied to oral expression. When confronted with evil, the heroes of Herbert's dramas become poets, even when neither their consciousness nor their language rises above their social footing. Such heroes include the inhabitants of a tenement house in *Drugi pokój* (The Other Room, 1958) and the residents of a northern Polish provincial town in *Lalek* (1963). In these plays, poetry is born from situations of existential tension and is usually expressed through dramatic monologues strongly infused with lyricism. Yet Herbert also makes rhythmic the characters' banal lines: he subjects them to phonetic instrumentalization, creating parallel syntactical structures and infusing them with images, metaphors, and symbols, thus adding semantic potential to individual words. By writing in this manner, Herbert achieved an effect that T.S. Eliot – one of his masters, whose postwar reception influenced the shape of poetic drama in Poland – called the "musicalization" of drama.

The Cave of Philosophers is set in Athens and presents the last three days of Socrates's life. Herbert sourced the basic theme of his work from Plato's dialogues, in particular from *Phaedo* and *Crito*, but the image of Socrates he constructs differs from the traditional one. The hero of Herbert's play maintains the ethical stance of the Greek philosopher by accepting an unjust verdict, rejecting the temptation to escape from prison, and drinking the hemlock with dignity. Unlike the historical Socrates, however, Herbert's version blends characteristics of the great philosopher of antiquity with those of a contemporary poet and creates one of the first great individualists in Polish postwar drama. What links these two different figures are poetry and existential philosophy, which was just then being discovered by Polish audiences through translations of Sartre and Camus. Herbert's Socrates learns mere hours before his death that the philosophy he espouses, encompassed by the equation "wisdom = goodness = happiness," does not stand up to life's trials. He is visited by a Council Emissary, who uses Socrates's own method of arriving at truth to prove an idea contrary to the philosopher's ideas. Not only that, but the consequence of his reasoning produces the evil that strikes the philosopher. Socrates's students, in turn, convince their master that wisdom cannot alter fate, nor knowledge alleviate fear. While Socrates meets the false proof of the Council Emissary with silence, he answers his students' arguments by challenging them to seek order in the world and not to confront its painful mystery. In *The Cave of Philosophers*, poetry turns out to be the proper instrument for exploring this mystery and perhaps also the source of salvation from evil and fear. Through monologues of great lyrical power, Herbert's Socrates probes the depths of evil and reveals the transcendental aspect of human existence, thus preparing for his death, which he meets in the manner of his ancient prototype. Nevertheless, in the play's final act he is tempted to rebel and experiences fear that Plato does not mention.

Other playwrights also engaged in this type of play with tradition, inspired mainly by the turn-of-the-century poetic dramas of Stanisław Wyspiański (1869–1907) and by the work of American poet and playwright T.S. Eliot. Among them was Karol Wojtyła (1920–2005), the future Pope John Paul II, who wrote three interesting poetic plays, including *Przed sklepem jubilera* (The Jeweller's Shop, 1960). Wojtyła's take on drama with a Christian provenance gave it an original form that, in lieu of a clear plot, focused on meditation on moral dilemmas and the divine laws governing human life. In this it reflected its author's stage experience at Teatr Rapsodyczny (the Rhapsodic Theatre), which was founded by the director Mieczysław Kotlarczyk in Nazi-occupied Kraków and which placed the strongest emphasis on the poetic and rhetorical qualities of the spoken word.

WITKACY IN THE THEATRE OF TADEUSZ KANTOR

When the doctrine of socialist realism ceased to be enforced in Poland, the avant-garde artists took to the floor. Under the new conditions, they took up the tradition of artistic experimentation founded by prewar artists like Stanisław Ignacy Witkiewicz (Witkacy). Witkacy was particularly inspiring for Tadeusz Kantor, a painter, stage designer, and director who launched his theatre Cricot 2 in 1956 with Witkacy's *Mątwa* (The Cuttlefish, 1922). Kantor was fascinated with Witkacy's hyper-realistic imagination and with his courage to undertake risky artistic endeavours, as well as by his catastrophic outlook, which resonated powerfully among people affected by war and Stalinism. Just as Witkacy had liberated drama from the strictures of verisimilitude, logic, illusion, and unity, so Kantor liberated theatre from the strictures of literature, focusing on discovering new means of theatrical expression. Each subsequent staging of Witkacy's plays served him as another experiment with theatrical form. *W małym dworku* (Country House, 1961) was a manifestation of "Theatre Informel": in this production, all elements of the performance were subordinated to chance and to the destructive impact of matter on the human body. This process was visually represented by the bodies of actors tumbling out of a wardrobe along with stuffed bags. In the production of *Wariat i zakonnica* (The Madman and the Nun, 1963), defined by Kantor as "Zero Theatre," the stage was dominated by an "Annihilation Machine" built entirely from chairs, which drowned out the actors and pushed them to the margins of the stage. Witkacy's *Kurka wodna* (The Water Hen, 1967) allowed Herbert to develop the rules of the "Happening Theatre," in which stage action is based on a series of loosely interconnected actions. The titular character moved among café tables in a bathtub, to which she invited the spectators. *Nadobnisie i koczkodany* (Dainty Shapes and Hairy Apes, 1973), in turn, played out in a cloakroom, where the audience awaited a performance that could not begin. In this way, Kantor performed his idea of the "Impossible Theatre." Finally, Kantor's most famous production, *Umarła klasa* (The Dead Class, 1975), from which his "Theatre of Death" emerged, was based on Witkiewicz's play *Tumor Brainiowicz* (1920) as well as a short story by Bruno Schulz titled "Emeryt" (The Pensioner, 1937).

Nevertheless, the shape of the new drama in Poland was determined largely by authors influenced by the grotesque, with Witkacy as their patron, rather than by the poetic current. Witold Gombrowicz (1904–69), Tadeusz Różewicz (1921–2014), and Sławomir Mrożek (1930–2013) were undoubtedly foremost among these authors, although their work did not exist in a vacuum; other important writers with avant-garde roots debuted after 1956, including the poets Miron Białoszewski (1922–83), Stanisław Grochowiak (1934–76), Ireneusz Iredyński (1939–85), and Tymoteusz Karpowicz (1921–2005), and the prose writer Janusz Krasiński (1928–2012). These artists in turn had their followers, such as Helmut Kajzar (1941–82) and Janusz Głowacki (1938–2017), who in the 1990s established a Broadway career with his play *Antygona w Nowym Jorku* (Antigone in New York, 1992).

Experience of Postwar Nihilism: Henryk from *The Marriage*

The three most important postwar Polish plays are without doubt Gombrowicz's *Ślub* (The Marriage, 1953), Różewicz's *Kartoteka* (The Card Index, 1960), and Mrożek's *Tango*

(1964). All three of these authors considered their master to be Witkacy, the prewar innovator of dramatic form founded in Expressionism and a grotesque aesthetic. Not surprisingly, the grotesque became the calling card of their plays, with its dissonant language, logical incoherence of dramatic action, and multilayered deformation of the represented reality. They parodied former dramatic models as a means to present the situation of the modern human being whose world has lost its ordering principle – a principle expressed in the past already at the level of convention. Michał Głowiński, an perceptive scholar of Gombrowicz's work, notes that such parody is *constructive* parody – its aim is not to ridicule tradition but to diagnose the present state of a disintegrating world.[3] The process of dismantling the metaphysical principles governing the universe began during the Renaissance, with Shakespeare's *Hamlet* as its most poignant expression in theatre. *Hamlet* is a tragicomic play about a hero whose intelligence and feelings prevent him from fulfilling his mission of avenging his murdered father. It comes as no surprise, therefore, that in writing *The Marriage* Gombrowicz parodied *Hamlet*. According to the Danish Prince, "time is out of joint" as a result of the treacherous murder of his father, but the crisis in the play is rather rooted in its hero's indecisiveness. Hamlet is uncertain whether to believe the message he has received from a Ghost appearing from beyond the grave, and he is aware that his mother and stepfather are deceiving him and that the world is governed by permanent treachery. The death of the wrongdoers, and even Hamlet's courage and self-sacrifice, change nothing. To control the world – that is, to impose an arbitrary order upon it – one needs a strong ruling hand. As it turns out, at the play's end that hand belongs to Fortinbras.

JERZY JAROCKI'S PRODUCTION OF GOMBROWICZ'S *THE MARRIAGE*

Witold Gombrowicz, who emigrated from Poland in 1939, was critical of the communist authorities. As a result, only his prewar short stories and the novel *Ferdydurke* were published in Poland, while his dramatic works were subject to censorship and rarely staged. Gombrowicz did not trust theatre directors, fearing that they would distort the sense of his precisely structured plays; for this reason, he commented extensively on them. Nevertheless, it was in Poland that they found their best director in Jerzy Jarocki (1929–2012), who staged *The Marriage* six times (also abroad) and worked out a masterful theatrical form for Gombrowicz's text. Jarcoki's 1991 production of the play at the Stary Teatr (Old Theatre) in Kraków took place on an empty, black stage that was itself a metaphor of Henryk's internal world. The drama's protagonist was played by the young, talented actor Jerzy Radziwiłowicz, whose face is known to audiences around the world thanks to Andrzej Wajda's renowned film *Man of Marble*. Playing Henryk is unusually difficult, since the hero appears on the stage as a figure who is dreaming up himself and all the other characters in the play while also retaining his full mental awareness. The world he dreams up constantly surprises him, but it is also subject to his creation and analysis, which the actor undertakes on the proscenium, with audience members acting as witnesses to his struggles. He is thus both the object and the subject of his own stage actions, continuously entering into relations with other characters that have formed him and that precisely correspond to Gombrowicz's concept of humanity. The sequence of grotesque interactions has a tragic dimension in *The Marriage* and takes on the form of a dark ritual, with Henryk as its self-proclaimed "priest."

Gombrowicz took a similar path, albeit he considerably expanded the scope of the treachery in his play, which affects its heroes at the level of thought, feeling, and even language. Thus in *The Marriage*, the author calls into being a royal court and makes its protagonist, Henryk, a Prince; however, the world represented therein is only an evocation of the internal conflicts of the hero, who is no more than "dreaming" his courtly drama while a soldier at a war front. In this way, Gombrowicz references the convention of subjective drama created by August Strindberg, but he also modernizes it in his play by parodying various dramatic conventions and meta-theatrical devices. Gombrowicz equips his play with numerous authorial commentaries and his hero with a heightened self-awareness that he is the creator of his own dream. In a way, Henryk becomes the director of the play's successive scenes, which thus acquire a hyper-theatrical character. He "dreams" his return to the family home and in this process fills an empty, dark stage with people and objects. The world represented in the play is thus a function of Henryk's consciousness, which Jerzy Jarocki expressed very well in his congenial production of *The Marriage* at Kraków's Stary Teatr (Old Theatre) in 1990. Played by the excellent actor Jerzy Radziwiłowicz, Henryk frequently approaches the proscenium, distancing himself from the rest of dramatic action and addressing the audience directly through monologues. The entire stage functions like a screen for his consciousness, with the people who appear on it being – like actors – only reminiscent of concrete people (his father, his mother, his fiancée) and the objects there only an imitation of the real world, in the manner of theatrical props. A degrading imitation at that, for Henryk dreams or imagines his house with his mother and father as innkeepers and his fiancée as a "barmaid." Henryk discovers that their status depends entirely on him, but the "dark" force slumbering within him, which degraded his home and family, does not readily submit to his will. On the contrary – it escapes him and even personalizes itself in the figures of the Drunk and his companions, who arrive at the inn and vulgarly offend his parents and fiancée. To oppose them, Henryk mobilizes within himself admiration for his Father; even as he is aware of the total artificiality of his words and gestures, he turns him from an innkeeper into a king.

The world in the play is elevated, and Henryk wants to fix it once and for all, despite the schemes of the Drunk, who functions in the play as the sphere of instincts in the human psyche. If the Drunk stands in for the id, then Henryk's Father represents the superego, the highest and divine authority, as Jan Błoński observes in his excellent reading of *The Marriage* as a "psychoanalytic tragedy."[4] The Drunk constantly undermines the Father's authority, which "weakens" Henryk. To defeat his opponent and take control of reality, this truly unique hero decides to marry his fiancée, rightly reasoning that a religiously understood sacrament of marriage has an absolute dimension that is independent of other people's will. There is one caveat, however: the sacrament of marriage is decided by God, whose earthly representative is the king, and thus the Father, and Henryk does not wish to receive a blessing from his father's hands. So he decides to officiate in his own marriage, which sounds absurd but is consistent with the logic of the play, in which the hero creates the world. Yet as this world is populated by other people who are also capable of "creating" situations and meaning, Henryk is doomed to see treachery everywhere. Like Macbeth, another tragic Shakespearean hero, he seeks to eliminate all of his opponents and turns into a tyrant who imprisons his own father and convinces his closest friend to commit suicide. The tyrant can terrorize a court, but he cannot control its thoughts, and since it is enough for one person to discredit the validity of the marriage in their thoughts, the entire endeavour makes no sense.

In the end, therefore, Henryk is defeated, and his defeat is the defeat of a modern man, as Henryk calls himself in one scene. *The Marriage* is a great metaphor that can be explained as follows: we live in a metaphysical vacuum that we fill in two ways – through subconscious life and death instincts that, as in Freud's theory, reveal themselves in our sexual drives and aggression; and through a conscious desire to "take control" of reality through the constant imposition of some form upon it. The tension between instincts and form decides the shape of human reality. In this "Interhuman Church" – as Gombrowicz notes in comments added to the play – in a world of fluid principles and values, people tyrannize one another and death remains its only absolute element.

The Anti-Romantic Romantic: The Hero from *The Card Index*

While Henryk is the universal figure of the modern nihilist, the hero of Różewicz's *The Card Index* reveals the condition of a generation that lived through the wartime hecatomb and permanently lost its sense of the value and meaning of life. In Polish postwar reality, such a hero was better understood than Henryk, in part because Różewicz constructed his play on remnants of the Romantic dramatic form with which Polish audiences felt close cultural affinity. The Polish Romantic hero also owes much to Hamlet – he is well-read and highly sensitive, a great individualist, as well as a bereft lover – but he is different in his decisive will to repair the world and to struggle for the freedom of his homeland and the happiness of the enslaved nation. Heroes such as Konrad from Adam Mickiewicz's *Dziady* (Forefathers' Eve) and Słowacki's eponymous Kordian do not belong to the world of the royal court; rather, their status is directly determined by the social and historical situation of gentry Poland, which at the end of the eighteenth century was subjected to brutal partitions by neighbouring states. These young noblemen are "aristocrats of spirit," however, who overcome their individual heartbreaks and take up the burden of responsibility for an entire nation, if not humanity. Both experience a characteristic transformation that, in the case of Mickiewicz's hero, is even marked with a name change. Both also become involved in conspiracies and wind up in a prison cell instead of a university hall, and eventually either in exile (Konrad), or in front of an execution squad (Kordian).

Precisely this type of character is synonymous with the dramatic hero in Poland. In naming his main character "Hero," Różewicz automatically locates *The Card Index* in the Romantic tradition, which revived in Poland during the 1950s due also to new productions of both *Kordian* and *Forefathers' Eve* (both of which were broadly forbidden during the Stalinist years because of their message of national sovereignty). It is not by accident that the set design for the first production of *The Card Index*, at the Teatr Dramatyczny (Dramatic Theatre) in Warsaw in 1960, included a portrait of Juliusz Słowacki hanging among contemporary theatre posters and announcements. Yet Różewicz references the Romantic tradition in a contrary, even parodic, manner: the stance of his Hero contradicts that of his Romantic predecessors. Instead of acting in the public interest, the man ostentatiously manifests his privacy and passivity. The space in which he acts is a bed, which he climbs out of only sporadically. Buried under the covers, he refuses activity of any kind, thus inspiring the indignation of the Chorus of Elders that is present in the room. The Chorus is vested with social authority, which the hero ignores, and is a sign of traditional theatricality, which *The Card Index* intentionally violates. A character who does not act destroys the rules of drama and undermines the sense of theatre performance, which is why not only the Chorus commenting from within the play, but also theatre critics, saw

The Card Index as an anti-drama and anti-theatre manifesto. Calling its Hero an anti-hero, they associated this play with the Western European theatrical current named the Theatre of the Absurd by Martin Esslin and represented in his book by Samuel Beckett and Eugene Ionesco.[5]

The inaction of the Hero in *The Card Index* has serious meta-dramatic consequences: the play loses its action, the remaining characters lose their status of being engaged in some kind of dramatic conflict, and the entire world becomes absurd. This is tellingly expressed by the image of a street running through the Hero's room. At the same time, dramatic tension does not disappear from the play; it arises within the Hero with every successive character that appears at his bedside, usually to remind him of his trespasses, compel his contrition, and demand redress. Różewicz composes the Hero's relationships with the remaining characters of this anti-play in the manner of a grotesque: the people who appear in his room are both living and dead – familiar and strange – and the ways in which they speak with one another are in no way related to the Hero's current social status (he is a middle-aged director of operettas). His parents thus treat him like a child, and a former neighbour like a pubescent teen. From this accumulation of grotesque microdramas a quite serious biography emerges, of a man who lived through the war and Stalinism (allusively evoked in one episode as the epoch of clapping with blood-stained hands) and who is now only with increasing difficulty performing his social role. The Hero's world has fragmented into pieces that he is unable to put back together into a sensible whole. Internally paralysed, he retreats from external life. The Hero's stagnation is disturbed by rare moments of rebellion, when the former, Romantic spirit of a warrior awakens inside him. At these times, he launches lengthy tirades against the people of his generation, which express powerlessness against despair. After one such tirade, he even makes an (unsuccessful) attempt on his own life. Różewicz counterposes the serious parts of the play with entirely trivial divulgences of the main character as he reads a newspaper, and with his grotesque attack on the Chorus that leaves it deprived of not only a voice but also their heads.

Różewicz's Hero, overwhelmed by passivity, embodies a deep crisis of the dramatic hero's subjectivity, which consists entirely of other people's perceptions, opinions, and judgments, with his official curriculum vitae (which he begins writing on several occasions) replacing his actual biography. The absurd vision that Różewicz builds on the stage turns out to be a metaphor for the disintegration of modern man's personality, articulated by the author also in his poetry. In a work with the telling title "To się złożyć nie może" (This Cannot Be Put Together), the poet presents a litany of activities that add up to human existence, with death as its only horizon: "Getting up in the morning / going to bed / choosing from a menu / trying on gloves / kissing / giving birth to children / walking / playing cards / playing the gramophone / drinking vodka / drinking black coffee / lubricating / brushing / massaging / decorating / wearing cotton wool on the shoulders / wearing rings / wearing mustaches / looking in the mirror / blinking / making faces / making a career / making this and that/ / this is dying …")[6]

A Conservative in a World without God: Arthur from *Tango*

Constructive parody is also the domain of Sławomir Mrożek's most important play. In writing *Tango*, Mrożek called on the eighteenth-century tradition of the comedy of manners, playfully reversing its conventions. The hero of this play is a well-educated young man named Arthur, who decides to marry his girlfriend Ala to spite his parents. The parents do not oppose the union, but consider it redundant since Arthur is already sleeping with Ala. Arthur is frustrated by his parents' liberal attitude towards marriage (the mother Eleonore openly cheats on her husband Stomil with the frequent house guest Eddie, which does not shock anyone), and he longs after a traditional family and social order, or – more broadly speaking – after form. It is this form that the sacrament of marriage is to restore. Unfortunately, Arthur does not believe in God, and his faith that an empty marriage ceremony will transform their shared life and organize the world does not sustain him for long. The young man has a breakdown, gets drunk, and gives up on marriage, even though Ala has already put on her wedding gown and the family their ceremonial clothes. At this moment of crisis, however, the hero of the play has no intention of letting go of his longings. At the play's climax, he tyrannizes his loved ones, threatening them with a gun while shouting nihilistic slogans.[7] The young tyrant must give way to the ruthless Eddie, who kills Arthur in cold blood in front of his family and takes over the "rule" of Stomil's household. In the play's finale, the conformist Uncle Eugene and Eddie dance the tango, with the dance symbolizing an alliance between tradition and violence.

THE ART OF THEATRICAL INTERPRETATION OF DRAMA: ERWIN AXER (1917–2012)

The flowering of Polish drama impacted the development of theatre in Poland. Indeed, dramatic theatre became the brand of Polish culture for many years, with highly talented directors staging new plays by Mrożek, Różewicz, and Iredyński not only in Poland but also abroad. The Teatr Współczesny (Contemporary Theatre) in Warsaw, under the direction of Erwin Axer, became a model for the artistic symbiosis between authors and theatre directors. Axer brought to the stage both Polish and foreign plays, establishing a deep dialogue between them in a way typical of remarkable directors. In 1962 he directed Bertold Brecht's *The Resistible Rise of Arturo Ui* (1941), and three years later Sławomir Mrożek's *Tango* (1965). He cast the great Polish actor Tadeusz Łomnicki (1927–92) in the role of Brecht's Arturo, and Wiesław Michnikowski (b. 1922) as Arthur in *Tango*. In the scene where the frustrated hero of Mrożek's play turns into a tyrant and delivers a monologue standing on top of a table, Michnikowski mimicked the facial expressions and gestures of Łomnicki, who himself had parodied Hitler in his performance of Arturo. In this manner, through a series of theatrical allusions, Axer interpreted Mrożek's work.

Mrożek parodied the domestic comedy by including a tragic ending that ran counter to its conventions; he was in fact writing a modern grotesque drama, with each character representing a different world view and model for social life. The tension between Stomil and Arthur basically articulates the conflict between twentieth-century liberals and conservatives, although Mrożek turns middle-class conventions on their head by making the young rather than the mature man into the conservative. In a communist Poland, this conflict reflected actual social divisions only to some extent. Stomil represents the prewar generation of avant-garde artists who had revolutionized both art and social life and who became part of the communist establishment in the postwar years (which the play does not state directly for reasons of censorship). Arthur, in turn, represents an ideological and political formation that was not officially represented (tolerated) in communist Poland. Yet the Polish audiences of *Tango* interpreted his rebellion as an allusion to an anti-revolutionary world view. In fact, the play's conflict was more legible in the West, where Mrożek emigrated and finished writing *Tango* (which since then has been regularly produced in theatres around the world). With Poland's return to democracy after 1989, Polish audiences read *Tango*'s conflict as a reflection of real tensions between progressives and traditionalists that, as in all of Europe, also divided Poland's political scene.

Yet *Tango* is not a political drama per se; rather, it is a dramatic diagnosis of the condition of the world after the end of religion and of great ideologies, when the natural need for social order finds no adequate ordering principles. Read in this manner, *Tango* transfers the problematic of *The Marriage* to the realm of familial and social conflicts. Arthur turns into Henryk's younger brother – a hero looking for ways to deal with a chaotic reality in which the only constant is death, and terror is the only means of maintaining order. At least so it seems to both heroes, who end up doubting the power of love as failed husbands-to-be, which on a philosophical level calls attention to the issue of the absolute in both dramas. Both Mrożek's *Tango* and Gombrowicz's *The Marriage* can be read as a dramatic treatises about the modern man, whose elimination of the divine element of love leads him straight towards nihilism and tyranny. It is in this veiled manner that Polish postwar drama tackled totalitarianism.

War and Realism during 1970s: The Hero as Scapegoat

Realism made a comeback in Polish playwriting in the 1970s, and even the masters of the grotesque deformation of the world – Różewicz at home, and Mrożek abroad – changed the style of their works. Różewicz's most important play of the period, *Do piachu ...* (Bite the Dust ..., 1979), is almost naturalistic in its depiction of life in a Polish partisan unit during the Nazi occupation. The partisans are encountered not during a heroic fight with the enemy, but at a forest camp in the course of their everyday activities. Różewicz amplifies the entirely non-heroic aspect of the war, accenting also the sharp division between officers and regular soldiers, who are treated as servants in the camp. The hero of *Bite the Dust ...* is the young, simple, illiterate partisan Waluś, who occupies the lowest rung in the unit's social hierarchy. When one day some soldiers rape a peasant woman and pillage her food supplies, the blame is assigned to Waluś, who is sentenced to death without an investigation. The boy, unaware of the verdict, spends his final hours in a cell like an animal destined for slaughter, and is then shot and buried in a shallow grave. Waluś is a true anti-hero of Polish drama, treated like Woyzeck in Georg Büchner's famous pre-Expressionistic play. Deceived, humiliated, and finally killed, Waluś is also the one character in the play with an elementary moral compass, which sharply distinguishes him from his colleague-oppressors. Różewicz juxtaposes the scene of his execution with that of pig slaughter and a field mass, creating a shocking and dramatic mosaic of human humiliation and holiness.

Różewicz's play waited for its premiere for a long time. It took place only in 1979, directed by the renowned Polish actor, Tadeusz Łomnicki. The delay was caused by protests of the Home Army combatants, who considered *Bite the Dust ...* defamatory of Polish partisan movements. It must be remembered here that, right after the war, communist propaganda labelled Polish soldiers fascists and locked them in prisons. Różewicz, however, did not write a political play. The story told in *Bite the Dust* ... served mainly to diagnose the human condition, which was degraded to a horrifying degree during the war. Różewicz does not throw accusations at the partisans, although he certainly criticizes the attitudes of the officers he presents. He does question, however, the system of values and the social hierarchy supported by that system, which collapsed under the weight of fratricidal crimes.

Interestingly, the figure of a simple and innocent human being – a man, a woman, a boy, a girl, a child – subjected to the pressures of a small social group, persecuted, tortured, driven to suicide or killed – appeared in the 1970s more frequently, also outside of a war context. The very young Blada in *Żegnaj, Judaszu* (Goodbye, Judas, 1971) by Ireneusz Iredyński, the warehouse worker in Zbigniew Herbert's radio play *Listy naszych czytelników* (Letters from Our Readers, 1972), Greta from *Dulle Griet* (1975) by Stanisław Grochowiak (1934–76), and Cinderella from Janusz Głowacki's *Kopciuch* (Cinders, 1979) are all manipulated and hounded by people with some kind of power: of a man over a woman, a supervisor over a worker, an administrator over a petitioner, a director of a young offenders' home over the underage convicts, a doctor over a patient, a judge over an accused. In all of these works, the playwrights analyse the same archaic mechanism: the persecution of an innocent, sacrificial victim – "the scapegoat." That mechanism revives in contemporary societies marked by the war.

War returns also to Sławomir Mrożek's play *Pieszo* (On Foot, 1980), in which representatives of Polish society meet at an abandoned train station at a unique moment – the end of the Nazi occupation and the beginning of communist rule, which the characters do not yet foresee. Among them is a young boy, Son, who is strongly reminiscent of the author himself. Born in 1930, Mrożek referred to himself as "a child of war," and in *On Foot* he reconstructed the wartime consciousness of his generation. That consciousness would be passed down, as is evident in the plays written by young authors in the early twenty-first century. It was historical plays, however, that became the real sign of the times during the 1970s and 1980s, having as their theme nineteenth-century conspiracies and national uprisings against the Russian partitioning power. In this regard, a new archetype appeared in the work of Polish playwrights – the young conspirator. To fully understand the meaning of plays by Jerzy Mikke (1920–99) and Władysław Terlecki (1933–99), however, we must note the political context is which they were created.

Historical Drama: The Mirror of Nineteenth-Century Heroes

At the turn of the 1960s and 1970s in Poland, two serious confrontations between society and the communist regime took place. In March 1968, students protested in Warsaw against the undemocratic government, prompted by the removal of Kazimierz Dejmek's production of Adam Mickiewicz's *Forefathers' Eve* from the National Theatre repertoire. The students gathered underneath the monument of Mickiewicz at the Warsaw University campus, where they were attacked by the militia; many of the protesters were severely beaten and some arrested and sentenced to prison terms. Two years later, in December of 1970, workers at the Polish shipyards in Gdańsk and Szczecin took to the streets to protest against drastically worsening social conditions. The authorities opened fire, killing and wounding many of them. These events profoundly altered the relationship between Polish society and its government, driven by the agenda of the Soviet Union. Over time, some intelligentsia and working-class circles began illegal oppositional activities. After subsequent workers' strikes in Radom in 1976, the Workers' Defence Committee was established in Poland, and the Polskie Porozumienie Niepodległościowe (Polish Independence Accord) abroad. The Polish democratic opposition organized aid for the persecuted and began publishing uncensored "samizdat" journals and books, which by definition were illegal. A time of intense underground activity began both in Poland and in the emigrant circles of Paris and London, and this led to the founding of Solidarity in 1980. This independent self-governing trade union – essentially the first mass social movement independent of the communist regime – brought together close to ten million people. It was dissolved by the authorities after just over a year. Then on 13 December 1981, martial law was introduced in Poland.

The period of clandestine activities the 1970s and 1980s was reminiscent of the epoch of anti-Russian independence conspiracies, which emerged during the nineteenth century on territories of the Russian Partition and led to the eruption of two anti-tsarist uprisings in Poland – the November Uprising of 1830 and the January Uprising of 1863. In the 1970s, literature, including drama, took up these historical themes in order to dialogue about the contemporary situation with readers and theatre audiences. The main question in this heated debate, conducted through allusions and thus tolerated by the censors, was whether Poles were still a nation capable of independence. Is independence achievable under conditions of general conformity, and if so, by what means and at what cost? Fictional characters in Polish drama now included heroes of Polish history presented in true or probable situations and speaking in the slightly archaic language of their epoch, but about issues commonly recognizable and important to contemporary audiences.

Jerzy Mikke's play *Niebezpiecznie, panie Mochnacki* (It's Dangerous, Mr Mochnacki) was published at the beginning of 1975 in *Dialogue*. Its titular hero is a political journalist and conspirator born at the beginning of the nineteenth century, a participant in the November Uprising and founder of the partisan press. The play's prologue references Mickiewicz's *Forefathers' Eve, Part III*, which features the figure of a mother pleading with a Russian police dignitary for mercy towards her son, who has conspired against the tsar. In Mikke's play, the mother of the imprisoned Maurycy Mochnacki turns to Polish officials for mercy. It is they who, on Russian authority, govern the Kingdom of Poland, a state carved out of Eastern Europe at the Congress of Vienna, without its own constitution and politically dependent on Russia, but with its own economy and education system, and even an army, albeit with a Russian commander-in-chief. The Polish Peoples' Republic was reminiscent of Congress Poland, especially after 1976, when a note about friendship with the Soviet Union was added to the Polish constitution.

There are no Russians in Mikke's play. Its action takes place between Poles: officials loyal to the foreign ruler, and professors and young rebels who refuse to be satisfied with a substitute for freedom, who conduct anti-Russian activities, and who decide to rise up. Mikke presents the moment the uprising begins from two perspectives, emphasizing the poor planning by the conspirators (who did not take steps to prepare their own government), and exposing the conformism and fear of Polish ministers, who scuttle the uprising and strip its leaders of authority. Such is the situation of Mochnacki, a strategic genius who nevertheless must subordinate himself to the rule of young military officers and who is victimized by Polish conformists as the "brain of the uprising." The treasury minister Prince Lubelski, in order to save his position, makes public a document in which the young Mochnacki, imprisoned and under police pressure, urges the authorities to use force against the rebelling students. This document disgraces Mochnacki, eliminating a truly exceptional individual from the uprising.

In 1975, Mikke recalls the figure of Maurycy Mochnacki in order to reveal complex tensions and problems that Poles faced in the first days of the November Uprising. The play, produced by Television Theatre and several Polish stages, was received as a warning to contemporary conspirators – isolated, prey to provocations of the secret police, unprepared for the dangerous game with the authorities – and as an accusation levelled at contemporary loyalists, who were decidedly more numerous in the 1970s. The conspirators could count on the support of "the street," however, as they discovered five years later at the Gdańsk Shipyards and in thousands of workplaces across Poland.

When Władysław Terlecki's *Dwie głowy ptaka* (The Two Heads of the Bird)[8] was published in *Dialogue* in 1981, no one suspected that the democratization process launched by Solidarity would end eleven months later with the dispatch of tanks onto the streets by the authorities and the arrest of thousands of activists. As in Mikke's play, its hero is a historical figure: Aleksander Waszkowski, the last leader of Warsaw during the January Uprising, who in 1863 acquired the military maps the insurgents needed as well as money from the state treasury earmarked for the purchase of arms. He was arrested by the tsarist authorities towards the end of 1864 and imprisoned in the Warsaw Citadel, a fortress built by the Russians after the failure of the November Uprising. Waszkowski was one of the last participants of the January Uprising to be executed at the Citadel, the setting of Terlecki's play. *The Two Heads of the Bird* is a drama about the defeat of a Polish patriot, and simultaneously of the nation, which was unable to rise to independence. The tsarist police charge Waszkowski with robbing the Royal Bank and expects that he will admit his guilt and sign a document that will allow the Russians to officially reclaim the rest of the money deposited in London. Knowing that he will not escape the noose, Waszkowski nevertheless signs his name, completely broken by Poland's situation. From the beginning, the tsarist policemen try to convince him of the end of all hope for independence, and it is to them that the last word of the play belongs – a call to opportunism as the only permitted form of participation for Poles in the life of a country defeated by Russia. Staged in December 1982, and thus during the martial law period, *The Two Heads of the Bird* left no hope for changing the situation. It did allow its spectators, however, to stare into the face of a defeated nineteenth-century conspirator and ask: Are we still capable of victory?

Holocaust Drama: The Ghetto and the Totality of Experience

Plays about the Jewish Holocaust were a continuation of historical drama in the 1980s, although they also constitute a separate and original thematic current in Polish drama. In 1988, *Dialogue* published no fewer than four works set in the Warsaw Ghetto – not accidently, given that all appeared on the occasion of the forty-fifth anniversary of the outbreak of the Warsaw Ghetto Uprising. This anniversary was celebrated in an unusual way; the political climate in Poland had changed in the mid-1980s and it was now possible to discuss topics previously forbidden or censored. The Holocaust was one such subject; until then, it had been subjugated to the official communist politics of history. For example, because of the leftist political orientation of its leaders, the story of the Warsaw Ghetto Uprising was incorporated into this politics. Everyday life in the ghetto, however, was officially downplayed, since it was organized mostly by prewar civil servants and thus was "inconvenient" for the communist authorities. The liberalization of life in Poland during the second half of the 1980s, compelled by the democratic opposition and samizdat publications, intersected with Holocaust studies conducted abroad. It is in the context of these studies that one should read plays such as *Gwiazda za murem* (The Star behind the Wall, 1988) by Jacek Stanisław Buras (b. 1945), *Słuchaj, Izraelu!* (Hear, O Israel!, 1989) by Jerzy S. Sito (1934–2011), *Szukam* (Seeking, 1988) by Joanna Kulmowa (b. 1928), and *Stół* (The Table, 1988) by Ida Fink (1921–2011).

THE HOLOCAUST THEATRE OF JERZY GROTOWSKI

The most horrifying vision of the Holocaust in Polish theatre was created by Jerzy Grotowski, a theatre director and innovator. In 1962, in his "Teatr Laboratorium 13 Rzędów" (Laboratory Theatre of 13 Rows) in Opole, he staged *Akropolis*, subsequent versions of which were performed around the world. It is considered a masterpiece of twentieth-century theatre. The performance was based on a dramatic poem by Stanisław Wyspiański from 1904, the action of which takes place during the special time of Easter (the night of Holy Saturday to Resurrection Sunday) at the Wawel Castle in Kraków, the centre of Polish historical consciousness. In the Wawel Cathedral, statues from the tombs of saints and Polish kings come to life, along with mythical and biblical figures from tapestries and carvings from the quire. By their means, the history of Poland mixes with scenes from Homer's accounts of the Trojan War and the biblical story of Jacob, creating a remarkable composition of the most important motifs of the European and Polish cultures. The main theme of *Akropolis* is resurrection understood as salvation from death and forgetting. In Grotowski's staging of *Akropolis*, however, this theme underwent a significant transformation, for the director moved the action of the play to Auschwitz, confronting the great myths of Western civilization with the experience of the Holocaust. The prisoners built a concentration camp on the stage, repeating the words of Wyspiański's drama at the same time. This repeat lesson from the history of humanity transformed the stage into a collective, ecstatic prayer that ended with a hymn to Resurrection, which acquired an ironic and tragic resonance given the circumstances. At the end of the performance, the "figure" of the Resurrected – in reality a ragdoll reminiscent of a killed human being – was carried by prisoners in a procession formation into a tomb evocative of a crematorium. Their death in the performance is answered only by words coming from offstage: "They have gone – and rings of smoke unreel." The stage design of the performance was the work of Józef Szajna (1922–2008), a theatre director and a former prisoner of Auschwitz.

http://www.grotowski.net/en/encyclopedia/akropolis

The action of these plays focuses on two events: the creation of the ghetto, into which the Germans crowded close to half a million people; and its liquidation, with the mass murder of Jews at the German concentration camp at Treblinka (100 kilometres northeast of Warsaw). "You will live behind a black wall, In hunger, filth and madness / And lice will eat you alive / And your laws will be harsh" – so announces an Officer in Scene 2 of Buras's *The Star behind the Wall*. Buras shows life on the precipice of death from the perspective of one Jewish family, whose members try to survive by various means, taking on whatever work is available, trading, and smuggling food in from outside the ghetto. Every day their situation worsens. The family of Rabbi Jehuda Rozenblat, like the vast majority of ghetto residents, becomes destitute and begins to starve. The exception is the rabbi's youngest daughter, Marysia, who is gifted with a beautiful voice and tries to sing despite the circumstances. She dreams of becoming a star and performs at the shabby "Eldorado" theatre, where the ghetto's shady financial élite gathers every evening. Singing literally keeps her alive, but at a high price. She does not suffer from hunger, but she loathes the company of blackmailers and prostitutes, takes to drinking, and falls into despair. Yet she does not leave the cabaret. Buras shows how, under the duress of fear, hunger, and despair, the survival instinct begins to crush morality, which pushed some ghetto residents even to murder.

The conflict experienced by the play's female protagonist is born of a great desire for life and an equally great desire to care for her loved ones. This care wins despite everything, and the girl does not take the opportunity to escape from the ghetto. In the poignant final scenes of the play, Marysia voices fragments of her diary and dedicates them to her unborn daughter. With her child in mind, she breaks open a vial containing poison, but the play's symbolic finale leads one to believe that she will go along with others to meet her death rather than commit suicide. Beforehand, in a gesture of defiance, she had taken off the demeaning armband with the Star of David. The tone of *The Star behind the Wall*, however, is melodramatic rather than tragic. The action of the play shows the humiliation, martyrdom, and death of Jews, but it is the theme of love, faith, and art that takes centre stage; indeed, the play has the form of a musical. Its 1988 stage production at Warsaw's Dramatic Theatre thus recovered the memory of both the Holocaust and past Jewish culture, in which music, dance, and singing were so important. The premiere of Buras's play coincided with growing interest in Jewish culture in Poland and was perceived as an opportunistic gesture. Over time, however, it has become clear that this dramatic and theatrical return to the Warsaw Ghetto was highly significant, for it made present and thus restored the tragedy of Polish Jewry to Polish collective memory.

Historical figures in the history of the Warsaw Ghetto are among the fictional characters of Buras's play. The first is Adam Czerniaków (1880–1942), a renowned scientist and prewar social activist, who served as chairman of the Judenrat, the Jewish council under German orders that organized life in the ghetto. Another is Janusz Korczak (1878 or 1879–1942), a notable writer, doctor, and educator who cared for orphaned children in the ghetto, organizing shelters and places where they could die with dignity, and who in the end accompanied his charges into the gas chamber. Characteristically, both characters also appear in Sito's *Hear, O Israel!* as the Chairman and Old Doctor, embodying the highest values: courage, wisdom, valour, perseverance, sacrifice, dignity, and – in the case of the "orphanage supervisor" Korczak – also calmness of spirit. Using the conventions of a dramatic epic, *Hear, O Israel!* attempts to show the totality of the experience of life (and constant death) in the ghetto to an even greater degree than *The Star Behind the Wall*. In its multidimensional design, it presents the world of the living and the dead, people and ghosts, contemporary and historical heroes. The play is framed by contemporary events set at the Nożyk Synagogue in Warsaw, which is visited by a cantor from the United States who wishes to conduct a service during a Jewish holiday; for this, however, he requires the presence of ten devout Jews. Since they are not to be found in Warsaw, the Cantor sends Szames, one of those present in the synagogue, to the cemetery to fetch the missing person from there in order to begin the prayer. The terrified Szames has an apocalyptic vision in which a destroyed, overgrown Jewish cemetery in Warsaw turns into the Valley of Jehoshaphat, where according to the Torah the dead gather for Judgment Day at the end of time. In Szames's vision, the Jews murdered during the war rise from the dead, filling the vacuum created by the Shoah. The time of "the final solution of the Jewish question" is revived along with them, as is Warsaw of 1939 – the play's setting is now that of the city under Nazi occupation.

Sito's play continues the tradition of poetic drama that dates back to Romanticism. The text of *Hear, O Israel!* is syncretic, encompassing various styles and genres as well as three languages (Polish, German, and Yiddish). The play is punctuated with Jewish songs and prayers, as well as individual accounts of witnesses to the events, the most important of which is *Adama Czerniakowa dziennik getta warszawskiego* (The Warsaw Diary of Adam Czerniaków). Published in Poland for the first time only in 1983 (the Hebrew translation of the diary appeared in Israel in 1968), the work deeply impacted the form of Sito's play. The struggles with Gestapo officers in defence of the Jewish people that Czerniaków describes day after day in his diary serve as the play's main dramatic thread. *Hear, O Israel!* is simultaneously a drama of the entire Jewish nation and of one human being placed in a tragic situation. In order to save the greatest number of Jews, Czerniaków cooperates with the Germans, whose mission is to kill them all. Successive scenes reveal the efforts and defeat of this remarkable character, whose heroism is stripped of pathos. Czerniaków represents the quintesential qualities of the ethos of the Polish intelligentsia: wisdom, humility, and consistency. He is responsible for the fate of the Jewish community, and he is also a Polish patriot; a portrait of Józef Piłsudski, the great prewar Polish leader, hangs on his office wall. Sito also tries to touch on the religious dimension of the Holocaust and includes in the play two symbolic figures: Josel and Ishmael, who like angels constantly accompany Czerniaków and express the spiritual aspect of his experience, right up until his death.

Holocaust Drama: Questions of Memory and the Critique of Language

Buras and Sito tried to grasp the totality of the ghetto experience in as objective a way as possible, by dividing their texts between multiple voices of Holocaust victims, perpetrators, and witnesses, including historical figures, and using a discourse that integrated different languages and multiple perspectives. For their part, Ida Fink, an Israeli prose writer writing in Polish, and the poet Joanna Kulmowa worked within an entirely different strategy of Holocaust literature. Fink's *The Table* focuses entirely on a single episode in the ghetto's history, recalled from memory. Moreover, the play's action is limited to one situation – namely, the interrogation of four witnesses to events that occurred in the Warsaw Ghetto's *Umschlagplatz* (Assembly Point) on the first day of the mass transport of Jews to Treblinka. Grumbach, Woman I, and Zachwacki all go through the selection and luckily escape the gas chamber. Woman II, who is interrogated last, was not in the square, but saw the execution of Jews who were discovered hiding from the transport. The witness accounts reveal the horror experienced by the Jews; however, it is not this horror but rather the memory of people who went through hell that is the main theme of *The Table*. The reconstruction of events in the ghetto in Buras's and Sito's plays progresses as if our knowledge of the Holocaust was complete and unequivocal, with access to it being the only issue. Fink questions this kind of assumption and calls into doubt the very possibility of constructing an objective image of the tragic past. In *The Table*, the Prosecutor questions the witnesses about the tiniest details of the events, such as the surnames of the Gestapo officers, their location, and the manner in which they conducted their selection, with each account differing significantly from the others. The terrified and humiliated Jews remember the same event in different ways, contradicting one another even in things as seemingly obvious as the size of the table at which the Gestapo sat. For the Prosecutor – who is, as we surmise, leading an investigation into Nazi crimes – this is a serious problem, since only exact and unanimous testimonies can be treated as evidence. This is particularly true of the testimony of Woman II, who is convinced of the guilt of the Gestapo but does not have first-hand proof of it as a witness, since she was hiding in a cellar at the moment of the shootings. *The Table* fits well into Holocaust studies, which aim to aggregate all possible testimonies to ensure that the tragic events are not forgotten, and which are likewise aware of the imperfections of human memory. Fink takes a critical approach to the process of event reconstruction and thereby delivers an important dramatic account of the Holocaust.

Another example of this critical current is Joanna Kulmowa's *Seeking*. The heroine of this poetic play is Gabriela, a "grey-haired older lady" in the first part of the play, and a little girl in the second. Part One is set in a hospital, where grotesquely adorned patients (in an abandonment of situational realism) are engaged in traditional childhood games like hide and seek, tag, and blind man's bluff. Their actions suddenly materialize places and situations from years past that can be traced to the heroine's biography. The hospital is transformed into a German concentration camp, a court, and a prison before becoming a hospital again. These metamorphoses of the represented world are momentary and follow the logic of sudden, childlike associations, which become a code for Gabriela's recurring trauma in the play. In Part Two, the action moves to a city in Occupied Poland, where those who so far have been provided with only a mask and a name become proper dramatic characters. The atmosphere of play continues to permeate this work's dramatic situations, however. The poetics of *Seeking* are deeply subversive. Kulmowa throws into complete disarray the previous order of her heroine's biography. Significant issues intermingle with entirely trivial ones, and the pathos of tragic events is tested by the grotesque. In Kulmowa's play, the Holocaust (and the fate of Poles who tried to save Jewish lives) is articulated through children's counting rhymes.[9]

Recalling the numerous lyrical parts of the plays by Buras and Sito, it is easy to grasp the essence of Kulmowa's artistic project. In *Seeking*, the principal motifs of the already stable narrative of the Holocaust undergo a surprising, even provocative transposition to another language. This changes how these motifs are perceived and experienced, for they are now in a sense outside of official conventions. Kulmowa makes apparent the ever-greater linguistic chasm that separates the experience of Holocaust victims from that of contemporary people who wish to understand it. The critical dismantling of communicative conventions around the subject of the Holocaust through the use of poetic games involving language, memory, and consciousness offers one of the more interesting answers to this problem. The power of Kulmowa's play arises not only from the originality of her imagination but also from the tradition of dramatic experimentation, undertaken primarily by Tadeusz Różewicz and, on a smaller scale, by the poet Miron Białoszewski (1922–83).

In the early 1960s, at his home-based Teatr Osobny (The Separate Theatre), Białoszewski staged, among other works, his grotesque microdrama *Peruga czyli Szwagier Europy*

(Peruga, or Europe's Brother-in-Law, 1958). Through the sudden, sometimes surreal associations and seemingly absurd actions of its two characters, the play synthesizes situational fragments of a social visit, childhood games, wartime bombings, and even, on some barely inferrable plane, death in a concentration camp. The very short dramatic text ends with a sequence of actions reminiscent of girlish play with multicoloured wigs. The game is played at a slowed-down pace, however, and with the participation of the adult heroine, who keeps nodding off to, and "waking up" from, sleep. Her totally bald head brings to mind Orthodox Jewish women, whom the author remembered from prewar Warsaw, while simultaneously recalling the image of shaved female prisoners at a concentration camp. The horror in Białoszewski's play is also built through rhythmically repeated sequences of words, among them a seemingly childish counting rhyme, "Z ciszy wszy się rodzą" (Lice Are Born of Silence). Joanna Kulmowa must have remembered it when uncanningly transforming the counting rhymes in her play.

Kulmowa's courageous, even radical idea is paralleled to some extent by the concept of *Nasza klasa* (Our Class, 2009) by Tadeusz Słobodzianek (b. 1955), which came out many years later but belongs to the current of Holocaust-centred Polish drama. The subject of *Our Class* is the crime against Jewish residents of Jedwabne, a small town in eastern Poland, during the summer of 1941. The perpetrators of the massacre of more than three hundred Jews, who were burned alive in a barn, were Poles inspired by and acting with the permission of German occupants. Słobodzianek's play took shape as a result of a debate among historians and journalists around the subject of Jedwabne, but it is far from a historical reconstruction of the tragic events. The author uses the poetics of a multivocal narrative about the shared life of Poles and Jews in his play, which stretches back to prewar days and leads right up to the present. Its narrators are the students of a single class at a prewar school, who in "a theatre within a theatre" perform successive episodes of their shared history. Słobodzianek's play deliberately references the legendary 1975 production of *Umarła Klasa* (The Dead Class) by Tadeusz Kantor (1915–90). In *The Dead Class*, a group of elderly people gathered in a classroom try to awaken their memories of childhood, but every gesture, movement, melody, and broken word stirs up instead associations with war, the Holocaust, and the death of an entire generation. While Kantor's performance has an aspect of unspeakable tragedy, however, Słobodzianek's *Our Class* leans towards satire. It is both a vehement accusation levelled at Poles and an attempt to find an answer to why the pogrom took place. The author points to the inveterate antagonism between Poles and Jews, emphasizing the Catholic mentality of Poles that, in his view, turns Jews into enemies of their faith; he also points to the nationalistic Polish culture, which is rooted in Romantic but greatly simplified models. The crimes committed against school friends activate the mechanism of revenge, which spans generations. After the war, victimized Jews enter the communist ranks and get back at Poles, locking them up in Stalinist prisons and sentencing them to death. Years later, in turn, the nationalistic wing of the communist party launches the persecution of Jews in Poland, forcing them to emigrate in 1968. The casting of Polish history as a Polish–Jewish war in *Our Class*, however, is a gross simplification.

Transformation *of* Drama – Transformation *in* Drama

The plays of Buras, Sito, Fink, and Kulmowa came out a year before sweeping political changes entirely transformed Polish reality. The drama of the 1990s tried to grasp the significance of this change, with collective and individual transformations becoming its main theme. The new reality impacted many dimensions of life, including political, economic, social, cultural, and spiritual. After more than half a century, the nations of Central and Eastern Europe were throwing off the yoke of communism and returning to the family of democratic free market nations. They had to make up rapidly for their civilizational delay as well as address problems from which they previously had been kept separate by the Iron Curtain. Playwrights searched for adequate metaphors with which to capture this fascinating process of transitioning from an "old" to a "new" world. They found these metaphors in images of a house for sale, of a city divided into two districts (of glass highrises and of putrid garbage), of a country hut in which the central place is taken up by a television set, and of an apartment block where a frustrated member of the Polish intelligentsia recites a Romantic poem.

Reliance on metaphor is characteristic of the varied drama of the 1990s: its creators called forth and transformed a variety of styles, poetics, and dramatic conventions, seemingly uncertain as to which one might best meet the challenges of the changing reality. They treated genre indicators in a modern way, that is, not as rules of composition but as formal markers of meaning, as conscious references to a chosen literary and theatrical tradition that concealed a certain understanding of the world and of human beings. The genre designation of their plays was thus provisional and fluid. The plays of the 1990s entered in sophisticated ways the post-Romantic tradition of hermeneutic play with conventions. Realistic drama toyed with comedy conventions, transforming itself into grotesquery, while grotesquery took on the form of a dramatic fairy tale or became a new form of mystery play. All of this was happening in full awareness that the game was being played with marked cards and for the highest of stakes – a chance to dramatically grasp the condition both of individuals and of an entire collective in an epoch of great change.

Let us look then at the heroes of drama during the times of transformation understood in a double – genre and sociocultural – sense of the word. Artur Grabowski (b. 1967) presents an allegorical image of the dismantling of the old world in *Czwarta osoba* (The Fourth Person, 1999). This allegory is encoded in the forced sale of a palace; in the new times, its prewar owners are no longer wealthy enough to maintain their family estate and must move out. The play's protagonists are three women – a grandmother, a mother, and a daughter – and an absent but constantly recalled man – their son, husband, and father, respectively. The relations between the absent Karol and each of the three women are entirely different, but all are underpinned by love, jealousy, and disappointment. As a result, the play initially follows a melodramatic convention. Karol's family has occupied one of the wings of the palace since it was nationalized after the war by the communist authorities. In the free Poland, the palace has been "reprivatized" – a keyword of the 1990s – but its owners are being forced to sell it to home-grown businessmen who are better prepared for life under capitalism. Karol's ancestral estate can be thus viewed as synecdochal of Poland itself: it was rescued with difficulty and then quickly sold to various former "processing plant directors" who "have some shares" and "sit on boards" and who make up the post-communist financial elite of the Third Republic. The play takes place the night before the move, a special night since it falls on Easter Sunday; thus the melodrama transforms itself into a mystery play, an effect that Grabowski roots in the tradition of verse drama represented primarily by the T.S. Eliot of *The Cocktail Party* (1950). The intense dialogue of the three women cleanses the relations between them, leading to a true – since internal – "reprivatization" of their lives, which until now have been entirely dependent on external factors. Grabowski's heroines thus "gain" themselves even as they lose their palace. The question the play poses in the end is: What kind of a world will they build in accepting this freedom?

Ewa Lachnit (b. 1957) formulated an answer to a similar question in *Człowiek ze śmieci* (Man of Garbage, 1996), striking a very bitter note. The play is written in the convention of an apocalyptic fantasy in which reality is divided between an exclusive district of glass houses and a malodorous slum reminiscent of Cairo's Garbage City or the outskirts of Santiago. Its inhabitants are likewise divided. The "glass" people – "Szklani" – are those working for huge corporations, banks, companies, and subsidized institutions; the "garbage" people are those who live outside the sphere of prosperity and a money-based economy. Among the destitute are representatives of all professions and social levels – workers, artists, and even professors – who refused to work for a corporation. In the name of freedom, they collect garbage and dig graves. The world created in Lachnit's play is a grand metaphor for the new social system in Poland, allusively touching on its greatest problems, especially the drastic division of society into the rich who get richer and the poor who get poorer. The play's heroes are the people living on the margins, or at the bottom of the system for which they once fought – a system that is now victimizing them.

Among the "garbage" people – the contemporary *les misérables* – lives Nestor, a charismatic leader and protector, who is well suited to the partly fairy-tale-like reality. This ex-musician and hippie anarchist serves as the saviour of the garbage heap, from which he wishes to transport everyone by boat to an imagined "other side." He earns money for this journey with street performances of "theatre from life" – a meta-theatrical device that underscores the stipulated nature of represented reality in Lachnit's play. But he can never earn enough, and meanwhile, the garbage heap steadily expands and police persecute its inhabitants. One of the wretched records the history of the marginalized people and like a castaway throws it in bottles into the river. His efforts will allow the world to discover that the professor's books still await publication, since erotica, prophecies, and horoscopes – the real publishing hits of the 1990s – must be published first. Nestor dies, and his burial on the garbage heap interrupts the beggars' dream of a better life. So ends the first play to criticize capitalism in the new epoch.

Lachnit's vision of social degradation resonates with the life of a frustrated member of the Polish intelligentsia presented by Marek Koterski (b. 1942) in *Dzień świra* (Day of the Wacko, 2002), a play that was later turned into a film and became a cinematic hit in Poland. Koterski condenses every possible obsession in his hero: social, familial, medical, professional, and sexual. Divorced, dependent on a grumbling mother, and scorned by his own son, Adaś Miauczyński leads the solitary and humiliating life of a Polish language and literature teacher and a homespun poet in a country where no one respects teachers or reads poetry. *Day of the Wacko* is the masterfully constructed lament of a sociopath who sees the world as a collection of primitive and spiteful people who are self-obsessed, dismissive of others, and devoid of empathy, and who sees society as a pack of wild beasts fighting voraciously for themselves. Koterski gathers a collection of human specimens around Miauczyński; stamped with nasty nicknames alluding to despicable traits or attitudes, these people represent a bitterly satirical cross-section of Polish society. Miauczyński is overwhelmed by a reality marked by aggression and constant tension; he needs a system for asserting control, which he implements to pathological perfection. His day is made up of hundreds of activities performed in a set order, and any departure from that order throws him off balance. The absurdity of the life of the Polish intelligentsia is further amplified by the protagonist's use of thirteen-syllable verse – identical to the one used by Adam Mickiewicz in writing the Romantic national epic *Pan Tadeusz* (Sir Thaddeus, 1833), which Miauczyński also recites. Koterski uses it not simply to describe the spiritual ascents of his hero, however, but also to describe his morning routine and night-time masturbation. The effect is grotesque, which perfectly expresses the protagonist's condition of a true loser, an intellectual who leads a pariah's life in the new Poland, as well as that of a rapidly changing world, which is beyond the grasp of any other convention.

Once again in the history of Polish drama, the grotesque turned out to be the most adequate language for a time of social and cultural crisis – for the dismantling of an old world and the construction of a new one, still unknown, its outlines barely perceptible. Prior to the war, this approach had its patron in Witkacy, and afterwards in Różewicz; tellingly, critics saw the figure of Miauczyński as a new embodiment of the Hero from *The Card Index*. During the 1990s, the language of the grotesque was used also by Sławomir Mrożek in *Miłość na Krymie* (Love in the Crimea, 1993), by Tadeusz Słobodzianek in *Sen pluskwy* (A Bedbug's Dream, 2001), and by Janusz Głowacki in *Czwarta siostra* (The Fourth Sister, 1999). All of these plays are set, in part or entirely, in the Moscow of cowboy capitalism, right after the fall of the Soviet Union.

The collision of two entirely different worlds, which came to exist side by side in Poland in the 1990s, is also the theme of *Requiem dla gospodyni* (Requiem for the Country Wife, 2000) by Wiesław Myśliwski (b. 1932). On the one hand, there is the world of traditional but already greatly strained peasant spirituality; on the other, there is the world and mentality of the most recent times, where people are completely cut off from their religious roots, morality and customs have changed, and primitive consumerism rules the days. The peasant house has often served as a site of such confrontation in Polish dramatic tradition, to mention only Stanisław Wyspiański's *Wesele* (The Wedding, 1901). Myśliwski, however, wrote "The Wedding à rebours"; he gathers contemporary Poles in a peasant house not for a wedding but for a deceased housewife's night-time wake. The play's protagonist, the old Host, invites the guests, prepares the house, and sets out food on the table, but no one comes to the wake since he does not provide any vodka. Only two daughters arrive, one with a friend, the other with a so-called fiancé. They are later followed, however, as in the evangelical parable about wedding guests invited in from the fields and the road, by accidental arrivals: tourists, a businessman with his girlfriend, a passing retiree, and some young people. It is they who replace the absent community of mourners, and it is for them that the night of the wake will prove life-changing.

Myśliwski uses the conventions of Symbolism, staging encounters of the living with the dead, mixing temporal dimensions, contravening physics (the television works without electricity), and introducing extraordinary figures such as the "seeing" Boleś, and the Young Man who observes "other worlds," all in the name of unsettling people who have lost their bearings in the materialistic reality of 1990s Poland. Their semi-farcical ritual, carried out by accident, in the end does have sense and brings results. The surface of a primitive world has been torn, exposing a completely different world, unknown to contemporary consumers and symbolized in the play by the sound of choral music. The people accidently gathered in the deceased's house begin to speak about truth and freedom, the most important themes of *Requiem for the Country Wife*.

The play premiered at the National Theatre under the direction of Kazimierz Dejmek, who understood Myśliwski's work very well. The director found in *Requiem*, and brought to life on stage, the national *topos* of the night of turning tides, during which Poles gather to engage in "countrymen's long talks in the night" (as Adam Mickiewicz wrote in the famous poem "Do Matki Polki" [To a Polish Mother]) in order to part in the morning transformed.[10] This *topos* is present in great works of various epochs and styles, beginning with Mickiewicz's *Forefathers' Eve* (1823–60) and continuing through Wyspiański's *The Wedding* and *Acropolis* (1904), Andrzej Wajda's film version of *Ashes and Diamonds* (1958), Jerzy Andrzejewski's novel *Miazga* (Pulp, 1979), Jerzy Kawalerowicz's *Austeria* (1983), which is based on a novel by Julian Stryjkowski, and Krzysztof Zanussi's film *Contract* (1980).

The metaphoric and multi-genre dramas of the 1990s, based on the contrast between the "old" world and the "new," should be read as a palimpsest. Their varied plots conceal an almost identical network of motifs that superbly describe a world of constant change, transition, and transformation, of endings and beginnings, as experienced by Poles during that epoch. There is the motif of a delayed or unsuccessful excursion, a dream trip into the unknown, and escape from one's former self; the motif of a forced but also awaited move to a new world; the motif of frustrating stagnation and longing for change, which either does not come or brings disappointment; the motif of a desperate attempt to reject an old identity in favour of a new, uncertain, momentary, and socially contested one; and finally, there is the motif of drawn-out old age, of prolonged decline, of life's decadence and of death, stretched out in time into a "before" and an ambiguous "after." It is through these motifs that playwrights were able to effectively express this epoch's experience of a painful and not always successful transition to a new life.

The Present: Polish "Brutalism" and Playing with Media

The most recent turn of the century brought a fundamental change to the dramatic paradigm in Poland. The writers debuting at this time spoke with their own voice, which critics quickly linked to that of the British Brutalists and German neo-Expressionists of the 1990s. The reception of works by Sarah Kane, Mark Ravenhill, and Marius von Mayenburg – at first literary, and soon also theatrical – strongly impacted the form of many Polish plays. The differences in the poetics of English and German drama did not play a significant role here. What counted was the shared aim of young artists who modelled themselves on Western writers, that aim being to radically and provocatively expose the progressive ethical and moral degradation of contemporary human beings in an increasingly materialistic world. In this regard, the Western current of new drama inspired also the authors of other post-communist nations of Central and Eastern Europe, such as the Serbian Biljana Srbljanović (*Family Stories*, 1998) and the Russian Nicolai Kolada (*Marilyn Mongol*, 1998). In Poland, it became a means of articulating disappointment with the social situation that had taken root ten years after the great systemic transformation – a situation that stunned both critics and audiences.

A wave of "brutalism" in drama swept through Poland under the sign of "Generation Porno." Such was the title of an infamous anthology of new Polish drama published in 2003 by Roman Pawłowski. In its introduction, the author characterizes the selected texts as follows: "An invasion of nihilism, which attacks all spheres of life and social groups, violence that rules mass imagination, crisis of emotional relationships and the family, disappointment with capitalism and free market economy, the triumph of consumerism as the main life model, and the fall of authority, including that of the Church – such is their content."[11] The heroes of these new plays mainly represented the young generation of Poles, rebellious teens from grey tenement blocks deprived of a real family, home, and perspectives, expressing their anger loudly and bluntly, and urging others to rebel. The anthology *Generation porno* closes with a play by Przemysław Wojcieszek titled *Zabij ich wszystkich* (Kill Them All, 2000), the opening parts of which have a tone characteristic of this current in Polish drama: "One must burn everything, right down to the ground. I drive into the centre of a city ablaze. Behind me stands a house in which I no longer wish to live."[12] Starting in the 1990s and continuing to this day, the ethical, intellectual, and agentive power of dramatic characters has constantly oscillated between the capabilities of a dangerous manipulator and the situation of a victim of social or domestic violence. For this type of hero, aggression directed at oneself and others offers the only means to push back against personal circumstances; perversely refined forms of this aggression came to dominate drama at the most recent turn of the century.

Since the first decade of the twenty-first century, new Polish plays have revealed another original tendency that can be linked to the achievements of both Polish and world drama from the beginning of the previous century. Brutal dramatic realism, near in its effect to documentary film or reportage, is giving way to much more refined literary constructions. Meta-theatrical devices multiply in these plays, and attempts are made to establish a subject external to the play's characters. In these instances, the playwright is in a sense playing on two instruments at once: he is speaking in other voices, which come from within the represented world, as well as in his own, which resonates on the outside in the form of authorial commentary and is accessible to the audience, which is invited to partake in the textual game. This type of technique has been influenced strongly by electronic media, the role of which has risen in tandem with systemic and cultural transformations in Poland. Polish contemporary drama happily parodies film and television formats, and by playing with conventions of reportage, television series, and reality shows, it calls attention to the artifice of the created situations, thus exposing the falsity of media messages. In so doing, it also aims to break the illusion of stage realism, creating the effect of a real theatrical situation through openly artificial means (e.g., by including the figure of a master of ceremonies). In this way, an unusual tension arises between the actors and the audience, so characteristic of post-dramatic theatre, the theory and practice of which has seeped into Poland from Germany.

One of the first among the debuting playwrights to use this type of technique was Wojciech Tomczyk (b. 1960) in *Wampir* (Vampire, 2002), which presents the actions of communist militia as a propagandistic performance of the authorities in front of the cameras. The play is about the investigation of the serial killings of women during the 1970s. The militia embarrasses itself by letting the perpetrator go free, after which it arrests innocent people and sentences them to death for the sole purpose of performing a public display of its effectiveness and strength. To convey the tragic absurdity of the actions of the functionaries, Tomczyk uses a convenient meta-theatrical device: he stages the entire play as a showcase performance of several actors playing out episodes of the investigation as it is being reconstructed. In the play's finale, the characters pretend they are making a film about a serial killer of women. Their actions turn out to be a repetition of a manipulated crime scene visit, during which an innocent person was forced to perform a murder. The stone used to kill a woman in the final scene of Tomczyk's play also breaks through the falsehood of the "staged" crime scene and the media forms that uphold it.

One could say that all new Polish drama is developing within a mediatized reality typical of contemporary times as well as in clear opposition to it. More and more, drama is becoming a space of sharp critique of the rules governing the "society of the spectacle." This critique concerns the mechanisms of constructing an image of the world through television, the press, the Internet, market-driven advertising, various performances of power, and the symbolic violence of official discourses. Theatre attempts to variously deconstruct these mechanisms; drama more often examines their underpinnings, directing the attention of its audiences to things that journalists and media specialists either do not want to show or *cannot* show. We thus arrive at a paradox characteristic of contemporary culture: the illusion of fictive – constructed and created – reality is broken by a dramatic fiction that brings true understanding by probing what is unofficial, taboo, traumatized, or subjected to political correctness or collective silence.

The Present: Disclosing the Hidden

Contemporary Polish drama is usually populated by characters denied high social standing – by normal and often excluded people subjected to and burdened by various pressures but not lacking in personality. Their crises, defeats, rebellions, and transformations touch the psychic and existential as well as spiritual foundations of their lives. The world view of new Polish drama is based not on a specific social theory but on the real misfortune that drags a human being down, takes away hope, strength, and freedom, pushes towards non-existence, and becomes the cause of a catastrophe but also – sometimes – elevates a person, urges that person towards rebellion, and allows him or her to notice other people and to change his or her own life. The task facing playwrights is to diagnose social conflicts that divide contemporary Poles, but also to penetrate the deepest and most painful regions of human experience. Various dramatic techniques are used to this end, which rely in large part on the dismantling of realism as conventionalized by television and film.

The tragic aspect of fate is examined in *Łucja i jej dzieci* (Łucja and Her Children, 2003) by Marek Pruchniewski (b. 1962), the most harrowing Polish play of the first decade of the new century. The author was inspired to write it by a news report about a young peasant woman accused of infanticide and stigmatized by her local community. When we meet her in the play, she is raising two children; as she gives birth to others, her mother-in-law kills them. The latter woman is jealous of her own son and does not accept her daughter-in-law, although in reality she is avenging a wrong done to her in her youth. The symmetry of the two women's misfortune in Pruchniewski's drama is terrifying. The mother-in-law lost her mother in a house fire, while the young mother, left unsupported by her immature husband, in the end sets herself on fire in the barn, gathering her invisible, murdered infants around her. Composed of short utterances that cut like a knife, Pruchniewski's play raises social questions, beginning with unemployment in small towns, from which Łucja and Jacek must move away, and ending with the model of a traditional Polish family. In this play, authoritarian mothers raise immature men who then persecute their wives, forcing them into submission or provoking them into a fight. The intensification of the misfortune experienced by the play's heroine leads further, however – namely, to the philosophical and religious question of *unde malum*. It is not by accident that the author places a choir of peasant women – reminiscent of the chorus in a Greek tragedy, but undermined by the attitude of the speakers – in front of the chapel not far from the church. In the play, the Church becomes a symbol not only of the shallow and superficial religiosity of the villagers, but also of the powerlessness of God with regard to human suffering and fear. It is from fear that hate passed down as legacy is born. Pruchniewski views this as the foundation of human relations.

An equally tragic perspective is outlined by Mariusz Bieliński (b. 1986) in *Nad* (Above, 2006). On the level of style, the play is an unexpected mix of brutal realism with philosophical and poetic meditation. It is apparent that its author carefully read the dramatic works of Karol Wojtyła, who surely, though, would have never included such shocking descriptions of murder. Bieliński's hero, Jakub, was unjustly accused of the murder of his neighbour when he was twenty years old, on the basis of his own father's testimony. The audience meets him at thirty-five years of age, after fifteen years spent in a prison cell; he is a mature, sensitive, and inquisitive man who reads a lot. Conversing with God about his fate, as a result of experienced injustice and after balancing all of the sides known to him, Jakub denies Him – who in the human imagination lives "above" – the right to exist. Jakub's poetic monologues include an authentic judgment of the world and open up a metaphysical dimension within the play, precipitating questions about divine justice and mercy, of which Jakub was brutally deprived.

Poetry also indicates here a hermeneutic space of tradition linked to the philosophical comedy of Calderón de la Barca's *Life Is a Dream*, in that Jakub is exonerated and freed after fifteen years, much like the Spanish prince, who was kept asleep in a tower and wakes up in his father's palace. Soon afterwards, however, like his prototype, he returns to the prison cell, this time for the right reason. Broken, he really does commit murder once freed, killing his own father. Revenge for wrongs done only multiplies them, and were it not for the love of Jakub's mother, the world of *Above* would turn into hell. Even so, the Poland of *Above* is not a kind country to those touched by misfortune.

Wojciech Tomczyk (b. 1960), the author of *Norymberga* (Nuremberg, 2006), looks at contemporary Poland from an entirely different perspective, yet his observations are equally shocking. The hero of his play, Stefan Kołodziej, is a colonel in the communist secret service, a person who investigated foreign agents but in practice murdered people inconvenient to the regime. This character injects history into new Polish drama, which is rare; and political history at that, which is rarer still; completely unique is that this political history is narrated by a secret service officer. One might suppose that close to two decades after the fall of the Polish Peoples' Republic, the subject of communist surveillance would be at home in Polish literature, theatre, and film. This has not been the case, however; indeed, appraisals of functionaries of the communist regime continue to provoke debate in Poland. In his play, Tomczyk touches on a truth commonly known but simultaneously subjected to social taboo – a shameful truth largely avoided by the official national media.

Nuremberg is a political and a psychological play in a realistic style that is, however, fractured from within by the attitude – seemingly absurd, but in fact deeply ironic – of the main character. Tomczyk is interested in the contemporary mind frame of a former secret service officer as well as in the consciousness of the young journalist Hanka, who visits him to talk about an entirely different colonel. She is writing an article about Ryszard Kukliński, an officer in the Polish Army who was also a spy for the West, who warned the United States about plans to introduce martial law in Poland. Instead of telling her about Kukliński, however, Kołodziej proposes that she write a denunciation of *him* for the Prosecutor's Office. Kołodziej admits his crimes and demands punishment for himself – more than that, he wishes for the trial of all communist criminals, in other words for another Nuremberg (the city where Nazi criminals were tried after the war). Although he takes responsibility even for the death of Hanka's father, the manipulated journalist lacks the courage to accuse him, and in the end even knowingly accepts the colonel's protection, from which she has already benefited for many years.

Nuremberg is a play that stirs up bitter melancholy among Polish audiences. In it, the truth about communist crimes that were never judged is articulated by one of their perpetrators. Moreover, his dramatic expiation may turn out to be another great manipulation. The play provokes existential anxiety. To what extent are our decisions independent, and in what degree are they foreseen, suggested, and planned by someone else? Are we the subject of experiences, or the object? Read metaphorically, *Nuremberg* is a play about power wielded secretly over people, about the fabrication of events and appearances that are naively taken for reality, and about deceit dressed as truth and evil parading as goodness. If any bonds exist within it, it is those between executioner and victim.

The subject of undisclosed guilt also organizes the plot of *Trash Story* (2008) by Magda Fertacz (b. 1975). The play is set in a house where a German family lived prior to the Second World War, and a Polish one afterward. The house is visited by the ghost of a murdered girl, Ursulka, who recalls the mass suicide that German women committed on hearing that the Soviet Army was approaching. The wartime misfortune of Poles, persecuted and killed by Germans, is juxtaposed with the misfortune of German wives, mothers, and daughters. The most poignant parts of the play are three intertwined monologues spoken by the heroines outside of the dramatic action; this breaks the illusion of the represented world in a manner typical of post-dramatic theatre. These monologues also build tension between their addressers and addresses. Equally provocative in the play's plot is the collation of the fate of a German SS officer who leaves the house on the river for the Eastern Front, with that of a contemporary Polish soldier who leaves his young wife to go fight in Iraq. Fertacz asks what these two figures have in common in order to expose the military ethos. On the bright side of that ethos, there is the chivalric code; on the other, there is pride, chauvinism, and aggression underpinned by fear and directed not only at opponents but also at loved ones, and especially wives. The cult of the soldier that rules the house on the river conceals a shameful truth about domestic violence and the self-destructive behaviour of family members. In this "trash story," the memory of war, filled with traumas and personified by the figure of the murdered Ursulka, penetrates the contemporary, painful experience of its young heroine, allowing hidden misdeeds to rise to the surface.

The subject of war returns also in *Między nami dobrze jest* (All Is Well between Us, 2008) by Dorota Masłowska (b. 1983). This play takes the form of an absurd skirmish, but not of individuals as much as of languages and of the stereotypical mentality of different generations. A grandmother, mother, and daughter live in a dilapidated Warsaw building neglected since the German occupation. It is a space of entirely real human degradation, as well as a symbol of the permanent catastrophe of which the heroines of this play appear to be completely unaware. This symbol rests on the grandmother's wartime "memory reel." When the war broke out, she was a young girl who went sunbathing and swimming on the Vistula with her friends. In her memory, recollection of her youth is superimposed on recollection of the historical catastrophe and totally overshadows it. The effect is tragicomic, since the thought of war arouses feelings of former happiness in the grandmother. Masłowska infuses the part of the Dejected Old Woman with a Romantic emphasis in order to immediately contrast it with the common style of her granddaughter (Little Metal Girl) – a style tinged with irony and even cynicism. Elderly idealization versus teenage vulgarization: this is how the two projections enclosed in language function in the play. They do not describe reality, but they do express the state of consciousness of the speakers, who have difficulty communicating with one another.

Reality in Masłowska's play is a disturbing metaphor of a world after a catastrophe, a world that lasts and even expands despite not actually existing; it consists only of what remained after its annihilation and now endures in sclerotic memory and increasingly grotesque language. This is made clear only in the paradoxical finale of the play, when the granddaughter – while describing wartime bombardment interchangeably with the Dejected Old Woman – finds the corpse of her own grandmother in the ruins and realizes that her life is only seeming, or virtual, like the lives of the characters in her favourite computer games. Bauman's metaphor of "liquid life," in which a key role is played by the commingled motifs of wartime ruin, contemporary waste, and pixilated computer images, effectively captures the condition of Masłowska's phantasmic figures. The heroine's room in the dilapidated house is a massive garbage pile of old packaging and advertising flyers that give the illusion of prosperity, even of life itself. What they actually signal, however, is "living-toward-the-refuse-dump," as Bauman would put it.[13] The author resorts to an excellent parody of advertising slogans that consists of adding "no" to the names of products and services in order to name the essence of contemporary make-believe life, or simply "non-life." The three female figures appear to represent the world of excluded, marginalized, and poor people, but first and foremost they represent life in non-reality, in some half-real, half-virtual cloud of packaging emptied of its content.

A clear rebellion against the barren, unreal life of consumers of rubbish propels *Cukier Stanik* (Cukier Brassiere 2008) by Zyta Rudzka (b. 1964). The play's title refers to a tailor shop where Dawid Cukier for many years made brassieres and corsets for the women of Warsaw. In the "new" Poland, the shop falls into decline as clients go to buy cheap underwear at megastores. The old tailor lives on his memories and suffers from depression. His sister, Mira, tries to help him out by going around stores and secretly taking apart the seams of Chinese bras, but this fails to save the shop. Other characters in the play undertake similarly desperate actions. Rudzka's characters are victims of Poland's transformation – they are its social "waste," people from the margins of the new economic system, undistinguished outsiders abandoned by their nearest relations. The author looks at them with compassion as well as a sense of humour, gifting each character with wit, cleverness, cheerfulness, optimism, a biting tongue, and sometimes considerable subtlety of feeling. The subjectivity if not the ontological essence of characters in Masłowska's play continually diminishes, whereas Rudzka's protagonists attain ever-fuller personhood. Rudzka intertwines the motifs of their personal lives in such a way as to make shared what was separate, find what was lost, heal what was painful, and fill with hope what was hopeless. From these isolated people, a new "recycled" family forms in front of the audience. They are linked by hope, imagination, and – play. This is all they have left. As one of the play's heroines states in the end, astutely diagnosing the present times: "God has died and so has Marx. And so we too feel unwell."[14]

The restoration of severed community bonds is a pervasive and significant theme in new Polish drama. *Popiełuszko* (2012) by Małgorzata Sikorska-Miszczuk (b. 1964) provides a good example. This play is in part a historical document, since it is about the charismatic Catholic priest killed in 1984 by the Polish communist secret service. At the same time, *Popiełuszko* can be read as a contemporary miracle play. This miracle is brought about by the martyrdom of a saint tranforming the heart of the witness to his murder. The author avoids any stylization: the connection to Middle Age drama arises only on the level of plot. Written in the convention of a post-dramatic debate that does not respect the unity of time and space, but only that of thought and imagination, *Popiełuszko* is primarily a voice of protest assigned to the character named Anti-Pole. The author uses this figure to attack social stereotypes of faith and faithlessness produced by Catholics and their anti-clerical opponents in public discourse, examining also the questionable position of the Church towards the persecuted priest (Cardinal Józef Glemp, who was then the Primate of Poland, also appears in the play and is implicated in the tragic events). Through a deeply personal dramatization of the priest's fate (in order to access his experience, Sikorska-Miszczuk even undertook a journey in the trunk of a car), the play removes the armour of social discourse from his figure, bringing it into the realm of individual experience. At the same time, contrary to tendencies in Western culture, which teaches conformism and associates the readiness to sacrifice one's life exclusively with Islamic fanaticism, she asks about the contemporary meaning of martyrdom. The issue she presents in her play sounds scandalous in the liberal culture of modernizing Poland: "Did Popiełuszko die also for me?" The Anti-Pole for a long time claims: "I have nothing to do with it!" The shared journey in the trunk of a car with a man condemned to die will completely transform him, however. The hero stops being "anti," without becoming "pro." He is free and, in his attitude, hatred gives way to compassion, aggression to gentleness, shame to pride, doubt to confidence, and weakness to strength. The bond with the murdered priest rebuilds his personhood.

A Manifold Portrait: Synthesis

When we remove the veil of mediated reality, which we ourselves create for power, money, or artificial comfort, we see the true faces of contemporary heroes: the faces of people who have been wronged, who are experiencing injustice, are subjected to social pressures, caught in the trap of history and politics, and lost in a labyrinth of memory and language. It is through their means that authors of new plays deliver a severe judgment of the world, in which familial and social bonds have deteriorated and moral codes have been forgotten. The current state of the world as diagnosed by contemporary Polish playwrights is defined primarily by anti-values: greed, materialism, the disappearance of solidarity and compassion, hatred, injustice, and aggression. While clearly delineating evil, downfall, and passivity, the playwrights confront their heroes with dramatic "either/or" situations, and they, in turn, with difficulty pass this test of morality, courage, and freedom. Many of them are overwhelmed by the weight of tragic events, injustices, complexes, and existential emptiness, in which they greatly resemble their predecessors. Looking them in the face, we can once again ask about the most important characteristics of the Polish postwar dramatic hero.

A single, synthetic view of Polish playwriting from 1945 until the present makes it apparent that the most characteristic portrait of such a hero was created by artists of the grotesque, avant-garde theatre of the 1950s and 1960s, which developed under the predicament of postwar trauma. That hero's condition and actions became a metaphor for a human being who, despite individual ambitions, loses a sense of uniqueness, separateness, and freedom. In extreme versions, he is incapable of expressing an individual "I" and of communicating with others. He becomes enslaved by absurd situations that he either creates or is forced into by other people. In the end, he loses the sense of an overarching, metaphysical order of the world and even of reality itself. In the structure of avant-garde drama, the disappearance of the basic determinants of subjectivity is signalled by the lack of the hero's name, by the loss of individual language and of influence over reality, and by the inability to act, understand, and establish one's selfhood.

An attempt to restore the hero as the conscious dramatic subject was undertaken, in turn, by realistic and psychological drama. Its postwar development paralleled that of the avant-garde current, taking on the form of a propagandistic trumpet of the Stalinist regime in the name of "socialist realism" between the years 1949 to 1956. Later on, the political situation in Poland forced authors of realistic and psychological plays to escape into the world of history –sometimes ancient or medieval – which served to disguise contemporary conflicts. A similar path, though with a different aim, was taken by authors of poetic drama, which first developed towards the end of the 1940s, and subsequently towards the end of the 1950s, after the doctrine of socialist realism ceased to be mandatory in Poland. Themes and motifs sourced in antique and biblical traditions played a key role in this dramatic practice. The renewal of tradition on the level of mythical or parabolic language led to a critical confrontation of contemporary human consciousness with a bygone image of the world and an old-time code of values.

A later current of politically allusive drama, written mainly with reference to the nineteenth-century history of Polish national uprisings, brought back the image of a man entangled in political conflicts and thus aware of principles, oriented towards the realization of his own aims, and on guard for shrinking freedoms, both personal and collective. The theme of war and the Holocaust, which re-emerged in the 1970s and 1980s, generated a portrait of a heroic protagonist on the one hand, and – on the other – of a person horrifyingly degraded in his humanity. The face of the anti-hero was not new to the manifold portrait created by Polish playwrights, having already been sketched out in the 1970s by writers exploring mechanisms of social exclusion. The passage of time that separated authors from the wartime catastrophe also provoked questions about the means of remembering and speaking about the extreme experience of the Holocaust. The dramatic hero of plays dedicated to this problem became a medium for reflecting on the past residing in memory, language, and the subconscious rather than being a fictional delegate of people touched by this historical tragedy.

In drama of the 1990s, which developed in entirely new historical and cultural circumstances, and in the most recent Polish plays, the ethical, intellectual, and agentive power of dramatic heroes constantly changes, oscillating between dangerous manipulation and (social, domestic, or political) victimization. For these heroes, aggression against themselves and others often becomes the only means of rebellion, with violence dominating the "new brutalist" drama at the most recent turn of century. Consolation and internal transformation of the hero rarely takes place in today's Polish drama, making an appearance only in exceptional plays that in various ways expand the realm of human experience. The newest drama shifts our attention from the picture-perfect reality projected by the media and towards the life of real people touched by misery. The brutalism that is part of the presentation of their fates meets with poetry, which almost literally straightens the spines of the miserable, raising them from their knees, and restoring their dignity and self-awareness. Such values are very fragile, however, and always threatened by another act of violence or manipulation. Consequently, the most recent drama does not carve a stone monument of its hero, sketching instead a portrait that is provisional and time-lapsed, or rather fractured. In looking at this manifold contemporary portrait closely, we can arrive at a deeper understanding of ourselves.

Jacek Kopciński
Institute of Literary Research of the Polish Academy of Sciences
Translated by Agnieszka Polakowska

NOTES

1 Turner, *From Ritual to Theatre*.
2 Censorship in the Polish People's Republic instituted a "list of prohibitions" not only of content, but also of people, and its existence was one reason why Polish literature after the war splintered into national and emigrant branches.
3 Głowiński, "Parodia konstruktywna."
4 Błoński, "'Ślub' jako tragedia psychoanalityczna."
5 Esslin, *The Theatre of the Absurd.*
6 Translated by Agnieszka Pokojska.
7 In a well-known 1965 production of *Tango* by director Erwin Axer at the Teatr Współczesny (Contemporary Theatre) in Warsaw, the actor playing Arthur mimicked Adolf Hitler's movements, known from German documentary films.
8 The play was an authorial adaptation of a story, included in the collection *Faces 1863* (*Twarze 1863*).
9 The title of Kulmowa's play is evocative of this in that "Szukam" is the phrase called out in the Polish version of hide-and-seek by the child designated as "it" as they start to look for those who are hidden. The counting rhyme used in the game and referenced by Kulmowa goes as follows: "Pałka zapałka dwa kije / kto się nie schowa ten kryje / kto nie schowany, ten zaklepany." In the play, however, it reads: "Pałka zapałka dwa kije / kto się nie schowa nie żyje, / a kto się schowa będzie żył, pójdzie za niego ten co krył." The sense of the rhyme's transformation reflects the realities of the Nazi persecution of Jews: the person who does not find a place to hide will die, the one that finds a hiding spot will survive, and the one who helps to hide someone will pay for it with their own life.
10 Mickiewicz, "To A Polish Mother," 137.
11 Pawłowski, *Pokolenie porno i inne niesmaczne utwory teatralne*, 5.
12 Ibid., 461.
13 Bauman, *Liquid Life*, 9–10.
14 Rudzka, *Cukier Stanik*, 2008, 48.

WORKS CITED

Bauman, Zygmunt. *Liquid Life*. Cambridge: Polity, 2005.
Błoński, Jan. "*Ślub* jako tragedia psychoanalityczna." In *Forma, śmiech i rzeczy ostateczne (Studia o Gombrowiczu)*. 113–40. Kraków: Znak, 1994.
Esslin, Martin. *The Theatre of the Absurd.* Garden City: Doubleday, 1961.
Głowiński, Michał. "Parodia konstruktywna (o *Pornografii* Gombrowicza)." In *Gry powieściowe. Szkice z teorii i historii form narracyjnych*. 279–303. Warszawa: PWN, 1973.

Mickiewicz, Adam. "To A Polish Mother." In *The Sun of Liberty. Bicentenary Anthology 1798–1998*. Polish–English Edition by Michael Mikos. 135–7. Warszawa: Wydawnictwo Energeia, 1998.

Pawłowski, Roman. *Pokolenie porno i inne niesmaczne utwory teatralne*. Kraków: Zielona Sowa, 2004.

Rudzka, Zyta. "Cukier Stanik." *Dialog* 7–8 (2008): 5–28.

Terlecki. Władysław. *Faces 1863* (*Twarze 1863*). Warszawa: Państwowy Instytut Wydawniczy, 1979.

Turner, Victor. *From Ritual to Theatre: The Human Seriousness of Play*. New York: Performing Arts Journal Publications, 1982.

POSTWAR AND POST-1989 DRAMA

Border States and Boundary Crossings (Tadeusz Różewicz)

If words are also deeds, as Ludwig Wittgenstein's aphorism reminds us, it is appropriate (and necessary) to give an account not merely of what plays are saying but also of what they are *doing* in propounding their arguments. The dramatic project of Tadeusz Różewicz (1921–2014) provides a powerful case in point. Perhaps best-known in the West for his poetry, Różewicz is also the author of seventeen full-length plays and numerous shorter pieces, many of which can still appear bafflingly elusive. In particular, the cultural work performed by these texts – by which I mean their active participation in the historically contingent processes of constituting, facilitating, or contesting the value and belief system of the writer's culture – invites if not compels closer attention.

It goes almost without saying that modern Polish drama and theatre have not been locked in a prison of moth-eaten concepts and forms. Ever since the 1820s, when Adam Mickiewicz (1798–1855) published the initial sections of *Dziady* (Forefathers' Eve, 1823–32) and Seweryn Malinowski (1777?–1850) turned this seemingly unperformable text into a path-breaking virtuoso performance, there has been no dearth of experimental initiatives by playwrights and theatre artists. In 1960, Różewicz burst onto this fast-expanding field of formal and conceptual innovation with *Kartoteka* (The Card Index). Its premiere has become the *locus classicus* of postwar Polish drama and theatre. It was the launching pad, directly or indirectly, for many dissenters from the dramatic mainstream in the 1960s; it has also served as an important influence on younger writers such as Janusz Głowacki (1938–2017), Marek Pruchniewski (b. 1962), and Michał Walczak (b. 1979).

Yet it would be misleading to suggest that Różewicz's contribution to drama has always placed him on the cutting edge or to presume that he turned to playwriting only in the late 1950s, after he had established his reputation as a poet. To gain a fuller and more complex understanding of his dramatic project, it is helpful to recognize that he has worked in mahogany as well as plain pine and that the trajectory of his writing has encompassed both poetry and drama from the 1940s onward. Prior to *The Card Index*, he had written two conventional plays in the realistic mode: *Będą się bili* (They Will Fight, 1948; excerpts published in 1950) and *Ujawnienie* (Coming Out, 1950; unpublished). *They Will Fight* addresses the attraction of Marxism as a way out of the crises of the 1930s; *Coming Out* focuses on the political and ethical dilemmas that soldiers in the anti-communist military underground, the Home Army, faced when confronted with the communist takeover of Poland in 1944–5.

After these two early plays, Różewicz began to experiment with dramatic techniques in *The Card Index* to challenge essentialist notions of subjectivity. He found inspiration and confirmation for this approach in the writings of his Western European contemporaries,

Samuel Beckett and Eugène Ionesco chief among them. After *The Card Index*, a new play by Różewicz appeared almost every year. Important works from the 1960s and 1970s include *Świadkowie albo nasza mała stabilizacja* (The Witnesses, or Our Little Stabilization, 1962), *Stara kobieta wysiaduje* (The Old Woman Broods, 1968), *Białe małżeństwo* (White Marriage, 1974), and *Do piachu* ... (Bite the Dust ..., 1979). By the early 1980s, his output had slowed down noticeably. He completed *Pułapka* (The Trap) in 1981 and wrote a new version of *The Card Index*, titled *Kartoteka rozrzucona* (The Card Index Scattered), in 1992.

Like many twentieth-century playwrights, from Eugene O'Neill and Tennessee Williams to Elfriede Jelinek, Różewicz is impatient with well-made dramatic structures and smooth dialogue. He has a poet's ear for the cacophony of human voices, and he recognizes the power of pauses and silences not just to expose linguistic fallibility but also to dislocate stable word sense meaning. His typical theme is the breakdown of a character's ritualized relationship to cultural rules and taboos, which in turn is reflected in a breakdown of language. At the same time, however, Różewicz differs from many of his contemporaries in that he does not merely abandon the black box of modern stage realism to experiment with dramatic and theatrical conventions, but consistently works at the limits of drama to re-envision concepts of the play text and performance. With the "generically conflicted" text (to borrow Paul Hamilton's translation of Friedrich Schlegel's "*Mischgedicht*") as his favoured genre, he explores how much might be done in a drama, how free it can be of its multiple constraints. His strategies range from pushing obsolescent forms to absurd extremes, through developing the meta-dramatic moment in which a play performs a critique of its own sufficiency, to inviting us to experience a radical uncertainty about what language can and cannot do. His dogged determination to push the boundaries of drama and to claim new territory for performance injects a risky, audacious, even outrageous quality into compositions such as *Akt przerywany* (The Interrupted Act, 1964) and *Przyrost naturalny* (Birth Rate, 1968). And while we do not yet have an appropriate rubric and sufficient terminology for these compositions, much of the significance of this body of work – along with its dramaturgical "bad" manners, "ungrammaticalities," and "loose ends" – lies precisely in its conceptual underpinnings.

What kind of cultural work do Różewicz's revisionary experiments perform? In the series of loosely linked mini-dramas that make up *The Card Index*, the protagonist, a Home Army veteran ironically named Hero, is haunted by those whom he remembers as well as by his different, younger selves, along with his delusions, self-deceptions, and bitter disappointments. But the Hero's splintered self remains elusive, and his search for coherence, stability, and communication with others is always thwarted by the fragmented and open-ended form of the play, which insists on being a work-in-progress. In *White Marriage,* in contrast, Różewicz uses a simulacrum of conventional family life to experiment with procedures that seem to defy dramatizable action: performative explorations of multivalent intertextuality, a postmodern feature made familiar under many guises, such as pastiche, grafting, and hybridization. A spectator may experience *White Marriage* simply as a risqué spectacle in which the characters act out their sexual fantasies, caprices, and repressions, but a closer analysis reveals that the text's riskiest game, one that is rife with ambiguity, is played out within a world of extensive literary quotations (from the works of Stanisław Korab Brzozowski, Wincenty Korab Brzozowski, Jan Lemański, Maria Komornicka, Tadeusz Miciński, Piotr Skarga, Juliusz Słowacki, Narcyza Żmichowska, and other writers), where statements refer not so much to *realia* as to the language that generates them. Viewed from this perspective, *White Marriage* pivots on an interrogation, through intertextual dynamics, of how meaning is created, how we determine what is true or false, and how we interpret and define reality.

The 1970s marked the emergence of Różewicz's sustained or "scandalous" engagement with what has been arguably the principal taboo topic in postwar European culture: the idea that a person can be both victim and victimizer. In one of his most controversial plays, *Bite the Dust* ..., he takes up this theme in the context of the Polish underground resistance during the Second World War. When the play opened in 1979, it touched off vehement protests by Home Army veterans, who were offended by the play's debunking of self-congratulatory heroic myths. In *The Trap*, based on the biographies of Franz Kafka and his sisters, Różewicz confronts spectators with yet another pitiless exploration of the nation's repressed past. Like Thomas Bernhard in *Heldenplatz* (1988), he is purposefully insensitive, even insulting to the spectators, who are determined not to see themselves as anything other than Hitler's first victims. Like Bernhard, he depends on calculated theatrical self-reflexivity to break the taboos that haunt his society's perceptions of the past. For example, he implicates the applauding audience in the ironic ending of *The Trap* in a way that anticipates the closing scene of *Heldenplatz*. In making the spectators' voyeuristic pleasure less innocent, both *The Trap* and *Heldenplatz* compel them to refocus their gaze back on themselves. In so doing, the two plays articulate an ethic of spectatorship that challenges the notion of spectatorship itself.

While some of Różewicz's plays have proved more durable (or "canonizable") than others, there are still large areas of his work as a dramatist that require close, iconoclastic, and sensitive investigation. His most challenging dramatic writings take themselves as their subject only to then struggle with themselves, as if against an undesired framework. In making visible a discontent with dramatic solutions, a discontent that nevertheless produces the drama of drama, these texts wrestle with both their angels and their demons. Framed in this way – as textual performances in their own right, rather than exclusively as materials for theatrical enactment – they hold implications not only for how we read modern and postmodern drama but also for how we conceptualize performance. In this, Różewicz becomes one of Mickiewicz's children, his metaphorical progeny, his afterlife.

Halina Filipowicz
University of Wisconsin at Madison

WORKS CONSULTED

Filipowicz, Halina. *A Laboratory of Impure Forms: The Plays of Tadeusz Różewicz.* New York: Greenwood Press, 1991.

– "What's Love Got to Do with It?: Adam Mickiewicz's *Forefathers' Eve, Part 4*, and the Art of Transgressing the Private/Public Divide." *New Perspectives on Polish Culture: Personal Encounters, Public Affairs*. Ed. Tamara Trojanowska et al. 13–31. New York: PIASA Books, 2012.

Niziołek, Grzegorz. *Ciało i słowo: Szkice o teatrze Tadeusza Różewicza.* Kraków: Wydawnictwo Literackie, 2004.

Piwińska, Marta. *Legenda romantyczna i szydercy.* Warszawa: Państwowy Instytut Wydawniczy, 1973.

Trojanowska, Tamara. "Home/lessness and the Discourse of Subjectivity in Gombrowicz's *The Marriage* and Różewicz's *The Card Index*." In *Framing the Polish Home: Postwar Cultural Constructions of Hearth, Nation, and Self.* Edited by Bożena Shallcross. 68–94. Athens: Ohio University Press, 2002.

– "Individuality and Otherness: Reading Różewicz Performing Kafka." In *Studies in Language, Literature, and Cultural Mythology in Poland: Investigating "The Other."* Edited by Elwira M. Grossman. 115–29. Lewiston: Edwin Mellen Press, 2002.

Poland – Local Universe (Sławomir Mrożek)

Throughout his youth, Sławomir Mrożek (1930–2013) had special ties to Kraków. The extraordinary atmosphere of that city – a blend of Italian Renaissance courtly culture and Viennese cabaret, of academic snobbery and *petit bourgeois* insularity – charmed the greatest of figures: Stanisław Wyspiański, the founder of modern theatre in Poland, and later Tadeusz Kantor, who showcased his neighbouring village of Wielopole to the world. Moreover, the region around Kraków constituted an exceptional empire with a shared sensibility, traces of which are still evident in cities within a day's journey of Vienna, from Zagreb to Lviv. It was in Kraków that Freud and Kafka as well as Ionesco and Cioran were born, and it was with them that Mrożek shared the salon of the Central European imagination.

In Kraków, the young provincial – a writer of cabaret sketches and a satirical cartoonist, as well as a skilful reporter – let himself get carried away by the fresh ideology of communism, and quickly made a brilliant career. This early success determined the trajectory of Mrożek's literary life; from here on, Poland would serve as the perpetual source of his inspiration, with relations between politics and the individual becoming a central theme in his writing. Kraków would leave an indelible mark on his style.

Central Europe is a shared label for countries located between Berlin and Kiev, and the Baltic and the Adriatic, that were initially supposed to fall under German cultural and economic expansion and that were later taken over by the multi-ethnic Austrio-Hungarian Empire. At the turn of the nineteenth and twentieth centuries, a community of artists and thinkers formed in these areas; that community was politically dominated yet spiritually independent and sourced in endemic traditions. In the second half of twentieth century, it found itself, in turn, under the control of the Soviet Union. This idiosyncratic historical experience led to a characteristic scepticism among Central European intellectuals towards the ideology of modernity, accompanied by a deep faith in Western values. This has found its expression in an aesthetic founded on linguistic irony and the grotesque deformation of genres, as well as in the tendency to use literary fiction as a carrier of philosophical discussions.

Mrożek's theatre debut came in 1958; he would follow it with more than forty more dramatic works. The earliest of his comedies were quickly and somewhat automatically relegated to the Theatre of the Absurd. The Absurd in Paris, however, is not the same thing as the reality of the Polish People's Republic – a reality that served as both a theme of tragicomedy and a model for it. Critics later replaced the concept of the "absurd" with that of the "grotesque," which has clear antecedents in this part of Europe and perfectly describes the feudal quotidian reality of the "progressive" communist system. On the stage, the conceptual grotesque turned out to resemble realistic sociopolitical satire; the simple, often schematic scripts worked beautifully, since their proper text was supplied by the context of everyday life that the audience brought to the theatre with them.

So, even though some of the logical paradoxes in Mrożek's plots may bring to mind the parabolic farces of Eugène Ionesco, and even though his aphoristic dialogue sometimes generates the poetic-philosophical aura we encounter in Samuel Beckett, the Polish writer is closer to the political engagement of Arthur Adamov or Fernando Arrabal, on the one hand, and to the surrealistic imagination of Roland Topor, on the other. That said, he is closest to those with whom he shares similar experiences: the Czech Václav Havel, the Hungarian István Örkény, and the Croatian Ivo Brešan. The grotesque-satirical style was popularized in Central and Eastern Europe to such a degree that it entered into the popular literature and everyday language of its inhabitants. The arguably deeper links between the author of *Tango* and the theatre of Friedrich Dürrenmatt and Max Frisch – artists interested primarily in the moral condition of the contemporary Western individual – would be noted by critics only later.

Mrożek's unique literary approach is more complicated, though. He happily ascends to a meta-literary level, enjoys overlaying the conventions of the comedy of manners with the responsibilities of a morality play, and assigns the task of conveying philosophical themes to a lowbrow farce. Also, he often plays games with literary styles and does not hide the conventionality of his characters. That said, when he writes less humorous plays, he directs his attention to his primary interest: the meeting of one human being with another.

Romantic drama is seen as both the beginning of modern Polish literature and as its most original achievement. It is dominated by a tendency to present events from the political history of a given nation as a model of human history in its spiritual and metaphysical dimensions. The nation is understood here not as an ethnic group but rather as a consciously created and cultivated cultural formation. It is precisely the universalism of the "romantic tradition" that turns it into a constant point of reference for Polish writers and theatre artists. The ritualistic and meta-theatrical form of stage performance inscribed in these poetic texts, their symbolic images and fragmentary structure, served as an inspiration for avant-garde playwrights and as a source of revolution in twentieth-century theatre.

In all of Mrożek's dramatic works, the hero, however idiosyncratic he is, functions not only as himself but also as the Human Being – the entire society, the entire nation, the entire humanity of Western civilization. He does not thereby lose his individuality; what *does* happen is that his fate and attitude take on a universal significance; put another way, they serve as an existential answer to a question contrived by political events. Also, the notion of the "political" refers here not to the Social Contract but rather to a collective Fate or a civilizational Myth. This tendency towards parable links Mrożek directly to Polish Romantic dramas, mainly those of Adam Mickiewicz (1798–1855), Juliusz Słowacki (1809–49), and, later, Stanisław Wyspiański (1869–1907). In turn, Mrożek's use of dramatic form as a vehicle for thought rather than emotion makes him a successor to the greatest of modern Polish dramatists – Stanisław Ignacy Witkiewicz (1885–1939; pen name Witkacy) and Witold Gombrowicz (1904–69).

The Metamorphoses of Dramatic Form

The deliberate complexity of Mrożek's dramas opens them up to highly diverse and often contradictory stagings. In fact, "the theatre of Mrożek" does not actually exist, since he is first and foremost a playwright. This means he does not just create "texts for the stage," but rather constructs full dramatic forms, which then metamorphosize. These transformations can be roughly conceived as circles encompassing ever grander themes and emotions.

Mrożek begins with a scene sketch built upon a single and simple idea, whether situational or story-based. *Na pełnym morzu* (Out at Sea, 1961) resorts to the motif of co-dependent castaways, who – surrounded by the elements, and after first engaging in a bitter political debate that discredits democracy – are capable only of eating one another. In *Strip-tease* (1961), an enormous hand reaches into the box stage, forcing two respectable citizens to expose themselves to each other. Moreover, it is not at all clear whether the absurd circumstances determine or merely enable this behaviour towards a fellow human being. The three monologues with a fox – *Lis filozof* (The Fox Philosopher, 1977), *Lis Aspirant* (The Fox Aspirant, 1978), and *Serenada* (The Serenade, 1977) – are all versions of the Enlightenment animal fable that has long been an allegorical genre "scene," here reworked by Mrożek for the stage. Even full-length plays such as *Policja* (The Police, 1958), *Dom na granicy* (House on the Border, 1967), *Indyk* (The Turkey, 1960), *Karol* (Charlie, 1961), and *Kynolog w rozterce* (Cynologist in a Dilemma, 1962) depend on the prolonged stretching of a "dramatic" situation that is in fact static but paradoxically convoluted nonetheless.

At times, the author gives a scene a disquieting depth, suggesting that the spectator's first impression is too facile and that some kind of "heart of darkness" is hidden within the human psyche or perhaps even somewhere beyond it. This is the case with *Zabawa* (The Party, 1962), an "arrangement" for the three voices of the Farmhands, who – frustrated by the lack of promised entertainment – respond to one another with short ripostes in the rhythm of the Polish folk dance *oberek*, and who literally – that is, word for word – escalate their reciprocal aggression.

Human nature – which seems to be Mrożek's main theme – is always presented somewhere on the continuum between strikingly clear and utterly unfathomable. At the very core of the universe we always find "our" picture of it – a cultured picture in a civilized frame, displaying members of a family dressed in their respective social uniforms. *Tango* (1964) catapulted Mrożek from a popular-in-Poland comedy writer into an international playwright; and although he would would later write pieces just as good, it is this play that has since served as his calling card. *Tango*, like many of his other comedies, uses a specific model of a family as a parable of a presently dominant social formation. In this particular parable, childrearing signifies the ethos of a ruling culture, which – being the creation of artists and philosophers – preserves the traces of a long process of gestation that we call civilization. The presence in Mrożek's plays of three signifying layers – psychological, sociological, and anthropological – renders his heroes neither "real" (for they are too schematic) nor symbolic (for they are too socially entangled); they are, however, unequivocally "literary," which is to say recognizable only through the prism of already known and here actualized character-models. The joining of linguistic pastiche with parody of the dramatic genre comes to fruition in works that arise from literary elements – *Krawiec* (The Tailor, 1977), *Garbus* (The Hunchback, 1975) and *Vazlav* (1982) – and that aim their ambition at no more and no less than a historiosophical treatise.

Emigranci (Emigrants, 1974) – a true psychomachia, intimate yet played out against a political background – is considered to be the next breakthrough in the writer's career after *Tango*. In a makeshift basement apartment in some Western metropolis meet a typically Mrożkian pair – a mendacious intellectual/political emigrant and an arrogant boor/economic emigrant. A coil of frustration and hope binds them tighter and tighter to the most sensitive parts of each other's psyches.

Clearly, Mrożek the Mocker is capable of creating characters who are human to the core. This happens in situations where two characters confront each other directly, most often in conditions of relative isolation. Such encounters constitute an entirely separate current in the author's dramatic thinking, one that is different from what we encounter in his stylized comedies. For Mrożek has an extraordinary awareness of form's dependence on its medium. His one-act plays are openly theatrical, since the trappings of a cage or a boat are a simple consequence of dealing with a black box stage. The domestic space of family dramas is ostentatiously revealed behind the fourth wall of a nineteenth-century proscenium stage, whereas political dramas are played out against the background of openly theatrical sets, displaying their stipulated nature in Brechtian fashion. While the trauma of exile and murder for hire in *Kontrakt* (Contract, 1986) could take place anywhere, it is best suited for the modern, empty stage, whereas the static, monotonous narration of *Alfa* (Alpha, 1984) clearly suggests a televised mode of realization, much like in *Portret* (The Portrait, 1987), which is constructed from short scenes. The made-for-radio *Rzeźnia* (The Slaughterhouse, 1973) turns its heroes into "musical" voices, acoustically demarcating their inner space of consciousness. Through these intimate dramas, in which the simple collision of popular clichés is replaced by an interpersonal encounter, Mrożek is clearing the path towards the mystery of the individual and perhaps even towards his own self, as happens in three film scripts: *Wyspa róż* (The Island of Roses, 1975), *Amor* (1978), and *Powrót* (The Return, 1994).

Many critics consider *Pieszo* (On Foot, 1980) to be Mrożek's most profound, perhaps even most perfected drama. Its story traces the end-of-the-war journey of a father and his teenage son though a war-torn Poland; the deeply human relationship that connects them contrasts with the schematic characters they encounter along the way. Into this epic construction the author weaves lyrical dialogues saturated with ambiguous yet highly suggestive symbolism, harmoniously balancing the two currents of his writing up until now: intimate drama, and philosophical dramaturgy. After the experiences of war, communism, emigration, and finally of a transformed Poland and Europe, the metamorphoses of Mrożek's dramatic forms generate a kind of synthesis.

In 1993, Mrożek wrote *Miłość na Krymie* (Love in the Crimea), a play constructed on simultaneously multiple registers. Its three acts represent three stages of the modern history of Russia, with each one stylistically referring to its given era's literature, and with the idea of "Russianness" itself serving as a metaphor for European history.

Characters exist seemingly in two worlds, with some of them waning, having exhausted their potential in history, and others returning under changed circumstances, untouched by time; yet all of them are concerned with the same thing – love. Types clearly drawn from literature thus speak as if they were real people who are conscious of their own artificiality, and on top of it all they repeatedly recite Shakespeare – in line with its author's recommendation – "as naturally as possible."

In this way the playwright retrieves the historical styles of drama, for they are imprinted with traces of History, meaning the styles in which people organized their dramas of human relations. Is it not then the old European Cogito that acts as Mrożek's hero? When it is alone with itself, it turns into pure Intellect and falls prey to aporias and paradoxes that inevitably reveal their ridiculous impotence; when it meets the Other, however, it transpires that it has always been a Conscience, at which point all jokes end. For metaphors, if they are taken seriously (and this is the tendency among Poles), usher forth from the theatre and towards the edge of a precipice – "between nothingness and infinity" – someone's singular life.

Artur Grabowski
Jagiellonian University, Kraków
Translated by Agnieszka Polakowska

Revolt of Memory (Tadeusz Kantor)

Tadeusz Kantor (1915–90) was one of Poland's foremost theatre artists of the second half of the twentieth century, whose work left a deep imprint on theatre and performance arts abroad. Jarosław Suchan, curator of the exhibition "Tadeusz Kantor. Niemożliwe" (Tadeusz Kantor – Impossible), states that "Kantor is to Polish art what Joseph Beuys was to German art, what Andy Warhol was to American art. He created a unique strain of theatre, was an active participant in the revolutions of the neo-avant-garde, a highly original theoretician, an innovator strongly grounded in tradition, an anti-painterly painter, a happener-heretic, and an ironic conceptualist. These are only a few of his many incarnations."[1]

Kantor studied at the Academy of Fine Arts in Kraków, where his work as a painter and stage designer evolved in constant dialogue with the dominant avant-garde movements such as constructivism, Dadaism, and Surrealism in the 1920s and 1930s. He survived the Second World War working as a decoration painter in the Słowacki Theatre in Kraków, while also engaging in clandestine theatre activities and staging Juliusz Słowacki's *Balladyna* (1839) and Stanisław Wyspiański's *Powrót Odysa* (The Return of Odysseus, 1907), the latter of which he would revisit towards the end of his career. In the postwar decades, when socialist realism flourished as the official aesthetic in Poland and other countries of Eastern Europe, Kantor still managed to take part in major artistic currents of the Western avant-garde by conducting his own "provocations" and experiments, all the while incessantly questioning the very idea of representation. Together with his Cricot 2 theatre company, founded in 1955, he presented many radical stagings of Stanisław Ignacy Witkiewicz (1885–1939, pen name Witkacy), which brought these works critical acclaim at theatre festivals in France, Italy, and Britain in the late 1960s and early 1970s.

In the mid-1970s, Kantor shifted his focus to a cycle of performances he titled the "Teatr Śmierci" (Theatre of Death, 1975–90). This marked the beginning of his sustained, almost obsessive engagement with historical trauma, memory, and forgetting. For Kantor, the stakes of memory were enormous. His memory-theatre served as a platform for interventionist cultural and political engagement, a form of repair and redress. Having experienced the Second World War and the Holocaust, he sought to represent and commemorate those staggering losses in the hope of a better future. Aware that the public appearance of collective memories in communist Poland was highly mediated by its power structures, Kantor constantly challenged the frames of intelligibility in his performances in ways that exposed and critiqued dominant representations of the Second World War in communist Eastern Europe. In so doing, he allowed the silenced, suppressed, and disavowed experiences of his audiences to emerge and become subject to the processes of grief and mourning, thus renewing his audiences' affective engagement with the dark side of Europe's twentieth-century history.

MOURNING AND MELANCHOLIA

In "Mourning and Melancholia" (1917 [1957]), Freud seeks to explain the distinction between a normal and a pathological affect occasioned by the death of an object of love. He argues that a successful work of mourning constitutes an articulated reaction to loss: the loss is recognized by the subject and separated from the body through the recognition of what has been lost. In contrast to mourning, melancholia is characterized by the inability of the subject to separate itself from the object (that is, by the ego's identification with the lost object) and an essential misrecognition of what has been lost. And while in both mourning and melancholia the subject dwells on the past, the melancholic appears unable to leave the past behind – grief does not end.

– Freud, "Mourning and Melancholia," 243–58

Umarła klasa (The Dead Class, 1975) opened at the Krzysztofory Gallery in Kraków on 15 November 1975. It was acclaimed by many critics as Kantor's masterpiece, bringing him and Cricot 2 international recognition and fame. In *The Dead Class*, working with closely intertwined personal memories and intertextual references to the works of Polish modernists (Bruno Schultz, Witold Gombrowicz, and Witkacy), Kantor reflects on the nature of time and human memory. As in his previous stagings of Witkacy's plays, he does away with the primacy of the text and the narrative character of theatrical representation. Instead, he emphasizes visual, oral, auditory, and other sensory elements and questions any firm boundaries between theatre and performance art. *The Dead Class* and the rest of his "Theatre of Death" productions thus constitute a distinct kind of post-dramatic theatre, now widely recognizable for its potent visual images, masterful theatricality, and strong emotional grip on audiences. According to the central theorist of this genre, Hans Thies Lehmann, Kantor can be seen as one of its main protagonists – along with Robert Wilson, Heiner Müller, and a handful of other artists and theatre collectives who came to prominence in the late 1980s and 1990s, such as the Wooster Group, Jan Fabre, Jan Lauwers, Reza Abdoh, and the Societas Raffaello Sanzio.

Post-dramatic theatre is marked by "a preference for the visual image over the written word, collage and montage instead of linear structure, a reliance on metonymic rather than metaphoric representation, and a redefinition of the performer's function in terms of being and materiality rather than appearance and mimetic imitation."[2] The observation about a performer's function in post-dramatic theatre rings particularly true in *The Dead Class*. As in the more explicitly autobiographical pieces that would follow, Kantor was physically present on stage in *The Dead Class*, simultaneously playing the role of a silent witness and a re-creator of represented events: the bygone school days, the vanished world of prewar Poland, and the catastrophic events that marked the twentieth century.

TRAUMA

In *Beyond the Pleasure Principle* (1920), Freud defines trauma as a breach in the protective shield of consciousness. According to Freud, the shock of something unexpected that suddenly attacks the subject from outside tears this filter; the subject is unable to master the excess of affect produced by the impact – and flooding results.

– Freud, *Beyond the Pleasure Principle*, 29–30

As Cathy Caruth, a prominent trauma theorist, elaborates, traumatic memory is a memory of an event that "is not assimilated or experienced fully at the time, but only belatedly, in its repeated possession of the one who experiences it."

– Caruth, "Introduction," 4–5

Wielopole, Wielopole, the second production from the "Theatre of Death," was developed in Florence in 1980 and got its title after the small town near Kraków where Kantor was born. "In the square," remembers Kantor, "stood a chapel with some sort of saint for the Catholic faithful. In the same square was a well near which Jewish weddings were held, primarily when the moon was full. On one side stood the church, the rectory, and the Catholic cemetery, and on the other the synagogue, the narrow Jewish lanes, and another cemetery, somewhat different. Both sides existed in a harmonious symbiosis."[3] As he relates on another occasion, however: "During the last war half of the town was destroyed, many houses were burnt down and the Jews deported."[4] *Wielopole, Wielopole* is thus clearly a performance of mourning understood in a Freudian sense, as a "working through" of the trauma of loss by remembering, repeating, and re-experiencing that loss. Yet this does not warrant a cathartic interpretation of the performance. If longing for a lost past is the performance's overt theme, then the struggle against forgetting and repression is its underlying impetus. That impetus is inscribed on the performance most powerfully in the scene of the death of the rabbi, whose character signifies the Jewish people and their experience during the Second World War. The scene starts when the rabbi joins the funeral cortege of his deceased friend, a Catholic priest, and starts singing a popular Jewish song: "Sha Sha Sha de Rebe / Gite / Sha Sha Sha bam reben / Stite / Der shames bad y tur / In di Rebezn oy is duisa / Oy Oy Oy / Oy Oy Oy."[5] Shot by a group of soldiers, the rabbi collapses to the ground. The dead priest helps him stand up, however, and the rabbi takes up his song again. The soldiers fire from their machine-guns again, and once again he falls to the ground; this action is repeated a number of times before the rabbi leaves the stage.

The structure of repetition in this scene turns the death of the rabbi into the central and most obsessive image of remembering in Kantor's *Wielopole, Wielopole*. This self-reflective exhortation to tell and repeat, to hold on to the past and on to death by "calling" it forth through cultural practice, is both a call to active intervention in the discourse of national remembrance and a mark of Kantor's aesthetics. In replaying this violent death on stage, Kantor is not merely returning to a traumatic moment. This repetitive and obsessive procedure is also a way of inducing anxiety, of forcing the spectator to re-experience the (traumatic) explosion of an irreparable past in a way that impedes emotional indifference. These insistent repetitions suggest that, if "rehearsed" and replayed often enough, the death of the rabbi – this "memory" that is so integral to the culture in which it is only diffusively "present" – could also become part of a collective trauma to be remembered and mourned.

Calling attention to the way that Kantor implicates the spectators in the production of images in *Wielopole, Wielopole* highlights the complex and still contested place of the Holocaust in Polish and European history and culture. Kantor's *Wielopole, Wileopole* and the rest of his memory-theatre can be seen as extending a moral hospitality to Poland's Jews who died in the war, and whose losses – in Poland as in the rest of Europe – were for decades folded into national narratives of mourning and loss without acknowledgment of the uniqueness of Jewish wartime experiences. In commemorating Polish-Jewish losses as a national trauma, Kantor's theatre can also be seen as a painful and also radical rethinking and reformulation of the notion of boundaries as means of regulating the exchange between the inside and the outside – between the (indigenous) self and the (foreign) other. In place of these boundaries, Kantor puts forward a vision of Polish identity that incorporates the historical reality of Poland as a set of multicutural communities.

Niech sczezną artyści (Let the Artists Die, 1985), the next performance from Kantor's theatre of personal confessions, also aimed to rescue the unnamed and still unaccounted-for from obscurity and oblivion and to thereby counter the disavowals that were constitutive of the public discourse of national remembrance in Poland until the late 1980s. The performance evokes the Second World War massacre of Polish prisoners of war in the Katyn Forest, which was carried out by the Soviet NKVD (People's Commissariat for Internal Affairs) in the spring of 1940. Most Poles never accepted the Soviets' denial that they had carried out the massacre, yet the Soviet authorities continued to insist on the Third Reich's responsibility for the crime until 1990. For Kantor, the need to mourn the Katyn massacre was heightened by the authorities' refusal to allow Poles to do so after the war; the communist regime suppressed the Katyn massacre for half a century. By placing this event on the stage in *Let the Artist Die*, Kantor allowed his audiences to encounter what had been "forgotten" – marginalized, excluded, even rendered unthinkable.

If the destructiveness of both world wars had a compelling gravity that attracted and challenged Kantor, then the personal aspect of Kantor's obsession with this thematic is best revealed in the penultimate piece from "The Theatre of Death," *Nigdy tu już nie powrócę* (I Shall Never Return, 1988). This is perhaps Kantor's most intimate piece, for it broaches the death of his father, a secular Jew who was killed by the Nazis at the beginning of the Second World War. A variety of emotional states inflects this piece, from melancholy, grief, alienation, and trauma to self-irony and self-mockery. Just as in other performances from Kantor's "late style" cycle, however, mourning – considered here as a practice of counter-memory that attends to that which has been negated, deemed unrepresentable on account of its traumatic nature, or silenced – remains central. *I Shall Never Return* was the last performance that featured Kantor live on stage; he passed away in December 1990 while working on *Dziś są moje urodziny* (Today Is My Birthday), which was performed posthumously.

Kantor will be remembered as one of the most inventive, articulate, and influential of twentieth-century European theatre makers. He sought theatrical forms for communicating experienced and inherited traumas of the Holocaust and other modern genocides. His theatrical praxis testifies to his unrelenting effort to invent a new theatrical language of memory capable of releasing the past from personal and collective oblivion. In this sense, it provides an example of a work of mourning in which the ghosts and phantoms of culture are to be entertained rather than exorcised. His performances reframe the question of mourning in ethical terms, functioning as resonant texts, a complicated web of temporality in which memory is not only taken in, introjected, or accrued, but also reworked, projected, and given back to a collective subject. In Kantor's work, the past is allowed to find a "place" within the identity of the remembering community. Informed by his commitment to witnessing and by the struggle for justice in the present, his legacy is also an attempt to do justice to history, to make sure that the atrocities of both the world wars will not recur, and thereby to create an opening onto a different future.

Milija Gluhovic
University of Warwick

NOTES

1 Quoted in Kitowska-Łysiak, "Tadeusz Kantor (1915–1990)," n.p.
2 Balme, "Editorial," 1–3.
3 Kantor, quoted in Pleśniarowicz, *The Dead Memory Machine*, 11.
4 Kantor quoted in Thibaudat, "Kantor Will Never Return to Wielopole," 183–4.
5 Kantor, *Wielopole/Wielopole*, 86.

WORKS CITED

Balme, Christopher. "Editorial." *Theatre Research International* 29, 1 (2004): 1–3.
Caruth, Cathy. "Introduction." *Trauma: Explorations in Memory*. 3–12, 151–7. Edited by Cathy Caruth. Baltimore: Johns Hopkins University Press, 1995.
Freud, Sigmund. *Beyond the Pleasure Principle* [1920]. In *The Standard Edition of the Complete Psychological Works of Sigmund Freud*, vol. 18. Translated and edited by James Strachey. London: Hogarth Press, 1953–74.
– "Mourning and Melancholia" [1917]. In *The Standard Edition of the Complete Psychological Works of Sigmund Freud.*, vol. 14. Translated and edited by James Strachey. 243–58. London: Hogarth Press. 1957.
Kantor, Tadeusz. *Wielopole/Wielopole: An Exercise in Theatre*. Translated by Mariusz Tchorek and G.M. Hyde. London: Marion Boyars, 1990.
Kitowska-Łysiak, Małgorzata. "Tadeusz Kantor (1915–1990)." In *All About Jewish Theatre*. 2002. http://archive.li/TUquI.
Pleśniarowicz, Krzysztof. *The Dead Memory Machine: Tadeusz Kantor's Theatre of Death.* Translated by William Brand. Aberystwyth: Black Mountain Press, 2004.
Thibaudat, Jean-Pierre. "Kantor Will Never Return to Wielopole." *Cricot 2 Theatre – Information Guide, 1989–1990*. Kraków: Cricoteca, 1990.

The Dramaturgy of Jerzy Grotowski

"Where do you come from, and where are you going?"

Book of Judith 10:12

Jerzy Grotowski (1933–99) was the first Polish theatre director to command significant international attention. In 1958 he co-founded the Teatr Laboratorium (Laboratory Theatre) with critic and dramaturge Ludwik Flaszen (b. 1930), and that company provided the collaborative platform for his theatrical career for over two decades. Working initially in relative obscurity in the provincial Silesian city of Opole, Laboratory Theatre first attracted attention abroad with its radical 1962 adaptation of *Akropolis* (1904), a rarely performed Symbolist play by the early-twentieth-century playwright and theatre reformer Stanisław Wyspiański (1869–1907). The international prestige of the Laboratory grew steadily with each subsequent production, culminating in *Apocalypsis Cum Figuris* (1969), an original piece freely inspired by various texts. Over time, the company became highly influential around the world, and had a signficant impact in Latin America, South Africa, and Japan, in addition to Western Europe and North America. In North America and Great Britain, Grotowski's theatre was by far the best-known and most influential export of twentieth-century Polish theatre up to that point in time. This success was based on the company's critically acclaimed tours, the appearance of Grotowski's collected writing in English (*Towards a Poor Theatre,* 1968), and the 1971 television broadcast of *Akropolis* in Britain and the United States. Of equal importance was the steadfast support of leading figures in American and British theatre such as Ellen Stewart, Joseph Chaikin, André Gregory, Richard Schechner, and Peter Brook.

Grotowski's work with the Laboratory Theatre before his quiet political defection from Poland to the United States in 1982 was the period of his greatest international fame. To refer to the phenomenon of "Grotowski" in this period is convenient shorthand for what was in fact the collaborative work of the director with dramaturge Ludwik Flaszen, the director's Italian protegé Eugenio Barba, the designers Jerzy Gurawski and Józef Szajna, and actors such as Ryszard Cieślak and Rena Mirecka.

Ludwik Flaszen, a well-established theatre critic in postwar Poland, was Grotowski's full partner in the founding and the artistic and intellectual leadership of the theatre from start to finish. In fact it was Flaszen who first proposed a shared theatrical venture to Grotowski. The character, history, and ultimate significance of Flaszen's relationship with Grotowski can be compared to that of the Russian critic and dramaturge Vladimir Nemirovich-Danchenko (1858–1943) with Konstantin Stanislavsky in the earlier founding and leadership of the Moscow Art Theatre.

The initial sensation created by *Akropolis* was the result of several factors: the unprecedented physical and vocal virtuosity of the actors, the production's specific embodiment of the principles of "poor theatre" (here as much a reflection of Szajna's aesthetics as of Grotowski's), and its Artaudian treatment of both the Holocaust and Wyspiański's lyrical play. The virtuosic performance of the actors combined with the production's specific visual, musical, and choreographic evocation of the Holocaust captured the attention of international critics and audiences alike.

The importance of *Towards a Poor Theatre* for the sustained international presence of Grotowski cannot be overstated. Decades after its first appearance in a Danish translation (the book was originally assembled by Eugenio Barba, who facilitated its publication in Denmark), the text today stands as a contemporary classic of performance theory read alongside the writings of Stanislavsky, Artaud, Brecht, Chaikin, Lecoq, and others. Barba's own writing and artistic work with his company the Odin Teatret in Denmark since 1964 was the earliest application of Grotowski's principles abroad, and today Barba's work stands as its own distinct contribution to contemporary theatre and performance studies. The experience of actual live performances by the Laboratory Theatre was always limited to a minuscule audience due to Grotowski's insistence on maintaining the intimacy of his staging on tour. As a result, the reputation and influence of Grotowski over time, particularly in the English-speaking world, has largely depended upon *Towards a Poor Theatre* and the television version of *Akropolis* (which included a detailed introduction by Peter Brook). Ironically, the book did not exist in a Polish edition until decades after its wide circulation abroad, and Grotowski for years disowned the video version of *Akropolis*.

In retrospect, Grotowski's work can be broadly divided into two major phases. First was his period of theatrical work with the Laboratory Theatre (1958–82). Through the early 1970s, this period was defined by a complex and defiant polemical approach to Polish culture and theatrical tradition. It is best exemplified by the practice of the "dramaturgical violation" of Romantic and Neo-Romantic classics such as Adam Mickiewicz's *Dziady* (Forefathers' Eve), Juliusz Słowacki's *Kordian*, and Wyspiański's *Akropolis*, alongside spare and startling interpretations of more familiar world classics: Shakespeare's *Hamlet*, Marlowe's *Doctor Faustus*, and Calderón's *The Constant Prince*. The complexity of Grotowski's critical engagement with Polish culture is revealed by his simultaneous acknowledgment of both the Romantic tradition of Mickiewicz and Słowacki, and the later work of the Polish interwar director/actor Juliusz Osterwa (1885–1947) and his company Reduta, as deep and integral inspirations for the Laboratory Theatre's ongoing work. Reduta's character as an *auteur* ensemble rigorously applying Stanislavsky's methods to the Polish Romantic repertoire provided Grotowski's link to both Polish and Russian sources. In collaboration with Flaszen and others, Grotowski combined a radical questioning of conventional theatrical practices in acting and scenography with a dramaturgy that interrogated metaphysical questions alongside specifically Polish ones. In this phase, Grotowski and the artistic team of the Laboratory Theatre functioned as engaged public intellectuals, expressing bitter and corrosive cultural critique through highly distilled theatrical analogy and metaphor.

GROTOWSKI, OSTERWA, AND REDUTA

A member of Poland's Communist Party, Jerzy Grotowski nevertheless strongly identified with the work of Juliusz Osterwa (1885–1947), a progressive Catholic and a radical innovator of the interwar Polish stage, and his company Teatr Reduta (Redoubt Theatre). Notwithstanding the suppression of the legacy of Reduta in communist Poland, Grotowski clearly identified with Osterwa's goals of rigorous actor training, communal living, and an ethos that combined social consciousness with spirituality. Osterwa's five stagings of Calderón/Słowacki's *The Constant Prince* anticipated Grotowski's renowned postwar production. Among Grotowski's earliest and most loyal supporters were Tadeusz and Irena Byrska of the original Reduta company, who were fervent Catholics, leftists, and anti-communist dissidents.

As Ludwik Flaszen's published writings and memoirs reveal, the then-banned work of the novelist and playwright Witold Gombrowicz (1904–69) was a significant influence for both the Laboratory Theatre founders.[1] This revelation unexpectedly connects two of the most powerful streams flowing between Polish theatre and the world at the time: Grotowski as communist Poland's most prestigious theatrical export, and Gombrowicz as one of the country's most visible émigré literary figures, whose work was widely published and performed abroad, but still suppressed in Poland of the 1960s. Gombrowicz's caustic critique of Polish culture in his *Dziennik* (Diary) was akin to the more focused tactical strikes of the Laboratory Theatre in their productions of national classics. Grotowski was a supreme man of the theatre who sought an escape from theatre after 1970; Gombrowicz, in contrast, evaded all contact with the working world of theatre, yet his writing and sensibility were irresistibly attractive to actors, directors, and opera composers. Perhaps the most important contrast between Grotowski and Gombrowicz as artists was that the former both benefited from and struggled against postwar Poland from within, while the latter paid for his artistic freedom and status of a dissident intellectual with displacement and dispossession. The intensity of Grotowski's off-stage intellectual and artistic engagement with Gombrowicz was thoroughly belied at the time by his public persona of a party loyalist. Flaszen's book suggests, however, that Gombrowicz's impact on the off-stage work of the Laboratory approached that of the Polish Romantics or Juliusz Osterwa.

While Grotowski publicly underplayed the significance of his own status as a Communist Party member, his work was only possible thanks to the privileges that came with this sustained association. The Laboratory's rigorous physical and vocal training depended on the comprehensive theatrical subsidies provided by Poland's communist establishment. At the same time, the dramaturgy of the Laboratory Theatre tested the assumptions and boundaries of Marxist philosophy, not to mention the official cultural theory and practice of Soviet-dominated Poland at the time. Indeed, Grotowski's international success generated considerable ambivalence among the country's communist cultural leadership. Despite the company's success abroad, Grotowski's theatre almost closed when it lost its original subsidized home in Opole. Only a last-minute invitation from the city of Wrocław resolved the crisis, and the company moved there instead. Like Brecht had done earlier in the German Democratic Republic, Grotowski had to walk a fine line between his artistic agenda and the performance of his roles as both an engaged public intellectual and an officially sanctioned and subsidized artist.

The general scepticism among Poland's theatrical establishment regarding Grotowski's work has long been reflected in his conspicuous absence from Poland's drama schools, both during and after communist rule. The harshness of Grotowski's critiques of postwar Polish theatre certainly earned him no love in many quarters. Moreover, his radical revisionist approach to Stanislavsky's training and practice was impossible to reconcile with its highly esteemed and officially sanctioned version that was the basis of drama school curriculums in Sovietized Poland. Grotowski and the Laboratory's *auteur* model of direction and company organization, while in step with experimental companies emerging around the world at the time, was incompatible with the country's extensive system of professional resident repertory companies. In the supremely partisan world of Polish theatre, resentment of Grotowski's unprecedented international success even while he maintained his base in the modest setting of Opole was surely also cause for suspicion. Finally, his quiet defection to the West in 1982, during the martial law period, was perceived as a betrayal by large segments of the Polish theatre community, particularly those involved with the highly visible actors' boycott of official theatre, television, and film production in protest against the martial law regime .

Grotowski's self-proclaimed departure from theatre preceded his departure from Poland, with the company spending the 1970s and early 1980s in pursuit of work variously described as "active culture" or "paratheatre." This phase of work was abandoned by Grotowski once abroad, yet hugely attractive to international participants, especially Americans such as the critic Margaret Croyden and the director André Gregory. In Poland, it found an important continuation in the early work of Włodzimierz Staniewski (b. 1950), Grotowski's former assistant, who founded and still directs the Ośrodek Praktyk Teatralnych "Gardzienice" (Centre for Theatre Practice "Gardzienice"). Grotowski's influence is also noticeable in the openly oppositional political work of the Teatr Ósmego Dnia (Theatre of the Eighth Day) in Poznań.

The second phase of Grotowski's career consisted of his work in exile, largely in the United States and Italy. Significant honours came to Grotowski abroad, including the realization of his "Dramat Obiektywny" (Objective Drama) project through the founding of an artistic and research program under that name at the School of Fine Arts at University of California at Irvine. He was also named to the faculty of the *Collège de France* in Paris and received Italian government subsidies for his Workcenter in Pontedera, which has continued to operate after his death under the direction of the American Thomas Richards. Here "Grotowski" as an individual artist, separated from his collaborators at the now defunct Laboratory Theatre, truly became his own brand for the first time.

GROTOWSKI, MICKIEWICZ, AND THE *COLLÈGE DE FRANCE*

Jerzy Grotowski became the first theatre director/theorist to be named to the *Collège de France* in 1997. Grotowski was also the first Pole to be so recognized since Adam Mickiewicz (1798–1855) became the college's first chair in Slavic literature and gained both popular fame and political notoriety for his lectures there in the 1840s. Mickiewicz's unorthodox mixture of religious mysticism and progressive politics made both the French government and the Roman Catholic Church uncomfortable and he was eventually removed from the position. Grotowski invoked Mickiewicz and the Polish Romantics as a defining influence throughout his career.

According to the conceptualizations of Richard Schechner and his followers in the field of performance studies, Grotowski's work in emigration was defined as "performance" rather than "theatre." Grotowski's own wide-ranging anthropological fieldwork in the 1970s and 1980s related to performance (often traditional ritual performance practice) placed him conceptually in the vanguard of performance studies as defined by Schechner and his disciples, and they in turn laid a firm claim to the critical discourse on his work in emigration. Grotowski initially described his comparative research around the world as "Teatr Źródeł" (The Theatre of Sources) and later as a search for "Objective Drama."

In Grotowski's "post-theatrical" work abroad there was a marked distancing from his Polish identity, his past Polish collaborators, Polish contemporary political reality, and the Polish roots of his artistic theory and practice. The heady and volatile dramaturgical mix of the erotic, the metaphysical, and the political, both explicit and tacit, in the work of the Laboratory Theatre was absent from Grotowski's work after 1982, though the shift in this direction was already clear following the success of *Apocalypsis Cum Figuris* in the mid-1970s. Without this mix, his work became increasingly private, intimate, and meditative.

Grotowski's emigration marked the end of his life as an engaged public intellectual both in Poland and abroad. His retreat as a public intellectual arguably required a simultaneous de-emphasis on the specifically Polish aspects of his work. His disciples and collaborators were no longer Poles, and they demonstrated little interest in engaging with Grotowski's Polish history and context, political or otherwise, as well as a limited capacity to do so. One must assume this is how Grotowski wanted it.

Abroad, Grotowski devoted himself to leading intensive physical and vocal workshops for actors and other performers. As part of his Objective Drama program at the University of California at Irvine he redefined his laboratory explorations one last time as "work on physical actions." This marked Grotowski's return to Meyerhold and the late work of Stanislavsky and to questions relevant to the physically based training of actors and performers ("working from the outside in"), if not to work directly related to rehearsing dramas for public performance. Grotowski's emphatic re-embrace of Stanislavsky in his late work in emigration (with Thomas Richards as the designated heir to his work) suggests an attempt to repeat the history of the successful earlier transplanting of Stanislavsky's training system and practice to the American theatre that began in earnest in the 1920s and 1930s. Starting in Irvine, and later in Pontedera, Grotowski's American and international disciples ultimately pursued an exploration of body and voice increasingly informed by eclectic performance practices from around the world. As an émigré artist, Grotowski became a private citizen and a master acting teacher with an experimental pedagogy, whose theatre research and practice is perhaps best encapsulated by the idea of a *laboratory studio*. In the end, Grotowski's performance research did not relate to any one existing theatre practice; it was a sustained quest with no known destination. In this way the work resembled a meditative discipline. Was this a failure of vision or an ultimate act of faith?

What united the various phases of Grotowski's work was ultimately his deep commitment to an integrity of process in the interpersonal arenas of training, workshops, rehearsal, and performance. The post-theatrical phases of Grotowski's work and his emigration amounted to a sustained search for a new destination, a search as much existential or spiritual as artistic. It was as a spiritual seeker that Grotowski ultimately parted ways with Marxist materialism and communist Poland. This was also how he proved himself possibly the most important late-twentieth-century heir to the spirit of Polish Romantics. But Grotowski's Polish voice proved inaudible in emigration, more elusive than the songs of the indigenous peoples he sought out and collected. The biblical question "Where are you going?" ultimately hovered unanswered over this period of his career. It is also this question that continues to confront Grotowski's disciples both in Poland and abroad.

Allen J. Kuharski
Swarthmore College

NOTE

1 See Flaszen, *Grotowski & Company*.

WORKS CONSULTED

Burzyński, Taduesz, and Zbigniew Osiński. *Grotowski's Laboratory*. Translated by Bolesław Taborski. Warszawa: Interpress, 1979.

Flaszen, Ludwik. *Grotowski & Company*. Translated by Andrzej Wojtasik and Paul Allain. Edited by Paul Allain. Hostebro–Malta–Wrocław: Icarus, 2010.

Grotowski, Jerzy. *Towards a Poor Theatre*. New York: Touchstone/Simon and Schuster, 1968.

Kowalska, Bożena, ed. *Józef Szajna i jego świat*. Warszawa: Wydawnictwo Hotel Sztuki/Galeria Sztuki Współczesnej Zachęta, 2000.

Kuharski, Allen. "Jerzy Grotowski's First Lecture at the Collège de France." *Slavic and East European Performance* 17, no. 2 (1997): 16–20.

– "Pierwszy wykład Jerzego Grotowskiego w Collège de France." Translated by Grzegorz Janiak. *Pamiętnik Teatralny* 1, no. 4 (2000): 370–3.

Richards, Thomas. *At Work With Grotowski on Physical Actions*. London: Routledge, 1995.

Wolford, Lisa. *Grotowski's Objective Drama Research*. Jackson: University Press of Mississippi, 1996.

Wolford, Lisa, and Richard Schechner, eds. *The Grotowski Sourcebook*. London: Routledge, 1997.

The Polish Essay: Between Realism and Nominalism

It is still much better known what [the essay] isn't than what it is.

Czesław Miłosz[1]

The Missing Link

In 1947, Kazimierz Wyka (1910–75), by that time the editor-in-chief of *Twórczość* (Creativity), one of the most prestigious monthly literary magazines in postwar Poland, published a few remarks titled "Porozmawiajmy o essayu" (Let's Talk About the Essay).[2] In it he defended the essay form against recent accusations made by Zygmunt Kałużyński, a second-rate but influential communist critic, that the essay, as practised in interwar Poland, was a formless, pointless, bourgeois, and irresponsible genre full of "cultured garrulousness."

Wyka had not set an easy task for himself. He recognized, as did other critics,[3] that "prior to 1918, there was nobody on the banks of the Vistula River to use this form." Regarding the interwar period (1918–39), he could list only four genuine Polish essay writers: Tadeusz Boy-Żeleński (1874–1941), Jan Parandowski (1895–1978), Jerzy Stempowski (1893–1969), and Bolesław Miciński (1911–43). Because of this scarcity, Wyka (himself a great essayist-to-be) warned the reckless critic he was addressing in "Let's Talk About the Essay" not to cut down a tree that is rarer in the Polish landscape than the English yew or the Swiss pine. He humorously proposed the establishment of a National Reserve for Extinct Literary Species in Polish Culture, in which the essay would hold pride of place.

Wyka was right. Before its popularity skyrocketed in the late 1950s,[4] the essay was hardly a privileged genre among Polish writers and reflections on it were pretty uncommon.[5] In 1939, after attending a PEN Club meeting in Warsaw at which the literary connoisseur and translator Stefan Napierski (1899–1940) diagnosed the death of the essay, Tadeusz Breza (1905–70) wrote a short article titled "Rozważania o essayu" (Remarks on the Essay) to defend the supposedly extinct genre. In it he points out that the peculiarity of the essay lies in the fact that its author peers at the world through "different lenses, often through altogether diaphanous fabrics," which allows him "to see common things and commonly known truths as unexpected and new."[6] These optical metaphors are well chosen, for in emphasizing the mediating character of the essay, Breza is trying to undermine one of the main premises of the Arnoldian model of criticism, the primary point of reference for many modern essayists.

In defining essay writing as "looking at art through the optics of life," Breza turns away from Matthew Arnold's "seeing things as they are,"[7] embracing instead Walter Pater's ideal of criticism as expressed in his preface to *The Renaissance* – namely, it is the act of figuring out "what effect does it [the object] really produce on me"[8] and how the perception of things changes their substance. In other words, the essay as defined by Breza is not an impersonal study conducted from a disinterested distance, but a biased examination of things caused by striking a distinctly personal chord.[9] This highly personal, impressionistic take on the essay remains, in Poland in particular, a basic feature of the genre. An excess of personal impressionism can, however, have an adverse effect on the form. This approach, which allows writers to withdraw from the public space into a world of private perceptions and would be very tempting in a country tormented by history, did not dominate the cultural landscape of Polish essay writing in the twentieth century.

> Rober Musil suggests that the essay is a mediatory form between two models of exposition: the expression of personal feelings and the search for impersonal truths: "The underlying problem presented itself to Ulrich not at all intuitively but quite soberly, in the following form: A man who wants the truth becomes a scholar; a man who wants to give free play to his subjectivity may become a writer; but what should a man do who wants something in between?"
>
> – Musil, *The Man Without Qualities*, 274

For and Against Life

Stanisław Brzozowski (1878–1911) was the first Polish philosopher to consciously use the term "essay" to qualify his intellectual production.[10] He was a unique writer: a novelist and a mostly self-taught philosopher, as well as a literary critic who single-handedly launched several intellectual campaigns against traditional Polish writers and the sentimental (so he argued) Polish cultural tradition in general. After being charged on the basis of forged documents with collaborating with the tsarist secret police (one could hardly find a more devastating accusation in Poland under the Russian partition), Brzozowski was forced into exile; he died in Florence in 1911.

Heavily influenced by Marx, Nietzsche, and Bergson, Brzozowski rejected the notion that the world has a fixed shape in which people are denied their creative functions. Instead, he perceived reality as being in incessant flux that determined all meaningful human activities: "The word has no absolute, trans-historical meanings. It is always a truncated and limited creation of life: truncated and limited even when considered as the work of the whole species, yet the only one. The human reality is relative, unfinished, and incomplete; there is no finished, complete, closed reality."[11] For Brzozowski, "all values and all of the qualities of values are the results and forms of cultural existence,"[12] meaning that an extra-temporal standard of values that would guide human existence from above does not exist. The opposite also applies: nothing can exist beyond human reach, and the creation of values and the negotiation of their applicability to shared cultural reality is our only task. Hence his famous statement: "What is not biography does not exist at all. What ascribes to itself a meaning that is more than biographical, more than specific and individual, is actually less real."[13] The content of any thought, instead of being dealt with as external to the way it is expressed, must be considered as intrinsically tied to modes of expression – as "a certain form of life and behavior"[14] and therefore as "a certain literature."[15] By the latter, Brzozowski meant not a separate field of *belles-lettres* but rather "the whole linguistic creation"[16] by which different forms of life take shape in culture, as Giorgio Agamben would say.

At the end of his critical career, Brzozowski distanced himself from the impressionistic, subjectively defined idea that essays are intimate transactions with readers. He began to think about essay writing as the creation of "clear ... intellectual objects"[17] that refer openly to the writer's existential and historical situatedness, thus placing him in life instead of closing him off in a purely cognitive space of thought. His late philosophical approach can be understood as a vehement attack on humanism as an ideology that explicitly postulates human nature as eternal and unchanging and that implicitly aims to impose its vocabulary on all cultural users, regardless of their position in a historically defined reality.

On the other side of the philosophical argument concerning the relationship between life and thought as shaped by the medium of an essay we meet Henryk Elzenberg (1887–1967), a philosopher and essayist only seven years Brzozowski's junior, who survived two world wars and was exiled by the communists to teach at a provincial university in Poland. As he writes in his diary:

> I used to have this ambition to enclose my thought in some ultimate formulas, to grasp it in a series of truths to which I could stick. I considered incongruity of two thoughts as a disqualifying and lethal property, and the same applied to the approximate and fluid character of thought. Today I know that each utterance displays only one aspect of my iridescent, nuanced thought, which weaves through contradictions like a stream, and which can reveal its essential content, irreducible to a formula, only through contradictions, constant approximations, metamorphoses and perpetual flux.[18]

What makes this philosophical and literary attitude possible is an essential discrepancy between *what* the world is and *how* we talk about it. According to Elzenberg, "the world and discursive thought are reciprocally incommensurate to one another."[19] As there is no symmetry between discourse and reality, there is also no communication (or there should not be) between two levels of reality: true reality and misleading appearances.

Although Elzenberg's intellectual position towards the infinite fluidity of thought seemingly resembles Brzozowski's, their particular philosophies of human involvement in the world could not be more contrasting. Unlike Brzozowski, Elzenberg was convinced of "an incurable dissonance between the world of serious and pure things (the world of beauty in the first place, specifically that of the cosmos) and this strange world of our human relations."[20] He locates human efforts to bridge this distance at the core of life: "What we call life on a daily basis provides only the raw material, and it is only ethical will, systematic thought, and art that create life out of this material."[21] Life is life only when the empirical experience in which we are enclosed "as a chick in an egg"[22] is overcome and we passionately "come out into the light."[23] This is why Elzenberg always understood philosophy as a "dynamite to detonate the empirical world."[24]

The distinction between these two philosophers matches the old distinction between nominalists and realists. Without going into detailed explanations of nominalism and realism, I will follow Richard Rorty's elegant definition: "Let me define 'nominalism' as the claim that all essences are nominal and all necessities *de dicto*. This amounts to saying that no description of an object is more true to the nature of that object than any other."[25] Nominalism posits that the intellectual grasp of reality is always determined by language and, consequently, by a particular existential position of a thinker. In contrast, realism is a belief that reality (both empirical and intellectual) exists independently of the ways it can be described, or that description has no impact on its object. From this point of view, nominalist essayists, like Brzozowski, are those who think of their writing practice as inescapably shaping the world. Conversely, realists like Elzenberg are those who believe that they faithfully describe reality without filtering it through their style. Nominalists would agree with the claim that in order to shape reality through writing, one must be existentially involved in the process, whereas realists would maintain that this involvement can bring only obstruction of a pure view of reality.

Although Brzozowski and Elzenberg both adopted the essay, or the essayistic strategy of writing, as a discursive tool to approach *true* reality, they differed radically in their understanding of this notion. For Brzozowski and for other contemporary nominalists, true reality is the unstoppable flux of historically determined human affairs, for which there is no final word and no definite vocabulary. For Elzenberg, a dedicated realist, true reality resides in the eternal world of values that humans can only attain (and not produce) when they stoically withdraw their passions from history. Both thinkers saw the essay, with its unfinished and tentative character, as the best device for approaching their respective truths. For Brzozowski, however, the open, non-conclusive form of the essay reflected the dynamic structure of reality ("the richness of life"),[26] whereas for Elzenberg, the approximating form of his essayistic writing proved the impossibility of capturing pure truth in a culture of misguiding appearances, to which all discourse must belong. Where Brzozowski saw no escape from language and history, Elzenberg viewed this escape as the only guarantee of reaching an undistorted form of truth.

To Give Life Back to Words

Born in the year of Brzozowski's death, Bolesław Miciński (1911–43) was the next writer to elevate the essay to the level of a serious philosophical medium. Miciński was a sophisticated writer and critic (and a PhD candidate in philosophy) whose principal aim was to loosen the rigid philosophical language imposed by analytical philosophers from the Warsaw/Lviv School: Kazimierz Ajdukiewicz (1890–1963), Tadeusz Kotarbiński (1886–1981), and Alfred Tarski (1901–83). His attempt to impart autonomy on the essay as a philosophical genre attacked the three main premises of analytical philosophy related to language: that the language of philosophy had to be a transparent medium for conveying thoughts, that it could not be prey to ambiguities, and that it could not be personally and emotionally tinged. According to analytical philosophers, the semantic clarity and univocity of philosophical language should be guaranteed through a highly conventionalized relation between signifier and signified and the total disappearance of an utterer from the utterance. Miciński was aware long before Adorno that philosophers' assaults on the essay were signs of "the degeneration of the human sciences." As he wrote to Jerzy Stempowski, whose intellectual lead he followed, about Polish analytical philosophers: "initially a relatively small bunch of asses imposed a certain style of writing on universities – one was not allowed to write differently for fear of 'lacking scientific rigor' ... Don't you think that professional thinkers caused greater harm to knowledge than pyromaniacs?"[27]

Miciński fought strongly against this mode of philosophical writing, but he did not embrace the opposite approach – that is, aestheticism, within which the writing subject, distanced from his own writing, also performs a kind of impersonal detachment. For Miciński, the essay was a principal form of thinking in word and flesh. In his posthumously published *Notes* he left the most fervent and explicit apology for the essay in Polish literature, presenting it as a privileged mode of philosophical writing. For him, the essay as a philosophical form, rather than being a neutral and transparent account of ideas, in fact offered an openly engaged and linguistically sophisticated exposition of the writer's experiences: "I would like for these notes, whose form will gradually set itself, to avoid all 'curiooosity' [*sic*], all 'grace,' 'charm,' 'skill,' all that could stink of aestheticism and intellectual rentiership. Perhaps I have nothing to fear: it is hard to say how deeply I experience each thought, how painful it is!"[28] He believed that any form of detachment or intellectual voyeurism departed from the core of human things, leading to a "life made easier, sweetened." He was certain that his personal salvation, understood in religious terms, was his only concern, which is why the essay regarded as a radically singular mode of writing was the only adequate medium for being in touch with all levels of individual existence:

> One of the tasks of philosophy is to restore life to words. Words are not only signs – they are not only the incarnations of independent beings – words are "beings" that contain the dynamic of not only expression, but also invention. A definitive philosophical vocabulary – the dream of contemporary neo-positivists – would amount to the murder of philosophy. The philosophical vocabulary is also a matter of choice. There are thus no words outside the human being … Were the ultimate codification of words aimed at by neo-positivists to succeed, there would be no two different books in the world. The vocabulary – an institution seemingly unarmed and objective – would despotically impose their content on all of the books that would like to live with it in peace … The definitive philosophical vocabulary is the coffin of philosophical invention, because it is not only words that follow thought, but also thought that follows words.[29]

Clearly, Miciński's philosophical program as delineated here is more or less nominalist. According to him, words do not refer to independent entities, nor do they form a "definitive vocabulary" (Miciński uses Rorty's signature category *avant la lettre*). According to this form of essayistic nominalism, nothing exists meaningfully prior to language. In contrast, the commonly exercised essayistic realism aims to express only what is already there, either in the world or in the writer's mind. For nominalism, reality does not get its meaning until it goes through several filters: it is simply there, but it does not yet mean anything to us. The essay, as the most incomplete and tentative mode of textual production, undermines ready-made thoughts based on ready-made words, and by shaking off the linguistic ground on which expression is made, it consequently revitalizes the thought. In the late 1930s, a time when Edmund Husserl diagnosed a severe crisis of European culture caused among many other factors by relativism and psychologism,[30] Miciński complained that "everybody writes in the same way without, however, being the same."[31] What makes a discourse existentially important is its dissimilarity to other discourses and the different tone it assumes when inviting readers to rethink well-established and familiar opinions.

Glimpses into Eternity

Despite his relentless insistence on the creative rather than solely referential use of words, Miciński was not a consistent nominalist. In the long run, he would never deny the objective existence of reality, that is, reality resistant to the discursive condition of meaning. The main tension within his essays exemplifies the main conflicts between the nominalist and realistic approaches within the twentieth-century Polish essay. On the nominalist side, language is an autonomous being in which creative thinking takes place, and not a transparent medium for conveying independently existing ideas. The realistic approach, by contrast, posits the world as existing regardless of any particular linguistic filter. Miciński required objectivity as the ultimate test for human existence, because the latter, he argued, would go astray and collapse if left solely to the egoistic practices of its users and their unrestrained will and desires. This requirement was evidently amplified by the severe political crisis that developed in Poland in the late 1930s that pitted the fascists and the communists against each other. Nevertheless, it was fuelled, first and foremost, by Miciński's Arnoldian urge to see things as they are, beyond "the chaos of unbridled imaginings."[32]

Miciński's admiration for the "unspeakable miracle"[33] of unmediated reality went hand in hand with his "furor eticus"[34]: a need to anchor his beliefs in a set of enduring values existing outside "the internal unrest."[35] This need may seem strange in a writer so invested in saving the individuality of man, but it becomes more comprehensible when one understands that, for Miciński, being an individual meant overcoming one's weaknesses and flaws, which always arise from being all too human, or too singular:

> One has to seize the psychic reality. One has to give it stasis in order for it to be as real as a landscape outside the window, as nature. One has to give it regularity: the symmetry of classical form. Words have to be enmeshed in the law of gravity – like objects. Feelings have to flow along charted orbits as regularly as heavenly bodies do.[36]

The essay, therefore, can be neither a direct expression of the soul (a "subjective" essay), nor an impersonal statement of facts (an "objective" essay). Instead, Miciński's approach to the form was an attempt to marry two seemingly contradictory positions – extreme nominalism and extreme realism – in an unbreakable continuum: from the self, through the essay, to reality. Moreover, these dimensions should be classically ordered so as not to allow in anything disturbing or too singularly inappropriate. Feelings, thoughts, and words have to transcend their accidental limits and open themselves to eternity, where all "ideal objects exist forever."[37] At the end of his life, Miciński unambiguously opted for an anti-historical and metaphysical (also Classical) realism, wherein the world, "as the object of ethics," exists independently from the fictions of our mind[38] but cannot be reduced to its material structure. Since individuals are constituted by more than mere mechanics of feelings or thoughts, the world is habitable only if the rules of its construction seem to be eternal and are not subject to change made by fragile humans.

Miciński's essential hesitation with regard to choosing between linguistic nominalism (to which he adhered by defying abstract, lifeless philosophy) and metaphysical realism (which attracted him because it promised stable values) mirrors a conflict that is crucial to Polish culture. In *Remarks on Politics*, written during the Second World War, he remarks that architecture is "the victory of intellect over matter," making it clear that the most fundamental image of "our constant internal fight" takes the form of a battle between "the constructive power of the intellect" and the degrading and debasing power of matter, which corresponds with "the dark, evil nature of man."[39] Miciński, with his late realism, adored individuality but must have abhorred singularity, given that the latter jeopardized, in its materiality and contingency, any urge for quasi-religious salvation (i.e., becoming free of human imperfection) or for belonging to a wider community.

By singularity I mean here a process of *becoming* a subject without a final structure, as in Brzozowski's understanding of life as immanent flux, or Miciński's refusal of a definitive vocabulary with which to define oneself. Individuality, in turn, refers to the final structure imposed on that process. While singularities are always unique, individualities are not. The former are purely idiomatic (to the extent that they are incommunicable), whereas the latter are collectively agreed upon and therefore representable. Individuality is what makes you a person, or a member of a group, and singularity is what makes you an unrepeatable "this," beyond any collective grasp. Individuality is easily subsumed within a larger framework, whereas singularity withdraws from that framework and stands aside from it.[40] This double-tension between individuality and singularity on the one hand, and realism and nominalism on the other, would determine the whole intellectual map of the Polish essay during the twentieth century. Individualists were more eager to adopt realism than singularists, for whom reality counted not as an objective space shared by similarly inclined individuals, but as an idiomatic and therefore unrepeatable existential project.

The Classical Desire

Miciński was far from alone in Poland in being tempted by realism. In 1951, before everything became nationalized and while a few private publishing houses were still in business, Jan Parandowski, a classical philologist, published a book-length essay on the conditions of successful literary creation:

> Sometimes it seems that the whole world supports the writer's mission, calling for a word that would secure durability of things and men. Literature is dedicated to arresting the devastating course of time. It suspends all that could have ever happened in the everlasting present ... The word is power. When written, it acquires an incalculable and unforeseeable power over thought and imagination, it rules over time and space. A writer who does not remember this is a bad writer; he is bad if he measures the life of his work with the transitory moment ... Who does not look at the work he is producing as *aere perennius* … should not pick up the pen, because he sows the chaff.[41]

The gist of Parandowski's proudly anti-historical book is clear: literature that looks after historical necessities and finds its justification only in the floating interests of the dominant class is doomed to perish. The stakes of the book are overtly political. Even though the author never mentions contemporary communist writers as his enemies, his book implicitly demolishes socialist realism as an official literary doctrine.[42] With Flaubert as "the patron" of his book, he instead reintroduces Classicism as one of the most persistent approaches to reality in Polish literature, and in essay writing in particular, during the second half of the twentieth century.

The Classical approach, mixed with metaphysical realism and anthropological individualism, is represented and defended by essayists as different as Parandowski, Stempowski, Miciński, Stanisław Vincenz (1888–1971), Zbigniew Herbert (1924–98), Paweł Hertz (1918–2001), Czesław Miłosz (1911–2004), Zygmunt Kubiak (1929–2004), Jarosław Marek Rymkiewicz (b. 1930), and Ryszard Przybylski (1928–2016). According to Paweł Hertz, it is "neither a school nor a literary movement, but, first of all, an attitude of [a writer] towards the world and himself."[43] This attitude is built on several oppositions, the basic aim of which is to evaluate and impose order on a changing, and therefore threatening world.

In the *Preface* to Stanislaw Vincenz's collection of essays, published by the Parisian Literary Institute in 1965, Czesław Miłosz wrote: "It so happened that two people, whose early youth coincided with the years preceding WWI, did what gardeners do when they crossbreed distant plants. They grafted the gentry *gawęda* [oral tale] onto their humanistic erudition and as a result produced what is usually called the essay. This foreign and too broad a term, however, does not comprise the distinctive, local features of this new creation." Those two people mentioned by Miłosz were Stanisław Vincenz and Jerzy Stempowski. Both belonged to the classically educated, polyglot Polish intelligentsia that lived in the multicultural Polish Borderlands, both survived two world wars, and both found refuge in Switzerland after 1945.

– Miłosz, "Przedmowa," 237

Classicism can be seen as a vast metaphysical enterprise for arresting time. It is aimed *against history* understood as a succession of changing circumstances and contradictory interests. It tries to combat time by reducing temporality to *the everlasting present*. There is no past that would be foreign to us, Classicists maintain, because we are capable of including all that has happened to humankind as an integral and meaningful part of our lives. As Józef Czapski (1896–1993) wrote about Jerzy Stempowski: "When [he] writes about the Peloponnesian War or the attempt of Mitilene to gain independence from Athens, we lose the feeling of separation between yesterday and today, because everything is today."[44] The radical anti-historicism of the Classical attitude also claims that "all cultural reality is extra-temporal" and, by the same token, implies an essential "unity of men across different cultures."[45] One consequence of this assumption is the Classical tradition, which sets universal models of behaviour; another is myths, which are the basic and indestructible literary patterns that control singular temptations. As Vincenz states, "myth is a symbol of what is, in contrast to what comes to be and passes."[46] There is no clearer metaphysical (Platonic in fact) distinction than this opposition between *being* and *becoming*. What really matters is what eternally exists, beyond any historicity and any contingency, and it is expressed faithfully only in myths moving unchangeably through time.

In what passes for the first Polish definition of the essay, written by Jerzy Stempowski in 1932, we read: "In its essence the essay is an attempt to singularly formulate the shades of thought that have no traditionally shaped contours, but that present themselves to us in a form not completely recognizable, unclearly tied with the accepted resources of positive knowledge. Its charm consists in the wit of constructions, which, built with a somewhat unwieldy material of the known and respected concepts, tightly adhere to the most unexpected and fantastic shades of a refined thought."

– Sendyka, *Nowoczesny esej*, 150

In another place (and time), Stempowski ironically remarked that he "would have no problem with writing an article on any topic more or less known to him that would be solely composed of quotes. As long as we do not forget to attribute all those quotes to their sources, we would not only receive our due remuneration, but, if we draw only from the best authors, we could also pass for a brilliant essayist."

– Stempowski, "Zagadnienie plagiatu," 5

Another distinction at play in Classicism is the one between *chaos* and *order*. Classicism needs ordering principles (such as myths) to impose order on the world in which chaotic forces dominate. As Ryszard Przybylski writes in "Główna brama" (The Main Entrance), the introductory essay of his collection *Mityczna przestrzeń naszych uczuć* (The Mythical Space of Our Feelings), "poets transfer diurnal and nocturnal affairs – theirs and ours – amongst which we incessantly get lost, into a mythical space so that we can see them in the sharp light of the black sun of our ancestors' wisdom."[47] Classicists need myths and a straighforward style to see the world without distortion and to think clearly. Józef Czapski wrote about Stempowski that "the virtue of his prose is the clarity of thought ordering the chaos of phenomena."[48] This order is not only horizontal and stylistic (expressed in a plain rhetoric of the essay), but also vertical and ethical, conveyed by an unchangeable hierarchy of values that might serve as signposts in turbulent times. "The classical attitude," according to Paweł Hertz, is that literature does not create the world; it "can only understand, pierce, order, and consolidate it."[49]

Moreover, as a rigorous metaphysical operation, Classicism cannot comply with the changing world. In contrast to existential immersion and engagement, it requires distance from the world, as a result of which the world becomes a spectacle observed from above by an individual untouched by the changes. This attitude was particularly well developed by Miłosz, who borrowed his Classical position from the French philosopher Simone Weil, whom he translated. According to Weil, "distance is the soul of the beautiful."[50] In Miłosz's essays and poetry, readers find a similar desire to watch reality from an unbiased perspective of "pure seeing" and to remember past things through the purifying screens of memory.[51]

Finally, Classicism prefers an individualistic and communal approach to any particular immersion in the fabric of life. According to Hertz, "classicism … is also the consciousness of what can remain, what is really important and essential. [A writer] acquires this consciousness by gaining access to any community that remains stable and marked throughout its changes. This community can be religious, or philosophical, cultural or national."[52] This aspect of Classicism was strongly emphasized by Zbigniew Herbert, the author of several essayistic travelogues:[53]

> I travel across Europe in order to find in the long and dramatic human history traces and signs of a lost community. This is why a Roman column from Tyniec, near Kraków, a tympanon from St. Petronela church near Vienna, and reliefs in the St. Trophim cathedral in Arles, have always been for me not only a source of aesthetic experience, but also of the realization that there exists a motherland larger than that of your own country.[54]

Classicist distinctions are more than obvious. On the one hand there is being, order, distance, allegiance to authority, individuality, and community; on the other, becoming, chaos, immersion, and singularity. Classicism, in emphasizing the first and rejecting the latter parts of these oppositions, makes it clear that there is definitely something more at stake in this confrontation than delineating one intellectual position among many others. In its urge to go beyond historically determined appearances, Classicism is a majestic call to turn back from any singular form of existential experience in order to find an efficient remedy for the vicissitudes of life, both personal and collective. Its cultural persistence may be explained by an assumption that "real life is elsewhere" – married in Poland to painful historical experiences of loss of national sovereignty – and this life as we know it – here and now, metaphysically and politically – cannot fully satisfy human beings.

"Who Am I in My Flesh?"

Shifting attention from the realistic belief in perennial values to the nominalist emphasis on unrepeatable experience led the Polish essay to two discoveries. The first consists of multiple appraisals of *the living body*, the second of limiting one's perspective to what is *little and local*.

Discoveries of the singular body were made mostly in response to all-embracing narratives of enlightened reason and a civil Body Politic, and put into artistic practice to dismantle the plainness of discourse – its logical continuity, subject's detachment from writing, clear-cut conceptuality, and individual roundness of statements. As the writing of one of the most inventive Polish essayists, Andrzej Falkiewicz, demonstrates, the essay should be an anti-Cartesian, fragmented space of uncertainty and dubious attribution, of constantly renewed attempts at "me-wholeness" (*mnie-całości*) or even "self-flesh" (*siebie-mięsa*)[55] to come to terms with a world exposed to chance and lack of order.

Talking about "the thinking corporeality," Falkiewicz described his own position in the following way:

> I am talking about a discovery of a concrete body, with its particularities, non-beauties, sickness, and anomalies – about the body that is always in the singular, a body that you are to the very core of your being. I am talking about full acceptance of your own body, me-body, incomparable and not compared to any other, not registered on the market. About your own body, accepted fully and without reservations.[56]

This meditation, enabled by "participation in the all-becoming drama of reality,"[57] is more than just a reflection on the contemporary discourse about the body. At one point Falkiewicz asks himself (and writes it all in capital letters):

> WHY, FOR INSTANCE, AM I DYING? WHO AM I IN MY FLESH? HOW DO THE MALE AND THE FEMALE MEET IN MY FLESH; TWO FEMALES; TWO MALES? IS THERE

> ANYTHING ELSE BENEATH THE FLESH, A DARK CREVICE FOR INSTANCE, AND WHO IS STAYING THERE? WILL HE DIE WITH ME? IS EROTIC PERCEPTION OF THINGS THE ONLY ONE POSSIBLE? WHAT KIND OF AS YET UNREVEALED WORK DO I HAVE TO DO BEFORE I START LOOKING AT THE WORLD?[58]

This total acceptance and taking over of the me-body is parallel to the denial of eschatology, teleology, or any other transcendent justification for existence: "Only with my own self can I confirm the Revelation." Or even stronger: "Who waits for Parousia, waits in vain. It does not sum up!"[59] From this perspective, life does not sum up: "No conclusions. I am just writing this down." It means that life can only happen in fragments, in ecstatic bouts of the writing body whose singularity looks for the universal (without which it could neither think nor write), and only from a limited bodily position in the world: "I smell my own sperm and look for a cosmic perspective."[60]

The same double-edged approach can be seen in the philosophy of the flesh developed by Jolanta Brach-Czaina in her two books: *Szczeliny istnienia* (The Crevices of Being, 1992)[61] and *Błony umysłu* (Membranes of the Mind, 2003). Brach-Czaina refuses to talk about "being as such," pointing instead to various concrete existential details, like cherry, sand, rat, plate, bud, sausage, newborn, or basic human activities, such as peeling a potato, eating a cherry, catching a bus, or making up a room. All of these concrete singular things and activities, if encountered on a sensual level, outside of the conceptual grip that we impose on things, allow us to escape the traps of reason. Brach-Czaina does not look for any extra-existential justification of life and does not believe in long-lasting values. Instead, she reveals the true facticity of human behaviour, whereby human beings share their fragile condition with other "existential concretes"[62] and take care of themselves and others. In this existential being-with-things, human beings open themselves to the "voices" of the minutest of objects, which call for refined understanding that is, in turn, "a reconciliation with the diversity of the world."[63] For the author, who writes in succinct, aphoristic paragraphs strengthened by striking images referring to down-to-earth existential situations, openness to the world is not intellectual, but corporeal: "In order to open ourselves up, we spontaneously transform ourselves into a fleshy crater, parted onto the world and ready to explode."[64] It is not by chance, then, that the basic vocabulary of *Crevices of Being* references the female experience of giving birth, especially in the chapter titled "Otwarcie" (Opening).

As contingent and singular beings on our way to individuation, we are irrevocably immersed in ordinary lives. Our existential description of life cannot avoid brutally concrete and painful everydayness that "combines obtrusive reality with transitoriness."[65] Brach-Czaina focuses on "bustling about" (*krzątactwo*), the specific phenomenon of being occupied with myriad issues, in order to maintain a living space that is in a constant state of disorder: "Bustling about belongs to the primary categories that seize presence in the world. It is a manner of being in the everyday. Of the bird, the human being, the insect, with no exceptions."[66]

Among Polish essayists, Falkiewicz and Brach-Czaina drifted farthest from the Classicist desire to escape human facticity. In their carnal philosophies, what counts most is not ideas, or the form-giving mind of a well-settled, individualistically formed subject. Rather, of primary importance are the shaky and provisory human attempts to cope with existential matters on the level of singularities that are almost unrepresentable.[67] In their books, form and matter radically diverge: the former is rejected at the outset as a disembodied illusion, while the latter is praised as the real, painful, and non-shareable environment of (wo)men.

Conclusion

In 1994, five years after Poland regained independence, one of the most active essayists of the second half of the century, Ryszard Przybylski, published *Pustelnicy i demony* (Eremites and Demons), a volume of essays about Early Christian ascetic monks. Three of the essays deal with "traumas": "Uraz Materii" (Trauma of Matter), "Uraz Ciała" (Trauma of Body) and "Uraz Mowy" (Trauma of Speech). In his Introduction, Przybylski confesses:

> Having been accustomed throughout my entire life to despise the filthy social order, I decided to go to the Desert ... in order to occupy myself with the wisdom born from silence of long deceased monks at a time when the sins of language contaminate with the "poison of asps" [Romans 3: 13] the lips of many of our compatriots. For the more miserable our time is ... the more we need to talk with the masters who created our tradition, as sacred as it is necessary. I flee away, therefore, as people frustrated by the vulgarity of contemporary social life tend to do, to an oasis of beautiful texts left behind by extraordinary eremites, who once saw their world as being equally trivial and unattractive.[68]

It is characteristic that the first two modernist philosophies of the essay, developed by Walter Pater (*Plato and Platonism: A Series of Lectures* [1893]) and György Lukács ("On the Nature and Form of the Eassay" in *Soul and Form* [1911]), were unmistakably Platonic. Pater sees Platonism as "a habit, namely, of tentative thinking and suspended judgment," but first and foremost he fosters Plato's "aspiration towards a more perfect Justice, a more perfect Beauty, physical and intellectual, a more perfect condition of human affairs, than anyone has ever yet seen" (175). Lukács, having defined Plato as "the greatest essayist" (28) and viewing all "the Platonists' writing" as essays, described succinctly the path thought should follow to qualify as "essayistic": "from the accidental to the necessary" (39).

This ascetic move based on the triple-trauma can serve as a metaphor of the main essayistic trend in Polish literature of the twentieth century. Przybylski, a partisan of Classicism in Poland, scorns the unavoidable contingency of human existence, looking in many directions to find "notes to eternity."[69] What he terms as "the filthy social order" is an apt description of communism in Poland, but more importantly, it points to what I have called an anti-historicist attitude in Polish essay writing: a Platonic conviction that human existence can lead to truth only if the whirlpool of contradictory opinions can be suspended and the united trinity of the Good, the Beautiful, and the True may be revealed above the corporeal level of life. This Platonism, akin to the same tendency in Western modernist essay writing,[70] promised to find real life somewhere other than in the life tormented by historical events. Given that Polish culture was marked by the loss of state sovereignty since Enlightenment, it needed to develop symbolic strategies of compensating for this loss; it needed to build parallel communities through literature and art more than it needed to diversify critical attitudes and promote dissident philosophies.

Stanisław Brzozowski's vehement assault on the Polish tradition of complacency and self-congratulativeness thus inaugurated a new, more critical phase of Polish criticism. It gave birth to a new essayistic form that was influenced by three different yet connected traditions: the Marxist tradition of *Homo faber*, a human being – creator of his own life; the Bergsonian tradition of life as a constant flux; and the Nietzschean tradition of imparting meaning to an inhuman, meaningless universe. Those three resources allowed Brzozowski to deconstruct Polish Romantic Platonism and to offer a new vision of existence, one that almost all essayists who have embraced the nominalist position have since followed.

As we have seen, the Polish essay during the twentieth century oscillated between two extremes. On the one hand, it tried to suppress human facticity in the medium of universal ideas, preferably shared within a larger, national, or otherwise imagined community (which I call the realist temptation). On the other hand, the genre is marked, from Brzozowski to Brach-Czaina, by scepticism about the very possibility of suspending the singularity of its practitioners in the act of writing, which always stands in testimony to their existential position (I call this position nominalist). What is crucial here is that the essayistic quarrel between Classicism and Romanticism, which had been constitutive of the Polish literary tradition since the first decades of the nineteenth century and which took different forms in the twentieth century (realism versus nominalism, individualism versus singularity, etc.), has never been seduced by the temptation of communism. The reason for its resistance was communism's denial of both the past and everlasting values, and of the unshakeable value of a particular personal experience. If Classicism was lured by a collective temptation, it was that of a collective, archetypal subconscious rather than the collective consciousness of social realists and their political comrades. And if Romanticism was seduced by historical agency, it was definitely its obsession with singularity that did not allow for its marriage with communism in Poland. This is why the main discussion that took place in and through the Polish essay in the twentieth century – the discussion between realist Classicism and nominalist Romanticism – had open political undertones. Its real goal was to undermine the basic distinction made by the communists between social engagement in favour of socialism in Poland, and individualistic egotism that was seen as a sign of a corrupted self. Focusing on an ongoing dialogue between Classicist realism and Romantic nominalism, the Polish essay carved out an area separate from the political space, establishing a framework for philosophical discussion that is still pertinent in a neoliberal world, even if relations between social engagement and individual drives are now completely reversed.

Michał Paweł Markowski
University of Illinois at Chicago

NOTES

1 Miłosz, *Ogród nauk*, 192. In the following discussion, "essay" refers to a multiform activity of non-fictional (literary and philosophical) writing, including memoirs, aphorisms, and reviews, rather than a single genre of expository prose defined by a fixed set of textual properties.

2 Wyka, "Porozmawiajmy o essayu," 299–302. It is worth noting that Wyka wrote his essay at a time when the Polish equivalent of the English word "essay" – *esej* – was not yet in circulation.

3 Jarosław Iwaszkiewicz, a poet and an essayist, noted in 1938 that "the essay form" was "quite foreign to the Polish mind." ("Wiadomości Literackie," [Literary News] 1938). The same conviction was expressed in the 1970s by Czesław Miłosz: "Between 1918 and 1939 in Poland, essay as a literary genre was a meal for a very few gourmands" (Miłosz, *Ogród nauk*, 192).

4 "Essays, essays, and essays! Half of the writing Poland is plagued by essays." This is how the critic Ludwik Flaszen (b. 1930) commented on the invasion of the essay in the late 1950s, a time of greater freedom in public life relative to the preceding period of Stalinism, when socialist literary doctrine subsided. See Flaszen, "Na oleju grzechów naszych," 171.

5 As Wyka himself noted in "Dwugłos o Bolesławie Micińskim" (his and Tadeusz Breza's review of Miciński's long philosophical essay *Podróże do piekieł* [1937]), "he located his essays on the borderland, almost virginal in Poland, between literature and philosophy," *Ateneum*, 144–6.

6 Breza, "Rozważania o eseju," 114.

7 Arnold, *Culture and Anarchy,* 56.

8 Pater, "Preface," in *The Renaissance*, 20.

9 See Breza, "Rozważania o eseju," 107, 108, 110.

10 See Markiewicz, "Wstęp," iii.

11 Brzozowski, *Pamiętnik*, 65.

12 Ibid.,165.

13 Ibid., 142.

14 Ibid., 83.

15 Ibid., 98.

16 Ibid., 98.

17 Ibid., 38.

18 Elzenberg, *Kłopot z istnieniem*, 280.

19 Ibid., 363.

20 Ibid., 357.

21 Ibid., 378.

22 Ibid., 361.

23 Ibid., 361.

24 Ibid., 352.

25 Richard Rorty, "Being That Can Be Understood Is Language," 24.

26 Brzozowski, *Pamiętnik*, 31.

27 Miciński, *Pisma*, 542.

28 Ibid., 191.

29 Ibid., 195–6.

30 See Husserl, *Die Krisis der europäischen Wissenschaften.*

31 Miciński, *Pisma*, 196.

32 Miciński, "Portrait of Kant," 180.

33 Miciński, *Pisma*, 73.

34 Ibid., 393.

35 Ibid., 91.

36 Ibid., 91.
37 Ibid., 133.
38 "If you once write a poem about chirping birds, you will never really hear them again; once you write a poem about the green grass, the grass loses its color. You become blind and deaf." Miciński, *Pisma*, 402.
39 Ibid., 161–3.
40 My understanding of this distinction is close to Gilles Deleuze's argument as laid down in his late text *Pure Immanence*.
41 Parandowski, *Alchemia słowa*, 18–19, 364–5.
42 Socialist realism was proclaimed in the Soviet Union in 1934 and introduced as an official literary doctrine in Poland in 1949.
43 Hertz, "O klasycyzmie," 45–6.
44 Czapski, "Przy Sybillach Królowych," 28.
45 Both quotes come from Stanisław Vincenz's essay "Uwagi o kulturze ludowej," 203, 192.
46 Vincenz, "Krajobraz jako tło dziejów," 362.
47 Przybylski, *Mityczna przestrzeń naszych uczuć*, 10.
48 Czapski, "Przy Sybillach Królowych," 28.
49 Hertz, "O klasycyzmie," 47.
50 Weil, "Beauty," 379.
51 For example, see "To jedno" (This Only), in Miłosz, *Poezje wybrane / Selected Poems* (bilingual edition), 308–9.
52 Hertz, "O klasycyzmie," 45.
53 Of which "Barbarian in the Garden" and "Labyrinth on the Sea" are included in Zbigniew Herbert, *The Collected Prose*.
54 Herbert, "Holy Iona," 20.
55 Falkiewicz, *Takim ściegiem*, 312–13.
56 Falkiewicz, *Być może*, 152, 154.
57 Falkiewicz himself calls this participation "Romantic" and contrasts it with Classicism, in which "the shape of the world has already been given." *Takim ściegiem,* 134.
58 Ibid., 306.
59 Ibid., 310.
60 Ibid., 329.
61 Very soon after the book was published in Poland, it started to be called the "Bible of Polish Feminism."
62 Compare it with Heidegger's concept of *Faktizität* (facticity) as developed in Heidegger, *Being and Time*, 82.
63 Brach-Czaina, *Szczeliny istnienia*, 27.
64 Ibid., 25.
65 Ibid., 64.
66 Ibid., 73.
67 Other Polish practitioners of the existential essay include Jan Kott (his late essays), Tadeusz Komendant, Krzysztof Rutkowski, Aleksander Nawarecki, Stefan Szymutko, Marek Bieńczyk, Michał Paweł Markowski, and Wojciech Nowicki.
68 Przybylski, *Pustelnicy i demony*, 5–7.
69 Przybylski, *A Swallow's Shadow: an Essay on Chopin's Thoughts,* 11.
70 For the first two major Platonic philosophies of the essay, see Pater, *Plato and Platonism*; and Lukàcs, "On the Nature and Form of the Essay."

WORKS CITED

Arnold, Matthew. *Culture and Anarchy.* Edited by Samuel Lipman. New Haven: Yale University Press, 1994.

Brach-Czaina, Jolanta. *Szczeliny istnienia.* Kraków: eFKa, 1999.

Breza, Tadeusz. "Rozważania o eseju." In *Nelly. O kolegach i o sobie.* 109–15. Warszawa: Czytelnik, 1970.

Brzozowski, Stanisław. *Pamiętnik.* Lwów: Księgarnia Polska B. Połonieckiego, 1913.

Czapski, Józef. "Przy Sybillach Królowych." In *Kultura* 11 (1961): 27–31.

Deleuze, Gilles. *Pure Immanence: Essays on a Life.* 2nd ed. New York: Zone Books, 2005.

Elzenberg, Henryk. *Kłopot z istnieniem. Aforyzmy w porządku czasu.* Kraków: Znak, 1963.

Falkiewicz, Andrzej. *Być może. Być – w stu trzydziestu czterech odsłonach.* Gdańsk: słowo-obraz/terytoria, 2002.

– *Takim ściegiem.* Wrocław: Wydawnictwo Dolnośląskie, 1991.

Flaszen, Ludwik. "Na oleju grzechów naszych." In *Kosmopolityzm i sarmatyzm. Antologia powojennego eseju polskiego.* Edited by Dorota Heck. 171–4. Wrocław: Ossolineum, 2003.

Heidegger, Martin. *Being and Time.* Translated by J. Macquarrie and E. Robinson. New York: Harper and Row, 1962.

Herbert, Zbigniew. *The Collected Prose 1948–1998.* Edited by Alissa Valles. New York: Ecco, 2010.

– "Holy Iona, czyli kartka z podróży." In *Mistrz z Delft i inne utwory odnalezione.* Edited by Barbara Toruńczyk. 19–20. Warszawa: Zeszyty Literackie, 2008.

Hertz, Paweł. "O klasycyzmie." In *Świat i dom. Szkice i uwagi wybrane.* Warszawa: Państwowy Instytut Wydawniczy, 1978.

Husserl, Edward. *Die Krisis der europäischen Wissenschaften und die transzendentale Phänomenologie. Eine Einleitung in die phänomenologische Philosophie.* The Hague: Nijhoff, 1954.

Kott, Jan. *Four Decades of Polish Essays.* Evanston: Northwestern University Press, 1990.

Lukàcs, György. "On the Nature and Form of the Essay." In *Soul and Form.* Translated by Anna Bostock, edited by John T. Sanders and Katie Terezakis. 16–34. New York: Columbia University Press, 2010.

Markiewicz, Henryk. "Wstęp." In Stanisław Brzozowski, *Eseje i studia o literaturze.* I–XCII. Wrocław: Zakład Narodowy im. Ossolińskich, 1990.

Markowski, Michał Paweł. *Die Chronik des polnischen Essays 1951–2000.* Kraków: Villa Deciusa 2000.

Miłosz, Czesław. *Ogród nauk.* Kraków: Wydawnictwo Literackie, 2013.

– *Poezje wybrane / Selected Poems* (bilingual edition). Kraków: Wydawnictwo Literackie 1996.

– "Przedmowa do *Po stronie pamięci.*" In *Zaczynając od moich ulic.* 236–42. Paryż: Instytut Literacki, 1985.

Miciński, Bolesław. *Pisma, Eseje, artykuły, listy.* Edited by Anna Micińska. Kraków: Znak, 1970.

– "Portrait of Kant." In *Four Decades of Polish Essay.* Translated by Jadwiga Kosicka, edited by Jan Kott. 148–81. Evanston: Northwestern University Press, c1990.

Mitova-Janowski, Katia. "Polish Essay." In *Encyclopedia of the Essay.* Edited by Tracy Chevalier. 666–8. London: Fitzroy Dearborn, 1997.

Musil, Robert. *The Man without Qualities*, vol. 1. Translated by Sophie Wilkins. New York: Vintage Books, 1996.

Parandowski, Jan. *Alchemia słowa.* Warszawa: Gebenthner, 1951.

Pater, Walter. *Plato and Platonism: A Series of Lectures*. New York: Macmillan, 1893.
– *The Renaissance: Studies in Art and Poetry: The 1893 Text*. Edited by Donald L. Hill. Berkeley: University of California Press, 1980.
Przybylski, Ryszard. *Mityczna przestrzeń naszych uczuć*. Warszawa: Sic!, 2002.
– *Pustelnicy i demony*. Kraków: Znak, 1994.
– *A Swallow's Shadow: An Essay on Chopin's Thoughts*. Translated by John Comber. Warszawa: Fryderyk Chopin Institute, 2011.
Rorty, Richard. "Being That Can Be Understood Is Language." *London Review of Books* 22, no. 6 (16 March 2000): 23–5.
Sendyka, Roma. *Nowoczesny esej. Studium historycznej świadomości gatunku*. Kraków: Universitas, 2006.
Stempowski, Jerzy. "Zagadnienie plagiatu." *Wiadomości Literackie* 52 (1936): 5.
Vincenz, Stanisław. "Krajobraz jako tło dziejów." In *Z perspektywy podróży*. 360–414. Kraków: Znak, 1980.
– "Uwagi o kulturze ludowej." In *Po stronie dialogu*, vol. 1. 190–213. Warszawa: Państwowy Instytut Wydawniczy, 1983.
Weil, Simon. "Beauty." In *The Simone Weil Reader*. Edited by G.A. Panichas. 377–80. New York: McKay, 1977.
Wyka, Kazimierz. "Porozmawiajmy o essayu." In *Szkice literackie i artystyczne*, vol.1. 299–302. Kraków: Wydawnictwo Literackie, 1956.
Wyka, Kazimierz, and Tadeusz Breza. "Dwugłos o Bolesławie Micińskim." *Ateneum* 2 (1938): 144–6.
Zawadzki, Andrzej. *Nowoczesna eseistyka filozoficzna w piśmiennictwie polskim pierwszej połowy XX wieku*. Kraków: Universitas, 2001.

Trial and Error: Between Criticism and Essayism (Karol Irzykowski)

"Since my thoughts are really precious to me and I do not want them to be attacked by missiles of the most primitive kind, I do not send them out into the world without armouring them first, and even equip them with weapons of offence."[1] This quote, taken from the final pages of Karol Irzykowski's celebrated novel *Pałuba* (The Hag, 1903), sheds light on some essential features of Irzykowski's approach to writing, particularly within the genre of the essay. To begin with, the assertive and belligerent tone of the final part of *The Hag* (characteristically titled "Szaniec *Pałuby*," i.e., "The Rampart of *The Hag*") prefigures the military metaphors that abound in Irzykowski's large body of literary criticism and essays from the 1920s and 1930s. Titles like *Walka o treść* (The Struggle over Content,1929) and *Lżejszy kaliber* (Lighter Caliber, 1938) suggest that Irzykowski conceived of literary communication (and human interaction in general) in terms of conflicts, duels, and polemics rather than as a constructive dialogue between benevolent partners. The pugnacious tone of some of these books and essays should not be taken to mean, however, that Irzykowski was merely a rabble-rouser and provocateur, with little to offer by way of new values and ideas. More a method than a goal in itself, Irzykowski's constant polemic with his opponents' opinions was predominantly a tool for delineating and developing the author's own propositions – a strategy that has aptly been called "polemical digressiveness" (Nycz) or "radicalized dialogism" (Panek).[2]

As a genre that foregrounds the process of thinking, the essay is known for its questioning and tentative character. More often than not, Irzykowski's intellectual "trials" take the form of criticism directed against existing ideas and values. In addition to Irzykowski's characteristically militant tone, the above-quoted statement from *The Hag* exhibits the critical-intellectual mode that would become a dominant feature of Irzykowski's essays in the first three decades of the twentieth century. Significantly, while *The Hag* – Irzykowski's prose debut – served primarily as a metafictional attack on the artistic practices of the Young Poland period, Irzykowski's subsequent work would widen its polemical focus from fiction writing to literary and cultural criticism in the broadest sense.

Irzykowski's conception of his critical output is inextricably linked to his profound anthropocentrism as a writer. Unwilling to accept any values or absolutes originating outside man's experience or that threaten his individuality, Irzykowski considered the realm of creativity to be the most important – if not the only – site of negotiation for values and ideas. "Cultural work," he stated in the prewar article "Świat pracy a świat emocji" (The Realm of Work and the Realm of Emotions, 1907),

> aims to uncover everywhere, under various respectable disguises, hidden ossifications, to destroy them, and to clear the road for the refreshing impact of original elements of mutation.

> Undeniably, in our days one of these hidden ossifications, or – as [Stanisław] Brzozowski calls them – these carrions that decompose under festoons of flowers, is artistic ossification. Everyone senses this, yet so far the struggle with this ossification has been, by and large, merely illusory, a new means for conserving the old error.[3]

More often than not, Irzykowski's omnipresent authorial voice refrains from discussing art in purely aesthetic terms (e.g., "good" versus "bad" art). Instead, his approach is to "test" the cognitive and axiological potential of the works of art of a given epoch. This partly explains why so many of his critical writings abound in terms like "false," "error," and "mistake" – terms usually applied to artistic ideas and values that have been subjected to "ossification," "petrification," and even "fossilization" and are thus ripe for overturning. Irzykowski's pursuit of originality and inventiveness is another key element in his writings of the interwar period. More than any other literary critic of his day, Irzykowski was allergic to – and implacable towards – writers and artists who dared to repeat, let alone plagiarize, established ideas and opinions. Irzykowski's critical method relies on a two-step process of ergocentric analysis or "decomposition," as he liked to call it, followed by "re-composition," where the critic proposes alternative artistic solutions. As such, criticism (understood as the testing of the existing order and its hierarchies) and essayism ("trying" something yet unknown) appear to be two sides of the same coin.

Irzykowski's texts abound in terms such as "critique" and "criticism," yet scarcely make explicit references to the essay as a literary form. As early as *The Hag*, however, his work displays a certain predilection for terms that express tentativeness, most notably "*próba*" (trial, attempt). The term "essay" itself makes rare appearances in the introduction to his volume of film theory *Dziesiąta Muza. Zagadnienia estetyczne kina* (The Tenth Muse: Esthetic Issues of Cinema, 1924) and in *Beniaminek. Rzecz o Boyu-Żeleńskim* (Little Benjamin: On Boy-Żeleński, 1933).

As the above-quoted passage from "The Realm of Work and the Realm of Emotions" indicates, when Irzykowski was beginning his critical writing, he felt a strong affinity for the work and ideas of his contemporary, the critic and philosopher Stanisław Brzozowski (1878–1911). Arriving on the Polish literary scene at the turn of the century, both Irzykowski and Brzozowski took issue with the Young Poland movement and combined forces to intellectualize Polish social and cultural life. Among the "ossifications" that Irzykowski criticized in the aforementioned article (written, in part, to defend Brzozowski's own views on the matter) was the "convenient dualism that makes easier the resolution (the naming!) of difficult aesthetic problems: like content/form, intellectual and moral questions/aesthetic questions, the realm of ideas/the realm of emotions, social qualities/artistic qualities."[4] Well aware of the inadequacy of so-called word-postulates – that is, the lofty, transcendental concepts such as "truth," "love," and "beauty" that tend to govern human behaviour – Irzykowski questioned artificial categories and simplifying labels that distorted "real life" or "the truth about life." While the perceived dualism between content and form is at the polemical heart of Irzykowski's interwar volume *The*

Struggle over Content, other dichotomies figure prominently in his earlier, elaborate critique of the artistic practices of Young Poland titled *Czyn i słowo. Glossy sceptyka* (Deed and Word: Comments of a Sceptic, 1913).

One issue of particular importance to Irzykowski as a critic was the abrupt shift from "decadentism" ("art for art's sake") to "heroism" ("art for society's sake") that some of his contemporaries made in the aftermath of the 1905 Revolution in Russia. For Irzykowski, as he wrote in the 1907 article "Dwie rewolucje" (Two Revolutions), this socio-ethical turn was an all too easy retreat into outdated cultural reflexes and showed a superficial understanding of the tenets of modernism in general, and of decadentism in particular. Rather than perpetuate such "false" dichotomies, Irzykowski envisioned a reconciliation of the two currents – decadentism and heroism – in what he termed "intellectual activism"; here, a critical awareness of cultural decline ("decadentism") would go hand in hand with a commitment to "revolutionary" thinking ("heroism"). In a similar vein, Irzykowski took issue with the widespread conception of history as a circular movement, or as a pendulum swinging between opposite poles (reflected in the various "neo" labels then in vogue). Instead, most notably in his article "W kształt linii spiralnej" (In the Form of a Spiral Line, 1913), he proposed that historical "progress" moved in a spiral.

While Irzykowski's prewar criticism revolved around the Young Poland current, his later writings turned to the generation that arrived on the Polish literary scene after the First World War, a generation that Irzykowski ironically nicknamed "Youngest Poland." The specifically Polish contexts in which these polemics arose make Irzykowski's critical output less accessible to a contemporary – and even more so a foreign – readership, and obscure some of its more general underpinnings. Nevertheless, these concrete (con)textual references are both the basis and the strength of his authorial approach, which focused on particulars and topical examples rather than on building an all-encompassing, and inevitably generalizing, conceptual framework. Along with the critical-essayistic mode of his writings, it helps explain why his intellectual position has been categorized as "pragmatism," or even "irrational rationalism" (i.e., rejecting systemic and systematic thinking in favour of tentative reflection).[5] It also allows one to consider Irzykowski in the same light as Georges Sorel, Friedrich Nietzsche, Georg Simmel, Henri Bergson, and other modernist essayists known for their deep suspicion of systematic reasoning, however much they diverged on numerous ideological and artistic points.

By making aesthetic criticism central to his intellectual activities and foregrounding the "refreshing impact of original elements of mutation" in his evaluation of art, Irzykowski anticipated a number of important developments in twentieth-century critical theory.

Victor Shklovsky introduced the concept of "*ostranenie*" (usually translated as "defamiliarization") in his famous essay "Art as Device" from 1917. Starting from the idea that repeatedly performed acts lead to a form of habituation (especially in the realm of perception), Shklovsky claims that art and its various devices and techniques allow us to counter this process of automatization. By making the artistic form "strange" and "difficult" (in comparison to existing and established forms of expression), poetic language is capable of deautomatizing the reader's perception and shifts the focus of attention from the knowledge of an object to its activated and renewed perception.

Irzykowski's ideas about "ossification" and "refreshing mutation" were echoed, to some extent, by the Russian Formalist School, in particular by Victor Shklovsky, who analysed the dynamic between "automatization" and "defamiliarization."[6] It would be a mistake, however, to reduce Irzykowski's legacy to his aesthetic criticism, groundbreaking though it may be. His concern over the socially and psychologically conditioned mechanisms that hamper the "crystallization" and "fermentation" of new ideas and values (to use his own terms) is just one facet of his legacy. His anthropocentric convictions prompted fierce debates over contemporary discourses that reduced human beings to "automatons," mere pawns to be sacrificed for the future benefit of the collective. His convictions shine through in the celebrated 1918 essay "Filozofia koralowa a religia" (Coral Philosophy and Religion), in which he ironically minimizes the enormous loss of life in the First World War: "We are eternal because we are a society of corals after all, constantly growing one above another and branching off like trees in the ocean of being ... Death has become a trifle, the dead are nothing but the excrement of a huge body."[7] A staunch opponent of war in the real world, the belligerent critic Irzykowski appears in these pages in one of his more pessimistic guises, as he indicts the misguided spirit of collectivism that would cause so much destruction in the decades to come.

Kris Van Heuckelom
Catholic University of Leuven

NOTES

1 Irzykowski, *Pałuba*, 576. All translations from the Polish are mine.
2 Nycz, "Wynajdywanie porządku," 156–7; Panek, *Krytyk w przestrzeniach literatury i filozofii,* 76.
3 Irzykowski, *Wybór*, 66.
4 Ibid., 68.
5 See Burek, "Cztery dyskusje Karola Irzykowskiego," 129–82.
6 See Nycz, "Wynajdowanie," 165–82; and Sienkiewicz, "Zamiast wstępu," 9–28.
7 Irzykowski, "Filozofia koralowa a religia," 101.

WORKS CITED

Burek, Tomasz. "Cztery dyskusje Karola Irzykowskiego. Prolegomena." In *Problemy literatury polskiej lat 1890–1939,* vol. 1. Edited by H. Kirchner and Z. Żabicki. 129–82. Wrocław: Ossolineum, 1972.

Irzykowski, Karol. "Filozofia koralowa a religia." In *Alchemia ciała i inne szkice oraz aforyzmy.* 98–105. Wrocław: Towarzystwo Przyjaciół Polonistyki Wrocławskiej, 1996.

– *Pałuba. Sny Marii Dunin.* Kraków: Wydawnictwo Literackie, 1976.

– *Wybór pism krytycznoliterackich.* Wrocław: Ossolineum, 1975.

Nycz, Ryszard. "Wynajdywanie porządku. Karola Irzykowskiego koncepcje krytyki i literatury." In *Język modernizmu. Prologomena historycznoliterackie.* 155–90. Wrocław: Wyd. Uniwersytetu Wrocławskiego, 2002.

Panek, Sylwia. *Krytyk w przestrzeniach literatury i filozofii.* Poznań: Poznańskie Studia Polonistyczne, 2006.

Sienkiewicz, Barbara. "Zamiast wstępu. Irzykowski – krytyk Lessinga." In *Między rewelacją a repetycją. Od Przybosia do Herberta.* 9–28. Poznań: Poznańskie Studia Polonistyczne, 1999.

Metaphysics of Experience: (Czesław Miłosz)

Czesław Miłosz (1911–2004) published around a dozen essay collections over a period of more than fifty years. Among them are such fundamental works as the essays he wrote in Nazi-occupied Warsaw, published many years later as *Legendy nowoczesności* (Legends of Modernity, 2005), which constitute a diagnosis of European culture on the brink of the "European civil war" (as he called the Second World War); *Zniewolony umysł* (The Captive Mind, 1953), the still relevant study that discusses the temptations and seductions of writers and intellectuals by Marxism; *Rodzinna Europa* (Native Realm, 1958), the poet's attempt at an intellectual autobiography; and *Ziemia Ulro* (Land of Ulro, 1977), which analyses the erosion of religious imagination in European civilization. In all of his essay collections, Miłosz's reflections on poetry and literature are intertwined with political and philosophical diagnoses, incursions into theology, and reminiscences about people, prewar Poland, and the United States during the second half of the twentieth century. In line with genre conventions, Miłosz's essays fuse a variety of themes, matters, and styles.

Although he is undoubtedly a master of the essay craft, Miłosz seems to have regarded this form primarily as a utilitarian vehicle, a helpful means of laying out his views and convictions. As he wrote about his early essay writing many years later in *Ogród nauk* (Garden of Sciences, 1979), the important point is to "weave the process of argumentation into the very fabric of style," thus steering the reader towards "a specific vision," but – as he emphasizes – "somewhat obliquely."[1] This spatial metaphor favoured by Miłosz appears also in his foreword to *Native Realm*, where the author identifies with Charles Baudelaire's admiration for the drawings of his contemporary Constantin Guys, a French artist who chronicled the life of a nineteenth-century metropolis and the Parisian *beau monde*. Miłosz writes: "His eulogy of crinolines, powder, and rouge is very wise, because one can get at man only obliquely, only through the constant masquerade that is the extension of himself at a given moment, through his historical existence."[2]

It is this conviction that provides Miłosz with the ingredients for his essayistic alchemy, in which notable details and anecdotes that evoke the atmosphere of a particular time are amalgamated with reflections and generalizations that impart them with meaning. Hence Miłosz's writing method is characterized by shifts in perspective, reminiscent of the zoom lens function in a camera: his work reveals what is near and what is far away, juxtaposing sweeping panoramic vistas with dramatic close-ups, with additional use of perspectival illusions (*trompe d'oeil*) that draw on the effect of *anamorphosis*. In so doing, Miłosz tells us that things are not always what they seem. This means of presentation liberates essayistic discourse from the chains of abstract or shallow philosophizing, thus allowing the reader an easy entry to its riches. In Miłosz's essays the world is given a spatial and historical depth that happily marries the subjective and the objective. The individual perspective is maintained, however; indeed, it becomes indispensable: "In order to grasp reality, one needs a protagonist," Miłosz notes, "as well as an organizing principle."[3]

The essayist's historical imagination provides such a principle, and it is through this imagination that the "will to reality," so greatly admired by Witold Gombrowicz in Miłosz's work, manifests itself.[4] This historical imagination allows Miłosz to resist the temptations of narcissism, which is so frequently present in the postmodern essay. To write obliquely thus means to write indirectly (in other words: with respect for the complicated nature of reality), though it does not mean writing without principles. Miłosz never abandons his strong convictions, nor does he shy away from formulating a personal stance, not even when he shares his doubts with his readers. In this sense, perhaps, he is not the best example of a twentieth-century "essayistic person," if this term is understood to mean a proclivity for reflecting among/upon ever-proliferating question marks, the condition of someone who compulsively ponders the existence of boundaries or ultimate answers. Miłosz's essays reveal a strong axiological perspective, a "sense of hierarchy" on which he constantly calls. Miłosz the essayist speaks against culture and literature that are solely preoccupied with their own, intrinsic, self-referential matters. "A purely artistic culture is a cage in which the chase after one's own tail takes place," he writes in *Land of Ulro.*[5] With similar decisiveness, he speaks against postmodernity's fluid philosophical understanding of reality and truth (meaning the concurrence of judgments with reality). He maintains that these tendencies have borne evil fruits in literature, art, and poetry – namely, the abandonment of mimetic aesthetics, that is, of the principle of imitation, and thus the ability and will to express reality.

There is little proselytizing in Miłosz's stance, however. Quite the contrary: he is too aware of the depth of his own pessimistic world view and the magnitude of his doubts to feel comfortable in the role of a teacher. Miłosz's conscious choice to speak in the name of reality and truth, made despite his awareness of its shortcomings, is rooted in aesthetic and philosophical reasons rather than moral ones. Following the Classical tradition, he stubbornly believes that by choosing to side with goodness and beauty one increases one's chances of taking the side of the truth. He was aware of the cultural devastation – not only in communist Poland, but also in the West – that resulted from the triumphs of relativism and from the erasure of a sense of hierarchy that allows us to distinguish between the significant and the insignificant, the high and the low. In several of his books – most prominently in *The Land of Ulro* – he describes this "realm of spiritual pain,"[6] suggesting a range of remedies for such a condition. In light of the intellectual paradigms of postmodernism, Miłosz's conservative position seems utterly eccentric, a type of creative anachronism.

It is only appropriate at this point to note a peculiar paradox in Miłosz's essayistic writing: Why does this anti-postmodern writer turn out to be so difficult upon close reading, and quite perplexing? Briefly speaking, although Miłosz explores the nature of human evil and the mystery of metaphysical evil throughout history (for he believes in the substantiality of evil), he resists the temptation of philosophical nihilism. Instead, he locates certainty in the realm of Pascal's Gambit, just as postmodern philosophers today position it in a crypto-teleological realm, where their metaphysics of absence reside. It is out of Pascal's Gambit that Miłosz's hope grows, supporting a faith in *apokathastasis*, namely, the belief in the return to a state of primeval harmony once history comes to its end. This is also a consequence of the fact that, in his thinking about the world, Miłosz is aware of the contradictions in which we are inevitably implicated by merely living in it; if he ends with a full stop, he does so knowing that the period is like a stone thrown into a rapid current – it will never stop the flow of interpretation.

Miłosz's thinking also feeds on logic, in which the principle of non-contradiction often loses its axiomatic value. A number of contradictions appear as antinomies in his essays. For example, while he eulogizes the beauty of the world and praises human existence on "this Earth of wonder,"[7] he simultaneously often writes about his hatred towards life and the imperfect Creation, which is tainted with evil. He admits of the need for order but reminds his readers that such a desire cannot be fulfilled. He writes extensively about immorality of art and ambiguity of artistic choices; about the alienation that preconditions communal ties; and about the mystery of destiny, which makes the presence of evil prerequisite for the manifestation of good. His conviction about the importance of mindfulness and contemplation in the process of directing the modern mind, infected with "motion malady,"[8] towards eternal truths, exists alongside a belief that these truths can be grasped in the midst of historical events and through an adoration of the moment. Taking things further still: Miłosz stands on the side of reason, but he also considers the victory of the scientific world view as a lethal threat on a universal scale; he maintains that only a restored religious imagination can provide salvation and a chance at escaping the crisis. His metaphysical project is based on the architectonics of an early Christian imagination, yet he is also the author of this statement: "heresy is the salt of our times."[9] While he affirms the advantages of orthodoxy, it is the "homeless, searching, and not necessarily Christian"[10] faith that triggers his respect. In light of the widely discussed decline in secular thinking by such contemporary scholars as Peter L. Berger, Charles Taylor, and Jurgen Habermas, Miłosz's course of thought is acquiring new interpretative contexts, and this anachronistic and conservative writer is turning out to be quite current.

In his writings about literature, Miłosz deliberately takes an old-fashioned stance. He wants to be a poet from before the "linguistic turn" of the last century, when the language of poetry became autonomous, signifying and simultaneously establishing its own conditions of signification, and thus constituting its own reality. Miłosz wants to believe in the connection between language and the world and to write intelligible poems that communicate important matters. His awareness of linguistic traps and of the chasm between language and being, however, forces him to accept his defeat in this matter, for he is chasing the inexpressible. Therefore, as in his essay "O moim zamiarze" (Of My Intention) from *Widzenia nad zatoką San Francisco* (Visions from the San Francisco Bay, 1969), he defends literature that speaks about reality even as he constantly deliberates upon its failure.

Such contradictions cease to baffle once we come to appreciate that Miłosz believes that all poetry and art have them at their core. More than that: it is only faith that enables the conception of the world as anointed with meaning. For this reason, and despite what I have initially stated, perhaps Miłosz is, after all, "an essayistic man": someone for whom what is permanent, innocuous, and unchanging appears always in the guise of that which is ephemeral, provisional, and fluid. The belief in the presence of meaning is a metaphysical gambit, with life being an endless interpretation of the conditions of this risky gamble, a never-ending negotiation and fulfilment of the contract. The essay is a fitting genre for such operations, for – as Walter Hilsbecher wrote in his essay about the essay – "the absolute is the constant temptation of an essayist."[11]

Marek Zaleski
Institute of Literary Research of the Polish Academy Sciences / University of Warsaw
Translated by Joanna Niżyńska and Tamara Trojanowska

NOTES

1 Miłosz, *Ogród nauk*, 146.
2 Miłosz, *Native Realm: A Search for Self-Definition*, 4.
3 Miłosz, *Ogród nauk*, 36.
4 Gombrowicz, *Diary*, vol. 1, 20.
5 Miłosz, *The Land of Ulro*, 156.
6 Miłosz. *The Land of Ulro*, 32.
7 Miłosz, "An Appeal," 268.
8 The verse "Cause of that malady" appears in a poem titled "To Raja Rao," 254.
9 Miłosz, "Traktat moralny," 290.
10 Miłosz, "Państwo wyznaniowe?," *Gazeta Wyborcza*, 8.
11 Hilsbecher, "Esej o eseju," 133.

WORKS CITED

Gombrowicz, Witold. *Diary*, vol. 1. Translated by Lillian Vallee. New Haven: Yale University Press, 2012.

Hilsbecher, Walter. "Esej o eseju." In *Tragizm, absurd i paradoks*. Translated by Sławomir Błaut. 127–37. Warszawa: PIW, 1972.

Miłosz, Czesław. "An Appeal." In *New and Collected Poems 1931–2001*. 268–70. New York: HarperCollins, 2001.

– "To Raja Rao." In *New and Collected Poems 1931–2001*. 254–6. New York: HarperCollins, 2001.

– *The Land of Ulro*. Translated by Louis Iribarne. New York: Farrar, Straus and Giroux, 1984.

– *Native Realm: A Search for Self-Definition*. New York: Doubleday, 1968.

– "Państwo wyznaniowe?" *Gazeta Wyborcza*, 11 May 1991.

– "Strefa chroniona." In *Ogród nauk*. 143–55. Paris: Instytut Literacki, 1979.

– "Traktat moralny." In *Wiersze*. 284–98. Kraków: Wydawnictwo Znak, 1993.

THE ESSAY

History of Ideas (Leszek Kołakowski)

Leszek Kołakowski (1927–2009) is a singular figure in Polish culture. He was an authority figure for many in Poland (though never for all) for almost his entire life – a rare example of a renowned philosopher who actually influenced politics and contributed to political transformations. This outstanding thinker, essayist, and writer also represents the fate of the Polish intelligentsia after 1945. His significance for Polish culture lies in four areas: his emblematic biography and position as an authority figure; the categories and metaphors he brought into intellectual circulation; the role of his philosophical oeuvre; and, finally, his literary talent.

BIOGRAPHY

Leszek Kołakowski was born in 1927 in Radom. He studied philosophy in Łódź, where he joined the Communist Party in 1945. After 1953 he lectured at Warsaw University. He was expelled from the party in 1966 and two years later he was stripped of the right to lecture and publish, which effectively forced him to emigrate. After short visits and lectures in Paris, Montreal, and Berkeley, he settled in England, where he resided until the end of his life, teaching at All Souls College at Oxford University between 1972 and 1995. He was an official representative in exile for some opposition circles, and to him is attributed the idea of creating free trade unions in communist Poland. In 2003 he became the first recipient of the John W. Kluge Prize of the Library of Congress (an American equivalent of the Nobel Prize in the Humanities). He died in 2009 in Oxford.

Kołakowski's intellectual journey followed a path characteristic of a substantial part of the postwar Polish intelligentsia. He began his literary and philosophical career in the 1950s as a Marxist of revolutionary temperament (in the area of philosophy), sometimes brutally criticizing acclaimed philosophers with non-communist outlooks (for instance, Władysław Tatarkiewicz [1886–1980]). During this period he was an authority figure for young communists, distinguished even then by his intellectual horizons and superb polemical style. He was particularly severe in his critique of the Catholic Church, although his polemics stood out – in contrast to many attacks of communist political writers – for having a good grasp of both theology and official Church documents.

His stance and opinions began to evolve towards the end of the 1950s, a process that lasted approximately until the mid-1960s. The turning point in relations between Polish intellectuals and communism came with Nikita Khrushchev's 1956 iconic speech addressing, among other things, Stalinist crimes in the Soviet Union. High hopes regarding the new authorities – initially thought of as more liberal – were deflated the same year, however, when it become clear that the communists did not intend to either reform the country or share in its rule. In Kołakowski's case, of additional significance was the growing antipathy of the communist authorities towards his views and writing, for the philosopher did not always follow the directives of the Party, especially in relation to Marxism. During this period, he became an intellectual leader for the so-called revisionists – a group of intellectuals who reinterpreted the philosophy of Marx by referencing primarily early philosophical works of the author of *Capital* and contrasting them with his later, more politicized writings.

At the same time, relations with the Catholic Church were changing, both for Kołakowski and (a little later) for some of Poland's leftist intellectuals. At first, the philosopher's stance towards religion became neutral, and later even sympathetic, although he avoided making unequivocal declarations.

After 1968, the year he emigrated, having been expelled from the Party and the university in connection with the "March events," Kołakowski became an intellectual authority figure for the anti-communist opposition. In an essay important to these circles titled "Tezy o nadziei i beznadziejności" (Theses on Hope and Hopelessness, 1971), he argued that communism is by nature despotic and non-reformable, meaning that one cannot count on its disintegration and must, through one's own actions, take lessons from "the most simple precepts – those which forbid silence in the face of knavery, servile subservience to those in authority, accepting alms with humility or other similar attitudes. Our own dignity gives us the right to proclaim out loud the old words 'freedom,' 'justice,' and 'Poland.'"[1] Declarations like these ensured that until 1989, when the Berlin Wall fell, Kołakowski would be a formative presence in Poland, even if he was speaking as an émigré. After 1990, Kołakowski – now published in Poland without restrictions – became a powerful figure in public discourse, somewhat paradoxically considering his own aversion to the labelling of his opinions and the fact that his stance leaned ever more strongly towards conservatism. This was a time for celebrating Kołakowski, however, rather than for the careful analysis of his work.

Such a complex biography led to numerous paradoxes in the reception of Kołakowski's writings. To this day he is treated by some as a Marxist who did not account sufficiently for his past ideological engagement. At the cusp of the 1950s and 1960s, when he began to change his position on religion, he was criticized by some groups with ties to the Catholic Church and simultaneously by the authorities and the regime's publicists. These paradoxes were only deepened by differences in Kołakowski's Polish and foreign reception. In the West, the philosopher was – and is to this day – perceived as an expert on and critic of Marxism, for which he was sometimes the target of sharp polemics from Western leftist circles. During the 1990s and in the twenty-first century, despite maintaining a moderate conservative stance, he was still treated by right-wing circles as an heir to communist ideology and a critic of religion.

Another complication with the reception of Kołakowski's writing stems from the evaluation of his philosophical work. Some academics view him as more of an essayist or a writer than a philosopher, because of his writing style and his involvement in public discourse as well as the fact that he was not a traditionally oriented academic, but rather a critical commentator on various concepts and a historian of ideas. At the same time, due to the quality of his writings and his academic positions at renowned universities (Oxford University and the University of Chicago), he is the best-known Polish philosopher and has a rock-solid intellectual legacy. Kołakowski is thus a rare – in Polish culture – example of a philosopher who not only described reality but also had a real (albeit indirect) impact on it.

Metaphors and Categories

Kołakowski brought a number of resonant metaphors and important categories into intellectual circulation. The most important of them is undoubtedly the opposition between the priest and the jester, which refers to diametrically different means of engaging in critical reflection. The priest strengthens absolutes and cultivates traditional values, whereas the jester – advocated by the philosopher – "reveals the shakiness of the seemingly unshakeable and casts doubt on the seemingly obvious, the self-evident, the incontrovertible; it ridicules accepted common sense and discovers truths in absurdities."[2]

Another of Kołakowski's categories that is active to this day stems from the title of one of his essays: "Jak być konsereatywno-liberalnym socjalistą" (How to Be a Conservative–Liberal Socialist).[3] The intriguing notion of reconciling these polarities can even be approached as a program, as a position of peculiar compromise and, simultaneously, as a critical and sometimes self-ironic distancing from all labels, especially those viewed as contrary. To some extent this distancing may stem from the philosopher's own experience: since he had succumbed to communist ideology and was also the victim of Nazism (his father was killed by the Nazis), it is possible that Kołakowski considered sharp criticism and the avoidance of polarities to be the safest stance from which to defend oneself against ideological asphyxiation. At the same time, he considered the validity of such a position. In one of his most important historio-philosophical works, *Świadomość religijna i więź kościelna* (Religious Consciousness and Church Ties, 1965), he described the situation of unorthodox seventeenth-century thinkers from the perspective of their relationship to dogmas and institutions. This work has often been interpreted as a deeply personal philosophical parable, the actual object of which is to contemplate the dilemmas of disloyal revisionists with regard to Marxist orthodoxy. Kołakowski, then, developed a specific mode of thinking and writing about contemporary problems that allowed him to sidestep censorship even while revealing the universality of certain dilemmas.

Kołakowski as a Philosopher

Internationally, Kołakowski is most valued as the author of the monumental work *Main Currents of Marxism: Its Origins, Growth, and Dissolution* (1978). This wide-ranging presentation of Marxist thought reaches the conclusion that its murderous character was embedded in it from the start; thus it cannot be defended with the argument that communism is a perversion of a supposedly noble ideology. Marxism, that is, was always ignoble. The philosopher ends his deliberations as follows:

> Marxism has been the greatest fantasy of our century … At present Marxism neither interprets the world, nor changes it: it is merely a repertoire of slogans serving to organize various

interests ... The self-deification of mankind, to which Marxism gave philosophical expression, has ended in the same way as all such attempts, whether individual or collective: it has revealed itself as the farcical aspect of human bondage.[4]

But Kołakowski had attained his high rank among philosophers much earlier than this. Together with Jerzy Szacki (1929–2016), Bronisław Baczko (1924–2016), Barbara Skarga (1919–2009), and Andrzej Walicki (b. 1930), he co-founded the Warszawska Szkoła Historyków Idei (Warsaw School of Historians of Ideas), which studied ideas from the perspective of their ideological underpinnings, which often went unrecognized by their creators. Such studies demonstrated the immutability or repetition of certain ideas. For a significant part of his academic career, Kołakowski was a philosopher of religion, who analysed past means of interpreting and reinterpreting Christianity (especially those of the seventeenth century) as well as contemporary Catholic doctrine and the problems and paradoxes of religious reflection. After an initial critique of religion in the 1950s, Kołakowski crossed over in the second half of the 1960s to the position that mythical thought, including religious thought, is the foundation of all world views, including rationalism (in *Obecność mitu* [The Presence of Myth, 1966, published 1972]). This led him to surmise that we should neither give up this perspective, nor assume that we will be able to establish a position free of *mythos*. Kołakowski can thus be viewed a herald of post-secular thought.

His meta-rational position, from which he analysed various forms of rationalism, is accompanied from his earliest writings by the conviction that despite truth's unknowability, the search for it cannot be forsaken (articulated most explicitly in *Husserl i poszukiwanie pewności* [Husserl and the Search for Certitude, 1975]). Searching for truth, according to Kołakowski, is a human response to an indispensable existential need and constitutes a foundation of our culture. It is from this perspective that he critiqued modernity for its totalizing tendencies, but also postmodernity for its strongly relativistic character.

Kołakowski's contribution to philosophical culture through the popularization of philosophical concepts is also worth underscoring. He was able to use his authority, especially towards the end of his life, to popularize the history of philosophy (e.g., *Mini wykłady o maxi sprawach* [Mini-Lectures on Maxi-Issues, 2003]; *O co nas pytają wielcy filozofowie* [What Are Great Philosophers Asking Us, 2004]) and chosen philosophical currents (e.g., in the anthology *Filozofia egzystencjalna* [Existential Philosophy, 1965], in *Filozofia pozytywistyczna* [Positivist Philosophy, 1971] and in *Bergson* [1985]). His effectiveness in this regard flowed from his ability to synthesize ideas as well as from his literary talent.

Kołakowski as a Writer

Kołakowski wrote literary texts almost from the very beginning of his career. Notably, however, the greatest part of his literary output belongs to period of his ideological transformations, namely from the end of the 1950s until the mid-1960s. It seems that literature allowed him to test ideas in a less binding form, stripped of the categorical nature of academic discourse and with room for free speculation, ambivalence, and semantic nuance. Hence, Kołakowski's literary style of writing reflected both the need for artistic expression and the desire to question the legitimacy of discursive philosophy and to thus expose its limitations.

Kołakowski always cared about style and had a great sense of the reader, as a result of which he reached a varied audience. The distinctive characteristics of his style are irony (his titles are an example – see inset) and auto-irony and a tendency towards archaisms and clarity of expression (as well as an aversion to philosophical terminology). These are most evident in his later output. Kołakowski could also brilliantly parody various styles – philosophical in particular.

It is worth paying attention to the changing role of irony in Kołakowski's work. Initially it serves a satirical critique (mainly of religion and the Catholic Church); later it more frequently has a defensive character, when the philosopher is either defending himself against attacks – for example, in *Moje słuszne poglądy na wszystko* (My Correct Views on Everything, 1999) – or distancing himself from the contemporary world:

> So many components of our civilization not only have been condemned to death, but effectively guillotined, yet afterwards – we see them still, alive and well. How many times has it been announced with a tragic look that the novel has given up the ghost? Not so: new novels are constantly created – after the execution – and some of them are actually good ... The end of history, the end of love, the end of ideology ... corpses everywhere, cemeteries all around, but afterward after all a resurrection.[5]

Irony functions best, however, when Kołakowski confronts contrary opinions while situating himself outside the polemic (e.g., in the introduction to *Main Currents of Marxism*).

INVENTION AND (SELF)IRONY: THE POETICS OF TITLES

Antysemici. 5 tez nienowych i przestroga (Anti-Semites – Five Theses that Are Not New, and a Warning, 1956); *Nieskromny komentarz do skromnej encykliki papieża Jana XXIII* (An Immodest Comment to the Modest Encyclical of Pope John XXIII, 1961); *Moje słuszne poglądy na wszystko* (My Correct Views on Everything, 1974); *Jak być konserwatywno-liberalnym socjalistą?* (How to be a Conservative–Liberal Socialist?, 1978); *Moje życie ze szczególnym uwzględnieniem szalonego wręcz powodzenia u kobiet* (My Life with Particular Emphasis on Outright Insane Success with Women, 1978); *Komentarz do komentarza Heideggera do domniemanego komentarza Nietzschego do komentarza Hegla o potędze negatywności* (A Comment on Heidegger's Comment on Nietzsche's Alleged Comment on Hegel's Comment on the Power of Negativity, 1990).

The range of genres of Kołakowski's texts is impressive: short and long poems (mainly occasional in character), dramas and monologues, fables and other parabolic forms, and finally various kinds of parodic and pastiche texts. The most accomplished on a literary level are three volumes – *13 bajek z Królestwa Lailonii* (Tales from the Kingdom of Lailonia, 1963) and *Klucz niebieski albo opowieści budujące z historii świętej zebrane* (The Key to Heaven, 1964) – which were published together in English translation in 1989; and *Rozmowy z Diabłem* (Conversations with the Devil, 1965). Kołakowski's tales are philosophical parables that play with popular notions and follow the Enlightenment model of Voltaire's philosophical tales. *The Key to Heaven* is a collection of apocryphal reinterpretations and commentaries of biblical stories presented from the perspective of a rationalist and a sceptic. *Conversations with the Devil* consists of several monologues, also apocryphal, delivered by historical figures (such as Héloïse and Luther) and – in the "Great Sermon of Priest Bernard" – by the devil (and titular preacher) himself.

> Perhaps the most salient feature of Leszek Kołakowski's work, and one that characterizes him best, is his attitude towards truth and certainty. He writes in his preface to *My Correct Views on Everything*: "None of the dilemmas is properly solved. Everything is left ambiguous. I want to believe that this is not just a result of my ineptitude, but perhaps also of the incurable ambiguity of reality itself."
>
> – Agnieszka Kołakowska in Kołakowski, *Is God Happy? Selected Essays*, xiii

Thematically, Kołakowski's literary work is largely a reflection of his strictly philosophical writings. It constitutes, however, an intriguing and (in Poland) rare example of an effective reconciliation of various discourses. It also makes up a significant part of the output of Kołakowski, who is himself an indisputable phenomenon in Polish culture. In the introduction to the last collection of texts prepared during his life, Kołakowski summed up his writing as follows:

> As with almost everything that I have written … I cannot arrive at final conclusions in matters of greatest importance and always stumble on issues that have to be by-passed with the awkward and absconding saying "on the one hand …, but on the other hand …" Perhaps it is an affliction, or rather a defect of the author's mind, but perhaps it is after all … an affliction of existence. With this I end.[6]

Maciej Michalski
University of Gdańsk
Translated by Agnieszka Polakowska

NOTES

1 Kołakowski, "Hope and Hopelessness," 52.
2 Kołakowski, "The Priest and the Jester," 260.
3 Kołakowski, "How to be a Conservative-Liberal Socialist: A Credo" in *Modernity on Endless Trial*.
4 Kołakowski, *Main Currents of Marxism: Its Origins, Growth, and Dissolution*, vol. 3: *The Breakdown*, 523, 530.
5 Kołakowski, "Nasza wesoła apokalipsa. Kazanie na koniec wieku," 47.
6 Kołakowski, "Zastrzeżenie albo ostrzeżenie," *Czy Pan Bóg jest szczęśliwy i inne pytania*, 5.

WORKS CITED

Kołakowski, Leszek. "Hope and Hopelessness." *Survey: A Journal of East and West Studies* 17, no. 3 (1971): 52.

– "How to Be a Conservative–Liberal Socialist: A Credo." In *Modernity on Endless Trial*. 225–7. Chicago: University of Chicago Press, 1990.

– *Is God Happy? Selected Essays*. Translated by Agnieszka Kołakowska. London: Penguin Books, 2012.

– "Kapłan i błazen." In *Pochwała niekonsekwencji: pisma rozproszone z lat 1955–1968*. Vol. II. Edited by Zbigniew Mentzel. 263–93. London: Puls, 1989.

– *Main Currents of Marxism: Its Origins, Growth, and Dissolution*, vol. 3 (*The Breakdown*). Translated by P.S. Falla. Oxford: Clarendon Press, 1978.

– "Nasza wesoła apokalipsa. Kazanie na koniec wieku." In *Moje słuszne poglądy na wszystko*. 41–52. Kraków: Znak, 1999.

– "The Priest and the Jester." In *The Two Essays of Spinoza and Other Essays on Philosophers*. 239–62. South Bend: St Augustine's Press, 2004.

– "Tezy o nadziei i beznadziejności." In *Czy diabeł może być zbawiony i 27 innych kazań*. 285–99. London: Aneks, 1984.

– "Zastrzeżenie albo ostrzeżenie" [Introduction]. In *Czy Pan Bóg jest szczęśliwy i inne pytania*. Edited by Zbigniew Mentzel. 5. Kraków: Znak, 2009.

Hermeneutics of the Marginal (Jolanta Brach-Czaina)

In *Świat bez kobiet* (World Without Women, 2001), one of the most important works of Polish feminism, Agnieszka Graff recommends Jolanta Brach-Czaina's *Szczeliny istnienia* (The Crevices of Being, 1992) in the following manner: "A cult essay about bustling about, giving birth and dumplings. A philosophical book, which apparently does not have anything in common with feminism ... but without it – no can do."[1] Indeed, *The Crevices of Being* and its continuation *Błony umysłu* (Membranes of the Mind, 2003) became uncommonly popular. Their language, both poetic and reminiscent of a treatise, is now recognizable and intelligible to many feminists who – taking it as their own – have supplemented or repudiated it.

> The direct impact of Brach-Czaina's philosophy on Polish feminism is not self-evident. The movement's most important voices, conflicts, and activities – to recall Kinga Dunin, Agnieszka Graff, Kazimiera Szczuka, and, among the younger generation, Agnieszka Mrozik – have long focused on political issues that are absent from *The Crevices of Being*, such as the right to abortion, the redefinition of gender roles, equality in the labour market, and the stronger representation of women in public life, as well as on the right to make strategic choices. These feminists situated themselves vis-à-vis actual sociopolitical problems that intensified after the mid-1990s. *The Crevices of Being* is often referenced, however, in the context of utopian themes, for example, of the existential ennoblement of women's domestic work or of the open subject that does not produce the sense of the abject.

The Crevices of Being was published in 1992, but emerged out of labour dating back at least to the mid-1980s. Arriving eleven years later, *Membranes of the Mind* only slightly modified the philosophical conceptualization and poetics presented in its predecessor. Although Brach-Czaina refers in it to the sociopolitical context from the beginning of the most recent century, albeit indirectly, she also makes an effort to evade it – to write after her own fashion despite the passage of time. This choice calls for respect, since the author avoids being pressured into certain thematic choices, as well as for criticism, in that she does not appear to notice the heavy weight of reality. Consequently, her essay writing can provoke ambivalent feelings.

Brach-Czaina's career is unusual also because she rarely (although perhaps more often of late) reaches for a distinctly feminist vocabulary; even her use of the word *woman* is rare. She frequently relies on experiences that are physiologically or traditionally feminine, such as childbirth, menstruation, cooking, cleaning, and laundry, yet she does not focus on these. Instead she builds great existential metaphors and brings about an ostentatious universalization, as the gender-neutral subjects of her sentences – "the one who births," "the one who bustles" – vividly express.

Brach-Czaina avoids auto-interpretation, and it is only in the introduction to *Membranes of the Mind* that she writes directly about the strategy she adopted many years earlier: "In contemporary culture the voracious question about the relation between a human being and the world demands a woman's reply, even though it is meant for everyone – formulated from a feminine point of view, but universal. For a period of time."[2] Her output is part of the current of cultural feminism, with a strong motif of ecofeminism; it converges on many points with views expressed by, among others, Mary Daly, Marilyn French, Susan Griffin, Julia Kristeva, Hélène Cixous, and Luce Irigaray. It encloses a project both anthropological and ethical, one that remains in opposition to traditional conceptualizations of the subject as much as it does to the subject's contemporary deconstructions.

Brach-Czaina proposes a philosophical perspective on three aspects of human experience. First, its existential background – activities elusive of our reflection, banal and repetitive, the sense and value of which we do not notice, and which are neutral and transitory in their effect, such as breathing or eating or washing dishes. Second, those activities that can provoke repulsion and fear, from which we often turn away our eyes, such as the act of cleaning up vomit, bodily decomposition, childbirth, or absurd evil. Third, the existence of animals, plants, and objects that blind ignorance forces us to separate from our own existence and to hierarchize. The philosopher considers all of these things to be a massive conglomerate of "significant details" – concretes that communicate their meaning to us and have an immanent metaphysical dimension. According to Brach-Czaina, we lose much by not understanding that dimension, through isolating ourselves from the world and by locating meaning beyond that which exists. Her feminism and universalism is thus a type of hermeneutics: "The silence of being – or rather the false impression of silence – stems also from the deafening hubbub of human thought and speech, the noise that we raise on the planet."[3] The subject that practises and is shaped by this hermeneutics is open to heterogeneity and affirms shared domains. It does not split anything up, does not impose itself on the world, does not have set boundaries, does not hierarchize, and does not wish to rule; it constitutes a continuum with the world, it is a process, it courageously develops itself, it links oppositions, and it does not know dualities or conflicts.

An important part of this project concerns the search for language of experience – often that of women – that has remained beyond language thus far and as such has not really existed. The declaration of difference, the potential mystique of femininity, however, is immediately turned and transformed into a mystique of that which is common but rejected by both static, Western rationalism and the contemporary culture of "flashes, sounds and images,"[4] which is trying to persuade the subject of its disintegration.

Brach-Czaina's philosophy depends on the performative function of writing; it is created in suggestive, poetic texts that have their own rhythm and are vivid and intertextual, made dense by metaphors and allusions. These texts are spiral in composition, with key thoughts and phrases returning in supplemented and expanded forms and demanding the return to the concept of *écriture feminine*. Their tone is part aphoristic, part religious. Brach-Czaina contrarily stylizes her text after a tractatus, meditation, prayer, or gospel, weaving in micro-citations and strongly marked words from the history of philosophy, the Bible, Catholic liturgy, and carols. She does not hesitate to assert that this or that is of a particular nature, that our fate is such and such, and that we should act in this or that way. She does not hesitate to speak of mystery, revelation, the confession of faith and sin – to use language that she calls non-rational, tautological, and paradoxical. It is clearly a kind of a literary game –the communicativeness of her essays does not suffer as a result, and neither does their crystalline construction.

Brach-Czaina draws inspiration from both existentialism and phenomenology. She poses questions that are characteristic of existentialism – for example, about the place of the individual human being in the world, about the responsibility that ensues from freedom, and about our being in time and constantly becoming. She utilizes the phenomenological method of direct analysis of reality's manifestations. Her essays oscillate between paraphrase and pastiche of this most popular of philosophical languages during the 1980s. She uses it in the service of "low" themes and phenomena, however, which were never the object of interest for the "great" existentialists and other philosophers.

Best known are two of the essays from *Cracks of Existence*. The first one, "Otwarcie" (Opening), is an explication of childbirth as a "preverbal existential initiation"[5] that is accessible to everyone. Within it is contained an unconditional acceptance, an opening onto all possibilities, including evil, and the transgression of oneself. "Fear and suffering, which animate our activity and force us to push, are from the beginning written into the foundations of our being."[6] The tautology of birth depends on the fact that the effort put into it points to the value of existence that rests "on the hard ground of pain, which we know well." This is not a throwaway formula – we give birth, and we evolve ourselves at all times. Birth teaches resignation from will, which is wilfulness; binding us with animals, it proves that the distancing from nature is an illusion and that the rejection of bloated individual consciousness under a biological imperative allows us to experience success, not failure.

The second famous essay, "Krzątactwo" (Bustling About), is dedicated to minor, obvious activities that are necessary but stripped of significance and that fill our everyday lives. Since we spend our lives bustling about, it would be helpful to know the sense of these activities – to be conscious of cleaning as a battle against death, as the creation of order against amorphism and chaos, as an effort to hinder the earth that "buries us along with our houses, although the falling clusters cannot be heard even as, despite our protests, they pound on the lid."[7] Bustling about, which we share with animals – for instance, a spider or a beetle – is our driving force, and the dignity of this act should be appreciated. In other essays, Brach-Czaina writes about the "gravitas of rags," testifying to the impossibility of separating cleanliness from dirt, or about the "metaphysics of meat,"[8] meaning the element of meatiness that makes us part of a bloodthirsty and sacrificial community whose members eat others and themselves are eaten as they participate in the unceasing metamorphosis of death into life.

Perhaps her most daring essay is about the sanctity of evil, which according to her is not a defect that is impossible to remove, but rather an important element of experience.

Moral prohibitions and the dispensation of justice are all too frequently a form of revenge and aggression and thus increase the sum of evil while allowing us to maintain a pure conscience. Here the author of *The Crevices of Being* goes furthest in her reflections: she is interested in situations where an extreme act of cruelty takes place – an absurd murder of an accidental, innocent victim, including the mass evil of the Holocaust. In line with this philosophy, the suffering of a victim – even if no one, including the victim itself, is aware of it – "reveals the pure value of existence,"[9] which in more favourable circumstances is obscured by the value of those circumstances. Cognizance of this value "is worth the price of being stricken by evil tending toward our annihilation."[10] The tormentor with each blow intensifies the existence of the tormented, and the tormented is untouchable, "chosen by fate."[11] And again, this does not have to be a human being – "it could be a tormented rat."[12] In this way, Brach-Czaina attempts to cross over the aporia of post-Holocaust literature and to save the victims through the cessation of "whimpering" over them.

Would it perhaps be better, however, to try and prevent suffering – which Brach-Czaina considers to be impossible – rather than to give it meaning? This question, which arises frequently in the process of reading, concerns the utopia that the philosopher designs while balking at its previous forms. She does not trust the progressive vision of evolution and does not believe in the elimination of evil, but she yearns after a "renewal,"[13] imagining and evoking change. An immense change, even if accomplished on a micro-scale, in the intimate sphere and through subtle hermeneutic means. She does not deal, however, with social, political, or economic conditions, and on principle she does not see the need for legal solutions and institutional interventions. She is not troubled even by the fact that it would be difficult to join in public discourse and articulate the everyday problems of Polish women using her language. It is as if she were already living in a different world. The closest that Brach-Czaina gets to the issue of the restrictive anti-abortion bill is when she euphemistically describes the properties of the Black Hollyhock and other plants that "induce menstruation."[14] With each year the isolation of this writing strategy chosen in the mid-1980s appears to deepen – Black Hollyhock is not sufficient for women to be able to make decisions about their own lives.

Jolanta Brach-Czaina could also be instrumentalized in an anti-feminist way. The feminine mystique with its central praise of childbirth may provide symbolic exaltation while serving real subordination rather than an existential renewal. The characteristics that Brach-Czaina considers feminine, natural, even physiological and that she wishes to universalize could equally well be seen as the result of cultural training. "The one who births" or "the one who bustles" is still frequently economically and socially disabled in Poland, and it so happens that this person is a woman. Since childbirth and bustling about are such significant activities, it may be concluded that women should be proud of their position. Since they have obtained physiological gratification, there is no sense in demanding it in another form. Moreover, within Brach-Czaina's sterile world there are no strong, existing influences (for instance, market forces). Perhaps it is precisely the discomfort and ambiguity generated by Brach-Czaina's approach that may constitute the greatest value of her philosophy.

Eliza Szybowicz
Literary critic
Translated by Agnieszka Polakowska

NOTES

1 Graff, *Świat bez kobiet*, 279.
2 Brach-Czaina, *Błony umysłu*, 6.
3 Brach-Czaina, *Szczeliny istnienia*, 8.
4 Brach-Czaina, *Błony umysłu*, 57.
5 Brach-Czaina, *Szczeliny istnienia*, 29.
6 Ibid., 34.
7 Ibid., 72.
8 "Powaga ścierek" (Gravitas of Rags) and "Metafizyka mięsa" (Metaphysics of Meat) are the titles of the two chapters in *Szczeliny istnienia* (The Crevices of Being). Przemysław Czapliński writes about Brach-Czaina's philosophy in the context of body, cleanliness, dirtiness, and otherness in Polish contemporary culture in *Polska do wymiany*, 357–9.
9 Brach-Czaina, *Szczeliny istnienia*, 121.
10 Ibid., 121.
11 Ibid., 121.
12 Ibid., 117.
13 Brach-Czaina, *Błony umysłu*, 116.
14 Ibid., 51.

WORKS CITED

Brach-Czaina, Jolanta. *Błony umysłu*. Warszawa: Sic!, 2003.

– *Szczeliny istnienia*. Warszawa: Państwowy Instytut Wydawniczy, 1992.

Czapliński, Przemysław. *Polska do wymiany. Późna nowoczesność i nasze wielkie narracje*. Warszawa: Wydawnictwo W.A.B., 2009.

Graff, Agnieszka. *Świat bez kobiet: płeć w polskim życiu publicznym*. Warszawa: Wydawn. WAB, 2001.

Poland's Autobiographical Twentieth Century

When taken as a starting point, Ryszard Nycz's differentiation of four discourses in Polish modern literature – fictional, documentary, autobiographical, and essayistic – reveals that the first of them, over the course of the twentieth century, gradually lost its importance to the benefit of the other three, with autobiographical discourse (genres such as diaries, memoirs, and letters) playing the most significant role among them.[1] In very general terms, this process can be described as a transition from a fiction-centric to an autobiographical model of Polish literature.

Significant here is the historical context of Polish twentieth-century experiences, including the restoration of Poland's independence in 1918 after more than a century of partitions, followed by two world wars, the Holocaust, mass economic and political emigration, and postwar life in a country of "real socialism," governed by a communist party. Autobiographical genres with a clear authorial voice proved best at expressing these experiences. Indeed, one could say that rejection of impersonal (omniscient) narration has been an important characteristic of both Polish and Central European modern literature. Seen through a prism of autobiographical genres, Polish modern literature reveals both its original and universal aspects.

In describing the autobiographical and (to some extent) documentary tendencies in Polish literature, three factors are of particular importance. The first is the increasing significance of everyday, common writing practices and genres, often undertaken by people who are far from professional writers, along with the impact of these on professional literati. The second is the evolution of autobiographical genres themselves, which have acquired an ever more literary character, as is best visible in intimate diaries. The third and last phenomenon is the feminization of autobiographical genres. Polish twentieth-century literature, after being dominated during the nineteenth century by the masculine voice, has acquired a stronger feminine component. The female voice is being heard across a range of genres, and in autobiographical writing it now occupies a central place.

Polish twentieth-century writing is no longer the exclusive domain of professional writers. The five-volume work *The Polish Peasant in Poland and America*, published in the United States between 1918 and 1920 by sociologists William Thomas and Florian Znaniecki, was based almost exclusively on autobiographical materials such as letters and diaries. The authors used these as source materials for their study; they also published 764 of the letters, as well as more than half of the six-hundred-page diary that Władysław Wiśniewski wrote at their request. The author of *Pamiętnik emigranta* (Life Record of an Immigrant) was a Polish peasant who, with many others like him, immigrated to the United States at the beginning of the twentieth century.[2] As a consequence of appearing in print, autobiographical notes of non-professional writers acquired an autonomous value. This was the beginning of the "biographical method" that henceforth became a speciality of Polish twentieth-century sociology; it also served as the symbolic introduction to Polish letters of autobiographical documents by non-writers, whose role over the course of the century would grow and gradually change the meaning of terms such as *writer*, *writing*, and *literature*.

An important part of this process was played by memoir-writing contests, which were organized throughout the twentieth century in Poland by scientific institutes, social organizations, and journal editors as well as, after its founding in 1969, by the Towarzystwo Przyjaciół Pamiętnikarstwa (The Friends of Memoir-Writing Society). Several dozen such contests were held during the interwar period (1918–39). Their popularity fell after 1945 before rising sharply again after 1960. Over the course of the century, the total number of such contests reached approximately 1,600 – undoubtedly a world-scale phenomenon.

The first such contest – for memoirs by physical labourers – was organized by Florian Znaniecki in 1921, right after his return from the United States. In the 1930s, more such contests would be organized by the Instytut Gospodarstwa Społecznego (Socio-Economic Institute), headed by Ludwik Krzywicki; these spotlighted memoirs by peasants, the unemployed, or emigrants.[3] After the war, memoir contests were aimed at specific professions (doctors, teachers, miners, the militia, etc.) or had as their subject historical events (first and foremost Second World War experiences).[4] These postwar contests were "ideologized," in that they emphasized the negative aspects of the prewar capitalist system along with the positive changes brought about under communism. For this reason, there was no room therein for experiences related to (for example) the Soviet prisons and gulags, the Warsaw Uprising, the postwar anti-communist partisan brigades and their repression by the communist authorities, or anti-communist activities by the opposition in Poland. This situation continued right up to and throughout the Solidarity movement and the martial law period. Autobiographical writings about these experiences remained buried in family archives for many years or were collected in the archives of Polish emigration centres in England, France, and the United States. Their compilation in Poland would begin only after 1989, usually alongside ever more numerous oral history collections. These latter recordings constitute, after diaries and memoirs, another important means for preserving historical experiences of significance to the Poles.

All of this points to the democratization of Polish writing, as well as the pervasiveness of historical experiences in it, especially those related to the Second World War, approached from the perspective of "history from below." Moreover, these phenomena underscore the acquisition of literary value by practices and genres previously situated outside of literature. During the 1930s, the memoirs of peasants, workers, the unemployed, and emigrants were printed in thick, solid volumes. The introduction to one of these volumes – of selections from a peasant memoir contest – was written by a renowned Polish writer, Maria Dąbrowska (1889–1965). Her contribution likely secured for the volume the prize for the best book of 1936, awarded by *Wiadomości Literackie* (Literary News), the most important literary journal in Poland at that time. A year earlier, the Golden Laurel of the Polish Academy of Literature for notable contributions to Polish literature had been awarded to Jakub Wojciechowski; his several-hundred-page-long memoir, which he submitted to a contest, was published in 1930 as *Życiorys własny robotnika* (A Worker's Own Biography) and generated great critical interest.

Historical events undoubtedly spurred people to keep diaries and journals. During the Second World War, the number of people who kept diaries and journals rose despite the harsh conditions. These materials were written in occupied cities, ghettos, prison camps, concentration and extermination camps, and on the war fronts, even though it was dangerous to do so and writing materials were hard to come by. They were often written, moreover, by people who had never kept a journal before.

Of unique importance are the journals and other autobiographical writings of Jews in ghettos, in hiding, and even in extermination camps, written in Polish, Yiddish, or Hebrew. Jacek Leociak in *Tekst wobec Zagłady. O relacjach z getta warszawskiego* (Text in the Face of Destruction: Accounts from the Warsaw Ghetto Reconsidered) calls attention to a real "writing phenomenon" that testifies to the difference between Jewish experience in the ghettos and what was taking place outside their walls. As Emanuel Ringelblum also notes in *Kronika getta warszawskiego* (The Warsaw Ghetto Chronicle):

> The Jew took up writing. Everyone wrote: journalists and writers, but also teachers, public men, young people – even children. Most of them kept diaries where the tragic events of the day were reflected through the prism of personal experience. A tremendous amount was written; but the vast majority of the writings was destroyed during the annihilation of Warsaw Jewry during the resettlement days. All that has remained is the material we have preserved in our Ghetto archive."[5]

The ghetto archive mentioned by Ringelblum is the famous archive created on his initiative and called the Ringelblum Archive today, which consists of materials about the Holocaust collected and hidden in tin boxes and milk canisters in three different underground locations on the grounds of the Warsaw Ghetto, two of which were discovered after the war. Today's Ringelblum Archive holds around 2,000 documents, including many diaries, journals, letters, and reports.

Two Jewish wartime diaries written in the Warsaw Ghetto merit particular attention. The first is by Adam Czerniaków (1880–1942), the head of the Warsaw Ghetto's Jewish Council. His notes on the period September 1939 to June 1942 constitute a record of the ghetto's daily functioning and its management by the council. They also express an increasing tension between the desire to serve one's own community and the necessity to enforce German orders, which culminated in Czerniaków's suicide an hour after his final diary entry on 23 June 1942.[6] The other is the diary of Chaim Kaplan (1880–1942/3), an eminent Jewish teacher who, despite his own worsening situation ("it's been five days since I had real food in my mouth"), treated writing (as did Victor Klemperer in Germany) as a peculiar "historical mission that one must not abandon."[7]

In diaries like those of Czerniaków and Kapłan, existential and social and even historical motivations are much more important than literary ones. Jews kept diaries and journals in order to "describe all of the atrocities," to testify to a time of murder and violence, to "raise an alarm and shake up the world's conscience," and finally to prepare materials that would serve as the foundations for indictments in postwar tribunals.[8] The situation is somewhat different in the case of diaries of children and teenagers, which inadvertently became testimonials of the Holocaust. These notes about everyday matters, family, friends, books, and first loves become permeated more and more by descriptions of the cruelty and terror of the Holocaust. Such is the case with the diaries of Dawid Rubinowicz (the Bodzentyn Ghetto near Kielce, 1927–42), Dawid Sierakowiak (the Łódź Ghetto,

1924–43), Renia Knoll (the Kraków Ghetto, 1927–?), and Rutka Laskier (the Będzin Ghetto, 1929–43). While the diary of Anne Frank is considered to be a unique record of the Holocaust from the perspective of a teenage girl, many of her peers in Poland kept similar journals.

A very clear characteristic of the numerous Jewish (and not only Jewish) diaries and journals kept during the war in Poland is the clash between the everyday and the extreme – the human and the inhuman. This comes to the fore not only in their contents but also their material form. For example, the lack of standard materials for writing in the Warsaw Ghetto meant that their authors used paper containers, labels and recycled documents instead. The diary of one member of a Jewish family hiding for some time in a small dugout covered with branches on one of the river islands around Sandomierz in southern Poland was written with a nib made from a fingernail. The notes of *Sonderkommando* prisoners from the Auschwitz–Birkenau extermination camp constitute perhaps the most shocking example of the encounter between daily and extreme reality in both the Holocaust text and its material form. Forced to service gas chambers and crematoria, they buried their notes in pits filled with human remains and ashes from crematory ovens, which interacted with the paper and changed its consistency. "I buried it under the ashes" – Załmen Gradowski writes – "thinking it the surest place, which will certainly be dug up in order to find the traces of millions of exterminated people ... The journal and other journals laid in graves, soaking in the blood from not always completely burned bones and pieces of meat."[9]

In the journals kept by Poles during the war, the encounter between daily and extreme reality is registered differently: the need to survive moves into the foreground. This type of journal becomes part of a personal, dynamic identity that exists in time and is both continuous and changeable, constituted ever anew. An important characteristic of these journals is the extension and ordering of memory. In this context, a missing record (the lack of an entry) can appear terrifying and be interpreted – as happens in Zofia Nałkowska's diaries – as a "lacuna in life's history."[10] Just as frequently, a journal serves the effort, renewed on a daily basis, of determining one's own future and selfhood. The diarist does not describe only his or her own life, and does not discover only him or herself; rather, he or she constitutes him or herself as he or she is. The diary of Zofia Nałkowska (1884–1954) is one example of such a journal.

Nałkowska was a prominent Polish author even before the Second World War, when she called for the emancipation of women and wrote, among others, the renowned psychological novel *Granica* (The Frontier, 1935). Her collection of short stories *Medaliony* (Medallions, 1946), written after the war, provides a harrowing description of the Holocaust. Nałkowska kept a diary for almost her entire life, from the age of twelve until her death at seventy, amassing sixty-seven notebooks. Her entries from the wartime years (1939–44), first published in a separate volume, are a unique part of her diaristic output. For Nałkowska, wartime occupation was, first and foremost, an experience of the strangeness and otherness of life. The social order had suddenly been shattered, basic products were lacking (Nałkowska and her sister, a sculptor, operated a cigarette store), and "horrific changes in the very essence of existence" were taking place. Nałkowska does not take a distanced position, but rather identifies with the fate of other inhabitants of occupied Warsaw in her diary. At the same time, she undertakes the effort of "rediscovering herself in the horror of the world" and of "holding onto her identity" in a situation where "everything happens 'wholesale,' everything is experienced collectively."[11] After the war,

Nałkowska thought of her diary more and more in terms of a life and memory archive. This merged with her belief that it is precisely personal and family archives that are the true traces of lived, experienced reality and, simultaneously, that they are the sources of literature that wants to address this reality. Consequently, both in her own works and in those of others, Nałkowska looked for the means by which a document of life, an archive of memory, or a trace of experience transforms itself into literature. Literature, as envisioned in Nałkowska's diary and realized in her other works, makes present and rescues reality, however horrific it may be.

The diary of Andrzej Trzebiński (1922–43) provides another example of a Polish wartime journal. Trzebiński was a young poet, writer, playwright, and journalist, an activist in the clandestine nationalistic organization Konfederacja Narodu (Confederation of a Nation), and an editor of the underground publication *Sztuka i Naród* (Art and Nation); he is also one representative of the so-called Columbus generation – Poles born around 1920, many of whom, including Trzebiński, lost their lives during the war. Like Nałkowska, Trzebiński wrote his diary in occupied Warsaw and experienced the war as a time of great creativity. For him, artistic and intellectual problems were deeply personal; discovering a sense of the world and of history was synonymous with finding the sense of his own life; creating an artistic program meant creating foundations for individual existence; and "I" and "history" were intimately linked.

The war, with its constant threat of death, elicited a state of unceasing psychological determination in Trzebiński. He kept a journal mainly to keep a grip on himself, to instil order within himself, to caution himself, to spur himself to even greater effort, to assign himself ever new tasks, and, afterwards, to account for their realization. The shaping of his own character and the shaping of a vision of Polish culture were for Trzebiński part of a single process of identity creation. The second part of his journal is primarily a diary of ideas, which links his writing to an important tradition of Polish twentieth-century intellectual diaries. Within this tradition, one notable example is Stanisław Brzozowski (1878–1911) – a pre-eminent Polish thinker during the first decade of the twentieth century, as well as a writer and essayist with an anti-positivist and anti-naturalist stance, who wrote his *Pamiętnik* (Memoir, 1913) during the final year of his life (it was published posthumously). Another example can be found in Henryk Elzenberg (1887–1967), a philosopher and ethicist who kept a philosophical journal throughout his entire adult life (starting in 1907); it was published for the first time in 1963 as *Kłopot z istnieniem. Aforyzmy w porządku czasu* (The Trouble with Being: Aphorisms in Time).

A third and final example of a Polish diary from the time of occupation is that of Andrzej Bobkowski (1913–61), who experienced the war as a great liberation. A young graduate of the Warsaw School of Economics, he travelled to Paris just before the Second World War and decided to stay there. His diary *Szkice piórkiem* (Sketched with a Quill Pen, 1956), published also in French as *En guerre et en paix*, is a colourful record of a cycling escapade from Paris to Carcassone and back, and of everyday life in occupied Paris. These experiences awakened in Bobkowski a sense of absolute freedom. The war, which frequently stirred up chaos and helplessness or anxiety and mobilization, released in Bobkowski an almost ecstatic fascination with life, experienced primarily on a sensual level: "Most important is NOW and one must not be afraid to suck this now dry, and then to throw it away and think about how to best use the next NOW."[12] Bobkowski did not allow external events to determine the internal course of his life. Thus, there exists a clear distance between "I" and "history" in his diary. His sense of individual identity is shaped in opposition to all forms of collective identity. The author of *Sketched with a Quill Pen* consequently rejects all cultural identifications – with Poland, France, and Europe, and with world views, ideologies, or politics. He takes the position of an outsider who does not hesitate to firmly formulate his pro-American and anti-Soviet opinions. It is known today, from a comparison between the manuscript of *Sketched with a Quill Pen* (written between 1940 and 1944) and its book form (first published in its entirety in 1956), that Bobkowski changed the tone of his text while preparing it for publication in the second half of the 1950s. He omitted his critique of American models that accompanied his critique of Soviet models in the original version, and he deleted anti-Semitic passages that were initially present. Disappointed with Europe, Bobkowski moved to Guatemala after the war, where he opened a model-making hobby store that was his main source of income for the rest of his life.

> I was lying down on the handlebars, taking sharp bends, leaning with the entire bicycle. There was something intoxicating about this. At a certain point I felt very clearly that I was no longer bothered by anything. Now, as I write this, I feel that something within me broke. Perhaps a break with the past had occurred. Finally. I am free within all this commotion … The entire ballast of thought under normal conditions, the ballast of the past, had fallen away.
>
> – Bobkowski, *Szkice piórkiem (Francja 1940–1944)*, 30–1

Bobkowski would not have published his *Sketches with a Quill Pen* were it not for Jerzy Giedroyć (1906–2000). An officer with II Corps under the command of General Władysław Anders, Giedroyć, like most Poles who fought on the Western Front during the Second World War, chose to remain in exile after the war. In 1947 he founded the political and cultural journal *Kultura* (Culture) as well as the Literary Institute Publishing House in Rome; both were shortly thereafter moved to Maisons-Laffitte near Paris. Over the course of fifty-three years, Giedroyć edited 637 issues of the monthly journal, and several hundred books were published by the house under his direction. In this capacity, Giedroyć played an important role in Polish postwar literature, especially with regard to autobiographical genres. Numerous memoirs and diaries were published in *Culture* and through the Literary Institute, including those of Jerzy Stempowski (1893–1969), Andrzej Bobkowski, Witold Gombrowicz (1904–69), and Gustaw Herling-Grudziński (1919–2000).

The Polish centre in Maisons-Laffitte was also a hub of Polish epistolography – so much so that today, historians of literature refer to the extensive net of correspondence created by Jerzy Giedroyć as "the Epistolary Republic." His correspondence includes more than 200,000 letters; a portion of these have been published in more than a dozen volumes. Over many years, Giedroyć corresponded with several hundred important personalities in Polish cultural and political life. Among the writers, in addition to those just mentioned, were also Czesław Miłosz (1911–2004), Konstanty Jeleński (1922–87), and Juliusz Mieroszewski (1906–76). The published volumes of Giedroyć's correspondence with these authors, as well as their correspondences with one another, despite being strongly tied to their contemporary context, are read today as collections of sophisticated essays and journalistic writing, often approaching the qualities of *belles-lettres*.

Maisons-Laffitte was home not only to *Culture* and Jerzy Giedroyć, but also to other extraordinary personalities. One of them was Józef Czapski (1896–1993), a prominent Polish painter and writer who, as a Polish officer, became a Soviet prisoner at the beginning of the Second World War. He was one of the few who managed to avoid the Katyn massacre. He later related his experiences in *Wspomnienia starobielskie* (Reminiscences of Starobyelsk, 1945). Once released from "the inhuman land," as he titled another book about this experience (*Na nieludzkiej ziemi*, 1949; in English, 1951), he became Giedroyć's brother-in-arms in the West. After the war, he helped him establish the Literary Institute in Maisons-Laffitte, where he lived for half a century, until his death, painting and writing his diary there. His is perhaps the most important diary even written by a Polish painter – if nothing else, it is the most extraordinary and beautiful. (Other Polish painters who kept diaries include Józef Mehoffer [1869–1946], Ferdynand Ruszczyc [1870–1936], Tadeusz Makowski [1882–1932], Jan Cybis [1897–1972], and Jerzy Stajuda [1936–92].)

Czapski's diary comprises 274 workbooks, notebooks, and specially ordered journals encompassing the period 1942 to 1992. Its entries are in the four languages in which Czapski was fluent: French, German, Russian, and Polish. It includes more than written entries: it also encompasses – and equally so – drawings, sketches, and watercolours, as well as letters, photographs, press clippings, and typescripts, which are glued to its pages. In its entirety, the diary is a combination of an intimate journal, a painter's sketchbook, and an artist's archive. Word and image comprise here a unified whole. As images encroach, the written entries lose their linearity; the images themselves are hemmed in by words, which often combine with or permeate them. We are dealing with a unique, personal testament of the activity of intellect, hand and eye. This is singularly conveyed by its last entries, made by the elderly painter as he is losing his sight and written in ever larger letters with straight lines. Czapski used his diary as a means to sublimate his spiritual life, with painting and writing as its main elements. Painterly and literary matters are treated therein as existential issues that infiltrate the everyday experience of the diarist. The diary serves as a kind of externalized conscience of the artist.

When it came to literature, the Literary Institute in Maisons-Laffitte was the most important centre of Polish emigration and thus also of epistolography. But it was not the only centre. Mention is due also to centres of Polish emigration in London, where Mieczysław Grydzewski (1894–1970) edited the important weekly *Wiadomości* (News), in New York, and in Munich, where Radio Free Europe was located, directed for many years by Jan Nowak-Jeziorański (1914–2005), himself the author of many important letters.

The lack of press freedom in Poland, first during the partitions (1795–1918) and later during the communist period (1948–89), and the split of Polish culture into domestic and exilic branches, meant that to some extent correspondence took on the functions of a free press. It served as a space of discussion, criticism, and exchange of ideas within which programs and concepts could be formulated. As a result, Polish writers left enormous numbers of letters behind them, which today – ever more often and owing to their merits – are either included in the sphere of contemporary literature or treated as its closest neighbour. Sometimes an intensive correspondence was engaged in as if "in place of literature," becoming over time, after the death of its authors, an argument for treating them as writers. Such was the case with Andrzej Bobkowski: he wrote a wartime diary, a handful of short stories and essays, and one play; but it was his many letters, published in successive book volumes, that led to his recognition as an outstanding Polish twentieth-century writer.

In Polish twentieth-century literature, the diaries of writers occupy a central place, largely because, as a type of writing tied to daily practices, they became an increasingly literary genre. The diary, being fragmentary, dynamic, deeply personal, and tied to its moment, proved well suited to expressing Polish twentieth-century experiences. Polish writers quickly discovered the genre's usefulness for a new approach to history, one that linked their own biographical experience to literary creation. Diaries, as Józef Czapski wrote, allow us to "perceive the most general questions through the prism of one's own intimate inner world."[13] This approach allows us to see twentieth-century reality – even when it is a reality of terror and dread – in a personalized form, one that exists in the feelings, thoughts, and attitudes of the experiencing subject and that is embedded in its memory. The dynamics of reality, personal experience, and memory in the diaries of Polish writers are symptomatic of modern Polish literature in general.

The turning of the non-literary into literature depends not only on the content of the diaries, however, but also on their initial (pre-publication) material form and the communicative context in which they function. The first type of twentieth-century writers' diaries are those written without thought of publication. These are primarily of use value for their authors, and this is not necessarily tied to their literary activities; they function, for instance, as a form of self-discipline or self-therapy, and they contain abbreviated notes about ongoing activities, including literary work. Diaries of this type are strongly contextualized, are usually kept for a specific period of time in workbooks, notebooks, or calendars, do not contain deletions or corrections, and are not copied. Left in the archives of a writer, they are published after the diarist's death.

The best example of such a diary is that of Stefan Żeromski (1864–1925), an outstanding Polish writer of the early twentieth century who wrote, among others, the novels *Ludzie bezdomni* (Homeless People, 1900), *Popioły* (Ashes, 1902–3), and *Przedwiośnie* (The Coming Spring, 1925). His diary was written before the end of the nineteenth century (1882–91), in workbooks, while he was a middle school student in Kielce and later a veterinary student in Warsaw. He used the diary to record his love conquests and school torments as well as the raptures accompanying his first literary creations, and abandoned it when he became a full-fledged writer. He did not consider publishing it while alive and placed a fifty-year moratorium on its posthumous publication, although this condition proved possible to sidestep: the first, abridged edition of Żeromski's diary appeared in 1953–6. Thus, his diary played the role of an "initiation ritual" that opened the way for a student and a lover to become a writer.

In the second category are diaries that accompany the literary activities of writers in twentieth-century Poland. These diaries help their authors crystallize their opinions about the world and literature and recognize their own place in society. They are frequently copied, usually on a typewriter, with occasional changes, corrections, and edits made to the manuscript, and with diary fragments published during the author's life. The language of such diaries comes close to literary language, meaning that it rises above the merely communicative. These diaries are most often kept for an extended time; once started, they usually end with the death of the author. Typical examples of this type of diary are the already mentioned *Diaries* of Zofia Nałkowska and those of Maria Dąbrowska (1889–1965), Jarosław Iwaszkiewicz (1894–1980), Mieczysław Jastrun (1903–83), Jan Józef Szczepański (1919–2003), Miron Białoszewski (1922–83), and Sławomir Mrożek (1930–2013).

Zofia Nałkowska and Maria Dąbrowska kept diaries throughout their adult lives, the former for fifty-eight years (1896–1965) and the latter for fifty-one (1914–65). They wrote them, like Żeromski, in workbooks, notebooks, and notepads. Over time, both women placed more and more significance on their diaries, publishing fragments from them while alive and viewing them as part of their literary legacy. In reading their own diaries later on, both of them introduced addenda and corrections to their texts. Among the diaries of Polish twentieth-century writers, those of Nałkowska and Dąbrowska hold a vital place.

Dąbrowska's diaries were notable publishing events in Poland.[14] She was one of the most important twentieth-century Polish women writers. Before the war, among other works, she wrote an important collection of stories about the lives of Polish peasants, *Ludzie stamtąd* (People from Yonder, 1926), as well as a saga about the Polish gentry, *Noce i dnie* (Nights and Days, 1932–4); later, she became a prominent member of the Polish postwar intelligentsia. Her handwritten diary fills eighty notebooks of various kinds. Moreover, large parts of her diary exist in a second version, since Dąbrowska decided to type them from the manuscript during the war, giving them a more literary shape; undoubtedly, she was thinking about future readers (she transcribed almost 1,600 pages). She also crossed and blocked out many parts of the original, handwritten diary. It is apparent today that this writing and rewriting of her diary, tied to the tension between everyday writing practice and literature, to some extent served to replace a novel that remained unfinished after the war. The diary was written "instead of the novel."

At the same time, the double-materiality of her diary is evidence of one of the most important processes in Polish twentieth-century literature – its personalization and embedding in the author's quotidian experiences. Transcription becomes a means to create literature. In oscillating between literature and a record of the everyday, Dąbrowska's diary occupies a border space on the literary map. This borderland, as can be seen from today's perspective, is shifting more and more towards the centre of Polish twentieth-century literature. Her diary also reveals other tensions, those stemming from the complications of the political situation in Poland and the resulting contradictions between the private and public stances of Polish writers during that time. It is not by accident that diaries played such an important role in writers' activities. In Poland, they allowed writers to react on an ongoing basis to life in a communist and totalitarian state that limited the freedoms of its citizens, including their freedom of speech, and to maintain a semblance of balance under those conditions.[15]

The contradictions in attitudes encountered in Dąbrowska's diary are most visible in matters related to world views and ideologies. She was part of a leftist and anti-nationalistic intelligentsia that was also pro-independence and patriotic. She was critical of the Catholic Church and maintained an anti-clerical stance while remaining open to new developments within the Polish and world church (for instance, she had high hopes for the papacy of John XXIII). Even though her diary contains anti-Semitic remarks, Dąbrowska protested sharply against anti-Semitism and not only befriended Jews but also actively helped them during the war. She had no doubt that Poland would lose its independence after the war and become a zone of Soviet occupation. In her diary, she expressed her outrage at the creeping Sovietization with rare force, and made it clear that she was aware of both the criminal (imprisonment, torture, murder) and the propagandistic methods used by the communists. But at the same time, she did not openly oppose the new authorities, accepting invitations to congresses, conventions, and official gatherings held by the communist leaders Bolesław Bierut and Józef Cyrankowicz. In the reforms carried out by the communist authorities, she saw flawed and costly but nevertheless real changes leading Poland towards a modern society.

The third type of diaries written by writers are literary diaries intended for publication, most often in literary and cultural journals first, and later in book form, still during their author's lifetime. Here, private entries and literary outlines give way to general considerations of literature, the writer's world view, or philosophical reflections. An important place in such diaries is occupied by writers' reactions to current literary, intellectual, social, and political phenomena, the articles and books they have read, and the films and plays they have seen. This form of the diary amounts to a literary genre. Two exemplary realizations of this model are Witold Gombrowicz's *Dziennik* (Diary) and Gustaw Herling-Grudziński's *Dziennik pisany nocą* (Journal Written at Night).

Both works were written is exile. Witold Gombrowicz lived in Argentina from 1939 until 1963 and in Berlin and France upon his return to Europe. Gustaw Herling-Grudziński, after his imprisonment in the Soviet gulag for part of the war, lived in Rome after the war, then moved to London and in 1952 to Munich, where he worked for the Polish broadcasting station Radio Free Europe. In 1955, after his marriage to the daughter of Benedetto Croce, he moved back to Italy and settled in Naples. Both writers maintained close contacts with Jerzy Giedroyć: Gombrowicz chiefly through correspondence, Herling-Grudziński also on a personal level, first as his comrade-in-arms in General Anders's army, then as a close colleague in Rome, and later, while he lived in Naples, as the editor of *Culture*. Both Gombrowicz's *Diary* and Herling-Grudziński's *Journal* were first published there in instalments.[16] Indeed, Gombrowicz's *Diary* would not exist without Giedroyć, for it was the editor of *Culture* who convinced the writer residing in Buenos Aires after the war to write and publish his literary diary in his journal.

Both diaries were first handwritten (more precisely, jotted down on loose pages) and then immediately afterwards transcribed on a typewriter (like other literary works). This allowed for ongoing copying and continuous revising. In both diaries, the literary and the personal are interwoven in an original and unique manner. Gombrowicz turns his diary into a "form of presence" for his readers, the quintessence of his understanding of literature as a "form of existence." Herling-Grudziński's *Journal*, for its part, amounts to a "private writerly microcosmos" of sorts, a creative formula expansive enough to gradually absorb all aspects of the author's literary activities (book editions of the journal include Herling-Grudziński's short stories and essays).

It is often believed that André Gide was the first writer to publish from his diary during his lifetime, initially in the *La Nouvelle Revue Française* and subsequently in the 1930s *Oeuvres completes* edition of his work. However, his entire diary was not published until many years after his death. Gombrowicz, in contrast, instead of publishing fragments of his diary on an occasional basis, decided to write it "right in front of the eyes" of his readers, so to speak. The tension between the private and the public is nevertheless always present within it (Gombrowicz makes note of the "dishonest honesty" with which he writes it). The immediately published *Diary* is not an intimate diary, to be sure, but neither is it intimacy's complete negation, or its parodic imitation. Gombrowicz transforms an intimate diary into a literary one, reformulating the genre by turning it into literature. We now know that the author also kept a different kind of a journal, which he called *Kronos* (Chronos, 2014), in which he recorded in monthly intervals the events of most importance to him, relating to health, finances, publishing matters, and sexual relations (both heterosexual and homosexual in nature). In a sense, *Chronos* constitutes the invisible lining of the published *Diary*.

> Referencing the significance of Adam Mickiewicz, the most important writer of Polish Romanticism, at the very beginning of his diary, Gombrowicz writes: "My attitude to Poland is a consequence of my attitude to form: I would like to elude Poland as I elude style, I would like to soar above Poland, as above style, here and there, my task is the same ... A hundred years ago, a Lithuanian poet forged the shape of the Polish spirit and today, I, like Moses, am leading the Poles out of slavery of that form. I am leading the Pole out of himself."
>
> – Gombrowicz, *Diary*, 44

Witold Gombrowicz's *Diary* is one of the most important Polish literary works of the twentieth century in terms of the originality of both its form and problematic. Gombrowicz is a harsh critic of Polish attitudes, in which national issues, rooted in simplified, stereotypical continuations of Polish Romantic traditions, overshadow existential concerns, and in which collective responsibilities coalesce into a collective form that puts pressure on the individual, subordinating it to the demands of the community. Gombrowicz, who very much enjoyed living in cafés, turns his diary into a sort of a conversation around the café table, where he expounds on his opinions, carries out debates, and evaluates and comments on various issues. At stake in the process is not an abstract tournament of ideas (so disliked by Gombrowicz), but rather a performative personal clash. This builds on his theory of form, according to which people continuously create one another in interpersonal relations. Their being towards one another is a kind of eternal duel. Gombrowicz's *Diary* is also a duel with its readers. The famous beginning added to its book edition – "*Monday* I. *Tuesday* I. *Wednesday* I. *Thursday* I" – can be interpreted as a blueprint of his presence for the readers. Gombrowicz is concerned primarily with creating a new communicative situation between a writer and his readers, hence his diary aims less at delivering a message than at the very act of communication, understood as an existential act.

The central existential and communicative category for Gombrowicz is *pain*: "It is on pain and on nothing else that the entire dynamic of existence depends. Remove pain and the world becomes a matter of complete indifference."[17] For Gombrowicz, pain is a moment of irreducible and inexpressible presence of one living being vis-à-vis another (whether human towards human, or human towards animal). Pain is a communication without a communiqué, a context without text. Pain is incomprehensible and inexpressible, but it exists. Gombrowicz designs a model of literary communication that utilizes a peculiar "effect of presence" (through analogy with Barthes's "effect of reality"), which depends on the following proposal, made to the reader, for how to read his diary: "Read me in such a way as to make present my pain, through which I myself will become present to you."

In twentieth-century Poland, women are central to the genre of diaries and journals. To the diaries of Zofia Nałkowska and Maria Dąbrowska one can add those of Maria Iwaszkiewicz (a translator and the wife of Jarosław Iwaszkiewicz, 1897–1979), Anna Kowalska (a writer and Dąbrowska's friend, with whom she had a homoerotic relationship, 1903–69), and Agnieszka Osiecka (poet and songwriter, 1936–97). The female voice is clearly present also in memoirs and autobiographical narratives. This is the domain of not only female writers, and the wives and daughters of writers, but also women who became writers thanks to their life stories. Women bring to Polish autobiographical writing a perspective on history that is distinctly personal and private, and often also familial. Within their autobiographical narrations, the category of memory (the fate of individuals and families) is as important as that of history (the fate of the collective). In addition, autobiographies of women are oriented towards the concrete and include details that are often missing in the memoirs of men.

A very noticeable characteristic of twentieth-century women's memoirs and autobiographies – especially of those whose authors were born into the gentry – is the experience of the end of a particular kind of a world. From an individual and familial perspective, this entails the loss of the ancestral home and of the places and things to which one is accustomed; on a broader scale, it encompasses changes to borders and another loss of Poland's sovereignty after the Second World War. In the memoirs of women, the twentieth century – a time of revolution and of two world wars – is recorded as a time when the world lost its stability, as exemplified by Maria Czapska's (1894–1981) *Europa w rodzinie* (Europe in the Family, 1970), Karolina Lanckorońska's (1898–2002) *Wspomnienia wojenne 22 IX 1939–5 IV 1945* (War Memoirs, 2001), and Anna Szatkowska's (1928–2015) *Był dom...* (There Was a House ..., 2006). Women perceive the war as a cataclysm, a caesura between an old and a new world, which from then on is a world of newly defined, gendered social roles. Miron Białoszewski wrote in *Pamiętnik z powstania warszawskiego* (A Memoir of the Warsaw Uprising, 1970) that the war was a time of a peculiar matriarchy. Women had to take on most male roles and tasks, including the responsibility for supporting their families.

The wartime heroism of women was realized in the realm of everyday life and in the joining of everyday activities with activities of a patriotic nature, which meant engaging in combat and conspiracy (Lanckorońska and Szatkowska). This constitutes a necessary corrective to the popularized image of the heroic world of fighting men. As Tatiana Czerska writes: "Personal narrations of women bring a different truth about survival: without pathos, or the sense of calling and sacrifice in the name of great values and issues. We are faced with evidence of thankless, often punishing work, of everyday effort at resisting despair, resignation, and depression."[18]

The motif of wandering, exile, and imprisonment appears very frequently in the autobiographical stories of women that pertain to the war and the postwar period. This peculiar nomadism is one of the most important experiences related in these stories. An important place is reserved here for experiences in concentration camps, both Soviet (*Po wyzwoleniu 1945–1956* [After Liberation 1945–1956, 1985] by Barbara Skarga [1919–2009]) and German, primarily Auschwitz and Ravensbrück (*Z otchłani: wspomnienia z lagru* [From the Abyss: Gulag Memoir, 1946] by Zofia Kossak [1889–1968]; Lanckorońska's *War Memoirs*; and *I boję się snów* [And I'm Afraid of Dreams, 1961] by Wanda Półtawska [b. 1921]). These works reveal that even under conditions of enslavement and extreme exhaustion, women were capable of maintaining their dignity and mutual solidarity, although their accounts also articulate significant differences (for instance, in attitudes towards homoerotic relations), both in relation to one another and in comparison to accounts by men. Significantly, basic human values appear as a frame of reference in the camp narratives of women more often than in those of men, and these values are always accompanied by concrete actions and practical attitudes. Women attach greater significance to the physical aspects of their extreme trials. For example, they focus more on skill in attending to battle wounds, and on basic sanitary procedures during the Warsaw

Uprising, as well as on the physical humiliations, rape, and sexual violence that women were exposed to during and right after the war.

In women's memoirs, accounts of postwar displacement focus on the experience of emigration and the need to start a new life outside of Poland. This is true for emigration right after the war, motivated by resistance to life in a new, communist Poland and fear of repressions for "conspiratorial" activities in the Home Army, as is the case in Kossak's *Wspomnienia z Kornwalii* [Memories from Cornwall, 2007]), Lanckorońska's *War Memoir*, and Szatkowska's *There Was a House...*, as well as for later phases of emigration, such as that caused by anti-Semitism during the postwar decades. The latter is best exemplified by Eva Hoffman's *Zagubione w przekładzie* (Lost in Translation, 1989). Hoffman is a Polish American journalist and writer of Jewish descent, who lived in Poland for the first fourteen years of her life (1945–59) and subsequently emigrated to North America with her parents. In *Lost in Translation*, a book first published in English in the United States and translated into many languages since, Hoffman describes her happy childhood and early youth in Kraków, her teenage years in Canada, her studies at prestigious American universities, and her work on the editorial board of the *New York Times*. But the book's most important thread is its record of life experienced in two languages, and its expansive reflections on the influence of language and its related cultural context on individual identity and communicative relations. Hoffman offers examples of important decisions (for instance, about marriage) that are different in their consequences depending on the language in which they are made. This leads her to formulate a conclusion about the necessity "of translating herself."

A separate current in female autobiography, one that gains momentum towards the end of twentieth century and continues into the present, comprises books that inscribe an individual fate onto a reconstructed family history, sometimes reaching back many generations. Among them are the books of Hanna Malewska (1918–83) (*Apokryf rodzinny* [Family Apocrypha, 1965] and Maria Czapska's *Europe in the Family*, published in the 1960s, as well as those published in the twenty-first century, such as *W ogrodzie pamięci* (In the Memory Garden, 2001) by Joanna Olczak-Ronikier (b. 1934) and *Proszę bardzo* (You're Welcome, 2009) by Anda Rottenberg (b. 1944). The books by Olczak-Ronikier and Rottenberg reconstruct their family histories (in the first instance Jewish, in the second Jewish-Russian) based on family archives (photos, notes of various kinds, reminiscences, diaries, letters, documents, and keepsakes). Numerous photos reproduced in both books (and in the first case also letters, documents, and family heirlooms) play as important a role as the text itself. To some degree, this is a throwback to the *silva rerum*, the multifaceted home chronicles of the nobility, and to the tradition of memoir writing practised by women in noble families. These contemporary books, however, are no longer addressed to one's relatives but rather to the reader. The subject of identity exploration through a return to one's Jewish roots is important in both books. A similar experience is related in memoirs and autobiographical books written by men. The numerous autobiographic books of Michał Głowiński (b. 1934) are one clear example. Saved from the Holocaust as a boy, Głowiński became an eminent literary theorist and historian after the war, describing his experiences most completely in the autobiography *Kręgi obcości* (Circles of Strangeness, 2010), and focusing on his memories of the ghetto in *Czarne sezony* (Black Seasons, 1999; in English, 2005).

The cultural advancement of women in the twentieth century, tied among other things to changes in the family model and in women's presence in public life, provides an important context for memoirs and autobiographies by women, including those by Olczak-Ronikier and Rottenberg. In both instances, and in many others, readers encounter women who have attained professional success. Olczak-Ronikier is a writer, screenwriter, and co-founder of the famous Kraków cabaret Piwnica pod Baranami (Cellar Under the Rams); Rottenberg is an outstanding art critic and historian and the long-time head of the Zachęta National Gallery of Art in Warsaw. Rottenberg's book also includes motifs of motherhood, of searching for a missing, drug-addicted son and of mourning him, and of taking stock of one's life.

Autobiographical genres during the twentieth century in Poland are of pivotal significance for at least three reasons. First, their fragmentary, documentary, and personalized character has helped decentre fiction in modern Polish literature. Second, the historical experiences of Polish people during the twentieth century have been most fully recorded in forms such as journals, letters, and diaries. Third, due in part to the influence of autobiographical forms, Polish modern literature has completely transformed its understanding of subjectivity, in terms of both the text's author and characters represented in it. The voices of previously silenced or marginalized groups and collectives – workers, peasants, women, children, Jews, and homosexuals – are now being heard with unprecedented resonance. Along with other literary genres, autobiographical forms now co-create the polyphony and internal differentiation that define Polish writing in the twentieth and twenty-first centuries.

Paweł Rodak
Sorbonne Université / University of Warsaw
Translated by Agnieszka Polakowska

NOTES

1 Ryszard Nycz, "Literatura nowoczesna: cztery dyskursy."
2 See Thomas and Znaniecki, *The Polish Peasant in Europe and America.*
3 See Krzywicki, *Pamiętniki bezrobotnych*; Krzywicki and Dąbrowska, *Pamiętniki* chłopów; Krzywicki, *Pamiętniki emigrantów. Francja*; Krzywicki, *Pamiętniki emigrantów. Ameryka Południowa.*
4 See Adamczyk, Dyksiński, and Jakubczak, *Pół wieku pamiętnikarstwa*; and Gołębiowski Grad, and Jakubczak, eds., *Pamiętniki Polaków 1918–1978.*
5 Sloan, ed., *Notes from the Warsaw Ghetto*, xxi.
6 See Czerniaków, *The Warsaw Diary.*
7 Katsh, ed., *Scroll of Agony*, 383–4.
8 See Leociak, *Tekst wobec Zagłady*, 97–129.
9 Gradowski [letter], in Smoleń, *Wśród koszmarnej zbrodni*, 131–2.
10 Nałkowska, *Dzienniki 1899–1905*, 154.
11 Nałkowska, *Dzienniki 1939–1944*, 74, 366, 357, 434, 166.
12 Bobkowski, *Szkice piórkiem*, 30–1, 93.
13 Czapski, "Ja," in *Czytając*, 166–7.
14 Five volumes in 1988; seven volumes between 1996 and 2000; thirteen volumes in 2009.
15 While living in Warsaw, Dąbrowska maintained contact with Polish émigré circles, especially those in Paris and London, by reading their publications and corresponding with Jerzy

Stempowski and Giedroyć, among others, as well as by visiting Maisons-Laffitte. This did not prevent her from being particularly critical towards the work of emigrants, although she considered Gombrowicz to be the greatest of postwar writers.

16 The former from 1953 to 1969; the latter from 1971 to 2000.

17 Gombrowicz, *Diary*, 699.

18 Czerska, *Między autobiografią a opowieścią rodzinną*, 58.

WORKS CITED

Adamczyk, Stanisław, Stanisław Dyksiński, and Franciszek Jakubczak. *Pół wieku pamiętnikarstwa*. Warszawa: Ludowa Spółdzielnia Wydawnicza, 1971.

Bobkowski, Andrzej. *Szkice piórkiem (Francja 1940–1944)*. Londyn: Kontra, 1985.

Czapski, Józef. *Czytając*. Kraków: Znak, 1990.

Czerniaków, Adam. *The Warsaw Diary of Adam Czerniakow: Prelude to Doom*. Translated by Stanislaw Staron and the staff of Yad Vashem. Edited by Raul Hilberg, Stanislaw Staron and Josef Kermisz. Chicago: Ivan R. Dee. Published in association with the US Holocaust Memorial Museum, Washington, D.C., 1999.

Czerska, Tatiana. *Między autobiografią a opowieścią rodzinną. Kobiece narracje osobiste w Polsce po 1944 roku w perspektywie historyczno-kulturowej*. Szczecin: Wydawnictwo Naukowe Uniwersytetu Szczecińskiego, 2011.

Dąbrowska, Maria. "Słowo wstępne." In *Pamiętniki chłopów*, vol 2. ix–xvi. Warszawa: Instytut Gospodarstwa Społecznego, 1936.

Gołębiowski, Bronisław, Mieczysław Grad, and Franciszek Jakubczak, eds. *Pamiętniki Polaków 1918–1978. Antologia pamiętnikarstwa polskiego*. Warszawa: Ludowa Spółdzielnia Wydawnicza, 1983.

Gombrowicz, Witold. *Diary*. Translated by Lillian Vallee. New Haven: Yale University Press, 2012.

Katsh, Abraham Isaac, ed. *Scroll of Agony: The Warsaw Diary of Chaim A. Kaplan*. Translated by Katsh. New York: Macmillan, 1965.

Krzywicki, Ludwik. "Przedmowa." In *Pamiętniki bezrobotnych*. v–xxxvii. Warszawa: Instytut Gospodarstwa Społecznego, 1933.

– "Przedmowa." In *Pamiętniki emigrantów. Ameryka Południowa*. v–xxv. Warszawa: Instytut Gospodarstwa Społecznego, 1939.

– "Przedmowa." In *Pamietniki emigrantów. Francja*. v–xxix. Warszawa: Instytut Gospodarstwa Społecznego, 1939.

Krzywicki, Ludwik, and Maria Dąbrowska. "Przedmowa." In P*amiętniki chłopów*, vol. 2. v–viii. Warszawa: Instytut Gospodarstwa Społecznego, 1935–6.

Leociak, Jacek. *Tekst wobec Zagłady. (O relacjach z getta warszawskiego)*. Wrocław: Wydawnictwo Leopoldinum Fundacji dla Uniwersytetu Wrocławskiego, 1997.

Nałkowska, Zofia. *Dzienniki 1899–1905*. Edited by Hanna Kirchner. Warszawa: Czytelnik, 1975.

– *Dzienniki 1939–1944*. Edited by Hanna Kirchner. Warszawa: Czytelnik, 1996.

Nycz, Ryszard. "Literature nowoczesna: cztery dyskursy." In *Poetyka doświadczenia. Teoria – nowoczesność – literatura*. 182–207. Warszawa: Wydawnictwo IBL PAN, 2012.

Sloan, Jacob, ed. *Notes from the Warsaw Ghetto: The Journal of Emmanuel Ringelblum*. Translated by Jacob Sloan. New York: Schocken Books, 1974.

Smoleń, Kazimierz. *Wśród koszmarnej zbrodni: notatki więźniów Sonderkommando*. Oświęcim: Wydawnictwo Państwowego Muzeum, 1975.

Thomas, William Isaac, and Florian Znaniecki. *The Polish Peasant in Europe and America: Monograph of an Immigrant Group*. Chicago: University of Chicago Press, 1918.

Transformations of Polish Reportage

It is becoming increasing clear that reportage is being treated today as literature both by those who write it and by those who read it. The self-understanding of its creators is of particular significance here, since it signals an important shift within the genre. Why is their outlook so important? The simple answer is that although the most accomplished reportage writers have always (which in Poland means since the 1930s) aspired to "literariness," by and large they had no illusions that the world of literature would treat them as its own. The opposition between "document" and "literature" that arises from time to time (and that every epoch settles anew and according to its own measures) located them firmly on the side of journalistic fact-based writing. Now, for the first time, the middle and youngest generations of reportage writers do not have to aspire to this mythical "literariness," for they have an inherent sense of belonging to it. In their understanding, reportage has entirely emancipated itself from journalism, crossing over to literature's side, and if it still becomes entangled in old divisions, it is now in opposition to the newspaper genre.

It is striking that contemporary perspectives on reportage are beginning to resemble those on "high" literature, which was once seen by its defenders as threatened by the development of mass culture and later by the invasion of new media. "They call it an aristocratic genre. It requires time, thorough documentation, costly business trips ... and demands patience and a constant search for form" – so contends the author of a survey conducted in 2005 among Polish reportage virtuosos and the editors of the most respected weekly publications.[1] Thus, reportage today does not connote either the need to keep up with events as they occur, or to conduct exposés of how things really are, or to dig up facts and interpret them wisely. Indeed, it seems that reportage can no longer exist outside of the sphere of literary values. That it can still be called reportage despite this arresting fact calls for an explanation. "For cannot reportage be literature?," asks Wojciech Tochman: "Does reportage lose its nature and identity only because it is good, exemplary, and its author cares about form and language?"[2]

In this state of affairs, the main culprit is not difficult to identify: it is the now almost total disappearance of reportage from weekly magazines, newspapers, and their weekly supplements, compelled by relentless competition with television and the Internet. Vividness, immediacy, and photographic faithfulness is as much the driver of this competition as speed of coverage (synonymous in the most important cases with live streaming). Almost all the participants in the above-mentioned survey experienced various pressures that forced them out of the press: limitations on length of features and deadlines that could not be met, a painful sense that readers did not care, and the unprofitability of the labour it took to prepare a solid text. The removal of reportage from the press signifies the cutting of its journalistic umbilical cord, and the shedding of demands for first-hand immediacy; as a result, reportage has been forced to find other reasons for being.

Of course, this departure from journalistic reality compelled by the development of new media is a common occurrence, as can be easily illustrated with examples from other literatures.[3] But to understand why Polish reportage has developed the way it has, we must understand how the new generation of Polish reportage, in rebuilding the genre after an almost decade-long break caused by martial law and its consequences, was prepared for contemporary challenges by masters of the previous generation. To that end, we must return to the 1970s, the final decade – due to historical circumstances – when the genre functioned without the presence of electronic media. These were also the best years of Polish reportage of the communist period, when it equalled – in the hands of Hanna Krall (b. 1935), Krzysztof Kąkolewski (1930–2015), and Ryszard Kapuściński (1932–2007), among others – the achievements of the first, prewar generation of Polish practitioners of the genre.

I.

Of particular significance for the future of Polish reportage was its rapprochement with testimony – an important type of writing for Polish literature due to its close connections with historical experience. The strength of testimony, like the strength of reportage, arises from the personal presence of the author in the text – including a first and last name, as well as an actual biography that confirms the credibility of communicated content. Yet the account of a witness – who usually becomes a participant in an important event owing to chance and necessity rather than choice, and who does not need to know or understand the entirety of this experience, but only to provide a reliable account of his or her own fragment – is very partial from the point of view of reportage. The reporter's task is interpretive with respect to the related event or phenomenon, and most often that task includes choosing and researching the subject. But for vast swathes of twentieth-century experience – especially with regard to the Second World War – the testimonies of victims, precisely as documents of survival, became a fundamental source of knowledge and understanding, if not a moral directive. This established new criteria of reliability that constitute a challenge for other kinds of writing.

The challenge of testimony was taken up by reportage only in the 1970s. Why so late? The answer seems to lie in the transformations of testimony itself. By then, as a result of confronting the personal experiences of authors with knowledge from other spheres of war martyrology and twentieth-century experiences in general, testimony had transformed itself into testimony of an age and of history. As a settling of not only personal but also universal accounts, it found itself on the level of literary activity that, due to its sense or meaning, belongs to literature, if only "literature of fact", regardless of the type of writing it represents. This is confirmed by the popularization of the term "testimonial literature," a category that includes, among others books, *Mój wiek* (My Century, 1977; in English, 1988), which emerged from the conversations of Czesław Miłosz (1911–2004) with Aleksander Wat (1900–67); *Rozmowy z katem* (Conversations with an Executioner, 1978 – incomplete; 1992 – complete; in English, 1981) by Kazimierz Moczarski (1907–75); Miron Białoszewski's (1922–83) *Pamiętnik z Powstania Warszawskiego* (A Memoir of the Warsaw Uprising, 1970 – incomplete; 2014 – complete; in English, 1991), and the works of Henryk Grynberg (b. 1936).

Testimony thus had a literary hue and range during the 1970s, and in this form affected Hanna Krall, Ryszard Kapuściński, and Krzysztof Kąkolewski, fundamentally changing their writing. Each of the mentioned writers used the inspiration of testimony in their own way, as is confirmed by the fact that transformations of reportage are the work of great literary personages – of their own understanding and practice of this genre.

Hanna Krall is closest to what is particularly important and characteristic of testimony in the 1970s. Earlier, she was known for her ability to find and reveal through patient and intimate conversations private worlds seemingly created to spite great history. She has since changed her approach in order to excavate and ennoble experiences that have been pushed into the shadows, or – as she likes to say – into the blackness of history in its official interpretations. In *Zdążyć przed Panem Bogiem* (Shielding the Flame, 1979; in English, 1986), she enticed to conversation Marek Edelman (1919 or 1922–2009), the last commander of the Warsaw Ghetto Uprising, who had remained silent for thirty years (since the publication of *Getto walczy* [The Ghetto Fights, 1946; in English, 1990]). In waiting so long to speak, Edelman ensured that he would consider his experience from a new, broader perspective – indeed, from the perspective of a witness to an age.

In texts written after August 1980, published mainly in the collection *Trudności ze wstawaniem* (Problems with Getting Up, 1988), Krall moved towards a more rigorous subordination of reportage to the formula of testimony. In the process she crossed the boundary from reportage (as she had practised it until then) into literature and presented the protagonists of new, historically weighty events. This shift restricts her role as an author to writing down what these contemporary creators of history say about themselves – or what can be said in their name – from the perspective of their fragmentary but deeply personal involvement in collective experiences. This removal of transparent interpretive measures is compensated for by the choice and montage of the statements as well as their linguistic form, which sometimes comes close to refined stylization. Some of these accounts have turned out to be tailor-made for the stage.

Two of Krall's novels, *Sublokatorka* (Subtenant, 1985) and *Okna* (Windows, 1987), mark an important phase in this transformations of her writing. In them, she takes up the challenge of testimony – and of her ideas about it – but now in her own name: as someone who survived the Holocaust as a child and who, as a mature documentarian, is living through martial law. In the end, however, she gives the spotlight to others. After these two novels, Krall returned permanently to writing reportage, although now subordinated entirely to the mission of testimony: the remembrance of the Polish-Jewish past and of the Holocaust. By reconstructing successive individual stories of victims and survivors who can testify to what occurred, in a sense she speaks for those who cannot speak for themselves.

A very different answer to the challenge of testimony in the 1970s is found in the writing of Ryszard Kapuściński, who was a "front page newsman" at the time, reporting on wars and revolutions in various hot spots around the globe. For Kapuściński, conversation was an important phase of "material collection." It lost its significance, however, in later phases – during the actual writing and formulating of the report's message, initially from the perspective of an engaged participant, and later from that of a helpless observer of the undeserved suffering of humanity involuntarily embroiled in history's unexpected turns. The author sought common ground in solidarity with his subjects by creating a situational resemblance between his and their circumstances – for example, by placing himself, too, at the mercy of fate and chance. He often allowed himself to be surprised by an unexpected coincidence, to come across a place by chance, to become lost, to see something totally unplanned, and even to become a participant in an event, in defiance of the journalist's role and at a risk to his life. Knowledge acquired in this manner, when intended to be passed on to others, is marked by a certain partiality, but also by a credibility that stems from removing the distance characteristic of a professional observer. Moreover, it is Kapuściński's means of repaying his moral debt to those who allowed his participation in their fate.

The literariness of Kapuściński's writing grows in tandem with his engagement with the aims, problems, and dilemmas of testimony, as well as with the creation of his self-image as a non-professional witness of and participant in events. But his writing never transforms itself, even temporarily, into a new or different form of *belles-lettres* prose. In the beginning it comes close to the kind of personal, fact-based literature that was created at this time by "plot-weary" writers trying to liberate themselves from what they perceived as worn-out literary and ideological fictions. The first collection of Kapuściński's reportage, *Wojna futbolowa* (The Soccer War, 1978; in English, 1992), consists of texts written between 1958 and 1976 and of two sketches for "unwritten books" that link the reports together. These sketches strengthen the personal interpretive perspective of the collection through reminiscence of Kapuściński's journalistic adventures, consideration of who he was at different moments in time and of the circumstances in which he wrote a given text, as well as by revealing his new, still unfulfilled creative goals. As a result, this selection of reportage also becomes a consistent testimony of the writer's past interactions with the world.

Different yet again, and perhaps most momentous in its consequence, was the encounter between testimony and Krzysztof Kąkolewski's writing. Kąkolewski did not make his reportage a tool for attesting to the truth of someone's experience (as Krall did), nor did he attempt to transform himself into a witness-participant of someone's experience (as Kapuściński did). His writing from the 1960s and 1970s, renowned then and somewhat forgotten today, was distinctive for its author's position as a tenacious stalker of suprising, even shocking truths. Kąkolewski's relationship with the protagonists of his report could be highly active, and he sometimes even turned them into partners in a shared search for truth, but he never intentionally identified with or submitted to them. The protagonist always remained to some degree his opponent, someone from whom the truth had to be squeezed through sheer tenacity, and this often meant resorting to investigative tricks, a kind of aggression, and a passion for demystification. Kąkolewski's approach allowed him to reach the extraordinary that hid within each event and character and that engaged his interest, whatever the reasons. His search for the extraordinary was rooted in his understanding of reportage: for him, the postulate of unconditional fidelity to "fact" – understood as concrete detail – accompanied the conviction that such fidelity permitted competition with *belles-lettres* prose, provided the writer found what would exceed the imagination of a *belles-lettres* writer. According to Kąkolewski, the literariness of reportage needed to be unpacked from the accidents of life instead of emerging from a surplus of generalizations, or simply from invention.

The Second World War and postwar complications became more and more Kąkolewski's source of extraordinary – "true to life" – stories. For instance, in tracing the later fate of Jews from Bodzentyn, he picked up the thread of Dawid Rubinowicz's memoir where it had been snapped along with its author's life. Even when dealing with subjects at the heart of war testimony, however, he restricted himself as much as he could to factual accuracy, without abandoning either a moral message or identification with the victims. Thus, he focused on unearthing and collecting documents, on tracking down scarce and difficult-to-access witnesses, and on archiving their accounts; he then used these kinds of materials to reconstruct fates and events that should not be forgotten. In this sense, his project was a battle with forgetting – a typical one for testimonial literature.

In the 1990s and after, Kąkolewski's writing, which set out to expose collective falsehoods and to gather testimonies and witnesses to historical truth, became ideologicalized and acquired a tinge of political polemic. He responded to the spirit of that time by exploiting the regained freedom of speech to settle accounts with the deceptions of the Polish People's Republic. At stake were the most obvious of lies, including those that had been made concrete by either literature or by communist propaganda. He tackled the first type of (literary) lie in *Diament odnaleziony w popiele* (Diamond Found in the Ashes, 1995), in which he daringly reconstructed the actual events and fates of the real-life people on which Jerzy Andrzejewski (1909–1983) supposedly based his most popular novel, *Popiół i diament* (Ashes and Diamonds, 1948). To unmask the falsehoods of communist propaganda, in turn, in *Umarły Cmentarz* (Dead Cemetery, 1996), Kąkolewski evaluated, with the assistance of Joanna Kąkolewska, the communist presentation of the Kielce Pogrom, concluding that the event's presentation was intentionally hostile to and skewed against Poles.

Taking up the challenge of testimony fundamentally transformed the writing of the three authors discussed here; it also sharply separated their writing from 1970s reportage, elevating it to a level where connection to current events and problems was less important than establishing a long-term perspective encompassing the memory of generations and the problematic of great civilizational changes. This approach freed these authors from the chains of immediacy and allowed them to develop as writers. It was around this time that Krall, Kapuściński, and Kąkolewski came to be seen as the "great triad," the leading artists of the formation that had been created by the 1956 generation and that had bequeathed to their successors a model known as the "Polish school of reportage." Actually, it is more precise to see that school as three different schools – founded by three masters – that were taken up once more after the break of the 1980s and that forced the entire genre to move into the regions of literature.

II.

It goes without saying that the period of Solidarity and of martial law, and the imprisonments, internments, conspiracies, and social resistance that went along with it, all contributed to the growing appeal of testimony in Poland. What was happening was a genuine, "made in Poland" story, and it is well known that such stories call for the testimony of writers. As Włodzimierz Bolecki wrote in 1983, following the imposition of martial law, one could expect to see "the further expansion of the genre of diary, journal, memoir, recorded commentary, and even chronicles."[4] It is not coincidental that during this predicted eruption of documentary writing there was no room for reportage. The demand was growing for participant accounts and for testimony that would preserve memories of experiences and achievements, and reportage as it was then understood was documentation of a secondary order, so to speak – it relied on second-hand accounts. The conditions necessary for the practice of the genre were unfavourable after 13 December 1981, at any rate, and this continued to be the case until the early 1990s. In the meantime, reportage could either learn how to become testimony or cease to exist altogether.

It turned out that the journalists who were just beginning their careers were best prepared for this challenge. It is entirely possible that the needs of the moment actually helped them reconcile fascination with the perspective and possibilities of individual testimony with the elementary requirements of journalistic topicality and social import, leading to the creation of polyphonic stories that reproduced the experiences of chosen communities. The process involved collecting as many individual accounts as possible – usually in audiotape form – and then editing them into one multivocal, cohesive narrative encompassing the most important moments that were revealed in individual stories. A focus on collective experiences – usually, the experiences of particularly significant groups, or of groups representative of society at the time – made the historical dimension of a narrated story possible to grasp. Allowing actual participants to speak helped preserve privacy, contingency, and internal motivations at the same time as it secured the differentiation of specific points of view within the collective telling its own story.

Yet neither circumstances nor time restraints nor even the desire to satisfy society's awakened subjectivity can explain the growing popularity of reportage as polyphonic testimony. It grew by taking on various forms, primarily because the sphere of reality that demanded discovery, understanding, and demystification grew denser and could be reached precisely through collective testimony (of concern, after all, was collective experience), often produced by the last surviving witnesses. At stake was the past – the most recent one of the Polish People's Republic – for instance, the workers' protests of June 1956 in Poznań,[5] and the more distant one, which nevertheless persisted throughout the communist period both at home and among emigrant communities, and which now appeared to be irrevocably ending together with the waning epoch of "real socialism." The sense that this was its inevitable end was born in August 1980, as a result of workers' strikes and the birth of Solidarity, which restored confidence in the ability of Poles to resist subjugation. This faith was not dulled by the dreary 1980s, which in some ways, due to the underground press and ease of publication abroad, made it easier to expose the truth about silenced people and falsified facts from the past. For example, between 1982 and 1984, Teresa Torańska (1944–2013), who had previously been interested in the socially critical "view from below" (the title of her 1979 debut, *Widok z dołu*), conducted a series of conversations with the leading dignitaries of the Stalinist period, among them Jakub Berman, Edward Ochab, and Roman Werfel. The resulting collection testified not so much to the times when the new regime was being established, as to the communist mentality. Published as *Oni* (Them: Stalin's Polish Puppets, 1985), it became one of the most celebrated books of the 1980s. It also launched an entire series of psychological portraits constructed by Torańska through collections of conversations with representatives of groups created at the intersection of politics and history: the activists of the opposition and the first "Solidarity" (*My* [We, 1994]), the second generation of "them" – the party activists of the 1960s and 1970s (*Byli* [Bygones, 2006]), and the generation of March '68 emigrants (*Jesteśmy. Rozstania '68* [We Are, 2008]).

The past, as an inexhaustible reservoir of "blank pages," events, and people unknown or little-known that demand to be represented anew, is a still active source of reportage – that is historical testimony of usually multivocal character. This is only one of two reasons for its popularity, however. The second, which is becoming clearer in tandem with the receding problematics of the 1980s, is the literary potential contained in reportage. This is revealed by the various creative operations that need to be performed on collected materials, operations that include choosing fragments from particular recordings, giving them proper linguistic form and stylistic cohesion, harmonizing multiple voices representing different points of view, and finally (in the most cohesive compositions) discovering, or imparting through the editing process, the dynamic of a narrated history. It is difficult to tell how these operations benefited from the novelistic technique of points of view, or from the high regard for narrative polyphony popularized by Bakhtin's studies on Dostoyevsky and used – as in the term "polyphonic reportage novel" – to denote a hybrid form.[6] Multivocal testimony was also easily inspired by American "new journalism" in its objectifying version, aimed at a collage, in which a journalistic narrative was linked with the accounts of event participants and witnesses, and sometimes with documents, letters, or diaries.[7]

In a situation that disavowed the right of reportage to exist on the grounds of strict immediacy, its ability to shift its interest to history combined with its ability to assimilate oral history, collage, and literary testimony opened a significant opportunity for the genre. Marek Miller (b. 1951) is the best example here. He started by founding a group of a dozen or so members, called the Laboratorium Reportażu (Reportage Laboratory), and with its help collected more than forty stories about the strike of August 1980 from journalists who had been able to access the Gdańsk Shipyard. Here, the Great Strike was not made directly present through either the events or the protagonists; instead it was repeatedly reflected in the mirrors of diverse sensibilities. What these reflections shared determined the key points of the collective experience, giving order and dynamic to the entire narrative that reconstructed the difficult road to victory. The differences visible especially at the beginning, at the moment of arrival at the strike (from different realities and by different means), to some degree mapped real social differences, but they were gradually lost along with the discovery of one's courage and feelings of solidarity, and in the end disappeared within the euphoric moment of experiencing the collective. The historic aspect of the strike was thus presented not only through what was said about it, but also by the transformation that took place in its narrators, for every one of them left the shipyard different from when they arrived.

Subsequent books by Miller and his group (which evolved from a barely formalized "workshop" to a "school" to a "Reportage Laboratory" functioning as post-graduate studies at the University of Warsaw's Faculty of Journalism) pertain, in line with the above-mentioned general tendency, to past topics either nearing closure or already closed. The expansive narrative of *Filmówka* (Film School, 1992), for example, tells the history of the National Film School in Łódź and is constructed exclusively from the statements of several dozen artists, professors, and prominent graduates; these are edited and arranged into chronological and thematic blocks. The book aims to answer the question of how it was possible during a time of "real socialism" to build and maintain an independent art school that was considered among the best in the world by the film industry. The school continues to exist (it celebrated its fiftieth anniversary in 1998), but it was clear that it was different already in the 1990s, more ordinary, and that it was no longer a unique phenomenon with a unique atmosphere. *Arystokracja* (Aristocracy, 1998), in turn, narrates the war and post-war fates of seven aristocratic families (the Branickis, Krasickis, Lubomirskis, Potockis, Radziwiłłs, Sobańskis, and Zamoyskis) and consists of accounts and family reminiscences of their representatives, especially the dozen or so of those who survived deportation by the NKVD to a labour camp in Krasnogorsk (an almost entirely unknown event).

The example of both these books makes it clear that when dealing with the past, polyphonic reportage prefers as its theme worlds with their own distinct ethos, incomprehensible to the uninitiated and possible to narrate solely from within. It serves primarily to revive this past, to render it dynamic and proximate to the reader as a participant in a great narration-conversation, one that encompasses multitudes of people and many decades and that exists only on the pages of these books. Inevitably, the method heightens the role of all creative literary techniques, since they make it possible to gather vast spans of time and human experience in a cohesive form.

The true test of Miller's method and school will come with the realization of the monumental project "Europe According to Auschwitz."[8] The project commenced during the 1990s and aims at narrating Auschwitz differently than it has been thus far. It is intended to be a collective narration based largely on the not yet used accounts of Polish prisoners from the camp archives (around 3,000 of them, read by consecutive years of Reportage Laboratory students) as well as on German testimonies. It will constitute, one could say, a confrontation with the source, in the sense of a return to the experience that turned testimony into a foundational narrative of the twentieth century.

Miller's explorations signal a more widespread tendency, to mention only the biographical novel, which offers interesting terrain for transforming testimonies of ongoing history into a multivocal reconstruction of important corners of the past. Much as with other examples discussed, the authors of these undertakings, on discovering the value of live, multifaceted testimony, did not wish to give up it up when turning towards figures from the past. For example, Joanna Siedlecka (b. 1949), the author of biographies about, among others, Gombrowicz (*Jaśnie panicz: O Witoldzie Gombrowiczu* [His Young Lorship: About Witold Gombrowicz, 1987]) and Witkacy (*Mahatma Witkac*, 2014), started out by writing reportage collections. Among these is *Jaworowe dzieci* (Sycamore Children, 1988), a collage of conversations with a dozen or so families of people who had been detained, imprisoned, or in hiding during the years 1983–5, which centres on the fate of children who were thereby suddenly deprived of care. Barbara Stanisławczyk (b. 1962) is best known now for the multivocal narrative about Marek Hłasko *Miłosne gry Marka Hłaski* (Love Games of Marek Hłasko, 1997), but she is also the co-author (with Dariusz Wilczak) of *Pajęczyna* (Spiderweb, 1992), the first truly polyphonic story about the world of the security services, as told by officers in the organization and tape-recorded. There are, of course, other justifications for narration through witnesses, such as the need to utilize their memory and knowledge before they are gone, or to capture their unique character in order to add colour to the represented and obsolescent past reality.

The incursion of reportage writers into the biographical novel, which has long been at home in literature, is probably best explained by – and confirms – the general direction of transformations in reportage, and has undoubtedly modernized the genre and made it more attractive. It was clear to see that authors who began with more traditional forms of literary biography were following the example of writers just discussed. Agata Tuszyńska (b. 1957), for instance, in *Długie życie gorszycielki* (A Long Life of a Scandalizer, 1999), her book about the feminist interwar writer Irena Krzywicka (1899–1994), relies almost exclusively on a montage of recorded and written accounts about her subject. In two of her other books touched by the spirit of testimony – *Rodzinna historia lęku* (A Family History of Fear, 2005) and *Ćwiczenia z utraty* (Exercises in Loss, 2007) – she conducts an auto-vivisection of familial history and attests to the process of her husband's death, using the Holocaust as the background in both cases.

Of the three models of reportage that were inspired by testimony in the 1970s, Kąkolewski's was the first to attract followers; it was made current by the need to give collective testimony under the conditions of martial law, and continued – in a different form – after the situation changed. This model is characterized by a focus on discovering and reviving the past and on exposing past lies; by the importance it places on conversation and the use of documents; by the decisive role it assigns to authorial construction and montage; by a fairly clear pursuit of objectivism in representation; and by the independent status of representation from authorial intention. These characteristics are more easily perceptible when looking at continuations of Ryszard Kapuściński's model.

III.

In the context of written reportage, there is no point looking for successors to Kapuściński from the 1970s, since he was only then becoming a witness and starting to highlight his participation, including exposure to all the dangers of armed conflict. This mode of testimony has since become primarily the domain of war correspondents – namely, television crew members, camera operators, and photojournalists. It is the somewhat later Kapuściński that is of importance to reportage writers today – the one who transformed himself from a witness into an anthropologist and who recast the moral dilemmas of the witness-participant as the dilemmas of engaging with people of other cultures. This happened only after a ten-year break, in books written during and after the 1990s. These books were a reaction to the world's changing situation after the fall of communism – the moment called "the end of history" following Fukuyama, and that Kapuściński suggested should be considered at most as a holiday from history. The latter concluded that the age of cataclysmic events, which had commenced with the First World War, had come to an end, and a period in which conflicts ceased to be eventful began instead. In these new conditions, events could not be understood without probing their depths and paying attention to the greater processes encompassing entire civilizational formations. For the author, the radical emancipation of non-European cultures (under the banner of the "dethronement of Europe") and the rising significance of great cultural formations as basic factors of historical development became the measure of the times.

Kapuściński and Aesopian Readings: Kapuściński's travels constantly expanded the image of the world for Polish readers, leading to an ever deeper understanding of what was shared in the experiences of the nations of Africa, South America, and the Near East at that time. Books written at the end of the 1970s made identification with issues in distant countries particularly likely since they looked for more general rules in the great historical processes they described – processes such as the duration and the decline of anachronistic dictatorships (*Cesarz* [The Emperor, 1978]), or the rise, progress, and collapse of revolutions (*Szachinszach* [Shah of Shahs, 1982]). The great popularity of *The Emperor* in Poland was the result of a widespread tendency to see, in the figure of the Ethiopian ruler, Edward Gierek, the leader of the party having authoritarian control of Poland at that time; and to see, in the image of the Ethiopian court, the central committee of the Polish Workers' Party (PZPR), on which a similarly inevitable end was wished.

Kapuściński saw this change as fundamental and profound enough to radically alter his writing so as to follow its tracks. Beginning with *Imperium* (Empire, 1993), through his Africa book titled *Heban* (The Shadow of the Sun, 1998), to his unrealized plans for books about South America and the Pacific – the latter to be set in the Trobriand (Kiriwina) Islands of Bronisław Malinowski's anthropological discoveries – Kapuściński increasingly became a "translator of cultures," the author of comprehensive conceptualizations of cultural difference. He attained the effect of synthesis through resort to his perennial travels, reconstructing in his writing the process of his discovery of foreign lands as he experienced them first-hand. He reached into the stockpile of adventures, experiences, impressions, and reflections that he had not utilized in previous works (which focused on events), and drew on them during new journeys, which were now more anthropological than journalistic. He verified the image of the world emerging from those books and created a new image of himself, this time as an explorer of otherness and a proponent of dialogue with others, rather than a witness-participant in the world's historical upheavals. This is most apparent in *Podróże z Herodotem* (Travels with Herodotus, 2004), a writerly expedition to the sources of European culture during which the author discovers anew his personal, literary, cultural (European), and human identity.

It could be said that Kapuściński, following the logic of his own development, led Polish reportage out of the "age of history" and adapted it to an age of re-evaluation of the merits of traditional cultures, intercultural dialogue, and interest in the "other" and the "foreign." This adaptation also involved pulling reportage away from journalistic forms and opening it onto "deeper," universal themes.

In returning to writing after a break from it in the 1980s and giving his writing the shape of a personal narrative of a "translator of cultures," Kapuściński took into consideration not only the requirements of a new historical situation, but also the new situation of reportage itself, which stemmed from the invasion of electronic means of communication. "Reporters of image and sound," he wrote, "change our means of looking at the world, of talking about it. Camera and sound operators look not for the historical or political sense in an event, but rather – for a spectacle, an audio-drama, a theatre."[9] He predicted that reportage, should it wish to look for this political or historical sense, would have to leave the pages of newspapers and move onto the pages of books, thus becoming a form of "creative non-fictional writing."[10]

Schools and Generations: the most important and best-known authors of the last quarter of the century belong to the third generation of writers of the "Polish school of reportage." Since the 1930s, the school had been characterized by a particularly strong interest in the historical process, one stemming from Poland's recently regained independence. To this is tied its second characteristic – the blurring of boundaries between journalism and literature. The canons of modern journalism did not have time to form in Poland, and reportage developed through assimilation of the oral narrative with various literary traditions of non-fiction writing. Both characteristics added up to the strong Polonocentrism of the first generation of Polish reportage writers, which was overcome by the great figures of the second generation, such as Hanna Krall, Krzysztof Kąkolewski, and Ryszard Kapuściński. In the 1960s and 1970s they extended the existing interest in history to a universal problematic, revealed by the experiences and consequences of the Second World War. By taking up the inspiration and challenge of testimonial literature, they formed three distinct models of reportage, which have been continued and transformed by young Polish reportage writers at the most recent turn of the century.

The impact of Kapuściński's writing thus stems primarily from the fact that it provided an answer to a new historical and communicative situation in Poland during the 1990s. It helped, of course, that he was backed by the authority of being a world writer, and that his explorations resonated with transformations in world reportage. Moreover, in his editorial capacity at *Gazeta Wyborcza* (Electoral Newspaper), the most influential newspaper after 1989, he initially mentored, together with Krall, novice journalists. Among them were the future authors of *Duży Format* (Broadsheet), a weekly supplement to *Gazeta Wyborcza*, the only periodical that to this day still tries to be a "reporters' journal." Most important, however, was the fact that through his books and his authority he sanctioned the transformations of the reportage genre.

Artur Domosławski (b. 1967) belongs to the generation of Kapuściński's successors. After the death of his mentor, he wrote and published the biography *Kapuściński Non-Fiction* (2010), in which he challenged substantial aspects of Kapuściński's literary and biographical legend. His questioning of Kapuściński's use of literary modes in his model of reportage proved highly significant. This was coupled with accusations of an ethical and professional nature that referred to Kapuściński's breaking of the "non-fiction pact" – to his alleged confabulations and fictionalizations, and infidelity to fact. Combined with an expository approach to Kapuściński's private and public life during the communist period, the biography created an image of an unreliable man. All of this ensured a long and heated discussion of the book. Notwithstanding the drastically varied opinions it inspired, Domosławski's book became the catalyst for an important debate in Poland about the borders of non-fictional writing and the admissibility of privacy in a biography.

Even a cursory look at the work of the youngest reporters leads to the conclusion that a great number of them – in fact, many of the best – have followed in Kapuściński's footsteps. In part, they may even have been responding to his challenge to the young to go forth into the world, for it must be discovered, described, and defined anew in all of its diversity. Kapuściński's patronage of his successors is signalled by the striking regionalization of this newer reportage. The most interesting books of the younger authors pertain to South America, Africa, the Islamic Near East, Russia, the South Caucasus (formerly part of the Soviet Union), Afghanistan, and the Czech Republic. Each of these regions evokes Kapuściński's books and reportage cycles, or at least the dream of travelling there. More significant, however, is the fact that the territories of Kapuściński's great writerly achievements have been quite strictly divided between authors, for whom chosen regions of the world have often become a personal passion. They have committed many journeys and many years of their lives to their discovery. South America is the domain of Artur Domosławski and his *Gorączka latynoamerykańska* (Latin American Fever, 2004), which was written after ten years of travels across the continent. Africa drew Olga Stanisławska (b. 1967), with her two solitary journeys, one across and one down the length of the "Dark Continent," culminating in *Rondo de Gaulle'a* (De Gaulle Roundabout, 2002). The Islamic Near East calls forth, among others, Beata Pawlak (b. 1957) and her book *Piekło jest gdzie indziej* (Hell Is Somewhere Else, 2003), on which she worked for almost a decade. Russia has at least two faithful travellers. One of them is Jacek Hugo-Bader (b. 1957), the author of *W rajskiej dolinie wśród zielska* (Among the Weeds in Paradise Valley, 2003) and *Biała gorączka* (White Fever, 2009), consisting of reports from 2001 to 2009. The other is Mariusz Wilk (b. 1955), who had lived in northwestern Russia for almost twenty years, where he wrote a cycle of books that commenced with *Wilczy notes* (The Journals of a White Sea Wolf, 1998) and has ended – for the time being at least – with *Dom włóczęgi* (House of a Vagabond, 2014). The Caucasus and South Caucasus as well as Afghanistan are the domain of Wojciech Jagielski (b. 1960), who published two great books *Modlitwa o deszcz* (Prayer for Rain, 2002) and *Wieże z kamienia* (Towers of Stone, 2004) ten years after his equally remarkable debut and after countless travels through both regions. Mariusz Szczygieł's (b. 1966) book about the Czech Republic, *Gottland* (2006), appeared a decade after the author's debut.

Other names could easily be added to this group of authors who specialize in chosen regions and work for years on one book. This seems to contradict the message of Kapuściński's work; he created at least two syntheses of different cultural formations himself and was considering two more. Kapuściński, however, reinterpreted a stockpile of experiences he had collected during his lifelong travels, which he initially undertook without a special interest in the diversity of world cultures, but rather with the belief in the unity of humankind. He was yet to discover that the "Other" is truly other. The mentioned and unmentioned authors learned from the experiences of the later Kapuściński: if the world is really heteronymous and if no human, political, or social issue can be understood outside of its proper cultural context, the knowledge of which means arriving at its core, its hidden mysteries, than there is no way out – one has to commit oneself to exploring just one.

Be that as it may, all of these authors are characterized by inquisitiveness regarding the mutability of the world they choose to describe, a desire to create rapprochement between their narrative and this world, or else to turn it, as far as possible, also into this world's story about itself. This is clearly perceptible in books that address current events and issues. To give one example: Artur Domosławski's *Latin American Fever* exhaustively describes the political history of South America – from the Cuban Revolution to the most recent changes in Venezuela, Brazil, and Mexico. It is not unclear in the end, however, whether the author's interest in this history did not emerge out of a passion for politics in this part of the world, where it is an inseparable attribute of life without which it could neither be understood nor described. In addition, Domosłowski's narrative about political history is interwoven with stories of its more and less important participants: revolutionaries, exiles, conspirators, *favela* residents, and writers. Some of these stories are stylized after picaresque novels with a subtext of magical realism and come bearing baroque titles. The book also contains personal notes from subsequent visits and more than twenty short essays called "miniatures." Everything has been edited and mixed together in a way that allows it to be read as either a dynamic, "feverish" collection of diverse, interwoven, and cross-supplementing narrations, or along a constant theme, arriving at an image of the continent according to its political history, essayistic miniatures, local stories, and the author's reminiscences and reflections. It can be read in the manner of Cortázar's *Hopscotch* – as a "scale model." The most political book of one of Kapuściński's pupils is thus brimming with ambition to reproduce the "text" of a culture in which this politics takes place. Despite its clearly journalistic ambitions, it is also one of the most deliberate literary constructions encountered in reportage prose.

Analysis of Jagielski's books would lead to similar conclusions. In them, accounts of incomprehensible wars in Afghanistan and Chechnya morph into profound studies of the closed worlds of both cultures. Generally speaking, the anthropological and literary aspects of works by Kapuściński's successors are unquestionable. Not all of them, however, have as contemporary a theme as those of Jagielski or Domosławski. In such cases, questions arise: To what extent is this still reportage? To what extent do these authors uncover the world in its living connection with contemporary problematics? And what is their relevance? It seems, however, that such doubts are not warranted for the time being.

Olga Stanisławska's captivating, phantasmagorical book about Africa seemingly focuses entirely on experiencing the joy of close, intimate encounters with an "other" and the sorrow of separations. But it can also be read as tracking the calamity of contemporary Africa, namely its worsening water shortage, which is breaking up communities, especially nomadic ones, creating slums around springs, and causing wars over grazing rights. The picaresque stories of Jacek Hugo-Bader, who accesses with great skill various sealed enclaves of post-Soviet life in order to speak from the inside about their often terrifying ethos, make up what is likely the best book about the breakdown of the Soviet utopia into various microworlds, which are closed off from one another. Mariusz Szczygieł's dozen or so stories about Czech culture constitute an ominous narrative about the grinding of a small nation through the hand mill of twentieth-century history – a narrative that serves as one of the weightier reckonings with Europe's recent political experiences. Beata Pawlak's book, which begins with a fascination with the innocent signs of Islam's renaissance, transforms as a result of fatal events at the turn of the twentieth century into a narrative about wars, assassinations, and terror, and finds its conclusion in the tragic death of the author herself in a terrorist attack on 12 October 2002 in Bali.

If there is a threat to this renewed reportage, it perhaps has to do with the peculiar excess of space it leaves for the author, for interest in cultural diversity inevitably awakens curiosity about oneself, the person who recognizes and describes this diversity, and tests and determines his or her self in relation to it. This danger is confirmed by Mariusz Wilk's writing. Wilk initially dreamed about "reading" Russia's complexities through long-term observation of its Solovki microcosm and over time came to treat it as a space in which he can renew his acts of auto-reflection and self-discovery ad infinitum.[11]

IV.

Hanna Krall's significance in preparing Polish reportage for a new historical situation is no less than that of Kapuściński or Kąkolewski. Half of the most popular practitioners of this genre – those who are subjects of interviews and whose texts come with self-commentaries – point to Krall when asked about their "master." When asked about the important attributes of reportage writing, they indicate the fundamental significance of the choice of protagonist (preferably, it is someone ordinary and seemingly undistinguished), and of intimate conversation that allows the protagonist to open up and reveal some deeply buried truth. These characteristics evoke Krall's model of reportage.

The broad impact of this model became noticeable later than that of Kąkolewski's or Kapuściński's "school," although individual "students of Hanna Krall" could easily be identified at the beginning of the 1990s. It could hardly have been otherwise, given that the author of *Hipnoza* (Hypnosis, 1989) organized the reportage section in *Gazeta Wyborcza*, employing and editing the work of, among others, Mariusz Szczygieł, Wojciech Tochman (b. 1969), and Lidia Ostałowska (b. 1954). Beside the characteristic method of concentrating on "opening up" human beings, these now famous authors, as well as many others, are linked with Krall's tradition by a particular interest in the everyday, aimed at exposing what is hidden under the mundane, and what is remarkable, surprising, or unknown because it has not as yet been spoken about.

The early reportage of Wojciech Tochman is a good example. The co-founder of the "Itaka" foundation (a centre for missing people) sourced the majority of themes for his best reports, collected in his first book *Schodów się nie pali* (Don't Burn Down the Stairs, 2000), in the reality hidden behind people's disappearances and the ensuing search for them. Deciphering this reality often required investigative talents as well as a gift for extracting from people their most shameful secrets. Another example is Katarzyna Surmiak-Domańska (b. 1967), who began her mature career as a reportage writer by focusing on people who diverge from heterosexual and conventional norms and by revealing their presence in society and differences from one another. The protagonists of her texts (for instance, in *Beznadziejna ucieczka przed Basią. Reportaże seksualne* [Hopeless Escape from Basia: Sexual Reportages, 2007]) are transvestites, transsexuals, and homosexuals raising children, and they are presented from the perspective of their problems with identity and with finding their place in society. Even though she limits her explorations of identity complications to gender and sexuality, the author follows Krall's tradition of avoiding an outsider's perspective and stimulating the protagonists' self-reflection by allowing them to realize for themselves – in front of the author and the readers – the logic of their own, distinct fate.

Mastery at penetrating beyond the masks and self-defence postures of marginalized people was very quickly achieved by Lidia Ostałowska (b. 1954), who since 1991 has been creating a map of communities, social groups, and people struggling with problems of exclusion. Her reportages have been collected (partly and with delay) in the volume *Bolało jeszcze bardziej* (It Hurt Even More, 2012). At stake in her work are primarily those who were marginalized either by the mechanisms of transformation (villages after the dissolution of State Agricultural Farms; unemployed youth in working-class neighbourhoods in large cities), or as a result of family violence (e.g., a victim of incest). Others include those who marginalize themselves (a woman who commits infanticide, sufferers of post-abortion trauma), or who perceive themselves as underprivileged or aggrieved.

The multivariant nature of the theme of exclusion can be explained by the contemporary interest in primarily the *sense* of being excluded and, worse, overlooked, which is not limited to the clearly socially underprivileged. The authors are interested in aspects of the everyday that evade official structures of social life and official channels of social communication, and that hide in shadows of silence and ignorance that are only sporadically disturbed by drastic events. They try to overcome the barriers of silence and indifference by giving voice to those who have found themselves behind those barriers either as a result of a lack of social interest in uncomfortable issues, or by their own choice, out of shame or fear of public opinion.

At the juncture of interests in the everyday and in the marginalized, the main, leading theme of contemporary Polish reportage finally appears, idiomatically referred to as "Planet Province," "Poland B," or "non-Varsovian Poland." It's worth noting that it is this version of Poland that has attracted the attention of reportage writers – when it became a source of self-sufficient themes that were equal in importance and in literary appeal to themes previously taken up by them, which were marked by History writ large, whether this history was still in the making or already transitioning into the past. Some reportage writers tried to stay with historical themes for quite some time, and it was only an intense experience with the realm of everyday Poland that commanded their journalistic focus. Paweł Smoleński (b. 1959) thus debuted with an account of one of the two most important strikes of 1988, which opened the road to the Round Table Agreement and elections in 1989 (*A na hucie strajk. Opowieść dokumentalna* [Strike at the Ironworks: A Documentary Novel, 1989]). He then traced the dynamics of political and generational transformations (in *Szermierze Okrągłego Stołu. Zwątpienia i nadzieje* [The Swordsmen of the Round Table: Doubts and Hopes, 1989] and *Salon patriotów* [The Patriots' Salon, 1994]) and of the renewed Polish–Ukrainian disagreements (*Pochówek dla rezuna* [Burial for the Butcher, 2001]). Finally, he become a valued foreign correspondent reporting on intense moments in Israel and Iraq (*Israel już nie frunie* [Israel Is No Longer Flying, 2006] and *Irak. Piekło w raju* [Iraq: Hell in Heaven, 2004]). Then, in 2009, he surprised his readers with an unexpected return to national problems in the collection *Powiatowa rewolucja moralna* (The Regional Moral Revolution, 2009). Włodzimierz Nowak (b. 1958), in turn, after several years of fascination with the identity complications in the Polish–German borderlands and the historical inheritance of these regions, which he addressed in his *Obwód głowy* (Head's Circumference, 2007), focused almost exclusively on portraits of "non-Varsovian Poland." From his perspective, presented for instance in *Serce narodu koło przystanku* (The Nation's Heart at the Bus Stop, 2009), this surprisingly extensive region governs itself in its own way and is filled with dashed hopes as well as collective and individual dramas. Interest in "Planet Province" has been steadily increasing over the past decade, as confirmed by books such as *Prowincje* (Provinces, 2013) by Bogdan Białek (b. 1955), and by various television reports and documentaries. Its significance has been sealed with such anthologies as *20 lat nowej Polski w reportażach według Mariusza Szczygła* (20 Years of Poland in Reportage According to Mariusz Szczygieł, 2009), and by the several-hundred-page selection of reportage from the weekly *Polityka* (Politics), which consists almost exclusively of studies and analyses of provincial everyday reality. This extensive theme, while transformed and adapted to current times, was to a large extent established by Krall's school of reportage.

~

These remarks about ties between the new formation of Polish reportage and its predecessors aim to present a continuity of the genre's transformations – a continuity that has been maintained despite radical changes in Poland's historical situation and means of social communication. Another approach that would undoubtedly help fill out this outline of Polish reportage would involve looking at the genre's current situation through the lens of oppositions to its masters and focus on ways in which some remarkable young reporters have found and followed their own paths.

Zygmunt Ziątek
Institute of Literary Research at the Academy of the Polish Academy of Science
Translated by Agnieszka Polakowska

NOTES

1 Wyszyńska, "Życie zwielokrotnione," 42.
2 Tochman, "Twórcze pisanie niefikcyjne."
3 See Perez-Reverte, *Terytorium Komanczów*; Tarzani, *Powiedział mi wróżbita.*
4 Bolecki, *Widziałem wolność w Warszawie*, 11.
5 See Maciejewski and Trojanowiczowa, eds., *Poznański Czerwiec 1956.*
6 Miller, "Polifoniczna powieść reportażowa."
7 For more information see Durczak, *Contemporary American Literary Nonfiction.*
8 So far, only the first volume planned by the project has come out (Marek Miller, *Europa według Auschwitz. Litzmannstadt Ghetto* [Oświęcim: Państwowe Muzeum Auschwitz-Birkenau, 2009]). The book focuses on the Łódź ghetto and ends together with its liquidation.
9 Kapuściński, *Lapidaria*, 201.
10 Haszczyński, "Rasowy reporter."
11 Since 2015, Wilk has lived in Naples and possibly also at a distance from his Russian experience.

WORKS CITED

Bolecki, Włodzimierz. *Widziałem wolność w Warszawie. Szkice 1982–1987.* Warszawa: Wydawnictwo Przedświt, 1984.

Durczak, Jerzy. *Contemporary American Literary Nonfiction.* Lublin: Wydawnictwo UMCS, 1988.

Haszczyński, Jerzy, "Rasowy reporter." Interview with Ryszard Kapuściński. *Rzeczpospolita*, 11 March 2005. http://kapuscinski.info/rasowy-reporter.html.

Kapuściński, Ryszard. *Lapidaria.* Warszawa: Czytelnik, 2003.

Maciejewski, Jarosław, and Zofia Trojanowiczowa, eds. *Poznański czerwiec 1956.* Poznań: Wydawnictwo Poznańskie, 1981.

Miller, Marek. "Polifoniczna powieść reportażowa." *Studia medioznawcze* 2 (2011): 347–63.

Perez-Reverte, Arturo. *Terytorium Komanczów.* Translated by Joanna Karasek. Warszawa: Wydawnictwo Literackie Muza, 2001.

Tarzani, Tiziano. *Powiedział mi wróżbita. Lądowe podróże po Dalekim Wschodzie.* Translated by Jerzy Łoziński. Poznań: Zysk i S-ka, 2008.

Tochman, "Twórcze pisanie niefikcyjne." www.tochman.com.pl.

Wyszyńska, Małgorzata. "Życie zwielokrotnione." *Press* 5 (2005): 42–5.

The Four Elements of Reportage (Melchior Wańkowicz)

The position of Melchior Wańkowicz (1892–1974) in Polish literature is still unsettled, even though the author of *Bitwa o Monte Cassino* (The Battle of Monte Cassino, 1945–7) is seen, along with Ksawery Pruszyński (1907–50), as the father of Polish reportage. An inimitable, eloquent raconteur, known for his contrariness and his ability to combine contradictions, Wańkowicz usually preferred what he popularized as "the third place club" (in a title of one of his books: *Klub Trzeciego Miejsca*, 1949) rather than an easy compromise. For more than half a century of his writing career, he was considered an unconventional figure: the descendant of an ancient noble family who nonetheless exposed the weaknesses of his social sphere, a pioneer of modernity, and a businessman as well as – in today's idiom – a creative copywriter, who penned the famous advertising slogans "Lotem bliżej" (Closer with LOT) and "Cukier krzepi" (Sugar Fortifies). As a participant in the most difficult moments in twentieth-century history and a person tested by fate, Wańkowicz had a gargantuan appetite for life until its very end. Motivated by unrestrained passion in his professional work, he was unpredictable in interpersonal relations and unbridled in his writing. Literary criticism has always found it a challenge to corral him within monographic frameworks.

"Passionate exuberance" describes not only Wańkowicz's ebullient personality but also his entire oeuvre, with which it is permeated. The elements of earth, fire, water, and air function in his work as tried-and-tested interpretative categories that can carry diverse meanings, as Gaston Bachelard has shown in *On Poetic Imagination.* In the interpretations that best match Wańkowicz's poetics, earth is a metaphor for refuge and, more broadly, for homeland, and thus finds its best exemplification in works that deal with the familial sphere. The publication of *Szczenięce lata* (Puppy-Dog Years, 1934) – a tender story of childhood, the gentry traditions, and old-world values in the Borderlands – was a significant event in the history of Polish non-fiction literature. In subordinating this reportage to the tradition of the gentry oral tale (*gawęda*) – lush, colourful, and teeming with neolexic invention – Wańkowicz showcased the expressive potential of the reportage genre. His next significant publication to engage the subject of home, *Na tropach Smętka* (On the Trail of Smętek, 1936), tells of a kayaking journey to eastern Prussia, undertaken in 1935 along with his younger daughter in order to find the Polish element on these once-Polish territories. Instead, the travellers encounter local speech that "drips of German and worn-out profanities" and can constitute only "the Slavic manure, an under-bedding for German culture."[1] The innovative nature of this reportage stems from the coupling of the authorial narration with the observations of a child who, in directly experiencing a new reality, names it in a fresh and insightful way.

> Wańkowicz's life unfolded in the realm of "the magnificent borderland" … A descendant of the Borderlands' landowners, he grew up among people who were closer in customs and mentality to the eighteenth rather than to the nineteenth century … Was it perhaps the clash and simultaneously symbiosis of cultures and traditions that created especially favourable conditions for his development? Or maybe it was his breaking away from the peculiar atmosphere of noble estates that triggered a hidden energy? Wańkowicz often claimed that he owed a great deal to his roots and to the land where he was born and where he grew up. For him it was a source of memories, and the origin of his rich, colourful personality and of his closeness with nature.
>
> – Ziółkowska-Boehm, *King i Królik*, 6

Ziele na kraterze (Herbs at the Crater, 1951) – his most famous book dedicated to the familial thematic, which is bursting with humorous reportage – is in fact a story about family bonds and the catastrophe of war, as the fusion of the elements of earth and fire in the title metaphor aptly conveys. In broaching the subject of his daughter's tragic death in the Warsaw Uprising, Wańkowicz clearly modifies the nature of reportage narration. His builds this story of a family's wartime drama from literary representations rather than descriptions of his actual emotions and perceptual experiences. His description of Krysia's death calls forth the literary *topos* of a father grieving the death of a child. Sophisticated in composition, it has as its prelude a quintessentially Polish scene of joyous couples dancing their last mazurka on the eve of the great uprising.

In Wańkowicz's work, fire is more often a destructive force than a beneficial one. It symbolizes history writ large, in which the author of *Puppy-Dog Years* takes part with rare intensity, first as an involuntary witness, then as an participant in the twentieth-century upheavals. He had already encountered the 1917 revolutions: in February in Moscow, and in October in Saint Petersburg. He described them in *Opierzona rewolucja* (*Full-Fledged Revolution*, 1934), a book that was controversially received, especially among conservative circles, and which he later himself referred to as "Bolshevik." The yield of a six-day journey to Moscow in December 1933, it is surprisingly kind in its description of the Soviet Union, full of curiosity and understanding of the diktats of history. Suprisingly, for it is written, after all, by a son of an insurgent in the 1863 January Uprising who was exiled to Siberia, an artist born in the Russian partition who was sentenced to three months in a tsarist prison as a teenager and who soon afterwards was deprived of his family home in Kałużyce and, what is more, a writer who took part in the Polish–Russian War of 1920 that solidified Poland's independence. It was to this subject that Wańkowicz dedicated *Strzępy epopei* (Scraps of an Epic, 1923), a story evocative of Henryk Sienkiewicz in its style and reminiscent of the knightly epic poem tradition.

His reports from occupied Poland first collected in *Wrześniowym szlakiem* (The September Campaign, 1944) were written in the heat of the moment at the beginning of the Second World War in September 1939. This collection was later published as *Wrzesień żagwiący* (Scorching September, 1947), with the addition of two stories: "Hubalczycy" (Hubal's Men) – the history of the first partisan division of Major Henryk Dobrzański, aka "Hubal"; and "Westerplatte" – Major Henryk Sucharski's account of his defence of the famous bastion. In these reports, Wańkowicz categorically opposed diminishing the significance of the Polish defensive war in 1939 and presented the efforts of Polish soldiers as heroic instead. He considered the intellectual settling of accounts with prewar Poland undertaken by Polish intellectuals even while battles were still raging as premature. War appears again in *Dzieje rodziny Korzeniewskich* (Golgotha Road, 1944), which tells the tragic history of Polish exiles to Siberian gulags, and in the monumental *Battle of Monte Cassino* (1945–7), an eyewitness account glorifying the sacrifice of Polish soldiers during one of the bloodiest and most significant Second World War battles, one that made it possible for the Allies to overcome German defences and take Rome in 1944. The three-volume *Battle of Monte Cassino* is unique on a world scale – a fresco of war that presents a detailed and simultaneously epic vision of the battle. The fire motif also unfolds in his reflections on the subject of war reportage as a genre. His six-hundred-page compendium *Wojna i pióro* (War and Quill, 1974), about the work of war correspondents, contains short essays about the history and theory of war reportage and numerous remarks on the craft.

The element of fire rules over other interests of Wańkowicz's, such as the ones he explores in *COP – ognisko siły* (CID – Source of Power, 1937), which focuses on the Central Industrial Region (the largest economic project of interwar Poland), and in *Sztafeta* (Relay, 1939). In both instances, the author tries to stir the young generation to build a modern Poland and to light within them the desire to mobilize the civilizational force of a young country. His lively polemic also produced works that sparked controversy – for instance *Kundlizm* (Mongrelism, 1947), a collection of unpopular judgments about Polish vices. *The Third Place Club*, in turn, voiced a decisive critique of Polish émigré reality, presenting it as a social space built on appearances and illusions from which you can only extricate yourself at the price of public ostracism.

Another element – that of water – manifests itself in Wańkowicz's work through images of motion, changeability, travel, and – in most general terms – emigration. Uprooted from his family home, the writer was unable to put down permanent roots anywhere else. Motion reigned supreme in his unstable life, launching him around the world – he travelled to, among other countries, Mexico, Iran, Iraq, Egypt, Syria, Lebanon, Italy, Great Britain, the United States, and Canada. His mobility, while always tied to separation from a domesticated space, had various other causes: wartime wanderings, a passion for moving around, and a yearning to satisfy a thirst for knowledge, as well as the publicizing of his own writing. His North American travels are particularly significant. An early reportage, *W kościołach Meksyku* (In the Churches of Mexico, 1927) would be his only expression of an initial, unsatiated fascination with Mexico. Travels to the remaining countries of North America had greater impact on his creative biography.

The Canadian peregrination, which began in 1950 and was renewed after five years, was envisioned as a gigantic reading tour for Polish communities there. The creation of a "panorama of Polish fate" (with the initial forecast of five volumes reduced first to three and eventually to two) served as an additional goal. The rejuvenating force of postwar Canada helped the heroes of Wańkowicz's books rebuild their shattered lives, but it did not transform his own writing, as the author had hoped. The first part of the work – *Tworzywo* (Three Generations, 1954) – which narrates the fate of four Polish emigrants, was not successful;[2] the second, *Droga do Urzędowa* (The Road to Urzędowo, 1955), is rightly considered compositionally strained. The third, *Jak daleko?* (How Far Is It?) – remained in manuscript form. The Canadian journey influenced his creative biography in another way, however. By orienting his work towards belles-lettres, it led to reflection on the subject of the genre purity of reportage. It also allowed him to revive, after many years of war's dominance in his work, writing born of a passion for wandering, as well as to once again find the Polish reader and to feel, with time, a longing for a return to the homeland.

The trip to America that Wańkowicz took with his wife on the cusp of 1956–7 was different in character from his other journeys and perhaps the most meaningful. They embarked on a road trip around the United States in order to feel and learn to understand the continent that their only living daughter had chosen as her new homeland. They too were considering putting down roots there. The journey left its mark on his writing by initiating *W ślady Kolumba* (In Colombus' Footsteps) – a trilogy consisting of *Atlantyk-Pacyfik* (1967), *Królik i oceany* (Rabbit and Oceans, 1968), and *W pępku Ameryki* (In the Navel of America, 1969). Those works are perfectly attuned to the prevailing atmosphere in the United States at that time, as set by Jack Kerouac's cult novel *On the Road* (1957). In embracing this ultra-American myth of travel, Wańkowicz aimed to learn about the New World from its underpinnings, without prejudices or easy compromises. His senses were stifled, however, on contact with a technologized civilization; the culture of stability was not his element, after all.

In 1958, right after his American travels came to an end, he returned to Poland permanently, which seriously strained his relations with the Polish émigré community. Here it must be recalled that a part of the émigré community that remained abroad after the Second World War opposed the return of writers to the Polish People's Republic. It was thought that the regime might use their return for the purposes of propaganda, as proof of their acceptance of the political order imposed on Poland. Wańkowicz's readers in Poland, however, welcomed the returning émigré. A few years later, he became a signatory of "Letter of the 34," written by writers and scholars in defence of freedom of speech. In 1964, the seventy-two-year-old writer was accused of sending abroad information deemed defamatory to the Polish People's Republic and sentenced to three years in prison. This attracted the attention of the foreign press and left Polish authorities in an uncomfortable position. In the end, though the writer underscored his willingness to serve his prison sentence, that sentence was not carried out.

The element of air summons a transitoriness that, in Wańkowicz's writing, is conveyed through meta-literary remarks, especially ones pertaining to a creative approach to reportage. His creative method is exhaustively described in a number of works, including the slim collection *Prosto od krowy* (Straight from a Cow, 1965); the introduction to *Od Stołpców po Kair* (From Stowbtsy to Cairo, 1969) titled "O poszerzenie konwencji reportażu" (About the Expansion of Reportage Conventions); and the two-volume *Karafka La Fontaine'a* (La Fontaine's Carafe, 1972, 1981). The author admits to the use of literary fiction and – as with the famous conception of a "mosaic" that he popularized – to composing a new whole out of elements that were not necessarily connected in reality, but that fit well together in a narrative. Wańkowicz believed himself free to excerpt an episode of interest from any biography and include it in that of another figure in the name of making the world of his reportages more attractive. It is difficult to say with certainty today whether Wańkowicz was the first to take this approach to journalism, but he was undoubtedly the first to popularize and comment broadly on it.

Wańkowicz's writing has an elemental character, with its stylistic wildness, lack of compositional restraint, and textual overproduction, so to speak. Time has not been kind to it, however. In the 1970s, he still enjoyed above-average interest: he was able to fill thousands of seats in the Congress Hall with his readers, his radio and television talks were hugely popular, and his books were reprinted many times and sold in great numbers. Today the author of *Tworzywo* (Material, 1954) is mostly forgotten as a writer, and unjustly so, since he is an important link in the chain of contemporary literature. The Polish school of reportage, known around the world and associated mainly with Ryszard Kapuściński, Hanna Krall, Wojciech Tochman, and Mariusz Szczygieł, owes some of its rare energy to the unrestrained temperament of Melchior Wańkowicz, his personal view of the world, and his incontestable bravura in pushing the boundaries of reportage.

Beata Nowacka
University of Silesia, Katowice
Translated by Agnieszka Polakowska

NOTES

1 Wańkowicz, *Na tropach Smętka*, 49.
2 Wańkowicz, *Three Generations*.

WORKS CITED

Wańkowicz, Melchior. *Na tropach Smętka*. Warszawa: Wydawnictwo Literackie, 1988.
– *Three Generations*. Translated by Krystyna Cękalska. Toronto: Canadian Polish Research Institute, 1973.
Ziółkowska-Boehm, Aleksandra, ed. "Wstęp." In *King i Królik. Korespondencja Zofii i Melchiora Wańkowiczów 1914–1939*. 5–15. Warszawa: Wydawnictwo Książkowe "Twój Styl," 2004.

New Polish Idiom (Mariusz Szczygieł)

Mariusz Szczygieł is a well-known journalist and one of the most frequently translated of contemporary Polish authors. He enjoys particular popularity in the Czech Republic, the subject of three of his bestselling books: *Gottland* (2006), *Zrób sobie raj* (Make Your Own Paradise, 2010), and *Láska nebeská* (Heavenly Love, 2012). How is it possible that a Polish author achieved European renown thanks to books about Czechs?

Mariusz Szczygieł (b. 1966) – reporter, television journalist, writer, Czechophile, and "Czechologist." In 1985, in a Boy Scouts journal, *Na Przełaj* (Cross-Country), he published a feature about a homosexual prostitute – "Nie róbcie sensacji" (Don't Fuss) – that is considered to be the first report about the lives of homosexuals in the official communist press. A year later he launched the "Shrive" cycle, about to the lives of young gays and lesbians in Poland. Since 1990, he has worked for *Gazeta Wyborcza*, where in 1993 he published "Onanizm polski" (Polish Onanism), thus begining a public discussion about the autoerotic practices of Poles. Between 1995 and 2001 he hosted the talk show *Na każdy temat* (About Everything).

Book publications:

1996 – *Niedziela, która zdarzyła się w środę* (Sunday That Happened on Wednesday)
1997 – *Na każdy temat – talk show telewizyjny do czytania jako książka* (co-author: Witold Orzechowski; On Every Topic – A Talk Show to Read as a Book)
2006 – *Gottland* (published in English in 2014)
2010 – *Kaprysik. Damskie historie* (Caprice: Feminine Histories)
2011 – *Zrób sobie raj* (Make Your Own Paradise)
2012 – *Láska nebeská* (Heavenly Love)

The title *Gottland* is a deliberate provocation: the author knows that Polish readers associate the Czech Republic primarily with the popular singer Karel Gott, "the idiot of music," as he is called by Milan Kundera in the novel *The Book of Laughter and Forgetting*. At the time of *Gottland*'s publication, Szczygieł was known to the mass public exclusively as the witty host of *Na każdy temat* (On Every Topic), a popular television talk show that violated customary taboos tied to the sexuality of Poles. Decidedly fewer people associated him with writing and knew that prior to his career in television, he was a reporter for the biggest Polish newspaper, the author of many prize-winning texts, a pupil of the outstanding journalist Hanna Krall, and one of the most talented practitioners of the Polish school of reportage. The surprise of *Gottland*'s readers was thus double: Szczygieł, who was taken for "an idiot of television," turned out to be an excellent writer, and the Czechs – the comical "nation of idiots" – the heroes of poignant dramas.

Polish school of reportage: a term referring to young journalists who debuted toward the end of the twentieth century (such as Artur Domosławski, Jacek Hugo-Bader, Wojciech Jagielski, Mariusz Szczygieł, and Wojciech Tochman), who practise different types of reportage and who have been influenced by various predecessors such as Hanna Krall, Ryszard Kapuściński, Józef Kuśmierek, and Małgorzata Szejnert. The common denominator of their poetics consists of the following: (1) a broad understanding of social facts that extends to the sphere of customs and morals and that is considered a necessary departure point for reportage; (2) treatment of literariness and documentariness as equal means for representing reality; (3) the withholding of judgment, in tandem with representation of events aimed at generating a strong and morally clear judgment in the reader; (4) the ironic use of colonial poetics in descriptions of civilizational differences arising in Central Europe in connection with capitalism and democracy; and (5) the presentation of processes occurring in less developed regions (Mexico, South America, Asia) as possible indicators of global problems.

Poles like to make fun of Czechs, and vice versa. The historic ties between the two nations go back to the tenth century. Also, the Polish and Czech languages belong to the same, West Slavic language group, with many words that sound similar but mean something quite different, which gives rise to amusing misunderstandings. In addition, it seems to Poles that Czechs speak in diminutives, so Poles consider them childish and patronize them; Czechs, in turn, have the impression that Poles lisp and perceive them as uncouth or even primitive.

Despite their linguistic closeness, these two societies do not know much about each other and perceive each other mainly through the lens of stereotypes. Czechs traditionally "orientalize" Poland and see it as a country even more "Eastern" (read "backward") than it actually is. For Czechs, anything can serve as evidence of Poles' backwardness, but most often mentioned are the significant number of rural Poles, their traditional Catholicism, the strength of their noble traditions, their anti-Semitism, nationalism, and militarism, and the absence of a native middle class. The Poles, in turn, often "occidentalize" the Czechs, imagining them as significantly more "Western" (read "modern") than they actually are. For Poles, anything can serve as proof of this, but most often mentioned are the following: indifference to religion, middle-class traditions, tolerance towards behavioural codes, philo-Semitism, pacifism, a sense of humour, and common sense. From this perspective, Czechs are not longer a nation that really exists, but a phantasm. "God created Czechs in order to please the Poles," declares the author of *Heavenly Love*, which is an exceptionally accurate characterization of Poles' attitude towards Czechs.

The first two of Szczygieł's books describe the absurdities of Czech history and the "metaphysical uprootedness" of its people, but they can also be read as a polemic against

Polish vices, which include a tendency towards pathos (in *Gottland*) and clericalism (in *Make Your Own Paradise*). That is how they are viewed from Poland, where interest in Czech history and culture is rather slight. A certain imbalance rules their relations: Czechs are generally not interested in Poles, while Poles are interested in imagined rather than real Czechs. In these imaginings, when the need arises, the clever but cowardly crooks and plebeians without a sense of honour or respect for any values are revealed as warm, humorous, and open-minded people who know how to enjoy life and let others live (tacitly: in contrast to Poles). A negative stereotype is swapped for a positive one that has just as little to do with reality.

Gottland, Szczygieł's first book and the best of his "Czech" works, is a collection of articles published between 2000 and 2005 in *Gazeta Wyborcza* (Electoral Newspaper). It is a masterfully constructed palimpsest; almost all of its stories were previously told by Czech journalists and prose writers (they are known, for instance, to the readers of Milan Kundera's or Josef Škvorecký's novels). Szczygieł, however, is able to tell them better, certainly in a more accessible manner, than anyone before him. At a time when the sales of *belles-lettres* works seem to be declining (with the exception of the most conventionalized genres, such as crime, romance, and adventure novels), the "newspaper" provenance of *Gottland* has contributed greatly to its commercial success. Jiři Gruša once said in a conversation with the Polish journalist and translator Andrzej S. Jagodziński that Milan Kundera's novels of *The Unbearable Lightness of Being* type are "comic books" that allow the general Western public to absorb the historic experiences of Central Europe.[1] At present, this function is often fulfilled by non-fiction literature.

Among the protagonists of *Gottland* are the famous singer Karel Gott; Tomáš Baťa, the founder of a shoe company; Otakar Švec, the creator of Stalin's biggest monument in Prague; the actress Lída Baarová, who was Joseph Goebbels's mistress; Marta Kubišová, the singer with ties to the anti-communist opposition; Jan Procházka, the communist writer persecuted by his former comrades; and Zdeněk Adamec, who set himself on fire in Prague's Wenceslas Square in 2003, much like Jan Palach, who self-immolated there in January 1969. Szczygieł consistently presents readers with protagonists who – against (auto)stereotypes – resist the temptations of conformism. A significant exception here is the protagonist in "Łowca tragedii" (Hunter of Tragedies) a writer whose conformism eventually causes his personality to disintegrate.

The author of *Gottland* seems to be saying that "even Czechs have their fate." They are not generally perceived, even among themselves, as a nation with a dramatic history; their fortunes are rarely viewed through the lens of heroism, which apparently only characterizes the histories of "great nations" (not by accident, the most famous of Czech books is Hašek's *The Good Soldier Švejk*). The biographies of the protagonists of Szczygieł's reportages testify to something quite the opposite: they are all, without exception, incredibly dramatic, and it is not the "insufficiency of history" that provides the source of drama, but precisely its excess, symbolized by two twentieth-century totalitarianisms.

It is not surprising, therefore, that Czechs fell in love with *Gottland*; they read it the way Poles read the books by British historian Norman Davies – with a sense of pride that someone finally noticed and appreciated them. Readers in other countries, in turn, are charmed by Szczygieł's aphoristic style and by his deep empathy towards the book's protagonists, as well as by their truly extraordinary fortunes. What most intrigues the book's author, however, is not so much "Czech fortunes" as "Czech stories" – in other words, the tragicomic Czech narration style that offers an alternative to the solemnity of

Polish narration. Many Polish writers who debuted in the 1980s – a time when Czech writers like Milan Kundera, Bohumil Hrabal, Václav Havel, and Josef Škvorecký were conquering heroes in world literature – suffer from a peculiar inferiority complex in relation to these Czech authors. Szczygieł, a purebred reporter, turned this to his advantage by writing a "Czech reportage" instead of a "Czech novel." Never had there been such a book, not even in the Czech Republic.

Make Your Own Paradise and *Heavenly Love* followed the great success of *Gottland.* The first contains reports previously published in *Gazeta Wyborcza* (Electoral Newspaper), mainly on the subject of Czechs' relationship to God and institutionalized religion. Printed individually, these texts read like minor anecdotes, yet their amalgamation in a single volume had an unexpected effect: *Make Your Own Paradise* turned out to be unprecedented (on a European scale) post-secular reportage. The title of the book can be taken quite literally, as an interpretive direction and as an explanation of the Czech way of building a secular paradise. The condition of creating that paradise is the elimination of suffering. On the path to happiness thus conceived, one finds basic aspects of human life: the body, sexuality, and bonds with the living as well as with the dead.

Through anecdotes, records of conversations, observations of the Czech quotidian reality, and analyses of various texts, Szczygieł reveals successful methods for maximizing happiness by minimizing suffering. The body is "conquered" by being stripped of significance, through ridicule and through the neutralization of aesthetic criteria that normally force people to care about health and appearance. (In a society dismissive of the categories of beauty, attractiveness, or youth, it is not so much that everyone is beautiful, but rather that no one is ugly, badly dressed, unkempt, or old.) As they are portrayed by Szczygieł, Czechs have neutralized sexuality as a source of potential suffering by eliminating shame. The common perception that the Czechs are a nation of cowards – a perception especially prominent in Europe – is explained by the disarmament of the collective as a source of suffering. If the members of a collective do not feel responsible for the active defence of national pride, if they are able to laugh at their own history and mock all types of heroism, then the national bond – as a sensitive part of individual identity – disappears, and along with it national wounds and traumas, and nationalistic and xenophobic positions. The most poignant part of the book, one that is saturated with a vague melancholia, deals with the final issue – of bonds with the departed. In this section, Szczygieł describes ever more common "cold" burial customs: the prevalence of cremation, storage rooms filled with urns unclaimed by relatives, and the disappearance of the custom of visiting graves. These are mass behaviours, although some individuals do exhibit shame (for neglecting the dead) or suffering (over the death of a loved one). The erasure of prohibitions and precepts that generate a sense of shame for one's own body and for personal sexual proclivities, the neutralization of pathos related to belonging to an imagined community, and the loosening of bonds with the deceased are thus revealed as four steps on the road to paradise. This is why Szczygieł's book can be treated as post-secular reportage: it presents a society that believes in a path to collective happiness that sidesteps God and violence.

The next book in Szczygieł's oeuvre – *Heavenly Love* – is a collection of feuilletons that accompanied a series of the most popular twentieth-century Czech books and films that were sold as a supplement to *Gazeta Wyborcza*. The book consists of seventeen texts that were tied at the onset to specific works, among them Ota Pavel's *Death of Beautiful Does*, Hrabal's *I Served the King of England*, Hašek's *The Good Soldier Švejk*, Ladislav

Grosman's *The Shop on Main Street*, and Ladislav Fuks' *The Cremator*. While related to these works at their departure point, these feuilletons also make use of improvisation, free association, and anecdotes. In addition to concrete information about the novels themselves, therefore, Szczygieł includes anecdotes about, for example, President Havel's mistress, the fight of Helena Vondráčková's husband for his wife's dignity, the most famous of Czech bathroom graffiti, and the role of haemorrhoids in the history of literature.

In line with the author's declared intention, *Heavenly Love* is the last of his "Czech books." It seems that Szczygiel has concluded that Czechness, which allowed him to doff the mask of a television showman and turn himself into a European writer, is restricting his prospects for the time being.

Aleksander Kaczorowski, journalist
Przemysław Czapliński, Adam Mickiewicz University, Poznań
Translated by Agnieszka Polakowska

NOTE

1 Gruša, "Nie przestałem być czeskim pisarzem," 77.

WORKS CITED AND CONSULTED

Bauer, Zbigniew. *Dziennikarstwo wobec nowych mediów. Historia – Teoria – Praktyka.* Kraków: TAiWPN Universitas, 2009.

Glensk, Urszula, *Po Kapuścińskim. Szkice o reportażu.* Kraków: Universitas, 2012.

Gruša, Jiři. "Nie przestałem być czeskim pisarzem." In Andrzej S. Jagodziński. *Banici. Rozmowy z czeskimi pisarzami emigracyjnymi.* 69–80. Kraków: Oficyna literacka, 1988.

Sadowski, Witold. "Wersyfikacja reportażu." *Teksty Drugie* 5 (2005): 82–99.

Szczygieł, Mariusz. *Gottland.* Wołowiec: Wydawnictwo Czarne, 2006.

– *Láska nebeská.* Warszawa: Wydawnictwo Agora, 2012.

– *Zrób sobie raj.* Wołowiec: Wydawnictwo Czarne, 2010.

Szczygieł, Mariusz, and Wojciech Tochman. "Reportaż – opowieść o tym, co wydarzyło się naprawdę," In *Biblia dziennikarstwa.* Edited by Andrzej Skworz and Andrzej Niziołek. 294–306. Kraków: Znak, 2010.

Wójcińska, Agnieszka. *Reporterzy bez fikcji. Rozmowy z polskimi reporterami.* Wołowiec: Wydawnictwo Czarne, 2011.

From Soul to Science and Back Again: A Short Stroll through Polish Twentieth-Century Literary Theory

A decade ago, in his book *Europe East and West*, Norman Davies aptly observed:

> Like all English-speakers who have immersed themselves in the wonderful cosmos of Polish literature, I often wondered why it is not better known. The answer has to lie partly in the unfamiliarity of a difficult language, partly in the hostility of neighbours who would have been happy to see Polish culture suppressed, and partly in the coded allusions and allegories by which Polish classics convey their message. If one doesn't know the history of Poland's politics and society, one can't easily decipher the allusions even in translations. And, of course, the vast majority of educated Westerners are blissfully ignorant of Polish history. So for them the book remains closed.[1]

Although Davies's diagnosis pertains mainly to literature, the above statements retain their relevance also in reference to other aspects of Polish culture, including literary studies. Applied to literary theory and the methodology of literary studies, however, Davies's rumination has to be slightly modified. The rigours and precision of theoretical discourse undoubtedly make it an entirely consumable good that does not require special hermeneutic effort when proficiently translated into Western languages. Nevertheless, familiarity with the historical complications of this discourse as well as language barriers remain a significant challenge for researchers working outside of the Polish context. Fully legitimate is also the observation about limited awareness of the undertakings of Polish twentieth-century literary studies, and the great intellectual satisfaction derived from immersion in the "cosmos," as Davies puts it, of Polish theoretical reflection on literature. The author maintains that "studies by western scholars of the eastern half of [the European] continent have been discoloured by deep-seated assumption[s] about the extent and permanence of Eastern Europe's 'otherness.'"[2] In the realm of literary theory, one can find both a confirmation of this difference and its reverse – the proof of deep, pan-European, and even wider relations.

This stroll through Polish literary theory has a twofold rationale. In the first place, the original approaches that Polish literary theory offers open the prospect of a new problematic for literary studies, or of a new interpretation of already known issues. Second, these remarks are motivated by belief in the singularity of all locally developed literary discourses. The dynamic of interaction of various aspects of Polish literary discourse is unique and unrepeatable even when its specific conclusions are a variant of past literary deliberations. The catalogue of questions that Polish literary scholars like to address is curious in itself. The study of literature does not have a long history as a discipline, but in the kaleidoscope of the twentieth century it offers an interesting conglomerate of ideas that can be variously organized. Chronological order, usually the most obvious and difficult to omit, is from our perspective the least exegetical. Looking at the various oppositions that have impacted this discourse is more appropriate here.

The positivist beginnings of literary studies compel the most basic opposition between various genealogical – meaning extrinsic – research approaches (such as biographism, psychologism, sociologism, or comparative studies), which were supported in postwar Polish discourse by literary Marxism, and those research methods that are described in Polish literary scholarship as "internal" or intrinsic. "Internality" points to the intention of moving within (rather than outside of) the "world of literariness" in the analysis and interpretation of literary texts. This type of literary studies undoubtedly includes Roman Ingarden's phenomenology, on the one hand, and the formalist, structuralist, and semiotic concoction on the other. The conviction that the meaning of a literary work cannot be reduced to external and determining factors distinguishes the "ergocentric" approaches that dominate much of the period of interest here. As will soon become clear, however, oppositionist categories can also be applied to the relation between these two anti-genealogical discourses.

Ergocentric methods (studies): a collective term for approaches that diminish the role of external influences in the shaping of a literary text in favour of the self-sufficient and autonomous structure of interdependent textual elements. See Wellek and Warren, *Theory of Literature*, 74.

Another opposition of interest to a contemporary observer of Polish literary studies rests on the differentiation between two types of reflection on literature; the first type attempts to promote itself as the "exponent, sentry, and explorer of communal cultural tradition and the interdisciplinary centre of the entire (national) humanities," while the other works towards the image of literary studies as "a modern science, meaning an autonomous discipline with its own subject and method."[3] Both structuralist and phenomenological declarations can be contrasted with genealogical ones in this regard as well. Structuralists tried to legitimize the scientific nature of literary studies, while researchers grouped here under the term "genealogists" often saw themselves are guardians of an age-old tradition.

It is also tempting to view Polish literary studies from a perspective rooted in the opposition between "grand" and contrasting world views (e.g., between Marxism and personalism). Since literary discourse is culturally determined, is it not necessary to question how Polish literary theory has internalized its Christian cultural context, which is not infrequently underscored in Polish cultural self-characterizations? This approach, which is the most risky and is mostly foreign to Polish literary meta-discourse, will be carefully explored in the final part of this discussion.

The Great Hypotaxis

Essentially, the entire history of spiritual life in postwar Poland is relativized, in one way or another, to the several years of Stalin's and Bierut's rule. Regardless of whether the experience of those years is subsequently condemned, justified, or perceived as a warning – whether it is spoken of directly or using refined euphemisms – it inevitably appears as a reference point for current experiences.[4]

Remarks about Polish literary scholarship during the twentieth century require a brief look at Marxist literary discourse.[5] In the Marxist version, literary studies range between intensive critique of the discipline's past and aggressive propaganda of literary scholarship's new path. Stefan Żółkiewski (1911–91), the most aggressive "terroretician" (propagandist) of socialist realism, peremptorily announced in 1950: "Whoever considers literary forms in their historical development, separating them from social struggles, creates an illusory academic problematic. It is a methodological undertaking without any merit."[6] All literary scholarship that searched for the author's individuality or spirituality was thus denied any value, and the separation of art from "life" (narrowly understood as a political and economic situation) was rejected. Formalism and idiographism of any kind were also ridiculed, as was belief in the autonomy of literary processes. Furthermore, according to Marxists, the "museum of pathology" (as Żółkiewski calls it) of prewar literary scholarship was characterized by the "chaos and infertility" of rummaging conducted with "nonideological objectivism."[7] An entire formation of authoritative scholars of such rank as Roman Ingarden (1893–1970), Manfred Kridl (1882–1957), Wacław Borowy (1890–1950), and Stanisław Ossowski (1897–1963) was also dismissed. In the words of the leading ideologue of the period, "hostile are the words of bourgeois Polish literary studies, and hostile is its silence."[8]

The annihilation of literary scholarship's past was a necessary gesture of chiliastic delusion – of the conviction that history was beginning anew from a mythologized point zero that would give history its destined shape and final explanation. The implementation of the positive Marxist program (starting from around 1949 and continuing until the milestone Polish Literary Studies Conference in 1958) produced literary scholarship typified by extreme isomorphism; in other words, irrespective of the direction taken within the field of Marxist literary investigations, their form was strikingly similar. This isomorphism was mainly the function of a universal method of organizing the highly ideologized and persuasive Marxist discourse, which had a developed hypotaxis as its backbone. Syntactic hypotaxis, to recall, is a combination of the antecedent – *protasis* (or *principium*) – and the consequent – *apodosis* (or *reflexio*). The discursive practice of Marxism within literary studies manufactured tensions between a superordinate ideological principle and a subordinate empirical (in this case, literary) confirmation. The manner of constructing explanations, interpretations, or analyses of literary texts was made subordinate to the illusion of permanent inference from a principal premise. The critical text appeared as a combination of a series of implications – the logical equivalents of hypotactic relations – and this created the illusion of a scientific and all-encompassing description of literary "events" and "beings," the powerful rhetorical impact of which masked the gaps in its reasoning.

The "theory of reflection" is the only theoretical foundation of hypotaxis. As Henryk Markiewicz (1922–2013) explains: "Marxist theory of culture counts literature among so-called ideologies, in other words forms of social consciousness that aid our understanding and transformation of reality."[9] Ideology, in turn, in accordance with generally known findings, is part of the superstructure of the economic base, and in particular of the relations of production. "In agreement with Lenin's theory" – echoes Żółkiewski – "the work of art is a reflection of reality as a characteristic form of its cognition." Not every kind of reflection receives the imprimatur of Marxism, however. The imprecise category of "reflection" has degrees of "correctness" that are dependent on the "writer's class standing": "Only the position of progressive classes, even a partial rapproachement with it, makes possible the correctness of reality's reflection in art."[10] It is clear, therefore, that this version of reflection about literature becomes, in the first place, a procedure for verifying the writer's biography, and especially of locating him within the social structure. The isomorphism of Marxist literary studies is apparent also on the level of reflection – albeit only skeletal – on the structure of the literary work. The qualities and formal values of literature are pushed far onto the back burner of Marxist analysis and interpretation and reduced to a subservient role vis-à-vis the "objective" (according to Marxist ideologues) ideological and cognitive value of the work. "All types of formalism" – Jerzy Putrament (1910–86) writes – "represent bourgeoisie ideology. Objectively, on the ideological front, the formalist writer fights on the side of the bourgeoisie, sometimes more effectively than a conscious, programmatic fascist."[11]

The chiliastic aspect of Marxist research was a corollary of the absolutization of values tied to the researcher's *hic et nunc*. The only positive values were attached to the present moment of reflection. This was an acute and hyperbolic form of presentism of Marxist reflection on literature, one that affected every narration about the history of literature. The irony of the situation stemmed from the contrast between the persistence of this hyperbole and the postulate of "objectivism," since it was fervently argued that "there are no neutral departure points, with the scientific outlook on the world being decisive in all things."[12] In the choice between the positions of idealism and materialism, only the latter was to be uncontestably correct and binding. The polyphony of literary discourse was seen as superfluous.

It also has to be noted that Marxist literary discourse is ostentatiously accordant with the ideological party discourse.[13] According to Foucault's conceptualization, the latter constitutes "the field of concomitance," meaning that it

> includes statements that concern quite different domains of objects, and belong to quite different domains of objects, and belong to quite different types of discourse, but which are active among the statements studied here, either because they serve as analogical confirmation, or because they serve as a general principle and as premises accepted by a reasoning, or because they serve as models that can be transferred to other contents, or because they function as a higher authority than that to which at least certain propositions are presented and subjected.[14]

Faced with a literary text, a Marxist seeks the confirmation of already known and agreed-upon conclusions. Ideological functions steer both the choice of texts and their analysis. From the point of view of literary theory – and especially literary analysis and interpretation – the greatly limited hermeneutics of Marxist discourse do not cognitively enrich the discursive field; indeed, they do not even reinterpret "the field of concomitance." Instead, through a methodological and discursive mimicry, they subordinate the experience of literature to a number of phenomena that are external to it.

In the Mesh of Structure

Michał Głowiński (b. 1934), one of the most influential of the so-called Warsaw Structuralists (along with Janusz Sławiński [1934–2014] and Aleksandra Okopień-Sławińska [b. 1932]), recalls that the gravitation of his generation of researchers towards structuralism was in part a negative choice:

> I did not want to have anything to do with Marxism, the officially approved and ideologically oriented methodology; I studied during Stalinism, when Marxism was imposed upon us in an extremely vulgar version. We became interested in literary theory that was understood primarily as a theory of the literary work, text, or utterance. A broadly understood poetics formed its centre. At that time, we read voraciously the works of Russian formalists, classic by then, along with works of the Prague School scholars as well as publications by Polish authors that came out in Warsaw and Vilnius of the 1930s, and represented an early phase of structuralism, not yet well crystallized ... Very impactful were also the remarkable, world-class scholars who visited Poland, among them Roman Jacobson, Jan Mukařovsky, Roland Barthes, and A.J. Greimas.[15]

As the author admits, freedom from ideological obligations motivated the theoretical turn towards "intrinsic" methods of textual investigation, which made autonomous its artistic qualities and minimized the significance of its external obligations of representation.

It is difficult to overestimate the impact of structuralism on the development of Polish literary studies. Two aspects of home-grown structuralism deserve particular attention: its discursive grounding in the literary studies paradigm, and its problematic omnipotence. It should be noted here that structuralism in Poland is significantly stronger and more influential than many other cultural contexts of comparable morphology and dynamics.

> Structuralism's paradigmatic status was secured by institutional instruments such as conferences, publication series (e.g., "Z dziejów Form Artystycznych i Literackich" [From the History of Artistic and Literary Forms]), journals (*Teksty* [Texts] and *Teksty Drugie* [Second Texts]), canonical works (such as Sławiński's *Dzieło-Język-Tradycja* [Work–Language–Tradition, 1974]), and an influential research centre with renowned scholars and the means to overcome (to some extent) the barriers in academic contacts with the rest of the world (the Instytut Badań Literackich [Institute of Literary Research] in Warsaw).

This is true also today, at least in the sense of structuralism being a "key tradition" towards which one must take a stand, even if it is a negative one. In the Polish case, the structuralist transformation of literary studies has very deep roots. An important characteristic of the paradigm is its strong tendency towards "scientification" of the discipline, apparent in all aspects of the discourse: from the prominent role of literary theory, through (not infrequently illusory) stringent definitions of concepts and terms, to textual and rhetorical scientisms.

The second aspect of structuralism that has to be addressed here is its "omnipotence," meaning its tendency to annex various fields of literary inquiry: from the problems of literary communication (in both its broad and narrow understandings), through the theory of poetic language (including versification and stylistics), narrative theory, and genre studies, to "the sociology of literary forms." Post-structuralism is not as ambitious in its scope, focusing as it does on certain fragments of literary studies: the interpretation or ontology of the text, or the means of creation of a literary "I." It is hard today to imagine deconstructive versification, or Lacanian stylistics. The structuralist paradigm has not been implemented in all its potency with equal success in all areas of literary studies; that said, the categories of structure and system have a powerful ability to configure the object of study, something that semiotics illustrates particularly well. Even when the postulate of looking for dependencies, functions, relations, and binary oppositions is only partly and figuratively implemented, such undertakings have rhetorical and, to some degree, substantive consequences: they "structuralize" the field of inquiry. While many of the theoretical determinations of Polish structuralism can be linked to numerous foreign theoretical inspirations, the formation of an all-encompassing concept of literary studies may constitute a Polish phenomenon. Since Polish literary studies were going through a Marxist phase when structuralism was gaining ground in the West, structuralism in Poland benefited to some extent from the "delayed reception" of tendencies that shaped Western European literary studies.[16] Polish structuralism planted its roots in soil that had been fertilized by Russian Formalism,[17] its prewar reception in Poland, the Prague School, and a selection of ideas from dynamically developing Western literary theory: Roland Barthes's semiotics and theory of discourse, as well as elements of New Criticism.

A look at a few details of this new – in the 1960s and 1970s – theoretical framework may prove useful here. The "text" (also: linguistic message, utterance) and the "system" function as supercategories in structuralism, orienting the entirety of literary research endeavours. Their original linguistic understanding became, in line with the developing doctrine, more expansive and complicated, to the point of post-structuralist self-liquidation. From the concepts of Roman Jacobson, Jan Mukařovsky, and Felix Vodička, structuralism moved towards the "textual world" of discourse ruled by Michel Foucault, Jacques Derrida, Roland Barthes, and Julia Kristeva, along with many other figures of authority recognized, accepted, and esteemed in the subsequent decades of the 1980s and the 1990s. The categories of "text" and "system" freed the literary work from authorial intention and other genealogical traps, placing the researcher-structuralist in opposition to both Marxists and Positivists. The structural ordering and scientification of literary studies can be viewed through a prism of binary oppositions that mirror linguistic ones: in other words, the pairing of *parole* and *langue* known from linguistics finds a parallel in the opposition between "literary work" and "system."

An early text written by Sławiński at the beginning of the 1960s, titled "Wokół teorii języka poetyckiego" (On the Theory of Poetic Language), reveals some of the original characteristics of Polish structuralism. Taking the proposals of Karl Bühler and Roman Jacobson as his cue, Sławiński defines the literary work as an utterance (*parole*, the realization of a system) with a specific-to-it configuration of linguistic functions. Like every linguistic message (*parole*), it is implicated in a network of various dependencies, including the fundamental one of a language system. The departure point is thus the analysis of the linguistic sign and its functions, which are subsequently projected onto a literary text. These are as follows: the cognitive function, referring to the ability to make true or false statements about the facts of reality; the expressive function, referring to the ability of linguistic signs to express the experiences of the speaker; the impressive function, referring to the ability of a sign to affect the addressee; the phatic function, enigmatically characterized as the sign's ability to establish and maintain communication between a sender and a recipient (i.e., "hello"); the metalinguistic function, denoting the sign's orientation towards its determining system; and, finally, the poetic or aesthetic function.[18] This last function counters all of the remaining ones in a "dialectic negation," as Sławiński puts it, by aiming at the "inside" of the poetic communication, which creates another binary opposition within this system. The aesthetic function determines a certain "surplus of organization"[19] that cannot be reduced to the other, "external" obligations of a poetic or – more broadly – literary text (e.g., expressing emotions of the speaking subject or depicting the world).

In Sławiński's conceptualization, the functions of linguistic utterances are analogous to the functions of linguistic signs. The poetic (aesthetic) function of a linguistic utterance is of key importance to the idea of a literary work being a form of linguistic message. This function, which dominates other functions, ensures a characteristic "reification" of the message, understood as the "restriction of its role as a carrier of experiences, objects, and commands and the underlining of its role as a new 'thing,' the existence of which is an end in itself."[20] In addition, this "surplus of organization" replicates the information carried by a text, making it equivocal and displaying the utterance itself with some surplus that is not a requirement of the communication. The dominance of the poetic function "brings to a linguistic communication a particular kind of organization of the sequences of signs and meanings": it gives them the character of a system in which "the position of a sign is motivated by another sign," becoming a "codified message" – a structure. It is distinguished, therefore, by the order of both succession and "synchronism," thus constituting a "parole imitating langue."[21]

This description of a literary work, in which words are "astounded by other words," "shimmer" with meanings, or "play with their complex biography,"[22] has not lost its intellectual and rhetorical appeal. Sławiński's comparisons and metaphors still have cognitive merit and a discursive allure. This is especially true since Sławiński was able to avoid a pervasive weakness of early structuralism – namely, its neglect of diachrony (the historical developmental context of a literary text, as opposed to synchrony – its relation to the system) and its reduction of analysis and interpretation of literary texts to purely linguistic characteristics. The category of tradition as a "collection of rules and norms residing in the consciousness of writers and readers" appears in the same work from 1961.[23] Every poetic text – the author explains – stands in opposition to existing and already known forms of poetic information. Literary tradition is, in fact, the correlate of these limitations. Thus framed, the literary work is limited in its structure not only by the linguistic system but also by the system of literary tradition, which is more specific to literature and is the subject of Sławiński's particular attention in his subsequent works. This double-dependency of the literary *parole* would have its own, significant consequences in defeating another binary opposition – the one between the synchrony and the diachrony of the literary process.

As presented by Sławiński, tradition far exceeds the conventional storehouse of past works, becoming a systemic creation – a synchronic order that mediates the relations of the participants in the literary game of communication: the author, the text, and the reader. "Its entry into this arrangement is double: as a system of rules and tools of creation, and thus as a **system of resistances** between an utterance and its intention, as well as a **system of expectations** on the part of the reader."[24] Sławiński explains this latter, less obvious aspect of tradition's function through the category of literary norm and convention. Readers recognize certain devices and literary solutions as either "familiar or foreign," and this becomes the basis of their understanding of the text. The author's system of limitations, meaning the places already occupied by other literary texts, simultaneously constitutes the reader's system of expectations, as he or she encounters the text through recognizing its already known or decisively innovative solutions.

Sławiński analyses these issues in more breadth in a canonical text titled "Synchronia i diachronia w procesie historycznoliterackim" (Synchrony and Diachrony in the Historical–Literary Process," 1967). In it, he expresses a fundamental disagreement with some of the possible consequences of the structuralist perspective. Structuralism viewed the literary text as merely a structure exemplifying changes in the system – in *langue*. The *parole* of a specific work was thus not supposed to be the object of study, at least not in early versions of structuralist literary research (Sławiński references Franciszek Siedlecki here). "From this perspective, works of literature would be only externalizations of changes that have taken place [in the literary system, e.g., on the level of versification or genre – KK], their exponents rather than participants."[25] Sławiński argues that the "historical-literary process takes place in the realm of the literary langue, but only to the extent that it occurs simultaneously on the level of individual paroles."[26]

Sławiński gives traditions the status of a "characteristically literary" context, one that stands before all other contexts of a literary work (such as ideology, poetic school, literary current, or formulated poetics, as the author enumerates). This allows, to some degree, the preservation of the components of the genealogical approach, although only to the extent that they can be incorporated as norms and conventions into a new, autonomous, and *stricte* literary system of tradition. External reality, which constitutes the ultimate explicatory framework for genealogists, infiltrates the literary utterance in Sławiński's approach only through the amount of change in the created system of norms and conventions that compose the literary tradition. Naturally, the "systematicity" of this system has to be queried. What are the relations of these norms and conventions vis-à-vis one another? Are they binary as the elements of language? What is the catalogue of these norms and conventions, and what are the dependencies between a norm and a convention? How do lower-level elements constitute higher structures? Notwithstanding such questions, it has to be noted that Sławiński attempts to lay the foundations of the particular "grammar" of literary norms and outlines a number of rules of its functioning.

To begin with, from his perspective, each literary text is a configuration of idiomatic, untranslatable, and individual properties. The choice behind each of these properties, however, opens a "class" of potential but unused solutions. For example, the choice of eight-syllable lines as the versification form of an epigram (trifle) appears as a choice from among other forms that permit a similar kind of utterance – for instance, eleven- or thirteen-syllable lines. Positions "occupied" by specific literary realizations bring to mind the presence of "available" positions that *can* be used, thus illuminating a class of possible solutions within the reservoir of tradition. In Sławiński's conceptualization, a "norm" would be the boundary of such a class. Norms are organized hierarchically within the framework of "partial systems" of temporally differentiated "deposits" of tradition. Sławiński also functionalizes the terms "phenotype" and "genotype," which he borrows from Sebastian K. Szaumian's linguistics. These terms are well fitted to the outlined relationship between a work and a tradition understood as its primary modelling system. "Phenotype" refers to the work's "explicated structure … of characteristics," while "genotype" indicates "the implied structure of literary norms referenced in the work."[27] The DNA of a literary work is a form of replication of tradition's code – its evocation and modification.

In the end, however, an earlier formula, one that was adopted from Jacobson's analysis of historical phonology and that characterizes the state of tradition at a given moment as "the projection of diachrony into synchrony," remains the most inspiring. The logic and incisiveness of this conceptualization of the mechanics of movement within the field of literary "beings" and "events" cannot be denied. Sławiński's perceptiveness, manifested also in many of his other texts, remains of value to structuralist discourse outside its Polish variants. However, it is difficult today to embrace the final, overly categorical part of the author's discussion (as in all likelihood was the case during the time of structuralism's victorious offensive): "Only in exceptional circumstances is the tracing of individual innovations worthwhile to a historian of literature. He is concerned primarily with the general changes in the structure of tradition."[28] The responsibilities of the historian of literature are clearly subordinated here to the duties of a theoretician. Yet the analysis of "minor and dispersed advances brought about by individual choices of writers" proves necessary, since "everything begins with the latter," as the author adds almost with resignation.[29] It is the literary critic, rather than the historian or the theoretician of literature, who is assigned the task of concrete (and less constrained by theory) contact with the individual text. The contemporary incarnations of Polish literary theory will significantly blur those distinctions, gathering under the umbrella of post-structuralism a blend of roles and analytical instruments in the process of capturing textual meaning.

Awareness of the limitations of thinking about a literary work in categories of a static synchrony of elements activated only once within a configuration determined by a system led to an attempt to create a theoretical space that could enable the removal of these limitations. Such an undertaking necessitated the inclusion of systemically unpredictable, sociological aspects of the literary process: the author (expunged from the text due to genealogical fears), the reader (a historical and singularized individual), and the critic (who tries to represent both of these figures; a type of mediator). Sławiński called this space between sociology and historical poetics "the sociology of literary forms," tasking it with two obligations. The first was to research "the differentiation of the system of tradition understood as a correlate of literary culture, and thereby of the public," and the other was to reflect on "the semantic structure of a message that is understood as a model of a communicative situation and exists in a historically determined context.[30] To begin with, therefore, the sociology of literary forms considers literary culture in relation to the stratification of the public, and then concentrates on the systems of literary limitations that affect works created at different stages of literature's evolution. Clearly, categories that were once isolated from one another are forced to cooperate here. The initial expulsion of the "human" factor – non-systemic, unpredictable, and historical – and of actual, historically conditioned communication that was typical of early structuralism, gives way to efforts at reintroducing these "actors," this time in line with structuralist principles. On the one hand, the sociology of literary forms analyses "forms of literary life" in their literary embodiment, in other words as they are "translated" (as Sławiński puts it) into artistic solutions. On the other hand, "the methods of literary communication gain their equivalents in literary life."[31] If censorship is in effect in a given culture, therefore, authors attempt to find a suitable language of communication and to construct a new artistic form that is functional in this context. In so doing they also outline certain kinds of readerly behaviours that respond to the demands of this form. "In this way, the institution infiltrates the inside of creativity; the mechanism of its actions becomes, so to speak, built into the system of poetics' tenets."[32]

On the side of textual recipients, in turn, a group of readers appears who are "sensitive to the subtexts of works, persistent in searching for hidden connotations, [and] ready for active collaboration with the author in the process of moving from textual data to sometimes very distant systems of meanings."[33] Sociology of literary forms, for example, would encompass analysis of Norman Davies' text cited at the beginning of this discussion, in which he speaks about the challenges of understanding Polish Romantic literature experienced by readers outside the Polish context. Their unfamiliarity with literary forms shaped by pressures of communicating "over the heads" of censors and political opponents makes activating models of communication written into literary texts more difficult. Reflections on literary life as a space where such forms take shape belong to the field of study devised by Sławiński. His text "Sociology of Literature and Historical Poetics" is also to some extent a decisive discussion with the genealogical tendencies that form the negative context of the sociology of literary forms.

As it does in its other incarnations, structuralism in its Polish version opens many fascinating paths for the development of theoretical thought. The issue that remains to be decided is which direction to choose at the end of the battle with structuralism's residuum. Reflection on the structures that transgress the boundaries of texts created new languages and interpretations of the problematic of discourse. Sławiński's consideration of the sociology of literary forms contains many inspiring ideas about the discursive conditions of all "speech" that are sure to be explored by new generations of researchers. The independence of interpretation as an activity of literary studies that occupies a space between literary criticism, theory, and history, is today self-evident. This shift appears to be rooted both in the opposition to the idea of the text as *parole* actualizing the potencies of *langue*, and in the favourable reception of the structuralist respect for the complexity of a text and the complications of internal, functional dependencies of even the most minute of textual elements. The detailed nature and rationalism of structuralist discussions of texts has opened new perspectives for dealing with the "opaqueness" of an individual linguistic utterance in relation to its externality.

The Play of Quality and Value versus the Schematics of a Literary Work

In Polish theoretical and literary discourse, Roman Ingarden's work is almost always accompanied by adjectives such as "great," "exceptional," and "original." Despite its originality, solid philosophical foundations, and clear applicative potency, however, Ingarden's phenomenology has not come to dominate the discourse of literary studies. The universal high regard for this author, who has attracted numerous "adherents," does not change the fact that this current belongs to the history of literary studies' doctrines to a much greater extent than it constitutes a "key tradition" that actively shapes contemporary Polish thought about literature. The authors of the Polish textbook *Teorie Literatury XX wieku* (The Theories of Twentieth-Century Literature, 2007) do not devote much space to Ingarden's work, emphasizing his inattention to the "cultural entanglement of a literary work" as a reason for its loss of attractiveness: "Ingarden does not appear in literary theory anthologies today, although his pioneering position with reference to all reader-oriented theories is noted."[34] These remarks need to be met with some scepticism. *The Encyclopedia of Contemporary Literary Theories*, for instance, dedicates at least as much room to Ingarden as the Polish compendium.[35] Furthermore, the grounding of his theory in a broader cultural context is possible, even if it has not been explored as intensely as it deserves to be. The presence of Ingarden's thought and inspiration in the 1942 *Theory of Literature* by Wellek and Warren, in the reception theories of Wolfgang Iser and Hans Robert Jauss, and in the achievements of the Geneva School, all speak to the productivity of such an approach.

One factor limiting Ingarden's reception for literary scholars is the intellectual context of his work, which requires considerable philosophical grounding. If the litmus test of the potency of a given direction of literary studies is its ability to create historico-literary syntheses that popularize further detailed research, than the phenomenological history of Polish literature has not yet been written. It has to be acknowledged that a legitimate presentation of Ingarden's theory of the literary work would require a separate and extensive text, in which the philosophical context that served as the basis of his ontology is given its rightful place. Here, it is only possible to catalogue some of the inspiring ideas that entered Polish literary studies as a consequence of its reception of Ingarden's ontology. The author himself set his philosophy in a context penetrable to the non-philosophical mind. In *Man and Value*, he asks: "What, in the final reckoning, *are* all the strange objects which somehow go into making up the world man lives in: are they reality or fiction?"[36] He further adds:

> Philosophically untrained readers will hold that I am needlessly "breaking through the open door." For who could possibly doubt the existence of all these products of man's activity? At the same time, however, these same readers, under the influence of psychologism and psychologistic relativism (which among Polish academically trained people is still [1935] sustained as a special sort of *opinio communis*), will hold that these products are nothing other than certain human "apparitions" or, more generally, something "psychical." But if all these objects were essentially "psychical," they would be in ourselves, and not in the world around us. Yet, when we have to do with these objects in everyday living it seems to us that they make up one of the constituents of the surrounding world, and a constituent, at that, which is neither material nor psychical, but something of an entirely different nature, even though it appears within the framework of the material-psychical word (if we may put it that way).[37]

Ingarden's interest in the literary work is motivated by the search for arguments in his polemic with Husserl's transcendental idealism. Literature, architecture, music, and theatre are inescapably the domain of "intentional objects," the ontology of which allows Ingarden to ask and answer questions about the real and the ideal spheres of existence. Husserl's account of subjectivity as the basis for what objectively exists is negated within the framework of Ingarden's "second phenomenology," which does not accept that the existence of a real world depends on pure consciousness. This, in turn, allows it to escape "from the 'vicious circle' of the phenomena of consciousness."[38]

Husserl's work is part of the discussion about the existence of the real world. Following Franz Brentano, he distinguishes between acts of consciousness and objects belonging to the cognized world, concentrating chiefly on the acts. His method of "phenomenological reduction" is a tool for cognizing objects by "bracketing" away all their non-essential aspects, in other words separating what is directly given to consciousness as essential, natural, and obvious from epistemological presupposition. Phenomenology considers as real not only objects that can be empirically perceived, but also non-empirical, "ideal objects."

Although Husserl initially criticized both psychologism and naturalism, in his later works (*Ideas 1*) he displayed some idealistic tendencies, which Roman Ingarden, Husserl's disciple, vigorously opposed. In his later phase, Husserl presented the outer world as an "intentional object" ontologically founded by pure consciousness, arguing that what remains after "phenomenological reduction" are only consciousness's equivalents of cognized objects. Hence, the world exists "for somebody," not "in itself" – in other words, as a correlate or creation of cognizing consciousness, which constitutes in some interpretations transcendental idealism and psychologism.

In case this problematic appears convoluted and far removed from the routine of literary studies' endeavours, it must be added that the author's intentions are rooted in a world of values that is close to us all:

> Do we not come to be human beings who are radically different from the beasts precisely because we have created some new reality out of our surrounding – more than that, out of our world? And how diverse that reality is, for which the realm of so called "nature" is just a necessary substratum ... We are human beings because we surpass the biological conditions in which we have found ourselves, and build on their foundation a new, different world.
>
> But let us take one more, decisive step: All those things we call values – such as goodness, beauty, truth, justice, etc. – are not found in the psycho-biological substratum of our human world, but indeed emerge only in that superimposed reality we have created.[39]

Reflection on the phasic and stratified formation of the literary work, on its schematics or concretization, and on the nature of quasi-judgments and the cognitive virtues of a text, are incorporated in the end into this beautifully described effort at understanding the values that constitute the human domain. "Man stands on the fringe of two worlds – one world out of which he originated and which he surpasses with the greatest exertion of the spirit, and the other, which he approaches through his most prized creations – not being truly 'at home' in either."[40]

In the context of the Polish twentieth-century discourse of literary studies, phenomenological research occupies the same anti-psychological and anti-genealogical territory as structuralism. Both concepts also take a polemical stance towards Marxism. Nevertheless, the departure *and* arrival points of their study of ways of being, the specifics of organization, and the characteristics of a literary works stand a considerable distance from one another. The positive reception of some of Ingarden's views by the structuralist discourse is incontestable, yet the primary tendencies of searching for artistic and aesthetic values and qualities in phenomenology lead researchers to diverse areas of the humanities. While structuralism looks for ways of making reflection on literature objective and scientific, finding its primary support in linguistics and semiotics, phenomenologists see literature as a universe of specific, "intentional objects," with their value being the subject of special consideration. Whereas structuralism sees the realization of a supra-individual system within individual texts, phenomenology looks for means of grasping "the thing in itself." The basic question that binds and organizes Ingarden-inspired approaches is thus the issue of what constitutes a literary work – "Among what kind of objects is the literary work to be included – the real or the ideal?" – as well as what distinguishes it from both the real and the ideal objects.[41]

Replying to this question, the author writes: "The literary work is a purely intentional formation which has the source of its being in the creative acts of consciousness of its author and its physical foundation in the text set down in writing ... As such it is not a psychological phenomenon and is transcendent to all experiences of consciousness, those of the author as well as the reader."[42] As an "intentional object," it is heterogeneous: neither fully real, nor fully ideal, and at the same time not identifiable with either its linguistic materiality or the sum of its linguistic meanings. "The literary work" – adds Ingarden – "is a true wonder. It exists and lives and works on us, it enriches our lives to an extraordinary degree, it gives us hours of delight, and it allows us to descend into depths of existence, and yet it is only an ontically heteronomous formation which in terms of ontic autonomy is nothing."[43] What are its positive aspects? Traditionally, the presentation of a phenomenologist's views is initiated with a handful of terms from Ingarden's catalogue of the literary work's characteristics, with two-dimensionality being first and foremost among them. One of these dimensions is, naturally, the succession of phases of the text (words, sentences, compositional parts). While a painting can be encompassed with a single look, the literary text reveals itself to the reader gradually, in a sequence of parts that follow one another. Its reception requires the phasic "consumption" of all of its gradually revealing literary components.

The second dimension of a literary work relates to the coexistence, or concurrence, of its heterogeneous strata: the stratum of *word sounds* and of the higher-order phonetic formations built on them; the stratum of *meaning units*; the stratum of schematized *aspects*; and the stratum of *represented objectivities* and their vicissitudes.[44] The combination of these essentially heterogeneous elements of its structure distinguishes a work of literature from all other works of art. The concept of "the represented world" with its numerous ontological complications has proved especially useful and is perhaps most popularized in non-theoretical discourse. "Objects presented by literary work are derived from purely intentional objects projected by units of meaning."[45] Words and sentences create a complete, ontologically distinct "world" that includes various relationships and relations, processes and dependencies, as well as emotions, "subjective moments," and "emotional illustrations," which are present, for example, in pure lyric poetry. Ingarden describes the quasi-existence of this world with great care and detail, understanding that "the great majority of literary studies devote their attention to this stratum of the work."[46]

A distinguishing characteristic of all these strata is their specific schematism, which stems from the presence of "places of indeterminacy." This schematism is a function of the disproportion between the descriptive potential of language itself and the demands of the represented subject. Given the diversity and multiplicity of that subject's individual characteristics, its exhaustive description would require an endless number of sentences. Naturally, multiplying descriptive approximations of subjects to the point that their individual characteristics are exhausted is neither possible, nor – given the nature of aesthetic reception – desirable. Ingarden meticulously describes and explains the presence of "places of indeterminacy" in all of the strata of the text, aiming at a fundamental conclusion – the necessity of distinguishing between a work of art as an artistic object and its "concretization" (meaning the aesthetic object created in the act of reception undertaken by a concrete reader). During this process, "the places of indeterminacy" that are anchored in the real linguistic structure, called into existence by the authorial subject, are filled in by the reader's subjectivity. In addition, Ingarden underscores that concretization occurs in various "basic attitudes," starting with the naive one that characterizes an average reader, through different versions of practical attitudes, the scientific attitude, to the aesthetic attitude that is his clear preference as a means of activating the aesthetic values enclosed within a literary work. The foundation that stabilizes the aesthetic values of a work is formed by "aesthetically relevant qualities" established within each cross-section of the text: formal and constructive, sensual, harmonious, as well as metaphysical. As Ingarden phrases it, they make up "a polyphonic harmony of the aesthetic value qualities."[47]

The hierarchical ordering of material, formal, and – built atop of them – secondary values is the characteristic of every work of art. Ingarden dedicates a lot of attention to this aspect of a work of art (which scholars mention infrequently), opening the door to a construction of its universal, axiological theory. Aesthetic values are constituted through "aesthetic qualities," which are seen as ontologically and axiologically absolute and self-sufficient. At the foundation of the aesthetic values constituted in the process of concretization are the artistic values of the literary work, which are not absolute in character. From this perspective, the artistic process is significantly different from the one that can be reconstructed within the field of structural and semiotic theory. In the process of reception – concretization in the case of literary works – the primary aesthetic quality can be grasped by virtue of artistic values set in motion by the artist. Ingarden was aiming at devising a one-of-a-kind, rational system of aesthetic values. This has been seen as an extension of Władysław Tatarkiewicz's (1886–1980) "great theory of beauty," which he had based on "number, measure, proportion, [and] form."[48] In Ingarden's "second phenomenology," works of art are a space where metaphysical qualities, such as "the sublime, the tragic, the dreadful, the shocking" become manifest: "their revelation constitutes the summit and the very depths of existence."[49] To which he adds: "The literary work of art attains its high point in the manifestation of metaphysical qualities."[50]

There are many moments in this part of Ingarden's work that are difficult and that transgress the theory of literature, inclining towards philosophical aesthetics instead. This may be one reason why literary scholars do not probe these areas as enthusiastically as they do others. Yet it seems that this part of Ingarden's reflections contains many compelling, if perhaps unfashionable, rationales for our contemporary literary research. The trajectory of Ingarden's inquiries into the "world of literariness" that is of interest here leads from considerations of the structure of a literary work to the sphere of concretization, which in turn prompts contemplation of axiological expanses. The attractiveness of this conceptual potential is revealed, for instance, in Ingarden's "catalogues" of aesthetic and artistic values. They include categories of both "strong" and "weak" aesthetic values, among them, in the first case, "beauty, ugliness, tragedy, comedy, grandeur, triviality, naiveté, sophistication" and, in the latter, "prettiness, unsightliness, dread, playfulness"; they also include artistic values such as "novelty, masterful execution, individual invention, aptness, richness, symmetry, asymmetry, polysemy."[51] What would humanistic, particularly literary studies education look like if it were based in these types of deliberations? This kind of deeply axiologized reflection appears very well suited to the "ethical," or "cultural" turn announced in present-day Polish literary studies.

"Full" and "Empty" Discursive Places

In the panorama of literary theory viewed as part of Polish twentieth-century culture, the "great theoretical figures" of literary positivism, phenomenology, structuralism and semiotics, and finally post-structuralism (an array of diverse kinds of reflection on literature) are clearly outlined. The fundament of this theoretical discourse is manifold. It includes refined philosophical ideas as well as inspiration born of ideology or world view; it can be shaped by a set of scientific convictions of another discipline or by the intra-disciplinary dynamics of opposition and continuation. Transformations of this discourse were impacted equally by remarkable individuals and by groups of scholars that shared an idea or a reformative mission. The institutional anchor that allowed the dissemination of ideas both within academic circles (at conferences or through specialized publications) and outside of them – in the form of popularizing discourse (textbooks, dictionaries, historical models of literary interpretation) – determined to some extent the force of theory's influence as a paradigm of literary studies.

Nineteenth-century positivist thought initiated the then still undivided discipline of literary theory as part of university education, favouring scientific tendencies that were at that time understood as the search for genealogical relations. Translated into literary discourse, this meant answering the question of what constitutes the source of a "fact" identified as literary. The institutionally robust structuralism, along with elements of semiotics, was on the one hand motivated by opposition towards positivist and Marxist genealogy, which served as its intra-disciplinary inspiration. On the other hand, it also became a manifestation of the rejection of the world view imposed on literary studies by their political context. Finally, it was also the discourse's response to linguistic inspirations. Phenomenology in literary studies was constituted by the philosophical discipline of phenomenology.

The impact of highly creative individuals on Polish literary studies cannot be overestimated, especially in the case of Roman Ingarden, who worked and influenced the field from a place of relative isolation, and thus in a singular manner and without a clearly formed group of collaborators. At the same time, prominent individuals in the Warsaw structuralist group functioned both cooperatively and independently, leaving behind their distinct discursive mark. There is thus no single variable that determines the outcome of the equation, and no steady function or relation between the tone of literary theory at a particular moment in history and the contextual canvas that underpins it.

These fluctuations of Polish literary discourse with regard to both the subject of study and research methods are thought-provoking. The relatively short history of the discipline reveals its flexibility in meeting the challenge of the times. Generally speaking, however, the discourse of literary theory does not so much "reflect" the tendencies of the external world as "contemplate[] its own reflection" in the most broadly understood reality, modifying its shape in answer to reality's new questions. If this is indeed the case, there is a certain lack or gap in this game of challenges arising from "within" and "outside" of the discipline that must give us pause. Of interest here is the weak presence, especially in the recent period following the fall of communism, of these forms of literary discourse that would answer the challenges of reality seen in its transcendental aspect, in other words the collectively diverse and variously experienced forms of spirituality. Initially, this type of reflection did not find a prominent position in institutional literary studies owing to historical circumstances; and presently, the reason likely stems from the accelerated chase after new world trends that is propelled by an understandable sense of having to sort through the backlog of the previous epoch.

If recent proclamations of literary scholars are to be believed, the "cultural turn" in literary studies presses for "new languages of interpretation tied to anthropological, feminist, ethnic, postcolonial, and racial theories, as well as queer and gender studies."[52] It does not reserve a significant place, however, for the open participation in postmodern literary discourse of cultural reflection rooted in a specific type of transcendence, regardless of its provenance. It must be added here that considerations of this nature entice us onto very slippery terrain where no help is provided by a conceptual GPS, be it theoretical or simply terminological. It is enough to ask, for instance, what "Christian culture" should be understood to mean to become mired in centuries-old annals, endless discussions, and impenetrable borderlands. Jacek Woźniakowski once asked, "Is culture requisite to salvation?," and attempted to tackle various hermeneutics of the term "Christian culture," but ended his deliberations on a rather cautious note: "In speaking about Christian culture we are speaking of a difficult, Protean phenomenon, which cannot be programmed in detail and once and for all, and yet *cum fundamento in re*."[53] In the end, the author underscores the importance of fellowship with voices from the past: "Christian culture? It means that their thought is also our thought, that above time and space ... and whatever we might say in categories of sociology, we experience the irrefutable fact: despite all differences, we are connected to them in the most essential community."[54]

Why venture into these regions, then? From the perspective of those looking at Polish culture from "the outside," its Christian aspect constitutes one of its emphasized characteristics. It is pertinent to ask, therefore, whether this aspect inspires any answers in the discourse of literary studies. It is a thought-provoking paradox that over the past few decades there have been no texts within the field of literary studies addressing what appears to hold an incontrovertible position in Polish culture and is tied (in various and, strictly speaking, not necessarily religious ways) to the Christian aspect of the Polish "anthroposphere." Is there a substantial counterweight to the methodologies mentioned earlier?

Obviously, the discursive "emptiness" evoked in the section title is simply a rhetorical exaggeration that does not describe the reality of literary studies with sufficient precision. Following are a few examples of reflections on literature that escape previously introduced categorizations: "We search for these heroes in order to understand our own worth, to find our truest worth. We search for them in order not to feel alone."[55] Or: "The task of art, the task of literature, is to arrive at truth, to provide complex interpretations."[56] Or: "Lyric poetry is a mirror in which the human face is reflected most directly, most spontaneously … It seems to me … that lyric poetry has something in common with psychological tests that do not allow you to cheat, with the test result being the same even if the pictures are defiantly chosen for having the least correspondence to the test subject."[57] Most often, such writing would be classified simply as literary criticism, which removes the problem from the domain of literary theory. In the American context, this difference (almost) does not exist: "literary criticism" is part of "literary studies." Polish twentieth-century discourse, however, especially during the dominance of the structuralist paradigm, makes a fundamental distinction between the functions of these two branches of "the study of literature." In addition, these theoretical declarations do not necessarily translate into textual incarnations: the fabric of literary study texts is heterogeneous and woven from diverse languages that speak about literature. It is just as palimpsestic, therefore, as a literary text is in relation to various forms of natural language.

In the history of literary theory, the discursive formation that is responsible for finding the above-mentioned connections does not occupy an especially prominent place, regardless of the high value of its representative texts. Attempts to theorize these kinds of attitudes towards literature are not trivial. If they were to be included in thinking about literature and our responsibilities towards it, however, what categories would have to be set in motion? One can find examples of such endeavours in a sphere where two distant discourses – of literary studies and metaphysics – intertwine, such as personalistic criticism. In the constellation of names representative of this mode of reflection appear, undoubtedly, Ludwik Fryde (1912–42), Hieronim Michalski (1913–86), Tymon Terlecki (1905–2000), and Stanisław Brzozowski (1878–1911). After 1956, "a current crystallized within literary criticism that is convergent with the personalistic system of values, represented by Jan Błoński, Andrzej Kijowski, Jan Prokop, and the chief (in the early years) critic of *Więzi*, Jacek Łukasiewicz; a current that was neither sufficiently defined theoretically (its creators avoided literary theory), nor described by the historians of literature."[58]

Sketching a theoretical portrait of this theoretically averse current of engagement with literature benefits from a look at some of Tymon Terlecki's declarations about its relationship to "personalistic criticism" and the personalism of Emmanuel Mounier – the founder of the French journal *Esprit* and the author of *Manifeste au service du personnalisme*, which appeared in 1936. In his 1957 manifesto *Krytyka personalistyczna. Egzystencjalizm chrześcijanski* (Personalistic Criticism: Christian existentialism), Terlecki views formalism, historical materialism, and *Stammgesschichte* ("the ethnic spirit") as the negative frame of reference for personalistic approaches. His dislike of formalism is motivated by the conviction that the separation of the "artistic form" from the person – its "creative grounding" – is unacceptable. Viktor Shklovsky's statements that "a work of art is equal to the sum of technical processes used therein," and that "art develops through understanding of one's own technique"[59] are decisively negated by Terlecki, and contrasted with the belief that "the creative individuality and artistic technique, content, and form are inseparable."[60] Historical materialism, in turn, is discredited as a consequence of the lack of "personal creative impulse"[61] in its concepts of the base and the superstructure. Finally, the reduction of the artist to some form of embodiment of the spirit of the nation leads to the disapproval of the denatured characters in romanticizing concepts.

Terlecki looks for a positive tradition in the "history of ideas," setting in motion the category of reflection that in fact belonged to refuted Marxist concepts: "[personalistic] criticism under discussion here exhibits the closest affinity to the so-called 'history of ideas,' a history that studies the reflection of human individuality, or the reflection of time in its characteristic symptoms. Personalistic critique, however, hangs a bridge between individuality and the time in which it appears."[62] As Terlecki writes, the axis of personalistic criticism – its "centre point" – is the belief that "every creative act is a personal act, and every work a sign made by a human being and preserved in some kind of material."[63] A unique and irreproducible person serves as the "measure of all things." "The human being" – the author echoes Mounier – "is the only reality that we know and which we simultaneously create from the inside." What is more, this human being is not like Leibniz's *monad*, but rather a being "open onto other beings,"[64] a being "toward something," which distinguishes personalism from Romantic reclusiveness and egocentrism. "This movement beyond oneself and above oneself is both the content and the sense of a human being, and it is the source and the sense of human culture."[65] In this context, the author calls forth the term *l'engagement* popularized by *Esprit*, signifying the active relation with the surrounding world and opposition to all collectivistic and reifying images of humanity. The work of art, including a literary work, is seen here as a kind of *l'engagement*, "a movement from oneself to others."[66] It is a way out of the world of the unnamed into a world that bears a mark of a human being. In his characterization of the artist, Terlecki makes use of a quote from Brzozowski: "The artist is a human being consciously and freely elevating the self with its spirit to a level at which it becomes a form that is permanent and lasting in the face of history."[67]

The description of the role of a personalistic critic strikes strong genealogical notes. "Personalistic criticism desires to understand and explain that surge of energy that became the stimulus behind a work's creation."[68] At the same time, the critic attempts both to recognize the connections between the artist and the community within which a work is created, and to mediate in the process of its reception. The critic becomes a participant in the "drama" played out between the artist and the audience. "From this perspective, the ideal critic would open the work's farthest horizons for its readers, and – for its artist – the farthest perspectives in the world and in himself ... With his participation, both the creator and the consumer of art would become human beings in the highest, fullest sense of the word."[69] Unfortunately, the author does not provide a further explication of this poetic description. It is thus not entirely clear why the critic would be key to the artist's self-discovery. Is it because as the "ideal reader," following Eco, the literary critic sees more for recognizing "the subject of creative activity" – the role taken up by the artist in the process of creation? Is the artist aware of this role that flows from the need for *l'engagement*? And is the engagement of the critic not, *de facto*, a form of "interference" in the encounter of unrepeatable and individualized people?

Terlecki's essay does not go beyond a set of very general world view postulates interpreted from the perspective of the specific activity of critical textual interpretation. It does not contain more detailed explanations of the manner of existence of a literary work, or of the tools that would enable the penetration of its interior, which contains the unrepeatable efflorescence of the artist's personality. It is also not clear how to avoid the oversimplifications of biographism, in other words connecting what happened in the life of a human being directly to the represented world of a literary text. With the history of structuralist, semiotic, and post-structuralist experiences behind us, it is difficult to overestimate the weight of such questions and – especially – of the not yet conceived answers.

Krzysztof Dybciak, in reconstructing the opinions of prewar personalistic critics (the early Kazimierz Wyka and Ludwik Fryde) from a literary theory perspective, offers more concrete insights. He points to these critics' interest in traditional forms and "artistically unequivocal structures" and links it to the position of defending ethical values in the face of a crisis of values. The author identifies an entire constellation of rules of poetics affirmed in the personalistic context during the prewar period. Among them are purity of genre, constructivism, intellectualism, the structural unity of texts, the principle of mimesis, an apologia for objectivism, and finally tragedy and pathos.[70] The author also addresses the issue of personalism's supposed biographistic tendencies:

> A literary text is understood here as the individualized sign of a person, the message of this person created with the intention of establishing inter-human contact, and, down the line, the formation and solidification of some form of community of persons. The literary act is a personal act; the creative personality – or the inner author, its equivalent expressed in the categories of poetics – must stand at the centre of its interest.[71]

Dybciak activates the structuralist concepts of literary theory, applying the terms of Aleksandra Okopień-Sławińska's text about personal relations in literary communication and transposing the literary work into a literary message that is governed by laws of literary communication.[72] The distinctiveness of these procedures in the realm of personalism is marked by the "transition from an objective to a subjective attitude, from reified statics to personal dynamics, [and] from institutional determination to individual decision and initiative."[73]

The new "quality of literary studies" would be reached, in this analysis, through a new interpretation of interpretation. The existing set of literary research instruments would allow us to inspect the inside of a literary work, while aesthetic values analysed and interpreted in this way would find their interpretation broadened by the personalistic philosophy of interhuman contact, which *de facto* belongs to a different intellectual order, far exceeding the limits of literary studies. Personalistic theory of literature would be, in this context, a matter of choice among already existing analytical and interpretive tools. This would not lend itself to the extraction of novel theoretical ideas, which is certainly not an aspersion. The fusion of horizons of various disciplines speaks to the broadly propagated and practised interdisciplinarity of recent times. A poem by John Paul II, cited in the coda of reflections titled "Wertykalny wymiar Europy" (The Vertical Dimension of Europe), can represent this broadened context of literary studies:

Oh Man, on You I call, for You I search
in whom man's history finds its body.
I approach you saying, not "Come"
But simply "be."

Be there where not one trace is found
but where man once did dwell,
where heart and soul, desire, pain, will,
were consumed by emotions ablaze with holy shame.
Be as the eternal seismograph of things invisible but real.[74]

The authors of a Harvard report about the present state and the future perspectives of studies in the humanities write that "the Arts and Humanities teach us how to describe experience, how to evaluate it, and how to imagine its liberating transformation."[75] When we look at the past of Polish theory of literature, we find "recipes" that allow us to reach for all of the above enumerated virtues of the humanities: structuralism teaches us description and some forms of textual interpretation, and phenomenology leads towards wise evaluation, while personalistic endeavours give us a taste of the liberating, transformative power of literature.

Katarzyna Kasztenna
Independent Scholar, Canada
Translated by Agnieszka Polakowska

NOTES

1 Davies, *Europe East and West*, 171.
2 Ibid., 27.

3 Nycz, *Poetyka doświadczenia*, 18.
4 Sławiński, "Krytyka nowego typu," 130.
5 For further description of Marxist discourse in Polish literary studies, see Kasztenna, *Z dziejów formy niemożliwej*.
6 Żółkiewski, "Aktualny etap walki," 75.
7 Budzyk and Durr-Durski, "Stan badań i potrzeby nauki," 129.
8 Żółkiewski, *Stare i nowe literaturoznawstwo*, 78.
9 Markiewicz, *Materializm historyczny a nauka o literaturze*, 3.
10 Żółkiewski, "Aktualny etap walki," 28.
11 Quoted in Smulski, "Przewietrzyć zatęchłą atmosferę uniwersytetów," 102.
12 Żółkiewski, "Aktualny etap walki," 44.
13 Some aspects of discourse practices in the Marxist era are analysed in Sławiński, "Krytyka nowego typu."
14 Foucault, *The Archeology of Knowledge*, 58.
15 Głowiński, *Monolog wewnętrzny*, 64–5.
16 Lewiński, *Strukturalistyczna wyobraźnia metakrytyczna*, 115.
17 See also Karcz, *The Polish Formalist School*.
18 Sławiński, "Wokół teorii języka poetyckiego," 72. Sławiński's categories parallel those identified by Jacobson as, respectively, referential, emotive, conative, phatic, metalingual, and poetic.
19 Ibid., 73.
20 Ibid., 74.
21 Ibid., 78.
22 Ibid., 80–1.
23 Ibid., 83.
24 Ibid., 84.
25 Sławiński, "Synchronia i diachronia," 287.
26 Ibid., 287.
27 Ibid., 297.
28 Ibid., 298.
29 Ibid., 299.
30 Sławiński, *Dzieło – Język – Tradycja*, 62–3.
31 Ibid., 40.
32 Ibid., 39.
33 Ibid., 39.
34 Burzyńska and Markowski, *Teorie Literatury XX wieku*, 95.
35 See Makaryk, *Encyclopedia of Contemporary Literary Theory*.
36 Ingarden, *Man and Value*, 28. Translation of the Polish *Książeczka o człowieku* (1972).
37 Ibid., 31.
38 Szczepańska, *Estetyka Romana Ingardena*, 10.
39 Ingarden, *Man and Value*, 30.
40 Ibid., 30.
41 Ingarden, *The Literary Work of Art*, 9.
42 Ingarden, *The Cognition of the Literary Work of Art*, 14.
43 Ingarden, *The Literary Work of Art*, 373.
44 Ibid., 30.
45 Ibid., 218.
46 Ibid., 217.

47 Ingarden, "Z teorii dzieła literackiego," 47.
48 Gołaszewska, *Istota i istnienie wartości*, 15.
49 Ingarden, *The Literary Work of Art*, 290–1.
50 Ibid., 294.
51 See Gołaszewska, *Istota i istnienie wartości*, 172–4.
52 Burzyńska, "Kulturowy zwrot teorii," 87.
53 Woźniakowski, *Czy kultura jest*, 51.
54 Ibid., 51.
55 Łukasiewicz, *Szmaciarze i bohaterowie*, 9.
56 Ibid., 167.
57 Ibid., 12.
58 See Dybciak's foreword in Terlecki, *Krytyka personalistyczna*, 7. In his own book *Personalistyczna krytyka literacka. Teoria i opis nurtu z lat trzydziestych* (1981), Dybciak approached this problematic from the perspective of literary studies. See also Jarzębski and Juszczyk, eds., *Tymon Terlecki*.
59 Terlecki, *Krytyka personalistyczna*, 35.
60 Ibid., 36.
61 Ibid., 37.
62 Ibid., 42.
63 Ibid., 27.
64 Ibid., 28.
65 Ibid., 29.
66 Ibid., 30.
67 Ibid., 32.
68 Ibid., 32.
69 Ibid., 34.
70 See Dybciak, *Personalistyczna krytyka literacka. Teoria i opis nurtu z lat trzydziestych*, 70–80.
71 Ibid., 48.
72 Okopień-Sławinska, "Relacje osobowe w literackiej komunikacji."
73 Dybciak, *Personalistyczna krytyka literacka. Teoria i opis nurtu z lat trzydziestych*, 49.
74 John Paul II, "Easter Vigil, 1966," 175–6.
75 "The Teaching of the Arts and Humanities at Harvard College: Mapping the Future," 1. http://scholar.harvard.edu/files/jamessimpson/files/mapping_the_future.pdf.

WORKS CITED

Budzyk, Kazimierz, and Jan Durr-Durski. "Stan badań i potrzeby nauki o literaturze okresu kontrreformacji." In *O sytuacji w historii literatury polskiej. Wybór referatów wygłoszonych na Zjeździe Polonistów w dniach od 8 do 12 maja 1950 roku.* Edited by Jan Baculewski. Kraków: Państwowy Instytut Wydawniczy, 1951.

Burzyńska, Anna. "Kulturowy zwrot teorii." In *Kulturowa Teoria Literatur. Główne pojęcia i problem.* Edited by Michał Paweł Markowski and Ryszard Nycz. 41–92. Kraków: Universitas, 2006.

Burzyńska, Anna, and Michał Paweł Markowski. *Teorie Literatury XX wieku.* Kraków: Wydawnictwo Znak, 2007.

Davies, Norman. *Europe East and West.* London: Jonathan Cape, 2006.

Dybciak. Krzysztof. *Personalistyczna krytyka literacka. Teoria i opis nurtu z lat trzydziestych.* Wrocław: Zakład Narodowy im. Ossolińskich, 1981.
Foucault, Michel. *The Archeology of Knowledge and the Discourse on Language*. Translated by A.M. Sheridan Smith. New York: Pantheon Books, 1972.
Głowiński, Michał. *Monolog wewnętrzny Telimeny i inne szkice*. Kraków: Wydawnictwo Literackie, 2007.
Gołaszewska, Maria. *Istota i istnienie wartości*. Warszawa: Państwowe Wydawnictwo Naukowe, 1990.
Ingarden, Roman. *The Cognition of the Literary Work of Art*. Translated by Ruth Crowley and Kenneth R. Olson. Evanston: Northwestern University Press, 1973.
– *The Literary Work of Art: An Investigation on the Borderlines of Ontology, Logic, and Theory of Literature. With an Appendix on the Functions of Language in the Theater*. Translated by George G. Grabowicz. Evanston: Northwestern University Press, 1973.
– *Man and Value*. Translated by Arthur Szylewicz. Washington, DC: Catholic University of America Press, 1983.
– "Z teorii dzieła literackiego." In *Problemy teorii literatury*. Seria 1. Prace z lat 1947–64. 7–51. Wrocław: Zakład Narodowy im. Ossolińskich, 1987.
Jarzębski, Jerzy, and Andrzej Juszczyk, eds. *Tymon Terlecki. Pamięć i sumienie emigracji*. Przemyśl: Państwowa Wyższa Szkoła Wszecheuropejska, 2009.
John Paul II. "Easter Vigil, 1966." In "The Vertical Dimension of Europe." *Memory and Identity: Personal Reflections*. 173–8. London: Weidenfeld and Nicolson, 2005.
Karcz, Andrzej. *The Polish Formalist School and Russian Formalism*. Kraków: Jagiellonian University Press; Rochester: University of Rochester Press, 2002.
Kasztenna, Katarzyna. *Z dziejów formy niemożliwej. Wybrane problemy historii i poetyki polskiej powojennej syntezy historycznoliterackiej*. Wrocław: Towarzystwo Przyjaciół Polonistyki Wrocławskiej, 1995.
Lewiński, Dominik. *Strukturalistyczna wyobraźnia metakrytyczna. O procesach paradygmatyzacji w polskiej nauce o literaturze po 1958 roku*. Kraków: Towarzystwo Autorów i Wydawców Prac Naukowych Universitas, 2004.
Łukasiewicz, Jacek. *Szmaciarze i bohaterowie*. Kraków: Spłeczny Instytut Wydawniczy Znak, 1968.
Makaryk, Irena R. *Encyclopedia of Contemporary Literary Theory: Approaches, Scholars, Terms*. Toronto: University of Toronto Press, 1993.
Markiewicz, Henryk. *Materializm historyczny a nauka o literaturze. Szkic informacyjny*. Wrocław: Zakład Narodowy im. Ossolińskich, 1950.
Nycz, Ryszard. *Poetyka doświadczenia.Teoria – nowoczesność – literarura*. Warszawa: Wydawnictwo IBL, 2012.
Okopień-Sławinska, Aleksandra. "Relacje osobowe w literackiej komunikacji." In *Semantyka wypowiedzi poetyckiej. (Preliminaria)*. 84–98. Wrocław: Zakład Narodowy im. Ossolinskich, 1985.
Sławiński, Janusz. *Dzieło – Język – Tradycja. Prace wybrane*, vol. II. Kraków: Universitats, 1998.
– "Krytyka nowego typu." In *Teksty i teksty*. 130–52. Warszawa: Polska Encyklopedia Niezależna Pen, 1990.
– "Synchronia i diachronia w procesie historycznoliterackim." In *Problemy teorii literatury*. Seria 2. Prace z lat 1965–74. 284–99. Wrocław: Zakład Narodowy im. Ossolińskich, 1987.
– "Wokół teorii języka poetyckiego." In *Problemy teorii literatury*. Seria 1. Prace z lat 1947–64. 69–85. Wrocław: Zakład Narodowy im. Ossolińskich, 1987.

Smulski, Jerzy. "Przewietrzyć zatęchłą atmosferę uniwersytetów." In *Wokół literaturoznawczej polonistyki doby stalinizmu*. Toruń: Wydawnictwo Naukowe Uniwersytetu Mikołaja Kopernika, 2009.

Szczepańska, Anita. *Estetyka Romana Ingardena*. Warszawa: Państwowe Wydawnictwo Naukowe. 1989.

Terlecki, Tymon. *Krytyka personalistyczna. Egzystencjalizm chrześcijanski*. Warszawa: Biblioteka Więzi, 1987.

Wellek, Rene, and Austin Warren. *Theory of Literature*. New York: Harcourt, Brace, 1956.

Woźniakowski, Jacek. *Czy kultura jest do zbawienia koniecznie potrzebna*. Kraków: Społeczny Instytut Wydawniczy Znak, 1988.

Żółkiewski, Stefan. "Aktualny etap walki o marksistowskie literaturoznawstwo w Polsce." In *O sytuacji w historii literatury polskiej: Wybór referatów ogłoszonych na Zjeździe Polonistów w dniach od 8 do 12 maja 1950r*. 7–51. Kraków: Wydawnictwo PIW, 1951.

– *Stare i nowe literaturoznawstwo. Szkice krytyczno-naukowe*. Wrocław: Wydawnictwo Zakładu Narodowego im. Ossolińskich, 1950.

Negotiating the Aesthetic: The Politics of Polish Postwar Cinema

Released in 1947, the film *Zakazane piosenki* (Forbidden Songs), directed by Leonard Buczkowski (1900–67), marked the re-emergence of Polish cinema after its imposed cessation during the Second World War. The conditions of the film's production and presentation, which included numerous interventions by censors, demonstrate the origins of the political and cultural negotiations that pervaded the postwar era of Polish cinema. Moreover, the film's content and its formal structure point to a series of textual negotiations that would permeate all cinematic production in Poland over the coming decades.

Forbidden Songs depicts Poles' everyday experience of the Second World War and the German occupation. Its simple narrative serves as a pretext for presenting war songs that were sung as a symbolic form of resistance to the Nazi occupiers. Aesthetically, the film both references the prewar model of Polish popular cinema and looks towards the postwar model of politically engaged cinema, which would soon adopt the dogmatic forms of socialist realism. The former manifests itself through the film's melodramatic narrative, which presents war songs in a manner specific to the form of the musical; the latter gains its explicit expression in the propagandistic dialogue and formulaic construction of its characters. *Forbidden Songs* also demonstrates an internal tension between cinematic realism and staginess. Its musical sequences, shot mostly on location and often featuring real street singers, convey a sense of authenticity, whereas the scenes that develop the protagonist-centred narrative, filmed in a studio with professional actors delivering politically charged dialogue, come across as contrived and artificial. The aesthetic and ideological contradictions that characterize this film would pervade Polish films for many years. Leonard Buczkowski and Ludwik Starski (1903–84), the film's screenwriters, were simply the first to learn the bitter lesson that aesthetic compromise had become a prerequisite for a wide range of artistic activities in the newly emerged communist state.

In its attempts to reconcile various aesthetic impulses, the cinematic text of *Forbidden Songs* foreshadowed a significant tension that was yet to develop within Polish national cinema. This tension arose from the ongoing negotiations among the national, the modernist, and the popular tendencies in postwar vernacular cinema. I propose to conceive of the national tendency as a broad and inclusive category comprising all signifying practices that define and redefine a nation. Such practices question what and who constitutes a nation, as well as its function and importance. In Polish postwar cinema, films that revive a national mythology rooted in a vernacular cultural tradition as well as those that rely on communist cinematic propaganda in privileging class over nation belong to the same general discourse on the national. I identify the modernist tendency primarily through a critical interrogation of cinematic representation, which may take the form of either radical realism or self-reflexive experiments that deconstruct traditional narrative and visual conventions. Finally, popular films are intended to reinforce the dominant ideological order through the transparent use of familiar forms and generic conventions.[1]

The hegemonic representational strategy characterizing each phase in the historical development of Polish cinema emerged from various regulatory mechanisms of a political, economic, and cultural nature, which I now briefly delineate. To begin with, the period of postwar restoration that lasted from 1945 to 1949 attempted to bridge a gap between prewar popular cinema and postwar propaganda cinema in accordance with the needs of the new communist regime. After 1949, when the totalitarian aesthetic doctrine of socialist realism was imposed on all public forms of art, including Polish cinema, the propagandistic imperative prevailed, as visible in the work of such directors as Maria Kaniewska (1911–2005), Jan Rybkowski (1912–87), and Leonard Buczkowski. During the period of political relaxation that followed Stalin's death, which came to be known as "the October Thaw" (or simply "the Thaw"), the Polish film school (e.g., Andrzej Wajda [1926–2016], Andrzej Munk [1921–61], Kazimierz Kutz [b. 1929]) initiated the engagement of Polish cinema with the national tradition. That movement also made a tentative foray onto the terrain of modernist filmmaking, mostly via its interrogation of alternatives to the narrative and visual conventions of classical cinema, as exemplified by the films of Tadeusz Konwicki (1926–2015), Jerzy Kawalerowicz (1922–2007), and Wojciech Has (1925–2000).

This adventure did not last long: by 1961, the political authorities had halted the modernist exploration and representation of both the past and the present, calling instead for more traditional forms: standard realism and familiar genres. During the 1960s – often referred to as the years of "small stabilization" (after the title of a play by Tadeusz Różewicz [1921–2014]) – popular forms once again achieved relative hegemony (e.g., with the films of Stanisław Bareja [1929–87], Tadeusz Chmielewski [1927–2016], and Sylwester Chęciński [b. 1930]). Towards the end of the decade, a new generation of filmmakers (e.g., Jerzy Skolimowski [b. 1938], Witold Leszczyński [1933–2007], and Walerian Borowczyk [1923–2006]) emerged and attempted to reinvigorate the field of formal modernist experimentation; these films remained, however, on the margins of mainstream popular cinema and of the historical cinema of nationalistic propaganda that rapidly developed following the anti-Semitic events of 1968.

In the second half of the 1970s a new cinematic current with an interest in the national appeared: the Cinema of Moral Concern. Unlike the Polish film school, which was mostly concerned with the past, however, this movement – exemplified by such directors as Krzysztof Zanussi (b. 1939), Krzysztof Kieślowski (1941–96), Agnieszka Holland (b. 1948), and Janusz Kijowski (b. 1948) – engaged with the social and political dilemmas of contemporary reality. In the liberating climate brought on by the birth of the Solidarity movement in 1980, some filmmakers from the Cinema of Moral Concern (e.g., Janusz Zaorski [b. 1947], Wojciech Marczewski [b. 1944], Ryszard Bugajski [b. 1943]) decided to direct the camera's interrogatory eye towards the relatively recent Stalinist period. Alas, the introduction of martial law in 1981 halted these fiery inquisitions of the present and the past; most of the films made during this period ended up "shelved" for most of the decade.[2] Consequently, the cinema of the 1980s escaped into the realm of the popular, with the works of Juliusz Machulski (b. 1955), Radosław Piwowarski (b. 1948), and Waldemar Krzystek (b. 1953) paving the path for a real explosion of this mode of cinema in post-communist reality, as seen in films by Władysław Pasikowski (b. 1959), Maciej Ślesicki (b. 1966), and Jacek Bromski (b. 1946).

Welcomed by most young viewers, but often rejected or derided by critics and older audiences as flagrant "Americanization," popular cinema was the first and strongest effort to reposition Polish film culture within world cinema. This often escapist entertainment had to compete with lavish adaptations of the Polish literary canon, or with historical epics often depicting those parts of the national past that had previously been erased from public discourse (e.g., Jerzy Kawalerowicz's *Quo Vadis*, Jerzy Hoffman's *With Fire and Sword*, and Andrzej Wajda's *Katyń*). Recently, modernist film projects have become more difficult to realize than ever before. Nevertheless, a strong tradition of art cinema and a widely shared conviction that film is art rather than entertainment have secured them a modest but significant existence in contemporary film practice, with the work of Małgorzata Szumowska (b. 1973), Mariusz Grzegorzek (b. 1962), and Dorota Kędzierzawska (b. 1957) providing good examples of such practice. More importantly, the coexistence within a single text of the modernist and the popular aesthetic in much of recent cinema (e.g., the films of Wojciech Smarzowski [b. 1963], Marek Koterski [b. 1942], Borys Lankosz [b. 1973]) has become ever more pronounced, signifying both an effort to rejuvenate national cinema and a response to the postmodern condition of contemporary art.

Instead of offering a historical trajectory of Polish cinema by examining its most significant works, directors, and movements – which is the most common critical strategy for a comprehensive survey – I propose to scrutinize the three main tendencies of Polish cinema – the national, the modernist, and the popular – separately. I will focus in particular on how they have functioned in selected cinematic texts to negotiate the political pressures and demands of the postwar totalitarian regime and its aftermath.

The National (Memory)

The national has manifested itself throughout the history of Polish postwar cinema in various forms and configurations. For the purpose of this essay, I will focus on the issue of memory – on the way it has been cinematically negotiated to construct and maintain an ideologically desired notion of national community. Specifically, I will discuss how postwar cinema has regulated processes of both remembrance and forgetting of the Second World War and the Holocaust, as these have been, and indeed remain, the most contested sites of memory in Polish postwar cinema, if not in all of Polish culture.

The ideological struggles concerning cinematic representations of the Second World War began during the postwar restoration of the Polish film industry between 1945 and 1948. The endless reworking and re-editing of *Forbidden Songs* in order that it might "properly" represent the war experience instantiates this symbolic battle concerning the depiction of the past. The formation of the Polish United Workers' Party in 1948 transformed Poland into a totalitarian, one-party state based on an exclusive model of the nation. Socialist realism, an aesthetic doctrine imposed on Polish art in 1949, responded eagerly to the new communist government's political need to appropriate the war memory in order to legitimize its own ascent to power. To that end, the official account of Poles' participation in the Second World War favoured the Polish Army that had been established under Soviet auspices while drastically diminishing the significance of the military forces that fought alongside the Western Allies. Specifically, an organized act of "forgetting" was directed at the military activities of the Home Army, an underground military force of the Polish government-in-exile that kept fighting in Poland throughout the German Occupation. Until 1956, the political authorities either denied the military achievements of the Home Army or presented them as criminal acts targeted at communists. The most efficient cinematic strategy to suppress this part of memory was to avoid the subject matter of the war experience altogether and to focus instead on the contemporary struggle to build a new communist reality. This strategy can be found in films such as *Niedaleko Warszawy* (Not Far from Warsaw, 1954) by Maria Kaniewska and *Przygoda na Mariensztacie* (An Adventure at Marienstadt, 1954) by Leonard Buczkowski. Instead of remembering, socialist realist films celebrated the present – or, more accurately, its propagandistic project.

Stalin's death in 1953 and the consequent political relaxation, metaphorically christened "the October Thaw," ignited a reconsideration of the national past. The cinematic movement of the Polish film school significantly contributed to this debate. Its emergence in the late 1950s represented for Polish cinema a radical break with the schemata of the previously dominant model of socialist realism. Impersonal cinematic propaganda was replaced by films that offered an individualized vision of reality, whether it was Andrzej Wajda's Romantic Expressionism, Andrzej Munk's grotesque and ironic gaze, or Kazimierz Kutz's realism. All of these directors dealt primarily with the Polish experience of the Second World War. Their films represent post-traumatic cinema in a double-sense: they address the trauma of the war experience itself as well as the trauma of the Stalinist regime's methodical bid to erase some of its aspects.

Tadeusz Lubelski was the first Polish critic to note this post-traumatic aspect of the Polish School films when he stated that they represented "the strategy of a psychotherapist."[3] He claimed that Wajda's *Popiół i diament* (Ashes and Diamonds, 1958) was the best example of this approach, with the film representing an attempt to reunify the Polish nation, which had been fractured by the totalitarian doctrine of communism and especially by efforts to repress the nation's collective memory. Maciek Chełmicki, the film's protagonist (exquisitely played by Zbigniew Cybulski [1927–67], who was dubbed the Polish James Dean and who, like Dean, died young in an accident), embodied the disappointments and bitterness felt by many Poles during the postwar years (especially those who had been members or supporters of the Home Army). The film, the action of which takes place over twenty-four hours during the last day of the Second World War, can be viewed as an attempt to symbolically represent this turning point in Polish history as an ancient Greek tragedy, complete with catharsis. From this perspective, the absurd and accidental death of Maciek at the end of the film symbolizes the political discrimination against, if not the conscious annihilation of, former soldiers of the Home Army in the actual political reality of postwar Poland. The exceptional expressive power of this final scene, in evoking feelings of pity and terror, forced many Polish viewers to confront these sentiments and, in the process, to relive and address the trauma of their own political and existential alienation.

Notwithstanding the unique potential of *Ashes and Diamonds* to address the collective Polish trauma in 1959, many years later the film was subjected to a vehement ideological critique. In his book *Polskie, arcypolskie* (Polish, All Too Polish, 1987), Andrzej Werner, a respected literary and film critic, accused Wajda of ideological opportunism as well as aesthetic and political compromise.[4] While the content of the film's narrative might warrant such an interpretation and ideological disapproval, Werner and his followers seemed intent on ignoring the affective power of the film and its imagery.

A description of two scenes featuring two protagonists who represent oppositional ideological and political orders in the film can help elucidate this contradiction between the ideological and the affective.[5] The first scene revolves around Szczuka, who genuinely believes in communism, as he recollects together with a friend their experiences – and the comrades who died – during the Spanish Civil War. In the second scene, it is Maciek along with his friend and commanding officer, Andrzej, who are shown remembering their fallen Home Army brothers-in-arms. In the first scene, Szczuka and his friend reminisce about the old days while sipping wine and listening to Spanish music on a gramophone in a hotel room. Although their tales prove that the past is still vitally real for them, it is also apparent that it is hermetically sealed off from the present day; in the face of the fierce exigencies of Polish political reconstruction, their memories come across as irrelevant.

The second "memory scene" is a reversal of the first one. Maciek and Andrzej are sitting in a hotel bar, while in an adjacent room a young woman sings the song "The Poppies on Monte Cassino," which commemorates the Polish soldiers who fought in the West during the war. The deep staging and deep focus used in the scene depict the characters against the backdrop of the other room, which is crowded with people listening to the song. Although the two young men are compositionally isolated from the other patrons, the spatial layout of the scene along with its soundtrack links them to the drama of the national community. The song is a direct evocation of a collective commemoration of those who perished far from their homeland, and it prompts Maciek's and Andrzej's own memories of the war. At one point, Maciek notices glasses filled with spirit on the bar. He sniffs them intently, like an animal, and then rapidly asks: "Do you remember the spirit at Rudy's place?" When Andrzej initially cannot remember, or denies remembering the night, Maciek curls his body animalistically and shouts "No?" as he slides the glasses one by one towards his friend and proceeds to ignite their highly concentrated content. This time Andrzej cannot resist the evocative power of the image, which excavates his memory of the evening and sets off their commemoration of their dead comrades. As Maciek lights each glass of spirit, Andrzej speaks a name of one of the deceased, as if they were performing the ancient ritual of calling forth the dead, who can appear only as flames. The scene thus presents a modern variant of Catholic "All Souls' Day" customs, reminiscent of Forefathers' Eve, the ancient Slavic ritual dedicated to commemorating the dead that was memorialized in the play of the same name by the Polish national poet, Adam Mickiewicz (1798–1855). Tellingly, Szczuka's evocation of memory and loss is not supported by the plethora of cultural signifiers with which Wajda invests the scene with Maciek, thus giving the latter a distinct "affective" advantage.

Maciek's death on a heap of garbage in the film's final scene is another moment of exceptional affective power. His ultimate defeat is devoid of heroism. His curled body twitches spasmodically as if he were a tiny, defenceless animal. The overwhelming sense of pity for this young man that still characterizes my experience of this scene is likely shared by many of the film's viewers. Certainly, this deep emotional affinity with the protagonist who loses because he lacks any political pragmatism would have been expected and especially significant for the Polish audience at the end of the 1950s; Wajda's film acknowledged those who had been excluded, or, at the very least, marginalized by postwar communist public discourse. The fact that the action of *Ashes and Diamonds* takes place during the first day of Poland's liberation and that the film ends with the death of its protagonist makes its message disconcertingly ambiguous. In 1959, it resonated poignantly with the manifest sentiments of many Poles, who felt that the end of the war marked the beginning of a new occupation, this time at the hands of a Soviet-controlled Polish government.

It needs to be emphasised that these post-traumatic images and narratives of Wajda's *Ashes and Diamonds* and his other films performed an integrative function for Poles throughout the period of communism. War and postwar trauma worked in this context as a unifying force for the beleaguered nation. It could be further said that Wajda's films functioned as cinematic variants of an Andersonian "imagined community," actively (re) creating the idea of Poland as a nation founded on shared suffering.[6] Indeed, the mythologization of individual and collective suffering has served as the lynchpin of the notion of Polishness since the period of Romanticism.

This particularity of Polish identity inevitably affected, among other things, the collective memory of the Holocaust. The collectively cultivated memory of Polish suffering eclipsed the extermination of the Jews and, furthermore, facilitated the process of repressing Polish indifference to the genocide – indeed, their contribution to it. Polish postwar cinema has provided a significant arena for various ideological appropriations of the Holocaust. Immediately after the war, the mass extermination of Jews was seen as merely one aspect of general wartime atrocities, since the war was interpreted as primarily a conflict between Communism and Nazism within the Soviet Bloc, which downplayed the ethnic aspects of the war.[7] The most conspicuous example of this perspective can be found in *Ostatni etap* (The Last Stage, 1948), a film made by Wanda Jakubowska (1907–98), who herself had been a prisoner in Auschwitz. Aleksander Ford (1908–80) addresses the issue of the extermination of Jews in a more direct fashion in *Ulica graniczna* (Border Street, 1949), yet their social class identity predominates over their ethnic one. The film openly admits to the problem of anti-Semitism in Poland but ascribes it exclusively to the middle class and thus conveniently relegates it to the prewar period of capitalist Poland. In contrast, working-class heroes are always willing to help their Jewish neighbours, affirming in a sense that postwar communist Poland has been cured of the disease of anti-Semitism. Even if that had been the case, the theme of the Holocaust was left virtually untouched during the period of socialist realism. After Stalin's death in 1953 and during the October Thaw of 1956, films dealing with the Holocaust were sporadically made; while infrequent, they testify to its constant, significant, and troublesome presence in Poles' collective memory. The Polish indifference towards the Jews' fate and complicity with the German perpetrators during the war was not been sufficiently recognized in them, however. Even when acknowledged, Polish guilt is often absolved, so to speak, by reciprocal Polish suffering and death. This approach to the issue became part of the narrative thrust in many of Wajda's films dealing with the Holocaust, including his debut *Pokolenie* (A Generation, 1955), where it was employed in a very conspicuous manner.

Among Polish films dealing with the Holocaust, Andrzej Munk's *Pasażerka* (The Passenger, 1961–3) addresses the specific problem of how this event can and should be remembered. Munk's film career was brief but significant: he is often regarded as Wajda'a counterpart within the Polish film school due to his predilection for ironic and grotesque imagery, and his work testifies to a constant and conscious preoccupation with the problems of memory and its filmic modes of representation. *The Passenger*, left unfinished because of Munk's untimely death, employs a flashback narrative structure to interrogate the postwar memory of Auschwitz. The remembering subject is, importantly, a former Nazi female camp guard. There are three flashbacks that bring Liza's past into the present, although they do not add up to a singular, complete story owing to the many inconsistencies and contradictions between them. By means of this flashback narrative structure, Munk demonstrates how the character of an oppressor trims and selects parts of memory to suppress images of the Jews exterminated at Auschwitz. Their deaths are narratively and visually pushed far into the background.

The narrative and visual marginalization of the Holocaust in Munk's film poses vital questions. Did *The Passenger* contribute to the process of downplaying the extermination of Jews during the Second World War in Polish postwar public discourse? Or did Munk, himself a Jew, understand well before the debate on the representability of the Holocaust emerged and developed that a full and complete representation of the event was impossible? Unfinished by its author and offering three flashbacks with conflicting renditions of the past, *The Passenger* contests the possibility of a complete and singular representation of the Holocaust. Instead, the film relocates the event to the present as a site of various competing and often incompatible memories.

With the emergence of the first Solidarity movement and the general demand to liberate historical discourse from the shackles of communist ideology, a significant number of films that dealt more directly with the Holocaust experience emerged. The turning point in the Polish postwar discourse on the Holocaust came in 1987, when the Catholic weekly *Tygodnik Powszechny* (The Universal Weekly) published Jan Błoński's essay "Biedny chrześcijanin patrzy na getto" (A Poor Pole Looks at the Ghetto). The publication opened a nation-wide debate about the Polish postwar repression of Holocaust memory and collective responsibility for it.[8] Polish cinema responded to this debate with a large number of films that explored the subject by investigating the Poles' attitude towards the Holocaust and examining the survivors' responses to their wartime past. Between 1987 and 2009, almost one hundred films (features as well as documentaries) dealing with this subject were made in Poland,[9] which testifies to the sudden eruption of repressed memory. Among these films, of special importance was a 2001 documentary film *Sąsiedzi* (Neighbours), made for Polish Television network by Agnieszka Arnold (b. 1947). It concerns Polish participation in (and instigation of, as it also claims) the Jedwabne massacre of local Jews in 1941, the same event that Jan Tomasz Gross examines in his book *Neighbours*, in which he openly addresses Polish complicity in and support for the Holocaust.[10]

Among all of the Polish films about the Holocaust made after 1989, *The Pianist* (2002) by Roman Polański (b. 1933) and *In Darkness* (2012) by Agnieszka Holland exemplify a new, reconciliatory approach to the subject. Directed by two famous Polish èmigrè filmmakers, both films are big-budget international co-productions with international and highly acclaimed casts. Both of them seem to deliberately disengage from the previously dominant discourse on the Holocaust in Polish cinema: they are open about Polish hostility or indifference towards Jews, yet – in contrast to most of the Polish films made after 1989 – these attitudes are not juxtaposed with images of Polish suffering to capitalize on the latter's redemptory value. Polański and Holland, both of Jewish descent, tell stories about Jewish survival and the part that Poles played in it in an ambiguous manner. The previously dominant paradigm of "conflated suffering" has been replaced with more ordinary, perhaps even banal attitudes of help and betrayal. Both Polański and Holland attempt to address the past from an individual rather than a collective perspective; they avoid representing either "Polish guilt" or "Jewish suffering," instead foregrounding the singularities of both characters and narratives. They confirm the need to address the national past even as they deliberately produce a subjective and thus inevitably limited vision of it. Such consciously limited perspectives on history and on the act of memory are being used with increasing frequency by the younger generations of filmmakers. Perhaps this signals the liberation of Polish memory politics from the absolutist, totalitarian regimen of the second half of the twentieth century.

The Modernist: Realism versus Self-Reflexivity

John Orr distinguishes two principal movements in contemporary modernist cinema: the first is linear, leading "towards establishing … the luminous validity of the image," whereas the second is cyclical, stimulating "the increasing dislocation of the image, the bracketing and the unmasking of its problematic nature."[11] According to Orr, modernist cinema has been driven by two opposing impulses – trust in and distrust of the cinematic image – with this tension developing into its two main aesthetic strategies of realism and self-reflexivity. A modernist variant of cinematic realism prefers open, often episodic narrative structures, the lack of cause-and-effect logic, an absence of clearly explained psychological motivations for characters, long takes that reduce the inevitably manipulative work of editing, and deep focus that visually conveys the ambiguity of represented reality. The effect of cinematic self-reflexivity, in turn, is obtained through the use of non-continuous editing that foregrounds the constructed nature of cinematic representation, episodic narrative structure (often divided into chapters in order to emphasize narrativity), various "alienation effects" (for instance, characters looking directly into camera), and intertextual references. To summarize the difference in Orr's terms, modernist realism attempts to minimize the process of cinematic mediation to constitute "the luminous validity of the image," whereas self-reflective modernist cinematic practice foregrounds all possible forms of this mediation to attain a "dislocation of the image."[12]

Both branches of modernism thus understood are present in Polish postwar cinema, but neither evolved into a separate cinematic "new wave" as happened elsewhere in Europe.[13] There are many reasons for this. Most important among them is the deep engagement of vernacular cinema with national subject matter. Such a thematic focus tends to prioritize narrative content over cinematic form. In consequence, the filmmakers who have made attempts to contest the principle of narrative transparency in order to engage with more universal subject matter have inevitably been marginalized.[14] Both critics and viewers frequently respond to formal cinematic experiments as an escape from vital national matters. Thus, it may explain why most of the Polish filmmakers interested in exploring cinematic form, such as Roman Polański, Jerzy Skolimowski, Andrzej Żuławski (1940–2016), and Walerian Borowczyk, left Poland to continue their careers abroad.[15] Others, such as Wojciech Has and Grzegorz Królikiewicz (1939–2017), accepted their secondary position within vernacular cinema. This "secondary position" refers not just to (the lack of) critical recognition or popular acclaim, but also to the limits on financial resources that were distributed by state agencies at that time.

Polish postwar cinema has nevertheless made significant contributions to European cinematic modernism that still wait to be fully recognized. In the following discussion I briefly address the relative absence of realism in Polish cinema and then take a closer look at the most original and productive examples of self-reflexivity. When examining the problem of realism in Polish cinema, it might seem natural to begin with socialist realism. Despite its name, however, the movement offered a vision of a utopian communist paradise rather than a depiction of an existing reality. Using methods of conventional cinematic realism, as most cinematic propaganda tends to do, the socialist realist films portrayed a world that, in fact, never existed and, moreover, would never come to be.

In the late 1950s and early 1960s, meaning the period of the Polish film school and its aftermath, Wajda, Munk, Skolimowski, Has, and many others began to interrogate the possibilities of realism in their films, frequently juxtaposing realism with non-realistic aesthetics, as has been noted by critics. In examining Wajda's output, for example, Orr claims that "it is never really easy to label him a realist, a modernist or a romantic because nothing quite fits."[16] In a similar vein, Ewa Mazierska notices a constant tension between realistic and non-realistic elements in Skolimowski's films, recognizing a variety of inspirations from Surrealism, Absurdism, Expressionism, and Romanticism.[17] Likewise, Maria Kornatowska regards Has's films as also drawing upon various modernist traditions such as Symbolism, Surrealism, and Absurdism.[18] These critical opinions prove that realism in Polish cinema has always been undermined by other aesthetic strategies and thus has never evolved into an entirely autonomous cinematic movement.

Polish School of Documentary Film: a postwar current of critically minded documentary film in Poland. After 1955, documentary film became part of the process of social emancipation and an important element of the anti-Stalinist "thaw," which liberated reality from the grip of propaganda. The school's first films were still burdened by didacticism – for instance, Jerzy Hoffman and Edward Skórzewski's *Uwaga, chuligani!* (Look Out, Hooligans!, 1955). Later, documentary film moved beyond a purely journalistic or interventionist role. The shortest definition of the genre appears in Kieślowski's *Amator* (Camera Buff, 1979): "to film what is there." As the film shows, however, while initially a revelation, filming "what is there" ceases to suffice with time. At the turn of the 1960s and 1970s, quiet, lightweight cameras became available to documentary filmmakers, who also discovered the possibility of exposing the dramaturgy of reality. What makes the Polish School of Documentary Film distinctive is the simultaneous appearance of ethical doubts and awareness of film's new limitations. The documentary filmmaker Paweł Łoziński contends that the making of a documentary is "a careful observation of the ordinary world, seemingly unattractive, in a way that allows the spectator to look at it as a mirror." (As cited by Tadeusz Sobolewski in "Kino-oko Pawła Łozińskiego," an insert to a DVD series *Polska szkoła dokumentu. Paweł Łoziński*, Wydawnictwo Narodowego Instytutu Wizualnego, 2009.)

Kazimierz Karabasz (b. 1930) was a key figure of the documentary school and its greatest purist. His films find life's hidden drama by observing the most ordinary of people and events, such as a rehearsal of a streetcar drivers' orchestra (the famous and award-winning *Muzykanci* [The Musicians, 1960]), a meeting of philatelists or pigeon breeders, or the operations of a railway junction. Karabasz inherited the conviction that the drama of life itself can be captured without disturbing the membrane of reality from Italian Neorealists like Roberto Rossellini and Cesare Zavattini. He was aware, however, that reality is not a given. Kieślowski, his student, dealt with this dilemma differently. He looked for a synthesis using formal concepts. It was not the observation of life, but rather a certain idea, that served as his departure point. In the documentary film *Gadające głowy* (Talking Heads, 1980), for instance, forty-four people ranging from a child to a centenarian in some sense constitute a single, collective human being searching for the meaning of life. Likewise, the films of

Marcel Łoziński (b. 1940; father to Paweł) both describe and serve as models or metaphors for concrete situations. Such films include *Jak żyć* (How to Live, 1977), *Ćwiczenia warsztatowe* (Workshop Exercises, 1984), *89mm od Europy* (89mm from Europe, 1993), and *Wszystko może się przytrafić* (Anything Can Happen, 1995). Their creator's approach is characterized by distrust of the human being and society and of the film medium itself: the act of filming is never entirely innocent, and the possibilities for falsifying reality are endless.

The relative underdevelopment of realism in Poland has been due to various factors, the most important being a weak tradition of vernacular literary realism. While recognizing Bolesław Prus's (1847–1912) achievements within the realm of literary realism, it still needs to be acknowledged that there are no Polish counterparts to Balzac, Dickens, or Stendhal. This deficit of realism is the result – among many other factors – of the weak development of capitalism in nineteenth-century Poland, in contrast to most of Western Europe; a Polish middle class did not emerge in that century as a dominant cultural presence and thus could not serve as both the object and subject of realism in either literature or art in general. This already weak tradition was further eroded during the period of socialist realism, when conventional realism was used to further the aims of communist propaganda. The Cinema of Moral Concern attempted to reinvigorate trust in the cinematic image and its ability to depict reality in order to unearth the various pathologies of an already degenerate communist system. The urge to interrogate political and social reality, however, did not leave much space for probing the problems of cinematic representation.

Krzysztof Kieślowski's career demonstrates the gradual evolution of his modernist tendencies. Initially a documentarist and later a prominent proponent of the Cinema of Moral Concern, he began his artistic trajectory in the 1960s with a strong belief in the "luminous" nature of the cinematic image, but his late films, especially his Three Colours trilogy, are clear examples of the process of "dislocation of the image." His *Camera Buff* marks the turning point in this aesthetic trajectory. Before assessing this film, however, I need to discuss the earlier negotiations between realism and self-reflexivity in Polish cinema.

The first attempts to undermine the reproductive aspect of the cinematic image occurred during the period of the Polish film school in films with contemporary themes. Some critics referred to these films as the movement's "existential strand," whereas others viewed them as a vernacular "new wave." The most representative examples of these are Tadeusz Konwicki's *Ostatni dzień lata* (Last Day of Summer, 1958), Jerzy Kawalerowicz's *Pociąg* (The Night Train, 1959), and Roman Polański's *Nóż w wodzie* (Knife in the Water, 1961). With minimalist narratives and downplayed editing, the films appear rather realistic, but this effect is often undermined by their careful frame composition, which produces a self-contained space. This enframed space functions here as an entity rather than as a fragment of an unlimited spatial continuum typical of the realist model of cinematic representation. As a consequence, the symbolic value of the cinematic image comes at the expense of its indexical value. The characters in these films are locked within meticulously composed frames that become either a symbol for their inhibited emotions and existential doom, or abstract canvases on which past traumas are projected.

Jerzy Skolimowski's debut *Rysopis* (Identification Marks: None, 1964) also undermines the realistic aspect of cinematic representation by means of spatial devices. Its protagonist Leszczyc (played by Skolimowski himself), a vernacular variant of a *flâneur*, moves across urban space freely, yet his movement does not propel narrative development or evolve into a progressive linear trajectory. He moves aimlessly between his apartment and various, apparently random places. The repetitiveness of his pendulum-like movement causes the cinematic space in this film to take the form of a vortex, demonstrating its conceptual rather than realistic character. Skolimowski continues to realize and significantly extends the ambitious spatial project initiated in *Identification Marks: None* in his later film *Ręce do góry* (Hands Up!, 1966/1985), the main action of which takes place in a freight train that never leaves the station. In fact, in most of his Polish films, the director establishes realism in order to ultimately undermine it, transforming their diegetic space into a symbolic stage on which either past traumas or spectacles of power are acted out.

The juxtaposition of realistic cinematography with a highly artificial and theatrical *mise-en-scène* is another strategy used to "dislocate the image." The most conspicuous examples of this artistic strategy can be found in Has's films, which are often rooted in Expressionist and Surrealist imagery. For example, in the opening scenes of his debut *Pętla* (The Noose, 1957), the director consistently uses the realistic device of the sequence-shot in a manner that not only captures the real flow of time but also enhances the artificiality of the diegetic reality produced by the theatrical setting. Prolonged tracking shots reveal an abundance of metaphorical props, most significantly a telephone wire entangled with a noose that foreshadows the suicide of the film's alcoholic protagonist. The room in which the action takes place is expressionistically lit with sharp *chiaroscuro*, evoking, as it were, a Manichean world in which good and evil struggle over the "soul of man." Deep-focus photography establishes a spatial link between the various elements of *mise-en-scène*, thereby rendering the fictional reality consistent and coherent. Simultaneously, the frequent use of internal framing and mirror-reflection shots throughout the film discloses the process of signification at work. The mirror images are of special importance here since they introduce the motif of a double, split identity while producing, moreover, a modest variant of the *mise-en-abyme* effect, which injects an element of self-referentiality into cinematic representation and thus subverts its realist aspect.

In *Rękopis znaleziony w Saragossie* (The Saragossa Manuscript, 1964), Has offers a narrative equivalent of *mise en abyme*. His employment of a "Chinese box" narrative structure hinders the construction of a consistent and coherent diegesis. The multiplication of various stories that remain unfinished shifts the viewer's attention from the content of these stories to the way in which they are related, with the focus falling on the act of storytelling and its paradoxes rather than on the fictional realities that emerge from it. Consequently, the cinematic image becomes less and less attached to reality; there are too many stories presented by means of these images to allow any of them to become ontologically privileged. In *The Saragossa Manuscript*, the narration produces a self-contained circular structure within which the referential value of the cinematic image becomes irrelevant. The film exemplifies one of the most radical instances of dislocation of the image in Polish cinema. Its reproductive potential is finally annihilated in the film's final scene, when the protagonist, Alfons van Vorden, observes his own double walking away as he looks out through an inn window.

Krzysztof Kieślowski's *Przypadek* (Blind Chance, 1981) also uses narrative devices – specifically, a modular type of narrative – to dislocate the cinematic image. It presents the viewer with three variants of its protagonist's life, all of which are crucially dependent on whether he catches or misses a particular train. Witek's constant and numerous returns to a certain place and situation, such as the train station, further the pattern of circularity used by Has in *Saragossa Manuscript*.[19] This narrative device is typical of a forking-path narrative, which according to Allan Cameron "focuse[s] upon crucial events in the fabula, and the various outcomes that may result from (often very minor) differences in these events."[20] While Kieślowski's film employs most of the cinematic techniques typical of stylistic realism (e.g., handheld camera, on-location shooting, long takes), its modular narrative destabilizes the consistency of cinematic representation. The small differences in the three repetitions of the train station scene on which the narrative hinges obstruct the process of constructing a singular and consistent diegesis. Kieślowski radically opposes realistic cinematography and modernist narrative. Thus, cinematic realism is rendered as a mere aesthetic convention.

The epistemological uncertainty of *Blind Chance* results from the use of a modular narrative pattern that serves as an external interrogative framework for the cinematic image and its ontology. Conversely, one of Kieślowski's earlier films – the already mentioned *Camera Buff* – questions the validity of the cinematic image from within a singular narrative. Its unambiguous plot follows a cause-and-effect pattern that does not give rise to either spatial or temporal ambiguities. Its protagonist Filip Mosz is equipped with a sufficient dose of psychological and emotional motivation to facilitate the viewer's spectatorial allegiance and affinity. Like *Blind Chance*, *Camera Buff* employs the techniques and devices of realism even while expressing a constant distrust of the cinematic medium and a deep scepticism about its ability to capture and represent reality. Arguably, its protagonist's story metaphorically recapitulates the whole history of cinema, or rather the history of its conceptualization; in some ways, Filip is an incarnation of the Vertovian "man with a movie camera" who (re)discovers all the possibilities and limitations of the medium.

The protagonist of *Amator* is a married man who works in a small factory in a provincial town. To mark the birth of his first child, he buys an 8 mm camera, in a sense following the path initiated by the Lumière Brothers in the short *Repas de bébé* (1895), the first historic example of a home movie. Filip's first films conform perfectly to the earliest model of a "cinema of attraction" with its emphasis on "showing things" and its total lack of concern for creating a narrative.[21] Gradually, he moves towards a cinema of "narrative integration."[22] However, his work becomes subject to the principle of ideological appropriateness and appropriation. When his boss asks him to film a factory party, Filip chooses to include in his footage minor "behind the scenes" episodes, for example of artists getting paid for their performance, or of a pigeon sitting on a windowsill, with the latter footage captured while a "behind closed doors" meeting from which Filip and his camera have been barred is taking place. Using the power of film editing, he undermines the "master narrative" of the factory's prosperity with a collage-like structure of seemingly disconnected motifs and images, rejecting any preconceived hierarchy of objects to be recorded. This subversion does not go unnoticed upon the film's reception: Filip is asked to re-edit the film to exclude materials deemed problematic by the authorities.

One of Filip's films almost literally epitomizes André Bazin's idea of cinema as a phenomenon that is inextricably linked to a "mummy complex."[23] As the French critic claims, reality leaves its imprint/trace on celluloid, which lies at the base of cinema's ontological realism. In Kieślowski's film, this takes the form of a self-reflexive thematic motif. One day, Filip films his neighbour's mother looking out of her apartment window and soon after, she unexpectedly dies. Overwhelmed with grief and unable to accept his sudden loss, the neighbour comes to Filip and asks to see the randomly shot footage of his late mother. One single long take, with no camera movement or reframing, just a spatio-temporal continuum of reality rendering its trace on a strip of celluloid, demonstrates the power of film to "mummify," in Bazin's terms, time.[24] All Bazinian metaphors of the cinematic image – as a death mask, a fulfilment of the "mummy complex," a fingerprint of reality, an embalming of time – seem to find perfect incarnation in this scene from Filip's/Kieślowski's film.

The metaphysically powerful cinematic image soon proves to be prone to various types of ideological manipulation. Paradoxically, this is entirely due to the "truthfulness" of the recorded image. One of Filip's uncompromising, *cinéma vérité*–like films that epitomizes his zealous pursuit of the "truth" results in a friend losing his job, which practically ruins his life. At this point, Filip realizes the potentially dangerous gap between the ethical and epistemological dimensions of cinema. Far from being complementary, as he had previously believed, these two dimensions can, in practice, contradict each other. The film's final scene presents Filip as he directs the camera lens towards himself, turns it on, and says: "My name is Filip Mosz."

The ambiguity of this ending of *Camera Buff* does not bring narrative closure. Instead it dislocates the cinematic image by merging the filming subject with a filmed object. As Joseph Kickasola aptly notices, the film's final scene is "a POV [point-of-view shot] divorced from Filip himself."[25] Subjectivity supplants the objectivity that is so often associated with the cinematic reproduction of reality. Moreover, Filip's introduction of himself to the camera suggests that he is about to record his confession, or his own story. It can be surmised that he now believes that the cinematic apparatus is perhaps better suited to the penetration of an inner rather than an external reality. The camera appears here as akin to an X-ray or MRI machine; it is not merely a tool to facilitate mere reproduction of a facile reality, but reveals a reality that is hidden to the human eye. The final scene asks a crucial question concerning the potential and power of the movie camera: What is it good for? Filip does not yet have an answer to this question. He needs to consider it once again, as does every generation of filmmakers working under given social and historic circumstances, and – like every filmmaker – he needs to arrive at his own answer to the Bazinian question of 'What is cinema?'

The Popular: Between Complicity and Subversion

Notwithstanding Anita Skwara's often quoted phrase "Film Stars Do Not Shine in the Sky over Poland,"[26] which metaphorically signifies an absence of popular commercial cinema in postwar Poland, such cinema has, in fact, been present all along, albeit in a variant different from the dominant form of Hollywood cinema. The most important difference between Polish and American popular cinema concerns the means of their production. Specifically, Hollywood films were financed with (huge) investments of private or corporate money, whereas Polish productions were made with very moderate state funding, which determined, among other things, certain aspects of the quality of cinematic entertainment. Despite these differences, the two models of cinema have played an analogous function, which is to maintain and solidify the dominant ideology. Whereas Hollywood popular cinema has perfected the ability to almost completely hide its ideological work from the viewer, Polish cinema has often ostentatiously foregrounded this function, as is typical of propagandistic art. Thomas Schatz argues that the ideological task of Hollywood popular cinema is to facilitate and enhance the stability of the socio-political-cultural order; to that purpose, it presents endless possibilities for that order's restoration and demonstrates how the whole "melting-pot" of American society can be imbued with certain foundational values. With regard to this twofold function of Hollywood cinema, Schatz divides popular genres into two groups: those that work to re-establish a social order (westerns, crime movies, gangster films) and those that work to bring about social integration (musicals, melodramas, comedies).[27]

In its mainstream form, Polish postwar popular cinema developed these same two generic branches, although the "social integration" genres dominated the genres of "social order," for reasons I will address in due course. Among the first group of films, the comedy – or rather a communist variant of romantic comedy – gained a special currency. Unlike the unhappy endings of melodrama, which allow viewers to cathartically release their unfulfilled desires, the "happily ever after" endings of comedies were a perfect fit with the officially promoted ideas of "a brave new world." The comedy-romance genre also flourished due to its strong vernacular tradition in prewar cinema. While films made before 1939 worked towards the integration of a post-partition Polish society, communist comedies were meant to help found a new communist society consisting of people from various social backgrounds, with a variety of war experiences and representing conflicting political beliefs. Among the many fault lines that split Polish society after the Second World War, of greatest importance was the one that divided the proponents from the opponents of the newly imposed political order of communism and Poland's social alliance with the Soviets. As such, that line was often addressed by both popular and art cinema. Social, political, and cultural divisions were also emerging along the lines of gender, class, and ethnicity, however. To explore the ideological function of comedy-romance genres in more specific terms, therefore, I will briefly discuss how Polish popular cinema addressed the emerging tensions between genders and nationalities.

Socialist realism demonstrates the efficiency with which cinematic conventions of popular cinema tackled the problem of communist redefinitions of gender politics. Two films, Buczkowski's *An Adventure at Marienstadt* and Jan Fethke's *Irena, do domu* (Irena, Go Home, 1955), provide useful examples of an ideological appropriation of the traditional model of femininity that was previously elaborated within national discourse. Both films were made by prewar filmmakers and employed the generic conventions of comedy and romance made familiar to viewers in the "good old days before the war." The casting of the most popular prewar comic actor, Adolf Dymsza (1900–75), in the leading male role of Fethke's film significantly added to this familiarizing effect. Both films demonstrate how Polish society responded – or was supposed to respond – to the new gender politics brought by communism, with its demand that traditional notions of femininity and masculinity be reconsidered. Their narratives involve the propagandistic theme of women entering the job market, an eventuality heralded by the films as a step towards emancipation, but in reality necessitated by economic conditions. In an effort to achieve wide spectatorship, both films presented the problem of women's emancipation within a familiar framework of the "eternal battle of the sexes" rather than as an ideological and political issue.

For their emancipatory tales, Fethke and Buczkowski used the same narrative pattern: a female protagonist overcomes numerous difficulties and obstacles in order to pursue a professional career, which, however, is not her sole aim, as she also desires to be (re)united with her lover. Her wish comes true at the end of both films. The positive resolution of a heterosexual romance is a prominent device in many socialist realist romances and comedies, as well as one of the most frequently used narrative patterns in genres of "social integration." Its vernacular variant follows this generic principle by means of containing female sexuality in a safe and desirable form. For this aim, two models of femininity are opposed to each other. Positive female characters first repress their sexuality and then sublimate it in the form of professional competition with men. Finally, this displaced energy is relocated to and appropriated by heterosexual romance that is complicit with the patriarchal order. In contrast, the "bad" female figures have full access to their sexuality, but they are ultimately punished, either literally or metaphorically, by being eradicated from the fictional reality. Consequently, these films reproduce the fearful and suppressive myths regarding female sexuality inherent in the patriarchal ideology they presume to question.

Polish cinema from the period of the "small stabilization" in the 1960s often employs the narrative schemas of "social integration" genres to address the problem of national tensions, and especially to tackle the ideological demands of the forced Polish–Soviet alliance. Tadeusz Chmielewski's *Gdzie jest generał?* (Where Is the General?, 1964) extrapolates the political imperative of Polish–Soviet "friendship" into generic patterns of comedic romance. Free from the excesses of propagandistic messages, the film did not arouse undesirable resentment in its viewers. The generic conventions of romance and the "happy ending" turned out to be the most efficient and persuasive strategy for creating a positive cinematic image for the politically imposed liaison. The huge popularity of the Polish–Soviet romantic couple from the TV series *Czterej pancerni i pies* (Four Tankmen and the Dog, 1966–70), directed by Konrad Nałęcki (1919–91), is sufficient proof of this; the passionate love affair between the blond Janek Kos and the red-haired Red Army girl Marusia served as convincing evidence of the values of the Polish–Soviet alliance. Significantly, in both *Where Is the General?* and *Four Tankmen and the Dog*, it is a Polish man who functions as the object of desire of a Russian/Soviet woman. In both films, it is the female who initiates the romance, a thematic motif that reveals a narcissistic aspect of Polish culture and Polish masculinity.[28]

The "socially integrative" generic scenarios of communist popular cinema do not offer a reversed variant of the Polish–Soviet romance. When a relationship between a Polish woman and a Soviet man does occur – which is rare indeed – it is in a melodrama such as Buczkowski's *Przerwany lot* (Interrupted Flight, 1964), with its unhappy romantic resolution. This narrative acknowledgment of the social unacceptability of a marriage between a Polish woman and a foreigner – specifically, a Soviet man – also points to the narcissism present within both Polish patriarchy and nationalism. For this and other reasons, it has been necessary to neutralize and integrate the "foreign" into the national body of communism. Stanisław Bareja's film *Żona dla Australijczyka* (A Wife for an Australian, 1965) presents a model narrative of "national integration." In this comedy-romance, a Polish immigrant to Australia returns to his "old country" to find a wife. When he finally meets a perfect candidate, however, she refuses to leave her motherland. Enchanted by both the beauty of his beloved and the blossoming charm of the "new" Poland, he decides to stay. Thus, the would-be husband becomes the prodigal son who finally returns to an abandoned motherland to be reintegrated into the national community. Likewise, Sylwester Chęciński's *Sami Swoi* (All among Ourselves, 1967) prominently features the thematic motif of the reintegration of a Polish émigré from the United States. Although Polish comedies and romances differ significantly from their Hollywood counterparts, they still perform the same social and ideological function described by Robert Stam as "a 'cultural ritual' to integrate a conflictual community."[29] In postwar Poland, these reconciliatory narratives worked to create the illusion of a national consensus that was, in reality, absent from political and social life.

Polish communist cinema did not fully develop the genres of "re-establishment of social order." There are some examples of such films within socialist realist cinema, in which either foreigners or people linked to the prewar bourgeoisie endanger the social order of communist Poland only to be defeated in the end, thus ensuring the eventual sustainability of the status quo. Neither viewers nor critics found these propagandistic spy dramas to be appealing, however. Likewise, crime films made in the 1960s never matched the popularity of contemporaneous comedies and romances. There are two reasons for the relative underdevelopment of such films. First, the crime novel tradition was distinctly absent in Polish popular culture, and access to Western literature of this kind was very limited after the Second World War. Second, communist propaganda was adamant that there was no organized crime in postwar Poland. Obviously, then, there could be no such thing as a realistic crime film. For a long time and with few exceptions, crime films thus functioned as a *terra incognita* in Poland, only to rapidly emerge in post-communist times, a phenomenon to which I will return shortly.

As I have already demonstrated, popular cinema was complicit with the dominant ideology of communism until the 1970s. When the totalitarian order began to erode, a new type of popular cinema emerged that is best represented by Marek Piwowski's (b. 1935) *Rejs* (Cruise, 1970) and Stanisław Bareja's *Poszukiwany, poszukiwana* (Wanted, 1973), *Co mi zrobisz, jak mnie złapiesz* (What Will You Do When You Catch Me, 1978), and *Miś* (Teddy Bear, 1981). These absurdist comedies, which included elements of social and political satire, presented their Polish audiences with fictional worlds in which neither "social integration" nor "re-establishment of social order" could occur. Tellingly, they portrayed the social, political, and cultural disintegration of Polish society under the communist regime. Communist popular cinema had thus evolved, to paraphrase Schatz's taxonomy of Hollywood films, into an idiosyncratic generic form of "social disintegration and disorder."

Bareja's work demonstrates this (r)evolution within Polish communist popular cinema. His early films, made in the 1960s, were comedies of "social integration" and thus complicit with a dominant model; whereas his last feature film *Teddy Bear*, and the 1980s TV series *Alternatywy 4* (Alternative Street, No. 4, 1983, premiered in 1986–7), are commonly regarded as model examples of cinematic absurdism and political subversion. Neglected for years by both film critics and his peers, Bareja has recently achieved the status of a cult filmmaker who grasped the true spirit of life under communism. This is largely because of his knack for merging hyperrealism with the absurdities of everyday life. When examined in chronological order, his films exhibit a gradual decline in the importance of conventional cause-and-effect narrative structures. Temporal and spatial contingencies crumble with each successive film, and the characters' motivations simultaneously become more and more inconsequential. This modernist narrative amorphousness is juxtaposed with the pictorial realism of the cinematic image and a mixture of everyday and stylized dialogue. In Bareja's films, eroded narrative structures undermine pictorial realism. Episodic narratives represent communist reality as scattered fragments that do not add up to a larger whole. This aesthetic device signifies the impossibility of creating or apprehending a coherent world based on the principle of causality. This representation of communism shows it to be immune from the laws of causality and logic. Instead, it is rendered as absurd.

Polish popular cinema, be it of the genre of "social integration" or, more rarely, of "social order," has located its fictional worlds within a familiar contemporary Polish landscape in order to enhance their persuasive potential. However, there are also films that do not fit this model in that they depict a non-existent space, thereby establishing an alternative reality to the one experienced in real life. Mazierska uses the example of a sci-fi film by Marek Piestrak (b. 1938), *Test pilota Pirxa* (The Test of Pilot Pirx, 1979) to explain this artistic strategy. According to her, this film creates a fictional, non-determined space that can be seen as an example of a Foucauldian "heterotopia": a heterogeneous space that is a site for the extrapolation of indefinite otherness.[30] The comedies of Juliusz Machulski (b. 1955) are also examples of cinematic heterotopias. In *Seksmisja* (Sexmission, 1983), the dystopian world governed by women is an isolated space within a real world that retains its essentially patriarchal nature. There are three distinct spaces within the film's diegesis: the first is an artificial space of totalitarian matriarchy, the second an anarchist space of female contestation, and finally, at the film's end, there is a patriarchal master space that is instrumental for the restoration of social order. Despite the hierarchical ordering of these diegetic spaces, they retain the potential to subvert one another due to their simultaneous coexistence. Another variant of a heterotopian space is present in Machulski's *Vabank* (1982) and its sequel *Vabank 2, czyli riposta* (1985), two comedies in which the action takes place in an indistinct prewar reality. The diegetic space of the films is neither utopian nor real. It is constructed according to the cinematic tradition of a crime/gangster comedy, yet this is achieved by means of a deliberate pictorial realism. These films thus create an imaginary alternative to the reality of Poland under martial law. It is only within these heterotopian spaces created by the popular cinema of "late communism" that the generic "re-establishment of social order" can be exercised.

After the collapse of communism, the generic formulas of "social order" could finally be realized within the realistic space of the then flourishing popular police/gangster drama. These films focused mostly on the ethical dilemmas that emerged after the collapse of communism. Notwithstanding its evident affinity with the American gangster genre, Władysław Pasikowski's *Psy* (Dogs, 1992) vigorously addresses contemporary social and political changes in a different way than its Hollywood predecessors. The classic Hollywood gangster movie typically presents the social order that is to be regained as based on some form of existent and legitimate moral order. Conversely, *Dogs* only offers the re-establishment of a moral order while simultaneously emphasizing the absence of the social one; as the film's narrative demonstrates, the contemporary social-political reality is too degenerate and too chaotic to be ordered. Its protagonist, a former secret service officer, experiences a moral awakening and accepts the punishment for his misdeeds, yet he proves to be utterly ineffectual in curing the pathologies of social and political reality.

Krzysztof Krauze's *Dług* (The Debt, 1999) is aesthetically closer to the model of art cinema despite its crime theme, and also develops the motif of the re-establishment of a moral order. As with Pasikowski's film, its narrative demonstrates such re-establishment to be impossible, largely due to the impotence of public institutions and authorities. Nevertheless, even within this amorphous social and political reality of rampant post-1989 capitalism there is a space for moral judgment; the protagonist admits his guilt and accepts his prospective punishment. This moral redemption substitutes for the generic formula of "social order" to indicate that the latter cannot be re-established during a time of political, social, and economic transition. Both Pasikowski's film and Krauze's seem to claim that a moral reawakening must precede any societal change if such a change is to occur at all. Hence, the main premise of the crime/gangster/police dramas of "social order" is violated within Polish post-communist cinema, which presents the ideal of social order as unattainable in a post-communist social and political reality that is regulated not by the virtuous principles of democracy, but rather by the "dog eat dog" precepts of unbridled Western capitalism.

Around the most recent turn of the century, the perceived unattainability of "social order" began to be compensated for by nostalgic cinematic visions of the national past offered in a vernacular variant of "heritage cinema," which Mazierska describes as "a cluster of lavish historical or costume films, typically based on masterpieces of Polish literature."[31] Among these films, two stand out: *Pan Tadeusz*, Andrzej Wajda's adaptation of Adam Mickiewicz's canonical epic poem, and Jerzy Hoffman's *Ogniem i mieczem* (With Fire and Sword), both made in 1999 and identified by Mazierska as examples of "a conservative, reactionary ideology."[32] Indeed, both films offer a nostalgic vision of the Polish past. I would argue, however, that in *Pan Tadeusz* this occurs in a self-conscious fashion, whereas in *With Fire and Sword* there is a striking contradiction between the narrative and visual discourses that significantly destabilizes its supposed ideological consistency.

In Wajda's film, the national past is presented as an act of memory performed by the author of the literary original, who is featured as a character in and the narrator of the film's story. The idealistically depicted Polish past is thus doubly denaturalized. First, in line with Mickiewicz's poem, the cinematic images represent a nineteenth-century Lithuania, which was part of the partitioned Poland at the time of the story. Second, these images are marked as essentially the product of the narrator's memory; the difference between the past and the present is shown through contrast – between light and dark, and between the monochromatic blueness of a Parisian flat and the blossoming colours of Soplicowo, a quintessential gentry manor where the main action takes place. As the historian Simon Schama notes, in *Pan Tadeusz* Mickiewicz was celebrating a world he knew to be already extinct.[33] The same can be said of Wajda and his film.

The cinematic rendition of *With Fire and Sword* provides material that reveals the ideological complexities of the discourse on Polish national identity and its positioning within post–Cold War Europe. On the one hand, the film's narrative, centred on a Polish hero, presents a pre-modern and homogenous image of Polishness based on traditional and indeed conservative religious and patriotic values. On the other hand, the narrative strategies and visual devices used to represent Ukrainian Cossacks and Tartars imbue them with a sensuality that is notably absent from the Polish characters. The narrative agency of the Polish hero is undermined by the affective power of these images of the "Other," which in turn reveals the uncertainty surrounding the national subject and Polish masculinity.

While interrogating and negotiating the relationship between Polish masculinity and that of the archetypal "Other," *With Fire and Sword* employs the narrative device of a love triangle, a strategy typical of melodrama. In so doing, Hoffman's film is part of a wider current, since the previously marginalized genre of melodrama returned with great intensity during the first decade of the twenty-first century. This recent flourishing of melodrama, a genre commonly perceived as feminine, interrupts and disrupts the post-1989 hegemony of male-oriented crime/police/gangster films. Furthermore, melodrama is often regarded as a generic response to rapid and radical social changes, and thus its revival in Poland reflects the seismic economic, social, political, and cultural shifts that followed the collapse of the Berlin Wall. The emotional excess produced by melodramatic narratives and imagery serves as a vent for the collectively experienced tension and fear caused by new realities, which challenge the traditional notion of Polishness rooted in the Polish gentry and Romantic traditions as well as its communist variants.

A melodramatic return to the past occurs also in two recent and successful melodramas: *Mała Moskwa* (Little Moscow, 2008) by Waldemar Krzystek and *Różyczka* (Little Rose, 2010) by Jan Kidawa-Błoński (b. 1953). Krzystek's film tells the story of a tragic romance between a Russian woman and a Polish officer, while the protagonists of Kidawa-Błoński's film represent both the Stalinist regime and the political opposition to it. In both cases, therefore, current social and political frictions are displaced onto past struggles. Both films feature various types of opposition and conflict, including national and political concerns, as well as issues related to class, gender, and economics. Another component of the genre's adjustment to the Polish context is the establishment of a male protagonist as a central figure in these two films; even if the narrative seemingly privileges the female characters, it is a male hero who serves as the crux of the melodramatic affect. In *Little Moscow*, the whole story is presented through the memory of its male protagonist. In *Little Rose*, almost the entire narrative presents the female protagonist as experiencing an emotional and moral dilemma, yet it is the character of a secret police agent, an *ubek*, who is left tormented by a genuine internal drama at the end of the film, when it transpires that even though he participated heavily in the 1968 anti-Semitic movement, he himself is a Jew. The film's final scene, with its melodramatic narrative surplus, impacts the emotional response of the viewer. The female protagonist is shown in a state of advanced pregnancy, and thus her previously fragmented feminine identity regains its ideologically desired integrity. She will be a mother, and that sufficiently and profoundly defines her social position within the body of the nation. He, along with other Polish Jews, is shown as embarking on a train to Vienna. A close-up of his face reveals both his vulnerability and an uncertainty regarding his future in exile. Quite unexpectedly, in Polish melodrama it is a male figure who becomes a vehicle for the expression of both guilt over the past and anxiety for the future.

Conclusion

Responding to constantly changing political circumstances, Polish postwar cinema has oscillated between ideological complicity and subversiveness. This has manifested itself in all three of its dominant strands – national, modernist, and popular. Limited by political censorship, films addressing national issues searched for an aesthetic means to communicate with its audiences, address Poland's historical traumas and repressed memories of the past, and negotiate the political, social, and cultural dilemmas of contemporaneity. Simultaneously, state funding supported cinematic experiments to a moderate extent, since such films conveniently assigned less importance to their subject matter. They were also made to prove the superiority of a communist system of film production over that of bourgeois cinema, which was driven entirely by financial profit. The communist authorities also strove to assist popular cinema, as long as it conveyed an ideological message that was properly supportive of the political system.

According to most vernacular film criticism, the most vital part of Polish postwar cinema is to be found in its art cinema, with its preoccupation with the national subject, as represented at its best by Wajda, Munk, and Kieślowski. As a consequence, other cinematic phenomena linked with cinematic modernism, such as the films by Wojciech Has, Grzegorz Królikiewicz, Tadeusz Konwicki, Jerzy Skolimowski, and Walerian Borowczyk, have been significantly marginalized within critical discourse both in Poland and abroad.

The collapse of communism in 1989 caused a radical change in the whole system of film production, distribution, and exhibition. Instead of the erstwhile political censorship, filmmakers were subjected to the tough demands of a domestic film market, which was now saturated with Hollywood productions. They responded to these changes in a twofold manner: the younger generation attempted to establish a vernacular model of popular cinema, whereas older filmmakers wanted to use their newfound political freedom to address previously repressed parts of national memory. A significant trend towards "heritage cinema" also emerged, which attempted to combine the national and the popular. In more recent Polish cinema (since 2000), the popular, the modernist, and the national currents seem to be more clearly separated from one another than in the past, due mostly to changes in modes of film production and distribution. The general imperative to produce films for targeted audiences has resulted in a rather strong compartmentalization of post-communist cinema. Some filmmakers, however, such as Wojciech Smarzowski, Krzysztof Krauze, and Waldemar Krzystek, merge various cinematic conventions, adjusting them to their own authorial aims. Of special importance in this context is the common employment of popular genres to interrogate the national past. It is not Romanticism in either its heroic or ironic manifestations, but transnational generic codes that now serve as a meta-language capable of serious engagement with national, social, and political issues. A major shift in the cultural paradigm of Polish national cinema is thus finally taking place.

Elżbieta Ostrowska
University of Alberta

NOTES

1 It needs to be noted that it is difficult, perhaps impossible, to isolate a cinematic text that manifests only the national, or the modernist, or the popular; more often than not, these three impulses are intertwined. Moreover, they occur not only within a singular cinematic text, but also within the entire oeuvre of individual filmmakers, or in the works of a whole cinematic movement.
2 A common term used for a censor's decision to withdraw a film from distribution.
3 Lubelski, *Strategie autorskie*, 138–44.
4 See Werner, *Polskie, arcypolskie*.
5 For another analysis of these two "memory scenes," see Lubelski, *Strategie autorskie*, 167–9.
6 See Anderson, *Imagined Communities*. The privileging of sacrifice and suffering within discursive practices that "construct" the Polish nation dates back to Romanticism and is epitomized by the character of Konrad in Adam Mickiewicz's *The Forefathers' Eve*.
7 See Mazierska, "Double Memory," 226. See also Haltof, *Polish Film and the Holocaust*.
8 For an English translation of the essay as well as the public debate that its original publication provoked, see Polonsky, ed., *My Brother's Keeper?*

9 Skibińska, "Film polski o Zagładzie," 40–73.
10 See Gross, *Neighbors*.
11 Orr, *Cinema and Modernity*, 3.
12 Ibid.
13 For example, the French New Wave, the Czechoslovak New Wave, and the British "Angry Young Men" cinema.
14 A detailed examination of the issue is offered in a collective volume *Polish New Wave; The History of a Phenomenon that Never Existed*, ed. Barbara Piwowarska and Łukasz Ronduda.
15 In his article discussing these filmmakers' marginal position within Polish national cinema, Michael Goddard claims that for them "exile was the only available response to the impossibility of continuing their specific film practice in Poland" (Goddard, "The Impossible Polish New Wave and its Accursed Émigré Auteurs," 296).
16 Orr, "At the Crossroads," 2.
17 Mazierska and Skolimowski, *The Cinema of a Nonconformist*, 71.
18 Kornatowska, "'Yet we do not know what will become of us,'" 39.
19 The comparison concerns narrative structures in both films and not their protagonists as narrative agents.
20 Cameron, *Modular Narratives in Contemporary Cinema*, 71.
21 Gunning, "The Cinema of Attractions," 57.
22 Ibid., 60.
23 Bazin, "The Ontology of the Photographic Image," 159.
24 Ibid.
25 Kickasola, *The Films of Krzysztof Kieslowski*, 128.
26 Skwara, "'Film Stars Do Not Shine,'" 220.
27 Schatz, "Film Genre and the Genre Film," 571.
28 Rammel, "'Dobranoc ojczyzno kochana,'" 77.
29 Stam, *Film Theory*, 127.
30 Mazierska, "International Co-productions," 483–503; Foucault, "Of Other Spaces," 229–36.
31 Mazierska, *Polish Postcommunist Cinema*, 63.
32 Ibid., 89.
33 Schama, *Landscape and Memory*, 56.

WORKS CITED

Anderson, Benedict. *Imagined Communities: Reflections on the Origin and Spread of Nationalism*. London and New York: Verso Books, 2006.

Bazin, André. "The Ontology of the Photographic Image." In *Film Theory and Criticism*. Edited by Leo Braudy and Marshall Cohen. 159–62. New York and Oxford: Oxford University Press, 2009.

Cameron, Allan. *Modular Narratives in Contemporary Cinema*. Hampshire and New York: Palgrave Macmillan, 2008.

Foucault, Michel. "Of Other Spaces." In *The Visual Culture Reader*. Translated by Jay Miskowiec, edited by Nicholas Mirzoeff. 237–44. London: Routledge, 1998.

Goddard, Michael. "The Impossible Polish New Wave and Its Accursed Émigré Auteurs." In *A Companion to Eastern European Cinemas*. Edited by Anikó Imre. 291–310. Malden: Wiley-Blackwell, 2012.

Gunning, Tom. "The Cinema of Attractions: Early Film, Its Spectator, and the Avant-Garde." In *Early Cinema: Space, Frame, Narrative*. Edited by Thomas Elsaesser and Adam Barker. 56–62. London: BFI Publishing, 1990.

Gross, Jan Tomasz. *Neighbors: The Destruction of the Jewish Community in Jedwabne, Poland*. Princeton: Princeton University Press, 2001.

Haltof, Marek. *Polish Film and the Holocaust: Politics and Memory*. New York and Oxford: Berghahn Books, 2012.

Kickasola, Joseph G. *The Films of Krzysztof Kieslowski: The Liminal Image*. New York and London: Continuum, 2004.

Kornatowska, Maria. "'Yet we do not know what will become of us': On the Artistic Output of Wojciech Jerzy Has." In *Polish Cinema in Ten Takes*. Edited by Ewelina Nurczyńska-Fidelska and Zbigniew Batko. 35–43. Łódź: Łódzkie Towarzystwo Naukowe, 1995.

Lubelski, Tadeusz. *Strategie autorskie w polskim filmie fabularnym lat 1945–1961*. Kraków: Rabid, 2000.

Mazierska, Ewa. "Double Memory – the Holocaust in Polish Film." In *Holocaust and the Moving Image*. Edited by Toby Haggish and Joanna Newman. 225–35. London: Wallflower, 2005.

– "International Co-productions as Productions of Heterotopias." In *A Companion to Eastern European Cinemas*. Edited by Anikó Imre. 483–503. Malden: Wiley-Blackwell, 2012.

– *Polish Postcommunist Cinema: From Pavement Level*. Bern: Peter Lang, 2007.

Mazierska, Ewa, and Jerzy Skolimowski. *The Cinema of a Nonconformist*. New York and Oxford: Berghahn Books, 2010.

Orr, John. *Cinema and Modernity*. Cambridge: Polity Press, 1993.

– "At the Crossroads: Irony and Defiance in the Films of Andrzej Wajda." In *The Cinema of Andrzej Wajda: The Art of Irony and Defiance*. Edited by John Orr and Elżbieta Ostrowska. 1–14. London: Wallflower Press 2003.

Piwowarska, Barbara, and Łukasz Ronduda, eds. *Polish New Wave: The History of a Phenomenon That Never Existed*. Warsaw: Adam Mickiewicz Institute, Center for Contemporary Art, Ujazdowski Castle, 2008.

Polonsky, Antony, ed. *My Brother's Keeper: Recent Polish Debates on the Holocaust*. Oxford: Routledge, 1990.

Rammel, Iwona. "'Dobranoc ojczyzno kochana, już czas na sen...' Komedia filmowa lat sześćdziesiątych." In *Syndrom konformizmu? Kino polskie lat sześćdziesiątych*. Edited by Alina Madej and Tadeusz Miczka. Katowice: Wydawnictwo Uniwersytetu Śląskiego, 1994.

Schama, Simon. *Landscape and Memory*. New York: A.A. Knopf, 1995.

Schatz, Thomas. "Film Genre and the Genre Film." In *Film Theory and Criticism*. 7th ed. Edited by Leo Braudy and Marshall Cohen. 691–702. New York and Oxford: Oxford University Press, 2009.

Skibińska, Alina. "Film polski o Zagładzie." *Kwartalnik Historii Żydów* 1 (2010): 40–73.

Skwara, Anita. "'Film Stars Do Not Shine in the Sky over Poland': The Absence of Popular Cinema in Poland." In *Popular European Cinema*. Edited by Richard Dyer and Ginette Vincendeau. London: Routledge, 1992.

Sobolewski, Tadeusz. "Kino-oko Pawła Łozińskiego." Insert to a DVD series. *Polska szkoła dokumentu. Paweł Łoziński*. Wydawnictwo Narodowego Instytutu Wizualnego, 2009.

Stam, Robert. *Film Theory: An Introduction*. Oxford: Blackwell, 2000.

Werner, Andrzej. *Polskie, arcypolskie*. London: Polonia, 1987.

History and Grand Narratives (Andrzej Wajda)

Andrzej Wajda (1926–2016) was one of the most acclaimed Eastern European filmmakers of his generation, along with Hungarian director Miclós Jancsó, Czech director Milos Forman, and Soviet director Andrei Tarkovsky. Wajda was a true *auteur*; his films reflected his personal style and vision, and he frequently turned to the same themes in film after film. Wajda's creative signature can be found in all aspects of his work, from his screenplays to the formal features of cinematography, film design, editing, sound effects, and film score.

Wajda directed more than fifty film and television productions, in which the most frequently recurring themes were Polish history (particularly the Second World War), contemporary politics, and the universal leitmotifs of love, passion, and death. Many of his films were based on works of Polish literature, particularly those that engage with questions of national discourse. In sixty years of filmmaking, he examined the most important and controversial events in Polish history. He also engaged with the problematics of Polish national identity, probing its various meanings, both collective and individual, particularly in the context of historical upheavals. Embedded in these larger issues, the individual narratives of Wajda's protagonists – mostly young people with tragic outlooks – unfolded in terms of the moral cost of living.

Polish film school: a phenomenon that can be interpreted as a reaction of the first cohort of graduates of the Łódź Film School (founded on 8 March 1948) to the recently ended Second World War. Its most important artists and works include the films of Andrzej Wajda (1926–2016); Andrzej Munk (1921–61) with *Eroica* (1957), *Zezowate szczęście* (Bad Luck, 1960; also known as Cross-Eyed Luck) and *Pasażerka* (Passenger, 1963); Kazimierz Kutz (b. 1929) with *Krzyż Walecznych* (Cross of Valour, 1958) and *Nikt nie woła* (Nobody's Calling, 1960); and Stanisław Lenartowicz (1921–2010) with *Zimowy zmierzch* (Winter Dusk, 1956). The screenplays of Jerzy Stefan Stawiński (1921–2010) and the cinematography of Jerzy Lipman (1922–83), Mieczysław Jahoda (1924–2009), and Jerzy Wójcik (b. 1930) also played a significant role in history of this formation. Cinematography in particular accounts for a defining characteristic of the current, namely, the "thinking images" (*myślące obrazy*) aimed at conveying a maximum of information and at circumventing censorship, which was much more sensitized to words than to the visual aspects of art. In their visual aspect, the films of this school frequently reference *film noir* – in their use of backlighting, for instance, or by the inclusion of ceilings within frames to convey the entrapment of characters in a space from which they will not escape. They also reference Italian Neorealism by presenting great historical events through the prism of average people's lives and – from a technical perspective – by filming on location.

Wajda belonged to a generation of Polish filmmakers whose consciousness was defined by the Second World War, a generation that included Wojciech Jerzy Has (1925–2000), Jerzy Kawalerowicz (1922–2007), Kazimierz Kutz, Andrzej Munk, and Stanisław Różewicz (1924–2008). The war was at the centre of both his debut film, *Pokolenie* (A Generation, 1955), and its follow-up, *Kanał* (Canal, 1957). The latter earned him international recognition and multiple awards at Venice and other film festivals. Wajda's preoccupation with the war also informed *Popiół i diament* (Ashes and Diamonds, 1958), *Lotna* (1959), *Samson* (1961), and *Krajobraz po bitwie* (Landscape after Battle, 1970). Years later, he would return to the subject of the Second World War in films that were at once nostalgic and revisionist. In *Miłość w Niemczech* (A Love in Germany, 1983), a film about a wartime relationship between a German woman and a Polish forced labourer, Wajda explored the intersection of passion and national identity. In 1986, he adapted Tadeusz Konwicki's novel *Kronika wypadków miłosnych* (A Chronicle of Amorous Incidents); that film is an elegy to the lost youth of Wajda's generation. Following Poland's transition to democracy, he participated in the renewed national discourse about the Holocaust with the films *Dr. Korczak* (1990) and *Wielki Tydzień* (Holy Week, 1995). Similarly, with *Pierścionek z orłem w koronie* (The Crowned-Eagle Ring, 1992) and *Katyń* (2009), Wajda contributed to ongoing historical revisionism regarding the Soviet Union's role in wartime and postwar Poland.

All of these films explore national identity at the intersection of the public and the private. It is here that Wajda drew out unpleasant truths, such as the wartime cooperation between the Soviet Union and Nazi Germany, and Poles' clandestine business dealings with the Nazis. Full of familiar national symbols, yet at the same time uneasy with deeply engrained notions of Polish patriotism and valour, these films tell stories about a scarred generation who grew up too quickly only to be destroyed in the brutal reality of war.

In other films, Wajda turned his attention to the political and social realities of life under Communism; these films include *Człowiek z marmuru* (Man of Marble, 1976), *Bez znieczulenia* (Without Anaesthetic, 1978), *Człowiek z żelaza* (Man of Iron, 1981) and even *Danton* (1982). Although it is set during the French Revolution, the last film lends itself to interpretation as a direct commentary on the history of communism and Solidarity in Poland. Wajda can thus be grouped together with filmmakers like Krzysztof Kieślowski (1941–96), Krzysztof Zanussi (b. 1939), and Agnieszka Holland (b. 1948), all of whom are associated with the Cinema of Moral Anxiety, a movement that highlighted the political and moral dilemmas of Poles living under the crumbling communist system of the 1970s and 1980s. In *Man of Marble*, for example, the protagonist, Birkut, loses his job, apartment, and social status and ends up in prison, all because of his search for a friend who has mysteriously disappeared after being interrogated by the Stalinist secret police. Though disillusioned with the communist system, Birkut nevertheless remains faithful to the idea of social and political engagement. Only in *Man of Iron*, the sequel to *Man of Marble*, do we learn that Birkut was killed in the workers' protests in Gdańsk in 1970. A similar situation, transposed to an intellectual milieu, is presented in *Without*

Anaesthetic. The protagonist, Jerzy, loses his job as a journalist after giving an eloquent speech about freedom and democracy on state television, an act that triggers his persecution by the communist government. Later, when he dares to promote the work of a young and controversial writer, Jerzy loses his teaching position at Warsaw University. In both films, Wajda exposes the pervasive abuses of power by Polish apparatchiks.

Besides being a master of national cinematic narratives, Wajda was a skilled interpreter of literary works, especially those dealing with existential questions. He adapted several short stories by Jarosław Iwaszkiewicz (1894–1980) – *Brzezina* (The Birchwood, 1970), *Panny z Wilka* (The Maidens of Wilko, 1979), and *Tatarak* (The Sweet Rush, 2008) – all of them about the interplay of life and death instincts – Eros and Thanatos. His cinematography was at its most striking in these films, which take up eternal and universal questions of love, passion, illness, mortality, and the fragility of human relations. Set in Polish villages and small towns, they portray characters whose lives are nearing an end and examine their present and their past with profound empathy. In *The Birchwood*, for example, two brothers, Bolesław and Stanisław, are able to reconcile their differences in the face of Stanisław's impending death from tuberculosis. In *The Maidens of Wilko*, the protagonist, Wiktor, begins to understand the passage of time when he revisits his childhood home and friends and realizes that life, like the river he has crossed to get to his old village, has quietly and surreptitiously flowed past him.

The aesthetics of Wajda's films, particularly their *mise-en-scène* and colour palette, show his familiarity with Polish and European fine art, which he studied in his youth at the Kraków Academy of Fine Arts. *The Birchwood*, for instance, recalls the work of Polish Symbolist painters such as Jacek Malczewski (1854–1929); *Ashes and Diamonds*, in turn, begins and ends with a sequence reminiscent of Ferdynand Ruszczyc's modernist masterpiece *Ziemia* (The Earth). The film opens with an image of a field being ploughed and ends with a character dying on top of a garbage dump; the final scene both recalls the ploughed field from the film's beginning and serves as a metaphor for the ash heap of history. In *Ashes and Diamonds*, the promise of spring and rejuvenation implied by Ruszczyc's painting gives way to futility and hopelessness. Wajda's cinematography also frequently alludes to Western European art. The black-and-white evacuation scenes in *Canal* – of soldiers during the Warsaw Uprising being led through the city's sewers – gesture towards the Surrealism of Luis Bunuel's early films as well as his *Los Olvidados* (1950), while the senselessness of the soldiers' march towards certain death is expressed through lines from Dante's *Divine Comedy*. In *Landscape after Battle*, by contrast, musical quotations play a major role, with Vivaldi's *Four Seasons* expressing the chaos and excitement that accompanies the release of Polish prisoners from a concentration camp by American troops.

Wajda's numerous screen adaptations of literary works allowed him to explore the relationship between literary and cinematic languages and were aided by his instincts as a close reader and by his painterly eye. His textual sources included Stanisław Wyspiański's *Wesele* (The Wedding, 1972), Władysław Reymont's *Ziemia obiecana* (The Promised Land, 1974), Adam Mickiewicz's *Pan Tadeusz* (1999), Stefan Żeromski's *Popioły* (Ashes, 1965), Aleksander Fredro's *Zemsta* (Revenge, 2002), Joseph Conrad's *The Shadow Line* (1976), Fyodor Dostoevsky's *The Possessed* (1988), and Nikolai Leskov's *Lady Macbeth of Mtsensk* (1962). Even beyond such adaptations, Wajda's larger cultural and historical vision was based primarily on his readings of literature. At the same time, a large segment of Wajda's audience learned to read Polish literature through his films. His powerful cinematic images imprinted themselves so indelibly on the popular imagination that it became nearly impossible to read any classic he had adapted without recalling these images.

Wajda was also praised for his formal innovations, notably in the two films in which he responded to the French New Wave, *Wszystko na sprzedaż* (Everything for Sale, 1968) and *Niewinni czarodzieje* (Innocent Sorcerers, 1960), as well as the more recent *Tatarak* (Sweet Rush, 2009). The first two films included such experimental features as fragmentary narrative, the overlapping of fictional and documentary forms, self-reflexive gestures towards the filmmaking process, and the disruption of acting conventions. In *Everything for Sale*, Wajda tested the limits of self-reflexive, autobiographical filmmaking by focusing on his relationship with Zbigniew Cybulski (1927–67), an iconic Polish actor who had worked with Wajda in the 1960s and died prematurely in a train accident. The film depicts Wajda's own milieu, as well as a more general view of 1960s Poland, and at the same time foregrounds the filmmaking process by showing the director at work with his cast and crew within the film's diegetic world. *Sweet Rush,* by contrast, is an intertextual mosaic composed of three narratives: the fictional story of a terminally ill married woman, Marta, and her passion for a much younger man who dies in an accident; the onscreen confessions of Krystyna Janda (b. 1952), the actress who plays Marta, about the illness and death of her real-life husband, the renowned cinematographer Edward Kłosiński (1943–2008); and, finally, the meta-narrative in which Wajda directs Janda in her role as Marta.

During a long and distinguished career, Wajda shaped the collective imagination of several generations of Polish filmgoers. Through his engagement with Poland's historical traumas and their recent re-evaluations, as well as his adaptations of Polish literary classics, he became the iconic cinematic interpreter of Poland's collective experiences both historical and cultural. He also created a distinctive and easily recognizable visual language to articulate national traumas and complexes. This language resonated with inherited cultural symbols and beliefs while at the same time questioning and reformulating them. Wajda owes his prominence in Polish cinema to this distinctive language as well as to the empathy he showed his characters, who came from every social background and with whom many of his viewers could identify, and he has undoubtedly become the face of Polish cinema abroad.

Janina Falkowska
University of Western Ontario

WORKS CONSULTED

Falkowska, Janina. *Andrzej Wajda: History, Politics, and Nostalgia in Polish Cinema.* Oxford and New York: Berghahn Books, 2007.

– *The Political Films of Andrzej Wajda.* Oxford and Providence: Berghahn Books, 1996.

Falkowska, Janina, with Marek Haltof. *The New Polish Cinema.* Trowbridge: Flicks Books, 2003.

Michałek, Bolesław. *The Cinema of Andrzej Wajda.* London: Tantivy, 1973.

Miczka, Tadeusz. *Inspiracje plastyczne w twórczości filmowej i telewizyjnej Andrzeja Wajdy.* Katowice: University of Silesia Press, 1987.

Nurczyńska-Fidelska, Ewelina, and Piotr Sitarski, eds. *Filmowy i teatralny świat Andrzeja Wajdy*. Kraków: Wydawnictwo Uniwersytetu Łódzkiego, 2003.

Orr, John, and Elżbieta Ostrowska, eds. *The Cinema of Andrzej Wajda: The Art of Irony and Defiance*. London: Wallflower, 2003.

Wajda, Andrzej. *O polityce, o sztuce, o sobie*. Warszawa: Prószyński i S-ka, 2000.

Neither East, nor West (Jerzy Skolimowski)

Searching for parallels between the life and work of an artist is regarded as an old-fashioned approach nowadays, yet it is difficult to avoid it when analysing the films of Jerzy Skolimowski (b. 1938). The director often cast himself in his films (as well as his girlfriend, wife, and children) and shot some of them in his own house. He also drew on episodes from his own life – for example, his boxing career in *Walkower* (Walkover, 1965). Furthermore, autobiographism is reflected not only in the content of his films but also in their mode of narration and their aesthetics. In Skolimowski's case, therefore, it makes sense to follow Susan Sontag's directive: "One cannot use the life to interpret the work. But one can use the work to interpret the life."[1] Indeed, the autobiographical trope is all the more useful when it comes to examining Skolimowski's elusive presence in Polish cinema. After making four full-length fiction films in Poland in the 1960s, which brought him recognition and international acclaim as a leading representative of the cinematic New Wave outside of France, he emigrated and spent more than twenty years abroad. Emigration would not have estranged him from his Polish audience had it not been for the limited distribution of his foreign films in Poland. This was due not to political censorship, but rather to the relative lack of success of these films abroad. Unlike his fellow émigré, Roman Polański (b. 1933), Skolimowski came across as a "Pole struggling abroad" and not as someone who had "made it."

Jerzy Skolimowski on:

His early life in Czechoslovakia: "[Milos] Forman was the boss of our dormitory," he reveals. "On the next bed to me was [director] Ivan Passer. I shared school papers with Václav Havel. I helped him with drawings and, in exchange, he did my Latin and Greek."

His poetry writing and boxing: "Maybe the boxing was to balance the fact that poetry wasn't an extremely masculine occupation."

His friendship with Roman Polański: "Roman was living in Belgravia," he recalls. "I was very impressed. He introduced me to the London scene." This included the Playboy Club: "Suddenly, I was on a dancefloor with those bunnies. As a young man, I had a wild life – as Roman did, too. We were similar in our adventures."

His sixteen-year hiatus in film making: "Remember that I am not only a film-maker but also a painter," he says of his absence. "Practically the whole break, I was busy painting. I had considerable success. It wasn't wasted time."

http://www.theguardian.com/film/2009/mar/11/1

The view that Skolimowski belongs to the (short) history of Polish New Wave cinema seemed confirmed on his return to Poland in the early 1990s, based on the reception of *30 Door Key* (1991), his film adaptation of Witold Gombrowicz's novel *Ferdydurke* (1937). The result was literary in the worst sense of the word: instead of offering an original interpretation of the novel, it clumsily and without lucidity tried to render the content of the book, adding to the impression that Skolimowski had lost his talent while abroad. The director must have agreed with this criticism, for he retired from directing and devoted his time to painting instead, and to acting occasionally in other people's films. After a hiatus of seventeen years, however, he surprised audiences in Poland and abroad with a new cycle of films consisting, so far, of three productions: *Cztery noce z Anną* (Four Nights with Anna, 2008), *Essential Killing* (2010), and *11 Minutes* (2015). The second of these features achieved significant international success and prompted a re-examination of Skolimowski's entire oeuvre. Since then, retrospectives of his work have been presented at several prestigious film festivals and some of his best films made abroad, such as *Deep End* (1971) and *Moonlighting* (1982), have been released on DVD and Blu-ray. He has also attracted the attention of a new generation of film historians, becoming the subject of both academic essays and monographs.

Listening to Oneself

Skolimowski's films closely correspond to the model of "accented cinema." This is due to his privileging of lonely and alienated characters, his referencing of personal experiences, and his use of internal monologues to address the audience. This correspondence is not surprising given that the director spent much of his creative life abroad. What is peculiar, however, is that he started to make "accented" films even before he left Poland and continued to use this form after returning to his homeland.

> **Accented cinema**: a term coined by Hamid Naficy in *An Accented Cinema: Exilic and Diasporic Filmmaking* to account for the specificity of exilic and diasporic filmmaking. "Accented cinema," like "accented speech," refers to those who use the mainstream language in a specific way that reveals their outsider or marginal status.

Lonely and alienated characters populate his first feature film, *Rysopis* (Identification Marks: None, 1964), as well as the subsequent *Walkover*, *Moonlighting*, *Success Is the Best Revenge* (1984), and *Essential Killing*. Their loneliness and alienation arises from being in a new place, not speaking the language, and being an outcast or a criminal. Skolimowski's alienated protagonist barely communicates with those whom he encounters during his wanderings through the city, and when communication does happens, the dialogue is superficial or disrupted. People do not understand him, and he hardly tries to remedy this situation. The clearest sign of the distance between him and others is that nobody addresses him by his first name. In some instances, in fact – for example, in *Bariera* (Barrier, 1966) and *Essential Killing*, as well as in Polański's *Nóż w wodzie* (Knife in the Water, 1962), which Skolimowski co-scripted – we never learn the name of the protagonist (the screenplays provide only descriptions such as "Boy"' or "Student").

Unable or unwilling to communicate with others, the protagonist in a film by Skolimowski immerses himself in the sounds of the world. In *Identification Marks: None* and *Walkover*, he frequently stops and listens to the banal sounds of radio ads or the conversations of restaurant patrons. His attentive listening distinguishes him from his "fellow travellers," who are usually uninterested in such sounds, and this brings him closer to himself and the city. While the motives for his actions are not transparent, Skolimowski manages to convey to the audience his physical awareness of walking and listening. In this respect he can be compared to a rap artist, although the latter comes across as an insider who knows his "hood" perfectly well, while Skolimowski's protagonist is always an outsider. This focus on walking and listening, rather than on showing the character in action and overcoming obstacles – the norm for both Hollywood and socialist realist cinema – along with the compression of the film's action to one or two days, creates a certain paradox. On the one hand, we know little about the lives of Skolimowski's characters, as critics have noted when they describe Leszczyc, the hero of his first two films, as opaque or abstract. On the other hand, we are always in close proximity to the character, able almost to hear him breathing, because the camera never leaves him. He is in the centre of every episode.

Skolimowski tends to privilege hearing over sight, in line with Henri Lefebvre's claim that hearing is more intuitive and closer to our bodies than sight: we absorb sounds with our bodies in the same way a sponge absorbs water.[2] By this token, hearing is a better way to learn about oneself. On the most literal level, in order to learn about ourselves through sight, we need a medium, such as a mirror or somebody's eyes. When we use hearing as a tool for self-exploration, however, we do not need any mediator.

Neither East nor West

Skolimowski frequently uses the motif of wandering to reflect on the protagonist's disappointment with the political system in which he finds himself. The director's critical attitude towards state socialism in his early Polish films, such as *Barrier* and *Ręce do góry* (Hands Up!, 1966), is typical of the New Wave generation. His unwillingness to compromise with the censors cost him his job and forced him to leave Poland and seek work abroad. Emigration, however, only made him more sensitive to the injustices of other political and economic systems. Skolimowski is at his best as a political director who links the East with the West, as happens in *Moonlighting* and *Essential Killing*.

Moonlighting is a story about Polish workers hired to renovate the London house of a wealthy Polish man, most likely a member of the *nomenklatura*. In the film, Poland during martial law is compared with Thatcher's England. The builders engage in "moonlighting" because of the poor wages in Poland and the high value of Western currency. In London, the Polish brigade works according to harsh rules: limited freedom of movement, low wages, and no strikes. Such rules were introduced under the Thatcher government to redress the balance of power between capital and labour. Soon they became the norm for neoliberal capitalism in every country, a shift that can now be observed also in Poland, both in practice and in official discourses on work. The heroic figure of the miner or shipyard worker has been pushed off the pedestal to make way for new kinds of heroes: managers and entrepreneurs. Following Slavoj Žižek's observation, in *Moonlighting* manual labour has become the site of obscene indecency to be concealed from the public eye.[3]

Skolimowski's film is prophetic in drawing attention to the physical distance between the places where manual labour is performed, on the one hand, and where it is planned, controlled, and exploited, on the other. He shows that maintaining distance between the exploited worker and the exploiting capitalist works to the advantage of the latter by freeing him from involvement in production and from any moral or aesthetic displeasure that such involvement might bring. References to the introduction of martial law in Poland are intermingled with those to Thatcherite politics and rhetoric. Skolimowski shows that the ruthless competition for scarce jobs reduces social cohesion and, especially, solidarity with foreigners. Although London in *Moonlighting* is full of posters proclaiming the solidarity of English people with Poles suffering as a result of the military coup, the actual attitudes of British people towards Polish workers in the film come across as bigoted. In the end, the London neighbours of the Polish "Boss" call the hired workers "communists" and demand that they leave England immediately.

Essential Killing offers a no less depressing assessment of global political and social realities. Here, a Muslim fighter of undisclosed ethnicity and nationality who is engaged in combat against American soldiers, possibly in Afghanistan, is captured, tortured, and transported to a secret location in Europe, possibly Poland (the film was inspired by an event that took place not far from where Skolimowski lives). Once there, the "enemy combatant" manages to escape, and he spends the rest of his life running and hiding from his captors. Physical survival is the most he can accomplish, however, and even that requires him to live like an animal, much like Agamben's *Homo sacer*. The film indicts the brutal methods adopted by the United States in the infamous "War on Terror" while also pointing to Poland's diminished agency in the context of the Western sphere of influence. One of the film's scenes shows a mute woman, a contemporary incarnation of the Polish "lady of the manor," offering shelter to the Muslim man, which can be read as a sign of solidarity between the colonialized and the marginalized in global politics. Yet this solidarity cannot counterbalance the military might of the America and NATO – the Muslim fighter is sentenced to death.

The comprehensive rejection of the political reality offered by Skolimowski in his films can be linked to his affinity for Polish Romanticism. The injustice and marginalization experienced by Poles under the partitions of the nineteenth century rendered them reluctant to improve their position through integration with existing political structures. This attitude continued into later periods of Polish history. Instead of setting out to improve their situation, Poles conjured up an ideal land that existed either in heroic myths or in a projected future. This explains their propensity for nostalgia as well as for ill-fated uprisings. In this context it has to be remembered, however, that Skolimowski also criticizes the Romantic attitude, denouncing its gestures as ineffectual and Poles' heroic memories as fake.

Screen Happiness

Is there a way out of their misery for Skolimowski protagonists? The screen seems to be the only place where they can find happiness, however temporary. His films are self-referential, as indicated both by his inclusion of films within films and by his protagonists' cinematic mode of looking and living. Examples of the latter can be found in *Identification Marks: None*. One of the film's early scenes shows a welder doing some roadwork at night; the light from his torch illuminates the wall of a building as the film's protagonist passes by. In the words of one critic, the effect is a "sort of natural cinematographic projection."[4] We do not know whether this image brings Leszczyc joy, but it does signals his ability to see beyond the materiality of things and to become transported by the power of his imagination. Indeed, these abilities are foregrounded by the film whenever Leszczyc puts on different masks to present himself as someone different to the people he meets.

In *Le Départ* (The Departure, 1966), Marc, a hairdresser, dreams about becoming a racing-car champion and does everything he can to achieve this goal, including stealing a car. Although his efforts are ultimately futile, he nevertheless finds fulfilment of sorts when looking at a series of photographs his girlfriend brings to their hotel room. As they project the slides onto the wall, the images merge with Marc's shadow. When the slides start to burn because the projector is too close to the lamp, the photographic images fuse with Marc's image on the wall. For Marc, this projection proves illuminating. After a long search for his "right" place, he finds it on the screen and realizes that it can be found anywhere and nowhere. Finally, in *Cztery noce z Anną* (Four Nights with Anna, 2008), the character is happiest when he looks at his beloved woman from his window through a kind of natural screen. From a distance, the otherwise plain-looking woman comes across as beautiful. It is only when he attempts to overcome the physical distance between them that he loses her and everything in his life collapses.

Such faith in the power of screen images harks back to cinema's "second youth" of the 1960s, which might appear naive today. Skolimowski, however, dignifies it by conveying it with subtlety. His is the cinema of a cineaste aimed at a fellow cineaste.

Ewa Mazierska
University of Central Lancashire

NOTES

1 Sontag, *Under the Sign of Saturn*, 111.
2 Lefebvre, *Rhythmanalysis*, 27–37.
3 Žižek, *Did Somebody Say Totalitarianism*, 133.
4 Ronduda and Piwowarska, "Skolimowski, Królikiewicz, Żuławski, Uklański," 26.

WORKS CITED

Lefebvre, Henri. *Rhythmanalysis: Space, Time, and Everyday Life*. London: Continuum, 2004.
Naficy, Hamid. *An Accented Cinema: Exilic and Diasporic Filmmaking*. Princeton: Princeton University Press, 2001.
Ronduda, Łukasz, and Barbara Piwowarska, eds. "Skolimowski, Królikiewicz, Żuławski, Uklański." In *Nowa Fala: Historia zjawiska, którego nie było*. 24–47. Warszawa: Instytut Adama Mickiewicza, CSW Zamek Ujazdowski, 2008.
Sontag, Susan. *Under the Sign of Saturn*. New York: Doubleday, 1991.
Žižek, Slavoj. *Did Somebody Say Totalitarianism? Five Interventions in the (Mis)Use of a Notion*. London: Verso, 2001.

Poetics of Chance (Krzysztof Kieślowski)

Krzysztof Kieślowski (1941–96) is one of the few filmmakers in world cinema who has created a body of work so closely bound up with personal experience and so consistent that it appears like a journey planned in advance. In this regard, his creative path can be compared to that of Bergman or Rohmer. Kieślowski was able to overcome the barriers posed by censorship in the Polish state film industry before 1989, and later, when he worked for French producers, he did not give in to the censorship of the marketplace. He continued to realize his own artistic project until the end. In 1995, exhausted from producing sixteen films in a single decade, including *Dekalog* (The Decalogue, 1988), he parted ways with cinema. He felt fulfilled as an artist, and he desired, in his word, "peace." He died of heart failure in 1996.

In film circles, Kieślowski's nickname was "the engineer"; he referred to himself as a "craftsman." Yet his world view was also that of a writer: cinema served him as a platform for posing – to himself and his audience – fundamental philosophical questions, which arose from his own biography as well as from the pressures of life in postwar Poland. Like the earlier generation of the "Polish School" filmmakers (Andrzej Wajda and Andrzej Munk), Kieślowski had a sense of both the significance of his work and of the importance of contact with an audience. In defining the goals of his filmmaking in "Głęboko zamiast szeroko" (Deeply Rather Than Broadly, 1980), he speaks of "looking for a way that would impart to the audience of my films emotions similar to mine."[1] For Kieślowski, human connection is of fundamental importance, and it is his characters' pursuit of identification with another human being that accounts for the metaphysical quality of his cinema. It is telling that the director speaks of "emotions" rather than "social consciousness." He does not wish to go along with the crowd, and like the hero of his film *Amator* (Camera Buff, 1979), he turns the camera towards himself.

At the beginning of *Camera Buff*, the titular "amateur," as the Polish title has it, is satisfied with filming "what is there," yet he does so with a critical eye that quickly turns towards showing "the world not represented." Such was the title of the New Realism manifesto – *Świat nie przedstawiony* – published by two young poets, Adam Zagajewski (b. 1945) and Julian Kornhauser (b. 1946), in 1974. Kieślowski began his work in cinema with the equally revolutionary intent of exposing the reality that official propaganda had falsified: *Robotnicy '71* (Workers '71, 1971), a documentary film directed with his peers, focuses on the Workers' Council elections at the Gdańsk Shipyards – the place where "Solidarity" would be born a decade later. Its production was a lesson in *Realpolitik* for Kieślowski; made in good faith as a "letter to the authorities," the film was taken away from its creators and re-edited, a clear indication that the ruling élites could never be expected to play fair.

In the parable of "the amateur," Kieślowski implicates his own entanglement in the double-game played by filmmakers during the 1970s as they attempted to manipulate the system while simultaneously benefiting from the privileges the state film industry offered. The emblematic final gesture of *Camera Buff* – Kieślowski turns the camera lens towards himself in order to speak not so much about "the world not represented," but rather about his adventure in that world – was an attempt to escape the trap of the system, to pull away from it and to trust the film medium and the possibilities hidden within it. The fulfilment of these possibilities – the "ardent act" of Kieślowski's cinema in which his world view and aesthetics are most fully articulated – would come to fruition in *Przypadek* (Blind Chance, 1981).

Initially treated as a dissenter interested in the problem of social inequality within real socialism, Kieślowski gradually revealed the metaphysical aspirations that had been present in his films from the outset. The protagonists of his early films – *Personel* (Personnel, 1975) and *Spokój* (The Calm, 1976) – undergo a bitter social initiation, discovering the injustice of a social life in which they cannot find a place for themselves. In that system, accusations of treason become inescapable, as happens to the heroes of *The Calm*, *Camera Buff*, *Blind Chance*, and *Bez końca* (No End, 1985). In order to be just, one must locate oneself outside the system and perhaps even outside life, in which the yearned-for "calm" is never attained. In *The Calm*, which was made for television and banned by the censors for featuring a workers' strike, the first of Kieślowski's metaphysical images appears: an unexplainable film frame of running horses on the screen of a turned-off television set.

Zbigniew Preisner (b. 1956) is a self-taught composer initially associated with the literary cabaret in Kraków. After being invited by Krzysztof Kieślowski to compose the score for *No End*, he became part of the director's creative team, which also included Krzysztof Piesiewicz. The three friends worked closely together until the end of Kieślowski's life. Preisner's international career was one result of their collaboration; he scored eighty films and published his own compositions. His role in Kieślowski's films, especially in *Decalogue* (9), *The Double Life of Veronique* (1991), and *Three Colours*: *Blue* (1993), was of special significance, however. Music becomes the heroine of these films in some sense, having more than just an aesthetic value. In the words of the musicologist Iwona Sowińska, it "has an existential value, it is a means of living life" (Sowińska-Rammel, "Czułe miejsca," 157).

Performed in front of the spectator, the music is part of the story and becomes a metaphysical argument and a symbol of ties that exceed individuality. Its status as subject in these films is underscored by the mystification surrounding its authorship, which is assigned to Van den Budenmayer, a fictional Dutch composer from the turn of seventeenth and eighteenth centuries. The figure was conceived by Kieślowski, adapted by Preisner, and referenced from film to film.

Kieślowski's later films – *Camera Buff*, *Blind Chance*, and *No End* (which deals with the martial law period) – constitute the subsequent stages of the director's journey outside the framework set by Poland's political system and history. In those films, Kieślowski remains an incisive observer of people and social life, but his field of vision has expanded to include what is invisible and inexplicable. Other-worldly characters begin to appear in his films, as if they were representatives of an untestable transcendence who simultaneously are and are not. Their examples include the deceased attorney's ghost in *No End*, who is invisible to the living, and the mysterious character who reappears throughout *The Decalogue*. Depending on the viewer, the latter enigmatic figure can represent God, a guardian angel, the author, or simply a witness, and expresses the dilemma that Kieślowski confronts his audience with in each part of *The Decalogue*. In the gaze of this figure, there is both vigilance and helplessness – moral judgment as much as empathy – which reflects the spectrum of available audience positions.

Piotr Sobociński (1958–2001) was a promising cinematographer who started to work on ambitious, big-budget productions in America after receiving an Oscar nomination for his work on Kieślowski's *Three Colours: Red* (1994). He died suddenly, on the threshold of his career, of a heart attack. Kieślowski gave him a unique opportunity to work on films from the moment of their conception. Sobociński was raised on the set of Wajda's and Has's films, for which his father Witold was the cinematographer, and he had a self-confessed sense of "the terrible devaluation of the film image" in which "refined technological solutions are used without cause" (Sobociński, "Sfilmowane déjà vu," 46). His work on *Three Colours: Red* was a remarkable attempt to bring depth to the film image. The film's spectator gradually recognizes that under a layer of coincidence lies a hidden script of the events. Reality adjusts itself, so to speak, to a model that exists outside of time. Sobociński used a rich palette of means that are far from arbitrary to suggest to the audience the existence of a hidden underpinning of events – the phenomenon of *déjà vu*.

In his subsequent films – *Podwójne życie Weroniki* (The Double Life of Veronique, 1991), *Trzy kolory. Niebieski* (Three Colours: Blue, 1993) and *Trzy kolory. Czerwony* (Three Colours: Red, 1995) – Kieślowski looks for means to include the unrecognized side of reality in the "represented world" without recourse to symbolic figures. This is tied to changes in optics; initially, during the 1970s, the cinematography of his films had a raw, documentary texture reminiscent of the Czech "New Wave" cinema or the films of Ken Loach. In his late films that were produced in France, a delicate net of associations with links to music, light, and colour is superimposed on the image of reality instead. In *Blue*, glints of blue and black shimmer with meanings, sometimes evoking depression and death, and sometimes spirit and grace. The real and transcendental worlds are thus joined together, shown as the obverse and reverse sides of the same reality.

Kieślowski as a religious director? His theological credo can be found in *Blind Chance*, where the young protagonist in one of the hypothetical variants of his fate – as a newly baptized Catholic and member of an opposition movement – prays: "God, now that everything has already taken place, I ask only that you be!" According to Costica Bradatan, an American scholar of Romanian descent, the sense of the prayer "God, be!" depends on "creating a place for God who is not yet here."[2] This place must remain empty, occupied by no one. The filmic "theology" of Kieślowski is thus turned towards the future, not as a lament over the "death of God" but as a preparation for a God not yet born. In this manner, Kieślowski builds solidarity with an audience from which no one is excluded.

Against the background of Poland during the 1970s and 1980s – a bipolar world limited by ideology on the one side and by religion on the other – Kieślowski's position was separate and not always understood. It was treated in political categories, whereas he was already post-political. He remained opposed to communism, but he also distanced himself from all mass, revolutionary social movements. Although he was the director of *The Decalogue*, he refused to be locked in by religious formulas. He kept his distance from Catholicism; religious in his own way, he did not identify with any specific church.

In one of his masterworks, the documentary survey *Gadające głowy* (Talking Heads, 1980), the director asks forty-four people, from a one-year-old child to a hundred-year-old woman, two questions: "Who are you?" and "What would you wish for?" A priest answers: "I am on the precipice of two mysteries, for on the one hand there is a natural reality – the fact that I am human. The other reality, however, in which I am deeply rooted, concerns matters of faith. And this brings me great joy and great happiness, to me personally as well as to others, by virtue of the fact that I can help them to be better, to be happier." In this declaration about the double-character of reality that enlarges human freedom and allows a new solidarity to develop, it is possible to notice an idea held dear by Kieślowski himself, as long as the word (religious) "faith" is replaced with the word "cinema." *Talking Heads* is an excellent example of a compositional method used by the director in both documentary and feature films: the film begins as a sociological survey but becomes a short treatise on mankind. People representative of the entire social spectrum of contemporary Poland, each in his or her way, generate hope that may be illusory but without which life loses its meaning. In a way, *Talking Heads* come together into the figure of a single, collective human being.

The gesture of connecting characters appears to be a key to Kieślowski's cinema. A certain characteristic visual motif recurs in his films, for instance at the end of *Decalogue* (2) and in the final scenes of *Three Colours: Blue*. In a single take, complicated camerawork brings together the drama's separated protagonists, binding them to one another (in the case of the latter film, the scene is accompanied by a hymn about love) while grasping the drama from a transcendental perspective.

Krzysztof Piesiewicz (b. 1945) The meeting between Krzysztof Piesiewicz and Krzysztof Kieślowski in 1982 was a turning point in the life of both men. Piesiewicz was a defence attorney at the state trials of "Solidarity" activists during the martial law regime. Kieślowski wanted to film these proceedings, but his only success in this instance was that he began an enduring friendship with Piesiewicz. Seeing that Piesiewicz did not completely fit the role of a lawyer and that he perceived life in terms of drama, Kieślowski asked him whether he wanted to become an artist. It was their friendly conversations, confessions, and arguments that provided the director with screenplay materials for *No End*, *Decalogue*, *The Double Life of Veronique*, and *Three Colours* (seventeen screenplays in the course of a decade). These stories were told in an innovative manner, through "splashes" that brought into confrontation different planes of reality, including metaphysics. They expressed moral dilemmas that could not be resolved, reflecting Piesiewicz's experiences with the law as well as his opposition to the death penalty. Despite Piesiewicz's public engagement – he was one of the prosecutors in the case against the murderers of the priest Jerzy Popiełuszko in 1984, and became a senator after 1989 – the films that he made with Kieślowski were programmatically apolitical and areligious. They went against Poland's patriotic and religious fervour and opposed a world divided into "them" and "us." Kieślowski's decision to retire from cinema and his subsequent premature death were heavy blows for Piesiewicz. The screenplays that he started with Kieślowski and finished on his own were not successful. Moreover, his political career as a senator was ended by a criminal provocation that was meant to disgrace him and was possibly an act of political revenge.

In Kieślowski's work, the foundational issue of religion, namely the communion of man with God that gives significance to initiation rituals by allowing participants to discover their unity with others, is expressed through the cinematic phenomenon of projection and identification – the ability of the viewer to "incarnate" another person on the screen. The protagonists of *The Double Life of Veronique*, *Three Colours: Blue*, and *Three Colours: Red* begin to look at the world through another's eyes, and different characters interpenetrate each other. In *Three Colours: Red*, the camera – like the eye of a director, who is represented in this film by the Judge – joins together two strangers. In this manner, the old Judge "interpenetrates" young Auguste, who experiences a love that the Judge himself did not live through. *The Double Life of Veronique* poses questions at the border between science fiction and philosophy: Do human duplicates exist? Can people take the place of other people? Do I and this other constitute a unity? "Are you I?"

In his masterwork *Blind Chance*, Kieślowski throws down the gauntlet on his divided homeland and, in a sense, bids it farewell. He first forces young Witek, with whom he identifies, to live through two parallel variants of his fate. As chance would have it, in each instance Witek finds himself on the opposite side of the socio-political barricade while maintaining the same integrity: one time he is a young communist-reformer, the other a Catholic dissident. Only the third, most courageous variant, however, in which Witek remains himself, really happens. This does not mean that he rebels against the system. To the contrary, he already knows that he cannot allow himself to become involved: he becomes an apolitical doctor.

In each variant of this "game," a death in an airplane catastrophe awaits Witek; in each one he is also unjustly accused of treason. Is there no prize to be won? The terrifying scream "No!" fills the screen in the scene where the plane catastrophe is shown, but the message is found elsewhere in the film. Seemingly by chance, Kieślowski juxtaposes an image of a dying old woman who is visited by Witek-the-doctor with that of jugglers practising in her courtyard. They perform their circus act with such perfection that no one in the world can equal them. In this moment, Witek/Kieślowski reaches the fullness of experience; he sees the world as it is, with all of its suffering, which is no longer masked by any ideology. This juxtaposition of disinterested perfection with suffering, death, and the absurd is very telling. In such company, perfection does not lose its value or sense, and it is towards such perfection that Kieślowski strove in his films.

Tadeusz Sobolewski
Cultural Critic, Poland
Translated by Agnieszka Polakowska

NOTES

1 Kieślowski, "Głęboko zamiast szeroko."
2 Bradatan, "The Terror of History," 177–96. Reprint: "On Transcendence and History," 425–46.

WORKS CITED

Bradatan, Costica. "The Terror of History in Krzysztof Kieslowski's Blind Chance." In *Kino polskie – interpretacje: historia – ideologia – polityka*. Translated by Tomasz Kłys, edited by Ewelina Nurczyńska and Konrad Klejsa. 177–96. Łódz: Wydawnictwo Uniwersytetu Łódzkiego, 2008.

– "On Transcendence and History in Krzysztof Kieslowski's Blind Chance." *East European Politics and Societies* 22, no. 2 (2008): 425–46.

Kieślowski, Krzysztof. "Głęboko zamiast szeroko." *Dialog* 26, no. 1 (1981): 109–11.

Sobociński, Piotr. "Sfilmowane déjà vu." *Kino* 315 (September 1993): 22–3, 46.

Sowińska-Rammel, Iwona. "Czułe miejsca. O muzyce w filmach Kieślowskiego." In *Kino Krzysztofa Kieślowskiego*. Edited by Tadeusz Lubelski. 153–61. Kraków: Universitas, 1997.

Not Quite *Alla Polacca* (Wojciech Jerzy Has)

Luis Bunuel, a master of cinematic Surrealism, was fascinated by Wojciech Jerzy Has's *Rękopis znaleziony w Saragossie* (The Saragossa Manuscript, 1964). Francis Ford Coppola and Martin Scorsese, after watching the same film, considered its director to be a "painter of cult cinema."[1] Jerry Garcia, the lead singer of The Grateful Dead, associated Has's film with an acid trip.[2]

The cinema of Wojciech Has (1925–2000) is a remarkable phenomenon that engages and challenges key traditions in the medium. From the traditions of Polish cinema he inherited his preoccupation with literature; from the Polish film school, of which some of his films are considered to be a part, he adopted the "thinking image," that is, a way of visualizing of meaning that simultaneously limits reliance on words. He employed these thinking images in order to outsmart the censors – a way to express visually what could not be expressed verbally.[3] Among other innovations was his non-declarative approach to history. Has was interested in characters who experience politics "between the kitchen and the living room," as Maciek (Zbigniew Cybulski) puts it in *Szyfry* (The Codes, 1966). His films also tend to emphasize the value of an epistemological quest, in which the heroes of his films engage at all costs. And finally, his female characters are both enigmatic and captivating.

During the German Occupation, Has studied at the underground Academy of Fine Arts in Kraków, where he attended the classes of the well-known Polish modernist painter Józef Mehoffer (1869–1946), among others.[4] After the war, he graduated from the Academy of Fine Arts and the Prafilmòwka (literally, Pre-Film School), a year-long introductory course in filmmaking. Contrary to expectations, it was literature and not visual arts that Has claimed as his main source of inspiration: "My idea of film making comes from literature. Visual arts did not have a significant influence. What counts foremost is the desire to translate into image that layer of literature that is not cinematic."[5] Throughout his career he adapted a wide variety of literary texts, including the novel on which *The Saragossa Manuscript* is based; written in French by Jan Potocki (1761–1815), a Polish eighteenth-century aristocrat, it was first published in Polish translation in 1847. Among other Polish authors who caught Has's cinematic eye were Bolesław Prus (1847–1912), Poland's greatest nineteenth-century novelist (*Lalka* [Doll, 1968]); Bruno Schulz (1892–1942), the Polish-Jewish visionary of the interwar period (*Sanatorium pod Klepsydrą* [The Hourglass Sanatorium, 1973]); and the "young, angry" Marek Hłasko (1934–69) (*Pętla* [The Noose, 1957]). Has also adapted Anton Chekhov (*Nieciekawa historia* [An Uneventful Story, 1982]) and James Hogg (*Osobisty pamiętnik grzesznika przez niego samego spisany* [Memoirs of a Sinner, 1985]). For all of his work with film adaptation, critics, such as Alicja Helman, see Has as creatively unfaithful to literature, pointing out that he greatly deviated from literary texts and filtered the experience of literature through the sensibility of a painter and the temperament of a filmmaker.[6]

> Adaptation is adaptation. I have no regard for literalism. Generally, it is faithfulness to the Author's intentions that counts. The changes that are made in the process of transferring a literary work to the screen do not affect the work itself. They do not damage the original. It continues to exist in an unchanged form. Film is an inscription of happening, an inscription of actions. You have to look at something, see something.
>
> – Wojciech Has, cited in Kornatowska, "Nie lubię niespodzianek na planie," 64–5

Thus, *The Hourglass Sanatorium* is not only a screen adaptation of Schulz's world but also a cinematic story about the necessity of radically altering one's optics in order to enter Jewish culture. Access to this culture appeared irrevocably lost to Polish society after the events of 1968, a year when, as a consequence of the anti-Semitic smear campaign that arose from frictions and shuffles within the party leadership, many intellectuals and artists of Jewish descent left Poland.[7] Has paid for his stubborn interest in this "ideologically unsound" subject matter and for his attempt to restore and recall Jewish culture – an unerasable element of Polish culture – with several years of silence.[8] Following *The Hourglass Sanatorium*, his next film – *An Uneventful Story* – premiered only in 1983. Has never made political films *per se*, although in his own way he voiced his opinions about issues he considered important. In such films as *Pożegnania* (Farewells, 1958), *Jak być kochaną* (How to Be Loved, 1962) and *The Codes*, he privileged the intimate and the private over the general and the historical, a move atypical for the Polish film school current to which these films belong.

A similar approach to Has's adaptation of literature in *The Sanatorium* appears in *Saragossa Manuscript,* although in this case the film becomes a philosophical essay about the quest for knowledge pursued even at the risk of dangerously blurring the boundaries between dreams and reality. The main character, Alfons van Worden (played by Zbigniew Cybulski, a cult Polish actor of the time), a captain in the Wallonian Guard, is beguiled by Mauretian princesses and the sheik of Gomelez and accepts the challenges of such a quest. In his debut film, *The Noose*, Has turns a literary account of an alcoholic's demise into a tale of premeditated self-destruction. Kuba (Gustaw Holubek, who, like Zbigniew Cybulski, created his most interesting roles under Has's direction) commits suicide not because he cannot stop drinking but because he has no one to live for. Even his lover, Krystyna (the icy Aleksandra Śląska), does not believe in him anymore and treats him as excuse for charity rather than as a source of passion. Indeed, there is little passion in Has's world, and love does not brings much good either.

> Looking at … Has' films, the spectator must take the position of the viewer of a painting, who is first struck by the *otherness*, the subjectivism of the vision of the world represented

> on canvas, and only later by the similarities ... A film by Has can be assimilated or rejected, but it cannot be received on the same principle that is used in watching thousands of well-made films. Has' films are created on the same principle as a poem, essay, or a painting – they demand of the spectator a certain specific ability in deciphering the image, and cannot be treated as all other films.
>
> – Eberhardt, *Wojciech Has*, 6–7

Has's cinema is one of thinking images, in which what matters most is translated into visual rather than verbal imagery – it is shown rather than told. In one instance, it is the reflection in a mirror in which van Worden sees his own self. In another, it is the dead eye-pupils of the conductor on the train on which the main character of the *Sanatorium*, Józef, is travelling, which portend that the world he is about to enter is neither entirely visible nor fully alive. And in *The Noose*, it is the tangle of tracks and streetcar routes that reflects Kuba's entanglement and reveals the impossibility of living in such reality. The most verbal of Has's films is *How to Be Loved*. In an internal monologue lasting more than ninety minutes, Felicja (played by Barbara Krafftówna), relates her story of unfulfilled love. Felicja is an actress whose theatrical debut in the role of Ophelia has been made impossible by the war. Her devastating experiences and emotional disillusionments enable Has to show wartime history "between the kitchen and the living room."

In *How to Be Loved*, Felicja hides her beloved throughout the war, and in order to do so, she works in a German theatre, which marks her as a collaborator. She does this only to be told in the end that she has merely imprisoned her beloved, and that it is her fault that he cannot now be a good actor and has been branded "an informant during occupation," just as she has been branded "a whore." The past catches up with Felicja during her trip to Paris, where she is invited by a listener who is fascinated by a character she created for a radio play – radio is the only medium besides children's theatre in which she has been allowed to work since the war ended. She torments herself with memories that confirm that what she did was not worth it; but at the same time, she tells herself and wants to believe that "no one respects oneself when they truly love." She defines love as something between "nightly fallings onto cement" and "daily runs to fortune tellers."

Has was interested in precisely this aspect of history: the collision between politics at large and the private individual, who pays the highest price despite striving not for heroism, but for survival. The story of Felicja, who is crushed by the war and stripped of both intimacy and dignity, is contrasted in the film with a story of an RAF pilot, who dispenses platitudes about "being in one's own place." Yet in the end he too is revealed to be a broken man – for unknown reasons, his son has committed suicide. In Has's world, no one really is happy. In *How to Be Loved*, one can find everything that differentiates the cinema of Has from all other Polish films of that time – an interest in the collision between the private and the historical (and advocacy for the first); juxtaposition of life under the Nazi occupation with the wartime experience of those living in different circumstances, for whom the absurdity of some conspiratorial situations is inpenetrable; focus on the individual, and on politics and history only insofar as they interfere in human lives; and a highly self-aware heroine.

Has largely created women's cinema. His heroines are stronger than his heroes – they can withstand more, as Felicja does in dealing first the poverty of wartime and then with the humiliating postwar condemnation of her colleagues. In *Wspólny pokój* (Shared Room, 1959), Teodozja (Beata Tyszkiewicz) fights for the life of her sick lover and adamantly believes in his recovery until the end. Lidka (Maja Wachowiak) from *Farewells* will weather even the regime change and will not be frightened by the Bolsheviks; although she knows "it will not be much fun,"[9] she will take care of herself and the boy now reunited with her, whom she knew before the war.

The women of Has's cinema also know more: like the heroines of *Saragossa Manuscript*, the mistresses of ceremony and the organizers of van Worden's initiation; like Mrs Wąsowska in *The Doll*, who is reconciled to the fact that she will not be loved by the one she wants, but is by the same token convinced of her freedom; and like Magdalena from *Farewells*, who is aware that the past cannot be corrected. It is not surprising, in fact, that Has's women know more, for in his world they symbolize death. This is particularly true of heroines in films made after *The Hourglass Sanatorium*. Such representation of women echoes the modernist *topos*, in which Eros and Thanatos are inextricably linked and together have a face of a woman.

Has made History writ large accessible and his heroes humane through the conventions of melodrama (in *Farewells* and *How to Be Loved*) or of a thriller (as in *The Codes*). It was only after 1989 that Polish cinema started to catch up on "Has's lesson."[10] In describing Has's work, scholars often use terms such as Expressionism, Onirism, Surrealism, or Existentialism, but all of these labels should be treated only as suggestions. The cinema of Has is of autonomous value – it can be understood and delighted in without knowledge of its literary prototypes. For in Has's case, two temperaments – of a man of word and of a man of image – were confronted with each another. Despite the artist's own reservations, his films prove that the latter (after all) has won.

Katarzyna Taras
Cardinal Stefan Wyszyński University, Warsaw
Translated by Agnieszka Polakowska

NOTES

1 Grodź, *Katalog Międzynarodowego*, 410.
2 Kornatowska, "Niezwykłe podróże Wojciecha Hasa," v.
3 A good example of this practice is the famous take of shot glasses filled with distilled alcohol and set aflame in Andrzej Wajda's *Popiół i diament* (Ashes and Diamonds), which is denoted in the screenplay as the eating of herring salad. As mentioned by Janusz Morgenstern in Tadeusz Bystram's and Stanisław Zawiśliński's documentary film *Między prawdą a wyobraźnią. Opowieści twórców polskiej szkoły filmowej*.
4 Słodowski, Wijata, *Rupieciarnia marzeń*, 6–7. Has's sensitivity to female characters, their beauty and emotions, may have something to do with the influence of Mehoffer's famous paintings of women.
5 Ibid., 52.
6 Helman, *Twórcza zdrada*, 1998.
7 The moment of intensification of anti-Semitic feelings and the atmosphere of all-encompassing suspicions are represented in Jan Kidawa-Błoński's film *Różyczka* (Little Rose, 2010). *Little Rose* is influenced by Has's approach to the relationship between cinema and

Polish history and follows Has's precepts to project the historical upon the personal. In the case of *Little Rose* such projections takes the form of melodrama.

8 "I had to fall silent for eight years despite having plenty of projects. It was a work accident, so to speak. I do not want to comment upon it since I do not like having a crown of thorns pressed upon my head" (Słodowski and Wijata, *Rupieciarnia marzeń*, 12).

9 Ibid., 6.

10 Proof that the lesson has been diligently made up for are Waldemar Krzystek's *Mała Moskwa* (Little Moscow, 2008), Borys Lankosz's *Rewers* (Reverse, 2009), the already mentioned *Little Rose*, Jan Jakub Kolski's *Wenecja* (Venice, 2010), and finally Wojciech Smarzowski's *Róża* (Rose, 2011).

WORKS CITED

Eberhardt, Konrad. *Wojciech Has*. Warszawa: WAiF, 1967.

Grodź, Iwona. *Katalog Międzynarodowego Festiwalu Filmowego Era Nowe Horyzonty*, 22 July–1 August 2010.

Helman, Alicja. *Twórcza zdrada. Filmowe adaptacje literatury*. Poznań: Ars Nova, 1998.

Kornatowska, Maria. "'Nie lubię niespodzianek na planie' – conversation with W.J. Has." In *Debiuty polskiego kina*. Edited by Marek Hendrykowski. Konin: Przegląd koniński, 1998.

– "Niezwykłe podróże Wojciecha Hasa." In *Era Nowe Horyzonty. Międzynarodowy Festiwal Filmowy Wrocław* 22 July–1 August 2010. Twórcy z charakterem [free supplement *Charaktery*].

Słodowski, Jan, and Tadeusz Wijata. *Rupieciarnia marzeń*. Warszawa: Skorpion, 1994.

Poetry of the Discarded (Dorota Kędzierzawska)

When we walk nondescript streets gazing at decrepit buildings with paint peeling from walls lit by warm, yellowish light, or we enter the ugly interiors of provincial Polish towns following runaway boys and girls who are somehow managing to preserve their innocence, or when we peep into an old woman's dilapidated house and catch her conversing happily with her dog, we are in the world of Dorota Kędzierzawska (b. 1957), one of the outstanding Polish film directors of the past two decades. Coming of age in the late 1970s, she belongs to the generation of filmmakers who experienced communism but whose careers began in the post-communist Poland of the 1990s. She enrolled in Cultural Studies at Łódź University (1976–8) and then studied directing at the Moscow Film School (WGIK) and the Łódź Film School (1981–5). So far, her major feature films include *Koniec świata* (The End of The World, 1988), *Diabły, diabły* (Devils, Devils, 1991), *Wrony* (Crows, 1994), *Nic* (Nothing, 1998), *Jestem* (I Am, 2005), *Pora umierać* (Time to Die, 2007), *Jutro będzie lepiej* (Tomorrow Will Be Better, 2010), and a biographical documentary *Inny świat* (Another World, 2012).

Together with Agnieszka Holland (b. 1948), Barbara Sass (1936–2015), Urszula Urbaniak (b. 1962), Magdalena Łazarkiewicz (b. 1954), and a few others, Kędzierzawska is one of the few women directors in the still male-dominated Polish cinema.[1] Her authorial style and cinematic interests, however, make her a truly unique voice among all contemporary Polish filmmakers. The hallmarks of her style are captivating images, lingering narratives, sparse dialogue, extraordinary use of colour, slow tempo, focus on detail, and intimate camerawork. The quality of her films that defines her artistic position is the urge to foreground socially marginalized groups. The director observes the world from local vantage points – from a village somewhere in the Polish countryside (*Devils, Devils*), a provincial town (*Crows*), or an old house (*Time to Die*). All her protagonists occupy marginal positions in society, whether it is an orphanage runaway in *I Am*, an old woman in *Time to Die*, or a girl drawn to a group of Romani, as well as the Romani themselves, in *Devils, Devils*.

Kędzierzawska's films deal with deeply rooted social, generational, ethnic, and gender prejudices, suppressed and treated as taboos by Polish culture. They depart from the history-oriented, heroic, and patriarchal traditions of most postwar Polish cinema characterized by Romantic heroism, as it is manifested in the works of such iconic Polish filmmakers as Andrzej Wajda (1926–2016). Kędzierzawska resists the system of cultural values that prioritizes the "higher good" and a grand historical narrative over the individual. She prefers to highlight individual needs and local spaces. Her artistic vision privileges the non-heroic mode, which she expresses through slow, aleatory, lingering story lines, care for detail, openness of the film frame, and use of non-professional actors. Her photographic effects, including her masterful structuring of every scene and colours that are often dimmed and diluted with warm, grainy overtones, result from her cooperation with Arthur Reinhart (b. 1965), who has been the director of photography for almost all her films (apart from *Devils, Devils*, filmed by Zdzisław Najda). Reinhart's cinematography enhances the individualistic and authorial character of her films. In their statement on Kid Film, their website, they stress the aesthetic and artistic quality of cinema.[2] And indeed, visual perfection, the meticulous treatment of detail, rhythm, timing, and music, and the director's ability to work with professional and non-professional (child and adult) actors all contribute to the striking quality of their work together.

The interplay of light and shadows creates the *chiaroscuro* effect, deepening the intensity of each frame both in landscape shots and in character close-ups. The light effects (as in the city shots of *Crows*) that enhance or obliterate the detail in the frame, together with unusual camera angles, create an intimate connection between the viewer and the image on the screen. At the same time, the interplay of light and shadow estranges the characters and enhances their sense of alienation. Light and dark effects such as the moon shining on a boat against the almost palpable dark blue sky (*I Am*) and the silhouettes of two little girls on a seashore (*Crows*) contribute to Kędzierzawska and Reinhart's unsurpassed cinematic aesthetics of eerie beauty reminiscent of Caspar David Friedrich's paintings.

In Kędzierzawska's work, narratives are usually uncomplicated and executed through slow and meandering action. In *Devils, Devils*, for instance, things happen, but as Ewa Mazierska points out, the film's "main stylistic method [is that of] fragmentation."[3] Many other films (such as *Time to Die* and *Tomorrow Will Be Better*) can be approached as cinematic poems or ballads. In *Crows*, Kędzierzawska's second full-length feature, the story is simple: an older girl kidnaps a little girl for a day in order to play "mother" and fulfil her need for love and care. Yet neither the action nor the dialogue drives the narrative, and the film is really composed like a long poem in blank verse made of individual scenes, images, and sounds.

The director embraces slowness, minimalist dialogue, and long periods of silence, employing language as an artistic tool rather than as a driving force of communication and action. She inscribes its idiosyncratic features as a part of the characters' individuality (as in *Devils*), but she also explores the emotive and poetic functions of language relating to atmosphere, feelings, and mood, thus building a broader non-verbal milieu.[4] Verbal exchanges function mostly as sound, contributing to the overall atmosphere of each film. We often do not hear full, meaningful utterances, but only scraps of sentences, disjointed, blurred mumblings, and murmurs. Maleństwo, the little three-year-old girl from *Crows*, speaks her own baby talk, which is often not fully comprehensible. Often the very physicality of language production and the corresponding emotional charge is what matters in the film. Kundel (Mongrel) from *I Am* communicates with his girlfriend in a hushed tone, and we do not hear full sentences. It is not *what* is said, but *how* it is said – the tone of voice, along with facial expressions, gestures, and emotions – that carries meaning. *Time to Die* explores still another communicative situation that does not require a human subject at all: the dog is almost the sole interlocutor of "Granny," and they communicate effectively and lovingly, but the dog, of course, uses no human language. The paraphernalia of speech and the very fact of making contact matter more than the strict "message" contained in words.

By challenging customary forms of expression, Kędzierzawska's films test the viewer's participatory potential and expectations. The lack of traditional dialogue and action brings to the fore structural elements of the narrative, including the object/subject relationship, the composition of scenes, and colour, mood, and detail, thus demanding more interaction from the viewer. The Kid Film website declares that "addressing sensitive and 'seeking' spectators" is its mission.[5] By contrasting the aesthetic and emotional content of the screen narrative, the director creates the effect of incongruity as a form of estrangement, thus inviting her audience to willingly engage in a different, indeterminate, and more emotional mode of communication.

Such was the case with one of the most journalistic of Kędzierzawska's films, *Nothing*, which addresses the problem of abortion and the responsibility for newly created life. The untranslatability of the main female character's emotions – triggered by a failed abortion that led her to kill her newborn child – led to many misunderstandings in the film's reception, especially among male critics.[6] In court, when asked to explain her deed, the protagonist Hela provides only this answer: "Nothing." And indeed, no language can express her struggle and humiliation in the face of an indifferent society, unjust laws, and a male jury that is unwilling to understand her predicament. No explanation would matter anyway. Thus, the climactic moment of the film descends into a heavy and foreboding silence.

The untranslatability of the protagonist's experience is amplified in *Nothing* by the tension between the aesthetic and narrative realms. The photography, even when the camera slides over the crumbling walls of an apartment building, creates an unusual aesthetic effect. Equally admirable are the *chiaroscuro* effects bringing forth various hues of brown, with only occasional streaks of light enhancing the pregnant woman's sombre mood of entrapment, anguish, and despair. Thus through the interplay between the hopelessness of the situation and the sublime beauty of the photography, the film, especially in its final sequences, strikes a deeply tragic cord.

The tension permeating Kędzierzawska's cinematic narratives is often created by an emphasis on detail. One of the best examples is *Time to Die*, a film about an elderly woman living alone in an old house on the outskirts of a town. The black-and-white photography and the meticulous camerawork full of close-ups contribute to the almost documentary quality of the film. In the opening scene, the camera moves very slowly over the face of Danuta Szaflarska (1915–2017), an iconic Polish actress, who at the age of ninety-two plays the main character, "Granny." It traces the deep lines on her face and her white hair. When amidst the wrinkles it pauses on her eyes, they do not express fatigue or the lack of will to live, as could be expected; on the contrary, they project vividness, perceptiveness, and spark. The whole face radiates an unusual, unforgettable beauty.

> **Photosensitive Poland** is a project that promotes ambitious Polish "auteur" films in places where, without us, such films never would have gone (i.e., where there are no movie theatres). It's a shame that the network of small theatres has disappeared from the Polish map. Every one of those small cinemas had its own aura. Films were shown morning to evening, as long as there were at least three viewers at each screening. Sometimes you had to buy three tickets for them to show the film … I remember how in high school and college we would go to the screenings in a big group and then afterwards discuss the films for quite a while … It seems to us that the viewers of "Photosensitive Poland" are really the truest type of audience: they are thirsty for a good film, they have greater energy and desire for

discussion. And they talk honestly ... These screenings are basically like family gatherings – totally different from the atmosphere of meetings with audiences at the festivals, where practically no one knows anyone else. In these small towns and villages people know one another, they get together. Sometimes during post-film discussions very personal issues come up. The same questions never appear twice; every conversation is different, has a different temperature. The comments and reflections expressed during these discussions are really incredibly insightful. This audience often notices things that critics don't.

http://www.dwutygodnik.com/artykul/4292-zeby-nie-narzekac.html

An overarching question that Kędzierzawska addresses in all her films is that of otherness. Starting with her first full-length feature, *Devils, Devils*, and its leading character Mała (Little One), most of her main protagonists such as Wrona (Crow) from *Crows*, Kundel (Mongrel) from *I Am*, Hela from *Nothing*, an old woman from *Time to Die*, and the three boys from *Tomorrow Will Be Better* are the ultimate Others – they are rejected by society and also accept their predicament. Thus otherness becomes their only form of being in the society. At the same time, by accepting their otherness they remain free in a deep existential sense. When in the very last sequence of *I am* Kundel is asked "Man, what are you doing in this world?," he thoughtfully answers: "I am." Kundel and other characters confront the questions of freedom on a more mundane level as well, by breaking free of the strict social order and unjust laws, traditions, habits of reasoning, and confined spaces that limit their physical and personal freedom. Many are on the run or are literally runaways, but again they embrace that state as one more attribute of their otherness.

As a filmmaker, Kędzierzawska consistently chooses the margin or the edge, as Tony Judt puts it,[7] and in order to be heard, whether as a woman-director or a concerned artist, she remains there on principle. The main feature of that margin is its indefinability. Like Kędzierzawska's dim, blurred film frames, the margin represents the state of diffusion and murkiness; it opposes "the world proposed by TV soap operas" and does "not want to give easy answers."[8] Kędzierzawska's films relentlessly remind their audiences that the greatest threat to freedom is to be engulfed by the mainstream. So in order to retain one's voice one must speak from the margin. From that position she has been incessantly posing difficult but at the same time fundamental questions about the relationship of Polish post-communist society (or any other society) to its own deeply suppressed cultural issues, which include xenophobia, poverty, greed, religion, selfishness, all forms of social exploitation (especially child and family abuse), and the position of such institutions as church, family, and school in society.

Krystyna Iłłakowicz
Yale University

NOTES

1 In her excellent study of Kędzierzawska, Ewa Mazierska calls her an "ambivalent feminist" and quotes numerous statements by the director in which Kędzierzawska positions herself outside

the discourse of feminism. Mazierska states that "when [she] interviewed [Kędzierzawska] in the summer of 1999 she was utterly dismissive of the concept of women's cinema, claiming that she neither understood what 'woman's' cinema means, nor had any particular interest in or knowledge of films made by fellow women artists." Mazierska, "Dorota Kędzierzawska: Ambivalent Feminist," 204–5.

2 "About Us." *Kid Film*, http://kidfilm.businesscatalyst.com/.

3 Mazierska, "Dorota Kędzierzawska," 210.

4 On the functions of language, see Jacobson, "Linguistics and Poetics."

5 "About Us." *Kid Film*.

6 See Horton, "New Perspectives on European Film."

7 See Judt, "Edge People," 102.

8 "About Us." *Kid Film*.

WORKS CITED

"About Us." *Kid Film*. http://kidfilm.businesscatalyst.com.

Horton, Andrew James. [home page]. *Kinoeye: New Perspectives on European Film*. 2001–11. http://www.kinoeye.org.

Jakobson, Roman. "Linguistics and Poetics." In *Style in Language*. Edited by Thomas Sebeok. 350–77. Cambridge, MA: MIT Press, 1960.

Judt, Tony. "Edge People." *New York Review of Books*. 60, no 17 (2013): n.p.

Mazierska, Ewa. "Dorota Kędzierzawska: Ambivalent Feminist." In *Women in Polish Cinema*. Edited by Ewa Mazierska and Elżbieta Ostrowska. 205–20. New York: Berghan Books, 2006.

Popular Culture in Poland

What Is Popular Culture?

In *Inventing Popular Culture*, John Storey calls attention to two significant issues that help us understand what popular culture means. First, the meaning of this social category changes in relation to who we include in it and what role we assign to it in social life. Second, *popular culture* is a concept created not by the people but by intellectuals. Moreover, it is a concept created not in order to describe the life of the people but rather in order to produce this social category, negotiate its status, and enforce the way it is perceived.[1]

Treating Storey's remarks as an appeal for a more ideologically neutral and descriptive definition of popular culture, one can attempt to define the concept through the category of *popularity*. For something to be popular, it has to fulfil a number of conditions. To begin with, it needs to be commonly known, which is to say that it depends on both mass and network communication media. Another aspect of popularity is voluntariness, that is, the right to choose, but also the ability to make choices. These abilities are the result of life's democratization and of achieving such a level of fulfilment of needs that they no longer impose themselves as absolute necessities. Yet another aspect of popularity is polyfunctionality; in other words, what becomes popular is viewed as having diverse meanings and significance, such that it can be used in many different ways.

Doda (stage name of Dorota Rabczewska, b. 1984) is a *polyfunctional* and thus extremely popular singer in Poland. For some people she is a remarkable vocalist, for others a sexual object; for others still she is living proof that the American Dream is real and accessible to everyone. Yet another part of her audience sees her as the embodiment of kitsch and bad taste and as the strongest evidence for the increasing moral decay of entertainment.

The next aspect is closely linked with the last one – what becomes popular is universal enough to allow individuals to communicate their own distinctiveness and to understand the differences of others. The existence of this tool of (self-)discovery appears to be necessary in complex, diversified societies looking for effective means of making key differentiations that enable people to move and act effectively within a given reality. The final aspect of popularity is that it must be capable of delivering diversified pleasures.

Pleasure, as Roland Barthes notes, appears where the individual experiences satisfaction sourced in the control of both the desire and the means of its fulfillment.[2] The category of pleasure and the earlier noted aspects of popularity make it clear that popular culture is a modern phenomenon, present only in modernized societies. For only in such societies do individuals have choices and the necessary means for making them; only in such societies are they obligated to be subjects and thus to control their behaviour and surroundings; and only in such societies does the experience of pleasure become an important social obligation.

Popular culture: a type of culture that provides diversified pleasures to socially diverse individuals. The conditions of the delivery of such pleasures are the universal recognizability and polyfunctionality of its goods, the freedom to use them, and the possibility of expressing oneself through them in a way that is understandable to others.

Development of Popular Culture in Poland

The development of popular culture in Poland had a specific and somewhat different character than it did in the West. Decisive in this respect were primarily factors political in nature (such as extended periods of oppression in the nineteenth and twentieth centuries, including the partitions and the Second World War, and the dominance of socialist doctrine in the postwar period), as well as delayed (in part due to these factors) social modernization. The specific structure of Polish society also played a significant role in this development. It had a predominantly peasant character in the prewar years, then underwent several transformations in the postwar period as capitalism gave way to socialism, which flipped, often recklessly, back to capitalism after 1989. Except for short periods of relative prosperity, Polish society functioned in a state of permanent scarcity, and this too had a strong impact on how its popular culture developed. The priorities were to build the infrastructure for a functioning society and to fight for everyday survival. By necessity, leisure time and entertainment mattered less – which does not mean, however, that these aspects of life did not matter to Poles.

The character of Polish popular culture was also determined by its functioning within a state that not only lacked society's approval but was treated by that society as an opponent. During the partitions, Poland was ruled by three foreign powers: Russia, Prussia, and Austria-Hungary; during the Second World War it was occupied by Germany and the Soviet Union; and after the war, against the wishes and convictions of many Poles and by forcible means, it became a socialist state. As a consequence of all this, the official version of popular culture became a vital tool of propaganda – put another way, culture was something directed *against* the masses. Having to function within antagonistic political systems, in turn, led to a peculiar duality of social life, which was supported by one set of rules and values in the private sphere and by another in the public one. This dimorphism produced a duality also in popular culture. A cultural current evolved that did not require the mediation of mass media; instead it took the form of subversive fashions, contestation of customs, and urban folklore, and spread through word of mouth and other private channels.

The last driver of popular culture in Poland worth noting here is the selective isolation of Polish society, especially during the socialist period. This isolation stemmed from strict controls on cross-border movements, the monopoly of state institutions over the exchange of cultural goods, and censorship. All of this, combined with the enmity of a large part of society towards the socialist system, culminated in a paradoxical phenomenon: an unconditional love for all that was Western, and in particular for American pop culture. This love manifested itself as an enthusiastic reception of everything from the West; a celebration of the smallest of its cultural goods, which were always obtained with difficulty through informal market exchanges; and a well-developed market, also within the official economic system, for substitutes for Western cultural products.

Prewar History of Popular Culture in Poland

Despite many differences between the development of popular culture in Poland and in the West, its initial phases were similar, albeit less dynamic and varied in Poland. At the turn of nineteenth and twentieth centuries, popular culture was the domain of two new social categories – namely, the bourgeoisie and the intelligentsia, and later also the lower-middle and working classes. The principal media of popular culture at this time were the press and literature, along with public entertainments such as theatre productions (including open-air ones, on café terraces and in marketplaces), curiosity shows (e.g., panopticons, waxworks, panoramas, and dioramas), circuses, fairs, and peepshows. Popular culture thrived in public places – for instance, in city gardens and parks (such as the Saxon Garden, the Krasiński Garden, and Royal Baths Park in Warsaw, and the Planty Park in Kraków), in cafès, confectionary shops, and restaurants, and in ballrooms and dance halls. These places popularized new fashions and provided individuals with opportunities to peek at the lives of others and to draw upon other models of behaviour and being. Cabarets were another important means for disseminating popular culture.

> The most important Polish **cabarets of the interwar period** were Kraków's Zielony Balonik (Green Balloon), founded in 1905 in Jan Michalik's café by Jan August Kisielewski and Tadeusz Boy-Żeleński, as well as Warsaw's Qui Pro Quo, established in 1919, whose stars included Eugeniusz Bodo, Hanka Ordonówna, Mieczysław Fogg, and Adolf Dymsza, with Julian Tuwim and Marian Hemar, among others, writing its texts.

Cinema was equally important to popular culture's development, instantly grabbing hold of Poles' imagination. The first permanent cinema was established towards the end of the 1890s in Łódź, but the real growth of cinemas came during the 1920s. By the time the Second World War broke out, there were almost nine hundred cinemas in Poland. Most of the earliest Polish films were adaptations of great works of Polish literature (for example, *Pan Tadeusz* [Sir Thaddeus]; *Moralność Pani Dulskiej* [The Morality of Mrs Dulska]; and *Ziemia Obiecana* [The Promised Land]); some, however, were pure entertainment (including *Ada, to nie wypada* [Ada, This Is Not Proper]; *Zapomniana Melodia* [Forgotten Melody]; *Czy Lucyna to dziewczyna?* [Is Lucy a Girl?], and many others). Radio was developing equally rapidly. Polish Radio broadcast its first program in 1925 and became an important channel for both information and entertainment. Also worth noting is the dynamic growth of the press – including the tabloid press, which trafficked in sensation – and of comic books.

The best example of **prewar comics** is the series about the adventures of Koziołek Matołek (Matołek the Billy-Goat), a character created by Kornel Makuszyński and Marian Walentynowicz. Launched in 1933, the comic narrated the world travels of the likable goat Matołek in search of Pacanów – supposedly a place where goats could get shoed – and has gone through many editions. It was also the basis for an animated series in the 1960s titled *Dziwne przygody Koziołka Matołka* (The Strange Adventures of Koziołek Matołek), and in 2010 a European Fairytale Capital bearing his name was created in Pacanów (Europejskie Centrum Bajki im. Koziołka Matołka).

The Second World War

For obvious reasons, entertainment was put on the back burner during the Nazi and Soviet occupation (1939–45). During those years, daily survival was paramount and there were no means to produce entertainment or to participate in it. Polish radio was forced off the air, and the population boycotted *en masse* the entertainment controlled by the Germans, the purpose of which was indoctrination. Yet popular culture did not cease to exist; instead, it took the form of political folklore that comforted and provided hope, and which was aimed against the occupiers. This was the role of the taunting songs performed by street singers and in private homes (some of which were preserved in Leonard Buczkowski's 1947 film *Zakazane piosenki* [Forbidden Songs]), of slogans and graffiti painted on city walls, of privately told jokes, and of satirical publications released by the underground state. The war meant, however, not only the destruction of infrastructure that made the production and distribution of cultural goods possible (especially printing presses, radio networks, and cinemas and theatres), but first and foremost the emigration or death of many outstanding artists and producers, as well as the loss or destruction of priceless cultural works.

Postwar Period (1945–1954)

Production novel (*produkcyjniak*): a derisive term for literary and film works created in Poland in the late 1940s and early 1950s. These works glorified the effort of building a socialist society and utilized black-and-white formulas that allowed readers/viewers to immediately recognize heroes and villains and that were supportive of the new order and critical of its alternatives. Among their shared characteristics were the setting of the action – usually a great building site or a factory – as well as didacticism with regard to instilling new attitudes and loyalty towards the socialist state. Some classic examples in film are *Dwie Brygady* (Two Brigades, 1950, production overseen by Eugeniusz Cękalski) and Maria Kaniewska's *Niedaleko Warszawy* [Close to Warsaw, 1954]), and, among novels,

Jan Wilczek's *Numer 16 produkuje* (Number 16 Produces, 1949), Witold Zalewski's *Traktory zdobędą wiosnę* (Tractors Will Conquer Spring, 1950), and Aleksander Ścibor-Rylski's *Węgiel* (Coal, 1950).

These years in Poland were mainly a time of accelerated modernization linked to the rebuilding of the country following the ravages of war, as well as to introduction of the new, socialist system. Except for a short period right after the war, socialist realism became the dominant aesthetic doctrine, and entertainment was subjected to its rules. Accordingly, culture became subservient to the economic system, and given that the purpose of socialist realism was to shape social consciousness, it turned into a tool of indoctrination and propaganda.

Quite clearly, then, the popular culture of this period was popular only in name. From the perspective of the monopolizing power, it was meant not to entertain but rather to support the creation of a new society. It thus included poems and songs that spurred people to work hard and that canonized as heroes those who exceeded work norms. It also generated iconic forms of propaganda, largely in the form of posters and murals, as well as new types of literature and film that later on would be scornfully named "production works" (*produkcyjniak*). Moreover, new means for disseminating culture were introduced, such as rallies, march-pasts, parades, commemorative gatherings, and theatre productions put on in factories. The point of all of this was to foster in individuals a sense of unity, shared fate, and membership in a wonderful new society. The popular culture of this time was usually devoid of aesthetic value, highly schematic, and simple enough for all to understand. It is worth noting, however, that the state, besides instrumentalizing culture, was engaged in activities that raised the cultural competencies of Poles through intensive educational initiatives and the creation of a cultural infrastructure. While undoubtedly positive in their effects, these processes also enabled cultural homogenization and denationalization, as well as the elimination of the multiculturalism that was so characteristic of prewar society in Poland.

The Thaw and the 1960s

A television signal was sent in Poland for the first time in October 1952, but only in 1961 were daily television broadcasts begun. A second television channel devoted exclusively to entertainment appeared in 1970 as Program Two.

The death of Joseph Stalin in 1953 began a slow retreat from the use of culture as a propaganda tool under the state's strict control. Although this loosening of state controls was interrupted several times (especially in 1968 and 1970), the principles of Stalinism were never to return. The authorities at the time, headed by Władysław Gomułka, engaged in a somewhat schizophrenic politics that allowed for greater freedom of world views and behaviours while trying to reroute society onto the socialist path. Consequently, this time is remembered for its heavy use of socialist buzzwords in the mass media, intensified visual propaganda in public spaces, and spectacles of hatred directed at people viewed as enemies of the system ("red diaper babies" [*bananowa młodzież* in the Polish context], revisionists, students, and Jews). It was also a time of significant changes in social customs and of greater scope for individual freedoms, however. The development of mass media, and in particular of television, was undoubtedly one of the more pertinent factors behind these transformations.

> During the communist years, the journal *Przekrój* (Cross-Cut) not only tried to inform its readers about significant issues in Western culture but also promoted ambitious literature and film, taught good manners, and made the newest fashions more accessible while also offering advice on how to obtain them in times of economic scarcity. This publication was undoubtedly responsible for fostering a uniquely Polish type of intelligentsia – namely, well-educated individuals who were culturally literate and active but who were also resigned to the system and, instead of trying to change it, "did their own thing."

Television became an important tool of propaganda, largely through news programs about ongoing successes in the construction of socialism. It also had a different side – an entertaining one. Various types of programs were on offer from the beginning, including advice shows aimed mainly at farmers but also at a general audience. Some of these programs achieved cult status (Adam Słodowski's *Zrób to sam* [Do It Yourself], for example). Audiences also enjoyed popular scientific programs (such as *Eureka*), ambitious cultural commentary (*Pegasus*), and the first talk show, *Tele-echo*, broadcast between 1962 and 1981 and hosted uninterruptedly by the charismatic Irena Dziedzic (b. 1925). Also popular were game shows like *Kółko i krzyżyk* (Tic Tac Toe) and *Wielka Gra* (The Great Play), the latter of which ran from 1962 to 2006. In a class of its own was a unique undertaking called *Teatr telewizji* (Television Theatre). Since its inception, its Monday evening broadcasts have created an archive of over more than 4,000 theatre productions. Theatre programming has also been enriched by *Teatr Sensacji "Kobra"* (Sensational Theatre "Cobra"), which has broadcast lightweight mysteries every Thursday since 1956, and by ambitious literary cabarets such as *Kabaret Starszych Panów* (Elderly Gentlemen's Cabaret), which broadcast from 1958 to 1966.

Television series were an important form of television at this time, and this led to the birth of celebrity culture. The most important of these series were war-themed shows such as *Czterech pancernych i pies* (Four Tankmen and a Dog), an adventure story about a fictional Rudy 102 tanker crew, and *Stawka większa niż życie* (Stakes Greater Than Life), about a Soviet mole in the German *Abwehr*, going under the alias J-23 and the name of Hans Kloss. These series attracted huge audiences, and although they distorted history and had a decidedly propagandistic character, they also provided expertly constructed stories that pulled the viewer in with fast action, vividly drawn characters, and attractive lead actors. The latter enjoyed star status, and children staged scenes from these famous shows in the course of backyard play.

The development of other media supportive of popular culture during this period should not be overlooked. Some of them were significant agents of modernization. The weekly magazine *Cross-Cut*, published since 1945, is most important in this context. Magazines with titles like *Przyjaciółka* (Girlfriend) and *Kobieta i życie* (Woman and Life) also played a modernizing role; directed primarily at housewives, they promoted new ways of managing a household and modern family models. Another notable medium in the development of popular culture was literature, especially of the less ambitious, pocketbook kind. An excellent example of such books is the famous *Seria z Tygrysem* (Series with a Tiger), published by the Ministry of National Defence since 1957, which in paperback format narrated selected episodes from the Second World War in a sensational manner.

The first mature manifestation of **jazz culture** in Poland was the International Jazz Festival, launched in 1956 in Sopot. Two years later the first Jazz Jamboree, a true jazz holiday that takes place annually to this day, was held in Warsaw. The International Jazz Festival in particular has left its mark on history, mainly because its 50,000-strong audience made up of young people manifested, for the first time, values openly different from socialist ones – individual freedom, individualism of lifestyle, and distaste for official culture.

A characteristic trait of this phase of popular culture was the explosion of culture created for and by youth, and focused initially around student life and jazz, and later around rock'n'roll, in Poland also called "bigbit."

The thaw years allowed contemporary jazz to escape the private and semi-private spaces in which it had functioned since the war. Although rock'n'roll was being played earlier in Poland, its first concert was performed by the group Rhythm and Blues (founded by Franciszek Walicki, the father of bigbit in Poland) on 24 March 1956 in the Rudy Kot (Ginger Cat) Club in Gdańsk. Initially, most of the songs played were covers first made famous by Western bands, but as this movement developed it became more musically and lyrically independent, resulting in the explosion of Polish "bigbit" groups and performers, such as Niebiesko-Czarni (Blue-Blacks), Polanie, Czerwone Gitary (Red Guitars), Skaldowie, Czerwono-Czarni (Red-and-Blacks), Karin Stanek, and No To Co (So What). This movement brought with it distinct fashions for youth (longer hair, narrow trousers, especially jeans, tall boots, miniskirts, sunglasses, and short suit jackets and skinny ties, among others), as well as greater liberty in manners and behaviour.

Western music was rarely made available by official media and was thus often accessed through unconventional means. Records were brought in from abroad by the few Poles who travelled at that time, and counterfeit singles were produced in small, private studios without consideration of licensing rights. *Polska Kronika Filmowa* (Polish Film Chronicle) showcased, among other global events, worldwide Beatlemania. Another illicit source of music pleasure came via Western radio stations whose signals were strong enough to reach Poland, such as Radio Luxemburg. The Rolling Stones performed the most famous concert of this period. They gave two performances on 13 April 1967 in the Congress Hall at the Palace of Culture – one of the most important symbols of Poland's subservience to the Soviet Union. The end of the decade saw the appearance of a new enemy of socialist power – the hippies, a movement that the ruling party tried to squelch not only because of their appearance but also because of their "unproductive" lifestyle.

Student culture developed with equal intensity during this period. Many of today's well-known artists debuted and developed their talents within its framework, which was also the crucible of many groups and institutions that have continued to shape Poles' cultural life. Student culture had a dissident character, yet it was able to win comparative independence that allowed for the creation of meaningful culture, often highly critical of the socialist state.

The state created a number of institutions during this period that, as means to control leisure time, circulate ideas, and impact educational activities, also shaped the lifestyles, intellectual fads, and behavioural models of that time. Among them were the so-called Café Clubs that opened in cities and villages, where – beside eating and drinking – you could read current books and periodicals, play games (chess, checkers, cards), develop your talents and skills, meet creators of culture, and, above all, lead an intense social life. Meanwhile, the Fundusz Wczasów Pracowniczych (FWP; Foundation of Workers' Vacations) was organizing employee vacations and leaves. Almost every workplace developed its own resort facilities, in which a specific folklore flourished, intensely promoted by instructors of culture and education. In the cities, the network of Pracownicze Ogródki Działkowe (Workers' Allotment Gardens) was expanding, and companies were conducting their own cultural activities.

Among the most important **song festivals** in Poland were the National Festival of Polish Song in Opole, founded in 1963, and the Festival of Song, held in Sopot since 1961, which gathered artists from abroad, most often from the Eastern Bloc. Two other famous festivals had an extremely ideological character: the Festival of Soviet Song, founded in 1965 in Zielona Góra, and the Festival of Military Songs, the first of which was held in 1968 in Kołobrzeg.

The huge festivals organized by the authorities and transmitted through the media were another influential form of popular culture. Admittedly, they flourished only in the 1970s, but the majority were launched in the 1960s. The culture they presented had a stamp of official approval, but within their framework also appeared bands playing "bigbit" music and experimenting with hippie culture. The socialist authorities delighted in festival culture and organized annual "Dni Kultury, Oświaty, Książki i Prasy" (Days of Culture, Education, Press and Book), as well as parades, fairs, and performances on national holidays and during the September Harvest celebrations (*dozhinki*). The latter in particular were an occasion for the authorities to demonstrate the value they placed on village life, inhabitants, and traditions. During these ceremonies, party secretaries were gifted a loaf of bread by the farmers, and people watched folklore performances and bragged about their harvests. One of the most famous political protests took place during one such celebration in 1968, when Ryszard Siwiec immolated himself during the Harvest festivities held at the 10th Anniversary Stadium in Warsaw as a protest against the Polish military intervention in Czechoslovakia.

Sport was another form of pop culture. Particularly dynamic was the development of soccer, in the service of which massive stadiums were built (e.g., the 10th Anniversary

Stadium in Warsaw, and the Silesian Stadium in Chorzów), which also served as sites for commemorative gatherings and propaganda events. Cycling, boxing, track and field, and winter and motor sports also flourished. Also, attention was now being paid to the development of "physical culture." The authorities put the motto "healthy body–healthy mind" into practice by founding sport clubs and promoting tourism and active leisure.

The most characteristic **sport event** of this period, which perfectly illustrated the state's tendency to use sport for propaganda purposes, was Wyścig Pokoju (The Peace Race). This annually organized bicycle tour with a route that joined symbolically friendly countries – Poland, East Germany, and Czechoslovakia, and later also the Soviet Union – was an ideologically important endeavour that also gave rise to authentic emotions. Related through the press, radio, and later also television, the event attracted huge audiences and fertilized the public's imagination.

The 1970s

This period began with the dramatic events of December 1970, when the military and militia bloodily suppressed workers' protests against price increases. One consequence of these events was the supersession of Władysław Gomułka in his role as First Secretary of the PPR by Edward Gierek. The Gierek Epoch, as the 1970s are now referred to, can be divided into several periods. The first, which lasted until 1976, was a time of economic prosperity, the Westernization of Polish society, and its first taste of consumerism, albeit in highly substitutive forms. During this period, the economy developed rapidly and housing, the communication infrastructure, and pop culture all expanded, albeit most often funded by Western loans. In the second half of the 1970s, Poland had to deal with a deepening economic crisis that reached its apogee with the outbreak of protests in 1976, and reached it again in the early 1980s. Rising opposition would culminate in the Solidarity "carnival" of 1980–1.

Polish soccer players perfectly suited the atmosphere of success of the first half of the 1970s. Called "Orły Górskiego" (Górski's Eagles) after the surname of their coach, they achieved their greatest international successes at the Olympic Games in 1972, where they won a gold medal, and at the World Cup in 1974, where they took third place. Their tie against England on 17 October 1973 during the World Cup elimination round became an important element of national mythology. Often called "the miracle at Wembley," this match has set a high bar ever since for the Polish national soccer team.

The 1970s were a time of rapid growth of mass communication, especially television, which to an ever-greater degree organized the imagination of Poles and shifted their interests towards entertainment full of glitz and spectacle. During these years, television co-organized the biggest music festivals and variety performances. It also broadcast Western crime series and films, concert performances of the stars of that time (Halina Frąckowiak, Maryla Rodowicz, 2+1, Anna Jantar), and cabaret and satirical programs such as *Spotkania z balladą* (Encounters with a Ballad), *Cabaret TEY*, Gallux Show, Studio Gama, and *Teraz leci kabarecik* (Now On: Cabaret). Simultaneously, television was heavily promoting higher culture through programs such as *Pegaz* (Pegasus), *Camerata*, *Sam na Sam* (One on One), and *Twarze teatru* (The Faces of Theatre).

Symptomatic of the 1970s was the increasing availability in Poland of **products symbolic of the West**, such as Coca-Cola and Pepsi (domestically produced since 1972 and 1975, respectively), chewing gum, original jeans, whisky, and rock music records (available in the special foreign exchange stores Pewex and Baltona.) Paradoxically, they were a significant means of propaganda that testified to the dynamic development of the socialist system.

A number of cult series were produced in the 1970s: *Czterdziestolatek* (The Forty-Year-Old), *Janosik*, *Karino*, *Stawiam na Tolka Banana* (I'm Betting on Tolek Banan), *Gruby* (Fatty), *Podróż za jeden uśmiech* (A Trip for a Smile), and comedies such as *Nie ma róży bez ognia* (There's No Rose without Fire), *Co mi zrobisz jak mnie złapiesz* (What Will You Do When You Catch Me), *Nie lubię poniedziałku* (I Don't Like Mondays), and *Sami swoi* (Our Folks). This joyful atmosphere of incessant entertainment was strengthened by news programs announcing the latest in economic successes, displaying new inventions and scientific discoveries, and promoting domestic motor vehicles (the famous Fiat 125 and 126p, and later FSO Polonez) as well as fashions by native designers like Barbara Hoff and Grażyna Hase.

New types of entertainment appeared at this time as well. One of the more significant was the discotheque, which had its beginnings in the late 1960s. In their early years, discos had little in common with typical dance events; they were hosted by radio presenters playing Western rock music on record players. Later on, discos popped up all over Poland, often on private initiative, and transformed themselves into purely entertainment venues playing Western disco, funk, and Polish pop music. During the 1970s, rock music thrived, with a crop of new groups like Kasa Chorych (The Health Fund), Budka Suflera (Prompter's Box), Klan, SBB, Exodus, Krzak (Bush), Kombi, and Porter Band. Youth magazines like *Na przełaj* (Cross Country), *Świat Młodych* (Youth World), and *Razem* (Together), as well as comic books, imprinted themselves on the imagination of new generations. Those who grew up then will undoubtedly remember *Captain Żbik; Tytus, Romek and A'Tomek*; *Kajko and Kokosz*; *Jonka, Jonek and Kleks*; and the series *Przygody Kwapiszona* (Adventures of Kwapiszon). After 1976, the growing ranks of comic fans could enjoy the journal *Relax*, which focused solely on their favourite genre.

In the context of the growing oppression in communist Poland, the dynamic growth of **science fiction** is worth remarking upon. The journal *Fantastyka* (Fantasy) was founded in

1982 (and would continue until 1990), printing stories, excerpts of novels, and comics by both Polish and Western science fiction artists. Alongside appeared *Komiks-fantastyka* and *Little Fantastyka*. Very popular at the time were also the dystopian novels of Janusz Zajdel, the futurological work of Stanisław Lem, and the apocalyptic films of Piotr Szukin (such as *The War of the Worlds: Next Century* and *O-Bi, O-Ba: The End of Civilization*).

This happy period ended quite quickly with the onset of huge economic problems and social unrest. Once again, society's attention shifted towards the struggle for material survival.

1980s

Orange Alternative (Pomarańczowa Alternatywa): a happening movement created by "Major" Waldemar Frydrych in the early 1980s in Wrocław and linked to the contestation traditions of the 1960s, and especially to the actions of the Dutch Provo movement. Its members enacted in reality their leader's imagined idea of "socialist surrealism" by painting images of dwarves on city walls and organizing street happenings that ridiculed the militia.

The 1980s began with a celebration of freedom, with Solidarity as its most important symbol. The successes of the August 1980 strikes and the concessions made by the authorities with regard to many social issues were reason for hope that civil liberties would be broadened. Unfortunately, those hopes proved futile. In December 1981, martial law was imposed on the entire country; it would last until August 1983. This time of repressions and arrests meant that cultural life decelerated, partly because artistic communities boycotted official institutions. At the same time, a well-developed political folklore appeared, and there was strong growth in politically and patriotically engaged songs (represented by artists such as Jacek Kaczmarski, Przemysław Gintrowski, Stefan Brzoza, and Andrzej Kołakowski, among others), and in underground radio stations and publications. Specific social displays became popular (e.g., beards, and the wearing of stretched-out sweaters and check shirts, along with electronic resistors in lapels). Also, the role of the church expanded as it brought under its protection those artists who were boycotting the regime's culture.

Mainly, however, the 1980s saw the rapid growth of youth culture, organized around radical music and subcultural movements, whose Mecca was the Jarocin Festival. This radical current has often been viewed as a kind of safety valve for channelling social discontent, but the mark it left on Polish culture is prominent enough that it is difficult to downplay its impact. It was made up largely of a multiplicity of subcultures, each presenting young people with music created by their peers, as well as fanzines, radical fashions in clothing, stimulants, and a community based on listening to and exchanging music and designing one's own clothes and hairstyles.

Alongside the radical current, a mainstream movement also developed, focused on rock music and supported by domestic record companies and agencies. It possessed all the characteristics of idol culture: unquestionable stars (groups such as Oddział Zamknięty [Closed Ward], Perfekt, Lady Pank, Maanam, Republika, Lombard, TSA, and Turbo), music posters reprinted in popular publications, the first scandals connected to the raunchy behaviour of pop idols, ecstatic crowds during concerts, and huge runs of records that sold out at lightning speed.

Businessmen whose fortunes grew daily, and who expressed their wealth through ostentatious consumerism, became the new social heroes of the 1990s. This social category has been represented in many pop cultural productions. Good examples include Jerzy Gruza's series *Tygrysy Europy* (Tigers of Europe) and *40-latek. 20 lat później* (The Forty-Year-Old: Twenty Years Later), as well as films such as Waldemar Szarka's *Żegnaj Rockefeler* (Goodbye Rockefeller) and Feliks Falk's *Kapitał, czyli jak zrobić pieniądze w Polsce* (Capital, or How to Make Money in Poland).

In the second half of the 1980s, the Westernization of Polish culture and customs intensified owing to the spread of satellite television and video players, as well as business trips to – and help arriving from – the West. This period was marked by a fascination with *Conan, Rambo, Lemon Popsicle*, Bavarian porn, and the pop stars of that time (such as Sabina, C.C. Catch, and Modern Talking), and by a passion for Italo-disco, aerobics, teased hairstyles, leg warmers, and shoulder pads. The saturation of visual space with previously unencountered images from the West triggered a rethinking of the cultural offerings of domestic media. Films with brave erotic scenes appeared in cinemas (for example *Tabu* [Taboo], *Łuk Erosa* [Bow of Eros], *Widziadło* [Apparition], and *Medium*), while television attempted to compete with VCRs and satellite TV with its first soap opera *W labiryncie* (In the Labyrinth), evening soft-porn shows *Różowa seria* (The Pink Series), and programs showing Western music videos (*Bazaar*). The new media not only transformed Polish tastes but also infected the imagination of Poles, fostering new standards of acceptability in clothing, hairstyles, home design, and customs. One can risk the thesis that the pop culture revolution sped up the systemic change of 1989.

1990s to the Present

The systemic change of 1989 and the subsequent period of great transformation – the transition from socialism to capitalism – began the process of normalization in culture, but also of gluttonous consumerism. It was a time when everything that had been limited in availability – primarily Western pop culture – was intensively tasted and tested. It was also a time of another social breakdown, with entrepreneurs rising as a powerful new group while workers, farmers, and the intelligentsia fell increasingly into poverty. The popular culture of the 1990s, having been freed from previous state dictates, was becoming highly diverse and ever more commercialized. The first private TV stations (Polonia 1, Polsat, TVN) and radio stations (Radio ESKA, Zet, RMF FM) began operations, and the magazine market expanded once again.

> The increasingly **ludic treatment** of local colour is visible in many television series set in small towns, whose local atmosphere is an important draw for viewers. Among the more significant productions of this type that enjoy immense popularity are *Ranczo* (Ranch), *Dom nad rozlewiskiem* (House by the Backwater), *Ojciec Mateusz* (Father Matthew), and *Szpilki na Giewoncie* (High Heels on Giewont).

In addition, previously inaccessible music became available, and the growing erotic market offered Poles both Western and domestic pornography. The most recent years have been a time of "normalization" in Polish culture: the Internet has become the most important medium, and the "global mainstream," along with its glocal variations, is now the most important cultural form. A network-based culture of participation and with it the blogosphere, social portals, and computer game culture have developed quickly, including in the Polish context. Much like in the West, there has been a radical thematization of television, and television channels are proliferating as a consequence. No less noteworthy is the expansion of a strongly formulized consumer culture signalled by the spread of huge shopping centres and entertainment multiplexes. At the same time, the media are being tabloidized, and a gossip press has developed, complete with portals aimed at domestic celebrity culture.

This "normalization" does not mean that Polish culture has started to simulate global pop culture. Poles are taking a more ludic approach to local culture, creating their own new, local traditions and transforming them into entertainment. The "theme villages" that have been established in small towns and villages across Poland are a good example of this phenomenon; so is the saturation of culinary culture with local specialties; and so is the growing enthusiasm for festivals and fairs. Another local expression of pop culture is its strong pop-historic and pop-patriotic current, as manifested by the explosion of various reconstructive groups that organize on-location re-enactments of important historical events; yet another is the appearance of comic books and music exploring Poland's past. Meanwhile, a specific "fashion for Poland" is visible in demonstrations of national affiliation during mass events. In addition, especially today, content that had been expunged from history textbooks and social memory by censorship and martial law is making a comeback. This is true especially of events such as the Warsaw Uprising and the Battle of Westerplatte that began the German invasion of Poland in September 1939. The memory of these events is evoked today in the form of interactive exhibits (e.g., at the Museum Powstania Warszawskiego [Warsaw Rising Museum]), comic books, computer games, graffiti and murals, music videos, and public historical reconstructions. All of these share a retrospective tendency to celebrate war as an event that spurs traits of particular value to Polish society (heroism, patriotism, friendship, loyalty) – traits that these productions tell us are lacking in present-day Poland.

Another example of the ludification of local culture is Polish hip-hop, which has been developing since the 1990s and is now extraordinarily diverse. A key aspect of it is the "little homeland," which refers to the housing complex, neighbourhood, or hometown and the familiar people who live there – "buddies" whom one respects, towards whom one is loyal, and on whom one can always count to provide protection from the threatening world beyond the enclave. Domestic folklore and traditions are rarely referenced by hip-hop, yet many of its expressions contain a similar yearning for a world with a human scale, an authentic world where the bonds between people are strong – a world so hard to find in modern times.

In another form of retrospection, the socialist era has been transformed into a sort of cultural warehouse of characters, objects, events, cultural goods, and trends. Because they are so local, these cultural products clash with global pop culture. This popularization of the past has aroused controversy and given rise to accusations that it is propagating communism and mocking the suffering of Poles under totalitarianism; but it also has many adherents, largely from the ranks of those for whom this form of remembrance is an exercise in nostalgia. Even younger generations are attracted; for them, the world of communist Poland is fascinating for being so different from their own. Yet another phenomenon in contemporary Polish pop culture is the return to traditional forms of cultural participation: café-clubs, intimate bars and restaurants, independent cinemas and film clubs, theatre, festivals, and private meetings and parties – all of these are making a comeback. Some would view all of the above phenomena as signs that Polish society is being "retraditionalized." It seems more accurate, however, to see them as signs that neo-tribal communities are beginning to appear in a domestic context, as Michel Maffesoli would put it.[3] These communities' members are linked by similar interests and yearnings and by the possibility of their realization, as well as by the need to belong to a community.

Karwowski's arch: a specific architectural feature made by removing internal apartment doors and rounding the upper edges of the space in which they hung. They owe their popularity to the series *The Forty-Year-Old*, whose titular hero, in response to his wife's aspirations, renovates their highrise apartment to make it resemble a gentry manor.

Leading Motifs of Polish Pop Culture

Looking at some of the leading motifs in Polish pop culture allows us to grasp its specificity as well as to see some of the consistent elements of the Polish world view and way of experiencing reality. One example of such a motif is signalled by the notion "-polo" and designates those products of Polish popular culture in which some universal and worldwide genre or convention is used as a carrier of local cultural traditions. This form of cultural remixing appeared as early as during socialist realism, when attempts were made to create works "national in form and socialist in content," as well as later, whenever authorities searching for legitimacy reached for folk culture. This tradition has returned today by way of music groups exploring Polish highlander folklore (Golec uOrkiestra; Brathanki; Zakopower); it is also present in the revival of banquets and banquet music (Banquet Song Galas and Silesian Banquets come to mind, organized in the mid-1990s), and in the ludic elements that accompany weddings, village dances, and discotheques.

Disco Polo: A specific genre of music born in Poland during the 1980s that immediately became a mass phenomenon. The repertoire of groups who play this music consists of wedding songs and new versions of folk songs, often bawdy in nature, but not without references to values of great importance to Poles, such as family, children, love, and home. Its music is very simple, created with the help of synthesizers and drum machines.

Barbecues with family and friends are among the most popular ways to spend free time in Poland. This leisure activity, which has American roots, was brought to Poland by people who had emigrated to or temporarily worked in Germany. Poles set up grills in home gardens, in garden allotments, on lawns, or on apartment balconies. It is no accident that grills are hugely popular in Poland, for they evoke the "household hearth" and atavistic bonds with one's loved ones.

This current has been deeply rooted in the Polish lifestyle since at least the 1970s. It reflects a fondness for Sarmatian and gentry traditions. It influences house decor: a love of wood (wainscotting) and oriental touches (patterned carpets, heavy curtains, military regalia, heraldic portraits, devotional objects, and crystal). It also colours social customs, which favour the carnival with its periodic reversal of the existing order. It actualizes the collective through often ecstatic celebrations filled with moments of loss of control. In recent years, advertising has often exploited local traditions for the sake of tourism and product sales, using slogans like "Dobre, bo polskie (Yummy 'Cause Polish), "Polskie Jadło" (Polish Fare), "Pyzy babci Tereni" ("Granny Terenia's Potato Dumplings), and "Krakowski kredens" (Kraków's Pantry), to name a few. Such phenomena seem to have their origins in the yearning of Poles for a world on a human scale – a local homeland in which life is predictable, safe, and controllable.

The lyrics to one of the songs by the disco-polo group Bayer Full signal the crucial role both of the national collective and of the family in Polish culture: "Bo wszyscy Polacy to jedna rodzina. Starszy czy młodszy, chłopak czy dziewczyna" (For all the Poles are one family / Older or younger, fellow or filly,). In regard to the latter, its central place in Polish culture has not been weakened even by the recent and rapid transformations in the family model, which is moving towards more egalitarian unions and more informal affective-sexual relationships. As elsewhere in the world, the family provides the fodder for soap operas (such as *Klan* [Clan], *M jak Miłość* [L like Love], *Zaklęta* [Enchanted], *Złotopolscy* [The Złotopolski Family], and *Rezydencja* [Residence]) and comedy series (such as *Rodzina zastępcza* [The Foster Family], *rodzinka.pl* [family.pl] and *Świat według Kiepskich* [The World According to the Kiepskis]), Indeed, this was also the case for older television series, such as *Rodzina Kanderów* (The Kander Family), *Dom* (House), *Wojna domowa* (Civil War), and *Rodzina Leśniewskich* (The Leśniewski Family). The family and its often tragic fate, which is often intertwined with great historical events, has been the subject of many feature films (e.g., in the work of Kazimierz Kutz [b. 1929]). Poles highly value family in their daily lives, spending leisure time and holidays in the company of close relatives. Singlehood is still viewed with suspicion, though acceptance of it is gradually rising.

The importance of **the line-up** (or the queue) is evidenced by the popularity of the board game named "Kolejka" (Line-Up), produced in 2011 by the Institute of National Remembrance (IPN), which was followed by a second game, "Ogonek" (Little Tail), in 2013. The object of the game is to acquire the greatest number of consumer goods in competition with other players, whose pawns are lined up in queues. More than 40,000 units of "Line-up" have been sold, and in 2013 it was acclaimed the board game of the year.

The deep religiosity of Poles partly accounts for the cult of the family, but equally important here have been the brutal challenges faced by Poles over the past century, during which the family circle was the only refuge from an antagonistic outside world. This seemingly positive role played by the family brought with it also something that Banfield has termed "amoral familism," namely, a tendency to apply double moral standards in interpersonal relationships depending on the familiarity or otherness of the people involved.[4] The family performed an important survivalist function, in that it ensured the continuation of many traditions, specific values, and customs; at the same time, though, the cult of the family is undoubtedly responsible for the prevalence of nepotism and the propensity for treating the outside world as bad and dangerous in Poland.

Waiting and anticipation are also prominent motifs in Polish pop culture. As Leopold Tyrmand astutely observes, "under communism, a person spends their life [in] line."[5] Indeed, Polish daily life, especially during the communist period, was subject to the logic of a specific form of socialization embodied in the queue formed in expectation of the arrival of scarce consumer products. Not accidentally, therefore, many films feature the motif of people awaiting the delivery of goods, arguing over their place in the line, attempting to trick others waiting for the same delivery, and even (in the series *Alternative St. # 4*) a homemade humanoid robot whose primary task is precisely to wait in line.

The statue of **Christ the King** in Świebodzin was built in 2010 on the initiative of a local parish priest, Sylwester Zawadzki. The statue is 33 metres tall and is the tallest statue of Christ in the world. Its size generated a heated discussion about the forms in which Polish religiosity manifests itself, as well as a flood of Internet memes deriding the megalomania of the enterprise.

Line-ups also reference a deeper and more widespread phenomenon of waiting for, anticipating, and waiting out – of Poles waiting for independence, prosperity, and democracy as well as for the end of war, socialism, and martial law, but also for an apartment or a car voucher, for a taxi or a delayed train, for a passport or a job, for the decision of an indolent bureaucrat or an eternally postponed verdict of the court, for an operation or a hospital bed, for a place in a sanatorium, a preschool, or a kindergarten, for a miracle or the end of the world. The experience of waiting is ubiquitous in Polish society and underscores Polish people's lack of control over basic parameters of their existence, the fact that they function in the context of an unstable and unpredictable system in which much depends on luck, fate, accident, someone's goodwill or mercy, contacts and deals. This experience explains the huge popularity of television shows of interventional character, such as Elżbieta Jaworowicz's *Sprawa dla reportera* (A Case for a Journalist), broadcast on a public channel since the mid-1980s. It also explains why one of the most important icons of pop culture is a journalist, first with a microphone and later with a video camera. This hero of the collective imagination attempts, in the name of the people, to make the system more predictable and just, or at least to reveal its true nature.

The Ulhan imagination (*Ułańska fantazja*): a term used by Polish people to describe the national tendency to undertake actions that have slim chances at success, are incredibly risky, and stem from a momentary elation and the desire to do something extraordinary, as well as the need to prove one's subjectivity in situations that have stripped it away.

The experience of permanent anticipation created a specific mentality rooted in the conviction that even the most immediate world is governed by forces beyond one's influence. This mentality can manifest itself in fervent religiosity, which often leads to stubborn attempts to leave the mark of God on public spaces. Excellent examples of this include the hundreds of statues of John Paul II, crosses hanging in public buildings, the gigantic Basilica of Our Lady of Licheń (in Licheń), and the gargantuan figure of Christ in Świebodzin. This mentality is also made apparent when faith in fate and coincidence becomes the basic mode of relating to reality, and when resignation – the conviction that nothing will ever change – becomes the core of one's life. All of these motifs have been worked through in Polish popular culture, with the last two being of particular importance. The films of Krzysztof Kieślowski, such as *Przypadek* (Blind Chance) and *Podwójne życie Weroniki* (The Double Life of Veronique), are powerful examples of a fate-oriented world view, while Marek Koterski explores the fatalistic mindset in films such as *Życie wewnętrzne* (Inner Life), *Nic śmiesznego* (Nothing Funny), *Dzień świra* (Day of the Wacko), and *Wszyscy jesteśmy Chrystusami* (We're all Christs).

Another clearly present theme in Polish pop culture is laddishness (*chłopięcość*). This motif features as the hero a rebellious young man prone to an adventurous lifestyle, one who does not shy away from violence yet is simultaneously kind and just, very often acting in defence of the weaker and the afflicted. This motif strongly emphasizes the value of adventure and experience, of masculine rough friendship, of intensity in experiencing the world accompanied by nobility of conduct and often intense feelings. Laddishness is also a form of a particular heroism, stripped of martyrdom and suffering, taking the form of a somewhat wild "Uhlan imagination" – of desperate yet somehow also joyful confrontations with something one hundredfold more powerful. This motif, which features prominently in popular films as well as, for instance, in comic books, presents war as an adventure and the pursuit of criminals as an exciting and colourful activity; it also encompasses the theme of journeying and wandering. The theme of laddishness can be found in significant Polish pop culture series like *Czterej pancerni i pies* (Four Tankmen and a Dog), *Stawka większa niż życie* (A Stake Larger Than Life), *Janosik*, *Stawiam na*

Tolka Banana (I'm Betting on Tolek Banan), and *07 zgłoś się* (07, Over), as well as in many films, such as *Tramwajada* (Tramiade), *Nad rzeką, której nie ma* (By a River That Does Not Exist), *Psy* (Pigs), and *Wszystko co kocham* (All That I Love). Laddishness is most fully embodied by iconic figures in Polish pop culture such as Zbigniew Cybulski (1927–67), a cult actor who died tragically in a train accident; the writer Marek Hłasko (1934–69); and, in the present day, the theatre and film actors Bogusław Linda (b. 1952) and Paweł Małaszyński (b. 1976). This current is also the source of fashion for army boots, US Army jackets, knapsacks and backpacks, leather bomber jackets, and dark glasses.

Załatwianie **(handling)**: the bypassing of bureaucratic regulations and laws through social connections, nepotistic deals and relations, or corruption.

Kombinowanie **(finagling)**: the acquisition of scarce goods through (often, but not always) barely legal means, from sources outside the official market.

Radzenie sobie **(making do)**: the ability to meet basic needs despite absence of means that would make it possible, through recourse to inventiveness and innovative use of available resources and of substitutes.

Laddishness also encompasses a lifestyle, perhaps even a culture, that grew around wandering and hiking, which were closely tied to both the hippie movement and dissident circles, but also to official tourism developed by the state. This culture manifested itself in sung poetry (*poezja śpiewana*) and tourist songs, as well as in various fashions such as smoking a pipe, growing a beard, and wearing hiking boots, flannel shirts, and woollen highlander sweaters. Laddishness also refers to a tendency to celebrate the urban hooligan as a hero of the people who battles the authorities. He often takes the form of the urban survival artist, a prominent figure in works of city folklore (e.g., the anonymous *Ballada o Paramonowie* [Ballad of Paramonow]), poetry, and songs (e.g., the work of Stanisław Grzesiuk [1918–63] and Kazik Staszewski [b. 1963]), as well as in literature, especially the books of Leopold Tyrmand (1920–1985).

The motif of laddishness in the Polish context is somewhat synonymous with the yearning to live on one's own terms within a system that bends individuals to collective action, uniformity, and strong traditions. The attractiveness of this model during the times of the PPR, primarily among young people, attested to the search for modes of being more expansive than those offered by the state. This model led to a strong politicization of the everyday (expressed by the length of hair, type of clothing and shoes, colloquial language, and ways of spending free time). At the same time, however, it created a social enclave that the system could control, within which rebellion and discord could be contained.

Another motif that is just as heavily exploited in Polish popular culture is resourcefulness, or cunning. This motif celebrates what for many Poles is the most important national characteristic: the ability to overcome any circumstance through cleverness, resourcefulness, and everyday know-how. It is strongly marked in social custom: handling, finagling, and making do are considered especially valuable survival skills. This motif also has a dignifying character – being clever, resourceful, and "entrepreneurial" allows for the recovery of subjectivity and provides a sense of control over one's own life. Not incidently, urban folklore is full of examples of this sort of cleverness: popular are stories about a Varsovian crook who sold the Palace of Culture to an American businessman, street songs praising this ethos in the style of "Nie ma cwaniaka nad warszawiaka" (There's No Charlatan Like a Varsovian), and legends about fortunes being made in the Eastern Bloc on the sale of Biseptol (a popular antibiotic) as birth control pills. This ethos is also present in many films, embodied in urban survivalist characters who can come out on top in any situation. Their actions may not always be completely legal, but they themselves are noble at the core, harming only those whom they consider their enemies.

The pantheon of **"Polish artful dodgers"** (cwaniaki) includes the hero of Kazimierz Sławiński's novel *Przygody kanoniera Dolasa* (Adventures of Gunner Dolas, 1967), on which Tadeusz Chmielewski's film trilogy *Jak rozpętałem drugą wojnę światową* (How I Unleashed World War II) is based; and Henio Lermaszewski (played by Zbigniew Buczkowski, a non-professional actor who specializes in similar roles), a Varsovian con artist from the TV series *Dom* (House), which tells the postwar fates of Poles from the perspective of one Varsovian apartment house.

This motif also appears in nostalgic recollections of making do in times of scarcity, especially during the PPR period. Mass-produced clothing was ingenously altered; private, home-based manufacturers (*prywaciarze*) developed substitutes for scarce products. The paradox here is that the state was able to exert some control over this adaptive strategy. Even though there was no music market to speak of, public radio was able to generate lists of hits; chocolate was replaced by pseudo-chocolate products, and orange jam by a pumpkin preserve with orange peel, while dollars were imitated by commodity coupons issued by the National Bank of Poland.

An interesting thread of Polish pop culture is selective xenophilia, meaning a powerful interest in the foreign, notwithstanding a belief in one's own superiority. Selective xenophilia was largely a reaction to the isolation in which Polish society functioned as a consequence of low and state-controlled mobility; but it was also as the result of complex and often painful relations with one's closest neighbours. A symptom of selective xenophilia is an exoticizing interest in otherness – in foreigners, and in people of a different race or religion. This does not, however, mean willingness to assimilate others.

We must point out here that aspect of selective xenophilia that relates to Poland's long history of tragic relations with Germany and Russia. With regard to Germany, Poles envy their standard of living, their economic efficiency, and their civilizational development; with regard to Russia, Poles admire their cultural wealth, as well as their romantic world view and their imagination. Yet these positive attitudes are accompanied by a tendency to endlessly scratch at barely healed wounds, by a drive to identify those guilty of past crimes, and by attempts to build a Polish identity while leaning on the role of a victim who is helpless but also heroic and always standing on the right side of the line.

During the postwar period, **anti-Semitic currents** were markedly present in the events of March 1968, when the Arab–Israeli War became a pretext for removing people of Jewish descent from state and university structures, public institutions, and consequently also the country. They are also present in contemporary soccer wars, conducted by fans of the Łódź clubs Widzew and ŁKS, during which the word "Jew" as well as ethnic slurs serve as the ultimate insults. Thus the expression "You, Jew" is equivalent to a scornful challenge thrown at an opponent.

A similar principle applies to the enormous interest, especially in the present day, in Jewish folklore, traditions, music, and literature, countered at times by poorly concealed anti-Semitism and by raising the figure of the Jew to name what is unwanted, undesirable, hostile, and deserving of exclusion.

Selective xenophilia is also evident in the popularity of home-grown exoticism, most often performed by local artists. It takes the form of a simulated worldliness, a cosmopolitanism, the inauthenticity of which is betrayed by excess, ornamental richness, and formal mannerisms. The best examples of this syndrome are singular phenomena of Polish pop culture such as the group Tercet Egzotyczny (Exotic Trio) and the singer Violetta Villas, whose presence in the grey reality of PPR provided audiences with highly desirable yet simultaneously safe culture shock.

An interesting current in Polish popular culture, especially postwar, was "ambitious entertainment" (*ambitna rozrywka*). It was used to counter mass culture, which was viewed as a Western product. Ambitious entertainment was a form of critique of popular culture undertaken from elite positions yet at the same time integral to that culture. This double-logic perfectly reflected the authorities' ambivalent attitude towards leisure, entertainment, and consumerism. These were seen as distancing the individual from issues of importance to the system, and as diminishing their engagement in building that system (socialist, but also resting on traditional, patriotic, and Catholic values), but also as useful propaganda tools that could help model individual attitudes.

Ambitious entertainment was created by the intelligentsia and reflected its way of experiencing the world and the values it preferred. At the same time, it was not meant solely for the intelligentsia, but for all social classes, and in that sense its purpose was to educate those of low cultural capital, imposing on them a proper model of a "cultured being" and cultural participation. In this respect, ambitious entertainment was a clear example of symbolic violence – of the colonizing relation of the state towards society, of the state's educational ambitions and its efforts to bring culture to places where, supposedly, it has not yet been ("under the thatched roof," to the village, to working communities).

Sung poetry: a genre in which a poem (frequently longer in form, such as a ballad or a narrative poem) is set to specially composed music. It draws on many traditions: romantic songs, cabaret, and urban folklore, but especially on street ballads and songs of the kind sung by, for instance, Edith Piaf. It is often related to poetic song and to the works of folk and folk rock artists – for example, Bob Dylan, Simon and Garfunkel, Leonard Cohen, Suzanne Vega, Jacques Brel, and Georges Brassens. At the turn of the 1950s and

1960s, many prominent Polish artists made sung poetry an important genre of stage art. They included Tadeusz Chyła (1933–2014, stage debut 1954), a painter who became famous as a ballad singer; Ewa Demarczyk (b. 1941; stage debut 1961), who earned world renown with performances of, among others, Julian Tuwim's poem "Grande Valse Brillante," Miron Białoszewski's "Karuzela z madonnami" (Carousel with Madonnas), and Krzysztof Kamil Baczyński's war poems; and Marek Grechuta (1945–2006; stage debut 1967), who performed the poetry of Bolesław Leśmian and Tadeusz Nowak and the texts of Stanisław Ignacy Witkiewicz. Sung poetry is closely connected to the work of bards such as the Pole Jacek Kaczmarski, the Russian Bulat Okudzhava, and the Czech Jaromír Nohavica, all of whom comment on reality in elaborate texts with independently composed music.

Within the framework of ambitious entertainment fell literary cabarets that consciously referenced prewar traditions; pop music with poetic aspirations (the songs of Agnieszka Osiecka, Seweryn Krajewski, Wojciech Młynarski, Magdalena Umer, and Edyta Gepert); texts of well-known poets (e.g., Marek Grechuta); "actor's songs" (*piosenka aktorska*) popularized by the huge festival in Wrocław; and sung poetry (*poezja śpiewana*), with its Mecca in Kraków.

Ambitious entertainment also meant specific cultural fashions, first for existentialism, and later for Witold Gombrowicz, Sławomir Mrożek, and Ibero-American literature; systematic reading of *Przekrój* (Cross-Cut) and *Literatura na świecie* (World Literature); love of the "Polish school of posters" and the work of Jerzy Duda-Gracz and Franciszek Starowiejski; and passion for the theatrical stagings of Adam Hanuszkiewicz, Kaziemierz Dejmek, Józef Szajna, and Konrad Swinarski. It also encompassed leading a modern lifestyle: hygienic, sexually aware, and surrounded by both the newest of civilizational spoils and by historical memorabilia. It appears that some behaviours characteristic of this traditional ethos of the intelligentsia have been taken up today by the seemingly cosmopolitan hipsters, who, to showcase how loosely rooted in the social structure they are, display their liking for particular books and cinema and spend their time in contemporary café-clubs and at house parties. What previously would have been called ambitious entertainment, today is designated as *niche*, *alternative*, or *indie*.

Marek Krajewski
Adam Mickiewicz University, Poznań
Translated by Agnieszka Polakowska

NOTES

1 See Storey's preface to *Inventing Popular Culture* for an overview of the ideas that he explores throughout the book, ix–xii.
2 Barthes, *The Pleasure of the Text*, esp. 51–3.
3 Maffesoli, *The Time of the Tribes*. For a brief summary of the main concepts treated throughout the book, see Rob Shield's forward, pp. ix–xii.
4 Banfield, *The Moral Basis of a Backward Society*, especially chapter 5, "Predictive Hypothesis," 85–103.
5 Tyrmand, *Rosa Luxemburg Contraceptives Cooperative: Primer on Communist Civilization,* 139.

WORKS CITED AND CONSULTED

Banfield, Edward C. *The Moral Basis of a Backward Society*. Glencoe: Free Press, 1958.

Baranowki, Bohdan, Julian Bartyś, and Tadeusz Sobczak, eds. *Historia kultury materialnej Polski w zarysie*, vol. 6. Wrocław: Zakład Narodowy im. Ossolińskich, 1979.

Barker, Chris. *Cultural Studies: Theory and Practice*. 2nd ed. London: Sage, 2003.

Barthes, Roland. *The Pleasure of the Text*. Translated by Richard Miller. New York: Hill and Wang, 1975.

Berger, Peter Ludwig. *The Capitalist Revolution: Fifty Propositions about Prosperity, Equality, and Liberty*. New York: Basic Books, 1986.

Bołdak-Janowska, Tamara. *Co dobrego było w peerelu?* Olsztyn: Borussia, 2009.

Brylewski, Robert. *Kryzys w Babilonie. Autobiografia (rozmawia Rafał Księżyk)*. Kraków, 2012.

Chwalba, Andrzej, ed. *Obyczaje w Polsce. Od średniowiecza do czasów współczesnych*. Warszawa: Wydawnictwo Naukowe PWN, 2004.

de Certeau, Michel. *The Practice of Everyday Life*. Translated by Steven Rendall. Berkeley: University of California Press, 2002.

Eisler, Jerzy, et al., eds. *Polska 1944/45–1989. Życie codzienne w Polsce 1945–1955. Studia i materiały*, vol. 5. Warszawa: Instytut Historii PAN, 2001.

Fiske, John. *Introduction to Communication Studies*. 3rd ed. New York: Routledge, 2011.

Godzic, Wiesław. *Znani z tego, że są znani. Celebryci w kulturze tabloidów*. Warszawa: Wydawnictwa Akademickie i Profesjonalne, 2007.

– ed. *30 Najważniejszych programów TV w Polsce*. Warszawa: Trio, 2005.

Groński, Ryszard Marek. *Kabaret Hemara*. Warszawa: Inne, 1989.

Halawa, Mateusz. *Życie codzienne z telewizorem*. Warszawa: Wydawnictwa Akademickie i Profesjonalne, 2006.

Hall, Stuart. ed. *Representation: Cultural Representation and Signifying Practices*. London: Sage, 1997.

Jenks, Chris. *Culture*. 2nd ed. New York: Routledge, 2005.

Kisielewska, Alicja, ed. *Bohater. Idol. Osobowość medialna*. Białystok: Wydawnictwo Uniwersytetu w Białymstoku, 2004.

Kłoskowska, Antonina. *Kultura masowa. Krytyka i obrona*. 4th ed. Warszawa: Wydawnictwo Naukowe PWN, 2011.

Knyt, Agnieszka, and Alicja Wancerz-Gluza. *Prywaciarze 1945–1989*. Warszawa: Ośrodek Karta, 2004.

Kot, Wieslaw. *PRL jak cudnie się żyło!* Poznań: Wydawnictwo Publicat, 2008.

Koziczyński, Bartek. *333 popkulturowe rzeczy ... PRL*. Poznań: Wydawnictwo Vesper, 2007.

Krajewski, Marek. *Kultury kultury popularnej*. Poznań: Wydawnictwo Naukowe Uniwersytetu Adama Mickiewicza, 2005.

– *POPamiętane*. Gdańsk: słowo/obraz terytoria, 2006.

Lash, Scott, and Celia Lury. *Global Culture Industry: The Mediation of Things*. Cambridge: Polity, 2007.

Maffesoli, Michael. *The Time of the Tribes: The Decline of Individualism in Mass Society*. Translated by Don Smith. London: Sage, 1996.

Majewski, Tomasz, ed. *Rekonfiguracje modernizmu. Nowoczesność i kultura popularna*. Warszawa: WAiP, 2009.

Marszałek, Rafał. *Kino rzeczy znalezionych*. Gdańsk: słowo/obraz terytoria, 2006.

Milewski, Stanisław. *Codzienność niegdysiejszej Warszawy*. Warszawa: Iskry, 2010.

Miłosz, Czesław, ed. *Kultura masowa*. Kraków: Wydawnictwo Literackie, 2002.
Pelka, Anna. *Teksas-land. Moda młodzieżowa w PRL*. Warszawa: Trio, 2007.
Pikulski, Tadeusz. *Prywatna historia telewizji publicznej*. Warszawa: Muza, 2002.
Pleskot, Patryk. *Wielki mały ekran. Telewizja a codzienność Polaków w latach sześćdziesiątych*. Warszawa: Trio, 2007.
Prasek, Cezary. *Życie towarzyskie w PRL*. Warszawa: Bellona, 2011.
Przybyszewska Urszula. *Przemiany uczestnictwa kulturalnego społeczeństwa polskiego w świetle badań socjologicznych*. Warszawa: Instytut Kultury, 1982.
Rychlewski, Marcin, et al., eds. *Mała encyklopedia obciachu*. Poznań: Vesper, 2008.
Stevenson, Nick, ed. *Culture and Citizenship*. London: Sage, 2001.
Storey John. *Inventing Popular Culture: From Folklore to Globalization*. Malden: Blackwell, 2003.
Sulima, Roch. *Antropologia codzienności*. Kraków: Wydawnictwo Uniwersytetu Jagiellońskiego, 2000.
Świda-Ziemba, Hanna. *Młodzież PRL. Portrety pokoleń w kontekście historii*. Warszawa: Wydawnictwo Literackie, 2011.
Szarota, Piotr. Od *skarpetek Tyrmanda do krawata Leppera. Psychologia stroju dla średniozaawansowanych*. Warszawa: Wydawnictwa Akademickie i Profesjonalne, 2008.
Szpakowska, Małgorzata, ed. *Obyczaje polskie. Wiek XX w krótkich hasłach*. Warszawa: W.A.B., 2008.
Szubert, Małgorzata. *Leksykon rzeczy minionych i przemijających*. Warszawa: Muza, 2003.
Toeplitz, Krzysztof Teodor. *Mieszkańcy masowej wyobraźni*. Warszawa: Państwowy Instytut Wydawniczy, 1970.
– *Sztuka komiksu. Próba definicji nowego gatunku artystycznego*. Warszawa: Czytelnik, 1985.
Tyrmand, Leopold. *Rosa Luxemburg Contraceptives Cooperative: Primer on Communist Civilization*. New York: Macmillan, 1971.
– *Dziennik 1954*. London: Puls, 1999.
Veblen, Thorstein, and Frentzel-Zagórska, Janina. *Teoria klasy próżniaczej*. Warszawa: Muza, 2008.
Young, Robert J.C. *Postcolonialism: A Historical Introduction*. Oxford: Blackwell, 1999.
Zblewski, Zdzisław. *Leksykon PRL*. Kraków: Znak, 2000.

Between Personal and Collective Memory: History and Politics in Polish Comics

Comic books have long been considered products of mass culture. They have had a global reach, facilitated by popular translations and film adaptations.[1] Often relegated to the category of "low" literature, comics have long fought for recognition as a legitimate literary and artistic form. Similarly, their fans have frequently been denigrated and seen as second-class readers.[2] With the emergence of the term "graphic novel," which is gradually becoming an umbrella term for the entire genre, the "funnies" have slowly been turning into a sanctioned form of "high" literature.[3] According to some scholars, this new nomenclature has the potential to "rescue comics from their critical neglect, as well as to recognize the emergence of specifically adult comics and book length works."[4] Nonetheless, to some extent comic books continue to be viewed as a form of light entertainment, associated mostly with young and inexperienced readers, while paradoxically becoming an important educational resource used in classrooms around the world. Teachers consider the comic book to be an invaluable resource in history teaching. Art Spiegelman's *Maus* (1986), for example, is commonly read in courses on the Holocaust and genocide.[5]

Indeed, *Maus* has simultaneously transformed history writing and the history of comics, addressing important questions about the limits of representation, the workings of memory, the ethical dilemma stemming from retelling a painful past, and, more broadly, the relationship between aesthetics and history.[6] Other graphic narratives portraying experiences of war, conflict, and genocide continue mapping sensitive areas of family, national, and world histories, particularly Marjane Satrapi's story of growing up in revolutionary Iran told in *Persepolis* (2000), Joe Sacco's travels to some of the world's hot spots presented in *Palestine* (1996) and *Safe Area Goražde* (2000), and Jean-Phillipe Stassen's *Deogratias* (2000), which offers a harrowing depiction of the Rwandan genocide.[7] The success of these narratives suggests that, like any other graphic or literary form, the comic book provides an ideal platform for exploring complex historical themes, while its hybridity might offer a testing ground to probe the limits of historiography, besides constituting a site where *representations* of war and genocide are questioned, challenged, and undermined.[8]

An extended version of this article appeared as "'Long Live Poland!': Representing the Past in Polish Comic Books," *Modern Language Review* 109, no. 1 (2014): 178–98.

Polish Comics before and after 1989

Comics appeared in Poland shortly after independence in 1918, functioning initially in the form of panel cartoons published in magazines and newspapers, and having a humorous and satirical content. It was, however, the 1930s work of Kornel Makuszyński (1884–1953) and Marian Walentynowicz (1896–1967) called *Koziołek Matołek* (Matołek the Billy-Goat) that marked the actual beginning of the genre in Poland. Aimed at children and recalling adventures of a clumsy goat, the story quickly became a favourite of the nation, making it one of the most popular children's books of all time.[9] In the immediate aftermath of the Second World War, particularly after 1948, comics rapidly became a potent tool of Stalinist indoctrination. Newspapers and youth magazines published comic strips that praised socialist heroes, such as shock workers and peasants, and that demonized actual or imagined enemies of the system, including imperialist spies working to damage Polish interests. All of these stories fashioned one-dimensional realities based on binary oppositions of good socialism and evil imperialism.[10] According to Jerzy Szyłak, these works – blatant communist propaganda, ineptly drawn and scripted – appealed mostly to young and uncritical readers.[11] In the early 1950s, following a period of heightened anti-American propaganda, the term *komiks* and the genre itself began to be associated with Western culture and frowned upon by communist authorities. It was only after the Polish October of 1956, when the regime loosened its grip on cultural production, that comics were restored to their status of legitimate entertainment, free from overt state propaganda.[12]

The rapid expansion of television in the late 1960s brought important changes for other forms of popular culture in communist Poland. The dissemination and visibility of comics increased, shifting to an independent format of magazine-like books, described as *zeszyty komiksowe* or "comic notebooks." This new format reinvigorated the interest of the ruling authorities in the genre, and numerous comic series adhering to the state-controlled vision of Poland's past were published, especially in the early 1970s, such as *Kapitan Kloss* (Captain Kloss) and *Podziemny front* (The Underground Front). Often based on popular television programs, these series emphasized the struggle against Nazi oppressors and the involvement of Red Army and aligned Polish troops in fighting the enemy during the Second World War. Inconvenient topics such as the role of the Home Army and the border shifts following the war were either omitted or distorted to match communist historiography.[13] Michał Słomka shows that comic books at the time used uncomplicated plots, while their aesthetics tended to remain a matter of secondary concern as long as the publications served their main purpose – namely, the legitimation of power. He also asserts that propagandistic and educational principles formed the basis on which "historical" comics in Poland developed; this factor greatly affected the genre's standing after the fall of communism.[14]

Following the workers' protests in 1970 and the subsequent takeover of the leadership by Edward Gierek, the country experienced a short period of economic and cultural revival. Poland opened up to Western influences, and this enriched the comics market. Reprints of French- and English-language strips such as *Astérix* and *Tarzan* were appearing in satirical periodicals, including the popular weekly *Szpilki* (Pins). In 1975 the first issue of the home-grown comic magazine *Relax* came out, and although it was modelled on the Franco-Belgian magazines *Tintin* and *Spirou*, it published and promoted works by Polish artists alone.[15] Szyłak maintains that the overall quality of this monthly was uneven, ranging from high-calibre strips by some of the most accomplished illustrators such as Grzegorz Rosiński (b. 1941) and Janusz Christa (1934–2008) to poorly drawn pieces of communist propaganda that eulogized certain aspects of Poland's past. Nevertheless, *Relax* made an outstanding contribution to popularizing the genre, demonstrating its potential to readers and energizing the comics community as a whole.[16]

In the 1980s two important comics that alluded to Poland's contemporary political situation came to the fore. Despite representing two distinct types of the genre, science fiction and horror respectively, *Funky Koval* and *Wampirus Wars* were addressed to the adult reader well-versed in the complexities of double-speak (Aesopian language). Both series gained a significant following at the time but were largely forgotten in the period immediately after the fall of communism, when comics had become chiefly associated with banal propagandistic pieces of mediocre quality from a bygone era.

The democratic transition of 1989 led to the privatization of the publishing industry; this rendered comics a minority product and forced young artists underground. Despite the existence of successful publishers such as TM-Semic (1990–9), which specialized in American superhero comics, the genre remained practically invisible. Consequently, young artists turned to zines or fanzines, alternative low-circulation magazines that represented a variety of subcultures and were edited by fans. The 1990s also saw an emergence of comics festivals, most notably in Łódź and Warsaw, and the rise of specialist mainstream magazines aimed at stimulating a critical discussion about the genre, including *AQQ*, established in 1993 by Witold Tkaczyk and Łukasz Zandecki, and *Świat Komiksu* (The World of Comics), launched in 1998 by the Egmont Publishing House.[17]

The early 2000s saw the beginning of a short-lived comics boom, heralded by *Antologia komiksu polskiego: Najlepsi młodzi rysownicy* (The Anthology of Polish Comics: Best Young Graphic Artists, 2000). That anthology included a variety of genres ranging from children's graphic novellas to erotic comics, and introduced artists who had emerged during the International Festival of Comics and Games in Łódź, such as Przemysław Truściński (b. 1970); newspaper cartoonists, most notably Michał "Śledziu" Śledziński (b. 1978); and underground artists who had made their debut in fanzines, including Adrian Madej (b. 1977) and Benedykt Szneider (b. 1982). Three years later, *Wrzesień – Wojna Narysowana* (September: The War in Drawings) was published, providing a selection of short graphic narratives on the theme of the Second World War. Main themes included the September campaign, the Warsaw Uprising, and the Holocaust, while the artists themselves used a variety of conventions ranging from realism to fantasy.

In the mid-2000s a new type of graphic narrative of the past emerged that tackled themes that had been either forbidden or distorted under communism. At the same time, the production of historical albums became largely subservient to official narratives of Poland's traumatic and heroic past, particularly following the upsurge of support for the conservative Law and Justice Party. Graphic accounts adhering to such a vision of history mushroomed in Poland, especially between 2005 and 2010, as a result of generous state funding, the growing importance of certain publishing outlets, such as the Poznań-based Zin Zin Press, and an annual comics competition organized by the Warsaw Uprising Museum (Figure 1). This deliberate politicization of the genre made it once more a powerful tool of ideological struggle; fact-based plotlines were enforced to counter the propagandistic stories of the communist era. Though they still existed, alternative projects exploring either personal or fictionalized visions of the past were less likely to attract

Figure 1 Recent comics published by Zin Zin Press. Courtesy of Zin Zin Press.

government subsidies and were not as vital in shaping the popular view of national history. This is not to say there have been no works that offer a personalized take on Poland's past. In fact, in the past decade two outstanding accounts have emerged that explore life under communism and that provide an unconventional examination of the interaction between personal and collective memory. As the analysis below will show, these works build on the tradition of graphic memoir; one is a genuine example of the genre, while the other uses the stylistics of memoir to explore the vicissitudes of history.

The Memory of Communism in Graphic Memoirs

Recently the graphic memoir has become one of the most popular comic genres in the world. Marjane Satrapi's highly acclaimed *Persepolis: The Story of a Childhood* (2000) sold more than 400,000 copies in France and over one million worldwide, winning several prizes and being made into a film in 2007. Praised for its accessible representation of Iranian culture and history told from the perspective of a child, the memoir is also a story of exile and a salient commentary on the Middle Eastern world. Together with other graphic autobiographies, such as Craig Thomson's *Blankets* (2003) and Alison Bechdel's *Fun Home* (2006), *Persepolis* paved the way for new narratives of childhood and adolescence. In the Polish context, *Marzi*, scripted by Marzena Sowa (b. 1979) and illustrated by Sylvain Savoia, is unquestionably the best example of the graphic memoir.[18] Originally written in French and published in six volumes by the Belgian publisher Dupuis between 2005 and 2011, the story is a chronicle of growing up in Stalowa Wola, a small town in southeastern Poland.

Like *Persepolis*, the memoir was written in exile, albeit self-imposed, in France and Belgium. And like Satrapi, Sowa created her literary alter ego, Marzi, in an attempt to revisit her childhood, lived against the backdrop of momentous historical changes. Born in 1979, Marzi is an only child in a working-class family witnessing her country in the process of extricating itself from communism. Like any other little girl of her time, she is preoccupied with small matters – she longs to own a Barbie doll and eat lots of chocolate, while admitting plainly many years later: "I didn't want to carry the weight of my nation, nor search for our identity. In truth, I didn't care. I had no desire to settle History's accounts, to try to figure out who was good and who was bad. I wanted to get away from all that."[19] Despite her attempts to detach herself from the vicissitudes of history, her script shows an acute awareness of the complex intertwining of her family life and the life of her nation under communism, on the brink of independence, and post-1989. As such, alongside telling her deeply personal story, Sowa represents Polish realities of the 1980s and early 1990s.

We meet Marzi one winter as she watches a carp swim in the bathtub before it is butchered by her father and eaten for Christmas Eve dinner, a ritual performed by countless families in Poland. Gradually we learn more about Marzi's life in a highrise apartment block, a symbol of the country's rampant urbanization and standardization of life under communism, under which everyone lives in an identical flat (albeit available in two variants) and has the same brand of Soviet-produced refrigerator, very little space, and even less privacy.[20] Although her everyday life is seldom rosy, with long queues in shops, food rationing, and mean shopkeepers, she seems to be having a happy childhood, one in which rationing is overcome by growing fruit and vegetables on a piece of ancestral land in the country, by gifts from abroad (mostly from Czechoslovakia and the United States), and by occasional deliveries of scarce products, such as oranges.[21] Her free time is spent playing with friends on the staircase or going to the countryside; her leisure activities are visibly influenced by her Roman Catholic upbringing. For example, we see Marzi re-enact the Pope's 1979 Polish pilgrimage from documentary slides she was given by her mother, take her first communion, and attend mass in a country church at Easter.[22] She also imagines what talking to God would be like; one of the panels bears a resemblance to Satrapi's fantasy of being "the last prophet."[23]

Most of the time Marzi is only an unsuspecting observer, but she becomes more aware of politics when important events unfurl before her eyes and begin to affect the life of her family. In the spring and summer of 1988 her father, a worker at the local steel mill, takes part in a series of strikes in which workers demand the relegalization of Solidarity. The strike, which lasts eleven days, is one of the most important acts of workers' resistance in the late 1980s. This is when the little protagonist experiences history in the making and loses some of her innocence as she attempts to understand both her father's and her fatherland's plight: "We're all in the same boat, say the adults, and we're beginning to feel seriously seasick. We need more arms to speed up our progress, to reach land. And not just any land, but the one that'll suit all of us. One that's the way we want it to be. Open and free, a real home!"[24]

She learns quickly that national history is closely intertwined with private history, most notably when she experiences the exhilaration of seeing her father leave the factory after the strike, while the workers celebrate the successful outcome of negotiations, having secured a promise that their demands will be met. The round table talks open in February, and the first parliamentary elections are held in June 1989. At this point Marzi's narrative shifts to include insights on freedom, showing at times Sowa's adult perspective when, for example, she tries to explain the battle her nation has just finished fighting and to define its future trajectory: "They repeated the news on the radio, on TV. Everyone was talking about it. We were trapped in a nightmare but it's over now and we have to learn to talk about it as the past."[25] Here the memoir presents a modern, forward-looking vision of a nation that is not afraid to stand on its own two feet, take responsibility for itself, and make the most of its newly gained freedom without looking back.

Sowa's representation of Poland's past is deeply personal and personalized. Lending a voice to her younger autobiographical self, she presents the complexities of Polish history without letting the child's perspective restrict her thematic choices. In depicting iconic events of the 1980s, she avoids providing an over-historicized chronicle of the times by always keeping the story of her growing up at the centre of the narrative. Thus, national history tends to be treated here as the background to a personal narrative rather than the main focus of the story, as was the case with the state-sponsored albums discussed above. Sowa's memoir steers clear of the mainstream narratives of the past fostered by the political élites in present-day Poland; by focusing on the perplexities of childhood in general, it maintains a more universal appeal. Perhaps this is one reason why *Marzi* has been so popular with its original French-speaking audiences.

Sylvain Savoia's colour illustrations make this memoir a happy one, breaking the stereotypes of greyness and dreariness of Polish life under communism and captivating the reader's imagination. Panels of the same size are used consistently throughout the story, so that they resemble photographs neatly stacked in a family album. According to Dana Mihailescu, this technique is meant to indicate the gradual development of both the life of the Sowa family and that of Polish society under communism.[26] The extensive captions can be compared to those found in family albums, making *Marzi* an important artefact documenting personal history, the role of family in one's upbringing, and the impact of politics on the life of a child.

As a graphic novel that brings Polish realities of the 1980s closer to the Western reader, *Marzi* offers a positive, life-affirming representation of a childhood behind the Iron Curtain, one in which people's values, including family and friendship, turn out to be similar to those of their Western counterparts. Since finishing her work on the series, Sowa has published another graphic novel, this time in collaboration with Sandrine Revel, that tells an endearing fictionalized story of growing up in Stalinist Poland.[27]

Marzi is certainly the most popular graphic account representing the communist past, but it is not the only one. In recent years, some interesting fictional accounts have also appeared. One of them is Jacek Frąś's mini–graphic novel *Stan* (2006), which looks at how the life of a little boy changes on one earth-shattering day under martial law. Although the author does not give away much, it is possible to infer that the plot is set on the night of 1–2 September 1982 in the small copper-mining town of Lubin in lower Silesia. We are told that the boy's name is Andrzej and that his father, Tomasz, has sustained a head injury while at work in the local mine. The novel recounts Andrzej's race to the hospital where his father has supposedly been taken. It is after curfew, and on the way he meets several militia officers patrolling the streets. One of them tells him that during a demonstration in town, Tomasz was killed by a shot to the head by a crazed officer named Bikerski. When the boy reaches the hospital, he finds his father alive, resting with his head bandaged. They embrace, happy to see each other. Meanwhile, Andrzej's mother reports him missing.

Up to this point, the story of Andrzej's night-time dash is interspersed with documentary-like, six-panel pages presenting his father's friends and colleagues sharing their memories of him. It is clear from these reminiscences that years have passed, the boy has grown up, and his father is now dead. These accounts supplement the story of Andrzej's childhood distress; they also provide a commentary on the narrative strategies used in the graphic novel. Throughout the main body of the comic, the boy's identity is performed visually in the third person, since the lack of captions makes it difficult to identify him as the narrator. It is only through the documentary-like memories of other people who address him as they speak that we learn that he is also the person collecting their accounts, and as such controls the overall narrative. The information he provides is intentionally sparse, and the narrative's climax is provided only on the penultimate page, which is a splash page – one of two in the entire comic. It presents the boy hiding in his neighbour's wardrobe and holding on to his father's photograph. At the bottom of the page we can see a speech bubble conveying the neighbour's words: "He was in my wardrobe all this time" (Figure 2).[28] The splash combines minimalistic script and artwork and renders most of the earlier narrative a product of Andrzej's imagination and an expression of bereavement following his father's tragic death. Its simplicity and paucity magnify the sense of loss experienced by the little boy and provide a powerful closure to the story. The final page, also a splash, serves as a form of graphic postscript, showing Andrzej with his father and sister, standing with their backs to the reader. Here the narrator uses captions for the first time in the comic and admits that he had known of his father's death from the very beginning but will never accept it, and instead continue his quest to find him.

Although Frąś's graphic novel can be read as a universal story of loss and anguish following the sudden death of a parent, the historical context is crucial here, for it provides the trigger that sets the events in motion. Indeed, his narrative alludes to the events of 31

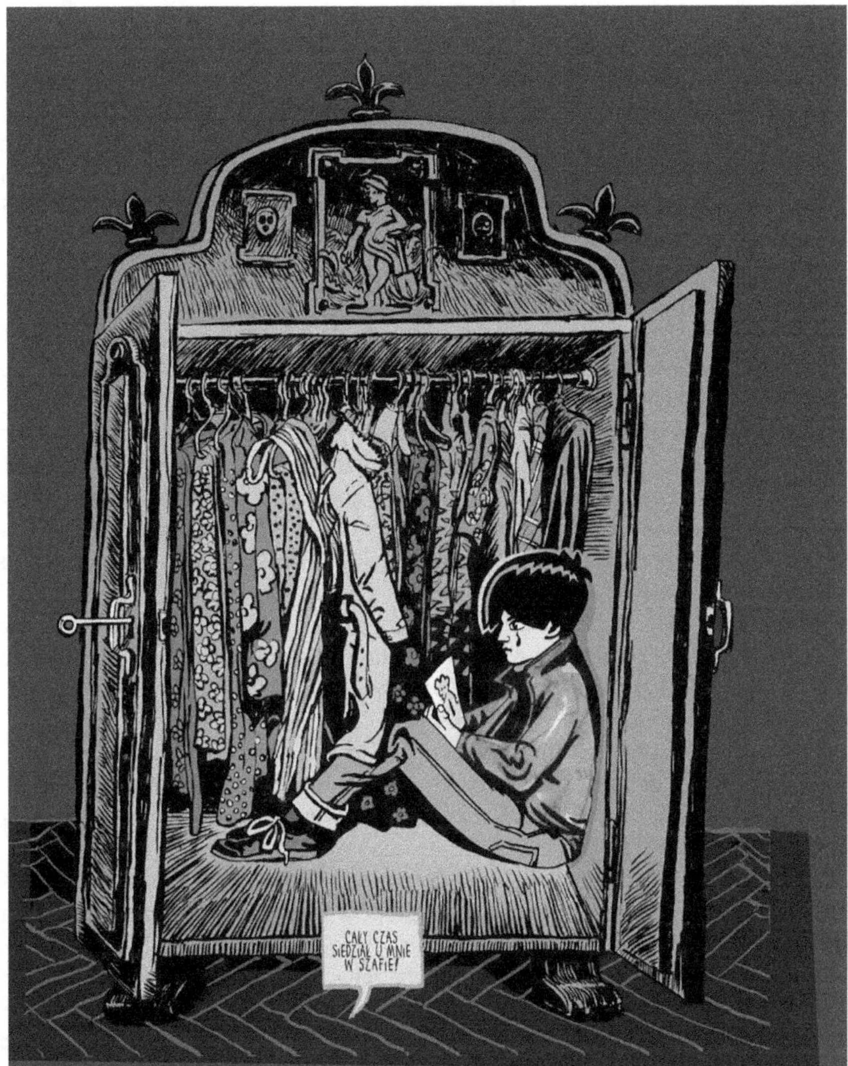

Figure 2 Jacek Frąś, *Stan*, in Przekrój (suppl.), 6 December 2006, p. 19. Courtesy of Jacek Frąś.

August 1982, when the inhabitants of the small town of Lubin came out onto the streets to commemorate the second anniversary of Solidarity, which had been suspended with the imposition of martial law in December 1981. During the peaceful demonstration, three young men were killed, two of them married with children. Though based on these true events, *Stan* avoids literality. Frąś understands that there is no one "correct" version of history, but instead a collection of memories that different people have of a particular event, its victims, and their deaths. By intertwining Andrzej's story with recollections of his father's friends, the comic emphasizes the impossibility of creating a unitary narrative of the past. Needless to say, Tomasz himself is an artistic and literary creation, perhaps a synecdochic representation of the three men or a metaphor for all the victims of the martial law years. This subjectivity and plurality of cultural memory are well expressed in the choice of general theme for the novel. The album steers clear of big history and instead presents events that normally remain on the margins of mainstream narratives of the period of martial law. It looks at local histories while avoiding their potentially politicized interpretations. Frąś speculates, for example, on the possible causes of the tragedy as if accounting for the fact that those who shot at the demonstrators were never identified. This is how he invents Private Bikerski, a lightweight simpleton and laughing stock, who is responsible for Tomasz's death and whose motivations are anything but political. While refraining from judging the events at Lubin directly or providing one-dimensional answers to the tragedy, the artist uses his narrative to suggest that not all incidents of communist-era violence necessarily had their roots in ideology. In this way, he demythologizes one of the most powerful narratives in the Polish national discourse, stripping away its martyrological veneer.

The multiplicity of perspectives and openness to various interpretations of history are shown skilfully in the artwork. For example, Andrzej's childhood story is told in colour using predominantly dark shades, and employs panels of different shapes and sizes, depending on the situation. The narrative of the militia officer who tells the boy about his father's death is presented in red, mainly with caricatural, childlike drawings and irregular panel frames. This helps express the accidental and reckless nature of the shooting, represented on the textual level by the figure of Bikerski. Also, the reminiscences of Tomasz's friends are presented on pages consisting of six panels of uniform size, which use different shades of grey. As such, they express the purported documentary nature of those accounts, while the regularity of the panel frames signals the protagonists' emotional detachment that comes with the passing of time (Figure 3).

Stan is perhaps the greatest achievement of contemporary Polish comic art that deals with the theme of communism. This is no surprise, given that one of Frąś's earlier stories, *Kaczka* (The Duck, 2001) was praised for its unconventional take on the Warsaw Uprising and awarded the Prize for Young Talent at the Angoulême International Comics Festival. Despite the emergence of other fictional graphic narratives exploring the communist period from a child's perspective – most notably Michał Śledziński's *Na szybko spisane. 1980–1990* (Swiftly Drawn: 1980–90) and Marzena Sowa's new graphic novel *Dzieci i ludzie* (Children and People) – to date there have been no works to match Frąś's achievement. Nonetheless, his stories have not yet succeeded in attracting a wider readership, and they remain, to some extent, part of the alternative comic scene known to a narrow group of comic specialists and enthusiasts. This leads to broader questions about the strength of the historical trend in Polish comics and the future development of the genre.

Conclusion

In post-Communist Poland, creators of historical comic books have faced the difficult task of changing the cultural status and common perception of this hybrid genre. As a medium traditionally reserved for fun, propaganda, or fantasy, comics have had to reinvent themselves as a valid form of literary and artistic expression that is "serious" enough to tackle national history. However, this process has been inextricably bound up with the redefinition of national identity and the shifting of the cultural economy following the collapse of communism. Thus, while there is no dearth of historical comics in Poland,

Figure 3 Jacek Frąś, *Stan*, in Przekrój (suppl.), 6 December 2006, p. 13. Courtesy of Jacek Frąś.

most of these works have a didactic purpose and rarely yield satisfactory artistic results. It is the personalized graphic narratives, both autobiographical and fictional ones, such as Sowa's *Marzi* and Frąś's *Stan*, that are beginning to change the face of contemporary comic art in Poland, providing a fascinating take on the complex intertwining of personal and collective memory. As such, these works offer readers the possibility of critical engagement with well-known historical events, eliding the pathos and pomposity of some of the state-funded comics, and depicting a painful past without trivializing it. The two narratives discussed here are contributing to the development of a new generation of readers and artists, nurturing their visual imaginations and providing new models for comic book writing to follow. With any luck, these stories are harbingers of a wider revolution in Polish comic art and mark the beginning of a more open cultural debate about the past.

Ewa Stańczyk
University of Amsterdam / Trinity College, Dublin

NOTES

1 Labio, "What's in a Name?,"' 124.
2 Ziolkowska and Howard, "'Forty-one-year-old female academics,'" 163.
3 Despite having been readily embraced by publishers and readers alike, the use of the term "graphic novel" to describe the whole genre is still widely contested in scholarly circles. For example, Catherine Labio argues that the new term "sanitizes comics; strengthens the distinction between high and low, major and minor; and reinforces the ongoing ghettoization of works deemed unworthy of critical attention, either because of their inherent nature (as in the case of works of humor) or because of their intended audience (lower, less-literate classes; children; and so on)" (Labio, "What's in a Name?," 126). Despite recognizing the need for clearer distinctions in the existing nomenclature, this chapter will chiefly use the two broad terms "graphic novel" and "comic books." They will be understood here as fiction and non-fiction works of varying length that use sequential art and are published in book format, as opposed to in magazines.
4 Frey and Noys, "Editorial," 255.
5 See, for example, Decker and Castro, "Teaching History with Comic Books," 169.
6 See Chute, "'The Shadow of a Past Time,'" 201.
7 Satrapi, *Persepolis*; Sacco, *Safe Area Goražde*; Stassen, *Deogratias*.
8 Frey and Noys, "Editorial," 258–9.
9 Rusek, "Krótka historia opowieści obrazkowych w Polsce Ludowej," 31.
10 Ibid., 33.
11 Szyłak, *Komiks*, 133–4.
12 Rusek, "Krótka historia," 35.
13 Ibid., 38.
14 Słomka, "Polacy lubią brąz," 80–1.
15 Szyłak, *Komiks*, 137.
16 Ibid.
17 For a longer discussion of the situation of comic books in the early 1990s, see Jerzy Szyłak, *Komiks,* 170–3; and *Komiks w kulturze ikonicznej XX wieku,* 72–3.
18 In Poland it was published in a series of three books: *Dzieci i ryby głosu nie mają* (2007), *Hałasy dużych miast* (2008), and *Nie ma wolności bez solidarności* (2011). In this chapter I will use the English edition published as one album in 2011.
19 "Introduction," in Savoia and Sowa, *Marzi*, i–ii.
20 See, for example, ibid., 6–7, 40, 104.
21 Ibid., 14, 17–18, 28, 70.
22 Ibid., 34–5, 42–4, 55.
23 Ibid., 68; cf. Satrapi, *Persepolis*, 14.
24 Savoia and Sowa, *Marzi*, 187.
25 Ibid., 204.
26 Mihailescu, "The Legacy of Communism," 54.

27 Sowa and Revel, *Dzieci i ludzie*.
28 Frąś, *Stan*, 19.

WORKS CITED

Chute, Hillary. "'The Shadow of a Past Time': History and Graphic Representation in *Maus*." *Twentieth Century Literature* (2006): 199–230.

Constantino, Manuela. "Marji: Popular Commix Heroine Breathing Life into the Writing of History." *Canadian Review of American Studies / Revue canadienne d'études américaines* 38 (2008): 429–47.

Decker, Alicia C., and Mauricio Castro. "Teaching History with Comic Books: A Case Study of Violence, War, and the Graphic Novel." *History Teacher* (2012): 169–87.

Frąś, Jacek. *Stan*. In *Przekrój* (suppl.). 6 December 2006, 1–20.

Frey, Hugo, and Benjamin Noys. "Editorial: History in the Graphic Novel." *Rethinking History* 6, no. 3 (2002): 255–60.

Labio, Catherine. "What's in a Name? The Academic Study of Comics and the 'Graphic Novel.'" *Cinema Journal* 50, no. 3 (2011): 123–6.

Mihailescu, Dana. "The Legacy of Communism through a Child's Lens: The Thrusts of Emotional Knowledge out of Marzi's Poland." In *Literary and Visual Dimensions of Contemporary Graphic Narratives*. Edited by Mária Kiššová and Simona Hevešiová. 45–75. Nitra: Constantine the Philosopher University Press, 2012.

Rusek, Adam. "Krótka historia opowieści obrazkowych w Polsce Ludowej." In *45–89: Comics behind the Iron Curtain*. Edited by Michał Słomka. 31–41. Poznań: CENTRALA Central Europe Comics Art, 2009.

Sacco, Joe. *Palestine*. London: Jonathan Cape, 2001.

– *Safe Area Goražde: The War in Eastern Bosnia, 1992–95*. London: Jonathan Cape, 2007.

Satrapi, Marjane. *Persepolis: The Story of a Childhood and the Story of a Return*. London: Jonathan Cape, 2006.

Savoia, Sylvain, and Marzena Sowa. *Marzi: A Memoir*. Translated by Anjali Singh. London: Vertigo, 2011.

Słomka, Michał. "Polacy lubią brąz: czyli o heroizacji polskiej historii w komiksie. Zarys zagadnienia." In *Komiks a problem kiczu. 9 Sympozjum Komiksologiczne. Antologia referatów*. Edited by Krzysztof Skrzypczyk. 80–1. Łódź: Stowarzyszenie Twórców 'Contur', 2009.

Sowa, Marzena, and Sandrine Revel. *Dzieci i ludzie*. Poznań: CENTRALA Central Europe Comics Art, 2012.

Stańczyk, Ewa. "'Long Live Poland!!: Representing the Past in Polish Comic Books." *Modern Language Review* 109, no. 1 (2014): 178–98.

Stassen, Jean-Phillipe. *Deogratias: A Tale of Rwanda*. New York and London: First Second, 2006.

Szyłak, Jerzy. *Komiks*. Kraków: Znak, 2000.

– *Komiks. Świat przerysowany.* Gdańsk: słowo/obraz terytoria, 1998.

– *Komiks w kulturze ikonicznej XX wieku. Wstęp do poetyki komiksu.* Gdańsk: słowo/obraz terytoria, 1999.

Ziolkowska, Sarah, and Vivian Howard, "'Forty-One-Year-Old Female Academics Aren't Supposed to Like Comics!': The Value of Comic Books to Adult Readers." In *Graphic Novels and Comics in Libraries and Archives: Essays on Readers, Research, History, and Cataloguing*. Edited by Robert G. Weiner. 154–66. Jefferson: McFarland, 2010.

Media and Culture

Media – at the sound of this word, the imagination usually calls forth images of the print press, television, radio, and such notions as public debate, politics, or the Fourth Estate. These associations are appropriate, but they conjure up a narrow understanding of media, one that focuses on institutions. The world of media is significantly more complex than that, for it pertains to a fundamental human competence – the ability to communicate through symbols. These symbols and the means for understanding them are created by culture, but their creation and exchange between people requires the aid of media.

Sociologists define media as means that facilitate the formation of relations between people. Anthropologists know that, even though human beings are social creatures, entry into direct relations with the Other requires the conquest of anxieties.[1] This is a consequence of hundreds of thousands of years of evolution that have equipped *Homo sapiens* with a set of emotions, among which fear is the most important mechanism of defence against danger. Fear of the other – a representative of another tribe, clan, or nation – finds its primordial source in the evolutionary history of the species.

Fear, often a symptom of real danger, is easier to overcome in a community, in a group of people who understand and have empathy for one another. Techniques of togetherness were born of this need, and one of the most important – dance, as the coordinated, collective, rhythmic performance of sequences of movements in time and space – is known not only to humans.[2] Only humans, however, require that reality be symbolized in order to be consciously experienced, in other words translated from what they see into concepts and mental pictures.

These concepts and images come alive in social space when materialized through various media, for example in the form of figures painted in the Lascaux Caves, or of produced sounds. The conscious individual and social life of human beings occurs in a virtual space: "We tell stories about our real experiences and invent stories about imagined ones, and we even make use these stories to organize our lives. In a real sense, we live our lives in this shared virtual world."[3] Society inhabits the virtual space constituted by culture, and media provide the means that enable culture's sustenance and growth, thereby ensuring the continuance of community.

Media thus understood not only become mediators that aid interpersonal communication, but also play the role of an interface between different spheres of life, especially during times when societies are developing and increasing their organizational complexity. Culture, economy, technology, government, politics, and law all employ media and both shape and are shaped by media in the process of social communication.

Human need for symbolization is underpinned by a tension between creativity and stability, in other words between the desire for change, which constantly generates new views of the world, and the need to repeat symbolic orders that reinforce the existing structure, hierarchies, and power relations in a given community. From the beginning of human history, specialization has provided a means for reconciling these tensions. Analyses of prehistoric artworks indicate that they required a tremendous amount of work as well as the full commitment of the artist at the cost of other responsibilities. Apparently the cave inhabitants of the Ice Age thought it worthwhile to support specialists who "worked with symbols" – the first media people, such as artists and shamans – in order to reconcile the two contrary, above-mentioned goals: the constant creation of new symbols and representations of reality, and thus of knowledge, and the stabilization of social structure with the support of recurring elements of "cultural virtual reality."[4]

While this tension has no equilibrium point, technology is among the many factors that balance it. The invention of writing thus radically altered reality by making possible the separation of knowledge and symbols from their place of production. Signs written on clay tablets and papyrus rolls served as the glue that held together the first civilizations. The birth of great civilizations founded on the written word was undoubtedly one of the most significant turning points of the past ten thousand years of human history. For those living in the twenty-first century, however, a more recent and more important innovation was Johannes Gutenberg's moveable-type printing press, which radically shifted the balance between novelty and repetition towards novelty. Scholars of relations between society and technology use the notion of affordance – technology does not determine the purpose for which it will be used. In fact, it is often used against the intentions of its creators. It does, though, create a potential that makes some paths of cultural and social development more likely than others. Greg Urban contends that with print was born a modernity that relies on the rule of a metaculture of newness.[5]

Metaculture is a key concept in considerations of Polish culture and media. Urban defines it as a means by which culture speaks about itself and creates the conditions for its own sustenance and development. The pre-Gutenberg epochs were dominated by a traditional metaculture that relied on repetition. Both the media available at the time and the necessities arising from that availability favoured cultural forms that built on the repetition of traditional practices and rituals: the same forms of dance, the same myths told around the fire. Fidelity to tradition expressed in the most precise memorization of myth or rituals would guarantee the permanence of the fragile.

The metaculture of newness in which innovation and constant change are held at a premium arose with mechanized printing. Print was originally intended to serve traditional culture – the mass production of Bibles was supposed to ensure the return of Christian doctrine to its sources (i.e., the word of the Bible). Something else happened instead: print unleashed a demand for reading *per se* that the Bible alone was unable to fulfil. As a consequence of this demand, there appeared a supply of new publications, and thus new forms of culture began to develop, such as the novel, of which Miguel Cervantes's *Don Quixote* from the turn of sixteenth and seventeenth centuries is an excellent example. In that novel one learns not only of the adventures of a knight-errant, but also that even then culture which relied on mass replication had to contend with its pathologies: piracy and plagiarism.[6] In response to these issues, new institutions were created and tasked with deciding whether subsequent books met the criteria of newness and quality. When repetition was held at a premium, it was necessary to have institutions that guaranteed the accuracy of repetition. The modern epoch, by contrast, brought about the need to evaluate whether new texts were actually new, or only poor copies of previously published content.

The metaculture of newness permeated other spheres of life – science, technology, and other areas of culture. The need to evaluate that newness could be fulfilled only by "new" media (i.e., new from the historical perspective at the time); these media were aimed at "news" – in other words, the print press. By happy coincidence, the technology that led to the development of the metaculture of newness also made possible the institutional development of this metaculture in the form of the press. Print technology made its way to Poland in 1473 through Kraków, where the first printing press commenced operation. It was necessary to wait for the first Polish newspaper until 1661, when *Merkuriusz Polski Ordynaryjny* (The Polish Common Mercury) appeared in Kraków,[7] and continued on a weekly basis in order to "inform with excellence on note-worthy events both in the homeland and in the entire world, namely Europe and the Christendom."[8]

The *Mercury* was founded on the initiative of the royal court: Jan Kazimierz (John II Casimir), the King of Poland and the Grand Duke of Lithuania, wanted to introduce *vivente rege* elections (the election of a successor to the throne during the predecessor's reign) in order to avoid the chaos of an interregnum period. Obviously, the point of this institutional reform was to allow the living king plenty of influence over who his successor would be. But the nobility were accustomed to "golden freedom" and had no intention of making any concessions in this vein. Stripped of many of the attributes of real authority, the ruler of the Commonwealth decided to influence the minds of the political spheres by creating an instrument suited to that task – almost as if he had studied modern theories of media power.[9]

The newspaper, which appeared every week starting on 3 January 1661, was more than a propaganda tool; it also presented information from the war front with Moscow as well as from abroad. The adventure most likely ended on 22 July 1661, when the reform project failed during a Sejm meeting in Warsaw. The circulation of *Merkuriusz* was undoubtedly small, estimated today at between 100 and 300 copies. Its reach and readership are unfortunately unknown, as is its impact on public opinion in the Commonwealth, which had entered a period of permanent crisis of political identity in the decades since the first free election to the throne in 1572. The elected king had ceased to be a guarantor of the continuity of the "political body,"[10] and this void was not filled by democratic public opinion, for this would have required the existence of media that allowed for the creation of political positions and the defining of public interests. The ruling magnates and nobility were not interested in this form of deliberative democracy. The failure of the *Mercury* and the lack of popularity of other press projects revealed that the country of the Sarmatians was still steeped in a metaculture of tradition and was not prepared to receive the metaculture of newness.

This anachronism and traditionalism is identified perfectly by Adam Mickiewicz in *Pan Tadeusz*:

> But such was then the blindness of the nation,
> None would believe the wisdom of the ages,
> Unless 'twere read in some French journal's pages.[11]

For residents of manor houses in Lithuania, the Borderlands, and Podlachia, the source of meaning was still found in tradition, in the repetition of rituals tested "through the ages," and in obeisance to the customs of forefathers. Not so for those youth who had come into contact with the wider world, or at least with Warsaw, where intellectual life began to bloom anew during Stanisław August Poniatowski's reign, as expressed by increased publishing activity and press readership. The weekly *Monitor* was so popular that some issues were reprinted, and *Zabawy Przyjemne i Pożyteczne* (Pleasant and Useful Entertainment) was copied by hand by its readers.[12] For readers of these titles, much like today among those who use Google, if something was not encountered in their favourite medium, it did not exist at all.

A newspaper reader became almost a different kind of a human being – something grasped (again) by Mickiewicz:

> 'Twas sad to hear the pale-faced puppies drawl
> Through noses – if they had a nose at all
> Stuffed with all kinds of pamphlets and gazettes
> Proclaiming new religions, laws, toilettes.[13]

Appetite for the press depended on broadened horizons and interest in the world. However, reaching for a newspaper also entailed a Faustian bargain: those who read periodicals, regardless of their content, became modern in the sense that they accepted the metaculture of newness, developed a dependency on regular doses of fresh news, and expected that each edition of a favoured paper would deliver something new instead of repeating already known ideas and facts.

Consequently, newspapers during the nineteenth century became a powerful force in cultural production, and not just in the former Commonwealth. Readers expected newspapers to deliver novelty, and this compelled publishers to look for sources of new, original content. Political life was not sufficient for this, especially since political communication was sharply restricted across the partitioned territories as a result of censorship. Consequently, the quickly developing capitalist economy became an important supplier of and audience for information. The mass of urban readers, however, also expected the press to entertain them.

The dislike of novelty that Mickiewicz observed and that was present in late-eighteenth-century culture had given way by the turn of the nineteenth and twentieth centuries to an entirely different spirit. Thus, Stanisław Wyspiański's *Wesele* (The Wedding, 1901) begins with a reference to media, which becomes part of the narration, when Headman stresses with pride, "We read the papers, even here! We know a thing or two –"[14] Even in the farthest corners of the country, in the villages and the most traditional of environments, the metaculture of newness was coming out on top, and the journalist, or media man, was becoming an important public figure.

This is not surprising, considering that

> in the second half of the nineteenth century the development of journals is so intense that the newspaper displaces the book at least in some circles of Polish society. Editors are well aware that a rebus, charade, sensational correspondence, columns, as well as serial novels are much more attractive options than a lyric or narrative poem. What is worse, the majority of newspapers are constantly searching for a proprietary formula out of concern for the number of subscribers, often changing their owners, profiles, addressees, or political orientation.[15]

There was surely no shortage at that time of those who were upset by the cultural changes tied to the development of the press, just as there is no shortage of critics of the Internet today. Many at that time saw those changes as a mark of decline. It is worth noting, however, that it was precisely the press that led to the development of a specific cultural form so characteristic of the nineteenth century: the novel. Bolesław Prus (1847–1912), Władysław Reymont (1867–1925), Stefan Żeromski (1864–1925), and Henryk Sienkiewicz (1846–1916) all printed their works in newspapers, and the newspapers' publication cycle drove them to constant creative effort. As soon as Sienkiewicz finished *Potop* (The Deluge, 1886), the audience demanded new adventures, never mind that he was exhausted and was mourning his wife's death. He had no choice but to take up his pen again and bring to life *Pan Wołodyjowski* (Colonel Wolodyjowski, 1888).

In creating the metaculture of newness, the press simultanously created the demand for new content and satisfied the need for it, in the process producing an entirely new formation: the modern nation. The Polish territories and society had been divided among neighbouring states, yet Poles retained their cultural identity and indeed became culturally modern. This was a consequence of searching, with the help of press and culture, for an answer to a key question: Who are we? What constituted the collective "we" that linked the Poles living in Warsaw, Kraków, and Poznań – meaning, respectively, under Russian, Austro-Hungarian, and Prussian partition? They were undoubtedly united by the fact that, in newspapers published independently in each of these cities, they read the same novels and embraced the same myths that reconstructed the times of Commonwealth's greatness. Simultaneously, they all also took up – as did Prus's *Lalka* (The Doll, 1890) and Reymont's *Ziemia obiecana* (Promised Land, 1899) – contemporary nineteenth-century problems that were similar across the board: the progress of capitalism, the transformation of the social structure, and the modernizing shift by means of which "all that is solid melts into air."[16]

Yet this construction of a modern "we" of Poles did not take place solely on a spiritual plane, in the virtual world of culture. A modern communication infrastructure was permeating society, at a different speed in each of the partitions but always with the same tendency. The press would not have had such a strong impact were it not for the development of the telegraph and the railway in the second half of the nineteenth century. The telegraph erased distance and ensured almost immediate access to information from around the globe. The railway made possible not only the transportation of people and products but also the distribution of periodicals. As it modernized society, the press was also modernizing itself, evolving into a media system – an increasingly professionalized and specialized part of social reality. It depended directly and primarily on readers, so publishers had a great stake in promoting universal education. To satisfy a growing mass of recipients, technical infrastructure had to be developed: printing houses, distribution systems, financial accounts, and the training of a cohort of journalists. But most importantly, the development of the press was impacted by political factors and censorship.[17]

Political restrictions were unable to stop the development of the press even in the Polish Kingdom after the January Uprising of 1863, when heightened censorship became an instrument of repression. Twenty periodicals were published there in 1864, mainly in Warsaw; twenty years later, there were 80; forty years later, in 1904, there were 140. Among them were dailies – only five in 1864, but nine by 1885 and fourteen by 1904.[18] A modern society was taking shape alongside the developing modern infrastructure and media system, integrated by a culturally promoted idea of a nation, but also divided by social class and ideology.

Due to the absence of political sovereignty, this new social stratification, in which the working and middle classes played an increasingly important role, was burdened with divisions stemming from different assessments of history and the catastrophe of partitions, as well as from divergent visions of the future. Poland's search for its own civilization was simultaneously a search for an answer to the question of what constituted the Polish "we." That search oscillated between two extremes: Occidentalism and its obverse.[19] At the beginning of the twentieth century, this model was superimposed on real social structures and informed the development of two major political ideologies, nationalism and socialism. These defined the most important political projects aimed at restoring Poland's independence and they subsequently shaped the Second Republic. The press, of course, played a key role in consolidating and popularizing these ideologies and in attracting new followers to them.

A sign of a new media reality had appeared even before the First World War, when Poland was still partitioned. In 1910 the *Ilustrowany Kurier Codzienny* (Illustrated Daily Courier) began publication, and over time it would develop into the most popular paper in the Second Republic. Aimed at a broad readership and not shy about politics, but also filled with sensationalism, it became a perfect expression of the evolution of the media system as an enterprise loyal only to readers and investors. Marian Dąbrowski (1878–1958), the architect of its success, became a Polish "Citizen Kane," a press magnate with huge financial, social, and political influence.

The press market was growing also in regions annexed by Prussia – albeit less intensively due to a fairly small class of intelligentsia – with Poznań as its most important publishing centre. The landscape of Polish media changed radically after the 1905 revolution in Russia, when a wave of political liberalization in the Russian Empire further stoked the already existing enthusiasm for news media in Poland. Political parties played a large role in this new expansion. The National Democratic Party bought up existing titles such as *Goniec Poranny i Wieczorny* (Morning and Evening Courier) and *Głos Warszawski* (Varsovian Voice), besides undertaking its own projects, notably the sensationalistic party paper *Gazeta Poranna 2 grosze* (2 Penny Morning Paper), which was launched in 1912 and aimed at a mass readership. The task of socialists in the Polish Kingdom was more difficult since they were subjected to more strident censorship and political repressions, a consequence of their anti-tsarist radicalism. Notwithstanding these challenges, the day before the war broke out in 1914, Varsovians could choose from among fourteen Polish-language newspapers.

The modern Polish nation that had been established by culture with the considerable support of the press was ready to regain its political sovereignty. Shared cultural identity, however, could not eclipse the differences that divided Polish society. These differences concerned both the strategy for establishing a future Poland and the foundations on which that entity was to rest. In the latter case, the question, put simply, was whether that nation would bring back the traditions of Piast's Poland, or those of the multicultural Jagiellonian Commonwealth? Choosing a strategy, in turn, was a political matter involving alliances between particular groups and defining your enemies. These differences were fully apparent by the time Poland regained its independence in 1918, and concerned even such symbolic moments as Independence Day. The date of 11 November was entered into national and state calendars, but it was contested by nationalists for overemphasizing Józef Piłsudski's camp. Regardless of the conflict over symbols, the Polish state had returned to the political map of Europe, although with still undefined borders and a multicultural society that was divided not only along ethnic lines, but also by those of mentality – a consequence of having been split between three very different empires for more than a century.

From the first days of the independent Second Republic, the media played a key role in the search for an answer to the question carried over from the nineteenth century about the "we" of Poles. At stake in this search, among other things, was Poles' attitude towards other societies. Other social groups – whether within Polish borders or in the new states bordering Poland – were engaging with the same issue. The answers that Poles formulated often conflicted with answers arrived at by Ukrainians, Lithuanians, and Jews living in Poland, and they were sometimes at odds also with answers that served the integration of new political entities such as Czechoslovakia.

The media played a significant role in these conflicts in that they organized public debate and cranked up emotions. By the time its independence was restored, six hundred press titles were being published on Poland's territories, half of them in Warsaw. Despite the difficult economic situation faced by a society only beginning to rebuild itself after war's devastations, within a decade there were a thousand press titles. Not only Poles but also members of minorities were able to read newspapers in their native tongue. Yet for at least the first decade of the interwar period, there were no publications with a nationwide reach to speak of; the development of such initiatives was thwarted by infrastructural shortfalls that made distribution impossible.

In 1918, rural residents constituted 64 per cent of Polish society, and it was they who were the majority of the illiterate masses – at that time, levels of illiteracy exceeded 30 per cent. The task of writing history and reproducing the myths that defined national identity fell to the intelligentsia, who were a mere 5 per cent of the society and came largely from the gentry and the nobility.

The myth of the Sarmatian nobility became the cultural foundation of Polish identity even though Polish society was dominated by the peasant class. Yet in feudal times, peasants had been stripped of both citizenship and voice. Sarmatian ideology even distinguished the occupants of villages condemned to serfdom as an anthropologically different species. Roman Dmowski's efforts to transform a people into a nation succeeded in political terms, yet the cultural codes of the National Democratic electorate, whose strength derived mainly from the middle class and the *petit bourgeoisie*, were not effective at displacing or even weakening the dominant myth. Similarly, the rising political aspirations of farmers in the Second Republic did not translate into a narration that could infiltrate the cultural code that dominated the national identity.

Modern Polish identity thus rested on a discursive dissonance – Poles represented themselves differently than their actual social substance would dictate. The dominance of a noble, "aristocratic" discourse became a source of stereotypes, from which external observers drew when defining the Polish national character. The Poland of lords, of hotheaded Sarmatians obsessed with honour and scornful of death, of knights and warriors fighting in the name of our freedom and yours – these clichés filled to the brim the symbolic toolboxes that Poles used when defining themselves, then as now; they were also used by foreign propagandists who, depending on their political interests, deployed them either to lampoon or to legitimate the presence of Poles in civilized salons.

Furthermore, the significance of culture is not solely symbolic or identity-based. An identity rooted in a "code of the nobility" was aligned perfectly with the material and organizational structure of Polish society, which invariably relied on re-creating the manor structure as a model of organizing economically valuable production, interhuman relationships, and social bonds. The valorization of the noble myth was possible only at the cost of erasing from public consciousness the fact that the material foundations of this myth had been secured by what amounted to agricultural slave labour.[20]

The aspects of identity that had been suppressed in social consciousness invariably returned as the Real, which constantly reproduced itself in the organizational and social structures of, first, the Second Republic, then the Polish People's Republic,[21] and, finally, the Third Republic.[22] This discursive dissonance does not express some psychological affliction unique to the Poles, however. In an excellent essay about the historical fate of small Eastern European nations, which analyses the convoluted political projects of Poles, Hungarians, and Czechs, István Bibó[23] traces their roots to an endemic anachronism – that is, an inability to perceive and adequately adjust to the spirit of the times. Societies touched by this affliction paid the highest price by being erased from the political world map.

This price was perhaps inevitable given the semi-peripheral status of Central European countries, which were too weak to develop fully autonomous political, social, and economic projects. After all, the manor form of organization used to exploit peasant labour, while a Central European invention, was also a response to economic pressure from Western Europe, which at the time was the centre of political power. Reality necessitated the adoption of realistic solutions, which did not align well with the pride and sense of self-worth of the spheres exerting ideological control over society. The Real had to be covered with a layer of cultural varnish; the grim, feudal Poland of farm estates, in which roughly 90 per cent of society had the status of slaves for several hundred years, exists today in the collective imagination as a country of golden freedom and horsemen in winged helmets. Understanding this tension between the Real and the image that exists both in the collective imagination and the dominant discourse is indispensible to understanding the public debates that have been ongoing since the nineteenth century. Each such debate repeats the same questions about the extent to which Poland can develop in an original way, and about the degree to which, as a semi-peripheral country, it is condemned to imitate more developed societies.

The media, as a system for organizing social communication, have always played a key role not only as transmitters of content but as generators of metaculture. When Gabriel Narutowicz (1865–1922) became the first president of the Second Republic in 1922, his election elicited a furious reaction among the National Democratic press, with Stanisław Stroński (1882–1955), one of the most renowned and talented journalists of the interwar period, leading the way. In the journal *Rzeczpospolita* (The Republic), he published an article titled ""Ich prezydent" (Their President) in which he argued that Narutowicz had become the head of state only because of ethnic minority votes and thus was not a fully legitimate president. Stroński not only undermined the validity of the election results; his vision of Poland also included depriving ethnic minorities of the opportunity to enjoy their full political rights. Stroński's hate campaign intensified until, tragically, the president was assassinated on 16 December 1922 by Eligiusz Niewiadomski. Even this did not end the escalation of tensions; the following day, Stroński published another text, "Ciszej nad tą trumną!" (Be Quiet Over this Coffin!), which shifted responsibility for the tragedy onto the political powers behind Narutowicz's election. This mode of expressing one's vision for a collective "we" – rejecting any participation of the "Other" in the collective, and undermining the legitimacy of the ruling powers – became standard in Polish public debate and politics.

Participation in the power discourse is among the media's most important prerogatives. They participate in that discourse on several levels, including directly, as the example of Stroński's journalism demonstrates. The authorities responded to Stroński's rhetoric with propaganda. Propagandistic activities engaged, among others, one of the most accomplished Polish reporters, Melchior Wańkowicz (1892–1974), who directed the Press Division of the Ministry of Internal Affairs from 1923 to 1926. *Sztafeta* (Relay, 1939), a collection of Wańkowicz's reports from the building sites of New Poland showing the country's unprecedented scale of modernization, can be considered a pinnacle achievement in the art of propaganda. The narrative ends at the moment when the Polish Army occupies Zaolzie; this is meant to express the nation's maturity and to serve as proof of Poland's success at modernizing itself. Its next project is to be an imperial one – to join in the colonization efforts in which the most advanced Western societies were by then taking part.[24]

A second level of media participation in the power discourse – its metacultural function by which it affects the development of other cultural forms – is less direct but, as has been previously noted, incredibly important for legitimizing perceptions of a collective identity – of that "we" as a subject of joint action. For example, during the nineteenth century, the press supported the dynamic development of the novel; when the fashion for serialized novels was exhausted in the twentieth century, the entertainment function was taken over by cinema as well as theatre, which fulfilled the cultural needs of a slowly consolidating middle class. The press stimulated cultural production through the mere fact of its existence and the cyclical logic of its activities. The growing number of publications spurred the development of new types of content, with newspapers requiring news and sensations not just from the world of politics. The passion for novelty was supported by cultural criticism – reviews written by often remarkable talents, which assessed whether a new film, performance, or book was worth paying attention to. In these ways, the press activated among its readers a demand for culture, turning them into spectators who constantly expected new writing.

The press in independent Poland did much to sustain political tensions around a fundamental argument over the identity of Poles. Setting aside the brutal conflicts arising from these tensions, the metacultural character of the media that helped to build a modern nation during the nineteenth century also helped, under conditions of independence, to build a modern culture in all its aspects: from a plebeian one that feasted on true crime accounts through popular cinema to high art. The appearance of radio in 1925 did not radically alter the media landscape of Poland. Initially a toy for the élites, radio began to acquire mass popularity in the 1930s, not by competing with newspapers, however, but rather by supplementing what the press was already offering. Thus, between 1932 and 1937, the consumption of newsprint paper increased by half, during which time the number of radio subscribers increased from 300,000 in 1933 to more than 500,000 by

1939 (the number of subscribers can be multiplied by five to arrive at the number of listeners).[25]

In summarizing Poles' encounters with the media prior to the Second World War, one cannot omit the phenomenon of the Catholic press, published under the auspices of the Roman Catholic Church. In May 1935, *Mały Dziennik* (The Little Daily) began to appear, circulated by the Franciscan Friars of Niepokalanów. This venture, launched by Maximilian Kolbe (1894–1941), joined sensationalism with a national and Catholic vision of the world; in that vision, prior to the war, anti-Semitism was an integral element. *The Little Daily* enjoyed Episcopal support and could count on distribution through the parish network. As a result, its circulation surged to 100,000 within a few months. Another Franciscan publication, the monthly *Rycerz Niepokalanej* (Knight of the Immaculate), had a circulation of 700,000.

The interwar aspirations of the Second Republic were crushed by the German invasion of September 1939. The discourse of power and ambition created in the virtual space of myths and ideologies maintained by media and culture turned out to be inadequate when faced with real historical forces, whose actors deployed a different calculus of power. The outbreak of the Second World War ended Poland's brief independence, and many cultural institutions that had begun forming in the nineteenth century, including the media, disappeared at that time. The war, and the ensuing German and Soviet occupation, marked a new reality also on the level of communication.

In an effort to legitimize their conquest, the aggressors reconstructed Poland's media on their own terms, funding the activities of propaganda rags (*gadzinówki*) that supported the occupiers' administrations. As early as 11 October 1939, the weekly "Nowy Kurier Warszawski" (New Warsaw Courier) was appearing in print runs of 300,000. The situation was similar in other cities, although the impact of titles like these on Polish society was insignificant, since Poles turned towards the underground press instead. The fact that such a press even existed under conditions of brutal repression is remarkable; the fact that it thrived, published by all forces and organizations involved in the liberation struggle, is close to miraculous. By the time the Warsaw Uprising broke out, an entire underground press had taken root; in August and September 1944, 130 titles were coming out in Warsaw, with "Biuletyn Informacyjny" (The Informational Bulletin) even reaching a circulation of 50,000.[26]

THE MOST IMPORTANT POLISH ÉMIGRÉ MEDIA, CULTURAL INSTITUTIONS, AND PRIZES:

Paris: *Wiadomości Polskie, Polityczne i Literackie* (Polish Political and Literary News, Paris/London, 1940–4); Instytut Literacki (Literary Institute, since 1947), with Jerzy Giedroyć's monthly *Kultura* (Culture, 1947–2000) and its annual literary prize (1954–99); *Zeszyty Literackie* (Literary Notebooks, 1983–90, in Warsaw since 1990); Editions Spotkania (1978–93) and its quarterly *Libertas* (1978). **London**: Mieczysław Grydzewski's *Wiadomości* (News, 1946–81) with its annual literary prize (1957–90); Krystyna and Czesław Bednarczyk's Publishing House Oficyna Poetów i Malarzy (Poets' and Painters' Press, 1950–92) and its quarterly *Oficyna Poetów* (Poets' Press, 1966–80); *Kontynenty* (Continents, 1959–64); Polonia Book Fund Ltd (1959–94); Polska Fundacja Kulturalna (Polish Cultural Foundation, since 1950); Puls Publications (established in 1977 in Łódź; in London 1982–90; in Warsaw 1991–3); *Aneks* (The Annex, 1973–90; previously in Uppsala). **New York**: Kazimierz Wierzyński and Jan Lechoń's *Tygodnik Polski* (Polish Weekly, 1943–6); Polish Institute of Arts and Science; Alfred Jurzykowski Foundation (since 1960) with its annual prize (1964–98). **Munich**: an important hub of émigré life due to Radio Free Europe, with its own literary prize and an all-day Polish broadcast (1952–90; in Warsaw from 1990 to 1994). **Berlin**: *Przekazy* (Transmissions, 1982–4); *Pogląd* (Opinion, 1982–90); *Archipelag* (Archipelago, 1984–7). **Geneva**: Kościelski Foundation Prize (since 1962). **Montreal**: Polish Institute of Arts and Sciences in Canada and the Wanda Stachiewicz Polish Library at McGill University (since 1943). **Toronto**: The Canadian-Polish Research Institute (since 1956); Polish Publishing Fund; W&N Turzański Foundation (1988–2015). The émigré prizes were not limited to émigré writers and were often awarded to writers from Poland.

The Polish press was also developing in exile, taking up the painful task of accounting for the defeat of the September Campaign and, once again, envisioning a future Poland. The resulting visions did not stand a chance of being realized, however, once Poland found itself within the Soviet Union's sphere of influence as a result of the Yalta Conference. Using the Yalta agreements and its military power, Moscow set the parameters for the future development of a new state: the Polish People's Republic.

The period of the PPR does not submit to easy descriptions. It adopted various unique strategies in the areas of culture, social life, and media whose many nuances and idiosyncrasies get overlooked when approached from an unequivocal stance. It goes without saying that the communist government of the PPR arrived on the tips of Soviet bayonets, had an initially totalitarian character, and remained authoritarian as a system until the end. Yet it is also true that for many years the communist system in Poland enjoyed considerable social legitimization that did not stem solely from fear. The PPR brought on a social revolution that irrevocably broke with Poland's feudal inheritance, shaping at the same time a new socio-economic system that did not differ that much from the abolished one. The PPR authorities belonged to the communist Polish United Workers' Party, yet the most difficult, often bloody battles fought by this party were precisely against workers who did not accept its hegemony. It was also workers who brought about the triumph of Solidarity in 1980. Only one in four workers supported the falling system by 1988; among intelligentsia and the public managerial sector, that support was 50 per cent. All expressions of social and cultural life were subject to licensing and state control, but at the same time, Polish cinema, literature, and theatre flourished. Within this complex, paradoxical reality, the role of the media was, of course, no less paradoxical. It was subject to censorship, but this did not stop the development of great talents and journalistic careers. For example, Ryszard Kapuściński (1932–2007) was an employee of the PPR media system, but this did not prevent him from reaching world-class heights; his reportages are indispensible to understanding the revolutions that shook developing countries in the 1960s and 1970s.

In a simplified picture of media in non-democratic or quasi-totalitarian countries, it is assumed that the press, radio, and television serve only propagandistic aims. Propaganda is, of course, an important aspect of the media, but authoritarian discourse is more complex than this. No power, not even a totalitarian one, can rely solely on force for its legitimacy. A much more important source of legitimacy is cognitive acceptance of the existing regime, and that acceptance does not depend solely on persuading the people that the system is the best in the world despite its evident deficiencies.

The cognitive acceptance of the existing regime depends also on the conviction that the structures of social communication that serve the aims of identity construction, social bonding, and metacultural development meet all the requirements of normal, commonly accepted practice. What is interesting is that the standard of such normality was determined not by the centre in Moscow but by the civilizational centre in the West, which served as source of technological progress, cultural models (especially regarding mass culture), and consumer trends.[27] Socialist consumption did not differ from capitalist consumption beyond the fact that, due to a central planning system, it was officially supposed to be less wasteful than the free market system for allocating resources and setting prices. In reality, precisely the opposite was the case.

This divergence of theory and practice was a principal theme of media debates that continued throughout the PPR era, with ritually recurring motifs: shortage of twine for reaper-binders during harvest, unloaded citrus-filled cargo ships waiting in ports before Christmas, and so on. The task of the socialist media was twofold: in a standard, journalistic way they revealed the pathologies that had developed during the process of building the system of "social justice," admittedly within the parameters set by political climate and by the censorship apparatus. At the same time, however, they cooperated in hiding especially uncomfortable aspects of reality to help prevent the system's foundations from being undermined.

The more acquiescent of media institutions, such as *Trybuna Ludu* (People's Tribune) and *Żołnierz Wolności* (Freedom's Soldier), the official newspapers of the United Polish Workers' Party, also participated in witch hunts against those who could be blamed for the difficulties the system encountered. This included ritual condemnations of "loafers" and instigators and of party members whose class-consciousness was underdeveloped. Operating within the media reality of the PPR required appropriate journalistic competency but also knowledge of how the game was played by journal and broadcast editors in the print and electronic media. One picked up *People's Tribune* only to learn what the party line was; that knowledge then made it easier to interpret articles in the weekly newsmagazine *Polityka* (Politics), whose content had been redacted by the censors to reflect the party line, but without indicating the extent of this intervention.

The source of legitimacy for an authoritarian system is not the single voice of all licensed media, but a polyphony signifying that social emotions clash with one another within a public space controlled by the authorities; those voices are controlled, and therefore are not fully free, but neither are they completely subjugated to the centre's will. Regardless of the binding political regime, modern society is a complex structure that depends on a supply of personnel with a high level of intellectual competency. The dynamic space of culture, science, and media is a condition of their development and reproduction. In the end, no power is a monolith; inner tensions ensure that its control of social space cannot be absolute. It is precisely within this space of ambiguity that the media system of the PPR, judged to be the most interesting one in all the Soviet Bloc, developed. Its development between 1944 and 1989 can be analysed in various ways.

Media as the means of social communication are by definition sensitive to historical events and social, political, and cultural contexts; this makes it necessary to periodize their evolution. Indeed, Polish postwar history allows us to identify the distinguishing functions of media during each of its discrete periods. The years 1944 to 1947 were, in effect, a time of civil war, during which the Moscow-sponsored Polish Workers' Party eliminated the remnants of a democratic order. The communists established their own media system (based mainly in the press and to a smaller degree in radio right after the war) while simultaneously eliminating publications by the political opposition and the Church (which at the time were still legal). The communists repressed their competition through censorship and by restricting the freedoms of the most inconvenient opponents, as well as through direct control of the paper supply, distribution channels, and printing houses. As a result, even legal titles often struggled to reach their readers.

Still, we have to remember that the communists' aim was not simply to wipe out the opposition; they also hoped to build legitimacy for the new socialist reality. This goal was advanced in part through diverse and quite subtle publishing policies. One architect of these policies was Jerzy Borejsza (1905–52), the founder of the Czytelnik (Reader) Publishing Cooperative, whose article "Rewolucja łagodna" (The Gentle Revolution), published in the weekly *Odrodzenie* (Revival) in 1945, presented the authorities' rules of liberal cultural politics.

> After the catastrophic war that was sealed with the tragedy of the Warsaw Uprising of 1944, Poland faced the task of rebuilding its **intelligentsia**: after all, 37 per cent of Poles with a higher education died during the war (and there was no excess of such people in the Second Republic), along with 30 per cent of those with a high school diploma. These losses were amplified by decisions to remain in exile made by many of the refugees who had emigrated to the West in 1939 or who had escaped the Soviet Union with the army of General Anders.

It was precisely significant cultural openness, supported by such initiatives as the popular cultural weekly *Przekrój* (Cross-Section), that helped build a new intellectual elite. These élites did not fully support communism, but they also took at face value gestures suggesting that the "dictatorship of the proletariat" would not be a dictatorship of simpletons, but a system open to high and refined culture. The new intelligentsia was often the product of social advancement and needed cultural institutions and practices that would confirm the validity of their aspirations and accomplishments; they also needed to affirm that former farmhands could rise not only to factory work but also to the ranks of intelligentsia.

The liberal cultural politics within the framework of communist-controlled media were suspended in 1948. Victory in the civil war, which had pacified the democratic opposition and crushed the armed underground, assured the communists of their complete power. In December 1948 the Polish Socialist Party was absorbed by the communist Polish Workers' Party to create the United Polish Workers' Party. In the Soviet Union, Josef Stalin once again heightened his terror, and he expected the satellite states to take a similarly harsh approach. In tandem with the political turnaround, a reversal took place in the politics of culture and media. The aesthetic of socialist realism was imposed on culture, and the media were submitted to full communist control, as were all autonomous forms of social life, whose last enclaves could be found in the structures of the Catholic Church. The years 1948 to 1956, known as the Stalinist period, were the grimmest time in the postwar history of Poland, marked as they were by restrictions on all freedoms and by brutal repressions and the physical extermination of actual and suspected enemies of the totalitarian order. In the cellars of the Department of Security perished not only former soldiers of the armed underground but also communists who had been insufficiently sensitive to unpredictable changes in the political climate.

The next, more optimistic period dawned after Stalin's death in 1953, although the actual thaw began only three years later. Its first act – a workers' revolt in June 1956, in Poznań – while it ended with bloody carnage, nevertheless resulted in a breakthrough that bore fruit in the fall. Władysław Gomułka came to power and with his firm stance towards the Soviet Union demonstrated that, while he was a communist, he was also a patriot focused on maximizing national sovereignty within the framework of socialism. The October events generated a breeze that refreshed the space of culture and the media. The refurbished weekly *Po prostu* (Simply Put) became an icon of those days, fulfilling the function of a free tribune. It was joined by the quickly remodelled weeklies *Sztandar Młodych* (The Banner of Youth) and *Politics*, as well as by the re-released Catholic *Tygodnik Powszechny* (Universal Weekly). The social sphere was boiling over; several months of thaw resulted in a creative pool of people who would define the unique and high standard of Polish media for decades to come – people like Ryszard Kapuściński, Marian Turski (b. 1926), Dariusz Fikus (1932–96), Krzysztof Kąkolewski (1930–2015), Mieczysław F. Rakowski (1926–2008), and Jerzy Turowicz (1912–99).

The anti-Stalinist social revolution was accompanied by a technological revolution. In 1955, an experimental television program was broadcast; normal service started a year later, and the first news program two years after that. The ever-increasing numbers of TV sets were a clear indication that television would soon become the most important medium for information, propaganda, and cultural production. In 1958 there were only 84 subscribers; two years later there were 425,000, and by 1968 there were 3.4 million. The position of radio stabilized at this time. The development of both of these electronic media relied not only on expanded coverage but also on longer broadcast times and (eventually) on increasing the number of available stations. Over time, radio and television became the media of metaculture; along with audience numbers and extended length of broadcasts grew the demand for content, such as serials, music, and broadcast journalism. Although the energy of the October thaw was quickly suppressed, the revolutionary spirit survived in the metacultural dimension.

In developing new media, especially television, the communists set in motion an instrument of cultural modernization regardless of the degree of control they maintained over the media. The Rolling Stones concert in Warsaw in 1967 was of similar significance for Poland's internal transformation; so was the first pilgrimage of John Paul II in 1979. The sclerotic power structure headed by Gomułka was unable to meet the aspirations of a society that was being transformed by mass culture and that was expecting mass consumer goods and social liberalization to arrive along with that culture. The student protests in March 1968, many of which were instigated by children of the PPR élites, heralded a structural fissure. In this regard, the Polish March was structurally similar to that year's Prague Spring and the May Days in Paris. Modern societies in the capitalist West and the socialist East found themselves at a crossroads. Czechoslovakia attempted to modernize and democratize its socialist system, knowing that it would otherwise fall into social senility. That experiment was crushed, brutally; indeed, the PPR's military helped pacify the Czechs after dealing with protests by Polish students and participating in the anti-Semitic purge of intellectuals.

> By the end of Gierek's decade, Polish television had close to 8 million subscribers (and was thus already a common medium), and the press market had stabilized at a level of 2,400 titles with a cumulative circulation of 29.9 million in 1980.

Force, however, could not halt the delegitimization of the system, a process to which metaculture contributed strongly, with the help of new media and mass culture. After the bloody suppression of the shipyard strikes in 1970 and the subsequent change of leadership in the PPR, the authorities attempted to buy the people's respect and trust with consumer goods. Gomułka's successor, Edward Gierek, played the role of a pro-Western communist and defined "socialist normality" anew as meaning a better supply of goods, acceptance of Western lifestyles, liberalization of social customs, and the expansion of mass culture. A clear indicator of the last was the evolution of television, signalled by the introduction of a second, entertainment channel with a more modern programming formula.

Consumption by means of the state's own credit did not correct the system's structural faults. Throughout the 1970s, Polish media engaged in passionate discussions about how to rationalize the system and escape the contradictions of the planned economy. During the 1970s this was still believed to be possible, but that faith evaporated in 1976. The workers' strikes that year stripped communist authorities of all their legitimacy. Society responded to the repression of those strikes by organizing independent structures: the Workers' Defence Committee was founded, as was the Movement for Defence of Human and Civil Rights. Meanwhile, an independent underground publishing movement began to form. All of this culminated in 1980 with the birth of Solidarity. So began a sixteen-month carnival of freedom.

The energy of that carnival was reflected in changes in the state-controlled media and in new initiatives taken up within the framework of the Independent Self-governing Trade Union ("Solidarity"). Access to the most important media – radio and television – was a key issue in the constant skirmishes between Solidarity and the authorities. Another was the honesty of those media. The authorities resisted relinquishing control over strategic aspects of social communication, and in doing so, they revealed that they were unwilling to compromise beyond a certain point – with that point being giving up their power. A system that was utterly compromised both morally and culturally could respond to this social ferment in only one way – with violence. Martial law was introduced on 13 December 1981 by Wojciech Jaruzelski, who became the First Secretary of the Communist Party, as well as Poland's prime minister and the commander-in-chief of the Polish Army. This secured the system's survival for eight more years, but at a tremendous social cost that included mass political and economic emigration, repressions, and growing anomie. The media system re-created after martial law ended in 1983 had been cleansed of "subversive elements"; many of the most valuable editors had left their editorial boards as a result of a political house-cleaning. Those who did not move abroad sought shelter and sustenance working for non-political publications such as *Przegląd Techniczny* (The Technical Review).

Meanwhile, a massive underground publishing movement was developing, with close to 1,400 titles appearing after martial law was proclaimed in 1981. This cannot be taken to mean that they impacted the mass imagination, although they certainly shaped the discourse of the now more numerous oppositional élites. Still, society was changing under the influence of culture, and mass culture in particular. One form of contestation of existing reality was the youth music scene and the phenomenon of punk rock.

Independent publishing movement: often also referred to as *second circulation*; *underground publishing houses*; *samizdat* or *independent publishing*; *the self-publishing movement*; *independent culture*. This was a publishing infrastructure set up outside of state control and censorship. While *samizdat* initiatives were often launched after the Second World War, they were greatly spurred by the events of 1976. After the workers' strikes at Ursus, Radom, and Stalowa Wola, and subsequent legal actions against the striking workers, the Workers' Defence Committee was established along with its publication *Komunikat KOR*. The first independent political journal *U progu* (At the Threshold) was founded at this time. By 1977 there were more than a dozen underground newspapers, and the publishing house Niezależna Oficyna Wydawnicza NOWA (The Independent Publishing Press NEW) had been established. From 1976 to 1989 (when censorship was abolished), more than five hundred independent publishers functioned in Poland. Between them, they published the most important works of Polish émigré literature – for instance, the banned works of Witold Gombrowicz, Czesław Miłosz, Gustaw Herling-Grudziński, Józef Mackiewicz, Józef Czapski, and Leszek Kołakowski – as well as various titles from world literature – by Aleksandr Solzhenitsyn, George Orwell, Aldous Huxley, Bohumil Hrabal, Milan Kundera, Josef Škvorecky, Karl Popper, Hannah Arendt, and Raymond Aron, among others.

In the second half of the 1980s, after failed attempts at economic reform, the state functionaries understood that their system could no longer sustain itself. The deepening economic crisis pointed towards a looming catastrophe that could be avoided only through radical reforms backed by new sources of legitimacy, such as were at the disposal of groups in the democratic opposition and in the underground structures of Solidarity. Negotiations initiated in 1988 led to the Round Table Talks in the spring of 1989 and later to partly free elections on 4 June (the same day that the Chinese Communist Party violently suppressed a gathering of students and workers in Beijing's Tiananmen Square). Could anyone have predicted that these negotiations would end with the fall of communism in the entire Eastern Bloc? But the key task facing Poland's transformation in 1989 was to build legitimacy for the changes. This rested on the conviction that the period of apparently normal socialism – which, as it turned out, was abnormal – had come to an end, and that the (economic, capitalist, democratic) transformation would clear a path towards a world of *actual* normalcy: "Normalcy was one of the foundational myths of the new reality. It seems that this myth stated that 'normal' is the opposite of 'totalitarian,' and thus that freedom constitutes a self-regulating system that allows to exist (to act, live, create, work, and earn) normally."[28]

All of the forces joined in the construction of the myth of normalcy: both old and new intellectual and cultural élites participated in the process, which took place largely in the realm of culture and the media. Suddenly free of censorship, both culture and the media diversified, yet the more diverse they became, the more alike they grew in declaring that there was no alternative to the transformation being undertaken by Poland. Their consensus was that the economic shock therapy prescribed by the finance minister, Leszek Balcerowicz, and the government of Tadeusz Mazowiecki was necessary, even if it would be costly. It should be emphasized, however, that an unavoidable consequence of that therapy was millions of people falling into a Polish underclass on the margins of society, where poverty continues to this day, reproducing itself from generation to generation. Such inequalities and spheres of exclusion have grown in recent decades in *all* developed countries. It seems that this is the norm under neoliberal capitalism.

A more significant problem for Poland and the Poles was that earlier discussions about the Polish "we" were reignited. While structurally the society was split into winners and losers by the transformation, in a cultural sense the spectrum of the divisions is broader, even if dominated by a simplistic separation of society into liberal and conservative "modernizers." This division was fuelled by the Smolensk tragedy on 10 April 2010, when the plane carrying President Lech Kaczyński and other Polish dignitaries to a commemorative ceremony at Katyn, the site of the Second World War mass execution of Polish officers by the Soviet Union, crashed while landing at the Russian airport, killing all on board. This tragedy raised serious concerns about existing state structures, among other things. But it did not lead to the modernization of those structures. Instead, the discourse around it exacerbated the cultural wars already taking place within the increasingly polarized and sectarian media.

Alongside old debates about identity and Poland's civilizational position, which have been reappearing since the beginning of twentieth century, a new dimension of social space, culture, and media – the Internet – has been developing. Symbolically born along with the Polish Third Republic, it debuted as a popular medium in 1991. Poles quickly got on board this new technology; the first Internet portal – *Wirtualna Polska* (Virtual Poland) – was created in 1995, at a time when similar initiatives were beginning to appear in the West. Initially treated as a toy for the select few, the Internet soon became both a symptom and a carrier of new culture and metaculture.

The society of television and mass culture did not fit socialist modernity. In much the same way, the society of the Internet does not fit "normal" modernity, which consists of reheating addled cutlets taken out of a freezer of national symbols, and of a cargo cult, namely, the mindless importation of institutional solutions. An alternative society has been developing beyond the borders of official media circulation, within an unrepresented reality that does not exist for the élites and the politicians. It manifested itself in the winter of 2012 on the streets of dozens of cities, using as a pretext the ACTA agreement – a multinational treaty addressing the counterfeiting of goods and computer piracy. We have discovered that a map is not a territory and that social order as expressed in institutional organizations and in the images of reality created by culture and the media has little in common with real social structures and actual cultural practices. The world as it is imagined and represented by the cultural and media élites is only a fragment of a larger, unrepresented world. It turns out that regained freedom has not meant a return to normalcy, but rather has driven us once again into a trap of discursive dissonance.

Edwin Bendyk
Collegium Civitas, Warsaw
Translated by Agnieszka Polakowska

NOTES

1 See Luhmann, *Love as Passion.*
2 See McNeill, *Keeping Together in Time.*
3 Deacon, *The Symbolic Species,* 22.
4 Cook, *Ice Age Art.*
5 Urban, *Metaculture*, xiii.
6 See Johns, *Piracy.*
7 See Myśliński in Jabłonowski, *350 lat prasy polskiej.*
8 Przyboś, "Merkuriusz Polski," 3.
9 For more on these theories, see Castells, *Communication Power.*
10 For more on this concept. see Sowa, *Fantomowe ciało króla.*
11 Mickiewicz, *Pan Tadeusz*, 26.
12 Jan Tomkowski in Jabłonowski, *350 lat prasy polskiej,* 22.
13 Mickiewicz, *Pan Tadeusz*, 24.
14 Wyspiański, *The Wedding*, 21.
15 Tomkowski in Jabłonowski, *350 lat prasy polskiej,* 25.
16 Marx and Engels, *Communist Manifesto*, 63.
17 Jakubowska in Jabłonowski, *350 lat prasy polskiej,* 52.
18 Habielski, *Polityczna historia.*
19 For more on this subject, see Jedlicki, *Jakiej cywilizacji Polacy potrzebują.*
20 Hryniewicz, *Polityczny i kulturowy kontekst*, 142.
21 Magala, *Walka klas w bezklasowej Polsce,* 61.
22 Hryniewicz, *Stosunki pracy w polskich organizacjach*, 38.
23 Bibó, *Bieda východoeurópskych malých štátov.*
24 See Wańkowicz, *Sztafeta.*
25 Habielski, *Polityczna historia,* 99.
26 Ibid., 157.
27 For the analysis of these trends, see Wallerstein, *Utopistics.*
28 Czapliński, *Efekt bierności*, 6.

WORKS CITED

Bibó, István. *Bieda východoeurópskych malých štátov. Výbrané štúdie*. Višegrád: Kalligram, 1996.

Castells, Manuel. *Communication Power*. New York: Oxford University Press, 2013.

Cook, Jill. *Ice Age Art: The Arrival of the Modern Mind.* London: British Museum, 2012.

Czapliński, Przemysław. *Efekt bierności. Literatura w czasie normalnym*. Kraków: Wydawnictwo Literackie, 2004.

Deacon, Terrence W. *The Symbolic Species: The Co-evolution of Language and the Brain.* New York: W.W. Norton, 1997.

Habielski, Rafał. *Polityczna historia mediów w Polsce w XX wieku.* Warszawa: Wydawnictwa akademickie i profesjonalne, 2009.

Hryniewicz, Janusz T. *Polityczny i kulturowy kontekst rozwoju gospodarczego.* Warszawa: Wydawnictwo Naukowe Scholar, 2004.

– *Stosunki pracy w polskich organizacjach.* Warszawa: Wydawnictwo Naukowe Scholar, 2007.

Jabłonowski, Marek. *350 lat prasy polskiej*. Warszawa: Instytut Informacji Naukowej i Studiów Bibliologicznych Uniwersytetu Warszawskiego, 2012.
Jedlicki, Jerzy. *Jakiej cywilizacji Polacy potrzebują. Studia z dziejów idei i wyobraźni XIX wieku*. Warszawa: W.A.B./Wydawnictwo CiS, 2002.
Johns, Adrian. *Piracy: The Intellectual Property Wars from Gutenberg to Gates*. Chicago: University of Chicago Press, 2009.
Luhmann, Niklas. *Love as Passion: The Codification of Intimacy*. Translated by Jeremy Gaines and Doris L. Jones. Cambridge, MA: Harvard University Press, 1986.
Magala, Sławomir. *Walka klas w bezklasowej Polsce*. Translated by Jarosław Dąbrowski. Gdańsk: Europejskie Centrum Solidarności, 2012.
Marx, Karl, and Friedrich Engels. *Communist Manifesto*. Translated by Samuel Moore. New York: Pocket Books, 1964.
McNeill, William H. *Keeping Together in Time: Dance and Drill in Human History*. Cambridge, MA: Harvard University Press, 1995.
Mickiewicz, Adam. *Pan Tadeusz*. Translated by Kenneth R. MacKenzie. New York: Hippocrene Books, 1992.
Przyboś, Adam, "*Merkuriusz Polski* z 1661 roku. Pierwsze polskie czasopismo." *Mówią wieki* 1 (1961): 1–3.
Sowa, Jan. *Fantomowe ciało króla. Peryferyjne zmagania z nowoczesną formą*. Kraków: Universitas, 2011.
Urban, Greg. *Metaculture: How Culture Moves through the World*. Minneapolis: University of Minnesota Press, 2001.
Wallerstein, Immanuel Maurice. *Utopistics, or, Historical Choices of the Twenty-First Century*. New York: New Press, 1998.
Wańkowicz, Melchoir. *Sztafeta. Książka o polskim pochodzie gospodarczym*. Edited by Błażej Brzostek and Aleksandra Ziółkowska-Boehm. Warszawa: Prószyński i S-ka, 2012.
Wyspiański, Stanisław. *The Wedding*. Translated by Noel Clark. London: Oberon Books, 1998.

Subject Index

Page numbers in **bold** *indicate the main discussion of a topic.*

Name Index

www.ingramcontent.com/pod-product-compliance
Lightning Source LLC
LaVergne TN
LVHW082005060826
844660LV00028B/1237

* 9 7 8 1 4 8 7 5 2 4 5 9 3 *